Arid-land ecosystems: structure, functioning and management

Volume 1

THE INTERNATIONAL BIOLOGICAL PROGRAMME

The International Biological Programme was established by the International Council of Scientific Unions in 1964 as a counterpart of the International Geophysical Year. The subject of the IBP was defined as 'The Biological Basis of Productivity and Human Welfare', and the reason for its establishment was recognition that the rapidly increasing human population called for a better understanding of the environment as a basis for the rational management of natural resources. This could be achieved only on the basis of scientific knowledge, which in many fields of biology and in many parts of the world was felt to be inadequate. At the same time it was recognised that human activities were creating rapid and comprehensive changes in the environment. Thus, in terms of human welfare, the reason for the IBP lay in its promotion of basic knowledge relevant to the needs of man.

The IBP provided the first occasion on which biologists throughout the world were challenged to work together for a common cause. It involved an integrated and concerted examination of a wide range of problems. The Programme was co-ordinated through a series of seven sections representing the major subject areas of research. Four of these sections were concerned with the study of biological productivity on land, in freshwater, and in the seas, together with the processes of photosynthesis and nitrogen fixation. Three sections were concerned with adaptability of human populations, conservation and ecosystems and the use of biological resources.

After a decade of work, the Programme terminated in June 1974 and this series of volumes brings together, in the form of syntheses, the results of national and international activities.

INTERNATIONAL BIOLOGICAL PROGRAMME

Arid-land ecosystems: structure, functioning and management

Volume 1

EDITED BY

D. W. Goodall
R. A. Perry
with the assistance of
K. M. W. Howes
*Division of Land Resources Management,
CSIRO, Wembley, Western Australia*

CAMBRIDGE UNIVERSITY PRESS

CAMBRIDGE
LONDON·NEW YORK·MELBOURNE

Published by the Syndics of the Cambridge University Press
The Pitt Building, Trumpington Street, Cambridge CB2 1RP
Bentley House, 200 Euston Road, London NW1 2DB
32 East 57th Street, New York, NY 10022, USA
296 Beaconsfield Parade, Middle Park, Melbourne 3206, Australia

© Cambridge University Press 1979

First published 1979

Printed in Great Britain at the University Press, Cambridge

Library of Congress Cataloguing in Publication Data
Main entry under title:
Arid-land ecosystems.
   (International Biological Programme; 16)
   Includes index.
   1. Desert ecology. 2. Desert research.
   I. Goodall, David W., 1914–   II. Perry, R. A.
   OH541.5.D4A74   574.5'265   77–84810
   ISBN 0 521 21842 x

Contents

Contents

Table des matières

Содержание

Contenido

xviii

List of Collaborators

G. T. Austin	Department of Biological Sciences, University of Nevada, Las Vegas, Nevada, 89154, USA
F. C. Bell	School of Geography, University of New South Wales, P.O. Box 1, Kensington, N.S.W. 2033, Australia
J. L. Charley	Department of Botany, University of New England, Armidale, N.S.W. Australia
P. Chouard	Phytotron CNRS, 91190, Gif-sur-Yvette, France
I. R. Cowan	Department of Environmental Biology, Research School of Biological Sciences, Australian National University, P.O. Box 475, Canberra City, A.C.T. 2601, Australia
J. B. Cragg	Faculty of Environmental Design, The University of Calgary, 2920 24 Avenue, Calgary, Alberta, Canada
C. S. Crawford	Department of Biology, The University of New Mexico, Albuquerque, N.M. 87131, USA
E. J. DePuit	Department of Animal and Range Sciences, Montana State University, Bozeman, Montana 59715, USA
M. C. Drew	Agricultural Research Council, Letcombe Laboratory, Wantage, Oxfordshire, United Kingdom
E. A. Fitzpatrick	School of Geography, University of New South Wales, P.O. Box 1, Kensington, N.S.W. 2033, Australia
M. Fuchs	Agricultural Research Organization, Department of Agricultural Meteorology, Volcani Centre, Bet Dagan, Israel
D. W. Goodall	CSIRO, Division of Land Resources Management, Private Bag, P.O., Wembley, 6014, Western Australia
R. D. Graetz	CSIRO Division of Land Resources Management, Private Bag P.O. Deniliquin, N.S.W. 2710, Australia
R. K. Gupta	Central Soil and Water Research and Training Institute, 218 Kaulargh Road, Dehradun, India
N. F. Hadley	Zoology Department, Arizona State University, Tempe, Arizona, USA
D. R. Johnson	Department of Biological Sciences, University of Idaho, Moscow, Idaho 83843, USA

List of collaborators

R. N. Kaul	UNESCO Project Manager, Institute for Applied Research on Natural Resources, Baghdad, Iraq
V. A. Kovda	Institute of Agrochemistry and Pedology, Academy of Sciences of the USSR, Moscow 117234, USSR
H. N. Le Houérou	Department of Environmental Science and Plant Production, Sahel Programme, B.P. 60, Bamako, Mali
O. A. Leistner	Botanical Research Institute, Private Bag X101, Pretoria 001, South Africa
W. A. Low	CSIRO, Division of Land Resources Management, P.O. Box 77, Alice Springs, Northern Territory 5750, Australia
W. G. McGinnies	College of Earth Sciences, University of Arizona, 1201 East Speedway, Tucson, Arizona 8571, USA
J. A. MacMahon	Dept of Biology and Ecology Center, Utah State University, Logan, Utah 84322, USA
H. Meidner	Department of Biology, University of Stirling, Stirling FK9 4LA, Scotland
J. J. Mott	CSIRO, Division of Tropical Crops and Pastures, Cunningham Laboratory, St Lucia, Queensland 4067, Australia
M. J. O'Farrell	Department of Biological Sciences, University of Nevada, Las Vegas, Nevada, 89154, USA
C. B. Osmond	Department of Environmental Biology, Research School of Biological Sciences, Australian National University, P.O. Box 475, Canberra City, A.C.T. 2601, Australia
R. A. Perry	CSIRO, Division of Land Resources Management, Private Bag, P.O. Wembley, 6014, Western Australia
E. R. Pianka	Department of Zoology, University of Texas, Austin, Texas 78712, USA
I. Prakash	Central Arid Zone Research Institute, Jodhpur, India
S. E. Reichert	Department of Zoology, University of Tennessee, Knoxville Tennessee, USA
O. J. Reichmann	Department of Biology, University of Utah, Salt Lake City, Utah 84112, USA
L. E. Rodin	Komarov Botanical Institute, USSR Academy of Science, Leningrad, USSR
V. Roig	Casilla de Correo 507, Correo Central, Mendoza, Argentina

E. M. Samoilova   Department of Pedology, Moscow State University, Moscow 117234, USSR

R. K. Schreiber   Department of Biological Sciences, University of Idaho, Moscow, Idaho 83843, USA

J. S. Singh   Department of Botany, Kurukshetra University, Kurukshetra, India

J. J. Skujins   Department of Biology, Utah State University, Logan, Utah, 84322, USA

D. C. P. Thalen   UNESCO Associate Expert, Subdepartment Vegetation Survey, International Institute for Aerial Survey and Earth Sciences, P.O. Box 6, Enschede, Netherlands

M. J. Trlica   Range Science Department, Colorado State University, Fort Collins, Colorado 80521, USA

F. W. Went   Laboratory of Desert Biology, Desert Research Institute, University of Nevada, Reno, Nevada 89507, USA

N. E. West   Range Science Department, Utah State University, Logan, Utah 84322, USA

O. B. Williams   CSIRO Division of Land Resources Management, P.O. Box 1666, Canberra City 2601, Australia

Preface

The anonymous author of a recent article, reflecting on UNESCO's many years of research on natural resources, began by quoting Francis Bacon: *Naturae enim non imperatur, nisi parendo.* These words, even in translation, remain linguistically impressive and important: 'We cannot command nature except by obeying her.' Within a few years of its establishment in 1946, UNESCO, acting as though it had taken Bacon's aphorism to heart, initiated a worldwide programme on arid lands. The numerous volumes and papers which have emerged from thirty years of study have indicated some of the ways in which these fragile ecosystems can be utilized and at the same time safeguarded against destruction. IBP's Arid Lands programme followed many of the pathways established by UNESCO and it is important to remember that IBP itself has had UNESCO's support from its inception.

Whilst arid lands defy precise definition, they cover a large part of the earth. A conservative estimate puts their area at about one-eighth of the land surface of the globe. If semi-arid areas are included, the total reaches one-third of the world's land surface with, perhaps, one-tenth of the world's population dependent on it for survival.

Characterized by long periods without precipitation and by extreme temperature gradients, arid lands impose considerable restraints on the organisms which inhabit them. Above all, their ecosystems, as recent years have demonstrated so clearly in the Sahel, are subject to severe and, in some cases, irreversible destruction. The Arid Lands Theme in IBP was shaped to establish a firm basis of integrated knowledge on which to base the future management of arid lands.

Studies on arid lands within the Terrestrial Productivity section of IBP were defined as Theme 3 in the following terms: 'Arid Lands present important problems to man's rational use of natural resources. In these areas vegetation is in sensitive balance with an irregular and limited water supply and, in general, consumers are either nomadic (or migratory) or are capable of high protein production during favourable periods. The balance of arid zone communities with the environment is so precarious that man has devastated large areas of the world by unwise management practices. The IBP aim is to further our understanding of the structure and functioning of these arid zone communities, so that we may be better able to predict the consequences of man's efforts to utilize the natural resources of these areas.'

In 1969, eleven National IBP Committees were prepared to contribute projects to the Theme. Some of the projects never materialized and only the USA mounted a major coordinated biome study. Nevertheless, world coverage was extensive and it was no easy matter to organize the synthesis of many different lines of enquiry. The Steering Committee which guided this final phase of IBP's arid lands investigations consisted of: Dr D. W. Goodall (USA – now in Australia), Professor M. Evenari (Israel), Professor M. Kassas (Egypt), Professor L. A. Rodin (USSR), Dr V. Roig (Argentina), Dr R. K. Gupta (India) and Dr R. A. Perry (Australia). The latter member acted as Convener. In 1972, the Committee met twice – in Leningrad in June and in Logan, USA, in September. A Symposium was to have been held in New Delhi in 1973 but the meeting had to be cancelled through lack of funds. However, the plan proposed for that meeting under the title *Arid Ecosystems and Management* represented an important step in the preparation of the synthesis volumes.

At Leningrad it was proposed to have three volumes: the first concerned with the description and structure of arid land ecosystems with some emphasis on ecosystem processes; the second was to be devoted to ecosystem dynamics both short-term and long-term; the final volume was to take as its theme the all-important subject of the management of arid lands and was to deal with the practical aspects of management and the utilization of optimization models. These overall plans, as happened with early proposals in other biome studies, foundered through lack of funds. Once the field investigations for IBP had been completed, some individuals had to take up other activities and were unable to contribute in a major way to the final synthesis.

At the Logan meeting the plan, as a consequence, had to be reduced in size and, in my opinion, the synthesis has gained rather than lost by the twin processes of attrition and compression. The two volumes which have now emerged present a succinct view of the extensive problems associated with arid lands. Of special interest is the approach to modelling which has been followed in this Theme. The very nature of arid lands lent substance to Goodall's view stated some years ago in a meeting at Montreal: 'The dynamics of most ecosystems constitute a succession of transients, and they are never in anything resembling a steady state.' Thus modelling in the Arid Lands Biome has included a number of sub-models built to answer specific questions, whereas elsewhere in IBP attempts were made to create large models capable of answering a multiplicity of questions. Wherever modelling has been discussed in IBP, the small-model vs large-model approach has been heatedly contested. I cannot disguise my own sympathies for Goodall's insistence on the necessity for concentrating efforts on sub models and, of course, on their improvement and validation especially in relation to measuring productive capacity.

Again quoting Goodall: 'Prediction is the acid test of a set of hypotheses about the real world; the pure gold survives, the counterfeit is rejected

xxvi

and must be replaced.' His ideas influenced much of the thinking in the Arid Lands Biome studies. In all his modelling studies, Goodall never lost sight of the importance of fundamental biological knowledge for he considers that attempts '. . . to understand the dynamics of an ecosystem without taking biological individuality into account is doomed to failure'.

No programme is ever completed to the satisfaction of its participants. There have been many moments of despondence in the synthesis phase as gaps emerged in our knowledge of the basic components of arid land ecosystems. Information essential for the development of a broadly based general theory was lacking.

The absence of a firm data base cannot be attributed to an absence of funding or to a shortage of scientific personnel although these deficiencies did contribute in some measure. There is another reason for the 'information gap' – the piecemeal approach to many environmental problems. These two volumes on Arid Lands, together with other IBP Biome volumes now in press or in the final stages of preparation, emphasize the need for a holistic approach to the investigation of ecosystems and related environmental problems. In fact, the exposure of gaps in our present knowledge can be looked upon as one of the major successes of the programme! Topics which now require detailed study have been defined and some have already become parts of two major international operations: the desertification studies of UNEP (United Nations Environment Program) and UNESCO's *Man and the Biosphere*. The latter is combining the predominantly biological approaches of IBP with social and economic studies.

J. B. CRAGG
Killam Memorial Professor

Introduction

R. A. PERRY

Arid lands comprise a significant proportion of the land surface of the world and support about 300 million people. The history of man's use of arid lands is, in general, a sad record of progressive, man-induced deterioration of the natural resource base and of generally low and declining living standards for the human population. Developing ways to reverse this trend in resource degeneration and to raise the living standards of the increasing human population supported on these resources is an important challenge to mankind. One pre-requisite to meeting the challenge is a sound knowledge of the natural ecosystems. It is to this objective that the IBP arid-land studies reported in this, and a succeeding volume, are addressed.

Arid-land studies are part of only one of the themes of the International Biological Programme. Throughout the world the main contribution to this sub-theme, in terms of research specifically funded and identified with the IBP, was from the USA. However, a very considerable amount of research in other countries had similar objectives and so is relevant to the IBP although not identified specifically with it. These two volumes have drawn on information from all relevant research and thus include much more than the results of IBP studies.

The subject matter of the two volumes is organised into five major topics; two are included in the first volume and three in the second volume.

The first section of Volume 1 describes in detail the structure of the arid ecosystems in terms of climate, soils, geomorphology, hydrology and flora and fauna. Unfortunately South America is not covered because, despite very considerable and repeated attempts, the editors were unable to find an author willing to prepare the chapter. The areas which are described include North America, north Africa, south Africa, Australasia, southwest Asia and central Asia. In the second section of Volume 1 the processes which operate within, and control, the ecosystem are dealt with individually. The section is subdivided into four parts which deal with aspects of atmospheric soil, plant, and animal processes.

The interaction of the various components of the ecosystem is covered in the first section of Volume 2 and this is followed in the second section by an integration of the composite and interactive processes as they influence the short- and long-term dynamics of the whole system. Over the IBP period modelling has played an increasingly important part in the integrative views of ecosystem functioning and three chapters are devoted

1

Introduction

to this topic. The third section in Volume 2 deals with the impact of man on the arid areas and the various options available for management of the arid lands. A final chapter is included in Volume 2 to pull together the contributions to both volumes and to indicate areas where further research could improve our knowledge and management of the arid lands.

PART I

Description and structure of arid ecosystems

1. General description of desert areas

W. G. McGINNIES

General characteristics of the desert biome

Dry climates are the most extensively developed over the land surface of the earth of all of the great climatic groups, occupying, according to Köppen (1954), 26% of the continental area. Of this total, 14% is steppe and 12% is desert.

The bulk of the desert area lies between 15° and 35° latitude, in both the northern and southern hemispheres although extending to 55° N latitude in some areas. The dry climates of the continents occur in five great provinces separated from one another by oceans or by wet equatorial zones. Of these five provinces, the North African–Eurasia province is larger than all the remaining dry areas of the world combined. It includes the world's largest desert, the Sahara, and a series of other hot deserts and semi-arid areas continuing eastward through the Arabian peninsula along the Persian Gulf to Pakistan and India. To the north lie the milder cool-winter dry areas of the Mediterranean coast and Iran, while farther northward and eastward lie the vast deserts and steppes of the USSR, China, and Mongolia, with subfreezing winters and warm or hot summers. In east Africa there are the hot lowlands of the Somali–Chalbi, which bear certain affinities to much of the southern part of the Arabian Peninsula.

Under Köppen's classification the desert areas of northern Africa, Arabia, and the southern part of Asia are BWh (desert, average annual temperature under 18 °C). Meigs (1963) shows these same areas as extremely arid or arid, and ranging from hot areas to warm areas with cold winters. The UNESCO–FAO map (UNESCO, 1963), shows true desert regions surrounded by desert regions in both the Sahara and the Arabian Peninsula, and in the Iranian Desert, desert regions interrupted and surrounded by regions of lesser aridity. The map also shows a desert region in Pakistan and India separated from the Iranian desert regions by an area with more favorable moisture conditions.

The Mediterranean climate, with its emphasis on winter rainfall originating in mid-latitude cyclones, applies to a region that extends from western Africa eastward along the northern fringe of the continent and north of the core of the Sahara through the Middle East and into the Iranian Desert. The climate of this region is related to the shift of the

5

intertropical convergence zone and therefore also falls in the general field of tropical meteorology.

Reasons for the aridity are very complex for the entire sector from the Somali–Chalbi north-eastward across the Arabian Sea and the southern Arabian peninsula into Pakistan. The mountainous nature of surrounding areas, thermal low pressure, coastal upswelling and the monsoon circulation of the Indian subcontinent in summer combine to produce an environment in which rainfall is rarely recorded.

The south African dry province consists chiefly of the narrow elongated coastal desert of the Namib, the Karroo and Kalahari and steppe uplands.

The Australian dry province occupies a large portion of the continent, with hot climates prevailing in the northern half and mild climates in the southern.

The south American dry province is confined to a strip along the west coast and an area on the east side of the Andes toward the southern portion of the continent.

The North American dry province resembles the North Africa–Eurasia province in variety of sub division types, although the sub-divisions are much smaller. Dry upland areas analogous to those of Iran, Turkestan, and upland Arabia, make up much of the province of the United States and Mexico. A small area bordering the Gulf of California is comparable to the Sahara by virtue of its scanty and irregular precipitation.

Causes of aridity

A general discussion of the weather systems of deserts is not possible because these arid lands are found over a wide range of latitudes and come under the influence of nearly all the major wind and pressure belts. A variety of weather systems prevail and a variety of reasons for aridity exist. Aridity arises from three general causes acting individually or in combination. One of these causes is the separation of the region from oceanic moisture sources by topography or by distance. Part of the desert area of the United States and the Monte–Patagonian Desert to the leeward of the Andes in South America is a result of the aridifying effect major mountain barriers have on air masses which move over them. One of the causes of the Takla–Makan, Turkestan, and Gobi deserts of Central Asia is the great distance from major moisture sources.

A second general cause of aridity is the formation of dry, stable air masses that resist convective currents. The Somali–Chalbi desert probably owes its existence to a stable environment produced by large-scale atmospheric motions. Deserts dominated by the eastern portions of subtropical high-pressure cells originate in part from the stability produced by these pressure and wind systems. Aridity can also result from the lack of storm systems, the mechanisms that cause convergence, create unstable environments, and provide the upward movement of air which is necessary for precipitation. The paths, frequencies, and degrees of development of mid-latitude cyclones or tropical cyclones are crucial factors in the production of rainfall. The deserts of the subtropical latitudes are particularly sensitive to the climatology of cyclones. The Arabian and Australian deserts and the Sahara are examples of regions positioned between major wind belts with their associated storm systems.

The heart of the tropical dry climates is in the vicinity of latitudes 20 to 25° N and S, with the average positions of their extreme margins at approximately 15° and 30°. They are more or less coincident with the dry, subsiding air masses of the subtropical anticyclones. Ordinarily the dry climates do not extend to the eastern margins of the continents, humid climates characteristically taking their places on the eastern margin.

The low-latitude deserts, dominated as they are by the subtropical anticyclones, probably are the most nearly rainless regions of the earth. Since they occupy regions of dry, stable, settling and diverging air masses, conditions are unfavorable for the development of convectional showers.

General, widespread rains are almost unknown over large parts of the hot deserts, most of the precipitation coming in violent convectional showers that do not cover extensive areas. The wadis, entirely without water during most of the year, may become torrents of muddy water filled with much debris after one of these flooding rains. Because of the violence of tropical desert rains and the sparseness of the vegetation cover, temporary local runoff is excessive, and consequently less of the total fall becomes effective for vegetation or for the crops of the oasis farmer. Much of the precipitation that reaches the earth is quickly evaporated by the hot, dry desert air.

Skies are normally clear in the low-latitude deserts so that sunshine is abundant. Annual ranges of temperature in the low-latitude deserts are larger than in any other type of climate within the tropics. It is the excessive summer heat, rather than the winter cold, that leads to the marked differences between the seasons.

During the high-sun period, scorching, desiccating heat prevails. Midday readings of 40 to 45 °C are common at this season. During the period of low sun the days still are warm, with the daily maxima usually averaging 15 to 20 °C and occasionally reaching 25 °C. Nights are distinctly chilly with the average minima in the neighborhood of 10 °C.

The usual characteristics of tropical desert – high temperatures, low relative humidity, and little cloud cover – are modified to a considerable degree along the western littorals of several of the low-latitude deserts, where cool ocean currents parallel the coasts. The presence of cool currents is especially marked along the desert coasts of Peru and northern

Description of arid ecosystems

Chile and the west coast of south Africa. Although along these cool coasts rainfall is extremely low and the drought conditions may extend to within a few degrees of the equator, they are regions of high relative humidity and abundant fog.

Because of clear skies and dry atmosphere, desert climates tend to be severe for their latitude, having relatively extreme seasonal temperatures and consequently large annual ranges. Most marked, however, are the large daily ranges; clear cloudless skies and relatively low humidity which permits an abundance of solar energy to reach the earth by day but also allows a rapid loss of energy at night. Large diurnal ranges in deserts are also associated with the meager vegetation cover, which permits the barren surface to become intensely heated by day. Deserts acquire, but can also lose heat rapidly.

Rainfall is always meager. In addition it is extremely variable from year to year. The dependability of precipitation usually decreases with decreasing amount. No part of the earth is known for certain to be absolutely rainless, although at Arica, in northern Chile the rainfall over a period of 17 years was only 0.5 mm. During the whole 17 years there were only three showers heavy enough to be measured.

Relative humidity (with a few exceptions) is low in dry climates. Potential evaporation is extremely high.

Dry regions are inclined to be windy places, there being little frictional retardation of the moving air by the low and sparse vegetation cover. Because of the strong and persistent winds, desert air is often murky with fine dust.

Characteristics of individual deserts

Deserts can be classified in several ways, for example, warm deserts and cold deserts, coastal and continental, or by geographical location.

One listing is that used by the author in *Deserts of the World* (McGinnies, 1968) as follows:

Kalahari–Namib (southern Africa)
Sahara (northern Africa)
Somali–Chalbi (northern Africa)
Arabian Desert (western Asia)
Iranian Desert (western Asia)
Thar (western Asia)
Turkestan Desert (central Asia)
Takla Makan and Gobi (central and eastern Asia)
Australian Deserts
Monte–Patagonian Desert (South America)
Atacama–Peruvian (South America)
North American Deserts

8

Although this listing is not identical with that used by the Synthesis authors, it does serve as a basis for broad descriptions and comparisons of the various desert areas.

The Namib Desert extends from about 9° S to 33° S in the Republic of South Africa. Its width is about 165 km in most places. The extreme desert extends less than half the total length.

The Kalahari occupies Botswana and eastern South West Africa, from the Okavango River in the north to the northern border of South Africa in the south. The northern part is not considered true desert and is referred to locally as 'thirstland'. From 22° S to the Orange River, the Kalahari is more truly desert, receiving only little and unreliable rainfall in summer, and supporting scattered small trees, bushes and, in occasional wet years, summer grasses.

The Sahara, largest desert in the world, extends from the Atlantic coast of Africa to the Red Sea. It measures more than 5000 km from east to west and 1300 to 2000 km from north to south. The total area of the Sahara is between 8 and 9 million km².

The Somali–Chalbi Desert extends along a narrow band along the African shores of the Red Sea and Gulf of Aden southward along the east coast bordering the Indian Ocean to just south of the equator.

The Arabian Desert includes the nations of the Arabian peninsula and Jordan, Iraq, Israel, Syria, and a small part of Iran. Roughly a rectangle, its longer axis extends from southeast to northwest through the Arabian peninsula to the Mediterranean Sea. It includes the Syrian, Saudi, Aden and Tihama Deserts, and the very dry Rub'al Khāli.

Four phytogeographic regions have been recognized in the Asian continent: these are the Irano–Turanian, the Dzungaro–Kazakhstan, the 'Central Asiatic' or Mongolian, and the Tibetan. The last includes the high-elevation cold deserts of Pamir and Tibet.

The Iranian Desert, which includes parts of Iran, Afghanistan, and Pakistan is one of the smallest desert areas and one of the least known. It includes five major units: the Dasht-e-Kavir in the northwest, the Kavir-i-Namak in the north, the Dasht-e-Lut in the southwest, the Dasht-i-Naomid in the east, and the Dasht-i-Margo in the southeast.

The Turkestan Desert is bounded on the west by the Caspian Sea, and on the south by the mountains bordering Iran and Afghanistan, on the east by mountains bordering Sinkiang, and on the north by the Kirgiz Step. The region is an immense undrained basin with parts below sea level.

Desert and semidesert comprise the most extensive natural region of China; covering more than 1.75 million km² and extending to the middle of the Kwang Ho (Yellow River) in the east. The Gobi, largest desert in Asia, lies in Outer Mongolia (Mongolian Peoples' Republic) and mainland China's Inner Mongolian Autonomous Region. The deserts of Outer Mongolia change gradually, going northward into desert steppes and then into steppes. To the southwest of the Gobi lies the Takla–Makan; between them and south of the Gobi lie other desert areas, including notably the Bei Shan (Pieshan, Beichan), Tsaidam, Ala Shan (Ala-Chan), and Ordos.

The Patagonian Desert extends the entire length of Argentina, bordering the eastern face of the Andes Mountains to the west, and stretching eastward an average distance of about 600 km into the plains, and extending southward all the way to the sea. It forms a coastal desert and steppe for 1700 km.

The North American Desert extends southward from central and eastern Oregon, embracing nearly all of Nevada and Utah except the higher mountains, into southwestern Wyoming and western Colorado, reaching westward in southern California to the eastern base of the Sierra Nevada, the San Bernardino Mountains, and the Cuyamaca Mountains. From southern Utah, the desert extends into northeastern Arizona and western and southwestern Arizona. Desert areas extend southward along the eastern coast of northern Baja California, in the lee of the mountain ranges of Sierra de Juárez and Sierra de San Pedro Mártir. South of these ranges it extends across the peninsula as far south as the northern end of Sierra de la Giganta; farther southward it is limited to the Pacific coast. On the mainland it occupies the lowland of the state of Sonora, Mexico. The desert area extends into low elevations in New Mexico and western Texas. In Mexico it extends through eastern Chihuahua and nearly all of Coahuila and southward into central Mexico.

Climatic characteristics

The Somali–Chalbi area is under the intertropical convergence influence, but the rainfall is related to orography, thermal low pressure, and coastal upswelling.

The Kalahari–Namib Desert of southern Africa is a transition zone with tropical summer rains on its equatorward margins and winter cyclonic rainfall on its poleward borders.

The Namib Desert receives an average of less than 5 cm of rainfall but benefits from sea fogs and dews, and in areas it supports a scanty vegetation. The essential characteristic of the climate is its cloudiness, which results from a cold ocean current.

The Sahara is not only the largest desert, but also includes some of the hottest and driest areas and the greatest expanses of sand. The Sahara has a mediterranean climate in the north and a tropical climate in the south. The southern Sahara falls in the intertropical convergence zone with warm winters, hot summers, and a predominantly irregular and scanty summer rainfall. The Sahara has great uniformity from west to east; the north-to-south differences are similar in the west, the center and the east.

The Arabian Desert has been classified 'sub-desertic' to 'true desert'. The southern portion is much like the Sahara, with a small area of extreme aridity along the southwest coast of the Arabian Peninsula and a larger area in the southeast. Practically all of the peninsula is arid or extremely arid.

A mediterranean influence and winter precipitation govern in the northern third; scanty rainfall occurs any season of the year in the southern half. The southern portion is hot in all seasons; moving northward the winters gradually become milder, but without much, if any, relief from the summer heat.

The Iranian Desert has primarily a mediterranean climate with winter rainfall produced by cyclonic storm systems. The winters are cool and the summers hot.

The climate of the Irano–Turanian regions is subtropical, continental, and arid. The total annual precipitation is 100–200 mm with the maximum season being March–April. The spring is humid and warm.

The Thar, sometimes called the Indian Desert, includes the arid portions of western India and eastern Pakistan. Some authors identify the area eastward to the Aravalli Range and southward into Sind as arid. There is some question, however, as to how much of this area is naturally arid and how much of this arid appearance has resulted from the activities of man.

The Thar is a transition zone between major wind belts. Mid-latitude cyclones produce moderate amounts of winter precipitation in the northern and western portions, while the eastern portion receives its rainfall from the monsoon circulation that dominates the subcontinent in the summer. The monsoon movement of moist air terminates in western India, resulting in a small and irregular rainfall in the Thar. Summers are hot and winters warm throughout the area.

Except in the far north, the Turkestan Desert has a Mediterranean type of moisture distribution but with colder winters than in typical mediterranean climates. Throughout the area winters are mostly cold and the summers hot or very hot. The average precipitation varies from 75 to 200 mm, falling in winter or spring, leaving the summer months without precipitation.

The Takla–Makan and Gobi deserts can be considered as a unit. This is an area separated from major moisture sources by the orographic barriers or by great distance. The Tibetan plateau, roughly 3000 km in length with a mean elevation of about 4000 m, forms an effective barrier to moist air moving northward from the Indian Ocean. Mountain barriers and distance are important to the exclusion of moisture from sources to the west.

The Takla–Makan, in common with other Central Asian deserts, owes

11

its dry climate to the high mountains and great distance separating it from moisture sources. It is an area of hot summers and cold winters with no particular seasonality for the scanty precipitation. A large portion of the Takla–Makan is extremely arid. The remainder of the area is arid as far as can be determined from available records.

The climate of the Dzungaro–Kazakhstan region is moderately continental and moderately arid. The total annual precipitation is 80–150 mm with a spring–summer maximum. Spring is cool and wet.

Vegetation in the Central Asian deserts, grows at an altitude ranging from 300 m below sea level in the Turfan Depression to about 2000 m in the high desert. Mean annual precipitation seldom exceeds 100 mm and may be as low as 50 mm.

The driest parts are eastern Kashgaria, Bei Shan, and Tsaidam. In the Turfan and Hami Depressions, both of which are below sea level, the summers are hotter than in the tropics and the frost-free season is 240 days; elsewhere the vegetation must contend with extremely low winter temperatures (January means range from -6 to $-19\,°C$) and warm summers.

The climate of the Mongolian region is temperate, extra arid, and sharply continental. The precipitation season is related to the arrival of the eastern Chinese monsoon, the total is 10–100 mm and the maximum precipitation falls in the summer. The spring is dry, cold and windy.

The vegetation of the Gobi receives a rainfall varying from 50–80 mm in the western Gobi to 170 mm in the east; 80% of the rainfall occurs in summer, mostly in July and August. Temperatures affecting the plants range from -25 to $44\,°C$ with strong diurnal and yearly variations.

The vegetation of more than half of Australia must contend with arid conditions with less than 250 mm of rainfall per year. One fifth of the continent receives less than 125 mm. Although the deserts of Australia do not reach the dry extremes of some others, they are nevertheless sizeable and important.

The arid land of Australia is affected by tropical weather in the north and by midlatitude cyclones in the south. The climate is of the monsoonal type in the north and mediterranean type in the south. The entire area has mild winters and warm to hot summers.

The coastal deserts to South America, west of the Andes, owe their existence to the combined effects of the cold ocean currents and the stable eastern portion of a subtropical high-pressure cell.

The Atacama is the driest coastal desert in the world; with a precipitation at Arica and Iquique of less than 1.00 mm. At the southern limits of the Atacama, the annual rainfall is 64.5 mm. To the north the desert of Chile merges into the Peruvian coastal desert extending northward nearly to Equador.

12

The Peruvian coastal desert becomes slightly less arid northward as does the Atacama southward. The whole area has a mild climate year around with little variation in temperature from summer to winter. Heavy fogs and high humidity are the rule. The Peruvian portion is a narrow band dissected by more than forty transverse valleys.

The Monte–Patagonian desert of Argentina and Bolivia, occupying intermountain valleys where moist air currents rarely penetrate, can be thought of as a rainshadow desert. Precipitation, which occurs mostly in the summer, is generally less than 200 mm. Winters are cool and summers are mild.

The Patagonia Desert is the only high-latitude east coast desert in the world, and has no counterpart among the Earth's deserts. It owes its dryness to the Andes Mountains, which form a barrier to the rain-bearing air masses from the west, and to the cold Falkland current off the east coast.

The climate is cold temperate, very dry, and windy. Precipitation varies from 150 to 300 mm falling principally during the warm season.

The deserts of North America span a latitude range of about 20°, extending from the Tropic of Cancer on the south to about 40° N. Mountain barriers are most important on the northern boundaries and continue to be a factor as far south as Baja California. The seasonal shift of the wind belts from winter to summer brings moisture from the Gulf of Mexico, extending westward across Mexico and northward into the southwestern US. Its westward extent is to about the Arizona–California border and to parts of Baja California. In summer, the Pacific region of the desert comes under the influence of a stable eastern portion of a sub-tropical high pressure cell. The southern portion of the North America deserts has a summer maximum rainfall, the northern and western regions have winter maximum, and the intermediate regions, such as central Arizona, receive some precipitation in both seasons.

There is an extremely arid area around the north end of the Gulf of California with limited extension northward in California, including Death Valley. The Chihuahuan and Sonoran Deserts have a mild to hot climate and the Great Basin Desert has cold winters and warm summers.

Geomorphology and soils

The physical features of the Afro–Asian deserts, including physiography and soils, have much in common. They all have relatively small sandy areas (10% or less of total area), some mountainous areas, and large expanses of relatively flat land.

The Sahara embraces a variety of landscapes, including mountain massifs, great flat areas of stone and gravel, and huge expanses of sand. The

13

elevated plateaus, or *hammadas*, are often very extensive. Extensive sand dune areas called *ergs* have been formed from wind-blown sand. The largest of these *ergs*, located in the Libyan Desert, embraces an expanse of sand as large as France.

For the Sahara as a whole, sandy and stony materials are dominant, vegetative cover is very sparse, and susceptibility to wind-erosion is high.

The coastal-zone strip of the Somali–Chalbi Desert consists chiefly of raised coral reefs. Inland are extensive eolian and alluvial deposits and limestone areas. In the west and south are large areas of crystalline rocks, and volcanic rocks of various ages. The soils of the Somali–Chalbi are largely undeveloped. Stony plains are common, but sand dunes are largely restricted to coastal areas.

The Arabian peninsula has a basement of crystalline rocks that reaches an altitude of more than 3000 m in the western highlands. It is overlaid in places with sedimentary rocks and by great sand desert areas, including the great An Nafud or (Nefud) in the north and the Rub'al Khāli in the south-central area. Generally the Arabian Desert consists of sandy and stony materials, with fine-textured saline sediments occurring extensively in the lower Mesopotamian plain and in the plains of central Saudi Arabia. Sand dunes of the *erg* type occur in a broad arc extending from southern Jordan through northeastern and eastern Saudi Arabia to the vast expanse of the Rub'al Khāli.

Soils of the Iranian Desert are generally coarse-textured and un-developed. Commonly they are calcareous throughout the profile, deep except on rough, broken land, very low in organic matter, frequently covered with desert pavement.

For the Thar as a whole, the entire desert consists of level to gently sloping plains broken by some dunes and low, barren hills, interspersed with sandy and medium- and fine-textured surface materials. Soil salinity is high in the uncultivated fine-textured soils and much of the irrigated land. Sand dunes occur within the Thar Desert area of the Indus plain and more widely outside the plain.

The Turkestan Desert includes extensive sand dunes, loessial or alluvial plains, fine-textured depressions or river terraces, and flood plains. Stony and gravelly soils are confined to the footslopes of the mountains on the south and east and the plateaus in the northwest.

Two great sandy expanses are included: the Kara-Kum (meaning black sands), covering about 350000 km^2, and the Kyzyl-Kum (meaning red sands) covering about 200000 km^2.

The desert areas of Asia represent diverse conditions. The mean elevations are: Dzungaria, 150–600 m; Takla–Makan, 600–1200 m; and Tsaidam, 2700–3100 m. Some of the oldest geological formations are represented, with some sedimentary deposits and extensive Quaternary materials including alluvial and extensive eolian deposits. The Bei Shan and Ordos, like the Kazakh hilly area, are very ancient dry land areas (from the Cretaceous). The areas with the largest expanses of sands are the Dzungarian, Takla–Makan, and Ala Shan. 'Gobi' surfaces of varying types are widely distributed. Rocky and pebbly deserts predominate in this part of the world, in contrast to the Turkestan Desert. In general, the area lacks external drainage and receives very little rainfall; mean annual precipitation seldom exceeds 100 mm and may be below 50 mm.

Soils of the Takla–Makan Desert vary from coarse-textured sandy and gravelly material, with surface stones (gobi) on the footslopes of the mountains to sandy to medium-textured alluvial fans and plains becoming fine-textured in the river flood plains, and finally to the dunes of loose sand in the center.

The soils of the Dzungaro Kazakhstan are gray-brown, the vegetation growth shows a slight summer depression. Fewer ephemerals grow in this region than in the Irano–Turan.

The Gobi is a repeating sequence of mountains, gravelly and stony footslopes, plains, and gentle slopes and depressions, giving a mountain-and-basin landscape with some basins up to 30 km across. Sand dunes are extensive in some parts of the Gobi and may be found nearly anywhere on the plains; they are not nearly as extensive, however, as within the Takla–Makan. In addition to the widespread sand dunes, brown gobi soils are the most extensive types. The soils are coarse-textured, with lime accumulations in the subsoil. Saline soils occur in the many closed depressions and sodium-affected soils are common on the slopes.

The landscape of arid Australia gives the appearance of a vast plain interrupted by occasional desert mountains, large and small tableland and sand dunes with many saline depressions and flood plains of intermittent streams. The dominant soil colors are red and reddish-brown.

The sand dunes which are common, are fixed by a fairly dense vegetative cover. Soils include sand plains, coarse-textured and deep brown soils, red and brown hardpan soils, deep red earths of medium to fine texture, and saline and sodium-affected soils.

The Atacama section of Chile is characterized by coastal ranges rising to elevations of 900 to 1100 m. East of this is a depression consisting of a series of undrained basins 40–80 km wide. The floors of these basins are made up of alluvial fans from material washed down the canyons from the Andes. Soils of northern Chile include skeletal soils of mountains and plains, recent alluvial soils of the river valleys and old lacustrine soils.

The Monte–Patagonian Desert is located in the rain shadow of the Andes Mountains. The northern portion, the Monte, is an area of mountains, valleys, and extensive depressions occupied by saline deposits. The southern portion, the Patagonian Desert, consists of low tableland dissected by stream valleys.

No permanent streams reach the ocean from this area. The main landscape types are muddy depressions, salt pans, dunes, slopes, bad-lands, permanent rivers, mountain torrents, brackish soils, alluvial cones and tablelands. The soils grade from coarse to medium-textured toward the plains; in the valleys the soils are generally gravelly or sandy with saline soils occupying the small (and large) closed basins.

The terrain of the Patagonian Desert consists of extensive plateaus more than 1500 m high in many places. The plateaus slope toward the sea and end in cliffs along the coast. Because of the gravelly surface, wind erosion is slight in spite of the continuously strong winds. Low-lying soils tend to be marshy and remain wet throughout the year.

Together with the great variation in climate physiography and geology in the North American Deserts there is also a great diversity of soils. Sand dunes and hummocks are smaller and cover much smaller portions of the desert areas in North America than in desert areas of north Africa and Arabia.

Comparison of various deserts

The expanse of the Afro–Asiatic desert belt is astounding. A traveler could go from a point at the western coast of Africa to the western part of India and be in desert almost all the way. Throughout this trip he would encounter similar vegetation with many genera of plants represented across the entire area. To the north in Asia, he would find desert conditions with a few interruptions extending through Turkmeniya into Outer Mongolia and China to within a few hundred kilometers of the Yellow Sea. Along the southern route he would recognize many of the plant families familiar from the southwestern deserts of North America, and on the northern route he would find many of the plant families of the Great Basin represented.

There are few succulents in the Sahara and those that do occur belong to a different family from those in North America. In southern Africa, there are many succulents of great variety largely belonging to the family Euphorbiaceae, which has few succulent members in the United States.

The desert areas of Asia and of Africa have much in common; certain conditions of climate, terrain and soils occur in the deserts of both continents. The floristic regions of Afro–Asia are extensive, for example the Saharo–Sindian Region extends from the western Sahara in Africa far eastward into India.

In Australia, the traveler would be surprised to find the lack of spiny plants, and that the *Acacia* spp. are different in appearance from their relatives elsewhere. He would also find the principal grass of the desert (*Triodia basedowii*) substituted for the common shrubs of other deserts.

Between the deserts of North and South America, a traveler would find a great deal in common, even to the same species in some cases. Perhaps the greatest noticeable difference would be in the much greater development of the cushion type of growth in some of the arid areas of South America.

The fact that these desert areas have a great deal in common gives support to the concept that they can be considered as a unit, although a large one, with common characteristics when only major conditions are considered.

There may be some real differences, but many of the so-called differences reported in the literature are due to the differences in terminology used by various researchers. For example, a researcher in Africa may set the limit of the 'desert' at an annual precipitation of 100 mm, another in the United States at 300 mm. A comparison of vegetation between these two areas would show differences but likewise a comparison between the vegetation at the isohyets of 100 to 300 mm in the Unied States would show great differences. On the other hand, a comparison of vegetation at the 200 mm isohyets in Africa, the Palestine area, India, South and North America would show great physiognomic similarity, and many of the same families of plants would be found to be important in all the areas.

The Sahara is essentially a desert of herbs and small shrubs, with larger shrubs and trees appearing where moisture is most abundant. Ephemerals are common, particularly in the northern portion. Halophytes are found in the saline areas. A large portion of the central part of the Sahara is almost devoid of any plant life.

The vegetation of the Somali–Chalbi resembles that of the warmer parts of the Sahara and the southern Arabian Desert. Scanty vegetation grows in the area where annual precipitation falls below 100 mm and the dry period lasts six months or more. In areas where conditions are more favorable, the shrubs are larger, more closely spaced, and intermixed with grasses. Where average annual rainfall reaches or exceeds about 200 mm, shrub and tree savannas are found.

The same general type of vegetation as that found in the Sahara extends eastward across Asia and India. There is general agreement that this is a phytographical region with common characteristics. It has been called the Saharo–Sindian Region, extending from the Atlantic coast of North Africa through the Sahara, the Sinai Peninsula, extratropical Arabia, southern Iraq, Iran, West Pakistan, Afghanistan, and into India to Sind. The Arabian Desert also includes two other phytogeographical regions, the Irano–Turanian and Sudano–Deccanian. The former includes deserts and steppes in the cooler part of the desert and the latter in the tropical portion. In the north *Zygophyllum dumosum* is the key plant along with a large number of winter annuals and some succulent perennials. In the southern part the vegetation consists largely of ephemeral plants that grow

17

only following rains. Perennials include many halophytes but almost no true succulents. Some vegetation is found in the driest portion, even in the Rub'al Khāli.

The major phytogeographical regions are the Irano–Turanian and Saharo–Sindian. The vegetation tends towards Mediterranean types on the west. Many of the desert areas at the higher elevations with cold winters are dominated by *Artemisia herba-alba* communities similar in appearance to those found in the Great Basin Desert of the United States. In the south where the summers are very hot the plant population is quite scanty. The Irano–Turanian vegetation shows a clear spring maximum and a summer depression period. Ephemerals and ephemoeroids grow over much of the region.

The Thar lies near the eastern end of the Saharo–Sindian Region. The vegetation is influenced strongly by edaphic conditions, with communities varying distinctively among sand, gravel, and rock areas. Trees and shrubs appear to be more common, especially on open soils, than is average for the Saharo–Sindian.

The vegetation of the Turkestan Desert depends upon an average precipitation varying from 75 to 200 mm which falls in late spring and early autumn, leaving the summer and winter months without precipitation. The temperature range is great. The vegetation varies with soil conditions. *Poa bulbosa* is the dominant spring plant in the clay desert portion, which is the driest of all habitats. The stony deserts, which are also unfavorable for plant growth, support a sparse stand of small shrubs. The salt-desert areas have shallow water tables and an extremely scanty vegetation dominated by halophytic shrubs and a few summer annuals.

Of the Gobi and Takla–Makan group, organic life is most developed in the Ordos. Only in the deserts of Dzungaria does the vegetation approach the character and abundance of that in eastern Kazakhstan. Many other areas are barren. Adjacent to the flowing streams, there is a lush *tugai* vegetation. Elsewhere, the vegetation is sparse. The valley of the Tarim River contains dense sand and in some places impassable forests similar to the tugais of the Amy Dar'ya as they might have been before the trees were felled.

The sand deserts, which make up the greatest part of the area, support sparse herbaceous vegetation where moisture is low and a scanty woody vegetation on the more stabilized dunes. Halophytic vegetation occurs in the old valley, lake depressions, and river deltas.

The plant forms of the Mongolia region are predominantly brush and low brush. There is little grassy vegetation and ephemerals are almost completely absent. The vegetation growth in the south clearly decreases in the spring and summer. In the northern deserts of this region, only the spring decrease takes place.

The vegetation of the Gobi has eastern and western affiliations with the latter dominating. The vegetation of the Gobi plains is characterized by shrubs and semishrubs. On unstabilized dunes, grasses and some widely spaced shrubs are found. The vegetative cover is greatest on stabilized dunes and is dependent upon depth to the water table.

The most characteristic plants of Australian deserts are perennial evergreen tussock grasses called 'spinifex' and small trees and shrubs belonging to the genus *Acacia*. In depressions and on more saline soils, salt bushes and various members of the Chenopodiaceae are characteristic.

The Atacama–Peruvian Desert is almost without vegetation except along streams. On slopes moistened by mist or drizzle during the winter a sparse stand of *Tillandsia* sp. may exist with a few lichens in association. *Lomas*, barren mist-bathed slopes with ephemeral vegetation; occur between 150 and 1500 m above sea level.

Much of the Monte has a cover of resinous bushes, with Zygophyllaceae bushes being dominant. Many species are totally or partially aphyllous. Trees, if present at all, are found on river borders where they form gallery forests. Perennial grasses are limited to moist places.

The vegetation of the Patagonian Desert is dominated by widely spaced clumps of xerophytic grasses and low, cushion-type shrubs.

The vegetation of the North American Deserts is of two general types, sagebrush and saltbushes in the cooler portions, and mixed shrubs and succulents in the warmer portions. The southern deserts have large communities dominated by *Larrea tridentata* (creosote bush) with mixed stands of vegetation including large shrubs and small trees and a variety of succulents on the upper slopes.

References

Köppen, W. (1954). Classification of climates and the world patterns. In: *An introduction to climate*, 3rd edition (ed. G. T. Trewartha), pp. 225–6 and 381–3. McGraw-Hill, New York.

McGinnies, W. G. (1968). *Deserts of the World – An appraisal of research into their physical and biological environment*. University of Arizona Press, Tucson.

Meigs, P. (1953). World distribution of arid and semi-arid homoclimates. In: *Review of Research on arid zone hydrology*. Arid Zone Programme, **1**, 203–9. UNESCO, Paris.

UNESCO (1963). Bioclimatic map of the Mediterranean zone, explanatory notes. *UNESCO Arid Zone Research*, **21**.

Manuscript received by the editors March 1975.

2. North American deserts: their floral and faunal components

J. A. MACMAHON

Introduction

The problems of defining 'desert' are particularly well represented in North America, where the lands termed desert are seldom within the extremely arid zone of Meigs (1953). About 55% of the North American deserts are semi-arid, 40% arid and only 5% extremely arid.

In this discussion I define as desert the areas outlined in Fig. 2.1, realizing that in some cases, as an Egyptian colleague once said 'to me this is not a desert but a veritable botanical garden'.

For my purposes, four deserts are recognized: the Great Basin Desert, best represented in Utah and Nevada, but extending northward; the Mohave Desert, a local subdivision of extreme aridity in California, S. Nevada, and a small section of Arizona; the Sonoran Desert of Arizona, and the Mexican states of Sonora and Baja California; the Chihuahuan Desert barely entering the United States in New Mexico and Texas, and best developed in the Mexican states of Chihuahua, Coahuila, Durango, Zacatecas, San Luis Potosi, and Nuevo León.

The map (Fig. 2.1) of North American deserts is a 'best guess' based on literature and field verification of the distribution of both plant and animal components of the desert biota – a total community approach. This is somewhat different from most maps (e.g., Shreve, 1942) which rely only on plant distributions and usually on a few key species. Lowe (1955) extended the conventional Sonoran desert boundaries using animal data. I expanded on this in Barbour, MacMahon, Bamberg & Ludwig (1977), and attempt to use this philosophy for the boundary definitions of all deserts here. Specific details of boundary determination will be treated after the Vegetation and Fauna sections.

Physiography

Most of the North American desert region falls within one of the sub-divisions of the Basin and Range Province (Fig. 2.2), an area of well over 1 036 000 km².

The province is generally surrounded by parts of the main United States and Mexican Cordilleras (Fig. 2.2), and bisected into the Sonoran Desert and Mexican Highland Sections in Mexico by the Sierra Madre Occidental.

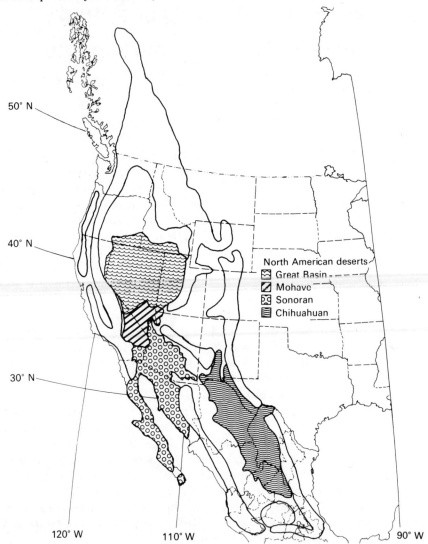

Fig. 2.1. Map of the deserts of North America. Boundaries are determined by plant and animal distributions. See text section 'The map' for a detailed justification. Areas of Cordilleras are outlined. Compare to Fig. 2.2.

The southern boundary in central Mexico is marked by a combination of the rich agricultural depression, the Bajío Province, and the Transverse Volcanic Cordillera.

The name of the province derives from its characteristic alternation of desert basins and adjacent mountains. The basins range from below

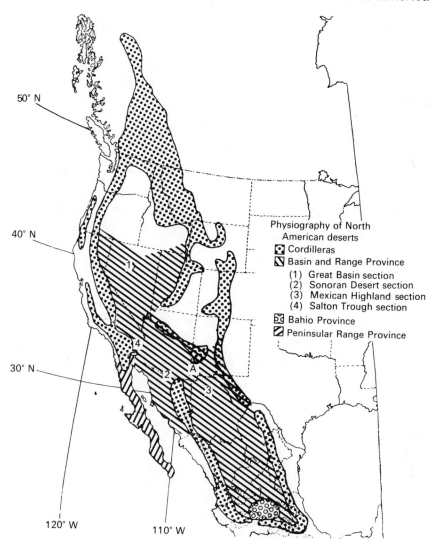

Fig. 2.2. Map of some regions of physiographic significance for a discussion of North American deserts. Sources of data include Fenneman (1931), Hunt (1974), Leopold (1959), West (1964). 'A' is the Deming Plain.

sea level (Death Valley, −86 m, and the Salton Sea, −71.7 m) to over 1525 m in parts of the Great Basin and southern sections of the Mexican Highland. The mountains may be up to 2500 m above the basins. Many of the basins are closed and have internal drainages from the surrounding mountains which may create seasonal *playa* lakes during the wet seasons and dry lakes and/or salt flats during dry periods. The ratio of the area

23

of basins to that of the surrounding mountains varies, but is generally over 1:1 and reaches 4:1 in many sections of the Sonoran Desert.

The origin of the Basin and Range Province may be traced to its development as a series of geosynclines beginning in the Precambrian and extending into the Mesozoic. During the Cretaceous the province was folded, faulted, and uplifted and an erosional sequence was begun which deposited to the east. In the Paleocene and Eocene, North America became essentially free of the marine embayments which during the Cretaceous extended from the Gulf of California to the Arctic Ocean; in the Rockies faulting and volcanism had uplifted tall mountains. During the Oligocene block faulting occurred, creating the basins and ranges. In addition, by middle Tertiary times extensive volcanic activity occurred in various places throughout the province. In late Tertiary mountains continued to lift and erode, and with the effects of Pleistocene activities provide the current landscape – mainly still in flux.

Of the subdivisions of the province (Leopold, 1959; Hunt, 1974) the Great Basin (about half of the province), Sonoran Desert, Salton Trough and Mexican Highland sections contain desert elements (Figs. 2.1 and 2.2).

The Great Basin section contains mainly northward-trending mountains of fair length. The valley floors may be more than 1525 m below the surrounding peaks. The mountains vary in their composition. Those to the north and east contain large amounts of Paleozoic limestone while those in the west contain sandstones and shales of volcanic rock derivation.

Two large adjacent pluvial basins are present in the northern part of the section. The Lahontan Basin butts against the Sierra Nevada, is generally covered by alluvium and contains mountains of Triassic or Jurassic rocks interspersed with more recent volcanics. The Bonneville Basin extending eastward to the Wasatch front in Utah is similar to the Lahontan, that is, much of the area is covered with alluvium. Three large lakes (Great Salt Lake, Utah Lake, Sevier Lake) persist.

Along the southern edge of the Great Basin section, Death Valley drains an area of over 23 000 km². Most of the remaining portion is drained by the Colorado River.

The Sonoran Desert section is composed of mountains, lower than those in the Great Basin section, derived from metamorphic rocks which due to their erosional resistance, have slopes of 20° or greater. Valleys seldom exceed elevations of 650 m. The southern portion of the section drains to the Gila and Colorado Rivers, or in Mexico directly to the coast. The northwestern portion has closed valleys.

The Mexican Highland Section (Central Plateau of many authors) contains the Chihuahuan desert and is characterized by high (up to 1525 m) valleys, surrounded by block-faulted mountains. The highest portions of this section are in the south (Jalisco to western Hidalgo), the lowest northward along the Rio Grande at the United States border.

Drainage systems are moderately well developed. The Arizona portion drains to the Gila River; New Mexico, Chihuahua, Coahuila and Nuevo León drain to the Rio Grande (Sanders, 1921; West, 1964).

The Salton Trough Section is limited in extent. A discussion of its physiography is found in Hunt (1974).

The only additional physiographic province of importance in a discussion of deserts is the Peninsular Range Province extending from the transverse ranges of southern California to the tip of Baja California, Mexico. The history of this area is dealt with in detail by Durham & Allison (1960). While I treat the Baja California deserts as an extension of the Sonoran desert, they exhibit many unique biological characteristics, due mainly to their peninsular character.

A physiographic feature of much of the Basin and Range Province is the development of *bajadas*, sloping alluvial fans, extending from the ranges, frequently coalesced into extensive areas occupying the basins. At low elevations in the Sonoran desert, *bajadas* may occupy 75% of the valley area (Shreve, 1942).

The effect of particle sorting down the length of a *bajada* is to accumulate coarse-grained to rock-sized soil particles at the top and sandy or even silty soils in the valleys. Such texture gradients regulate, to some extent, the plant and animal components of communities.

On the upper *bajadas*, in the areas of distinct alluvial sections arising from each drainage, the slope against the mountain may be from 6° to 9°. The lower *bajada*, by definition, is that area of coalesced alluvial fans, in the valley, which seldom rises more than one degree above the flood plain or *playa* (Dunbier, 1968).

Climate

The basic climate of each of the desert types is somewhat different. In fact the lay names for the deserts, that is, hot and cold deserts, allude to gross differences. Cold desert refers to the Great Basin, characterized by its northern position, higher elevation and predominantly winter moisture input (over 60%) in the form of snow.

The more southern hot deserts derive their moisture as rain either in the winter (Nov.–April, Mohave); the summer (May–Oct., Chihuahuan); or have a biseasonal rainfall in both the winter and the summer (Sonoran).

Aside from the seasonal timing differences, the origin and nature of hot-desert rainfall patterns varies. The winter rain of the Mohave and Sonoran deserts derives from Pacific Ocean cool westerly air currents with imbedded cyclones which provide rain of moderate intensity but long duration (a few hours to several days) (Hastings & Turner, 1965).

The summer rains of the Chihuahuan and Sonoran originate in cyclonic tracts in the Gulf of Mexico and move northwesterly as small, isolated, but extremely intense thunderstorm cells.

The biseasonality of the Sonoran desert rainfall (particularly in Arizona) and the progressive monoseasonality (winter rainfall to the north and west, summer to the southeast) is elegantly shown by a Fourier analysis where mean monthly rainfall is fitted by least squares to two sine curves (Bryson, 1957).

The predictability of the winter rainfall in any area is great compared to the summer rainfall (Turnage & Mallery, 1941).

The total rainfall (or rainfall plus snow equivalent) can be misleading. In the Great Basin, where moisture is mainly in the form of snow, much of the water enters the soil during the plant's dormant period and thus becomes unusable. In areas of cyclonic summer rains, the intense, short-duration rain may be dissipated by sheet flow across the soil surface and moved in the form of 'flash floods' through deep arroyos. This sequence allows little soil moisture recharge over most of the desert surface.

In the hot deserts, as the mean annual rainfall decreases, the year-to-year variation increases. For example Jaeger (1957) cites the example of Bagdad in the Mohave desert, which has a mean rainfall of 57.91 mm per year. During the period February 1917 to January 1920 only one month had any measurable rainfall, yet later a 12-month period had 251.46 mm.

Temperatures show fewer desert-by-desert patterns than rainfall. The obvious latitudinal and altitudinal gradients affect the distribution of desert communities.

The extreme high is probably reached in Death Valley (57 °C). Winters in hot deserts are moderate. The Great Basin may have a number of successive winter days below 0 °C. The average growing season can vary from 137 days in Reno, Nevada to 365 days in Guaymas, Sonora. No section of the North American desert is consistently above freezing. For example, in January 1937 a cold spell extending beyond the southern boundary of the Sonoran Desert to the Sonora–Sinaloa border damaged many temperate plant species (Turnage & Hinckley, 1938).

Temperature and rainfall data for a spectrum of desert sites are presented in the form of simplified Walter (1971) climatic diagrams and a summary table (Fig. 2.3; Table 2.1).

Soils

Discussions of North American desert soils are doomed to superficiality. When we remember the basic causes of soil-forming processes, i.e., parent

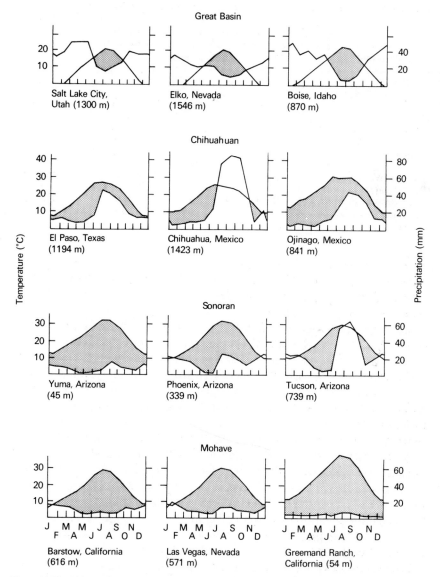

Fig. 2.3. Simplified climatic diagrams (Walter, 1971) representing four North American desert types. Elevations are in parentheses after the name of the United States Weather Bureau reporting station. Stippled areas represent periods when water is limiting.

Table 2.1. *General climatic data for some North American desert sites*

Locality	Annual precipitation (mm)	Average no. of days of precipitation	Average January temperature (°C)	Average July temperature (°C)
Great Basin				
Salt Lake City, Utah	408.2	91	−1.7	25.0
Reno, Nev.	179.8	49	0.0	21.7
Mohave				
Las Vegas, Nev.	104.9	26	7.2	30.0
Barstow, Calif.	114.3	18	7.8	30.0
Sonoran				
Tucson, Ariz.	267.5	23	10.0	30.6
Yuma, Ariz.	85.9	15	12.8	29.4
Chihuahuan				
El Paso, Texas	222.5	50	7.2	27.8
Ciudad Lerdo, Durango	244.1	33	13.9	26.7

material, climate, flora, fauna, topography, time, and of course man, and consider the diversity of each of these factors independently in the total extent of the North American deserts, the enormity of the task is clear.

My brief discussion will highlight the general processes and will be couched in terms of both older familiar soil terms and the recently evolving US Soil Conservation Service Comprehensive System.

Because the soil-forming process is still active in North American deserts we recognize two broad categories of soils. First are the genetic Aridisols. These soils contain subsurface layers of varying character including: (1) concentrated silica clay minerals – argillic; (2) sodium concentrations such that 15% of the exchangeable cations are replaced by sodium – natric; (3) an altered light-colored fine-textured layer, low in organics – cambic; (4) a 15-cm or greater salt layer more soluble in cold water than gypsym – salic; (5) a similar 15 cm layer with more than 15% $CaCO_3$ – calcic; (6) the same as (5), but with more than 5% gypsum and in which multiplication of gypsum percent by layer thickness (inches) gives more than 60% inches – gypsic; (7) a horizon cemented by silica such that water and acid will not slake – duripan (Fuller, 1974).

The second category includes all of those soils derived so recently that structure has not developed. These are very characteristic of, though, not confined to, desert zones. The common types of these are frequently termed: Lithosols – thin soils recently formed from parent material; Regosols – originating from unconsolidated parent material rather than massive rock (Lithosols), and including wind-blown deposits such as loess, volcanics and sand; Alluvium – water-transported soils not affected by soil processes (Stevens, 1964).

The abruptness of desert mountains in the Basin and Range Province keeps soil-formation processes active most of the time. Upper parts of *bajadas* are frequently Lithosols and as you go down, the force of water lays out Alluvium. Some *bajadas* and adjacent valleys are sufficiently stable that soil-forming processes are well advanced. In other areas Lithosols persist (e.g., many mountain slopes in the Chihuahuan desert contain such zones of rhyolitic origin (Rzedowski, 1966)).

The evaporation milieu of valleys which receive the characteristic internal drainages of the province cause the accumulation of calcium (Calcisols), gypsum or sodic (Solonetz) materials. These with other azonal types (sand dunes) may occur anywhere in the province.

The basins in the center of the province are driest (lower Great Basin and Sonoran Desert Sections) and increase in moisture both north and south.

There is a similar curve of temperature, i.e. the hottest basins are in the central part of the province. Basins are cooler to the north and south (at least into the Chihuahuan).

The Sonoran and Mohave Deserts and the northern half of the Chihuahuan have Red Desert soils (Aridosols). These are formed on deep valley fills of medium to coarse texture. The red color derives from the greater hydration of iron compounds in the arid heat. In the more mesic cooler southern Chihuahuan (remember elevation increases in the southern half of the Mexican Highland Section), Gray Desert soils, with calcareous horizons at various depths develop (Stevens, 1964).

In the Mohave–Great Basin area, desert soils grade northward into Sierozems of northern Nevada and Oregon. Sierozems differ from desert soils in their *B*-horizon clay accumulation (Fuller, 1974).

Three other phenomena of North American (and other areas also) desert soils should be pointed out. First, many areas, composed of cobbles or pebbles on the surface (desert pavement) (Springer, 1958) are covered by a patina of dark material on the rocks and adjacent soil surface. This 'desert varnish' is a black, hydrated ferromanganese oxide. The processes forming such varnishes start out geochemically but 'later involve the cation-scavenging properties of colloidal, hydrated MnO_2, as affected by chemolithotrophic bacteria' (Bauman, 1976). The process is similar to that forming deep-sea nodules.

Secondly, many desert communities, from all desert types, are covered by crusts composed of algae and lichens. These crusts fix nitrogen (Cameron & Fuller, 1960; Rodgers, Lange & Nicholas, 1966; MacGregor

& Johnson, 1971; Snyder & Wullstein, 1973). The dynamics of these crusts and the affect that their disturbance has on desert soil fertility is a topic of great interest.

Thirdly, the subsoil accumulation of calcium carbonate can become so dense that a thick petrocalcic layer, caliché, may form. The effect of this on desert plants has long been recognized (Shreve & Mallery, 1933).

Vegetation

At the outset of the biological sections it should be stated that I believe that the essential nature of communities is that they are the sum of a series of species, each of which has been able to get to – and survive in – that particular plot of earth. This is the 'individualistic' or 'continuum' bias (Gleason, 1939; Curtis & McIntosh, 1951; Whittaker, 1965; McIntosh, 1967).

This view causes me to consider formations, associations, etc., as convenient points along continua of species distributions, which we can use for purposes of discussion, rather than believing that these are discrete entities in nature. In short, if a species can get somewhere and survive there it will be part of that community. I am not surprised then to see Chihuahuan desert associations of plants in a Sonoran desert area which contains Sonoran desert animals, as I have in the Tucson, Arizona area (see also Whittaker & Niering, 1964, 1968).

The same reasoning is true for the evolution of 'floras'. Many species happen to be evolving together, but their relationships change spatially and temporally and we need not believe that all the species of a contemporary community were components of the same or even a closely similar paleocommunity. A similar viewpoint was expressed by Mason (1947) and Johnson (1968). McDonough (1963) alludes to this for current desert species.

Obviously the expressed viewpoint flavors every part of my discussions of biological topics, both plant and animal, and my treatment of the works of others.

General composition

The three hot deserts are so characterized by the distribution of creosote bush *Larrea tridentata* that, as an approximation, their aggregate distribution is similar to a *Larrea* distribution map (Benson & Darrow, 1954; Yang, 1970; Hastings, Turner & Warren, 1972).

Interestingly each of the three hot deserts has a different *Larrea* polyploid; diploid in Chihuahuan, tetraploid in Sonoran and hexaploid in the Mohave (Yang, 1970).

30

Fig. 2.4. Views of four North American desert types: (A) Mohave desert, Death Valley, California – mainly creosote bush (*Larrea tridentata*), some *Franseria*; (B) Sonoran desert, Organ Pipe Cactus National Monument, Arizona – note diversity of life forms and presence of a tall (>3 m) synusium; *Larrea tridentata*, lower left corner; *Opuntia bigelovii*, center; saguaro and organpipe cacti in background; (C) Great Basin, Curlew Valley, Utah – note monotonous aspect of big sagebrush (*Artemisia tridentata*) stands – some shadscale (*Atriplex confertifolia*) and winter snow between plants; (D) a Chihuahuan desert, Texas – note luxuriant shrubs (*Larrea*) left center, ocotillo (*Fouquieria splendens*) right center, and cacti (*Echinocereus*) foreground. Photos (A) and (C) by Neil West, (B) John Andre, (D) by Frederic Wagner.

Table 2.2. *Characteristic Sonoran desert plants. List is not meant to be comprehensive, merely to include genera or species likely to be encountered. Sources of data include: personal field notes; Hastings, Turner & Warren (1972) and Shreve & Wiggins (1964)*

Perennial shrubs	
Creosote bush	*Larrea tridentata* (Zygophyllaceae)
White bursage	*Franseria (Ambrosia) dumosa* (Asteraceae)
Bursage	*F. deltoidea*
Ocotillos	*Fouquieria splendens* or *macdougalii* (Fouquieriaceae)
Squawberry	*Lycium* sp. (Solanaceae)
Desert ratany	*Krameria* sp. (Krameriaceae)
	Jatropha sp. (Euphorbiaceae)
Jojoba	*Simmondsia chinensis* (Buxaceae)
Desert hackberry	*Celtis pallida* (Ulmaceae)
Cheesebush	*Hymenoclea* sp. (Asteraceae)
Brittlebush	*Encelia* sp. (Asteraceae)
	Sapium biloculare (Euphorbiaceae)
Desert zinnia	*Zinnia pumila* (Asteraceae)
Subtrees	
Paloverde	*Cercidium* sp. (Fabaceae)
Ironwood	*Olneya tesota* (Fabaceae)
Mesquite	*Prosopis glandulosa* (Fabaceae)
Boojum	*Idria columnaris* (Fouquieriaceae)
Elephant trunk	*Bursera* sp. (Burseraceae)
Acacias	*Acacia* sp. (Fabaceae)
Perennial grasses	
Fluffgrass	*Erioneuron pulchellum* (Poaceae)
Tobosa	*Hilaria mutica* (Poaceae)
Succulents(allCactaceae)	
Saguaro	*Cereus (Carnegeia) giganteus*
Cardon	*Cereus (Pachycereus) pecten-aboriginum*
	Opuntia dozens of cholla and beavertail types
Organpipe	*Cereus (Lemaireocereus) thurberi*
Senita	*Cereus (Lophocereus) schottii*
Barrel cactus	*Ferocactus* sp.
Fishhook cactus	*Mammillaria* sp.
Annuals	
Plantain	*Plantago insularis* (Plantaginaceae)
	Pectocarya heterocarpa (Boraginaceae)
Bird's foot trefoil	*Lotus* sp. (Fabaceae)
	Chaenactis carphoclinia (Asteraceae)
	Eriophyllum sp. (Asteraceae)
Phacelia	*Phacelia* sp. (Hydrophyllaceae)

The Great Basin Desert has no one species which is very abundant yet confined to its boundaries. Big sagebrush, *Artemisia tridentata* (Fig. 2.4*c*), so characteristic of this desert occurs south to Los Angeles Co., Calif., north into areas of Canada clearly not desert and at upper elevations in the Great Basin in association with spruce–fir forests. The other 'indicator' species, shadscale (*Atriplex confertifolia*), occurs into south-central Arizona and southern California.

Table 2.3. *Characteristic Mohave desert plants. Rejoinder as in Table 2.2.*
Data from field notes

Perennial shrubs	
Creosote bush	*Larrea tridentata* (Zygophyllaceae)
White bursage	*Franseria* (*Ambrosia*) *dumosa* (Asteraceae)
Squawberry	*Lycium* sp. (Solanaceae)
Brittlebush	*Encelia farinosa* (Asteraceae)
Indigo bush	*Dalea fremontii* (Fabaceae)
Goldenhead	*Acamptopappus shockleyi* (Asteraceae)
Desert ratany	*Krameria parvifolia* (Krameriaceae)
Subtrees	
Joshua tree	*Yucca brevifolia* (Liliaceae)
Succulents	
Beavertail	*Opuntia basilaris* (Cactaceae)
Mohave yucca	*Yucca schidigera* (Liliaceae)
Annuals	
Evening-primrose	*Oenothera* sp. (Onagraceae)
Sand-verbena	*Abronia turbinata* (Nyctaginaceae)
Gilias	*Gilia* sp. (Polemoniaceae)
Phacelias	*Phacelia* sp. (Hydrophyllaceae)
Wild buckwheat	*Eriogonum* sp. (Polygonaceae)

NOTE: Some 'subtrees' along washes, e.g., *Prosopis pubescens* (Fabaceae) and *Chilopsis linearis* (Bignoniaceae); Grasses and succulents rare.

It is necessary then to list (Tables 2.2–2.5) some species characteristic of each of the deserts, realizing that few of them have ranges conterminous with the particular desert and that any one site may be a potpourri of species depending on a myriad of biotic and abiotic factors.

Despite the infidelity of species to desert boundaries we can make some generalizations.

The Sonoran Desert (Fig. 2.4b) seems well differentiated by the dominance of several plant types. First, cacti of various forms; these include the opuntias (flat-padded beavertails; cylinder-padded chollas), the large tree-like (to 12 m) saguaros (Fig. 2.4b) and cardons (*Cereus*), the medium height but large organpipe (Fig. 2.5a) and senita and a host of small species. Secondly, there are numerous 'subtrees', i.e., very tall (to 10 m) shrubs with single bases, such as *Cercidium, Jatropha, Olneya,* some acacias, and *Prosopis*. The abundance of subtrees is greatest on the upper to middle parts of *bajadas* and increases as you go south to the Rio Mayo, the desert–thorn scrub transition (Gentry, 1942; Shreve & Wiggins, 1964).

Thirdly, there are so many shrub species that this desert, more than the others, is subdivided into local associations based on flora (Shreve & Wiggins, 1964; Hastings *et al.*, 1972).

The Mohave Desert (Fig. 2.4a) is probably a transition between the Sonoran and the Great Basin. It is singled out here because its physiognomy is one of a single, or at most two, low (< 1 m) synusia. Cacti, while

33

Table 2.4. *Characteristic Chihuahuan desert plants. Rejoinder as in Table 2.2. Sources of data include: personal field notes; Ochoterena (1945); Miranda & Hernandez (1963); Gomez-Pompa (1965); Rzedowski (1966) and McCleary (1968)*

Perennial shrubs	
Creosote bush	*Larrea tridentata* (Zygophyllaceae)
Apache plume	*Fallugia paradoxa* (Rosaceae)
Tarbush	*Flourensia cernua* (Asteraceae)
Sandpaper plant	*Mortonia scabrella* (Celastraceae)
White thorn	*Acacia constricta* (Fabaceae)
Crucifixion-thorn	*Koeberlinia spinosa* (Koeberliniaceae)
Guayule	*Parthenium* sp. (Asteraceae)
Candelilla	*Euphorbia antisyphilitica* (Euphorbiaceae)
Ocotillo	*Fouquieria splendens* (Fouquieriaceae)
Sumac	*Rhus trilobata* (Anacardiaceae)
Sotol	*Dasylirion wheeleri* (Liliaceae)
Leather plant	*Jatropha spathula* (Euphorbiaceae)
Silverleaf	*Leucophyllum* sp. (Scrophulariaceae)
Subtrees	
Mesquite	*Prosopis glandulosa* (Fabaceae)
Perennial grasses (Poaceae)	
Muhly	*Muhlenbergia* sp.
Dropseed	*Sporobolus* sp.
Buffalo grass	*Buchloe* sp.
Burrograss	*Scleropogon* sp.
Succulents	
	Cereus (Myrtillocactus) geometrizans (Cactaceae)
Lechuguilla	*Agave lecheguilla* (Agavaceae)
Palmilla	*Yucca elata* (Liliaceae)
	Opuntia many beavertail species (Cactaceae)
Fishhooks	*Echinocactus* sp. (Cactaceae)
Hedgehogs	*Echinocereus* sp. (Cactaceae)
	Yucca sp. a number of species
Annuals	
Wild buckwheat	*Eriogonum* sp. (Polygonaceae)
Spurge	*Euphorbia micromera* (Euphorbiaceae)
	Bahia sp. (Asteraceae)
	Iva ambrosiaefolia (Asteraceae)
Desert marigold	*Baileya multiradiata* (Asteraceae)

NOTE: 'Subtrees' mainly along washes – *Yucca* and *Agave* give appearance of subtrees; *Koeberlinia* sometimes a subtree.

present, are not as diverse with respect to species or lifeforms as in the Sonoran. Subtrees are essentially absent, with the exception of the tree-like *Yucca brevifolia* – Joshua tree (Fig. 2.5b). The annuals flora is very rich (any one site having as many as 70 species). The extreme aridity causes some of the greatest aspect dominance contrasting high and low rainfall winters.

Table 2.5. *Characteristic Great Basin desert plants. Rejoinder as in Table 2.2. Sources of data include personal field notes and Billings (1949)*

Perennial shrubs	
Big sagebrush	*Artemisia tridentata* (Asteraceae)
Horsebrush	*Tetradymia glabrata* (Asteraceae)
Mormon tea	*Ephedra viridis* (Ephedraceae)
Hop-sage	*Atriplex spinosa* (Chenopodiaceae)
Bitterbrush	*Purshia tridentata* (Rosaceae)
Rabbitbrush	*Chrysothamnus nauseosus* (Asteraceae)
Shadscale	*Atriplex confertifolia* (Chenopodiaceae)
Black sagebrush	*Artemisia spinescens* (Asteraceae)
Blackbrush	*Coleogyne ramosissima* (Rosaceae)
Winterfat	*Eurotia (Ceratoides) lanata* (Chenopodiaceae)
Greasewood	*Sarcobatus* sp. (Chenopodiaceae)
Perennial grasses	
Galleta	*Hilaria jamesii* (Poaceae)
Squirreltail	*Sitanion hystrix* (Poaceae)
Speargrass	*Stipa speciosa* (Poaceae)
Annuals	
Cheatgrass	*Bromus tectorum* (Poaceae)
Wild buckwheat	*Eriogonum* sp. (Polygonaceae)
	Vulpia octoflora (Poaceae)
	Halogeton glomeratus (Chenopodiaceae)
	Bassia hyssopifolia (Chenopodiaceae)
Russian-thistle	*Salsola kali* (Chenopodiaceae)
Shield-cress	*Lepidium perfoliatum* (Brassicaceae)

Succulents and subtrees are rare or absent.

The Great Basin (Fig. 2.4c) contains few shrub species. This causes a monotonous aspect, particularly where *Artemisia* and *Atriplex* predominate. Grasses (*Agropyron, Oryzopsis, Poa* and *Sitanion*) are abundant and increase northwardly and with elevation. The annuals flora is dominated by old-world imports (*Bassia, Descurainia, Kochia, Lepidium, Halogeton, Bromus*).

The Chihuahuan occurs on predominantly limestone soils. The high elevation, moderate rainfall (for deserts), of most sites, favours high shrub density, moderate diversity and fair stands of grasses. Liliaceous plants (*Yucca* (Fig. 2.5c) and *Dasylirion*) are diverse, abundant and conspicuous as are agaves (Agavaceae). Few subtrees occur except along washes. Cacti are very diverse in terms of species, but less so in lifeform than in the Sonoran. This generalization breaks down somewhat in the south, where large cacti occur (Rzedowski, 1955).

A comparison of the twelve dominant plants of each desert shows only *Larrea, Fouquieria* (Fig. 2.5d) and *Prosopis* common to the Sonoran and Chihuahuan. I agree with Shreve (1942) that this gives an exaggerated view of the floristic *dissimilarity*.

Fig. 2.5. Four typical plants of North American deserts. (A) Organ pipe cactus, *Cereus*
(*Lemaireocereus*) *thurberi*, characteristic tall cactus of the Mexican portion of Sonoran
Desert. Lifeformwise this species is somewhat similar to cactus species in the southern
portion of the Chihuahuan Desert. (B) Joshua tree, *Yucca brevifolia*, indicator species of
higher elevations of Mohave desert. (C) Palmilla, *Yucca elata*, a common Chihuahuan yucca
on higher or mesic sites. Tree form typifies several species in Mexican section of the desert.
Note the tobosa (*Hilaria mutica*) swale around plant. (D) Ocotillo (*Fouquieria splendens*)
occurs throughout Sonoran and Chihuahuan deserts. May occur as solid stands or a major
dominant in many parts of Chihuahuan. Background subtree (*Cercidium microphyllum*),
foreground small shrub (*Franseria* (*Ambrosia*) *deltoidea*).

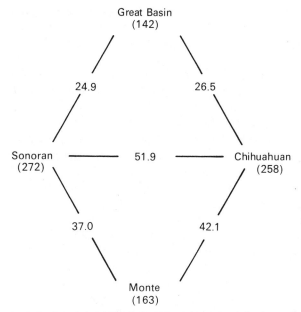

Fig. 2.6. Generic similarity of three North American deserts and the Argentinian 'Monte'. Similarities (numbers on lines) are calculated as the coefficient of similarity (Preston, 1962) of floras. Total number of genera is in parentheses. Data from Rzedowski (1973).

For all of the deserts, species lists *per se* are deceptive. The desert areas of North America, with minor breaks, extend unbroken from south-eastern Oregon to central Mexico. It is not surprising then that species distributions form a continuum with few *absolute* breaks.

The floral similarities of three North American and one South American desert types, at the generic level, are shown in Fig. 2.6. The Sonoran and Chihuahuan are most similar to each other and each is more similar to the distant Argentinian 'Monte' than either is to the Great Basin.

Vegetation subdivisions

While in this section I do not attempt to discuss every vegetation type ever suggested, I do attempt to include most variants recognized in major vegetational reviews of the United States and Mexico.

The Great Basin Desert is most frequently divided into two types, sagebrush associations and shadscale associations (Fautin, 1946; Billings, 1949).

The sagebrush (Fig. 2.4c) association is generally more northern, higher in elevation and on more mesic, less saline sites with brownish soils. The dominant species, big sagebrush (*Artemisia tridentata*) frequently makes up 65–90% of the community. Bitterbrush (*Purshia tridentata*) and black-brush (*Coleogyne*) are common associates, as are some perennial grasses (e.g., *Agropyron*) (Küchler, 1964).

The shadscale association occurs on dry or saline sites with Gray Desert soils. The association butts against the *Larrea*-dominated Mohave sites in the south. Associates of shadscale (*Atriplex confertifolia*) are *Artemisia spinescens*, *Ephedra* sp., *Eurotia lanata*, *Grayia spinosa*, *Lycium* sp. and *Sarcobatus baileyi* (Billings, 1945, 1949).

The ranges of these seven shrub species overlap in an area of 250 by 100 km in west central Nevada. Since all characteristic species of the association are not conterminous, the constituents of the association change from place to place. This variable definition is the problem alluded to previously and an example of the rationale for using best, average distributions for boundary definitions.

The Mohave Desert is seldom subdivided other than into those low-elevation, hot sites not containing joshua tree (*Yucca brevifolia*) (Fig. 2.5 *b*) contrasted to higher elevation, cooler, upper *bajada* sites where joshua tree persists and other yuccas flourish (Shelford, 1963). Some hot, local areas contain very unusual and striking plant groupings, e.g. the nearly pure stands of desert holly (*Atriplex hymenelytra*) in Death Valley (Hunt, 1966, 1975).

The Sonoran Desert, as mentioned, is frequently subdivided on the basis of vegetation. This has been done on the basis of vertical zonations along the gradients of *bajadas*, for example, the paloverde–saguaro community on the upper *bajadas* contrasted to creosote bush–bursage lower down (Lowe, 1964; Whittaker & Niering, 1964). Such gradients, particularly since they involve the addition or loss over short distances of conspicuous elements (tall cacti and subtrees), are important in community definitions. It is difficult to define boundaries in this case and all such variants are termed Lower Sonoran life zones.

Superimpose on the *bajada* gradient the north–south gradient of rainfall and temperature from Arizona to the Rio Mayo, Sonora, Mexico and the concomitant plant species shifts and one discovers that, while the community physiognomy is similar, many species replacements occur. Frequently this involves congeners, e.g. *Cercidium microphyllum* and *C. floridum* exchange on *bajadas*, *C. praecox* becomes abundant in Sonora, some Sonoran sites contain the rather limited *C. sonorae* and southern Baja California has the endemic *C. peninsulare*.

Other similar shifts involve not only the types of species replacement and overlaps mentioned, but may also involve intrageneric life-form shifts, e.g., *Jatropha cardiophylla*, *J. cinerea*, *J. cordata*, *J. cuneata*, *J. vernicosa* and the various *Cereus* species (Shreve & Wiggins, 1964; Hastings *et al.*, 1972).

One conspicuous trend, alluded to before, is that as you go south from Arizona, subtrees increase in density and diversity and there are more species of tall cacti.

Despite these broadly overlapping species gradients, Shreve & Wiggins (1964) identify several general Sonoran subsections.

The Lower Colorado Valley region lies around the top of the Gulf of California and extends slightly into extreme western Sonora and extreme eastern Baja California. The area is dominated by *Larrea–Franseria dumosa* communities, and is the most simple part of the nonpeninsular Sonoran desert.

The Arizona Upland region is mainly a section covering the eastern half of the Sonoran Desert in Arizona. This is an area more diverse in terms of species and life forms than the Lower Colorado Valley, and is the 'typical' Sonoran Desert of the United States (Fig. 2.4*b*). Here the vegetation gradients of *bajadas* define local associations.

The Plains of Sonora region lies between the foothills and the coastal strip in central Sonora. It is a zone of low relief, and regular surface. The senita and organpipe cacti, brittlebush (*Encelia*) and the ironwood (*Olneya*) are the most characteristic forms. Many chollas also occur.

The Foothills of Sonora region is defined on the west by a line from Arizpe to Guaymas, on the east and north by the mountains and in the south by the Rio Mayo or Rio Yaqui. As Shreve & Wiggins (1964) state, this is the least desert-like region. There is a strong influence of the thorn-scrub coming from the south. Many subtrees (*Bursera odorata*, *Jatropha cordata*, *Cercidium*, and others) occur. Shrubs are also important, giving the vegetation a dense aspect (Gentry, 1942).

Aside from the small section of the northeastern Gulf Coast which belongs to the Lower Colorado Valley region, Baja California contains three Sonoran regions.

The Central Gulf Coast region is a section of the Gulf Coast of Baja extending from Isla Angel de la Guarda to San Jose del Cabo. In addition a portion of the coast of Sonora, across the Gulf, extending from the Rio Magdalena to the mouth of the Rio Yaqui is included.

The physiognomy of the two separate regions is similar. Species composition overlaps, yet each geographic area has some species not shared with the other.

Generally the region is one of low and unpredictable rainfall. Shreve & Wiggins (1964) give as the unique feature the fact that many of the subtrees have 'trunks of exaggerated diameter'. These include: *Bursera microphylla*, *Jatropha cinerea* and *Idria columnaris*. While this is true, these species are usually not dominants – the more normal *Olneya*, *Cercidium*, etc., prevail. Additionally, none of the 'characteristic species' is confined to the region, e.g., I have collected *B. microphylla* in the Sierra Estrella near Maricopa, Arizona. Certainly *Idria* is much more characteristic of other parts of Baja California (Humphrey, 1974).

Description of arid ecosystems

The Vizcaino region occupies the central third of the Pacific Ocean coast of the Baja peninsula. The area is one of light winter rainfall. High humidity permits the dominance of lichens and the epiphyte *Tillandsia recurvata* (also common in the extreme southern sections of the Chihuahuan).

Various leaf succulent species (*Agave*) are abundant. *Franseria chenopodifolia* occurs widely, as does boojum (*Idria columnaris*). Detailed descriptions of the vegetation and photographs are given by Humphrey (1974).

The Magdalena region occupies the southern third of the peninsula's Pacific Coast. Boojum does not occur in this area and leaf succulents are less common. Several endemic species occur, e.g. *Cercidium peninsulare* and *Fouquieria peninsulare*. Shreve & Wiggins (1964) suggest that the most representative plants are *Lysiloma candida* and *Machaerocereus gummosus*.

Subdivisions of the Chihuahuan desert are not as clearly defined as one is led to believe they are in the Sonoran. Generally, authors have recognized only two or three subdivisions (Brand, 1936; Muller, 1939, 1947; Shreve, 1942; Leopold, 1950; Miranda & Hernandez, 1963; Gomez-Pompa, 1965; Rzedowski, 1966). Part of the problem comes from the confusion of complex soil mosaics, i.e. gypsophilic dune areas, slopes of rhyolitic origin, rocks of limestone origins, etc.

The three most often mentioned zones, physiognomically defined, include a microphyllous desert scrub (*Larrea* and *Flourensia cernua*) (creosote-bush desert of Leopold) which includes, depending upon soils, arroyos, etc., *Acacia constricta* and other *Acacia* sp., *Condalia*, *Celtis*, *Lycium* sp. and in the extreme southern Mexican section some of the large cactus, *Myrtillocactus geometrizans*, and the large *Yucca filifera*.

This formation is the main type in New Mexico and parts of Texas. Many beaver-tail opuntias are common, and locally *Parthenium* sp., *Mortonia scabrella* and *Jatropha dioica* or *Koeberlinia spinosa* may predominate.

The second formation (Rzedowski; 1966) is a rosettophyllous desert scrub which includes *Agave lecheguilla*, *Yucca carnerosana*, *Euphorbia antisyphilitica*, *Parthenium argentatum*, *Hechtia glomerata*, and *Dasylirion* sp. Cover may be 50%. This same formation was called 'Cactus Zone' by Leopold (1950). In some areas this formation takes on a number of tall shrubs or subtrees.

The third vegetation formation is the crassicaulescent formation which is dominated by large cacti (*Opuntia leucotricha*, *O. streptacantha*, and *Myrtillocactus*). These communities occur on rhyolitic and basaltic soils and on alluvium. Legumes of some sort are codominants. These include *Mimosa biuncifera*, *Prosopis*, *Acacia* sp., and in places, *Cassia*.

There is no community in the United States quite like the crassicaulescent formation. The other two formations, with mainly the same domi-

40

nant species occur in New Mexico (mainly microphyllous) and Texas (microphyllous and rosettophyllous). Few localities within the United States contain these communities at their highest development.

The vegetation at the southern boundary of the Chihuahuan and somewhat on the southeast and southwest sides, blends into a thorn-scrub sharing many similarities, at the genus level, with the Sonora–Sinaloa thorn scrub. I would reemphasize here the close generic affinities of the Sonoran and Chihuahuan floras (Fig. 2.6). As we will see later, their origins are close and their histories are seldom completely separate.

Azonal vegetation

Many local areas contain species which are adapted to extreme local conditions. These species, or their relatives, are frequently of wide occurrence wherever the unusual condition occurs. In desert areas, sand dunes, areas of high salt concentration, and the borders of washes are of this type.

In the Chihuahuan Desert, the local areas of gypsophilous soils or sand dunes (e.g., White Sands National Monument, New Mexico) are azonal situations (Emerson, 1935; Johnston, 1941; Waterfall, 1946). These contain a total of twenty-eight gypsophilic species including *Muhlenbergia villifora, Dicranocarpus parviflorus, Nama carnosum, Dalea filiciformis,* and *Coldenia hispidissima.*

Sand dunes generally, depending on their stability, contain a variety of grasses. Sand sage *Artemisia filifolia* occurs in sand areas from Utah to Chihuahua. Mesquite, *Prosopis glandulosa*, does quite well in sand areas and is a dominant in its prostrate form over large areas of sand in New Mexico and Mexico.

Wash or arroyo borders may harbor trees or subtrees in desert areas where such plants could not otherwise exist. In the North American deserts common species of these situations include mesquite, *Prosopis glandulosa*; desert willow, *Chilopsis linearis;* apache plume, *Fallugia paradoxa*; the introduced *Tamarix pentandra*; and arrow weed *Pluchea sericea*. Various *Acacia* species may also be abundant along washes (Gardner, 1951).

Saline areas are frequently in basins with internal drainage, or in local depressions. In either situation *playas* may develop.

The vegetation of saline areas varies from tobosa swales (*Hilaria mutica*) to large areas of saltbush desert (various *Atriplex* species).

In some situations widely distributed salt-tolerant plants occur. These include species of *Salicornia, Suaeda, Kochia, Allenrolfea, Distichlis, Sarcobatus* and *Hordeum* (Branson, Miller & McQueen, 1967; Ungar, 1974).

Description of arid ecosystems

Origins of the vegetation

In Eocene through Miocene times there were no mountains between the Pacific Ocean and the Rockies. The Basin and Range Province was a plain with rolling hills and minor mountains.

In the Miocene the northern part (above about 40° latitude) of the province was occupied by the Arcto-tertiary geoflora (Chaney, 1947). (Although it should be noted that controversy about the geofloras exists, these are problems more with earlier periods than those of importance to a discussion of deserts. For a discussion of the controversy see Wolfe, 1969, 1972, 1975.) South of 40° the landscape was covered with the oak woodlands of the Madro-tertiary geoflora (Axelrod, 1958). With such low topographic relief both vegetations probably overlapped broadly.

During Pliocene and Pleistocene the Cascade–Sierra Nevada mountain axes developed, creating a rainshadow in the Great Basin Section of the Province.

To the south since the Eocene there has been a decrease in rainfall (MacGinitie, 1958) and the development of isolated local rainshadows (Axelrod, 1967) or even edaphic drought zones (Axelrod, 1972). Xerophytic plants of these areas were preadapted to desert conditions.

In the Sonoran Desert and Mexican Highland Sections, rainshadow effects were not too important. These desert areas depend more on subsiding subtropical dry air which causes the northern and southern global desert bands (Logan, 1968).

Parts of Baja California derive their aridity from the effect of coastal currents.

By the time the Cretaceous seas left, the area up to 55° latitude in the Great Basin contained tropical and subtropical elements. Canada contained Arcto-tertiary floras generally similar to contemporary eastern United States.

Of course elevational effects permitted migration of these forests far southward in the Cordilleras. This situation caused the interfingering of Neotropic-tertiary and Arcto-tertiary elements through the Eocene.

During the Oligocene the Madro-tertiary flora (Axelrod, 1958) was distinguishable and probably occupied low-lying areas with semiarid climates. Genera of this flora included *Acer*, *Bursera*, *Cercocarpus*, *Prosopis*, and others (MacGinitie, 1953; Darrow, 1961). All indications are that extensive grasslands were established in North America by this time.

By Miocene times the drying continued above 40° latitude in the Great Basin. Temperate conifer and hardwood forests persisted. South of 40° latitude the Madro-tertiary flora, in areas that would become today's hot deserts, contained some of the progenitors of the current desert floras developing as the Neotropic–Madro-tertiary flora transition.

42

The Pliocene period, with its mountain building and associated rain-shadows, emphasized the Basin and Range aridity. This caused a north-ward movement of the Madro-tertiary elements into areas previously too moist. Recent dating studies suggest that this northward movement of arid forms may have occurred millions of years earlier, i.e. lower Miocene (Evernden & James, 1964).

No modern desert flora, related to the hot deserts, was known, but it is believed (Axelrod, 1950; Darrow, 1961; Johnson, 1968) that the current Great Basin Desert species were developing at middle elevations.

A number of contemporary Sonoran Desert species have equivalents in the Mohave Desert during the Miocene and Pliocene. These include *Acacia greggii, Acalypha californica, Baccharis sarothroides, Bursera microphylla, Cercidium floridum, Condalia* sp., *Lycium* sp., *Prosopis glandulosa*. These forms may have been displaced from the Mohave by the advent of climatic changes forming the current cool, winter rainfall dominated systems.

Johnson (1968) suggests that 'the presence of annual plants, some apparently adapted to cool moist conditions for germination and others to warm moist conditions, is also taken as evidence supporting a long existing distinction between the two deserts'.

Axelrod believes that eventually the genera *Chrysothamnus, Eriogonum, Grayia, Salvia,* and *Tetradymia* originated on the margin of the southwardly retreating Neotropic-tertiary flora. Simultaneously in the northern Great Basin Arcto-tertiary shrub derivatives, able to withstand dry sites, occupied the drier forest sites. These forms include genera common in contemporary sagebrush and shadscale communities, e.g. *Atriplex, Artemisia, Eurotia*.

The fossil data suggest that by, or during the Pliocene, most of the families (or infrafamilies) which are now arid or semiarid endemics within North America had either developed in place (Agavaceae, Canotiaceae, Fouquieriaceae, Koeberliniaceae, Krameriaceae, Simmondsiaceae) or made the 'long jump dispersal' from South America (Solbrig, 1972; Raven & Axelrod, 1974). The latter is the case for all of the amphitropical disjunctions of forms common to the Argentinian 'Monte' and the Sonoran–Chihuahuan complex. The generic similarity of these two floral areas is greater than the North American hot deserts are to the proximate Great Basin (Rzedowski, 1973 and Fig. 2.6).

Desert genera with no populations occurring in between the Neotropical and the Nearctic arid areas include *Allenrolfea, Coldenia, Condalia, Encelia, Flourensia, Franseria, Gutierrezia, Larrea,* and others.

Pleistocene times brought with the glaciation the alternating pluvial (cool, moist) and interpluvial (warm, dry) periods. There is abundant evidence of these trends (Martin, 1963; Martin & Mehringer, 1965; Wright, 1971).

43

Description of arid ecosystems

The extremes of cooling and expansion of boreal elements drove arid desert elements into either local savannah areas or into larger refugia southward in Mexico (see Figure in Savage, 1960). Obviously, the Sierra Madre split the arid zone into Mexican Highland and Sonora–Sinaloa subsections. Coastal California and peninsular Baja California may also have provided refuge. For some species, differentiation took place in isolation, for others, separated populations were compatible when they remet. These possibilities are represented by the well studied flora and fauna of Baja California (see entire symposium 1960, *Systematic Zoology* **9**, 47–232).

Another mode of flora origin is that of species developing in place in North America from mesic forms in mountains. This group would be expected to have more species outside the desert, to have its whole fossil record North American, and to have a large number of endemics (no close relatives north or south). Johnson (1968) includes in this group *Linanthus*, *Mimulus*, *Astragalus*, *Gilia*, *Phacelia*, *Eriogonum*, and *Calochortus*.

It is clear that various genera have quite different origins, got to the deserts at different times, had different histories in and fidelities to deserts and in recent times have been differently affected by contemporary environments. The deserts we see are the result of independent populations edited by time and the environment to produce present 'communities'.

Biology

In this section, as in the parallel animal section, my goal is to treat *some* biological attributes of North American desert species. The attributes of greatest interest are those which seem to affect the distribution of the species. Additionally I attempt to include reference to important biological studies of some characteristic species.

Soils

The intimate relation between the plant and the soil obviously affects community composition. We need not review again extremes such as salt flats, gypsum dunes, etc.

Studies reveal differences in species along *bajada* soil gradients (Yang & Lowe, 1956; Niering, Whittaker & Lowe, 1963; Whittaker, Buol, Niering & Havens, 1968; Barbour & Diaz, 1973).

The general trend is that as one goes up the *bajada* (increasing soil coarseness) *Larrea* decreases in cover, going from 60% or more of the cover to being codominant with several (up to six or eight) other species. Additionally upper parts of *bajadas*, especially in the Sonoran, have a greater diversity of lifeforms. Klikoff (1967) attributed similar changes

44

to moisture stress patterns. Barbour & Diaz (1973), while seeing changes in moisture gradients, found that coarse soils vs fine, under similar moisture regimes, still affect the vegetation as stated.

Where shrub density increases on such gradients, and where the species have loose-knit canopies (e.g. *Larrea* and *Cercidium* as opposed to *Franseria*), annuals density increases (Halvorsan & Patten, 1975). It should be pointed out that species like *Franseria* and *Larrea* have toxic chemicals (Muller, 1953; Muller & Muller, 1956) thought to be capable of killing annual seedlings, but these seem not to be effective in nature. The positive effect of some shrubs on annuals was attributed to increased organic matter at their bases (Muller, 1953). One study showed fewer annuals in hummocks developed under *Larrea*, *Prosopis* and *Cercidium*. This effect was reported to be caused by greater water repellency (Adams, Strain & Adams, 1970).

In the Great Basin, Mitchell, West & Miller (1966) found no correlations between plant distribution and some soil physical properties across a stark vegetation change from monospecific stands of *Atriplex nuttallii* to a monospecific stand of *Eurotia lanata*. Similar results occurred in studies of more Great Basin species (Gates, Stoddart & Cook, 1956). Fautin (1946) alludes to soil characteristics as controls of plant species composition in the Great Basin.

The development of a petrocalcic soil layer (caliche) (Gile, Peterson & Grossman, 1966) may modify plant distributions (Shreve & Mallery, 1933). In the Chihuahuan, as the caliche became better developed the density of *Larrea* decreased and *Krameria parvifolia* increased (Burk & Dick-Peddie, 1973).

Calcium content, regardless of caliche, is also significant. Rzedowski (1955) compared Chihuahuan plants characteristic of calcareous and igneous soils. The igneous substrate flora contained large cacti (*Myrtillocactus geometrizans*, *Lemaireocereus* and some *Opuntia* sp.). Yuccas, agaves and *Parthenium* occurred on calcareous soils. Anthony (1954) found most small desert *Opuntia* species on calcareous soils. Whittaker & Niering (1968) describe an essentially Chihuahuan Desert plant assemblage from a limestone area in the middle of the Sonoran Desert. Beatley (1975) found *Coleogyne ramosissima* confined to limestone soils in the Great Basin.

Moisture and temperature

The effect of increasing moisture in desert systems is initially to increase plant density and productivity. Ultimately, too much water obviously destroys desert communities.

It has been suggested that the Mohave–Great Basin transition is caused

Description of arid ecosystems

by the marked increase in rainfall (and decreased temperature) eliminating *Larrea* (Beatley, 1974a; 1975). Beatley (1974a) also showed that for the northern Mohave, *Larrea* cover increases with rainfall over the low- to intermediate-rainfall ranges and decreases with increasing rain in high-rainfall areas. Barbour & Diaz (1973) record increases in *Larrea* cover and density with rainfall on a Sonoran transect. They found no correlation in species richness to moisture. This noncorrelation probably is not true in the southern Sonoran where the desert areas are invaded by thorn scrub species in slightly more mesic sites.

An interesting effect of increased moisture was shown by Johnson, Vasek & Yonkers (1975). They studied road-edge plants in the Mohave and showed increases in diversity, biomass and density at the road edge. These observations were attributed to collection of road runoff. The observations were true for annuals and perennials. *Larrea* responded as we would predict, i.e., growth was enhanced with moisture increase in this low-rainfall area.

Temperature, rainfall amounts, and timing greatly affect the dynamics of annuals (Went, 1949; Juhren, Went & Phillips, 1956; Tevis, 1958a, b; Klikoff, 1966; Beatley, 1967, 1969a, 1974b). These are mainly effects on germination. Similar germination effects occur for desert perennials (Turner, Alcorn, Olin & Booth, 1966; Wallace, Romney & Ashcroft, 1970; Barbour, Diaz & Breidenbach, 1974; Humphrey, 1974).

Dispersion patterns

Desert plants are said to be clumped – because of shade and soil organic matter requirements; regular, because of root competition and allelopathy; or simply random.

Each of these patterns has been described for North American desert species.

For *Larrea*-dominated communities Woodell, Mooney & Hill (1969) suggest that *Larrea* is regular. Barbour (1969, 1973) does not find such consistent patterns in his studies or those of Wright (1970). In fact, regular dispersion pattern is less common than others. My own work, in Barbour *et al.* (1977), shows that plants may be random or clumped depending on the dispersion metric you use. The various measures define dispersion at quite different scales.

Anderson (1971) argued that, regular or not, root competition for water was not likely to be the cause for the patterns. King & Woodell (1973) offered comments in refutation of Anderson. Barbour (1973) summarizing the allelopathic data sees no allelopathic effects to explain regularity either.

For other species we have seen clumping of annuals and shrubs (Muller, 1953; Muller & Muller, 1956; Halvorsan & Patten, 1975).

46

Perennials like *Idria* and *Cereus* frequently germinate under other perennials (Turner *et al.*, 1966; Humphrey, 1974) and thus show contagion. Wallace & Romney (1972) show contagious distributions for most perennial species they studied in the Mohave–Great Basin transition. McDonough (1965) found clumped dispersion for cacti in normal stands and random dispersion for declining stands.

Yeaton & Cody (1976), based on evidence from nearest-neighbor distances, suggest competition between all intra- and interspecific nearest-neighbor pairs for *Opuntia acanthocarpa*, *O. ramosissima* and *Yucca schidigera* in the Mohave.

Succession

It has generally been stated that succession does not occur in North American deserts (Muller, 1940; Shreve, 1951).

Wells (1961) demonstrated successional tendencies for a Nevada ghost town. Some trends of replacement were noted on the Nevada Test Site after nuclear cratering (Shields & Wells, 1962; Wallace & Romney, 1972).

These observations do not change the general principle. Normal disturbance of well-developed desert plots probably opens areas to colonization by the resident species. When one goes to more mesic areas e.g. Great Basin and desert transitions, succession may well occur.

In well-developed deserts the conditions are sufficiently extreme so that only desert plants could survive, compete, and therefore succeed themselves.

It should be pointed out that the conditions we perceive today may not be the conditions necessary for the establishment of the vegetation we observe, i.e., the current community cannot successfully replace itself. Many desert species are long-lived (Chew & Chew, 1965; Hastings & Turner, 1965). They may have germinated under conditions different from those existing now. Changes in vegetation where new species, adapted to current conditions, replace species residual from previous times is not strictly succession. The replacement of native species by introduced species is also not strictly succession (e.g. in Curlew Valley in northern Utah non-native annuals (*Bassia*, *Halogeton*, *Descurainia* and *Lepidium*) replace *Artemisia* and *Atriplex* in disturbed sites).

Topics such as above- and below-ground productivity or phytosociology are consciously ignored herein. IBP volumes are in preparation covering below-ground ecosystems and productivity. The paper by Barbour *et al.* (1977) summarizes phytosociological data on *Larrea*-dominated (hot-desert) communities for North America and South America.

Description of arid ecosystems

Table 2.6. Comparison of mammalian faunas of North American deserts

Inclusion in a desert implies that the species is characteristic of that desert and can be observed there with fair probability. Species marked with an X do not occur only in that desert, the absence of an X does not mean the species is entirely absent from that desert. Distributions are based on personal field collections and the following publications: Baker (1956); Hall and Kelson (1959); Anderson (1972); US IBP Desert Biome Validation Site data and data collected for MacMahon (1976). Bats have not been included.

Species	Sonoran	Mohave	Chihuahuan	Great Basin
Soricidae				
Desert shrew (*Notiosorex crawfordi*)	X	X	X	
Leporidae				
Blacktail jackrabbit (*Lepus californicus*)	X	X	X	X
Antelope jackrabbit (*L. alleni*)	X			
Cottontails (*Sylvilagus* sp.)	*audubonii*	*audubonii*	*audubonii*	*idahoensis; audubonii*
Sciuridae				
Ground squirrels (*Spermophilus* sp.)	*tereticaudus*	*tereticaudus*	*spilosoma*	*townsendii*
Antelope squirrels (*Ammospermophilus* sp.)	*harrisii*	*leucurus*	*leucurus*	*leucurus*
Least chipmunk (*Eutamias minimus*)				X
Geomyidae				
Valley pocket gopher (*Thomomys bottae*)	X	X	X	X
Heteromyidae				
Pocket mice (*Perognathus* sp.)	*penicillatus; baileyi; amplus*	*penicillatus; longimembris*	*flavus; nelsoni; penicillatus; merriami*	*parvus; longimembris*
Kangaroo mice (*Microdipodops*)				X
Kangaroo rats (*Dipodomys* sp.)	*spectabilis; deserti*	*deserti*	*spectabilis; nelsoni; ordii*	*ordii; microps*
Merriam's kangaroo rat (*D. merriami*)	X	X	X	X
Cricetidae				
Cactus mouse (*Peromyscus eremicus*)	X	X	X	X
Deer mouse (*P. maniculatus*)	X	X	X	X
White-footed mouse (*P. leucopus*)	X		X	
Grasshopper mice (*Onychomys* sp.)	*torridus*	*torridus*	*torridus*	*leucogaster*
Desert woodrat (*Neotoma lepida*)	X	X		X
Whitethroat woodrat (*N. albigula*)	X	X	X	
Sagebrush vole (*Lagurus curtatus*)				X
Canidae				
Coyote (*Canis latrans*)	X	X	X	X
Kit fox (*Vulpes macrotis*)	X	X	X	X
Gray fox (*Urocyon cinereoargenteus*)	X	X	X	X

48

Species	Sonoran	Mohave	Chihuahuan	Great Basin
Mustelidae				
Badger (*Taxidea taxus*)	X	X	X	X
Felidae				
Bobcat (*Lynx rufus*)	X	X	X	X
Tayassuidae				
Collared peccary	X		X	
(*Tayassu tajaçu*)				
Antilocapridae (Bovidae)				
Pronghorn				
(*Antilocapra americana*)	X	X	X	X

Fauna

General composition

The three hot deserts have some striking similarities in their fauna. For each of them at a normally diverse locality ('typical') one would find about 10–12 mammal species, 10–15 bird species, 10–20 reptile and amphibian species and 300–500 arthropod species.

While the species similarity from desert to desert varies, the guilds or functional groups (e.g., mammals) are amazingly similar (MacMahon, 1976).

Inspection of the lists of characteristic vertebrates of each desert (Tables 2.6–2.8) show that the same is true for all vertebrates. The array of forms for mammals includes: 3–5 heteromyid rodents (seed-eaters), a diurnal ground squirrel, an insectivorous mouse (*Onychomys*), a pocket gopher, a desert mouse (*Peromyscus* sp.), the ubiquitous *Peromyscus maniculatus*, usually a small rabbit (*Sylvilagus*) and a hare (*Lepus*), and two carnivores, usually from an array of foxes, coyote, bobcat, and perhaps a skunk and a badger.

If there is a considerable grass component (e.g., some sections of the Chihuahuan and the Great Basin) in the vegetation, two more mammals might be added: harvest mouse, *Reithrodontomys*, and a vole or a cotton rat (*Sigmodon*).

For the hot-desert birds one generally finds the cactus wren, verdin, black-tailed gnatcatcher, one or two thrashers, a dove, a quail, some sort of flycatcher, the roadrunner, a sparrow or two, an owl, and perhaps a raven. In addition to these species there are very important seasonal migrants to the desert. Warblers and finches of various types are periodically abundant and probably have impact on the systems (Cody, 1971). Some favorable sites may have species lists of over 250 species at one time or another, e.g. Organ Pipe Cactus National Monument, Arizona.

Reptiles and amphibians generally include the gopher snake, desert

49

Table 2.7. *Comparison of bird fauna of North American deserts. Bases for species inclusion or exclusion as in Table 2.6*

Distributions are based on personal field collections and the following publications; van Rossem (1945); Hensley (1954); Dixon (1959); Raitt & Maze (1968); Hubbard (1973); Oberholser (1974); Tomoff (1974); Behle (1976) and US IBP/Desert Biome Validation Site reports.

Species	Sonoran	Mohave	Chihuahuan	Great Basin
Kestrel (*Falco sparverius*)	.	X	.	X
Scaled Quail (*Callipepla squamata*)	X	.	X	.
Gambel's Quail (*Lophortyx gambelii*)	.	X	.	.
Mourning dove (*Zenaida macroura*)	X	X	X	.
White-winged dove (*Zenaida asiatica*)	X	X	.	.
Roadrunner (*Geococcyx californicus*)	X	X	X	.
Elf Owl (*Micrathene whitneyi*)	X	.	X	.
Burrowing Owl (*Speotyto cunicularia*)	.	X	.	X
Lesser nighthawk (*Chordeiles acutipennis*)	X	X	X	.
Poorwill (*Phalaenoptilus nuttallii*)	X	X	X	.
Gila woodpecker (*Centurus uropygialis*)	X	.	.	.
Ladder-backed woodpecker (*Dendrocopus scalaris*)	X	X	X	.
Ash-throated flycatcher (*Myiarchus cinerascens*)	X	X	X	.
Raven (*Corvus corax*)	X	X	*C. cryptoleucas*	X
Verdin (*Auriparus flaviceps*)	X	X	X	.
Cactus wren (*Campylorhynchus brunneicapillus*)	X	X	X	.
Mockingbird (*Mimus polyglottos*)	X	X	X	.
Curve-billed thrasher (*Toxostoma curvirostre*)	X	*T. leconti*	X	.
Crissal thrasher (*T. dorsale*)	X	X	X	.
Sage thrasher (*Oreoscoptes montanus*)	.	.	.	X
Black-tailed gnatcatcher (*Polioptila melanura*)	X	X	X	.
Phainopepla (*Phainopepla nitens*)	X	X	X	.
Loggerhead shrike (*Lanius ludovicianus*)	X	X	X	.
Black phoebe (*Sayornis nigricans*)	X	X	*S. sayus*	.
Horned lark (*Eremophila alpestris*)	.	.	.	X
Scott's oriole (*Icterus parisorum*)	X	X	.	.
Summer tanager (*Piranga rubra*)	X	X	.	.
Pyrrhuloxia (*Pyrrhuloxia sinuata*)	X	.	X	.
House finch (*Carpodacus mexicanus*)	X	X	X	.
Sage sparrow (*Amphispiza belli*)	.	X	.	X
Black-throated sparrow (*A. bilineata*)	X	X	X	X

tortoise, long-nosed snake, night snake, glossy snake, kingsnake, a racer, one or two rattlesnakes, a blind snake, the western whiptail, perhaps one other *Cnemidophorus*, a horned lizard, a *Sceloporus* sp., a gecko, and the side-blotched lizard, one of the best-studied desert vertebrates (Tinkle, 1967; Turner, Medica & Kowalewsky, 1976). You would be likely to see more species in a shorter time in the Sonoran Desert and parts of the Mohave than you would in the Chihuahuan.

The species lists for the Great Basin are somewhat deceptive. Many more species occur in the Great Basin area than you would be likely to see at any one time.

On typical Utah sagebrush plots I have seen a chipmunk, a kangaroo rat, *Peromyscus maniculatus*, a *Perognathus*, sage thrasher, sage sparrow, horned lark, Great Basin rattlesnake (*Crotalus viridis lutosus*), sagebrush lizard, a horned lizard, gopher snake and striped whipsnake – a depauperate assemblage.

South in Nevada and in sandy areas of the Lahontan Basin species density of vertebrates is greater. Tables 2.6–2.8 summarize vertebrate distribution data.

Arthropods and their desert-by-desert distribution are difficult to generalize about and the critical data for discussions such as these are contained in specialized taxonomic monographs and in the minds of field entomologists. Results of the IBP studies will somewhat offset this, but these are not currently available.

My approach then is to consider groups I have encountered frequently in deserts and then to seek sources about these forms rather than attempting a rigorous literature review.

Conspicuous insects include the abundant tenebrionid beetles. In Rock Valley, Nevada, Elbert Sleeper of the US IBP/Desert Biome recorded total densities of over 3000/ha including five species. Ahearn (1971) also found high densities of five tenebrionid species (three species were common to the two studies) in a Sonoran desert site near Phoenix, Arizona.

Long-horned beetles (Cerambycidae) are common and characteristic of the North American desert. Linsley (1958) states that 22% of all North American cerambycids are a Sonoran element, '...centering in south-western United States and northern Mexico'. Most of these are of ancient origin and 'are characteristic of the Lower Sonoran Life Zone of Merriam'. Obviously a strong desert representation.

An interesting derivative of the Sonoran groups are several genera (e.g., *Crossidius*, *Tetraopes*, and *Mecas*) which occur in the Great Basin and are associated with roots of *Artemisia* and *Chrysothamnus*.

Meloid beetles, while not as dense in terms of species as some other families are conspicuous desert elements. *Pyrota postica* commonly feeds on *Larrea* in the Chihuahuan. Hurd & Linsley (1975a) state that 'Among

Table 2.8. *Comparison of reptile and amphibian faunas of the North American deserts. Bases for species inclusion or exclusion as in Table 2.6. Distributions are based on personal field collections and maps in Stebbins (1966)*

Species	Sonoran	Mohave	Chihuahuan	Great Basin
Ambystomidae				
Tiger salamander	X	X	X	X
(*Ambystoma tigrinum*)				
Pelobatidae				
Couch's spadefoot	X	X	X	
(*Scaphiopus couchi*)				
Scaphiopus sp.	*hammondi*		*bombifrons*	*intermontanus*
Bufonidae				
Colorado River toad	X			
(*Bufo alvarius*)				
Red-spotted toad	X	X	X	
(*B. punctatus*)				
Green toads (*Bufo* sp.)	*retiformis*		*debilis*	
Kinosternidae				
Sonora mud turtle	X		X	
(*Kinosternon sonoriense*)				
Testudinidae				
Desert tortolse	X	X		
(*Gopherus agassizi*)				
Gekkonidae				
Leaf-toed gecko	X			
(*Phyllodactylus xanti*)				
Banded gecko	*variegatus*	*variegatus*	*brevis*	
(*Coleonyx* sp.)				
Xantusidae				
Desert night lizard	X	X		
(*Xantusia vigilis*)				
Iguanidae				
Chuckwalla	X	X		
(*Sauromalus obesus*)				
Desert iguana	X	X		
(*Dipsosaurus dorsalis*)				
Zebra-tailed lizard	X	X		X
(*Callisaurus draconoides*)				
Earless lizards	X		X	
(*Holbrookia* sp.)				
Fringe-toed lizard	X			
(*Uma* sp.)				
Leopard lizard	X	X	X	X
(*Crotaphytus wislizenii*)				
Collard lizard	X	X	X	X
(*C. collaris*)				
Desert spring lizard	X	X	X	X
(*Sceloporus magister*)				
Crevice spiny lizard			X	
(*S. poinsetti*)				
Sagebrush lizard		X		X
(*S. graciosus*)				
Tree lizard	X	X	X	
(*Urosaurus ornatus*)				
Side-blotched lizard	X	X	X	X
(*Uta stansburiana*)				
Horned lizards	*solare*		*modestum*	*douglassi*
(*Phrynosoma* sp.)				

Table 2.8. (*cont.*)

Desert horned lizard (*P. platyrhinos*)	X	X		X
Teiidae				
Western whiptail (*Cnemidophorus tigris*)	X	X	X	X
Helodermatidae				
Gila monster (*Heloderma suspectum*)	X	X		
Leptotyphlopidae				
Western blind snake (*Leptotyphlops humilis*)	X	X	X	
Boidae				
Rosy boa (*Lichanura trivirgata*)	X			
Colubridae				
Yellow-bellied racer (*Coluber constrictor*)		X		X
Leaf-nosed snake (*Phyllorhynchus* sp.)	X			
Coachwhip (*Masticophis flagellum*)	X	X	X	X
Striped whipsnakes (*Masticophis* sp.)	*bilineatus*	*taeniatus*	*taeniatus*	*taeniatus*
Western patch-nosed snake (*Salvadora hexalepis*)	X	X	X	X
Gopher snake (*Pituophis melanoleucus*)	X	X	X	X
Glossy snake (*Arizona elegans*)	X	X	X	
Trans-pecos rat snake (*Elaphe subocularis*)			X .	
Common kingsnake (*Lampropeltis getulus*)	X	X	X	
Long-nosed snake (*Rhinocheilus lecontei*)	X	X	X	X
Small burrowing colubrids	*Chilomenisus cinctus;* *Chionactis occipitalis*		*Ficimia cana*	
Night snake (*Hypsiglena torquata*)	X	X	X	X
Lyre snakes (*Trimorphodon* sp.)	*lambda*		*vilkinsoni*	
Elapidae				
Arizona coral snake (*Micruroides euryxanthus*)	X	X		
Viperidae				
Rattlesnakes (*Crotalus* sp.)	*tigris;* *molossus;* *atrox;* *cerastes;* *mitchelli;* *scutulatus;* *ruber*	*cerastes;* *mitchelli*	*molossus;* *atrox;* *scutulatus*	*viridis*

numerous beetles associated with *Larrea*, meloids are perhaps the most commonly encountered. A number of brightly colored species (*Lytta*) occur on various desert plants, particularly composites (Werner, Enns & Parker, 1966).

Bees are common in deserts. Some of the best studied are the eighty-four species in eight families which occur on *Larrea* (Hurd & Linsley, 1975*b*). Twenty-two of these species in five families and nine genera are *Larrea* oligoleges. Interestingly few of these are coextensive with the entire *Larrea* distribution. Many other hymenopterans, particularly parasitic forms are also encountered.

Wheeler & Wheeler (1973) list eighty-one species of North American desert ants of which thirty are restricted to the hot deserts.

In aerial photographs of some northern Utah desert sites, harvester ant discs may cover up to 20% of the land surface in local areas.

In hot deserts, four to six species may commonly occur and be significant in the removal of seeds from seed reserves – particularly annual species. Colony densities may exceed 20/ha (Whitford, Johnson & Ramirez, 1976). The effect of seed consumption by ants may have floristic effects on the community, out of proportion to the total energy consumed, due to seed species selectivity (Tevis, 1958*c*; Chew, 1974).

Orthopterans (Tinkham, 1948) are interesting in that several hot-desert species have protective coloration matched to *Larrea*. Among these are acridids including the grasshoppers *Bootettix punctatus* and *Ligurotettix coquillette* (both widely distributed with *Larrea*), *Clematodes larreae* and *Conaclea huachucana*, and the creosote bush katydid *Insara covilleae* (Rehn, 1958; Hurd & Linsley, 1975*a*; Otte & Joern, 1975). Several phasmids (e.g. *Diapheromera*) and mantids (*Stagmomantis limbata*) are also encountered. Finally, mention should be made of the polyphagid roach genus *Arenivaga* – a hot-desert form which has been studied out of proportion to its community importance (Edney, 1974).

Many hemipterans and homopterans occur but are less conspicuous. An exception is the seasonally abundant desert cicada *Diceroprocta apache* (Heath & Wilkin, 1970).

Termites (Isoptera) are important influents in hot deserts (Haverty & Nutting, 1974). Several species occur in any one area and may be among the most important detritivores. They seem not to perform, to the same extent, similar functions in the Great Basin.

Arachnids are prominent in hot deserts. Few studies relate to specific areas. Exceptions are Chew (1961) for a Sonoran–Chihuahuan transition site and Allred & Beck (1967) for a Great Basin–Mohave transition site in Nevada.

In a general comparison of his 1967 site to a site in southern Idaho, Allred (1975) found twice as many spider species in Nevada i.e., a ratio of 42:94. Only seven species were common to both sites.

An interesting group in the Mohave and the Sonoran is the family Diguetidae. This monogeneric family occurs in all of the hot deserts of the United States and in the 'Monte' of Argentina – a strong *Larrea* distribution analogue (Gertsch, 1958; Gerschman de Pikelin & Schiapelli, 1962).

Scorpions and solpugids (Muma, 1970) are locally common in hot deserts. Genera like the large *Hadrurus* (Vejovidae) are common and confined to the Sonoran (Williams, 1970). Nine species of scorpions and twenty-eight solpugids occur on a Mohave–Great Basin transition site (Allred, 1975).

An unusual, but periodically and locally abundant, arthropod of the Chihuahuan and Sonoran is the desert millipede *Orthoporus ornatus* (Causey, 1975). This species may be important in desert ecosystems (Crawford, 1976).

Edney (1974) reports that workers at Deep Canyon Research Center in California have obtained 245 families, 796 genera and 1160 species of arthropods. This number might occur in many hot-desert localities, but it would take an intensive program to collect them. Nonetheless the Great Basin appears to have fewer species at any locality. Curlew Valley in northern Utah, probably has about 900 species. Fautin (1946) in a short-term study accumulated 197 species of arthropods in 150 genera and 76 families.

Great Basin species of significance include the sagebrush defoliator *Aroga websteri*, a gelechiid moth which occurs locally at high densities. Many tenebrionid beetles occur, perhaps the two most common are *Eleodes hispilabris* and *E. obscura*.

Fautin (1946) reported that homopterans occurred in greater abundance and frequency than any other groups of insects. My experience is the same. This may be true for hot deserts, but many forms are not obvious and it takes exhaustive sampling to obtain them.

Fautin (1946) found 23 species of spiders over a diversity of vegetation types. This is more than the 20 hot-desert species Chew (1961) records, but Chew demonstrated higher densities. My own spider collections include up to 42 species in northern Utah mixed-sagebrush communities.

A few scorpions and solpugids occur in the Great Basin; generally they are abundant nowhere. The most common species is *Vejovis boreus* (Gertsch & Soleglad, 1966).

I have not addressed myself to aquatic organisms. Two groups should be mentioned.

First, there is a distinct and diverse fauna and flora associated with the ephemeral *playas*. Recently W. Whitford and his group at New Mexico State University have extensively studied one *playa* in the Chihuahuan Desert. Results of their work are in preparation. A general review of desert limnology is provided by Cole (1968).

Description of arid ecosystems

The second group I should mention are those physiologically plastic cyprinodont fish occupying areas in all of the hot deserts. The best studied species are in the genus *Cyprinodon*. *Cyprinodon macularius* occurs in the Sonoran, a few species including *C. bifasciatus* occur in the Chihuahuan. In the Mohave, several isolated *Cyprinodon* populations, warrant taxonomic recognition (e.g. *C. radiosus*, *C. diabolis*, *C. nevadensis*, *C. salinus*). These probably developed as residual isolates of the Pleistocene Lake Manly.

Other spring and intermittant stream forms occur in the North American deserts (Deacon & Minckley, 1974).

Faunal subdivisions

Dice (1943) divided North America into biotic provinces. A biotic province '... covers a considerable and continuous geographic area and is characterized by the occurrence of one or more important ecologic associations that differ at least in proportional area covered, from associations of adjacent provinces. In general, biotic provinces are characterized also by peculiarities of vegetation type, ecological climax, flora, fauna, climate, physiography, and soil.'

In fact, since Dice's work, animal ecologists have used the biotic province concept more than plant-oriented workers.

Recently Hagmeier & Stults (1964) (corrected by Hagmeier, 1966) used a mammalian-species similarity analysis to define mammal provinces.

The final map does not differ much from Dice's outline and does not coincide well with my concept of the distribution of deserts, or even their possible subdivisions based on animal distribution patterns.

Hagmeier's Columbian and Artemisian provinces are the northern and southern Great Basin Desert respectively; the Yaquinian is Sonoran–Chihuahuan transition; the Mapimian, a combination Chihuahuan-grassland; the Mohavian splits part of the Sonoran Desert and misses part of the Mohave.

The reason their scheme does not fit desert community patterns better, is that mammal-species similarity alone is considered. Species depend on many factors – past evolutionary history, dispersal opportunity, gene pool plasticity and the opinion of a taxonomist, etc. The contention here is that total community overlap is more significant than similarity of any one taxon, e.g. mammals. In the present case, on the one hand many mammal species have low desert-fidelity and therefore their occurrence in other community types blurs the desert patterns; on the other hand some local areas have high degrees of endemism.

Using data from the total Middle American vertebrate fauna, Stuart (1970) derives biotic provinces which coincide with the Chihuahuan Desert and some adjacent grass- and tree-dominated areas (Chihuahuan–Zaca-tecas), the nonpeninsular Sonoran Desert (Sonoran), and the aggregate of all of Shreve & Wiggins' (1964), Baja regions, except the Lower Colorado Valley (San Lucan). Thus there is a good fit to my desert boundaries with the exception of the endemic-rich San Lucan (Baja).

These three zones essentially contain similar groups of vertebrates (generic level) and, as will be seen, are differentiated by closely related species, isolated in the three historical refugia coinciding with these provinces.

Breaks in the faunal areas of North American deserts seem to occur at several levels of resolution. The first (gross) separates hot and cold deserts. This is caused by the commonality of many birds in hot deserts, and also a few mammals and ectotherms, including insects (Tinkham, 1948) (see Tables 6–8).

The second (intermediate) level of differentiation sets off Sonoran desert, Chihuahuan, Mohave, Great Basin, and the endemics of Baja.

The third level (detailed) includes all of the above, but might also recognize the northern Great Basin and two Chihuahuan subdivisions – the typical 'northern' section and one farther south characterized by *Neotoma goldmani*, *Ammospermophilus interpres* and *Perognathus nelsoni*. Few other organisms would have coincident patterns with this distribution (Dalquest, 1953; Baker, 1956; Urban, 1959; Baker & Greer, 1962).

I opted for the intermediate level, ignoring Baja endemism, for purposes of mapping desert distribution.

Animals demonstrate fewer geographical associations, at any level of analysis, which could be considered subdivisions of the four desert types. Of course this is partly the reason I use them for boundary recognition of the deserts.

None of this negates obvious local 'community' differences like those on various soil types. For example, in hot deserts there is almost always a desert-adapted *Peromyscus*; whether it is *P. eremicus* or *P. crinitus* or some other form frequently depends on local soil type (Ryan, 1968). An ecological difference between the two Great Basin *Microdipodops* species is that *M. pallidus* is somewhat random with regard to soil choice while *M. megacephalus* chooses sandy soils (Ghiselin, 1970).

Origins of the fauna

Origins of North American desert faunas will be based primarily on a discussion of papers by Savage (1960); Findley (1969); Hubbard (1973); Blair, Hulse & Mares (1976) and inferences drawn from the vegetation material presented above.

Description of arid ecosystems

Unlike many plants (Fig. 6), the relationships between vertebrates of the 'Monte' and North American deserts is remote. Only 4.5% of the species and 11.5% of mammalian genera are shared; lower vertebrates (ectotherms) are worse (6.8% genera and no species shared) (Blair *et al.*, 1976).

Many North American desert mammal species occur widely outside of the deserts (60 of 83) while 32 of 67 ectotherms are endemic to the Sonoran or occur in the Sonoran and Chihuahuan.

It is reasonable to look for autochthonous (Nearctic) origins for many desert animals, where their center of species density is the North American deserts, or where they are derivable from forms found adjacent to deserts. Desert animals of this type include *Peromyscus*, *Citellus* and *Perognathus* from the Miocene; *Neotoma*, *Onychomys*, *Thomomys* and *Taxidea* from the Pliocene; *Lepus*, *Sylvilagus*, *Dipodomys*, and *Microdipodops* from the Pleistocene (Savage, 1958). These genera include over 70% of the desert species in any locality with the exception of the Great Basin with its strong Eurasian influence (e.g. *Eutamias* and *Lagurus* from the Pliocene).

Regardless of the time or place of the ultimate origins the increasing aridity of the Basin and Range Province was undoubtedly 'working on' a fairly modern 'desert' fauna by mid-Pliocene. This is substantiated by the mammals above and the fact that the bird genera *Callipepla*, *Lophortyx*, *Geococcyx*, *Auriparus*, and *Oreoscoptes* are undoubtedly remnants of this Pliocene assemblage (Hubbard, 1973).

Additionally, while evidence is not direct (i.e., fossils) the history of reptiles and amphibians in the west, as inferred from their current distribution patterns, follows closely, like the birds and mammals, the floral sequence (Brattstrom, 1955, 1958; Peabody, 1959).

This means that desert elements evolved early (Pliocene on) and during the Pleistocene were moved around numerous times even to the point of many forms being displaced south into Mexico or isolated in scattered savannah localities in the United States.

Faunal elements were driven into central Mexico (Chihuahuan), Baja California (endemics), or the Sonora–Sinaloa (Sonoran) coast at glacial maxima. They existed in these desert refugia and subsequently during interglacials moved northward, eastward and/or westward. Other refugia existed. Two, coastal California and peninsular Florida, had some influence on current desert species. A widely distributed arid-grassland species could be driven south separating into two isolates – Mexican Highland refugium and peninsular Florida. Such differentiation probably explains the field sparrow complex *Spizella wortheni* endemic to the Chihuahuan and *S. pusilla* in southeastern United States and the similar Chihuahuan *Aimophila cassinii* and southeastern United States *A. aestivalis* (Hubbard, 1973).

During the pluvial period the desert fauna of the west (Sonoran) was periodically separated from the east (Chihuahuan) while boreal faunas migrated downward and occupied previously arid areas. In the interpluvials, as now, the Deming Plain (Fig. 2.2*a*) was open, allowing faunal connection between Sonoran and Chihuahuan elements (Findley, 1969).

This would allow range expansion for some species, thus we find forms that occur in all hot deserts and some adjacent grasslands (e.g. *Dipodomys merriami*). For other species, related (sibling) pairs of species, with complementary distributions might develop (e.g., *Lepus callotis–L. alleni, Ammospermophilus harrisii–A. interpres, Onychomys torridus–O. leucogaster*) and birds such as the four-species *Toxostoma curvirostre* complex, the three-species *Toxostoma dorsale* complex, the three-species *Callipepla* (*Lophortyx*) complex, etc. Also some forms might, after range contraction, never expand much but merely remain (e.g., *Spermophilus spilosoma* and *S. tereticaudus*) in a subsection of the arid zone.

The difference in mammal and ectotherm endemism patterns (more endemic ectotherms) may be related to ectotherms being forced into more extreme arid areas of Mexico (thus farther south) while the more mesic adapted (wide-ranging) mammals were closer to contact in the pluvials and therefore had their separated populations reunited faster and for longer periods during interpluvials.

During the current interpluvial the isolated Sonoran and Chihuahuan endemics (birds, mammals and ectotherms) seem to be meeting in the area of the Deming Plain (Lowe, 1955; Findley, 1969; Hubbard, 1973) just as proposed for interglacials longer ago.

Interestingly, essentially Sonoran and essentially Chihuahuan reptiles seem not to overlap much on the Sonoran–Chihuahuan Border (see Map Discussion), mammals overlap some, and the bird species of the two deserts overlap greatly.

This may be due to the reptiles and mammals being less vagile than birds (cannot reunite populations as fast) and the mammal components of the two deserts having less distance to travel (being displaced less because of the broader ecological tolerances) during the interglacials and therefore being able to reunite populations faster due to proximity not vagility.

Biology

The species densities and their alleged causes have been discussed for many North American vertebrates and essentially no invertebrates.

For mammals Simpson's (1964) contour map of species density shows high densities for mountainous areas and a drop across the deserts. This desert depression pattern shows up on a north–south transect traversing hot deserts, and an east–west transect across the Great Basin. The general north–south trend is one of species density increase. Despite the desert depressions, hot deserts show higher species densities than the Great Basin. Cook (1969) found similar trends for birds. Kiester (1971) showed no desert depression for reptiles, simply a continuous north–south increase from the Canadian to Mexican borders. For amphibians, Kiester's data suggest an east–west oriented desert depression i.e., a north–south species density transect through the Basin and Range Province increases little.

It should be noted that these are total mammals etc. Individual taxa of lower rank (e.g., families) may not follow the trends (Cook, 1969).

Kiester (1971) suggests an inverse relationship between mammal and reptile species density. In a detailed study of Texas reptiles and amphibians, Rogers (1976) found no such correlation.

Pianka (1966, 1967) correlated the diversity of lizard species of the North American flatland desert with the climatic variability and diversity of plant life-forms, two potentially interactive factors. Thus in the lower-rainfall and consequently high-variability hot deserts, more lizard species occur. Pianka's (1967) map shows an obvious species density break correlating with hot vs cold deserts.

Later Pianka (1971) demonstrated that lizard species density does not increase as fast as bird species density in North American deserts. Lizards are somehow contained more. There are fewer guilds in North American desert lizards than others studied and there is a negative correlation between species density and extent of overlap of members of the lizard community (Pianka, 1975).

Desert bird species diversity in any desert site seems to depend on vegetation structure, particularly physiognomic (life form) diversity (Hensley, 1954; Raitt & Maze, 1968; Tomoff, 1974). Population density follows a similar trend and also, to some extent, tracks rainfall (Raitt & Maze, 1968). Physiognomic diversity is not the same as floral height diversity used to analyze bird communities successfully in other biomes (see review by Recher, 1971). Interestingly no desert species uses *Larrea* for nesting. On occasion black-throated sparrows nest at their bases (Tomoff, 1974). Many bird species use cacti and subtrees (Anderson & Anderson, 1973; Tomoff, 1974).

Brown (1975) recently summarized the data bearing on desert mammal species densities. He suggests that biogeographic barriers limit faunas in some isolated basins. Where there is easy biogeographic access, species density depends on productivity, particularly that of seeds. In addition there is an effect of competition in structuring the community. His overall contention is that species densities are related to the degree of overlap of community members. These observations are consistent with previous work (Beatley, 1969*b*; Brown & Lee, 1969; Rosenzweig & Winakur, 1969;

Rosenzweig & Sterner, 1970; Brown, Lieberman & Dengler, 1972; Brown & Lieberman, 1973; Rosenzweig, 1973).

Another point is that structurally similar communities with biogeographic openness and similar productivity have similar functional groups. This is consistent with my observations (MacMahon, 1976).

None of these generalities offsets local factors which cause species losses, or replacement. These local factors can include: the presence of one plant species, e.g., the relation between cholla (*Opuntia*) and woodrats (*Neotoma*) (Brown *et al.*, 1972); the change in habitat structure by artificial or natural means e.g., loss of *Dipodomys microps* and replacement with *D. merriami* after disturbance in the Mohave Great Basin transition (Beatley, 1976*a*); the presence of another effective species, regardless of the habitat, e.g., Rosenzweig, Smigel & Kraft (1975) reported that when a single badger (*Taxidea taxus*) moved into a plot, for a period no *Dipodomys* occurred; periodic changes in native but not introduced plant seed availability (Beatley, 1976*b*); or local soil factors (Hardy, 1945).

Recently several workers have documented seasonal and yearly changes in desert mammal communities and correlated these to various factors (MacMillen, 1964; Chew & Chew, 1970; French *et al.*, 1974; Schroeder & Rosenzweig, 1975; Whitford, 1976; Montgomery & MacMahon, 1978).

There are good reasons to believe that desert animals may have competitive relationships with other, very distantly related, taxa which affect distribution and species composition. An example is the relationship between harvester ants and seed-eating rodents (Brown, Grover, Davidson & Liebermann, 1975). Transient seed-eating birds might also have effects. Similar scenarios can be envisioned for relationships between such forms as ground-dwelling lizards and arachnids such as scorpions and solpugids, or spiders.

In habitats like deserts, where forms of life are on the edge of their adaptive potential, a combination of factors, seemingly frivolous to us, may regulate the community.

That such interactions are coevolved is frequently shown for animal–plant pairs (e.g. insects and plants) and less often for animal–animal interactions. The very starkness of the desert permits us to perceive such possibilities more clearly.

The map

Fig. 2.1 differs from several other maps proposed for North American deserts. Differences between my concept and that of others are usually related to my use of plant and animal distribution data, rather than relying on plants alone. Animal distribution data come from papers mentioned in the various subsections of this paper and the headings of the flora and fauna tables (2–5 and 6–8). In this section I will explain the boundaries of my representation of North American deserts.

Since all areas are not controversial, let me point out both the problem areas and those of agreement. I will use as my basic reference the Shreve (1942) map. This figure has been replicated so often that it is surely the standard. A second major representation that I will consider is that of Jaeger (1957).

In the northern Great Basin, *Artemisia tridentata* goes farther north than the boundary indicated, but characteristic association with *Atriplex confertifolia* drops off in southeastern Oregon (Franklin & Dyrness, 1973); the mammals *Dipodomys microps, Neotoma lepida, Peromyscus crinitus, Ammospermophilus leucurus*, and the reptiles *Cnemidophorus tigris, Phrynosoma platyrhinos, Crotaphytus wislizenii, C. collaris*, and *Crotalus viridis lutosus* all have their northern distributions approximately at this boundary. Those Great Basin desert species extending farther north are not confined to 'desert' associations e.g., *Sceloporus graciosus*, which occurs in pine forests and also Douglas fir, *Perognathus parvus* and *Sylvilagus idahoensis* extending into steppes.

Southwestern Wyoming, the Red Desert of some authors (Jaeger, 1957), has a desert physiognomy, some Great Basin plants (Billings, 1949) but few animals. Great Basin species notably absent are the mammals *Thomomys bottae, Spermophilus townsendii, Lepus californicus, Sylvilagus idahoensis, Neotoma lepida, Microdipodops megacephalus, Perognathus longimembris, Dipodomys microps*, and the reptiles *Cnemidophorus tigris, Crotaphytus wislizenii, Phrynosoma platyrhinos, Hypsiglena torquata, Crotalus viridis lutosus, Crotaphytus collaris, Rhinocheilus lecontei* and *Masticophis taeniatus*. Great Basin species that do occur have distributions greatly outside desert zones e.g., *Lagurus curtatus, Dipodomys ordii*, and *Sylvilagus audubonii*.

Because so many animals are absent I exclude this area from the Great Basin Desert.

The eastern and western boundaries of the Great Basin and the Mohave are determined by the mountain ranges and essentially all of the desert plant and animal boundaries coincide to a high degree.

The exception to the above statement is the Colorado Plateau Section referred to as the Painted Desert (Jaeger, 1957).

The Painted Desert area is excluded from the map, again because it lacks a characteristic Great Basin fauna. Examples include the mammals *Spermophilus townsendii, Microdipidops* sp., *Perognathus parvus*, essentially no *P. longimembris, Dipodomys merriami* and *Onychomys torridus*. Reptiles which are otherwise characteristic of the Great Basin include *Rhinocheilus, Callisaurus* and *Phrynosoma platyrhinos*.

The southern Great Basin–Mohave boundary here is well represented by the northward extension of *Larrea* (Yang, 1970; Beatley, 1975).

Mammals observing similar boundaries include species of the Great Basin not going into the Mohave (e.g., *Spermophilus townsendii, Microdipodops, Dipodomys ordii, Onychomys leucogaster, Lagurus curtatus*). The other case, Mohave desert species not getting into the Great Basin include: *Spermophilus tereticaudus, Peromyscus eremicus, Arizona elegans, Gopherus agassizi, Coleonyx variegatus, Xantusia vigilis, Sauromalus obesus, Heloderma suspectum, Leptotyphlops* and *Bufo punctatus*.

The northern Sonora–southern Mohave boundary is not as clear as northern Mohave boundary. Vegetationally one series of good indicators include the subtrees and saguaro (see Benson & Darrow, 1954) which do not enter the Mohave. I know of sites in northwestern Arizona containing saguaro, junipers (*Juniperus*), joshua trees, *Larrea*, and abundant grasses. There is then a real transition and nothing is too well delimited.

Animals contributing to the choice of boundaries include the mammals *Ammospermophilous harrisii* and *Neotoma albigula*, not ranging much into the Mohave. The reptiles *Urosaurus ornatus* and *Lichanura* are similarly limited. The spadefoot toad *Scaphiopus intermontanus* is generally absent from the Sonoran.

Most of the boundary areas of the Sonoran and the Chihuahuan deserts are well defined in Mexico by vegetation and animals. Both vegetations blend into thorn scrubs in the south and loose characteristic species with increasing altitudes. Interestingly, my Chihuahuan outline, developed independently using animals and plants, is closely similar to that shown by Henrickson & Straw (1976). The southern Sonoran boundary is somewhere between the Rio Mayo and the Rio Yaqui. Shreve (1942) used the Rio Yaqui. My data from the area show that the transition is very gradual through that section (see also Hastings *et al.*, 1972). Animals that prompt me to choose the more southern boundary are the mass of reptiles and amphibians (Bogert & Oliver, 1945) and the mammals *Lepus californicus, Ammospermophilus harrissii, Spermophilus tereticaudus, Thomomys bottae, Perognathus baileyi*, and *Taxidea taxus*.

The final boundary to consider is the meeting of the Sonoran and Chihuahuan. I have followed Lowe (1955) and his use of animal distributions. The subtree distribution reinforces this (Benson & Darrow, 1954; Hastings *et al.*, 1972). The *Larrea* polyploid pattern is also similar (Yang, 1970). Interestingly, again independently, Henrickson & Straw (1976) use the same Chihuahuan border.

Main differences in my general map and others are to: (1) eliminate southwestern Wyoming and the Painted Deserts from the 'desert biome'; (2) limit the extent of the Great Basin northward in Idaho and Oregon;

(3) join the Chihuahuan and Sonoran on the Arizona–New Mexico border; (4) extend the Sonoran slightly southward to just north of the Rio Mayo.

In retrospect, the weakest part of the map is the southern boundary of the Chihuahuan. Much of the desert area south of the state of Chihuahua is scattered and difficult to depict at the scale of this map.

Man

The history of man in the deserts of North America is one filled with controversy.

One of the more interesting exchanges involves the sequence of climates during the last 12000 years. The nature of the classic post-glacial sub-divisions of Antevs (1955) have recently been challenged by Martin (1963).

Briefly, Antevs recognized three subdivisions: the Anathermal 9000 B.P.–7000 B.P., a period like today initially, then growing warmer – Great Basin lakes were higher than now; the Altithermal 7000 B.P.–4000 B.P., an arid time, warmer than now – Great Basin lakes disappear; the Medi-thermal 4500 B.P.–present – a moderately warm arid to semi-arid time – Great Basin lakes reborn.

Martin's (1963) boundaries differ in age, he has 11000 B.P.–8000 B.P. for Anathermal and 8000 B.P.–4000 B.P. for Altithermal. Also Martin believes that from Pleistocene to 8000 B.P. it was warm and arid with an increasing summer rainfall pattern. From 4000 B.P. to present it was warm and arid with no summer rainfall pattern except the period 2500 B.P.–1000 B.P. An implication of Martin's work is that the Great Basin lakes would have been low quite a long time ago, more than 10000 years. Antev's work would have Lake Bonneville at an elevation higher than Danger Cave, 9500 years ago. Jennings (1957) has dates of occupation of Danger Cave 11000 years ago. Martin's postulates seem more plausible.

I might point out that Antev's approach is geomorphological and Martin's palynological. Malde (1964) using both data sets suggests '...the altithermal was at first rather arid and then gradually became wetter'. Irwin-Williams & Haynes (1970), in an outstanding review, infer cooler and more moist conditions in the period 9500 B.P.–7500 B.P., than those existing today.

The earliest dates for man in the deserts are also open to discussion. Certainly he was hunting large mammals in the southwest by 13000 years ago. This date marks the time of the Clovis points. There may have been a 'pre-projectile' period but this is by no means certain. Dates for camps at Tule Springs, Nevada of 23800 B.P. (Harrington & Simpson, 1961) have been questioned (Schulter, 1965).

There are few data to suggest that large animals still existed in the desert areas other than southern Arizona (Naco and Lehner sites), when man was hunting there (Baumhoff & Heizer, 1965).

The date for Nevada sites, particularly Gypsum Cave, while tempting, are not definite enough to show man hunting the large animals (Martin & Plog, 1973).

Despite the doubts about hunting man in the deserts, it is fairly clear that the Clovis tradition (Paleo-Indian) was gone by about 8000 B.P.–6000 B.P. This time also marks the end of the Pleistocene faunas, supporting the suggestion of Martin (1967) that man may have been a proximate cause for the extinctions of the megafauna.

It should be noted that this time period also coincides with increasing aridity and one could argue, as have Baumhoff & Heizer (1965), that the drying may also have caused species loss. At any rate there is a distinct change from hunters to gatherers in the Great Basin and the hot deserts, including the Mexican portions (Baja, Sonora, Coahuila) (Aveleyra, 1964) which were intruded from the North.

In the whole of the Basin and Range Province (Desert West of anthropology) from about 9000 B.P. to 2000 B.P. the Desert Culture (Archaic) developed as a widespread uniform culture (Jennings, 1964). This was true not only for the United States but also Mexico including Baja (Massey, 1961) and at least as far south as Coahuila.

The Desert Culture had some differentiation very early in the Plateau regions and by 6000 B.P. was differentiating somewhat in the southwest. It is thus possible to recognize both a Southwest and a Great Basin tradition (Reed, 1964).

It is important to state that the Desert Culture occurred over a wide variety of habitat types, not merely desert.

The best data suggest that the Desert Culture developed in the Intermountain area, perhaps from Big Game Hunters (Paleo-Indians). It is clear that this was a nonfarming, nonherding culture who must hunt and gather. With the meager resources available in the arid lands much of the time was consumed by these activities. Martin and Plog (1973) suggest that the scant resources caused the people to be adaptable, finding ways to exploit every possible resource. Corn, first known about 5000 B.P. from the southern part of their area, may have been just another source of food for the people.

By about the time of Christ the Great Basin area and the hot-desert Southwest area cultures had diverged to a point where we can recognize separate traditions. The divergence started about 4000 B.P.

To summarize, there was a general tradition which I refer to as the Desert Culture (Intermontane Tradition of Jennings (1964)), derived from Paleo-Indians about 12000 B.P., occurring everywhere in the Basin and Range Province. Early on, by 9000 B.P., this was differentiated into a

Table 2.9. *Summary of gross geological, climatic and floristic changes taking place in the Basin and Range Province from the late Cenozoic Era through the Mesozoic Era. Material collated from Axelrod (1950, 1958); Darrow (1961); Martin & Mehringer (1965); Hunt (1974); Raven & Axelrod (1974)*

Time	Geology	Climate	Flora
Cretaceous	Marine embayment from Gulf of California to Arctic Ocean; uplifting in Rocky Mountains; Province Mountains uplifted and erode to east	Tropical to warm temperate	Neotropic- and Arcto-tertiary floras developed
Paleocene–Eocene	Seas subside; faulting and volcanism in Rockies	Early: increased warming extending northward Late: some subhumid areas develop in Central Rockies	Early: Neotropic-tertiary flora migrates north Late: Floras of northern and southern Great Basin differentiate
Oligocene	Volcanic activity; block faulting forms characteristic Basin and Range aspects. Structural valleys form	Increasing aridity; local arid zones present	Madro-tertiary flora develops on arid edges of Neotropic-tertiary flora
Miocene	Sierra Nevada axis defined; volcanism in area to be southern deserts	More aridity; northern Great Basin 880–1250 mm/yr equally distributed over the year; 380–635 mm/yr southern Great Basin	Arcto- and Madro-tertiary floras meet in central Nevada
Pliocene	Province becomes more basin-like by uplifts e.g., San Bernadino Mountains.	Local drying – edaphic and topographic aridity	Probable 'long jumps' of South American groups to arid North America; Mohavia splits into Mohave and Sonoran parts
Pleistocene	Final Sierra Nevada uplift and tilt	Alternating sequences of cool moist and warm dry	Alternate pluvial and interpluvial, occupation of refugia

Table 2.10. *Generalized comparison of North American Deserts*

	Great Basin	Mohave	Sonoran	Chihuahuan
Season and type of water input:	Winter – snow	Winter – rain	Spring and summer – rain	Summer – rain
Elevation (m):	610–1350	80–610	0–610 m	610–1350
Latitude (°N):	37–43	35–37	27 (24 Baja)–35	22–34
Plants:	*Atriplex confertifolia;* *Chrysothamnus* sp.; *Artemisia tridentata*	*Larrea; Ambrosia* sp.; *Yucca brevifolia*	*Larrea; Ambrosia* sp.; Subtrees (leguminous); Cactaceae (tall)	*Larrea;* Agavaceae; Liliaceae; Cactaceae
Extent:	Nevada, W. Utah	S. Nevada, S.E. California	Arizona, Sonora, Baja California	Minor New Mexico and Texas, N.E. Mexico (Mexican Highland)
Affinities:	Eurasia; Arcto-tertiary geoflora	North and South America; Madro-tertiary geoflora	North and South America; Madro-tertiary geoflora	North and South America; Madro-tertiary geoflora
Cause:	Rainshadow	Rainshadow	Subtropical high; Coastal current (Baja)	Subtropical high

Description of arid ecosystems

Plateau subculture (particularly in the Northwest) and another portion which covered all of the desert areas (e.g., Danger Cave). By 4000 B.P. an additional subdivision occurred. This last one separated the Great Basin desert groups (e.g., Lovelock) from the more hot-desert group e.g., Hohokam. Within each of these areas there were additional cultures developing e.g., Mogollan vs Hohokam in Arizona. Martin (1963) called the Desert Culture in Arizona the Cochise.

The transition to these latter cultures is marked by the people establishing semi-permanent habitations, erecting storage facilities, using unfired clay vessels etc.

The really distinctive southwestern element was the advent of pottery and dwelling in clustered villages. This of course is tied to the ability to produce rather than hunt food.

By 800 A.D. Hohokams in Arizona developed complex and sophisticated irrigation systems similar to those in use today by the Salt River Project.

During their Sedentary period (900 A.D.–1200 A.D.) Hohokams withdrew from outer areas and concentrated their populations. The classic period of the Hohokam (1200 A.D.–1400 A.D.) was 'the Golden Age of southern Arizona'.

During this period the Hohokam lived mainly at the confluence of rivers e.g., Salt, Gila, Verde. Bohrer (1970) suggests that agriculture was two crops a year. A winter crop watered by winter river runoff and a summer crop watered by rains.

Bohrer (1970) developed an index of crop seed vs native seed concentration in samples. A decreasing crop-seed proportion indicates agricultural failure. This was the case close to the end of the Hohokam. Their disappearance is not documented.

Pima and Papago tribes, linked by their unusual language, are thought to be Hohokam derivatives.

By aboriginal times the desert cultures of the Sonoran were composed of Piman (including Pimas, Papagos, Subaipuris, Sobas, and Lower Pimas); Cahitan (Yaquis and Mayos (Coastal Mexico)); Yuman; Seris and in Baja California, the Kamia, Diegueno and Cochimi (Fontana, 1974).

By 1521 Cortez entered the Sonoran desert (Dunbier, 1968). The intrusion of European man was an ecological event of extreme consequence to the North American deserts. Many traces of the past were obliterated as a consequence of white man's occupation. Part of the remaining heritage of the Pimas is the fact that the main urban centers of the Sonoran Desert (Phoenix, Tucson, Caborca, Magdalena) were once Pima villages.

The use of North American deserts by historical man varies from the essentially subsistence cultures of some Indian groups, to the technological societies of other cultural groups.

There has been a history of over grazing and abuse of desert–grassland transitional areas. The result is to develop more hectares of desert, which for agricultural purposes are less useful (Buffington & Herbal, 1965).

Changes in vegetation during the last eighty years have been beautifully documented for Arizona by Hastings & Turner (1965). They infer that these are man-caused changes. Similar changes have been documented for the Great Basin in a series of essays by Cottam (1961) and for the Chihuahuan (Buffington & Herbal, 1965; York & Dick-Peddie, 1969).

Many management studies are going forward. A discussion of these is outside of the scope of this work.

To finish, let me note that native deserts have many useful functions. It is not necessary to treat every hectare of the North American deserts as a potential grazing land.

Plants of desert origin have many uses. Cruse (1973) lists desert species that can provide, for man's use, pharmaceuticals (alkaloids, steroids, and hypoglycemic extracts). In addition, feeds (see Duisberg, (1952) for *Larrea*) enzymes, fiber, gums, essential oils, foods, cleansers, fats, oils and waxes are known – not to mention artist's woods. This has been underlined for shrubs by McKell (1975).

A specific example is jojoba (*Simmondsia chinensis*). Sherbrooke & Haase (1974) review its past and potential uses. It is a species successfully cultured and economically feasible in commercial production. Jojoba oil can be used in place of whale oil for delicate machinery, as a food, and in modern medicine.

There is another aspect of deserts which is very useful. As an area of recreational activities they are sparsely populated, aesthetically pleasing, and to some of us spiritually uplifting.

Of course, even this use can be overdone. A case in point is the impact of offroad vehicles on the flora, the fauna, and the structure of desert soils (Stebbins, 1974).

The North American deserts have persisted at least since Pliocene. Some important events and characteristics of North American deserts are shown in Tables 2.9 and 2.10. Only time will tell if they have been subjected to a new environmental factor outside of their tolerance range – modern man.

Acknowledgments

Douglas Anderson, Donna Baranowski, Frank Parker, Charles Passavant, Donald Phillips, Bette Peitersen and David Schimpf aided me in many ways. Linda Finchum endured my cryptic handwriting and turned it into words. This paper is a contribution from the US/IBP Desert Biome, funded by National Science Foundation Grant GB-32139.

69

Description of arid ecosystems

Addendum

Since the completion of the manuscript, several titles of direct interest have become available. They cannot be worked into the body of the text but are given here for reference purposes.

Beatley, J. C. (1976). Vascular plants of the Nevada Test Site and Central-Southern Nevada: ecologic and geographic distributions. *United States Atomic Energy Council*, TID-**26881**.

Burk, J.H. (1977). Sonoran desert vegetation. In: *Terrestrial vegetation of California* (eds. M. G. Barbour & J.Major), pp. 869–89. Wiley, New York.

Chew, R. M. (1977). Some ecological characteristics of a desert-shrub community in southeastern Arizona. *American Midland Naturalist*, **98**, 33–49.

Cressman, L. S. (1977). *Prehistory of the far west*. University of Utah Press, Salt Lake City.

Johnson, H. B. (1976). Vegetation and plant communities of southern California deserts – a functional view. In: *Symposium proceedings: Plant communities of Southern California* (ed. J. Latting), pp. 125–52. Special Publication, **2**, California Native Plant Society, Berkeley.

Mabry, T. J., Hunziker, J. H. & DiFeo, D. R. Jr. (eds.) (1977). *Creosote bush: biology and chemistry of Larrea in new world deserts*. US/IBP Synthesis Series 6. Dowden, Hutchinson & Ross, Stroudsburg, Pennsylvania.

Morafka, D. J. (1977). A biogeographical analysis of the Chihuahuan Desert through its herpetofauna. *Biogeographica*, **9**, 1–313.

Mulroy, T. W. & Rundel, P. W. (1977). Annual plants: adaptations to desert environments. *BioScience*, **27**, 109–14.

Orians, G. H. & Solbrig, O. T. (eds.) (1977). *Convergent evolution in warm deserts*. US/IBP Synthesis Series 3. Dowden, Hutchinson & Ross, Stroudsburg, Pennsylvania.

Otte, D. (1976). Species richness of New World desert grasshoppers in relation to plant diversity. *Journal of Biogeography*, **3**, 197–209.

Otte, D. & Joern, A. (1977). On feeding patterns in desert grasshoppers and the evolution of specialized diets. *Proceedings of the Academy of Natural Sciences of Philadelphia*, **128**, 89–126.

Raitt, R. J. & Pimm, S. J. (1976). Dynamics of bird communities in the Chihuahua Desert, New Mexico. *Condor*, **78**, 427–42.

Schmidly, D. J. (1977). *The mammals of Trans-Pecos Texas*. Texas A & M University Press, College Station.

Simpson, B. B. (1977). *Mesquite: its biology in two desert ecosystems*. US/IBP Synthesis Series 4. Dowden, Hutchinson & Ross, Stroudsburg, Pennsylvania.

Vasek, F. C. & Barbour, M. G. (1977). Mohave desert scrub vegetation. In: *Terrestrial vegetation of California* (eds. M. G. Barbour & J. Major). Wiley, New York.

Wells, P. V. & Hunziker, J. H. (1976). Origin of the creosote bush (*Larrea*) deserts of southwestern North America. *Annals of the Missouri Botanical Garden*, **63**, 843–861.

References

Adams, S., Strain, B. R. & Adams, M. S. (1970). Water-repellent soils, fire and annual plant cover in a desert scrub community of south-eastern California. *Ecology*, **51**, 696–700.

Ahearn, G. A. (1971). Ecological factors affecting population sampling of desert tenebrionid beetles. *American Midland Naturalist*, **86**, 385–406.

Allred, D. M. (1975). Arachnids as ecological indicators. *Great Basin Naturalist*, **35**, 405–6.

Allred, D. M. & Beck, D. E. (1967). Spiders of the Nevada Test Site. *Great Basin Naturalist*, **27**, 11–25.

Anderson, A. H. & Anderson, A. (1973). *The cactus wren*, p. 226. University of Arizona Press, Tucson.

Anderson, D. J. (1971). Pattern in desert perennials. *Journal of Ecology*, **59**, 555–60.

Anderson, S. (1972). Mammals of Chihuahua: taxonomy and distribution. *Bulletin of the American Museum of Natural History*, **148**, 149–410.

Antevs, E. (1955). Geologic climatic dating in the West. *American Antiquity*, **20**, 317–35.

Anthony, M. (1954). Ecology of the Opuntiae in the Big Bend region of Texas. *Ecology*, **35**, 334–47.

Aveleyra, L. (1964). Primitive hunters. In: *Handbook of middle-American Indians* (ed. R. C. West), pp. 384–412. University of Texas Press, Austin.

Axelrod, D. I. (1950). Evolution of desert vegetation in western North America. *Carnegie Institution of Washington Publication*, **590**, 215–306.

Axelrod, D. I. (1958). Evolution of the Madro-tertiary geoflora. *Botanical Review*, **24**, 435–509.

Axelrod, D. I. (1967). Drought, diastrophism and quantum evolution. *Evolution*, **21**, 201–9.

Axelrod, D. I. (1972). Edaphic aridity as a factor in angiosperm evolution. *American Naturalist*, **106**, 311–20.

Baker, R. H. (1956). Mammals of Coahuila, Mexico. *University of Kansas Museum of Natural History Publication*, **9**, 125–335.

Baker, R. H. & Greer, J. K. (1962). Mammals of the Mexican state of Durango. *Publication of the Museum, Michigan State University*, **2**, 25–154.

Barbour, M. G. (1969). Age and space distribution of the desert shrub *Larrea divaricata*. *Ecology*, **50**, 679–85.

Barbour, M. G. (1973). Desert dogma re-examined: root/shoot productivity and plant spacing. *American Midland Naturalist*, **89**, 41–57.

Barbour, M. G. & Diaz, D. V. (1973). *Larrea* plant communities on bajada and moisture gradients in the United States and Argentina. *Vegetatio*, **28**, 335–52.

Barbour, M. G., Diaz, D. V. & Breidenbach, R. W. (1974). Contributions to the biology of *Larrea* species. *Ecology*, **55**, 1199–1215.

Barbour, M. G., MacMahon, J. A., Bamberg, S. A. & Ludwig, J. A. (1977). The structure and distribution of *Larrea* communities. In: *Creosote bush biology and chemistry of Larrea in new world deserts* (eds. T. Mabry, J. Hunziker & D. Di Feo). US/IBP Synthesis Series 6. Dowden, Hutchinson & Ross, New York.

Bauman, A. J. (1976). Desert varnish and ferro-manganese oxide nodules: con-generic phenomena. *Nature*, **259**, 387–8.

Description of arid ecosystems

Baumhoff, M. A. & Heizer, R. F. (1965). Postglacial climate and archaeology in the Desert West. In: *The Quarternary of the United States* (eds. H. E. Wright & G. D. Frey), p. 922. Princeton University Press, New Jersey.

Beatley, J. C. (1967). Survival of winter annuals in the northern Mohave Desert. *Ecology*, **48**, 745–50.

Beatley, J. C. (1969a). Biomass of desert winter annual plant population in southern Nevada. *Oikos*, **20**, 261–73.

Beatley, J. C. (1969b). Dependence of desert rodents on winter annuals and precipitation. *Ecology*, **50**, 721–4.

Beatley, J. C. (1974a). Effects of rainfall and temperature on the distribution and behaviour of *Larrea tridentata* (creosotebush) in the Mojave Desert of Nevada. *Ecology*, **55**, 245–61.

Beatley, J. C. (1974b). Phenological events and their environmental triggers in Mojave Desert ecosystems. *Ecology*, **55**, 856–63.

Beatley, J. C. (1975). Climate and vegetation pattern across the Mohave/Great Basin Desert transition of southern Nevada. *American Midland Naturalist*, **93**, 53–70.

Beatley, J. C. (1976a). Environments of kangaroo rats (*Dipodomys*) and effects of environmental change on populations in southern Nevada. *Journal of Mammalogy*, **57**, 67–93.

Beatley, J. C. (1976b). Rainfall and fluctuating plant populations in relation to distribution and numbers of rodents in southern Nevada. *Oecologia*, **24**, 21–42.

Behle, W. H. (1976). Mohave desert avifauna in the Virgin River valley of Utah, Nevada and Arizona. *Condor*, **78**, 40–8.

Benson, L. & Darrow, R. A. (1954). *The trees and shrubs of the south-western deserts* (2nd edition). University of Arizona Press, Tucson.

Billings, W. D. (1945). The plant associations of the Carson Desert region, western Nevada. *Butler University Botanical Studies*, **7**, 89–123.

Billings, W. D. (1949). The shadscale vegetation zone of Nevada and eastern California in relation to climate and soils. *American Midland Naturalist*, **42**, 87–109.

Blair, W. F., Hulse, A. C. & Mares, M. A. (1976). Origins and affinities of vertebrates of the North American Sonoran Desert and the Monte Desert of northwestern Argentina. *Journal of Biogeography*, **3**, 1–18.

Bogert, C. M. & Oliver, J. A. (1945). A preliminary analysis of the herpetofauna of Sonora. *Bulletin of the American Museum of Natural History*, **83**, 301–425.

Bohrer, V. L. (1970). Ethnobotanical aspects of Snaketown, a Hohokam village in southern Arizona. *American Antiquity*, **35**, 413–30.

Brand, D. B. (1936). Notes to accompany a vegetation map of northwest Mexico. *University of New Mexico Bulletin, Biological Series*, **4**, 5–27.

Branson, F. A., Miller, R. F. & McQueen, I. S. (1967). Geographic distribution and factors affecting the distribution of salt-desert shrubs in the United States. *Journal of Range Management*, **20**, 287–96.

Brattstrom, B. H. (1955). Pliocene and Pleistocene amphibians and reptiles from southeastern Arizona. *Journal of Paleontology*, **29**, 150–54.

Brattstrom, B. H. (1958). New records of Cenozoic amphibians and reptiles from California. *Bulletin of the Southern Californian Academy of Science*, **57**, 5–12.

Brown, J. H. (1973). Species diversity of seed-eating desert rodents in sand dune habitats. *Ecology* **54**, 775–87.

Brown, J. H. (1975). Geographical ecology of desert rodents. In: *Ecology and evolution of communities* (eds. M. L. Cody & J. M. Diamond), pp. 1315–41. Belknap Press, Massachusetts.

Brown, J. H. & Lee, A. K. (1969). Bergman's rule and climatic adaptation in woodrats (*Neotoma*). *Evolution*, **23**, 329–38.

Brown, J. H. & Lieberman, G. A. (1973). Resource utilisation and coexistence of seed-eating desert rodents in sand dune habitats. *Ecology*, **54**, 788–97.

Brown, J. H., Lieberman, G. A. & Dengler, W. F. (1972). Woodrats and cholla: dependence of a small mammal population on the density of cacti. *Ecology*, **53**, 310–13.

Brown, J. H., Grover, J. J., Davidson, D. W. & Lieberman, G. A. (1975). A preliminary study of seed predation in desert and montane habitats. *Ecology*, **56**, 987–92.

Bryson, R. A. (1957). The annual march of precipitation in Arizona, New Mexico and northwestern Mexico. *University of Arizona, Institute of Atmospheric Physics, Report on Meteorology and Climatology*, **6**.

Buffington, L. C. & Herbal, C. H. (1965). Vegetational changes on a semi-desert grassland range. *Ecological Monographs*, **35**, 139–64.

Burk, J. H. & Dick-Peddie, D. A. (1973). Comparative production of *Larrea divaricata* Cav. on three geomorphic surfaces in southern New Mexico. *Ecology*, **54**, 1094–1102.

Burt, W. H. (1938). Faunal relationships and geographic distribution of mammals in Sonora, Mexico. *Miscellaneous Publications of the Michigan Museum of Zoology*, **39**, 1–77.

Cameron, R. E. & Fuller, W. H. (1960). Nitrogen fixation by some soil algae in Arizona soils. *Soil Science Society American Proceedings*, **24**, 353–6.

Causey, N. B. (1975). Desert millipedes (Spirostreptidae; Spirostreptida) of the southwestern United States and adjacent Mexico. *Occasional Papers of the Museum, Texas Technological University*, **35**, 1–12.

Chaney, R. W. (1947). Tertiary centers and migration routes. *Ecological Monographs*, **17**, 139–48.

Chew, R. M. (1961). Ecology of the spiders of a desert community. *Journal of the New York Entomological Society*, **69**, 5–41.

Chew, R. M. (1974). Consumers as regulators of ecosystems: an alternative to energetics. *Ohio Journal of Science*, **74**, 359–70.

Chew, R. M. & Chew, A. E. (1965). The primary productivity of a desert shrub (*Larrea tridentata*) community. *Ecological Monographs*, **35**, 355–75.

Chew, R. M. & Chew, A. E. (1970). Energy relationships of the mammals of a desert shrub (*Larrea tridentata*) community. *Ecological Monographs*, **40**, 1–21.

Cody, M. L. (1971). Finch flocks in the Mohave Desert. *Theoretical Population Biology*, **2**, 142–58.

Cole, G. A. (1968). Desert limnology. In: *Desert Biology*, vol. 1 (ed. G. W. Brown), pp. 423–86. Academic Press, New York.

Cook, R. E. (1969). Variation in species density of North American birds. *Systematic Zoology*, **18**, 63–84.

Cottam, W. P. (1961). *Our renewable wild lands: a challenge*. University of Utah Press, Salt Lake City.

Crawford, C. S. (1976). Feeding-season production in the desert millipede *Orthoporus ornatus*. *Oecologia*, **24**, 265–76.

Cruse, R. R. (1973). Desert plant chemurgy: a current review. *Economic Botany*, **27**, 210–30.

Curtis, J. T. & McIntosh, R. P. (1951). An upland forest continuum of the prairie forest border of Wisconsin. *Ecology*, **32**, 476–96.

Dalquest, W. W. (1953). Mammals of the Mexican state of San Luis Potosi. *Louisiana State University Studies, Biology Series*, **1**, 1–229.

Darrow, R. A. (1961). Origin and development of the vegetational communities of the Southwest. In: *Bioecology of the arid and semi-arid lands of the Southwest* (eds. L. M. Shield & L. J. Gardner), pp. 30–47. New Mexico Highlands University Bulletin.

Deacon, J. E. & Minckley, W. L. (1974). Desert Fishes. In: *Desert Biology*, vol. 2 (ed. G. W. Brown), pp. 385–488. Academic Press, New York.

Dice, L. R. (1943). *The biotic provinces of North America*. University of Michigan Press, Ann Arbor.

Dixon, K. L. (1959). Ecological and distributional relations of desert scrub birds in western Texas. *Condor*, **61**, 397–409.

Duisberg, P. C. (1952). Development of a feed from the creosotebush and determination of its nutritive value. *Journal of Animal Science*, **11**, 174–80.

Dunbier, R. (1968). *The Sonoran Desert, its geography, economy and people*. University of Arizona Press, Tucson.

Durham, J. W. & Allison, E. C. (1960). The geologic history of Baja California and its marine faunas. *Systematic Zoology*, **9**, 47–91.

Edney, E. B. (1974). Desert arthropods. In: *Desert Biology*, vol. 2 (ed. G. W. Brown), pp. 312–84. Academic Press, New York.

Emerson, F. W. (1935). An ecological reconnaissance in the White Sands, New Mexico. *Ecology*, **16**, 226–333.

Evernden, J. F. & James, G. T. (1964). Potassium–argon dates and the Tertiary floras of North America. *American Journal of Science*, **262**, 945–74.

Fautin, R. W. (1946). Biotic communities of the northern desert shrub biome in western Utah. *Ecological Monographs*, **16**, 251–310.

Fenneman, N. M. (1931). *Physiography of western United States*. McGraw-Hill, New York.

Findley, J. S. (1969). Biogeography of southwestern boreal and desert mammals. *Miscellaneous Publications, Kansas Museum of Natural History*, **51**, 113–28.

Fontana, B. L. (1974). Man in arid lands: the Piman Indians of the Sonoran Desert. In: *Desert Biology*, vol. 2 (ed. G. W. Brown), pp. 489–528. Academic Press, New York.

Franklin, J. F. & Dyrness, C. T. (1973). *Natural vegetation of Oregon and Washington*. USDA General Technical Report. PNW-8. Washington, D.C.

French, N. R., Maxa, B. G., Hill, H. O., Aschwander, A. P. & Kaaz, H. W. (1974). A population study of irradiated desert rodents. *Ecological Monographs*, **44**, 45–72.

Fuller, W. H. (1974). Desert soils. In: *Desert Biology*, vol. 2 (ed. G. W. Brown), pp. 31–102. Academic Press, New York.

Gardner, J. L. (1951). Vegetation of the creosotebush area of the Rio Grande Valley in New Mexico. *Ecological Monographs*, **21**, 379–403.

Gates, D. H., Stoddart, L. A. & Cook, C. W. (1956). Soil as a factor influencing plant distribution on salt deserts of Utah. *Ecological Monographs*, **26**, 155–75.

Gentry, H. S. (1942). Rio Mayo plants. A study of the flora and vegetation of the valley of the Rio Mayo, Sonora. *Carnegie Institution of Washington Publication*, **527**, 1–316.

Gerschman de Pikelin, B. S. & Schiapelli, R. D. (1962). La familia Diguetidae (Araneae) en la Argentina. *Physis (Florence)*, **23**, 205–8.

Gertsch, W. J. (1958). The spider family Diguetidae. *American Museum Novitates*, **1904**, 1–24.

Gertsch, W. J. & Soleglad, M. (1966). The scorpions of the *Vejovis boreus* groups (Subgenus Paruroctonus) in North America (Scorpionida, Vejovidae). *American Museum Novitates*, **2278**, 1–54.

Ghiselin, J. (1970). Edaphic control of habitat selection by kangaroo mice (*Microdipidops*) in three Nevada populations. *Oecologia*, **4**, 248–261.

Gile, L. H., Peterson, F. F. & Grossman, R. B. (1966). Morphological and genetic sequences of carbonate accumulation in desert soils. *Soil Science*, **101**, 347–60.

Gleason, H. A. (1939). The individualistic concept of the plant association. *American Midland Naturalist*, **21**, 92–110.

Gomez-Pompa, A. (1965). La vegetacion de Mexico. *Boletin de le Sociedad Botanica de Mexico*, **29**, 76–120.

Hagmeier, E. M. (1966). A numerical analysis of the distributional patterns of North American mammals. II. Re-evaluation of the Provinces. *Systematic Zoology*, **15**, 279–99.

Hagmeier, E. M. & Stults, C. D. (1964). A numerical analysis of the distributional patterns of North American mammals. *Systematic Zoology*, **13**, 125–55.

Hall, E. R. & Kelson, K. R. (1959). *The Mammals of North America*, 2 Volumes, 1083 pp. Ronald Press, New York.

Halvorsan, W. L. & Patten, D. T. (1975). Productivity and flowering of winter ephemerals in relation to Sonoran Desert shrubs. *American Midland Naturalist*, **93**, 311–19.

Hardy, R. (1945). The influence of types of soil upon the local distribution of some mammals in southwestern Utah. *Ecological Monographs*, **15**, 71–108.

Harrington, M. R. & Simpson, R. D. (1961). Tule Springs, Nevada: with other evidences of man in North America. *Southwest Museum Paper*, **18**.

Hastings, J. R. & Turner, R. M. (1965). *The changing mile: An ecological study of vegetation change with time in the lower mile of an arid and semi-arid region.* University of Arizona Press, Tucson.

Hastings, J. R., Turner, R. M. & Warren, D. K. (1972). *An atlas of some plant distributions in the Sonoran Desert.* University of Arizona, Institute of Atmospheric Physics, Technological Report on Meteorology and Climatology of Arid Regions, No. 21. Tucson.

Haverty, M. I. & Nutting, W. L. (1974). Natural wood-consumption rates and survival of a dry-wood and a subterranean termite at constant temperatures. *Annals of the Entomological Society of America*, **67**, 153–7.

Heath, J. E. & Wilkin, P. J. (1970). Temperature responses of the desert cicada *Diceroprocta apache* (Homoptera, Cicadidae). *Physiological Zoology*, **43**, 145–54.

Henrickson, J. & Straw, R. M. (1976). *A gazeteer of the Chihuahuan Desert region.* California State University, Los Angeles.

Hensley, M. M. (1954). Ecological relations of the breeeding bird population of the desert biome in Arizona. *Ecological Monographs*, **24**, 185–207.

Hubbard, J. P. (1973). Avian evolution in the arid lands of North America. *Living Bird*, **12**, 155–96.

Humphrey, R. R. (1974). *The boojum and its home.* University of Arizona Press, Tucson.

Hunt, C. B. (1966). *Plant ecology of Death Valley, California.* U.S. Geological Survey, Professional Paper No. 509.

Hunt, C. B. (1974). *Natural regions of the United States and Canada.* W. H. Freeman, San Francisco.

Hunt, C. B. (1975). *Death Valley: geology, ecology, archaeology.* University of California Press, Berkeley.

Hurd, P. D. & Linsley, E. G. (1975*a*). Some insects other than bees associated with *Larrea tridentata* in the southwestern United States. *Proceedings of the Entomological Society of Washington,* **77,** 100–20.

Hurd, P. D. & Linsley, E. G. (1975*b*). The principal *Larrea* bees of the southwestern United States (Hymenoptera: Apoidea). *Smithsonian Contributions to Zoology,* **193,** 1–74.

Irwin-Williams, C. & Haynes, C. V. (1970). Climatic change and early population dynamics in the southwestern United States. *Quaternary Research (New York),* **1,** 59–71.

Jaeger, E. C. (1957). *The North American Desert.* Stanford University Press, Stanford, California.

Jennings, J. D. (1957). Danger Cave. *University of Utah, Anthropological Paper,* **27,** 1–328.

Jennings, J. D. (1964). The Desert West. In: *Prehistoric Man in the New World* (eds. J. D. Jennings & E. Norbeck), pp. 149–74. University of Chicago Press, Chicago.

Johnson, A. W. (1968). The evolution of desert vegetation in western North America. In: *Desert Biology,* vol. 1 (ed. G. W. Brown), pp. 101–40. Academic Press, New York.

Johnson, H. D, Vasek, F. C. & Yonkers, T, (1975). Productivity, diversity and stability relationships in Mohave roadside vegetation. *Bulletin of the Torrey Botanical Club,* **102,** 106–15.

Johnston, I. M. (1941). Gypsophily among Mexican desert plants. *Journal of the Arnold Arboretum,* **22,** 145–70.

Juhren, M., Went, F. W. & Phillips, E. (1956). Ecology of desert plants. IV. Combined field and laboratory work on germination of annuals in Joshua Tree National Monument, California. *Ecology,* **37,** 318–30.

Kiester, A. R. (1971). Species density of North American amphibians and reptiles. *Systematic Zoology,* **20,** 127–37.

King, T. J. & Woodell, S. R. J. (1973). The causes of regular pattern in desert perennials. *Journal of Ecology,* **61,** 761–5.

Klikoff, L. G. (1966). Competitive responses to moisture stress of a winter annual of the Sonoran Desert. *American Midland Naturalist,* **75,** 383–91.

Klikoff, L. G. (1967). Moisture stress in a vegetational continuum in the Sonoran desert. *American Midland Naturalist,* **77,** 128–37.

Küchler, A. W. (1964). Potential natural vegetation of the conterminous United States. *American Geographic Society, Special Publication,* **36.**

Leopold, A. S. (1950). Vegetation zones of Mexico. *Ecology,* **31,** 507–18.

Leopold, A. S. (1959). *Wildlife of Mexico.* University of California Press, Berkeley.

Linsley, E. G. (1958). Geographical origins and phylogenetic affinities of the cerambycid beetle fauna of western North America. In: *Zoogeography* (ed. C. L. Hubbs), pp. 229–320. American Association for the Advancement of Science, Publication No. 51. Washington, D.C.

Logan, R. F. (1968). Causes, climates and distribution of deserts. In: *Desert Biology,* vol. 1 (ed. G. W. Brown), pp. 21–50. Academic Press, New York.

Lowe, C. H. (1955). The eastern limit of the Sonoran Desert in the United States with additions to the known herpetofauna of New Mexico. *Ecology,* **36,** 343–5.

Lowe, C. H. (1964). Arizona landscapes and habitats. In: *The vertebrates of Arizona* (ed. C. H. Lowe), pp. 3–132. University of Arizona Press, Tucson.

McCleary, J. A. (1968). The biology of desert plants. In: *Desert Biology*, vol. 1 (ed. G. W. Brown), pp. 141–94. Academic Press, New York.

McDonough, W. T. (1963). Interspecific associations among desert plants. *American Midland Naturalist*, **70**, 291–9.

McDonough, W. T. (1965). Pattern changes associated with the decline of a species in a desert habitat. *Vegetatio*, **13**, 97–101.

MacGinitie, E. D. (1953). Fossils of the Florissant beds, Colorado. *Carnegie Institution of Washington Publication*, **599**, 1–188.

MacGinitie, E. D. (1958). Climate since the Cretaceous. In: *Zoogeography* (ed. C. L. Hubbs), pp. 61–79. American Association for the Advancement of Science, Publication No. 51. Washington, D.C.

MacGregor, A. N. & Johnson, D. E. (1971). Capacity of desert algal crusts to fix atmospheric nitrogen. *Proceedings of the Soil Science Society of America*, **35**, 843–4.

McIntosh, R. P. (1967). The continuum concept of vegetation. *Botanical Review*, **33**, 130–73.

McKell, C. M. (1975). Shrubs – a neglected resource of arid lands. *Science*, **187**, 803–9.

MacMahon, J. A. (1976). Species and guild similarity of North American desert mammal faunas: a functional analysis of communities. In: *Evolution of desert biota* (ed. D. W. Goodall), pp. 134–48. University of Texas Press, Austin.

MacMillen, R. E. (1964). Population ecology, water relations and social behaviour of a southern California semi-desert rodent fauna. *University of California Publications in Zoology*, **71**, 1–59.

Malde, H. E. (1964). Environment and man in arid Arizona. *Science*, **145**, 123–9.

Martin, P. S. (1963). *The last 10,000 years; a fossil pollen record of the American Southwest*. University of Arizona Press, Tucson.

Martin, P. S. (1967). Prehistoric overkill. In: *Pleistocene extinctions, the search for a cause* (eds. P. S. Martin & H. E. Wright), pp. 75–120. Yale University Press, New Haven.

Martin, P. S. & Mehringer, P. J., Jr. (1965). Pleistocene pollen analysis and biogeography of the Southwest. In: *The Quaternary of the United States* (eds. H. E. Wright & D. G. Frey), pp. 433–52. Princeton University Press, Princeton, N.J.

Martin, P. S. & Plog, F. (1973). *The archaeology of Arizona*. Natural History Press, Garden City, New York.

Mason, H. L. (1947). Evolution of certain floristic associations in western North America. *Ecological Monographs*, **17**, 203–10.

Massey, W. C. (1961). The survival of the dart-thrower on the peninsula of Baja California. *Southwestern Journal of Anthropology*, **17**, 81–93.

Meigs, P. (1953). World distribution of arid and semi-arid homoclimates. *UNESCO Arid Zone Research*, **1**, 203–9.

Miranda, F. & Hernandez, X. E. (1963). Los Tipos de vegetacion de Mexico y su clasificacion. *Boletin de la Sociedad de Botanica Mexico*, **28**, 29–179.

Mitchell. J. E., West, N. E. & Miller, R. W. (1966). Soil physical properties in relation to plant community patterns in the shadscale zone of northwestern Utah. *Ecology*, **47**, 627–730.

Montgomery, S. J. & MacMahon, J. A. (1978). Rodent-habitat relationships in Great Basin shrub communities. (Submitted to *Oecologia*.)

Muller, C. H. (1939). Relations of the vegetation and climatic types of Nuevo Leon, Mexico. *American Midland Naturalist*, **21**, 687–729.

Muller, C. H. (1940). Plant succession in the *Larrea–Flourensia* climax. *Ecology*, **21**, 206–12.

Muller, C. H. (1947). Vegetation and climate of Coahuila, Mexico. *Madrono*, **9**, 33–47.

Muller, C. H. (1953). The association of desert annuals with shrubs. *American Journal of Botany*, **40**, 53–60.

Muller, W. H. & Muller, C. H. (1956). Association patterns involving desert plants that contain toxic products. *American Journal of Botany*, **43**, 354–61.

Muma, M. H. (1970). A synoptic review of North American, Central American and West Indian Solpugida (Arthropoda: Arachnida). *Arthropods of Florida*, **5**, 1–62.

Niering, W. A., Whittaker, R. H. & Lowe, C. H. (1963). The saguaro: a population in relation to environment. *Science*, **142**, 15–23.

Oberholser, S. C. (1974). *The bird life of Texas*, 2 Volumes, 1069 pp. University of Texas Press, Austin.

Ochoterena, I. (1945). Outline of the geographic distribution of plants in Mexico. In: *Plants and plant science in Latin America* (ed. F. Verdoom), pp. 261–5. Chronica Botanica, Waltham, Mass.

Otte, D. & Joern, A. (1975). Insect territoriality and its evolution, population studies of desert grasshoppers on creosote bushes. *Journal of Animal Ecology*, **44**, 29–54.

Peabody, F. E. (1959). Trackways of living and fossil salamanders. *University of California Publications in Zoology*, **63**, 1–72.

Pianka, E. R. (1966). Convexity, desert lizards and spatial heterogeneity. *Ecology*, **47**, 1055–9.

Pianka, E. R. (1967). On lizard species diversity: North American flatland deserts. *Ecology*, **48**, 333–51.

Pianka, E. R. (1971). Lizard species density in the Kalahari. *Ecology*, **52**, 1024–9.

Pianka, E. R. (1975). Niche relations of desert lizards. In: *Ecology and evolution of communities* (eds. M. L. Cody & J. M. Diamond), pp. 292–314. Belknap Press, Massachusetts.

Preston, F. W. (1962). The canonical distribution of commonness and rarity. *Ecology*, **43**, 185–215.

Raitt, R. J. & Maze, R. L. (1968). Densities and species composition of breeding birds of a creosotebush community in southern New Mexico. *Condor*, **70**, 193–205.

Raven, P. H. & Axelrod, D. I. (1974). Angiosperm biogeography and post-continental movements. *Annals of the Missouri Botanical Gardens*, **61**, 539–673.

Recher, H. F. (1971). Bird species diversity: a review of the relation between species number and environment. *Proceedings of the Ecological Society of Australia*, **6**, 135–52.

Reed, E. K. (1964). The greater southwest. In: *Prehistoric man in the New World* (eds. J. D. Jennings & E. Norbeck), pp. 175–92. University of Chicago Press, Chicago.

Rehn, J. A. G. (1958). The origin and affinities of Dermoptera and Orthoptera of western North America. In: *Zoogeography* (ed. C. L. Hubbs), pp. 253–98. American Association for the Advancement of Science, Publication No. 51. Washington, D.C.

Rodgers, R. W., Lange, R. T. & Nicholas, D. J. D. (1966). Nitrogen fixation by lichens of arid soil crusts. *Nature (London)*, **209**, 96–7.

Rogers, J. S. (1976). Species density and taxonomic diversity of Texas amphibians and reptiles. *Systematic Zoology*, **25**, 26–40.

Rosenzweig, M. L. (1973). Habitat selection experiments with a pair of coexisting heteromyid rodent species. *Ecology*, **54**, 111–17.

Rosenzweig, M. L., Smigel, B. & Kraft, A. (1975). Patterns of food, space and diversity. In: *Rodents in desert environments* (eds. I. Prakash & P. K. Ghosh), pp. 241–68. Junk, The Hague.

Rosenzweig, M. L. & Sterner, P. W. (1970). Population ecology of desert rodent communities: body size and seed-husking as bases for heteromyid coexistence. *Ecology*, **51**, 217–24.

Rosenzweig, M. L. & Winakur, J. (1969). Population ecology of desert rodent communities: habitats and environmental complexity. *Ecology*, **50**, 558–72.

van Rossem, A. J. (1945). Birds of Sonora. *Occasional Papers of the Museum of Zoology, University of Louisiana*, **21**, 1–379.

Ryan, R. M. (1968). *Mammals of Deep Canyon Colorado Desert, California*. The Desert Museum, Palm Springs.

Rzedowski, J. (1955). Nota sobere la flora y la vegetation de San Luis Potosi II. *Ciencia (Mexico)*, **15**, 89–96.

Rzedowski, J. (1966). Vegetacion del estado de San Luis Potosi. *Acta Cientifica Potosina*, **5**, 5–291.

Rzedowski, J. (1973). Geographical relationships of the flora of Mexican dry regions. In: *Vegetation and vegetational history of northern Latin America* (ed. A. Graham), pp. 61–72. Elsevier, New York.

Sanders, E. M. (1921). The natural regions of Mexico. *Geographical Review*, **11**, 212–26.

Savage, D. E. (1958). Evidence from fossil land mammals on the origin and affinities of western Nearctic fauna. In: *Zoogeography* (ed. C. L. Hubbs), pp. 97–103. American Association for the Advancement of Science, Publication No. 51. Washington, D.C.

Savage, J. M. (1960). The biogeography of Baja California and adjacent seas: Evolution of a peninsular herpetofauna. *Systematic Zoology*, **9**, 184–212.

Schroder, G. D. & Rosenzweig, M. L. (1975). Perturbation analysis of competition and overlap in habitat utilisation between *Dipodomys ordii* and *Dipodomys merriami*. *Oecologia*, **19**, 9–28.

Schulter, R. (1965). Tule Springs expedition. *Current Anthropology*, **6**, 110–11.

Shelford, V. E. (1963). *The ecology of North America*. Illinois University Press, Urbana, Illinois.

Sherbrooke, W. C. & Haase, E. F. (1974). Jojoba: a wax-producing shrub of the Sonoran desert. *University of Arizona Arid Lands Information Paper*, **5**.

Shields, L. M. & Wells, P. V. (1962). Effects of nuclear testing on desert vegetation. *Science*, **135**, 38–40.

Shreve, F. (1942). The desert vegetation of North America. *Botanical Review*, **8**, 195–246.

Shreve, F. (1951). Vegetation of the Sonoran Desert. *Carnegie Institution of Washington Publication*, **591**, 1–129.

Shreve, F. & Mallery, T. D. (1933). The relation of caliche to desert plants. *Soil Science*, **35**, 99–113.

Shreve, F. & Wiggins, I. L. (1964). *Vegetation and flora of the Sonoran Desert*. Stanford University Press, Stanford, California.

Description of arid ecosystems

Simpson, G. G. (1964). Species density of North American recent mammals. *Systematic Zoology*, **13**, 57–73.

Snyder, J. M. & Wullstein, L. H. (1973). The role of desert cryptogams in nitrogen fixation. *American Midland Naturalist*, **90**, 257–65.

Solbrig, O. (1972). The floristic disjunctions between the 'Monte' in Argentina and the 'Sonoran Desert' in Mexico and the United States. *Annals of the Missouri Botanic Gardens*, **59**, 218–23.

Springer, M. E. (1958). Desert pavement and vesicular layer of some soils in the Lahontan Basin, Nevada. *Soil Science Society American Proceedings*, **22**, 63–6.

Stebbins, R. C. (1966). *A field guide to western reptiles and amphibians*. Houghton-Mifflin, Boston, Massachusetts.

Stebbins, R. C. (1974). Off-road vehicles and the fragile desert. *American Biology Teacher*, **36**, 203–208 & 294–304.

Stevens, R. L. (1964). The soils of Middle America and their relation to Indian people and cultures. In: *Handbook of Middle American Indians* (ed. R. C. West), Volume 1, pp. 265–315. University of Texas Press, Austin.

Stuart, L. C. (1970). Fauna of Middle America. In: *Handbook of Middle American Indians* (ed. R. C. West), vol. 1, pp. 316–62. University of Texas Press, Austin.

Tevis, L., Jr. (1958*a*). Germination and growth of ephemerals induced by sprinkling a sandy desert. *Ecology*, **39**, 681–7.

Tevis, L., Jr. (1958*b*). A population of desert ephemerals germinated by less than one inch of rain. *Ecology*, **39**, 688–94.

Tevis, L., Jr. (1958*c*). Interrelations between the harvester ant *Veromessor pergandei* and some desert ephemerals. *Ecology*, **39**, 695–704.

Tinkham, E. R. (1948). Faunistic and ecological studies of the Orthoptera of the Big Bend region of Trans-Pecos Texas, with special reference to the orthopteran zones and faunae of midwestern North America. *American Midland Naturalist*, **40**, 521–662.

Tinkle, D. W. (1967). The life and demography of the side-blotched lizard (*Uta stansburiana*). *Miscellaneous Publication of the Museum of Zoology*, **132**, 1–182.

Tomoff, C. S. (1974). Avian species diversity in desert scrub. *Ecology*, **55**, 396–403.

Turnage, W. V. & Hinckley, A. L. (1938). Freezing weather in relation to plant distribution in the Sonoran Desert. *Ecological Monographs*, **8**, 529–50.

Turnage, W. V. & Mallery T. D. (1941). An analysis of rainfall in the Sonoran Desert and adjacent territory. *Carnegie Institution of Washington, Publication*, **529**.

Turner, R. M., Alcorn, S. M., Olin, G. & Booth, J. A. (1966). The influence of shade, soil and water on saguaro seedling establishment. *Botanical Gazette*, **127**, 95–102.

Turner, F. B., Medica, P. A. & Kowalewsky, B. W. (1976). *Energy utilisation by a desert lizard* (Uta stansburiana). US/IBP Desert Biome Monograph, **1**, 1–57. Logan, Utah.

Ungar, I. A. (1974). Inland halophytes of the United States. In: *Ecology of halophytes* (eds. R. J. Reimold & W. H. Queen), pp. 235–306. Academic Press, New York.

Urban, E. K. (1959). Birds from Coahuila, Mexico. *University of Kansas, Publications of the Museum of Natural History*, **11**, 443–516.

Wallace, A. & Romney, E. M. (1972). Radioecology and ecophysiology of desert plants at the Nevada Test Site. *United States Atomic Energy Council*, **TID-25954**. Springfield, Virginia.

Wallace, A., Romney, E. M. & Ashcroft, R. T. (1970). Soil temperature effects on growth of seedling of some shrub species which grow in the transitional area between the Mohave and Great Basin Deserts. *Bioscience*, **20**, 1158–9.

Walter, H. (1971). *Ecology of tropical and subtropical vegetation.* Oliver & Boyd, Edinburgh.

Waterfall, U. T. (1946). Observations on the desert gypsum flora of southwestern Texas and adjacent New Mexico. *American Midland Naturalist*, **36**, 456–65.

Wells, P. V. (1961). Succession in desert vegetation on streets of a Nevada ghost town. *Science*, **134**, 670–1.

Went, F. W. (1949). Ecology of desert plants. ii. The effect of rain and temperature on germination and growth. *Ecology*, **30**, 1–13.

Werner, F. G., Enns, W. R. & Parker, F. H. (1966). The Meloidae of Arizona. *Technical Bulletin Arizona Agricultural Experimental Station*, **175**, 1–96.

West, R. C. (1964). Surface configuration and associated geology of Middle America. In: *Handbook of Middle American Indians* (ed. R. C. West), vol. 1, pp. 33–83. University of Texas Press, Austin.

Wheeler, G. C. & Wheeler, J. (1973). Ants of Deep Canyon. In: *Philip L. Boyd Deep Canyon Research Center Reports.* University of California, Riverside.

Whitford, W. G. (1976). Temporal fluctuations in density and diversity of desert rodent populations. *Journal of Mammalogy*, **57**, 351–69.

Whitford, W. G., Johnson, P. & Ramirez, J. (1976). Comparative ecology of the harvester ants *Pogonomyrmex barbatus* and *Pogonomyrmex rugosus*. *Insectes Sociaux*, **23**, 117–31.

Whittaker, R. H. (1965). Dominance and diversity in land plant communities. *Science*, **147**, 250–60.

Whittaker, R. H. & Niering, W. A. (1964). The vegetation of the Santa Catalina Mountains, Arizona. i. Ecological classification and distribution of species. *Journal of the Arizonan Academy of Science*, **3**, 9–34.

Whittaker, R. H. & Niering, W. A. (1968). Vegetation of the Santa Catalina Mountains, Arizona. iv. Limestone and acid soils. *Journal of Ecology*, **56**, 523–44.

Whittaker, R. H., Buol, S. W., Niering, W. A. & Havens, Y. H. (1968). A soil vegetation pattern in the Santa Catalina Mountains, Arizona. *Soil Science*, **105**, 440–50.

Williams, S. C. (1970). A systematic revision of the giant hairy-scorpion genus *Hadrurus* (Scorpionida: Vejovidae). *Occasional Papers of the Californian Academy of Science*, **87**, 1–62.

Wolfe, J. A. (1969). Paleogene floras from the Gulf of Alaska region. *United States Geological Survey Open-File Report*, p. 114.

Wolfe, J. A. (1972). An interpretation of Alaskan Tertiary floras. In: *Floristics and Paleofloristics of Asia and eastern North America* (ed. A. Graham), pp. 201–33. Elsevier, New York.

Wolfe, J. A. (1975). Some aspects of plant geography of the northern hemisphere during the late Cretaceous and Tertiary. *Annals of the Missouri Botanic Gardens*, **62**, 264–79.

Woodell, S. R. J., Mooney, H. A. & Hill, A. J. (1969). The behaviour of *Larrea divaricata* (creosote bush) in response to rainfall in California. *Journal of Ecology*, **57**, 37–44.

Wright, H. E., Jr. (1971). Late Quaternary vegetational history of North America. In: *Late Cenozoic glacial ages* (ed. K. K. Turekian), pp. 425–64. Yale University Press, New Haven.

Description of arid ecosystems

Wright, R. A. (1970). The distribution of *Larrea tridentata* (D.C.) Coville in the Avra Valley, Arizona. *Journal of the Arizonan Academy of Science*, **6**, 58–63.

Yang, T. W. (1970). Major chromosome races of *Larrea divaricata* in North America. *Journal of the Arizonan Academy of Science*, **6**, 41–5.

Yang, T. W. & Lowe, C. H. (1956). Correlation of major vegetation climaxes with soil characteristics in the Sonoran Desert. *Science*, **123**, 542.

Yeaton, R. I. & Cody, M. L. (1976). Competition and spacing in plant communities: the northern Mohave Desert. *Journal of Ecology*, **64**, 689–96.

York, J. C. & Dick-Peddie, W. A. (1969). Vegetation changes in southern New Mexico during the past 100 years. In: *Arid Lands in perspective* (eds. W. G. McGinnies & B. J. Goldman), pp. 157–66. University of Arizona Press, Tucson.

Manuscript received by the editors January 1977

3.   North Africa

H. N. LE HOUÉROU

Introduction

North Africa in this paper is taken to include the following countries from west to east, Morocco, Algeria, Tunisia, Libya and Egypt (UAR).

Arid land is understood in a broad meaning, that is the areas receiving less than 400 mm of average rainfall. The Arid zone, *sensu lato* is in turn divided into two areas:

(*a*) arid, *sensu stricto*, with average precipitations between 100 and 400 mm;
(*b*) desertic or Saharan with average precipitations below 100 mm.

These boundaries are not arbitrary; they will be explained in the chapters dealing with climate, vegetation and land use. The arid and desertic areas within each country are shown in Table 3.1.

Origins

Geology

The geological history of North Africa is rather simple in its broad outline when considered in a paleogeographic perspective. During all the sedimentary times, North Africa stood at the border of the African continent (Saharan Shield) and of the mesogean syncline occupied by the Tethys sea. The geological history is thus a succession of transgressions and regressions of the Tethys on and from the Saharan shield. There are three main geological provinces:

(*a*) the Saharan shield made out of three Precambrian folded metamorphic complexes with intrusive rocks in the first two;
(*b*) the northern Sahara made out of horizontal or subhorizontal sedimentary layers of marine (transgressions) or continental (regressions) deposits;
(c) the Atlas mountain province (southern Morocco and Mauritania), folded during the Hercynian orogenesis (Carbonifero-Permian) and the Atlas orogenesis of Oligocene age.

The continental sediments predominate in the south towards the Saharan shield and include Cambrian to Jurassic–Cretaceous 'continental intercalary' deposits (nubian sandstones of Libya and Egypt). Marine sediments predominate towards the north (northern Sahara and Maghreb

83

Table 3.1. *Arid and desertic zones in north Africa.* (Sources: Le Houérou, 1965, 1969a, c; Ionesco, 1965)

Countries	Total area (1000 km²)	Non-arid non-desert		Arid sensu stricto		Desert		Arid and desert	
		(1000 km²)	%[1]	(1000 km²)	%[1]	(1000 km²)	%[1]	(1000 km²)	%[1]
Morocco	447	197	44.2	120	26.8	130	29.0	250	55.8
Algeria	2381	181	7.6	200	8.4	2000	84.0	2200	92.4
Tunisia	155	37	23.9	55	35.4	63	40.7	118	76.1
Libya	1760	5	0.2	90	5.1	1665	94.7	1755	99.8
Egypt (UAR)	1000	0	0.0	30	3.0	970	97.0	1000	100.0
Total	5743	420	7.3	495	8.7	4828	84.0	5323	92.7

[1] Percentage of the total area of the country.

countries). The main transgressions took place during the Cambrio-Silurian period, the middle and upper Cretaceous (Cenomanian, Senonian) and during the early Cenozoic era. Cretaceous and Eocene terrains (limestones and shales mainly) occupy huge areas in the northern Sahara and the Atlas zone; so do the continental nubian sandstones of Libya and Egypt.

The position of North Africa, located between the Tethys and the African continent, also explains the importance of lagunary deposits of anhydrite, gypsipherous shales and salty quaternary alluviums.

Geomorphology

The arid zone of North Africa is a classic example of arid-land geomorphology. The ranges of hills and mountains of the Atlas chain, developed in a pure Jurassic tectonic style, show erosion forms in accordance with their lithology and structure. These ranges are separated by wide synclines in which huge Quaternary pediments have developed, often covered by a thick calcareous crust (caliche) of early and middle Pleistocene. As endoreism is the general rule, the lower parts are occupied by Quaternary alluvia, which is often saline (playas). They are called *Sebkha* or *Chott* and correspond to the Asian *Takyrs*.

The Sahara has four main types of land forms:

(*a*) the rocky and stony, steep-sloped hills or mountains (Ahaggar, Tibesti, Adrar, etc.);

(*b*) the *Reg* (*Serir* in the eastern Sahara), which are gravelly-pebbly subhorizontal plains swept off by aeolian erosion. These *Regs* may have various origins: flat structural surfaces of rather soft rocks; old pediments reshaped by aeolian erosion; detritic, coarse, alluvial deposits; they are accordingly divided in 'autochthonous' and 'allochthonous' *regs*;

(*c*) the *Hammada*, correspond to structural, almost flat surfaces, covered with large flagstones of limestone, sandstone or basalt;

(*d*) the *Erg* or *Sandseas* are massifs of dunes of various sizes and forms from the small, crescent-shaped, mobile *barkhans* to the huge fixed *ghourds*, 50 to 200 m high with a deep rocky skeleton.

The rocky mountains and *Hammadas* represent about 10% of the desert area (0.48×10^6 km²), the *Regs* cover about 68% (3.28×10^6 km²) while the *Ergs* occupy 22% (1.06×10^6 km²). Contrary to what many laymen imagine, sand dunes represent less than 25% of the Sahara.

Table 3.2(*a*). *Rainfall in the desert zone (mm)*

	J	F	M	A	M	J	J	A	S	O	N	D	Year
Egypt													
Port Said	18	12	9	5	3	1	0	0	0	3	11	16	78
Suez	5	3	3	2	2	0	0	0	0	1	4	4	24
Cairo	5	4	4	2	2	0	0	0	0	2	2	4	25
Dakhla	0	1	0	0	0	0	0	0	0	0	0	0	1
Libya													
Beni Walid	6.7	3.7	8.3	6.0	5.6	0.3	0.0	0.0	7.0	8.5	7.0	14.4	71.0
Rhadamès	6.0	5.0	4.0	13.0	1.0	0.0	0.0	0.8	0.0	2.0	7.0	4.0	43.0
Sebah	2.0	2.0	0.8	0.6	0.2	0.0	0.0	0.0	0.0	0.7	0.2	0.0	8.0
Kufra	0.3	0.0	0.0	0.0	0.2	0.0	0.0	0.0	0.1	0.3	0.0	0.0	0.9
Tunisia													
Tozeur	10.0	8.0	13.0	10.0	5.0	3.0	0.2	2.0	7.0	9.0	12.0	10.0	89.0
Fort Saint	6.7	3.0	4.1	1.3	2.7	1.0	0.0	0.0	1.5	2.4	4.1	4.0	30.8
Algeria													
Ghardaia	9.0	4.0	7.0	4.0	5.0	4.0	1.0	2.0	5.0	7.0	13.0	7.0	68.0
Tamanrasset	3.9	1.1	0.8	1.3	6.6	3.6	3.1	9.5	7.4	1.9	1.1	1.8	42.6
Bechar	7.0	7.2	12.7	7.5	2.3	2.9	0.4	3.6	6.6	13.8	11.6	9.6	85.2
Djanet	4.7	1.7	1.2	1.8	3.5	3.0	0.1	0.4	3.8	1.3	1.9	1.6	25.0
In Salah	2.9	0.8	2.1	1.1	0.3	0.1	0.0	0.7	0.1	1.3	2.3	3.9	15.6
Tindouf	4.4	2.0	5.2	2.1	0.1	0.0	0.2	5.2	8.5	9.8	8.9	6.1	52.5
Aoulef	0.4	0.4	1.1	0.1	0.5	0.0	0.0	1.1	0.1	2.0	2.0	1.5	9.2
Morocco													
Bou Denib	5.4	4.2	11.1	8.2	4.2	4.7	0.9	6.9	10.6	17.2	12.7	13.8	99.9
Ouarzazate	4.3	6.9	11.5	6.5	4.5	1.0	1.1	7.8	21.6	13.3	11.3	17.7	107.5
Zagora	0.8	2.4	5.4	7.0	0.6	1.6	0.5	4.0	11.8	8.2	5.6	11.8	59.7

Climate

The arid zone of North Africa may be divided into three main climatic zones:

(*a*) arid zone, *sensu stricto*, or steppic northern zone with a mediterranean climate and winter rains; average annual rainfall is more than 100 mm;

(*b*) northern desert zone with winter rains and less than 100 mm average rainfall;

(*c*) central zone with very rare rains which may fall in any season. This zone constitutes a transition towards the southern Sahara characterized by summer rains.

This classification proposed by Emberger (1938) uses both climatic and phytogeographic criteria.

Table 3.2(*b*). *Average rainfall in the northern steppic zone (mm and number of days)*

Stations	J	F	M	A	M	J	J	A	S	O	N	D	Year
Alexandria	48	24	11	3	2	0	0	0	1	6	33	56	184 mm
	10	7	4	1	1	0	0	0	1	2	6	10	42 days
Benghazi	67	40	19	5	2	0	0	0	3	17	47	66	266
	12	10	5	2	1	0	0	0	1	4	8	12	54
Sirte	42	28	13	3	2	1	0	0	7	16	26	34	172
	7	5	3	1	1	1	0	0	1	3	5	6	33
Tripoli	61	34	26	115	5	1	0	0	15	37	43	76	313
	11	7	5	3	2	1	0	0	2	5	7	11	54
Gabès	22	17	21	10	9	1	0	2	14	30	34	15	175
	4	3	4	3	2	2	0	1	3	4	4	4	34
Sousse	43	34	30	22	18	6	1	5	50	43	37	38	327
	9	7	8	6	5	4	1	3	5	6	7	8	69
Gafsa	17	13	22	16	10	8	2	4	14	14	18	14	152
	3	3	3	3	3	1	1	1	\3	3	3	3	30
Kairouan	27	26	35	26	24	12	5	8	37	31	30	25	286
	6	5	6	5	5	3	1	2	5	5	5	5	53
Barika	25	24	26	14	21	13	2	3	24	20	30	22	224
	5	4	5	3	3	2	1	1	3	4	4	4	39
Laghouat	12	12	16	12	19	12	5	7	23	17	18	14	167
	3	3	3	3	4	2	2	2	4	3	4	3	36
Djelfa	34	28	29	21	35	22	6	10	31	23	34	35	308
	7	6	7	5	6	5	2	3	5	5	6	6	63
Aflou	31	33	38	32	28	25	9	11	24	45	30	33	342
	5	7	7	5	6	5	4	4	4	7	7	7	68
Ain Sefra	10	10	14	9	15	28	8	7	15	29	29	18	192
	2	2	3	3	4	3	2	4	4	4	4	2	37
Berguent	13	17	22	22	23	9	4	7	18	25	18	19	197
Midelt	10	24	22	34	24	12	6	8	22	22	26	16	226
Marrakech	24	30	37	33	15	7	2	3	10	20	34	27	242
	4	5	5	5	3	1	1	1	2	4	6	5	33
Agadir	37	28	26	20	4	1	0	0	6	21	40	43	226
	3	3	3	2	1	1	0	0	1	2	4	4	24

Rainfall

Phytogeographic and agronomic criteria define the boundaries of the northern steppic zone as the 100 and 400 mm annual isohyets. The 400 mm isohyet corresponds to the northern limit of the steppic vegetation which includes steppes of *Stipa tenacissima*, *Artemisia herba-alba*, *Helianthemum lippii*, *Artemisia campestris*, and other similar species. This isohyet also corresponds to the lower limit of profitable cereal cultivation and mixed farming in dryland areas. The lower limit of 100 mm corresponds to the northern border of typical desert plant communities and species such as *Calligonum comosum*, *Cornulaca monacantha* and

Description of arid ecosystems

Moltkia ciliata. The 100 mm isohyet also corresponds to the absolute lower limit of farming without irrigation, including the use of runoff water (wadi agriculture). These limits were discussed at length by Le Houérou (1959, 1969c).

The annual and monthly variability in rainfall is high and increases inversely with average annual rainfall. Below the 400 mm isohyet annual rainfall may vary by a factor of four and below the 100 mm isohyet the factor may be ten to twelve. The seasonal maximum can occur in autumn, spring or winter depending on the area. This is the main difference between North African precipitation regimes and the Near Eastern regime where the bulk of the precipitation falls in winter. However, eastern Libya and Egypt have a Near Eastern pattern. Details of monthly rainfall for a number of areas in the northern steppic and desert zones are shown in Table 3.2 (*a* and *b*).

Rainfall gradient

At a given latitude rainfall increases about 5–10% per 100 m increase in elevation depending on exposure and other local conditions.

Evolution of rainfall

Weather records cover more than 100 years in several places but no systematic trend in rainfall evolution can be drawn from them. There are series of years with above-average rains and other series with below-average precipitations. We are at the present time in a 'dry series' which began in the 1960s. At Tripoli (Libya) for instance the ratio of rainfall in 1957 to rainfall between 1879 and 1971 is 0.77. If the average rainfall, expressed as mm, is divided by 5 the result gives an estimate of the number of rainy days (0.1 mm or more rain).

Temperatures

The mean annual temperature along the coast and at the border of the Sahara varies from 18 to 20 °C but falls to 12–14 °C above elevations of 1000 m. From an ecological viewpoint, average daily or monthly temperatures have little meaning. It is the average maxima and minima which occur regularly which are significant to plant and animal life. The average daily minimum of the coldest month (January) and the average daily maximum of the hottest months (July or August) are particularly important. The average daily minimum of January is correlated with the presence or absence of frost, the number of frosty days and frost intensity in the following way:

88

Average daily minimum temperature (°C)	
> 9	No frost, very warm winters
9 to 7	Frost exceptional or very rare, warm winters
7 to 5	5–10 days of light frost, mild winters
5 to 3	10–20 days of light frost, temperate winters
3 to 1	20–30 days of frost, cool winters
1 to −2	30–60 days of frost, cold winters
−2 to −5	60–120 days of heavy frost, very cold winters
< −5	More than 120 days of frost, high mountains

The above divisions are derived from studies of the distribution of plant communities.

Along the coast the average daily minimum temperature varies between 7 and 10 °C and there is no frost; however, temperatures decrease with continentality and elevation. The gradient is about 5–8 °C per 1000 m difference in elevation, depending on continentality and local conditions. The average daily maximum temperature is about 30 °C along the coast, 35–38 °C in the hinterland and 40–45 °C in the Sahara.

Evapotranspiration

Annual evapotranspiration, either measured or computed through various formulae (Penman, Turc), varies from 1400 mm at the northern border of the steppic zone to 1600–1800 mm in the central and southern Sahara. Daily rates range from 1–2 mm in January to 8–10 mm in the middle of the summer and account for about 60% of the evaporation measured in a 'class A' pan or 80% when measured in a 'colorado' pan.

Hot winds

Hot winds (*Sirocco, Ghibli* or *Chergui*) blow for 20–90 days per year, especially in spring and autumn. Relative humidity falls to 10–15% during these dry spells. If they occur in spring, these hot winds are very detrimental to crops and native vegetation which may dry out in a very few days.

Climatic synthesis

The climates of the North African arid and desert zone may be classified by using average rainfall in conjunction with average minimum temperature in January. This is similar to the scheme proposed by Emberger

Average rainfall (mm)	
300–400	Upper arid mediterranean climate
200–300	Middle arid mediterranean climate
100–200	Lower arid mediterranean climate
50–100	Upper Saharan mediterranean climate
20–50	Lower Saharan mediterranean climate
< 20	Eu-Saharan climate (not mediterranean)

(1955) but average rainfall has replaced 'Emberger's Index'. If a matrix is constructed, using these rainfall zones and the average daily minimum temperature in January, it can be seen that nearly all the combinations exist.

Average annual rainfall (mm)	Average daily minimum temperature (°C)					
	> 9	9–7	7–5	5–3	3–1	1––2
300–400	−	+	+	+	+	+
200–300	+	+	+	+	+	+
100–200	+	+	+	+	+	+
50–100	+	+	+	+	+	?
20–50	+	+	+	+	+	−
< 20	+	+	+	+	+	−

Where + is an existing combination and − a non-existing combination.

These combinations are not arbitrary climatic divisions, they correspond to a series of plant communities (Le Houérou, 1959) whose climatic limits are within the threshold criteria defined above. The plant communities are referred to as the stages and substages of vegetation which are discussed below (see pp. 97–9).

Hydrology

As in all arid zones, North African hydrology is characterized by intermittent streamflow following rains. Temporary rivers, *oueds* or *wadis* (equivalent to the *arroyos*) run for only a few hours after a rain. Rainfall of 10–20 mm is sufficient to cause some flow. Between 5% and 10% of the precipitation runs off as streamflow and is often lost as it spreads in the salt flats or *sebkhas* (*playas*).

In the zones located on the border of the higher elevations (2000–4000 m) of Morocco and Algeria some streams are perennial, at least in the upper part of their course: for example, the *oueds* Draa, Moulouya, Sous,

Tensift and Chelif. The same applies, of course, to the Nile, rising in the high, rainy mountains of central and east Africa. Large tracts of the Sahara, where average rainfall is below 20 mm, have no streamflow. For example, the eastern Sahara of Libya and Egypt, Tenere and Tanezruft in Algeria and the Majhat Al Kubra in Mauritania.

Aquifers in the arid zone are fed in four ways:

(*a*) percolation from higher rainfall areas on the mountains bordering the arid zone;

(*b*) runoff from the mountains and pediments of the arid zone and per- colation in the endoreic depressions;

(*c*) runoff on the mountains and *regs* of the desert and percolation in the endoreic depressions;

(*d*) percolation in the sandy areas.

These sandy areas, *ergs* or sandseas, are usually located in, or at, the border of great depressions where runoff from the *regs* or pediments also percolate. This is why the superficial aquifers and consequently the oases are almost always located at the border of the large sandy massifs.

Some aquifers are partially or totally fossil, that is to say partially refilled or not refilled at all. The first case is that of the 'continental intercalary' of southern Algeria and Tunisia. The second case is the large aquifer of the Kufra region in Libya, at the border of Egypt, Sudan and Chad.

Soils and erosion

Soil distribution is closely linked to geology, geomorphology, climate, vegetation and land use.

Soil units may be classified as follows (French classification and US 7th Approximation).

Arid zone (rainfall between 100 and 400 mm)
    Evolved soils

Calco magnesimorphic soils

Rendzinas $\begin{cases} \text{Black} \\ \text{Grey} = \text{Rendolls} \\ \text{Red} \end{cases}$

Degraded rendzinas

Rendzinas on limecrust = Mollic calciorthids with calcic horizons

Brown calcareous soils $\begin{cases} \text{non-vertic} = \text{Eutrochrepts} \\ \text{vertic} \end{cases}$

Gypsic soils = Mollic calciorthids with gypsic horizon.

Description of arid ecosystems

Vertisols and paravertisols $\begin{cases} \text{Topomorphic} = \text{vertisol} \\ \text{Lithomorphic} \end{cases}$

Isohumic soils or brown steppic soils and
Sierozem = Mollic camborthids = Mollic calciorthids
Sesquioxides soils or red and brown mediterranean soils equivalent to
   dystichrepts and eutrochrepts
Halomorphic soils
   Saline soils = Salorthids (Solontchacks)
   Saline soils with alkali (sodic Solontchacks) = Salorthids (sodic)
Hydromorphic soils (gley and pseudogley)
   with calcareous concretions = calciaquolls
   with gypsic concretions
   with saline concretions, saline phase or aquepts or aquents
   with sulfureous concretions

Unevolved soils – non-climatic

Lithosols – lithic subgroups, shallow classes
Regosols = orthents and psamments
Fluvia deposits = fluvents (calcareous)
Colluvial deposits
Aeolian deposits
   sand = psamments
   loess

Desert zone (rainfall below 100 mm)

Evolved soils are limited to the halomorphic and hydromorphic classes
shown above in the halomorphic and hydromorphic soils.

Unevolved soils – climatic

Lithosols (aeolian erosion)
   Hammada (flagstone pavements)
   Regs (pebbly plains)
      Autochthonous
      Allochthonous
      Fech – (loose pulverulent sodium sulfate or carbonate, or calcium
       carbonate)
Regosols (Aeolian deposits)
      Sand veils
      Sand patchwork
      Microdunes or Rheboub

Barkhans
Nebkas or Hummocks
Cordon dunes

Some of these soil units are rare or very rare, for example, the calco magnesiomorphic soils, vertisols and paravertisols and the sesquioxide soils, which are located at the northern border of the arid zone (upper arid mediterranean climate). Others cover huge areas, such as lime crust on the pediments of the arid zone, halomorphic soils in the endoreic depressions, and *regs* and sandy deposits in the desert zone.

From an ecological and agronomic viewpoint, the main soil factor in the arid zone is water balance, as it is closely correlated to ecosystem productivity. In this respect, the most significant soil characteristics are:

topographic or geomorphologic position (runoff or run in);
texture (infiltration rate and field capacity);
depth (storage capacity);
toxicity;
permeability of the upper layer (water intake).

The productive soils are those which are able to store water during the short rainy periods and to release it afterwards to vegetation during the long dry periods. That is to say the soils which, owing to their hydro-dynamic characteristics, are able to reduce the climatic drought. This is merely an expression of Liebig's law of the 'minimum'.

Erosion

Water erosion predominates in the arid zone, whereas the desert zone is mostly affected by wind erosion. In the arid zone, water erosion removes 0.5–1.5 mm of top soil per year, which amounts to 6–20 t of soil material ha^{-1} yr^{-1}. However, soil removal by wind erosion has been measured at over 70 t ha^{-1} yr^{-1} on cultivated sand steppes of southern Tunisia (Floret & Le Floch, 1972). This erosion is accelerated by mismanagement practices such as over-grazing, uprooting of woody species for fuel and cereal cultivation in the arid zone.

Erosion contributes to desertization of tens of thousands of hectares of arid steppes every year (Le Houérou, 1968, 1969*a*, *b*, *c*).

Flora and vegetation

The phanerogamic flora

The phanerogamic flora of arid and desert zones of North Africa includes about 2000 species of which about 1200 are found in the Sahara (le Houérou, 1959). The main botanical families represented are Composi-

Description of arid ecosystems

tae, Gramineae, Caryophyllaceae, Leguminosae, Cruciferae and Umbelliferae. These six families account for 50–60% of the flora. The most common genera, which include about 200 species, are *Astragalus*, *Silene*, *Euphorbia*, *Ononis*, *Helianthemum*, *Linaria*, *Centaurea* and *Erodium*. The rate of endemism is high (about 20 genera and 200 species) especially at the species, subspecies and variety level.

Many genera are represented by a single species. Jaccard's factor (number of genera:number of species) is about 0.5. In the phanerogamic flora about 70% of the species are considered as mediterranean, 20% Saharo–Sindian (including tropical species), and 10% Pluri-regional (cosmopolitan). These proportions vary from each stage and substage of vegetation to the next: for instance in the upper arid mediterranean substage the proportions are 85, 10 and 5% and in the lower Saharan mediterranean substage of vegetation these proportions become 18, 80 and 2% respectively (Le Houérou, 1959).

The vegetation

The flora and vegetation of arid and desert zones of North Africa have been studied, in depth, since 1620 and research on the flora was already active during the 18th century. The four volumes of *Flora Atlantica* by Desfontaines, published between 1798 and 1800, contained 1500 species. The bibliography now amounts to several thousand references and a meaningful synthesis would therefore call for hundreds of pages! To deal with such a synthesis in the space of a few pages may seem an almost impossible task even (and perhaps particularly) for somebody familiar with the subject. I will therefore restrict discussion to very broad phytogeographic features after having briefly described the main types of vegetation structure and physiognomy.

If greater detail of the flora is required the descriptions by Ozenda (1958), Nègre (1961), Quezel & Santa (1962, 1963), Le Houérou (1959) and Tackholm (1974) are useful references.

Physiognomy and structure (see Le Houérou, 1969c)

The following physiognomic and structural types of vegetation are found in arid North Africa.

Forest

A vegetation having trees over 5 m high and over 100 stems ha⁻¹ is considered as forest. The true forests are very rare and are located in the upper arid substage of vegetation (300–400 mm average annual rainfall) within

94

the arid mediterranean zone. They are almost always open forest and there is always an understorey of shrubs (see arid mediterranean stage).

Matorral

The matorral is equivalent to the American term 'chaparral' and comprises evergreen tall shrubs or small trees. Structure is very complex and numerous types of matorral are recognized depending on height, density and ground cover. They always correspond to degraded forests (see pp. 97–8, upper and middle substages of arid mediterranean stage).

Erme

Erme is short vegetation of forbs and grasses including many unpalatable species. *Asphodelus* spp., thistles, *Peganum harmala*, *Thapsia garganica*, *Ferula* sp., *Euphorbia* spp. and *Cleome arabica* are all common species. Erme is a post-pastoral vegetation resulting from heavy, long-term overgrazing which frequently occurs around villages, wells, etc.

The steppe

The steppe is a short, open, treeless vegetation dominated by perennial species with various proportions of bare ground. Plant cover may be anywhere from 5% to 80%. Three main types of steppes can normally be distinguished.

The gramineous steppes are physiognomically dominated by perennial grasses and are usually located on shallow or sandy soils and in middle arid, lower arid and Saharan stages of vegetation.

The crassulescent steppes are dominated by crassulescent, halophilous species, the majority belonging to the Salsolaceae. These crassulescent steppes should not be confused with 'succulent steppes' which have succulent, non-halophilous species, such as cactoid Euphorbiae, cacti and *Caralluma* spp., which belong to the tropical region and are restricted to south-western Morocco within North Africa.

The chamaephytic steppes are characterized by the dominance of short shrubs or half shrubs, 0.2–0.5 m high, corresponding to Raunkiaer's 'chamaephytes'. Chamaephytic steppes cover over 25 million hectares in North Africa.

Description of arid ecosystems

Pseudo steppes

The vegetation of the pseudo steppes is taller than that of the steppe. Shrubs, 0.5–3.0 m high are dominant. This type of vegetation is found in well-watered places such as dunes, flooded areas and along the stream network. The pseudo steppes are totally different from matorral in their botanical composition, habitat, structure and physiognomy.

Pseudo sylves

This is an extremely rare type of vegetation found in the large dunes of the Great Eastern Sandsea (Grand Erg Oriental) and in the Edeyen of Ubari (Fezzan). It comprises very scattered small trees (2–8 m high) of *Calligonum azel* and *Calligonum arich* with a few individuals of *Aristida pungens*, *Retama raetam*, *Genista saharae* and *Calligonum comosum*.

Pseudo savannas

These are found in the Sahara, along the main streams and on terraces. They comprise a tree layer of *Acacia raddiana* and/or *Maerua crassifolia*, *Balanites aegyptiaca* and *Zizyphus spina christi*, which cover 0.01–10% of the ground. Between the trees there is a denser cover of tall perennial grasses: *Panicum turgidum*, *Rotboellia hirsuta*, *Pennisetum dichotomum*, *Cymbopogon schoenanthus*, and small shrubs such as *Aerva persica*.

Meadows

Meadows occur in areas having permanent moisture in the top-soil. The soils and water are often somewhat saline with a conductivity of 2–10 mhos. These meadows occupy very restricted areas and occur only in the upper and middle arid substages of vegetation within the arid zone. They are almost absent in the lower arid and Saharan stages, but common in the semi-arid to humid mediterranean stages of vegetation.

Lawns

Lawns are defined as short grass or grasslike formations with complete ground cover. They have a marked seasonal rhythm; green in winter and spring and dry in summer. Lawns occur only in the upper arid substage of vegetation within the arid zone. They usually occur in non-arid areas and on rendzina soils. Dominant species are perennial grasses, numerous rosette-shaped Compositae and low-growing Lamiaceae.

96

Hygrophilous formations

These are associated with free water. The typical vegetation is mainly cosmopolitan genera such as *Typha*, *Phragmites*, *Carex*, *Cladium*, *Scirpus* and *Cyperus*.

Littoral marshes

In the arid and desertic zones of North Africa, mangroves of *Avicennia* are restricted to the Red Sea coast of Egypt (Kassas, 1957). Classical halophytes occur in other littoral salt marshes, for example: *Halimione portulacoides*, *Salicornia herbacea*, *Inula crithmoides*, *Tamarix gallica*, *Spergularia marginata*, *Aeluropus littoralis*.

Stages and substages of vegetation

As mentioned previously, the arid and desert vegetations of North Africa may be classified in stages and substages of vegetation corresponding to the various climates and sub-climates.

Arid mediterranean stage

This stage corresponds to the arid mediterranean climate with average annual rainfall between 100 and 400 mm. It is divided into upper, middle and lower.

Upper substage (300–400 mm average rainfall). The primeval vegetation is forest. Along the coast, where winters are warm or mild, this substage was dominated by *Tetraclinis articulata*. Other species present include *Olea europaea*, *Ceratonia siliqua*, *Chamaerops humilis*, *Periploca laevigata*, *Rhus pentaphyllum*, *Withania fruticosa* and *Pistacia lentiscus*. In western Morocco (Safi, Essaouia areas), *Argania spinosa* is co-dominant with *Tetraclinis articulata*.

In the hinterland, with cool or cold winters, the primeval forest was dominated by *Pinus halepensis*. Other species present include: *Juniperus oxycedrus*, *Juniperus phoenicea*, *Genista cinerea*, *Retama sphaerocarpa*, *Spartium junceum*, *Genista microcephala*, *Stipa tenacissima*, *Phillyrea angustifolia*, *Centaurea tenuifolia*, *Hippocrepis scabra*.

These primeval forests are almost always degraded into garrigues or matorrals and the latter are often further degraded into steppes of *Stipa tenacissima* on shallow soils; *Artemisia herba-alba* on silty or clayey soils and *Artemisia campestris* on sandy soils.

The upper limit of this substage corresponds to the upper limit of the steppic vegetation (400 mm) which, in this case, is always a 'secondary steppe'. Annual productivity of above-ground phytomass is about 1000–1200 kg ha in the forest and matorral and 800–1000 kg ha in the steppes (Le Houérou, 1969c).

Middle substage (200–300 mm average annual rainfall). The primeval vegetation is forest and relics can still be found in remote places. These forests were dominated by Aleppo pine and, perhaps, *Tetraclinis* sp. along the coast. In southwestern Morocco, there are still about 0.4×10^6 ha of *Argania spinosa* open forest in the Agadir–Taroudant area. However, relics of Aleppo pine aree extremely rare (Le Houérou, 1969c); the remaining matorrals are dominated by *Juniperus phoenicea* with the following associated species: *Pistacia atlantica, Rosmarinus officinalis, Rhamnus lycioides, Globularia alypum, Olea europaea, Genista microcephala, Thymus hirtus, Rhus tripartitum, Cistus libanotis, Periploca laevigata, Thymus capitatus, Stipa tenacissima.*

The primeval forest and derived matorral are generally degraded into steppic communities similar to those for the upper substage with the addition that *Anabasis oropedlorum* may be present on very degraded shallow soils.

Although the main dominating species of these steppes are the same as in the upper substage the botanical compositions are very different (Le Houérou, 1969c; Le Houérou, Claudin & Haywood, 1975). Similarly, productivity is different and about 50% lower than in the upper substage.

Lower substage (100–200 mm average annual rainfall). There is no evidence of a primeval forest vegetation in this substage, except in the depressions and along the stream network (*Acacia raddiana* and *Pistacia atlantica*). The original vegetation on the pediments was probably a gramineous steppe. The main species are *Artemisia herba-alba* and *Hammada scoparia* on silty or shallow soils; *Rhanterium suaveolens* and *Stipa lagascae* on sandy soils; *Thymelaea hirsuta* and *Artemisia campestris* on sandy shallow soils (eastern Libya and northern Egypt); and *Hammada schmittiana* and *Thymelaea microphylla* on sandy, gypseous soils. Annual aboveground phytomass production of these steppes is about 200–400 kg ha^{-1}, about 50% of the productivity observed in the middle arid substage.

Mediterranean Saharan stage of vegetation (less than 100 mm annual average rainfall)

The limits between this stage and the arid stage was discussed by Le Houérou (1959; 1969c), and Quezel (1965). It corresponds to well defined eremitic plant communities which barely extend beyond the 100 mm isohyet. This stage is sub-divided into upper and lower stages.

Upper Saharan (50–100 mm annual average rainfall). The vegetation on the *regs* and pediments is distributed on a 'diffuse' pattern (Monod, 1954), whereas in lower mediterranean Saharan and in Saharan vegetation it is distributed on a 'contracted' pattern and is restricted to runnels and stream networks, the *regs* being bare or, at least, void of perennial species. The main plant communities are: *Anthyllis henoniana–Gymnocarpos decander* on shallow soils and *regs*; *Salsola sieberi–Traganum nudatum* on gypseous *regs*; *Moricandia arvensis–Cymbopogon shoenanthus* and *Hammada schmittiana–Anabasis articulata* on sandy, gypseous *regs*; *Hammada scoparia* on silty *regs*; *Aristida pungens–Ephedra alata* on dunes; *Retama raetam–Calligonum comosum, Acacia raddiana–Ziziphus lotus* on wadis; *Fredolia aretioiodes* on *regs* in the Western Sahara; *Aristida pungens–Moltkia ciliata* on dunes; *Cyperus conglomeratus–Cornulaca monacantha* on coarse sands.

Productivity is low, irregular and highly variable from one plant community to the next and from one year to the next. Average aboveground phytomass production is 100–200 kg ha^{-1} yr^{-1} but the range is from 0 to 600 kg ha^{-1} yr^{-1}.

Lower Saharan (20–50 mm annual average rainfall). As mentioned above vegetation is restricted to depressions and dunes. The main plant communities are: *Zilla spinosa–Pulicaria crispa, Salsola baryosma–Hyoscyamus muticus, Salsola tetragona–Traganum nudatum, Aristida pungens–Calligonum comosum, Artemisia judaica–Astragalus pseudotrigonus, Asteriscus graveolens–Anvillea radiata, Acacia raddiana–Panicum turgidum* and *Randonia africana–Antirrhinum ramosissimum.*

There are also numerous temporary communities of ephemeral plants. *Fagonia* spp. are usually present with such species as *Plantago ciliata, Brocchia cinerea, Ormenis lonadioides, Ammosperma cinereum, Volutaria saharae* and *Trigonella anguina.*

Average productivity has little meaning here. It is assumed that over 10 years the total aboveground production would be about 500 kg ha^{-1}.

Eu Saharan (less than 20 mm average annual rainfall)

Perennial vegetation is virtually restricted to the main wadis which rise in the mountains of adjacent areas. Huge areas, amounting to a total of about 1.0×10^6 km^2, in the Tenere, the Tanezruft, and the Libyan desert are practically devoid of vegetation. In the Majabat al Kuba, the western 'empty quarter' of southern Mauritania, Monod (1958) found only seven species of phanerogams over 0.2×10^6 km^2, whereas Quezel (1965) found

99

Description of arid ecosystems

50 species over 0.15×10^6 km² in the Djourab and 20 over 0.2×10^6 km² in the Tenere.

The vegetation of the high mountains of the Sahara

The high mountains, over 1500 m (Ahaggar, Tassili, Tibesti, Ennedi), have a particular flora and vegetation comprising a mixture of mediterranean, tropical autochthonous, and African mountainous elements, for example: *Cupressus dupreziana–Olea laperrini, Myrtus nivellei–Ficus salicifolia, Boscia salicifolia–Acacia laeta* and *Cordia garaf–Grewia tenax*. Steppic vegetation occurs at the higher elevations and includes species such as: *Artemisia herba-alba–Pentzia monodiana, Artemisia tilhoana–Ephedra tilhoana* and *Helichrysum monodianum–Dichrocephala tibestica*.

Animals

Many large animals disappeared about 100 years ago, others have become very rare.

Mammals

Carnivora

Fennecus zerda, the fennec, is still common in some parts of the Sahara. *Canis aureus*, the jackal, is still common in the arid zone and northern Sahara. *Hyaena hyaena barbara*, the hyena, is found only in the northern Sahara and is very rare.

The large carnivores: *Panthera pardus*, the leopard: *Acinomyx jubatus*, the cheetah: *Panthera leo*, the lion disappeared 100 to 150 years ago, though in the semi-arid forest of Morocco there are still a few leopards.

Hyracoidea

Procavia capensis bounhioli, the rock dassie or hyrax, is still encountered in colonies in the high mountains of central Sahara.

Artiodactyla

Addax nasomaculatus, the addax, has almost disappeared from the Sahara. Twenty years ago, one specimen was reported in the Fezzan but there are still a few herds in the western Sahara. The same applies to the *Oryx algazel (Oryx tao)*, the gemsbock. *Alcelaphus buselaphus* the bubal hartebeest, has totally disappeared. *Gazella dama mhorr*, the dama gazelle, has disappeared except in the western Sahara. *Ammotragus lervia lervia*, the barbary sheep, has become very rare in the mountains of northern Sahara where it used to be common 30 to 50 years ago. *Capra*

100

ibex nubiana, the nubian ibex, of Upper Egypt and Sinai has almost disappeared. *Gazella dorcas*, the dorcas gazelle, was very common in all the arid zone of North Africa 20 years ago but is now very rare and can only be found in the Sahara. The other gazelles: *Gazella cuvieri*, atlas gazelle, the *Gazella leptoceros*, dune gazelle or rhim gazelle, are extremely rare.

Lagomorpha

Lepus capensis aegyptius, the hare, is still common in the arid steppe although heavily hunted.

Rodentia

Rodents are very common in certain types of ecosystems especially in the crassulescent, halophilous steppes and the sandy steppes of the arid zone.

Psammomys abesus may have a density of 50–100 ha^{-1}. Other rodents although less abundant are not rare: *Hystrix cristata*, a porcupine of the mountainous areas, is hunted for its flesh; *Ctenodactylus gundi*, is still common in the mountains of southern Tunisia and in Libya and is also hunted for its flesh; *Elyomys quercynus*, common in the non-arid zones, is rather rare in the arid areas; *Jaculus jaculus* and *Jaculus orientalis*, the jerboa, are still common in the arid zone. The same applies to *Gerbillus campestris*, *Gerbillus nanus garamantis*, *Gerbillus pyramidum*, *Gerbillus gerbillus* and *Pachyuromys duprasi*, *Meriones shawi* and *Meriones libycus* are common and are reservoirs for the plague's Yershin's bacillus.

Birds

The ostrich, *Struthio camelus*, used to be common and was hunted in southern Algeria and Tunisia 100 to 150 years ago. It has now almost disappeared except for a few individuals in the western Sahara. Smaller birds are so numerous that it would be impossible to list them here. However, they have been extensively studied and detailed descriptions can be found in Heim de Balsac (1936), Etchecopar & Hüe (1964) and Niethammer (1971).

Reptiles

Testudo kleinmanni, the land tortoises, are not rare and geckos are very common. *Uromastix acanthinurus*, the 'dhob' is not rare in the stony deserts, whereas the varans, *Varanus griseus*, prefers the sandy steppes, and the skink, *Scincus scincus*, lives in the dunes of the northern Sahara.

Description of arid ecosystems

One of the most common snakes in sandy habitats is the horned viper, *Cerastes cerastes*. The deadly *Vipera lebetina* is not rare in the stony hills of the arid zone while the cobra, *Naja haje*, is very common in certain types of sandy steppes and especially in the *Ziziphus lotus* hummocks. An extensive list of reptiles in the northern Sahara is given by Gauthier (1967).

Insects

Insects are extremely numerous especially in sandy habitats. The locust, *Schistocerca gregaria*, used to play an important economic role but their periodic invasions have been curbed by efficient control and international cooperation. The insects of the arid and desertic zones of North Africa are detailed by Pierre (1958). Grasshoppers and locusts are reviewed in detail by Uvarov (1954, 1966).

Man and the desert

Livestock industry

The livestock industry is by far the largest agricultural and economic industry in the steppic areas of north-western Africa. The numbers of animals kept on the steppic ranges, excluding those kept in irrigation farming, are shown in Table 3.3. The total livestock population, converted into sheep equivalents, is 45×10^6 adult sheep. This corresponds to an animal density of 0.9 sheep ha^{-1}. In practice, it is less because transhumance in the semi-arid zones in summer and in the northern Sahara in winter time, results in the livestock being fed partly outside the arid zone. The actual stocking rate is about 0.5 sheep ha^{-1}, which is still very high, about twice what it should be on a long-term sustained productivity basis.

Livestock numbers vary enormously, depending on the series of dry and rainy years. The numbers may vary by a factor of five between years and in the driest parts the factor may be as high as seven (Le Houérou, 1962). The human population to livestock ratio is about 1.7 sheep equivalents per person in the arid zone as a whole, and 2.5 sheep per person in the rural population.

History of land use and management

Prehistoric relics bear witness to man's presence in North Africa for several hundred thousand years, since the Pebble Culture. Several prehistoric civilizations had their origin there, notably in the present arid and desert zones: Chellean–Acheulean (lower Paleolithic), Aterian (middle Paleolithic), Ibero–Maurusian and Capsian (upper Paleolithic), and

102

Table 3.3. *Livestock numbers in the arid zone* (*in thousands*)

Country	Cattle	Sheep	Goats	Camels
Algeria	250	6000	2000	175
Egypt	100[1]	2000	1200	125
Libya	120	2200	1400	260
Morocco	800	12000	4000	100
Tunisia	200	2500	500	150
Total	1470	24700	9100	810

[1] Estimated number.

Saharan Neolithic (Balout, 1955). During the Neolithic and protohistoric times of the Egyptian empires (5000 to 500 B.C.) the Sahara was a sort of savanna occupied by cattle herders, similar to the Fulani. All kinds of wildlife were present and the Sahara was then comparable to the situation of the present east African savannas.

The oriental civilizations notably the Phoenicians, developed in North Africa about 800 B.C., then came the Greeks (Egypt, Eastern Libya), and the Romans. Agriculture was developed very early, not only along the Nile but even in Libya, Tunisia and Algeria. For example, Massinissa, King of Numidia (Eastern Algeria and Western Tunisia), exported more than 2000 t of wheat to Rome and Greece between 200 and 170 B.C., Carthaginian merchants dealt with much larger amounts of that commodity (Camps, 1960).

Under Roman domination, agriculture prospered and became diversified; North Africa became one of the main granaries of Rome with a special, state-controlled, wheat trade organization, the *Annona*. Vineyards and olive-tree plantations extended over several million hectares, of which a great proportion was located in the arid zone between the present 100 mm and 400 mm isohyets. At the border of the Sahara a prosperous 'wadi agriculture' developed and can still be observed in areas receiving as little as 50 mm of annual rainfall. Beni Walid, in western Libya, is an example.

Runoff waters were extensively used everywhere in the arid zone, as witnessed by the relics of man-made terraces and dams that can still be seen, even in the remotest and almost desertic areas. It is assumed, from the density of relics, that population between the third and the seventh centuries A.D. was at least as high as today. Toward the middle of the seventh century the Arab conquerors took over all North Africa from the Red Sea to the Atlantic ocean.

The civilization of nomadic shepherds developed primarily in the steppes of the arid zone or in their semi-arid northern margins. This is probably because the plains of areas located in more humid climates, toward the northern shores, were infested with malaria. Conditions suitable for the development of this disease prevailed when drainage and agriculture were abandoned at the end of the Roman and Byzantine domination. The nomadic population was constantly battling the agricultural settlers, whom they forced to retreat to mountain hideaways such as the Atlas mountains of Morocco and Algeria, Jebel Aures (south-eastern Algeria), Jebel Matmata (southern Tunisia) and Jebel Nefusah (south-western Libya). In these remote and arid mountains the Berbers developed rather sophisticated land-use practices making the best possible use of any rain. This is sometimes referred to as 'wadi agriculture'. A similar form of 'desert agriculture' developed in the Near East and notably in the northern Negev and Jordan during the Nabatean period, 700 B.C. to 200 A.D. (Evanari, Shanan, Tadmor & Aharoni, 1961; Evanari, Shanan & Tadmor, 1971).

Other Berber populations sought refuge in the mountains of the central Sahara (Ahaggar, Tassili, Air, Adrar) and developed there a type of complex and sophisticated nomadic, feudal civilization represented by the Tuareg society. The nomadic population engaged in endless tribal disputes for twelve centuries over ownership of grazing lands, grain fields and oases. In combination with epidemics and famines, these conflicts produced a certain equilibrium between the capacity for production in the steppes and the density of human and animal populations. Contrary to what has been and is often still stated, the traditional nomadic society was approximately in equilibrium with natural resources on which they entirely depended; any mistake in land use was followed by reduction of the land's carrying capacity for human and animal populations. Hence, they had to learn sound land-use practices in order to survive. This equilibrium was broken after the colonial conquests of the nineteenth century with the establishment of peace, security, guaranteed food supply, improved hygiene and medicine (vaccination, sulfonamides, antibiotics). The result is a population explosion (Table 3.4) which has been offset only to a small degree by progress in agricultural techniques.

Since the beginning of this century the population of the arid zones has increased nearly sixfold (Table 3.4), but the agricultural and shepherd's techniques have remained almost unchanged. The population density is extremely variable, reaching 80–100 people km^{-2} in the Moroccan Atlantic zone, the Tunisian Sahel and the eastern high plains of Algeria (almost urban densities are found in the Nile Valley and Delta). In the high steppes of western Algeria and eastern Morocco and the predesertic zones of central and eastern Libya the population density drops to 5 to 15 people km^{-2}, but in certain localities it reaches 100 to 200 inhabitants km^{-2}, such as on the Island of Djerba and Djerid in Tunisia, the Tafilalet of southern

Table 3.4. *Population, estimates and projections (in thousands)*

Country	1900	1950	1965	1970	1975	1985	2000
Algeria	2000?	8750	11540	13280	16000	19600	30000
Egypt	6000?	20000	30000	35000	42500	51000	75000
Libya	500	1030	1620	1875	2250	3200	4800
Morocco	2000	8950	13260	15600	19300	24500	58000
Tunisia	1000	3550	4650	5180	6000	6900	10500
Total	11500	42280	61070	70935	86050	105200	178300

Morocco. The increase of population in arid zones is comparable and even slightly higher than for the various countries as a whole. The annual rate of population growth is: Morocco–Algeria 3.5%; Tunisia 2.8%; Libya, Egypt 3.0%. This means that population doubles every 20 years in Morocco and Algeria; every 23 years in Egypt; and every 25 years in Tunisia. The consequences of this exponential population growth on the environment has been analysed by Le Houérou (1968, 1969*a*, *b*, *c*, 1971*a*, *b*, 1973*a*, *b*). They may be summarized as follows: (*a*) The surface of land cultivated for cereals (wheat and barley) has increased at approximately the same rate as population and the increase in food supply to meet population growth has been obtained by clearing new land in the mountains and the arid steppes. This has resulted in accelerated erosion over several tens of thousands of hectares every year. Algeria alone loses 40 000 hectares by water erosion annually (Greco, 1966) and about as much by wind erosion (Le Houérou, 1968). (*b*) Overgrazing is common (average stocking rate over the arid zone is about 0.5 sheep-equivalent per hectare). This generalized overgrazing has resulted in a sharp decrease in productivity of natural ecosystems. The current actual production is of about 25% of what it could be under appropriate management practices (Rodin *et al.*, 1970; Le Houérou, 1968, 1971*a*, *b*). (*c*) Clearing forests and forest remnants for firewood leads to 'steppization' (Le Houérou, 1969*c*). Clearing the woody half-shrubs from the steppe for fuel leads to 'desertization' (Le Houérou, 1968; Pabot, 1962; Kassas, 1970; Floret & Le Floch, 1972; Le Houérou, Claudin & Haywood, 1975; and others).

The pressure on the land by an exponential population growth is the major, if not the only, ecological problem of arid land in North Africa today.

References

Balout, L (1955). *Prehistoire de l'Afrique du Nord*. Arts et métiers graphiques, Paris.
Camps, G. (1960). Massinissa, ou les débuts de l'histoire. *Libyca*, **8**, 1–320.

Description of arid ecosystems

Emberger, L. (1938). La définition phytogéographique du climat desertique. In: *La vie dans la région desertique nord-tropicale de l'ancien mond*, pp. 9–14. Société Biogéographie, Paris.

Emberger, L. (1955). Une classification biogéographique des climats. *Travaux de l'Institut Botanique (Montpellier)*, **7**, 3–43.

Etchecopar, R. D. & Hüe, F. (1964). *Les oiseaux du Nord de l'Afrique, de la mer Rouge aux Canaries*. Boubée, Paris.

Evanari, M., Shanan, L., Tadmor, N. H. & Aharoni, Y. (1961). Ancient agriculture in the Negev. *Science*, **133**, 976–96.

Evanari, M., Shanan, L. & Tadmor, N. H. (1971). *The Negev – The challenge of a desert*. Harvard University Press, Cambridge, Mass.

Floret, C. & Le Floch, E. (1972). *Désertisation et ressources pastorales dans la Tunisie présaharienne*. Ministry of Agriculture, Inrat, Tunis.

Gauthier, R. (1967). Ecologie et éthologie des reptiles du Sahara Nord occidental. *Annales du Musée Royale de l'Afrique Centrale, Tervuren, Belgique, series 8*, **155**, 1–83.

Greco, J. (1966). *L'érosion, la défense et la restauration des sols en Algérie*. Ministere de l'agriculture et de la reforme, Algeria agricole, Algeria.

Heim de Balsac, H. (1936). Biogéographie des mammifères et des oiseaux de l'Afrique du Nord. *Bulletin Biologique de la France et de la Belgique*, Supplement 21.

Ionesco, T. (1965). Considérations bioclimatiques et phytoécologiques sur les zones arides du Maroc. *Cahiers de la recherche Agronomique*, **19**, 1–130.

Kassas, M. (1957). On the ecology of the Red Sea coastal land. *Journal of Ecology*, **47**, 187.

Kassas, M. (1970). Desertification versus potential recovery in circum-Saharan territories. In: *Arid Lands in Transition* (ed. H. E. Dregne), pp. 123–39. American Association for the Advancement of Science, Washington, D.C.

Le Houérou, H. N. (1959). Recherche écologiques et floristiques sur la végétation de la Tunisie méridionale. *Memoirs Hors Series Institut Recherches Sahariennes, Algeria*.

Le Houérou, H. N. (1962). *Les pâturages naturels de la Tunisie aride et désertique*. Paris. Institut de Science Economique Appliquée.

Le Houérou, H. N. (1965). *Improvement of natural pastures and fodder resources. Report to the Government of Libya*. Expanded Technical Assistance Programme, Report No. 1979. F.A.O., Rome.

Le Houérou, H. N. (1968). La désertisation du Sahara septentrional et des steppes limitrophes (Libye, Tunisie, Algérie). *Conseil de Tutelle Colloque Hammamat et Annales Algerie de Geographique*, **3** (6), 2–27.

Le Houérou, H. N. (1969a). North Africa: past, present, future. In: *Arid lands in transition* (ed. H. E. Dregne), pp. 227–78. American Association for the Advancement of Science, Washington, D.C.

Le Houérou, H. N. (1969b). *Principes, méthodes et techniques d'amélioration fourragère et pastorale en Tunisie*. F.A.O., Rome.

Le Houérou, H. N. (1969c). La végétation de la Tunisie steppique. (Avec référence aux végétations analogues d'Algérie, de Libye et du Maroc). *Annales de l'Institut National de la Recherche Agronomique de Tunisie*. No. 42.

Le Houérou, H. N. (1971a). Les bases écologiques de la production pastorale et fourragère en Algérie. Division of Plant Protein Production, F.A.O., Rome.

Le Houérou, H. N. (1971b). An assessment of the primary and secondary production of the arid grazing lands ecosystems of North Africa. *Ecophysio-*

logical foundation of ecosystems productivity in arid zone (ed. L. E. Rodin), pp. 168–72. Nauka, Leningrad.

Le Houérou, H. N. (1972). The useful shrubs of the Mediterranean basin and of the Sahelian belt of Africa. In: *Wildland Shrubs, their Biology and Uses*, pp. 26–36. Utah State University Press, Ogden, Utah.

Le Houérou, H. N. (1973*a*). *Ecological foundations of agricultural and range development in Western Libya*. Division of Plant Protein Production, F.A.O., Rome.

Le Houérou, H. N. (1973*b*). Ecologie, démographie et production agricole dans les pays méditerranéens du tiers monde. *Options Mediterranées*, **17**, 53–61.

Le Houérou, H. N., Claudin, J. & Haywood, M. (1975). La végétation du Hodna (Algérie). *Rapport Technique No. 6*. F.A.O., Rome.

Monod, T. (1954). Modes contractés et diffus de la végétation saharienne. In: *The Biology of Deserts* (ed. J. L. Cloudsley-Thompson), pp. 35–44. Institute of Biology, London.

Monod, T. (1958). Les parts respectives de l'homme et des phénomènes naturels dans la dégradation des paysages et le déclin des civilisations à travers le monde méditerranéen L.S., avec les déserts et semi-déserts ajacents, au cours des derniers millénaires. *Bibliographie 70, Union National pour la Conservation de la Nature (Comptes Rendu), 7è Réunion Technologique, Athènes.*

Nègre, R. (1961). *Petite flore des régions arides du Maroc occidental.* Centre National de la Recherche Scientifique, Paris.

Niethammer, G. (1971). Die fauna der Sahara. In: *Die Sahara und ihre Randgebiete*, Band 1, Physiographie (ed. H. Schiffer), pp. 499–587. Weltforum Verlag, Munchen.

Ozenda, P. (1958). *Flore du Sahara septentrional et central.* Centre National de la Recherche Scientifique, Paris.

Pabot, H. (1962). *Comment briser le circle vicieux de la desertification dans les régions séches d'Orient.* Mimeograph, F.A.O., Rome.

Pierre, F. (1958). *Ecologie et peuplement entomologique des sables vifs du Sahara nord occidental.* Centre National de la Recherche Scientifique, Paris.

Quezel, P. (1965). *La végétation du Sahara, du Tchad à la Mauritanie.* Fisher, Stuttgart.

Quezel, P. & Santa, S. (1962). *Nouvelle flore de l'Algérie et des régions désertiques méridionales, part 1.* Centre National de la Recherche Scientifique, Paris.

Quezel, P. & Santa, S. (1963). *Nouvelle flore de l'Algérie et des régions désertiques méridionales, part 2.* Centre National de la Recherche Scientifique, Paris.

Rodin, L., Vinogradov, B., Mirochnichenko, Y., Pelt, M., Kolenov, H. & Botschantzev, V. (1970). *Etudes géobotaniques des pâturages du secteur ouest du Département de Médéa de la Republique Algérienne Démocratique et Populaire.* Nauka, Leningrad.

Tackholm, U. (1974). *Student's flora of Egypt.* (2nd Edition.) University of Cairo Press, Cairo.

Uvarov, B. P. (1954). The desert locust and its environment. In: *The biology of deserts* (ed. J. L. Cloudsley-Thompson), pp. 85–9. Institute of Biology, London.

Uvarov, B. P. (1966). Grasshoppers and locusts. In: *Handbook of Acridiology.* Cambridge University Press. Cambridge.

Manuscript received by the editors January 1975

4. Southern Africa

O. A. LEISTNER

Introduction

The region dealt with here agrees largely with the desert or arid warm climatic zone as delineated by Schulze (1947) and Preston-Whyte (1974). It can be very roughly divided into the coastal Namib Desert and the inland Karoo and Kalahari regions. Average annual rainfall over the region is less than 250 mm.

Arid lands occupy only small areas in the southwest of both Angola and Botswana but cover between a third to a half of the surface of South West Africa and South Africa.

Physiography and geomorphology

The land surface is typical of an arid erosion cycle in that it has entirely internal drainage. It can be divided as follows (Wellington, 1955):

(*a*) marginal lands, comprising Namib desert and lower Karoo;
(*b*) escarpment transition zone, comprising broken regions, such as Kaokoveld and Richtersveld;
(*c*) plateau with Kalahari and upper Karoo.

Marginal lands
Namib Desert

The narrow coastal strip is generally known as the Namib (Koch, 1961; Logan, 1969), although the portion south of the Orange River, which can be regarded as transitional desert, is often referred to as the Namaqualand coast belt. Four main land forms are distinguished:

(*a*) gravelly to sandy flats sometimes with isolated barchan dunes;
(*b*) mobile sand dunes up to 300 m high (Stengel, 1971) (see Fig. 4.1);
(*c*) rocky outcrops, hills or mountains;
(*d*) a narrow, sandy, littoral strip along much of the coast.

Longitudinally, the Namib can be divided into three belts (Spreitzer, 1966):

(*a*) the Coastal or Outer Namib, which extends inland for 30–50 km, where fog and moist sea breezes occur regularly;
(*b*) the Inner Namib, about 30–50 km wide, with a typical desert climate;
(*c*) the Anterior, Pro-Namib or Vornamib which is about 10 km wide and merges into the escarpment zone.

Fig. 4.1. *Stipagrostis sabulicola* on Namib dunes. Photo: W. Giess.

Tanqua or Ceres Karoo

This region of flat to slightly undulating plains is badly 'tramped out' and the sandy clay soil has been eroded away in many parts to expose the bare shale (Acocks, 1953).

Great Karoo

Wind-blown sand occurs locally, especially in the west, but the typical surface consists of undulating stony plains with slightly decomposed shales and sandstones.

Little Karoo

This region consists of a series of arid areas more or less separated by less arid hills and mountains. The country is rocky with level to undulating plains, stony hills and riverbeds filled with deep sandy loam.

Escarpment transition zone

Wide zones of broken country are associated with the escarpment along much of its course (see Fig. 4.2). From north to south the following main regions are distinguished.

Fig. 4.2. Escarpment zone. In foreground *Commiphora saxicola*. Photo: W. Giess.

Kaokoveld

This is a rugged, hilly to mountainous area dissected by numerous dry rivers which are often wide, open features (Abel, 1954). Plateaux and table mountains of Karoo age and granitic or gneissic hills and mountains stand above the plains.

Namib transition

Here the escarpment is not well marked and inselbergs of granite and Karoo sediments are typical of the area.

Lower Orange River tract

Most of this region is a sandy and rocky wasteland with deep canyons and gorges.

Richtersveld

This region south of the Orange is characterized by rugged hills and mountains of granites, gneisses, schists and shales, and by riverbeds filled with deep loose sand.

111

Description of arid ecosystems

Namaqualand upland and Karoo escarpment

In Namaqualand, the escarpment is marked by dome-shaped granite and gneiss hills and further south by the Roggeveld Mountains, which are east of the Tanqua Karoo. The east–west oriented Nuweveld Mountains, north of the Great Karoo, mark the rest of the escarpment.

Plateau

The plateau can be divided into the Kalahari basin and the peripheral uplands between the margins of the basin and the escarpment. Three main areas can be distinguished.

Kalahari

This region is covered by more or less vegetated, reddish to greyish sand dunes which overlie calcrete-topped, Kalahari beds. These calcareous formations may be exposed in dune valleys, around pans and along riverbeds (Leistner, 1967; Leser, 1971).

Namaland and Bushmanland

This is a vast peneplain, occasionally broken by hills and tablelands (Logan, 1972). The flats are often covered with shallow, coarse sand, while pebbles and boulders form extensive 'desert pavements'. In southernmost Bushmanland many large brackish or salty pans are found.

Upper Karoo

The surface is predominantly tabular having been formed largely out of the almost horizontal beds of the Karoo System. Koppies and table mountains rise abruptly from stony to sandy plains.

Geology

Precambrian formations form an important part of the structure of the region (Haughton, 1969; Truswell, 1970).

Kheiss and Abbabis system

The oldest rocks are highly metamorphosed and folded sediments and lavas for which ages between 1.0×10^9 and 1.7×10^9 years have been determined.

112

Gariep system

This underlies the region around the mouth of the Orange River and northward into the Namib. It is composed of quartzite, limestone, schist and tillite and was possibly folded about 0.6×10^9 years ago.

Damara system

This covers a large portion of South West Africa north of 24° S and is made up largely of quartzites, limestones and schists. The orogeny has been dated at between 0.65 and 0.50×10^9 years.

Nama system

This system, of possible lower Palaeozoic age, occurs over much of the central plateau of southern South West Africa. It is a largely unfolded, horizontal marine deposit and consists typically of quartzites, sandstones, shales and limestones.

Cape system

It is found in the extreme southwest and south of the region, and has a base of probably Ordovician age. Sandstone and shales are its main components.

Karoo system

This system forms the entire plateau area south of the Precambrian belt in the Orange River region. It also occurs in the southeastern parts of South West Africa and in small patches further north in the Kaokoveld and Angola. The system is almost entirely of continental origin and dates from about 0.30×10^9 to 0.18×10^9 years ago. It consists predominantly of sandstone and shale and is riddled with sheets and dykes of dolerite. This hard rock has contributed to the formation of the very characteristic tabular mountains and ridges. Four main series are distinguished:

(a) Dwyka, the tillite base of the system, which is evidence of the wide-spread glaciation that occurred in Gondwanaland some 0.35×10^9 to 0.30×10^9 years ago;

(b) Ecca, well known for its plant fossils, especially of the genus *Glossopteris*;

(c) Beaufort, which has yielded a wealth of animal fossils, extending over a large area in the upper and the Great Karoo;

(d) Stormberg, composed of a mass of terrestrial sediments overlain by a succession of lava flows.

113

Description of arid ecosystems

Post-Karoo

During the early Tertiary, rivers apparently drained into the Kalahari basin and deposited clay, calcareous marls, sand and gravel bands which form the primary Kalahari beds. These are capped by calcrete and silcrete and are today largely covered by sand. Tertiary marine beds are scattered over a broad coastal plain more or less parallel to the Atlantic. These consist of sandstone, limestone and silcrete and are also covered by sand in many areas.

Climate

The subcontinent is situated largely within the southern subtropical high-pressure belt and is skirted to the south by the circumpolar westerly airstreams (Weather Bureau, 1965). The arid regions lie in the western half of the subcontinent which derives most of its atmospheric moisture from the Indian Ocean on its eastern shores.

Climatic classification

Three main climatic zones can be distinguished (Jackson, 1951):

(a) cool, almost rainless coastal zone of the Namib merging southwards into less extreme desert with winter rains;

(b) extremely hot desert receiving less than 125 mm average annual rainfall; this zone includes the rest of the Namib and the lower Orange River region;

(c) desert with less extreme aridity receiving 125 to 250 mm average annual rainfall; the remainder of the region is included in this zone.

Rainfall

Amount and seasonality

Rainfall ranges from 250 mm in the east to 50 mm or less towards the west coast. In the interior, the precipitation is mainly due to convectional showers and falls during summer and autumn (see Fig. 4.3a and b). Towards the west, in the southern part of the region, the sparse rainfall occurs mainly during winter (see Fig. 4.3c and d), while in the northern half the coastal regions receive their rain during the summer months (see Fig. 4.3e and f).

114

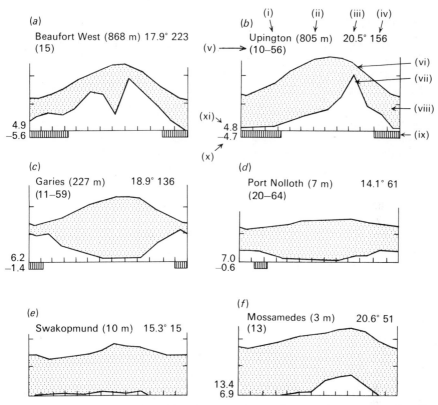

Fig. 4.3. Climate diagrams (for explanation see Upington diagram): (i) Name of station; (ii) altitude (m); (iii) mean annual temperature (°C); (iv) mean annual precipitation (mm); (v) number of years of observation; (vi) curve of mean monthly temperature; (vii) curve of mean monthly precipitation; (viii) dry season; (ix) months with absolute daily minimum temperatures under 0 °C; (x) mean daily minimum temperature of *coldest* month; (xi) absolute minimum temperature; horizontal scale, months – June to June; left vertical scale, mean monthly temperature calibrated in 10 °C; right vertical scale, rainfall calibrated in 20 mm. (After Walter & Leith, 1960.)

Variability

Relative variability of the rainfall is about 25–30% in the east and increases rapidly westward attaining a maximum of 80% on the coast. Single showers can account for as much as the normal annual precipitation.

Humidity

The air is generally very dry and the mean annual relative humidity in the early afternoon is around 30% in the interior, increasing to 40% in the coastal regions and 60% or more in the close proximity of the Atlantic. Mean monthly relative humidity is generally highest during winter.

115

Description of arid ecosystems

Cloud and fog

Cloudiness is normally at a maximum during the morning hours in the winter rainfall area, including parts of the Central Namib (Schulze, 1969) but an afternoon maximum is normal for most of the summer rainfall area. The cold Benguela current along the Atlantic coast cools the atmosphere to such an extent that moisture from the ocean moves onto the continent almost exclusively in the form of local fog (Logan, 1969). Fog generally advances inland in the late afternoon to a distance of 10–50 km. At Swakopmund, on the Namib coast, fog occurs on about 120 days per year (Stengel, 1971). Condensation from low clouds and fog plays a large part in supporting life in the coastal desert.

Sunshine

The average annual duration of bright sunshine is more than 80% of the daylight hours in most of the region. Along the coast of South West Africa the average duration may drop below 50% in some places owing to fog and low clouds.

Temperatures

These are subject to great seasonal and diurnal variation. The average daily maximum temperature is about 35 °C in January and 18 °C in July with extremes of 46 °C and 32 °C respectively. Average daily minima are about 17 °C in January and 3 °C in July; extremes can reach 5 °C and −10 °C respectively. One of the hottest regions in South Africa is the lower Orange River valley. Soil temperature at a depth of 10 cm at 14.00 hours is generally in excess of 40 °C.

Hydrology

All rivers have a very widely fluctuating flow and only two 'exotic' streams are perennial, the Kunene and the Orange. Riverbeds, even though they may carry floods only once in ten years or less, are important aquifers. Five river systems are distinguished (Wellington, 1955).

The Orange River system. The largest within the region. Layered Karoo sandstones which are widespread, are excellent aquifers. The Orange loses more than 10% of its flow during its course through the region.

Kalahari basin. The four large rivers of the Nossob–Molopo system drained into the Orange until the Molopo channel was blocked by dunes

116

(Lewis, 1936). Today the system is endoreic. Where the thickness of unconsolidated sand exceeds 6 m there is little possibility of water infiltration and recharge of underground water supply. Much of the crustal water is of fossil origin (Jennings, 1971).

Kunene system. This river drains only a small part of the coastal belt and loses much of its flow by evaporation and percolation in the region.

South coastal system. Several of the permanent rivers derive from the inland arid region where they run only intermittently.

West coastal system. Most rivers crossing the Namib seldom or never reach the sea because of low rainfall and riverbeds blocked by wind-blown sand. Occasional floods occur in rivers rising in the escarpment zone or on the plateau. Most towns and settlements are provided with water pumped from underground reserves in riverbeds.

Soils

Raw mineral soils

The Namib is covered by raw mineral soils or 'pre-soils' (Ganssen, 1963). Areas of mobile sand dunes occur in southern Angola (Diniz, 1973) and the central Namib. Regions of this desert not covered by dunes have grey desertic soils or detritus without soil formation. Calcareous crusts are found locally and, in the fog belt, halomorphic formations are encountered.

Weakly developed, mainly grey or brown soils

The weakly developed soils on loose sediments found in the Namaqualand coast belt extend into the southern Namib (Van der Merwe, 1962; D'Hoore, 1964). Grey littoral to near-littoral sands occurring in the coastal regions south of the Orange belong mostly to the Fernwood, Clovelly and Oakleaf forms as defined by Van der Eyck, Macvicar & De Villiers (1969). Undifferentiated lithosols and litholic soils, derived from miscellaneous rocks cover most of Namaland and Karoo, and soils of Mispah and Oakleaf form have been identified. Saline or alkali soils occur over large areas of southern Bushmanland and the eastern Karoo.

Arid or semi-arid reddish brown soils

The soils in the arid portion of the Kalahari are classified as continental red or brown shifting sand or aeolian psammitic regosols (Loxton, 1962).

117

Description of arid ecosystems

Soils of this type belong to the Hutton and Clovelly form (Van Rooyen & Burger, 1974). Similar but non-shifting sands are found in parts of Bushmanland. Surrounding the Kalahari is a wide zone defined as lithosols on calcareous crust.

Flora

Floral elements

Two major floral elements or floristic kingdoms are distinguished in Africa, south of the equator. The Cape Floral Region, Capensis or Southern Flora which is largely confined to the winter rainfall region in the southwest of the continent; and the Palaeotropical Kingdom, Palaeotropis or Tropical Flora.

The extent of the arid lands coincides very closely with that of the Karoo–Namib phytogeographical region which is included in Palaeotropis (Werger, 1973). Towards the winter rainfall area in the southwest the number of species with Capensis affinity increases.

Endemism

The highest number of endemic species are found on the border zone between Palaeotropis and Capensis. Acocks (1953) considers the Karoo flora to be a product of the interaction of these two floral kingdoms. The most pronounced centres of endemism are found in the region where summer and winter rainfall areas overlap. Three such centres, characterized mainly by succulents, especially of the families Mesembryanthemaceae and Crassulaceae, are the Little Karoo, the Van Rhynsdorp centre and the Gariep centre in the lower Orange River region (Nordenstam, 1969). The summer-rainfall arid lands are rather poor in endemics and, like *Welwitschia*, they are often of a relict nature (Exell & Gonçalves, 1973).

Origin

Desert conditions appear to have occurred continually somewhere on the continent since the Cretaceous, providing arid region floras and faunas the opportunity to develop and persist (Kaiser, 1926; Koch, 1962; Dyer, 1966). The vegetation patterns, however, must have changed repeatedly as a result of variations in temperature and humidity. These changes in vegetation were responsible for the evolution of many new taxa (Van Zinderen Bakker, 1967). They may also explain the disjunct amphitropical distribution areas of many African arid region plants (Engler, 1921; Monod, 1971).

118

The number of phanerogams in the region is estimated to be between 4000 and 5000. The families best represented are Asteraceae, Poaceae, Aizoaceae (including Mesembryanthemaceae), Liliaceae, Fabaceae and Scrophulariaceae (Werger, 1973).

Vegetation

Structure and habitat

Three basic types can be distinguished (Acocks, 1953; White, 1973).

(*a*) Dwarf and succulent shrub which consists typically of chamaephytes accompanied by desert grasses. Succulents are important to dominant along the coast, in areas where winter rains predominate and along much of the escarpment and the Orange River. Regions with summer rain are mostly dominated by non-succulents; grasses tend to predominate on deep soils and woody and succulent species on shallow rocky soils.

(*b*) Savanna or 'bushveld', grassland with interspersed tall shrubs and/or trees, is found in the Kalahari.

(*c*) Dry riverine forest is confined to the banks of perennial streams and to the courses of normally dry riverbeds.

Regional description

   Littoral zone

A strip of psammophytic–halophytic vegetation is found along the coast (Acocks, 1953; Barbosa, 1970; Giess, 1971). Sand accumulates into hummock dunes around perennials such as *Zygophyllum clavatum* and species of *Psilocaulon* and *Salsola*. Plants in the immediate vicinity of the sea include the grass *Paspalum dilatatum* and species of genera such as *Arthrocnemum* and *Salicornia*.

In the Strandveld (coastal vegetation) which occurs south of the Orange, species of southern affinity become prominent, for example, the shrubs *Salvia nivea* and *Eriocephalus racemosus* and grass species of the genera *Ehrharta* and *Chaetobromus*.

   Coastal plains

Gravel and sand plains

These plains cover vast areas which are often almost completely barren. Apart from lichens, growing on stones or unattached, most vegetation

119

is restricted to depressions and drainage lines. The lower surface of translucent pebbles is often covered by algae which receive their light through the stone and their moisture from fog condensing on the pebbles (Vogel, 1955; Louw, 1972).

The dominant grass genus is *Stipagrostis* with numerous species such as *Stipagrostis subacaulis* and *Stipagrostis uniplumis*. The grass cover increases steadily eastwards and the sub-desertic Pro-Namib may be covered by almost pure stands of *Stipagrostis obtusa* and *Stipagrostis ciliata*.

The halophytic succulent shrubs *Arthraerua leubnitziae* and *Zygophyllum stapffii* are characteristic of the fog belt of the central Namib. Beyond this belt halophytes are largely restricted to localities in, or near, riverbeds where slightly saline soils occurs. *Welwitschia mirabilis* is found in different vegetation formations from almost barren plains to fairly dense scrub or grassland with scattered trees (Giess, 1969; Walter 1971). After rains, annual succulents like *Mesembryanthemum cryptantham* and *Aizoanthemum mossamedense* may cover vast areas.

Towards the south, perennial succulents, chamaephytes with succulent leaves and semi-succulents gain gradually in importance.

Rocks

Succulents and lichens are particularly common in rocky areas. Hard rocks, like quartzite and marble, provide suitable conditions for small succulents such as *Lithops* spp., *Othonna* spp., *Anacampseros* spp. and *Trichocaulon* spp. Taller succulents which are also found on softer rocks, include species of *Euphorbia* and *Aloe*.

Sand dunes (see Fig. 4.1)

The mobile dunes, which may be up to 300 m high, are almost completely barren. The plants which grow are hard, perennial grasses such as *Eragrostis cyperoides* and *Stipagrostis sabulicola*. The thorny, leafless *Acanthosicyos horrida* (Cucurbitaceae) grows on low dunes in the fog belt, usually in drainage lines.

Inland regions below the escarpment

Regions receiving rain in winter or throughout the year

Succulents are important in this area although their prominence is partially the result of selective overgrazing which favours the often unpalatable succulent species (Acocks, 1953, 1964). Two main regions are distinguished, the Tanqua or Ceres Karoo and the Little Karoo.

Tanqua or Ceres Karoo. This is an old farming area which, in parts, has been reduced to almost total desert. Succulents, especially of the Mesembryanthemaceae, predominate. Representatives include shrubby species of *Ruschia, Lampranthus* and *Aridaria* as well as stemless species of *Pleiospilos* and *Conophytum.* Many of the common succulents, such as *Cotyledon wallichii* and *Augea capensis,* are unpalatable or poisonous to stock. Chamaephytes and shrubs include *Galenia africana,* several species of *Salsola, Lycium arenicolum* and species of *Gnidia.* Common annuals are *Tribulus terrestris, Amellus strigosus* and *Felicia bergerana.*

Little Karoo. Tall shrubs are important, the most typical species being *Euclea undulata* (Ebenaceae). Other shrubs or trees include *Rhus undulata, Pappea capensis* (Sapindaceae), *Schotia speciosa* (Caesalpiniaceae). Some common chamaephytes are *Eriocephalus ericoides, Felicia muricata, Nestlera humulis* and species of *Pteronia.* Among the succulents the Mesembryanthemaceae are particularly well represented by dwarf shrubs of genera like *Ruschia, Drosanthemum* and *Lampranthus* and by stemless dwarfs of the genera *Gibbaeum* and *Glottiphyllum.* Succulents of other families include *Crassula argentea* and *Cotyledon paniculata.* Grasses, occurring commonly in rested areas, include several species of *Stipagrostis* such as *Stipagrostis brevifolia, Ehrharta calycina* and the annual *Enneapogon desvauxii.*

Regions receiving rain in autumn or late summer

Great Karoo. In contrast to the other low-lying arid lands, succulents are relatively scarce. Dwarf shrubs are dominant while shrubs are largely restricted to riverbeds. Grasses are only conspicuous in areas protected from injudicious grazing (Acocks, 1953, 1964). Among the most important chamaephytes are species of the following genera of Asteraceae: *Pentzia, Eriocephalus, Pteronia, Felicia* and *Chrysocoma.* Genera of other families represented among dwarf shrubs include *Galenia, Zygophyllum, Drosanthemum, Trichodiadema* and *Hermannia.* Examples of shrubs found outside riverbeds are *Rhigozum obovatum, Lycium arenicolum* and *Asclepias filifolia.*

Escarpment and plateau

Escarpment zone and Orange River region (see Fig. 4.2)

Arborescent, semi-succulent to succulent plants, varying in height from less than 1 m to 5 m or more, are characteristic of the region. In the north, representatives of this growth form include species of *Commiphora, Cyphostemma, Sesamothamnus* and *Moringa.* In the central region

Description of arid ecosystems

around the Orange River *Aloe dichotoma* is common, while in parts of the southern escarpment *Crassula paniculata* is conspicuous. Characteristic tall succulent *Euphorbia* species include *Euphorbia venenosa* in the north and *Euphorbia avasmontana* along the Orange.

Among trees and shrubs *Colophospermum mopane* and *Terminalia pruinoides* are typical for Angola and the Kaokoveld and *Euphorbia guerichiana* for most of South West Africa. Tall woody species of the lower Orange region include *Euclea undulata* and *Adenolobus gariepensis* while further east, species like *Acacia mellifera* ssp. *detinens* and *Phaeoptilum spinosum* may be common.

Low shrubs and perennial herbs characteristic of the Orange River region include *Kissenia capensis* (Loasaceae) and *Codon royeni* (Hydrophyllaceae) and grasses like *Setaria appendiculata* and *Aristida engleri*. South of the Orange River, grasses belonging to genera of southern affinity, such as *Ehrharta* and *Pentaschistis*, predominate. Dwarf shrubs and perennial herbs of the Acanthaceae such as *Barleria cyanea* and species of *Petalidium* are important in the summer-rainfall region to the north where they appear to replace the smaller succulents.

Within the winter-rainfall area small and dwarf succulents are common to abundant, especially in the region around the lower Orange. Families best represented are Mesembryanthemaceae, Asclepiadaceae, Crassulaceae and Euphorbiaceae. In the regions receiving winter rains, especially Namaqualand, annuals may be abundant in spring and cover large areas in dense stands. Particularly well represented are Asteraceae with species of *Dimorphotheca*, *Arctotis* and *Cotula* and Brassicaceae of the genus *Heliophila* (Eliovson, 1972).

Typical of the desert transition zone along the escarpment, especially in the southern half of South West Africa, are desiccation-tolerant or 'resurrection' plants such as *Myriothamnus flabellifolius*, the grasses *Eragrostis nindensis* and *Oropetium capensis* and the water plant *Lindernia intrepida* (Gaff, 1971; Gaff & Ellis, unpublished).

Plateau

Two main regions are distinguished, the Karoo with generally shallow soils and the Kalahari with deep sandy soils.

Arid Karoo (with less than 200 mm average annual rainfall). The most characteristic plant of the region, which comprises Namaland and Bushmanland, is the shrub *Rhigozum trichotomum* (Bignoniaceae). The dominant grasses belong to the genus *Stipagrostis* (Acocks, 1953, 1964; Giess, 1971). Trees and tall shrubs are largely confined to deeper drainage valleys although species such as *Parkinsonia africana*, *Boscia albitrunca* and

122

Acacia mellifera ssp. *detinens* may occur on the plains, especially in sandy depressions. The commonest dwarf shrubs belong to the genera *Pentzia*, *Salsola*, *Eriocephalus*, *Pteronia*, *Chrysocoma* and *Leucosphaera*. Widely occurring perennial grasses are *Stipagrostis obtusa*, *Stipagrostis ciliata* and *Eragrostis nindensis*. The very hardy chamaephytic *Stipagrostis brevifolia* dominates in some areas in the west. The commonest annual grass is the small, tufted *Enneapogon desvauxii* and other species include *Aristida congesta* and *Schmidtia kalihariensis*. Annuals of other families, often very abundant after rain, include species of genera such as *Helichrysum*, *Heliophila* and *Sesamum*.

Karoo (with more than 200 mm average annual rainfall). Grasses are fairly prominent but species like *Eragrostis lehmanniana* and *Aristida congesta*, which are neither very palatable nor very drought-resistant, tend to dominate. More permanent grasses, largely restricted to protected areas, include *Eragrostis obtusa*, *E. curvula* and *Stipagrostis obtusa*. Shrubs of the genera *Lycium* and *Rhigozum* grow mainly at the foot of hills and on flood plains, while the characteristic shrub of hills is *Rhus undulata* var. *burchellii*. Dwarf shrubs include *Eriocephalus ericoides*, *Plinthus karooicus* and several species of the genera *Salsola* and *Pentzia*. Succulents, mostly unpalatable to stock, may become important in overgrazed areas. Examples are species of *Ruschia* and *Psilocaulon*.

Kalahari. Dunes and sandy flats are largely covered by a very open shrub or tree savanna, sparse dwarf shrub formations occur on calcrete outcrops while riverbeds and pans support very open grass communities (Leistner, 1967; Wild & Grandvaux Barbosa, 1968; Leser, 1971, 1972). Habitat and plant communities are closely correlated (Leistner & Werger, 1973):

(*a*) Dune crests are dominated by the shrub-like *Stipagrostis amabilis* accompanied by other grasses like *Eragrostis trichophora* and virgate shrubs of the genus *Crotalaria*.

(*b*) Dune valleys with red sand: *Asthenatherum glaucum*, *Hirpicium echinus* and *Dicoma schinzii* are typical.

(*c*) Dune valleys with pinkish to greyish calcareous sand: dwarf shrubs such as *Monechma incanum* are important and the shrub *Rhigozum trichotomum* may be codominant.

(*d*) Exposed calcrete: dwarf shrubs of the genera *Aizoon*, *Barleria*, *Zygophyllum* and *Pentzia* and grasses like *Enneapogon scaber* are typical.

(*e*) Compact calcareous sand is often dominated by *Stipagrostis obtusa* and *Rhigozum trichotomum*, accompanied by inconspicuous species like the annual fern *Ophioglossum polyphyllum*.

(*f*) Clayey lower parts of riverbeds: typical species include *Panicum coloratum*, *Geigeria pectidea* and *Psoralea obtusifolia*.

(g) Central portions of pans support an ephemeral community of two species: *Sporobolus coromandeliana* and *Trianthema triquetra* ssp. *parvifolia*.

Trees are largely confined to riverbeds and the crests of dunes which offer favourable moisture conditions (Leistner, 1961).

Riverbeds and drainage valleys (see Fig. 4.4)

The vegetation along the two perennial rivers, and both in and along the dry riverbeds with more or less permanent groundwater, is characterized by trees. Best represented is the genus *Acacia* with *Acacia albida* mainly in the north, *Acacia erioloba* chiefly in the central regions and *Acacia karroo*, which is by far the commonest tree or shrub, south of the Orange (Acocks, 1953). Other common tall woody species in the region include *Colophospermum mopane, Combretum imberbe, Euclea pseudebenus* and *Zizyphus mucronata*. The palm *Hyphaene ventricosa* is confined to the north and *Salix capensis* to the area from the Orange southwards.

Shallow drainage lines support mainly annuals; the number of perennials, especially woody species, increases with an increase in the size of the channels. Small riverbeds and drainage valleys in the north support shrubs like *Balanites welwitschii* and *Maerua schinzii*. *Adenolobus pechuelii* occurs mainly in the Orange River region while *Rhus pyroides* and *Euclea undulata* are typical of the south. Perennial grasses often found in the northern Namib include *Sporobolus robusta* and *Asthenatherum* (= Danthonia) *mossamedense* (Giess, 1962; Matos & Sousa, 1970), *Stipagrostis sabulicola* and *Eragrostis spinosa* may dominate in the central Namib while *Panicum coloratum* and *Eragrostis bicolor* are often abundant in Kalahari and Karoo (Acocks, 1953; Leistner, 1967). *Phragmites australis* and *Typha latifolia* ssp. *capensis* are restricted to moist localities. Species associated with saline conditions include the very characteristic tree *Tamarix usneoides*, shrubs like *Suaeda fruticosa* and the grass *Odyssea paucinervis* (Knapp, 1973).

Widely distributed exotics include *Nicotiana glauca*, a shrub or small tree, the short-lived *Argemone subfusiformis* and several species of *Datura*.

Fauna

Zoogeography

The region falls entirely within the South West Arid zone (Davis, 1962) which is part of the Ethiopian Zoogeographical Region (Darlington, 1957). This zone has the most distinctive fauna of the arid lands south of the

Fig. 4.4. Bed of the Kuiseb River showing riverine forest. Photo: W. Giess.

Sahara (Bigalke, 1972c). The greatest degree of endemism is recorded for the Namib, especially for the shifting, almost barren dunes. Groups with many endemic species include Acridoidea, Tenebrionidae (Koch, 1962) and Arachnidae (Lawrence, 1967). Numerous animals (and plants: see the section on Origin of flora) have disjunct amphitropical distribution areas and many closely related species pairs occur with one member in the South West Arid and the other in the Somali Arid zone (Monod, 1971). Balinsky (1962), Wells (1967), Verdcourt (1969) and others have postulated that the two arid regions must have been connected at one or more stages in the past by an 'arid' or 'drought corridor' during periods with higher temperatures and greater aridity than at present.

Davis (1962) demonstrates a close correlation between vegetation and the distribution of Muridae. Other animals with distribution patterns obviously linked to vegetation include termites (Coaton & Sheasby, 1972) and grasshoppers (Brown, 1972). Edaphic factors play a decisive role in the distribution of animals. Numerous species are confined to rocky areas (for example, rock-scorpions and klipspringers), others to firm ground (for example, the gecko *Ptenopus carpi* and the suricate *Suricata suricatta*) and yet others to sand (for example, the burrowing scorpion *Opisthophthalmus concinnus* and the lizard *Angolosaurus skoogi*). A much more mesic fauna is found in the long, linear oases formed by the riverbeds than in the surrounding areas. They serve as migration routes and act as a base from which animals may exploit the desert (Cloudsley-Thompson & Chadwick, 1964).

Adaptations

Most animals avoid strong insulation and heat and low humidity by either going underground, by being nocturnal or both. Many species have a high heat-tolerance and the majority seldom, if ever, drink. Most species are either carnivorous or make use of juicy vegetable matter or both. Moisture derived from fog and dew is utilized by feeding on moist material at night or in the morning (Tschinkel, 1973). Some animals absorb or drink water which has condensed on their bodies.

The most striking adaptations to a life in arid lands are usually found in species living in sand. These adaptations are mostly concerned with locomotion (Koch, 1961; Haacke, 1964) and the protection of body openings (Lawrence, 1959; Mertens, 1972). Species inhabiting the very loose, almost fluid Namib dunes are referred to as ultra-psammophilous (Koch, 1962; Newlands, 1972).

Main animal groups

The groups best-represented are insects, arachnids, reptiles, birds and mammals.

Insecta

Thysanura

Silver-fishes, especially of the genus *Lepisma*, are extremely numerous in the Namib (Lawrence, 1959) and probably form the animal basis of an important food chain (Cloudsley-Thompson, 1968).

Acridoidea

Grasshoppers. The region is characterized by a very rich grasshopper fauna in which geophilous and often stone-resembling forms are particularly well represented. The majority subsists largely on dwarf shrub vegetation and may thus be referred to as 'bushhoppers' (H. D. Brown, personal communication). Certain species appear to feed more or less exclusively on a particular plant species and this may partly explain a frequent correlation between vegetation and the distribution of hoppers (Brown, 1967, 1972). Few species occur in truly desert regions, probably because the eggs will not hatch without the stimulus of rain (H. D. Brown, personal communication).

126

Locusts. In contrast to grasshoppers, locusts have both a solitary and a gregarious phase during which they may congregate to form vast swarms (Dirsh, 1965; May 1973). Of the four species found in southern Africa only two have their permanent breeding area within the arid lands (Lea, 1964; Botha, 1969, 1970):

(*a*) *Locustana pardalina*, the brown locust, occurs over much of the region in its solitary phase but the outbreak area, in which the gregarious phase arises, is relatively small. In the past, plagues arising in the region used to spread over the whole of southern Africa.

(*b*) *Schistocerca gregaria flaviventris*, the southern African desert locust. Solitary individuals are widespread, but outbreak areas are largely confined to the southern Kalahari, as defined by Leistner (1967), and the Namib transition zone.

Isoptera

The distribution of termites is often closely correlated with vegetation types (Coaton & Sheasby, 1972).

Kalotermitinae. The dry-wood termites establish their colonies directly on dead wood. Colonies of *Epicalotermes*, found in driftwood in the Namib, seem to draw all the moisture they require from fog.

Hodotermitinae. Harvester termites forage for grass and leaves on the surface and drag the cut vegetation into their nests. *Hodotermes mossambicus* consumes approximately 25% of the aggregate hay yield produced in years of average rainfall. By their activities they accelerate the encroachment of Karoo shrublets into grassland (Coaton, 1971).

Coleoptera

Beetles, especially of the family Tenebrionidae, are the insects best adapted to desert life (Cloudsley-Thompson & Chadwick, 1964).

Tenebrionidae. The relative number of species, and even absolute numbers of these beetles increases progressively as conditions become more and more adverse to other forms of life. In the ultra-desertic parts of the Namib they play a dominant and basic role. Almost 200 species are endemic to the truly desertic Namib alone, a number apparently far in excess of other deserts (Koch, 1962).

Dune-dwellers usually have an enlarged gripping surface on their feet enabling them to dive into and 'swim' in the quasi-fluid sand on steep dune

Fig. 4.5. *Stenocara phalangium*, diurnal tenebrionid of the Namib sand and gravel plains. Photo: Dr L. Schulze-Prozesky.

slopes (Koch, 1961). Examples of such sand-divers are members of the genera *Cardiosis* and *Lepidochora*.

The interdune plains are inhabited by a completely different set of species most of which are adapted to fast running or burrowing. Some species have very long legs which make rapid movement possible and also carry the body high above the hot surface (see Fig. 4.5 of *Stenocara phalangium*).

Various activity distributions of tenebrionids can be ascribed to daily temperature cycles and there also appears to be a great seasonal variation in activity (Holm & Edney, 1973).

All members of the family are omnivorous and in arid regions they are particularly attracted by any substance with high water-content. The ultra-psammophilous species of the shifting Namib dunes no longer depend on active plant life but exist on organic detritus transported by the wind and on moisture derived from fog and dew (Koch, 1962). It appears that some forms can imbibe moisture which condenses on their bodies (Holm & Edney, 1973).

Arachnida

Scorpions, solifugids and certain families of spiders are particularly well suited to arid lands. The arachnid fauna of the south west African deserts comprises a larger number of peculiar autochthonous genera than the fauna of any other area of comparable size in Africa (Lawrence, 1967).

Araneae

The number of spiders which live on or beneath the ground surface increases with increasing aridity (Lawrence, 1960). Groups which are represented include (Lawrence, 1964):

(*a*) Dune spiders (Sparassidae) like *Cerbalus* spp., which exist mainly on prey larger than insects, such as small geckos (Lawrence, 1966);

(*b*) Trap-door spiders, such as *Stasimopus* spp., which live in underground tubes closed by stopper-like doors;

(*c*) Jumping spiders (Salticidae) which hunt down their prey like large carnivores;

(*d*) Orbweb-spiders (Argyopidae) which catch their prey in wheel-shaped webs.

Scorpionidae

About 160 species of scorpions, a quarter of all species known, occur in southern Africa and most of these are found in the arid western regions (Lawrence, 1955, 1971). Two families are represented:

(*a*) Buthidae (Stinging scorpions), like *Parabuthus* spp., which have slender pedipalps and thick, powerful tails with large poison glands;

(*b*) Scorpionidae (Cape scorpions) with strong pedipalps and thin tails; they are represented by *Hadogenes* spp., rock-scorpions, with dorso-ventrally compressed bodies and pedipalps, and by *Opisthophthalmus* spp., a large genus of burrowing scorpions, some of which live on loose sand dunes and have been described as ultra-psammophilous (Newlands, 1972).

Solifugae

The number of sun-spider species in southern Africa increases from the mesic to arid regions and reaches a climax in the deserts. One hundred species are known from South West Africa alone (Lamoral, 1973). Examples are *Solpuga* spp., a group of extremely active, savage species and *Chelypus* spp., and *Hexisopus* spp., which lead a subterranean existence and feed probably exclusively on termites (Lawrence, 1971).

Acarina

The sand tampan, *Ornithodorus savigny*, appears to be the only African species able to dig itself into deep sand (Theiler, 1964). The mite *Microcaeculus namibensis*, lives under exfoliating flakes on granite boulders in the Namib (Piffl, 1965).

Reptilia

Adaptations for a sandy habitat recorded in Namib reptiles are at least as striking and as numerous as those known in species from the Sahara (Mertens, 1972).

Gekkonidae

Some striking representatives are the large ground gecko (*Chondrodactylus angulifer*) (see Fig. 4.6), three species of *Ptenopus* with pronounced vocal ability (Haacke, 1969) and the web-footed *Palmatogecko rangei* which lives in loose sand dunes in the Namib.

Scincidae

Skinks are represented by members of the genus *Typhlosaurus* which are legless and live permanently under the sand surface, and also by numerous species of *Mabuya* such as *Mabuya striata* which lives under the bark and in holes in the trunks of trees. Some species rely completely on termites for their food (Huey, Pianka, Egan & Coons, 1974).

Lacertidae and Cordylidae

Examples are the two diurnal, vegetarian 'sand divers', *Angolosaurus skoogi* and *Aporosaurus anchietae*, both recorded from the Namib sand dunes (Hamilton & Coetzee, 1969; Louw, 1972).

Viperidae

Bitis arietans, the puff adder, is probably the most widespread snake in the region, *Bitis peringueyi*, the sidewinding Namib adder (Brain, 1960), is confined to the fog belt, while the horned adder, *Bitis caudalis* occurs widely in sandy areas. The dwarf python (*Python anchietae*) is specific

Fig. 4.6. Suricate (*Suricata suricatta*) feeding on *Chondrodactylus angulifer*. Photo: National Parks Board, South Africa.

to the Pro-Namib and the highly venomous Cape Cobra (*Naja nivea*) is common in most of the region.

Aves

Some 850 species of birds have been recorded from southern Africa (McLachlan & Liversidge, 1972) and roughly 300 of these occur in the arid lands. Best represented among birds confined to the region are larks, while other families with several endemic species are thrushes and chats, fly-catchers and warblers.

Temperature tolerance and control

Although birds generally have a high tolerance to elevated body temper-atures, most species seek the shade during the hottest hours (Maclean, 1974). Some species are known to shelter in gerbil burrows and the ant-eating chat, *Myrmecocichla formicivora*, may resort to its underground nest which is often dug into the walls of antbear holes occupied by numerous other animals. Birds nesting on the open ground such as plovers, korhaans

131

and sandgrouse are exposed to the sun throughout the day. In contrast to most other species, ostriches maintain their body temperature at a constant level by panting and by making use of convective and radiant cooling.

Coloration

In many species the plumage coloration matches the colour of the ground on which they live (Willoughby, 1969). In the Kalahari, lark species with a red tinge are found on red dunes and grey species on the grey calcrete (Maclean, 1974).

Feeding and drinking

Most species are insectivorous or carnivorous and independent of drinking water. Free water is mainly drunk by seed-eating species such as doves, finches and canaries, many of which are restricted to the vicinity of open water. The seed-eating sandgrouse (*Pterocles* spp.) are capable of flying up to 160 km in one day and can thus range far, even in the dry season. Ostriches live in the Namib without resorting to surface water by feeding on succulent and moist plant material.

Breeding

For most desert birds, rain, or some associated phenomenon, appears to be the main signal (*Zeitgeber*) to start breeding. Some species lay eggs within six days following rain. They will then continue to breed as long as favourable conditions last. Species which do not require rain as a stimulus for breeding include vultures. The poor condition of game animals during bad seasons may even increase their rate of reproduction.

Mammalia

Orders particularly well represented are Carnivora, Artiodactyla and Rodentia (Roberts, 1951).

Insectivora

This order is represented by elephant-shrews such as *Macroscelides proboscideus*, which lives under extreme desert conditions (Sauer & Sauer, 1971); shrews such as *Crocidura* spp. and the Namib golden mole *Eremitalpa granti*, the only mammal endemic to that region (Coetzee, 1969).

Carnivora

These animals are well adapted to desert life as they are mostly nocturnal and eat food with a high moisture content, including juicy plant material.

Hyaenidae. *Hyaena brunnea*, the brown hyaena and *Crocuta crocuta*, the spotted hyaena, are today largely confined to uninhabited regions and reserves. Although often regarded as mainly scavengers, both species may be active predators (Eloff, 1964; Mills, 1973).

Felidae. Three large cat species still occur, although mostly or exclusively within reserves:

(*a*) Cheetah (*Acynonyx jubatus*), now threatened by extinction;
(*b*) Leopard (*Panthera pardus*), known to exist without drinking water for nine months or more (Smithers, 1971);
(*c*) Lion (*Panthera leo*), which makes good use of succulent fruit such as the tsama (*Citrullus vulgaris*) (Eloff, 1973*a*). In the Kalahari small mammals such as porcupines are an important food item (Eloff, 1973*b*).

Canidae. The black-backed jackal (*Canis mesomelas*) occurs throughout the region including all habitats of the Namib (Coetzee, 1969). The bat-eared fox and the Cape fox live largely on arthropods, small reptiles and, occasionally, birds.

Mustelidae. The striped polecat (*Ictonyx striatus*) occurs widely, including all main Namib habitats and the ratel or honey badger (*Mellivora capensis*) is still found in many areas.

Viverridae. The carnivorous suricate (*Suricata suricatta*) (see Fig. 4.6) is very common but generally restricted to warrens which they often share with *Xerus inauris*, a ground squirrel, which lives on vegetable matter. The gregarious yellow mongoose (*Cynictis penicillata*) also frequently shares its burrows with suricates and ground squirrels (Smithers, 1971).

Tubulidentata

The aardvark or ant-bear (*Orycteropus afer*) feeds mainly on termites and ants which it laps up with its long sticky tongue. Many other animals such as hyaenas, porcupines and reptiles make use of its extensive burrows (Smithers, 1971).

Description of arid ecosystems

Hyracoidea

The widely distributed rock-dassie (*Procavia capensis*) is predominantly a browser, largely restricted to rocky hillsides. In the Karoo, where most of its natural enemies have been eliminated, it increases at an alarming rate and competes with sheep for grazing (Milstein, 1971).

Perissodactyla

Rhinocerotidae. The black rhinoceros (*Diceros bicornis*) is today restricted to southern Angola and northern South West Africa where an estimated 90 specimens still occurred in 1966 (Joubert, 1971).

Equidae. About 7000 specimens of the Hartmann zebra (*Equus zebra hartmannae*) still exist in the escarpment zone of South West Africa and Angola.

Artiodactyla

Bovidae. Vast numbers of antelopes once occurred in the region and even today most of the original species are still reasonably well represented. The klipspringer (*Oreotragus oreotragus*) is largely restricted to rocky areas while the steenbok (*Raphicerus campestris*) is almost ubiquitous. *Sylvicapra grimmia*, the common or grey duiker, also occurs in considerable numbers (Bigalke & Bateman, 1962). The kudu, *Tragelaphus stripsiceros*, is unique among the larger antelope, because there is good evidence that its range is increasing. One reason for this phenomenon is that the dense, tall bush which these animals prefer, is spreading in the moister areas as a result of farming activities. *Antidorcas marsupialis*, the springbok, is probably the most abundant and widespread medium-sized game animal, occurring typically in open country, especially dwarf shrub vegetation, short grassland and low shrub savanna (Bigalke, 1972a, b). They are gregarious and still occur in herds of over one thousand. Under favourable conditions their numbers may increase by more than 30% within one year (Bigalke, 1972a). Apart from gemsbok they are the only antelope found in all habitats of the Namib (Coetzee, 1969). Gemsbok, *Oryx gazella*, (see Fig. 4.7) are the largest mammal recorded for all habitats in the Namib, including rocky slopes (Coetzee, 1969). They are generally independent of water as they supplement their diet with fruit, roots and tubers which they dig out with their front hooves. The largest antelope in Africa is the eland, *Taurotragus oryx*. They can migrate over large distances and seem to feed on almost any available species of plant (Smithers, 1971).

134

Fig. 4.7. Gemsbok (*Oryx gazella*) on calcrete outcrop dominated by *Rhigozum trichotomum*. Photo: National Parks Board, South Africa.

Lagomorpha

The Cape hare (*Lepus capensis*) is widely distributed, occurring even in almost barren parts of the Namib, while the red rock hare (*Pronolagus randensis*) is closely confined to rocky areas.

Rodentia

Bathyergidae. The Namaqua dune-mole, *Bathyergus janetta*, lives in coastal dunes and the Damara mole-rat, *Cryptomys hottentottus damarensis* is found in sandy regions further inland.

Hystricidae. The porcupine (*Hystrix africae-australis*) occurs in much of the region with the exception of the most arid Namib.

Sciuridae. Xerus inauris, the ground squirrel, is found in open country from the Namib gravel plains to beyond the eastern borders of the region.

Muridae. The distribution of murids is generally very closely correlated with habitat and has been successfully employed to define biotic zones

135

Description of arid ecosystems

in Africa (Davis, 1962). Some twenty-four species occur in the area and five are endemic to it. Fifteen species are known from the Namib, which makes the Muridae the mammal family best represented in that desert. Among the commonest members are two gerbils, the Namaqua gerbil, *Desmodillus auricularis*, and the pigmy gerbil, *Gerbillus paeba*. The Karoo-rat, *Parotomys brantsii* which lives on succulents, seeds and young branches of shrubs, may do extensive damage to vegetation. *Parotomys littledalei*, is endemic to the Namib where it lives in coastal hummock dunes and feeds on succulent shrubs (Coetzee, 1969). *Petromyscus collinus*, is confined to rocky areas while the tree rat, *Thallomys paedulcus* is dependent on stands of trees.

Land use

Prehistory and early history

Early Stone Age implements bear witness to the presence of man in the region several hundred thousand years ago. Artefacts of Later Stone Age are associated with the remains of a beach-combing people, the Strandlopers. Explorers of the seventeenth century described nomadic pastoral Hottentot tribes and Bushmen who were exclusively hunters and food-gatherers. Vast numbers of game, perhaps exceeding the present population of domestic livestock, were present. During the 18th and 19th century man began to disturb the natural ecosystems by large-scale hunting and farming.

Ranching and deterioration of vegetation

By far the most important farming activity is extensive small-stock ranching, especially with sheep. In the most arid farming areas mainly non-wool breeds are kept, such as Karakul (which produce a total of 3×10^6 to 4×10^6 pelts per annum) and mutton-producing Dorpers. Cattle play a role in the long-grass areas of the Kalahari while goats are kept in small numbers throughout the region. The long-term average carrying capacity is estimated at between 8.6 and 2.5 hectares per small stock unit. The minimum size for an economical farming unit is given at between 4000 and 14000 ha (Department of Agricultural Technical Services; Mostert, Roberts, Heslinga & Coetzee, 1961).

The deterioration of vegetation as a result of overstocking sketched by Dyer (1955) is continuing (Hildyard, 1971). Selective grazing results in unpalatable and poisonous species increasing while edible plants become scarce. Karoo dwarf shrubs, such as the bitter *Chrysocoma tenuifolia* and taller shrubs like *Acacia mellifera* ssp. *detinens* replace the grass cover, phenomena respectively referred to as Karoo encroachment and bush encroachment.

In order to halt this deterioration the Stock Reduction Scheme was introduced in 1969. The scheme provides farmers with financial compensation on the basis of the number of livestock reduced and the area withdrawn from grazing (Verbeek, 1971).

Irrigation

Relatively small areas under irrigation, along the Orange and in several other regions, produce mainly lucerne, wheat, fruit and cotton.

Reserves and protected areas

Most parts of the region receiving an average annual rainfall of less than 100 mm are largely uninhabited and are set aside as nature reserves or are otherwise protected. Within Angola, more than half the surface of the arid lands lies within national parks or reserves (Teixeira, 1968). The largest of these is the Iona National Park with a surface of almost 1.6×10^6 ha. Most parts of Botswana receiving less than 250 mm average annual rainfall are within existing or proposed game reserves (Blair Rains & Yalala, 1972). In South West Africa most of the Namib is covered by the following protection areas: Skeleton Coast Park (1.64×10^6 ha), Namib Desert Park (1.41×10^6 ha) and the diamond areas in the southern half of the country covering 5.18×10^6 ha, which are for all practical purposes game reserves (Joubert, 1974). Within South Africa, the Kalahari is the best protected region, as the Kalahari Gemsbok National Park covers 0.96×10^6 ha. Other vegetation types are inadequately protected and the South African IBP CT Working Group has recommended the establishment of conservation areas in the Karoo and the Richtersveld.

Wildlife management and game farming

The utilization of game may be a means of increasing productivity without damage to the environment (Bigalke, 1966). Game ranching is receiving growing attention (Pollock, 1969) and the management of wild animal species is becoming scientifically based.

The springbok was found to have high potential as a farming animal (Skinner, Von la Chevallerie & Van Zyl, 1971) and about ten years ago some 370 000 were counted on South African farms. Eland are not difficult to domesticate and are better adapted to a hot, semi-arid environment than domestic cattle (Skinner, 1971).

137

Description of arid ecosystems

Acknowledgments

I wish to thank Dr R. C. Bigalke, Dr H. D. Brown, Dr W. G. H. Coaton, Dr B. de Winter, Dr D. Edwards, Mr W. Giess, Mr O. P. M. Prozesky and Dr L. Schulze-Prozesky for advice. As they had no access to the final draft they are in no way responsible for any omissions or mistakes. Mariette, my wife, took care of the typing.

References

Abel, H. (1954). Beiträge zur Landeskunde des Kaokoveldes (Südwestafrika). *Deutsche Geographische Blätter*, **47** (1–2), 1–120.

Acocks, J. P. H. (1953). Veld types of South Africa. *Memoirs of the Botanical Survey of South Africa*, **28**, 1–192.

Acocks, J. P. H. (1964). Karoo vegetation in relation to the development of deserts. In: *Ecological studies of Southern Africa* (ed. D. H. S. Davis), pp. 100–112. Junk, The Hague.

Balinsky, B. I. (1962). Patterns of animal distribution on the African continent (Summing-up talk). *Annals of the Cape Provincial Museums*, **2**, 299–310.

Barbosa, A. G. (1970). *Carta Fitogeografica de Angola*. Instituto de Investigaçao Científica de Angola, Luanda.

Bigalke, R. C. (1966). Some thoughts on game farming. *Proceedings of the Grassland Society of Southern Africa*, **1**, 95–102.

Bigalke, R. C. (1972*a*). Observations on the behaviour and feeding habits of the springbok, *Antidorcas marsupialis*. *Zoologica Africana*, **7**(1), 333–59.

Bigalke, R. C. (1972*b*). Symposium on animal behaviour – summing up. *South African Journal of Science*, **68**, 218–20.

Bigalke, R. C. (1972*c*). The contemporary mammal fauna of Africa. In: *Evolution, mammals and southern continents* (ed. A. Keast, F. C. Erk & B. Glass). State University of New York Press, Albany.

Bigalke, R. C. & Bateman, J. A. (1962). On the status and distribution of ungulate mammals in the Cape Province, South Africa. *Annals of the Cape Provincial Museums*, **2**, 85–109.

Blair Rains, A. & Yalala, A. M. (1972). The Central and Southern State Lands, Botswana. *Land Resource Study*, **11**, 1–118.

Botha, D. H. (1969–1970). Locusts and their control in South Africa. *Farming in South Africa*, August, pp. 45, 46, 53; September, pp. 52, 53, 55; October, pp. 37, 39, 40; November, pp. 110, 111, 116; December, pp. 17, 19, 33, 34; January, pp. 18, 19, 29.

Brain, C. K. (1960). Observations on the locomotion of the South West African adder, *Bitis peringueyi* (Boulenger), with speculations on the origin of sidewinding. *Annals of the Transvaal Museum*, **24**, 19–24.

Brown, H. D. (1967). A new grasshopper allied to *Shelfordites* Karny from South West Africa (Orthoptera: Acridoidea). *Cimbebasia*, (A) 1, 3–22.

Brown, H. D. (1972). Revision of the genus *Brownacris* Dirsh, 1958 with descriptions of new species (Orthoptera: Acridoidea). *Annals of the Transvaal Museum*, **28**, 47–77.

Cloudsley-Thomson, J. L. (1968). The Merkhiyat Jebels: a desert community. In: *Desert Biology* volume 1 (ed. G. W. Brown, Jr), pp. 1–20. Academic Press, New York.

Cloudsley-Thompson, J. L. & Chadwick, M. J. (1964). *Life in deserts*. G. T. Foulis, London.

Coaton, W. G. H. (1971). Termites (Order Isoptera). In: *Animal life in southern Africa*, eds. D. J. Potgieter *et al.*, pp. 90–95. Nasou, Cape Town.

Coaton, W. G. H. & Sheasby, J. L. (1972). Preliminary report on a survey of the termites (Isoptera) of South West Africa. *Cimbebasia Memoir*, **2**, 1–129.

Coetzee, C. G. (1969). The distribution of mammals in the Namib Desert and adjoining escarpment. *Scientific papers of the Namib Desert Research Station*, **40**, 23–36.

Darlington, P. J. (1957). *Zoogeography. The geographical distribution of animals*. John Wiley, New York.

Davis, D. H. S. (1962). Distribution patterns of southern African Muridae. *Annals of the Cape Provincial Museums*, **2**, 56–76.

Department of Agricultural Technical Services. *Ontwikkelingsprogram van die winterreënstreek*. Unpublished report, Pretoria.

D'Hoore, J. L. (1964). *Soil map of Africa*. Commission for Technical Co-operation in Africa. Publication 93.

Diniz, A. C. (1973). *Características mesologicas de Angola*. Missao de Inqueritos Agricolas de Angola, Nova Lisboa.

Dirsh, V. M. (1965). *The African genera of Acridoidea*. Cambridge University Press, Cambridge.

Dyer, R. A. (1955). Angola, South West Africa, Bechuanaland and the Union of South Africa. *UNESCO Arid Zone Research*, **6**, 195–218.

Dyer, R. A. (1966). Impressions on the subject of the age and origin of the Cape Flora. *South African Journal of Science*, **62** (6), 187–90.

Eliovson, S. (1972). *Namaqualand in flower*. Macmillan, Johannesburg.

Eloff, F. C. (1964). On the predatory habits of lions and hyaenas. *Koedoe*, **7**, 105–12.

Eloff, F. C. (1973 *a*). Water use by the Kalahari lion *Panthera leo vernayi*. *Koedoe*, **16**, 149–54.

Eloff, F. C. (1973*b*). Lion predation in the Kalahari Gemsbok National Park. *Journal of the Southern African Wildlife Management Association*, **3** (2), 59–63.

Engler, A. (1921). *Die Pflanzenwelt Afrikas*, volume 3. Wilhelm Engelmann, Leipzig.

Exell, A. W. & Gonçalves, M. L. (1973). A statistical analysis of a sample of the flora of Angola. *Garcia de Orta, Série de Botânica*, **1** (1–2), 105–28.

Gaff, D. F. (1971). Desiccation-tolerant Flowering Plants in Southern Africa. *Science*, **174**, 1033–43.

Ganssen, R. (1963). *Südwest-Afrika, Böden und Kultur*. Reimer, Berlin.

Giess, W. (1962). Some notes on the vegetation of the Namib Desert. *Cimbebasia*, **2**, 1–35.

Giess, W. (1969). *Welwitschia mirabilis* Hook. f. *Dinteria*, **3**, 1–55.

Giess, W. (1971). A preliminary vegetation map of South West Africa. *Dinteria*, **4**, 1–114.

Haacke, W. D. (1964). Descriptions of two new species of lizards and notes on *Fitzsimonsia brevipes* (Fitzsimons) from the Central Namib Desert. *Scientific Papers of the Namib Desert Research Station*, **25**, 1–15.

Haacke, W. D. (1969). The call of the barking geckos (Gekkonidae, Reptilia). *Scientific Papers of the Namib Desert Research Station*, **46**, 83–94.

Hamilton, W. J. & Coetzee, C. G. (1969). Thermoregulatory behaviour of the vegetarian lizard, *Angolosaurus skoogi*, on the vegetationless northern Namib Desert dunes. *Scientific Papers of the Namib Desert Research Station*, **47**, 95–104.

Description of arid ecosystems

Haughton, S. H. (1969). *Geological history of Southern Africa*. Geological Society of South Africa, Cape Town.

Hilldyard, P. (1971). Water and the veld situation in South Africa. *Proceedings of the Grassland Society of Southern Africa*, **6**, 16–19.

Holm, E. & Edney, E. B. (1973). Daily activity of Namib Desert arthropods in relation of climate. *Ecology*, **54** (1), 45–56.

Huey, R. B., Pianka, E. R., Egan, M. E. & Coons, C. W. (1974). Ecological shifts in sympatry: Kalahari fossorial lizards (*Typhlosaurus*). *Ecology*, **55**, 304–16.

Jackson, S. P. (1951). Climates of southern Africa. *South African Geographical Journal*, **33**, 17–37.

Jennings, C. M. H. (1971). Note on hydrological research in Botswana with special emphasis on research in the hydrogeological field. *South African Journal of Science*, **67**, 12–21.

Joubert, E. (1971). The past and present distribution and status of the Black Rhinoceros (*Diceros bicornis* Linn. 1758) in South West Africa. *Madoqua*, ser. *1* (**4**), 5–32.

Joubert, E. (1974). The development of wildlife utilization in South West Africa. *Journal of the Southern African Wildlife Management Association*, **4**, 35–42.

Kaiser, R. (1926). *Die Diamantenwüste Südwestafrikas*. Reimer, Berlin.

Knapp, R. (1973). *Die Vegetation von Afrika*. Gustav Fischer, Stuttgart.

Koch, C. (1961). Some aspects of abundant life in the vegetationless sand of the Namib Desert dunes. *Journal of the South West African Scientific Society*, **15**, 8–33, 76–92.

Koch, C. (1962). The Tenebrionidae of southern Africa. XXXI. Comprehensive notes on the Tenebrionid fauna of the Namib Desert. *Annals of the Transvaal Museum*, **24**, 61–106.

Lamoral, B. H. (1973). The arachnid fauna of the Kalahari Gemsbok National Park. Part 1. A revision of the species of 'mole solifuges' of the genus *Chelypus* Purcell, 1901 (Family Hexisopodidae). *Koedoe*, **16**, 83–102.

Lawrence, R. F. (1955). Solifugae, scorpions and pedipalpi, with checklist and keys to South African families, genera and species. In: *South African Animal Life*, vol. 1 (eds. B. Hanstrom, P. Brinck & G. Rudebeck), pp. 152–262. Almquist & Wiksell, Uppsala.

Lawrence, R. F. (1959). The sand-dune fauna of the Namib Desert. *South African Journal of Science*, **55**, 233–9.

Lawrence, R. F. (1960). Some observations on the Arachnid fauna of South West Africa. *South African Museums Association Bulletin*, **7**, 67–72.

Lawrence, R. F. (1964). *A conspectus of South African spiders*. Science Pamphlet 369, Department of Agricultural Technical Services, Pretoria.

Lawrence, R. F. (1966). New dune spiders (Sparassidae) from the Namib Desert, South West Africa. *Cimbebasia*, **17**, 3–15.

Lawrence, R. F. (1967). The zoogeography of some desert Arachnida from S.W. Africa. *Palaeoecology of Africa*, **2**, 75–6.

Lawrence, R. F. (1971). Spiders and other Arachnida. In: *Animal Life in Southern Africa* (eds. D. J. Potgieter *et al*), pp. 210–7. Nasou, Cape Town.

Lea, A. (1964). Some major factors in the population dynamics of the brown locust *Locustana pardalina* (Walker). In: *Ecological studies in Southern Africa* (ed. D. H. S. Davis), pp. 269–83. Junk, The Hague.

Leistner, O. A. (1961). Zur Verbreitung und Ökologie der Bäume der Kalahari-dünen. *Journal of the South West African Scientific Society*, **15**, 3.

Leistner, O. A. (1967). The plant ecology of the southern Kalahari. *Memoirs of the Botanical Survey of South Africa*, **38**, 1–172.

Leistner, O. A. & Werger, M. J. A. (1973). Southern Kalahari phytosociology. *Vegetatio*, **28**, 353–99.

Leser, H. (1971). *Landschaftsökologische Studien im Kalahari sandgebiet um Auob und Nossob*. Steiner, Wiesbaden.

Leser, H. (1972). Geoökologische Verhältnisse der Pflanzengesellschaften in den Savannen des Sandveldes um den Schwarzen Nossob und um Epukiro (Östliches Südwestafrika, Westliche Kalahari). *Dinteria*, **6**, 1–41.

Lewis, A. D. (1936). Sand dunes of the Kalahari within the borders of the Union. *South African Geographical Journal*, **19**, 22–32.

Logan, R. F. (1969). Geography of the Central Namib Desert. In: *Arid Lands in Perspective* (eds. W. G. McGinnies & B. J. Goldman), pp. 127–43. University of Arizona Press, Tucson.

Logan, R. F. (1972). The geographical division of the deserts of South West Africa. *Mitteilungen der Basler Afrika Bibliographien*, **4** (6), 46–65.

Louw, G. N. (1972). The role of advective fog in the water economy of certain Namib desert animals. In: *Comparative physiology of desert animals. Symposia of the Zoological Society of London*, **31**, 297–314.

Loxton, R. F. (1962). The soils of the Republic of South Africa; a preliminary reclassification, *South African Journal of Science*, **58**, 45–53.

McLachlan, G. R. & Liversidge, R. (1972). *Roberts Birds of South Africa*. C.N.A., Johannesburg.

Maclean, G. L. (1974). Arid-zone adaptations in southern African birds. *Cimbebasia*, (A) **3**, 163–76.

Matos, G. Cardoso de & Sousa, J. N. Batista de. (1970). *Reserva Parcial de Mocâmedes. Carta de Vegetaçâo e Memoria Descritiva*. Instituto de Investigaçao Agronomica de Angola, Nova Lisboa.

May, I. R. (1973). The locust threat of Africa. *Occasional Papers of the Africa Institute*, **34**, 1–20.

Mertens, R. (1972). Die Anpassungsmerkmale der Namib-Reptilien: ein Vergleich mit denen anderer Wüsten. *Mitteilungen der Basler Afrika Bibliographien*, **4** (6), 96–113.

Mills, G. (1973). The brown hyaena. *African Wild Life*, **27**, 150–53.

Milstein, P. le S. (1971). The value of our birds. In: *Birdlife in Southern Africa* (ed. K. Newman), pp. 205–16. Purnell & Sons, Johannesburg.

Monod, T. (1971). Remarques sur les symmétries floristiques des zones sèches nord et sud en Afrique. *Mitteilungen der Botanischen Staatssammlung München*, **10**, 375–423.

Mostert, J. W. C., Roberts, B. R., Heslinga, C. F. & Coetzee, P. G. F. (1971). *Veldt management in the O.F.S. region*. Department of Agricultural Technical Services Bulletin 791. Government Printer, Pretoria.

Newlands, G. (1972). Notes on psammophilous scorpions and a description of a new species (Arachnida: Scorpionides). *Annals of the Transvaal Museum*, **27**, 241–54.

Nordenstam, B. (1969). Phytogeography of the genus *Euryops* (Compositae). *Opera Botanica*, **23**, 1–77.

Piffl, E. (1965). *Microcaeculus namibensis* nov. spec., ein Vertreter der Caeculiden (Arachnoidea, Acari) aus der Namibwüste Südwestafrikas. *Scientific papers of the Namib Desert Research Station*, **28**, 1–12.

Pollock, N. C. (1969). Some observations on game ranching in southern Africa. *Biological Conservation*, **2**, 18–24.

Preston-Whyte, R. A. (1974). Climatic classification of South Africa: a multivariate approach. *The South African Geographical Journal*, **56** (1), 79–86.

Description of arid ecosystems

Roberts, A. (1951). *The mammals of South Africa*. Trustees, 'The mammals of South Africa' Book Fund, Johannesburg.

Sauer, E. G. F. & Sauer, E. M. (1971). Die Kurzohrige Elefantenspitzmaus in der Namib. *Namib und Meer*, **2**, 5–43.

Schulze, B. R. (1947). The climates of South Africa according to the classifications of Köppen and Thornthwaite. *South African Geographical Journal*, **29**, 32–42.

Schulze, B. R. (1969). The climate of Gobabeb. *Scientific Papers of the Namib Desert Research Station*, **38**, 5–12.

Skinner, J. D. (1971). Productivity of the eland: an appraisal of the last five years' research. *South African Journal of Science*, **67**, 534–9.

Skinner, J. D., Von la Chevallerie, M. & Van Zyl, J. H. M. (1971). An appraisal of the springbok for diversifying animal production in Africa. *Animal Breeding Abstracts*, **39** (2), 215–24.

Smithers, R. H. N. (1971). *The mammals of Botswana*. National Museums of Rhodesia, Salisbury.

Spreitzer, H. (1966). Beobachtungen zur Geomorphologie der zentralen Namib und ihrer Randgebiete. *Journal of the South West African Scientific Society*, **20**, 69–94.

Stengel, H. W. (1971). Die tyd staan nie stil in die Namibwoestyn nie. *South African Journal of Science*, **67**, 103–8.

Teixeira, J. Brito (1968). Angola. *Acta Phytogeographica Suecica*, **54**, 193–7.

Theiler, G. (1964). Ecogeographical aspects of tick distribution. In: *Ecological studies in Southern Africa* (ed. D. H. S. Davis), pp. 282–300. Junk, The Hague.

Truswell, J. F. (1970). *An introduction to the historical geology of South Africa*. Purnell, Cape Town.

Tschinkel, W. R. (1973). The sorption of water vapor by wind-borne plant debris in the Namib Desert. *Madoqua, ser. 2*, **2** (63–68), 21–4.

Van der Eyck, J. J., Macvicar, C. N. & De Villiers, J. M. (1969). Soils of the Tugela Basin. *Natal Town and Regional Planning Reports*, **15**.

Van der Merwe, C. R. (1962). Soil groups and subgroups of South Africa. 2nd edition, *Department of Agricultural Technical Services Science Bulletin No.* 231.

Van Rooyen, T. H. & Burger, R. du T. (1974). Plant–ecological significance of the soils of the central Orange River Basin. *South African Geographical Journal*, **56** (1), 60–6.

Van Zinderen Bakker, E. M. (1967). Upper Pleistocene and Holocene stratigraphy and ecology on the basis of vegetation changes in Sub- Saharan Africa. In: *Background to evolution in Africa* (eds. W. W. Bishop & J. Desmond Clark). University of Chicago Press, Chicago.

Verbeek, W. S. (1971). The need to safeguard and extend the pasture resources for animal production in South Africa. *Proceedings of the Grassland Society of Southern Africa*, **6**, 12–5.

Verdcourt, B. (1969). The arid corridor between the north-east and south-west areas of Africa. *Palaeoecology of Africa*, **4**, 140–4.

Vogel, S. (1955). Niedere Fensterpflanzen in der südafrikanischen Wüste. *Beiträge zur Biologie der Pflanzen*, **31**, 45–135.

Walter, H. (1971). *Ecology of tropical and subtropical vegetation*. Oliver & Boyd, Edinburgh.

Walter, H. & Leith, M. (1960). *Klimadiagramm–Weltatlas*. Fischer, Jena.

Weather Bureau (1965). *Climate of South Africa. 8. General survey*. W.B. 28. Government Printer, Pretoria.

Wellington, J. H. (1955). *Southern Africa. A geographical study*, vol. 1. Cambridge University Press, Cambridge.

Wells, L. H. (1967). N.E.–S.W. 'Arid Corridor' in Africa. *South African Journal of Science*, **63**, 480–1.

Werger, M. J. A. (1973). Notes on the phytogeographical affinities of the southern Kalahari. *Bothalia*, **11**, 177–80.

White, F. (1973). Vegetation map of Africa. *Kirkia*, **9** (1), 20–21.

Wild, H. & Grandvaux Barbosa, L. A. (1968). *Vegetation map of the Flora Zambesiaca area. (Flora Zambesiaca Supplement.)* M. O. Collins, Salisbury, Rhodesia.

Willoughby, E. J. (1969). Desert coloration in birds of the central Namib Desert. *Scientific papers of the Namib Desert Research Station*, **44**, 59–68.

Manuscript received by the editors December 1974

5.   Ecosystems of Australia

O. B. WILLIAMS

Introduction

Australia, a continent of 7.7×10^6 km^2, has 44% of its land surface in desert. An additional 37% of Australia is vegetated with semi-arid tussock grassland and shrub communities. The ecosystems of arid Australia to be described are those in both the desert and in the surrounding semi-arid crescent (see Fig. 5.1; R. M. Moore, 1973).

Most of Australia's inhabitants, 14 million in 1976, live in the non-mountainous parts of the remaining 19% of the continent; this includes the majority of Australian scientists. Research institutions in arid Australia are few and resident staff, as distinct from visiting scientists, probably number less than 50.

Aridity, a major feature of the Australian environment, receives little public attention from within Australia, possibly because of the small rural population and the fact that most of the 14% who are rural dwellers live in the higher rainfall regions of eastern, south-eastern and south-western Australia.

In arid Australia there is only one large, non-mining town, Alice Springs in the Northern Territory, with more than 10000 inhabitants. Large, old-established mining centres include Broken Hill in New South Wales, Mt Isa in Queensland and Kalgoorlie in Western Australia. Recent mining centres developed in Western Australia include Robe River, Tom Price, Pannawonica, Goldsworthy, Kambalda and Paraburdoo. Apart from mining, industries of the arid interior are not substantial in terms of total Australian production. For example, the sheep and cattle industries only become significant when flocks and herds in the wide zone of the semi-arid crescent are included.

Many hundreds of kilometres separate the deserts and shrublands from the larger urban centres and the major communication corridors tend to follow the coastline. The summer in Australia coincides with the major vacation period as is the case in Europe and the United States; however the coastal mountain ranges and numerous beaches are close to urban centres and are more pleasant environments than the extremely hot, distant desert. The Australian winter is mild compared with the winter of northern Europe and America, with snow limited to a small area in the south-east of the continent. In winter, the arid interior is less attractive than ski resorts in south-eastern Australia, and the tropical and sub-tropical coastline. Tourist pressures on the ecosystems of arid Australia

145

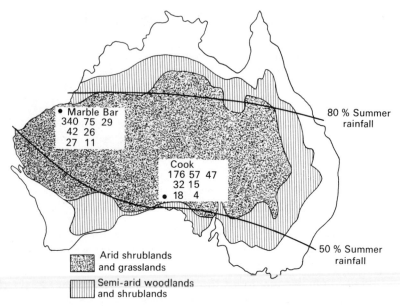

Fig. 5.1. Arid shrublands and grasslands with surrounding semi-arid crescent of eucalypt low woodlands, shrub woodlands and shrublands. The percentage of rainfall falling in the 6 summer months is indicated and the numbers for Marble Bar and Cook refer to: Line 1 – mean annual rainfall (mm), percentage rain October–March and mean number of rainy days; Line 2 – mean monthly maximum and minimum temperatures (°C) for hottest month; Line 3 – mean monthly maximum and minimum temperatures (°C) for coldest month. (After R. M. Moore, 1973.)

are localized and centre on a few features such as Ayers Rock in central Australia and the Flinders Ranges in South Australia.

In addition, frequent attempts by pastoral entrepreneurs to utilize Australia's arid lands over the past century have been costly in terms of capital, human effort and endurance, and deterioration of the soil and vegetation resources. Because educational curricula deal with these aspects in historical, geographical and economic terms the lack of public interest is more likely to be avoidance than ignorance or lack of awareness.

This chapter expressly provides an introduction to a very wide range of Australian biological studies pertaining to arid ecosystems. The aim is to provide the background for the later specialist contributions and allow comparisons with the general descriptions of arid lands in other countries. The references have been chosen, not only to illustrate particular points and views of biologists, but also to facilitate the entry of non-Australian readers to the Australian literature through extensive bibliographies.

Physical description

Land forms and geology

The major land forms of arid Australia have been described and illustrated by Mabbutt (1965, 1969, 1971); Hills, Ollier & Twidale (1966); Mabbutt & Sullivan (1970); amongst studies of landforms in particular arid regions are those in Jennings & Mabbutt (1971) by Twidale for the Flinders Ranges and Wopfner & Twidale for the nearby Lake Eyre basin, Mabbutt for central Australia, Mulcahy for the south-west of Western Australia (see also Mulcahy, 1973), Butler for the Riverine Plain of south-east Australia (see also Butler *et al.*, 1973) and Jennings for the karst area adjacent to the Great Australian Bight.

No review deals exclusively with the geology of arid Australia; Johnstone, Lowry & Quilty (1973) treat the south-west of Western Australia, most of which can be classified as arid. Brown, Campbell & Crook (1968) use a stratigraphical approach in what is one of the major contributions to the geology of the continent and the arid regions are treated at some length.

Australian arid lands comprise extensive plateaux, averaging 300 m above sea level, with associated sedimentary basins; this land surface has been subjected to deep lateritic weathering in the past (Tertiary). Subsequently this weathered surface has been modified by erosion, by burial with extensive alluvial deposits and by reworking and regional accession as a consequence of aeolian activity.

In addition to plateaux there are several local ranges which rise above them, notably the Macdonnell Range in central Australia. Flinders Ranges in South Australia and the Hamersley Range in the Pilbara region of Western Australia.

Drainage

The drainage is of two major types, being either external direct to the sea or internal to drainage sumps within the continental mass. The major external system is the Murray–Darling which rises in the high rainfall divides of eastern Australian, traverses the arid interior and finally reaches the sea in a mesic region of South Australia. This is the only non-ephemeral river system in Australia. Amongst the less extensive systems, of the external type are those that drain the Isa Highlands and Barkly Tablelands of northern Australia into the Gulf of Carpentaria and those that drain the western plateaux into the Indian Ocean; these latter may have apparently uncoordinated upper reaches featuring salt lakes (Mulcahy & Bettenay, 1972).

The most extensive of the internal drainage system drains into Lake

Description of arid ecosystems

Eyre which is a large saline *playa* lower than sea level; an impressive example of this internal system is given by the so-called 'Channel Country', a complex of anastomosing stream beds to the north-east of Lake Eyre which experiences substantial flows each summer and is extensively flooded one year in five as a result of deep cyclonic depressions swinging across the watersheds of the contributing rivers in northern and north-central Queensland. Lake Eyre has been filled several times in the last 100 years.

Short outwash systems flood out from local highlands such as the Macdonnell Ranges and disappear after a short distance into the continental dune fields.

Riverless areas of arid Australia have low relief and land surfaces of high permeability; examples are the jointed limestone of the Nullarbor Plain and extensive sand deserts.

Soils

The pattern of soils in arid Australia can be related to several aspects of the land form development. Erosional modification of the deeply weathered plateaux has yielded soil materials which are generally low in minerals required for plant growth: extensive areas of soils are related to alluvial depositions and the development of clay pans; aeolian activity has given rise to alluvial plains with calcareous aeolian clays and quartzose sandy deposits.

The soils resulting from these processes may be classified into three broad classes: red, brown and grey clays; red sands and earths; calcareous earths and clays.

The red, brown and grey clays cover large areas of north-western and south-western Queensland and northern and south-western New South Wales; in Queensland there are extensive areas of undulating lowlands which are the product of erosional modifications of weathered sedimentary rocks; elsewhere these soils are generally associated with alluvial plains.

The red sands occur most extensively in continental dune fields and relicts of deeply weathered land surfaces which have been relatively unaffected by erosion. In the latter case they are interspersed with extensive red earths which relate to deep weathering and local alluvial deposition. Red sands and red earths predominate in south-west Queensland, north-west New South Wales and central Australia; they are the major soils of arid Australia.

Calcareous earths and clays cover substantial areas of South Australia and south-west New South Wales; they overlie elements of the deeply weathered plateaux or alluvial plains.

Soils forming a minor proportion of arid Australian landscapes include

148

hard alkaline duplex soils, red earths, particularly in alluvial plains; areas of saline alluvium are associated with salt lakes and the so-called stony downs of eastern Australia appear to be local alluvial plains merging with the bevelled slopes of the plateaux.

In the scheme developed by Northcote (1971) the red sands would have the principal profile form Uc1.2 and Uc 5.21; the red earths would be Gn 2.1, Um 5.3 and Uf 6.71. In the cracking clays Ug 5.37 would cover the principal profile form. Northcote *et al.* (1975) use this same notation in their description of Australian soils. The full descriptions of the morphology of all soil groups in Australia, together with supporting laboratory data and colour illustrations of representative profiles will be found in Stace *et al.* (1968).

Soil fertility

Soil fertility is a relative term; the nutrient status of soils in arid Australia is adequate for the development of the type of indigenous vegetation seen at the time of European settlement, but they are infertile in the sense that, with water non-limiting, they rarely allow the potential yield of crop and introduced pasture species to be expressed (Winkworth, 1967). Irrigated crops or forages on arid soils require the same fertilizers in similar or larger amounts to crops and forages grown in the humid zone and there is no reason to suppose that deficiencies of nitrogen, phosphorus, sulphur, and copper, zinc and molybdenum in humid Australia are less pronounced in the ancient soils of arid Australia. The levels of nitrogen and phosphorus in Australian arid zone soils are substantially lower than in arid zone soils elsewhere (Charley, 1972). Jackson (1962) has suggested that these low nitrogen contents are an indirect effect of the low phosphorus status (see also Williams & Andrew, 1970). Because arid soils are low in nutrients it is likely that rare periods of continuous and abundant rain may produce less dry matter than expected (Trumble & Woodroffe, 1954).

European occupancy of arid lands has accelerated erosion and redistributed part or all of particular surface soils either locally in the form of sand hills as in western New South Wales or fresh alluvium as in the Gascoyne catchment of Western Australia or nationally and even internationally as red dust in cities and on glaciers in New Zealand. Scarce nutrients have been lost from arid ecosystems in this manner. Herbivore populations greatly in excess of pre-settlement number, concentrate plant nutrients in faeces and then redistribute them over the landscape; a small amount of nutrients in plants is exported in the animal product.

However there are differences in fertility between soils in arid Australia; alluvial soils of the flood plains are better able to support the growth of introduced grass species than are the adjacent sandplain soils (Winkworth,

1964). In general, clays are superior to red earths and sands. Within the one depositional system in south-western Queensland, red earths which are similar on physical criteria differ substantially in phosphorous levels; the growth of *Cenchrus ciliaris*, a grass known to be responsive to phosphorus, differs markedly on these two soils.

Subsoils are usually less fertile than surface soils, and in addition may contain chlorides and sulphates of sodium, calcium and magnesium to the point of toxicity for some plant species. Nutritionally, as well as physically, subsoils exposed by erosion are a poor medium for growth.

Soils and their water relationships

Soils in the arid zone do not appear to differ from those in mesic Australia in their reaction to rain and drought; opportunities for a deep profile to be wetted are infrequent in arid Australia. Soils in both regions have been totally dessicated by the same severe drought (Aitchison, 1971).

Infiltration rates after two hours for soils in central Australia (Jackson, 1962) range from 1.5 and 0.8 cm h^{-1} for fine-textured soils to 7.4 cm h^{-1} for red sands of a dune. The amount of water absorbed in two hours ranges from 1.9 cm in the fine-textured soil to 14.6 cm in the sand. An example of the infiltration characteristics of a red earthy sand at points 0.5 and 2.0 m from a trunk of *Acacia aneura* in a grove and at a point between groves (Slatyer, 1962) shows a decline in rate over a two-hour period from 3.6 cm h^{-1} to 2.3 cm h^{-1} near the trunk and 1.0 cm h^{-1} in the intergrove. In South Australia at Yudnapinna, Jackson (1958) has recorded infiltration values of 0.5 cm h^{-1} and 2.5 cm absorbed after two hours on a fine-textured soil; values on a coarse-textured soil reached 5.3 cm h^{-1} after one hour and 8.1 cm was absorbed in one hour. Winkworth (1967) comments that the depth of coarse-textured soils under spinifex grassland in central Australia is generally sufficient to absorb most of the rain that falls. Local runoff can occur (Winkworth, 1963) but would appear to be more a feature of finer-textured soils and exposed subsoils ('scalds'). Jones (1969) has noted that 2.5–7.5 mm of rainfall on certain scalds will produce less than 10% runoff in contrast to rains of 25 mm which may yield > 90% runoff. In a series of small ring infiltrometer observations on red earths in South Australia, Williams (unpublished) has obtained initial values ($\pm$S.E.) over the first 5 min of 10.2$\pm$2.0 cm h^{-1} on massive scalds, 21.1$\pm$2.5 cm h^{-1} on cracked scalds, 39.6$\pm$10.6 cm h^{-1} on the uneroded soil and 66.2$\pm$9.1 cm h^{-1} at a site where the coarse-textured surface soil from the scalds had accumulated. Initial soil moisture values were at their mid-summer low. The number of minutes taken for 7.6 cm of applied water to infiltrate into this sequence of soils was 297$\pm$40, 58$\pm$12, 28$\pm$5 and 8.5$\pm$2 respectively. The corrected minimum infiltration after five hours ranged from 0.5 to 1.0 cm h^{-1} and is similar to the values given by Jackson (1958).

Redistribution of rainfall in undisturbed arid landscapes can be substantial. For example, Goodspeed & Winkworth (1978) have noted that parts of an *Eragrostis eriopoda* grassland in central Australia may receive runoff which is equivalent to 16–47% of the incoming rain; in an *Acacia aneura* community, 80% of the rain falling on the treeless intergrove areas ran into the groves. The data taken in an area of pronounced gilgai micro-relief by Wilson & Leigh (1964) suggest that more than 60% of the incoming rain runs off the mounds and into nearby depressions.

There are few published field studies for the amount of available water held in representative soils of arid Australia. Winkworth (1970), using 2 years of records, has calculated 36 mm from −15 bar to maximum field moisture and 67 mm from minimum to maximum field values in the 81 cm profile of red earthy sand supporting an arid grassland of *Eragrostis eriopoda* in central Australia. In a three year study of soil moisture changes under three semi-arid grasslands at Deniliquin, New South Wales, Williams (1956) recorded values from −15 bar to maximum field moisture of 54 mm, 27 mm and 14 mm respectively for red-brown earth and brown and grey clays with massive surfaces; sandy loams with siliceous hardpan near the surface have given values of *c.* 20 mm. These are low values compared with 127 mm stored in the 1.5 m of a deep red-brown earth representative of the wheat lands of the Adelaide Plain (Butler & Prescott, 1955).

The normal depth of wetting in soils of arid Australia is not great and published values range from 1.5 m under *Acacia aneura* groves where runon is an important contributor (Slatyer, 1961), 1.3 m under *A. aneura* at Charleville (Pressland, 1978) and 45–60 cm in loams under *Maireana* shrubland (Carrodus & Specht, 1965) down to 5–10 cm in mounds of the galgai micro relief on grey clay (Wilson & Leigh, 1964).

Recently, exceptional periods of heavy and prolonged rain have produced deeply wetted profiles to greater than 3 m in mulga groves and to bedrock at 4 m in grey clay on the Barkly Tableland; the latter value is twice the depth of the neutron meter access tubes which were installed to cover what were known to be normal wetting and drying cycle (Winkworth, personal communication). Winkworth (1967) has recorded 250 cm depth of wetting under spinifex on red siliceous sands after 254 mm of rain had fallen in one day and Allen (1963) has reported a depth of wetting of 60 cm in grey clay after rainfall of 193 mm.

Jackson (1958) has noted that runoff at an arid site tends to be greater where domestic livestock are grazed. However quantitative information on the trampling effect of livestock in arid Australia is lacking. Descriptions of soils in northern New South Wales as they were before hard-footed domestic livestock (sheep and cattle) were introduced refer to the transformation of 'the land from its original soft, spongy, absorbent nature to a hard, clayey, smooth surface . . .' (Royal Commission, 1901, Q. 3157;

151

Description of arid ecosystems

quoted in part from Newman & Condon, 1969). In the same report (Royal Commission, 1901, Q. 12796) evidence is given of the removal of surface soil by wind erosion from 25% of a 188 000 ha pastoral lease. Soil erosion in arid Australia following pastoral settlement has been the subject of many studies, including those by Condon, Newman & Cunningham (1969a) for central Australia and Beadle (1948); James (1960); and Stannard (1963) for western New South Wales. Both wind erosion and water erosion, initiated by removal of vegetative cover, whether by grazing or tree and shrub cutting or trampling by livestock, and coincident drought have removed part or all surface soil from substantial areas of inland Australia. These processes still operate on a limited scale at a rate substantially in excess of long-term erosional rates. Elsewhere in the developed arid regions the rates have slowed over the past several decades, and appear to approximate the erosional rates of unsettled regions. However this steady state has been arrived at with a poorer soil resource base than when European settlement began (Newman & Condon, 1969).

Climate

The climate of the Australian continent has been described by Gentilli (1971, 1972) and Williams (1973a) has described the climatic component of direct relevance to pasture and the sheep and cattle industries. A concise account of the continent's climate together with tables and maps is available in the current *Year Book of the Commonwealth of Australia*. Gibbs (1969) has concentrated on the climate of Australia's arid zone and considered factors which might produce climate change.

Wind systems

Fleming (1978) has applied the systems, as described by Gentilli (1971), in an analysis of rainfall in arid Australia. The four pertinent systems are monsoon, tropical cyclones, mid-latitude fronts and inter-anticyclonic fronts.

Monsoon rains, preceded and succeeded by thunderstorms, penetrate about 500 km from the northern coastline to the arid interior where they are reduced to local convective thunderstorms. Tropical cyclones developed in the Coral, Arafura and Timor seas may cross the coastline in the course of their complex paths (Lourensz, 1977) and ultimately be reduced to rain depressions. Slow-moving depressions produce widespread heavy rain and rapid-moving depressions often produce intense, more restricted, rainfalls (Brunt, 1966). Mid-latitude fronts are associated with the 500 to 600 km/day procession of large oval anticyclones, or high pressures, from west to east across the continent. These anticyclones form

152

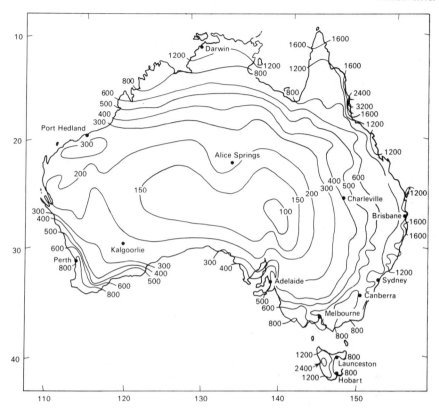

Fig. 5.2. Median annual rainfall (isohyets in mm).

over the Indian Ocean and cross Australia in latitude 37 to 38° S in summer and 29 to 32° S in winter. In winter, the rainfall associated with the line of the front is uniform and orographic effects can be substantial, but elsewhere rainfall is less uniform and lighter. In the summers of south-eastern Australia there can be a linear series of thunderstorms along the front, but rain seldom falls for longer than one hour because the fronts are narrow and rapid moving. The inter-anticyclonic front (or mid-tropospheric conveyor belt! (Fleming, 1978)) is an upper-level low, common but irregular in occurrence, and in eastern Australia is often associated with widespread moderate to heavy rainfall. In the Alice Springs area of central Australia, Eagleson & Goodspeed (1973) studied individual storm behaviour and tentative conclusions from this study include: storm type rather than season plays a primary role in determining the distribution of precipitation over an area, storm centres of convectional storms have an effective storm radius of 32 km or less, orographic influences are not well-defined, and convective storms have a wider range of

153

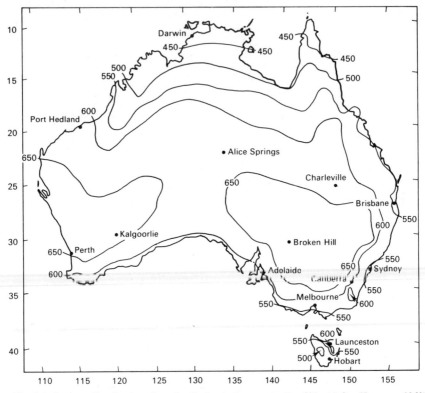

Fig. 5.3. Average distribution of total radiation in January (cal/cm²/day) (after Hounam, 1963).

time distributions than cyclonic storms but the latter are less variable from station to station.

The proportional contribution to monthly rainfall made by the rain-producing systems varies substantially between months and sites as exemplified by Gentilli (1971, p. 139). The usual cautions about placing undue reliance on mean annual rainfall data should be underlined, particularly for localities in arid Australia.

Rainfall

Rain is the only form of precipitation in the arid interior because snowfalls do not occur. A map of Australia showing the median annual rainfall is set out in Fig. 5.2.

In terms of annual rainfall, only 39% of the continent receives less than 250 mm. However the variability of inland Australia is 10% or more above the world average for places with the same annual rainfall. Fleming (1975)

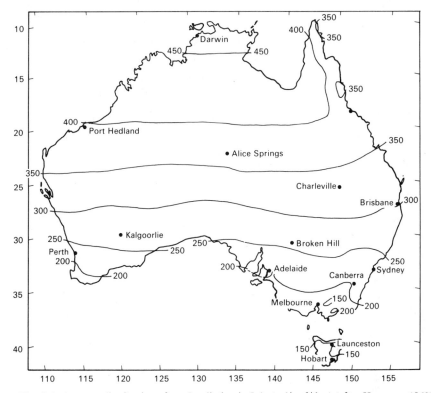

Fig. 5.4. Average distribution of total radiation in July (cal/cm²/day) (after Hounam, 1963).

has discussed rainfall variability in time categories from annual and seasonal to daily, hourly and storm events.

Maps and tables showing probabilities of rainfall on a monthly and annual basis for many hundreds of meteorological stations are available (Bureau of Meteorology, 1968). Examples of monthly rainfall expectancies for northern, central and southern regions of Australia are given by Williams (1973*a*). The extreme annual rainfall values for three representative stations are: Richmond, 108–1160 mm; Bollon, 180–1953 mm, and Deniliquin, 141–729 mm.

Long periods without rain are usual in the northern winter and the southern summer and are referred to as 'seasonal drought'. The absence of summer rains in northern Australia and of winter rains in southern Australia precipitate 'non-seasonal drought'; these can become critical for both the indigenous flora and fauna as well as the pastoral industry in the arid zone (Foley, 1957; Gibbs & Maher, 1967).

Lightning, thunder and occasional rain are produced by local thunder-

155

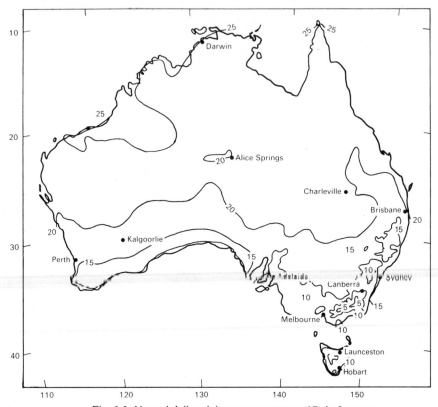

Fig. 5.5. Normal daily minimum temperature (°C) in January.

storms. Lightning from one storm, in conjunction with abundant dry grass has produced upwards of ten 'strikes' and fires in one district. Large fires, burning on several fronts which may each be of 5–10 km, rage for days or weeks over areas exceeding 1000 km² in unsettled or lightly settled inland districts. These fires are a natural feature, and pre-date European occupation (see Gill, 1975). Seasonal fire occurrence depends not only on rainfall but also on the type of vegetation providing the fuel (McArthur, 1972).

Solar Radiation, temperature and sunshine

The intensity of solar radiation of the earth's surface in midsummer is at its maximum at 30° S (Figs. 5.3 and 5.4), the equivalent of a power input of 700 W m⁻² for approximately 10 hd⁻¹. The mid-winter maximum is expressed in a band across the continent at the northern side of the arid

156

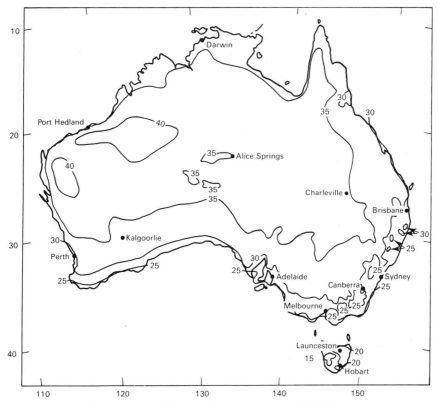

Fig. 5.6. Normal daily maximum temperature (°C) in January.

interior (Fig. 5.4). The outgoing terrestrial radiation from the earth's surface is high because of the dryness of the air.

Air temperatures in mid-summer are high over most of the continent, reaching particularly high levels in the interior (Figs. 5.6 and 5.7); the mean daily range is from 12 to 15 °C. At Port Hedland and Richmond (near Hughenden, Qld.) daily maxima can exceed 35 °C on 138 and 141 d yr^{-1} respectively, and at some northern stations a daily maximum exceeding 38 °C has been recorded on more than 50 successive days; Marble Bar (inland from Port Hedland) has exceeded this value on more than 100 successive days.

The distribution of mid-winter air temperatures (Fig. 5.7 and 5.8) in the interior is predominantly latitudinal and ranges from a mean maximum of 15 °C in the south to 25 °C in the north. The normal daily minimum is from 13 to 15 °C below this maximum, except near the coastline.

Frost occurrences are conventionally specified in terms of 0 °C for a

157

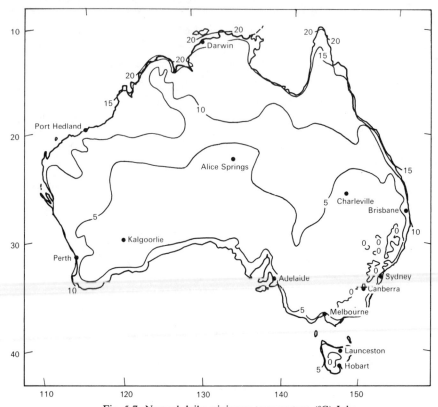

Fig. 5.7. Normal daily minimum temperature (°C) July.

heavy frost and 2 °C for a light frost. Latitude, altitude and nearness to the sea influence the frequency and severity of frosts; local topographic features in arid Australia are subdued and modify this general pattern only slightly. Duration and timing of frost periods (0 °C) are shown in Fig. 5.9.

The range from the highest maximum to the lowest minimum in one year may be 50 °C, but 40–45 °C is more usual.

The association of rain with concurrent and succeeding temperatures lower than average, for two or more days, is now considered to be ecologically significant.

The average hours of sunshine in the mid-summer month of January reach their maximum of 350 in south-eastern and south-western Australia; the northern arid zone reaches 250–275 hours because of cloud cover. In the mid-winter month of July this situation is reversed with 200–250 hours in the south and 275–300 hours in the north.

Changes in day-length assume importance in many biological phenomena and information on this is presented in Table 5.1 for locations in the

158

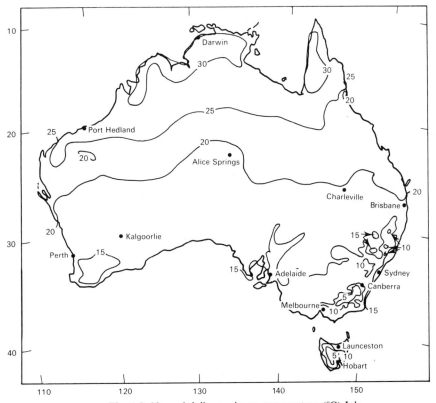

Fig. 5.8. Normal daily maximum temperature (°C) July.

northern, central and southern arid zone, together with northern hemisphere equivalents.

Evaporation

Average annual evaporation, as measured in the Australian standard tank, ranges from 1800 mm in the southern arid zone to 3300 mm at Oodnadatta (Fig. 5.10).

Hydrology

The underground-water components of arid-zone hydrology have been reviewed by Hills (1953); surface-water and ground-water resources have been reviewed by Fisher (1969) and water resources in the arid interior have been reviewed as part of the continental water resource study by the Australian Water Resources Council (1965).

159

Description of arid ecosystems

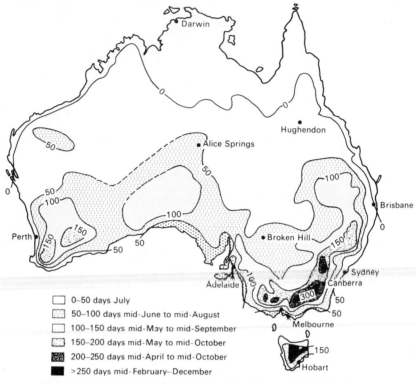

Fig. 5.9. Duration and timing of frosts (after Fitzpatrick & Nix, 1970).

Table 5.1. *Day-length (morning to evening civil twilights) in selected arid Australian latitudes with northern hemisphere equivalents*

Latitude °S	Location	Day-length (hr: min)			Day-length change (min/14 d)	
		Shortest	(difference)	Longest	Equinox	Solstice
20	Pt Hedland, Tennant Creek, Cloncurry (Mexico City, Sahara, Bombay Hanoi)	11: 43	(2: 27)	14: 10	17	3
30	Kalgoorlie, Maree, Bourke (Houston, Cairo, Delhi, Shanghai)	11: 06	(3: 54)	15: 00	28	5
35	Ouyen, Deniliquin (Los Angeles, Oklahoma City, Cyprus, Kabul, Tokyo)	10: 44	(4: 47)	15: 31	33	8

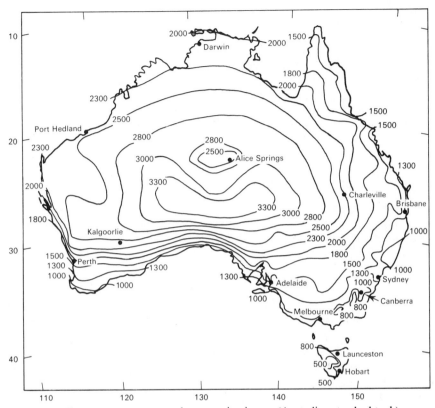

Fig. 5.10. Average annual evaporation in mm (Australian standard tank).

A comparison of average evaporation (Fig. 5.10) with median annual rainfall (Fig. 5.2) might suggest that there is no water to store. However, intense rainfall over a few hours greatly exceeds daily evaporation, and runoff generated on rugged topography can be stored in alluvial basins or in bolsoms (Quinlan, in Fisher 1969). Major intake areas to artesian and subartesian storages lie outside the arid zone, but there are possibly several intake areas for the Great Artesian Basin in the Finke River basin and in the Boulia area which operate during occasional flood flows. Several of the larger sedimentary basins each contain fresh ground-water in excess of the annual runoff from the continent; some of this ground-water is of Pleistocene origin.

Local intake into subsurface storages in the arid zone should have been substantial in 1973–74 because the 90-percentile value of rainfall was exceeded over all of the zone and a substantial region extending from south-western New South Wales to central Australia recorded its highest-ever annual rainfall. Rivers flowed in volume for unusually long periods and at Alice Springs the Todd River, to which folk-lore attributed a

161

continuous flow of 100 days, flowed continuously for more than 300 days. Substantial runoff was also generated within the smooth plains (Australian Water Resources Council, 1972) which cover 45% of the continent and which are estimated to produce a runoff of less than 12.7 mm per year. However, apart from economic considerations, there are few storage sites capable of being utilized to take advantage of these large, occasional to rare surface flows, and the main role of such flows will continue to be in ground-water recharge.

Climatic changes

Climatic change in the world's arid regions, including Australia, South America and South Africa has been reviewed by Butzer (1961). Gentilli (1971, pp. 189–211) has discussed the problems of cycles, trends, persistence effects and unusual runs in the Australian climatic information. There is considerable scientific interest in the climate of the late pre-European and early settlement periods because, to quote Gentilli (p. 197): 'Long-term variations, whether rhythmic or not, and even if quite small in magnitude, may affect areal distributions of organisms, especially if their wave-length or duration as the case may be, exceeds the life span of the individuals affected, because the species would tend gradually to follow their usual climatic environment in its spatial advance or retreat. There would thus be slow migrations of species and communities, with consequent alterations in the landscape.

Australian climatic records provide evidence of changes, which may perhaps not be part of any long-term trend or any cycle, but are very real and have noticeable consequences in the day-to-day weather and in the long-term changes in the biotic environment.'

Because climatic gradients in the Australian arid zone are gentle, small changes in climate affect vast areas. Gentilli (1971) has illustrated hydric recession in eastern Australia in the 1911–1940 period relative to the 1881–1910 period. In this case, summer rains decreased and winter rains increased, but the decrease in summer rains affected 2500000 km² compared with the 250000 km² affected by the winter increase. There is evidence that the discontinuous break in rainfall *c.* 1893–1894 in south-eastern Australia was associated with the increased strength of westerly anticyclones and their displacement to a more northerly track.

Recent trends in temperature and rainfall in Australia have been examined (Tucker, 1975) and the problems and types of study required in determining climatic change have been outlined; these studies include the analyses of past conditions, deterministic synthesis of climate and the assessment of the immediate consequences of realistic possibilities.

Biota

Vegetation, origin, general floristics and the arid zone formations

Current knowledge concerning the origin, distribution and elements of the Australian flora is contained in contributions by Gardner (1944); Crocker & Wood (1947); Crocker (1959); Burbidge (1960); Herbert (1966); Nix & Kalma (1971); Walker (1972*a*); Raven & Axelrod (1972, 1974); Marchant (1973); Good (1974); Johnson & Briggs (1975); Melville (1975); Smith (1975) and Beard (1976). Additional material of relevance to arid Australia will be found in Coaldrake (1967); Parsons (1969*a*, *b*); Specht (1972); and James (1973). Paleoclimate is treated by various authors in Walker (1972*b*), and in Mulvaney & Golson (1971), by Gill (1973) for a site in present-day arid Australia, and by Dodson & Wilson (1975) for a site 400 km distant in mesic south-eastern Australia.

In precis it can be said that plate tectonic theory rather than postulated land bridges has been increasingly involved to explain the origin and history of the present Australian flora. As the continent, with its sub-tropical rainforest, moved northwards into the circum-global arid zone the northern lands were first exposed to aridity; later, with the continuing northward movement the remaining biota were exposed to predominantly cyclonic and monsoonal influences. Presumably, in the millenia yet to come the mesic south of Australia will move into the arid belt and the north will experience a more consistent set of tropical conditions.

The flora of arid Australia consists of the Australian element of mainly sclerophyllous species which have diversified greatly from the ancient widespread (Gondwanic?) stock. Common genera include *Eucalyptus*, *Eremophila*, and *Acacia* or, to a lesser extent, grasses such as *Dichanthium*, *Themeda*, *Heteropogon*, and a cosmopolitan group of coastal origin including genera of halophytes such as *Atriplex*, *Maireana*, *Rhagodia* and grasses such as *Spinifex*. The invasive component in Australia appears to be much smaller than was originally thought and it is argued (Beadle, 1954, 1966; Beard, 1976) that sclerophylly is as much a product of the widespread impoverished (low-phosphorus status) soils, as of aridity.

Within present-day arid Australia the alternation of mesic and arid periods (see Gill, 1973) has given rise to an ebb and flow of plant species which is now manifest in spatial discontinuities (Crocker & Wood, 1947; Specht, 1972) and temporal discontinuities (Specht & Rayson, 1957; Williams, 1961; Holland, 1968).

Arid Australia has been defined by Good (1974) as the Central Australian Floristic Region. This region is equivalent to the Eremaean Floristic Zone of Burbidge (1960) and within this zone lies the Northern Botanical Province of South Australia described by Wood (1936) and Specht (1972). The vegetation of the inter-zone areas (Burbidge 1960), situated between the inner xeric and outer mesic regions of the continent, are mosaics of plant communities within which plant species are being sorted under the influences of the continuing interaction between climatic and edaphic components (Coaldrake, 1967) and the non-indigenous herbivores (Condon, Newman & Cunningham, 1969a, b; Williams, 1973b; Newsome & Corbett, 1976).

Of the endemic genera in arid Australia, about forty are specific to it; these genera are mainly in the families Chenopodiaceae, Compositae and Cruciferae. Endemic species include *Acacia aneura*, *A. harpophylla* and *Eucalyptus oleosa*. Specht (1972) points out that 63% of the genera of the Northern Province of South Australia have exotic affinities, mainly with the Malaysian flora, and 37% are endemic. The chief genera are *Acacia*, 50 species; *Eremophila*, 42 species; *Bassia*, 28 species; *Swainsona*, 26 species; *Maireana*, 22 species; *Atriplex*, 22 species and *Helipterum*, 21 species.

The major genera of Gramineae in arid Australia include *Triodia*, *Zygochloa*, *Aristida*, *Enneapogon*, *Eragrostis*, *Astrebla*, *Plectrachne*, *Dichanthium*, *Panicum* and *Chrysopogon*.

Alien species are uncommon in the arid zone, being mainly confined to disturbed areas around homesteads and townships, and along road sides, railway lines and routes used by travelling livestock; alien species are more common in semi-arid regions and in South Australia, for example, include representatives of Poaceae, Boraginaceae, Solanaceae, Asteraceae and Cucurbitaceae (Specht, 1972).

The major vegetation formations in xeric Australia are: semi-arid low woodlands as represented by *Acacia* shrublands and *Casuarina–Heterodendron–Callitris* low woodland, arid hummock grasslands and chenopodiaceous low shrubland or shrub steppe; between the xeric interior and the mesic fringe of the continent are *Eucalyptus* shrub woodland and tussock grasslands (Fig. 5.11).

These formations are defined and described by Leigh & Noble (1969); Moore, Condon & Leigh (1970); Perry (1970). Specht (1970) has presented a structural classification to which these formations can be related.

Leigh & Noble (1969) have published a map which shows the areas of arid-zone vegetation surveyed to that date. Further surveys since that time include far south-western Queensland (Boyland, 1974) and an area north of Broken Hill, New South Wales (Milthorpe, 1972). Specht (1972) has prepared a series of vegetation maps for South Australia utilizing both published and unpublished material; literature relevant to South Australian vegetation has been reviewed also. Leigh (1974) has reviewed the literature on composition and structure of arid and semi-arid vegetation as affected by the selective grazing of herbivores. Other extensive literature reviews are available (Davies, 1955; McGinnies, Goldman &

164

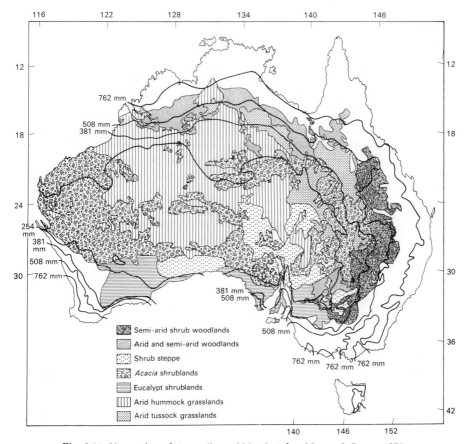

Fig. 5.11. Vegetation of Australian arid lands (after Moore & Perry, 1970).

Paylore 1968). A register of published papers and academic theses on the biota of arid and semi-arid Australia has been produced annually from 1968 (*Arid Zone Newsletter*, Melbourne: CSIRO); contributions to Australian plant ecology since 1956 have been covered in the monthly issues of the *Australian Science Index*.

Fauna, origin, present elements and distribution

Plate tectonic theory has been applied increasingly to explain the ancestral origins of the Australian fauna (Keast, 1959, 1972; Troughton, 1959; Raven & Axelrod, 1972). Main (1976) refers to the latitudinal shift of southern Australia from about 70° S during the Cretaceous to 30° S at present. With aridity came the drying of the central Australian lakes system, the development of soils of low nutrient status and their associated plants of

165

Description of arid ecosystems

either high-fibre, and low nutrition or high salt-content and good nutrition for herbivores. The present fauna of arid Australia consists of the evolutionary descendants from the cool high-latitude climate and an element which has emigrated to Australia since the continent reached its present positions; this latter element has evolved from Asian migrants which made their landfall on the beaches and includes rodents, agamid lizards, elapid snakes and some bird groups. Such invasions are continuing.

So far as migration within Australia, and particularly between eastern and western sides of the continent, is concerned, Paterson (1973) has drawn attention to studies suggesting the importance of rare long pluvial periods in the Pleistocene which apparently permitted successful migration of some faunal elements from the east (Main, 1968). (Also see Parsons (1969a) for evidence that the Nullarbor Plain could be by-passed to the south because of contemporaneous lowering of the sea-level in the Australian Bight.)

It is incorrect to write of a peculiarly Australian desert fauna (see Lowe, 1968), because in arid Australia there are many non-desertic meso- and micro-habitats, occasional rainfall events of considerable magnitude can occur; and because some species in the Australian desert are in fact desert-avoiding e.g. the euro, *Macropus robustus*, an occasional sequence of suitable rainfall events can lead to the development of excessively large populations. Davies (1968) has not only noted the close link between seasonal rainfall, the biology of mulga (*Acacia aneura*) and the breeding of the emu, *Dromaius novaehollandiae*, but has drawn attention to the importance of scattered light rain and its concentration in run-on areas where abundant forage can be produced (Davies, 1973a). A similar situation has been demonstrated by Newsome (1965b) for the red kangaroo, *Megaleia rufa*. Lindgren (quoted in Davies, 1973b) has shown that because of spatial variability in rainfall, Bourke parrots *Neophema bourkii* need not have flown a single flight of more than 130 km between 1935 and 1966 to procure seed of their preferred grass.

Strategies of land use by native animals have been described by Davies (1973b) who has also reviewed the movement behaviour for a number of animals including the emu, which has moved up to 550 km in 9 months, the red kangaroo which has been recorded 240 km from where it was tagged (Bailey, 1971) and the euro, which did not move more than 1 km from its cave shelter (Ealey, 1967).

In addition to the pluvial patchiness in arid Australia there is the patchy nature of fire. An apparent single burn up to 1000 km long can be a composite of many smaller fires. Further in one district different seral stages in pyric succession may coexist, each exhibiting different faunal assemblages.

As Keast (1972) has pointed out, there are difficulties in comparing

166

continents and deserts in terms of faunal richness and diversity. In general terms, most of the Australian deserts differ from those elsewhere because they are vegetated and have a marsupial fauna; Pianka (1969) has compared lizards and birds in Australian and American deserts, showing the preponderance of the former in Australia. Australian deserts also appear to support a wider range of frog species (Main, 1968), goannas, elapid snakes, ants and termites than elsewhere.

Regional studies on the fauna of arid Australia are not common, the tendency being to treat groups such as mammals (Finlayson, 1961); marsupials (Brown, 1974); macropodidae (Calaby, 1970); lizards (Pianka, 1969); invertebrates (Wood, 1970) or species of particular interest such as kangaroos (Newsome, 1965a, b; Griffiths & Barber, 1966; Ealey, 1967; Frith & Calaby, 1969; Bailey, 1971) and desert birds (Serventy, 1971; Fisher, Lindgren & Dawson, 1972).

However there is a regional study of the fauna at a site in north-western New South Wales (Bailey, 1972; Hall, 1972; Myers & Parker, 1972).

The composition and historical zoogeography of the modern vertebrate fauna have been reviewed by Simpson (1961); Storr (1964); Main (1968) and Calaby (1969). Newsome (1971) and Newsome & Corbett (1978) have discussed the interactions between wildlife and domestic livestock. Marshall (1968) has presented a colourful account of the influence of European man and associated domestic animals on the native fauna (see also Marlow, 1958); Frith (1973) has discussed the management of wildlife in Australia. The control of rabbit and kangaroo populations, long sought by pastoralists, has led to a large amount of biological research. Amongst the many excellent studies relevant to management of these animals are those reported recently by Myers & Parker (1975a, b) and by Wilson (1975).

Brief accounts of the native vertebrate fauna and naturalized species of the continent have been given by Fennessy (1970) and Frith (1970). According to Frith, the present vertebrate fauna includes about 400 reptiles, 229 mammals and 700 birds. The mammals include 2 monotremes, 119 marsupials and 108 placentals of which more than 50 are rodents and 50 are bats. All families and genera of the monotremes and marsupials are endemic. Approximately 75% of the genera of rodents and 30% of the genera of bats are endemic. There are at least 25 introduced birds and 12 introduced mammals, in addition to domestic livestock.

Not all of these vertebrates are found in arid Australia. For example, Keast (1959) estimated that 10% of the avifauna would be in arid habitats compared with 40% in grassland communities with scattered trees. For marsupials, the relationship with vegetation type is less clear cut; approximately 17% of marsupials are found on the grassplains and 12% are found in the desert (Keast, 1972). The echidna, *Tachyglossus aculeatus*,

Description of arid ecosystems

a monotreme, inhabits both rainforest and stony areas in the central Australian desert, but there any many species belonging to genera such as *Perameles, Isoodon, Thylacomys* and *Chaeropus* which are limited to the interior.

Keast, Crocker & Christian (1959) contains contributions on the avifauna (see also Serventy & Whittell, 1951; Slater, 1970, 1974; Macdonald, 1973; Kikkawa 1974), reptiles, fresh water fishes, diptera, grasshoppers and locusts, termites, mollusca, freshwater crustacea, marsupials (see also Tyndale-Biscoe, 1973), wild ducks, frogs, Merino sheep (see also Moule, 1968), sheep blowflies, and the rabbit (see also Fenner & Ratcliffe, 1965).

The Australian Aboriginal is not indigenous to Australia, having come from Asia at least 20000 and probably 30000 years B.P. (Bowler, Jones, Allen & Thorn, 1970). Thorne (1971); Kirk (1971) and Tryon (1971) have discussed the evidence bearing on racial affinities and derivation as exemplified by osteological material, by genetic markers and by linguistic analysis. The dingo, *Canis familiaris dingo* probably came with later migrants; the earliest known dating gives the dingo an entry time of more than 3000 years, but less than 7000 years B.P. (Mulvaney & Golson, 1971).

Between the review by Tindale (1959) of the *Ecology of primitive aboriginal man in Australia* and the publication of *Aboriginal Man and Environment* edited by Mulvaney & Golson, (1971), substantial contributions have been made to the understanding of the pre-European environment. Aboriginal peoples appear to have been in a deteriorating environment for possibly the last 15000 to 17000 years in arid Australia (Bowler, 1971; Pels, 1971; Wright, 1971) but an improving environment in the south-eastern highlands (Costin, 1971). Merrilees *et al.* (1973) have presented an appreciation of the environment and culture of past and present aboriginal man in south-western Australia.

Tindale (1959) is credited with first drawing attention to the evolutionary impact of aboriginal fires on the continental fauna and flora, a point of view now accepted by most terrestrial ecologists (see Jones, 1969; Calaby, 1971; Main, 1976). Gill (1973) has described the ecology of a site in semi-arid south-western New South Wales and drawn attention to the building up of an ecosystem over a period of 2 million years, the stability of the soil over a large area for a period of at least 2000 years and the marked erosion initiated and continued by European man in his occupancy of less than 200 years.

European man visited the coasts of Australia decades prior to the colonization at Sydney Cove in 1788, but it was from this date that European man made his impact on the flora and fauna of the continent.

The major European activity affecting the flora and fauna of arid Australia was, and still is, the grazing of domestic livestock (Moore, 1962;

168

Williams, 1962; Barnard, 1969; Peel, 1973; Chapman, Williams & Moule, 1973; Williams, 1973*b*). Newsome (1971) has discussed possible mechanisms involved in competition between the indigenous fauna and animals introduced by European settlers, including provision of permanent water for livestock in areas where no permanent, and even no temporary water was available. The depredations of the introduced European rabbit, *Oryctolagus cuniculus* have been described by Fenner & Ratcliffe (1965) and Rolls (1969).

The reduced fire-incidence, a product of fire-protection measures aimed at eliminating damage to fences and buildings, and the reduced amounts of forage fuel produced because of consumption by herbivores, erosion and pasture deterioration appear to favour the development of woody plants as in parts of the Cobar–Byrock area of New South Wales. This increase in woody plants can be expected to change both the domestic and the native fauna.

The initiation and acceleration of erosional processes in arid communities and the subsequent changes in plant and animal populations are recent in Australia, and have been described, for example by Cotton (1901) quoted by Newman & Condon (1969); Ratcliffe (1936, 1937); Beadle (1948); Moore (1953*a*, *b*); Cobar–Byrock Committee (1969); Condon *et al.* (1969*a*).

Reconstruction of the fauna in the early settlement era is not possible (Calaby, 1969) but I am trying to reconstruct a number of semi-arid plant communities for which descriptive location-specific records are available. However the most fruitful studies in the field of resource depletion and deterioration are likely to be made in contemporary pedology and geomorphology. A more quantitative expression of soil loss than photographs of exposed tree-stumps and buried fences, and maps showing degrees of erosion is required.

Plant communities of arid Australia

Classification and distribution

The major plant communities in arid Australia in terms of life form, height and projected foliage cover of the tallest stratum (Specht, 1970) are hummock grasslands, tussock grasslands, chenopodiaceous low shrubland, and *Acacia* open scrub to low woodland; semi-arid communities are *Eucalyptus* open scrub ('mallee') with grassy or shrubby understorey, a small area of *Casuarina–Heterodendron* low woodland, and *Eucalyptus* low woodland to shrubby woodland (see Fig. 5.11).

A complex of riverine and internal drainage communities occupies a small area of considerable ecological significance; these include *Eucalyptus* fringing woodland, closed scrub (*Muehlenbeckia* sp.) and open herbland (saltmarsh).

Description of arid ecosystems

Specht (1972) has classified and described the arid vegetation of South Australia in these terms and Specht, Roe & Boughton (1974) have used this classification in their assessment of the conservation status of arid (and non-arid) formations.

Maps showing the distribution of Australian plant formations have been prepared by R. J. Williams (1955, see also Specht, 1970); Cochrane (1967); Moore & Perry (1970). The approximate area of the plant formations defined by R. J. Williams (1958) and Specht (1970) is given by Specht *et al.* (1974); a useful summary at the subformation level is also available (Leigh & Noble, 1969).

An attempt to apply the scheme of vegetation classification developed under the aegis of UNESCO (1973) to Australian arid and semi-arid vegetation has been unsuccessful. The isolation of this flat, near-waterless and infertile continent, without hard-footed herbivores and animals capable of use for transportation or draught purposes, and the absence of nomadic herdsmen or cultivators has in the presence of Australian aboriginal man produced a unique floristic and faunal assemblage which defies conventional international classification.

In the following pages the major formations of arid Australia and research undertaken in them will be described.

Hummock grassland

This distinctive arid formation is represented by a community known as 'spinifex' grassland. In fact, the community is dominated variously by the genera *Triodia*, *Plectrachne* and *Zygochloa*; the genus *Spinifex* is not represented. *Triodia* and *Plectrachne* hummock grasslands have been described generally by Specht (1970) and Perry (1970); the *Zygochloa* grasslands are not as extensive and descriptions are regional as in Specht (1972) or site-specific as in Wiedemann (1971).

Regional descriptions for hummock grasslands include those by Blake (1938), Perry & Lazarides (1964) and Boyland (1974) for western, north-western and south-western Queensland; Crocker (1946) and Eardley (1946, 1948) for the western and Boyland (1970) for the eastern Simpson desert; Perry (1960) and Perry & Lazarides (1962) for central and northern Australia; Chippendale (1958, 1963) for central and western parts of the Northern Territory; Specht (1972) for northern South Australia and Gardner (1944) Speck (1963), Beard (1968, 1969) and Keay & Bettenay (1969) for the eastern region and Burbidge (1942, 1959) for the Pilbara region of Western Australia. James (1960) has described a small outlier in northern New South Wales.

The most detailed ecological studies of *Triodia* and *Plectrachne* hummock grasslands are those by Winkworth (1967), who investigated their botanical composition, structure and biomass in relation to climate, soil-

170

water and soil nutrients; Winkworth concluded that the vegetation was a stable edaphic climax subject to, and adapted to, repeated burning. Burbidge (1943a) has described the successional changes which follow burning of *Triodia pungens* communities in Western Australia. Zimmer (1940) has described successional stages for a *Triodia* understorey in northern Victorian *Eucalyptus* (Mallee) open scrub. Wiedemann (1971) following his phytosociological analysis of the vegetation of a site in the western Simpson Desert concluded that species groupings tended to form continua rather than sharply defined communities. Soil factors such as texture, hardness and sand mobility were influential in their effect on species distribution. Keay & Bettenay (1969) estimated and correlated major nutrient element concentrations in hummock grass vegetation and the soils on which it was found.

The area of Australia classified as hummock grassland approximates 304 500 km² and its distribution is shown in Fig. 5.11. However the Simpson Desert, for example, is a complex of communities (Crocker, 1946) with *Triodia* and *Zygochloa* grasslands on crests, slopes and inter-dune corridors, *Astrebla–Atriplex–Bassia* open grassland to low shrubland around the margins of hills and tableland residues, and *Eucalyptus–Atriplex* open woodlands to low shrublands on floodplains. Further, in semi-arid environments the hummock grassland becomes a ground stratum under increasing densities of shrubs and trees (Blake, 1938; Holland & Moore, 1962).

In typical hummock grassland the grass plants are from 1–1.5 m diameter and 0.5 m high to 6 m diameter and 1.5 m high. In some *Triodia* spp. the centre of the hummock dies and the plants become rings 0.5 m wide and 9.5 m high, exceeding 5 m diameter. Hummocks are well spaced and the ground between them is bare, except for short periods after rainfall when there may be a cover of ephemeral species. Isolated groups of shrubs and small trees may be scattered over the landscape.

Detailed floristic information for hummock grasslands is available in Chippendale (1958, 1963); Winkworth (1967); Wiedemann (1971); Specht (1972) and Boyland (1974).

The soils on which hummock grasslands occur are classified in the scheme developed by Northcote (1971) as Uc 1, sandy soils of minimum development, Uc 1.2 siliceous sand, and Uc 5.21 red sands with earthy fabric.

Keay & Bettenay (1969) have examined a range of soil properties at sites within this formation and the concentration of nutrients in plant species at these sites (including nitrogen, phosphorus, potassium, sodium, calcium, magnesium and sulphur). Specht (1972) has noted the extremely low phosphorous content of the neutral to slightly acid soils under the hummock grasses (less than 0.010%).

T. basedowii is the common species on sandy soils where mean annual

171

rainfall is up to 350 mm. It is replaced in the north and west of arid Australia by dominant *T. pungens*. In southern Australia *T. irritans* tends to dominate; however, communities of hummock grassland are not extensive there and *T. irritans* is more frequently an understorey to *Eucalyptus* open scrub and *Acacia* shrublands. Burbidge (1943*a*, 1945*a*, 1946*a*) has reported on the taxonomy, morphology and anatomy of *Triodia* spp.

The aridity, remoteness and poverty of these grasslands for livestock production are the reasons for the small amount of research information on them. Although grazing value for domestic livestock is poor (Perry, 1960; Low, 1974), some *Triodia* spp. are acceptable to cattle (Chippendale, 1968) and areas of hummock grassland are in the mediocre to fair condition classes (Condon, Newman & Cunningham, 1969*a*, *b*; Dawson & Boyland, 1974), presumably because they are adjacent to more productive forage types which are less drought-resistant; the substantial areas of hummock grassland distant from better classes of country are unoccupied Crown land.

In the Pilbara district of Western Australia, sheep grazing has reduced the density of grass species of forage value which grow on the less infertile alluvial soils. The euro or hill wallaby, *Macropus robustus* has extended its range from climax *Triodia* grassland to these induced *Triodia* communities (Main, Shield & Waring, 1959; Ealey, 1967). Suijdendorp (1968) has devised a system of burning and deferment which can regenerate these valuable grass species and Williams & Suijdendorp (1968) have estimated the wool growth rates and liveweight of pregnant and non-pregnant Merino sheep on this regenerated grassland.

On a less xeric hummock grassland nearer the Pilbara coastline Storr (1968) has investigated the dietary preferences exercised by two kangaroo species, the marloo, *Megaleia rufa* and the euro, *Macropus robustus*, and Merino sheep. *Triodia longiceps* and *T. secunda* are the dominant perennial grasses on the heavier textured soils; *T. pungens* becomes dominant where the upper soil horizons become sandy.

The dietary preferences exercised by plumed pigeons of the genus *Geophaps*, which occurs in large numbers in the *Triodia* hummock grassland of central and northern Australia, are strongly directed towards the seed of drought-evading grasses and herbs rather than towards seed of the dominant *Triodia* and *Plectrachne* spp. (Frith & Barker, 1975).

Tussock grassland

These grasslands in arid Australia cover more than 500000 km² on clay plains and include the widespread *Astrebla* (Mitchell grass) open grassland in northern Australia and a small area of disclimax *Danthonia* grassland in southern Australia.

The *Astrebla* open grassland has been described by Perry (1970) and

Specht (1970). Recently, Orr (1975) published a detailed review on this grassland and *Astrebla* species. The distribution of *Astrebla* grassland is shown in Fig. 5.11.

Regional descriptions of Astrebla grasslands include those for Queensland by Francis (1935), Blake (1938), Davidson (1954), Holland & Moore (1962), Everist (1964), Perry & Lazarides (1964), Roberts (1972), Boyland (1974), and Everist & Webb (1975); for western New South Wales by Beadle (1948), James (1960), and Milthorpe (1972); for northern South Australia by Specht (1972), and by Perry & Christian (1954), Perry & Lazarides (1962); for central and northern Australia. Biddiscombe (1963) has described a less arid *Astrebla* grassland in northern New South Wales. Crocker (1946) has described sparse *Astrebla* communities in the western Simpson Desert.

Detailed experimental studies on *Astrebla* sites in northern Queensland have been reported by Davies, Scott & Kennedy (1938) who investigated the botanical composition and yield over a 12-month period, Weston & Moir (1969) who ascertained the yield, effect of defoliation and nutritional value of Astrebla spp.; Purcell & Lee (1970) who followed changes' in species populations in burnt and unburnt grassland, and Lorimer (1975) who used oesophageally fistulated sheep to estimate dietary selection over 3 years.

Studies in southwest Queensland include those by Roe (1941) and Roe & Allen (1945) on the effects of climate and grazing and the influence of exclosure on *Astrebla* grassland, Allen (1963) on soil moisture flux under the same grassland, and by Williams & Roe (1975) who presented life tables for species of *Astrebla*, *Eragrostis* and *Dichanthium* based on data for a 30-year period.

Other studies include those in central and northern Australia by Siebert, Newman & Nelson (1968) on the chemical composition of *Astrebla* spp. by Jozwik (1969, 1970) and Jozwik, Nicholls & Perry (1970) on *Astrebla* spp. on taxonomy and the effect of defoliation on primary and secondary tillering. Whalley & Davidson (1968, 1969) have investigated dormancy in mature plants of a number of perennial grasses, including *Astrebla* spp. Calder (1974) has reviewed much of this physiological work. Orr (1975) in his review of literature on *Astrebla* spp. includes a number of hitherto unpublished observations by Everist and others on germination conditions, establishment and growth.

In a typical *Astrebla* grassland the tussocks are from 0.5 to 1 m high, and frequently circular with a diameter of 10–50 cm; mature plants can break up into a number of individual parts. The ground between these tussocks is bare during the long dry periods, but is populated by annual grasses and non-grasses following adequate rains (Everist, 1935; Davidson, 1954).

Astrebla grasslands are seldom mono-specific although one species may

173

dominate extensive areas. *A. pectinata* is common in northern Australia in low to moderate rainfall regions and is present as far south as Broken Hill, New South Wales; *A. lappacea* is prominent on the rolling downs of Queensland and outcrops in pure stands in southwestern Queensland and in northern New South Wales. *A. elymoides* is present in most *Astrebla* tussock grasslands; it is associated with *A. pectinata* in southwestern Queensland. *A. squarrosa* occurs in drainage lines and depressions where rain accumulates. Associated perennial grasses include *Aristida latifolia* and *Dichanthium fecundum* in northern Australia; in southern Queensland *D. sericeum*, *Eragrostis setifolia* and *Panicum decompositum* are associates.

Soils which support *Astrebla* grassland are classified (Northcote, 1971) as Ug 5.24, Ug 5.25 (grey cracking clays with self-mulching characteristics), Ug 5.3 (brown soils of heavy texture) and Dr 1.32 (stony desert tablelands soils). Such soils do not usually have a high erosion potential. Though the self-mulching clays are generally accepted as possessing high phosphate levels, there are a number of low-phosphate soils which support *Astrebla* grasslands.

Blake (1938) and Holland & Moore (1962) amongst others, have commented on the ecological status of *Dichanthium sericeum* in *Astrebla* tussock grassland, and recently Williams & Roe (1975) have been able to illustrate in demographic terms the type of irruption that occurs; the attrition of a mature *Astrebla* grassland under grazing and exclosure has also been documented. It is generally agreed that *Astrebla* grassland is climax, rather than disclimax.

The northern *Astrebla* grasslands are used by sheep and by cattle; the southern grasslands have been used by sheep alone (Bird, 1953), but the number of cattle there has been greatly increased in recent years.

Information on wool growth rates and reproduction of Merino sheep, the present dominant herbivore, is available for both northern and southern *Astrebla* grassland (Dolling, 1960; Queensland Dept. of Agriculture, 1963; Brown & Williams, 1970). In practice, experiments and observations have been prompted by concern over poor animal production, drought and doubts as to the viability of the grassland and its associated pastoral industry, the ingress or increase of undesirable plant species and a desire for better management of the grassland resource.

Deterioration of *Astrebla* grasslands has been variously attributed to climate and to excessive grazing and trampling. Newman & Condon (1969) have pointed to the resiliance of the grassland under all except gross disturbance. Condon *et al* (1969a, b) estimated that 57% of *Astrebla* grassland in central Australia was in very good condition, 31.1% was in good condition and the remainder was in fair condition. Dawson & Boyland (1974) have assessed the *Astrebla* grasslands of far south-west

Queensland as fair to good condition with a stable to slight downward trend under present use. The development of particular disclimax communities under grazing has been noted by Beadle (1948), James (1960) and Milthorpe (1972). Williams & Roe (1975) have documented a major decline in *Astrebla* spp. which is attributable to an unfavourable climate for recruitment in both the presence and absence of grazing. The ecological status of *Eragrostis setifolia* in *Astrebla* grasslands of northern New South Wales (James, 1960) at Cunnamulla, Queensland (Williams & Roe, 1975), and in the northern downs of Queensland and the Burt Plain in central Australia (Chippendale, 1968) is perplexing, but its dietary importance for domestic herbivores and kangaroos (Newsome, 1971) is beyond doubt.

The *Danthonia caespitosa* grassland in southern New South Wales, though much studied, is not extensive; however, there are species within it that occur over large tracts of the inland. This grassland was classified and mapped by Beadle (1948) as the *Chloris–Danthonia* association, but its status is rather that of a disclimax from *Atriplex nummularia* and scattered *Acacia pendula* which formed a shrub or semi-arid woodland before and during the early period of European pastoral occupation (Moore, 1953 *a*, *b*; Leigh & Noble, 1972). Biddiscombe (1963) has reported an *Acacia pendula–Atriplex nummularia* alliance in northern New South Wales in which *D. caespitosa* can occur.

The grassland is short, seldom greater than 20 cm, with a basal area of perennial bunch grasses of mainly *Danthonia caespitosa* Gaud., some *Stipa variabilis* Hughes and occasional *Enteropogon acicularis* (Lindl.) Lazarides at approximately 1–2% of the ground surface. Associated perennial and annual species belong to two phenological groups; those that grow in the cool season with the bloom period in spring, and those that grow in the warm season with one or more bloom periods during the summer. Warm-season species are generally of the indigenous flora and cool-season species are both indigenes and naturalized species.

Up to 60 species occur per 20 m², including the perennial grasses and representatives of genera such as *Maireana, Bassia, Chenopodium* and *Rhagodia*. Annual naturalized species of *Medicago, Trifolium, Hordeum* and *Vulpia* occur; the morphology of annual species in relation to grazing has been reviewed by Moore (1974). Standing crop approximates 15000 kg/ha with 30 cm annual rainfall.

The grassland and the factors involved in the occurrence and the phenology of species within it have been described and defined in experimental studies by Williams (1955, 1956, 1961, 1971) and Wilson & Leigh (1964).

Soils are generally grey self-mulching clays of considerable depth (Ug 5.24 and 5.25). Some *Danthonia* grasslands are on soils with contrasting (duplex) texture profiles (Dr 2.33).

175

Description of arid ecosystems

The influence of grazing by sheep on botanical composition has been studied in normal and in drought years (Williams, 1968, 1969, 1974); the diet selected by Merino sheep has been ascertained by Robards, Leigh & Mulham (1967) and the seasonal variation in wool growth of Merino sheep on this grassland has been estimated (Reis & Williams, 1965; Wilson & Leigh, 1970). The water consumption by sheep on this grassland has been studied in shaded and non-shaded treatments (Wilson, 1974). Information on dietary selection and animal production are also available for the related *Maireana aphylla–Stipa variabilis–Danthonia caespitosa* community (Leigh & Mulham, 1966; Leigh, Wilson & Mulham, 1968).

The demography of the three perennial grasses *Danthonia caespitosa*, *Stipa variabilis* and *Enteropogon acicularis* has been published in the form of survivorship curves and life table (Williams, 1970; Williams & Roe, 1975).

A range of exotic and indigenous plant species that were thought to offer improved forage in amount, quality or seasonal production, has been tested in comparison with the *Danthonia* grassland (Williams, 1963; Leigh & Mulham, 1964). Not only did additional culture practices, such as the use of gypsum as a soil amendment and fertilizer fail to show to advantage, but the two most successful species were *Atriplex nummularia* and *A. vesicaria*, components of the original vegetation.

Animal production systems using Merino wether sheep and *A. nummularia* plantations in conjunction with grassland have been tested (Leigh, Wilson & Williams, 1970) and the soil salinity and soil properties under and between bushes has been described (Sharma & Tongway, 1973; Sharma, 1973).

Faunal changes were noted early in the settlement era (Williams, 1962) and the disclimax *D. caespitosa* grassland would appear to favour the red kangaroo, *Megaleia rufa* (Frith, 1964).

Chenopodiaceous low shrubland

Low shrubland dominated by species of the family Chenopodiaceae, and particularly of the genera *Maireana, Atriplex, Bassia, Rhagodia* and *Chenopodium* (the saltbushes and blue bushes) cover an extensive area (308 000 km^2 or 5%) of Australia. Most of this area is in South Australia. The formation occurs on soils ranging from lithosols to deep self-mulching clays and from xeric habitats to drainage lines and occluded depressions Small patches of this arid shrubland occur from latitude 19° S–35° S.

Generally the shrubland consists of grey, blue grey to dull green, well spaced shrubby plants with isolated clumps or individual small trees of *Acacia* spp. Boundaries between chenopodiaceous low shrubland and the arid low and medium woodlands dominated by *Acacia* and *Eucalyptus* spp.

are imprecise because a slightly-modified low shrubland becomes an understorey. For convenience, in this review some experimental material on species of Chenopodiaceae which has been derived from sparse low woodland is included in this section.

Regional descriptions of the chenopodiaceous low shrubland include those for Queensland by Collins (1924); Blake (1938) and Boyland (1970, 1974); for New South Wales by Beadle (1948), James (1960), Stannard (1963) and Milthorpe (1972); for the Northern Territory by Perry (1960), Perry & Lazarides (1962) and for Western Australia by Gardner (1944), Beard (1969) and Johnson & Baird (1970). The literature on South Australian low shrublands is extensive and classification, floristics, maps and bibliography compiled by Specht (1972) should be consulted; soil-surface lichens have been investigated by Rogers & Lange (1972) and Rogers (1972*a, b*). Regional descriptions of particular value because of their experimental significance include those for Koonamore Vegetation Reserve (Osborn, 1925; Wood, 1936; Carrodus, Specht & Jackman, 1965) and for the north-west pastoral district (Murray, 1931; Crocker & Skewes, 1941; Jessup, 1951; Lay, 1972).

Semi-arid low shrubland dominated by *Atriplex* and *Maireana* spp. continues to be heavily used by the pastoral industry and experimental studies are rare on other than eroding or eroded sites.

Erosion is common and pasture deterioration is continuing in Queensland (Dawson & Boyland, 1974). In New South Wales the erosional status of *Atriplex* and *Maireana* low shrublands has been described by Beadle (1948) and defined for particular districts by James (1960); Stannard (1961, 1963) and Milthorpe (1972). In South Australia and central Australia the erodibility of soils and deterioration of low shrublands have been reported (Osborn, Wood & Paltridge, 1935; Crocker & Skewes, 1941; Jessup, 1951; Lay, 1972; Condon *et al.*, 1969*a, b*).

The reaction of *Atriplex vesicaria* plants to grazing was illustrated by Osborn, Wood & Paltridge (1932) who recognized zones of grazing severity around stock watering places and described the growth forms of *A. vesicaria* in these zones. Leigh & Mulham (1971) assessed the effect of various intensities of defoliation by sheep on the persistence of *A. vesicaria* in a natural stand; complete defoliation, even when followed by supplementary watering, led to death of the plant. Williams (1972) in a study of *Atriplex vesicaria* and *Maireana pyramidata* noted that sheep grazing has caused changes in plant cover, a reduction in both sexual and asexual reproduction and an unbalanced sex ratio which favoured male bushes.

The influence of sheep grazing on the stability of *A. vesicaria* low shrubland in south-western New South Wales has been documented by Wilson Leigh & Mulham (1969) for a range of stocking rates. Hall, Specht & Eardley (1964) assessed the effect of excluding sheep for almost three decades on a range of species in degraded *A. vesicaria* low shrubland at Koonamore. Unfortunately it was not possible to control rabbits at all times and they were a potent influence on the regeneration of woody species (see also Johnson & Baird, 1970). Using composite survivorship curves for *A. vesicaria*, Crisp (1975) has calculated the half-life to be 11 years; *Maireana sedifolia* communities appear to be even-aged and old, recruitment at Koonamore has been negligible and the half-life is in the range 150–300 years. Death of such communities is predictable and is likely to be spectacular. In Western Australia, Wilcox (1974) has documented the changes in species occurrence over a 7-year period in a degraded shrubland.

In a series of studies on the dietary selection exercised by sheep when grazing various *A. vesicaria* low shrublands, Leigh & Mulham (1966, 1967) established that grasses and herbs growing between the *A. vesicaria* bushes were preferred to it in both winter and summer. Estimates of the nutritional value of the forage and animal production were made in one of these experiments by Wilson *et al.* (1969) and comparisons have been made with animal production on other semi-arid communities (Wilson & Leigh, 1970). Water consumption and water turnover of sheep grazing on *A. vesicaria* low shrubland has been estimated by Wilson (1974); the behaviour of sheep and the availability of water on this shrubland has been studied by Squires (1970) and Squires & Hindley (1970).

The chenopodiaceous low shrublands occur on a wide range of soils. Communities dominated by *Atriplex vesicaria* may be on stoney shallow duplex soils (Dr. 1.13, 1.33) and on grey-brown and red calcareous earths (Um 5.11, Gc 1.12) with communities dominated by *Maireana sedifolia*, *M. astrotricha* and *M. pyramidata*. The grey self mulching clays (Ug 5.24, 5.25) and duplex soils (Dr 2.33) are populated by *A. vesicaria* and *A. vesicaria–Maireana aphylla*. Samphire communities grow on loamy calcareous or siliceous soils (Um 1.1, 1.2); non-cracking clays (Uf 6.61) and grey clays which exhibit seasonal cracking (Ug 5.17; Ug 5.5).

Specht (1972) has commented that plant communities containing these semi-succulent shrubs are common on soils in which calcareous, gypseous and saline materials are close to the surface, the soils tend to be alkaline and the phosphorus levels are reasonably high (0.14–0.043%). Carrodus & Specht (1965) have investigated the factors controlling the relative distribution of *A. vesicaria* and *M. sedifolia*; the depth to which the soil is wetted by normal rainfall is the prime causal factor (see Jessup, 1969).

Keay & Bettenay (1969) have analysed the soils of selected saline areas in arid Western Australia, not all surface soils were high in soluble salts. Levels of acid-soluble phosphorus, potassium and sodium were higher than in the remaining wide range of soils examined by them; they also noted that in the leaf material for 11 representatives of the Chenopodiaceae the

178

sums of the four cationic concentrations (K^+, Na^+, Ca^+, Mg^+) vary by a factor of two only, whereas the concentrations of Na^+ and K^+ vary by a factor of approximately six. In South Australia, Jessup (1969) examined the chloride and total soluble salt profiles and related them to soil moisture fluxes and plant uptake under an *Atriplex vesicaria–Maireana astrotricha* low shrubland and two degraded forms of it. Studies in western New South Wales include those on plant mineral composition and nutrient cycling by Beadle, Whalley & Gibson (1957), Charley & McGarity (1964), Charley & Cowling (1968), R. M. Jones (1969), Rixon (1970) and Charley 1972; on pattern analysis by Anderson (1970) and on quantitative aspects of productivity and root growth of *Atriplex* spp. by Jones, Hodgkinson & Rixon (1970) and Jones & Hodgkinson (1970). Sharma (1973) and Sharma & Tongway (1973) have reported investigations into water use and the effects of *Atriplex* spp. on soils in a former shrubland area now grass-dominant.

Reclamation of eroded low shrubland has been investigated mainly on duplex soils in western New South Wales with studies on natural reclamation, ploughing and waterponding (Stannard, 1961, 1962; Jones, 1966*a*, *b*, 1967; Newman, 1966 and Cunningham, Quilty & Thompson, 1974); the use of gypsum as a soil ameliorant (Muirhead, Jones & Williamson, 1974) and the sowing of indigenous and exotic species (Muirhead & Jones, 1966; Alchin, 1974). Regrettably, the erosion and removal of the surface soil from many arid communities not only exposes massive subsurface horizons but also permanently depletes the soil nutrient pool (Newman, 1974). The reclamation of saline soils by a variety of salt-tolerant shrubs has been reviewed by Malcolm (1972).

The germination of chenopodiaceous species which may be of value in the regeneration of depleted stands has been studied by Burbidge (1945*b*, 1946*b*), Beadle (1952) and by Jones (1968).

Acacia *woodland*

This formation probably covers 2 million km^2 of the continent and is represented by sub-formations that range from low woodland of 5–10 m height through tall shrubland to dense scrub of 2–8 m height.

The main *Acacia* species include *A. aneura*, *A. sowdenii*, *A. pendula*, *A. cambagei*, *A. georginae*, *A. brachystachya*, and *A. kempeana*. Associated tree species include *A. excelsa*, *A. loderi*, *Casuarina cristata*, *Heterodendron oleifolium*, *Callitris* spp. and shrub species include representatives of the genera *Cassia*, *Dodonea*, *Eremophila*, *Hakea* and *Myoporum*.

The ground layer of chenopodiaceous shrubs in Western Australia, South Australia and western New South Wales is displaced by grasses across northern Australia. At tree densities of < 1/ha the woodland is, for all practical purposes, either a chenopodiaceous shrubland or grassland.

The *Acacia aneura* dominant communities occupy approximately 1 500 000 km². The remaining 25% of the *Acacia* woodlands are classified variously as *A. cambagei–A. harpophylla*, and *A. georginae* and associated *Acacia* spp. communities in northern Australia, parts of Queensland, and north-western New South Wales, *A. cambagei–Eucalyptus microtheca* communities in south-western Queensland and northern South Australia, *A. sowdenii* and *A. linophylla–A. ramulosa* communities in South Australia.

Acacia aneura woodlands in Queensland have been described by Blake (1938), Everist (1949, 1972), Holland & Moore (1962), Burrows & Beale (1970) and Boyland (1973, 1974). A small area in northern Queensland has been described by Perry & Lazarides (1964). Regional descriptions include those in New South Wales by Collins (1923, 1924), Beadle (1948), Condon (1949), James (1960) and Milthorpe (1972); in South Australia by Crocker & Skewes (1941), Jessup (1951), Hall *et al.* (1964) and Specht (1972); in central and northern Australia by Christian & Perry (1954) and Perry & Lazarides (1962), and in Western Australia by Gardner (1944), Melville (1947), Wilcox (1960, 1974), Speck (1963) and Beard (1968, 1969).

Boyland (1973) has described the structure and floristics of *Acacia aneura* woodland on five landscapes in south-western Queensland in terms of landscape types which range from dissected residuals through sandplains to dunefields. Families which contribute substantially to the botanical composition of the woodland in terms of genera and species include Gramineae (32 genera/68 species) Leguminoseae (9/39), Chenopodiaceae (8/32), Compositae (17/26) and Myoporaceae (2/15). Specht (1972) has published a species list with estimates of abundance for *A. aneura–A. brachystachya* communities in South Australia where there appear to be fewer Gramineae relative to Chenopodiaceae.

The occurrence of characteristic mulga groves with moderate to dense stands of *A. aneura* and inter-grove areas with few, if any trees, has been described for central Australia by Perry (1960) and Jackson (1962); for Western Australia by Litchfield & Mabbutt (1962) and for south-western Queensland by Dawson & Ahern (1973) and Boyland (1973).

Mott (1972a, 1973) and Davies (1973a) have described the perennial and annual vegetation associated with the creek systems and their interfluviatile plains in *Acacia aneura* woodlands in the Murchison region of Western Australia. Mott (1972a, b) has investigated the important annual species component and the autecology of representative species, whilst Davies (1973b) has explored the flowering and fruiting of perennial species and soil water availability links with the ecology of the emu, *Dromaius novahollandiae* and other indigenous fauna.

The taxonomy of the *Acacia aneura* complex has been discussed by

180

Pedley (1973) who also discusses species which are closely related to it; these include *A. catenulata, A. clivicola, A. ramulosa* and *A. brachystachya*. The distribution of *A. aneura* has been examined on a continental scale by Nix & Austin (1973) in relation to the water regime.

The biology of *A. aneura* has been reviewed briefly by Winkworth (1973) who includes original observations on growth-rate and their direct link with soil moisture recharge, mineral nutrition, as well as the information on seed formation by Davies (1968) and Preece (1971a) and on germination by Preece (1971b).

Soil moisture relationships of *Acacia aneura* communities in central Australia have been investigated by Slatyer (1961, 1965) and reviewed by Winkworth (1973); in south-west Queensland. Pressland (1973) has related rainfall partitioning of rainfall, stem flow and soil infiltration characteristics to tree survival and production. Winkworth (1970) has described the soil water regime of an intergrove area dominated by *Eragrostis eriopoda* Benth. in central Australia.

Death of *Acacia aneura* and lack of recruitment have been widely reported (Collins, 1924; Beadle, 1948; Condon, 1949; Jessup, 1951; Hall, *et al.* 1964; Lange, 1966; Chippendale, 1963). Beard (1968) reported death due to drought in the Gibson desert but also noted recruitment. Condon *et al.* (1969a) made similar observations in central Australia. Burrows (1973) in a long-term study has noted substantial seedling populations in variously thinned mature stands in south-western Queensland; he concluded that both continuous recruitment and intermittent mass regeneration occurred. However, removal of mature trees and intervention by termites and sheep can prevent regeneration (Watson & Gay, 1970; Watson, Lendon & Low, 1973). Cunningham & Walker (1973) in north-western New South Wales found that recruitment was uncommon and the ensuing populations were short-lived. Under-shrubs regenerated and these could possibly convert a viable grazing enterprise into an uneconomic unit over a short period. C. W. E. Moore (1969, 1973) has described these less desirable shrub communities and the possibility that dense stands of *A. aneura* could develop, and commented on methods of control. Burrows (1972, 1974) has described the biology of one of these shrubs, *Eremophila gilesii* F. Muell. in a monospecific community, given estimates of its productivity and compared its nitrogen and phosphorus economy with that of other shrub species.

At Koonamore Vegetation Reserve in South Australia there has been little recruitment to the *A. aneura* population over the past 100 years (Crisp 1975). Recruitment resumed from 1965 when a successful rabbit destruction programme coincided with heavy summer rainfall. A maximum life span of 250–300 years has been calculated for *A. aneura* (Crisp 1975) and for the associated *A. burkittii* (Crisp & Lange, 1976).

Perry (1970) reported that thinning of *Acacia aneura* in the groves in

Description of arid ecosystems

central Australia reduced the yield of ground-layer species but stimulated *A. aneura* regrowth; contour furrowing on the intergrove areas to retain rainfall further reduced these yields.

Management procedures involving a reduction in the density of mature trees have been reported by Beale (1973) who found that attainment of maximum pasture yield was at tree densities that provided very little leaf or drought supplementation. The variation and levels of productivity of the ground layer species *A. aneura* in Western Australia have been cited in a review by Wilcox (1974); emphasis is given to the influence of the erratic rainfall on productivity and phenology of the dominant *Acacia*.

Studies on ground layer grasses by Wilcox (1973) in Western Australia have shown the relative insensitivity of *Danthonia bipartita* (now *Monochather paradoxa*) either to seasonal deferment or to stocking rate. *Neurachne mitchelliana* (now *Thyridolepis mitchelliana*) increased in number with winter use and summer deferment at both stocking rates used in the experiment. Christie & Moorby (1975) and Christie (1975*a*, *b*, *c*) have compared the physiological responses of *T. mitchelliana* (also *Astrebla elymoides* and *Cenchrus ciliaris* L.) to the external phosphorus supply, temperature and soil water deficit. Ross & Lendon (1973) have estimated plant productivity and soil moisture extraction in central Australia for another perennial grass of the *A. aneura* woodland, *Eragrostis eriopoda*.

Replacement of *A. aneura* with productive grassland is possible only in mesic environments on the eastern fringe of the Queensland woodland (Burrows, 1970). Silcock (1973) working near Charlesville in a semi-arid environment has described the natural pattern of germination and establishment of grasses in dense *A. aneura* woodland and in disclimax grassland cleared many years previously. Additional treatments included clearing of the woodland and disturbance of the grassland; mass germination of indigenous species occurred infrequently and sites with shade or litter were favoured.

Holland & Moore (1962) have described a considerable range of changes in botanical composition that have occurred following thinning or removal of the upper strata, fire and grazing in the south-eastern part of the *A. aneura* woodland in Queensland.

Information on the frequency of occurrence of grass species in burnt woodland has been published by Moore (1973).

O'Donnell, O'Farrell & Hyde, (1973) have assessed the value of various exotic and indigenous pasture species tested for long term grazing use in Western Australia, Northern Territory and Queensland (see also Ebersohn, 1969, 1970).

Soils supporting *A. aneura* woodland have been described in regional surveys by Jessup (1951, 1960); Northcote (1960, 1966); Northcote *et al.* (1967, 1968); Isbell *et al.* (1967); McArthur & Wright (1967); Bettenay,

Churchward & McArthur (1967), and Dawson & Ahern (1974). Information on the chemical properties of six representative profiles in south-western Queensland has been published (Dawson & Ahern, 1973); Keay & Bettenay (1969) have presented information on soil properties and the concentration of nutrients in plants on mulga plains.

A. aneura woodland occurs on a wide range of soils ranging from lithosols, Um 1.4, Um 1.2 through shallow loamy red earths, Um 5.51, Um 5.41, Um 5.31, loamy red sands Gn 2.12, Um 5.52, acid to neutral sandy red earths, Um 5.21 and siliceous sands, Uc 1.2 to texture contrast over alluvia Dr 2.12, Dr 2.13.

Erosion in north-western New South Wales has followed the removal of *A. aneura*; wind sheeting with moderate to plentiful drift on light-textured soils and water erosion on lithosols and shallow soils in undulating and hilly topography has been reported (James, 1960). Morris (1939) and Pidgeon & Ashby (1940) have described regeneration on eroded soils which formerly supported *A. aneura* woodland near the mining centre of Broken Hill.

A. aneura communities in south-western Queensland show evidence of severe deterioration of the vegetation as well as widespread and destructive sheet erosion (Dawson & Boyland, 1974).

In South Australia, Lay (1972) resurveyed the area of 50000 km^2 over which Jessup (1951) had made estimates of the density of three cheno-podiaceous shrubs and found that there had been significant loss of these plants; Lay related the extent of such loss to the numbers of livestock supported by a particular watering point. *A. aneura* was the only species studied which showed significant regeneration.

In central Australia, Condon *et al.* (1969*a*, *b*, *c*) have assessed the soil erosion status of *A. aneura* woodland as good to fair, with wind-sheeting as the dominant erosional type; in Western Australia, Wilcox & Speck (1963) have described extensive erosion and surface sealing of shallow soils due to continuous stocking and consequent deterioration of the ground layer from valuable perennial grasses to drought-evading ephemerals.

Sheep and cattle have utilized both the ground layer vegetation and the edible shrubs and trees for from 50 to over 100 years. Sheep are grazed at stocking rates of from 1:30 ha in parts of western Australia to 1:2 ha in southern Queensland in a good season and 1:5 ha in a poor season. Low (1972) has noted cattle densities of 1:140 ha and 1:220 ha in woodland at Alice Springs, Northern Territory. Everist (1969) has described the use of *A. aneura* for drought-feeding and methods of cutting branches so as not to kill the trees. Chemical analyses of leaf material from ground layer species, shrubs and tree components of *A. aneura* woodland (Griffiths & Barker 1966; Griffiths, Barker & McLean 1974; Siebert *et al.* 1968;

183

Description of arid ecosystems

Newman 1969; 1973) and a limited number of digestibility estimates (Harvey 1952; Norton *et al.* 1972; Wilson 1974) have been made, but dietary studies are few in *A. aneura* communities (Leigh, 1974, Low, Birk, Lendon & Low, 1973). Estimates of animal production in *A. aneura* communities are scanty, but include observations on wool production and reproductive performance (Williams & Suijdendorp, 1968; McMeniman & Holle, 1973; Morrissey, 1973).

The survey of the sheep industry in the Charleville district by Bird (1953) concentrates largely on the *A. aneura* woodlands and factors affecting sheep and wool production

The faunal component of *A. aneura* woodlands has not been studied intensively, but there have been studies on particular species by Davies (1973*a*, *b*) for a site in Western Australia, by Newsome (1971); Newsome & Corbett (1976); Low *et al.* (1973) for central Australia and by Bailey, Hall, Myers & Parker (1972); Hall (1972) and Myers & Parker (1972) for sites in western New South Wales.

The remaining *Acacia* woodlands include the *A. sowdenii* and *A. linophylla A. ramulosa* woodlands of South Australia (Crocker & Skewes, 1941; Specht, 1972) the *A. cambagei* woodlands of semi-arid Queensland (Blake, 1938, Holland & Moore, 1962; Perry & Lazarides, 1964; Boyland, 1970) and the *A. georginae* communities of central and northern Australia (Christian & Perry, 1954; Perry & Lazarides, 1962).

Detailed investigations include those on soil water relationships of *A. sowdenii* communities by Jackson (1958), some preliminary observations on the reaction of the chenopodiaceous shrub stratum to grazing (Trumble & Woodroffe, 1954), and the population ecology of four *Atriplex* spp. under grazing by sheep (Barker & Lange, 1970).

Casuarina–Heterodendron *and* Callitris *low woodlands*

These woodlands are located in the south-eastern part of the continent with their major occurrence in New South Wales, elsewhere they occur as scattered communities. *Casuarina stricta, Heterodendron oleifolium* and *Callitris columellaris* F. Muell, often inter-grade with other wide-spread communities such as those in which *A. aneura* is prominent.

Regional descriptions of the *Casuarina–Heterodendron* low woodland in New South Wales include those by Beadle (1948), Stannard (1958, 1963) and James (1960); by Specht (1972) for South Australia and Holland & Moore (1962) for south-eastern Queensland. Carrodus *et al.* (1965) describe mixed communities on the Koonamore Vegetation Reserve.

Callitris low woodland in Northern Victoria has been described by Zimmer (1946), and the New South Wales and Queensland *Callitris* woodlands have been described by Beadle (1948), James (1960) and Holland & Moore (1962).

184

A community in which *Casuarina descaisneana* is prominent has been described for northern South Australia, central Australia and Western Australia (Perry & Lazarides, 1962; Keay & Bettenay, 1969).

Little has been published on the structure and dynamics of these communities and on the biology of individual species. A notable exception is the inland form of *Callitris columellaris* (syn. *C. glauca* and including *C. huegelii* – the taxonomic status is not clear), a tree which provides timber of value for building construction and for fences.

The *Casuarina–Heterodendron* low woodland may have a sparse or a dense shrub understorey depending on previous management. These shrubs include *Acacia homalophylla*, *A. loderi*, *Eremophila sturtii*, *Cassia nemophila* var. *platypoda* and *Myoporum platycarpum*. Grass species include *Stipa variabilis*, *Enneapogon avenaceus*, *Chloris truncata*, *Eragrostis dielsii* and *Sporobolus caroli*. Williams & Roe (1975) have illustrated in demographic terms an irruption of *S. variabilis* in this woodland. There can be a strong chenopodiaceous element, with genera such as *Bassia* predominating. According to Moore *et al.* (1970) this woodland and the *Acacia sowdenii–Myoporum platycarpum* woodland in South Australia are related; there are strong ties also with *Casuarina cristata–Heterodendron oleifolium* communities in South Australia (Specht, 1972), though these latter generally exhibit a strongly developed shrub layer of *Maireana* spp. (Barker, 1970).

Dry-matter loss and gain has been estimated by Maconachie & Lange (1970) for canopies of *Acacia sowdenii*, *Heterodendron oleifolium*, *Myoporum platycarpum* and two *Cassia* spp. in South Australian low woodland.

Soils supporting the *Casuarina–Heterodendron* woodlands are brown calcareous earths (Gc 1.12, Gc 1.22) and grey-brown and red calcareous earths (Um 5.11). The *Casuarina decaisneana* woodland with hummock and tussock grasses grows on red sands (Uc 5.21, Uc 1.23). Jackson (1958) has provided analytical information and infiltration data for soils of the Yarramundi association upon which the mixed *Acacia sowdenii–C. cristata* woodland with chenopodiaceous shrub layer is growing at Yudnapinna in South Australia. The depth of penetration of 5 cm of water ranges from 60 to 80 cm in these soils compared with 30 cm in heavy-textured soils with *Maireana* low shrubland. Keay & Bettenay (1969) have provided analytical information for soils underlying *Acacia decaisneana* communities and for foliage of plants growing on them.

Erosion in the north-west of New South Wales mainly takes the form of wind erosion and James (1960) has mapped and described small areas of scalding and also of drift and dune activations, and large areas of wind-sheeting. In the adjoining region of east Darling, Stannard (1963) mapped and described a similar erosional situation.

The major land use in these woodlands is the grazing of Merino sheep.

Description of arid ecosystems

The effects of grazing in the early historical period have been described in terms of changes in soil structure and permeability, erosion and destruction of the ground layer vegetation, and the ingress or increase of shrubs in place of the original ground layer (Royal Commission, 1901; Cobar–Byrock committee, 1969).

In arid southern Australia large quantities of a *Santalum* sp. were selectively cut for incense production and for firewood (in Parsons, 1970).

Wilson, Leigh, Hindley & Mulham (1975) have compared the diets of goats and sheep on a semiarid *Casuarina–Heterodendron* woodland in which there were a number of undesirable shrub species; the sheep showed preference for ground-layer species and the goats generally preferred browse.

Barker & Lange (1969) have assessed the possible effects of stocking on plant populations in a *Casuarina cristata–Maireana sedifolia* community for species of major and of minor occurrence in a large paddock served by one watering point.

Callitris woodland in arid Australia, is generally situated on sandhills (Uc 5.12); occasionally on skeletal soils (Uc 6.11). The community can be represented by dense stands of small trees or by scattered large trees with an understorey of non-chenopodiaceous shrubs or a ground layer of hummock or tussock grasses; occasionally this ground layer is dominated by annual or ephemeral drought-evading species.

Invasion, encroachment or irruption of *C. columellaris* has been reported early and frequently following European settlement (New South Wales Legislative Assembly, 1881; Royal Commission, 1901; Williams, 1962; Cobar–Byrock committee, 1969) as has a reduction in more arid parts (Collins, 1924; Beadle, 1948).

Studies on *C. columellaris* and closely related forms include those on succession and regeneration (Pryor, 1942; Zimmer, 1944), aspects of seed production and seed fall (Zimmer, 1942; Hawkins, 1966), the influence of sheep and rabbit grazing on seedling survival (Johnston, 1968), mortality and conservation (Sims & Carne, 1947), and estimates of growth from tree rings (Lange, 1965).

Eucalyptus *open scrub*

The *Eucalyptus* spp. in this formation exhibit the 'mallee' habit; the word is aboriginal and its use in Australian botanical and geographical literature dates from 1848. Mallees are many-stemmed Eucalypt shrubs from 2 to 8 m high with large underground rootstocks. Leaves are carried only at the end of the branches and give the canopy a characteristic umbrella-like appearance. The understorey varies considerably and can consist of either sparse sclerophyllous shrubs (*Cassia, Eremophila, Myoporum* spp.) and

186

scattered tussock grass, chenopodiaceous shrubs (*Atriplex, Maireana* spp),
or hummock grasses (*Triodia* spp).

Eucalyptus open scrub extends from small eastern outliers in central
western New South Wales through northern Victoria and across southern
South Australia to Western Australia. (Moore & Perry, 1970; Barrow &
Pearson, 1970; Rossiter & Ozanne, 1970).

Regional descriptions include those for New South Wales by Beadle
(1948) and Stannard (1958, 1963); for Victoria by Patton (1951), Zimmer
(1946) and Connor (1966), for South Australia by Specht (1972) and for
Western Australia by Gardner (1944). These communities can cover large
uniform areas, or be in the form of belts on ridges or grow on sandy
islands surrounded by *Acacia* low woodland.

Detailed studies on the distribution of various mallee-type Eucalypts
have been made in south eastern Australia by Parsons (1969*a, b*) and with
particular attention to the Nullarbor Plain as a possible barrier to migration
(see Burbidge, 1952), and on Victorian species (Parsons & Rowan, 1968).
Parsons (1968*a, b*, 1969*a, b*) has also assessed the ecological amplitude
and factors concerned with the distribution of a number of mallee-type
Eucalypts. Goodall (1953) used an area in the Victorian *Eucalyptus* open
scrub for studies on classification and distribution of plant species, and
Noy-Meir (1971) undertook a multivariate analysis of a large complex
region in south-eastern Australia in which communities dominated by
mallee-type Eucalypts occupied the greater part; he noted the importance
his analyses attributed to the vertical distribution of available soil
moisture.

Regeneration by means of seedlings and lignotubers occurs after fire
(Zimmer, 1940); the climatic effects on reducing the seedling population
after the normal cool-season germination include the following dry
summer and grazing by domestic herbivores and rabbits (Parsons, 1968*c*).
The deleterious effect of rabbits on seedlings of *Eucalyptus* and other
species has been recorded in an exclosure study near Hattah Lakes in
northern Victoria (Cochrane & McDonald, 1966). Holland (1968) noted
that regeneration of the Eucalypts was by the setting of new shoots by
established lignotubers rather than from the germination of seeds: The life
expectancy of the Eucalypt shrubs is of the order of 500 years compared
with from 6 months to 5 years for ground-layer plants. Holland was able
to demonstrate that the new seasonal shoot growth in these Eucalypt and
other shrubs commenced at about the time that the ground layer plants
have attained maximum above-ground biomass.

The soils that support *Eucalyptus* open scrub are solonized brown soils
(Gc 1.12, Gc 1.22), leached sandy soils (Uc 2.2, Uc 2.3) and leached brown
soils (Uc 5.11, Uc 5.12). Detailed soil surveys and associated chemical
analyses are available for these soils because of their use for irrigated

Description of arid ecosystems

horticulture, as for example in Northcote & Boehm (1949), and Skene & Sargeant (1966). Ives (1973) has listed many of these surveys in his short bibliography.

Soil erosion follows removal of the trees and shrubs for what is marginal wheat growing and these landscapes are at risk in drought years as also are the abandoned wheatlands now used for grazing.

Scrub-clearing for grazing use is not economic in this arid community and existing cleared areas have their origin in speculative cropping or in the high wool prices and cheap labour of 100 years ago. Barrow & Pearson (1970) describe the arid sector of the pastoral industry where Merino sheep are grazed on the predominantly chenopodiaceous under-storey or on grasslands now composed of native perennial grasses and exotic annual species. Beadle (1948) describes these disclimax communities in south western New South Wales.

The faunal component of *Eucalyptus* open scrub is noteworthy (see Victorian Mallee Symposium, 1966). Ives (1973) has listed eighty references to mammals, amphibians, reptiles, insects and birds. Prominent in the bird studies are those by Frith (1962*a*) on the Mallee Fowl (*Leipoa ocellata* Gould). Conservation of this mound building bird has started (Frith, 1962*b*). Some native species have increased since settlement; the echidna *Tachyglossus aculeatus* is one of these.

Eucalyptus populnea *woodlands*

These communities have been classified by Moore *et al.* (1970) as semi-arid shrub woodlands which extend from central Queensland at latitude 23° S southwards to approximately 35° S in New South Wales, and in which *Eucalyptus populnea* can be the only tree, or may be associated with other tree species. Moore *et al.* summarize the occurrence of tree species over this wide geographical range in relation to changes in soil characteristics, particularly surface texture and depth. Holland & Moore (1962) illustrate this complexity and the additional effects of selective tree- and shrub-removal in a study area situated in south-western Queensland.

Regional descriptions are given in Blake (1938), Beadle (1948) and Stannard (1958, 1963).

These woodlands have been grazed by sheep and cattle for the past 100 years and marked changes have occurred in some communities. Heavy grazing pressure, erosion and the absence of fire to control woody species have led to the present thick shrub understorey and depauperate ground layer. Graphic descriptions of this process have been published (Royal Commission, 1901 – Minutes of Evidence) the current situation in central western New South Wales has been assessed (Cobar–Byrock committee, 1969) and the research approach and information on treatment effects

188

described (Moore, C. W. E. 1969, 1973). In south-western Queensland, Moore, R. M. & Walker (1972), Walker, Moore & Robertson (1972) and Moore & Walker (1974) have described experiments designed to reduce tree density and encourage development of the ground layer for use by sheep.

Soils underlying the Eucalypt woodlands range from the grey and brown cracking clays (Ug 5.2, Ug 5.3) through red earths (Gn 2.1) and duplex soils (Dr 2.3) to deep sands (Uc 1.2).

Erosion is severe, particularly on the hard, often gravelly red earths and on the duplex soils; various ameliorative measures have been tried, including furrowing and water spreading (Cunningham, 1967; Cobar–Byrock committee, 1969).

The carrying capacity of uneroded and open woodland approximates to 1 sheep/2.4 ha/year, but with severe sheet-erosion or with a thick shrub understorey the carrying capacity is 1 sheep/27 ha/year.

Faunal studies are limited to those by Griffiths & Barker (1966) and Griffiths *et al.* (1974) on the diet selected by the grey kangaroo (*Macropus giganteus* Shaw) and red kangaroo (*Megaleia rufa* Desmarest) in a paddock in which an *E. populnea* woodland was the major community.

Eucalyptus *frontage woodlands*

These woodlands are situated on the extensive flood plains of creeks and rivers throughout arid Australia (Moore *et al.* 1970). Four *Eucalyptus* species are prominent in either pure or mixed stands. *E. camaldulensis* occurs in both northern and southern Australia (Specht, 1972), ranging in form from massive forest types along permanent rivers to twisted small isolated trees in intermittent water courses of the desert. Associates include the other three Eucalypts, *E. microtheca* and *E. ochrophloia* in the north and *E. largiflorens* in the south.

Regional descriptions include those for frontage communities in Queensland by Blake (1938), Holland & Moore (1962), Boyland (1970) and by Dawson (1974); New South Wales communities have been described by Collins (1924), Beadle (1948), Stannard (1958), James (1960) and Biddiscombe (1963). Specht (1972) has classified these frontage woodlands in South Australia as woodlands; Perry & Lazarides (1962) describe the communities in central Australia in which *E. microtheca* and *E. camaldulensis* occur.

Frontage communities have been heavily used by domestic livestock and this use is being maintained because of the ground layer response to periodic flooding caused by rains in distant catchments and because of the readily available water in an otherwise waterless country. The understorey has been substantially modified by grazing and trampling (Beadle, 1948);

189

these frontages were the major stock routes in the early pastoral era (Williams 1962).

Recruitment of these *Eucalyptus* spp. is spasmodic and is associated with heavy and prolonged flooding. Recently, dense thickets of *E. microtheca* have developed on flood plains in northern New South Wales and southern Queensland. Stannard (1958) has noted thickets of *E. camaldulensis* and *E. largiflorens* in western New South Wales. Similar stands have been noted along embankments constructed in flood plains. By contrast, populations at the extremities of flood plains are depauperate, and in the continued absence of appropriate flood conditions will cease to be a component of the vegetation.

Eucalyptus camaldulensis produces timber of commercial importance in southern Australia and its occurrence, regeneration and growth under these conditions has been investigated (Boomsma, 1950). Less is known of the other three *Eucalyptus* spp. Because soil moisture is apparently of the utmost importance for germination, establishment and longevity of all four Eucalypts in semi-arid Australia, they are generally found in the grey and brown cracking clays (Ug 5.24, Ug 5.25, Ug 5.3) adjacent to, or bordering water courses.

Erosion is marked wherever the soils are other than cracking clays; duplex soils seldom have their surface horizon intact. Examples of erosion are given in Beadle (1948) for western New South Wales and Condon *et al.* (1969*a*, *b*) for central Australia. In spite of the poor to mediocre condition of the frontage woodland, heavy use by the pastoral industry is being maintained.

European settlement in arid Australia

European settlement of arid Australia started only when the better-watered regions were occupied. Each arid region in turn was exploited. Failures were frequent, and are continuing to the present, in what is, at best, marginal land.

Land tenure in arid Australia has been reviewed briefly by Heathcote (1969) who draws attention to the more detailed studies by Roberts (1924), King (1957) and Heathcote (1965*a*, *b*). Barnard (1969) has reviewed aspects of the economic history and drawn attention to the studies of Cain (1961, 1962) and Bauer (1962). Ives (1973) has listed 100 references that deal somewhat unevenly with the history and land settlement of the Mallee region in south-eastern Australia.

Of particular significance is the question posed by Heathcote (1969, p. 206) '...can we say for certain that the vegetation of the arid lands is a renewable resource?' and, proceeds to quote Campbell's suggestions (1966, p. 16), that (possibly) the lands of central Australia can only be economically used for pastoral purposes as a slow mining proposition. In other words, pasture deterioration might be inevitable if the land is to be used at all (see also Waring, 1973). Such reasoning certainly gives point to the arguments advanced for the conservation of adequate arid land ecosystems (Costin & Mosley, 1969; Everist & Webb, 1975).

Acknowledgments

It is a pleasure to acknowledge the assistance given me during the preparation of this review by Dr E. Bettenay, and Mr M. Churchward of the CSIRO Division of Land Resources Management, Perth, Western Australia; Mr B. E. Butler, CSIRO Division of Soils, Canberra. A.C.T.: Dr R. M. Moore, CSIRO Division of Land Use Research, Canberra, A.C.T. and Dr J. Calaby and Dr A. E. Newsome, CSIRO Division of Wildlife, Canberra, A.C.T.

References

Aitchison, G. D. (1971). Soil aridity during occasional drought in south-eastern Australia. *Proceedings of the Symposium on Soils and Earth Structures in Arid Climates, Adelaide, 1970.* Institution of Engineers, Sydney.

Alchin, B. M. (1974). Species trials in semi-arid south-western New South Wales. *Journal of the Soil Conservation Service New South Wales,* 30, 46–73.

Alexander, G. & Williams, O. B. (eds.) (1973). *The pastoral industries of Australia: practice and technology of sheep and cattle production.* Sydney University Press, Sydney.

Allen, G. H. (1963). Moisture penetration and plant growth in a Mitchell grass community following summer rain. *CSIRO Australia, Division of Plant Industry, Field Station Record,* 2, 55–7.

Anderson, D. J. (1970). Analysis of pattern in *Atriplex vesicaria* communities from the Riverine Plain of New South Wales. In: Jones (1970).

Australian Water Resources Council, (1965). *Review of Australia's water resources 1963.* Department of National Development, Canberra.

Australian Water Resources Council, (1972). In: *Hydrology of Smooth Plainlands of arid Australia. Hydrological Series No. 6.* Department of National Development, Canberra.

Bailey, P. T. (1971). The red kangaroo, *Megaleia rufa* (Desmarest) in north-western New South Wales. I. Movements. *CSIRO Australia, Wildlife Research,* 16, 11–28.

Bailey, P. T. (1972). Fauna of the Fowlers Gap–Calindary Area. I. Marsupial Fauna. In: *Lands of the Fowlers Gap–Calindary Area, New South Wales,* pp. 153–9. University of New South Wales, Research Series No. 4.

Bailey, P. T., Hall, L. S., Myers, K. & Parker, B. S. (1972). Fauna of the Fowlers Gap–Calindary Area. In: *Lands of the Fowlers Gap–Calindary Area, New South Wales.* University of New South Wales, Research Series No. 4.

Barker, S. (1970). Quandong Station, South Australia. A field context for applied rangeland research. *Transactions of the Royal Society of South Australia,* 94, 179–91.

Barker, S. & Lange, R. T. (1969). Effects of moderate sheep stocking on plant populations of a black oak–bluebush association. *Australian Journal of Botany*, **17**, 527–37.

Barker, S. & Lange, R. T. (1970). Effects of moderate sheep stocking on plant populations of a black oak–bluebush association. *Australian Journal of Botany*, **17**, 527–37.

Barnard, A. (1969). Aspects of the economic history of the arid-land pastoral industry. In: Slatyer & Perry (1969).

Barnard, A. (ed.) (1962). *The simple fleece: Studies in the Australian Wool Industry*. Melbourne University Press, Melbourne.

Barrow, P. M. & Pearson, F. B. (1970). The mallee and mallee heaths. In: Moore (1970).

Bauer, F.H. (1962). Sheep-raising in northern Australia: A historical review. In: Barnard (1962).

Beadle, N. C. W. (1948). *The vegetation and pastures of western New South Wales, with special reference to soil erosion*. Government Printer, Sydney.

Beadle, N. C. W. (1952). Studies in halophytes. I. The germination of the seed and establishment of the seedlings of five species of *Atriplex* in Australia. *Ecology*, **33**, 49–62.

Beadle, N. C. W. (1954). Soil phosphate and the delimitation of plant communities in eastern Australia. *Ecology*, **35**, 370–75.

Beadle, N. C. W. (1966). Soil phosphate and its role in moulding segments of the Australian flora and vegetation with special reference to xeromorphy and sclerophylly. *Ecology*, **47**, 992–1007.

Beadle, N. C. W., Whalley, R. D. B. & Gibson, J. B. (1957). Studies in halophytes. II. Analytic data on the mineral constituents of three species of *Atriplex* and their accompanying soils in Australia. *Ecology*, **38**, 340–44.

Beale, I. F. (1973). Tree density effects on yields of herbage and tree components in south west Queensland mulga (*Acacia aneura* F. Muell.) scrub. *Tropical Grasslands*, **7**, 135–42.

Beard, J. S. (1968). Drought effects in the Gibson Desert. *Journal of the Royal Society of Western Australia*, **51**, 39–50.

Beard, J. S. (1969). The natural regions of the deserts of Western Australia. *Journal of Ecology*, **57**, 677–711.

Beard, J. S. (1976). The evolution of Australian desert plants. In: Goodall (1970).

Bettenay, E., Churchward, H. M. & McArthur, W. M. (1967). *Atlas of Australian Soils, Sheet 6*, Meekatharra–Hamersley Range Area, with explanatory data. CSIRO, Australia & Melbourne University Press, Melbourne.

Biddiscombe, E. F. (1963). *A vegetation survey in the Macquarie region, New South Wales*. CSIRO Australia, Division of Plant Industry Technical Paper No. 18. Melbourne.

Bird, A. R. (1953). A study of the factors responsible for the fluctuations of sheep numbers in the Charleville district of south-western Queensland, 1948–1949. *University of Queensland Papers*, **1**, 43–85.

Blake, S. T. (1938). The plant communities of western Queensland and their relationships, with special reference to the grazing industry. *Proceedings of the Royal Society of Queensland*, **49**, 156–204.

Boomsma, C. D. (1950). The Red Gum (*Eucalyptus camaldulensis* Dehn.) Associ ation of Australia. *Australian Forestry*, **14**, 99–110.

Bowler, J. M. (1971). Pleistocene salinities and climatic change: evidence from lakes and lunettes in south-eastern Australia. In: Mulvaney & Golson (1971).

Bowler, J. M., Jones, R., Allen, H. & Thorn, A. G. (1970). Pleistocene human remains from Australia: a living-site and human cremation from Lake Mungo, western N.S.W. *World Archaeology*, **2**, 39–60.

Boyland, D. E. (1970). Ecological and floristic studies in the Simpson Desert National Park, south western Queensland. *Proceedings of the Royal Society of Queensland*, **82**, 1–16.

Boyland, D. E. (1973). Vegetation of the mulga lands with special reference to south western Queensland. *Tropical Grasslands*, **7**, 35–42.

Boyland, D. E. (1974). Vegetation. In: *Western Arid Region Land-Use Study, Part I*. Queensland Department of Primary Industries, Division of Land Utilization, Technical Bulletin No. 12.

Brown, D. A., Campbell, K. S. W. & Crook, K. A. W. (1968). *The geological evolution of Australia and New Zealand*. Pergamon Press, Oxford.

Brown, G. D. (1974). Biology of marsupials of the Australian arid zone. *Journal of the Australian Mammalian Society*, **1**, 269–88.

Brown, G. D. & Williams, O. B. (1970). Geographical distribution of the productivity of sheep in Australia. *Journal of the Australian Institute of Agricultural Science*, **36**, 182–98.

Brunt, A. T. (1966). Rainfall associated with tropical cyclones in the north-east Australian region. *Australian Meteorological Magazine*, **14**, 85–109.

Burbidge, N. T. (1942). Ecological notes on the De Grey–Coogan area, with special reference to physiography. *Journal of the Royal Society of Western Australia*, **29**, 151–61.

Burbidge, N. T. (1943*a*). Ecological succession observed during regeneration of *Triodia pungens* R. Br. after burning. *Journal and Proceedings of the Royal Society of Western Australia*, **28**, 149–56.

Burbidge, N. T. (1943*b*). A revision of the Western Australian species of *Triodia* R. Br. *Journal of the Royal Society of Western Australia*, **30**, 15–33.

Burbidge, N. T. (1945*a*). Morphology and anatomy of the Western Australian species of *Triodia* R. Br. I. General morphology. *Transactions of the Royal Society of South Australia*, **69**, 303–8.

Burbidge, N. T. (1945*b*). Germination studies of Australian Chenopodiaceae with special reference to the conditions necessary for regeneration. *Transactions of the Royal Society of South Australia*, **69**, 73–85.

Burbidge, N. T. (1946*a*). Morphology and anatomy of the Western Australian species of *Triodia* R. Br. II. Internal anatomy of leaves. *Transactions of the Royal Society of South Australia*, **70**, 221–34.

Burbidge, N. T. (1946*b*). Germination studies of Australian Chenopodiaceae with special reference to the conditions necessary for regeneration. II. (a) *Kochia sedifolia* F. Muell, (b) *K. pyramidata* Benth., (c) *K. georgii* Diels. *Transactions of the Royal Society of South Australia*, **70**, 110–19.

Burbidge, N. T. (1952). The significance of the mallee habit in Eucalyptus. *Proceedings of the Royal Society of Queensland*, **62**, 73–8.

Burbidge, N. T. (1959). *Notes on plants and plant habitats observed in the Abydos–Woodstock area, Pilbara, district, Western Australia*. CSIRO, Australia, Division of Plant Industry Technical Paper No. 12.

Burbidge, N. T. (1960). The phytogeography of the Australian region. *Australian Journal of Botany*, **8**, 75–212.

Bureau of Meteorology, (1968). *Review of Australia's water resources. Monthly rainfall and evaporation 1: Data tabulations*. Bureau of Meteorology, Melbourne.

Burrows, W. H. (1970). New pasture plants in the mulga zone. *Queensland Agricultural Journal*, **96**, 321–4.

Description of arid ecosystems

Burrows, W. H. (1972). Productivity of an arid zone shrub (*Eremophila gilesii*) community in south-western Queensland. *Australian Journal of Botany*, **20**, 317–29.

Burrows, W. H. (1973). Regeneration and spatial patterns of *Acacia aneura* in south west Queensland. *Tropical Grasslands*, **7**, 57–68.

Burrows, W. H. (1974). A study of the phenology and germination of *Eremophila gilesii* in semi-arid Queensland. In: *Plant Morphogenesis as the Basis for Scientific Management of Range Resources*. Proceedings of the Workshop of the US–Australia Rangelands Panel. Berkeley, California, 1971, pp. 150–59. USDA Misc. Publ. No. 1271.

Burrows, W. H. & Beale, I. F. (1970). Dimension and production relations of mulga (*Acacia aneura* F. Muell.) trees in semi-arid Queensland. *Proceedings of the XI International Grassland Congress, Surfers Paradise*, pp. 33–5. Queensland University Press, St. Lucia.

Butler, B. E., Blackburn, G., Bowler, J., Lawrence, C. R., Newell, J. W. & Pels, S. (1973). *A geomorphic map of the Riverine Plain of south-eastern Australia*. Australian National University Press, Canberra.

Butler, P. F. & Prescott, J. A. (1955). Evapotranspiration from wheat and pasture in relation to available moisture. *Australian Journal of Agricultural Research*, **6**, 52–61.

Butzer, K. W. (1961). Climatic change in arid regions since the Pliocene. In: *A History of Land Use in Arid Regions* (ed. D. Stamp). UNESCO, Paris.

Cain, N. (1961). Companies and squatting in the Western Division of New South Wales 1896–1905. *Economic Records*, **37**, 183–206.

Cain, N. (1962). Companies and squatting in the Western Division of New South Wales, 1896–1905. In: Barnard (1962).

Calaby, J. H. (1969). Australian mammals since 1770. *Australian Natural History*, **16**, 271–5.

Calaby, J. H. (1970). The vertebrate. In: *The Last of Lands* (eds. L. J. Webb, D. Whitelock & J. Le Gay Brereton). Jacaranda Press, Melbourne.

Calaby, J. H. (1971). Man, fauna, and climate in aboriginal Australia. In: Mulvaney & Golson (1971).

Calder, D. M. (1974). Morphogenesis and management of perennial grasses in Australia. In: *Plant Morphogenesis as the Basis for Scientific Management of Range Resources*. Proceedings of the Workshop of the US–Australia Rangelands Panel, Berkeley, California, 1971. USDA Misc. Publ. No. 1271.

Campbell, K. O. (1966). Problems of adaptation of pastoral businesses in the arid zone. *Australian Journal of Agricultural Economics*, **10**, 14–26.

Carrodus, B. B. & Specht, R. L. (1965). Factors affecting the relative distribution of *Atriplex vesicaria* and *Kochia sedifolia* (Chenopodiaceae) in the arid zone of South Australia. *Australian Journal of Botany*, **13**, 419–33.

Carrodus, B. B., Specht, R. L. & Jackman, M. E. (1965). The vegetation of Koonamore Station, South Australia. *Transactions of the Royal Society of South Australia*, **89**, 41–60.

Chapman, R. E., Williams, O. B. & Moule, G. R. (1973). The wool industry. In: Alexander & Williams (1973).

Charley, J. L. (1972). The role of shrubs in nutrient cycling. In: McKell *et al.* (1972).

Charley, J. L. & Cowling, S. W. (1968). Changes in soil nutrient status resulting from overgrazing and their consequences in plant communities of semi-arid areas. *Proceedings of the Ecological Society of Australia*, **3**, 28–38.

Charley, J. L. & McGarity, J. W. (1964). High soil nitrate levels in patterned saltbush communities. *Nature*, **201**, 1351–2.

Chippendale, G. M. (1958). Notes on the vegetation of a desert area in central Australia. *Transactions of the Royal Society of South Australia*, **81**, 31–41.

Chippendale, G. M. (1963). Ecological notes on the 'Western Desert' area of the Northern Territory. *Proceedings of the Linnaean Society of New South Wales*, **88**, 54–66.

Chippendale, G. M. (1968). The plants grazed by red kangaroos, *Megaleia rufa* (Desmarest) in central Australia. *Proceedings of the Linnean Society of New South Wales*, **93**, 98–110.

Christian, C. S. & Perry, R. A. (1954). Vegetation of the Barkly region. In: *Survey of the Barkly Region, 1947–48*, pp. 78–112. CSIRO Australia, Land Research Series No. 3.

Christie, E. K. (1975*a*). Physiological responses of semi-arid grasses. II. The pattern of root growth in relation to external phosphorus concentration. *Australian Journal of Agricultural Research*, **26**, 437–46.

Christie, E. K. (1975*b*). Physiological responses of semi-arid grasses. III. Growth in relation to temperature and soil water deficit. *Australian Journal of Agricultural Research*, **26**, 447–57.

Christie, E. K. (1975*c*). Physiological responses of semi-arid grasses. IV. Photosynthetic rates of *Thyridolepis mitchelliana* and *Cenchrus ciliaris* leaves. *Australian Journal of Agricultural Research*, **26**, 459–66.

Christie, E. K. & Moorby, J. (1975). Physiological responses of semi-arid grasses. I. The influence of phosphorus sample on growth and phosphorus absorption. *Australian Journal of Agricultural Research*, **26**, 423–36.

Coaldrake, J. E. (1967). Quaternary climates in north-eastern Australia and some of their effects. *Proceedings of the Royal Society of Queensland*, **79**, 5–58.

Cobar–Byrock Committee, (1969). *Report of the inter-Departmental Committee on scrub and timber regrowth in the Cobar–Byrock district and other areas in the western division of New South Wales*. Government Printer, Sydney.

Cochrane, G. R. (1967). *A vegetation map of Australia: some explanatory notes*. G. W. Cheshire, Melbourne.

Cochrane, G. R. & McDonald, N. H. E. (1966). A regeneration study in the Victorian mallee. *Victorian Naturalist*, **83**, 220–6.

Collins, M. I. (1923). Studies in the vegetation of arid and semi-arid New South Wales. Part I. The plant ecology of the Barrier district. *Proceedings of the Linnean Society of New South Wales*, **48**, 229–66.

Collins, M. I. (1924). Studies in the vegetation of arid and semi-arid New South Wales. Part II. The botanical features of the Grey Range and its neighbourhood. *Proceedings of the Linnean Society of New South Wales*, **49**, 1–18.

Condon, R. W. (1949). Mulga death in the west Darling country. *Journal of the Soil Conservation Service of New South Wales*, **5**, 1–8.

Condon, R. W., Newman, J. C. & Cunningham, G. M. (1969*a*). Soil erosion and pasture degeneration in central Australia. Part I. Soil erosion and degeneration of pastures and top feeds. *Journal of the Soil Conservation Service of New South Wales*, **25**, 47–92.

Condon, R. W., Newman, J. C. & Cunningham, G. M. (1969*b*). Soil erosion and pasture degeneration in central Australia. Part IV. *Journal of the Soil Conservation Service of New South Wales*, **25**, 295–321.

Description of arid ecosystems

Connor, D. J. (1966). Vegetation studies in north-west Victoria. 2. The Beulah–Hopetoun area. *Proceedings of the Royal Society of Victoria* **79**, 579–95.

Costin, A. B. (1971). Vegetation, soils and climate in Late Quaternary south-eastern Australia. In: Mulvaney & Golson (1971).

Costin, A. B. & Mosely, J. G. (1969). Conservation and recreation in arid Australia. In: Slatyer & Perry (1969).

Crisp, M. D. (1975). 'Long-term change in arid-zone vegetation at Koonamore, South Australia.' Ph.D. Thesis, Botany Department, University of Adelaide.

Crisp, M. D. & Lange, R. T. (1976). Age-structure, distribution and survival under grazing of the arid zone shrub, *Acacia burkittii*. *Oikos*, **27**, 86–92.

Crocker, R. L. (1946). The Simpson Desert Expedition, 1939. Scientific Reports No. 8. The soils and vegetation of the Simpson Desert and its borders. *Transactions of the Royal Society of South Australia*, **70**, 235–58.

Crocker, R. L. (1959). Past climatic fluctuations and their influence upon Australian vegetation. In: Keast, Crocker & Christian (1959).

Crocker, R. L. & Skewes, H. R. (1941). The principal soil and vegetation relationship of Yudnapinna Station, north-west South Australia. *Transactions of the Royal Society of South Australia*, **65**, 44–60.

Crocker, R. L. & Wood, J. G. (1947). Some historical influences on the development of the South Australian vegetation communities and their bearing on concepts and classification in ecology. *Transactions of the Royal Society of South Australia*, **71**, 93–136.

Cunningham, G. M. (1967). Furrowing aids revegetation at Cobar despite the worst drought on record. *Journal of the Soil Conservation Service of New South Wales*, **23**, 192–202.

Cunningham, G. M., Quilty, J. A. & Thompson, D. F. (1974). Productivity of waterponded scalds. *Journal of the Soil Conservation Service of New South Wales*, **30**, 185–200.

Cunningham, G. M. & Walker, P. J. (1973). Growth and survival of mulga (*Acacia aneura* F. Muell. ex Benth) in western New South Wales. *Tropical Grasslands*, **7**, 69–78.

Davidson, D. (1954). *The Mitchell grass association of the Longreach district.* Botany Department Papers III. University of Queensland Press, Brisbane.

Davies, J. G. (1955). The ecology arid and semi-arid zones of Australia. In: *Plant Ecology: Reviews of Research*, pp. 114–34. UNESCO, Paris.

Davies, J. G., Scott, A. E. & Kennedy, J. F. (1938). The yield and composition of a Mitchell grass pasture for a period of twelve months. *Journal of the Council for Scientific and Industrial Research*, **11**, 127–39.

Davies, S. J. J. F. (1968). Aspects of a study of emus in semi-arid Western Australia. *Proceedings of the Ecological Society of Australia*, **3**, 160–66.

Davies, S. J. J. F. (1973a). Land use by emus and other wildlife species in the arid shrublands of Western Australia. In: Hyder (1973).

Davies, S. J. J. F. (1973b). Environmental variables and the biology of native Australian animals in the mulga lands. *Tropical Grasslands*, **7**, 127–34.

Dawson, N. M. (1974). Land Systems. In: Technical Bull. No. 12, Queensland Department of Primary Industries (1974), pp. 74–83.

Dawson, N. M. & Ahern, C. R. (1973). Soils and landscapes of mulga lands with special reference to south-western Queensland. *Tropical Grasslands*, **7**, 23–34.

Dawson, N. M. & Ahern, C. R. (1974). Soils. In: Technical Bull. No. 12, Queensland Department of Primary Industries (1974).

Dawson, N. M. & Boyland, D. E. (1974). Resource use. In: Technical Bull. No. 12, Queensland Department of Primary Industries (1974).

Dodson, J. R. & Wilson, I. B. (1975). Past and present vegetation of Marshes Swamp in south-eastern South Australia. *Australian Journal of Botany*, **23**, 123–50.

Dolling, C. H. S. (1960). Efficiency of wool production in a semi-arid environment. *Proceedings of the Australian Society of Animal Production*, **3**, 69–76.

Eagleson, P. S. & Goodspeed, M. J. (1973). *Linear systems techniques applied to hydrologic data analysis and instrument evaluation.* CSIRO Australia, Division of Land Use Research Technical Paper No. 34.

Ealey, E. H. (1967). Ecology of the euro, *Macropus robustus* (Gould) in north-western Australia. 1. The environment and changes in euro and sheep populations. *CSIRO (Australia) Wildlife Research*, **12**, 9–25.

Eardley, C. M. (1946). The Simpson Desert Expedition, 1939 – Scientific Report No. 7. Botany – Part I: Catalogue of plants. *Transactions of the Royal Society of South Australia*, **70**, 145–74.

Eardley, C. M. (1948). The Simpson Desert Expedition, 1939 – Scientific Report No. 7. Botany – Part II. The phytogeography of some important sandridge deserts compared with that of the Simpson Desert. *Transactions of the Royal Society of South Australia*, **72**, 1–29.

Ebersohn, J. P. (1969). A reconnaissance collection in four homo-climates for herbage plants with potential in semi-arid north-eastern Australia. *Tropical Grasslands*, **3**, 1–11.

Ebersohn, J. P. (1970). Herbage production from native grasses and sown pastures in south-west Queensland. *Tropical Grasslands*, **4**, 37–41.

Everist, S. L. (1935). Response during 1934 season of Mitchell and other grasses in western and central Queensland. *Queensland Agricultural Journal*, **43**, 374–87.

Everist, S. L. (1949). Mulga (*Acacia aneura*) in Queensland. *Queensland Journal of Agricultural Science*, **6**, 87–139.

Everist, S. L. (1964). The Mitchell grass country. *Queensland Naturalist*, **17**, 45–50.

Everist, S. L. (1969). *Use of fodder trees and shrubs.* Advisory leaflet 1024, Queensland Department of Primary Industries, Division of Plant Industry.

Everist, S. L. (1972). Continental aspects of shrub distribution, utilization and potentials, Australia. In: McKell *et al.* (1972).

Everist, S. L. & Webb, L. J. (1975). Two communities of urgent concern in Queensland: Mitchell grass and tropical closed forests. In: *A National System of Ecological Reserves in Australia* (ed. F. Fenner). Australian Academy of Science, Report No. 19.

Fenner, F. & Ratcliffe, F. N. (1965). *Myxomatosis.* Cambridge University Press, London.

Fennessy, B. V. (1970). Native fauna. In: Leeper (1970), pp. 152–62.

Finlayson, H. H. (1961). On central Australian mammals. Part IV. The distribution and status of central Australian species. *Records of South Australian Museum*, **14**, 141–91.

Fisher, C. D., Lindgren, E. & Dawson, W. R. (1972). Drinking patterns and behaviour of Australian desert birds in relation to their ecology and abundance. *Condor*, **74**, 111–36.

Fisher, N. H. (1969). Water resources. In: Slatyer & Perry (1969).

Fitzpatrick, E. A. & Nix, H. A. (1970). The climatic factor in Australian grassland ecology. In: Moore (1970). pp, 3–26.

Description of arid ecosystems

Fleming, P. M. (1978). Types of rainfall and local rainfall variability. In: *Studies of the Australian Arid Zone. Part* III. *Water in rangelands*, (ed. K. M. W. Howes). CSIRO, Melbourne.

Foley, J. C. (1957). *Droughts in Australia*. Bulletin of Bureau of Meteorology, Australia. No. 43. Melbourne.

Francis, W. D. (1935). The Mitchell grasses of the Warrego district of western Queensland. *Queensland Agricultural Journal*, **43**, 270–81.

Frith, H. J. (1962*a*). *The Mallee Fowl*. Angus & Robertson, Sydney.

Frith, H. J. (1962*b*). Conservation of the mallee fowl, *Leipoa ocellata* Gould (Megapodiidae). *CSIRO (Australia) Wildlife Research*, **7**, 33–49.

Frith, H. J. (1964). Mobility of the red kangaroo *Megaleia rufa. CSIRO (Australia) Wildlife Research*, **9**, 1–19.

Frith, H. J. (1970). The herbivorous wild animals. In: Moore (1970), pp. 74–83.

Frith, H. J. (1973) *Wildlife Conservation*. Angus & Robertson, Sydney.

Frith, H. J. & Barker, R. D. (1975). Food of the plumed pigeons *Geophaps plumifera* and *G. ferrugia. Australian Wildlife Research*, **2**, 63–76.

Frith, H. J. & Calaby, J. H. (1969). *Kangaroos*. Cheshire, Melbourne.

Gardner, C. A. (1944). The vegetation of Western Australia with special reference to the climate and soils. *Journal of the Royal Society of Western Australia*, **28**, 11–87.

Gartner, R. J. W. & Anson, R. J. (1966). Vitamin A reserves of sheep maintained on mulga (*Acacia aneura*). *Australian Journal of Experimental Agriculture and Animal Husbandry*, **6**, 321–5.

Gentilli, J. (1971). *Climates of Australia and New Zealand*. World Survey of Climatology, vol. 13. Elsevier, Amsterdam.

Gentilli, J. (1972). *Australian Climate Patterns*. Nelson (Australia), Melbourne.

Gibbs, W. J. (1969). Meteorology and climatology. In: Slatyer & Perry (1969).

Gibbs, W. J. & Maher, J. V. (1967). *Rainfall deciles as drought indicators*. Bulletin of Bureau of Meteorology, Australia, No. 48. Melbourne.

Gill, A. M. (1975). Fire and the Australian flora: A review. *Australian Forestry*, **38**, 1–25.

Gill, E. D. (1973). Geology and geomorphology of the Murray River region between Mildura and Renmark, Australia. In: *Memoirs of the National Museum of Victoria. No. 34*.

Good, R. (1974). *The geography of the flowering plants*, (4th edition). Longman, London.

Goodall, D. W. (1953). Objective methods for the classification of vegetation. I. The use of positive interspecific correlation. *Australian Journal of Botany*, **1**, 39–63.

Goodall, D. W. (ed.) (1976). *Evolution of Desert Biota*. University of Texas Press, Austin.

Goodspeed, M. J. & Winkworth, R. E. (1978). Fate and effect of runoff. In: *Studies of the Australian Arid Zone, Part* III. *Water in Rangelands*. (Ed. K. M. W. Howes) CSIRO, Melbourne.

Griffiths, M. & Barker, R. (1966). The plants eaten by sheep and by kangaroos grazing together in a paddock in south-western Queensland. *CSIRO (Australia) Wildlife Research*, **11**, 145–67.

Griffiths, M., Barker, R. & McLean, L. (1974). Further observations on the plants eaten by kangaroos and sheep grazing together in a paddock in south-western Queensland. *Australian Wildlife Research*, **1**, 27–43.

Hall, L. S. (1972). Native birds. In: *Lands of the Fowlers Gap–Calindary Area, New South Wales*. University of New South Wales, Research Series No. 4.

198

Hall, E. A. A., Specht, R. L. & Eardley, C. M. (1964). Regeneration of the vegetation on Koonamore Vegetation Reserve, 1926–1962. *Australian Journal of Botany*, **12**, 205–64.

Harvey, J. M. (1952). The nutritive value of some Queensland fodders. *Queensland Journal of Agricultural Science*, **9**, 169–84.

Hawkins, P. J. (1966). *Callitris columellaris* (cypress pine): seed production and seed-fall studies. *Australian Forestry Research*, **2**, 3–16.

Heathcote, R. L. (1965*a*). *Back of Bourke: A Study of Land Appraisal and Settlement in Semi-Arid Australia*. Melbourne University Press, Melbourne.

Heathcote, R. L. (1965*b*). Changes in pastoral land tenure and ownership, an example from the Western Division of New South Wales. *Australian Geographical Studies*, **3**, 1–16.

Heathcote, R. L. (1969). Land tenure systems: past and present. In: Slatyer & Perry (1969).

Herbert, D. A. (1966). Ecological segregation and Australian phytogeographic elements. *Proceedings of the Royal Society of Queensland*, **78**, 101–11.

Hills, E. S. (1953). The hydrology of arid and sub-arid Australia with special reference to underground water. *UNESCO Arid Zone Research*, **1**, 179–202.

Hills, E. S., Ollier, C. D. & Twidale, C. R. (1966). Geomorphology. In: *Arid Lands, a Geographical Appraisal* (ed. E. S. Hills). Methuen, London; UNESCO, Paris.

Holland, A. A. & Moore, C. W. E. (1962). *The vegetation and soils of the Bollon district*. CSIRO Australia, Division of Plant Industry, Technical Paper No. 17.

Holland, P. G. (1968). Seasonal growth of field layer plants in two stands of mallee vegetation. *Australian Journal of Botany*, **16**, 615–22.

Hounam, C. E. (1963). Estimates of solar radiation over Australia. *Australian Meteorological Magazine*, **41**, 1–14.

Hyder, D. N. (ed.) (1973). *Arid Shrublands*. Proceedings of the 3rd workshop of the US–Australian Rangelands Panel (Tucson, Arizona, 1973). Society for Range Management, Denver, Colorado.

Isbell, R. F., Thompson, C. H., Hubble, G. D., Beckmann, G. G. & Paton, T. R. (1967). *Atlas of Australian soils, Sheet 4*. Brisbane–Charleville–Rockhampton–Clermont area. With explanatory data. CSIRO and Melbourne University Press, Melbourne.

Ives, A. (1973). *The Mallee of South-Eastern Australia: a Short Bibliography*. Dept. of Geography, Monash University, Clayton, Victoria.

Jackson, E. A. (1958). *A study of the soils and some aspects of the hydrology at Yudnapinna Station, South Australia*. CSIRO (Australia) Division of Soils, Soils and Land Use Series No. 24.

Jackson, E. A. (1962). *Soil studies in Central Australia: Alice Springs–Hermannsburg–Rodinga Areas*. CSIRO (Australia) Soil Publication No. 19.

James, J. W. (1960). Erosion survey of the Paroo–Upper Darling region. *Journal of the Soil Conservation Service New South Wales*, **16**, 185–206.

James, S. H. (1973). Animal and plant speciation studies in Western Australia: cytogenic aspects of the speciation process in plants. *Journal of the Royal Society of Western Australia*, **56**, 36–43.

Jennings, J. H. & Mabbut, J. A. (eds.). (1971). *Landform studies from Australia and New Guinea*. Australian National University Press, Canberra.

Jessup. R. W. (1951). The soils, geology and vegetation of north-western South Australia. *Transactions of the Royal Society of South Australia*, **74**, 189–273.

Jessup, R. W. (1960). The stony tableland soils of the south-eastern portion of the

Description of arid ecosystems

Australian arid zone and their evolutionary history. *Journal of Soil Science*, **11**, 188–96.

Jessup, R. W. (1969). Soil salinity in saltbush country of north-eastern South Australia. *Transactions of the Royal Society of South Australia*, **94**, 69–78.

Johnson, E. R. L. & Baird, A. M. (1970). Notes on the flora and vegetation of the Nullarbor Plain at Forrest, W.A. *Journal of the Royal Society of Western Australia*, **53**, 46–61.

Johnson, L. A. S. & Briggs, B. G. (1975). On the Proteaceae – the evolution and classification of a southern family. *Botanical Journal of the Linnean Society*, **70**, 83–182.

Johnston, T. N. (1968). The effect of sheep and rabbit grazing on regeneration of white cypress pine. *Australian Forestry Research*, **4**, 3–12.

Johnstone, M. H., Lowry, D. C. & Quilty, P. G. (1973). The geology of south Western Australia – a review. *Journal of the Royal Society of Western Australia*, **56**, 5–15.

Jones, R. (1969). Fire-stick farming. *Australian Natural History*, **16**, 224–8.

Jones, R. (ed.) (1970). *The biology of* Atriplex. CSIRO, Division of Plant Industry, Canberra.

Jones, R. & Hodgkinson, K. C. (1970). Root growth of rangeland chenopods: morphology and production of *Atriplex nummularia* and *Atriplex vesicaria*. In: Jones (1970).

Jones, R., Hodgkinson, K. C. & Rixon, A. J. (1970). Growth and productivity in rangeland species of *Atriplex*. In: Jones (1970).

Jones, R. M. (1966a). Scald reclamation studies in the Hay district, N.S.W. I. Natural reclamation scalds. *Journal of the Soil Conservation Service of New South Wales*, **22**, 147–60.

Jones, R. M. (1966b). Scald reclamation studies in the Hay district, N.S.W. II. Reclamation by ploughing. *Journal of the Soil Conservation Service of New South Wales*, **22**, 213–30.

Jones, R. M. (1967). Scald reclamation studies in the Hay district, N.S.W. III. Reclamation by ponding banks. *Journal of the Soil Conservation Service of New South Wales*, **23**, 3–17.

Jones, R. M. (1968). Studies on the germination and emergence of old man saltbush (*Atriplex nummularia* Lindl.). *Journal of the Soil Conservation Service of New South Wales*, **24**, 271–8.

Jones, R. M. (1969). Scald reclamation studies in the Hay district, N.S.W. IV. Scald soils, their properties and changes with reclamation. *Journal of the Soil Conservation Service of New South Wales*, **25**, 104–20.

Jozwik, F. X. (1969). Some systematic aspects of Mitchell grasses (*Astrebla* F. Muell.). *Australian Journal of Botany*, **17**, 359–74.

Jozwik, F. X. (1970). Response of Mitchell grasses (*Astrebla* F. Muell.) to photoperiod and temperature. *Australian Journal of Agricultural Research*, **21**, 395–405.

Jozwik, F. X., Nicholls, A. O. & Perry, R. A. (1970). Studies on the Mitchell grasses (*Astrebla* F. Muell.). *Proceedings XI International Grasslands Congress*, Surfer's Paradise, pp. 48–51. Queensland University Press, St. Lucia.

Keast, A. (1959). The Australian environment. In: Keast *et al.* (1959).

Keast, A. (1972). Australian mammals: zoogeography and evolution. In: *Evolution, Mammals, and Southern Continents* (eds. A. Keast, F. C. Erk & B. Glass). State University of New York Press, Albany.

Keast, A., Crocker, R. L & Christian, C. S. (1959). *Biogeography and ecology in Australia*. Monographiae Biologicae, VIII. Junk, The Hague.

200

Keay, J. & Bettenay, E. (1969). Concentrations of major nutrient elements in vegetation and soils from a portion of the Western Australian arid zone. *Journal of the Royal Society of Western Australia*, **52**, 109–18.

Kikkawa, J. (1974). Comparison of avian communities between wet and semi-arid habitats of eastern Australia. *Australia Wildlife Research*, **1**, 107–16.

King, C. J. (1957). *An outline of closer settlement in New South Wales. Part I. The sequence of land laws 1788–1956*. Department of Agriculture, Sydney.

Kirk, R. L. (1971). Genetic evidence and its implications for aboriginal prehistory. In: Mulvaney & Golson (1971).

Lange, R. T. (1965). Growth ring characteristics in an arid-zone conifer. *Transactions of the Royal Society of South Australia*, **89**, 133–7.

Lange, R. T. (1966). Vegetation of the Musgrave Range, South Australia. *Transactions of the Royal Society of South Australia*, **90**, 57–64.

Lay, B. (1972). 'Ecological studies of arid rangelands in South Australia.' M.Sc. Thesis, University of Adelaide, South Australia.

Leeper, E. W. (ed.) (1970). *The Australian environment* (4th edition, revised). CSIRO & Melbourne University Press, Melbourne.

Leigh, J. H. (1974). Diet selection and the effects of grazing on the composition and structure of arid and semi-arid vegetation. In: *Studies of the Australian Arid Zone II. Animal Production*. (ed. A. D. Wilson). CSIRO, Melbourne.

Leigh, J. H. & Mulham, W. E. (1964). The performance of introduced dryland species on three soil types in the southern Riverine Plain. *CSIRO Australia, Divison of Plant Industry, Field Station Record*, **3**, 9–20.

Leigh, J. H. & Mulham, W. E. (1966). Selection of diet by sheep grazing semi-arid pastures of the Riverine Plain. II. A cotton bush (*Kochia aphylla*)–grassland (*Stipa variablis–Danthonia caespitosa*) community. *Australian Journal of Experimental Agriculture and Animal Husbandry*, **6**, 468–74.

Leigh, J. H. & Mulham, W. E. (1967). Selection of diet by sheep grazing semi-arid pastures on the Riverine Plain. III. A bladder saltbush (*Atriplex vesicaria*)–pigface (*Disphyma australe*) community. *Australian Journal of Experimental Agriculture and Animal Husbandry*, **7**, 421–5.

Leigh, J. H. & Mulham, W. E. (1971). The effect of defoliation on the persistence of *Atriplex vesicaria*. *Australian Journal of Agricultural Research*, **22**, 239–44.

Leigh, J. H. & Noble, J. C. (1969). Vegetation resources. In: Slatyer & Perry (1969).

Leigh, J. H. & Noble, J. C. (1972). *Riverine Plain of New South Wales: its pastoral and irrigation development*. CSIRO Australia, Division of Plant Industry, Canberra.

Leigh, J. H. Wilson, A. D. & Mulham, W. E. (1968). A study of Merino sheep grazing a cotton bush (*Kochia aphylla*)–grassland (*Stipa variabilis–Danthonia caespitosa*) community on the Riverine Plain. *Australian Journal of Agricultural Research*, **19**, 947–61.

Leigh, J. H., Wilson, A. D. & Williams, O. B. (1970). An assessment of the values of three perennial chenopodiaceous shrubs for wool production of sheep grazing semi-arid pastures. In: *Proceedings of the XI International Grassland Congress, Surfers Paradise*, pp. 55–9. Queensland University Press, St. Lucia.

Litchfield, W. H. & Mabbutt, J. A. (1962). Hardpans in soils of semi-arid Western Australia. *Journal of Soil Science*, **13**, 148–59.

Lorimer, M. S. (1975). 'Forage selection by sheep grazing Mitchell grass pasture.' M. Agr. Sc. Thesis, University of Queensland.

Lourensz, R. S. (1977). Tropical cyclones in the Australian region, July 1909 to June 1975. Meteorological Summary, Bureau of Meteorology, Canberra.

Low, B. S., Birk, E., Lendon, C. & Low, W. A. (1973). Community utilization by cattle and kangaroos in mulga near Alice Springs, Northern Territory. *Tropical Grasslands*, **7**, 149–56.

Low, W. A. (1972). Community preference by free-ranging shorthorns in the Alice Springs district. *Proceedings of the Australian Society of Animal Production*, **9**, 381–6.

Low, W. A. (1974). Behavioural aspects of the ecology of arid-zone mammals, with particular reference to cattle. In: *Studies of the Australian Arid Zone. II. Animal production*. (ed. A. D. Wilson). CSIRO Melbourne.

Lowe, C. H. (1968). Appraisal of research on fauna of desert environments. In: McGinnies *et al.* (1968).

Mabbutt, J. A. (1965). Landscapes of arid and semi-arid Australia. *Australian Natural History*, **15**, 101–10.

Mabbutt, J. A. (1969). Landforms of arid Australia. In: Slatyer & Perry (1969).

Mabbutt, J. A. (1971). The Australian arid zone as a prehistoric environment. In: Mulvaney & Golson (1971).

Mabbutt, J. A. & Sullivan, (1970). Landforms and structure. In: Moore (1970).

McArthur, A. G. (1972). Fire control in the arid and semi-arid lands of Australia. In: *The Use of Trees and Shrubs in the Dry Country of Australia* (eds. H. Hall. *et al.*). pp. 488–575. Australian Government Publishing Service, Canberra.

McArthur, W. M. & Wright, M. J. (1967). *Atlas of Australian Soils, Sheet 9.* Kimberley area. With explanatory data. CSIRO & Melbourne University Press, Melbourne.

MacDonald, J. D. (1973). *Birds of Australia: a summary of information*. A. H. & A. W. Reed, Sydney.

McGinnies, W. G., Goldman, B. J. & Paylore, P. (eds.) (1968). *Deserts of the world. An appraisal of research into their physical and biological environments*. University of Arizona Press, Tucson.

McKell, C. M., Blaisdell, J. P. & Goodin, J. R. (eds.) (1972). *Wildland Shrubs – their Biology and Utilization*. USDA Forest service, General Technical Report INT-1.

McMeniman, N. P. & Holle, R. (1973). The reproductive performance of maiden ewes in the mulga zone of south-western Queensland. *Tropical Grasslands*, **7**, 157–62.

Maconochie, J. R. & Lange, R. T. (1970). Canopy dynamics of trees and shrubs with particular reference to the arid-zone topfeed species. *Transactions of the Royal Society of South Australia*, **94**, 243–8.

Main, A. R. (1968). Ecology, systematics and evolution of Australian frogs. In: *Advances in Ecological Research 5* (ed. J. B. Cragg). Academic Press, London and New York.

Main, A. R. (1976). Adaptation of Australian vertebrates to desert conditions. In: Goodall (1976).

Main, A. R., Shield, J. W. & Waring, H. (1959). Recent studies on marsupial ecology. In: Keast *et al.* (1959).

Malcolm, C. V. (1972). Establishing shrubs in saline environments. In: McKell *et al.* (1972).

Marchant, N. G. (1973). Species diversity in the south-western flora. *Journal of the Royal Society of Western Australia*, **56**, 23–30.

Marlow, B. J. (1958). A survey of the marsupials of New South Wales. *CSIRO (Australia) Wildlife Research*, **3**, 71–114.

Marshall, A. J. (1968). On the disadvantages of wearing fur. In: *The Great Extermination*, (ed. A. J. Marshall), pp. 18–54. Panther Books, London.

Melville, G. F. (1947). An investigation of the drought pastures of the Murchison district of Western Australia. *Journal of the Department of Agriculture of Western Australia*, **24**, 1–29.

Melville, R. (1975). The distribution of Australian relict plants and its bearing on angiosperm evolution. *Botanical Journal of the Linnean Society*, **71**, 67–88.

Merrilees, D., Dix, W. C., Hallam, S. J., Douglas, W. H. & Berndt, R. M. (1973). Aboriginal man in south-western Australia. *Journal of the Royal Society of Western Australia*, **56**, 44–55.

Milthorpe, P. L. (1972). Pastures and pasture lands of the Fowlers Gap–Calindary area. In: *Lands of the Fowlers Gap–Calindary Area, New South Wales*. University of New South Wales, Research Series No. 4.

Moore, C. W. E. (1953 a). The vegetation of the south-eastern Riverina, New South Wales. 1. The climax communities. *Australian Journal of Botany*, **1**, 485–547.

Moore, C. W. E. (1953 b). The vegetation of the south-eastern Riverina, New South Wales. 2. The disclimax communities. *Australian Journal of Botany*, **1**, 548–67.

Moore, C. W. E. (1969). Application of ecology to the management of pastoral leases in north-western New South Wales. *Proceedings of the Ecological Society of Australia*, **4**, 39–54.

Moore, C. W. E. (1973). Some observations on ecology and control of woody weeds on mulga lands in north-western New South Wales. *Tropical Grasslands*, **7**, 79–88.

Moore, R. M. (1962). The effect of sheep grazing on Australian vegetation. In: Barnard (1962).

Moore, R. M. (ed.) (1970). *Australian Grasslands*. Australian National University Press, Canberra.

Moore, R. M. (1973). Australian arid shrublands. In: Hyder (1973).

Moore, R. M. (1974). Morphogenesis and management of annual range plants in Australia. In *Plant Morphogenesis as the Basis for Scientific Management of Range Resources*. Proceedings of the 1st Workshop of the US/Australia Rangeland Panel, Berkeley, California, 1971. USDA Misc. publication No. 1271.

Moore, R. M. & Perry, R. A. (1970). Vegetation of Australia. In: Moore (1970).

Moore, R. M. & Walker, J. (1972). *Eucalyptus populnea* shrub woodlands: control of regenerating trees and shrubs. *Australian Journal of Experimental Agriculture and Animal Husbandry*, **12**, 437–40.

Moore, R. M. & Walker, J. (1974). Interrelationships among trees, shrubs and herbs in Australian shrub woodlands. *Proceedings XII International Grassland Congress, Moscow*.

Moore, R. M., Condon, R. W. & Leigh, J. H. (1970). Semi-arid woodlands. In: Moore (1970).

Morris, M. (1939). Plant regeneration in the Broken Hill district. *Australian Journal of Science*, **2**, 43–8.

Morrissey, J. G. (1973). Animal production and reproduction in the mulga zone of Western Australia. *Tropical Grasslands*, **7**, 163–8.

Mott, J. J. (1972a). 'The autecology of annuals in an arid region of Western Australia.' Ph.D. Thesis, University of Western Australia, Perth.

Description of arid ecosystems

Mott, J. J. (1972b). Germination studies on some annual species from an arid region of Western Australia. *Journal of Ecology*, **60**, 293–304.

Mott, J. J. (1973). Temporal and spatial distribution of an annual flora in an arid region of Western Australia. *Tropical Grasslands*, **7**, 89–98.

Moule, G. (1968). Sheep and wool production in semi-arid pastoral Australia. *World Review of Animal Production*, Part 1: 40–50; Part 2: 46–58.

Muirhead, W. A. & Jones, R. M. (1966). Species trials in the semi-arid south-west of New South Wales. II. Native shrub trials in the Hay district. *Journal of the Soil Conservation Service of New South Wales*, **22**, 138–46.

Muirhead, W. A., Jones, R. M. & Williamson, D. R. (1974). Response of scalds to gypsum on the Riverine Plain, New South Wales. *Journal of the Soil Conservation Service of New South Wales*, **30**, 112–19.

Mulcahy, M. J. (1973). Landforms and soils of south Western Australia. *Journal of the Royal Society of Western Australia*, **56**, 16–22.

Mulcahy, M. J. & Bettenay, E. (1972). Soil and landscape studies in Western Australia (1) The major drainage divisions. *Journal of the Geological Society of Australia*, **18**, 349–57.

Mulvaney, D. J. & Golson, J. (eds.) (1971). *Aboriginal Man and Environment in Australia*. Australian National University Press, Canberra.

Murray, J. B. (1931). A study of the vegetation of the Lake Torrens Plateau, South Australia. *Transactions of the Royal Society of South Australia*, **55**, 91–112.

Myers, K. & Parker, B. S. (1972). Introduced animals. In: *Lands of the Fowlers Gap–Calindary Area, New South Wales*. University of New South Wales, Research Series No. 4.

Myers, K. & Parker, B. S. (1975a). A study of the biology of the field rabbit in climatically different regions in eastern Australia. VI. Changes in number and distribution related to climate and land systems in semi-arid New South Wales. *Australian Wildlife Research*, **2**, 11–32.

Myers, K. & Parker, B. S. (1975b). Effect of severe drought on rabbit numbers and distribution in a refuge area in semi arid north-western New South Wales. *Australian Wildlife Research*, **2**, 103–20.

Newman, D. M. R. (1969). The chemical composition, digestibility and intake of some native pasture species in central Australia during winter. *Australian Journal of Experimental Agriculture and Animal Husbandry*, **9**, 599–602.

Newman, D. M. R. (1973). The influence of rainfall on the nutritive value of a semi-arid mulga pasture in south-west Queensland. *Tropical Grasslands*, **7**, 143–7.

Newman, J. C. (1966). Waterponding for soil conservation in arid areas in New South Wales. *Journal of Soil Conservation Services New South Wales*, **22**, 18–28.

Newman, J. C. (1974). Effects of past grazing in determining range management principles in Australia. In: *Plant Morphogenesis as the Basis for Scientific Management of Range Resources*. Proceedings of the 1st workshop of the US-Australian Rangelands Panel, Berkeley, California, 1971, pp. 197–206. USDA Misc. Publication No. 1271.

Newman, J. C. & Condon, R. W. (1969). Land use and present condition. In: Slatyer & Perry (1970).

Newsome, A. E. (1965a). The abundance of red kangaroos, *Megaleia rufa* (Desmarest), in central Australia. *Australian Journal of Zoology*, **13**, 269–87.

Newsome, A. E. (1965b). The distribution of red kangaroos, *Megaleia rufa* (Desmarest) about sources of persistent food and water in central Australia, *Australian Journal of Zoology*, **13**, 289–99.

Newsome, A. E. (1965*c*). Reproduction in natural populations of the red kangaroo, *Megaleia rufa* (Desmarest), in central Australia. *Australian Journal of Zoology*, **13**, 735–59.

Newsome, A. E. (1971). Competition between wildlife and domestic livestock. *Australian Veterinary Journal*, **47**, 577–86.

Newsome, A. E. & Corbett, L. K. (1977). The effects of native, feral and domestic animals on the productivity of the Australian rangelands. In: *The Impact of Herbivores on Arid and Semi-arid Shrublands*. Proceedings of the 2nd workshop of the US–Australian Rangelands Panel, Adelaide, 1972. Australian Rangelands Society, Perth.

Nix, H. A. & Austin, M. P. (1973). Mulga: a bioclimatic analysis. *Tropical Grasslands*, **1**, 9–21.

Nix, H. A. & Kalma, J. D. (1971). Climate as a dominant control in the biogeography of northern Australia and New Guinea. In: Walker (1972*b*), pp. 61–92.

Northcote, K. H. (1960). *Atlas of Australian Soils. Sheet 1*. Port Augusta–Adelaide–Hamilton area. With explanatory data. CSIRO & Melbourne University Press, Melbourne.

Northcote, K. H. (1966). *Atlas of Australian Soils*. With explanatory data. CSIRO & Melbourne University Press, Melbourne.

Northcote, K. H. (1971). *A Factual Key for the Recognition of Australian Soils*. (3rd edition). Rellim Technical Publications, Glenside, South Australia.

Northcote, K. H., Bettenay, E., Churchward, H. M. & McArthur, W. M. (1967). *Atlas of Australian Soils. Sheet 5*. Perth–Albany–Esperance Area. With explanatory data. CSIRO & Melbourne University Press, Melbourne.

Northcote, K. H. & Boehm, E. W. (1949). *The soils and horticultural potential of portion of the Coomealla Irrigation Area, New South Wales*. CSIRO Australia Soils and Land Use Series 1.

Northcote, K. H., Hubble, G. D., Isbell, R. G., Thompson, C. H. & Bettenay, E. (1975). *A description of Australian soils*. CSIRO, Melbourne.

Northcote, K. H., Isbell, R. F., Webb, A. A., Murtha, G. G., Churchward, H. M. & Bettenay, E. (1968). *Atlas of Australian Soils. Sheet 10*. Central Australia. With explanatory data. CSIRO & Melbourne University Press, Melbourne.

Norton, B. W., Rohan-Jones, W.G., Ball, F. M., Leng, R. A. & Murray, R. M. (1972). Nitrogen metabolism and digestibility studies of Merino sheep given kurrajong (*Brachychiton populneum*), mulga (*Acacia aneura*) and native pasture (*Stipa* spp.). *Proceedings of the Australian Society of Animal Production*, **9**, 346–51.

Noy-Meir, I. (1971). Multivariate analysis of the semi-arid vegetation in south-eastern Australia: model ordination by component analysis. *Proceedings of the Ecological Society of Australia*, **6**, 159–93.

N.S.W. Legislative Assembly. (1881). Reports by district and other surveyors as to spread of pine and other scrubs. *NSW Legislative Assembly*, **3**.

O'Donnell, J. F., O'Farrell, R. & Hyde, K. W. (1973). Plant introduction and reseeding in the mulga zone. *Tropical Grasslands*, **7**, 105–10.

Orr, D. M. (1975). A review of *Astrebla* (Mitchell Grass) pastures in Australia. *Tropical Grasslands*, **9**, 21–36.

Osborn, T. G. B. (1925). On the ecology of the vegetation of arid Australia. 1. Introduction and general description of the Koonamore Reserve for the study of the saltbush flora. *Transactions of the Royal Society of South Australia*, **49**, 290–7.

Osborn, T. G. B., Wood, J. G. & Paltridge, T. B. (1932). On the growth and reaction to grazing of the perennail saltbush, *Atriplex vesicaria*: an ecological study of the biotic factor. *Proceedings of the Linnean Society of New South Wales*, **57**, 377–402.

Osborn, T. G. B., Wood, J. G. & Paltridge, T. B. (1935). On the climate and vegetation of the Koonamore Vegetation Reserve to 1931. *Proceedings of the Linnean Society of New South Wales*, **60**, 392–427.

Parsons, R. F. (1968a). Ecological aspects of the growth and mineral nutrition of three mallee species of *Eucalyptus*. *Oecologia Plantarum*, **3**, 121–36.

Parsons, R. F. (1968b). Effects of waterlogging and salinity on growth and distribution of three mallee species of *Eucalyptus*. *Australian Journal of Botany*, **16**, 101–8.

Parsons, R. F. (1968c). An introduction to the regeneration of mallee eucalypts. *Proceedings of the Royal Society of Victoria*, **81**, 59–68.

Parsons, R. F. (1969a). Distribution and paleogeography of two mallee species of *Eucalyptus* in southern Australia. *Australian Journal of Botany*, **17**, 323–30.

Parsons, R. F. (1969b). Physiological and ecological tolerances of *Eucalyptus incrassata* and *E. socialis* to edaphic factors. *Ecology*, **50**, 386–90.

Parsons, R. F. (1970). Mallee vegetation of the southern Nullarbor and Roe Plains, Australia. *Transactions of the Royal Society of South Australia*, **74**, 227–42.

Parsons, R. F. & Rowan, J. N. (1968). Edaphic range and cohabitation of some mallee eucalypts in south eastern Australia. *Australian Journal of Botany*, **16**, 109–16.

Paterson, H. E. (1973). Animal and plant speciation studies in Western Australia. Animal species studies. *Journal of the Royal Society of Western Australia*, **16**, 31–6.

Patton, R. T. (1951). The Mallee. *Victorian Naturalist*, **68**, 57–62.

Pedley, L. (1973). Taxonomy of the *Acacia aneura* complex. *Tropical Grasslands*, **7**, 3–8.

Peel, L. J. (1973). History of the Australian pastoral industries to 1960. In: Alexander & Williams (1973).

Pels, S. (1971). River systems and climatic changes in south-eastern Australia. In: Mulvaney & Golson (1971).

Perry, R. A. (1960). *Pasture lands of the Northern Territory, Australia*. CSIRO Australia, Land Research Series No. 5.

Perry, R. A. (1970). The effects on grass and browse production of various treatments on a mulga community in central Australia. *Proceedings of the XIth International Grassland Congress, Surfers Paradise*, pp. 63–5. Queensland University Press, St. Lucia.

Perry, R. A. (1970). Arid shrublands and grasslands. In: Moore (1970).

Perry, R. A. & Christian, C. S. (1954). *Vegetation of the Barkly region*. CSIRO Australia, Land Research Series No. 3, pp. 78–112.

Perry, R. A. & Lazarides, M. (1962). *Vegetation of the Alice Springs area*. CSIRO Australia, Land Research Series No. 6, pp. 208–36.

Perry, R. A. & Lazarides, M. (1964). *Vegetation of the Leichhardt–Gilbert area* CSIRO Australia, Land Research Series No. 11, pp. 152–91.

Pianka, E. R. (1969). Notes on the biology of *Varanus candolineatus* and *Varanus gilleni*. *Western Australian Naturalist*, **11**, 76–82.

Pidgeon, I. M. & Ashby, E. (1940). Studies in applied ecology. I. A statistical analysis of regeneration following protection from grazing. *Proceedings of the Linnean Society of New South Wales*, **65**, 123–43.

Preece, P. B. (1971a). Contributions to the biology of mulga. I. Flowering. *Australian Journal of Botany*, **19**, 21–38.

Preece, P. B. (1971b). Contributions to the biology of mulga. II. Germination. *Australian Journal of Botany*, **19**, 39–49.

Pressland, A. J. (1973). Rainfall partitioning by an arid woodland (*Acacia aneura* F. Muell.) in south-western Queensland. *Australian Journal of Botany*, **21**, 235–45.

Pressland, A. J. (1978). Soil moisture distribution and evapotranspiration of a mulga (*Acacia aneura* F. Muell.) scrubland in south western Queensland. In *Studies of the Australian Arid Zone, Part III. Water in Rangelands* (ed. K. M. W. Howes). CSIRO, Melbourne.

Pryor, L. D. (1942). Plant succession and pine regeneration. *Australian Forestry*, **6**, 87–96.

Purcell, D. L. & Lee, G. R. (1970). Effects of season and of burning plus planned stocking on Mitchell grass grasslands in central western Queensland. *Proceedings XI International Grasslands Congress, Surfers Paradise, Australia*, pp. 66–9. Queensland University Press, St. Lucia.

Queensland Dept. of Agriculture (1963). *Annual Report of the Queensland Department of Agriculture and Stock, 1962–63*. Brisbane.

Queensland Department of Primary Industries (1974). *Western Arid Region Land-Use Study, Part I*. Division of Land Utilization, Technical Bulletin No. 12. Brisbane.

Ratcliffe, F. N. (1936). *Soil drift in the arid pastoral areas of South Australia.* CSIRO (Australia) Pamphlet No. 64.

Ratcliffe, F. N. (1937). *Further observations on soil erosion and sand drift, with special reference to south-western Queensland.* CSIRO (Australia) Pamphlet No. 70.

Raven, P. H. & Axelrod, D. I. (1972). Plate tectonics and Australian paleobiogeography. *Science*, **176**, 1379–86.

Raven, P. H. & Axelrod, D. I. (1974). Angiosperm biogeography and past continental movements. *Annals of Missouri Botanical Gardens*, **61**, 539–673.

Reis, P. J. & Williams, O. B. (1965). Variations in the sulphur content of wool from Merino sheep on two semi-arid grasslands. *Australian Journal of Agricultural Research*, **16**, 1011–20.

Rixon, A. J. (1970). Cycling of nutrients in a grazed *Atriplex nesicaria* community. In: *The Biology of* Atriplex (ed. R. Jones). CSIRO, Division of Plant Industry, Canberra.

Robards, G. E., Leigh, J. H. & Mulham, W. E. (1967). Selection of diet by sheep grazing semi-arid pastures of the Riverine Plain. IV. A grassland (*Danthonia caespitosa*) community. *Australian Journal of Experimental Agriculture and Animal Husbandry*, **7**, 426–33.

Roberts, B. R. (1972). *Ecological studies on pasture condition in semi-arid Queensland.* Department of Primary Industries, Queensland (Mimeographed).

Roberts, S. H. (1924, reissued 1968). *History of Australian Land Settlement 1788–1920.* Macmillan (Australia), Melbourne.

Roe, R. (1941). Studies on the Mitchell grass association in south-western Queensland. 1. Some observations on the response of Mitchell grass pastures to good summer rains following that 1940 drought. *Journal of the Council for Scientific and Industrial Research*, **14**, 253–9.

Roe, R. & Allen, G. H. (1945). *Studies on the Mitchell grass association in south-western Queensland. 2. The effect of grazing on the Mitchell grass pasture.* Bulletin 185, CSIR, Melbourne.

Rogers, R. W. (1972a). Soil surface lichens in arid and subarid south-eastern Australia. II. Phytosociology and geographic zonation. *Australian Journal of Botany*, **20**, 215–27.

Rogers, R. W. (1972b). Soil surface lichens in arid and subarid south-eastern Australia. III. The relationship between distribution and environment. *Australian Journal of Botany*, **20**, 301–16.

Rogers, R. W. & Lange, R. T. (1972). Soil-surface lichens in arid and subarid south-eastern Australia. I. Introduction and floristics. *Australian Journal of Botany*, **20**, 197–213.

Rolls, E. C. (1969). *They All Ran Wild: The Story of Pests and the Land in Australia.* Angus & Robertson, Sydney.

Ross, M. A. & Lendon, C. (1973). Productivity of *Eragrostis eriopoda* in a mulga community. *Tropical Grasslands*, **7**, 111–16.

Rossiter, R. C. & Ozanne, P. G. (1970). South-western temperate forests, woodlands, and heaths. In: Moore (1970).

Royal Commission, (1901). *Report of the Royal Commission to inquire into the condition of the Crown tenants, Western Division of New South Wales.* Government Printer, Sydney.

Serventy, D. L. (1971). Biology of desert birds. In: *Avian Biology* (eds D. S. Farmer & J. R. King), pp. 287–339. Academic Press, New York.

Serventy, D. L. & Whittell, H. M. (1951). *Handbook of the Birds of Western Australia* (2nd edition). Lamb Publications, Perth.

Sharma, M. L. (1973). Soil physical and physico-chemical variability induced by *Atriplex nummularia*. *Journal of Range Management*, **26**, 426–30.

Sharma, M. L. & Tonway, D. J. (1973). Plant-induced soil salinity patterns in two saltbush (*Atriplex* spp.) communities. *Journal of Range Management*, **26**, 121–5.

Siebert, B. D., Newman, D. M. R. & Nelson, D. J. (1968). The chemical composition of some arid zone pasture species. *Tropical Grasslands*, **2**, 31–40.

Silcock, R. G. (1973). Germination responses of native plant seeds to rainfall in south-west Queensland. *Tropical Grasslands*, **7**, 99–104.

Simpson, G. G. (1961). Historical zoogeography of Australian mammals. *Evolution*, **15**, 431–46.

Sims, H. J. & Carne, R. S. (1947). Mortality of Murray pine trees in the Victorian mallee. *Australian Journal of Science*, **9**, 188–9.

Skene, J. K. M. & Sargeant, I. J. (1966). *Soils and land use near Swan Hill.* Victorian Dept. Agriculture, Technical Bulletin No. 20.

Slater, P. (1970). *A Field Guide to Australian Birds. Non-Passerines.* Rigby, Adelaide.

Slater, P. (1974). *A Field Guide to Australian Birds. Passerines.* Rigby, Adelaide.

Slatyer, R. O. (1961). Methodology of a water-balance study conducted on a desert woodland (*Acacia aneura* F. Muell.) community in central Australia. *UNESCO Arid Zone Research*, **16**, 15–24.

Slatyer, R. O. (1965). Measurements of precipitation interception by an arid zone plant community (*Acacia aneura* F. Muell.). *UNESCO Arid Zone Research*, **25**, 181–92.

Slatyer, R. O. & Perry, R. A. (eds.) (1969). *Arid lands of Australia.* Australian National University Press, Canberra.

Smith, J. M. B. (1975). The living fragments of the flora of Gondwanaland. *Australian Geographical Studies*, **13**, 3–12.

Specht, R. L. (1970). Vegetation. In: Leeper (1970).

Specht, R. L. (1972). *The Vegetation of South Australia* (2nd edition) Government Printer, Adelaide.

Specht, R. L. & Rayson, P. (1957). Dark Island heath (Ninety-Mile Plain, South Australia). 1. Definition of the ecosystem. *Australian Journal of Botany*, **5**, 52–85.

Specht, R. L., Roe, E. M. & Boughton, V. H. (1974). *Conservation of Major Plant Communities in Australia and Papua New Guinea* (eds. R. L. Specht, E. M. Roe & V. H. Boughton). CSIRO, Melbourne.

Speck, N. H. (1963). *Vegetation of the Wiluna–Meekatharra area*. CSIRO Australia, Land Research Series No. 7, 143–61.

Squires, V. R. (1970). Grazing behaviour of sheep in relation to watering points in semi-arid rangelands. *Proceedings of the XIth International Grasslands Congress, Surfer's Paradise*, pp. 880–84, Queensland University Press, St. Lucia.

Squires, V. R. & Hindley, N. L. (1970). Paddock size and location of watering points as factors in the drought survival of sheep on the central Riverine Plain. *Wool Technology and Sheep Breeding*, **17**, 49–54.

Stace, H. C. T., Hubble, G. D., Brewer, R., Northcote, K. H., Sleeman, J. R., Mulcahy, M. J. & Hallsworth, E. G. (1968). *A Handbook of Australian Soils*. Rellim Technical Publications, Glenside, South Australia.

Stannard, M. E. (1958). Erosion survey of the south-west Cobar peneplain. Part II. Soils and vegetation. *Journal of the Soil Conservation Service of New South Wales*, **14**, 30–45.

Stannard, M. E. (1961). Studies on Kiacatoo regenerated area. I. Soils, vegetation and erosion. *Journal of the Soil Conservation Service of New South Wales*, **17**, 253–63.

Stannard, M. E. (1962). Studies on Kiacatoo Regeneration Area. II. The effect of stocking on recovery. *Journal of the Soil Conservation Service of New South Wales*, **18**, 10–20.

Stannard, M. E. (1963). Erosion survey of the central east-Darling region. III. Vegetation. *Journal of the Soil Conservation Service of New South Wales*, **19**, 17–28.

Storr, G. M. (1964). Some aspects of the geography of Australian reptiles. *Senckenbergiana biologica*, **45**, 577–89.

Storr, G. M. (1968). Diet of kangaroos (*Megaleia rufa* and *Macropus robustus*) and merino sheep near Port Hedland, Western Australia. *Journal of the Royal Society of Western Australia*, **51**, 25–32.

Suijdendorp, H. (1968). 'A study of the influence of management practices on "Spinifex" (*Triodia pungens*) grazing.' M.Sc. (Agric.) Thesis, University of Western Australia.

Thorne, A. G. (1971). The racial affinities and origins of the Australian aborigines. In: Mulvaney & Golson (1971).

Tindale, N. B. (1959). Ecology of primitive aboriginal man in Australia. In: Keast *et al.* (1959).

Troughton, E. Le G. (1959). The marsupial fauna: its origin and radiation. In: Keast *et al.* (1959).

Trumble, H. C. & Woodroffe, K. (1954). The influence of climatic factors on the reaction of desert shrubs to grazing by sheep. In: *Biology of Deserts* (ed. J. L. Cloudsley-Thompson). Institute of Biology, London.

209

Description of arid ecosystems

Tryon, D. T. (1971). Linguistic evidence and aboriginal origins. In: Mulvaney & Golson (1971).

Tucker, G. B. (1975). Climate: is Australia's changing? *Search*, **6**, 323–8.

Tyndale-Biscoe, H. (1973). *Life of Marsupials*. Edward Arnold, London.

UNESCO (1973). *International classification and mapping of vegetation*. Ecology and Conservation Series No. 6. UNESCO, Paris.

Victorian Mallee Symposium (1966). *Proceedings of the Royal Society of Victoria*, **79**, (2).

Walker, D. (1972*a*). Bridge and barrier. In: Walker (1972*b*).

Walker, D. (ed.) (1972*b*). *Bridge and barrier: the natural and cultural history of Torres Strait*. Proceedings of the Torres Strait Symposium. Australian National University Press, Canberra.

Walker, J., Moore, R. M. & Robertson, J. A. (1972). Herbage response to tree and shrub thinning in *Eucalyptus populnea* shrub woodlands. *Australian Journal of Agricultural Research*, **23**, 405–10.

Waring, E. J. (1973). Economic and financial constraints in the operation of livestock enterprises on arid shrublands. In: Hyder (1973).

Watson, J. A. L. & Gay, F. J. (1970). The role of grass-eating termites in the degradation of a mulga ecosystem. *Search*, **10**, 43.

Watson, J. A. L., Lendon, C. & Low, B. S. (1973). Termites in mulga lands. *Tropical Grasslands*, **7**, 121–6.

Webb, L. J. & Tracey, J. G. (1972). An ecological comparison of vegetation communities on each side of Torres Strait. In: Walker (1972*b*).

Weston, E. J. & Moir, K. W. (1969). Grazing preferences of sheep and nutritive value of pasture components in a Mitchell grass association in north western Queensland. *Queensland Journal of Agricultural and Animal Sciences*, **26**, 639–50.

Whalley, R. B. D. & Davidson, A. A. (1968). Physiological aspects of drought dormancy in grasses. *Proceedings of the Ecological Society of Australia*, **3**, 17–19.

Whalley, R. B. D. & Davidson, A. A. (1969). Drought dormancy in *Astrebla lappacea*, *Chloris acicularis* and *Stipa aristiglumis*. *Australian Journal of Agricultural Research*, **20**, 1035–42.

Wiedemann, A. M. (1971). Vegetation studies in the Simpson Desert, N.T. *Australian Journal of Botany*, **19**, 99–124.

Wilcox, D. G. (1960). Studies in the mulga pastoral zone. 1. The grazing of manderrie grass associations. *Journal of the Department of Agriculture of Western Australia*, **1**, 475–9.

Wilcox, D. G. (1973). Growth and reaction to grazing in *Danthonia bipartita* and *Neurachne mitchelliana*. *Tropical Grasslands*, **7**, 117–20.

Wilcox, D. G. (1974). Morphogenesis and management of woody perennials in Australia. In: *Plant Morphogenesis as the Basis for Scientific Management of Range Resources*. Proceedings of the 1st Workshop of the US/Australia Rangelands Panel, Berkeley, California, 1971, 60–71. USDA Misc. Publ. 1271.

Wilcox, D. G. & Speck, N. H. (1963). Pastures and pasture lands of the Wiluna–Meekatharra area. In: *Lands of the Wiluna–Meekatharra Area, Western Australia, 1958*. CSIRO Australia, Land Research Series, No. 7.

Williams, C. H. & Andrew, C. S. (1970). Mineral nutrition of plants. In: Moore (1970).

Williams, D. G. (1972). 'Ecological studies on shrub-steppe of the western Ruiesina, New South Wales.' Ph.D. Thesis, Australian National University, Canberra.

Williams, O. B. (1955). Studies in the ecology of the Riverine Plain. 1. The gilgai microrelief and associated flora. *Australian Journal of Botany*, 3, 99–112.

Williams, O. B. (1956). Studies in the ecology of the Riverine Plain. ii. Plant–soil relationships in three semi-arid grasslands. *Australian Journal of Agricultural Research*, 7, 127–9.

Williams, O. B. (1961). Studies in the ecology of the Riverine Plain. iii. Phenology of a *Danthonia caespitosa* Gaudich. grassland. *Australian Journal of Agricultural Research*, 12, 247–59.

Williams, O. B. (1962). The Riverina and its pastoral practices, 1860–1869. In: Barnard (1962).

Williams, O. B. (1963). Row pastures for a semi-arid environment. *CSIRO Australia, Division of Plant Industry, Field Station Record*, 2, 41–54.

Williams, O. B. (1968). Studies in the ecology of the Riverine Plain. iv. Basal area and density changes of *Danthonia caespitosa* Gaudich. in a natural pasture grazed by sheep. *Australian Journal of Botany*, 16, 565–78.

Williams, O. B. (1969). Studies in the ecology of the Riverine Plain. v. Plant density response of species in a *Danthonia caespitosa* Gaudich. grassland to sixteen years of grazing by Merino sheep. *Australian Journal of Botany*, 17, 255–68.

Williams, O. B. (1970). Population dynamics of two perennial grasses in Australian semi-arid grassland. *Journal of Ecology*, 58, 869–75.

Williams, O. B. (1971). Phenology of species common to three semi-arid grasslands. *Proceedings of the Linnean Society of New South Wales*, 96, 193–203.

Williams, O. B. (1973a). The environment. In: Alexander & Williams (1973).

Williams, O. B. (1973b). Environmental, biological, and managerial constraints to the production of sheep and cattle in Australian shrublands. In: Hyder (1973).

Williams, O. B. (1974). Vegetation improvement and grazing management. In: *Studies of the Australian Arid Zone. II. Animal Production*. (ed. A. D. Wilson). CSIRO, Melbourne.

Williams, O. B. & Roe, R. (1975). Management of arid grasslands for sheep: plant demography of six grasses in relation to climate and grazing. *Proceedings of the Ecological Society of Australia*, 9, 142–56.

Williams, O. B. & Suijdendorp, H. (1968). Wool growth of wethers grazing *Acacia aneura–Triodia pungens* savanna and ewes grazing *Triodia pungens* hummock grass steppe in the Pilbara district, W.A. *Australian Journal of Experimental Agriculture and Animal Husbandry*, 8, 653–60.

Williams, R. J. (1955). Vegetation regions (maps and notes). In: *Atlas of Australian Resources*. Department of National Development, Canberra.

Wilson, A. D. (1974). Water consumption and water turnover of sheep grazing semi-arid pasture communities in New South Wales. *Australian Journal of Agricultural Research*, 25, 339–47.

Wilson, A. D. & Leigh, J. H. (1970). Comparisons of the productivity of sheep grazing natural pastures of the Riverine Plain. *Australian Journal of Experimental Agriculture and Animal Husbandry*, 10, 549–54.

Wilson, A. D., Leigh, J. H., Hindley, N. L. & Mulham, W. E. (1975). Comparison of the diets of goats and sheep on a *Casuarina cristata–Heterodendron oleifolium* woodland community in western New South Wales. *Australian Journal of Experimental Agriculture and Animal Husbandry*, 15, 45–53.

Wilson, A. D., Leigh, J. H. & Mulham, W. E. (1969). A study of Merino sheep grazing a bladder saltbush (*Atriplex vesicaria*)–cottonbush (*Kochia aphylla*) community on the Riverine Plain. *Australian Journal of Agricultural Research*, 20, 1123–36.

Description of arid ecosystems

Wilson, G. R. (1975). Age structures of populations of kangaroos (Macropodidae) taken by professional shooters in New South Wales. *Australian Wildlife Research*, **2**, 1–9.

Wilson, J. & Leigh, J. H. (1964). Vegetation patterns on an unusual gilgai soil in New South Wales. *Journal of Ecology*, **52**, 379–89.

Winkworth, R. E. (1963). Some effects of furrow spacing and depth on soil moisture in central Australia. *Journal of Range Management*, **16**, 138–42.

Winkworth, R. E. (1964). Phosphate responses in some central Australian soils by seedlings of exotic perennial grasses. *Australian Journal of Experimental Agriculture and Animal Husbandry*, **4**, 26–9.

Winkworth, R. E. (1967). The composition of several arid spinifex grasslands of central Australia in relation to rainfall, soil water relations and nutrients. *Australian Journal of Botany*, **15**, 107–30.

Winkworth, R. E. (1970). The soil water regime of an arid grassland (*Eragrostis eriopoda* Benth.) community in central Australia. *Agricultural Meteorology*, **7**, 387–99.

Winkworth, R. E. (1973). Eco-physiology of mulga (*Acacia aneura*). *Tropical Grasslands*, **7**, 43–8.

Wood, J. G. (1936). Regeneration of the vegetation on the Koonamore Vegetation Reserve, 1926 to 1936. *Transactions of the Royal Society of South Australia*, **60**, 96–111.

Wood, T. G. (1970). Micro-arthropods from soils of the arid zone in southern Australia. *Search*, **1**, 75–6.

Wright, R. V. S. (1971). The archaeology of Koonalda cave. In: Mulvaney & Golson (1971).

Zimmer, W. J. (1940). Plant invasions in the mallee. *Victorian Naturalist*, **56**, 143–7.

Zimmer, W. J. (1942). A transect study of the flight of seeds of the Murray Pine. *Victorian Naturalist*, **59**, 142–3.

Zimmer, W. J. (1944). Notes on the regeneration of Murray Pine (*Callitris* spp.). *Transactions of the Royal Society of South Australia*, **68**, 183–90.

Zimmer, W. J. (1946). *The flora of the far north-west of Victoria. Its distribution in relation to soil types, and its value in the prevention of soil erosion.* Forests Commission of Victoria, Bulletin No. 2.

Manuscript received by the editors June 1975

6. South-west Asia

R. N. KAUL and D. C. P. THALEN

Introductory remarks

The region here referred to as south-west Asia covers the whole or parts of the following countries: India, Pakistan, Afghanistan, Iran, Iraq, Turkey, Syria, Jordan, Lebanon, Israel and the states situated on the Arabian Peninsula. Large areas can be classified as arid or semi-arid in all countries except Lebanon.

It should be emphasized that the available data for most of this region are fragmentary. Relatively small areas have been studied, in great detail, and vast stretches still remain unexplored or poorly inventoried. For this reason and because of the variation in environmental conditions over such a large area, we have subdivided the region in some sections of this paper, namely (a) Indo-Pakistan, (b) Iran and Afghanistan, (c) Middle East ('Middle East' has often been applied without sharp delineation of the region, but here it is used only for Iraq, part of Turkey, Syria, Jordan and Israel) and (d) Arabian Peninsula. This compilation is based mainly on the personal knowledge of the region and on review papers in the separate fields.

Regional geographies of Fisher (1950) and Cressey (1960) form a good introduction. The bioclimatic and vegetation maps of UNESCO–FAO (1963, 1969) with their explanatory notes provide a general basis for climate and plant cover, while the recent volumes of Zohary (1973) are the best guides for geobotanical aspects. For land use, the comprehensive review on the region by Whyte (1961) is perhaps the best guide, while the other volumes of the UNESCO Arid Zone Series also contain valuable information. Detailed bibliographies for south-west Asia can be found in Field (1953, 1955, 1956, 1957 and 1959), in Kaul (1970) and, for the desert areas, in McGinnies, Goldman & Paylore (1968). More specific references are given in the separate sections of this paper.

Geology and geomorphology

The geological history of extensive parts of south-west Asia, especially of the countries around the Persian Gulf, has been fairly well investigated. This is mainly because of the mineral resources, particularly oil, found in the area. In the near future revenues from oil sales may provide the countries concerned with means to develop their arid zones to a degree which, until now, has been considered unrealistic. Much of the geological

Description of arid ecosystems

information, however, has not been published and there are detailed accounts available for only a few countries. For example Wolfart (1967) and Bender (1968).

The present landform is a result of crustal movements that caused folding, fracturing, uplift and submergence. This was followed by other processes such as volcanic activity, erosion and sedimentation. In this paper the landforms of the three subregions, Middle East and Arabia, Iran and Afghanistan, and Indo-Pakistan are described.

Middle East and Arabia

During the Precambrian, this area was part of a huge continent that included part of Africa and consisted of a complex of igneous and metamorphic rocks. Northern India and part of north-west Arabia were covered by sea. Well-developed Cambrian deposits of limestone and other sedimentary layers found in the northern and eastern part of the Middle East (along the Zagros mountains, Palestine and central Iran) indicate local subsidence of part of the continent in the Palaeozoic era. The position of later deposits suggest that the Silurian was relatively quiet but during the Devonian considerable deposition of sediments took place when parts of the northern region, for example western Turkey and parts of Armenia and Iran, were folded.

Warping movements in the Asia Minor region during the Carboniferous age uplifted part of the northern area, giving rise to extensive low-lying land bordering the shallow sea and the formation of one of the world's largest cool basins. Further south, transgression of the sea followed down-warping over parts of the present north-west Syria, Iraq, Jordan, and north and central Arabia. The exact extension of the sea is not known. During the Permian further flooding occurred, most of the northern and eastern parts of south-west Asia were submerged under that great Tethys Sea (Fig. 6.1).

This geosyncline characterizes the northern, central and western parts of the Middle East for the major part of the Mesozoic from Triassic to middle Cretaceous times. A series of fold movements then affected southern Turkey and Iran in the north-western Zagros and in the upper Cretaceous the Gulf was further sloped by folding. In early Tertiary times the Tethys Sea still occupied most of the northern part of the area under discussion, while the southern part formed the extensive continental block, Gondwanaland. In the trough of the Tethys Sea, sedimentary material had accumulated in large amounts and limestone, chalk and sandstone were formed on an extensive scale. The large geosyncline had a basement of less resistant rock and when earth movements occurred during the Miocene orogeny compression and distortion resulted in the

214

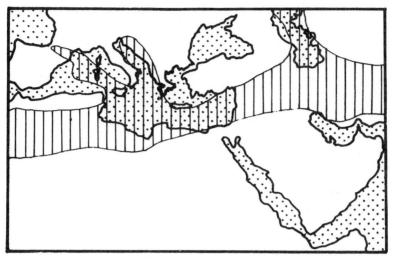

Fig. 6.1. Sketch of the Tethys Sea (vertically hatched) and Gondwanaland in early Permian times. Present seas are stippled. (After Schuchert, from Fisher, 1956.)

development of mountain chains. Zohary (1973) provides a summary of outstanding landforms, presently encountered in the Middle East.

(a) *The great crystalline Nubo-Arabian massif.* Mainly confined to south and south-west Arabia, southern Sinai and southern Palestine. 'It forms mostly a rugged mountainous landscape with no orderly tending ranges and no integral hydrographic system' (Zohary, 1973).

(b) *Volcanic landforms.* Areas covered with lava flows, basalt boulders, tuffs and alluvial basalt plains. In Arabia they may be overlying the crystalline massif. In Yemen, basalt reaches a thickness of 800–2000 m. Volcanic landforms are also found in south-west Syria, eastern Galilee and parts of Turkish Armenia.

(c) *Mountains of the folded zone.* Pontus, Taurus, Elbourz and Zagros are the most important formations, together with the mountains in the west (Syria, Lebanon and Palestine) near the Mediterranean.

(d) *Calcareous plateaus.* Well-developed in the steppe and desert areas and mostly forming the hammadas and desert pavements. They are perhaps the most widespread landform in the subregion, being found in Arabia, south Iraq, Sinai, Palestine, Syrian deserts and central Anatolian steppe.

(e) *Nubian Sandstone uplands.* Covering over half of the peninsula including the Rub'al Khāli and Great Nafud deserts. Southern Iraq, southern Sinai and Palestine are also included.

The shallow sands covering impermeable layers are particularly important for plant growth.

215

Description of arid ecosystems

(*f*) *Coastal plains*. Found in Arabia along the Red Sea (Tihamah) and locally along the Persian Gulf (Kuwait, southern Iraq); along the Mediterranean from the Jebel Liban to northern Sinai and along parts of the Turkish coast in south and west Anatolia.

(*g*) *Valleys and depressions*. Largest are the permanent valleys of the great rivers (Tigris, Euphrates, Jordan etc.), smallest are the local depressions and small wadis found all over the deserts. Because of their water accumulation they are important areas for plant growth.

Iran and Afghanistan

The four main distinct physiographic provinces of the country are (*a*) mountains, (*b*) plateau, (*c*) Khuzestan region and low-lying southern coastal plain, and (*d*) Caspian Sea coastal area. Of these four regions, the central plateau is the most important in relation to the arid zone.

The Zagros and Elburz mountain ranges enclose the large triangular area of central and east Iran. This area is the central plateau of Iran. Its own secondary ranges gradually slope down to become deserts, and extend into southern Afghanistan and Pakistan. The plateau is dissected and includes mountains and foothills, isolated hills, lake basins and several alluvial plains. Elevation ranges from 500 to 2500 m. The basins are surrounded and partly subdivided by mountain ranges from which large outwash fans and alluvial plains extend and grade into lake and playa deposits. The total area can be subdivided into four major geomorphological units (Dewan & Famousi, 1964):

(*a*) the high plateau of north-west central Iran, including the Urmia basin (1200–2500 m);
(*b*) the Isfahan–Sindabad basin (1000–1200 m);
(*c*) the salt-desert basin (Masileh–Kavir) (600–1000 m);
(*d*) the Lut desert basin (500–600 m).

India and Pakistan

Three broad geological regions can be recognized in the north-western part of the Indo-Pakistan subcontinent: the stable block of peninsular India; the young folded Himalaya with its continuing ranges to the east and west; the intervening Indo-Gangetic plain. All three regions are represented in the arid zone of the subcontinent. Eastern Rajasthan represents the peninsular block; the Sulaiman, Kirthar and Mekran ranges represent the young folded mountains and the Indus plain is representative of the third part of the division.

In the arid zone of the Indo-Pakistan subcontinent Archaean rocks occur

216

mostly in Rajasthan: Mesozoic rocks are exposed in a few patches in western Rajasthan and in the central axes of the Sulayman and Kirtha ranges, while Tertiary rocks are well exhibited in the mountain ranges of Baluchistan as well as being exposed in a few patches in Rajasthan near Jaisalmer. The entire Indus valley and a considerable part of western Rajasthan are covered with sub-recent and recent deposits.

The relief of the three geological regions is intimately related to the geological structure and to the long periods of base levelling, all regions have distinct land-forms. The youthful relief of the folded Baluchistan hills discloses a complicated picture of anticlines and synclines. The Indus Plain with flat and featureless agraded surfaces contrasts sharply both with the Baluchistan hills and with Western Rajasthan with its peneplained surfaces (Kaul, 1970).

Western Rajasthan

The Aravalli Range forms the north-western part of the stable block of the Deccan Peninsula. Its underlying geology is complex but most of western Rajasthan is covered by Quaternary formations, which have concealed the solid geology of this area. The aeolian deposits belong to Pleistocene and recent times. Wadia (1960) thinks that the sand in Rajasthan originated during post-glacial desiccation from the atmospheric weathering of rocky outcrops and the action of the south-west monsoons. The sand consists predominantly of quartz with grains of felspar and hornblende which are uniformly rounded by attrition. Western Rajasthan is mostly a sand- and alluvia-covered peneplain with infrequent local rocky outcrops. The most striking topographic feature is the Aravalli range which extends 640 km from the northern Gujerat plain north-eastward to Delhi. This range sharply defines the eastern limit of the arid and the semi-arid zone. The more humid conditions that prevail near the Aravalli mountains probably prevented the extension of aridity towards the east and the Ganges valley. Wherever there are gaps in this range, sand has advanced to the east of it.

Baluchistan

The desolate country of Baluchistan with its arid basins and hills forms the western part of the arid zone. The outer zone, bordering the Indus plain, is characterized by a succession of sharp anticlinal folds mostly composed of Eocene and Oligocene limestones, with sandy siwalik sediments in the intervening synclines and on the outer border. The middle zone is formed of highly folded sandstones, shales and clays in close-set, parallel ridges. The rocks of the middle zone are mostly of Oligocene age, often hard and resistant to erosion, the chief exception being the friable clay of the hills near the Makran coast. The inner (western) zone of Baluchistan is formed of ridges of various rocks, including volcanics, separated by desert basins. The Sulaiman and Kirthar ranges rise steeply from the Indus plain and clearly define the Baluchi hill country with steep slopes and great local relief, where level land is at a premium. The parallel mountain ranges of Baluchistan enclose valleys whose bottoms are covered with recent and sub-recent deposits of hill wash and alluvium derived from the adjoining ridges.

Indus plain

The plain is formed of Pleistocene and more recent alluvial deposits, which vary considerably with massive beds of both clay and sand, sometimes with calcareous concretions and silt. Blown sand occupies a considerable part of the Sind Sagar Doab and occurs also in a narrow belt along the foot of the Sulaiman and Kirthar ranges. These sand deposits are loessic in origin and were deposited for the most part after the Pleistocene. Empirically the Indus Plain can be divided into three sub-regions: the nearly flat land of the Indus Delta; plains predominantly formed of older alluvium; plains covered with loessic deposits.

The delta is formed of new alluvium and is characterized by numerous deserted channels whilst along the coast are abundant cracks and inlets. The greater part has long remained waste land with a few patches under cultivation. However, it is now being brought under large irrigation works. The second subregion of the Indus Plain includes alluvial plains along the valleys that are dunefree. Along the channels of the rivers there are narrow strips of floodplains which are subject to annual floodings. The third subregion of the Indus Plain, which coincides largely with the Sind Sagar Doab, is covered by a continuous spread of sand dunes. The sand of these dunes is probably derived to a large extent from the barren hills of Baluchistan and the river banks which are being continually renewed (Bharadwaj, 1961).

Climate

Global, regional and local factors all affect climatic conditions in south-west Asia. Local effects are mainly due to topographical features and the global and regional effects have been discussed by Bauer (1935) and Sutcliffe (1960). There is an extreme diversity, ranging from cold and cold temperate climate in the cold arid zone of India to tropical climate. Temperatures may range from below 0 °C to more than 50 °C and mean annual precipitation from 10 to 365 mm. In certain areas no precipitation at all may

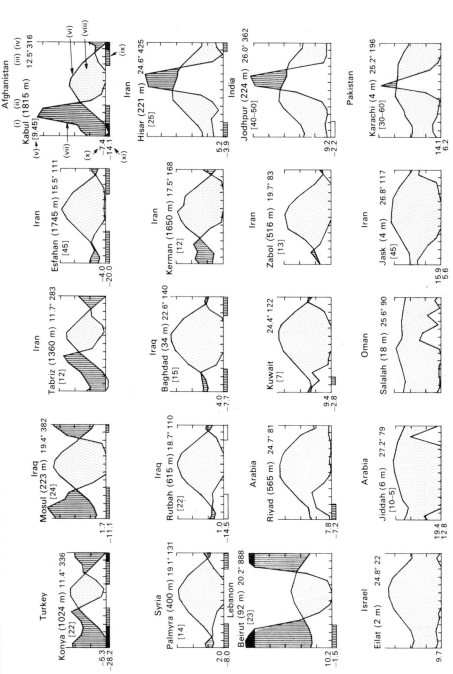

Fig. 6.2. Climate diagrams for representative stations in south-west Asia (for explanation see Kabul diagram): (i) Name of station; (ii) altitude (m); (iii) mean temperature (°C); (iv) mean annual precipitation (mm); (v) curve of mean monthly temperature; (vi) number of years of observation; (vii) curve of mean monthly precipitation; (viii) dry season; (ix) months with absolute daily minimum temperatures under 0 °C; (x) mean daily minimum temperature of *coldest* month; (xi) absolute minimum temperature. (After Walter & Leith, 1960.)

219

occur over several consecutive years. Available data from the areas with most extreme conditions are few as they are usually uninhabited. The climatic picture of the region is far from complete (Reitan & Green, 1967) and existing reviews are, with the exception of Israel and India, based on data from too few years and stations. The bioclimatic map of the Mediterranean produced by UNESCO–FAO (1963) and the study of Perrin de Brichambaut & Wallen (1963) on the agroclimatology of the arid zones of the Near East provide some detail of the desertic and sub-desertic regions. Zohary (1973) discussed the main climatic features of the individual countries of the region, excepting Afghanistan and Indo-Pakistan.

To include the topographical influences in a limited space, the following brief description is arranged almost country by country and illustrated by representative climadiagrams after Walter & Lieth (1960), presented in Fig. 6.2.

Turkey

The Syrian frontier, the plains of the Ourfa region and western Turkey have a hot, dry mediterranean climate. In most other areas of Turkey the climate is cold and often harsh with four to eight dry and cold months. On the heights overlooking the Black Sea, south-west of Ankara and the southerly slopes of Taurus and Kurdistan, there are not more than four cold and dry months. Ankara itself has only one month of frost, and east of Ankara the winter climate gradually becomes more severe in the cold, steppic zone of Turkey.

Israel, Jordan and Syria

From the Gaza area northwards, there is a belt of hot and dry mediterranean climate, more or less parallel with the coastline, but east of the coastal range and including Jerusalem, Damascus, Homs, Aleppo and Urga regions.

The desert boundary touches the coast on the south of the Sinai peninsula, passes close to the Mediterranean littoral, includes the Dead Sea and after passing close to the highlands of Hashemite Jordan runs northwards to a point south of Palmyra and then more or less along the 32nd parallel towards Iraq.

Between the boundaries of the desert and the mediterranean climates of the coast, a sub-desert climate with mediterranean bias is universal, extending to a sizeable area in Syria.

Arabian Peninsula

The Peninsula is one vast desert except for certain coastal areas and the mountain areas of the Yemen, Hadramaut and Hadjar (Oman).

In the east of the Peninsula, on the Hadjar uplands, the climate is hot and dry mediterranean.

A belt of attenuated sub-desert climate begins on the coast of the Red Sea in the Mastura neighbourhood, and then swings away from the coast to skirt the massifs of the Yemen and Hadramaut. The same pattern is found to the east of the Peninsula on the Hadjar uplands.

The main coastal climate of Arabia, except in the less arid Mecca region and in the extreme south-east, is accentuated sub-desert. On the southern coast of Arabia the climatic bias is markedly tropical and atmospheric humidity is high but the climate nevertheless remains accentuated sub-desert. On the coast itself summers are very dry but at higher altitudes dryness occurs mostly during the winter. The same type of climate prevails on the inland-facing slopes of all the massifs girdling the desert region and includes almost the whole of the peninsula. It reaches down to the coast at the northern end of the Red Sea and in the south-east on the Sea of Oman. The Nefud, the Dahna desert and the central basin are so arid as to rank as true deserts.

Iraq

The zone flanking the foothills in the north, the Mosul and Kirkuk regions and the Iranian frontier to the neighbourhood of Zorbatiya have a hot and dry mediterranean climate. The rest of the country is definitely arid with particularly high summer temperatures down-river from Mosul.

The climate along the middle course of the Tigris is mainly attenuated sub-desert, whereas accentuated sub-desert conditions prevail in the valley of the Euphrates and continue from the junction of the two rivers down to the coast of the Arabian Gulf. The boundary line of the desert climate cuts through Lake Khammar to the east and passes between the Tigris and Euphrates valleys. At Ad Diwaniy it crosses the Euphrates and then runs westwards roughly along the 32nd parallel. The presence of the rivers enables the extreme aridity of the climate to be countered by irrigation.

Iran

Inland, in the three great depressions (Dasht-I-Kavir to the north, the Dasht-I-Lut in the centre and the marshy Chil Kounar in the south), a desert climate prevails. The depressions are surrounded by regions of sub-desert climate with a mediterranean bias. In the north, under the Elburz range, the mediterranean area is a narrow belt but it broadens to the west and predominates in the south occupying all the eastern part of the country, running on into the arid regions of Afghanistan and Pakistan. On the highest ground, where winters are severe, the climate is cold sub-desert. The south coast, in contrast, is extremely hot with insignificant rainfall but the climate, due to very high atmospheric humidity, is accentuated sub-desert with a mediterranean bias.

Large areas have a hot and dry mediterranean climate. For example, the head of the Persian Gulf; the country around the mountain massifs of the west, south of the Elburz range, notably in the Teheran region; throughout the Mached and Kariz regions of the northeast on the Afghanistan frontier. In the mountain massifs of Iran there are a range of cold climates. In the vast massifs of the west, the climate, in general, is steppic with four to eight cold and dry months. This is a harsh climate in which only pastoralism is practicable but in the valleys between the ranges on the moderately high ground of north-west Iran and in the foothills around the Elburz, the climate is less extreme and plants will grow for eight months or more.

Afghanistan

Over most of the area the climate is arid. The hot and dry mediterranean climate prevails over most of the eastern part as well as at low altitudes along the frontiers with Iran and the USSR. Throughout the rest of the country the climates are arid owing to the length of the dry season in the hot lowlands, the cold season in the uplands, or the combination of severe winters and dry summers in a large part of the country.

In the Kandahar desert and the deserts on the Iranian and Pakistan frontiers, the dry season is 12 months long. Surrounding these deserts there is a broad belt of sub-desert climate with the mediterranean bias over all the low country to the west and south. Through the rest of the country cold climates prevail, usually cold sub-desert with over eight months of frost and dry weather but conditions are less severe in the areas bordering the USSR and Pakistan with from four to eight months dry and frosty.

Pakistan and India

West Pakistan and north-west India, with the exception of the high tablelands of Baluchistan and the Indo-Gangetic plains, about 150 km south of the Himalayas, are arid. In western Baluchistan the climate is mainly desert with mediterranean bias and forms one system with the deserts of Iran and Afghanistan where a desert climate with tropical bias predominates throughout the middle basin of the Indus.

In the west, the belts of sub-desert climate surrounding the deserts are of a mediterranean bias, attenuated in the relatively humid coastal areas and on the high tablelands and accentuated where they meet the desert climate in the low-lying warm areas of the south-west. The Thar desert area is surrounded by a vast zone of sub-desert climate with tropical bias, which also predominates in most of the Punjab, Rajasthan and the south coast. The aridity decreases from west to east, because of more abundant and better distributed rainfall.

The hot and dry mediterranean climate prevails in the central ranges of Baluchistan (Kalat Plateau) and the hills of the west of the Indus basin.

Hydrology

As for all arid zones, water is the most valuable resource in south-west Asia.

Water supply in the arid areas can come from three sources:

(*a*) rainfall directly occurring in the region;
(*b*) surface water flowing with rivers into the region;
(*c*) useable groundwater.

Arid areas by definition have a low rainfall, generally speaking so low that water is the limiting factor for the various life processes, ranging from mere survival to sustained high cropping. Surface water and groundwater, therefore, often play a decisive role in the determination of production capacity. It is interesting to note that, without the irrigation water derived from rivers supplied with water from catchment areas outside the actual arid region, in the mountains of Himalaya, Zagros etc., almost the whole region would have the appearance of one vast desert and steppe area. The water resources are briefly discussed for the subregions; Middle East, Arabian Peninsula, Iran–Afghanistan, and Indo-Pakistan.

Middle East

A comprehensive review of the water resources of the Middle East is given in Clawson, Landsberg & Alexander (1971). Important river systems are the Tigris and Euphrates with their tributaries and, to a minor extent, the Jordan, and further north, the Litani and Orontes. The twin rivers Tigris and Euphrates together drain a basin of over $784000\,km^2$. About half of it, $359000\,km^2$, lies in Iraq; $162000\,km^2$ in Turkey; $71000\,km^2$ in Syria; $146000\,km^2$ in western Iran and $46000\,km^2$ in Saudi Arabia. The last two figures refer to the Karun river basin and desert land, respectively.

The Euphrates flows from central Turkey via Syria to Iraq, where the river joins the Tigris at Qurna to form together the Shatt-al-Arab. About 40% of the drainage area above the plain is in Turkey and 15% in Syria.

Description of arid ecosystems

In Turkey, the water is collected in a mountainous area, in Syria in hills and plains, while the 45% drainage area in Iraq contributes only through wadis which discharge only a few days each year. Precipitation for the catchment areas is 400–1500 mm annually for the headwater area in Turkey, 150–400 mm for the middle reaches in Syria, and 120 mm for the lower reaches in Iraq. The Tigris also rises in Turkey. In contrast to the Euphrates, the river receives a high percentage of its water in Iraq from tributaries originating in the Zagros mountains: the Khabur (1418 km), Greater Zab (1180 km), Lesser Zab (1070 km), Adhaim (880 km) and Diyala (740 km) rivers. Development of the most efficient and economic use of the twin river water resources is of the utmost importance to Iraq, Turkey and Syria. Increased flood control, temporary storage of seasonal peak flow for later irrigation and division of water amongst the countries are of interest to them and have been the subject of many reports.

Arabian Peninsula

The vast Arabian continent, nearly as large as all of Western Europe, is an extremely arid area. Saudi Arabia covers the major part of the 3 million km^2 of the peninsula. Average annual precipitation for Saudi Arabia has been estimated at about 75–100 mm (Drouhin, Ambroggi & Kroon, 1963). In the states of the south-west, however, the amount is higher. Yemen for instance has sites with annual rainfall in the range from virtually 0 to 1000 mm. There are no perennial rivers but the continent is intersected by a system of wadis, often with an ill-defined beginning or end. Each of these wadis has its drainage area, sometimes covering thousands of square kilometers, but they contain water only rarely, often only a few days a year. Flow can be high for brief periods. In Wadi Hanifah near Riyad a discharge of 4.16×10^6 m^3 was measured over 24 hours with a peak of 1700 m^{3}s^{-1}. It is, therefore, possible to find areas flooded that are known as extremely arid. Only streams at the fringe of the continent reach the sea and then only occasionally (Fig. 6.3). All other water accumulated by run-off in wadis is transported to shallow basins where it evaporates quickly. A large amount also percolates to deeper layers. In the south-western part of the continent and in the mountainous region the higher precipitation can be stored in basins by dam construction. High evaporation, however, will be the limiting factor for economically justified storage.

Permeable outcrops make up an important part of the sedimentary deposits which cover two-thirds of Saudi Arabia. There is little seepage but aquifers are recharged over vast areas with considerable quantities of water. Fresh-water basins at greater depth also occur as a result of

224

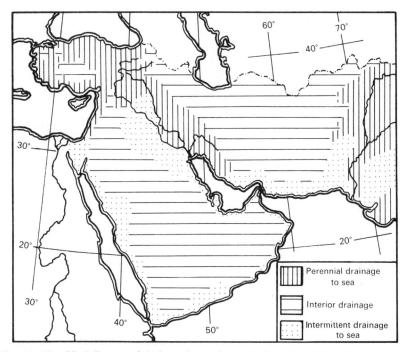

Fig. 6.3. Simplified diagram of drainage in south-west Asia (adapted from Cressey, 1960).

storage of water from similar processes during geological ages. Therefore two types of groundwater resources are available:

(a) shallow aquifers in areas of wadi alluvial deposits which have limited thickness. This source can only be tapped for domestic use or for stock watering;

(b) main aquifers of the lower part of the sediment. These are well distributed throughout the country and at depths that permit exploitation.

Water resources in this part of the world (both surface and groundwater) are limited and their potential use is restricted by the arid climate. Only domestic use, exploitation as stock watering points and very local irrigated agriculture seem possible.

Iran and Afghanistan

The 1.65×10^6 km² of Iran, with the exception of the Zagros and Elbrus mountain regions, receives a very low rainfall. The major part of the country receives less than 200 mm annually and a large part less than

225

Description of arid ecosystems

100 mm. Total precipitation has been estimated at between 3.0 and 4.0×10^{11} m^3 for the whole country (Gablot, 1963). Unlike its neighboring countries, Iran does not receive any major river from outside its territory. The northern slopes of the Elbrus which receive over 1000 mm of rainfall, drain to the Caspian Sea and most of the rain and snow that falls in the Zagros is drained to the Persian Gulf. The drainage of both Iran and Afghanistan is almost completely by interior basins (see Fig. 6.3). The only major river is the Karun in the west, which forms the Shatt-al-Arab basin together with the Tigris and Euphrates. In the extreme south a number of rivers drain a limited area to the Persian Gulf. Of the total precipitation mentioned above only an estimated 12–16% is transported by rivers, the remainder is lost in evaporation or by seepage. Water for irrigation is supplied by the few rivers and from wells, but in Iran thousands of hectares and hundreds of villages receive their water from underground infiltration tunnels (qanats or karez). They are found mainly in Iran and Afghanistan but also in other countries in the region. Cressey (1960) estimates that 20% of the water for the cropped area of Iran comes from these qanats.

India and Pakistan

Four distinct hydrological regions are recognized in the north-western arid zone of the Indo-Pakistan subcontinent, they are the Indus Plain, coastal tributaries, the Luni Basin and the Banas Basin.

The total Indus drainage area comprises over 0.85×10^6 km^2. Rivers of the Indus Plain are the Indus and its main tributaries Kabul, Jhelum, Chenab, Ravi and Stulej. They all flow in spring and early summer after monsoon-rainfall and snowmelting and have a peak discharge in July or August. Discharge in November to February may be as low as one-tenth of the peak value. About half the annual flow of the rivers on the Indus Plain is used for irrigation or lost by seepage and evaporation. Therefore, there is still scope for future surface-water development.

The Indus Plains (16.0×10^6 ha) form an extensive aquifer. Hydrological equilibrium in this aquifer, recharged from rivers and rainfall mainly in the north, was disturbed when large scale systematic irrigation started and an estimated 0.8×10^6 ha was affected by waterlogging and salinity. However, the majority of the area has groundwater suitable for direct application.

The Luni has its source in the Aravalli Range, its total length is nearly 805 km and the basin area is approximately 57000 km^2. As far as Balotra the water is fresh, but downstream it becomes more and more saline. The greatest peculiarity of the Luni in western Rajasthan is that it tends to increase its width rather than deepen the bed, because the floods develop

226

so rapidly and in such a short time that they have no time to scour the bed. The rainfall in the basin is non-uniform and erratic but the basin still provides the main drainage for the area.

In the Indian desert, groundwater occurs in appreciable amounts only in alluvial deposits, sand dunes, and the three youngest consolidated formations. Some water is also found along the joints and bedding plains in the Vindhya formation. The Indian desert and the Indus Basin are virtually cut off from the Ganga and the Punjab alluvial basin by the extension of the Aravalli Range. There is consequently no continuous groundwater basin extending from the Himalayan foothills to parts of Rajasthan or even to Multan. Moreover, the groundwater which spills over the Loharu–Shahpura ridge moves south-westwards into the Indus basin by passing the elevated tract of western Rajasthan (Auden, 1950).

Soils

Excepting Israel, arid-zone soils in the region have either not been studied at all or not in detail. From the scarce available information which is discussed in the following pages one tends to conclude that some soils differ from one another in only one or two particulars, others differ fundamentally in every respect and have no common characters. Relatively broad areas have similar soils; elsewhere there may be an intimate pattern of strongly contrasting soils.

The Middle East and the Arabian Peninsula

The soils of this sub-region have been studied mainly in the context of agricultural production and consequently there is little information on the steppe or desert soils. For reference the following studies can be mentioned: Turkey – Oakes (1957); Syria and Lebanon – Muir (1951) and Reifenberg (1953), Wolfart (1967); Jordan–Moormann (1959), Grüneberg (1965), Bender (1968); Iraq–Buringh (1960) and Altaie, Sys & Stoops (1969); Israel–Dan, Yaalon, Koyumdjisky & Raz (1962) and Ravikowitch (1967). Clawson, Landsberg & Alexander (1971) reviewing the agricultural potential of the Middle East produced a soil map for Syria, Lebanon, Israel, Jordan and Iraq, based on data provided by World Soil Geography Unit of the Soil Conservation Service, US Department of Agriculture. Their discussion of the soils is mainly for individual countries. Zohary (1973) brought together soils data from the area and discussed them in geo-botanical terms.

Zohary (1973) divided the soils into: (*a*) steppe and desert soils (including Sierozems, brown steppe soils, loess and loess-like soils, hammada, reg or desert pavements, saline soils, hydromorphic soils and sands) and

Fig. 6.4. Extensive flat, almost plantless stony plain, representative of large areas in the Middle Eastern deserts.

(*b*) forest soils (with Chestnut soils, Brown Forest soils, Terra Rossa, Rendzinas and alluvial soils). Clawson *et al.* (1971) use broadly the same groups and make a subdivision into about 100 mapping units.

Over half of the area under discussion is occupied by desert soils, comprising the hammadas, desert pavements, sands and saline soils. Most typical of the region are the first two groups. They appear in extensive flat or undulating gravelly plains, intersected by stream beds. They are plantless or bear a cover of very scattered low shrubs accompanied by annuals (Fig. 6.4) during the rainy season. The hammada is a desert substrate consisting of coarse boulder-like stones formed *in situ* on flat hill- and mountain-tops and slopes.

Regs or desert pavements are alluvial–colluvial desert areas consisting of non-residual soil material originally transported by wind and water from adjacent, more elevated sites. The hammada profile is barely differentiated. Stones or highly gypsiferous or saline clay may form the subsoil where soil moisture is extremely low. Regs have two easily distinguishable features; the mesas, remnants of former plateaus, and wadis, intersecting the flat areas, collecting the run-off water. The regs have usually been formed from alluvial fans situated at the outlet of watercourses that transport the material from the higher elevated areas. The fine particles are blown away and a compact pebble cover is formed under which profile

Fig. 6.5. Example of an inland saline depression (Boara salt-lake at the border of Iraq and Syria) where salt is being collected at the surface for commercial purposes.

development may take place. The desert areas under such stony covers are very common in northern Arabia, the Syrian desert and southern Palestine.

Sands may appear as sand dunes, sandy hammadas or sand flats. The most extensive formations are found in Arabia; both the large deserts, Rub'al Khāli and Great Nefud, are sand deserts. Dunes here cover some 30% of the total area and may reach a height of over 100 m. Other sand areas are in the interior of Palestine, locally in the Jezira in north-west Iraq and parallel to the Euphrates in the southern desert of that country. The sand has various origins; igneous rocks and Nubian sandstone being the most common. The sandy soil has been formed *in situ* or brought in by wind and water (including streams or sea currents). The sandy regions may have a number of micro-habitats, sometimes very suitable for plant growth because of the mulching effect of the upper layers over the deeper stored moisture. The mobility of the sand on the other hand is a disadvantage and only plants with very deep root systems can survive.

Saline soils occur in vast stretches, for example, the Mesopotamian Plain, as a result of poor irrigation practices applied to the land over thousands of years. Another group are the inland salinas in the Jezira Desert of Iraq and Syria (Fig. 6.5) and the hot-desert salinas in the coastal

229

belts of the Red Sea, the Arabian Sea, the Dead Sea region, etc. A distinction can be made between automorphic formations and hydro-morphic formations. The first group is formed as a result of local climatic conditions combined with the lithological constitution of the substratum. Examples are the Lower Jordan Valley, the Dead Sea basin and the halomorphic hammadas in the extreme deserts. The second group, the hydromorphic formations owe their salinity to intensive evaporation and the deposition of a salt layer on or near the soil surface. The saline soils vary widely in their physico-chemical composition, but soluble salts are mostly chlorides of sodium, calcium and magnesium and sodium sulphate. They are grouped as solonchaks that may be further differentiated in various types as Buringh (1960) did for Iraq.

Sierozens, brown soils and loess-like soils occupy vast stretches of the steppes. They generally bear a rich plant-cover under grazing or marginal dry farming. Sierozems, a group of grey to greyish-brown soils, vary greatly in depth, texture and content of organic matter, depending on topography, lithology, etc. They are usually found between the 200 and 300 mm isohyet in Syria and Iraq and are covered with dwarf shrub formations (*Artemisia herba-alba*). Agriculture is unstable and dependent upon the annual precipitation.

Brown steppe soils are formed under more favourable conditions (250 to 350 mm isohyets) but are very simlar to the Sierozems. The surface layers are brownish clays usually highly calcareous with limestone par-ticles and pebbles. They are widespread in Anatolia, in the Jezira and Mosul–Kirkuk region of Iraq and have been reported from the north-western fringe of the Syrian Desert. The natural vegetation in Anatolia is either the dwarf-shrub steppe (*Artemisia* spp. and *Astragalus* spp.) or the forest steppe with scattered trees (*Quercus* spp., *Crataegus* spp.). Dry-land farming and orchards are widespread on this soil.

Loess and loess-like soils have been transported by wind from more extreme deserts and deposited in plains and inter-mountain valleys. A fine-grained soil, of clay to silt texture with fine sand, is laid down almost without profile differentiation but with a relatively high fertility for the steppe region. These soils are found in the Sinai, Palestine, north-eastern Syria and near the foothills of Iraq.

Forest soils (Zohary, 1973) have developed under more humid condi-tions. Generally speaking they are found in areas with climatic conditions ranging from humid to semi-arid. They fall outside the scope of an arid lands review.

Chestnut soils have developed in parts of Turkey and the Kurdistan mountains of Iraq under high precipitation on slopes and in valleys. They have a high production potential and usually consist of a greyish granular surface, a brownish subsoil and stony calcareous lower horizons. *Quercus* spp. and *Pinus* spp. are the natural vegetation.

Fig. 6.6. Gully erosion and salinisation of the exposed underlying soil layers. The last stages of land degradation through mismanagement.

Brown Forest soils are commonly found under deciduous and coniferous forest in Turkey, Northern Kurdistan and the high ranges of Mount Lebanon. They have developed at high altitudes (1200–2200 m) under warm humid to sub-humid conditions. Cutting of the forests has largely reduced this soil-type.

Terra Rossa is most characteristic for the Mediterranean territory of Palestine, Lebanon, Syria and Turkey. The soils, derived from limestone mainly, have an *A–C* profile and bear a vegetation of various types of sclerophyllous evergreen maquis, more or less degraded.

Rendzina soils have a humiferous, shallow upper layer and the usually calcareous surface horizon is often dark coloured in contrast to its parent rock. They may be formed under a range of climatic conditions from sub-humid to semi-arid and are often derived from soft limestone, surface crusts, chalks etc. The natural vegetation in the region (Palestine, Lebanon, Syria and Turkey) is *Pinus halepensis*, *Pinus brutia* and Mediterranean maquis, but as a rule this cover has been destroyed to enable cultivation to take place.

Alluvial soils are fine-textured, often transported, soils which fill up plains, depressions and valleys. There is a steady influx of new matter and no clear horizons are formed. As a result the vegetation is usually similar to that on the parent material. They can be deep and are excellent for cropping if sufficient water is provided.

Description of arid ecosystems

The factors affecting productivity of the soils suitable for cropping in the region are:

(a) the soils are relatively well supplied with nutrients, except nitrogen, reflecting the low organic matter content in the arid areas. Phosphorus may not always be adequate for sustained high crop production, but potassium is as a rule found in ample amounts.

(b) excess limestone, nearly always 'over' supplies calcium and magnesium;

(c) gypsum, widely present in the subsoil, dissolves when the soils are put under irrigated agriculture leading to an uneven surface topography and difficulties in even application of water.

(d) many soils have poor physical characteristics. The high percentage of clay-size particles produces heavy soils, sticky and difficult to work when wet, deeply cracking when dry. Over large areas the soil-layer is shallow. Insufficient soil conservation practices allow erosion to take place on a large scale until the underlying rock is exposed (Fig. 6.6).

(e) generally speaking it is not the soil resource itself that is the limiting factor for higher production but the combination of the harsh arid environment and man's poor management practices.

Iran and Afghanistan

Soils of Iran have been classified and described by Dewan & Famousi (1964), while for soils of the arid zones of Afghanistan the publication of Saxena (1962) gives some information. Based mainly on this work, a brief account is presented on the soil associations in the arid and semi-arid zones of this sub-region, including their most important characteristics and their potential use.

Desert and red desert soils are formed through severe moisture deficiency. The soil is calcareous throughout and usually has a calcium carbonate zone close to the surface. The soil reaction is always alkaline and there is often accumulation of soluble salts in the profile. The soils are well drained and do not contain any humus. In their natural condition, they have a low productivity but with irrigation they can be highly productive.

Sierozems have been mapped in Iran on nearly level to moderately sloping areas. In several areas these soils occur in association with desert soils forming an intricate pattern with them. Texturally, they range from coarse to fine. Lime accumulation is normally close to the surface, though the whole profile is calcareous and pH varies around 8. The organic matter does not usually accumulate and is almost always below 0.5%. Drainage is slow from the surface and moderate internally. The substratum is permanently dry. Under natural conditions these soils have fair pasture production and low returns from barley and wheat. Excellent yields of a variety of crops can be expected under irrigation with the application of nitrogen and phosphorus.

Brown steppe soils are probably the predominant soils in Iran. These are brown to light brown, nearly neutral soils usually overlying a calcareous horizon. Generally they have a medium to fine texture, but all textural variations are found. In general, the sub-surface is of finer texture than surface horizons, but this also varies, depending upon the parent material. Permeability is often medium to low. Organic matter in the surface (10–20 cm) varies from 1% to 2%. Depth to the zone of lime concentration varies from 30 to 100 cm depending upon the region and the texture of the layer; pH varies from 7.4 to 8.4. The soils usually have medium to good natural drainage. On nearly level and on sloping lands the brown steppe soils are often under pasture, under rainfed moisture they provide moderate crop yields of barley and wheat. Under irrigation and fertilization these soils give very high yields of fruit, vegetables, cotton, sugar beets and wheat.

Chestnut soils are normally found on steep slopes or in rolling, hilly or mountainous areas. They are usually medium to heavy textured on the surface as well as in the subsoil and are moderately to well drained. The surface layer (10–15 cm) has high organic matter, while at greater depths (30–60 cm) there is adequate organic matter usually 3–4%. The topsoil is neutral to slightly alkaline. Lime accumulates at a depth of 50–150 cm and the percentage may vary considerably.

Desert soils (regosols) are common, especially in Dasht-i-lut, Kerman, Baluchistan and Seistan. Normally they are shallow to very shallow and light- to coarse-textured. Lime accumulation is generally close to the surface. The entire profile is usually calcareous, pH varies around 8, and organic matter is low. Under irrigation (qanats) good growth of horticultural crops is obtainable.

Sand dunes cover large areas of the plateau (Dasht-i-lut) and also the Kerman–Esfahan area in association with desert soils. Sometimes these soils are used to provide very poor ranges.

Desert soils – sierozem–solonchak soil associations cover large areas in the Great Salt Desert (Dasht-i-Kavir) or the Seistan Plain in south-eastern Iran. The soils in this association vary from shallow to deep, and from light- or coarse-textured to heavy-textured. Apart from the characteristics of desert and sierozem soils, extreme salinity of the surface and/or subsoil occurs. This salinity may be due to saline waters passing over the desert soils. The source of saline waters could be one of the saliferous and gypsiferous formations. The soils have moderate to slow internal drainage and moderate external drainage and include wastelands or poor range vegetation.

Description of arid ecosystems

Sierozem–regosol soils differ from desert soils in that they have slightly better moisture status. They occur fairly extensively in several desertic parts of the plateau of Iran. The soils belonging to this soil association are shallow to deep with varying degree of colluvium or sandy, wind-borne material on the surface. The textures of surface or sub-surface varies from coarse to medium-fine. Normally, these soils are very calcareous, have a pH of surface and sub-surface around 8 and are slightly saline. Drainage is good to excessive. They are used as poor rangelands but under irrigation orchard crops can be grown.

Brown soil–lithosol associations occupy about 6% of the total area of the country. These soils may vary from very shallow to moderately deep and occur on undulating to strongly sloping relief. Drainage varies from good to excessive. These are normally suited for poor to moderate range. In parts with favourable relief, crops such as wheat and orchards are grown under irrigation (from qanats or springs).

Highly saline desert soils – solonchaks occupy large areas in central, eastern and southern Iran. They are essentially wastelands, and are hardly used for grazing. In most cases these areas will remain wastelands, except in some localities where irrigation waters may produce low to medium yields of some crops such as barley, or fruit crops such as figs, and where drainage proves to be possible and economically feasible. In most cases it would be undesirable or uneconomical to reclaim them for crop-land.

Solonchaks, salt-marshes and mountainous land on saliferous and gypsiferous material are soils which have practically no agricultural value. They occur in large areas of central Iran, and many other parts of south and south-eastern Iran, including many of the deltaic districts where rivers like the Karkheh or the Karun form marshes near the sea. The Great Salt Desert and the highly saline soils occurring in several parts of Iran are included in this group. They are very seldom used for grazing. Generally these areas will remain wastelands.

India and Pakistan

The soils of western Rajasthan in the west and north-west of the Aravalli Ranges have been broadly classified as desert soils (Indian Council of Agricultural Research, 1953; Yadav, 1966). Wadia (1960) considers these soils as belonging to the whole complex of Indo-Gangetic alluvium extending from Assam to Sind. Later aeolian action and physical weathering of rock masses in the arid environment has given rise to deposition of sand dunes and sand sheets in the west and north-west of this subregion. Abichandani & Roy (1966) divide the Rajasthan desert into four physiographic regions (a) the sand dune and sand sheet deposits in the west and north-west bordering west Pakistan; (b) the comparatively dune-free area with rocky outcrops of Barmer Jaisalmer and Bikaner tract; (c) the rocky outcrops of Jalore Siwana, Nagour Mewar, Jodhpur, Phalodi and Bikaner, and (d) the central Luni and Jawai basins comprising old alluvial deposits of past river streams.

The soils of western Rajasthan can, by and large, be classified as sandy and of low fertility. They improve in fertility towards the east and north-east. In some parts the soils are saline and alkaline with unfavourable physical conditions and high pH values. The flat plains in the east and south-east of the sand dune deposits (see above) and large inter-dune areas are covered by aggraded alluvial deposits, mostly of coarse to medium texture. Physical weathering has predominated in the soil formation of this part of the arid zone of Indo-Pakistan.

Gupta (1968) examined a large number of soils from desert areas of western Rajasthan namely Jodhpur (Biae-ki-Bacri), Shergarh, Barmer, the Luni river, Jaswantpura, Mundar, Jaipur (grass farm), Calta, Bikaner (Philibagan), Bikaner (Suratgarh), Jaisalmer, Akoria Mosa, Bahakasar and Cutch Desert. He observed that in most of the aeolian sands the depth of sand deposits decreases from the west to the east, while the calcium oxide content of these deposits varies from 1.0% to 1.5%. In the case of sand dune deposits in the stabilized sandy areas, calcium oxide content is less. Over large parts of the sandy plains (as at Jodhpur) it is seen that calcium oxide content increases with depth and lime accumulates, resulting in the formation of Kankar pans of different degrees of indura-tion. This would suggest that the soils on the sandy plain and aggraded alluvial deposits have developed under alternate dry and wet conditions, the rain water during the wet spells having had sufficient time to leach the lime from the top layers down into the subsoil. The lime content in the subsoil at many places is more than ten times that in the topsoil. The phosphate content of the aeolian sand deposits and the aggraded alluvial deposits of this arid region compare favourably with those of some other alluvial soils. In most of the desert soils, phosphorus ranges from 0.22% to 0.04%. Nitrogen content is low, mostly ranging between 0.02% and 0.07%. This deficiency is, however, made up to a certain extent by the presence of fair amounts of nitrogen in the form of nitrates. Therefore these desert soils are reasonably fertile for agricultural crops and other plants when moisture is not deficient. Abichandani (1964) observed that pH of the desert soils and of the desert sands varies between 7.2 and 9.2, with the majority falling within the range 8.1–8.8 and that the carbon:nitrogen ratio of these soils generally ranges from 10:1 to 14:1. The salt content of the desert soil reaches toxic limits only at a few low-lying locations. Clay content generally varies from 2.5% to 8% except in low-lying locations where it may be 15% and more.

Jaya & Satyanarayan (1959) have studied the water-soluble boron contents of a few representative virgin soil profiles from Barmer, Cadra Road, Bandoar and Jaisalmer regions in western Rajasthan receiving less than 125 mm of rainfall, and from Pokaren Rann, Jodhpur, Mandore, Beriganga and Kailanz in central Rajasthan with rainfall above 250 mm. Texturally all the soils were coarse sands with pH varying between 7.9 and 8.6. The soluble salt content varied between 0.05% and 0.25% in the subsoil strata at low lying locations, as seen at Kailana. The water-soluble boron content of these soils was fairly high varying between 2.6 and 12.2 ppm. According to these authors, the surface and sub-surface soils of west Rajasthan contain, on average, 2.5 and 3.4 ppm of boron respectively.

The Bellary district in south India has black and red soils occurring side by side. Black cotton soils are alkaline (pH 8.7–9.5) and heavy-textured (clay 58%–65%), the soil depth varies from 45 cm to 120 cm underlain by impermeable murrum layers. The water-holding capacity of these soils is 60–65%, the infiltration capacity is poor (11 mm h^{-1}) and the soils have high base-exchange capacity. The nitrogen and phosphorus contents are low. The soils develop deep cracks during summer. Red soils show neutral reaction (pH 6.7–7.2) and are sandy loam in texture, with low water-holding capacity, high infiltration rate and low base-exchange capacity. The red soils are also low in nitrogen and phosphorus.

The soils of Pakistan are predominantly of alluvial origin with good permeability and fertility. In the arid zone in the Thal and Thar-Parkar areas, the soils belong to the Red and Grey desert and Sierozem great soil groups. The soils are calcareous, having excess of lime and other bases, and are generally characterized by a high mineral and low organic matter content. In some areas appreciable quantities of sodium salts are also present in the soil.

The soil characteristics of the cold arid zone have not been studied in any great detail.

Vegetation

A synthesis of the vegetation cover of south-west Asia has been part of the UNESCO–FAO project for the preparation of a 1:5000000 vegetation map of the Mediterranean Zone (UNESCO–FAO, 1969). No better basis can be used for the present account than the result of their effort. In Fig. 6.7 an attempt has been made to provide a generalized version of the map, which may give an overall view of mainly the physiognomic character of the south-west Asian arid-zone vegetation. The following account, presented by sub regions, attempts to provide additional information to that found in the map.

Arabian Peninsula

The vegetation of this vast arid area has been studied less than all other areas of south-west Asia under discussion. Some specific area studies are those of Vesey-Fitzgerald (1955, 1957a, b) and Popov & Zeller (1963). General compilations which include part of this area include McGinnies (1967), UNESCO–FAO (1969) and Zohary (1973).

Phytogeographically this area falls under two regions: the Sudanian and the Sahara–Arabian. Zohary (1973) gives the characteristic species for the two provinces of the Sudanian region, the Eritreo-Arabian and the Nubo-Sindian, represented in Arabia. The former is found in the south-western parts only, while the Nubo-Sindian province is less restricted and found along the coastal belts. The Eritreo-Arabian formations are similar to the areas of mountainous East Africa. The mountains show a distinct zoned vegetation with Afro-Alpine vegetation in the highest ranges (2500 to over 3000 m), composed, among others of *Rubus petitianus*, *Rosa abyssinica*, *Alchemilla cryptantha*, *Senecio* spp. and *Helichrysum abyssinicum* forming an open dwarf-shrub formation with many grasses and herbs in between. At lower elevations, montane forest types are encountered with *Juniperus procera*, and the woody herb *Euryops arabicus*, from 3000 to 2000 m, and evergreen forest or scrub a few hundred metres lower, dominated by such species as *Olea chrysophylla*, and *Tarchonanthus camphoratus*. *Acacia–Commiphora* bush formations (*Acacia asak*, *A. ethaica*, *A. senegal*, *A. flava*, *Commiphora schimperi*, *C. myrrha*) may be encountered between 500 and 1500 m, *Acacia nubica* and *Commiphora opobalsamum* may be encountered below 500 m. This formation can be regarded as the limit between forest, bush and savannah formations of the Eritreo-Arabian province and the pseudo-savannah and dwarf-shrub deserts in the Nubo-Sindian province, although no sharp boundary can be given. Much of the primary vegetation has been destroyed by over-exploitation.

In the lower ranges, on spurs and the gravel of eroded plains, 'orchard-like' bush formations are found with *Acacia ehrenbergia* in the valleys with tussocks of *Panicum turgidum*. In favoured places a stratified monsoon woodland may occur with *Acacia* spp., *Dobera glabra*, *Delonix elata* and *Hyphaene thebaica* in the upper storeys and shrubby species such as *Gymnosporia senegalensis* and *Anisotes trisulcus* in the second layer. Along wadis tall trees (*Tamarindus indica*, *Zizyphus spina-christi*) are found (Vesey-Fitzgerald, 1955).

Zohary (1973) quoting reports of FAO Expeditions, lists a number of communities from selected areas. Popov & Zeller (1963) reporting on southern Hijaz, Asir and Rub' al Khāli, mention a sparse vegetation even in parts of the Rub' al Khāli, where *Calligonum comosum* may be found

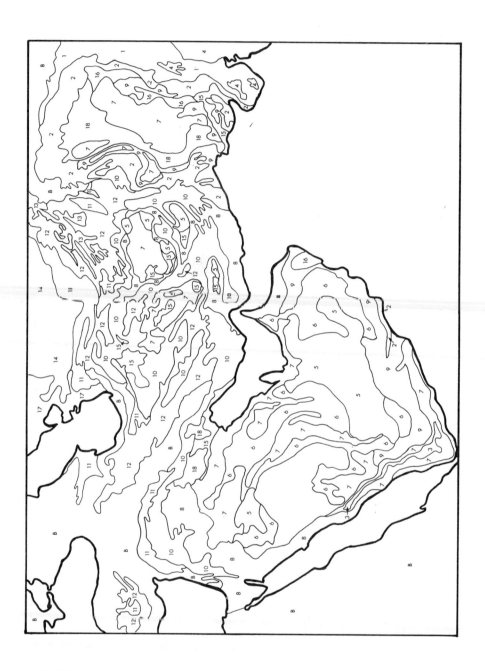

238

in the deep sands, together with the genera *Aristida*, *Tribulus* and *Fagonia*. On the plains, which are often saline, most of the vegetation belongs to the well-known halophytic genera *Haloxylon*, *Salsola*, *Seidlitzia* and *Suaeda*. In the wadis *Acacia seyal* and *A. tortilis* can be seen. The same authors have listed a number of plant communities of certain sites from an area approximately 25° to 28° N, 40° to 45° E. Many of the dominant species of these lists are the same, including *Haloxylon salicornicum*, *Zygophyllum coccineum*, *Rhanterium epapposum*, *Calligonum comosum*, *Helianthemum lippii*, the grass *Panicum turgidum* and herbs such as *Plantago* spp. and *Neurada procumbens*. Zohary concludes, 'the above-mentioned species are fairly common from the coastal belt of Aden in the south to the surroundings of Kuwait, whence it continues to the Southern Desert of Iraq and eastward to southern Iran, Baluchistan and Sind'. The same author points out that communities grouped under the Sahara–Arabian territory cover large areas, but are found in three main habitats: hammada and gravel deserts; sand flats and sand dune areas; saline areas, mostly found in undrained depressions, in oases and in the wadi outlets along the coast. Vesey-Fitzgerald's description (1957*b*), though qualitative, is the best source for vegetation data for the central and northern part of Arabia for which the habitats were classified by Zohary (1973). Six units have been mapped and described as the result of a vegetation survey of this vast area.

Fig. 6.7. Vegetation map of south-west Asia. (Generalised from UNESCO–FAO Vegetation Map of the Mediterranean Zone, 1969.)

I Mainly climatically determined formations
  A *Tropical and subtropical climates*
    1. Open dry forest
    2. Mountain thorny scrub and thorny subtropical pseudosteppe
    3. Upland and mountain savannah–woodland
    4. Dense dry forest
  B *Accentuated subdesert and hot desert, warm temperate and temperate climates*
    5. No vegetation or sparse ephemerophytes with few shrubs
    6. Ephemerophyte-dominated formations with shrubs in depressions
    7. Subdesert perennial steppe formations
    8. Mediterranean biased perennial (mainly shrub-) formations
    9. Tropical biased shrub and bush formations
  C *Mediterranean and attenuated subdesert climates*
    10. Arbuscular shrub pseudosteppe
    11. High steppe with or without trees or shrubs
  D *Cold climates with dry temperate summers*
    12. Plateau and submountain (tree-) steppes
    13. High mountain steppe and grassland
  E *Warm-summer, cold and cold temperate subdesert and desert climates*
    14. Steppe and desert formations on sand
II Edaphic formations
    15. Inland or coastal halophytic formations
    16. Formations of extensive dunes and sandy soils
    17. Formations on alkaline soils
III Introduced or transformed formations
    18. Vegetation transformed through longtime irrigation

Description of arid ecosystems

(a) Vegetation of the deep sands in the Great Nefud, Dahana crescent and Rub' al Khāli. Dominant perennial species are *Calligonum comosum* (greatly reduced locally by firewood gathering), *Artemisia monosperma*, *Monsonia nivea*, *Scrophularia deserti* and the grass *Panicum turgidum*. There are also a number of annual herbs and grasses, for example *Neurada procumbens*, *Aristida* spp., *Plantago* spp. and *Rumex pictus*. Large areas are bare, but depending on the amount of rain and local soil moisture conditions more abundant herbage can be seen around depressions and at the base of dunes.

(b) *Rhanterium epapposum* steppe, dominates the vegetation from about 30° to 25° N and is characteristic for gravel plains (locally overblown by a shallow sand layer) and places with more relief on slopes and in gullies. Other perennial shrubs are almost always absent, but herbage (mainly annual) may be abundant, including *Medicago aschersoniae*, *Plantago albicans*, *Neurada procumbens* and the grass *Aristida plumosa*. *Rhanterium* sp., together with *Haloxylon salicornicum* are the most common species of the sparse shrub vegetation of Kuwait (Kernick, 1966).

(c) Areas covered with the annual grass *Stipa tortilis* (= *S. capensis*) either below scattered shrublets or at places without perennial species. Vesey-Fitzgerald (1957b) mapped this unit, which also occurs mixed with *Rhanterium* sp. steppe, approximately in an extended triangle between Hofuf, Jauf and the southern border of Iraq and Kuwait. The characteristic habitat of the unit is a stony plain of grit and gravel, in shallow basins covered with a silty soil accumulated through run-off and wind erosion. For selected localities a variety of shrubs and woody herbs may be encountered, for example the aromatic Compositae *Artemisia herba-alba* and *Achillea fragrantissima*, in runnels leading to the pans *Anvillea garcini*, *Haloxylon salicornicum* and *Zizyphus nummularia* are frequently found. In sandy areas there are transitions to *Rhanterium* sp. with a variety of herbs. *Stipa* is then replaced by other grasses: *Aristida plumosa*, *Schismus barbatus*, *Cymbopogon schoenanthus* and *Chrysopogon aucheri*.

(d) Vesey-Fitzgerald (1957b) describes the vegetation of main drainage lines and 'sump' areas, which have a more differentiated vegetation due to variation in edaphic factors and, more important, better moisture conditions. Some characteristic perennials of the drainage channels are *Teucrium rigidum*, *T. polium*, *Zilla spinosa*, *Anvillea garcini*, *Astragalus* spp. and the grasses *Aristida* spp. and *Cymbopogon schoenanthus*. Annual species are numerous, including species of the genera *Trigonella*, *Medicago*, *Centaurea*, *Arnebia*, *Malva* and the grasses *Stipa* and *Phalaris*. Drought can inhibit growth of grasses and herbs for several years in certain areas. Such places may be covered only by valley saltbush associations, often Chenopodiaceae. Locally abundant and often differentiated by the degree of salinity, are *Haloxylon salicornicum*, *Agathophora alopecuroides*, *Anabasis* spp., *Seidlitzia rosmarinus* and *Atriplex* spp. At transitions of windswept salt pans to more sandy areas *Ephedra alata* is found with *Haloxylon persicum* (possibly *H. ammodendron*) on the sands.

(*e*) The associations described for the coastal area between the Dahana sand belt and the Persian Gulf, from Iraq to Abu Dhabi include the same species as quoted above from Zohary for the area from Aden to Kuwait. In addition saline depressions may have a peripheral zone with *Suaeda baccata* and *Bienertia cycloptera*, while shrubby *Tamarix* spp. can be seen on the mounds.

(*f*) The final unit is the coastal salt-bush associations along the Persian Gulf, the vegetation of a usually level and sandy beach. *Juncus maritimus* beds and cushions of the grass *Aeluropus lagopoides* are found north of 26°N with *Cressa cretica* on flats. Date palms (*Phoenix* spp.) form the conspicuous tree component. Stony and sandy areas bear the species mentioned already from Zohary's account, in saline environments mostly Chenopodiaceae and Zygophyllaceae. *Seidlitzia rosmarinus* and *Zygophyllum coccineum* and *Salsola* spp. are common together with patches of the grass *Panicum turgidum*.

Zohary (1973) thinks that areas of Vesey-Fitzgerald's *Stipa tortilis* steppe are the same or to a large extent similar to the associations of the Anabasetea known from adjacent countries. From the above account it can be noted that in the large and varied region of Arabia a considerable repetition of species and communities is found, as determined by the various habitat conditions. Topography, drainage, soil and the usually related degree of salinity become the major factors in an area where climatic conditions are more or less similar over extensive areas. Man and his livestock have reduced differences especially over the last decades since formerly inaccessible areas have been opened with the help of modern technology. Exploration for oil fields effects the exploitation of the vegetation cover through such factors as newly developed water sources used by the bedouins with their flocks. Studies of vegetation recovery in exclosures or at remote places may reveal the potential climax vegetation of certain habitats.

Middle East

Without any natural boundary conditions, the Arabian Desert extends across the border of Saudi Arabia into Iraq, Palestine, and with gradual changes, further into Syria. Of the four countries, the Palestinian area in particular has been thoroughly studied, but the other countries are also

241

well explored, especially floristically. More detailed vegetation descriptions have appeared over the last quarter of a century. Bibliographies are found in Zohary (1973), Kreeb (1961), Hadac (1966), Guest (1966) and McGinnies (1967). A first analysis of the vegetation of the central desert region, the Syrian Desert, was given by Zohary (1940), while the last compilation of knowledge on geobotanical aspects of the Middle East by the same author (Zohary, 1973), is the best up-to-date source of information for the present purpose. For general descriptive information on the vegetation of the individual countries the following authors may be mentioned: Iraq – Handel-Mazzetti (1914), Zohary (1946), Springfield (1954), Guest (1966), Al-Ani *et al.* (1970); Syria – Zohary (1940), Pabot (1955), Rodin (1959); Palestine – Eig (1946), Zohary (1947, 1962), Zohary & Orshan (1949), Zohary & Fienbrun (1951), Fienbrun & Zohary (1955). The countries are briefly discussed below based on data from the above references and personal observations.

Iraq

Excepting the mountainous area in the North, arid and semi-arid conditions are found all over the country. Iraq is usually divided in five physiographic regions: Zagros mountains, foothills, Lower Mesopotamian Plain, Jezira and Southern and Western Desert. The last three have an average annual rainfall below 200 mm, while the foothills area is a transition zone between desert on one side of the mountains and irrigated plains on the other, where more than 1000 mm annual rainfall has been recorded. Phytogeographically the following elements have been distinguished in the flora: (*a*) Saharo-Arabian, mainly in the Southern Desert, Western Desert and Mesopotamian Plain, (*b*) Irano-Truranian in the Iraqi Jezira and Foothills area, (*c*) Mediterranean (16% of the species according to Zohary), in the arid area mainly segetal and ruderal plants but further north some trees, shrubs and sub-alpine plants, (*d*) Sudanian, as a penetration area in the south-eastern corner (Zohary, 1973). On the Mesopotamian plain a vast area in the south is occupied by marshlands and lakes. Dominant species are *Phragmites communis* and *Typha angustata*, which are both used by the marsh Arabs and others for making mats and building houses. In the shallow lakes, floating *Salvinia natans* and *Nymphoides indica* form local colonies, while *Potamogeton* spp. are also found in deeper water. Along the shores *Juncus* spp. (*J. maritimus* and *J. acutus*) and *Cyperus rotundus* are found.

On the cultivated lands of the Plain a variety of weeds are found, most of them annual species (Springfield, 1954; and Zohary, 1946). Of the perennials *Prosopis farcta* and *Alhagi maurorum* are common all over the country. Although spiny and difficult to handle, both the species are of

Table 6.1. *Perennial cover types of Southern and Western Deserts of Iraq, as related to land form and soil type.* (After Al-Ani *et al.*, 1970)

Land form	Soil type	Range-cover type
	Western Desert	
Plain	Sandy	*Haloxylon salicornicum,* *Artemisia herba-alba*
	Fine, gravelly	*Haloxylon salicornicum,* *Ephedra alata*
	Fine, gravelly with slightly saline substratum	*Haloxylon salicornicum,* *Zygophyllum coccineum*
Wadi	Silty	*Artemisia herba-alba,* *Haloxylon articulatum*
	Sandy, sandy gravel	*Haloxylon salicornicum,* *Artemisia herba-alba*
	Saline, silty	*Halocnemum strobilaceum,* *Nitraria retusa*
Stone pavement (*hammada*)	In pockets where sand has accumulated	*Haloxylon salicornicum,* *Artemisia herba-alba*
Dunes	Sand	*Haloxylon ammodendron,* *Calligonum comosum*
	Southern Desert	
Plain	Sandy	*Rhanterium epapposum,* *Haloxylon salicornicum*
	Fine, gravelly	*Haloxylon salicornicum,* *Ephedra alata*
	Fine, gravelly with slightly saline substratum	*Zygophyllum coccineum,* *Cyperus conglomeratus*
Wadi	Silty	*Achillea fragrantissima,* *Anvillea garcini*
	Sandy, sandy gravel	*Anvillea garcini,* *Artemisia herba-alba*
	Saline, silty	*Halocnemum strobilaceum*
Stone pavement (*hammada*)	In pockets where sand has accumulated	*Haloxylon salicornicum,* *Artemisia herba-alba*
Dunes	Sand	*Haloxylon ammodendron,* *Panicum turgidum*

value as a source of fodder for the livestock, especially camels. A third species *Glycirrhiza glabra* is locally common especially in the north.

Over large areas agriculture in the Plain suffers from salinization, mainly as a result of thousands of years of flooding and (over)irrigation. The grass *Aeluropus* spp. and several Chenopodiaceae are common on these saline areas, for example *Cressa cretica, Aeluropus littoralis, Suaeda baccata, Salsola* spp., *Nitraria retusa, Seidlitzia rosmarinus* and *Halocnemum strobilaceum*. Al-Ani *et al.* (1970) tentatively recognized and described perennial covertypes of the Southern and Western Deserts of Iraq as related to land form and soil type (Table 6.1). This account, together with floristic descriptions by Guest (1966) and phytogeographical descriptions

243

of Zohary (1973) give an indication of the present and potential vegetation-cover of the Iraqi deserts. Two shrub species, *Haloxylon salicornicum* and *Rhanterium epapposum*, the most common ones of the southern desert, clearly indicate conditions similar to Arabia. Zohary regards these as Psammophilous communities and a transition between sub-Sudanian and Saharo-Arabian conditions. Guest (1966), in his discussion on the associations of the desert, lists them as the dominant species of two most important communities out of 25 communities given for the desert areas. Guest, in the same enumeration, gives three large shrubs as dominants of communities: *Haloxylon ammodendron, Calligonum comosum* and *Zizyphus nummularia*. The first two are found on deep sands and sand dunes but have largely been destroyed by fuel gatherers. *Z. nummularia* lines depressions and run-off gullies, often in stony areas near places where water stagnates after rains. In addition to the most important and widely distributed covertypes given in Table 6.1, a few more leading species, dominants of communities as listed by Guest for the desert areas, should be mentioned. In southern Iraq, as in Saudi Arabia, large tracts are found where the vegetation has been degraded by fuel cutting and overgrazing (Kaul, 1968; Kaul & Thalen, 1971). This has resulted locally in territories where *Stipa tortilis* becomes dominant, accompanied by the spiny *Astragalus spinosus* and some annual and/or inconspicuous species such as *Plantago ovata* and *Sawignia parviflora. Agathophora alopecuroides* is almost never dominant, due to its palatability, but it is a common associate in various communities. Two *Anabasis* species, *A. setifera* and *A. articulata* cover limited areas. The first one may have been more common once when grazing pressure was less, but there is some confusion about the distribution of the second species because of its similarity to the very widespread *Haloxylon salicornicum. Cornulaca* spp. (*C. leucantha, C. monocantha*) are often found together with *H. salicornicum*. The first species, protected by its spiny nature, may gradually replace the latter locally under heavy use. A last species to be mentioned is *Artemisia scoparia*, which may be found under a range of environmental conditions equally well as an associate of *H. salicornicum* on compact sandy soils or with *Artemisia herba-alba* on clay wadi beds. However, the species seems most common on soils of a medium texture in wadi beds and depressions which have been recently ploughed. At such locations *Zilla spinosa* and *Peganum harmala* are the common associates. Further north, across the river Euphrates, desert and semi-desert conditions gradually change into steppe. Zohary (1946, 1973) has discussed the use of these controversial terms for Iraq. In the Jezira, annual rainfall varies from about 150 mm in the south to over 300 mm further north.

Zohary (1973) mentions four characteristic habitats for the Iraqi part of the Jezira. This is followed below, with a brief mention of the vegetation cover. A first area is the north-western part with brown steppe soils; it is not sharply delineated from the foothills area. Rainfall is sufficient for dry farming, but too low for an arboreal vegetation. It has been suggested (see Guest, 1966) that the area was once covered by a grass steppe with scattered trees, among others, *Pistacia* spp. but almost the whole area is now under cultivation and one can only guess about the natural vegetation (Kaul, 1973). *Peganum harmala* and *Artemisia scoparia* are now common on abandoned fields and the spiny *Alhagi maurorum* and *Prosopis farcta*, widespread over the Mesopotamian Plain are also found here, especially on the silty soils in spring, together with a wealth of bulbous species. Occasionally *Artemisia herba-alba*, *Achillea conferta* and *Noea mucronata* may be seen, but at places lying waste for a number of years the low cover of the three following species is most common in the northern half of Jezira: *Poa sinaica* (= *P. bulbosa*), *Carex stenophylla* and *Ranunculus asiaticus* (see also Uvarov, 1933). These species also form the ground-layer if shrubs have developed.

The second area is one covered by gypseous soils in a shallow layer, found to the north of Wadi Tharthar. Locally the bedrock is exposed and because of heavy use only scattered patches of vegetation remain. A number of species mentioned above are also found here. *Artemisia herba-alba*, *Noea mucronata* and *Teucrium polium* are the most common sub-shrubs. In spring there is an open, annual cover.

The third area comprises local sandy stretches on which low dunes are forming, especially in the southern part of Jezira and along the Syrian border, *Haloxylon salicornicum* is common. Few relicts have been observed of *Calligonum comosum* but the larger woody perennials which are used for fuel, have disappeared.

Saline depressions are the last distinct habitat. There are saline areas around Wadi Tharthar but further north are the far more saline, inland salt-lakes such as the Boara depression at the border with Syria. *Haloxylon salicornicum* can be found near such places, but other Chenopodiaceae, for example *Salsola* and *Suaeda* spp., grow up to the white salt crust. *Tamarix* was found there and the grass *Aeluropus lagopoides*. The natural vegetation cover of Iraq as a whole reflects the impact of man's ruthless exploitation of a valuable resource. Only at remote or protected places can an impression be obtained of the production potential, particularly the lower-lying areas and wadi beds where rain-water accumulates (Thalen, 1972). An integrated plan of action affecting both the vegetation and its user, may, with much effort, bring back something similar to the valuable equilibrium of a hundred years ago, but for many places it will be too late (Kaul & Thalen, 1971).

Description of arid ecosystems

Syria

Forests occupy 5000 km² (2.7%) of Syria. They are scattered over the mountain ridges in the western part of the country (Antilebanon, Jebel Ansiriya). Another 70000 km² are under cultivation. This area receives an average annual rainfall of 300–600 mm, and extends from the extreme south (Jebel Druz) via the western part of the country, Damascus, Homs, Hama, Aleppo, to the Syrian Upper Jezira in the north. Almost the whole remaining part, the Syrian desert area, receives between 100 and 200 mm of rainfall. Zohary (1940) was among the first to make ecological vegetation studies of this desert area. In his mainly floristic and phytogeographical paper a review of earlier botanical exploration is included. Later authors such as Pabot (1955), and Van der Veen (1964, 1967), studied the area as a natural pasture and evaluated its forage value. These authors and Zohary (1973) are the main sources of reference here. The first autecological work on desert species by a Syrian author should also be mentioned (Sankary, 1971, Sankary & Barbour, 1972).

Phytogeographically almost the whole area of desert and steppe falls under the Irano-Turanian territory (Mesopotamian province), but near the mountainous areas in the south-west and north-west of the country, Mediterranean influences can be seen (Zohary, 1973). Pabot (1955), taking the distribution of the key species of the Syrian desert (*Artemisia herba-alba*) as an indicator of the *zone steppique* to the north and west, points out that about 70% (130000 km²) of the country is included in this zone. The cultivated area of 70000 km² mentioned above is included in the zone, partly because the river Euphrates and its effluent, the Khabour, dissect the area in the north-east, providing irrigation water. Other factors important in the large-scale pattern of plant growth are low mountain ridges and high plateaus, for example north of Palmyra. At such places rainfall may be above 300 mm locally and an open arboreal vegetation may occur with *Pistacia* spp., and *Rhamnus palaestina*.

Pabot (1955) states that the desert and steppe area may once have been covered with grasses (*Stipa* spp., *Agropyron* spp., *Festuca* spp.) and locally with trees (*Pistacia* spp., *Crataegus* spp., *Amygdalus* spp., *Prunus* spp., *Pyrus* spp., *Rhamnus* spp.). Trees and large shrubs were cut and burned, while overgrazing favoured the very short and spring-season species. Rodin (1959) listed 27 geobotanical 'regions', but this division is rather a listing of sites with their physical–geographical data. He classified the pastures in three groups: medium grass, short grass, and semi-shrub pastures. *Stipa barbata*, *Poa sinaica* and *Carex stenophylla* are the most important species of the first group. Cover of these species may be very dense apparently: Pabot gives 60–80% for *P. sinaica* and, including rhizomes, up to 100% for *C. stenophylla*. These two species, together with

246

ephemeral grasses, are given for the second group on clayey soils. Of the third group *Artemisia herba-alba, Salsola vermiculata,* and *Noea mucronata* grow on clay soils with crushed stones, while *Haloxylon articulatum, H. salicornicum, Anabasis* spp., *Cornulaca setifera,* and *Aristida* spp., are found on the sandy soils and sand, with *Artemisia herba-alba* and *Salsola* spp., as important associates. Mixtures of these species and *Achillea* spp., in several compositions, are given for temporarily flooded territories. Finally for salt marshes there are communities of *Aeluropus littoralis, Halocnemum strobilaceum* and, according to Pabot (1955) a few *Tamarix* species. Apart from these more common species, which are listed by Rodin, Pabot includes the species *Ephedra alata, Halogeton alopecuroides, Astragalus spinosus* and *Seidlitzia rosmarinus* amongst the common ones of the desert area.

From the foregoing it will be clear that the Syrian Desert areas have a great deal in common with the northern part of the desert areas of Iraq. This holds good not only with respect to climate and soils, but also regarding the destructive influence of man. As Pabot points out '. . . natural vegetation in real equilibrium with the complex of ecological factors is rarely encountered'. This is also illustrated by the species given as locally common, but more or less restricted to areas near villages or permanent camping sites, including, among others, *Peganum harmala, Achillea fragrantissima, Artemisia scoparia* and *Alhagi maurerum.* Floristic information on Syria and more detailed community descriptions can be found in the publications of Zohary (1940, 1973).

Palestine

From the phytogeographical point of view, most of the area under review belongs to the Mediterranean and Irano-Turanian territories, with only small areas forming part of the Saharo-Arabian territory (Zohary, 1962). Plant communities of the Mediterranean territory include various dwarf-shrub communities such as the *Thymetum capitati* on the pararendzina and kurkuar ridges of the Shephela. Semi-steppe batha communities with *Zizyphus lotus* on xerorendzina and grumusols are characteristic of the basalt mountains north of Beit Shean, while similar communities with species such as *Poterium spinosum, Ononis natrix* on brown lithosols and loessial brown soils occur in the foothills region. In the southern coastal plain, on dark-brown soils, the natural vegetation is entirely destroyed and replaced by the segetal *Prosopidetum farcatae.* Various degradation stages of evergreen maquis of the *Quercus calliprinos, Pistacia palaestina* and *Ceratonia* spp., *Pistacietum lentisci* associations occur on Terra Rossas and Rendzinas.

In the Irano-Turanian territory, the segetal *Achilleatum santolinae* is

247

Description of arid ecosystems

characteristic of the loessial brown soils and loessial sierozems; there is no arboreal climax, but isolated trees of *Acacia raddiana* and *Zizyphus spina-christi* occur here and there. The *Zizyphetum loti* with the tree *Zizyphus spina-christi* forms a wooded steppe on calcareous sierozems of the Beit Shean and Middle Jordan Valley.

Psammophytic communities such as *Artemisia monosperma*, *Cyperus mucronatus* associations on coastal sand dunes constitute Saharo-Arabian penetrations. The vegetation of the Judean desert, overlying lithosols, consists of very open dwarf-shrub communities such as *Chenoletum arabicae* and *Suaedetum asphalticae*.

Tropical relics of *Acacia albida* are encountered both in the southern coastal plain and the Middle Jordan Valley. The northernmost occurrence of the *Zizyphus spina-christi–Balanites aegyptiaca* is near Beit Shean.

Well developed hydrophytic communities, such as thickets of the *Tamaricetum jordanis* and small stands of *Populus euphratica* occur along the Jordan River.

Iran

Boissier's *Flora Orientalis* (1843–59) may be considered a good background for the flora of Iran. Boissier's work was followed by research by a number of botanists notably, Parsa (1943–59) and Rechinger (1963–70). The latter is editor of a new *Flora Iranica* of which a considerable part has already appeared. More recently McGinnies *et al.* (1968) published an excellent account of the present state of knowledge of vegetation of the Iranian desert environs, while Zohary (1973) has presented an up-to-date review.

Pabot (1964) recognized arid regions as those having precipitation of less than 100 mm, semi-arid having 100 to 250 mm, and dry sub-humid having more than 250 mm. The area described as arid includes the Dasht-e-Kavir and the Dasht-e-Lut, and covers 13% of the total area of Iran. The Great Salt Desert, the largest salt desert in the world, is absolutely devoid of vegetation. The semi-arid region represents about 61% of the Iranian land surface and includes a large part of the coastal area of the Persian Gulf and the Gulf of Oman, the Khurasan and Azerbeijan and central Iran. Elevation is mostly between 1000 and 2000 m.

On the basis of vegetation, the drier areas of Iran were categorized into desert, sub-desert, steppe, sub-steppe and xerophilous forest zone. In Iran, as in the whole of south-west Asia, the belt pattern of the vegetation is recognizable around the most arid desert centres. The pattern is best described by Boyko (1954) and also by Monod (1954, 1957). The pattern of belts is, however, strongly influenced by the orographical features surrounding the central parts: by the relatively high altitude of the inner

Table 6.2. *Main vegetation types of the semi-arid and arid zones of Iran,*
excluding modifications under direct human influence. (After Mobayen
& Tregubov, 1970)

Vegetation type	Area (km²)	Remarks
(1) Steppe vegetation of *Artemisia herba-alba*, *Astragalus* spp. and Gramineae (e.g. *Stipa* spp.); often floristically rich	756817	Extensive areas now under cultivation and even irrigation, rest under grazing; often deteriorated.
(2) Halophytic communities, among others *Halocnemum strobilaceum*, *Salsola* spp., *Aeluropus* spp., *Suaeda* spp., *Seidlitzia rosmarinus*, *Salicornia herbacea*	177720	Communities often in concentric circles around the saline depressions, depending on depth of the water table
(3) 'Ommanian vegetation', comprising *Acacia seyal*, *A. arabica*, *A. senegal*, *Zizyphus nummularia*, *Calotropis procera*, *Dalbergia sissoo*	146560	Subtropical, occupying a very hot and dry region, excepting near the Gulf-coast.
(4) Psammophytic communities, among others *Calligonum comosum* and *Aristida* spp.	56420	On dunes and moving sands, very poor vegetation, grazed, important for fixation.
(5) *Tamarix* communities, mostly *T. articulata*, but also *T. stricta*, *T. macrocarpa*	49600	In the south-east, almost desertic, often psammophytic and slightly halophytic in valleys.
(6) *Zygophyllum*-steppe with *Z. atriplicoides*, *Salsola arbuscula* etc.	30140	Bushy plants, often passing into *Artemisia* (type 1).
(7) *Haloxylon* communities, with *H. ammodendron*, *H. aphyllum* and *H. persicum*	17285	Mostly on sand; shrubs and small trees, important for reforestation and stabilization.
(8) *Anabasis* communities with *A. aphylla*, *A. hausknechtii*	4020	Transition between steppe and halophytes, grazed locally, cultivation.
Total area	1238562	
Without vegetation	23460	
Total other communities, outside the arid zone, mostly in the mountainous areas.	366760	
Total area of Iran	1628782	

plateau. Boyko (1955) presented a plant geographical map of Iran. The
UNESCO–FAO (1969) vegetation map of the Mediterranean zone shows
the distribution of different vegetation types in the Iranian desert in great
detail, largely extrapolated from physical features. Most recent is the
vegetation map (1:2500000) with explanatory notes by Mobayen & Tre-

Description of arid ecosystems

gubov (1970). These authors distinguished 25 types of potential vegetation and areas without vegetation. Eight types (listed in Table 6.2 as a representative example for south-west Asia) approximately constitute the arid and semi-arid zones. In their map, steppe vegetation of *Artemisia* and *Astragalus* spp. covers almost half of the country's total land-surface.

The interior of the southern units of the Iranian Desert belong to the hottest summer regions of the world with summer temperature over 54.5 °C. This climatic feature combined with frequent and very strong winds and the scant rainfall makes plant and animal life very difficult.

In the Baluchi region, the mean annual precipitation is under 300 mm and the plants have affinities with the Saharo-Sindian and subtropical regions. In spite of its extremely arid, and sometime desert-like appearance, the zone in Persian Baluchistan includes a large number of tree and shrub species that are rare in the rest of Iran (Pabot, 1964). The date palm is probably indigenous and *Zizyphus* spp. and *Acacia* spp. occur frequently. Among the trees and shrubs of this region are *Prosopis cineraria, Dalbergia sissoo, Diospyros tomentosa, Tamarindus indica,* and many shrubby or herbaceous Leguminosae, including such genera as *Indigofera, Tephrosia, Garagana, Crotolaria, Rhynchosia, Cajanus, Cassia* and *Taverniera*. The grasses are nearly all hot-region species belonging to the genera *Pennisetum, Cenchrus, Panicum, Sporobolus* and *Eragrostis*.

The Irano-Turanian region of Iran has rainfall which varies up to 500 mm but with a summer drought of at least three months; the winters are usually cold. The sub-desert zone has an annual precipitation under 100 mm; the steppe zone has cold winters and an annual precipitation between 100 and 250 mm.

The central Iranian sector harbours the most typical flora of Iran's steppes and deserts and constitutes the bulk of the Irano-Turanian territory in Iran. The Central Plateau is vegetationally the least explored. As in other deserts, relief is most decisive in determining the nature of plant communities. The poorly drained flats are inhabited by halophytic communities and the better drained ones by *Artemisia* spp. steppes, occurring in a variety of forms according to minor edaphic and topographic variations. Alternating with these flats are plantless or almost plantless gravel deserts and sand dunes.

The steppe flora in the vegetation zone with cold winters is dominantly an *Artemisia herba-alba* community. *Noea mucronata* is widespread and *Poa bulbosa* is abundant on non-eroded soils along with *Carex stenophylla; Aristida plumosa* is the dominant grass on sandy soils. Woody and young species of the genera *Astragalus, Acantholimon* and *Acanthophyllum* are generally quite common, especially above 1000 m. On slightly saline soils, the genera *Anabasis, Haloxylon, Salsola* and *Seidlitzia* are common. Legumes are not common, but occasionally *Onobryelis* spp. and *Trigonella* spp. can be seen, and the herbaceous genera *Astragalus* and *Cousinia* are fairly common. Annuals, often abundant in spring, are stunted and dry up very quickly. The sand dunes have their particular vegetation, which nearly always includes *Aristida* spp., *Calligonum* spp., *Pennisetum dichotomum* and *Cyperus conglomeratus*. There are a few trees in the steppe zone, including *Pistacia atlantica*. On rocky slopes *Amygdalus scoparia* and other bushy shrubs are found including *Pteropysym* spp., *Ephedra* spp. and *Lycium* spp. *Tamarix stricta* and *Haloxylon ammodendron* grow as trees on sand dunes. Other species of *Tamarix* are restricted to shrub form appearing in moist depressions, on salty land, and sometimes on very arid soils. In the latter case it is mainly *T. articulata*, indicating a deep-lying water source. *Populus euphratica* is seen in valley bottoms and *Zizyphus spina-christi* may penetrate into the southern slopes.

Afghanistan

Excepting a few floristic studies, Afghanistan remained (from the botanical point of view) *terra incognita* until the early 1940s when Linchevsky and Prozorovsky compiled an outline of the country's vegetation which was later re-written and translated (Linchevsky & Prozorovsky, 1949). Floristic information has since been provided by a few authors in a series of papers (Freitag, 1971) and in the published parts of the *Flora Iranica* (Rechinger, 1963–70). General descriptions have been given by Volk (1954) and Neubauer (1955), followed by the better documented information of Freitag (1971). The following account is based on data from this last author, who personally made observations throughout the country. A bibliography is found in Meher-homji, Gupta & Freitag (1973). The arid zone of Afghanistan with precipitation, on average, below 200 mm annually is located mainly in the western and south-western part of the country with a small part in the north. Natural vegetation in this region, not modified by the actions of man, is found only at remote and less accessible or protected places. The relicts and clearly related successional (degradation) stages, however, have provided Freitag (1971) with the material for a classification of the vegetation on a physiognomic–ecological basis. For the arid areas the following types are important:

> (1) *Calligonum–Aristida* communities on mobile sand dunes; (2) Chenopodiaceae dwarf shrub communities of extreme semi-deserts; (3) *Amygdalus* shrublands of moderate semi-deserts; (4) ephemeral communities of loess semi-deserts; (5) subtropically influenced shrub and grassland communities.

Description of arid ecosystems

All these types receive less than 300 mm annual precipitation. The perennial plant cover is low and hardly ever exceeds 25%. Trees are only occasionally encountered. The types and their subtypes are briefly discussed below.

(1) *Calligonum–Aristida* communities on mobile sand dunes. The most extensive areas are found in the Registan sand desert in the south and on offshoots of the Kara Kum in the north. Small trees and large shrubs such as *Haloxylon persicum*, *Calligonum* spp. indicate relatively better local moisture conditions. A variety of subtypes are found, with ground cover ranging from 1% to 25% depending on edaphic and micro-climatic conditions. *Aristida pennata* and *A. karelinii*, *Cyperus conglomeratus* and *Pennisetum divisum* are the hemi-cryptophytes listed. A good cover of annuals can be found, especially at the fringes where moisture conditions are better and consequently other species such as *Carex physodes* and *Sophora pachyclada* can be effective in natural dune fixation.

(2) Chenopodiaceae dwarf shrub communities of extreme semi-deserts. Such communities are encountered locally in different varieties all over the semi-desert areas with precipitation below 150 mm. The Chenopodiaceae component depends partly on the salinity of the topsoil. Freitag (1971) lists six subtypes for the lowland and two for the mountainous semi-desert areas, *viz.*

(a) *Haloxylon salicornicum* communities. Found on gypsiferous soils with an electrical conductivity of about 30000 mS, chloride contents up to 350 meq/l and many soluble sulphates. There has been little human influence, the cover is low, in runnels up to 20%, height 30–80 cm. Mostly shrubby species: *Haloxylon salicornicum*, *H. persicum*, *Salsola arbuscula*, *Seidlitzia rosmarinus*, *Cornulaca monacantha*, *Anabasis setifera*, *Ephedra scoparia*. Relatively few herbs and grasses are found (*Aristida* spp., *Astragalus* spp.). On thin sheets of sand overlying almost non-saline layers, other species were seen, e.g. *Calligonum* spp., *Aeluropus macrostachys*, *Fagonia bruguieri* and *Savygnia parviflora*.

(b) *Salsola–Salvia santolinifolia* communities. Similar habitat as (a) but under slightly higher precipitation (100–150 mm). Small shrubs dominant but largely reduced by grazing and cutting for fuel, cover 5–15%. Species: *Halocharis suffruticosa*, *Salsola subaphylla*, *Astragalus oligophyllus*, *Salvia trichocalycina*, *S. santolinifolia*, *Fortuynia bungei*, *Andrachne rotundifolia*, *Gaillonia bruguieri*, *Acantholimon longiflorum* etc. Most common annuals: *Halarchon vesiculosus* and *Gymnarrhena micrantha*; geophytes among others *Allium* and *Scorzonera* spp.

(c) *Zygophyllum–Cousinia arida* communities. Areas under precipitation as (a) and (b) but with colder winters. On young sierozems with low

252

salinity (1000–2000 mS). Shrubs and half-shrubs relatively little disturbed. Species among others *Zygophyllum tetrapterum, Ephedra scoparia, Salsola arbuscula, Cousinia arida, Artemisia* cf. *herba-alba.* Geophytes present, moderate annuals cover.

(*d*) *Reaumuria stocksii* communities. Mountain fringes in the south-west and isolated mountains in areas with precipitation below 120 mm and low soil salinity (less than 1000 mS). Low cover, little-disturbed. Species: *Reaumuria stocksii, Anabasis* cf. *setifera, Fagonia parviflora.* Few therophytes: *Brachypodium distachyon, Atriplex dimorphostegia, Plantago ciliata, Halocharis* spp.

(*e*) *Artemisia–Umbelliferae* communities. Only west of Herat, precipitation 100–150 mm, colder and longer winter, soils of fine sandy texture and low salinity. In April–May, 30% cover, later in the season more open. Species: *Artemisia* spp., *Ferula asa-foetida, F. badrakema, Salsola arbuscula, S. subaphylla, Krascheninnikovia ewersmanniana* etc. Hemicryptophytes and geophytes and numerous therophytes, e.g. *Stipa swozitsiana, Eremostachys regeliana, Iris songarica, Carex physodes* and *Allium* spp.

(*f*) *Seidlitzia–Salsola gemmascens* communities. Only found in the north. Area with hot summers and cold, but short, winters. Soils mainly fine sandy and with a moderate salt content (1500–4000 mS measured in April). Shrubs have disappeared in favour of annuals. Cover 5–25%. Species: *Seidlitzia rosmarinus, Salsola richteri, Tamarix ramosissima.* Many chamaephytes and therophytes, among others *Salsola* spp., geophytes *Carex physodes, Tulipa sogdiana, Dorema* sp. etc.

Semi-deserts in the mountainous area are found around Bemain, in the middle Ghrban valley, upper Amu-Darya valley and Gomal valley. Locally also on south slopes elsewhere. Composition changes with height and geographical situation. The following two communities are given:

(*g*) *Salsola maracandica* community. At 2000–2700 m elevation, precipitation 150–200 mm. Soils with soluble salts in the top-layer, e.c. 5000–15000 mS, mainly sulphates and chlorides, also HCO_3^- in high concentrations (5–13 meq/l). Species: Mainly dwarf shrubs to 30 cm, cover 5–15%. *Salsola* spp. *Anabasis macroptera, Arthrophytum* spp. and *Artemisia.* Other life-forms poorly represented, except therophytes.

(*h*) *Artemisia–Krascheninnikovia* community. At 2600–2900 m elevation and 150–250 mm precipitation on Sierozem with little salts. Dwarf shrubs to 25 cm covering 10–30%. Species: *Artemisia* sp., *Krascheninnikovia ewersmanniama* and *Acantholimon* spp. and many therophytes.

(3) *Amygdalus* shrublands of moderate semi-deserts. Located in belts in areas with 150–250 mm precipitation, at different elevations (mostly

between 950 and 1200 m in the west and south). Sulphates and chlorides have been washed from the soil, only gypsum is found at greater depth (electrical conductivity below 1000 mS). Shrubs of the genus *Amygdalus* (maximum ground cover 10%) of 5–150 cm height together with a dwarf-shrub layer (cover 10–25%) determine the physiognomy, but the shrub layer has often disappeared through intensive use. Two subtypes are given.

(*a*) *Amygdalus eburnea* and *A. erioclada* communities. The first species in the western part and to the south, up to the Hilmend valley, from there on to the east with the second. Other shrubs include *Pistacia khinjuk* and *Zygophyllum tetrapterum*. A number of dwarf shrubs can be found, differing between regions. Grasses include *Poa bulbosa*, *Stipa szowitsiana* and *Cymbopogon olivieri*, while also geophytes are listed and many therophytes, for example *Torularia* spp. and *Arnebia* spp.

(*b*) *Amygdalus brahuica* communities. Found at heights of 1800–2800 m in the dryer parts of east and central Afghanistan. Chamaephytes include *Gaillonia macrantha*, *Serriola orientalis*, *Astragalus jubatus*, *Artemisia* spp. and *Cousinia* spp. Other species are present only in limited number.

(4) Ephemeral communities of loess semi-deserts. Communities are found where rainfall is between 150 and 250 mm, usually with an electrical conductivity, which is highest in the 5 cm topsoil, of 1000 mS. Numerous therophytes and few hemi-cryptophytes and geophytes are characteristic of the community. There are no shrubs only sub-shrubs such as *Artemisia scoparia*, *A. turanica* and *Sophora pachycarpa*, the last one in transitions to the sandy desert. Rainfall and soil moisture content determine the cover which may range from 30% to 90% in spring. From May onwards, geophytes take over from the therophytes. Woody species may be absent through lack of moisture in the deeper layers, while most of the rainwater is consumed by the other species in the top layer, where they can develop under good soil and moisture conditions. Hemicryptophytes present were *Poa bulbosa*, *Cousinia alata*, *Anabasis* sp. and *Astragalus* spp., while *Carex* and *Gagea* were found amongst the geophytes. Of the numerous therophytes the following may be named: *Bromus* sp., *Leptaleum filifolium*, *Aegilops* spp., *Hordeum* spp., *Trigonella* spp., *Medicago* spp., *Astragalus* spp., and *Arnebia* spp.

(5) Subtropically influenced shrub and grassland communities. Semi-desert communities are found near Jalalabad and in the area around this town which have hot summers and a rainfall of 150–300 mm. They are mainly composed of hemi-cryptophytic grasses, spiny shrubs and sub-shrubs and even small trees. Intensive cutting has favoured *Rhazya stricta* and *Calotropis procera* which regenerate easily. Many types may be distinguished.

From the above account, derived from data presented by Freitag (1971), it will be clear that the vegetation cover of the arid zone of Afghanistan is extremely diverse. Locally, high production potential has been observed, but all over the country exploitation of the vegetation takes place without regard to the vulnerable environment. Cutting, overgrazing and fodder gathering for supplementary feeding are reported. Management strategies are urgently needed to prevent increasing depletion of the vegetation resource.

India and Pakistan

The core of the arid zone of the Indo-Pakistan subcontinent is in Pakistan with penetration into India in the east and the north. In addition, an arid island exists right in the middle of the inner Krishna River basin (Subba Rao & Subrahmanyam, 1962). The hot and cold arid regions of the subcontinent each have their characteristic vegetation.

The hot arid zones, which include the Thar Desert and the environs of Bellary in southern India, are fairly well described botanically and sufficient information is available on the flora and ecology for general purposes. Biswas & Rao (1953) point out that there are both climatic and edaphic influences and discuss the vegetation of three main community types: sand, gravel and rock communities. Satyanarayan (1963) has divided the vegetation into five formations.

(*a*) Mixed xeromorphic thorn forest. Plant communities growing on hills, consisting predominantly of thorny trees including those with evergreen leaves. Common communities on this land form are (i) the co-dominant *Acacia senegal–Anogeissus pendula* communities. The type varies from a low-statured thorn forest to a sparsely distributed scrub, but occasionally it assumes tree form especially where the moisture regime is good. (ii) the *Euphorbia caducifolia* community which appears to have grown where the original tree vegetation of *Acacia senegal* or *Anogeissus pendula* has been removed.

(*b*) Mixed xeromorphic woodland or wooded desert. This formation is dominated by thorny or spiny species mixed with either evergreen persistant leaves or green stems and branches. It occurs on flat alluvial plains with a hard *kanker* pan at varying depths. The principal species of this formation are *Salvadora oleoides, Prosopis cineraria, Acacia leucophloea, A. nilotica* ssp. *indica, Capparis decidus, Zizyphus nummularia, Cassia auriculata, Indigofera oblongifolia, Calotropis procera* and *Leptadenia pyrotechnica*. The climax community is not found in its optimum stage due to maltreatment for centuries by man and his livestock. *Salvadora oleoides–Prosopis cineraria* community is the climatic climax of the plains of Western Rajasthan and Cutch (Satyana-

255

rayan, 1963; Legris, 1963) while Chaudhri (1960) claims it as the climatic climax of the entire region (including hills) of Pakistan. Some common degraded communities of this formation are: *Prosopis cineraria–Zizyphus nummularia; Salvadora oleoides–Capparis decidua; S. oleoides–Cassia auriculata; Acacia leucophloea–Prosopis cineraria; Capparis decidua–Indigofera oblongifolia.*

(c) Dwarf semi-shrub desert. This formation includes an open assemblage of dwarf trees, generally not exceeding 3.5 m but dominated by shrubs. Plant communities of this formation are confined to flood plains and river beds. Common species of this formation are *Salvadora persica, Tamarix dioica* and *Acacia nilotica* ssp. *indica.* Along the river, in the annually inundated zone of Sind, *Populus euphratica* and *Butea monosperma* are also recorded along with the above species. The common community of flood plains is *Tamarix dioica–Salvadora persica.* The chief associates are *Aerva persica, Leptadenia pyrotechnica, Zizyphus nummularia, Tephrosia purpurea, Cenchrus* spp. and *Desmostachya bipinnata.*

(d) Psammophytic scrub desert. This formation is confined to aeolian deposits or stabilized sand dunes where the soils are deep, greyish brown, fine loamy sand, weakly to highly calcareous. The typical psammophilous species are *Calligonum polygonoides, Panicum turgidum, Acacia jacquemontii, Crotalaria burhia, Aerva persica, Cyperus arenarius, Cenchrus* spp. *Lasiurus sindicus.* The typical community of the north-west desertic region, which is full of high to medium dunes, is *Calligonum polygonoides–Panicum turgidum.* Density and frequency of these species vary according to land use. Old and well-stabilized dunes are generally occupied by small trees and shrubs of *Prosopis cineraria, Salvadora oleoides, Zizyphus nummularia* and *Tecomella undulata.* Other commonly occurring sand dune communities are *Crotalaria burhia–Leptadenia pyrotechnica–Aerva persica.*

(e) Succulent halophytic desert. This formation is characteristic of low-lying depressions and saline areas generally called 'Rann' or alkali flat. The open scrub community of halophytic chenopodiaceous plants dominates such sites. The characteristic halophytic species are *Haloxylon salicornicum, Suaeda fruticosa, Atriplex crassifolia, Salsola foetida, Zygophyllum simplex, Sporobolus marginatus, Aeluropus lagopoides* and *Cressa cretica.* Beyond the halophytic zone, shrubs of *Tamarix dioica* and *Salvadora persica* are found, apparently representing a higher stage of succession. Due to high salinity there is no definite community structure. At places *Suaeda fruticosa–Aeluropus lagopoides* and *S. fruticosa–Zygophyllum simplex* communities can be recognized.

Vegetation of the southern arid zone is classified as Southern Tropical Dry Deciduous Forest (Champion, 1936). The vegetation of plains consist of *Albizzia amara–Acacia nilotica* ssp. *indica* as the principal elements (Satyanarayan & Shankernaryan, 1964). *Hardwickia binata, Tectona grandis, Anogeissus latifolia* extend into the hills and form a deciduous forest when the natural vegetation is cut down or maltreated. *Euphorbia caducifolia* forms thick clumps. The plains communities under xeromorphic woodland formations are: *Prosopis cineraria–Acacia latorum* and *Albizzia amara–A. latorum.*

The temperate arid zone is little known botanically. Troll (1939) has given a short description of the habitat and listed the species in each microgeomorphic unit. The vegetation of the region has been grouped into three formations: sub-tropical semi-desert; alpine steppe and steppe of *Artemisia.* The plants under each formation have been listed according to the land-forms. The important tree and shrub species belonging to the three formations are:

(*a*) Subtropical semi-desert. On steep rocky slopes *Olea cuspidata, Rosa webbiana, Pistacia* sp., *Halophyllum griffithianum* and *Matthiola* spp., *Salsola* spp., *Rumex hastatus,* can be found. The dry river beds with sandy, loamy terraces are chiefly occupied by *Capparis spinosa, Salsola kali, Peganum harmala, Calotropis procera.* Bunched, woody grasses and shrub grow on permeable soils and moving sand. The grasses help to check sand drift. Some of the common species are *Capparis spinosa, Matthiola odoratissima, Zygophyllum* spp. and *Ephedra* spp. Vegetation on the water-courses is limited in distribution because of enormous changes in water content. The common species are *Tamarix gallica* var. *pallesii, Populus* spp., *Ficus palmata, Rosa moschata, Rumex* sp. and *Saccharum spontaneum.*

(*b*) Alpine steppe. The vegetation is concentrated along natural or artificial water courses and is in contrast with the open landscape. Typical trees and shrubs include *Rubus* spp., *Populus* spp., *Salix* spp., *Betula japonica, Clematis* spp., *Tamarix* spp., *Myricaria* spp., and *Hippophaë rhamnoides.* In swampy valleys, which are often cultivated, the vegetation is confined to stream beds. Thorny scrubs are common in high land valleys. The common species listed are *Carex* spp., *Taraxacum* spp., *Triglochin* spp., *Hippuris vulgaris* and *Ranunculus aquatilis,* and *Potamogeton* spp. near stream flows. Saline soils which are the former lake basins are occupied by halophytic vegetation like *Salsola kali, Triglochin* spp., *Glaux maritima, Chenopodium* spp. Sand dunes are occupied by *Sophora vicifolia, Oxytropis sericopetala* and *Onosma* spp. On the steep rocks and the ranges of high lands, a still more pronounced alpine vegetation exists but, in general plants do not attain good height. The species listed are *Gentiana waltonii, Selaginella involveus* and *Didissandra lanuginosa.*

(*c*) Steppe of *Artemisia.* Rocky terrain and gullies which occasionally

257

carry water are vegetated by *Juniperus* spp. *Rosa webbiana, Colutea arborescens, Prunus* spp., *Berberis* spp. and *Sophora* spp. The vegetation on areas with ground water is of steppe type and becomes conspicuous during July, with several species of the genera *Populus, Salix* and *Lonicera* along with *Ribes* and *Rosa*. The heath vegetation on the rocks includes *Ephedra intermedia, Quercus* spp., *Juniperus* spp., *Eremurus* spp., and *Astragalus* spp. Other succulent ground vegetation forms a dense cover with species like *Scutellaria prostrata* and *Hedysarum falconeri*. The grassy steppes of *Artemisia* are rich in humus content especially where the steppes do not abruptly change into humid coniferous forests. The characteristic species are *Leontopodium* spp., *Thymus serpyllum, Nepeta* spp., *Koeleria gracilis, Stipa* spp., *Dianthus* spp., *Gentiana* spp., and *Scorzonera* spp.

Human impact on vegetation

No restrictions have ever been imposed on the removal of the natural vegetation of arid and semi-arid zones in the region, and it has suffered accordingly. Cutting trees and shrubs for timber and fuel, free-range grazing and browsing by excessive numbers of uncontrolled domestic animals, indiscriminate burning of regenerating vegetation to facilitate their grazing and the exploitative methods of dry farming have all, operating in various intensities, caused the permanent disappearance of arboreal vegetation, especially in those areas of woodland situated on the borders of steppes and deserts. The advent of motor transport and the introduction of tractors has accelerated the process of devegetation, an example of which can be seen in the lower Jezira and desert region of Iraq.

White (1955) while discussing the consequences of human activity on natural vegetation, pointed out that the micro-climate becomes more arid as a result of the disappearance of woody plants and the reduction in the average height of the herbaceous cover. The action of wind on plants and soils thus become much more marked, temperature variations on and below the soil surface become greater, infiltration of water into the soil is affected, evaporation is more intense, and mesophilous species are replaced by more xerophilous species. The deterioration in micro-climates undoubtedly explains why many species, particularly the trees and shrubs, are no longer regenerating or regenerating very slowly (Kaul & Ganguli, 1963). Perhaps even more important is the reduction in effectiveness of the desert-fringe types of vegetation in acting as a protective barrier between the desert and the more mesophilous types of sub-humid and humid vegetation. The studies of Oppenheimer (1953) on ecological relationships and water expenses of Mediterranean forest vegetation provides useful information on this aspect. It would be interesting to see what would have happened if it were possible to discontinue the lopping, for fodder, of *Prosopis cineraria* in Western Rajasthan.

Pabot (1957) has attempted to indicate the original vegetation of the steppe region of Syria by reconstructing, diagrammatically, a hypothetical but reasonably well-founded succession, showing how the vegetation may have regressed and how it might progress back to actual or theoretical climax of steppe (*Pistasia atlantica*).

Zohary (1962) has described how heavy over-grazing of the more or less primary *Artemisia fragrans*, one of the important pasture resources of large areas of inner Anatolia, has produced non-pastoral communities with *Eryngium campestre*, *Euphorbia macrodada*, species of *Bromus*, *Ballota*, *Phlomis* and others. In Khurssan, north-eastern Iran, large tracts of *Artemisia herba-alba* were replaced by unpalatable *Peganum harmala*. Whereas in east Kerman, tragacanthic species of *Astragalus* and *Acantholimon* migrated from the mountains down to the cultivated fields, where some of them occur as weeds. West of Shiraz, excessive browsing has resulted in impenetrable and unbrowsable shrubbery consisting of various elements such as *Cerasus microcarpa*, *Berberis integerrima*, *Paliurus spina-christi* and *Crataegus aronia* (Zohary, 1962).

Pabot (1957) believes that in Afghanistan there were once open forests of *Pistacia khinjuk*, *P. atlantica* and *P. vera* in the less arid parts of the northern plain; bordering the plains there was *Juniperus excelsa*; in the mountains to the east of Kabul there was forest of *Quercus baloot* with *P. atlantica* and *Cercis griffithii* of which relicts still exist; and in the mountains near Kandhar forest of *P. atlantica*, some specimens of which are still to be found.

Animals

Man has been a ruthless exploiter of the animals in south-west Asia by unreasoned and uncontrolled killing, thereby depleting the wild animal resources. In addition, unlimited increases in livestock numbers have damaged the vegetation resource by grazing it right into the ground. The two aspects are briefly discussed below.

Wild animals

For many thousands of years there has been a delicate equilibrium between physical environment, vegetation cover and animal life, the animals using the plants not only as forage but also for cover. The carrying capacity and secondary production during those times will probably never be known. Estimates of the wild animal populations are too inaccurate to assess the value of this resource and it is impossible to describe the losses outlined below in quantitative terms. However, the processes that have taken place and the unfortunate consequences are clear enough. Although the number of large-animal species that can survive in the harsh arid environment is relatively low, the species that had adapted were usually found in good numbers. One hundred years ago large flocks of gazelles (*Gazella arabica*, *G. subgutturosa* and *G. dorcas*) were still roaming the Middle Eastern deserts and foothill regions and were preyed upon by asiatic lion (*Panthera leo persica*), cheetah (*Acinomyx jubatus*) and desert lynx (*Caracal caracal*). Several races of wild asses (*Equus hemionus*) grazed the vast steppe areas from the Near East to India. Even deep in the barren deserts of Arabia large animals found a suitable habitat. The long-horned Arabian oryx (*Oryx leucoryx*), a large white antelope, model for the famous 'Unicorn' is perhaps best known. Their meat, and that of the Arabian ostrich (*Struthio camelus*) and of the Houbara bustard (*Chlamydotis undulata*), supplemented the meals of the Bedouin.

The balance between vegetation, grazing animal and predator was broken over the last hundred years and with increasing intensity over the last fifty years. Each of the species mentioned has been pushed to the limit of survival or even extinction. The situation, that had been relatively stable within the fluctuations superimposed by the inconstant character of the arid climate, changed mainly as a result of two factors: the introduction of high-powered and automatic weapons and specially adapted vehicles, enabling areas that had been hardly accessible for man on horseback or camel now to be explored; newly drilled wells supplying the earlier limiting factor – water. The desert and steppe areas were opened up on a large scale and results for the wild animal resource were disastrous.

In the early 1950s, for instance, no one would have believed that the gazelles were a threatened species. Senseless killing with single parties killing over 300 gazelles a day occurred at an ever-increasing rate. All countries blame their neighbours for the hunting parties in which sometimes over a hundred cars took part. At present gazelles in the Middle East can be found only in the most remote areas, often rough stony terrain, inaccessible even for the well equipped cars. Talbot (1960) has collected valuable information on threatened species in the region and more recently the *Red Data Book* of the International Union for the Conservation of Nature and the volume of Fisher, Simon & Vincent (1969) based on it, have become an important source.

Representative of a number of species is the fate of the Arabian oryx. Habitat of this species is the gravel plain at the fringe of sandy areas. It feeds on the scattered shrubs, grasses and forbs in the area, but may move to the sands when disturbed. Its ecology is practically unknown. It has been reported from sites in the Rub' al Khāli up to 300 km from any known water and Bedouin believe that the oryx does not need to drink. As for

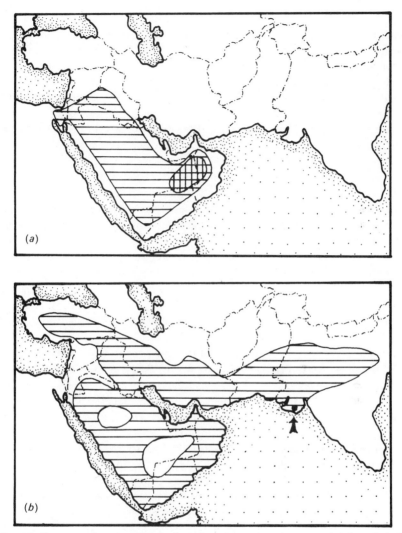

Fig. 6.8. Former and present distribution of (*a*) Oryx (*Oryx leucoryx*) and (*b*) Asiatic lion (*Panthera leo persica*) in south-west Asia. Area of distribution around 1800, horizontally striped; area of present distribution in (*a*) vertically striped, in (*b*) indicated by black dot (see arrow). (Redrafted after data from Talbot, 1960.)

many other desert animals, the inhospitable nature and remoteness of its environment has prevented gathering of detailed knowledge. Former and presumed present distribution are shown in Fig. 6.8. The limits of its range have never been satisfactorily determined, but the animal is known to have existed as far north as the Syrian Desert. During the nineteenth and early twentieth centuries the range was pushed back to Saudi Arabia, in

261

particular to its two extensive deserts, the Great Nafud and Rub' al Khāli, although occasionally records came from other areas, for example, from Jordan until about 1930. Increased human activity in the deserts and wide introduction of firearms (World War I), followed by the coming of the motor vehicle to the area, did their part. Traditionally the oryx had been hunted on foot or by camel and the species provided an opportunity for the desert dwellers to show their capability in the art of hunting. This is in sharp contrast to Talbot's report of hunting in early 1950s in which 300 vehicles were employed. Even the use of aeroplanes has been mentioned. Last reports of the oryx from the Great Nefud are from 1954 and at present it is believed that, at the most, a few hundred remain in a relatively undisturbed part of Saudi Arabia and Oman. Small breeding herds captured under great difficulties have shown promising results and may be used in the future to introduce the animal again in its original natural environment.

The Asiatic wild asses were once numerous over their vast territory from the western part of Asia to deep into India and Mongolia. At present the accepted races are extinct or endangered with extinction, including the two most important for south-west Asia. The Syrian race (*Equus hemionus hemippus*) roamed the Syrian Desert in the present Syria, Palestine, Arabia and Iraq. The last record was in 1927 from its last refuge, Jebel Sinjar. Destruction of the environment by cultivating former wild lands may have been an important factor for the extinction of this species. The distribution of the Persian wild ass (*E. h. onager*) has never been properly defined. It was abundant around the fringes of the Salt Desert and is still found in the salt steppe east of Gum as well as east and south of Meshed. The species seems now to be extinct in north and west Afghanistan. Wild onagers have been hunted and captured alive to be employed as beasts of burden, for their flesh and hides. The chase for wild onagers was a sport for the Persian nobility. Recent accurate estimates of their numbers are lacking but it is certainly below 1000 (Fisher *et al.* 1969). Their meat is considered delicious and despite measures of protection, shooting from cars is still practised.

Even more difficult to reconstruct is what happened to the large predators. Once the Asiatic lion was common from the Middle East to India (Fig. 6.8). In the Middle East the last ones were most probably shot in the mid-twenties near the gates of Baghdad. In Iran a couple of lions were seen in 1929 near Disful and there was another observation in 1938, but here too the species has most likely disappeared from the scene. The last known lion from Pakistan was killed in 1942 while in India its survival has been secured by establishing a reserve in the Giv Forest in the south-west of the Kathiawar Peninsula. The cheetah is becoming extinct in Asia. In 1950 and 1951 a few were shot near Tairif in Saudi Arabia and in 1952 a cub was captured in Syria. Nothing or little is known about the survival of the species in Iran and Afghanistan and in India where the last ones were shot in 1947 the species is most likely extinct now. The caracal is another species for which almost all information is lacking (Harrison 1964, 1968; Thalen 1973).

Slightly brighter is the future for the, at present, still rather common species like wolf (*Canis lupus*), striped hyena (*Hyaena hyaena*), jackal (*Canis aureus*) and fox species (*Vulpes vulpes* and *V. ruppelli*). They are less demanding in their habitat requirements, especially food, and may be living near human settlements partly on refuse and on young domesticated animals. A most important factor for their present survival is, no doubt, the fact that these species have not (yet) been the sole target of the hunting parties. Smaller mammals such as the hare (*Lepus europaeus*) and the jerboas (*Jaculus* spp.) are still common in the desert and semi-desert areas, but with the ongoing habitat destruction they will sooner or later follow the fate of the larger species.

For birds a complete analog course of events has been reported. The large steppe and desert species like the Arabian ostrich and bustards have disappeared as a result of intensive hunting, first only with guns or (in the case of the Houbara bustard) with the falcon, later with automatic weapons.

The Arabian ostrich may be considered extinct. The last confirmed report is a killing in 1933 at the border of Iraq and Saudi Arabia, while another probable record is from 1948 (Talbot, 1960). Even the sandgrouse (*Pterocles* spp.), once abundant all over the region, are decreasing in number as a result of the gun parties. The same may be true for many more species but information is usually too limited to show this for the deserts, or even to notice it. This holds also for the interesting fauna of reptiles, amphibians and certainly the lower fauna groups. Basic information is lacking but some idea can be obtained from case studies on regions or species (e.g. Mountfort, 1965). However, irreversible changes in environmental conditions that can be seen all over south or west Asia give little hope for the living conditions and survival of the interesting wild fauna of this region.

Extinction of species always is tragic, especially if it is a direct result of uncontrolled human action. In the arid areas of south-west Asia a practical point should be considered in the first place. The desert species that are endangered or have already been wiped out, have the ability to survive under conditions too hostile for almost any other large mammalian or avian life form. Their adaptation to this harsh environment could be of great value, if properly managed, in supplying protein to man in circumstances under which domestic livestock cannot survive. An important resource has been nearly depleted!

Description of arid ecosystems

Table 6.3. *Changes in number of sheep and goats in a few countries of the Middle East over a period of 25 years.* (Source: FAO Production Yearbook)

	Sheep (Thousands)			Goats (Thousands)		
	1940	1965	Change %	1940	1965	Change %
Jordan	200	987	+394	390	759	+95
Syria	3123	5422	+74	1800	832	−54
Iraq	6000	11040	+84	2200	1845	−16
Lebanon	36	90	+150	551	442	−20
Israel[1]	23	195	+748	23	152	+561
Total	9382	17734	+89	4964	4030	−19

[1] Estimates not for 1940, but for 1947.

Livestock

The area under discussion has seen some of the oldest civilizations in the world and evidence has been collected that here man changed his role from food-gathering by hunting and fruit collection to food production by primitive agriculture and domestication of animals. For many hundreds of years Bedouins, with their flocks of camels, sheep and goats, have roamed about the arid areas of south or west Asia. Some sort of equilibrium must have been present between livestock and wild animals at one side and the vegetation resource at the other. Although the number of nomads is decreasing (Johnson, 1969; Yacoub, 1971), the number of livestock is still increasing. Livestock statistics over longer periods for the countries are unreliable or not available and at best based on estimates. Only for the last few years are more reliable data available from a countrywide census or from sampling. Some important trends can be seen from Tables 6.3 and 6.4. In Table 6.3 it is shown, as an example, that in a quarter of a century in part of the Middle East the number of sheep almost doubled, while the number of goats decreased from about five million to four million. In Table 6.4 data have been compiled for the last twenty years. It can be seen that the trend for sheep holds good for the other countries in the region too. Most dramatic increases are given for Israel, Jordan and Lebanon, but the numbers are relatively small. Even countries such as Syria, Iraq and Iran almost doubled their numbers from 3, 9 and 18 to 6, 14 and 35 million, respectively, over a period of only 20 years. South west Asia now holds about 18% of the world sheep population and the majority is kept on the natural ranges. Most of them are breeds native to the region and they are primarily kept for their meat, but produce wool and milk too.

264

Table 6.4. *Summary of estimated livestock numbers (by country) in south-west Asia over the period 1950–1970.* (Source: FAO Production Yearbook vol. 25 (1971) Rome)

Approximate year (see note)	Thousands												Millions		
	India	Pakistan	Afghanistan	Iran	Iraq	Turkey	Syria	Lebanon	Jordan	Israel	Saudi Arabia	Yemen	Total SW Asia	Total World	SW Asia % of World
Sheep															
1950	36824	8330	14000	18000	9072	24282	2968	55	234	53	1098	10194	125.1	775.3	16.14
1960	40223	12890	19596	30320	10245	32863	4035	200	677	190	2288	11583	165.1	1007.1	16.39
1970	42800	15200	22900	35500	14000	36471	6200	218	664	189	3300	12615	190.1	1074.7	17.69
Goats															
1950	45196	10530	6000	11000	2732	18517	1325	430	300	74	750	810	97.7	291.4	33.53
1960	60864	14800	3644	13584	2223	22665	668	456	543	156	1400	809	121.8	360.1	33.82
1970	68000	19000	3300	12500	2500	19483	770	318	355	136	2050	870	129.3	383.0	33.76
Camels															
1950	638	466	350	450	181	107	75	2	10	2	265	123	2.7	10.3	26.21
1960	903	682	317	234	202	54	11	1	17	10	460	100	3.0	12.3	24.39
1970	1100	930	300	175	220	31	7	—	10	10	560	99	3.4	14.6	23.29
Horses															
1950	1514	475	195	358	290	1136	101	6	7	7	—	3	4.1	79.7	5.14
1960	1327	500	262	449	157	1247	67	3	7	15	—	3	4.0	67.2	5.95
1970	950	500	300	380	127	1049	70	3	2	10	—	3	3.4	66.3	5.13
Mules and Asses															
1950	1306	963	1030	1356	580	1800	219	32	38	20	22	7	7.4	48.4	15.29
1960	1149	951	1133	2171	638	2096	263	43	90	26	105	17	8.7	54.9	15.85
1970	1067	987	1300	2138	636	2104	296	28	53	21	135	28	8.8	56.6	15.55
Cattle and Buffaloes															
1950	196060	36390	2521	3499	1789	11060	489	75	66	55	110	1032	253.1	888.2	28.50
1960	226765	49330	2933	5703	1739	13783	456	100	59	228	230	1332	302.7	1131.9	26.74
1970	231100	56300	3735	5380	2210	13873	552	84	43	251	320	1472	315.3	1266.5	24.90

1950 is average value for the period 1947/48–1951/52. 1960 is average value for the period 1960/61–1964/65. 1970 is value for 1970/71.

Description of arid ecosystems

The demand for these livestock products has been increasing gradually over the past years as a result of the increase in population and higher income. Excepting India, Pakistan and Saudi Arabia, the goat population (about one-third of the world population) shows no marked upward trend and in some countries, like Jordan and Syria, the population even decreases. Most of these goats are also rangeland grazers and browsers. The goat has a very bad reputation in this part of the world for its role in destroying the vegetation. It is known for its ability to eat types of forage that sheep and cattle do not eat and to eat stems and very small leaves, even trees may be climbed. Management is here the key word. Properly guided, goats can be very valuable animals in the arid environment, living on types of forage that are unsuitable for sheep or cattle and producing milk, meat and hair. Unfortunately this well managed stage of livestock production is rarely encountered in this region.

The position of the camel (actually the one-humped camel *Camelus dromedarius*) is rapidly changing. Its invaluable role as the only means of transport across barren deserts is shared and taken over by mechanical transport, especially terraincars, heavy trucks and tankers. However, about 35 million camels, or one quarter of the world population is found in south-western Asia. Apart from transport, camels are kept for milk and meat, while camel-hair is also an important product. Especially in the field of meat production the species, with its low level of selection for forage, could be made more useful in the future in this part of the world where there is an ever-increasing meat demand. The other species mentioned in the table are less interesting because they are mainly kept in holdings. For a better understanding it may be mentioned that the figures for all countries given refer to the whole country and not to the arid regions only. For the Middle East, Clawson *et al.* (1971) have compiled invaluable data on livestock and livestock products.

Reviewing the livestock numbers for the region as a whole, it can be said that all types of livestock except horses have increased in number. Generally speaking the numbers have increased about 50% over the last 20 years. The most marked increase is in number of sheep. With the available livestock estimates it can be calculated if sheep and goats are counted as 0.25 units mules and assess as 0.5 units and other types as 1 unit, that the pressure on the resources of the natural ranges combined with the cultivated fodder in south or west Asia has increased from 1150 million to over 1600 million animal units over the last 20 years. The effect of this increase on the natural vegetation cover has been described previously but an important point is the gap between arable farming and livestock production (see Clawson *et al.*, 1971; Anon. 1971). Supplementation of the seasonally inadequate rations of the rangeland with high-quality fodder and concentrates, could give a very high economic return.

266

A number of other measures can be mentioned e.g. preventive veterinary care to keep the animals reasonably disease-free, improved breeding practices to upgrade present livestock strains, better marketing policies, etc., that will result in a higher output. Clawson *et al.* (1971) have estimated the livestock production potential for the Middle East, (*a*) taking into account the present situation, (*b*) assuming that livestock numbers would remain relatively constant, but output per head would be increased greatly, and (*c*) basing the rate of increase on experience from other parts of the world. Results are shown in Table 6.3, which is self-explanatory. Livestock production has, in south-west Asia, a long history. It needs a drastic rejuvenation.

References

Abichandani, C. T. (1964). Genesis, morphology and management of arid zone soils of Western Rajasthan, *Proceedings General Symposium on Problems of Indian Arid Zones*. UNESCO and Government of India, Ministry of Education, New Delhi.

Abichandani, C. T. & Roy, B. B. (1966). Rajasthan Desert – its origin and amelioration. *Indian Geographical Journal*, **41**, 35–43.

Al-Ani, T. A., Al-Mufti, M. M., Ouda, N. A., Kaul, R. N. & Thalen, D. C. P. (1970). *Range resources of Iraq. 1. Range cover types of Western and Southern Desert*. Technical Report no. 16. Institute of Applied Research and Natural Resources, Abu-Ghraib, Iraq. (Mimeo.)

Altaie, F. H., Sys, C. & Stoops, G. (1969). Soil groups of Iraq, their classification and characterization. *Pedologie*, **9**, 65–148.

Anon. (1971). Integration of the grain and livestock sectors in the Near East. *Monthly Bulletin of Agricultural Economics and Statistics*, **20** (2), 1–8. F.A.O., Rome.

Auden, J. B. (1950). Introductory report on the groundwater resources of western Rajasthan. *Bulletin of the Geological Survey of India* (*B*), **1**, 59.

Bauer, G. (1935). Luftzirkulation und Niederschlagverhaltnisse in Vorder-Asien. *Gerlands Beiträge zur Geophysik*, **45**, 38.

Bender, F. (1968). *Geologie von Jordanien*. Borhtraeger, Berlin.

Bharadwaj, O. P. (1961). The arid zone of India and Pakistan. In: *A History of Land Use in Arid Regions* (ed. L. D. Stamp), pp. 143–73. Arid Zone Research Series, XVII. UNESCO, Paris.

Biswas, K. & Rao, R. S. (1953). Rajputana desert vegetation. *Proceedings of National Institute of Science of India*, **19** (3), 411–21.

Boyko, H. (1954). A new plant – geographical subdivision of Israel (as an example for southwest Asia). *Vegetatio*, **5/6**, 309–18.

Boyko, H. (1955). Iran, Israel and Turkey. In: Plant ecology, reviews of research. *Arid Zone Research*, **6**, 40–76.

Buringh, P. (1960). *Soils and soil conditions in Iraq*. Report of the Iraq Ministry of Agriculture, Baghdad.

Butzer, K. W. (1958). Umweltfaktor in der grossen arabischen expansion. *Saeculum*, **8**, 359–71.

Champion, H. G. (1936). A preliminary survey of the forest types of India and Burma. *Indian Forest Records, Silviculture*, 1–286 & I–VIII.

Description of arid ecosystems

Chaudhri, I. I. (1960). The vegetation of the Kaghan valley. *Pakistan Journal of Forestry*, **10**, 285–94.

Clawson, M., Landsberg, H. H. & Alexander, L. T. (1971). *The agricultural potential of the Middle East*. Elsevier, New York.

Cressey, G. B. (1960). *Crossroads, land and life in southwest Asia*. Lippincott, Philadelphia.

Dan, J., Yaalon, D. H., Koyumdjisky, H. & Raz, Z. (1962). *The soils and soil association map of Israel*. Soil Conservation Department, Ministry of Agriculture and Department of Geology, Hebrew University, Jerusalem.

Dewan, M. L. & Famousi, J. (1965). *The soils of Iran*. F.A.O., Rome.

Drouhin, G., Ambroggi, R. & Kroon, A. (1963). *Report to the government of Saudi Arabia on future prospects for hydro-agricultural development*. Report no. 1638. F.A.O., Rome.

Eig, A. (1946). Synopsis of the phytosociological units of Palestine. *Palestine Journey of Botany* (Jerusalem). Series **3**, 183–246.

Field, H. (1953). *Bibliography of southwestern Asia, No. 1*. University of Miami Press, Coral Gables, Florida.

Field, H. (1955). *Bibliography of southwestern Asia, No. 2*. University of Miami Press, Coral Gables, Florida.

Field, H. (1956). *Bibliography of southwestern Asia, No. 3*. University of Miami Press, Coral Gables, Florida.

Field, H. (1957). *Bibliography of southwestern Asia, No. 4*. University of Miami Press, Coral Gables, Florida.

Field, H. (1959). *Bibliography of southwestern Asia, No. 5*. University of Miami Press, Coral Gables, Florida.

Fienbrun, N. & Zohary, M. (1955). A geobotanical survey of Trans-jordan. *Bulletin of the Research Council of Israel*, **5D**, 5–35.

Fisher, J., Simon, N. & Vincent, J. (1969). *The Red Book. Wildlife in danger*. Collins, London.

Fisher, W. B. (1950). The Middle East – A Physical, Social and Regional Geography. Methuen, London; Dutton, New York.

Freitag, H. (1971). Die natürliche Vegetation Afghanistans. Beiträge zur Flora und Vegetation Afghanistans I. *Vegetatio*, **22**, 285–344.

Gablot, H. (1963). Le probleme de l'eau en Iran. *Acta Geographica*, **48**, 25–36.

Grüneberg, F. (1965). The soils of Deir Alba area (Jordan Valley). Unpublished Report of German Geological Mission in Jordan. In: *Archives Bundesanst*. Bodenforsch, Hannover.

Guest, E. (ed.) (1966). *Introduction, Flora of Iraq*, Volume 1. Ministry of Agriculture, Baghdad, Iraq.

Gupta, R. S. (1968). Investigations on the desert soils of Rajasthan fertility and mineralogical studies. *Journal of the Indian Society of Soil Science*, **6**, 115–21.

Hadac, E. (1966). Bibliographia phytosociologia: Iraq (Part II). *Excerpta Botanica, Section B, Sociologica*, **7**, 102–4.

Handel-Mazzetti, H. Von (1914). Die Vegetationsverhältnisse von Mesopotamien und Kurdistan. *Annalen des Naturhistorischen Museums in Wien*, **28**, 48–111.

Harrison, D. L. (1964). *The mammals of Arabia* vol. I. Ernest Benn, London.

Harrison, D. L. (1968). *The mammals of Arabia* vol. II. Ernest Benn, London.

Indian Council of Agricultural Research (1953). *Final Report of All India Soil Survey*. Bulletin 73, Delhi.

Jaya, G. & Satyanarayan, Y. (1959). Distribution of trace elements in some soil profiles of arid and semi-arid regions of India. *Journal of Biological Science*, **2**, 110–15.

268

Johnson, D. L. (1969). *The nature of nomadism. A comparative study of pastoral migration in southwestern Asia and northern Africa.* Department of Geography Research Paper No. 118, University of Chicago, Chicago.

Kaul, R. N. (1968). *Range ecology.* Institute for Applied Research on Natural Resources, Abu-Ghraib, Iraq. UNESCO report 1127/MBS. RD/AVS, Paris.

Kaul, R. N. (1970). Indo-Pakistan. In: *Afforestation in Arid Zones* (ed. R. N. Kaul), pp. 155–209. Junk, The Hague.

Kaul, R. N. (1973). An integrated natural resources survey in northern Iraq. *Nature and Resources*, **9**, 13–18.

Kaul, R. N. & Ganguli, B. N. (1963). Fodder potential of *Zizyphus* in the scrub grazing lands of arid zones. *Indian Forester*, **89**, 624–30.

Kaul, R. N. & Thalen, D. C. P. (1971). *Range resources of Iraq. A problem analysis.* Technical Report no. 20. Institute of Applied Research of National Resources, Abu-Ghraib, Iraq.

Kernick, M. D. (1966). *Plant resources, range ecology and fodder plant introduction.* Report to the Government of Kuwait, F.A.O. Report No. TA 2181. F.A.O., Rome.

Kreeb, K. (1961). Bibliographia phytosociologia: Iraq. *Excerpta Botanica, Section B, Sociologia*, **3**, 78.

Legris, P. (1963). *La vegetation de l'Inde. Ecologie et Flore.* Travaux du Section Scientifique et Technique, Institut français de Pondicherry, No. 6. Pondicherry.

Linchevsky, I. A. & Prozorovsky, A. V. (1949). The basic principles of the distribution of the vegetation of Afghanistan. *Kew Bulletin*, 1949, 179–214.

McGinnies, W. G. (1967). *Inventory of research (1967) on vegetation of desert environments.* Inventory of geographical research on desert environments, vol. 6 (5). University of Arizona Press, Tucson.

McGinnies, W. G., Goldman, B. J. & Paylore, P. (eds.) (1968). *Deserts of the World.* The University of Arizona Press, Tucson.

Meher-homji, V. M., Gupta, R. K. & Freitag, H. (1973). Bibliography on 'plant ecology' in Afghanistan. *Excerpta Botanica, Section B, Sociologica*, **12**, 310–15.

Mobayen, S. & Tregubov, V. (1970). *Vegetation map of Iran. Scale 1:2,500,000 and explanatory guide* UNDP/FAO Project IRA 7, Bulletin no. 14.

Monod, T. (1954). Modes contracté et diffus de la vegetation Saharienne. In: *The Biology of Deserts* (ed. J. L. Cloudsley-Thompson), pp. 35–44. Institute of Biology, London.

Monod, T. (1957). *Les grandes divisions chorologiques de l'Afrique.* Conseil scientifique Africain, Publication No. 24, London.

Moormann, F. (1959). *Report to the Government of Jordan on the soils of East Jordan.* Report no. 1132. F.A.O., Rome.

Mountfort, G. (1965). *Portrait of a desert. The story of an expedition to Jordan.* Collins, London.

Muir, A. (1951). Notes on the soils of Syria. *Journal of Soil Science*, **3**, 68–88.

Neubauer, H. F. (1955). Versuch einer Kemreich der Vegetations Verhältnisse Afghanistan. *Annalen des Naturhistorischen Museums in Wien*, **60**, 77–113.

Oakes, H. (1957). *The soils of Turkey.* F.A.O. Report, Ankara.

Oppenheimer, H. R. (1953). An experimental study on ecological relationships and water expenses of Mediterranean forest vegetation. *Palestine Journal of Botany* (Rehovet) Series, **8**, 103–24.

Pabot, H. (1955). *Les pasturages du 'Desert Syrien'.* F.A.O., Rome.

269

Description of arid ecosystems

Pabot, H. (1957). *Rapport au Government de Syrie sur l'ecologie vegetale et ses applications.* F.A.O./ETAP Report No. 1093, Rome.

Pabot, H. (1964). Phytogeographical and ecological regions. In: *The Soils of Iran* (eds. M. L. Dewan and J. Famousi), pp. 30–40. F.A.O., Rome.

Parsa, A. (1943–1959). *Flore de l'Iran (La Perse)* (7 volumes). Danesh, Tehran.

Perrin de Brichambaut, G. & Wallen, C. C. (1963). *A study of agro-climatology in semi-arid and arid zones of the Near East.* Technical Note No. 56. World Meteorological Organisation, Geneva.

Popov, G. B. & Zeller, W. (1963). *Ecological survey report on the 1963 survey in the Arabian Peninsula.* F.A.O. Progress Report, UNSF/DL/ES/6.

Ravikovitch, S. (1967). *Soil map of Israel 1:250,000.* Survey Department, State of Israel.

Rechinger, K. H. (1963–1970). *Flora Iranica* (Flora des Iranischen Hochlands und der umrahmenden Gebirge: Persien, Afghanistan, Teile von West-Pakistan, nord Iraq, Azerbaidjan, Turkmenistan – appearing in parts by families). Nos. 1–72. Akademisch Druck unt Verlagsanstalt, Graz.

Reifenberg, A. (1953) (ed.). *The struggle between the desert and the sower.* Proceedings of an International Symposium, Jerusalem, 1952. Research Council of Israel, Special Publication, No. 2.

Reitan, C. H. & Green, C. R. (1967). Inventory of research on weather and climate of desert environments. In: *Deserts of the World* (eds. W. G. McGinnies, B. J. Goldman & P. Paylore), pp. 21–92. University of Arizona Press, Tucson.

Sankary, M. N. (1971). 'Comparative plant ecology of two Mediterranean type arid areas, in Syria and California, with emphasis on the autecology of twenty dominant species.' Ph.D. Thesis, University of California, Davis, USA.

Sankary, M. N. & Barbour, M. G. (1972). Autecology of *Haloxylon articulatum* in Syria. *Journal of Ecology,* **60,** 697–711.

Satyanarayan, Y. (1963). Ecology of the Central Luni Basin, Rajasthan. *Annals of the Arid Zone,* **2,** 82–97.

Satyanarayan, Y. & Shankaranarayan, K. A. (1964). Vegetation of Bellany district, Mysore State. *Annals of the Arid Zone,* **2,** 54–62.

Saxena, B. P. (1962). *Report au government de l'Afghanistan sur la mise en valeur des terres et des eaux.* Report no. 1586. F.A.O., Rome.

Springfield, H. W. (1954). *Natural vegetation in Iraq* Technical Bulletin of the Ministry of Agriculture, Baghdad.

Subba Rao, B. & Subrahmanyam, V. P. (1962). A climatic study of arid zones in the central Deccan. *Proceedings of the National Institute of Science (India),* **28**A, No. 4, 268–72.

Sutcliffe, R. C. (1960). The Mediterranean in relation to the general circulation. *UNESCO/WMO Seminar on Mediterranean Synoptic Meteorology.* Abhendlungen aus dem Institut für Meteorology und Geophysik der Freie Universitat, Berlin.

Talbot, L. M. (1960). *A look at threatened species.* A report on some animals of the Middle East and Southern Asia which are threatened with extermination. Fauna Preservation Society, London; for the International Union for the Conservation of Nature.

Thalen, D. C. P. (1972). A preliminary evaluation of biomass and production in the desert rangelands of Iraq. *Proceedings of the First Scientific Conference, Foundation of Scientific Research, Iraq, Baghdad.*

Thalen, D. C. P. (1973). The Caracallynx (*Cavacal Caracal Skhmitzi*) in Iraq, earlier and new records, habitat and distribution. *Bulletin of the Iraq Natural History Museum,* 1973.

270

Troll, Carl (1939). Das Pflanzenkleid des Nanga Parbat, Begleitworte zur Vegetations Karte der Nanga Parbat Gruppe (NW-Himalaya). *Wissenscheftliches Veroeffentlichungen der Deutschen Museum, Leipzig*, **7**, 151–80.

UNESCO–FAO (1963). Bioclimatic map of the Mediterranean Zone, explanatory notes. *Arid Zone Research*, **21**, 60.

UNESCO–FAO (1969). Ecological study of the Mediterranean zone, vegetation map of the Mediterranean Zone, explanatory notes. *Arid Zone Research*, **30**, 90.

Uvarov, B. P. (1933). Ecology of the Mosoccon Locust in Iraq and Syria and the prevention of its outbreaks. *Bulletin of Entomological Research*, **24**, 407–18.

Van der Veen, J. P. H. (1964). Some aspects of plant succession in the Wadij Al-Alazib range station and surrounding areas. *Proceedings of the 5th week of Science*, pp. 101–112. High Council of Science, Damascus.

Van der Veen, J. P. H. (1967). Preliminary results of a grazing trial in the Syrian Steppe. *Netherlands Journal of Agricultural Science*, **15**, 198–206.

Vesey-Fitzgerald, D. F. (1955). The vegetation of the Red Sea Coast south of Jedda, Saudi Arabia. *Journal of Ecology*, **43**, 477–89.

Vesey-Fitzgerald, D. F. (1957*a*). The vegetation of the Red Sea Coast north of Jedda, Saudi Arabia. *Journal of Ecology*, **45**, 547–62.

Vesey-Fitzgerald, D. F. (1957*b*). The vegetation of central and eastern Arabia. *Journal of Ecology*, **45**, 779–98.

Volk, O. H. (1954). Klima und Pflanzenverbreitung in Afghanistan. *Vegetatio*, **5/6**, 422–33.

Wadia, D. N. (1960). Salient features of geology of India in relation to soils of India. *Journal of the Indian Society of Soil Science*, **8**, 5–8.

Walter, H. & Lieth, H. (1960). Klimadiagramm–Weltatlas. G. Fischer, Jena.

White, R. O. (1955). Grazing resources. In: *International Arid Land Meetings*. American Association for the Advancement of Science, Washington.

Whyte, R. O. (1961). Evolution of land use in south-western Asia. In: *A History of Land Use in Arid Regions* (ed. L. D. Stamp), pp. 37–113. Arid Zone Research Series, XVII. UNESCO, Paris.

Wolfart, R. (1967). *Geologie von Syrien und dem Libanon.* Borntraeger, Berlin.

Yacoub, S. M. (1971). *Sedentarization and settlement of the nomadic populations in selected Arab countries.* Pamphlet No. AES.8, Faculty of Agricultural Science, American University, Beirut.

Yadav, J. S. P. (1966). Soils of the dry zone of India. *Indian Forester*, **86**, 274–95.

Zohary, M. (1940). Geobotanical analysis of the Syrian Desert. *Palestine Journal of Botany* (Jerusalem), Series 2, 46–96.

Zohary, M. (1946). The flora of Iraq and its phyto-geographical sub-divisions. *Direccion General de Agricultura Bulletin* No. 31, Government of Iraq.

Zohary, M. (1947). A vegetation map of western Palestine. *Journal of Ecology*, **34**, 1–19.

Zohary, M. (1962). *The plant life of Palestine.* Ronald Press, New York.

Zohary, M. (1973). *Geobotanical foundation of the Middle East.* Volumes I & II. Gustav Fischer, Stuttgart.

Zohary, M. & Fienbrun, N. (1951). Outline of vegetation of northern Negev. *Palestine Journal of Botany* (Jerusalem), Series 4, 90–104.

Zohary, M. & Orshan, G. (1949). Structure and ecology of the vegetation in the Dead Sea region of Palestine. *Palestine Journal of Botany* (Jerusalem), Series 4, 177–206.

Manuscript received by the editors January 1975

7. Productivity of desert communities in central Asia

L. E. RODIN

Introduction

The Arid Zone in Asia is a vast forage reserve which is used for cattle breeding in the Kazakhstan, in the Central Asia Republics and in the Mongolian People's Republic. The desert pastures are used by cattle practically the whole year round. This accounts for the interest the desert pastures have attracted from both the scientific and the practically oriented institutions. The pastures here are being assessed to determine their potential and to develop methods of rational utilization and improvement. An overview of the relevant investigations may constitute the subject of a separate study. In fact, this has been performed, to a certain degree, by Sovetkina (1938) who evaluated all types of pastures in Central Asia. Results contained in subsequent publications, numbering up to scores of titles in all, have been included in textbooks (Larin, 1960; 1969). However, development of scientifically substantiated, rational approaches to the utilization of the vegetation cover necessitated further scientific investigations on the biogeocoenological basis and on a broader scale.

Studies on the biological productivity of plant communities, and of the factors which govern it in the Arid Zone of the USSR, have been made by numerous research stations even before the start of IBP activities. Every station has been pursuing goals set up according to its particular programme. Among these there were different purposes aimed at solution of theoretical and practical problems. Results accumulated by stations prior to the IBP project have been published in numerous periodical press articles and in several multi-authored publications or monographs issued during the period of the IBP activities. In addition, reports presented at the meeting on biological productivity (1966) and at the two international symposia held in the USSR in 1968 and in 1972 have covered these results. See: *Methods of productivity studies in root systems and rhizosphere organisms*, International Symposium, Leningrad (1968); *Basic problems of biological productivity*, Leningrad (1969); *Biocomplex investigation in Kazakhstan*, Vols I, II, Leningrad (1969); *Pastures and hay meadows of Kazakhstan*, Alma-Ata (1970); *Vegetation of Central part of Karakum and its productivity*, Ashkhabad (1970); *Productivity of pastures of North Aral area*, Alma-Ata (1971); *Biological productivity and mineral cycling in the terrestrial plant communities*, Leningrad (1971); *Ecophysio-*

273

Description of arid ecosystems

logical foundation of ecosystems productivity in Arid Zone. International Symposium, Leningrad (1972); and others.

Investigations within the IBP Programme, which were more or less coordinated programmes and methodologies of the five research stations in the USSR and in one station in the Mongolian People's Republic (cooperative research of Soviet and Mongolian scientists), started in 1965 or later.

The IBP stations

All the research stations in the USSR are situated in the Asian desert region; the provinces are named according to Geobotanicheskoe raionirovanie SSSR, Leningrad, 1947. Some statistics relating to the six stations are given in Table 7.1.

Climate (K. I. Kobak)

All the IBP stations are located in the area of continental desert climate. The two most important climatic factors are the winter Siberian anticyclone and summer thermal depression. A very dry climate is common to all the stations. According to the classification proposed by A. A. Grigorjev and M. I. Budyko the dryness index (ratio of the evaporation, or feasible evaporation to the annual precipitation) is more than 3.00 while on the border of the southern and northern deserts it may rise to 8.00 or 9.00.

The M. Barsuki and Taukum Stations (46°05' N and 44°20' N, respectively) are situated in the semidesert and northern desert climatic zones which span the major part of the central Asian plains to the north from 43 to 44° N.

The Kyzylkum, Karrykul and Repetek Stations are located in the southern desert climatic zone and, according to B. P. Alisov, the Karrykul and Repetek Stations are found in the region of the southern-turan subtropical desert.

Temperature differences between the zones can be characterized by summing all temperatures above 10 °C for the period when mean air temperature is above this value. Using this criterion the M. Barsuki and Taukumy Stations are found in the 'warm' climate (the values for the M. Barsuki Station area being 3647 °C); while the other three stations are in the 'very warm' climate (the value for the Repetek Station being 5600 °C).

Different patterns of atmospheric circulation in the northern and southern deserts account for the differences in humidity in these areas. The differences are such that, in the southern deserts, cyclone activity is totally absent for the four summer months. The summer thermal depres-

274

Table 7.1. *Some indices of the environmental conditions of the desert stations*

Indices	M. Barsuki	Taukum	Kyzylkum	Karakum–Karrykul	Karakum–Repetek	Gobi
Longitude and latitude	46° 05' N 59° E	44° 20' N —	40° 45' N 63° 45' E	38° 14' N 58° 16' E	38° 14' N 68° 11' E	44° 12' N 103° 10' E
Height above sea level (m)	—	350–500	375	90	190	1000
Precipitation (mm)	120	217	95–103	148	114.5	130–150
winter–spring	90–100	160–180	70	123	113	45
summer–autumn	20–30	40–50	25	25	2	85[1]
Number of days with precipitation	10–15	30	47[11]	40–45	32	—
Temperature (°C)						
mean annual	—	9	15.2	15.6	16	3.8
mean July	—	25.5	30.8	31.9	32	21.4
mean January	—	-8.7	-1.5	0.4	1.7	-15.9
total > 10 °C	3647	3854–4303[2]	4560–4660[12]	5553	5600	2200
Duration of sunshine (h yr⁻¹)	—	2500–2900[3]	2800–2900	2850	3083	3200
Total radiation (kcal cm⁻²)	176[4]	180[4]	152[11]	148[5]	201[4]	120[6]
PAR,[13] period > 10° (kcal cm⁻²)	40–45	40.9	—	—	—	—
PAR,[13] period April–October (kcal cm⁻²)	51	50–55	—	—	—	—
Frostless period (days)	165	160	226	220–230	280	150
Beginning of vegetation (first shoots)	March–April	April	March–April	Feb.–March (Oct.)	Feb.–March (Nov.)	April–May
Mean annual wind velocity (m s⁻¹)	3.5	3.5	5.5	2.9	3.6	3.5
Depth of winter–spring humidifying (cm)	140–210	60–150	60–120	60–100[7]	70–150	—
Depth of ground waters (m)	10	2–40	20–30	20–25	4–7	—
Mineralization of ground waters (g l⁻¹)	—	1–2	1–4	14–30	3–5	—
Thickness of the soil profile (cm)	80–200	10–150	25–120	25–50	60–80	20–70
pH	6.4–6.8	7.9–8.6	7.2–8.0	7.8–8.2	6.0–8.1	—
Humus (%)	0.1–1.0	0.1–1.2	0.2–0.6	0.4	0.4–3.0	0.2
Microorganisms in soil (10⁶ cells g⁻¹)	—	0.05–0.2[8]	0.01[9]	—	2.0–8.0	—
Microorganisms in the layer 0–30 cm (kg m⁻²)	—	—	0.1–1.0[10]	—	0.3–0.4	—

(1) During June–August; (2) the sum of above-zero temperatures is given; (3) according to *The climate in Kazakhstan* (1959); (4) calculated according to T. G. Berlend; (5) according to data provided by the local meteostation; (6) according to data provided by the meteostation Dalan–Dzadagad; (7) on sands, on clay soils 50–60 cm; (8) in the layer 0–20 cm; (9) only microfungi; (10) only denitrifying bacteria; (11) papers by the Tashkent hydro-meteorological observatory, 1 (1961); (12) Babushkin L.P., Agrario-climatic regional division of Central Asia. *Proceeding of the Tashkent State University*, 236 (1964); (13) Photosynthetically Active Radiation.

sion ensues accompanied by the planetary frontal altitudinal zone to the north; in the zone of northern deserts, where the condensation level is lower, cyclones occur infrequently in the summertime.

Despite approximately similar annual precipitation, the pattern of precipitation is different between stations. At the M. Barsuki and Taukum Stations insignificant precipitation occurs during the summer months. In the area of the M. Barsuki Station, 20–30 mm of rain falls in June–September; at the Taukum Station, 40–50 mm of rain falls in the same period. The number of days when 0.1 mm or more rain falls is 10–15 at M. Barsuki and 30 at Taukum. Also at Taukum the major part of the rainfall can occur in spring or summer. In wintertime the northern deserts are affected by the winter Siberian anticyclone and practically no precipitation occurs there at that time.

In the southern deserts there is a very hot period with practically no rainfall from the middle of May until the middle of October. The rainfall in the Kyzylkum from June to September is only 10 mm; in the Karrykul, 5 mm; in the Repetek, 2 mm. The major precipitation in the southern deserts occurs in the cool season (October–May) as a result of vigorous cyclone activity. Moving from the northern to the southern regions there are steep increases in the mean annual air temperature: 3.8 °C in the Gobi (the Gobi station is about 1000 m above sea level); 9 °C in the Taukum; 14 °C in the Kyzylkum; 15.6 °C in the Karrykul and 16 °C in the Taukum; 30.4 °C in the Kyzylkum and 32 °C at the Repetek Station. In January these values are −15.9 °C in the Gobi; −8.7 °C in the Taukum; −2.7 °C in the Kyzylkum and +1.7 °C at the Repetek Station.

According to the classification proposed by M. I. Budyko, which is based on comparison of the severity of winters and the thickness of the snow cover, the M. Barsuki, Taukum and Kyzylkum are considered as regions characteristic of 'moderately mild winters' and the Karrykul and Repetek Stations are regions of 'mild winters'.

Vegetation of the communities studied

There are relatively few species in the areas around the stations but numerous life forms are present. Throughout this chapter plant names are given according to the flora of the USSR and to S. K. Czerepanov (1973). There is a general similarity of life-forms in the communities studied (Table 7.2).

In the natural communities, the shrubs (including 'trees' – both *Haloxylon* sp. and *Ammodendron conollyi*), semi-shrubs and semi-shrublets constitute some 15–25%; perennial grasses, 30–60%; ephemerals and other annual plants, 20–70%. In the anthropogenic communities in the Karrykul area, the shrubs and semi-shrubs constitute up to 38% of the whole

Table 7.2. *Composition of the life forms in some associations in the regions of the stations*

Region and association	M. Barsuki				Taukum			Gobi
	Ammodendron argenteum	Artemisia terrae-albae	Anabasis salsa	Mean data	Ephedra lomatolepis	Eurotia ceratoides	Artemisia terrae-albae	Agropyron fragile
Number of species in the formation or in the region of the stations	54[1]	300[2]	175[1]	200[2]	—	—	—	—
trees (%)	—	—	—	—	—	—	—	—
shrubs and shrublets (%)	6	—	—	—	14	—	4	10
semishrubs and semishrublets (%)	19	8–10	—	—	10	9	12	6
perennial grasses	56	20–25	—	—	55	49	60	48
ephemerals and other annual plants (%)	18	65	—	—	21	41	24	36
Number of species in the association	45	44	60	—	29	34	25	31

Region and association	Kyzylkum				Karakum		Repetek	
	Mean data	Artemisia turanica	Artemisia diffusa	Nanophyton erinaceum	Mean data	Karrykul	Haloxylon ammodendron	Reaumuria soongorica
Number of species in the formation or in the region of the stations	183	60	31	30	277	194[2]	135[2]	—
trees (%)	2	—	—	—	2	3	3	—
shrubs and shrublets (%)	3	3	—	3	12	15	10	11
semishrubs and semishrublets (%)	11	7	6	6	14	20	17	26
perennial grasses	25	5	32	16	22	30	—	43
ephemerals and other annual plants (%)	59	85	62	75	50	32	70	20
Number of species in the association	—	60	31	30	—	—	101	45

[1] Number of species in a formation; [2] number of species in the region of the station.

NOTE: Due to limitation of space only principal species are given.

Description of arid ecosystems

floristic composition. The *Reaumuria soongorica* community in the Gobi is noteworthy for its content of shrubs and semi-shrubs which amount to 37%, perennial grasses account for 43%, while annual plants contribute as little as 20%. The number of species which can be listed range from 25 to 45 and in certain instances even less.

Description and structure of vegetation in the communities studied
The Malye Barsuki (B. A. Bykov & N. G. Kirichenko)

Ammodendron argenteum–Artemisia tomentella–Agropyron fragile *associations*

Found on primitive sandy soils. Projected coverage is about 50%. *Ammodendron argenteum*, 1984 plants ha^{-1}; *Artemisia tomentella*, 18800 plants ha^{-1}; *Agropyron fragile*, *Astragalus ammodendron*, *Aristida pennata* and other species are abundant. Total, 45 species.

Artemisia terrae-albae–Rheum tataricum–Poa bulbosa *associations*

Projected coverage is about 37%. *Artemisia terrae-albae* about 150000 plants ha^{-1}; *Kochia prostrata*, 28500 plants ha^{-1}; *Poa bulbosa, Colpodium humile, Alyssum desertorum, Ceratocarpus arenarius, Leptaleum filifolium* and other species are abundant. There are 44 higher plant species in total. Lichens (7 species), make a considerable contribution to this association and account for 0.01 t ha^{-1} of absolute dry mass.

Anabasis salsa *associations with ephemerals*

Found on solonchak–solonetz soils. Projected coverage is up to 30%. *Anabasis salsa*, 60000 plants ha^{-1}; *Eremopyrum distans, Lepidium perfoliatum, Ceratocarpus arenarius* and other species are abundant. Total, 60 species. Lichens are also found.

The Taukum (L. Ya. Kurochnika & L. T. Osmanova)

Ephedra lomatolepis–Calligonum *sp. associations*

Found on primitive sandy soils mostly on the overgrown tops of hills and along depressions between the hills. Projected coverage is about 35%. *Ephedra lomatolepsis*, 114100 plants ha^{-1}; *Kochia prostrata, Carex physodes, Senecio subdentatus* and other species are sparse. Total, 29 species.

Eurotia ceratoides–Artemisia terrae-albae *associations*

Found on loamy calcareous soils in the depressions. Projected coverage of flowering plants is 35–50%. *Eurotia ceratoides*, 10000 plants ha^{-1}; *Artemisia terrae-albae*, 12600 plants ha^{-1}; *Carex physodes*, *Artemisia scoparia* are abundant, but *Colpodium humile* is sparse. Total, 34 species. It is characteristic of this area that *Tortula desertorum* is abundant and can contribute up to 80% of the projected coverage.

Artemisia terrae-albae–Kochia prostrata *associations*

Found on dense sandy soils. Projected coverage is about 50%. *Artemisia terrae-albae*, 61000 plants ha^{-1}; *Kochia prostrata*, 26000 plants ha^{-1}; *Agropyron fragile*, 9300 plants ha^{-1}; *Carex physodes*, *Colpodium humile*, *Oedibasis apiculata* and other species are abundant. Total, 25 species.

Agropyron fragile–Artemisia terrae-albae *associations*

Found on sandy soils. Projected coverage is about 40%. *Agropyron fragile*, 12700 plants ha^{-1}; *Artemisia terrae-albae*, 6200 plants ha^{-1}; *Kochia prostrata*, *Carex physodes* and other species are sparse. Total, 31 species.

The Kyzylkum (I. F. Mamotov)
Artemisia turanica & A. diffusa *associations with ephemerals*

Found on grey-brown loamy soils. Projected coverage is from 25 to 30%. *Artemisia diffusa*, 14200 plants ha^{-1}; *A turanica*, 1600 plants ha^{-1}; *Poa bulbosa*, *Carex physodes* and other species are abundant. Total, 23 species.

Artemisia turanica & A. diffusa–Salsola rigida & S. arbuscula *associations*

Found on grey-brown gypsum soils. Projected coverage is about 35%. *Artemisia turanica* and *A. diffusa*, 7705 plants ha^{-1} (4065 live and 3640 dead); *Salsola rigida*, 3804 plants ha^{-1} (60 dead plants included); *Carex physodes*, *Eremurus sogdianus*, *Goldbachia laevigata*, *Lachnoloma lehmannii* and other species are sparse. Total, 52 species. Frequently spots of *Tortula desertorum* surround dead shrubs.

Description of arid ecosystems

Nanophyton erinaceum *associations*

Found on grey-brown solonetz–solonchak soils. Projected coverage varies from 5 to 15%. Plants are very sparse, single plants are frequent. *Salsola gemmasens, Aellenia subaphylla* and other semishrublet species; *Gemanthus gamocarpus, Halimocnemis longifolia* and other species. Total, 17 species.

The Karakum–Karrykul (N. T. Nechaeva & K. G. Antonova)

Haloxylon persicum–Carex physodes *associations*

Found on stable sandy desert soils. Projected coverage is 30%. *Calligonum rubens, C. setosum, Salsola richteri* are also found among other species. Total, 50 species.

Calligonum rubens–Mausolea eriocarpa–Carpex physodes *associations*

Found on sandy desert soils. Projected coverage is 35%. *Calligonum setosum, Salsola richteri* and other species are also present. Total, 60 species.

Salsola arbuscula–Artemisia kemrudica–Carex physodes *associations*

Found on sandy desert soils. Projected coverage is 40%. *Calligonum rubens, C. setosum, Aristida pennata, Euphorbia cheirolepis* and others are also characteristic of this association. Total, 78 species.

All three communities of anthropogenic origin appeared some 80 to 100 years ago due to excessive pasture stress and cutting out of *Haloxylon persicum* for firewood; since 1960 these communities have been protected as reservations.

The community described below, presumably an original one, has also been protected since 1960 as a reservation.

Salsola gemmasens & Artemisia kemrudica–Gamanthus gamocarpus *associations*

Found on takyr-like clay soils. Projected coverage is 25%. There are also *Climacoptera lanata, Halimocnemis mollissima* and other species. Total, 42 species.

The Karakum–Repetek (Yu. M. Miroshnichenko, L. N. Novichkova-Ivanova, L. E. Rodin & R. Togyzaev)

Haloxylon ammodendron–Carex physodes *associations*

Found on desert sandy soils. Projected coverage is 90%. *Haloxylon ammodendron*, about 600 plants ha; *Ephedra strobilacea, Salsola richteri, Calligonum setosum, Aellenia subaphylla* and other species of shrubs and semishrublets, 200 plants ha^{-1}. The dominant *Carex physodes* is accompanied, to some extent, by *Anisantha tectorum, Malcolmia grandiflora, Papaver pavonicum, Kochia schrenkiana* and other ephemerals and annual plants (about 20 species). Total, 101 species. This community is characterized by spots of *Tortula desertorum* (projected coverage ranges from 2 to 3%) and development of soil algae.

The Gobi (T. K. Gordeeva, T. I. Kazantzeva, Z. G. Bespalova & T. A. Popova)

Reaumuria soongorica – Brachanthemum gobicum – Zygophyllum xanthoxylon *associations*

Found on extensively deserted, brown, desert-steppe, sandy and loamy-sand soils. Projected coverage ranges from 7 to 10%. *Reaumuria soongorica*, 3400 plants ha^{-1}; *Brachanthemum gobicum*, 980 plants ha^{-1}; *Salsola passerina*, 480 plants ha^{-1}; *Zygophyllum xanthoxylon*, 320 plants ha^{-1}. In addition there are occasional plants of *Nitraria sibirica, Potaninia mongolica, Stipa glareosa, Convolvulus ammanii* and other species. Total, 45 species (in some years 25–35 species).

In all the communities listed the principle parameters of their biological productivity, such as the phytomass potential, the annual production and the litter fall, as well as mineral cycling (elements of biological turnover) and the ash and nitrogen content were investigated. Climate, water relations, photosynthesis and respiration were also studied.

All of these parameters were assessed over season and the whole year. Limitation of space precludes full exposition of these results but it is planned to publish them separately. Here we present but a brief account of these parameters.

The phytomass

The absolute amount of the phytomass in various communities in different regions varies from about 5 to 34 t ha^{-1} (Table 7.3.). The highest values have been registered for *Ammodendron argenteum* and *Artemisia terrae-albae* communities in the M. Barsuki area and the *Haloxylon ammodendron* community in the Karakum–Repetek.

Table 7.3. *The phytomasss and dead organic matter (t ha⁻¹) recorded at five sites under various communities*

	M. Barsuki[1]				Taukum		
	Ammodendron argenteum	*Artemisia terrae-albae*	*Anabasis salsa*	*Ephedra lomatolepis*	*Eurotia ceratoides*	*Artemisia terrae-albae*	*Agropyron fragile*
Phytomass	34.22	33.74	8.26	12.84	10.32	7.45	6.03
leaves and assimilating shoots	4.33	1.46	0.61	1.03	0.96	1.32	0.57
the same (%)	13	5	7	8	9	18	10
woody tissue	4.80	4.45	0.63	2.22	0.44	0.98	0.56
the same (%)	14	13	8	17	4	13	9
roots	25.08	27.83	7.02	9.59	8.92	5.15	4.90
the same (%)	73	82	85	75	87	69	81
Dead material	3.97[2]	9.18	3.87	—	—	—	—
dead branches in the crown	3.97	0.96	0.03	—	—	—	—
dead plants and fallen plants	—	1.33	0.20	—	—	—	—
litter	—	1.90	0.64	—	—	—	—
leaves and shoots	—	1.20	0.40	—	—	—	—
branches	—	0.70	0.24	—	—	—	—
dead roots and other underground organs	—	5.00	3.00	—	—	—	—
Total amount of organic matter	39.19[2]	42.92	12.12	—	—	—	—
phytomass (%)	—	79	68	—	—	—	—
dead material (%)	—	21	32	—	—	—	—

	Kyzylkum				Karakum–Karrykul			Karakum–Repetek
	Artemisia turanica	Artemisia diffusa	Nanophyton erinaceum	Haloxylon persicum	Calligonum rubens	Salsola arbuscula	Salsola gemmascens	Haloxylon ammodendron
Phytomass	3.5	5.7	1.3	8.07	7.41	6.74	5.12	26.86
leaves and assimilating shoots	0.18	0.36	0.1	0.47	0.51	0.46	0.45	1.39
the same (%)	5	6	8	6	7	7	9	5
woody tissue	0.52	0.74	0.3	3.28	2.09	2.34	2.80	6.0
the same (%)	15	13	23	41	28	35	55	22
roots	2.8	4.6	0.9	4.32	4.81	3.94	1.87	19.47
the same (%)	80	81	69	53	65	58	36	73
Dead material	—	—	—	0.58	1.21	0.88	0.65	3.42[2]
dead branches in the crown	—	—	—	0.10	0.21	0.17	0.29	0.82
dead plants and fallen plants	—	—	—	0.19	0.47	0.28	0.14	0.64
litter	—	—	—	0.06	0.06	0.05	0.07	1.96
leaves and shoots	—	—	—	0.02	0.03	0.03	0.06	1.51
branches	—	—	—	0.04	0.03	0.02	0.01	0.33
dead roots and other underground organs	—	—	—	0.23	0.47	0.38	0.15	—
Total amount of organic matter	—	—	—	8.65	8.62	7.62	5.77	30.28[2]
phytomass (%)	—	—	—	93	86	88	89	—
dead material (%)	—	—	—	7	14	12	11	—

[1] The community utilized for practical purposes (grazing etc.). [2] Assessed partially. —, not determined; Authors: see Table 7.4.

Description of arid ecosystems

The phytomass structure, however, reveals significant peculiarities. Roots and other underground plant organs in natural communities constitute 70–85%; the assimilating organs, 5–18%; and the woody tissue (of perennial aboveground organs), 4–17%. These values, on the whole, are rather similar to those given in the paper by Rodin & Bazilevitch (1967) and in that by Rustamov (1972). Somewhat different are the anthropogenic communities in the Karakum–Karrykul where the phytomass structure is made up as follows: roots, 36–65%; assimilating organs, 6–9% and woody tissue, 28–55%.

In each case these differences can be accounted for by the ecologo-morphological peculiarities of the dominant species which determine the bulk of the phytomass.

A specific situation is seen in the *Reaumuria soongorica* community in the Northern Gobi, where the extremely sparse vegetation is characterized by insignificant aboveground phytomass which amounts to only 0.8 t ha^{-1}. Leaves and assimilating organs constitute 16% and the woody tissue, 84%.

Dead material

Absolute amounts also vary considerably (by an order of magnitude) from 0.6 to 9 t ha^{-1}. Within the limits of a region, however, these differences are much less: in the M. Barsuki 4–9 t ha^{-1}; in the anthropogenic communities 0.6–1.2 t ha^{-1}. The low absolute amount of the dead material in the latter communities is because the dominating plant species have not yet reached old age and there are few dead plants or branches. The ratios of the phytomass to the dead material in natural communities are similar, approximately 3:1 or 2:1, while in the anthropogenic communities of the Karakum–Karrykul this ratio is about 8:1. This is due to their relative youthfulness.

Annual production

It is only natural that the absolute amounts of the annual production vary considerably; they are, however, very similar in communities which have dominant species of the same life form (Table 7.4).

Comparison of the pattern of the annual production in separate communities can be made only with respect to the production of roots and of the whole aboveground mass. This is because of the incompleteness of the data available; in some cases there is no information as to the separate increment of leaves and of assimilating organs as well as about the increment of the woody tissue. Roots account for 65–85% of the annual increment in the natural communities and a little more than 50% in the anthropogenic communities of the Karakum–Karrykul region. Among the latter communities it is the *Salsola gemmasceus* community that is conspicuous for the extremely low proportion of roots in the total production. This is accounted for both by the specific features of the principal species itself and because the contribution of the ephemeral species in this community is very low (less than 0.1 t ha^{-1}). Where the proportion of the assimilating organs in the annual production of the community has been measured, it lies within the same order of magnitude, being approximately 15–30% of the total annual production (excluding the *Ephedra lomatolepis* community where the assimilating organs' production make up 41% of the total). The *Reaumuria soongorica* community in the Northern Gobi is a separate case where the annual production is extremely low; as little as 0.13 t ha^{-1} (aboveground parts only).

Litter fall

There is wide variation in the absolute amount of total litter fall in all the communities studied; 0.7–12 t ha^{-1} (Table 7.5). Comparison of the communities characterized by similar dominant species reveals similarities in these values. Thus, the natural communities dominated by semi-shrub species produce litter fall amounting to 3–7 t ha^{-1} (a particular case is the community where the dominating species is the evergreen shrub *Ephedra lomatolepis* whose litter fall is as low as 1.5 t ha^{-1}). In young anthropogenic communities of the Karakum–Karrykul region litter fall is low and very similar; 0.7–1.2 t ha^{-1}. Assimilating organs contribute 15–36% of the litter fall in the natural communities while the root fall amounts to 64–84%. In the anthropogenic communities of the Karakum–Karrykul region the input of the root fall is the lowest, 37–57%. The same holds true for the proportion of the root fall in the *Ephedra lomatolepis* communities.

The greatest amount of litter fall is, as expected, found in the communities with the highest phytomass accumulation, that is, the *Ammodendron argenteum* communities (12 t ha^{-1}) in the M. Barsuki and *Haloxylon ammodendron* (7 t ha^{-1}) in the Karakum–Repetek. These communities are also very similar in litter fall structure.

All of the peculiarities mentioned above support the general regularity highlighted in the review by Rodin & Bazilevitch (1967, Table 44).

Production of cryptogamic plants (L. N. Novichkova-Ivanova)

In the Repetek region the soil algae in the *Haloxylon ammodendron–Carex physodes* community have been studied and recorded. The number of species of algae is comparatively poor as opposed to the algal flora of other types of deserts. Some 50 species are found here, with a representative of the blue–green algae, *Microcoleus vaginatus*, and unicellular green algae predominant (Sdobnikova, 1959).

The algal biomass varies considerably between the different stations.

Table 7.4. *The contribution by trees, shrubs and grasses to annual production (t ha⁻¹) at five sites under a number of different plant communities*

	M. Barsuki			Taukum			
	Ammodendron argenteum	*Artemisia terrae-alba*	*Anabasis salsa*	*Ephedra lomatolepis*	*Eurotia ceratoides*	*Artemisia terrae-albae*	*Agropyron fragile*
Trees	0	0	0	0	0	0	0
leaves	0	0	0	0	0	0	0
woody tissue	0	0	0	0	0	0	0
roots	0	0	0	0	0	0	0
Shrubs, semi-shrubs	11.60	5.32	3.15	1.19	5.05	2.22	0.32
leaves, shoots	3.60	0.73	0.33	0.34	0.61	1.05	0.14
woody tissue	0.57	0.58	0.10	0.10	0.02	0.06	0.03
roots	7.43	4.01	2.72	0.75	4.42	1.11	0.15
Grasses	2.30	2.32	0.68	0.75	1.29	1.93	4.07
leaves, stems	0.73	0.73	0.28	0.45	0.39	0.30	0.50
roots	1.63	1.59	0.40	0.30	0.90	1.63	3.57
Above-ground layer (mosses, lichens, algae)	—	—	—	—	—	—	—
Total	13.90	7.62	3.83	1.94	6.34	4.15	4.39

	Kyzylkum			Karakum–Karrykul				Karakum–Repetek
	Artemisia turanica	*Artemisia diffusa*	*Nanophyton erinaceum*	*Haloxylon persicum*	*Calligonum rubens*	*Salsola arbuscula*	*Salsola gemmascens*	*Haloxylon ammodendron*
Trees	0	0	0	0.09	0	0	0	3.27
leaves	0	0	0	0.05	0	0	0	0.72
woody tissue	0	0	0	—	0	0	0	0.45
roots	0	0	0	0.04	0	0	0	2.10
Shrubs, semi-shrubs	0.32	0.52	0.15	0.34	0.42	0.33	0.47	0.80
leaves, shoots	0.14	0.24	0.07	0.22	0.29	0.23	0.38	0.19
woody tissue	—	—	—	—	—	—	—	0.19
roots	0.18	0.28	0.08	0.12	0.13	0.10	0.09	0.42
Grasses	0.05	0.17	0.04	0.58	0.68	0.61	0.09	3.28
leaves, stems	0.04	0.12	0.03	0.20	0.22	0.23	0.07	0.24
roots	0.01	0.05	0.01	0.38	0.44	0.38	0.02	2.94
Above-ground layer (mosses lichens, algae)	—	—	—	—	—	—	—	0.22
Total	0.37	0.69	0.19	1.01	1.09	0.94	0.56	7.47

Authors: M. Barsuki, B. A. Bykov; Taukum, L. Ya. Kurochkina; Kyzylkum, A. D. Li, I. F. Momotov; Karakum-Karrykul, K. G. Antonova, S. D. Karshenas, N. T. Nechaeva; Karakum–Repetek; Y. M. Miroshnichenko, L. N. Novichkova–Ivanova, L. E. Rodin, R. Togyzaev.

Table 7.5. *Weight (t ha⁻¹) and percentage of the litter fall recorded at five sites, under various communities*

	M. Barsuki		Taukum				
	Ammodendron argenteum	*Artemisia terrae-albae*	*Anabasis salsa*	*Ephedra lomatolepis*	*Eurotia ceratoides*	*Artemisia terrae-albae*	*Agropyron fragile*
Total weight of litter fall	12.33	6.94	3.13	1.54	5.87	3.61	3.60
leaves and shoots (weight)	3.93	1.46	0.50	0.79	0.90	1.30	0.56
leaves and shoots (%)	32	21	16	51	15	35.7	15.5
woody tissue (weight)	0.39	0.44	0.03	0.02	0.01	0.01	0.03
woody tissue (%)	3	6	1	1	1	0.3	0.5
total weight of above ground plant parts	4.32	1.90	0.53	0.81	0.91	0.31	0.59
as % of the total litter fall	35	27	17	52	16	36	16
weight of root tissue	8.01	5.04	2.60	0.73	4.96	2.30	3.01
as % of the total litter fall	65	73	83	48	84	64	84

	Kyzylkum			Karakum-Karrykul			Karakum-Repetek	
	Artemisia turanica	*Artemisia diffusa*	*Nanophyton erinaceum*	*Haloxylon persicum*	*Calligonum rubens*	*Salsola arbuscula*	*Salsola gemmascens*	*Haloxylon ammodendron*
Total weight of litter fall	0.76	1.13	0.47	1.21	1.09	0.91	0.70	7.41
leaves and shoots (weight)	0.22	0.32	0.13	0.36	0.41	0.34	0.31	1.21
leaves and shoots (%)	29	28	28	30	37	37	44	16
woody tissue (weight)	0.06	0.05	0.03	0.33	0.06	0.06	0.13	0.64
woody tissue (%)	8	4	6	27	6	7	19	10
total weight of the above ground plant parts	0.28	0.37	0.16	0.69	0.47	0.40	0.44	1.85
as % of total litter fall	37	32	34	57	43	44	63	26
weight of root tissue	0.48	0.76	0.31	0.52	0.62	0.51	0.26	5.56
as % of the total litter fall	63	68	66	43	57	56	37	74

The highest values are registered in the subcrown spots of *Haloxylon ammodendron*. In favorable, humid springs, up to $20\,\mathrm{g\,m^{-2}}$ of dry matter are produced. In open areas under *Carex physodes* production is halved. The mean value for the whole community is about $0.03\,\mathrm{t\,ha^{-1}}$ (Table 7.6). Short-term variations in the amount of algal biomass are related to variations in humidity and temperature. There is, however, a certain time-lag between the onset of favorable humidity and temperature and an increase in biomass. The algae form hard films on the surface of sand and markedly reduce wind erosion. In addition the algae can fix nitrogen from the atmosphere and accumulate organic matter which is subsequently utilized by bacteria, soil invertebrates and microfungi. The importance of the algae is most pronounced in the takyr soils where they accumulate $0.5–1.4\,\mathrm{t\,ha^{-1}}$ of biomass while the annual production is probably considerably higher (Hollerbach, Novichkova & Sdobnikova, 1956). Quantitative estimates of the algal phytomass at other IBP stations have not been made.

The contribution of the *Tortula desertorum* moss is more evident in terms of primary production. Its synusia, which form a turf 2–3 cm thick, accumulate up to $4\,\mathrm{kg\,m^{-2}}$ of air dry organic matter. Considering the extensiveness of the coverage and the thickness of the turf the annual production of *Tortula desertorum* was estimated to be $0.19\,\mathrm{t\,ha^{-1}}$. Soil algae and moss contribute about 3% of the annual production in the *Haloxylon ammodendron* community (Table 7.7).

Soil microorganisms

Bacteria (I. S. Skalon)

A large number of species of bacteria are present in the sandy communities of deserts. In the *Haloxylon ammodendron–Carex physodes* community more than 55 species were found; species of the *Pseudomonas* genus dominated, *Bacillus megatericus* Trevisani and a number of other spore-forming *Bacillus* species; *Azotobacter chroococceum* Beijerinck; species of *Actinomyces*, *Proactinomyces*, *Mycobacterium*, *Bacterium*, *Chromobacterium*, *Clostridium*, *Sporocytophaga* and other genera were also found. The number of bacteria per gram of dry soil can be as high as 3–8 million. The biomass of microorganisms within the 0–20 cm soil layer is estimated for this community as $0.3–0.4\,\mathrm{kg}$ wet weight $\mathrm{m^{-2}}$. In October 1969 13 generations were recorded, while in April 1970 there were 10 generations. Therefore it can be seen that the biomass of microbes in soils may reach considerable values.

Table 7.6. *Biomass of algal synusia (kg ha⁻¹) in association of Haloxylon in the spring vegetative period during 1969, 1970 and 1972 at Karakum–Repetek Station (L. N. Novichkova-Ivanova, 1973)*

Location	Vegetation	Minimum for observation period	Maximum for observation period	Average for the vegetative period			Average for an observation period
				1969 cold spring	1970 humid spring	1972 dry spring	
Mound of *Haloxylon persicum–Calligonum* association	Open (uncovered) sand surface	0.001	0.24	0.009	0.03	0.12	0.08
	Under crown of *Haloxylon persicum*	0.008	3.05	—	1.7	0.04	0.43
Depression of *Haloxylon ammodendron–Carex physodes* & ephemerals association	Under *Carex physodes*	0.59	111.84	1.82	65.89	26.5	35.0
	Under crown of *Haloxylon ammodendron*	0.65	203.30	3.34	72.11	0.7	27.0

Table 7.7. *Some details of moss synusia (Tortula desertorum) in associations of Haloxylon ammodendron–Carex physodes and ephemerals at the Karakum–Repetek Station (L. N. Novichkova-Ivanova, 1973)*

Location	State of turf	Thickness of turf (cm)	Height of moss (mm)	Number of shoots per cm²			Weight[1] mg cm⁻²	Weight[2] t ha⁻¹
				Non-vegetating	Vegetating	Total		
Mound of *Ephedra strobilacea*	Old	2.5	2.0–3.0	74	—	74	400	0.8
	Medium	1.8	1.5–2.0	67	6	73	300	0.6
	Young	1.5	0.3–0.5	6	134	140	300	0.6
On slope of depression	Old	2.2	1.8–2.0	54	20	74	250	0.5
	Medium	1.3	0.1–0.3	93	16	109	150	0.3
	Young	0.9	0.3–0.5	110	—	110	100	0.2
Bottom of depression	weakly	0.9–1.0	0.1–1.0	40	—	40	100	0.2
	expressed	1.1–1.3	0.7–0.9	74	—	74	300	0.6

(1) Air dry weight. (2) Calculated for 2% of the area of the association covered with moss.

Soil microfungi (M. A. Litvinov & N. V. Smirnova)

Studies on the soil microfungi in the takyr soils, in the solonchaks and in the takyr-like solonchak soils revealed that the fungal flora is poor and uniform in its species composition. It is also quite different from the microfungal communities in soils of other geographical zones (Bazilevich *et al.*, 1952; Litvinov, 1956, 1968, 1969; Rodin & Bazilevich, 1956). Soil fungi in the root systems of *Haloxylon ammodendron*, *Carex physodes*, *Ephedra strobilacea* and *H. persicum* were studied on the Repetek reservation. Mycological analysis of the collection of microfungi comprising 138 strains revealed that the species composition of fungi obtained from the rhizosphere and from areas near roots in the soil layers comprised 13 and 14 species, respectively.

The greatest number of fungi was found in the soil areas near roots of *Haloxylon ammodendron*: there were 1 683 730 per gram of dry soil in the spring of 1973 while in the autumn of 1972 this number was as low as 515 100. Still lower were the numbers of fungi in the soil areas near roots of *Carex physodes*. The data obtained testify to the fact that fungi of the *Penicillium* genus dominate, in particular, *P. viridicyclopium*, which is found both in autumn and in spring. Among the fungi found, *Ulocladium botrytis* has also been observed in the soils of Egypt, India and Pakistan (Ellis, 1971). Quantitative proportions of various fungal species in the rhizosphere of desert plants may be dissimilar. With respect to quantitative characteristics the most prominent is a group of fungi of the *Penicillium* genus, second in abundance is a group of the *Fusarium* genus.

Fauna, quantity and biomass of animals (V. I. Kuznetzov, K. Ataev, A. G. Davletshina, V. G. Kaplin, L. V. Komarova & O. R. Sabirova)

Quantitative estimations of the animal population have been performed only in the Repetek reservation. The data presented here is for the reservation as a whole and for the *Haloxylon ammodendron* community, in particular.

There are about 200 species of vertebrates in the Repetek reservation. They include 29 mammals, 23 reptiles and more than 140 species of birds, The invertebrate fauna has not been investigated though insects alone are represented by more than 1000 species. Populations of animals vary considerably in number. For example, the population of *Rhombomys optimus* varied between 6–7 animals ha^{-1} in 1965 and no more than 0.5 ha^{-1} in 1969, while in 1936 and in 1950 there were 19–22 animals ha^{-1} (Stalmakova, 1954). Mammals are most numerous, less abundant are the reptiles and the lowest population number is registered for birds. Biomass of the insects is an order of magnitude higher than that of the mammals (Table 7.8).

Table 7.8. *Quantity (animals ha^{-1}) and biomass (kg ha^{-1}) of some groups of animals in the* Haloxylon ammodendron–Carex physodes *community (average values for the 1966–73 period) at the Karakum–Repetek station*

	Reptiles				Invertebrates	
Indices	Turtles	Others	Mammals	Birds	Crowns	Soils
Quantity	0.6	24.8	16.4	2.6	No data	No data
Biomass	0.5	0.8	1.4	0.06	10.1	15.0

In the Kyzylkum communities the entomofauna is evidently poorer. According to the data obtained by A. G. Davletshina (unpublished data) more than 500 species were registered in the Kyzylkum station area. Their number in separate communities varies considerably. In the *Artemisia turanica–Salsola rigida* community there are more than 100 species, and in the *Nanophyton erinaceum* community only 60 species. About 60 of the species are phytophagous.

Tropho-functional scheme of the sandy-desert biogeocoenosis
(A. B. Georgievsky & V. I. Kuznetsov)

A biogeocoenosis (BGC) is a complex, dynamic, self-regulating system. The definition 'tropho-functional' implies all kinds of possible interactions within the BGC so that the trophic relations are the determinants. Four structure–functional blocks can be distinguished which, operating together, provide for the stable turnover of matter and transformation of energy in the BGC (Fig. 7.1).

(*A*) *The abiotic environment* which includes solar energy, heat, gas and water masses, the substrate with the elements of mineral nutrition. This environment determines the volume and functioning of the other BGC blocks. The most important result of the reverse action is the formation of soils.
(*B*) *The producing block* is the source of the organic matter in the BGC. This block included (1) autotrophs (photo- and chemosynthesizing organisms) and, inseparably linked to the latter, (2) the phytotroph organisms which feed upon living plant parts. The phytotrophs not only consume plant material but, to a great extent, are responsible for the process of formation of living matter. This makes us consider the energy-producing unit to be not the plants themselves but a rather unified block of plants and phytotrophs. The effects the phytotrophs produce upon plants are diverse and they depend upon the nutritional

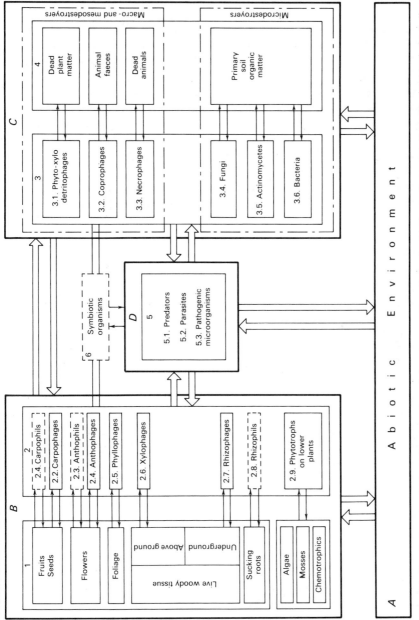

Fig. 7.1. Trophofunctional block diagram of sand desert ecosystem. Key: *A*, abiotic environment; *B*, producing block, including (1) autotrophs (2) phytotrophs; *C*, destroying block, including (3) saprotrophs, (4) dead organic matter; *D*, controlling block, including (5) controlling organisms, (6) symbiotic organisms. Arrows show the direction of exchange of information, matter and energy. Sub-blocks in broken lines are important for life autotrophs and heterotrophs. (A. B. Georgievsky & V. I. Kurnetsov.)

specialization of these organisms. With respect to this property a series of tropho-functional groups of the phytotrophs has been distinguished.

2.1. Carpophilic organisms. Terrestrial mammals and invertebrates (ants, carabids) which store seeds. In an arid BGC with sparse vegetation cover the contribution of animals to the distribution of seeds is small; wind is the major factor in dispersal of fruits and seeds.

2.2. Carpophagous organisms. This is a major group comprising mammals, birds and invertebrates as well as parasitizing microflora. These organisms extinguish the elevated concentration of seeds and fruits thereby limiting multiplication of plants and, consequently, serve to weaken the direct competition between plants and to maintain plant species diversity within the BGC.

2.3. Anthophilous organisms. This includes invertebrates from the orders Hymenoptera, Lepidoptera, Diptera and others. They act as pollinating agents in higher plants.

2.4. Anthophagous organisms. This group includes phytovorous mammals, reptiles and invertebrates. Specialized feeding on fully active flowers that could result in a noticeable effect upon the reproductive cycle of plants has not been observed.

2.5. Phyllophagous organisms. Numerous vertebrates and invertebrates which feed upon assimilating plant tissue as well as parasitic fungi.

2.6. Xylophagous organisms. A small number of species of vertebrates, invertebrates and fungi which feed on living perennial plant tissue.

2.7. Rhizophagous organisms. These include mammals and invertebrates which feed on tubers and underground plant parts; and parasitic fungi and achlorophyllous plants – parasites. The trophic activity of phyllophagous, xylophagous and rhizophagous organisms has been defined principally as injurious to the plants used as food. The recent data, however, viewed from the systems approach warrant different appraisal of the role these animals play in the BGC.

2.8. Rhizophilous organisms. Rhizosphere fungi and bacteria living in the area of the feeding roots. They function as a protection to these 'delicate' organs thus promoting uptake of various substances from soils.

2.9. Phytophagous organisms on lower plants. This group includes invertebrates and fungi as algaephagous organisms. In the sandy desert BGC these are sparse and sometimes unidentifiable. The phytotrophic organisms may be finally divided into two major functionally diverse groups. One can distinguish phytophilous organisms which are not only non-injurious to plants but are frequently beneficial. The phytophagous organisms, due to their trophic activity, accomplish a series of important functions in the BGC: they control the population density of plants;

favourably affect plant populations by speeding up the death of the weakened, ill and old plants; increase the yield of the primary production; considerably speed up the turnover of substances; serve to enrich the soils with substances required by plants; and alter the rate and direction of successional processes in vegetation during population 'explosions'.

Ancient higher and lower plants are little affected by the phytophagous organisms. This warrants our considering the rich abundance of the phytophagous organisms in the modern vegetation as an enhanced controlling mechanism developed by the BGC and directed towards the regulation of activity of the more vigorous higher plants.

(C) *The destroying block.* This group comprises the organic detritus (dead plant parts, both aboveground and underground; dead woody tissue of stems, branches, litter fall, as well as bodies of animals and dead microorganisms) and the destroyers of the detritus–saprotrophic organisms (see Fig. 7.1). Destruction proceeds in several stages. Macro- and mesodestroyers serve essentially to disintegrate and redistribute the detritus while the final utilization is performed by the microdestroyers. Activity of the latter is of primary importance for the BGC due to their dispersal and omnipresence. The function of this block is the earliest destruction of the organic matter with subsequent inclusion of the material produced into the soil.

(D) *The controlling block.* Intrapopulational mechanisms are known which control quantity and the state of populations when shifts in densities result in changes of physiological conditions of organisms and in their fertility. This mechanism is not a universal one. Most frequently a necessity arises in specific controlling influences of the other BGC components upon the heterotrophic organisms. These factors, on the one hand, comprise the conditions of the abiotic environment which determine spatial, temperature and time limits for the activity of heterotrophic organisms; on the other hand, the action of the complex of predators, parasites and pathogenic microorganisms. The latter are specific in their influences and are themselves subject to control influences. All of these factors listed affect the population of the heterotrophs not in a separate way but operate in a complex assembly forming a united mechanism of the biogeocoenisis control.

Apart from the antibiosis of the heterotrophic organisms mentioned above there can be a wide distribution of the opposite type of interactions, that is, a symbiosis which includes all the mutually profitable contacts of organisms within a BGC. In the modern BGC individual species practically never occur without their accompanying partners. Forming a single system with the host, the symbiotic organisms may be either grouped (Fig. 7.1) or present in a number of sub-blocks.

Conclusion

Phytomass accumulation, annual production and mineral cycling are a result of the exceptionally important activity of a few species. In the *Ammodendron argenteum* community some 89% of the annual production is contributed by five species (*Ammodendron argenteum, Artemisia tomentella, Kochia prostrata, Agropyron fragile* and *Astragalus ammodendron*). In the *Haloxylon ammodendron* community only two species, *Haloxylon ammodendron* and *Carex physodes*, produce 83% of the annual production and 89% of the ash content of the mineral elements.

In every association listed above several layers can be distinguished in the aboveground sphere and in the soils. Communities characteristic of the complex structure display high annual production and accumulate great amounts of phytomass.

Anthropogenic intervention causing destruction (or weakening) of only one layer invariably results in decrease both of the biological and economic productivity. Hence some practical measures can be proposed for the improvement of the serial communities disturbed by the anthropogenic intervention.

(*a*) Production would be increased by the introduction (by sowing or strip plantings) of a variety of plants which make the most effective use of the various layers of the aboveground sphere of the community and the various soil layers in various seasons.

(*b*) Various types of protection (reservation, rotation, lowering of the exploitation norms for pasture use, cutting-out and clearing for wood or for other needs) retain or maintain the normal multilayered structure of the community. This results in an increase in the agricultural productivity of the community.

(*c*) Sufficient water supply is the most important condition for the successful functioning of the desert biogeocoenoses. It is important, therefore, to use the limited water supply as effectively as possible. Among the measures available we can list treatment of the hard soils which conduct water poorly; reduction of water runoff; improvement of the mechanical properties of soils by addition of sands and decreasing the physical evaporation by application of mulches

Studies on water relations in desert plants show that these plants are adequately adapted to the severe stresses of the arid climate and even extreme fluctuations in the environmental conditions cause no destruction of the whole biogeocoenosis but only interfere with the proper functioning of separate structural elements. Extension of the root systems of numerous desert plants down to a considerable depth is not only an adaptation to insufficient water supply but has also a biological significance in that it diminishes root competition in between the plants which have more shallow root systems.

In the assimilating plant organs which fall off annually one observes predominant accumulation of the biohalogen elements (Na, Cl) while in roots of the desert plants the organogens accumulate to a greater extent (K, Ca, P). Therefore, the domination of roots in the organic matter and concentration of the majority of the nutrient elements in the roots, that is typical of the desert biogeocoenoses, may be considered as a reserve of natural soil fertility.

Finally, this warrants a conclusion that the principle way to improve and maintain highly productive, long-living and self-restoring biogeocoenoses in the arid zones is the creation of communities which have tree–shrub biomorphs with deep and extensive root systems and populations of other biomorphs (semishrublets, grasses, ephemeres, long-vegetating plants and annual plants) with different growth periods which would contribute to the multilayered (both above- and underground) structure.

References

Bazilevich, N. I., Hollerbach, M. M., Litvinov, M. A., Rodin, L. E., Steinberg, D. M. (1952). Biological factors in the takyr's formation at Main Turkmenian Canal (translated title). *Botanical Journal* (Leningrad), **38** (I), 3–30.

Ellis, M. B. (1971). *Dematiaceous Hyphomycetes.* Kew Gardens, Surrey.

Hollerbach, M. M., Novichkova, L. N. & Sdobnikova, N. V. (1956). Algae of takyrs (translated title). In: *Takyry Zapadnoi Turkmenii i puti ikh selskokhozyaistvennogo osvoeniya,* pp. 38–54. Moscow.

Larin, I. V. (1960). Pastbishcheoborot – sistema ispol' zovaniya pastbishch i ukhoda za nimi. Sel'khozgiz. *Pasture rotation as a system for range use and development* (translated title). Nauka, Moscow–Leningrad.

Larin, I. V. (1969). *Grassland management and range economy* (translated title). Leningrad.

Litvinov, M. A. (1956). Biotsenozy pochvennykh mikroskopicheskikh gribov na takyrakh. Biocoenoses soil microscopical fungi of takyrs (translated title). In: *Takyry Zapadnoi Turkmenii i puti ikh selskokhozyaistvennogo osvoeniya,* pp. 55–74. Moscow.

Litvinov, M. A. (1968). Microscopical fungi of plant rhizosphere in the steppe of Central Kazakhstan (translated title). In: *Novitates systematical plantarum non vascularium,* pp. 131–139. Leningrad.

Litvinov, M. A. (1969). Soil and rhizosphere–root microscopical fungi synusia (translated title). In: *Biocomplex investigation in Kazahstan, I, Plant and animal communities of the Central Kazakhstan Steppe and desert,* pp. 325–345. Leningrad.

Rodin, L. E. & Bazilevich, N. I. (1956). Takyrs of low-lying Karakum (translated title). In: *Takyry Zapadnoi Turkmenii i puti ikh selskokhozyaistvennogo osvoeniya*, pp. 280–297. Moscow.

Rodin, L. E. & Bazilevich, N. I. (1967). *Production and mineral cycling in terrestrial vegetation*. Oliver & Boyd, Edinburgh.

Rustamov, I. G. (1972). Phytomass quantitative characteristics and productivity of subshrublet communities of the Krasnovodsk Plateau. In: *Eco-Physiological foundation of ecosystems productivity in Arid Zones* (ed. L. E. Rodin), pp. 129–132. International Symposium June 7–19 1972. Nauka, Leningrad.

Sdobnikova, N. V. (1959). Some data on algae of Middle Asia sand desert (translated title). *Notulae systematicae sectione cryptogamica Instituti Botanici nominae V. L. Komarovii Academiae Scientiarum URSS, Leningrad*, **12**, 143–148.

Sovetkina, M. M. (1938). Pastbishcha i senokosy Srednei Azii. Range and haying of Middle Asia (translated title). Tashkent.

Stal'makova, V. A. (1954). Gryzuny Karakumov, ikh ekologiya i khozyaĭstvennoe znachenie. Rodents of Karakum Desert, their biology and economy (translated title). In: *Pustyni SSSR i ikh osvoenie*, pp. 756–82. Moscow–Leningrad.

Manuscript received by the editors October 1974

Addendum

Since the time of writing more detailed and up-to-date information has been collected and published by the authors. Much of this information can be found in:

Rodin, L. E. (ed.) 1977. *Productivity of vegetation in arid zone of the Asia.* (Synthesis of the Soviet studies for the International Biological Programme, 1965–1974). Nauka, Leningrad. (In Russian.)

8. Arid-land ecosystems – common features throughout the world

W. G. McGINNIES

The desert biome

In establishing the desert biome-type, Whittaker (1970) first defines biome as a major kind of community conceived in terms of physiognomy on a given continent. The biome differs from a (plant) formation in that the former includes both plants and animals. A grouping of convergent biomes of different continents constitutes a biome-type.

Structure of the ecosystem

Whittaker (1970) defines an ecosystem as a community and its environment treated together as a functional system of complementary relationships, and transfer and circulation of energy and matter.

Walter (1973) points out that an ecosystem is not a closed system since there is an inflow of external energy from solar radiation and of matter in the form of precipitation or from gaseous exchange, dust deposits and so on. At the same time, energy is lost in the form of heat, and loss of matter occurs as a result of gaseous exchange and water drainage.

The components of the ecosystem consist of producers, consumers and decomposers. The structure of these components will be considered in this section in a general way; the processes involved in the ecosystem are covered elsewhere.

Vegetation and climate

McGinnies (1968) pointed out the difficulties of establishing desert boundaries on the basis of climate, vegetation, geology or soils either individually or in combination. On the basis of vegetation, decisions must be made as to what criteria should be used. If based on physical conditions, there is a choice between situations where physical conditions permit no vascular plant growth or a line below which conditions make plant growth very difficult. The latter is usually accepted but there are differences of opinion as what degree of difficulty should govern.

299

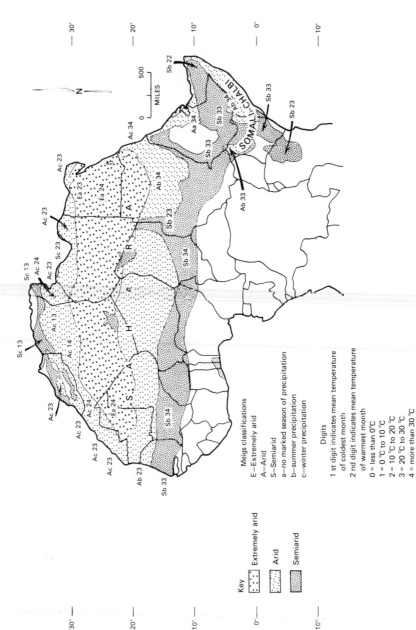

Key

Extremely arid

Arid

Semiarid

Meigs classifications

E—Extremely arid
A—Arid
S—Semiarid

a—no marked season of precipitation
b—summer precipitation
c—winter precipitation

Digits

1 st digit indicates mean temperature
of coldest month
2 nd digit indicates mean temperature
of warmest month

0 = less than 0°C
1 = 0 °C to 10 °C
2 = 10 °C to 20 °C
3 = 20 °C to 30 °C
4 = more than 30 °C

Fig. 8.1. Arid lands of northern Africa (after Meigs).

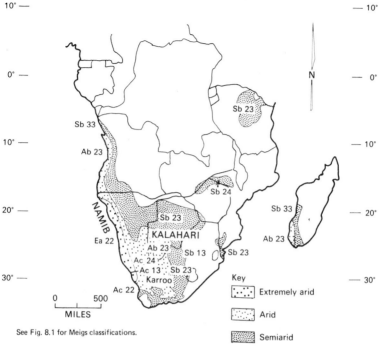

Fig. 8.2. Arid lands of southern Africa (after Meigs).

Shreve (1934) summarized the problems of defining desert as follows.

The very term 'desert' is a relative one, since the surface of the earth presents a great variety of arid areas, ranging from the most extreme rainless wastes of wind-blown sand or barren rock to regions with a moderate rainfall and a surprising amount of plant and animal life. Throughout this entire gamut of aridity the low and irregular rainfall is the most important item in the physical conditions. However, there is no particular minimum of rainfall and no other single criterion that will serve to distinguish a desert. Ten inches of rain in temperate latitudes will give better conditions than twenty inches in the subtropics. The altitude, the topographic features, the character of the soil, the proximity of the sea and the percentage of cloudiness all serve to modify conditions as much as differences in rainfall do. An adequate definition of desert must be a composite one, embracing both its causal and sequential features. It must be based on the degree to which a scanty and irregular water supply becomes an item of first moment in the life of plants and animals. Finally, its human aspects must be stressed, as has often been done by defining it as any region in which irrigation is essential to agriculture and to permanent settlement based on it.

According to Walter (1973), regions in which the potential evaporation is much higher than annual rainfall are termed arid. This is essentially the same criterion as that put forth by Trewartha (1954), Thornthwaite (1948),

301

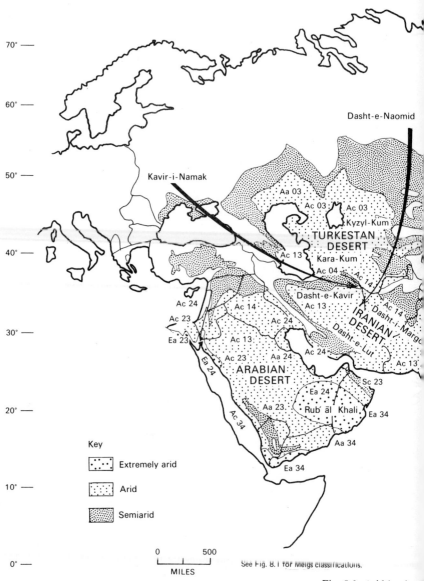

Key

∴ Extremely arid

⦂ Arid

▨ Semiarid

0   500
|___|___|
MILES

See Fig. 8.1 for Meigs classifications.

Fig. 8.3. Arid lands

70°

60°

50°

40°

30°

20°

10°

0°

...ia (after Meigs).

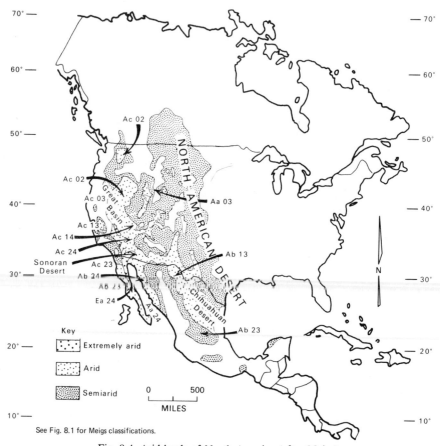

Fig. 8.4. Arid lands of North America (after Meigs).

and Meigs (1953). Thornthwaite and Meigs further state that the arid regions can be subdivided into semiarid and extremely arid.

Le Houérou (1970) considers zones with an annual average rainfall of more than 400 mm to be semiarid, subhumid or humid. Zones that receive less than 100 mm are considered as desert. He states that these limits are in satisfactory agreement with indices developed from more complex calculations such as those of de Martonne (1942), Thornthwaite (1948), and Gaussen (1963), and they correspond to Meig's maps (1953).

Aridity may be considered as an expression in a qualitative or quantitative manner of the dryness of an area. According to Reitan & Green (1968), aridity arises from three general causes acting individually or in combination. One of these causes is the separation of the region from oceanic moisture sources by topography or distance. Part of the desert

304

Fig. 8.5. Arid lands of South America (after Meigs).

area of North America and the desert to the leeward of the Andes arise from the drying effect on air masses moving over a major mountain barrier. The great distance from major moisture sources is one of the causes of aridity in the Takla-Makan, Turkestan and Gobi Deserts in central Asia.

A second cause of aridity is the formation of dry, stable air masses that resist convective currents. Deserts dominated by the eastern portions of subtropical high-pressure cells originate, in part, from the stability produced by these pressures and wind systems. The Arabian and Austra-

305

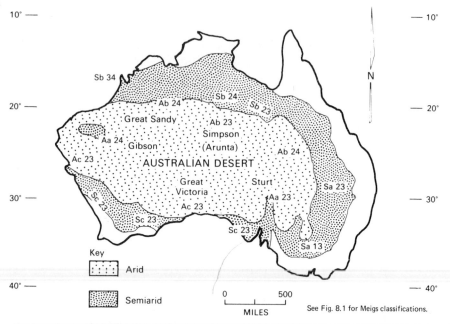

Fig. 8.6. Arid lands of Australia (after Meigs).

lian deserts and the Sahara are examples of deserts positioned between major wind belts with their associated storm systems.

Aridity is basically a comparison between water supply and water need. Water supply in general is the amount received from precipitation, while water need is measured in terms of evapotranspiration. Potential evaporation may be estimated by use of commonly observed climatological data. This method, while open to criticism, is the standard method in use in deserts where detailed information is not available. The best known index of aridity is that developed by Thornthwaite (1948). The index was used by Meigs (1953) in preparation of maps of the arid zone (Figs. 8.1 to 8.6).

Walter & Stadelmann (1974) further classified deserts on the basis of seasonality or rainfall into the following groups.

(a) Arid areas with two rainy seasons: north Venezuela, southwestern Somalia, Sonoran Desert, and Karroo region.
(b) Arid regions with winter rains: Mojave Desert, northern Libya, Mesopotamia, northern Chile and the northern Sahara.
(c) Arid regions with summer rains: Nubian Desert, Ordos Desert, central Australia, southern Peruvian region, southern Sahara.
(d) Arid regions seldom having rain which may fall at any time during the year: Lake Eyre basin.

306

(*e*) Fog deserts almost without measureable rainfall: southern Peruvian–northern Chilean region and Namib Desert.

(*f*) Deserts almost without rain and vegetation: central Sahara and southern Egyptian Desert.

With the exception of high-latitude polar deserts, Walter & Stadelmann (1974) classified arid regions on the basis of temperature as follows.

(*a*) Arid regions of the tropics with very little difference in the average monthly temperatures: islands of the South Caribbean Sea and north coast of Venezuela, the northern part of Somalia and the island of Socotra.

(*b*) Subtropical arid regions with considerable temperature fluctuation during the year and occasional frost: Sonoran Desert, Mojave Desert, Sahara–Arabian Desert region, southern Iranian Desert and the Thar Desert. In the Southern Hemisphere: southern Peruvian–northern Chilean region, Namib Desert, Karroo region and the desert regions of Australia.

(*c*) Arid regions of temperate zones which often have very cold winters: Great Basin (North America); the transitional regions north of the border line for date palm cultivation between the Syrian–Mesopotamian and the Iranian–Turanian Desert; the Kazakhstanian–Dzungarian Desert; the Tarim Basin with the Takla Makan Desert; Bei-sham; the Ala Shan Desert; the Ordos Desert and the Gobi Desert. In the temperate zone of the Southern Hemisphere the only arid region of this kind is Patagonia.

(*d*) Cold highland deserts, the Puna in the Andes Mountains; the Pamir and Tibet.

Whittaker (1970) distinguishes:

(*a*) tropical and subtropical deserts;

(*b*) warm–temperate deserts represented in North America by the widespread creosote bush (*Larrea*) communities and the floristically rich desert uplands of the Sonoran and Chihuahuan Deserts;

(*c*) cool–temperate desert scrub, including the Great Basin sagebrush (*Artemisia*) communities in the United States and the closely parallel communities in Asia;

(*d*) arctic–alpine deserts determined by the extreme cold of high latitudes and altitudes.

Kassas (1970) divides vegetation into three categories as related to precipitation:

(*a*) 'rainless' country where rainfall is not an annually recurring incident: plant growth may appear after rain and the type of growth is referred to as accidental growth form;

307

(*b*) where rainfall, though low and variable, is an annually recurring phenomenon, perennial growth is confined to especially favored habitats; wadis, depressions, high mountains, etc., the 'restricted type' of Walter (1973) or *mode contracté* of Monod (1954);

(*c*) in less arid areas, perennial plant life is widespread, although it is variable in density of cover and complexity of structure. This is the diffuse type.

The three vegetation types represent points on a continuum.

Land forms

Smith (1968) states that the broad outlines of desert relief are essentially similar to those of non-desert regions having similar geologic formations. Differences lie mainly in surface characteristics. Contours tend to be sharp and angular and transitions between topographic elements are abrupt. Water courses in general are dry most of the time and are limited in extent.

The following types of deserts are listed by Walter (1973):

(*a*) rocky desert or *hammada* mainly formed on plateaus or mesas from which all the finer products of weathering have been blown away;

(*b*) gravel desert or *serir* (*reg*) developed from heterogeneous parent rock;

(*c*) the sandy desert, *erg* or *ereg*, formed in large basin areas by deposition of sand, often forming dunes;

(*d*) dry valleys or wadis (oueds), known in America as washes or arroyos, are important features of all deserts;

(*e*) pans, *dayas*, *sebkhas* or *chotts*, are hollows or larger depressions in which silt or clay particles are deposited;

(*f*) Oases.

Soils

Desert soils are generally limited in topographic distribution, they occur mostly on flat to gently sloping surfaces and are absent from the steeper slopes and uplands where bare rock predominates. A prominent characteristic is the limited extent to which parent materials have been altered by the soil-forming processes. Vertical differentiation of the soil profile into distinctive horizons is not well developed. Chemical properties are essentially those of the parent material. The salt content may be high in local, poorly drained areas.

Dregne (1968) listed the terms applied to surface materials shown in Table 8.1.

Among other factors the amount of water accumulated in the soil determines the availability of water to plants, the amount of water in the

Table 8.1. *List of terms applied to surface materials.* (After Dregne, 1968)

Type of surface	Terms
Extensive plains of fine-textured material, with or without sand dunes	Clay desert, clay plain
Extensive sand dunes, usually 10 meters or more high with few non-sandy interdune areas	Dune field, *erg*, sand sea
Extensive saline depressions, usually fine textured	Salt flat, salina, *sebkha, chott, kavir*
Fine-textured depressions, large or small, usually moderately saline	*Playa, takyr,* pan, clay flats
Stony or gravelly surfaces	Desert pavement, stone pavement gibber, billy gibber, grey billy, stony table land, stony plain, *reg, serir (sarir), hammada, gobi*
Steep-sided water-courses in arid zones	Arroyo, wadi, *nullah, quebrado*

soil is dependent upon moisture derived from precipitation and on losses by evapotranspiration and deep percolation. In arid regions generally only the surface soils are moistened and the depth of penetration depends on the texture and field capacity of the soil. Penetration is least in clay soils and maximum in rocky soils, sandy soils are intermediate. Consequently, the same type of vegetation grows on a stable sandy soil with less rainfall than on a clay soil, and the favorable water-storage qualities of rocky soils in arid regions support a shrub and tree vegetation greater than that on adjacent fine-textured soils.

Moisture is the single most limiting factor for plant growth in desert soils (Fuller, 1974). Desert soils differ in their permeability to rainwater. Many are dry and hard, others are crusted. The beating action of raindrops compacts the surface reducing porosity. Grazing animals reduce plant cover and their hoofs compact the soil. Salts, especially sodium, cause soils to disperse, resulting in a low water-penetration and movement in the profile. Raindrop action keeps the surface layer dispersed. As a consequence, much of the rain that falls on sloping desert lands runs off and collects in basins where evaporation concentrates salts in an already salty soil.

Many desert soils are rich in micro-organisms (Fuller, 1974). Nitrogen-fixing *Azotobacter* and nitrifying bacteria are often abundant in desert soils. Algae are prominent in desert regions, the greatest number belong to the bluegreen and green groups. They may form crusts on desert soils and are most prominent where bare soil is exposed. While information on protozoa in desert soils is limited, they are known to occur widely. Actinomycetes and Streptomycetes are common in desert soils but fungi may generally be the least abundant population group in desert soils.

309

Description of arid ecosystems

Origin of plant and animal life

MacDougal (1909) noted that the total number of species within an arid region was not less than that in a closed tropical area, but the number of individuals was less.

In discussing aridity and evolution MacDougal considered the consequences of decreasing rainfall from humid toward arid conditions. He pointed out that in the present arid regions there is a variation in topography so that all areas are not affected in the same way. The change in precipitation from humid to drier conditions would result in the formation of long outwash detrital slopes or *bajadas* giving new habitat conditions; further differentiation would result in alkaline and saline areas.

Mountain summits would be least disturbed by the development of desert conditions. The original or pre-desert life forms would be able to maintain themselves on such elevated slopes with little adjustment and could provide the propagating stock from which more xerophytic forms could be developed.

Three types of vegetation might be related to such changes. First, some of the herbaceous forms might be able to survive during moist seasons and give rise to the modern ephemerals which are really mesomorphic plants surviving in an arid environment by shortening their growing season and escaping the dry season as seeds. The second type is one in which the leaves have been reduced, the branches sometimes reduced to spines and the root systems expanded. The spinose, stubby, and switchlike plants resulting are typical of enclosed basins throughout the world. The third type includes forms which have been modified along lines similar to the above, but in addition have developed storage capabilities in stems, branches, leaves or roots giving rise to such groups as cacti, euphorbias, agaves, yuccas, sotols and crassulas.

Shreve (1934) has pointed out that all the desert regions of the world have similarities in biological manifestations. Plants are very much the same in terms of structure, function and behavior in all deserts. Identical or very similar features in anatomy, physiology and adjustments to environment are repeated in far-separated regions and different continents. Shreve observed that there are very few plant species common to the arid lands of America, Africa, Asia, and Australia, and that deserts have been populated mainly by plants and animals from near at hand and only to a slight extent from other deserts. He noted that in many cases the same type of adjustment has been developed by unrelated stocks. Structural adjustments along parallel lines are found in several families and in widely distant areas of similar character. Examples are the euphorbias of Africa resembling the cacti of the Americas, *Aloe* resembling *Agave* and *Sarcocaulon* suggesting *Fouquieria*.

Axelrod (1950) stated that the present desert floras have their sources chiefly in Tertiary floras that occupied the regions which are now desert. The cold deserts have largely derived their species from Arcto-Tertiary floras and the warm deserts from Tropical-Tertiary floras. As gradually expanding dry climate restricted the Tertiary floras to moister regions, subhumid communities on the borders of the dry areas slowly expanded and through time have produced species adapted to successively drier climates.

In commenting on lack of fossil remains, Shreve (1936) stated that plant remains found in old lake beds or alluvium are apt to be misleading. He also observed that the poverty of the flora in the driest parts of the Sonoran Desert was due as much to the joint influence of aridity and temperature of winter as it was to aridity alone. He believed that many of the desert species had their origins in the south and that some had been limited by temperature in their northern extent.

Vegetation growth forms

Plant growth forms have been treated in various ways. Historically, the first system to receive wide consideration was that of Raunkiaer (1934) based upon the degree of protection afforded to the perenniating buds. This well known classification does not provide the most desirable break-down for the Desert Biome. Shreve's (1942) description of life forms of the North American Desert, as shown in Table 8.2, provides a classification that is generally applicable to all deserts.

Various authors have considered that variations in potential osmotic pressure provide a basis for the classification of plant structure within an ecosystem. Osmotic spectra have been developed from many thousands of determinations (Walter and Stadelmann 1974) in all climatic regions and different ecological conditions.

Adaptations of plants in arid environments listed by Whittaker (1970) include the following:

(*a*) deep or wide-ranging root systems;
(*b*) water-storage tissues;
(*c*) protective covering by wax, hairs and other coatings;
(*d*) reducing leaf surface by shedding leaves;
(*e*) use of green stems for photosynthesis;
(*f*) stomatal functions including 'reversed' action with carbon dioxide being taken in at night and fixed as malate which is then available as a carbon dioxide source during the day;
(*g*) tolerance of tissues to reduced water-content even to nearly air-dry conditions in some club mosses and ferns;

311

Table 8.2. *Life forms of the North American desert.* (After Shreve, 1942.)

	Genera
Ephemerals	
Strictly seasonal	
Winter ephemerals	*Daucus, Plantago*
Summer ephemerals	*Pectis, Tidestromia*
Facultative perennials	*Verbesina, Baileya*
Perennials	
Underground parts perennial	
Perennial roots	*Pentstemon, Anemone*
Perennial bulbs	*Allium, Hesperocallis*
Shoot base and crown perennial	*Hilaria, Aristida*
Shoots perennial	
Shoot reduced (a caudex)	
Caudex short, all or mainly leafy	
Leaves succulent	*Agave, Hechtia*
Leaves nonsucculent	*Nolina, Dasylirion*
Caudex long, leafy at top	
Leaves simple, semisucculent	*Yucca*
Leaves branched, nonsucculent	*Tnodes, Washingtonia*
Shoot elongated	
Plant succulent (soft)	
Leafless, stem succulent	
Shoot unbranched	*Ferocactus, Thelocactus*
Shoot branched	
Shoot poorly branched	
Plant erect and tall	*Pachycereus, Carnegiea*
Plant erect and low or semi-procumbent and low	*Pedilanthus, Mammillaria*
Shoot richly branched	
Stem segments cylindrical	*Cylindropuntia*
Stem segments flattened	*Platyopuntia*
Leafy, stem not succulent	*Talinum, Sedum*
Plant nonsucculent (woody)	
Shoots without leaves, stems green	*Canotia, Holacantha*
Shoots with leaves	
Low bushes, wood soft	*Encelia, Franseria*
Shrubs and trees, wood hard	
Leaves perennial	*Larrea, Mortonia*
Leaves diciduous	
Leaves drought deciduous	
Stems specialized	
Stems indurated on surface	*Fouquieria*
Stems enlarged at base	*Bursera, Idria*
Stems normal	
Stems not green	*Jatropha, Plumeria*
Stems green	*Cercidium, Euphorbia*
Leaves winter deciduous	
Leaves large	*Populus, Ipomoea*
Leaves small or compound	*Olneya, Prosopis*

Table 8.3. *The ecological methods by which plants and animals meet drought conditions.* (After Shantz, 1956.)

Plants	Animals
Drought-escaping	
Ephemerals which grow during moist seasons and live through dry seasons in the seed stage.	Animals that enter arid lands only when moisture is available – largely insects and other invertebrates.
Drought-evading	
Plants making economical use of limited soil moisture supply through wide spacing, reduced leaf and stem surface.	Burrowing animals, with night activity, that do not need to provide water for temperature control.
Drought-resistant	
Succulents that store water and are able to continue growth when soil moisture is not available. Not characteristic of extreme deserts.	Animals that resist drought through physiological processes by which they are able to concentrate their urine, lose little water in the feces, stop, perspiration, endure dehydration and still remain active – the camel is a fine example.
Drought-enduring	
Drought-dormant plants that estivate when drought occurs and continue growth when moisture is available. This includes many prominent desert seed plants and also algae, lichens, mosses and ferns.	Animals that estivate and any invertebrates that recover after desiccation. Also vertebrates such as ground squirrels and gophers that estivate during hot dry periods.

(*h*) high osmotic concentrations allowing water uptake from relatively dry soils;

(*i*) growth during seasons when water is available.

Animal components

The adaptation among desert animals listed by Whittaker (1970) includes the following:

(*a*) increasing water intake by eating plant tissue with high water content or by drinking dew;

(*b*) direct water uptake from the air (arthropods);

(*c*) use of metabolic water from respiration of food;

(*d*) reduction of water loss by excretion and egestion of concentrated urine and nearly dry feces;

(*e*) impermeable body coverings to reduce water loss;

(*f*) reducing water loss by inactivity, shade and underground shelters.

Shantz (1956) classified both plants and animals in arid lands on the basis

Description of arid ecosystems

of the ecological means by which they meet drought conditions as shown in Table 8.3.

Impacts of man

Grazing

Plants live in a precarious balance between their ability to survive and the austere resources that deserts provide. Under such conditions minor changes in the physical environment entail dramatic changes in plant life.

According to Cloudsley-Thompson (1970), one of the more effective ways in which man creates desert conditions is by felling trees for fuel, but even more important in creating erosion and desert conditions are overgrazing and the compacting of soil by domestic animals. Of all domestic animals the goat is chiefly responsible for enlarging the deserts of Asia and northern Africa. Kassas (1970) states that overgrazing may result in eradication of palatable species and encouragement of unpalatable species. Clearing for cultivation means wholesale destruction of natural plant growth and fire is a widespread ecological factor.

Hydrology

The infrequent precipitation in desert areas may be augmented by irrigation water from imported or groundwater sources. Stream sources may vary from small drainages with intermittent flows to large exogenous streams such as the Colorado River, Hwang Ho, Nile, and the many Andean streams in Peru and Chile. Groundwater is an important source of supply in all desert areas and may be derived from water stored during earlier more humid times, from local precipitation, or from underground or surface flow of exogenous streams.

According to Peterson (1970) the occurrence of water in, or at the edge of, desert areas permits sedentary agriculture, either for large areas where the supply is plentiful or for an oasis type of agriculture where quantities are limited. Oasis agriculture exists all over the arid world and varies from small patches to larger towns and villages. The water supply may be from artesian sources, dug wells, 'quanats', or from perennial streams.

Irrigation practices in the past have often resulted in deterioration of the soil through waterlogging or an increase in salt content. Typical areas are ancient Mesopotamia and to a lesser extent the modern Indus.

The ecological implications of man's use of water in desert environments are many. In some cases the irrigation increases the carrying capacity many times but often the end results of irrigation are a degradation of the environment resulting in decreased production, increased impact of disease and insects and even smog pollution.

314

Convergence of land use

Land-use problems are world wide in their extent. All the arid regions of the world have been subjected to major ecological disturbances resulting from the impact of man and agencies under his control.

While it is possible to improve resources in arid lands, such improvements are often accompanied by increases in population, making new demands on a naturally feeble environment and further altering the native flora and fauna. The meagerness of the products obtained give rise to extremely poor living conditions for the inhabitants.

As stated by Beltran (1956), arid zones offer intrinsic conditions which necessitate the greatest caution in considering any project affecting them. The margin of tolerance in arid regions is so small that any error may have serious consequences. Maintaining or improving living conditions should not rest exclusively on the improvement of domestic animals and plants nor on the introduction of new ones; it should also be based as far as possible on the rational ecological utilization of the elements native to the region. Full recognition should be given to the arid zone–wild plants and animals–human population–domestic plants and animals complex.

References

Axelrod, D. I. (1950). Studies in late Tertiary paleobotany. *Carnegie Institution of Washington Publication 590.*

Beltran, E. (1956). Plants, animals, and humans in arid areas. In: White (1956), pp. 419–23.

Brown, G. W. (ed.) (1974). *Desert Biology*, Volume II. Academic Press, New York.

Cloudsley-Thompson, J. L. (1970). Animal utilization. In: Dregne (1970), pp. 57–72.

Dregne, H. E. (1968). Surface materials of desert environments. In: McGinnies, Goldman & Paylore (1968), pp. 287–377.

Dregne, H. E. (ed.) (1970). *Arid lands in transition.* American Association for the Advancement of Science, Washington.

Fuller, W. H. (1974). Desert Soils. In: Brown (1974), pp. 31–101.

Gaussen, H. (1963). Bioclimatic map of the Mediterranean Zone. *UNESCO Arid Zone Research,* **21**.

Kassas, M. (1970). Desertification versus potential for recovery in circumsaharen territories. In: Dregne (1970), pp. 123–42.

Le Houérou, H. N. (1970). North Africa, past, present, future. In: Dregne (1970), pp. 227–78.

MacArthur, R. H. (1972). *Geographical ecology, patterns in the distribution of species.* Harper & Row, New York.

MacDougal, D. T. (1909). Influence of aridity upon the evolutionary development of plants. *The Plant World,* **12**, 217–31.

McGinnies, W. G., Goldman, B. J. & Paylore, P. (eds.) (1968). *Deserts of the world: an appraisal of research into their physical and biological environments.* University of Arizona Press, Tucson.

Martonne, E. de (1942). Nouvelle carte mondiale de l'indice d'aridite. *Annales de Geographie,* **51** (288), 242–50.

Description of arid ecosystems

McGinnies, W. G. (1968). Vegetation of desert environments. In: McGinnies, Goldman & Paylore (1968), pp. 381–566.

Meigs, P. (1953). World distribution of arid and semi-arid homoclimates. In: *Reviews of Research on Arid Zone Hydrology*, pp. 203–9. UNESCO, Paris.

Monod, T. (1954). Mode 'contracte' et 'diffus' de la vegetation Saharienne. In: *Biology of Deserts* (ed. J. L. Cloudsley-Thompson), pp. 35–44. Institute of Biology, London.

Peterson, D. F. (1970). Water in the deserts. In: Dregne (1970), pp. 15–30.

Raunkiaer, C. (1934). *The life forms of plants and statistical plant geography.* Clarendon Press, Oxford.

Reitan, C. H. Green, C. R. (1968). Weather and climate of desert environments. In: McGinnies, Goldman & Paylore (1968), pp. 21–92.

Shantz, H. L. (1956). History and problems of arid lands development. In: White (1956), pp. 3–25.

Shreve, F. (1934). The problems of the desert. *Scientific Monthly*, **40**, 199–209.

Shreve, F. (1936). The plant life of the Sonoran Desert. *Scientific American*, **42**, 195–213.

Shreve, F. (1942). The desert vegetation of North America. *Botanical Review*, **8**, 195–246.

Smith, H. T. U. (1968). Geologic and geomorphic aspects of deserts. In *Desert Biology*, vol. 1 (ed. G. W. Brown), pp. 52–100. Academic Press, New York.

Thornthwaite, C. W. (1948). An approach toward a rational classification of climate. *Geographical Review*, **38**, 55–94.

Trewartha, G. T. (1954). *An introduction to climate.* (Third edition.) McGraw-Hill, New York.

Walter, H. (1973). *Vegetation of the earth.* (Translated from the second German edition by J. Wieser.) English Universities Press, London.

Walter, H. & Stadelmann, E. (1974). A new approach to water relations of desert plants. In: Brown (1974), p. 310.

White, G. F. (ed.) (1956). *The future of Arid Lands.* American Association for the Advancement of Science, Washington, D.C.

Whittaker, R. H. (1970). *Communities and ecosystems.* Macmillan, New York.

Manuscript received by the editors March 1975

PART II

Component processes

9. Introduction

D. W. GOODALL

The major part of these volumes, dealing with the dynamics of arid-land ecosystems, is organized in terms of processes of increasing complexity, and involving interactions between increasingly more disparate parts of the ecosystem. The present section is concerned with the individual components of the ecosystem, biotic and abiotic, and the processes which they undergo.

The structure and dynamics of any ecosystem depend very largely on the biota which make it up. Each of the species plays a particular role within the system, limited by its environmental tolerances. The role and tolerances define the *niche* which the species occupies. The range of niches available and occupied in turn determines the biotic range within the ecosystem – its *diversity*, in other words.

The first contribution in this section discusses the niche structure and diversity of arid-land ecosystems. This serves as a preliminary to the chapters dealing with the processes in which the individual components of the biota are involved and which together determine the dynamics of the system as a whole. The atmospheric and soil processes determining the abiotic environment, and hence the range and nature of the niches available to the biota, are also discussed.

This section does not deal with processes involving interactions among the various components of the system. These will be discussed in the second volume, leading on to the dynamics of the system as a whole.

10. Diversity and niche structure in desert communities

E. R. PIANKA

Introduction

Do deserts generally tend to support communities that are either more or less diverse than communities in wetter areas? To what extent do desert communities possess characteristic patterns of resource partitioning and community structure? Are there general answers to these questions, or do they differ among various plant and animal taxa? Here I explore these questions, first briefly from a theoretical standpoint and then I examine the meager existing empirical evidence.

Some theoretical considerations

Species diversity

Diversity has been quantified in a wide variety of different ways (see, for example, Simpson, 1949; MacArthur & MacArthur, 1961; Pielou, 1969; MacArthur, 1972; Hill, 1973 and Peet, 1974). The two basic components of species diversity are simply the total number of species actually present and the degree to which they are equally important. Relative importance has been measured in a number of ways, ranging from abundances to biomass to the energetic importance within the community. In birds and lizards, at least, estimates of species diversity computed with various diversity indices are strongly correlated with the much simpler measure of the actual number of species present, termed species richness or species density (Tramer, 1969; Longuet-Higgins, 1971; Pianka, 1975).

MacArthur (1972) pointed out that species diversity in resource-limited, competitive communities is a simple function of three variables: (1) diversity of available resources or the overall size of the niche space, or hypervolume, (2) diversity of utilization of these resources by an average species or mean niche breadth, and (3) the extent to which resources are shared or the amount of niche overlap. All else being equal, community species diversity clearly should increase with increased diversity of available resources and increased niche overlap; conversely, as average niche breadth is enlarged, diversity must decrease unless there are concomitant changes in resource diversity and/or tolerable niche overlap. MacArthur also points out the importance of resource dimensionality or the number of different ways in which competition is avoided; again, all else remaining

Component processes

equal, an increased number of niche dimensions allows maintenance of a greater number of species. Increased niche dimensionality also results in a greater potential number of neighbors in niche space and hence a heightened potential for diffuse competition.

Optimal foraging tactics and niche breadth

A fairly substantial body of theory on optimal foraging predicts that niche breadth should generally increase as resource availability decreases (see for example, Emlen, 1966, 1968; MacArthur & Pianka, 1966; Schoener, 1971; MacArthur, 1972; Charnov, 1973). The reasoning behind this conclusion is that, in an environment with a scant food supply, a consumer cannot afford to bypass substandard potential prey items because mean search time per prey item encountered is long (expectation of prey encounter is low). Under this situation, a broad niche maximizes returns per unit expenditure and generalization is favored. In a food-rich environment, however, search time per item is low and a consumer encounters numerous potential prey items; under such circumstances, inferior prey types can be bypassed because expectation of finding a superior item is high. Hence rich food supplies should favor selective foraging and narrow niche breadths.

Deserts are less productive than other ecosystems owing to low water supply and should therefore support fewer potential prey items per unit area. A probable consequence of such a low prey density is that an average consumer will have a broad niche, which in turn should result in reduced species diversity in desert communities.

Spatial heterogeneity and environmental variability

Spatially complex habitats support richer communities than structurally simpler areas because there are more ways of exploiting the former. Many deserts, especially the more diverse ones such as the Sonoran desert, support a structurally complex vegetation which provides animals with ample opportunities for niche segregation involving differential use of microhabitats.

Deserts frequently have very variable precipitation regimes. Environmental variability can both enhance and limit diversity. To the extent that different species can adapt to particular subsets of conditions, temporal or seasonal heterogeneity can promote diversity (Hutchinson, 1961). Continually changing interactions between species may also facilitate persistence of a variety of species, provided that each enjoys a competitive advantage during some time period. By promoting a diversity of plant life forms, climatic variability can act to increase spatial heterogeneity and animal species diversity. Under some circumstances, however, members of a community may be unable to partition resources temporally. If an individual organism must be able to tolerate a variety of conditions in order to persist, environmental variability promotes generalization, broad niches, and hence lower species diversity.

Taxon-specific adaptations and historical events

Some anatomical and physiological traits confer an advantage upon particular taxa in appropriate environments. For example, lizards tend to be more diverse in deserts than elsewhere, probably partially as a result of their poikilothermy and consequent ability to capitalize on scant and variable amounts of primary productivity by becoming inactive and retreating underground during harsh periods. Thus lizards are in some senses 'predapted' for performance in hot and arid environments. Indeed, competition between lizards and birds may favor lizards under desert conditions (Pianka, 1967, 1973). Such complementary interactions between taxa can obscure trends in community structure and diversity when taxonomic subsets of the community are treated as a unit of study.

Accidents of history also profoundly shape community composition and, indirectly, species diversity. For example, Australian desert lizards have usurped some of the ecological roles played by snakes and mammals in deserts on other continents (Pianka, 1969a, 1973); moreover, the mammalian and snake faunas of the Australian deserts appear to be somewhat impoverished.

Empirical aspects

Plants

Plant species diversity generally varies independently of overall productivity (Whittaker, 1972). Data from the Great Smoky Mountains (Fig. 10.1) show that shrub diversity is highest on the more xeric ridges and peaks, while trees reach their highest diversity in more mesic canyons, draws, and ravines. In the same region, summer herbs attain high diversities under two disparate environmental conditions, namely in mesic low altitude cove forests and at high altitudes on xeric open slopes (Fig. 10.1).

Whittaker (1972) also points out that the Sonoran desert, with its bimodal annual march of precipitation, supports an exceedingly diverse array of plant communities in spite of its aridity and unpredictability. On Sonoran desert mountain slopes, species diversities of both perennials and annuals are higher than in most eastern forests. Perennials have adopted a wide range of plant life forms, apparently alternative ways of coping with unpredictable water availability. Annuals are very irregular in both

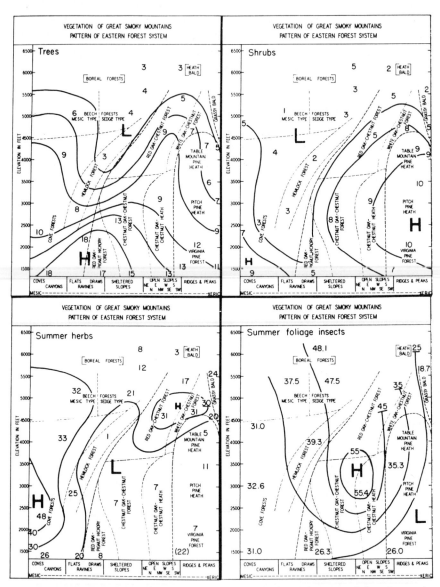

Fig. 10.1. Species diversity of trees, shrubs, summer herbs, and summer foliage insects in the Great Smoky Mountains. Diversity of each group of organisms is plotted along a xeric to mesic continuum against elevation. Diversity of the different groups vary with altitude and water availability, but high and low diversity situations differ markedly among groups. Contours outline number of trees, shrubs and summer herb species in 0.1 ha quadrats and alpha indexes for sweep samples of summer foliage insects. (From Whittaker, 1972.)

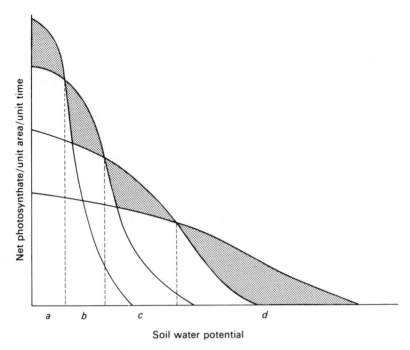

Fig. 10.2. Hypothetical relationship between net photosynthate per unit of leaf surface area per unit time and soil water potential for different types of leaves. The most mesophytic leaf type performs best under conditions of high soil water availability, marked *a* (low soil water potential), while the most xerophytic leaf type shown performs best over the range of conditions marked *d* (low water availability). Intermediate leaf types are more efficient photosynthesizers under intermediate conditions of water availability (marked with *b* and *c* in the figure). Shaded zones represent the soil water potential conditions under which the various leaf types are superior. (Adapted from Orians & Solbrig, 1977.)

their temporal and spatial patterns of appearance; many species of annual plants have evolved specific germination requirements and respond differentially to winter and summer rainfall. The bimodal annual pattern of rainfall clearly has allowed diversification of annual plant species, with a conspicuous dichotomy between summer annuals and winter annuals (Shreve, 1964). Certain plant communities in the Sonoran desert, however, are of very low plant species diversity, such as the almost 'pure' stands of creosote bush *Larrea divaricata* (Shreve, 1964; McCleary, 1968). Extreme aridity clearly must result in very low productivity and plant species diversity.

The high diversity of plant life forms on Sonoran desert slopes is probably a reflection of a variety of leaf tactics which have evolved in response to the great spatial and temporal variability of water availability in the Sonoran desert (Orians & Solbrig, 1976). Using cost-benefit

325

arguments, these authors contrast a continuum of leaf types, ranging from the relatively inexpensive deciduous 'mesophytic' leaf to the most costly evergreen 'xerophytic' leaf. Mesophytic leaves photosynthesize and transpire at a rapid rate, and hence require high water-availability (low 'soil water potential'). In contrast, xerophytic leaves cannot photosynthesize as rapidly when abundant water is available, but they are also able to extract water from relatively dry soil. Orians & Solbrig argue that each plant leaf tactic has an advantage at either different times or in different places (along washes, etc.), promoting plant life form diversity. During wet periods, plants with mesophytic leaves photosynthesize rapidly, but, under drought conditions they must drop their leaves and become dormant. During such dry periods, however, the slower photosynthesizers with xerophytic leaves are still able to function by virtue of their ability to extract water from dry soils. Of course, all degrees of intermediate leaf tactics exist, each of which may enjoy a competitive advantage under particular conditions of water availability (Fig. 10.2). Orians & Solbrig argue that the net annual profit per unit of leaf surface area determines the winning phenotype; moreover, even a relatively brief wet season may suffice to give mesophytic leaves a higher annual profit, thus accounting for the prevalence of high transpiration leaves along desert washes.

Lowe, Morello, Cross & Goldstein (1972) and Lowe *et al.* (1973) have correlated plant species diversity in the Sonoran and Monte deserts with various measures of soil texture (Fig. 10.3).

Insects

Sweep samples of summer foliage insects in the Great Smoky Mountains showed maximal insect species diversities at intermediate elevations in habitats intermediate along the xeric to mesic continuum (Fig. 10.1). Janzen & Schoener (1968) took sweep samples of insects from the under-storey of tropical forests along a moisture gradient during the dry season in Costa Rica. The absolute number of species increased with increasing moisture, as did insect species diversity, although somewhat more erratically.

Otte & Joern (1978) have studied species density and food-niche breadths of grasshoppers on numerous sites in deserts and along several desert–grassland ecoclines (Otte, personal communication). The number of grasshopper species is generally higher in more productive grasslands than it is in deserts (Otte & Joern, 1978).

Within deserts, the number of species of grasshoppers increases with the number of plant species (Fig. 10.4). In the Sonoran desert, both plant species numbers and grasshopper species density increase from low *Larrea* spp. flats towards higher slopes. Otte & Joern (1978) do not

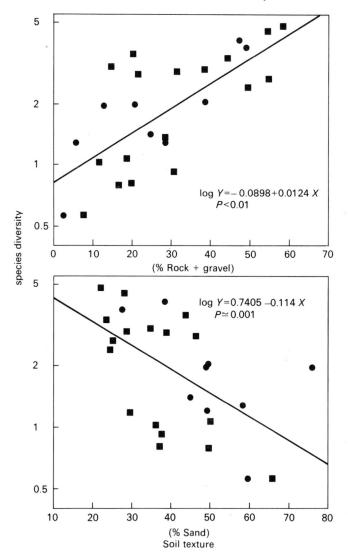

Fig. 10.3. Two plots of plant species diversity against two measures of soil texture for desert sites in Arizona (squares) and Argentina (dots). (From Lowe *et al.*, 1972, 1973.)

consider competition for food to be a major factor determining grass-hopper species richness, but they place much greater emphasis upon the available predator escape tactics. Thus, more diverse plant communities support a greater variety of grasshopper species because they offer grass-hoppers a wider variety of ways of camouflaging themselves from poten-tial predators. Otte & Joern consider it highly likely that grasshopper

327

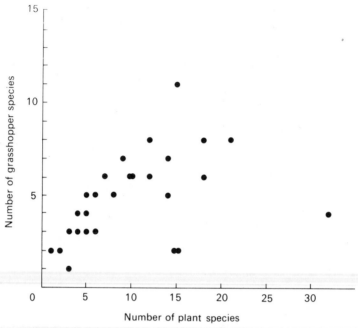

Fig. 10.4. Number of grasshopper species plotted against the number of plant species along an elevational gradient in the Sonoran desert of Arizona. (From Otte & Joern, 1978.)

communities are responding to increased structural complexity of the vegetation, rather than to plant species diversity, *per se*. Indeed, some plant species support more than one species of grasshopper, with different grasshopper species mimicking different parts of the plant (leaves, stems, etc.).

Somewhat surprisingly, grasshopper diets tend to be more restricted in deserts than in grasslands, with the result that average food niche breadth is narrower in deserts (Otte & Joern, 1978). Otte & Joern suggest that the high incidence of monophagy in deserts could be related both to high predictability of certain food plants in space and time and to decreased nutrient accessibility due to chemical and/or structural antiherbivore protective devices of woody perennials. However, they point out the great difficulty in determining whether the observed dietary specialization of desert grasshoppers is due primarily to crypsis-related factors or to adaptation to specific food plant secondary substances. Moreover, Otte & Joern note that predator escape tactics and foraging behavior are intricately interrelated and confounded; they state that no species of desert grasshopper forages away from foliage upon which it gains protection from potential predators.

In old fields in Michigan, species diversity of homopterans is strongly correlated with both plant species diversity and plant structural diversity

328

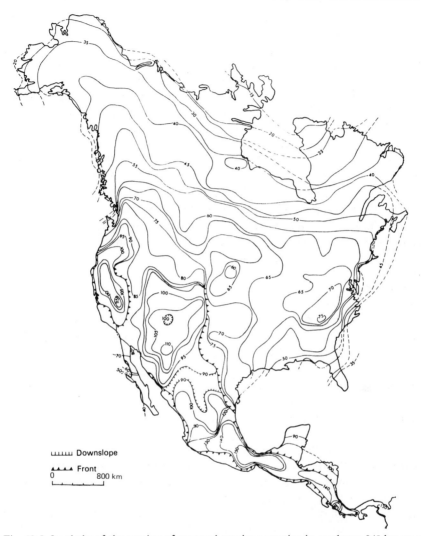

Fig. 10.5. Isopleths of the number of mammal species occurring in quadrates 240 km on a side over North America. (From Simpson, 1964.)

(Murdoch, Evans & Peterson, 1972), which are highly correlated themselves.

Mammals

Simpson (1964) plotted isopleths of mammal species density for the North American continent (Fig. 10.5). This map is based on numbers of species known to occur in large quadrats 240 km on a side; in topographically

329

Component processes

diverse regions, animals from several habitats are added together so that the figure includes both the between-habitat component of diversity as well as the within-habitat component. Nevertheless, desert areas in western North America are not conspicuously impoverished in numbers of mammal species. Indeed, mammal species density appears to be high in this area, perhaps largely because of the great topographic relief of the area and a consequent high between-habitat component of diversity. Simpson concludes that the observed pattern of mammal species density does not indicate a positive correlation with annual precipitation (and hence productivity), but rather suggests an *inverse* relationship. Indeed, there is a highly significant inverse correlation ($r = -0.59$, $P < 0.001$) between average annual precipitation and mammal species density in Simpson's quadrats within the continental US (Pianka, 1978). Within the state of Texas, the number of species of small mammals reaches maximal values in the far western trans Pecos area, which houses the Chihuahuan desert and is the driest and least productive part of the state (Rogers, 1976).

A number of fairly detailed studies of community structure and resource partitioning have been made on desert rodents (Rosenzweig & Winakur, 1969; Rosenzweig & Sterner, 1970; Brown, 1973, 1975; Brown & Lieberman, 1973). Rosenzweig & Winakur (1969) found little correlation between rodent species diversity and plant species diversity, but they did not attempt to evaluate the effects of precipitation or productivity upon rodent diversity. Rather, to account for observed patterns of rodent diversity, they constructed an index of habitat complexity that includes both various edaphic factors and aspects of vegetation structure.

Working with many of the same species of rodents on other study areas, Brown (1973, 1975) found that rodent species density was strongly correlated with both average annual precipitation and with the predictable amount of annual rainfall, as measured by the mean precipitation minus the standard deviation (Fig. 10.6). Hence, in these desert habitats the number of mammal species increases with increasing precipitation, even though on a more global scale (see Fig. 10.5 and above) mammal species richness decreases as precipitation increases.

Since local species density measures primarily the within-habitat component of diversity whereas total species density on a more global scale includes both the within-habitat and the between-habitat components, these contrasting results suggest that between-habitat turnover in mammal species must be greater in arid regions than in more mesic areas. (Note, however, that these patterns could merely reflect the extent to which average annual precipitation is inversely correlated with topographic relief and the resulting greater diversity of habitats per unit area.)

Larger species of heteromyid rodents husk seeds faster than smaller

330

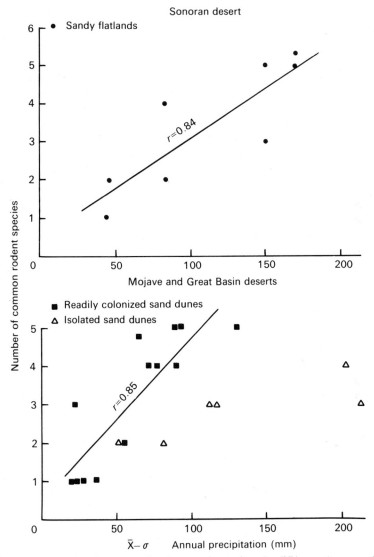

Fig. 10.6. Two plots of number of rodent species against the difference between the mean and the standard deviation in annual precipitation, which is a measure of the annual amount of predictable precipitation and productivity. (From Brown, 1975.)

ones, but smaller animals probably extract more energy per unit expenditure and should therefore have a competitive advantage in seed-husking ability (Rosenzweig & Sterner, 1970). These authors also indicate that seed selection is of dubious significance among coexisting heteromyids. Brown & Lieberman (1973) and Brown (1975), however, demonstrate that dif-

331

Component processes

ferent species of seed-eating desert rodents clearly partition seed resources by differentially harvesting seeds of various sizes and in different locations. Larger species tend to harvest more large seeds and various species forage at differing characteristic distances from desert shrubs. More productive habitats support a higher number of rodent species and niche overlap is greater. Brown & Lieberman (1973) interpret their results as demonstrating that species with similar resource utilization patterns can coexist in productive habitats thus promoting high diversity. They argue that ecologically similar species are excluded in less productive areas leading to lower diversity. Brown (1975) states that these rodents utilize an exceptionally wide range of seed sizes where, for historical reasons (biogeographic barriers), they occur in the absence of close competitors.

Actual evapotranspiration is strongly correlated with net above-ground primary productivity (Rosenzweig, 1968a). Using a partial correlation analysis to examine factors influencing body size of mammalian carnivores, Rosenzweig (1968b) found that actual evapotranspiration was a good predictor of body size in areas of low productivity such as deserts and tundra; moreover, these correlations persisted when the effects of latitude were held constant by partial correlation. Rosenzweig interpreted these results as indicating that body size of carnivorous mammals is limited by prey availability.

Birds

Cook (1969) analyzed species density of North American birds using 245 km square quadrats and found that the latitudinal gradient in bird species density is more pronounced than in mammals. Within the continental United States, bird species density is inversely correlated with long-term mean annual precipitation ($r = -0.64$, $P < 0.001$) and average annual actual evapotranspiration ($r = -0.58$, $P < 0.001$), which themselves are strongly correlated ($r = 0.88$) (Pianka, 1978). Thus birds follow the mammalian pattern.

In many (probably most) bird communities, bird species diversity is strongly correlated with foliage height diversity (MacArthur & MacArthur, 1961; Recher, 1969; Cody, 1970; Pianka & Huey, 1971). However, both MacArthur (1964) and Tomoff (1974) point out that species diversity of breeding birds in the succulent-rich Sonoran desert correlates rather poorly with foliage height diversity; Tomoff (1974) argues that particular plant life forms, especially various cacti, strongly influence bird species present at a particular site because of their importance as nest sites.

Cody (1974) studied the niche relationships and species diversity of eleven bird communities, including two on desert areas (Mojave and Sonoran deserts). Among the sites he studied, the two desert areas

332

supported an intermediate number of bird species (12 and 16, compared to a range of 5–20 on other areas). Bird species diversity on the desert sites was also intermediate (2.03 and 2.66, compared to a mean on non-desert areas of 2.03 with a range of 1.34–2.71). Within North America (8 sites), his two desert areas had low productivities (as measured by estimated actual evapotranspiration values of 177 and 291) when compared to six non-desert sites (mean is 353, range 275–473). Variance in rainfall during the breeding season was low on the desert sites (0.154 and 0.541; mean of non-desert areas is 0.913, range 0.099–2.036).

Habitat niche breadths increase with climatic predictability and tend to be slightly broader in desert birds than in non-desert species (see Fig. 29 in Cody, 1974) Cody found high niche overlap in bird communities on areas of high climatic predictability (low rainfall variability) including both desert communities and several non-desert ones. Habitat overlap tended to be lower in non-desert communities with less predictable climates. Cody's results do not suggest any fundamental differences between avian community structure in desert versus non-desert areas.

Independently-evolved desert avifaunas may differ in community structure; comparison of the niche structure and community organization of desert birds in Australia with the Kalahari desert of southern Africa shows some fundamental differences (Pianka & Huey, 1971). Compared with the Australian deserts, the Kalahari supports proportionately more species of ground carnivores, fewer arboreal species, but about the same number of ground herbivore species (Table 10.1). Lein (1972) has also noted some trophic differences between avifaunas of the different faunal regions. and emphasized the paucity of ground-feeding insectivorous birds in the Australian biogeographic region. Cody (1973, 1974) makes a case for convergence in both ecology and diversity between avifaunas of chaparral and matorral habitats in Chile and California, both areas with mediterranean-type climates.

Amphibians and reptiles, especially lizards

Kiester (1971) constructed species density maps for amphibians and reptiles in the continental US. As might be anticipated, amphibian species density is low in dry areas and correlates relatively well with average annual precipitation (see also Terentev, 1963, for a similar result from the Soviet Union). Species densities of both amphibians and reptiles show marked latitudinal gradients (Kiester, 1971). Within the continental United States, reptile species density is positively correlated with sunfall (Fig. 10.7) and *inversely* correlated with bird species density (Fig. 10.8) (Pianka, 1978). Moreover, reptile species density is positively correlated with long-term mean annual precipitation ($r = 0.33$) and average annual actual

Table 10.1. *The numbers of species of birds (N) in each of four niche categories are listed for nine Kalahari study areas and for eight structurally similar areas in the Western Australian desert. Percentages are given in parentheses. The two right-hand columns give the overall percentage of carnivorous and arboreal species*

N	Ground herbivores	Ground carnivores	Arboreal herbivores	Arboreal carnivores	Percentage carnivorous	Percentage arboreal
			Kalahari			
15	4.0 (27)	7.0 (47)	0.0 (0)	4.0 (27)	(73.2)	(26.7)
16	5.5 (34)	6.5 (41)	0.0 (0)	4.0 (25)	(65.6)	(25.0)
16	5.5 (34)	4.5 (28)	0.0 (0)	6.0 (38)	(65.6)	(37.5)
16	5.5 (34)	5.5 (34)	0.0 (0)	5.0 (31)	(65.6)	(31.2)
19	5.5 (29)	6.0 (32)	0.0 (0)	7.5 (40)	(71.0)	(39.4)
21	6.5 (31)	6.5 (31)	1.0 (5)	7.0 (33)	(64.3)	(38.1)
29	6.8 (23)	8.7 (30)	1.8 (6)	11.7 (40)	(70.7)	(46.6)
33	8.3 (25)	9.7 (29)	0.3 (1)	14.7 (45)	(74.2)	(45.4)
40	7.3 (18)	11.7 (29)	2.8 (7)	18.2 (46)	(75.0)	(52.4)
Means 22.8	6.1 (28)	7.3 (34)	0.7 (2)	8.7 (36)	(69.5)	(38.0)
			Australia			
15	6.2 (41)	3.8 (25)	0.0 (0)	5.0 (33)	(58.6)	(33.3)
16	4.2 (26)	2.8 (18)	0.0 (0)	9.0 (56)[1]	(73.8)[1]	(56.2)[1]
28	7.3 (26)	5.7 (20)	2.3 (8)	12.7 (45)	(65.6)	(53.4)
28	7.0 (25)	5.5 (20)	2.3 (8)	13.2 (47)	(66.8)	(55.3)
30	8.2 (27)	4.8 (16)	2.0 (7)	15.0 (50)	(66.3)	(56.6)
31	9.2 (30)	5.8 (19)	2.8 (9)	13.2 (43)	(61.2)	(51.9)
31	7.8 (25)	4.7 (15)	3.0 (10)	15.5 (50)	(65.1)	(59.6)
33	9.2 (28)	5.3 (16)	3.3 (10)	15.2 (46)	(62.2)	(56.0)
Means 26.5	7.4 (29)	4.8 (18)	2.0 (7)	12.4 (46)	(64.9)	(52.7)

[1] Probably an overestimate.

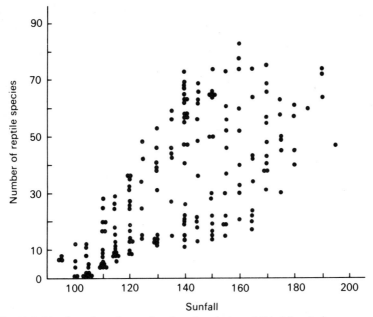

Fig. 10.7. Number of reptile species plotted against sunfall in kilocalories per square meter per year for 193 quadrates in the continental United States ($r = 0.66$, $P < 0.001$). (From Pianka, 1978.)

evapotranspiration ($r = 0.45$), in contrast to the numbers of species of mammals and birds, both of which are inversely correlated with average annual precipitation and actual evapotranspiration (see above and Pianka, 1978). The correlations between reptile species density and annual precipitation and actual evapotranspiration are greatly improved by partial correlation holding constant the effects of sunfall on reptile species density ($r_{xy \cdot z} = 0.76$ and 0.73, respectively). Evidently, physical factors regulating reptile diversity differ from those influencing avian and mammalian diversity (for a more detailed analysis see Schall & Pianka, 1978).

Over the last decade I have studied the niche relations and species diversity of desert lizards in some detail (see, for example, Pianka, 1966, 1967, 1969a, 1969b, 1971, 1973, 1974, 1975). Some 32 desert study sites at similar latitudes on three continents (North America, southern Africa, and Western Australia) support from 4 to 40 sympatric species of lizards. Below I limit discussion to numbers of lizard species because species diversity is very strongly correlated with species density ($r = 0.84$, $P < 0.001$); hence similar results would emerge from analysis of species diversity.

Although the study sites on the three continents have evolved independently of one another, presumably in response to similar selective

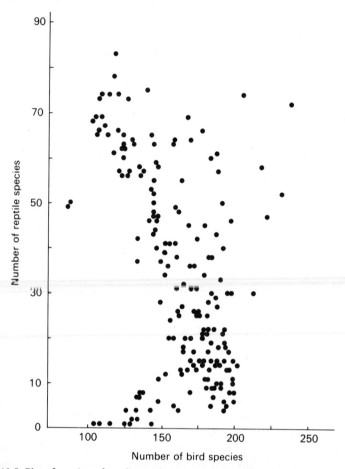

Fig. 10.8. Plot of number of reptile species versus number of bird species for the continental United States. The weak inverse correlation is statistically significant ($r = -0.397$, $P < 0.01$). (From Pianka, 1978.)

pressures, there are striking differences between continents in the diversity, composition, and structure of their lizard communities (Pianka, 1973, 1975). Different sites within North America support between 4 and 11 sympatric species of lizards (Pianka, 1966, 1967, 1975). In the Kalahari desert of southern Africa, from 11 to 18 lizard species occur together on any given study area (Pianka, 1971). The richest known saurofaunas occur in the Great Victoria desert of Western Australia, where as many as 18–40 lizard species are found in sympatry (Pianka, 1969a, 1969b, 1973, 1975).

Lizard species density is significantly correlated with both long-term mean annual precipitation ($r = 0.42$, $P < 0.05$) and the standard deviation in annual precipitation ($r = 0.68$, $P < 0.001$). The latter correlation remains

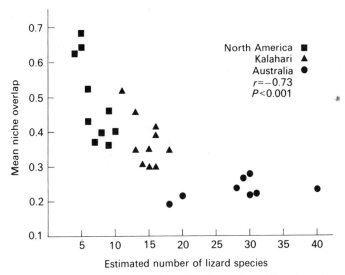

Fig. 10.9. Average niche overlap plotted against the number of lizard species on twenty-eight desert study areas on three continents. (From Pianka, 1974.)

significant ($r = 0.54$, $P < 0.01$) after partial correlation is used to hold constant the effects of long-term mean precipitation (however, the former correlation between lizard species density and long-term mean precipitation disappears when the standard deviation in precipitation is held constant by partial correlation).

Detailed analyses of the niche relationships of desert lizards in these saurofaunas (Pianka, 1973, 1974, 1975) show that average niche breadth does not vary markedly or consistently with numbers of species; however, niche overlap decreases as lizard species density increases (Fig. 10.9). Hence the number of coexisting lizard species in diverse lizard faunas is not facilitated by increased overlap, but rather reduced niche overlap contributes negatively to diversity. Niche overlap also varies inversely with standard deviation in annual precipitation (Pianka, 1974, 1975), but this correlation vanishes when the number of lizard species is held constant by partial correlation.

The relative importance of various niche dimensions in separating niches differs among continents. Food is a major dimension separating niches of North American lizards, whereas in the Kalahari, niche separation is slight on the trophic dimension and differences in microhabitat and time of activity are considerable. All three niche dimensions separate niches rather more equally in Australia. Resource diversity appears to be the major factor promoting differences in lizard species density within and between continents (Pianka, 1973, 1975).

Various historical phenomena have pronounced effects upon the struc-

337

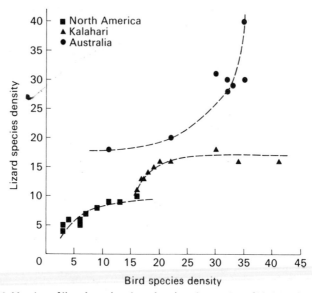

Fig. 10.10. Number of lizard species plotted against the number of bird species on twenty-eight desert study areas. Lizards increase faster than birds in Australia, whereas the reverse is true in North America and the Kalahari, where there appears to be a distinct upper limit on the number of lizard species. (From Pianka, 1975.)

ture of independently-evolved desert communities; historical differences in the interactions between taxa can profoundly influence the niche rela-tionships of component species. Some such interactions between taxa are quite evident while others can be exceedingly subtle. Part of the difference between the Kalahari and Australian deserts in numbers of lizard species can be attributed to differences in their avifaunas (Table 10.1). Thus, the reduced numbers of species of ground-foraging carnivorous birds in Australia may be a factor allowing increased lizard species density on that continent (Fig. 10.10). A more complete analysis of community structure that included both lizards and birds might be very revealing. As indicated above, Australian desert lizards have also usurped some of the ecological roles played by other taxa on other continents, including mammals, snakes, and perhaps some predatory arthropods (Pianka, 1969a, 1973, 1975). However, these mammal-like and snake-like lizard species contri-bute at most only a few species to the saurofauna of any particular area. Thus there are many more species of 'lizard-like' lizards in the Australian deserts. The influence of some historical differences remains obscure: for example, termites constitute some 40% of the diet by volume of Kalahari lizards, whereas they represent only about 16% of the total food eaten by lizards in North America and Australia (Pianka, 1973).

338

Conclusions

While the above very brief review of various empirical studies on just five major taxa is far from exhaustive, it clearly suggests major differences among these organismic groups in the factors influencing their niche structure and diversity. Moreover, reciprocal niche relations and interactions between taxa can play subtle, but sometimes profound, roles in shaping community structure. Whittaker (1975) emphasizes that different environmental factors influence diversity in different plant and animal groups; he concludes that species diversity of communities is an interesting property to observe and attempt to interpret, but that diversity is seldom really very predictable.

Few, if any, generalizations about diversity and niche structure in desert communities seem possible at present, but future studies on community structure and function could ultimately produce some general principles of community organization that might allow some such generalizations about desert communities.

References

Brown, J. H. (1973). Species diversity of seed-eating desert rodents in sand dune habitats. *Ecology*, **54**, 775–87.

Brown, J. H. (1975). Geographical ecology of desert rodents. In: *The Ecology and evolution of communities* (eds. M. Cody & J. Diamond). Belknap Press, Harvard University Press, Cambridge, Mass.

Brown, J. H. & Lieberman, G. A. (1973). Resource utilization and coexistence of seed-eating desert rodents in sand dune habitats. *Ecology*, **54**, 788–97.

Charnov, E. L. (1973). 'Optimal foraging: some theoretical explorations.' Ph.D. dissertation, University of Washington, Seattle.

Cody, M. L. (1970). Chilean bird distributions. *Ecology*, **51**, 455–64.

Cody, M. L. (1973). Parallel evolution and bird niches. In: *Ecological Studies No. 7* (eds. F. Di Castri & H. Mooney), pp. 307–38. Springer, New York.

Cody, M. L. 1974). *Competition and the structure of bird communities*. Princeton University Press, Princeton, New Jersey.

Cook, R. E. (1969). Variation in species density of North American birds. *Systematic Zoology*, **18**, 63–84.

Emlen, J. M. (1966). The role of time and energy in food preference. *American Naturalist*, **100**, 611–17.

Emlen, J. M. (1968). Optimal choice in animals. *American Naturalist*, **102**, 385–9.

Hill, M. O. (1973). Diversity and eveness: a unifying notation and its consequences. *Ecology*, **54**, 427–32.

Hutchinson, G. E. (1961). The paradox of the plankton. *American Naturalist*, **95**, 137–47.

Janzen, D. H. & Schoener, T. W. (1968). Differences in insect abundance and diversity between wetter and drier sites during a tropical dry season. *Ecology*, **49**, 96–110.

Kiester, A. R. (1971). Species density of North American amphibians and reptiles. *Systematic Zoology*, **20**, 127–37.

339

Component processes

Lein, M. R. (1972). A trophic comparison of avifaunas. *Systematic Zoology*, **21**, 135–50.

Longuet-Higgins, M. S. (1971). On the Shannon-Weaver index of diversity, in relation to the distribution of species in bird censuses. *Theoretical Population Biology*, **2**, 271.

Lowe, C. H., Morello, J. H., Cross, J. K. & Goldstein, G. (1972). Transect studies: comparative structure and variation of vegetation. In: *Origin and Structure of Ecosystems*, pp. 47–71. Technical report 72–6 'Papers presented at the annual meeting of the structure of ecosystems program', held in March, 1972, in Tucson, Arizona. University of Arizona Press, Tucson.

Lowe, C., Morello, J., Goldstein, G., Cross, J. & Neuman, R. (1973). Analisis comparativo de la vegetacion de los desiertos subtropicales de Norte y Sud America (Monte-Sonora). *Ecologia*, **1**, 35–43.

MacArthur, R. H. (1964). Environmental factors affecting bird species diversity. *American Naturalist*, **98**, 387–97.

MacArthur, R. H. (1972). *Geographical ecology. Patterns in the distribution of species.* Harper and Row, New York.

MacArthur, R. H. & MacArthur, J. W. (1961). On bird species diversity. *Ecology*, **42**, 594–8.

MacArthur, R. H. & Pianka, E. R. (1966). On optimal use of a patchy environment. *American Naturalist*, **100**, 603–9.

McCleary, J. A. (1968). The biology of desert plants. In: *Desert Biology* (ed. G. W. Brown), Chapter 5. Academic Press, New York.

Murdoch, W. W., Evans, F. C. & Peterson, C. H. (1972). Diversity and pattern in plants and insects. *Ecology*, **53**, 819–29.

Orians, G. H. & Solbrig, O. T. (1977). A cost-income model of leaves and roots with special reference to arid and semi-arid areas. *American Naturalist* **111**, 677–90.

Otte, D. & Joern, A. (1978). Feeding patterns among desert grasshoppers and the evolution of specialization. *Oecologia* (In press.)

Peet, R. K. (1974). The measurement of species diversity. *Annual Review of Ecological Systematics*, **5**, 285–307.

Pianka, E. R. (1966). Convexity, desert lizards, and spatial heterogeneity. *Ecology*, **47**, 1055–9.

Pianka, E. R. (1967). On lizard species diversity: North American flatland deserts. *Ecology*, **48**, 333–51.

Pianka, E. R. (1969a). Habitat specificity, speciation, and species density in Australian desert lizards. *Ecology*, **50**, 498–502.

Pianka, E. R. (1969b). Sympatry of desert lizards (*Ctenotus*) in Western Australia. *Ecology*, **50**, 1012–30.

Pianka, E. R. (1971). Lizard species density in the Kalahari desert. *Ecology*, **52**, 1024–9.

Pianka, E. R. (1973). The structure of lizard communities. *Annual Review of Ecology and Systematics*, **4**, 53–74.

Pianka, E. R. (1974) Niche overlap and diffuse competition. *Proceedings of the National Academy of Science U.S.A.*, **71**, 2141–5.

Pianka, E. R. (1975). Niche relations of desert lizards. In. *The Ecology and Evolution of Communities* (ed. M. Cody & J. Diamond), Chapter 12. Belknap Press, Harvard University Press, Cambridge, Mass.

Pianka, E. R. (1978). Reptilian species diversity. In: *Biology of the Reptilia* (eds. D. Tinkle & W. Milstead for C. Gans). Academic Press, New York.

340

Pianka, E. R. & Huey, R. B. (1971). Bird species density in the Kalahari and the Australian deserts. *Koedoe*, **14**, 123–30.

Pielou, E. C. (1969). *An introduction to mathematical ecology*. Wiley, New York.

Recher, H. F. (1969). Bird species diversity and habitat diversity in Australia and North America. *American Naturalist*, **103**, 75–9.

Rogers, J. S. (1976). Species density and taxonomic diversity of Texas amphibians and reptiles. *Systematic Zoology*, **25**, 26–40.

Rosenzweig, M. L. (1968a). Net primary productivity of terrestrial communities: prediction from climatological data. *American Naturalist*, **102**, 67–74.

Rosenzweig, M. L. (1968b). The strategy of body size in mammalian carnivores. *American Midland Naturalist*, **80**, 299–315.

Rosenzweig, M. L. & Sterner, P. W. (1970). Population ecology of desert rodent communities: body size and seed-husking as bases for heteromyid coexistence. *Ecology*, **51**, 217–24.

Rosenzweig, M. L. & Winakur, J. (1969). Population ecology of desert rodent communities: habitats and environmental complexity. *Ecology*, **50**, 558–72.

Schall, J. J. & Pianka, E. R. (1978). Geographical trends in numbers of species. *Science*. (In press.)

Schoener, T. W. (1971). Theory of feeding strategies. *Annual Review of Ecology and Systematics*, **2**, 369–404.

Shreve, F. (1974). *Vegetation of the Sonaran Desert*. Stanford University Press, Stanford, California.

Simpson, E. H. (1949). Measurement of diversity. *Nature (London)*, **163**, 688.

Simpson, G. G. (1964). Species density of North American recent mammals. *Systematic Zoology*, **13**, 57–73.

Terentev, P. V. (1963). Attempt at application of analysis of variation to the fauna of terrestrial vertebrates of the U.S.S.R., *Vestnik Leningradskovo Universiteta*, **21**, 19–26. (Translated by E. J. Maly and edited by E. R. Pianka, available as *Smithsonian Herpetological Information Services*, 1968).

Tomoff, C. S. (1974). Avian species diversity in desert scrub. *Ecology*, **55**, 396–403.

Tramer, E. J. (1969). Bird species diversity: components of Shannon's formula. *Ecology*, **50**, 927–9.

Whittaker, R. H. (1972). Evolution and measurement of species diversity. *Taxon*, **21**, 213–51.

Whittaker, R. H. (1975). *Communities and ecosystems*. 2nd Edition. Macmillan, New York.

Manuscript received by the editors May 1975

Atmospheric processes

11. Atmospheric processes – Introduction

R. O. GRAETZ and I. R. COWAN

To develop a cogent theme to this section it is necessary to define what is meant by 'arid ecosystems' in terms of physical environment. It best serves our purpose to regard arid lands as those whose functioning is largely determined by the time course of the amount and flow of water through them. The input of water to deserts is low, discrete, infrequent and stochastic. The nature of this input is reflected in the abiotic and biotic characteristics of the ecosystem.

The functioning of arid-land ecosystems will be treated by first considering the inputs of radiation and precipitation, which are independent of the surface conditions, and then dealing with the processes of physical transport which occur at the surface and both influence, and are influenced by, conditions obtaining there.

12. Radiation

E. A. FITZPATRICK

Controls under arid conditions

Because of its effect on radiation, the prevailing lack of cloud in arid regions ranks second only to the paucity of rainfall as a climatic feature of fundamental ecological significance. Much of the distinctiveness of arid environments is related to particular atmospheric and terrestrial charac- teristics which affect the various incoming and outgoing components of the radiation balance. Of the atmospheric characteristics, sparsity of cloud cover most of the time is of paramount importance.

During the day, the incoming flux of solar energy approaches a maximum for the latitude and time of year when there is little cloud; and, due to the characteristic dryness of natural surfaces, a large proportion of the available energy is expended in sensible heat rather than in the evaporation process. At night the absence of downward radiation from clouds leads to rapid cooling at the earth surface.

Another ecologically and hydrologically significant consequence of sparse cloud cover is the diminished effectiveness of the meagre rainfall that does occur. Commonly it happens that clear-sky conditions return quickly following individual falls of rain. With an early resumption of sunshine, water retained in the surface layer of soil is rapidly evaporated. This tends to limit greatly the number of occasions on which the surface soil remains moist longer than a few days.

According to Meigs' (1953) classification, arid climates occur mainly within the latitudinal limits of 10° and 40° in each hemisphere (see Fig. 12.1). However, extensions virtually to the equator are found along the eastern African coast in the Northern Hemisphere, and along the western South American coast in the Southern Hemisphere, and poleward exten- sions to about 50° occur in interior Asia and in Patagonia. With such large latitudinal span, there is a wide range in the seasonal régime of sun angle and day length, a factor that imparts considerable variety to the radiation climate of the arid zone even without consideration of atmospheric con- trols. Solar elevation angles and approximate day lengths at latitudes of 10°, 25° and 40° at the summer and winter solstice are shown in Table 12.1.

As a rough first approach, the effect of cloud in diminishing solar radiation at the earth surface can be ignored, and the attenuation due to scattering and absorption within the atmosphere under clear-sky condi- tions can be considered. In Table 12.2 three sets of radiation data are given for the solstice dates; all are expressed as daily totals of radiant energy

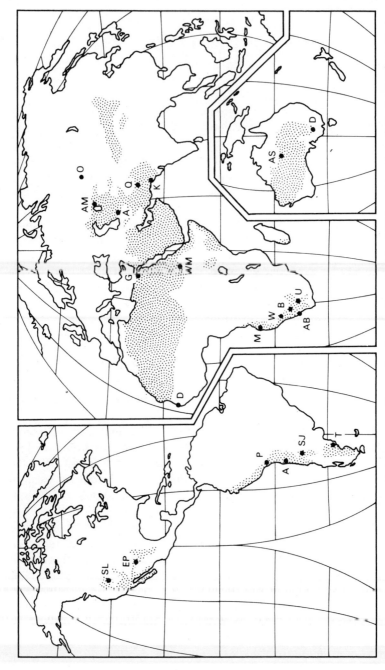

Fig. 12 1. World distribution of arid climates according to the classification of Meigs (1953), and location of all places referred to in the text.

Table 12.1. *Solar elevation and day length at the solstices for latitudes representing marginal and central parts of the arid zone*

	Summer solstice (22 June – N. Hemisphere, 22 Dec. – S. Hemisphere)		Winter solstice (22 Dec. – N. Hemisphere, 22 June – S. Hemisphere)	
Latitude	Solar elevation at noon	Day length	Solar elevation at noon	Day length
10° N or S	76° 33'	12 h 43 min	56° 33'	11 h 32 min
25° N or S	88° 27'	13 h 41 min	41° 33'	10 h 35 min
40° N or S	73° 27'	15 h 01 min	26° 33'	9 h 20 min

Table 12.2. *Daily extraterrestrial, direct, and global solar radiation with clear sky at the solstices for 10° intervals of latitude. All values in cal cm^{-2} day^{-1}*

	22 June			22 December		
Latitude	Extraterrestrial radiation	Direct solar radiation	Global solar radiation	Extraterrestrial radiation	Direct solar radiation	Global solar radiation
50° N	989	563	731	176	37	99
40° N	991	587	744	317	111	199
30° N	975	588	738	466	210	317
20° N	935	568	709	605	309	430
10° N	873	524	659	733	408	537
0°	790	462	590	843	493	630
10° S	687	382	503	933	560	705
20° S	567	290	403	999	606	757
30° S	436	196	296	1041	628	788
40° S	297	103	187	1059	627	795
50° S	165	34	92	1056	601	781

within the solar spectral range received on a horizontal surface. Extraterrestrial radiation represents what would be received if there were no atmosphere; direct solar radiation is that which is received only from within the angle subtended by the solar disk; and global solar radiation is the total solar radiation, both direct and diffuse, which is from the celestial hemisphere. Values of the daily extraterrestrial and direct solar radiation are taken from the Smithsonian Meteorological Tables (List, 1958) for which a solar constant of 1.94 cal cm^{-2} min^{-1} is assumed. The direct solar radiation values are based upon an assumed atmospheric transmission coefficient of 0.7 for a moderately turbid atmosphere. The method used here for determining values of global solar radiation is highly generalized (List, 1958, p. 40); it assumes that 9% is absorbed in the atmosphere (by water vapour and ozone) and that the amounts scattered forwards and backwards are equal. The values are an approximate indication of the seasonal extremes of global solar radiation under cloudless conditions across the latitudinal span of arid climates.

The most notable features of Table 12.2 are the near-constancy in the amounts of direct and global solar radiation over a broad range of latitudes in the summer hemisphere, and their rapid rate of change with latitude poleward of 20° in the winter hemisphere. Between 20° and 50°, the clear-day direct and global solar radiation totals that can be expected at the summer solstice are everywhere in excess of 550 and 700 cal cm^{-2} respectively, the values being somewhat higher for the southern latitudes because of shorter distance from sun to earth. The ranges of these two sets of values over the 30° latitudinal interval spanning the principal arid regions of the world do not exceed 40 cal cm^{-2}. This lack of contrast at differing latitudes within subtropical and middle latitudes of the summer hemisphere results from the compensating effects of increase in day length and decrease in solar elevation towards the pole.

In arid regions, as elsewhere, day-to-day differences in the total global solar radiation do occur even in the absence of cloud, because atmospheric absorption changes as the concentrations of water vapour and dust change. These concentrations are strongly governed by the origins of the air mass, atmospheric stability, wind strength and turbulence – in general terms, by the synoptic pattern. Data from arid stations in southern Africa given by Drummond (1958) for all cloudless days and for a more limited set of 'clearest' days show the latter to have daily totals of global solar radiation up to 7% higher. Taking data for a selection of arid stations (Table 12.3), I have compared the maximum of the daily totals for a given month, averaged over several years, with the absolute maximum for that month, and have found differences of the same order. It may be expected that the same would apply to differences *below* the mean value for all clear days. Thus under cloudless conditions daily totals of global solar radiation commonly differ by as much as 15% or 20% due to turbidity differences.

At many locations, particularly in the margins of arid regions and where there are strong monsoonal influences, distinct seasonal differences in solar radiation levels on clear days may be evident after the effect of changes in sun angle and day length are accounted for. These seasonal differences are related to contrasts in water vapour and dust concentrations in the prevailing air masses at different times of the year. Davies (1965) notes that at stations in West Africa the ratio of global solar radiation under cloudless sky conditions to extraterrestrial radiation declines from 0.91 in April to 0.76 in September, due to greater scattering and absorption over the wet-season period. Also there is a somewhat lesser

Table 12.3. *Mean annual total and relative duration of sunshine for 18 stations selected to represent eight major arid areas. Geographic coordinates, elevation and degree of aridity also included*

Arid area and station name	Latitude	Longitude	Elevation (m)	Degree of aridity[1]	Total sunshine[2] (h)	Total sunshine as percentage of maximum possible
Saharan
Giza, Egypt	30° 02′ N	31° 13′ E	21	E	3500	80
Dakar, Senegal	14° 44′ N	17° 28′ W	20	S	2800	64
Wad Medani, Sudan	14° 24′ N	33° 29′ E	405	A	3800	87
Central Asia
Omsk, USSR	54° 56′ N	73° 24′ E	94	S	1900	43
Aralskoe More, USSR	46° 47′ N	61° 40′ E	56	A	2450	56
Thar
Quetta, Pakistan	30° 11′ N	66° 57′ E	1799	A	3450	79
Karachi, Pakistan	24° 54′ N	67° 08′ E	4	A	3100	71
North American
Salt Lake City, USA	40° 46′ N	111° 55′ W	1329	A	3100	71
El Paso, USA	31° 48′ N	106° 24′ W	1194	A	3600	82
Atacama
Atacama Desert, Chile	(23° S)	(69° W)	(800)	E	4000	91
Parinacotta, Chile	18° 12′ S	69° 16′ W	4392	A	2500	57
Monte-Patagonian
Trelew, Argentina	43° 14′ S	63° 18′ W	39	A	2400	55
San Juan, Argentina	31° 36′ S	68° 33′ W	827	A	3000	68
Namib–Kalahari
Alexander Bay, S. Africa	28° 34′ S	16° 32′ E	21	A	2300	52
Uppington, S. Africa	28° 26′ S	21° 16′ E	814	A	3550	81
Mocemedes, Angola	15° 02′ S	12° 02′ E	44	A	2200	50
Australian
Deniliquin, Australia	35° 32′ S	144° 58′ E	102	S	2400	55
Alice Springs, Australia	23° 48′ S	133° 53′ E	546	A	3200	73

[1] Estimated from world maps of Meigs (1953). E, extremely arid; A, arid; S, semiarid.
[2] Estimated from world map of Landsberg (1965).

decline in this 'index of turbidity' in January and February, this being attributable to dust-laden 'harmattan' air covering the northern areas of West Africa at that time, and extending its effect southward by overriding moist maritime air. A study of turbidity over the United States based on sun photometer data from a network of 43 stations shows that the Rocky

351

Atmospheric processes

Mountains and arid plateaux of the southwest have low turbidity by comparison with the eastern half of the country, and that 'on the average, lowest turbidities are observed in polar continental air masses in winter, and highest in maritime tropical air masses in summer' (Flowers, Mc-Cormick & Kurfis, 1969). In Israel, Joseph & Manes (1971) found that there was a marked maximum in the mean level of atmospheric turbidity in spring and a smaller maximum in summer, and that these seasonal peaks coincided with high standard deviations in turbidity. This relationship according to the authors 'may well be an indication that the deviations from the regular annual march are due to occasional intrusions of air masses from southeastern directions with extremely high aerosol content (usually in spring), and air masses of polar origin with very low turbidities, as a rule in winter'. A more recent study by Mani, Chacko & Iyer (1973) in India reveals a very marked annual variation in turbidity over the subcontinent, with very high values in the summer pre-monsoon period, falling abruptly in the post-monsoon and winter seasons.

In the study of responses and adaptations of plants and animals to the radiation climate, intensities of radiation over short periods may be more significant than daily totals. Of particular interest are intensities at midday, from which the maximum total radiation load on an organism might be computed. The proportions of direct and diffuse solar radiation and the spectral composition are also important. Unfortunately data in these special forms are sparse, and even the more common data for global solar radiation are not usually presented in a form indicating variation in intensity through the day. Fig. 12.2 shows the diurnal course of mean global solar radiation at Alice Springs, Australia* for December and June. The curves were obtained by averaging three years of data summarized over hourly intervals (Bureau of Meteorology, n.d.). The intensities of global solar radiation are interesting as this station is representative of the central portion of the Australian arid region and is nearly on the Tropic line. The mean intensity shown in Fig. 12.2 is governed by the particular turbidity and cloudiness characteristics of this area, but is probably not much different from that at many places at low to moderate elevation within arid regions at the tropics. At noon in mid-December the sun is close to the zenith position and the mean intensity of global solar radiation is approximately 1.40 cal cm^{-2} min^{-1}, or about 0.7 of the extraterrestrial radiation flux. In mid-June the solar elevation at noon is approximately 43°, and the mean intensity is 0.85 cal cm^{-2} min^{-1}, or 0.66 of the extraterrestrial radiation. The curve for December in Fig. 12.2 displays an asymmetry to be expected in many areas. The afternoon levels are notably lower than at a comparable time before noon, and the trend of the curve is almost linear between 13.30 and 18.00 hours. This is due to increase

* Locations of all places referred to in the text are shown in Fig. 12.1.

352

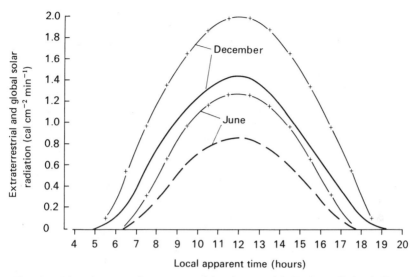

Fig. 12.2. Diurnal course of extraterrestrial and mean global solar radiation in December and June at Alice Springs, Australia.

in cloud in the afternoon, a common feature in both arid and humid climates.

An indication of expected intensities of either direct or global solar radiation under cloudless conditions can be obtained from theoretically based models that quantify the absorption and scattering with passage of radiation through the atmosphere (such as those of Robinson (1966) and Idso (1969, 1970)). The basic requirements for their application are a specification of the solar elevation or optical air mass (path length of solar beam through the atmosphere), precipitable water in the atmosphere (determined from radiosonde data or estimated from surface vapour pressure), and a measure of atmospheric turbidity, such as Ångström's (1929) 'turbidity coefficient'. Further adjustments for elevation above sea level, atmospheric ozone content and seasonal differences in distance from earth to sun are applied. Table 12.4 shows direct and global solar radiation intensities under cloudless conditions, determined from the model of Robinson (1966). Solar elevation angles were selected to be representative of midday conditions within the arid zone. The three amounts of precipitable water cover the range observed within the Australian arid region (Pierrehumbert, 1972), and similar amounts may be expected in other arid areas. The two reference levels of turbidity chosen are based on values of Ångström's (1929) turbidity coefficient, B, considered by Mani *et al.* (1973) to be appropriate for tropical continental air ('high turbidity' $B = 0.20$) and for polar continental and equatorial

Table 12.4. *Direct and global solar radiation fluxes estimated for various combinations of turbidity, precipitable water, and solar elevation according to Robinson's (1966) model. All values in* $cal\,cm^{-2}\,min^{-1}$

Precipitable water (cm)	Radiation type	Solar elevation			
		90°	70°	50°	30°
		Low turbidity ($B = 0.05$)[1]			
0.5	Direct	1.48	1.45	1.38	1.21
	Global	1.63	1.60	1.52	1.32
1.5	Direct	1.40	1.38	1.30	1.14
	Global	1.55	1.53	1.44	1.25
4.5	Direct	1.32	1.29	1.20	1.03
	Global	1.47	1.44	1.34	1.14
		High turbidity ($B = 0.20$)			
0.5	Direct	1.22	1.14	1.05	0.84
	Global	1.53	1.44	1.30	1.02
1.5	Direct	1.13	1.08	0.96	0.78
	Global	1.44	1.38	1.21	0.96
4.5	Direct	1.03	0.97	0.88	0.69
	Global	1.34	1.27	1.13	0.87

[1] Turbidity coefficient of Ångström (1929).

maritime air ('low turbidity' $B = 0.05$) over India. The values given in Table 12.4 are for sea level, average atmospheric ozone content, and mean distance from sun to earth. The values indicate that, for a given turbidity, the intensities of both direct and global solar radiation are reduced by 10% to 20% with an increase in precipitable water from 0.5 cm to 4.5 cm. For a given amount of precipitable water, the intensities of direct solar radiation are reduced by 20% to 35% with a change from 'low' to 'high' turbidity, and global solar radiation intensities are reduced by 5% to 25%; the reductions in both cases are greatest with the smallest angle of solar elevation. With a combined increase in precipitable water from 0.5 cm to 4.5 cm and in turbidity from 'low' to 'high' the direct radiation intensities are decreased by 30% to 45%, and global solar radiation intensities by 20% to 35%.

The differences in radiation intensity shown in Table 12.4 illustrate the importance of intrinsic properties of air masses, quite apart from the effects of cloudiness. No complete set of observational data were available to assess the reliability of values given in the table; however the direct solar radiation intensities given by Drummond (1958) for Drukkaros in the Kalahari arid area of Namibia (latitude 29° 52′ S; elevation 1585 m) agree well with the set of values for 'low' turbidity and 1.5 cm of precipitable water.

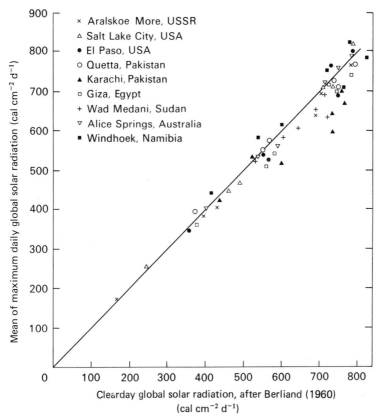

Fig. 12.3. Relationship between observed mean values of maximum daily global solar radiation at nine stations, and estimated global solar radiation according to the method of Berliand (1960). Points shown are for February, April, June, August, October and December.

As an alternative to calculating clear-day global solar radiation from known or assumed atmospheric transmission and precipitable water, a more empirical approach developed by Berliand (1960) can be used. Essentially, the method consists of plotting daily totals of global solar radiation over a number of years for stations within a specified narrow range of latitudes. Rectangular co-ordinates are used, the abscissa being the day of the year and the ordinate the observed level of global solar radiation. A smooth curve forming an upper envelope to the plotted points represents the limit of expected clear-day global solar radiation. From graphical analyses of this kind, Berliand (1960) has produced a table giving levels of global solar radiation on clear days for all months and at 5° intervals of latitude. To assess the reliability of Berliand's tabulated values specifically for arid conditions, published records of daily global solar

355

radiation for periods of three to six years (1967 to 1972) were obtained for a selection of arid stations (USSR Hydro-Meteorological Service, 1964 and on). The highest values in each month were noted and averaged over the period of the record. Comparable data were also obtained from Windhoek, Namibia; Alice Springs, Australia; and Giza, Egypt (Drummond, 1958; Hounam, 1963; Griffiths & Soliman, 1972). The relationship between observed means of the maximum daily global solar radiation in February, April, June, August, October and December and the 'predicted' totals for clear days from Berliand's table is shown in Fig. 12.3. In general they are in close agreement at these arid stations, although systematic errors are evident for some. The largest errors are for Karachi, Pakistan, where the 'predicted' values exceed the observed by about 100 cal cm^{-2} d^{-1} in February, April, June and August. As no additional climatic data were available for the particular days on which the highest daily global solar radiation occurred, it was not possible to identify a probable cause for the errors. From the limited data on which these assessments are made, it would appear that the tabulated values of Berliand (1960) are more reliable for arid stations at inland locations than for coastal stations (note, for example, the agreement for Quetta, Pakistan, as compared with Karachi).

The ratio of diffuse to global solar radiation varies within each day, from day to day, and seasonally with sun angle, turbidity, and particularly amount of cloud. Without cloud the diffuse component of solar radiation probably does not contribute more than about 15% of the total daily solar energy within the latitudinal limits of arid climates. Drummond (1958) gives mean daily values of diffuse and global solar radiation for all months at Windhoek, Namibia (22° 34' S) in the Kalahari arid area. The diffuse contribution is about 9%–11% when all cloudless days are considered, and about 7%–9% when only the 'clearest' days are included. When all days, with and without cloud, are included the percentage contribution is as high as 36% in February, which has only 65% of possible sunshine, and as low as 14% in July, when 94% of possible sunshine is received.

Cloudiness and sunshine in arid regions

World maps of mean cloud cover based on surface observations have long been available (for instance, Landsberg, 1945). These show that the principal subtropical desert areas usually have less than 30% average cloud cover. Some exceptions are notable, however. Mean cloudiness of up to 50% occurs over the arid western coastal regions of South America and southern Africa. Midlatitude arid regions of central Asia, interior western USA and Patagonia have up to 60% at some time during the year. By far the most extensive area with persistently small cloud cover (less than 10%)

is in the eastern Sahara and Arabia, and extends eastward as far as the Thar desert from May to November. Other much smaller areas with comparably small amounts of cloud but with greater seasonal variation are in the interior of southern Africa, Australia and the Sonoran area of southwestern North America. Recent studies based on pictures from *Tiros* meteorological satellites suggest that, although the amount of cloud in the world's cloudiest regions has probably been underestimated from surface data, values in the arid regions, and all areas dominated by oceanic anticyclones, are well represented in Landsberg's (1945) maps (Winston, 1969).

In appraising mean cloud-cover patterns it should be remembered that, for most climates outside the tropics, the frequency of days with differing amounts of cloud, ranging from fully overcast to clear, has a distinctive U-shaped distribution – that is, the mean amounts are less likely to occur than the extremes. Landsberg (1945) shows that the mean amount of cloud is positively correlated with the frequency of 'cloudy' days (days with more than 80% cover), and negatively correlated with the frequency of 'clear' days (days with less than 20% cover). On the basis of US data and evidence from other areas poleward of 20°, Landsberg suggests that the following can be taken as approximate relative frequencies of 'clear' days as compared with 'cloudy' days for differing percentages of mean cloud cover: 1:1 for 50%; 3:1 for 40%; 6:1 for 30%; 9:1 for 20%; and greater than 20:1 for 10% or less.

Total duration of sunshine is affected by day length as well as by the amounts of cloud cover. World maps showing total hours of sunshine for the year and for January and July have been provided by Landsberg (1965) from records at 1050 stations, together with additional estimated values based on an empirical relationship between the ratio of actual to maximum possible sunshine hours and mean cloud cover. Table 12.3 shows total hours of sunshine estimated from Landsberg's annual map for a selection of stations classed by Meigs (1953) as either 'extremely arid', 'arid', or 'semiarid'. The totals are also shown as a percentage of the maximum number of possible hours of sunshine (taken here to be $365.25 \times 12 = 4383$). Within the core areas of aridity in subtropical latitudes, total sunshine exceeds 3000 hr (70% of the maximum possible). At midlatitude arid stations (such as Aralskoe More, USSR and Trelow, Argentina), and also at coastal arid stations in southern Africa and the semiarid stations on the equatorward and poleward margins of the arid zone (such as Dakar, Senegal; Omsk, USSR; and Deniliquin, Australia) the duration of sunshine is considerably less, both in absolute and relative terms.

Representative magnitudes of global solar radiation

Although data are sparse in some areas, the geographic distribution of the mean annual total of global solar radiation and the basic form of its annual variation, are reasonably well established – at least where the incidence of cloud is not greatly complicated by strong topographic controls. Use of empirical relationships between the ratio of global solar radiation to extraterrestrial radiation, and the ratio of actual sunshine duration to maximum possible sunshine (or fractional cloud cover), facilitates the appraisal of spatial and temporal patterns. Because of errors resulting from the use of such relationships, and the intrinsic errors in the measurement of global solar radiation with many different types of instruments, an accuracy of better than 10% is probably not achieved in many areas. Fortunately, as has been noted by Budyko (1974), global solar radiation is one of the more conservative climatic variables, and quite representative means are obtained under most conditions without the necessity for observations over a very long run of years.

A number of maps at global scale have been published (for instance Black, 1956; Budyko, 1963; Landsberg, 1965; Löf, Duffie & Smith, 1966). The basic spatial patterns in these maps are generally in close agreement, although some differences shown in particular areas are evident. Fig. 12.4 shows the spatial pattern of mean annual global solar radiation according to Landsberg (1965). The map clearly reveals that the largest annual receipts are in the hot desert areas at latitudes about 20° to 25°. In these areas about 200 kcal cm^{-2} is received on average per year. By far the largest area with global solar radiation of this magnitude is the broad band extending across virtually the whole of the Sahara and Arabian Deserts. The map intends to show only broad spatial gradients, and it can be accepted that the true pattern is locally complicated by topographic control of cloudiness. Mean annual global solar radiation diminishes to about 100 kcal cm^{-2} at the poleward margins of the arid zone. Perhaps of greater direct ecological and biogeographical significance is the pattern of mean global solar radiation in mid-summer and mid-winter. This is shown in Figs. 12.5 and 12.6 the maps here being based upon Löf *et al.* (1966), who used observations at 668 stations and estimated values for 233 stations having long sunshine records. The maps require verbal elaboration only to the extent of noting the contrast between the basically concentric patterns around core areas with about 700–750 cal cm^{-2} d^{-1} within arid regions in the summer hemisphere, and the essentially zonal patterns in the winter hemisphere, where global solar radiation diminishes from about 400 cal cm^{-2} d^{-1} to about 100 cal cm^{-2} d^{-1} across the latitudinal span of the arid zone.

The form of the distribution of global solar radiation through the year

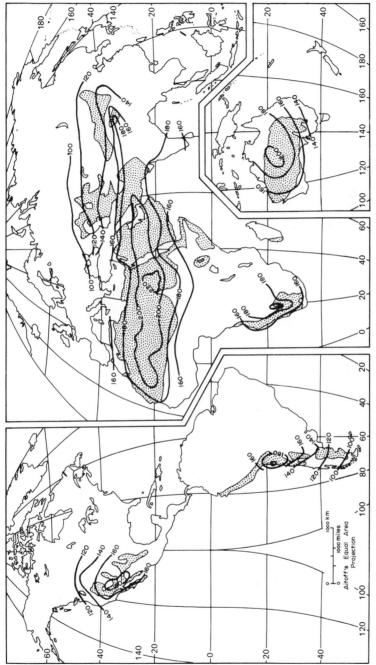

Fig. 12.4. Mean annual global solar radiation in kcal cm^{-2} yr^{-1} over arid and semiarid areas according to Landsberg (1965).

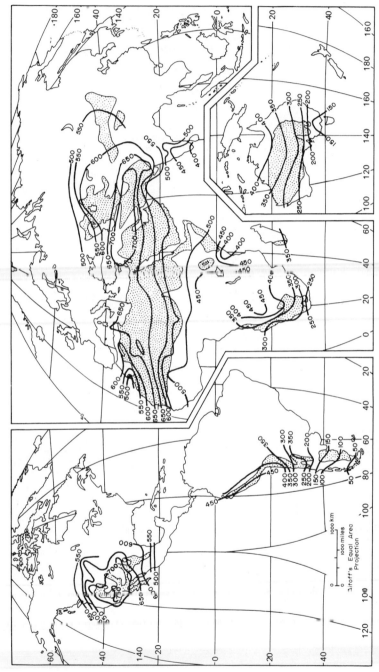

Fig. 12.5. Mean daily global solar radiation in cal cm^{-2} d^{-1} for June over arid and semiarid areas according to Löf et al. (1966).

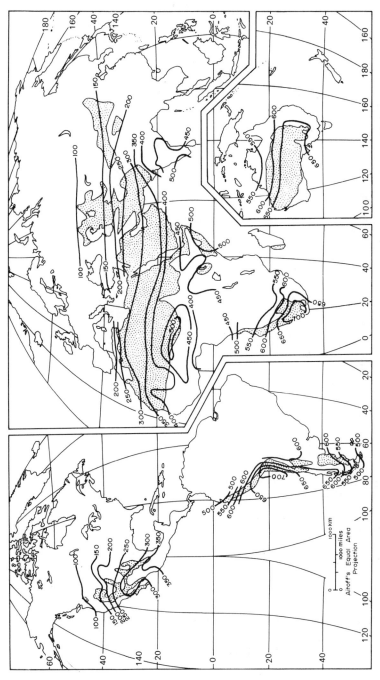

Fig. 12.6. Mean daily global solar radiation in cal cm⁻² d⁻¹ for December over arid and semiarid areas according to Löf et al. (1966).

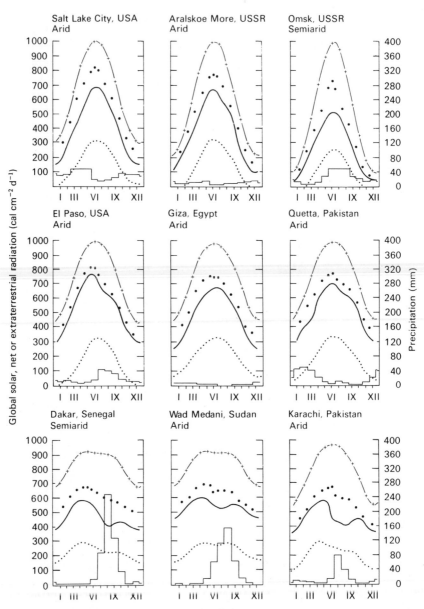

Fig. 12.7. Annual course of extraterrestrial radiation (broken line) mean global solar radiation (solid line), and estimated mean net radiation (dotted line) for nine Northern Hemisphere stations. Heavy dots indicate averages of highest daily global solar radiation occurring over a period from three to six years (1967–72), and histograms show mean monthly rainfall.

362

distinguishes different parts of the arid zone very clearly. Terjung (1970) has produced a global classification based on this attribute, particular attention being directed to the crest height and amplitude of the annual wave, and the characteristic shape of the curve. Through the central core areas of the arid zone, and extending to its poleward limit, the seasonal distribution is characterized by a unimodal curve of medium to high amplitude, reaching a peak close to the time of maximum observed solar energy input (normally June in the Northern and December in the Southern Hemisphere). Along the equatorial margins of the arid zone the amplitude of the annual curve diminishes, the maximum levels being somewhat lower because day-length is less, and minimum levels being considerably greater as a result of the combination of larger solar elevation angles and greater day length. The basic form of the curve also changes towards the equator, becoming asymmetrical or bimodal due to the combined effect of double passage of the sun across the zenith within the Tropics, and the usual summer maximum of cloud cover at these latitudes. These basic features are well portrayed in the diagrams of Fig. 12.7 where the solid-line curves show the annual course of mean daily global solar radiation at nine arid or semi-arid stations in the Northern Hemisphere. The data on which these curves are based were obtained by appropriately weighting and combining the means published by Löf *et al.* (1966) with records published by the USSR Hydro-Meteorological Service (1964 and on) and from one other source (Griffiths & Soliman, 1972). The diagrams also show the relationship between the mean daily global solar radiation and the extraterrestrial radiation (assuming the solar constant to be 1.94 cal cm^{-2} min^{-1}). The means of the highest recorded daily values (from records available between 1967 and 1972) and the long-term mean monthly rainfalls (Air Ministry Meteorological Office, 1960) are given also. Data for the mean annual global solar radiation, the crest and trough points on the curve, and the maximum and minimum ratios of global solar to extraterrestrial radiation (transmission ratio) are given in Table 12.5. The differing seasonal patterns are grouped according to latitude in Table 12.5 and depicted from top to bottom in Fig. 12.7. At latitudes greater than 40° N mean daily global solar radiation reaches levels well above 600 cal cm^{-2} d^{-1} at the two arid stations, Aralskoe More, USSR and Salt Lake City, USA, but is only slightly above 500 cal cm^{-2} d^{-1} at the more northerly and semiarid station of Omsk, USSR. The minimum levels at the two arid stations are between 100 and 200 cal cm^{-2} d^{-1}, but at Omsk, where day length at the winter solstice is only about 7 hours, and where solar elevation is about 12°, the minimum falls below 50 cal cm^{-2} d^{-1}. In all cases maximum and minimum values occur in June and December. As indicated by the transmission ratios, 60%–70% of the daily extraterrestrial radiation is actually received at ground level in the dry summer months

Table 12.5. *Mean global solar radiation and atmospheric transmission data for nine Northern Hemisphere stations within three selected intervals of latitude*

Latitudinal interval and station name	Mean annual global solar radiation (kcal cm^{-2})	Highest mean daily global solar radiation (cal cm^{-2}) (months I–XII)	Lowest mean daily global solar radiation (cal cm^{-2}) (months I–XII)	Highest transmission ratio[1] (months I–XII)	Lowest transmission ratio[1] (months I–XII)
Lat. > 40° N					
Omsk, USSR	97.2	521–VI	48–XII	0.55–III	0.35–X
Aralskoe More, USSR	142.4	671–VI	104–XII	0.67–VI	0.46–XII
Salt Lake City, USA	151.9	667–VI	157–XII	0.68–VII	0.50–XII
Lat. 30°–32° N					
El Paso, USA	191.8	704–VI	303–XII	0.75–IV	0.68–XII
Quetta, Pakistan	189.6	715–VI	307–XII	0.75–X	0.61–III
Giza, Egypt	176.4	667–VI	266–XII	0.68–VII	0.57–I
Lat. < 25° N					
Karachi, Pakistan	167.3	576–V	369–XII	0.69–II	0.45–VIII
Dakar, Senegal	172.7	579–IV	378–XII	0.64–III	0.44–VIII
Wad Medani, Sudan	171.3	595–IV	475–I	0.68–XII	0.58–VII

[1] Ratio of mean daily global solar radiation for the month to extraterrestrial radiation on median date of the month.

at the two arid stations, but only 45%–50% in December. At Omsk transmission ratios through the year never exceed 0.55, due to greater cloudiness and the increased path length (optical air mass) of the solar beam at high latitudes. A notable feature at all high-latitude stations is the great difference between the means of the largest amounts of global solar radiation on individual days in the summer months, and the means for all days. The means of the largest daily amounts are of about 700–800 cal cm^{-2}.

At the three arid stations in the range 30°–32° N, June and December are the months of maximum and minimum daily global solar radiation – as at higher latitudes. Amounts in winter are greater, though, being about 250–300 cal cm^{-2} d^{-1}. Transmission ratios of about 0.6–0.75 occur through the year; these values, and details in the shape of the curves also, are conditioned by cloudiness as evidenced by the association with mean rainfall. Mean values for days having the most solar energy during summer are about 700–800 cal cm^{-2} – about the same as at higher latitudes.

The curves for the three stations representing the equatorward margin

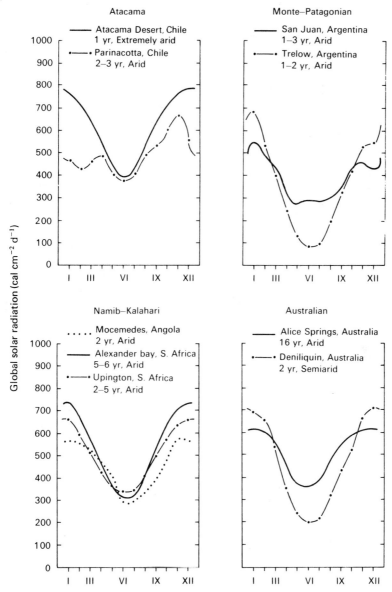

Fig. 12.8. Annual course of mean global solar radiation for four Southern Hemisphere stations.

of the arid zone have the common feature of being bimodal. The major maximum occurs in April or May. This is followed by a period of reduced radiation during the summer rainy period. This summer trough usually occurs between June and August, and is followed by a minor period of increased radiation preceding the annual minimum in December or January. With all days included, the average daily global solar radiation is about 550–600 cal cm^{-2}; the lowest about 350–450. Transmission ratios range from about 0.45 during the cloudy summer rainy period to about 0.70 at some time during the driest season. The averages of highest daily totals in each month (heavy dots in Fig. 12.7) reach about 650–700 cal cm^{-2} just prior to the onset of the summer cloudy period; even during this cloudier period some days receive about 600 cal cm^{-2}.

The characteristics of annual global solar radiation in the Southern Hemisphere generally resemble those in the North, except for the obvious seasonal reversal. Fig. 12.8 shows curves for a selection of arid or semiarid stations in four of the arid areas in the Southern Hemisphere. The data from which the curves have been constructed are from several sources (de Vries, 1958; USSR Hydro-Meteorological Service, 1964 and on; Löf *et al.*, 1966; Kalma, 1970). Only a few years of records were available for some stations, and minor irregularities in the form of some curves are probably related to this. Features in common with data for the Northern Hemisphere data are nonetheless evident – for instance, the poleward increase in amplitude and in maximum levels. The curves for the two stations in the Atacama arid area of northern Chile are particularly interesting because they show clearly how global solar radiation levels and seasonal régime may differ considerably at stations not far distant from one another if there are marked topographic influences on cloudiness.

Surface albedo and net radiation in arid lands

Conditions at the earth's surface markedly affect the partitioning of solar energy. Because these conditions are apt to be highly variable both in space and time, radiation balance components, other than the incoming fluxes, should be treated in a micro-environmental context (see Chapter 15 below). However, certain broad generalizations can be made about net radiation, because some of the surface and atmospheric properties which affect it are characteristic of arid zones. Typically, the proportion of incoming solar radiation that is directly lost by reflection at the earth's surface is greater in arid regions than in more humid areas because there is less vegetation. It is difficult to generalize about the surface albedo, however, because many arid landscapes consist of mosaic-like patterns, each element of which may have characteristic reflective properties. From a macro-scale viewpoint, the best measures of surface albedo are those that have a high degree of spatial integration so that the effect of purely localized reflective conditions is smoothed out.

Measures of albedo given in the literature fall generally within the range of 0.25 to 0.30. However measurements made from low-flying aircraft over various types of desert surface show a wider range. Kung, Bryson & Lenschow (1964) measured albedos from 0.18 to 0.29 for different types of surface and surface covers in western USA. Measurements from aircraft in Australia indicate that albedo levels for arid areas in that continent range from about 0.5 at a solar elevation of 10° to about 0.3 or slightly less at elevation angles above 30° (Paltridge, 1971, 1975). It can be accepted, then, that there is a considerable variation in surface albedo within arid regions, depending on the colour, texture and dryness of the soil, the height, form and density of the vegetation, the colour, texture and geometry of leaves, and the angle of solar elevation at a particular time. If any single value must be assigned to the albedo of a 'desert region', it is best set at about 0.28.

The upward and downward fluxes within the spectral range of terrestrial radiation which emanate from the surface and atmosphere are not often measured. These components of the radiation balance are usually assessed from theoretical considerations; use is made of the Stefan–Boltzmann law that the radiation emitted from a perfect radiator (a so-called 'black body') is proportional to the fourth power of its absolute temperature. Some difficulty arises from applying this law, however, not so much because the properties of natural surfaces differ greatly from those of a 'perfect radiator', but because neither earth surface temperatures nor atmospheric temperatures at various heights are normally known with any precision.

As a practical alternative to the separate determinations of upward and downward fluxes, various formulae can be used to estimate the net terrestrial radiation (that is, the difference between downward and upward fluxes) from such meteorological data as are commonly available (Ångström, 1916; Brunt, 1932; Swinbank, 1963). Of particular interest here is the fact that, usually, the excess of upward terrestrial radiation over downward atmospheric radiation during a complete day–night cycle is especially large in low-latitude desert regions. In these areas the net terrestrial radiation over a year may be -80 to -90 kcal cm^{-2}, the absolute value being about one-half of the total amount of global solar radiation normally received (Fig. 12.4). The comparatively high net loss of terrestrial radiation is the result of the intense flux of outgoing radiation which occurs from dry surfaces, which, during the daytime, may be as much as 20°–30° C warmer than the air at screen height, and the relatively small downward flux of radiation associated with the colder atmosphere and absence of cloud.

Because of the combination of large surface albedo and large net loss

367

of terrestrial radiation, the total net radiation (i.e. including wavelengths of both solar and terrestrial spectral ranges) is relatively small in arid regions. Therefore, whereas maps of mean global solar radiation (Figs. 12.4 to 12.6) show the major desert areas of the subtropics to have conspicuously large values, net radiation in these areas tends to be less than it is in adjoining land areas at comparable latitudes with wetter climates (Budyko, 1956).

It is important to recognize the marked effect of differing soil moisture on the net balance of radiation. A considerable decrease in the loss of terrestrial radiation occurs when the soil is moistened by rain or irrigation following a long dry period; therefore, if other components of the radiation balance are constant, the net flux of radiation increases. When the soil is wet surface temperatures are close to those of the ambient air throughout the day, because an appreciable amount of the incoming solar energy is converted into latent heat of evaporation; when the soil is dry, virtually all of the available energy is manifest in the increasing temperature of soil and atmosphere during the daytime hours. In addition, surface albedo is usually greater the drier the conditions (Bowers & Hanks, 1965).

Some net radiation or 'radiation balance' data given by Budyko (1974) are instructive. At Ashkhabad, USSR, in an arid area close to the border with Iran, the measured net radiation over an irrigated field during the months May to August was 8.2, 10.4, 10.5, and 10.0 kcal cm^{-2}. The corresponding levels for a desert site in the same locality are 5.4, 6.7, 6.4, and 6.1 kcal cm^{-2}. In another example given by the same author, midday levels of net radiation over an oasis and a dry semidesert surface are compared. At the former the net radiation was about 9.5 cal cm^{-2} min^{-1}; at the latter it was about 6.5 cal cm^{-2} min^{-1} – about 32% smaller.

Using the monthly values of the observed solar radiation for the nine stations included in Fig. 12.7 and Table 12.5, estimates were made of the net radiation, assuming an albedo of 0.28 and using a method for estimating net terrestrial radiation from air temperature (Swinbank, 1963) which has been applied in the Kimberley region of northwestern Australia (Fitzpatrick & Stern, 1965). Mean temperature data for these stations were obtained from Tables of Temperature, Relative Humidity and Precipitation (Air Ministry Meteorological Office, 1960). For reasons noted above, this use of mean air temperature is in keeping with circumstances provided by moist soil, and levels of estimated net radiation greater than those found over naturally dry surfaces will be obtained. Therefore these estimates are more appropriate to periods following rain or irrigation than to the prevailingly dry conditions. The annual curves of calculated net radiation are shown in Fig. 12.7 and a few features of these deserve special note. Firstly, for all stations, the net radiation at the time of maximum global solar radiation is approximately one-half the latter. From what has pre-

Table 12.6. *Estimated mean net radiation data and related variables for nine Northern Hemisphere stations within three selected intervals of latitude*

Latitudinal interval and station name	Estimated annual net radiation (kcal cm^{-2})	Highest estimated daily net radiation (cal cm^{-2}) (months I–XII)	Lowest estimated daily net radiation (cal cm^{-2}) (months I–XII	Mean annual precipitation (mm)	Latent heat equivalent of mean annual precipitation (kcal)	Budyko's radiative index of dryness[1]	Budyko's dryness class
Lat. > 40° N							
Omsk, USSR	36.31	266–VI	−39–I	318	18.76	1.93	Steppe
Aralskoe More, USSR	47.53	329–VI	−44–I	124	7.34	6.47	Desert
Salt Lake City, USA	58.08	319–VI	6–XII	414	24.43	2.38	Semi-desert
Lat. 30°–32° N							
El Paso, USA	72.17	347–VII	18–XII	221	13.04	5.53	Desert
Quetta, Pakistan	73.62	344–VI	46–XII	239	14.09	5.22	Desert
Giza, Egypt	76.91	336–VI	66–XII	28	1.65	46.61	Desert
Lat. < 25° N							
Karachi, Pakistan	77.39	267–VI	105–XII	196	11.54	6.70	Desert
Dakar, Senegal	84.02	280–V	163–XII	541	31.92	2.63	Semi-desert
Wad Medani, Sudan	90.75	296–V	176–XII	445	26.23	3.46	Desert

[1] Defined by Budyko (1956) as R_n/LP where R_n is the annual net radiation, L is the energy requirement for evaporation of a unit depth of water, and P is the precipitation.

viously been said, this is the approximate *upper* limit of the mid-summer net radiation to be expected with the albedo assumed here – that is when the net terrestrial radiation is minimal because of decreased surface temperature following wetting. Secondly, it is evident that the trends of net radiation over the year are more conservative than those of global solar radiation. Lastly, for the two higher-latitude stations in the USSR, net radiation during the winter months becomes negative – the combination of reflection and emission of radiation from the surface exceeds the incoming radiation. At Salt Lake City, USA, at about 40° N, the estimated net radiation in December is only slightly above zero.

Annual values of the estimated mean net radiation, and the maximum and minimum amounts during the year, are shown in Table 12.6. These values generally agree closely with those shown on world maps by Budyko (1963). As a measure of the dryness of climate Budyko (1956) proposed an index that expresses the mean annual net radiation in relation to the energy requirement for evaporation of the mean annual precipitation. The

Atmospheric processes

calculated values of this 'radiative index of dryness' are also given in the Table. According to Budyko, index values over 3.0 indicate 'desert' conditions, between 2.0 and 3.0 'semidesert' conditions, and between 1.0 and 2.0 'steppe' conditions. These defined degrees of aridity are generally in keeping with the result of Meigs' (1953) classification, which is based upon an accounting procedure in which monthly water balance is calculated using rainfall data and estimates of potential evapotranspiration.

References

Air Ministry Meteorological Office (1960). *Tables of temperature, relative humidity and precipitation for the world.* Her Majesty's Stationery Office, London.
Ångström, A. (1916). Über die Gegenstrahlung der Atmosphäre. *Meteorologische Zeitschrift*, **33**, 529–38.
Ångström, A. (1929). On the atmospheric transmission of sun radiation and on dust in the air. *Geografiska Annaler*, **11**, 156–66.
Berliand, T. G. (1960). Method of climatological calculation of global radiation (in Russian). *Meteorologiya i Gidrologiya, No. 6, 9–12.
Black, J. N. (1956). Distribution of solar radiation over the earth's surface. *Archiv für Meteorologie, Geophysik and Bioklimatologie, Serie B*, **7**, 165–89.
Bowers, S. A. & Hanks, R. J. (1965). Reflection of radiant energy from soils. *Soils Science*, **100**, 130–38.
Brunt, D. (1932). Notes on radiation in the atmosphere. *Quarterly Journal of the Royal Meteorological Society*, **58**, 389–418.
Budyko, M. I. (1956). The heat balance of the earth's surface. *Gidrometeorologicheskee Izdatel'stvo, Leningrad.* (English translation, Stepanova, N.A. 1958. Office of Technical Services, US Dept. of Commerce, Washington).
Budyko, M. I. (ed.) (1963). *Atlas of the heat balance of the earth* (in Russian). Akad. Nauk. SSSR, Presidium. Mezhvedomstvenni: Geofiz. Komitet. Moscow.
Budyko, M. I. (1974). *Climate and life* (English edition, ed. D. H. Miller). Academic Press, New York.
Bureau of Meteorology (no date). *Australian radiation records; 1953–56.* Melbourne.
Davies, J. A. (1965). Estimation of insolation for West Africa. *Quarterly Journal of the Royal Meteorological Society*, **91**, 359–63.
de Vries, D. A. (1958). Two years of solar radiation measurements at Deniliquin. *Australian Meteorological Magazine*, No. **22**, 36–45.
Drummond, A. J. (1958). Radiation and the thermal balance. *UNESCO Arid Zone Research*, **10**, 56–74.
Fitzpatrick, E. A. & Stern, W. E. (1965). Components of the radiation balance of irrigated plots in a dry monsoonal environment. *Journal of Applied Meteorology*, **4**, 649–60
Flowers, E. L., McCormick, E. A. & Kurfis, K. R. (1969). Atmospheric turbidity over the United States, 1961–1966. *Journal of Applied Meteorology*, **8**, 955–62.
Griffiths, J. F. & Soliman, K. H. (1972). The northern desert. In: *World Survey of Climatology*, vol. 10 *Climates of Africa* (ed. H. E. Landsberg), pp. 75–131. Elsevier, Amsterdam.

370

Hounam, C. E. (1963). Estimates of solar radiation over Australia. *Australian Meteorological Magazine*, No. **43**, 1–14.

Idso, S. B. (1969). Atmospheric attenuation of solar radiation. *Journal of Atmospheric Sciences*, **26**, 1008–95.

Idso, S. B. (1970). The transmittance of the atmosphere for solar radiation on individual clear days. *Journal of Applied Meteorology*, **9**, 239–41.

Joseph, J. H. & Manes, A. (1971). Secular and seasonal variations of atmospheric turbidity at Jerusalem. *Journal of Applied Meteorology*, **10**, 453–61.

Kalma, J. D. (1970). Estimating frequencies of daily amounts of global radiation over Australia. *Australian Meteorological Magazine*, **18**, 134–45.

Kung, E. C., Bryson, R. A. & Lenschow, D. H. (1964). Study of a continental surface albedo on the basis of flight measurement and structure of the earth's surface cover over North America. *Monthly Weather Review*, **92**, 543–64.

Landsberg, H. E. (1945). Climatology. In: *Handbook of Meteorology* (eds. F. A. Berry, E. Bellay & N. R. Beers), pp. 928–97. McGraw-Hill, New York.

Landsberg, H. E. (1965). Global distribution of solar and sky radiation. In: *World Maps of Climatology*, 2nd edition (eds. E. Rodenwaldt & H. J. Jusatz), pp. 1–6. Springer-Verlag, Berlin.

List, R. J. (1958). *Smithsonian meteorological tables*. Smithsonian Miscellaneous Collections, Vol. 114. Smithsonian Institution, Washington.

Löf, G. O. G., Daffie, J. A. & Smith, C. O. (1966). *World distribution of solar radiation*. Report No. 21 Engineering Experiment Station. Solar Energy Laboratory. University of Wisconsin, Madison.

Mani, A., Chacko, O. & Iyer, N. V. (1973). Atmospheric turbidity over India from solar radiation measurements. *Solar Energy*, **14**, 185–95.

Meigs, P. (1953). World distribution of arid and semi-arid homoclimates. *UNESCO Arid Zone Research*, **1**, pp. 203–10.

Paltridge, G. W. (1971). Solar and thermal radiation flux measurement over the east coast of Australia. *Journal of Geophysical Research*, **76**, 2857–65.

Paltridge, G. W. (1975). Net radiation over the surface of Australia. *Search*, **6**, 37–9.

Pierrehumbert, C. L. (1972). *Precipitable water statistics, Australia*. Monthly statistics of precipitable water between surface and 400 mb at 2300 GMT, 1958–1969. Bureau of Meteorology, Melbourne.

Robinson, N. (1966). *Solar radiation*. Elsevier, Amsterdam.

Swinbank, W. C. (1963). Long-wave radiation from clear skies. *Quarterly Journal of the Royal Meteorological Society*, **89**, 339–48.

Terjung, W. H. (1970). A global classification of solar radiation. *Solar Energy*, **13**, 67–81.

USSR Hydro-Meteorological Service (1964 and on). *Solar radiation and radiation balance data (the world network)*. A. I. Voeiker Main Geophysical Laboratory, Leningrad.

Winston, J. S. (1969). Global distribution of cloudiness and radiation as measured from weather satellites. In: *World Survey of Climatology*, vol. 4, Climate of the Free Atmosphere, (ed. H. E. Landsberg), pp. 247–80. Elsevier, Amsterdam.

Manuscript received by the editors January 1975

13. Precipitation

F. C. BELL

Precipitation processes

Spatial and temporal distributions of precipitation on a local scale are considerably influenced by the particular atmospheric processes responsible for the precipitation. Qualitatively these processes are the same in arid areas as in humid areas; but certain quantitative aspects, such as low frequency of occurrence and high space–time variability, tend to be characteristic of most arid areas.

Before precipitation can take place there must be adequate development of cloud, which usually requires the cooling of moisture-bearing air to its dew point. For the major forms of precipitation this is caused by a lifting of the air mass, producing adiabatic expansion and cooling. Adequate cloud development is not sufficient, in itself, to produce precipitation. It is also necessary for the very minute cloud droplets to aggregate sufficiently to fall and reach the ground before evaporating. Such aggregation is assisted by the presence of ice crystals which form sublimation centres (the so-called 'Bergeron–Findeisen process'), or by the presence of 'giant' condensation nuclei such as clay and salt particles. If the ice crystals or giant nuclei are very numerous, however, the aggregated drops tend to be greater in number but smaller in size, and in some cases they may be too small to produce precipitation. It has been suggested that excessive atmospheric dust may operate in this manner and thereby contribute to drought conditions (Linacre & Hobbs, 1976). It is possible that this effect is significant in some arid areas such as the Rajasthan Desert of India, where the atmosphere is particularly dusty and rain is less frequent than expected from theoretical considerations (Das, 1962).

The meteorological conditions associated with uplift of air to form cloud provide a convenient basis for classifying precipitation processes into the following categories:

(*a*) Local convective;
(*b*) Frontal cyclonic;
(*c*) Non-frontal cyclonic;
(*d*) Orographic and general convergence;
(*e*) Precipitation with little or no uplift.

Unfortunately, it is often difficult to make clear-cut separations between the above categories because the various processes frequently operate in combination, and similar space–time patterns may result from different

373

combinations of processes. Nevertheless this system of classification has advantages over other systems for the purposes of this paper.

Local convective precipitation

Local convective or thunderstorm precipitation may occur in almost all arid areas, particularly in summer and autumn months. It is the major type of precipitation in the low-latitude sections of the subtropical deserts, for example the southern Sahara, northern Australia and central Mexico. It is also responsible for more than half the total precipitation in some other desert areas, such as southern Israel (Sharon, 1972) and the Changtu province of China (Arakawa, 1969).

This type of precipitation is characterized by short bursts of high-intensity rain (> 15 mm h^{-1}) which may last from a few minutes to about an hour, within irregular periods of drizzle or no rain. Each burst corresponds with the sudden release of suspended water from vigorously ascending air in a 'local convective cell', as explained in detail in most meteorological text-books (for instance Byers, 1959). The area of intense rain at the surface is initially only 1 or 2 km^2, but it expands rapidly during the burst until it covers the whole core area of the cell, usually 5–10 km in diameter. Heavy hail may accompany the rainfall, but this is not common in the arid zone. Occasional falls of hail have been recorded in the desert margins of south-eastern Australia, South Africa, western India and the continental interiors of Asia and North America (Ludlam, 1963).

In addition to a moist air supply the initiation of local convective activity requires an unstable lapse rate – that is a rapid decrease of air temperature with height. Such temperature conditions are common in inland arid areas on summer afternoons because of surface heating by high rates of solar radiation. Instability leading to thunderstorms may also result from rapid cooling of higher layers of the troposphere, either through radiation from upper cloud surfaces or through movements of cold air aloft. Examples of this latter process are the frequent nocturnal thunderstorms in Texas and neighbouring semi-arid parts of the United States, which are attributed to diurnal low-level jet-stream activity (Court, 1974).

Cold ocean currents inhibit the development of moist, unstable air masses in certain coastal deserts, where local convective rainfall is consequently very rare. Examples of this are in the Peruvian and Atacama Deserts of South America, where climates are considerably influenced by the very cold Humboldt Current and deep off-shore upwelling. Here the aridity is so extreme that some places have allegedly never received rainfall in modern times (Rumney, 1968). In the northern part of the Peruvian Desert, however, there is occasionally a period of intense local convective rainfall in late summer when a branch of the equatorial countercurrent pushes warm water southwards, considerably raising ocean temperatures. Other arid coastal areas where thunderstorm activity is reduced because of cold ocean currents are in Namibia, California and the East African coast near Somalia.

Although high lapse rates are frequent in inland deserts, local convective precipitation is generally experienced only when moist airstreams reach the area. During these relatively infrequent occasions convective cells may develop and operate more or less concurrently throughout the area affected by the moist air. In subtropical deserts the spatial distribution of the cells is most commonly random, but under certain meteorological conditions a linear arrangement may be recognised. With randomly distributed cells the spatial patterns of daily or shorter duration rainfall show a typical 'spottiness'. This has been described and analysed by Sharon (1972).

Sharon's data for convective precipitation from a relatively dense network of gauges in Israel indicated a poor correlation of daily rainfalls for stations only 5 km apart ($r = 0.5$–0.6). The same data also revealed very few cases in which two or more cells affected any single station on one day, suggesting that the periods between cell formation are longer in arid regions than in humid regions. On the other hand, the spacing between cells in arid regions does not appear to differ much from the spacing in humid regions, as suggested in another study by Sharon (1974). In this latter work the average distance between active cells in a semi-arid part of Tanzania was found to be 40–60 km, which seems fairly typical of places in the humid zone.

Linear convection consists of groups of cells aligned in a particular direction, producing parallel 'streaks' of heavy rain within broader areas of light rain or drizzle. This may be associated with various meteorological conditions, especially frontal–cyclonic storms, which will be discussed later. Non-frontal linear convection is a notable feature of summer rain in some low-latitude sections of the subtropical deserts. Good examples are the 'disturbance lines' of the southern Sahara which move across Africa in a general east–west direction in the period from May to October (World Meteorological Organisation, 1956).

There is some evidence that individual convective cells persistently form in certain preferred localities or 'breeding grounds' where instability is readily initiated by conditions related to the nature of the terrain. However, according to Byers & Braham (1949), this tendency does not usually influence the spatial patterns of long-term average values.

Highly organised spatial arrangements of convective cells occur within large-scale cyclonic weather systems that sometimes bring precipitation to arid areas and which will be dealt with below. In these circumstances the localized features of individual cells often tend to be subdued because their dynamic processes are closely integrated with those of the larger systems.

375

Atmospheric processes

Frontal cyclonic precipitation

In the middle latitudes the most important storm and precipitation mechanism is the migrating 'wave cyclone' or 'frontal cyclone'. This is a large-scale weather disturbance that develops on a pronounced front (that is, the narrow transition zone between air masses of contrasting temperature) in association with jet-stream activity in the prevailing westerly airflow. A typical frontal cyclonic system may cause precipitation over an area thousands of kilometres in width, and its period of active life may be 5–10 days. It is common for two or three such systems to operate concurrently over a very large region, forming a 'family' of cyclones as described by Petterssen (1956) and Cole (1970). In general, the main tracks of these cyclones are over humid and sub-humid areas but from time to time they may bring precipitation to the arid zone, particularly in winter. The parts of the arid zone most likely to receive this type of precipitation are the poleward margins of subtropical deserts such as the northern Sahara, continental interiors of Eurasia and North America and high-latitude deserts such as Patagonia.

In desert areas, space–time patterns of frontal cyclonic precipitation are extremely variable, ranging from brief 'spotty' bursts similar to those of random local convection, to widespread, relatively uniform and steady rain or snow lasting for a day or longer at individual stations. In any particular storm the space–time pattern depends on the strength, speed of movement, stage of development and atmospheric moisture content of the system. Lighter, patchy rainfall or snow is more likely in desert areas than prolonged downpours, because the air masses tend to be depleted of much of their moisture when they reach these areas.

The low-pressure centre of a frontal cyclonic system is a broad area of rising air usually 200–400 km in diameter, moving in a general easterly direction at speeds varying from 300 to 1500 km d^{-1}. Within most of this area there is continuous precipitation of light-to-moderate intensity if the air inflow is sufficiently moist. Radiating from the periphery of the low-pressure centre (with a tendency to rotate about it) are usually cold and warm fronts, each of which may be 1000 km or more in length. For most of the system's life cycle the cold front extends equatorwards within a band of variable precipitation and unsettled weather. The warm front generally extends polewards from the system and also moves within a band of unsettled weather.

In frontal interaction some of the precipitation and unsettled weather may be attributed directly to 'upglide' of the warm air mass over the sloping surface of the cold air mass. If the uplifted warm air remains stable, stratus cloud may develop and produce steady or variable, low-intensity rain, drizzle or snow, depending on the temperature and moisture con-

376

ditions. If the air has latent instability then uplift is likely to produce cumulus cloud and convective cells, with typical spasmodic occurrences of high-intensity rain near the frontal line. Other linear clusters of convective cell activity may develop up to about 200 km from the surface position of the front. These include 'squall lines' which are usually aligned in the direction of the prevailing wind in the lower troposphere (Petterssen, 1956).

In the northern parts of the continental interiors of Eurasia and North America, frontal cyclonic storms are associated with outbursts of very cold polar air from higher latitudes during winter months. Such events may bring blizzards and violent snowstorms into arid and semi-arid sections of Dzungaria, Turkestan and similar middle-latitude areas. In many of these places the major part of the total annual precipitation is in the form of winter snowfalls, and the average duration of snow cover exceeds three months per year (Arakawa, 1969; Lockwood, 1974).

Non-frontal cyclonic precipitation

There are three types of cyclonic system that occasionally produce arid-zone precipitation with space–time patterns resembling those of frontal cyclonic systems, but which are quite different in their meteorological structure. These are (*a*) upper cold troughs and 'cut-off' lows; (*b*) continental heat lows; and (*c*) tropical cyclones.

Upper cold troughs may develop in any season when the upper troposphere westerlies have a strong meridional (north–south) component and a cold 'tongue' is extended aloft from the main body of polar air deeply into warmer air. Near the extremity of this system strong thermal contrast promotes the growth of a low-pressure trough, with resulting inflows of air from both cold and warm sectors. In some cases a substantial part of the cold tongue may separate to form an isolated 'cold pool' and below this a surface 'cut-off' low develops with similar dimensions to the low-pressure centres of frontal cyclonic storms.

Airstreams converging into upper cold troughs and cut-off lows may transport large quantities of atmospheric moisture long distances from their maritime sources, resulting in widespread inland rain which usually falls with moderate intensity over periods varying from 12 hours to 3 or 4 days. As described by Foley (1956), such systems are largely responsible for wet spells of 3 days or longer in the central and south-eastern parts of the Australian arid region. A study of data from Broken Hill, New South Wales, has shown that wet spells of this length are experienced on the average less than once per year but contribute 34% of the long-term total rainfall at that station (Bell, 1973).

Upper cold troughs and cut-off lows are evidently responsible for much

377

greater proportions of the total rainfall in the Egyptian and western Mediterranean coastal zone, as shown by Soliman (1953). In this region more than 80% of the days of rain are attributed to such conditions, but many of these rainfall events appear to be briefer and less intense than those of the Australian region. The same type of storm system may be expected to bring rare falls of heavy rain to Chile and Argentina (Schneider, 1971) and they undoubtedly could occur in many other parts of the arid zone.

Heat lows develop over the continental land masses in summer as a result of strong solar radiation which produces extensive areas of warm, buoyant air and general uplift. These systems may include the large 'permanent' lows over the interiors of Asia, North America and northern Africa in the period from May to September, and they also include smaller low-pressure centres that frequently form and dissipate during summer months in other areas such as northern Australia, southern Africa and Arabia. The associated atmospheric circulations generally direct very moist airstreams from warm maritime sources towards the interiors of the land masses and cause copious 'monsoonal' rainfall in many low-latitude coastal areas. At irregular intervals the configuration and strength of the circulation is such that moist air penetrates to normally dry areas, and these events correspond with periods of scattered summer convective precipitation as described earlier. On some occasions the smaller heat lows are particularly intense and situated wholly within the arid zone, resulting in rainfall that is more continuous and uniform in both time and space, and with convective centres present but less evident. This type of precipitation seems to be significant in the north-eastern section of the Australian arid area and also in parts of the Sahara (Griffiths, 1972).

Tropical cyclones or hurricanes are violent weather disturbances that require very warm ocean surfaces for their initiation and development. They are recorded mainly in summer and autumn months in certain low-latitude coastal areas, most of which are remote from the arid zone. In the outer margins of a few desert areas, however, there are very infrequent visitations of tropical cyclones that may bring enormous amounts of rain and highly destructive winds for several days. These areas are the normally dry coastlines around the Indian Ocean, especially north-western Australia and the Pakistan–Persian Gulf region.

An example of what may happen in such places during a cyclone was the 900 mm of precipitation recorded at Whim Creek, Western Australia in 1898 (Hunt, 1929). This fell as relatively steady, high-intensity rain over a period of 34 hours, and was about three times the average long-term yearly total.

Since a continual supply of near-saturated air from the ocean is necessary to maintain the vigour of a tropical cyclone, these storms usually decline rapidly in intensity when they pass over land surfaces. Nevertheless, some travel long distances inland, assuming general characteristics that make them almost indistinguishable from cut-off lows or heat lows. In this form they may bring widespread precipitation of moderate intensity to subtropical desert areas such as south-western Queensland and the Texas–New Mexico region.

Orographic and general convergence precipitation

Orographic precipitation is due to the forced uplift of moist airstreams as they pass over elevated land. In middle-latitude humid areas this mechanism often gives rise to drizzle or light, steady rainfall lasting many days, but such prolonged wet weather is very unlikely in the arid zone where moist airstreams are not persistent. On low-latitude seashores, warm, maritime airstreams may be so humid and unstable that a relatively slight rise from sea to land, augmented by increased frictional turbulence over the land, produces significant amounts of orographic precipitation. This effect contributes to the commonly higher rainfall along narrow coastal margins in both humid and arid zones.

Orographic influences are evident in many inland arid and semi-arid areas, where more precipitation is consistently recorded at higher altitudes. A typical example is the MacDonnell Range of central Australia where the mean annual rainfall is about 50 mm greater, and the general altitude about 700 m higher than the surrounding plateau surface. Other, more striking, examples are the 'islands' of steppe climate on the Ahaggar and Tibesti Highlands surrounded by some of the driest sections of the Sahara Desert (Griffiths, 1972).

In mountainous terrain, increases in precipitation with altitude do not apply to lee slopes and elevated areas sheltered from the prevailing airstreams. These places tend to receive significantly lower precipitation and are often areas of extreme aridity due to the so-called 'rainshadow' effect. Examples of such effects on both small and large scales may be found in many parts of the world. A particularly interesting case is the Szechuan province of China where there is a mosaic of small areas that change from humid to arid over distances of a few kilometres (Arakawa, 1969).

Orographic increases in total precipitation are not usually due to higher intensities of rainfall; in fact there may be decreases in intensity with altitude because of the reduced depths of local convective activity. In most cases longer periods of light rainfall and snow are recorded at higher altitudes, and these are usually the most significant contributions to orographic increases in precipitation (Wiesner, 1970).

Convergence precipitation occurs when moist airstreams are forced to

379

converge due to the shape of the land surface or to the configuration of the pressure patterns. Some air is consequently pushed upwards, resulting in condensation and precipitation with similar characteristics to orographic precipitation. There is usually strong convergence around cyclonic systems, and this contributes to the precipitation directly produced by such systems as discussed previously. Various degrees of airstream convergence also occur in places relatively remote from cyclonic centres, and in humid areas this often causes light- to medium-intensity rain for periods of six hours or longer. Similar conditions could be expected from time to time in most arid areas.

With both orographic and convergence precipitation, the rainfall intensity is not likely to be high if the uplifted air remains stable. As in the case of precipitation mechanisms mentioned previously, it is not uncommon for the uplift to stimulate instability and convective cell activity, particularly during summer months if the air is of tropical marine origin. When this happens the patterns of precipitation are similar to those of other local convective systems – that is randomly distributed centres of high-intensity rain within a broader matrix of low-intensity rain.

Precipitation with little or no atmospheric uplift

Land surfaces can receive relatively small amounts of moisture from the atmosphere under certain meteorological conditions that involve little or no uplift. In this category are included (*a*) light rain, drizzle and snow from layer clouds; (*b*) fog drip; and (*c*) dew and frost. Although these forms of precipitation and condensation are often quantitatively insignificant in humid areas, their regularity and seasonality may give them important physiological roles in the adaptation of living organisms to an arid environment.

Relatively long periods of light rain and drizzle may sometimes occur with deep formations of layer cloud (that is, stratus, altostratus and nimbostratus) with little vertical movement. This condition requires a continual horizontal inflow of moist air, and, because of the lack of an updraft, a steady stream of small drops can fall to the ground if the potential evaporation is low. Prolonged periods of light snowfall may result from virtually the same mechanism under appropriate temperature conditions. Such precipitation is most commonly experienced in middle and high latitudes and at high altitudes. It occurs in some parts of the arid zone, particularly in Asia and North America during winter months.

Fog is essentially stratus cloud that extends down to ground level. Vegetation and other objects projecting into dense fog often become so wet that 'fog drip' takes place, and this results in small localized accumulations of moisture. According to several authors (see, for instance, Rumney, 1968), persistent fogs in sections of the Atacama and Peruvian deserts are the main source of moisture for a grassy vegetation known as *loma*. Similar suggestions have been made about certain types of vegetation in arid areas near the Persian Gulf and Red Sea (Hills, 1966). Other parts of the arid zone affected by frequent fogs are in California, Mexico, and coastal districts of Namibia (Gentilli, 1958; Amiran & Wilson, 1973).

Meteorological conditions causing dense fog are also likely to result in dew, and the areas of frequent fog mentioned above are also areas of frequent dew. During winter months many other parts of the Arid zone experience early morning dew or frost, especially when nocturnal temperatures fall below 6 °C and average daily relative humidities approach or exceed 50%. Measurements of dewfall in Israel have indicated a yearly total of 30 mm, with significant values on more than 200 days (Slatyer & Mabbutt, 1964). Maximum daily readings under most conditions are unlikely to exceed 0.2 mm, with a theoretical upper limit of 0.9 mm as quoted by Slatyer & Mabbut (1964).

Occurrences of dew tend to be highly localized, with spatial distributions that reflect small variations in surface temperature and exposure to air movement. As mentioned by van Wijk & de Wilde (1962), there may be biologically important accumulations in certain favourable locations – for example, hollows that receive cold air drainage, and heaps of stones that lose excessive heat by nocturnal radiation and ventilation. Studies of the significance of dew concentrations in such 'cold islands' have been reported by Angus (1958).

Frost is formed in a similar manner to dew when screen temperatures fall below about 2 °C. As in the case of dew, susceptibility of a particular location to frost may depend on topographic and ground-surface factors as much as on synoptic weather conditions, with the result that certain gullies or hollows could be affected much more frequently than nearby rises. In the central and southern parts of the Australian arid zone, the number of days of frost varies from 5 per year up to about 100 (Foley, 1945; Bell, 1972*b*), and this is probably typical of the subtropical deserts. Greater frequencies are recorded in arid areas of higher latitude, for example in Kazakhstan, USSR, where yearly averages are 150–180 days of frost in addition to the 40–70 days of snow (Walton, 1969).

Variability of precipitation

Variability of hourly and other short-duration precipitation

Data on the actual amounts of precipitation that occur in short convective bursts are particularly scarce in arid areas because their proper collection usually requires automatic recorders (pluviographs) which have not been

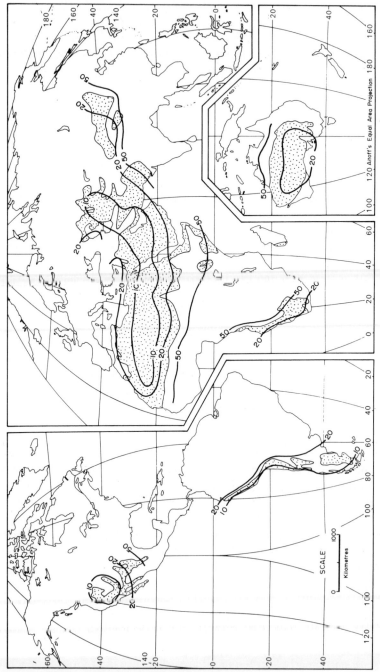

Fig. 13.1. Estimated 2-year 1-hour rainfall in mm (generalised).

Table 13.1. *Ratios for estimation of rainfall depth (with required return period and duration) from 2-year 1-hour values*

Return period (years)	Duration (min)				
	5	15	30	60	120
1	0.23	0.46	0.63	0.80	1.00
2	0.29	0.57	0.79	1.00	1.25
5	0.39	0.77	1.07	1.35	1.69
10	0.46	0.90	1.25	1.58	1.98
25	0.57	1.05	1.46	1.85	2.30
50	0.60	1.19	1.64	2.08	2.60
100	0.67	1.32	1.83	2.32	2.90

numerous until recent years. Various attempts have been made in most countries to estimate the frequencies of such intense precipitation because of their importance in the engineering design of culverts, bridges, water supply structures etc. A basic estimate for these purposes is the 2-year 1-hour value – that is, the depth of rainfall in one hour that is likely to be equalled or exceeded once every two years, on the average. Estimates of this value for arid areas are shown in Fig. 13.1, following studies by Reich (1963) with modifications by Bell (1972a). Reasonable estimates for other short durations and return periods may be made by multiplying the 2-year, 1-hour value by the empirically derived constants of Table 13.1, which evidently apply to many parts of the world where local convective precipitation is important (Bell, 1969).

It may be seen that the highest values in Fig. 13.1 are in the low-latitude margins of the subtropical deserts where atmospheric moisture, vigour of updraft and depth of convective cell development all tend to favour heavy rain from time to time. The smallest values are in areas of extreme aridity and in areas where relatively low surface temperatures restrict convective activity, such as South America and Kazakhstan, USSR. In areas of extreme aridity, two or three convective bursts may sometimes account for the entire seasonal rainfall, as suggested by comparisons of the values of Fig. 13.1 with those of the seasonal means shown in Figs. 13.2 and 13.3.

Based on theoretical models of the local convective mechanism, 'maximum probable' or extreme upper limits of 1-hour rainfall may be calculated by the procedures described in Wiesner (1970). For the Australian arid region these maxima range from approximately 180 mm at the poleward margins to 280 mm at the equatorward margins. Almost the same limiting values have been estimated for desert areas in the United States (Hershfield, 1961, 1962) and they are probably typical of the arid zone in other parts of the world. However, maximum hourly values lower

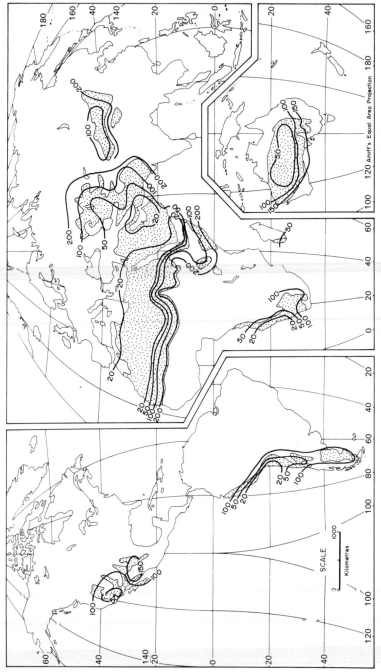

Fig. 13.2. Mean precipitation in mm for period April to September, inclusive (generalised).

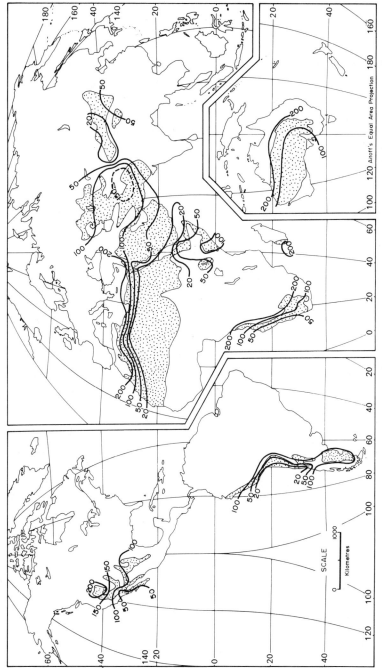

Fig. 13.3. Mean precipitation in mm for period October to March inclusive (generalised).

than 180 mm would be expected to apply to areas of extreme aridity and areas of restricted thunderstorm activity.

Variability of daily precipitation and periods without precipitation

Fig. 13.1 may be used to give very approximate estimates of the 2-year, 24-hour precipitation, based on studies similar to those of Hershfield (1962). In general, the ratio of the 2-year, 24-hour value to the 2-year, 1-hour value ranges from 2.0 to 3.0 in arid areas, depending on the relative significance of local convective storms. Where local convection is the dominant precipitation process, as in the low-latitude and central sections of the subtropical deserts, the ratios are usually between 2.0 and 2.3. On the other hand, areas of predominantly winter cyclonic precipitation, as in the Mediterranean region, would probably have ratios between 2.7 and 3.0.

Most areas of extreme aridity (mean annual precipitation < 25 mm) have experienced daily falls of rain that exceed the mean annual value. The probable maximum 24-hour precipitation in these areas is difficult to estimate but could be in excess of 300 mm, based on the studies for Australia and the United States mentioned previously (Weisner, 1970; Hershfield, 1961).

Daily falls exceeding the mean annual total have also been recorded in arid regions affected by tropical cyclones, even where these mean annual totals are as high as 450 mm. The probable maximum 24-hour value in such areas has been estimated at about 850 mm for both Australian and North American conditions, and this limiting value seems appropriate for other tropical cyclone areas such as Pakistan and the Persian Gulf.

In other low-latitude desert areas, maximum daily falls exceeding 50% of the mean annual total have been recorded at most stations. The probable maximum 24-hour values in these areas should vary from about 500 to 700 mm, depending on the remoteness of the location from maritime sources of moist airstreams. In higher latitude desert areas where winter cyclonic precipitation prevails, maximum daily falls between 25% and 60% of the mean annual total have been recorded at most stations. The probable maximum 24-hour values in these areas should range from about 350 mm to 450 mm.

The mean precipitation per wet day (that is, when precipitation > 0.2 mm) is a useful index of average daily rainfall conditions, and estimated values of this for the various desert areas are shown in Fig. 13.4. In most countries there are fewer wet days in the arid zone than in the humid zone, with the result that the calculated values of mean precipitation per wet day do not differ much between arid and humid areas in many parts of the middle latitudes. These circumstances do not generally apply to lower

386

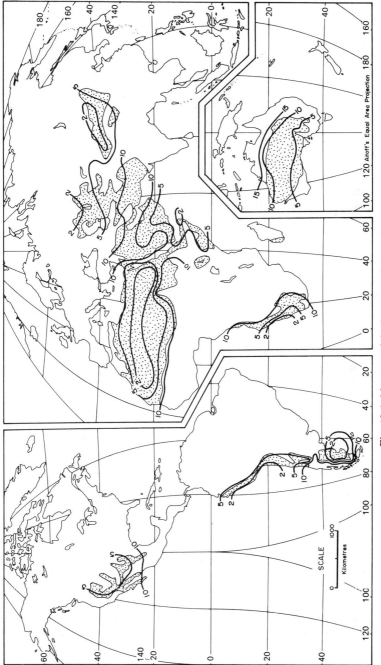

Fig. 13.4. Mean precipitation per wet day (mm).

latitudes, where rainfall is predominantly convective and the mean precipitation per wet day is distinctly smaller in the arid zone. The ranges of values shown in Fig. 13.4 are consistent with the suggestion in several publications that desert rainfall is comprised largely of isolated daily falls less than 12.5 mm (Slatyer & Mabbutt, 1964; Court, 1974).

At both northern and southern edges of the arid zone the average period between wet days is only 5–8 days in the wet season, and 20–50 days in the dry season. The actual periods between wet days vary greatly, however, and 4–6 months may be expected in some years at poleward margins, while rainless periods of 9 months or longer may be expected at equatorward margins. In drier parts of the arid zone the recorded longest periods without precipitation vary from about 12 months in central Australia and South Africa to more than 2 years for extensive areas elsewhere. In regions of extreme aridity such as the Atacama and eastern Sahara Deserts, periods exceeding 5 years without rain have been recorded (Griffiths, 1972; Rumney, 1968).

Annual and seasonal variability

Because of the general sparseness of precipitation data from the arid zone, it is not certain which place may correctly claim to be the driest in the world; but it would possibly be in the Atacama Desert of South America, or the eastern Sahara, or the Tarim Basin of China. In these three deserts there are substantial areas with mean annual totals of precipitation less than 10 mm. At the other extreme some low-latitude areas of the arid zone may have mean annual totals as high as 500 mm, while the poleward margins generally have values between 220 mm and 280 mm.

At any particular location, annual precipitation varies considerably in individual years, as may be seen in Fig. 13.5 which shows the average percentage departure from the mean. The highest variabilities are either in areas of extreme aridity such as the eastern Sahara, or in areas affected by tropical cyclones. The lowest variabilities are near the poleward margins of the subtropical deserts and in high-latitude deserts where precipitation is due largely to winter frontal–cyclonic influences. Significantly higher variabilities occur in most areas of predominantly summer convective precipitation.

In the central sections of the arid zone, and particularly in the areas of extreme aridity, precipitation is not strongly seasonal, as may be seen in Figs. 13.2 and 13.3. These diagrams also show the distinct winter cyclonic precipitation régime in the 'Mediterranean latitudes' between 25° and 40°. An exception is the Gobi–Tarim Basin in Asia where cyclonic storms rarely penetrate in winter because of 'blocking' by the persistent Siberian High and also because of topographic barriers to the west. The

388

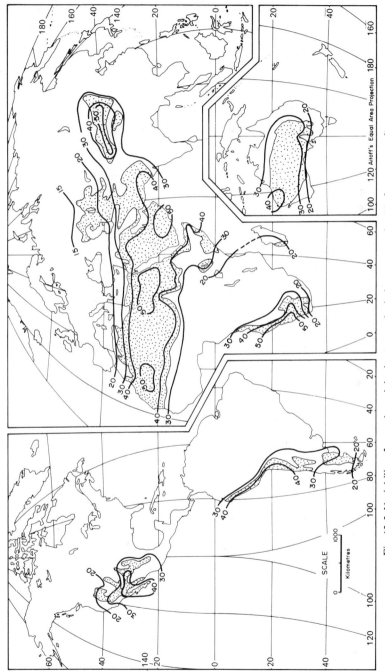

Fig. 13.5. Variability of annual precipitation (mean deviation expressed as % of mean annual).

same diagrams show the dry winter and the high summer convective rainfall in the equatorward sections of the subtropical deserts. A marked distortion of this pattern may be seen on the west coast of South America where convective activity is inhibited by the cold ocean current and the arid area is consequently extended to about 4° S, as explained previously.

Long-term trends and fluctuations

Notable climatic fluctuations over periods measured in centuries have been clearly established and well documented (see, for instance, Schwarzbach, 1963). The edges of the arid zone seem particularly sensitive to such fluctuations, as noted in various studies reviewed by Krauss (1958) and Veryard (1963).

Although reliable climatic data are not widely available for periods exceeding about 80 years, there is ample evidence to suggest that two significant climatic discontinuities or trend reversals have occurred since 1870. The first was during the decade 1890–1900 when a marked trend towards higher global temperatures commenced, and the second was during 1940–50 when temperatures stopped increasing and possibly commenced to decrease. Trends in precipitation appear to be associated with these temperature changes and have approximately the same times of reversal.

The period of rising temperatures apparently coincided with a period of expansion of the subtropical anticyclones, and also with a corresponding expansion of the subtropical deserts in both hemispheres (Krauss, 1958). The related changes in precipitation régimes seem most evident in the Southern Hemisphere, where a number of researchers have detected decreases in cyclonic winter–spring precipitation and/or increases in convective summer–autumn precipitation near the southern sections of the arid zone in South Africa and Australia (Deacon, 1953; Veryard, 1963; Wright, 1971; Bell 1972*b*). In general, these represent changes of 20% to 30% in long-term mean seasonal totals, although such differences are not consistent or significant in all areas. Precipitation trends of comparable orders of magnitude have been found in the arid zone of the Northern Hemisphere; but it is more difficult to interpret the spatial patterns of change in these areas because of the complex interactions between land-mass temperatures, anticyclone persistence and cyclone paths.

The mathematical analysis of trends is sometimes a controversial issue, and the calculated magnitudes of precipitation changes may depend considerably on the technique adopted. Since records are comparatively short and arid-zone precipitation variability is generally large, there is usually a high probability that any apparent trend may be attributed entirely to random fluctuations. Therefore, in many cases, what seems to be a definite trend is shown to be statistically insignificant when tested rigorously. Under these circumstances calculated long-term changes of precipitation in the arid zone should usually be interpreted with caution.

References

Amiran, D. H. K. & Wilson, A. W. (1973). *Coastal Deserts*. University of Arizona Press, Tucson.

Angus, D. E. (1958). Measurements of dew. In: *Climatology and Microclimatology*, pp. 301–3. UNESCO, Paris.

Arakawa, H. (1969). Climates of Northern and Eastern Asia. In: *World Survey of Climatology* (ed. H. E. Landsberg), vol. 8. Elsevier, New York.

Bell, F. C. (1969). Generalized rainfall–duration–frequency relationships. *Journal of Hydraulics Division, Proceedings of American Society of Civil Engineers*, **95, HYI**, 311–27.

Bell, F. C. (1972a). *Rainfall intensities in inland Australia*. Institute of Australian Geographers, Canberra.

Bell, F. C. (1972b). Climate of the Fowlers Gap–Calindary area. In: *Lands of the Fowlers Gap–Calindary Area, New South Wales*, Ch. 3. Fowlers Gap Arid Zone. Research Series No. 4. Institute of Rural Technology, University of New South Wales.

Bell, F. C. (1973). Climate of Fowlers Gap Station. In: *Lands of Fowlers Gap Station, New South Wales*, Ch. 3. Fowlers Gap Arid Zone Research Series No. 3. Institute of Rural Technology, University of New South Wales.

Byers, H. R. (1959). *General Climatology*. McGraw-Hill, New York.

Byers, H. R. & Braham, R. R. (1949). *The Thunderstorm*. United States Weather Bureau.

Cole, F. W. (1970). *Introduction to Meteorology*. Wiley, New York.

Court, A. (1974). The Climate of the conterminous United States. In: *World Survey of Climatology* (ed. H. E. Landsberg), vol. 2. Elsevier, New York.

Das, P. K. (1962). Mean vertical motion and non-adiabatic heat sources over India during the monsoon. *Tellus*, **14**, 212.

Deacon, E. L. (1953). Climate change in Australia since 1880. *Australian Journal of Physics*, **6**, 209–18.

Foley, J. C. (1945). Frost in the Australian Region. *Australian Commonwealth Bureau Meteorology Bulletin*, No. 32.

Foley, J. C. (1956). 500 mb contour patterns associated with the occurrence of widespread rains in Australia. *Australian Meteorological Magazine*, **13**, 1–17.

Gentilli, J. (1958). *A Geography of Climate*. University of Western Australia Press, Perth, Australia.

Griffiths, J. F. (1972). Climates of Africa. In: *World Survey of Climatology* (ed. H. E. Landsberg), Vol. 10. Elsevier, New York.

Hershfield, D. M. (1961). *Rainfall Frequency Atlas of the United States*. United States Weather Bureau Technical Paper No. 40.

Hershfield, D. M. (1962). Extreme rainfall relationships. *Journal of Hydraulics Division, Proceedings American Society of Engineers*, **88**, 73–92.

Hills, E. S. (1966). *Arid Lands*. Methuen, London.

Hunt, H. A. (1929). *Results of Rainfall Observations in Western Australia*. Commonwealth Bureau of Meteorology, Melbourne.

Krauss, E. B. (1958). Recent climatic changes. *Nature (London)*, **181**, 666.

Atmospheric processes

Linacre E. & Hobbs, J. (1976). *Australian Climatic Environment*. Wiley, New York.

Lockwood, J. G. (1974). *World Climatology*. Arnold, London.

Ludlam, F. H. (1963). Severe local storms. *Meteorological Monographs*, **5** (27), 1–32.

Petterssen, S. (1956). *Weather Analysis and Forecasting*. McGraw-Hill, New York.

Reich, B. M. (1963). Short-duration rainfall intensity estimates for regions of sparse data. *Journal of Hydrology*, **1** (1), 3–28.

Rumney, G. R. (1968). *Climatology and the world's climates*. Macmillan, New York.

Schneider, H. S. (1971). Tripos de tiempo de Chile Central. *Cuadernos Geograficos del Sur*, **1**, 77–93.

Schwarzbach, J. (1963). *The Climates of the Past*. Van Nostrand, New York.

Sharon, D. (1972). The spottiness of rainfall in a desert area. *Journal of Hydrology*, **17**, 161–75.

Sharon, D. (1974). The spatial pattern of convective rainfall in Sukumland, Tanzania – A statistical analysis. *Archiv für Meteorologie, Geophysik und Bioklimatologie, Series B*, **22**, 201–18.

Slatyer, R. O. & Mabbutt, J. A. (1964). Hydrology of arid and semi-arid regions. In: *Handbook of Applied Hydrology* (ed. V. T. Chow), pp. 24.1–24.46. McGraw-Hill, New York.

Soliman, K. H. (1953). Rainfall over Egypt. *Quarterly Journal Royal Meteorological Society*, **79**, 389.

van Wijk, M. R. & de Wilde, J. (1962). In: *The Problems of the Arid Zone*, pp. 83–113. UNESCO, Paris.

Veryard, R. G. (1963). A review of studies on climatic fluctuations during the period of the meteorological record. *UNESCO Arid Zone Research*, **20**, 3–15.

Walton, K. (1969). *The Arid Zones*. Hutchinson, London.

Wiesner, C. J. (1970). *Hydrometeorology*. Chapman and Hall, London.

World Meteorological Organisation. (1956). *Agroclimatology Survey of Semi-arid Area South of the Sahara. World Meteorological Organisation Technical Note* No. 86.

Wright, P. B. (1971). *Spatial and temporal variations in seasonal rainfall in south-western Australia*. Miscellaneous Publication 71/1, Institute of Agriculture, University of Western Australia, Perth, Australia.

Recommended texts for overview of Australian arid-land precipitation

Gentilli, J. (1971). Climates of Australia. In: *World Survey of Climatology* (ed. H. E. Landsberg), vol. 13. Elsevier, New York.

Gentilli, J. (1972). *Australian Climate Patterns*. Nelson, Melbourne.

Manuscript received by the editors January 1975

14. Atmospheric transport processes above arid-land vegetation

M. FUCHS

Introduction

The turbulent convection generated by the wind is the dominant mechanism of heat and mass exchange between the ground-surface and the air. The wind in the planetary boundary layer is controlled by the forces driving the general atmospheric circulation and the drag forces originating at the ground surface. The drag exerted by the ground depends upon the aerodynamic properties of the ground cover, which in turn relate to the geometrical and mechanical characteristics of the elements composing the ground cover.

Prandtl's mixing-length theory predicts that for air flow in aerodynamic equilibrium with the ground surface, under adiabatic conditions and no vertical divergence of momentum flux, the wind speed, u, increases logarithmically with height, $z-d$, measured above a datum reference level d (Sutton, 1953):

$$u = u^* k^{-1} \ln [1+(z-d) z_0^{-1}]$$ [1]

where $k \approx 0.4$ is the von Kármán constant, z_0 is an aerodynamic parameter of the ground cover known as the roughness length, and u^* is the friction velocity which is formally related to the shearing stress experienced by a parcel of air:

$$\tau = \rho u^{*2}$$ [2]

where ρ is the density of the air.

The shearing stress is then easily related to the wind speed as

$$\tau = 0.5 C_d \rho u^2$$ [3]

where C_d is the drag coefficient defined by:

$$C_d \equiv 2u^{*2} u^{-2} = 2k^2 \{\ln [1+(z-d) z_0^{-1}]\}^{-2}.$$ [4]

The only unknown parameters are the datum reference level and the roughness length. The datum reference level is by definition the hypothetical horizontal plane where the momentum sinks are concentrated. It is determined by a computational adjustment of the heights of the anemometers above an arbitrarily chosen level (usually the soil surface), until the wind-speed distribution, under adiabatic conditions, becomes

393

logarithmic. The extrapolation of the adjusted profile to zero wind speed yields the roughness length.

This straightforward approach has been criticized by Bradley & Finnigan (1973) because of a physically imprecise definition of the momentum sinks. This criticism is particularly valid for most natural-vegetation landscapes in arid environments. Here the scarcity of water in the layer of soil accessible to plant roots results in an open vegetation cover, with a large portion of the soil surface freely exposed to the wind. Since the smooth soil surface exerts a drag force much smaller than that caused by the vegetation, the morphological heterogeneity of the arid landscape has an aerodynamic counterpart. Consequently the first basic problem associated with the description of the wind in an arid environment is to scale the surface heterogeneity, define the ground surface in aerodynamic equilibrium with the wind, and assign a value for its roughness length.

The second difficulty is also a result of the drought condition. The reduction of evaporative heat dissipation caused by the shortage of water must be compensated by an enhanced sensible-heat transfer mechanism. The resulting thermal stratification of the lower atmosphere creates buoyancy forces which modify considerably the air motion and its convective properties.

Nonetheless, the mixing-length theory is well supported by experimental evidence, and widely used to describe the transport properties of the wind above homogeneous ground covers. Its application to the conditions prevailing in arid environments calls for modifications and empirical adjustments.

The first objective of this chapter is to discuss these revisions.

The Reynolds analogy (Sutton, 1953) links the convective transport of heat and mass to the momentum flux. However, the conversion of the Reynolds equations for fluxes into profile equations has to account for the specific transport properties of momentum, heat and mass at the sources and sinks of these quantities in the ground cover. The second objective of this chapter is to review the transport properties of the elements forming the ground cover, and to examine their relationship to the bulk exchange processes between the ground cover and the atmosphere.

Transport properties of the arid landscape

Momentum transport

The ground drag on the wind depends largely on the total area in contact with the air flow. The irregularly shaped cover of a forest constitutes a stronger air-momentum sink than a flat sand beach. The roughness length z_0 in [1] gives a measure of the momentum-sink strength of the ground cover. It is related to a weighted sum of the friction existing between

394

the solid contour area of the ground cover in contact with the air flow. However, the porosity of the cover needs also to be taken into consideration. In a very dense vegetation the higher portion of the canopy will absorb most of the air momentum, whereas the drag exerted by the lower canopy will be negligibly small. On the contrary, in an open canopy which is easily penetrated by the wind, the lower elements and even the soil surface contribute significantly to the total drag.

An analysis of the shearing-stress divergence inside a canopy by Cowan (1968) shows that the roughness length is a function of the adjusted height of the canopy $h-d$, the areas porosity a (total surface area of canopy per unit volume of space), and c, the drag coefficient per unit area of canopy element:

$$z_0 = (h-d) \exp-[4k^2(h-d)^{-1}(ca)^{-1}]^{1/3}. \qquad [5]$$

Estimates of c for the canopy of several crop species is 0.21, as compared with values of 0.25 to 0.30 derived for randomly oriented flat plates. Equation [5] implies that a has a uniform distribution in the ground cover. This assumption is practically never satisfied in the widely open vegetation which characterizes the arid environment. Consequently the validity of [5] is restricted to canopy providing a nearly continuous ground cover.

Lettau (1969) following Nikuradse's classical treatment of fluid flow in sand-roughened pipes relates the roughness length to the geometry of the discrete roughness elements of the ground surface:

$$z_0 = 0.5Sh\alpha \qquad [6]$$

where S is the silhouette area of an average roughness element across the average wind direction, h is its height above the ground and α is the average number of roughness elements per unit area. Assuming that the desert vegetation is a shrub formation with a silhouette area of 0.5 m^2 and a height of 1 m for the average shrub, and that the spacing between shrubs is 5 m, the resulting roughness length is 0.01 m. This value drops rapidly with increased spacing. At 10 m it is already of the same magnitude as the roughness length typical of a bare sand, indicating that the contribution of sparse vegetation to the total ground drag becomes small. This will be discussed further below.

If the density of the canopy increases to the point that the roughness elements merge into a continuous ground cover, [6] cannot be applied and should be replaced by [5]. A smooth transition between the two expressions obtains if the validity of [6] is limited to a ground cover with α^{-1} larger than $4S$.

Wind-profile data under near-adiabatic conditions over a flat desert in New Mexico (Campbell, Hansen & Dise, 1970) were used to check [6]. The terrain over a 4 km fetch consisted of small conical dunes colonized by shrubs of the genera *Larrea*, *Prosopis* and *Chilopsis*. The average obstacle, formed by the vegetation and accumulated sand, had a base diameter of 7.5 m and a height of 2 m. The average spacing between dunes, measured from an aerial photograph of the site, was about 10 m. Accordingly [6] yields $z_0 = 0.075$ m, which compares very well with the values between 0.05 m and 0.09 m derived from the wind profiles.

It appears that [6] provides an adequate estimate of the friction forces which develop in the air stream above an arid vegetation. However, the drag exerted by individual plants or parts of plants is ignored. Thus some important aspects of the mechanical effects of the wind on the vegetation remain unexplained.

An alternative approach is to consider the drag exerted by elements of the canopy, such as leaves, stems and fruits. Thom's investigation (1968) of the drag of leaves in a wind tunnel reconfirms the classical Blasius equation for flat thin plates in a laminar fluid stream parallel to the plate's surface:

$$c = 1.328 (Re)^{-0.5}, \tag{7}$$

$$(Re) = uDv^{-1} \tag{8}$$

where (Re) is the Reynolds number, D is a characteristic length for the leaf (D for an oval-shaped leaf is 0.6 times the largest leaf chord along the path of the air flow), and v is the kinematic viscosity of air. The active drag area used to derive [7] is the total area in contact with the fluid flow. Thom's measurements also confirm that when the air flow and the leaf are at an angle to one another, the drag coefficient increases sharply as a result of the body force causing the deflection of the air flow on the leaf surface. For air flow normal to the leaf surface the drag coefficient is an order of magnitude larger than predicted by [7], and assumes a constant value of 0.5 for $(Re) > 1000$. Although the mechanisms generating the friction force described by [7] and the body force are different, their physical effects are the same and usually compounded. In turbulent flow, skin friction becomes very small (Schlichting, 1960) so that its contribution to the drag in the natural atmospheric environment is probably minor.

For spherical shapes like fruits, succulent stems, spores and pollen (Schlichting, 1960) the drag coefficient is:

$$\left. \begin{array}{ll} c = 24(Re)^{-1} & (Re) < 1 \\ c = 18.5\ (Re)^{-0.6} & 1 \leqslant (Re) < 10^3 \\ c = 0.44 & 10^3 \leqslant (Re) \leqslant 2 \times 10^5 \\ c = 0.1 & 2 \times 10^5 < (Re) \end{array} \right\} \tag{9}$$

where D in (Re) is the diameter of the sphere and the active drag area is the silhouette area of the sphere $(1/4)\pi D^2$.

A similar expression (Schlichting, 1960) for transverse flow around long cylinders is:

$$
\left.
\begin{array}{ll}
c = 5.4 \ (Re)^{-0.25} & 4 < (Re) \leqslant 10^3 \\
c = 1 & 10^3 < (Re) \leqslant 10^4 \\
c = 1.2 & 10^4 < (Re) \leqslant 2 \times 10^5 \\
c = 0.3 & 2 \times 10^5 < (Re)
\end{array}
\right\} \qquad [10]
$$

where D in (Re) is the diameter of the cylinder and the active area is the silhouette area of the cylinder.

The drag force, ΔF, exerted by any particular part of a plant is given by:

$$\Delta F = 0.5 \, \rho s c u^2 \qquad [11]$$

where D in (Re) is the diameter of the cylinder and the active area is the appropriate from either [7], [9] or [10], and u is either measured in the immediate vicinity of the canopy part considered, or predicted from [1] and [6] provided the plant density is compatible with the range of validity of [6].

The summation of all the drag forces exerted by the parts of a plant yields the total drag force on the atmosphere. However, the summation process has to take into account the possibility of mutual aerodynamic sheltering between the various parts of the plant. Thom (1971) found that the total drag force in a fully developed bean canopy is:

$$F = p_d^{-1} \Sigma \Delta F \qquad [12]$$

where p_d is the shelter factor defined as the ratio of the drag coefficient obtained from the integration of [11] over the entire canopy to its actual drag coefficient.

Measuring the drag force of progressively thinned spruce shoots in a wind tunnel, Landsberg & Thom (1971) found:

$$p_d = 1.96 \, (S_e S^{-1})^{0.43} \qquad [13]$$

where S_e is the total silhouette area of all the individual elements composing the shoot, and S is the silhouette area of the complete shoot. Landsberg & Powell (1973) suggest that the shelter factor may decrease with wind speed, presumably because of the streamlining of the orientation of the leaves at higher wind speeds.

This aerodynamic sheltering may be extremely important for isolated desert shrubs with densely clustered leaves and twigs. In this case $(S_e S^{-1})$ is very large, and consequently the contribution of the individual foliage elements to the total drag exerted by the plant becomes insignificant. In support of this viewpoint, measurements by Hicks (1973) show that the drag in a regularly planted cordon vineyard is controlled by the bulk shape of the row structure, and is nearly independent of the drag by individual leaves. This result also provides a physical basis for the empirical relation

397

[6] put forth by Lettau (1969) to compute the roughness length for surfaces composed of an array of roughness elements.

Wind erosion

The discussions above are of course pertinent to the process of soil transport by wind in arid lands. This transport of material often occurs on a massive scale (Jackson *et al.*, 1973; Yaalon & Ganor, 1973) and may be natural or a man-induced process. Where the soil surface is bare, for example a desert sand-plain, the erodibility of the surface can be readily predicted by considering only the shear stress on the surface and a measure of particle size and/or coherence (Bagnold, 1941; Chepil & Woodruff, 1963; Hsu, 1971]. However, where there is vegetative cover, however sparse, there is need to partition the shearing stress between the two surfaces.

There have been various empirical approaches to predicting the partition of shearing stress from the properties of the windbreaks or vegetation elements (see, for instance, Chepil & Woodruff, 1963). Marshall (1970, 1971) investigated this partitioning of shear stress in a wind tunnel using arrays of solid objects of various sizes in various spacings. The sizes chosen were related to the dimensions of perennial shrubs from areas of semi-arid Australia where there has been a history of erosion through overgrazing. The results from these studies demonstrated critical values of various array and element parameters when the shearing stress on the intervening surface was negligible. These and other experimental results have been generalized through the analyses of Wooding, Bradley & Marshall (1973) for roughness elements in regular arrays, and it appears that the relationships determined by these workers can readily be related to arid landscapes.

Heat and mass transport

The Reynolds analogy used to link the heat and mass transfer to the momentum transfer in the air layer clear of the vegetation breaks down in the vicinity of the ground cover because the sinks and sources for momentum, mass and heat are not located on the same sites within the ground cover. Moreover, even at the skin of an element of the cover the transport mechanisms are dissociated, since there are no mass and heat equivalents for the body-force effects caused by momentum. It should therefore be expected that the transfer coefficients of a composite surface like the ground cover will assume different values for momentum, heat and mass. Since the transfer coefficient for momentum C_d, defined by [4], is related to the roughness length z_0, analogous surface parameters can be defined for heat z_H, and mass z_m (for water vapor, z_E). Bulk transport equations corresponding to [3] for sensible-heat flux density H, and water-vapor flux density E, are:

$$H = \rho c_p C_H u(T - T_0) \qquad [14]$$

$$E = C_E u(\chi - \chi_0) \qquad [15]$$

where c_p is the specific heat of air at constant pressure, T and χ are the temperature and water vapor concentration of the air at z, and T_0 and χ_0 are the surface values of these quantities. The transfer coefficients C_H and C_E (Garratt & Hicks, 1973) are:

$$C_H = k^2 \{\ln[1 + (z - d)z_0^{-1}] \ln[1 + (z - d_H)z_H^{-1}]\}^{-1} \qquad [16]$$

$$C_E = k^2 \{\ln[1 + (z - d)z_0^{-1}] \ln[1 + (z - d_E)z_E^{-1}]\}^{-1} \qquad [17]$$

where d_H and d_E are defined as the level of the hypothetical horizontal plane, where sinks and sources for heat or water vapor are concentrated. It should be pointed out here that [14] and [15] have very little practical value since T_0 and χ_0 are usually not measured. But the transport coefficients which they define have considerable theoretical importance for modeling the exchange of energy and mass between the vegetation and the atmosphere.

From the analysis of the variation of $\ln(z_0 z_p^{-1})$ (p standing for either H or E) with the roughness Reynolds number $\{(Re)^* = u^* z_0 \nu^{-1}\}$, Garratt & Hicks (1973) conclude that, for $(Re)^* < 100$:

$$z_H = \kappa(ku^*)^{-1} \qquad [18]$$

$$z_E = \delta(ku^*)^{-1} \qquad [19]$$

where κ and δ are the molecular diffusivities of heat and water vapor in air. At larger values of $(Re)^*$ there is a net branching of the values of $\ln(z_0 z_p^{-1})$. For continuous-canopy ground covers, $\ln(z_0 z_p^{-1})$ remains nearly constant around 1.6, corresponding to $z_p = 0.2z_0$. For ground covers with spaced solid roughness elements, $\ln(z_0 z_p^{-1})$ increases with $(Re)^*$:

$$\ln(z_0 z_H^{-1}) = 0.69(Re)^{*0.45}(Pr)^{0.8} \qquad [20]$$

$$\ln(z_0 z_E^{-1}) = 0.69(Re)^{*0.45}(Sc)^{0.8} \qquad [21]$$

where $(Pr) = \nu\kappa^{-1}$ is the Prandtl number, and $(Sc) = \nu\delta^{-1}$ is the Schmidt number. For oxygen or carbon dioxide fluxes [19] and [21] would apply with the appropriate values of δ and (Sc).

Since the arid vegetation is aerodynamically similar to arrays of spaced roughness elements, it is reasonable to assume that heat and mass transport

Atmospheric processes

will follow [20] and [21] respectively. Values of $\ln(z_0 z_H^{-1})$ for a vineyard, quoted from R. D. Graetz's 1972 doctoral thesis by Garratt & Hicks (1973), support this assumption.

At the level of a single plant organ, the heat or mass transfer by forced convection can be described as functions of (Re) and (Pr) or (Sc).

Wind-tunnel studies of the forced heat convection from leaves in laminar flow confirm the classical Pohlhausen equation for a one-sided flat rectangular plate of uniform surface temperature, expressed here in transfer-coefficient form as defined by [14]:

$$c_H = 0.664 (Re)^{-0.5} (Pr)^{-0.67} \tag{22}$$

provided the value of D used to compute (Re) is adjusted to account for the geometrical difference between the shape of the leaf and a rectangle (Parkhurst, Duncan, Gates & Kreith, 1968; Thom, 1968; Cowan, 1972).

The corresponding mass transfer coefficient c_m is:

$$c_m = 0.664 (Re)^{-0.5} (Sc)^{-0.67} \tag{23}$$

where m stands for the gas under consideration. Thom (1968) verified that [22] and [23], in contrast with [7], are nearly independent of the angle between the air stream and the leaf. Nevertheless, field measurements of the sensible-heat dissipation by leaves appear to be twice those predicted by [22] (Monteith, 1965; Parlange, Waggoner & Heichel, 1971). Often the assumption of uniform leaf surface temperature is not valid. An alternative boundary condition is to have a uniform heat flux on the leaf surface. But this has been shown to yield results numerically close to [22] and [23] (Parlange et al., 1971; Cowan, 1972). Measurements of c_H of metal discs in the natural wind by Pearman, Weaver & Tanner (1972) were systematically higher than [22]. Although the scatter of the values was larger than could be accounted for by experimental errors, they proposed:

$$c_H = 0.97 (Re)^{-0.5} (Pr)^{-0.67} \tag{24}$$

This result would indicate that the heat transfer coefficient depends upon turbulence in the air stream.

Convective heat dissipation from cylindrical shapes in transverse air flow can be approximated (see, for instance, Kreith, 1965) by:

$$\left. \begin{array}{ll} c_H = 0.9 (Re)^{-0.59} (Pr)^{-0.67} & (Re) \leqslant 10^3 \\ c_H = 0.2 (Re)^{-0.37} (Pr)^{-0.67} & 10^3 \leqslant (Re) < 10^5 \end{array} \right\} . \tag{25}$$

For spheres (see, for instance, Bird, Stewart & Lightfoot, 1960) we have:

$$c_H = (0.60 + 2.0 (Re)^{-0.5} (Pr)^{-0.33}) (Re)^{-0.5} (Pr)^{-0.67} . \tag{26}$$

Mass-transfer coefficients for cylinders and spheres can be estimated by replacing (Pr) in [25] and [26] by (Sc). Measurements of the evapora-

400

tion from these shapes by Powell, quoted by Monteith (1973), indicate that this procedure is acceptable.

When the plant organs are incorporated in an array, either in an isolated shrub or in a canopy, mutual interference modifies the transport phenomena as previously described for the drag force (Tibbals, Carr, Gates & Kreith, 1964). Landsberg & Thom (1971) found that [13] also applies for water vapor loss from a spruce shoot. However, present information on mutual sheltering between the elements of the foliage for heat and mass as well as momentum transfers remains sporadic. Field investigations of this subject are needed to further our quantitative understanding of the relationship between the desert vegetation and its atmospheric environment.

The buoyancy effect

In still air, the air density gradient, induced by either temperature gradients or gas concentration gradients, causes free convective transport processes. In this case the convective motion is characterized by the Grasshof number

$$(Gr) = gD^3 \nu^{-2} \ln(\rho_0 \rho^{-1}) \tag{27}$$

where g is the gravitational acceleration, and ρ_0 is the density of the air at the surface. In the atmosphere, the intensity of turbulence never allows pure free convection to take place. The turbulence is sustained by energy deriving from the drag force, and, in the case of strong density stratification of the air, by energy deriving from the buoyant forces as expressed by (Gr). Buoyant forces caused by gas concentration gradients are usually very small in the arid environment, therefore the importance of buoyancy can be measured by the ratio of the thermal buoyant energy production over the drag energy dissipation (see, for instance, Priestley, 1959):

$$(Rf) = gT^{-1} H(\rho c_p)^{-1} u^{*-2} (du/dz)^{-1} \tag{28}$$

where (du/dz) is the wind shear and (Rf) is the flux Richardson number.

We define the eddy viscosity K and the eddy heat diffusivity K_H by:

$$K = u^{*2} (du/dz)^{-1} \tag{29}$$

$$K_H = H(\rho c_p dT/dz)^{-1} = u^* T^* (dT/dz)^{-1} \tag{30}$$

where $T^* \equiv H(\rho c_p u^*)^{-1}$, and dT/dz is the potential air temperature gradient. Combining [28] with [29] and [30]:

$$(Rf) = K_H K^{-1}(Ri) \tag{31}$$

where $(Ri) = gT^{-1}(dT/dz)(du/dz)^{-2}$ is the gradient Richardson number. The Richardson numbers are indices of the atmospheric stability.

401

Atmospheric processes

The effect of the buoyancy is often measured by $\zeta = (z-d+z_0)L^{-1}$ where L is the flux Monin–Obukhov length (see Priestley, 1959):

$$L = \rho c_p \, Tu^{*3}(gkH)^{-1} = KK_H^{-1}L' \qquad [32]$$

where $L' = u^*T(du/dz)[gk(dT/dz)]^{-1}$ is the gradient form of the Monin–Obukhov length, which is used to define ζ'.

The Monin–Obukhov length is a scaling parameter which is independent of height in the atmospheric surface layer. Consequently ζ is linearly related to height and serves as a stability-corrected dimensionless height. This property of ζ extends to ζ' provided $K_H K^{-1}$ is assumed constant with height.

The buoyancy forces will cause a deformation of the logarithmic wind speed [1] and air temperature [14] distribution. These deformations are conveniently expressed in terms of dimensionless wind shear and temperature gradient by:

$$\phi = k(z-d+z_0)u^{*-1}(du/dz) \qquad [33]$$

$$\phi_H = k(z-d+z_0)T^{*-1}(dT/dz) \qquad [34]$$

where [34] implies that the shapes of the temperature and wind profile vary similarly.

Considerable theoretical and experimental efforts have been devoted to relating ϕ with either (Ri), (Rf), ζ or ζ'. The choice of the index is a matter of convenience, usually dictated by the available data. Since:

$$\zeta = K_H K^{-1}\zeta' = \phi(Rf) = \phi K_H K^{-1}(Ri) \qquad [35]$$

the relations found for one stability index can easily be adapted to the other stability indices.

Monin & Obukhov (1954) proposed to develop ϕ as a power series of ζ. Limiting the series to its first two terms:

$$\phi = (1+\beta\zeta) \qquad [36]$$

results in the so-called log–linear profile:

$$u = u^*k^{-1}\{\ln[1+(z-d)z_0^{-1}]+\beta(\zeta-\zeta_0)\} \qquad [37]$$

where $\zeta_0 = z_0 L^{-1}$. Values for β range between 2 and 10, and average about 6. The merit of [37] is its simplicity. However the crude approximation for ϕ in [36], reflected by the uncertainty of the β values, limits the validity of [37] to weakly unstable conditions, a situation rarely encountered in the arid environment.

In stable stratification $(0 < (Ri) < 0.15)$, McVehil (1964) showed that:

$$u = u^*k^{-1}\{\ln[1+(z-d)z_0^{-1}]+7(\zeta'-\zeta_0')\} \qquad [38]$$

fitted the observations well.

402

Swinbank (1964) suggested an exponential form for [36]. The resulting wind profile is more complex than [37], but nevertheless fails to predict the asymptotic behavior of ϕ for strong atmospheric instability, as derived from dimensional analysis.

One of the best-known relations based on dimensional analysis is the KEYPS function (Panofsky, 1963):

$$\phi = [1 - 18(Ri)]^{-0.25} \qquad [39]$$

where the form of the relationship derives from the dimensional arguments and the coefficient 18 is experimental.

The deformed wind profile can be reconstructed by integrating [33] (Lettau, 1962):

$$u = u*k^{-1}[\ln(1+(z-d)z_0^{-1})+\Phi] \qquad [40]$$

where:

$$\Phi = \int_d^z (\phi-1)(z-d+z_0)^{-1}\,dz. \qquad [41]$$

If it is assumed that $K_H K^{-1}$ does not vary with height, [35] and [39] establish Φ as a single-valued function of (Ri). This function had been tabulated by Lettau (1962), and has been reproduced in a more readily available reference (Tanner, 1968). Equation [40] gives a good account of the modification of the wind profile in an unstable atmosphere $[(Ri)<0]$, the usual daytime condition of the arid environment. However, it fails for the stable nighttime condition $[(Ri)>0]$, because [39] does not allow $(Ri)>0.0556$, a limitation contradicted by measurements of the Richardson number. In stable conditions the log–linear profile [37] should replace [40]. Since

$$\phi_H = K K_H^{-1}\phi \qquad [42]$$

the stability-corrected temperature profiles for the log–linear law and the KEYPS diabatic function respectively are:

$$T - T_d = K K_H^{-1}\{\ln[1+(z-d)z_0^{-1}]+7(\zeta'-\zeta_0')\} \qquad [43]$$

$$T - T_d = T*k^{-1}\{\ln[1+(z-d)z_0^{-1}]+\Phi_H\} \qquad [44]$$

where

$$\Phi_H = \int_d^z (K K_H^{-1}\phi-1)(z-d+z_0)^{-1}\,dz. \qquad [45]$$

Here T_d refers to a temperature extrapolated to $z = d$, and not to a measured value. To obtain Φ_H, compute ϕ from [39] and the given value of (Ri), then compute (Ri') from

$$(Ri') = 0.0556[1-(K K_H^{-1}\phi)^{-4}]. \qquad [46]$$

The value of Φ corresponding to (Ri') in Lettau's (1962) or Tanner's (1968) tabulation is the numerical value of Φ_H.

Atmospheric processes

Dyer & Hicks (1970) checked that a modification of the KEYPS function:

$$\phi = (1 - 16\zeta)^{-0.25} \tag{47}$$

$$\phi_H = \phi_E = (1 - 16\zeta)^{-0.50} \tag{48}$$

suggested by Businger (1966) for an unstable atmosphere, where ϕ_E is the deformation of the water vapor profile, is within a few percentage points of the experimental values. Dyer & Hicks (1970) also tabulated $(-\Phi)$ and $(-\Phi_{H,E})$ as a function of $(-\zeta)$ based upon their experimental determination of ϕ and $\phi_{H,E}$. Their values of Φ are less negative than those given by Lettau (1962), the largest discrepancies appearing when $-0.1 < \zeta < 0$. As $\zeta \to -1$, the two tabulations converge. The values of Φ_H in Dyer & Hicks (1970) differ by only a few percentage points from those derived from Lettau's table of Φ.

Businger, Wyngaard, Izumi & Bradley (1971), in one of the most comprehensive investigations of the flux-profile relationships, concluded that, for $\zeta < 0$:

$$\phi = (1 - 15\zeta)^{-0.25} \tag{49}$$

or in the KEYPS formulation:

$$\phi^4 - 9\zeta\phi^3 = 1 \tag{50}$$

and

$$\phi_H = 0.74(1 - 9\zeta)^{-0.5}. \tag{51}$$

For $\zeta > 0$, the log–linear model gives a good account of the experimental data:

$$\phi = 1 + 4.7\zeta \tag{52}$$

$$\phi_H = 0.74(1 + 6.35\zeta). \tag{53}$$

However, despite corrections accounting for overspeeding characteristics of the cup anemometer, they also reported $k = 0.35$ for the von Kármán constant, in flagrant contrast with the value around 0.4 almost universally accepted, and recently confirmed (Pruitt, Morgan & Lourence, 1973).

Closed-form integrations of [41] are feasible when ϕ and ϕ_H are given in the form of [49] and [51] respectively (Paulson, 1970):

$$\Phi = 0.5086 + 2\tan^{-1}(\phi^{-1}) - \ln[(1 + \phi^{-1})^2(1 + \phi^{-2})] \tag{54}$$

$$\Phi_H = 0.6931 - \ln(1 + 0.74\phi_H^{-1}). \tag{55}$$

Equation [54] follows closely the tabulated values of [41], but the values of Φ_H from [55] are closer to zero than those reported by Dyer & Hicks (1970) or those derived from Lettau's tabulation. The discrepancy is largely due to differences in the values of ϕ_H when $\zeta \to 0$, leading Businger et al. (1971) to postulate that the ratio of eddy diffusivities $K_H K^{-1}$ is 1.35 at $\zeta = 0$ rather than the smaller values usually quoted ($K_{H,E} K^{-1} = 1.1$ (Dyer & Hicks, 1970); $K_E K^{-1} = 1.13$ (Pruitt et al., 1973)). It is noteworthy that

404

Businger *et al.* (1971) recognize that their value of $K_H K^{-1}$ would be nearer to 1.0 if they had used $k = 0.4$, instead of 0.35.

The value of the diabatic correction for the temperature profile remains unsettled. It is unlikely that the controversy will be easily resolved since it arises from discordant values of ϕ_H when $\zeta \to 0$, a condition for which the absolute values of the sensible heat flux and of the temperature gradient are small and their measurement subject to considerable experimental errors.

The derivations of the diabatic corrections treat the ratio $K_H K^{-1}$ as an adjustment parameter which matches the various proposed forms of ϕ or $\phi_{H,E}$ to the experimental data. Although very little is known about the intimate physical processes macroscopically described by the eddy diffusivities, an acceptable explanation of why the ratio $K_H K^{-1}$ departs from unity, i.e. why eddies convey heat, mass and momentum differently, is that these quantities follow different paths in the atmosphere. This can occur if the transport processes at the sources or sinks of these quantities are different, as was shown in the discussion of the transport properties of the ground cover.

The eddy diffusivities are related to the bulk transfer coefficients:

$$\int_d^z K^{-1} dz = 2(C_d u)^{-1} \qquad [56]$$

$$\int_{d_H}^z K_H^{-1} dz = (C_H u)^{-1} \qquad [57]$$

where C_d and C_H are given by [4] and [16], corrected by Φ and Φ_H for the diabatic effect. Accordingly, under adiabatic conditions, $K_H K^{-1} = 1$, when $z_0 = z_H$. However, if $z_0 \neq z_{H,E}$, the similarity principle used to link the heat and water vapor transport to momentum transport needs to be modified to account for the true shape of the temperature and vapor density profile, down to the interface between atmosphere and ground cover.

Conclusion

Very few studies of the transport processes in the atmospheric surface layer have been carried out specifically to elucidate the relationship between the arid vegetation and its environment. Nonetheless theories based on information gathered chiefly in agricultural land can be applied to most arid vegetation.

The micro-environment of a leaf or a fruit is adequately understood by applying the relations between the dimensionless numbers developed in general transport theories. Numerical values of the transfer coefficients used to predict the shearing stress, mass and heat flux of plant organs may require some adjustment to account for the mutual sheltering effect and the turbulence of the atmosphere.

The description of the momentum transport may readily be obtained from wind-speed data using a roughness length derived from [6] and a correction accounting for the thermal stratification of the air. The choice of a particular diabatic correction is not very critical since most of the formulations discussed here do not differ by more than a few percentage points.

The flux-profile relationships for sensible heat transport and evaporation are not as well documented. It appears that many of the conflicting reports originate in misconceptions about the differences in the transport processes of momentum, heat and mass at the sources or sinks of these quantities. Nonetheless, the information published by Garratt & Hicks (1973) provides a good basis for modeling the basic exchange processes between the arid vegetation and its atmospheric environment.

References

Bagnold, R. A. (1941). *The Physics of Blown Sand and Desert Dunes*. Methuen, London.

Bird, R. B., Stewart, W. E. & Lightfoot, E. N. (1960). *Transport phenomena*. Wiley, New York.

Bradley, E. F. & Finnigan, J. J. (1973). Heat and mass transfer in the plant–air continuum. *First Australian Conference on Heat and Mass Transfer*, pp. 55–77. Monash University, Melbourne, Australia.

Businger, J. A. (1966). Transfer of momentum and heat in the planetary boundary layer. In: *Proceedings of the Symposium on Arctic Heat Budget and Atmospheric Circulation*, pp. 305–32. The Rand Corporation.

Businger, J. A., Wyngaard, J. C., Izumi, Y. & Bradley, E. F. (1971). Flux–profile relationships in the atmospheric surface layer. *Journal of Atmospheric Sciences*, **28**, 181–9.

Campbell, G. S., Hansen, F. V. & Dise, R. A. (1970). Turbulence data derived from measurements on the 32-meter tower facility: White Sands Missile Range, New Mexico. *Technical Report ECOM-5314*, US Army Electronic Command, Fort Monmouth.

Chepil, W. S. & Woodruff, N. P. (1963). The physics of wind erosion and its control. *Advances in Agronomy*, **15**, 211–302.

Cowan, I. R. (1968). Mass, heat and momentum exchange between stands of plants and their atmospheric environment. *Quarterly Journal of the Royal Meteorological Society*, **94**, 523–44.

Cowan, I. R. (1972). Mass and heat transfer in laminar boundary layers with particular reference to assimilation and transpiration in leaves. *Agricultural Meteorology*, **10**, 311–29.

Dyer, A. J. & Hicks, B. B. (1970). Flux–gradient relationships in the constant flux layer. *Quarterly Journal of the Royal Meteorological Society*, **96**, 715–21.

Garratt, J. R. & Hicks, B. B. (1973). Momentum, heat and water vapor transfer to and from natural and artificial surfaces. *Quarterly Journal of the Royal Meteorological Society*, **99**, 680–7.

Hicks, B. B. (1973). Eddy fluxes over a vineyard. *Agricultural Meteorology*, **12**, 203–15.

Hsu, S. A. (1971). Wind stress criteria in eolian sand transport. *Journal of Geophysical Research*, **76**, 8684–6.

Jackson, M. L., Gillette, D. A., Danielsen, E. F., Blifford, I. H., Bryson, R. A. & Syers, J. K. (1973). Global dustfall during the Quaternary as related to environments. *Soil Science*, **116**, 135–45.

Kreith, F. (1965). *Principles of Heat Transfer*. International Textbook Company, Scranton, Pennsylvania.

Landsberg, J. J. & Powell, D. B. B. (1973). Surface exchange characteristics of leaves subject to mutual interference. *Agricultural Meteorology*, **12**, 169–84.

Landsberg, J. J. & Thom, A. S. (1971). Aerodynamic properties of a plant of complex structure. *Quarterly Journal of the Royal Meteorological Society*, **97**, 565–70.

Lettau, H. H. (1962). *Notes on theoretical models of profile structure in the diabatic surface layer*. Final Report, No. DA-36-039-SC-80282, pp. 195–226. Department of Meteorology, University of Wisconsin, Madison.

Lettau, H. H. (1969). Note on aerodynamic roughness – parameter estimation on the basis of roughness-element description. *Journal of Applied Meteorology*, **8**, 828–32.

McVehil, G. E. (1964). Wind and temperature profiles near the ground in stable stratification. *Quarterly Journal of the Royal Meteorological Society*, **90**, 136–46.

Marshall, J. K. (1970). Assessing the protective role of shrub-dominated rangeland vegetation against soil erosion by wind. *Proceedings 11th International Grassland Congress, Surfers Paradise (Australia)*, 19–23. Queensland University Press, St. Lucia.

Marshall, J. K. (1971). Drag measurements in roughness arrays of varying density and distribution. *Agricultural Meteorology*, **8**, 269–92.

Monin, A. S. & Obukhov, A. M. (1954). Dimensionless characteristics of turbulence in the surface layer. *Akademiya Nauk SSSR Geofizicheskii. Instut Trudy*, **151**, 163–87.

Monteith, J. L. (1965). Evaporation and environment. In: *The state and movement of water in living organisms*. Symposia of the Society for Experimental Biology, Vol. 19, pp. 205–34. Cambridge University Press, Cambridge.

Monteith, J. L. (1973). *Principles of Environmental Physics*. Elsevier, New York.

Panofsky, H. A. (1963). Determination of stress from wind and temperature measurements. *Quarterly Journal of the Royal Meteorological Society*, **89**, 85–94.

Parkhurst, D. F., Duncan, P. R., Gates, D. M. & Kreith, F. (1968). Wind-tunnel modelling of convection of heat between air and broad leaves of plants. *Agricultural Meteorology*, **5**, 33–47.

Parlange, J. Y., Waggoner, P. E. & Heichel, G. H. (1971). Boundary layer resistance and temperature distribution on still and flapping leaves. *Plant Physiology*, **48**, 437–42.

Paulson, C. A. (1970). The mathematical representation of wind speed and temperature profiles in the unstable atmospheric surface layer. *Journal of Applied Meteorology*, **9**, 857–61.

Pearman, G. I., Weaver, H. L. & Tanner, C. B. (1972). Boundary layer heat

407

transfer coefficients under field conditions. *Agricultural Meteorology*, **10**, 83–92.

Priestley, C. H. B. (1959). *Turbulent Transfer in the Lower Atmosphere*. University of Chicago Press, Chicago.

Pruitt, W. O., Morgan, D. L. & Lourence, F. J. (1973). Momentum and mass transfers in the surface boundary layer. *Quarterly Journal of the Royal Meteorological Society*, **99**, 370–86.

Schlichting, H. (1960). *Boundary-Layer Theory* (4th Edition). McGraw-Hill, New York.

Sutton, O. G. (1953). *Micrometeorology*. McGraw-Hill, New York.

Swinbank, W. C. (1964). The exponential wind profile. *Quarterly Journal of the Royal Meteorological Society*, **90**, 119–35.

Tanner, C. B. (1968). Evaporation of water from plants and soil. In: *Water Deficits and Plant Growth* (ed. T. T. Kozlowski), Vol. 1, pp. 73–106. Academic Press, New York.

Thom, A. S. (1968). The exchange of momentum, mass and heat between an artificial leaf and the air flow in a wind-tunnel. *Quarterly Journal of the Royal Meteorological Society*, **94**, 44–55.

Thom, A. S. (1971). Momentum absorption by vegetation. *Quarterly Journal of the Royal Meteorological Society*, **97**, 414–28.

Tibbals, E. E., Carr, E. K., Gates, D. M. & Kreith, F. (1964). Radiation and convection in conifers. *American Journal of Botany*, **51**, 529–38.

Wooding, R. A., Bradley, E. F. & Marshall, J. K. (1973). Drag due to regular arrays of roughness elements of varying geometry. *Boundary Layer Meteorology*, **5**, 285–308.

Yaalon, D. H. & Ganor, E. (1973). The influence of dust on soils during the Quaternary. *Soil Science*, **116**, 146–55.

Manuscript received by the editors January 1975

15. Microclimate and evaporation

R. D. GRAETZ and I. COWAN

Introduction

The theme to be developed in this section has two parts. The linkage of the fluxes of radiant and thermal energy with those of water in systems with characteristically great temporal and spatial heterogeneity will be discussed, for it is this linkage which determines the envelope of environmental conditions, the microclimate, within which life must survive. Secondly, as a consequence of this, there is a coupling of the flow of metabolic energy with the characteristics of the hydrologic cycle within an arid ecosystem.

The energy balance

The dissipation of a major part of the radiant energy from the sun received in the terrestrial regions of the planet Earth takes place at the land surface. Here the incoming radiation is reflected or absorbed; the latter involves transformation to thermal energy which is in turn either conducted, convected or radiated away from the surface. It is the magnitude and the time course of the components of this balance that influence meteorological conditions on a global scale, and determine more completely the climate on a microscale. The generalized energy balance may be written

$$I(1-\rho)+L_d-L_u = R_n = G+H+\lambda E \qquad [1]$$

where I is the incoming solar radiation, both direct-beam and diffusely-scattered; ρ is the reflection coefficient or albedo of the underlying surface as a whole; L_d is the incoming long-wave radiation emitted from the clouds, dust, water vapour and carbon dioxide; and L_u is the upward flux of long-wave radiation emitted by the surface according to its temperature together with a very small component due to reflection of incoming long-wave radiation. These radiation terms together comprise the net flux of radiation, R_n, to the surface which is apportioned into the following components: G, the heat flux conducted into the soil; H, the flux of sensible heat convected into the atmosphere: and λE, the flux of latent heat also convected into the atmosphere. The magnitude of the energy flux into metabolic pools (via photosynthesis) is so small that it can be ignored in discussions of microclimate.

Overall, the most important independent factors in the energy balance of the vegetated landscape are precipitation, the incoming radiation flux and the atmospheric processes associated with the transfer of sensible and latent heat from the surface. These factors have been dealt with in the preceding chapters of this section. It is our task to show how, together, they determine the environments and affect the functioning of living organisms close to the ground surface. First however it is necessary to discuss how the natural variation in topographic and other land-surface properties may impose a lateral variability on the net results of transport processes which take place primarily in the vertical dimension.

Scales of heterogeneity in arid lands

In all the transfer processes discussed by Fuchs (Chapter 14, this volume) a simple one-dimensional model has been used. Our discussions, too, of heat and water transfer will rely on a similar simplification to provide the first-order approximation to conditions near soil and vegetative surfaces. It will be appreciated however that the arid landscape is very hetero-geneous, particularly in the horizontal distribution of soil and vegetation characteristics, topography, exposure, and so on. This lateral diversity is, in fact, exploited by living organisms. The imprint of this heterogeneity on the population of plants and animals is detectable even in wet times, and more so in dry times when retreat to refugia is vital to the persistence of many organisms (see, for instance, Roff, 1974a, b; Graetz, in preparation).

The most eloquent expression of the accumulated experience of field ecologists is that of Koller (1969): 'Plant life in the desert becomes possible only because rainfall is unevenly distributed in time and space, and because it generally becomes even more so by differences in soil surface topography and permeability.' Following this theme it is useful to assess the scales of heterogeneity in soil-water distribution, for these scales limit the validity of our treatment of physical transfer processes on a one-dimensional basis.

The largest of the scales is of the order of 1 km, and is due to the topographic differences arising from uplift, dissection and weathering, and the shedding of rain water by stony, bare hillsides to areas in the vicinity of valleys or stream beds. The magnitude of the redistribution of water can be very great – so large that historic man has used them as a basis for irrigated agriculture even in regions which appear relatively flat (Eve-nari, Shanan & Tadmor, 1971).

The next scale, of the order of 100 m, is manifested in the alignment of bands of vegetation across gentle slopes (Warrall, 1959; Boaler & Hodge, 1962, 1964; White, 1965, 1969). Such a pattern is common through-out arid lands, and it appears that in all cases there is a shedding of water from the bare intervals into the band of vegetation; the rainfall available to the vegetation may be two or three times as great as that precipitated on the area of soil occupied by the plant roots.

The third scale, of about 10 m or so, is associated with soil structures such as 'gilgais' or 'melon-holes' (McGinnies, Goldman & Paylore, 1968; Paton, 1974); variations in relief of 0.25–0.5 m are involved. These sunken soil structures collect overland flow and support, as a consequence, significantly more vegetation than the surrounds.

The smallest scale is about 1.0 m, and involves the heterogeneity of soil properties related to individual plants (see, for instance, Friedman, 1971) and the root systems of the plants themselves. Modifications of the water balance on this scale are due, for example, to stem and canopy channelling of water (see, for instance, Slatyer, 1961) and the presence or absence of lichen crusts increasing infiltration at the base of the plants.

All scales of heterogeneity can be related to the distribution of plants, and therefore animals. The largest is reflected in the behaviour of the large mammals (Cloudsley-Thompson & Chadwick, 1964) or flightless birds (Davies, 1973) and the smallest in the distribution of small vertebrates and invertebrates (Edney, 1974). Contrasts in humidity and temperature arising from a redistribution of water are less easily maintained in the atmosphere than in the soil, for time constants of mixing are of the order of seconds in the free atmosphere compared with days, or even months, in the soil.

The radiation balance of desert landscapes

Consideration of the terms in [1] allows the construction of a hierarchy of factors influencing the energy balance, and hence the microclimate of arid vegetated landscapes. In arid lands the levels of incoming solar radiation are high (Sellers, 1965; Fitzpatrick, Chapter 12, this volume). The albedos of arid land surfaces are also generally greater than those of landscapes characteristic of more mesic regions (Table 15.1). For example, a bare, dry *serozem*, a light-coloured desert soil, has twice the albedo (0.25–0.30) of a dry, dark-coloured *chernozem* (0.14) characteristic of more humid regions. Wetting, however, halves the albedo of both types.

The loss of long-wave radiation, L_u, is due to that emitted and that reflected. The relationship is

$$L_u = \epsilon \sigma T_s^4 + (1-\epsilon) L_d \qquad [2]$$

where ϵ is the emissivity of the surface, T_s the surface temperature, and σ is the Stefan–Boltzmann constant. The emissivity of vegetation is about 1.0; it is about 0.9 for most soils, and 0.7 for dry coarse sand (Bowers & Hanks, 1965; Hovis, 1965). That is, only some natural surfaces approximate to a 'black-body' radiator where [2] may be simplified to

$$L_u = \sigma T_s^4 \qquad [3]$$

411

Table 15.1. *Reflection coefficients (ρ) of land surfaces*

Arid landscapes	
Desert	0.25–0.30[1]
Sand dune (dry)	0.35–0.45[1]
Sand dune (wet)	0.20–0.30[1]
Desert wadi vegetation	0.36–0.39[2]
Dwarf desert shrubs	0.28–0.33[2]
Mesic landscapes	
Green meadows	0.10–0.20[1]
Deciduous forest	0.10–0.20[1]
Coniferous forest	0.05–0.15[1]
Cultivated crops	0.15–0.25[1]

Sources: [1] Sellers, 1965; [2] Stanhill, Hofstede & Kalma, 1966.

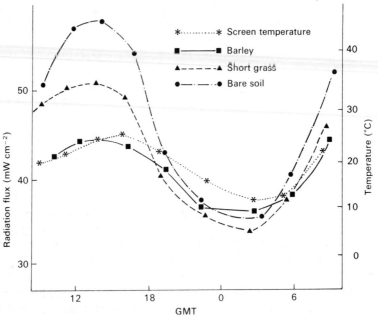

Fig. 15.1. A daily march of upward long-wave radiation flux (left-hand scale) and effective surface temperature (right-hand scale) for three surfaces compared with air temperature. (After Monteith & Szeicz, 1961.)

With any given solar radiation load the temperature of the surface and therefore the upward flux of radiation depend upon a complex of surface properties. The extent of the influence of ground cover is demonstrated in Fig. 15.1. Two major influences were involved in the differences shown. The energy absorbed by the crop surfaces was dissipated in the

Table 15.2. *Values calculated using the expression* $L_d = 5.31 \times 10^{-14} \cdot T_a$

Temperature (T_a) (°C)	Incoming long-wave radiation (L_d) (mW cm^{-2})
0	21.9
10	27.3
20	33.6
30	41.1
40	49.9
50	60.3

form of both latent and sensible heat. At the surface of bare soil, relatively little energy was converted into latent heat, and surface temperature was up to 20 °C more than air temperature. Also the differing roughness coefficients of the surfaces (barley > grass > soil) undoubtedly affected the turbulence of the atmosphere above, and in this way influenced the temperature of the surfaces relative to that at screen height.

In a humid atmosphere the downward flux of long-wave radiation is that which is emitted by the substantial amount of water vapour contained in approximately the lowest 200 m of the atmosphere. As the difference in temperature within a layer of this depth is not normally large, the effective temperature determining the rate of emission is not greatly different from screen air temperature (T_a). It is on this basis that Swinbank (1963) justified his empirical relation

$$L_d = 5.31 T_a^6 \times 10^{-14} \qquad [4]$$

Nevertheless Paltridge (1970) has shown that there are sometimes appreciable variations in the relationship between L_d and T_a, associated with the diurnal course of thermal stratification in the atmosphere. Also it is probable that Swinbank's relationship is in error in exceptionally dry climates when the downward radiation at the earth's surface is emitted by water vapour contained in a very substantial depth of the atmosphere. This formula would overestimate the downward flux during the daytime when surface temperature is greater than that in the atmosphere at some height.

Equation [2] incorporates an interaction, because L both affects, and is affected by, surface temperature, T_s. The average magnitude of L_u is greater in hot than in cold climates, and, because L_d is small in the absence of cloud, the net loss of long-wave radiation is a maximum in hot arid regions.

The contribution of I and L to the total energy balance of the surface

413

is demonstrated by an example of man's modification of the desert landscape. Severe overgrazing by domestic livestock of natural vegetation in the Sinai desert was associated with a very marked change in albedo and temperature (Otterman, 1974). The overgrazed sand plain area had, at the time of sampling, a computed albedo of 0.37, whilst that of the adjoining ungrazed area was 0.25, and surface temperatures were 40 °C and 45 °C respectively. The difference in temperature cannot be attributed entirely to the reduction of the incoming solar radiation load. As will be shown later, the magnitude and direction of surface temperature differences is also affected by other surface conditions.

In spite of dependence on temperature, diurnal variation in upward and downward fluxes of long-wave radiation, and in the balance of the two, is often not dramatic and is in any case relatively small compared with the diurnal variation of other components of the energy balance – particularly global radiation. Because of this, it is possible to express the net flux of radiation of all wavelengths as an approximate function of the short-wave radiation absorbed by the surface. The expression due to Gay (1971) is

$$R_n = (1+\lambda)(1-\rho)I + L_0 \qquad [5]$$

where λ and L_0 are empirically determined quantities, λ being the long-wave exchange coefficient and L_0 the extrapolated value of R_n when I is zero. The exchange coefficient λ is closely related to the concept of a heating coefficient developed by Monteith & Szeicz (1961) (see also Idso, Baker & Blad, 1969). It is implicitly dependent on the variation of net long-wave radiation with temperature, and the variation of temperature with incoming global radiation. In arid conditions it is normally negative. For data obtained from Soviet Central Asia, Gay found it to be -0.15; however specific values are unlikely to have any general validity even within a particular ecosystem type. Also, at a given locality λ will vary with soil water-content and turgidity of the vegetation, for reasons that will become apparent later.

Temperature and heat transfer in deserts

In truly arid areas all of the energy supplied to the surface as the net result of the radiation exchange is converted to thermal energy. If the soil surface is moist and vegetation is turgid a substantial proportion of the radiant energy is dissipated as latent heat associated with evaporation. For the moment, we shall concentrate attention on that part of the energy input which is dissipated as sensible heat.

In the short term, soil, and vegetation to a lesser extent, may act as a 'capacitor' in the energy-exchange system. Both are able to store substantial amounts of heat which can be released over short periods of time.

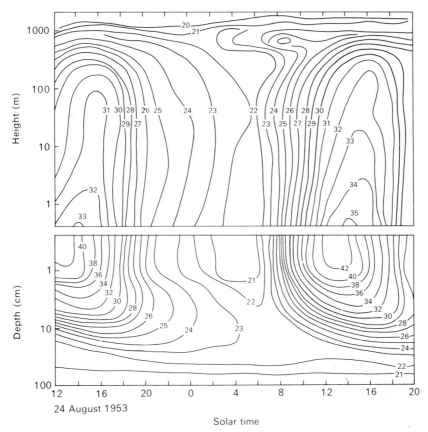

Fig. 15.2. Atmosphere (upper) and soil (lower) temperatures (°C) observed during the fifth period of the Great Plains Turbulence Field Program. (After Lettau & Davidson, 1957.)

For example, the capacity of the soil to store thermal energy during the day and release it at night serves to diminish the fluctuation of temperatures at the surface. But because of the small thermal conductivity and heat capacity in dry soils this effect is generally smaller than in more humid regions. Similarly the influence of vegetation is less in arid than in more humid areas because the biomass is smaller. The net effect of these considerations, together with the restricted rates of evaporation in arid regions, is that diurnal variations of temperature at the surface tend to be large.

The relative role of soil and atmospheric properties in determining the way in which energy is partitioned at the land surface, and the amplitude of the diurnal variation in temperature, may be demonstrated by an analysis due to Priestley (1959a, b). It strictly applies only if soil and atmosphere are each of infinite extent with uniform and constant thermal

415

Table 15.3. *Thermal properties of various media* (After Priestley, 1959*b*)

Medium	ρc_p	κ or K	$\rho_s c \sqrt{\kappa}$ or $\rho c_p \sqrt{K}$
New snow	0.03	0.006	0.002
Old snow	0.22	0.003	0.012
Dry sand	0.3	0.0013	0.011
Wet sand	0.4	0.01	0.04
Sandy clay (15% moisture)	0.6	0.0037	0.037
Organic soil	0.57	0.005	0.04
Wet marshy soil	0.7	0.003	0.038
Ice	0.45	0.012	0.05
Still water	1.0	0.0015	0.039
Ocean (moderately stable, strong currents)	1.0	50	7
Still air	3×10^{-4}	0.2	1.3×10^{-4}
Stirred air			
Stable	3×10^{-4}	10^3	0.01
Unstable	3×10^{-4}	10^7	1

properties, and the energy input is uniform over the whole (infinite) interface between the two. It provides only a rough indication of what really happens. Some of the complexities have been surveyed by Priestley (1959*b*).

The speed at which a given temperature disturbance at the soil/atmosphere interface is propagated into the soil or atmosphere is proportional to the square root of the thermal diffusivity of the medium, thermal diffusivity being the thermal conductivity divided by the heat capacity per unit volume. Because the turbulent diffusivity of the atmosphere in neutral conditions is about seven orders of magnitude greater than thermal diffusivity in soil, the diurnal temperature wave originating at the land surface is perceptible over a much greater depth of the atmosphere than in the soil. The effect is illustrated by the observations in Fig. 15.2. However, the rate at which heat is transferred into the medium depends not only on the speed of propagation of the disturbance, but also on the volumetric heat capacity of the medium. Combining both considerations, the amounts of heat entering the two media in a given time are in the ratio of their respective 'thermal admittances', these being

$$\rho_s c \sqrt{\kappa} \quad \text{and} \quad \rho c_p \sqrt{K}$$

for soil and atmosphere respectively, where ρ_s is soil density, ρ atmospheric density, c specific heat (subscript p signifying that pressure is held constant) and κ and K are the thermal diffusivities. Also, for a given

416

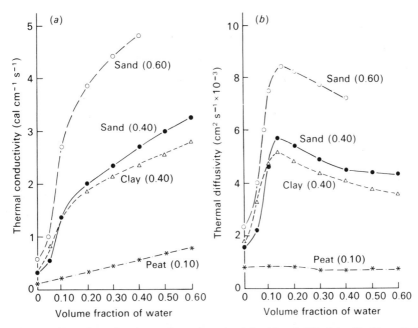

Fig. 15.3. The effect of water on thermal conductivity (*a*) and diffusivity (*b*). Note: (0.10), (0.40), and (0.60) = volume fraction of solid phase. (After Bauer, Gardner & Gardner, 1972.)

dissipation of heat at the interface, the rate of temperature increase at the interface is inversely proportional to the sum of the two admittances. Some thermal properties of the atmosphere, soil and other media are shown in Table 15.3. One notes that soil and air differ markedly in heat capacity and diffusivity (several orders of magnitude) but not nearly so much in admittance. Also thermal diffusivity of soil varies markedly with its water content (Fig. 15.3). Dry soil has a small thermal conductivity because soil particles do not make close contact; the addition of small amounts of water disproportionately increases the conductivity relative to the heat capacity (κ), but further increase in water content has the inverse effect and diffusivity decreases. For the atmosphere (see Table 15.3) the diffusivity is not constant but depends on wind speed, increases with height above the ground in the lowest 50 m or so, and is very sensitive to the temperature stratification (Fuchs, Chapter 14, this volume). In effect, much of the variation of K represents a reflex action according to whether radiant heat is being supplied to, or withdrawn from, the surface. In the first case the atmosphere responds by increasing its conductivity, and in the second case by reducing it; that is, the atmosphere accepts heat more readily than it gives it up. As the depth penetrated by a heat wave in a given time is proportional to $\sqrt{K}$, it can be seen that the heat released at the surface

417

Table 15.4. *Sharing of sensible heat between the atmosphere and an underlying medium.* (After Priestley, 1959a)

Surface	Day			Night		
	Ground share (%)	Air share (%)	Relative ΔT	Ground share (%)	Air share (%)	Relative ΔT
Air and new snow	2	98	1.4	20	80	11.5
Air and dry sand	10	90	1.3	52	58	6.6
Air and wet soil	28	72	1.0	80	20	2.9
Air and ocean	99	1	0.02	100	0	0.02

The K values used for the atmosphere are 10^5 cm^{2}s^{-1} by day and 10^3 cm^{2}s^{-1} by night. ΔT is the surface temperature change, being taken arbitrarily as unity for wet soil during the day. It is assumed that the amount of heat being shared is the same for all examples.

on a sunny day is distributed through a substantial depth of air, whereas that withdrawn from it at night during an inversion is confined to a much shallower depth. The effect of wind is particularly significant here. A strong wind does not change the order of magnitude of the already large value of K on a day of intense insolation, so that the surface temperature is not greatly affected. The relative effect of wind on the smaller value of K at night is considerably greater and more significant; stronger winds substantially increase the depth from which the heat is withdrawn, and correspondingly reduce the nocturnal decrease in temperature close to the surface.

Some results of actual calculations of heat-sharing and temperature changes at the interface between the atmosphere and various underlying media are shown in Table 15.4. This shows how markedly admittances affect heat-sharing and temperature response. Wet soils take up and give out a larger share of the heat than dry soils because their admittance is greater and they show smaller temperature changes (ΔT), especially at night. It is important to note that the analysis on which Table 15.4 is based is concerned only with fluctuations in heat flux and temperature during periods of a day or less, and is not applicable to the average values of these quantities, upon which the fluctuations are imposed.

The role of water

When water is available at the surface for evaporation it exerts a profound effect upon the energy balance. This is shown by the data in Fig. 15.4 which relates to a sparsely grassed site where, shortly after rain, the flux of latent heat into the atmosphere exceeds the sensible heat flux by a factor of two.

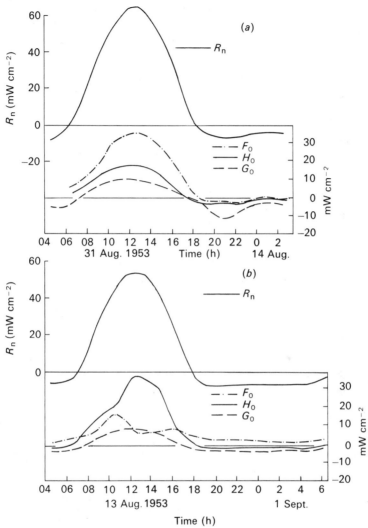

Fig. 15.4. The daily course of the energy budget on a prairie (Nebraska, U.S.A.) site; (*a*) soon after a fall of rain; and (*b*) after 15 rain-free days. F_0, H_0, G_0 and R_n are the fluxes of heat used in evaporation, sensible heat, ground heat and net radiation respectively. (After Lettau & Davison, 1957.)

Clearly, evaporation enhances the dissipation of heat at the land surface, and the temperature variation is thereby reduced. On a broad regional scale, it is often possible to relate airmass temperatures to the amount of water available for evaporation from the soil (and vegetation) surface, by use of rainfall data alone. Fig. 15.5 depicts the relationship between monthly rainfall totals and mean monthly maximum air temperatures at

419

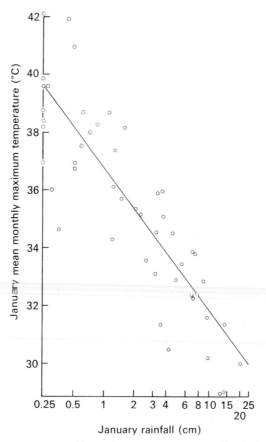

Fig. 15.5. January mean monthly maximum temperatures at Alice Springs (23.6° S 133.6° E), 1900–1949, related to January rainfall to illustrate the reduction in temperature by evaporation. (After Deacon, 1969.)

Alice Springs (23° 36′ S, 133° 36′ W). The relationship at this site in central Australia is not complicated by influence of cloud on radiation input or by effects of antecedent moisture conditions, because the January (mid-summer) rainfall occurs as brief, heavy showers.

The role of evaporation in affecting the energy balance and surface temperature can be explained in the following way. If heat is supplied to a closed system containing air and a small amount of liquid water, it is used both in heating the system and in providing the latent energy associated with the increased water vapour content of the air. The relative amounts of heat involved in these two processes depend only on the temperature of the system. We may write

$$\lambda E/H = \epsilon \qquad [6]$$

420

where ϵ has the values 0.7, 1.2, 2.0, 3.6, 5.9, 9.1, 13.8, for temperatures between 0 °C and 60 °C in ten degree steps. The quantity ϵ is equivalent to s/γ, where s is the slope of the vapour-pressure–temperature curve for water and γ the psychrometric constant – quantities introduced by Penman (1948) in his derivation of an equation for evaporation from land surfaces. If the atmosphere above a moist land surface were saturated then, neglecting the amount of heat passing into the soil, the radiant energy received at the surface would also be partitioned into latent and sensible heat in the ratio ϵ. Commonly, due to the circulation in the atmosphere, air above even quite extensive areas of moist land surface is not saturated and therefore ϵ is a minimum estimate of the partition ratio.

Let the increment in heat input into the atmosphere be ΔH; then the increment of latent heat dissipated is at least $\epsilon \Delta H$ and the variation of the total energy dissipated into the atmosphere is therefore at least $(\epsilon+1)\Delta H$. Making use of these minimum estimates, it follows that, for a wet land surface, the amounts of energy passing into the atmosphere and soil are in the ratio $[(\epsilon+1)\rho c_p \sqrt{K}](\rho_s c_s \sqrt{\kappa})$. The admittance of the atmosphere for enthalpy (the sum of sensible and latent heat) is $(\epsilon+1)$ times the admittance for sensible heat. For a given increment in net radiation the increment in temperature at the land surface is

$$\Delta T \propto \frac{1}{(\epsilon+1)\rho c_p \sqrt{K} + \rho_s c_s \sqrt{\kappa}} \qquad [7]$$

Reference to the magnitudes of ϵ we have quoted indicates how profoundly the partition of energy and the temperature variation at the surface is affected by the presence of water, particularly if the mean temperature is large.

As with the previous analysis of temperature fluctuations, it is to be emphasized that what has been argued here applies only to *fluctuations* of net radiation, heat and vapour fluxes, and temperature during periods of a day and less, and is not applicable to the average values of those quantities, upon which the fluctuations are superimposed. For example, whether or not dew is deposited at night can be thought of as the net result of a diurnal variation in vapour flux superimposed on the mean upward flux. However, the way in which the amount of water in soil and atmo- sphere affects the mean characteristics of the energy balance at a surface involves large-scale atmospheric processes which are beyond the compass of our discussion here. Attempts have been made to simulate the time- course of evaporation from bare soils (Sasamori, 1970; Rosema, 1974) using very large digital computers, with some success. In particular the work of Sasamori (1970) is interesting, for his simulations include drying phases of the soil. Whilst the physical interactions are not complex they require continuous updating during the passage of time. If the rate of evaporation from an initially wet soil is greater than the rate at which water can be conducted to the surface, then the soil water content near the surface decreases and the rate of evaporation falls. This process of 'dry mulching', which has been analysed by Philip (1957), has secondary effects in that the decrease in soil water content leads to an increase in albedo and a reduction in soil thermal conductivity. Therefore net radiation is reduced, but an increased proportion of the energy received during the day is conducted into the atmosphere. The net effect is to cause steep gradients in temperature and humidity near the soil/atmosphere interface, their magnitude being dependent upon the initial rate of water loss from the soil.

The microclimate at or near the surface is also influenced by the movement of soil water in response to temperature gradients. The mechanisms of this coupling between heat and vapour fluxes, which is important only in rather dry soil, have been discussed by Philip & de Vries (1957) and de Vries (1958). Rose (1968*a*, *b*, *c*) demonstrated, with a bare sandy soil in an arid climate (Alice Springs, Australia) under a high radiation load, that, whilst the direction of liquid water movement in the soil was predominantly upwards, the direction of the water vapour flux oscillated in response to the diurnal temperature gradient. The ecological significance of vapour diffusion in dry soils for plant and particularly animal communities has not yet been investigated. However, the rehydration of the surface soil layers at night would surely influence the behaviour patterns of small mammals and invertebrates (Porter, Mitchell, Beckman & de Witt, 1973). Similarly, this 'thermal distillation' could be expected to influence the germination of desert plant species. For example, Shur (1965) reported, in a laboratory study with *Citrullus colocynthis*, that the seeds imbibe water readily, but germination does not occur unless they are subjected to several cycles of wetting and drying. Whether this is effected in the field by fluctuations in soil water movement, and if this reaction of the seed to its environment has any survival value, has yet to be demonstrated.

The energy balance of leaves and canopies

A generalized picture of the energy balance of plants can be gained by considering the basic unit of exchange, the leaf, phyllode or cladode, and then proceeding to whole canopies. We will only be concerned with the simple canopies of isolated perennial desert plants. We may write the energy balance of a leaf as

$$I(1-\rho-\tau)+L_{d}-L_{u} = R_{n} = \lambda E+H+P+S \qquad [8]$$

where ρ and τ are the coefficients of reflection and transmission respectively, P is the photosynthetic energy flux, and S a heat-storage term. The radiation load on a leaf is influenced by its optical characteristics in the short-wave region, for some 90% of the incoming radiation from the sky is at wavelengths less than 0.4μm. Studies of the optical properties of leaves (Gates, Keegan, Schlecter & Weidner, 1965; Pearman, 1966; Wong & Blevin, 1967; Sinclair & Thomas, 1970) have shown that the presence of particular surface features, such as epidermal hair and wax cuticles, is associated with enhanced reflection. Variation in leaf pigmentation affects the transmission coefficient. The range of recorded values of these parameters is appreciable, but, surprisingly, there is little or no correlation with the physical nature of the habitat; species from mesic sites often possess very high values of ρ and τ. In a survey of arid-zone species, Sinclair & Thomas (1970) found one species, a perennial shrub, to be exceptional with $\rho = 0.51$ and $\tau = 0.14$, leading to the smallest absorption coefficient found amongst the species tested. The high reflectivity of these small ($1\,\text{cm} \times 1\,\text{cm}$), succulent leaves could be explained by the deposition of crystalline sodium chloride on the epidermis from collapsing vesiculate hairs. However, in the opinion of Sinclair & Thomas, little significance should be attached to small differences in optical characteristics of leaves with regard to the overall energy balance of the leaf. Far greater influence on the solar radiation load stems from differences in leaf orientation. In an environment where sunshine is intense and water availability, not light, is the primary limitation to growth, vertical leaves are effective in reducing the radiation load.

The long-wave balance of a single leaf is determined not so much by its intrinsic optical characteristics as by the nature of the leaf surroundings. The emissivity of leaves (ϵ) is almost unity, being in the range of 0.95 to 0.99 (Gates & Tantraporn, 1952). The exchange of thermal radiation between a leaf and a particular component in its surroundings, soil or other leaves, depends on the view factor, this being the fraction of radiation emitted by the leaf surface that is directly intercepted by the other component. In arid environments it may well be of considerable and unrecognized significance in the observed spatial configurations of leaves and canopies of desert shrubs and trees. These perennial plants persist in environments in which restricted water supply for evaporation is always correlated with high bare-soil temperatures ($50\,°\text{C}$–$60\,°\text{C}$) surrounding the canopy. Unfortunately view-factor analysis is very complex. Simplified expressions have been used by Aston & van Bavel (1972).

In considering the dissipation of the net radiation flux (R_n) at the leaf surface the photosynthetic energy flux (P) and the heat storage term (S) may be neglected as they account for less than 5% of R_n. The storage term will be insignificant when compared with $(H+\lambda E)$ for most leaves, the exceptions being the large succulent leaves of desert-dwelling species of such families as Aizoaceae, Portulacaceae, Euphorbiaceae and particularly the cladodes of the Cactaceae (Gates, Alderfer & Taylor, 1968; Gibbs & Patten, 1970).

To examine the inter-relationships between H and λE we use the electrical analogue of Cowan (1972) as a useful conceptual model. The loss of water vapour from leaves may be expressed as:

$$E = -\rho \frac{\Delta q}{r} \qquad [9]$$

where E is the mass of water lost per unit time per unit area of leaf, ρ is the density of air, Δq is the difference in specific humidity across any or all of the components in the pathway – such as leaf epidermis, leaf boundary layer – and r is the appropriate 'resistance' to transport. The transport of heat is:

$$H = \rho c_p \frac{\Delta T}{r} \qquad [10]$$

where H is the heat lost per unit area per unit time, c_p the specific heat of air, ΔT the temperature difference across a component of the path of transport and r the 'resistance' involved. Transforming [10] so that 'currents' and 'potentials' have the same dimensions as in [9],

$$\frac{H}{\lambda} = -\rho \frac{\Delta q_s}{er} \qquad [11]$$

where λ is the latent heat of vaporization of water and q_s is the specific humidity of air saturated at temperature T. The term ϵ represents the increase of latent-heat content of saturated air with increase in sensible-heat content which has already been referred to. The complete analogue, Fig. 15.6, gives the 'currents' E and H/λ in the circuit which consists of a current generator R_n/λ and potential sources $\rho\delta$ and $\rho\delta_0$, interconnected by several resistances. The current generated is in units of heat required to vaporize unit mass of water. If $\rho\delta$ and $\rho\delta_0$ are zero, R_n/λ is distributed between the transpiration, E, and heat flow, H/λ, in the inverse ratio of the total resistances in the pathways. For E these are r_1, the leaf (primarily stomatal) resistance, and r_w, the resistance encountered in the diffusion and convection of water vapour in the boundary layer of the leaf. For H/λ the resistance is er_h and r_h is the boundary layer resistance to heat transfer expressed in the form of [7]. As the difference between r_h and r_w is small we shall cease to distinguish between the two, and call either r. Lastly the potential source $\rho\delta$ is the deficit in absolute humidity, $\rho(q'-q)$, in the ambient atmosphere; $\rho\delta_0$ is related to the soil

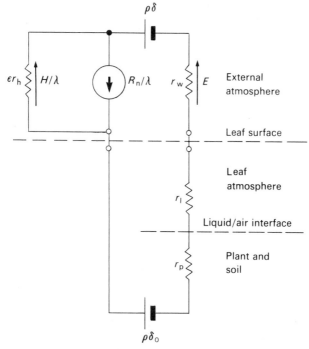

Fig. 15.6. The analogue of evaporation from a plant. (After Cowan, 1972.)

water potential and is negligible if soil water potential is sufficient to support living plants (Cowan, 1972). With the approximations indicated the solution of the circuit equations for water flow yields

$$E = \frac{\epsilon r \phi / \lambda + \rho \delta}{(\epsilon + 1)r + r_1} \qquad [12]$$

It may be verified that if $r_1 = \infty$, E becomes zero; if $R_n = 0$ then $E = -H/\lambda$. The complementary relation for heat transport is

$$H = \frac{(r+r_1) R_n \lambda \rho \delta}{(\epsilon + 1)r + r_1} = c_p \rho \frac{(T_1 - T_a)}{r} \qquad [13]$$

The second equality, which provides an expression for temperature difference between leaf and air, follows from [10].

The relative magnitudes of the radiation and humidity terms in [12] and [13] are of crucial importance. First we may note from an examination of [12] that evaporation rate increases with boundary layer resistance if

$$r_1 R_n > [1 + (1/\epsilon)] \lambda \rho \delta$$

425

Secondly, from [13] leaf temperature exceeds air temperature if

$$(r+r_1)R_n > \lambda\rho\delta$$

As r is small compared with r_1 for well ventilated leaves, and ϵ is large compared with unity at high temperatures, these two criteria are almost identical for isolated plants in a hot environment. We proceed on the basis that both evaporation rate and leaf temperature increase with boundary layer resistance if

$$r_1 > \lambda\rho\delta/R_n \quad \text{and vice versa.}$$

The boundary layer resistance to heat and water vapour, the reciprocal of r, of leaves depends upon the leaf shape, orientation and the wind flow. There are numerous expositions on this topic (see Fuchs, Chapter 14, this volume) and in general r diminishes with increasing windspeed and decreasing leaf size. Therefore small-area, narrow leaves tend to have low resistances within the range of wind speeds to be found in vegetation. In a hot dry environment under clear skies at midday we might adopt $\rho\delta \approx 40$ g m^{-3} and $R_n = 500$ W m^{-2}. With $\lambda \approx 2500$ J g^{-1} it follows that $\lambda\rho\delta/R_n = 2$ s cm^{-1}. This is close to the minimum value of leaf resistance in many plant species. Desert species which experience prolonged periods of water stress commonly operate with a greater leaf resistance; therefore one may surmise, following Parkhurst & Loucks (1972), that a small boundary resistance is advantageous in minimizing leaf temperature and evaporation rates. Many perennial desert shrubs and tree species have small leaves and open, well-ventilated canopies, a growth habit consistent with this analysis. On the other hand, ephemeral desert species, which function vegetatively only in restricted periods when soil water-content is adequate to maintain a rapid rate of transpiration, have a small leaf resistance. The argument that applies to 'drought-enduring' species does not hold for these 'drought-avoiding' species.

The coupling of water transport and carbon metabolism

So far we have discussed the influence of water, or lack of it, on the physical processes of energy transfer in the desert system. The interaction between the two exerts the profoundest influence on the climate to which plants and other organisms are exposed. We have also touched on the way in which that microclimate influences water loss from living plants. The rate of water loss is, in part, under physiological control, but the extent of physiological control is bounded by metabolic constraints associated with the existence of life itself. There can be no life without water flow. Water flow and growth are linked because both transpiration and assimilation are controlled by the stomatal mechanism in so far as it affects leaf resistance. It is this linkage that we discuss now.

Cohen (1970) has defined conditions in which plants may operate which would minimize transpiration ratio – the ratio of transpiration to assimilation. Plants are likely to do so when their supply of water is limited but is not available for use by competing plants or evaporated rapidly from the soil surface. Deep-rooted widely spaced perennial trees and shrubs are in this category. Shallow-rooted ephemeral species are not.

Noy-Meir (1973) has, using a simple but effective model or 'paradigm', discussed the types of linkage of plant growth to the temporal and spatial (depth of soil) distribution of water. The most obvious survival strategy for the drought-persistents is to have flexible coupling between transpiration and assimilation irrespective of other phenological behaviour, such as progressive leaf shedding (Evenari *et al.*, 1971). The extreme in this decoupling is permitted by the pathways for fixation of carbon dioxide found in the succulent plants, crassulacean acid metabolism (CAM) (Hatch, Osmond & Slatyer, 1971; DePuit, Chapter 21, this volume) which enables assimilation to proceed with the stomata open only at night when the potential for evaporation from the cladodes and leaves is minimal. For the remaining desert perennials possessing either the C_3 or C_4 metabolic pathways (DePuit, Chapter 21), some predictions of possible strategies can be made by considering the physics of the two exchange processes and the role of stomata in them. We shall assume that the rate of photosynthesis is at all times limited by the process of transfer of carbon dioxide into the leaf.

Transpiration and assimilation are not affected in exactly the same way by changes in leaf resistance. Transfer of carbon dioxide encounters, in addition to the leaf resistance, a boundary layer resistance and a 'resistance' r_i which is associated with transport and the process of carbon fixation inside the leaf. As shown by [12] the additional resistance to water vapour transfer is effectively $(\epsilon+1)r$. The ratio of the additional resistances to transfer of water vapour and carbon dioxide can be expressed as

$$\alpha = \frac{r_i r + 1}{\epsilon + 1} \qquad [14]$$

if the effects of the differing diffusion coefficients for carbon dioxide and water vapour are ignored. Cowan & Troughton (1971) have given slightly more complicated expressions allowing for the respective diffusion coefficients but [14] is sufficient for the purpose here. Its significance is this. If $\alpha > 1$ transpiration ratio increases with decreasing leaf resistance. That is to say, plants face the dilemma that faster growth is accompanied by disproportionately greater loss of water. If, on the other hand, $\alpha < 1$ the reverse is true and transpiration ratio diminishes with decrease in leaf resistance within the range in which photosynthesis is limited by transport of carbon dioxide rather than light intensity. Thus there is, in principle,

427

an optimum leaf resistance, diminishing with increasing light intensity, corresponding to minimum instantaneous transpiration ratio. The ratio α is likely to be less than unity in a hot environment (ϵ being large) and with species having a small internal resistance, r_i. The many species with C_4 carbon metabolism that inhabit arid environments typify these requirements. Plants relying on the Calvin cycle as their primary carboxylative mechanism, on the other hand, have internal resistances which are nearly an order of magnitude greater than those typical for C_4 plants, and for them α is probably close to or greater than unity in most environmental conditions. How might the differences in α affect the strategy adopted by stomata? A plant may achieve a more effective compromise by maintaining stomata on some leaves or parts of leaves closed, whilst those on the remaining leaves or parts of leaves are fully open, than it would by having a uniform stomatal aperture over the entire foliar surface. The transpiration ratio might be reduced, also, if stomatal resistance were to fluctuate in time about a mean value. Thus the ability to vary stomatal resistance in both space and time may be a desirable feature of some plant species in particular environments. On the other hand if α is greater than unity, the maximum rate of assimilation for a given rate of transpiration will be achieved with a uniform stomatal resistance.

De Wit (1958), in an analysis of crop yield and water use in arid conditions, found that transpiration ratio increased with increase in potential rate of evaporation, E_0. For the purpose here, potential rate of evaporation may be defined by [12] with r_i set equal to zero. The explanation put forward is that rate of transpiration increases with intensity of radiation and humidity deficit without limit, whereas photosynthesis becomes light-saturated and does not respond to humidity deficit at all. Noy-Meir (1973) suggests another reason, one which is more likely to be relevant to the discussion here. It is that the rates of assimilation and transpiration are perfectly coupled (that is, $\alpha = 1$), both being influenced by leaf resistance in the same way; but because rate of transpiration increases with increasing E_0, whereas rate of assimilation does not, transpiration ratio also increases. As Noy-Meir points out, de Wit's prediction has not been directly tested in natural arid communities. If it were valid then it might be expected that stomata would tend to close during periods when E_0 is particularly large – for instance, midday – and open at other times. The matter may be taken a little further.

We have suggested that, with C_4 species in a hot environment, transpiration ratio may diminish with decreasing leaf resistance (that is, $\alpha < 1$ in contradistinction to Noy-Meir's heuristic assumption quoted above). If then radiation intensity increases, transpiration ratio tends to increase in so far as E_0 is increased, but to decrease in so far as the plant opens its stomata in response to the increased availability of light for photosyn-

428

thesis. The net result of these opposed tendencies is difficult to estimate accurately for a reason which will be commented on shortly. However it seems possible that C_4 species in hot arid environments may not suffer to the same extent from the limitation implied by de Wit's finding for crop plants. For C_3 plants having $\alpha < 1$, there can be little doubt that transpiration ratio does increase rapidly with increasing intensity of radiation. There is some evidence, admittedly no more than circumstantial, that this analysis is reflected in the way in which stomata actually behave. The remarkable C_4 species *Tidestroemia oblongifolia* grows actively in Death Valley in California during the summer, with a leaf temperature approaching 50 °C; its rate of assimilation increases almost linearly with increasing intensity of radiation up to the largest intensities received, and it shows no sign of midday stomatal closure (Pearcey, Bjorkman, Harrison & Mooney, 1971). In contrast, species with C_3 carbon metabolism growing in the Negev Desert show a most pronounced stomatal closure in the middle part of the day (Schulze *et al.*, 1972, 1975).

The magnitude and diurnal variation of humidity deficit is a climatic attribute of great significance in relation to plant functioning, and is relevant to our discussion of the influence of radiation and potential rate of evaporation on transpiration ratio. The influence of humidity deficit relative to net radiation on rate of evaporation from a leaf is indicated by [12]. Let us assume $\rho\delta$ typically is about 40 g m^{-3} in a hot dry climate during the middle part of the day (this corresponds to a perfectly dry atmosphere at 35 °C). Let us assume the net radiation absorbed by a leaf is 500 W m^{-2} and that the boundary layer resistance is 0.2 s cm^{-1} (appropriate for a leaf about 2 cm broad with a wind speed of 1 m s^{-1}). Then, with ϵ being about 5, it follows that $\epsilon r R_n/\lambda$ is about 20 g m^{-3}. That is to say, the radiation term in [12] is one-half the humidity deficit term. In an extremely hot dry environment the fraction would be less. Evidently, any *independent* variation in net radiation causes a relatively smaller change in potential rate of evaporation and, to the extent that the latter *is* smaller, a relatively small effect on transpiration ratio. But in practice radiation and humidity deficit are not independent. The deficit is primarily a function of air temperature and is therefore affected by radiation in the ways indicated earlier in this chapter. It follows that the diurnal course of potential evaporation, and therefore the transpiration ratio of a given species, is dominated by the variation in net radiation but in a manner modulated by the thermal properties of soil and atmosphere and the availability of water for evaporation direct from the soil. Thus it is that the larger-scale physical processes involved in determining the gross energy balance of a land surface, which we considered first in this chapter, are fundamentally related to the discussion of the physiological functioning of plant leaves, with which we end it. The most dramatic example is provided by the behaviour of species having crassulacean acid metabolism. It is a well known phenomenon that the CAM mode of assimilation – that is, nocturnal fixation of carbon dioxide – is most pronounced when night temperatures are low and day temperatures are high (see Ting, 1971) – that is to say, when potential evaporation during the day is relatively much greater than at night, and there is therefore a considerable benefit to be derived in terms of minimizing transpiration ratio by means of CAM behaviour. It has been noted by Pearcy *et al.* (1971) that there are no CAM species present on the floor of Death Valley, California, where humidity deficit is substantial at night, although there are no other obvious biogeographical reasons for their absence. Without doubt, the particular nature of the inter-relationship between radiation and temperature in a given arid ecosystem is reflected in a multitude of ways in the species and behaviour of the plants which it supports.

References

Aston, A. R. & Bavel, C. H. M. van (1972). Soil surface water depletion and leaf temperature. *Agronomy Journal*, **64**, 368–73.

Baver, L. D., Gardner, W. H. & Gardner, W. R. (1972). *Soil Physics*. Wiley, New York.

Boaler, S.B. & Hodge, C.A.H. (1962). Vegetation stripes in Somaliland. *Journal of Ecology*, **50**, 465–74.

Boaler, S. B. & Hodge, C. A. H. (1964). Observations on vegetation arcs in the Northern Region, Somali Republic. *Journal of Ecology*, **52**, 511–44.

Bowers, S. A. & Hanks, R. J. (1965). Reflection of radiant energy from soils. *Soil Science*, **100**, 130–38.

Cloudsley-Thompson, J. L. & Chadwick, M. J. (1964). *Life in Deserts*. Foulis, London.

Cohen, D. (1970). The expected efficiency of water utilization in plants under different competition and selection regimes. *Israel Journal of Botany*, **19**, 50–54.

Cowan, I. R. (1972). An electrical analogue of evaporation from, and flow of water in plants. *Planta*, **106**, 221–6.

Cowan, I. R. & Troughton, J. H. (1971). The relative role of stomata in transpiration and assimilation. *Planta*, **97**, 325–36.

Davies, S. J. J. F. (1973). Environmental variables and the biology of native Australian animals in the mulga lands. *Tropical Grasslands*, **7**, 127–34.

Deacon, E. L. (1969). Physical processes near the surface of the earth. In: *World Survey of Climatology* (ed. H. Flohn), vol. II, pp. 39–104. Elsevier, Amsterdam.

de Vries, D. A. (1958). Simultaneous transfer of heat and moisture in porous media. *Transactions of the American Geophysical Union*, **39**, 909–16.

de Wit, C. T. (1958). *Transpiration and crop yields*. Instituut voor Biologisch Scheikundig Onderzoek van Landbougewasser, Mededelino 59. Wageningen, Netherlands.

Edney, E. B. (1974). Desert arthropods. In: *Desert Biology* (ed. G. W. Brown), vol. II, p. 312. Academic Press, New York.

Evenari, M., Shanan, L. & Tadmor, N. (1971). *The Negev: the challenge of a desert.* Harvard University Press, Cambridge, Mass.

Friedman, J. (1971). The effect of competition by adult *Zygophyllum dumosum* Boiss on seedlings of *Artemisia herba-alba* Asso. in the Negev Desert of Israel. *Journal of Ecology*, **59**, 775–82.

Gates, D. M. & Tantraporn, W. (1952). The reflectivity of deciduous trees and herbaceous plants in the infrared to 25 microns. *Science*, **115**, 613–16.

Gates, D. M., Alderfer, R. & Taylor, E. (1968). Leaf temperatures of desert plants. *Science*, **159**, 994–5.

Gates, D. M., Keegan, H. J., Schlecter, J. C. & Weidner, V. R. (1965). Spectral properties of plants. *Applied Optics*, **4**, 11–20.

Gay, L. W. (1971). The regression of net radiation upon solar radiation. *Archiv für Meteorologie, Geophysik und Bioklimatologie. Ser. B.*, **19**, 1–14.

Gibbs, J. G. & Patten, D. (1970). Plant temperatures and heat flux in a Sonoran Desert ecosystem. *Oecologia*, **5**, 165–84.

Graetz, R. D. Animal–plant interaction. In: *Arid-land ecosystems: structure, functioning and management*, vol. II (eds. R. A. Perry & D. W. Goodall). Cambridge University Press, Cambridge. (In preparation.)

Hatch, M. D., Osmond, C. B. & Slatyer, R. O. (eds.) (1971). *Photosynthesis and Photorespiration.* Wiley-Interscience, New York.

Hovis, W. A. (1965). Optimum wavelength intervals for surface temperature radiometry. *Applied Optics*, **5**, 815–18.

Idso, S. B., Baker, D. G. & Blad, B. L. (1969). Relations of radiation fluxes over natural surfaces. *Quarterly Journal of the Royal Meteorological Society*, **95**, 244–57.

Koller, D. (1969). The physiology of dormancy and survival of plants in desert environments. In: *Dormancy and Survival*, Symposia of the Society of Experimental Biology, **23**, 449–69. Cambridge University Press, Cambridge.

Lettau, H. H. & Davidson, B. (eds.) (1957). *Exploring the atmosphere's first mile.* Pergamon Press, New York.

McGinnes, W. G., Goldman, B. J. & Paylore, P. (eds.) (1968). *Deserts of the World.* University of Arizona Press, Tucson.

Monteith, J. L. & Szeicz, G. (1961). The radiation balance of bare soil and vegetation. *Quarterly Journal of the Royal Meteorological Society*, **87**, 159–70.

Noy-Meir, I. (1973). Desert ecosystems: environment and producers. *Annual Review of Ecology and Systematics*, **4**, 25–52.

Otterman, J. (1974). Baring high-albedo soils by overgrazing: a hypothesized desertification mechanism. *Science*, **186**, 531–3.

Paltridge, G. W. (1970). Day-time long-wave radiation from the sky. *Quarterly Journal of the Royal Meteorological Society*, **96**, 645–53.

Parkhurst, D. F. & Loucks, O. L. (1972). Optimal leaf size in relation to environment. *Journal of Ecology*, **60**, 505–37.

Paton, T. R. (1974). Origin and terminology for gilgai in Australia. *Geoderma*, **11**, 221–42.

Pearcy, R. W., Björkman, O., Harrison, A. T. & Mooney, H. A. (1971). Photosynthetic performance of two desert species with C_4 photosynthesis in Death Valley, California. In: *Annual Report of the Carnegie Institution, Department of Plant Biology 1970/71*, pp. 540–50. Stanford, California.

Atmospheric processes

Pearman, G. I. (1966). The reflection of visible radiation from leaves of some Western Australian species. *Australian Journal of Biological Sciences*, **19**, 97–103.

Penman, H. L. (1948). Natural evaporation from open water, bare soil and grass. *Proceedings of the Royal Society, London*, A **193**, 120–45.

Philip, J. R. (1957). Evaporation and moisture and heat fields in the soil. *Journal of Meteorology*, **14**, 354–66.

Philip, J. R. & de Vries, D. A. (1957). Moisture movements in porous materials under temperature gradients. *Transactions of the American Geophysical Union*, **38**, 222–32.

Porter, W. P., Mitchell, J. W., Beckman, W. A. & de Witt, C. B. (1973). Behavioral implications of mechanistic ecology: thermal modeling of desert ectotherms and their micro-environment. *Oecologia*, **13**, 1–54.

Priestley, C. H. B. (1959a). Heat conduction and temperature profiles in air and soil. *Journal of the Australian Institute of Agricultural Science*, **26**, 94–107.

Priestley, C. H. B. (1959b). *Turbulent transfer in the lower atmosphere*. University of Chicago Press, Chicago.

Roff, D. A. (1974a). Spatial heterogeneity and the persistence of populations. *Oecologia*, **15**, 245–58.

Roff, D. A. (1974b). The analysis of a population model demonstrating the importance of dispersal in a heterogeneous environment. *Oecologia*, **15**, 259–75.

Rose, C. W. (1968a). Water transport in the soil with a daily temperature wave. I. Theory and experiment. *Australian Journal of Soil Research*, **6**, 31–44.

Rose, C. W. (1968b). Water transport in the soil with a daily temperature wave. II. Analysis. *Australian Journal of Soil Research*, **6**, 45–57.

Rose, C. W. (1968c). Evaporation from a bare soil under high radiation conditions. *Transactions 9th International Soil Science Congress*, **1**, 57–66.

Rosema, A. (1974). Simulation of the thermal behaviour of bare soils for remote sensing purposes. Presented at *7th International Seminar on Heat and Mass Transfer in the Environment of Vegetation*, Dubrovnik.

Sasamori, T. (1970). A numerical study of atmospheric and soil boundary layers. *Journal of Atmospheric Sciences*, **27**, 1122–37.

Schulze, E. D., Lange, O. L., Buschbom, U., Kappen, L. & Evenari, M. (1972). Stomatal responses to changes in humidity in plants growing in the desert. *Planta*, **108**, 259–70.

Schulze, E. D., Lange, O. L., Evenari, M., Kappen, L. & Buschbom, U. (1975). The role of air humidity and temperature in controlling stomatal resistance of *Prunus armeniaca* L. under desert conditions. III. The effect on water use efficiency. *Oecologia*, **19**, 303–14.

Sellers, W. D. (1965). *Physical Climatology*. University of Chicago Press, Chicago.

Shur, I. (1965). Unpublished thesis cited in Koller (1969).

Sinclair, R. & Thomas, D. A. (1970). Optical properties of leaves of some species in arid South Australia. *Australian Journal of Botany*, **18**, 261–73.

Slatyer, R. O. (1961). Methodology of a water balance study conducted on a desert woodland (*Acacia aneura*) community *Arid Zone Research*, (*UNESCO*), **16**, 15–26.

Stanhill, G., Hofstede, G. I. & Kalma, J. D. (1966). Radiation balance of natural and agricultural vegetation. *Quarterly Journal of the Royal Meteorological Society*, **92**, 128–40.

Swinbank, W. C. (1963). Longwave radiation from clear skies. *Quarterly Journal of the Royal Meteorological Society*, **93**, 339–48.

432

Ting, I. P. (1971). Nonautotrophic CO_2 fixation and Crassulacean Acid Metabolism. In: *Photosynthesis and photorespiration* (eds. M. D. Hatch, C. B. Osmond & R. O. Slatyer), pp. 169–85. Wiley-Interscience, New York.

White, L. P. (1965). *Brousse tigrée* patterns in Southern Niger. *Journal of Ecology*, **58**, 549–53.

White, L. P. (1969). Vegetation arcs in Jordan. *Journal of Ecology*, **57**,461–4.

Wong, C. L. & Blevin, W. R. (1967). Infra-red reflectance of plant leaves. *Australian Journal of Biological Sciences*, **20**, 501–8.

Warrall, G. A. (1959). The Butana grass patterns. *Journal of Soil Science*, **10**, 34–53.

Manuscript received by the editors February 1975

16. Integration

R. D. GRAETZ and I. R. COWAN

This section has dealt with physical processes in the atmosphere which have a wide range of spatial and temporal scales. The broad characteristics of the time-course of solar radiation are primarily determined by the extra-terrestrial radiation which is incident at the top of the atmosphere; the manner in which it is depleted before reaching the earth's surface depends on the characteristics of air masses on a macro-scale. As the properties and movement of air masses on this scale are determined in turn by the solar energy absorbed at various levels in the atmosphere, including the land surface, there is an interaction between the two. It is the nature of that interaction which, together with the distribution of land masses, determines the fact that certain areas, those with which this volume is concerned, receive little and infrequent rainfall. This is the province of the climatologist and meteorologist. Some aspects of it have been discussed in Chapters 12 and 13, but the approach there has been primarily a pragmatic one – the specification of the characteristic inputs of radiation and precipitation in the drier areas of the earth's surface.

The net balance of radiation exchanged at the earth's surface is, on average, positive. The energy is transferred to the atmosphere as sensible and latent heat and is eventually re-radiated into space. The transport properties of the atmosphere, defined in terms of turbulent diffusivity in the slab of air close to the surface and convection coefficients for transfer in the vicinity of particular elements of the surface, determine not so much the amounts of sensible and latent heat which are dissipated, but the gradients of temperature and humidity in the lower part of the atmosphere which are required to support those fluxes (the fact that the interrelationship is usually written in the form flux = transport coefficient ×gradient gives the impression that it is the other way about). The magnitude of the turbulent diffusivity is in part determined by air movement at a height of several hundred metres in the atmosphere and in part by the aerodynamic roughness of the underlying surface. It is also affected by the temperature gradient, and therefore the relation between heat flux and temperature gradient is nonlinear. These are matters which are treated in Chapter 14.

The last chapter (15) endeavours to describe how the nature of the radiation field and the aerodynamic properties of the atmosphere together affect the microclimate near the land surface. The amount of soil water

435

Atmospheric processes

available for evaporation and the thermal properties of the soil exert major influences. Finally, the way in which that microclimate may affect the functioning of plant leaves is discussed. No apology needs to be offered for touching on physiological topics; there is no sharp division between physics and physiology, or boundary between environment and the organism.

Soil processes

17. Soil processes in arid lands

V. A. KOVDA, E. M. SAMOILOVA, J. L. CHARLEY and
J. J. SKUJINŠ

Introduction

Many surface formations of arid lands, such as calcareous, gipseous and saline soils, crusts and hardpans, are relics and date back to an earlier stage of the earth's history. They have been formed under physicogeographical conditions essentially different from the present ones. The pedogenic processes involved in their formation, as well as their present properties, are inconsistent with the present-day conditions of arid lands. The majority of such relict formations were formed during pluvial epochs, when geochemical migration and erosion were more active, and hydrogenic accumulation of secondary minerals more intensive. The humid epochs of the past caused the formation of great alluvial plains with ground waters at shallow depths, and with hydromorphic soils in which calcium carbonate, gypsum, easily soluble salts, sesquioxides and silica accumulated. Desert soils of central Asia, Africa and America have preserved some relict horizons of gypsum, calcium carbonate, and easily soluble salts (Kovda, 1946–7; Brown, 1956; Butzer, 1959; Perelman, 1959; Durand, 1963). In arid regions of Africa, Australia and Arabia ferruginous crusts are found extensively – relics of hydromorphic soils formed in humid tropical conditions of the past (Owen, 1954; Glazovskaya, 1971).

Silica crusts, formed as a result of the pluvial epochs, tropical weathering and geochemical migration, have been described in Australia, America and Africa (Kaiser, 1926; Kovda, 1954, 1971; Stephens, 1964). In deserts and semi-deserts of North America, Africa and other continents, soils of Neogene and Pleistocene age are extensive (Gile, 1967; US Department of Agriculture, 1970). Thus, many properties of arid soils are the result, not of present, but of ancient soil–geochemical processes. It is essential to distinguish properties resulting from processes in previous epochs which have been inherited by soils, and those resulting from present-day processes. Unfortunately up to now there have been very few studies of the ancient and present-day soil processes in arid lands, and only a small part of them have been directly connected with the International Biological Programme.

It is necessary to distinguish three types of arid-land landscapes:

(a) *automorphic landscapes*, which from the very beginning have been formed without any geochemical influence of underground waters. The water–salt budget of the landscapes is of the pure eluvial (leaching) type,

439

Soil processes

(b) *hydromorphic landscapes*, in the formation of which the most essential role has been taken by processes of hydromorphic accumulation of soluble and insoluble compounds, transported by ground and surface waters; and

(c) *neoautomorphic landscapes*, which had passed in previous geological time through a hydromorphic regime and have preserved some indications of palaeohydromorphism, but which at present belong to the neoeluvial type of water–salt régime.

Below are considered the soil processes of automorphic and neoautomorphic landscapes, and particularly those of hydromorphic landscapes of arid lands.

Pedogenesis in automorphic landscapes of arid lands (those without influence of ground waters)

Temperature dynamics

The heat-balance and temperature dynamics of arid soils in different climatic zones have a great deal in common. The dynamics of temperature are essentially identical in all deserts of the world (Petrov, 1973). In the heat régime of any desert two periods can be distinguished – summer heating and winter cooling of soils. The most intensively heated are the continental deserts of the tropics and subtropics. On the seaboard of the Red Sea the surface of the sandy desert soil is heated up to 83.5 °C; in the Sahara up to 81 °C; in Arizona more than 70 °C. The surface of takyr soils in clay deserts of Soviet Asia is heated up to 70 °C.

The desert soils of the temperate zone are characterized by the most marked fluctuation of maximal and minimal temperatures; the range reaches 120 °C. In Repetek (Karakum Desert of the USSR) the absolute minimum of the sand surface is −40 °C, the absolute maximum +79.4 °C. The range decreases exponentially as the depth increases. The temperature régime of sandy soil at Repetek is shown on Fig. 17.1.

In winter, desert soils of the temperate zone may freeze to a depth of 60 cm; in the subtropics and tropics negative temperatures on the soil surface are not observed, or very seldom. From the middle of winter onwards the soil begins to get progressively warmer. Optimum temperature and moisture conditions for vegetation on arid soils most often occur in spring – more seldom in summer, if the maximum precipitation falls during summer. In the course of summer the soil is heated to a temperature which prevents the development of plants. Towards the end of summer, surface temperature decreases, reaching a second biological optimum in autumn, or in winter. The lack of moisture in the soil at this time, however, prevents the growth of many plants.

Moistening of arid soils improves their heat conductivity and temper-

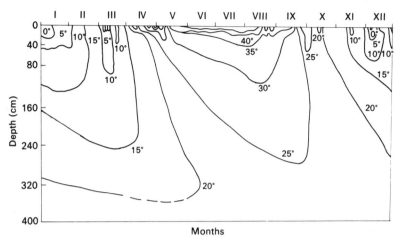

Fig. 17.1. The temperature (°C) régime of sandy soil of Repetek (Kyzylkum Desert).

ature conditions considerably. That is why the most favourable heat and water régime is observed in spring.

The temperature régime of arid soils is greatly influenced by slope and exposure. Investigations of Kassas & Imam (1957) have shown that the soils of south-facing slopes are considerably warmer than those of north-facing ones (Table 17.1). This leads to a greater specific diversity and productivity of the vegetation.

Water regime of soils

Peculiarities of the water régime of soils in arid areas are determined by the low quantity of atmospheric precipitation combined with intense evaporation. The second characteristic feature of the water régime is the high seasonal contrast. Against the background of extremely low humidity during the year, short periods of comparatively high moisture occur. These periods are accompanied by rapid development of vegetation and soil micro-organisms, diverse biochemical processes and weathering. These phenomena are displayed particularly distinctly in desert soils, and, less distinctly, in those of semi-desert.

The source of soil moisture in automorphic landscapes is atmospheric precipitation only. Condensation of water vapour from the atmosphere in continental deserts and semi-deserts is of no importance, amounting usually to about 15–20 mm and not exceeding 50 mm per annum, the greater part of which evaporates into the atmosphere (Petrov, 1973). In maritime deserts, moisture condensation from the atmosphere is so abundant that it is used for water supply and irrigation (Saa, 1963).

The potential evaporation of moisture in deserts of the temperate zone

441

Table 17.1. *Minimum and maximum soil temperature (°C) during the period January–July 1957 on slopes of different exposure (Cairo desert).* (Kassas & Imam, 1957)

	January		February		March		April		May		July	
Exposure	Max.	Min.	Max.	Min.	Max.	Min.	Max.	Min.	Max.	Min.	Max.	Min.
S	28.0	11.5	31.0	14.0	34.5	19.5	29.0	17.0	43.8	24.0	50.5	28.5
	32.2	11.4	28.4	14.6	30.0	18.6	27.0	16.0	43.8	23.4	47.5	28.0
N	18.0	8.5	21.5	11.5	28.0	17.0	26.4	14.5	39.5	22.5	43.0	27.5
	16.6	7.0	21.6	10.2	25.6	16.4	26.0	13.2	35.8	22.4	43.5	25.8

Table 17.2. *Moisture (% of dry soil) of surface (0–5 cm) soil horizon of Cairo desert.* (Kassas & Imam, 1957)

Relative altitude (m)	1956		1957	
	27 Nov.	13 Dec.	21 Jan.	17 Feb.
90.32	0.16	1.50	2.29	1.57
87.26	0.15	1.58	2.66	2.97
84.64	0.17	1.64	3.37	2.72
77.60	0.22	1.88	3.34	2.85
75.33	0.23	2.08	3.29	5.78

ranges up to 1500 mm yearly, and in subtropical and tropical deserts may reach 2000–2500 mm, and even 3000 mm.

The water balance of soils in arid lands is influenced by relief and parent rocks: moistening, evaporation, availability and dynamics of water in soils are determined by topography and by lithology.

Low-level depressions receive more water than the amount of rainfall. On the other hand, the tops and slopes receive considerably less moisture, returning it to the depressions and lower areas by run-off. Topography controls not only the quantity of moisture, but also the evaporation, which depends on exposure. Investigations by Kassas & Imam (1957) have also shown great differences in the amount of moisture received by desert soils at different altitudes (Table 17.2), even if the differences are slight.

The water régime and water balance of desert soils on different parent rocks have been studied by Hillel & Tadmor (1962) in the Negev Desert (Table 17.3, Fig. 17.2). Sandy soils have the most favourable water régime. They are wetted more deeply, have the largest store of available water, do not lose moisture by surface and ground run-off, and have low evaporation. Thus, 80% of stored moisture is used in the transpiration of plants. The most unfavourable water régime is that of clay and loess plains. In

Table 17.3. *Water régime and balance of soils in Negev Desert.* (Hillel & Tadmor, 1962)

Habitat	Maximum available water storage within root zone				Water balance for 'average' season[1]			
	Depth of penetration (cm)	Available range (%)	Available moisture (mm)	Total supply (mm)	Run-off (mm)	Deep penetration (mm)	Direct evaporation (mm)	Plant use (transpiration) (mm)
Loessial wadi	200	11.0	300	300–800	—	0–200	50	250–500
Rocky slope	70	3.0	40	100	15	5	30	50
Loessial plain	20–30	12.0	40	100	20	—	45	35
Tureibe sand	100	3.5	50–60	120	—	—	30	90

[1] The concept of an 'average' season in such a region is artificial and may be misleading since many seasons are likely to deviate greatly from this assumed average. The sole justification for the concept is that it permits simple comparison between habitats.

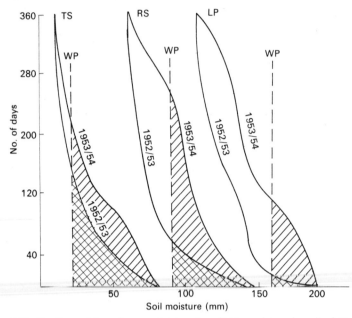

Fig. 17.2. Profile moisture storage: total and available moisture in soil of Negev Desert. Symbols: T.S., Tureibe sands; R.S., rocky slopes; L.P., loessial plain. Horizontal axis indicates the change of total soil moisture content to the depth of 150 cm, beginning in late Nov. to Nov. of the next year.

comparison with them, even the soils of rocky slopes have more favourable conditions. The natural stony mulch apparently retards run-off, prevents the formation of a continuous crust, and slows the rate of evaporation. Stones within the soil decrease the storage capacity and increase the depth of moisture penetration. On the other hand, the soils of clay and loess plains are covered by nearly solid crusts, poorly absorbing and rapidly evaporating moisture. Consequently, these soils lose much moisture unproductively; compared with run-off and evaporation rather little moisture is transpired.

The water régime of grey-brown desert soils has been investigated over many years in the west Kyzylkum of Soviet Central Asia (Khamzin, 1965). The annual amount of precipitation was 90–100 mm, of which 15% fell in summer and autumn. The water régime was of an unleached evaporational type. Maximum moisture accumulation in the soil occurred in February and March (88 mm), the smallest storage was in August and September (32 mm at a depth of 1 m). From June till November all the soils, except sandy ones, are devoid of available water. Even in spring the moisture content does not exceed 40–45% of the field capacity.

At the beginning of autumn, in spite of the lack of rain, the moisture content of deeper soil layers (100–200 cm) increases by several millimetres owing to the condensation of water distilled from deeper soil horizons. In consequence of the greater cooling of upper horizons in autumn, the vapour pressure of water is reduced much below that in the deeper part of the soil profile. As a result, an upward movement of water vapour, and its condensation in higher horizons, proceeds. After November the upper soil horizons become wet, following the rains. Moistening takes place, as a rule, to a depth of 70 cm, seldom to 1 m. Therefore if the ground watertable is deep (below 7–10 m) the subsoil horizons are practically air-dry in the zone above the watertable.

Data about differences in the water régime of sandy soils under stands of *Haloxylon aphyllum* Iljin and *Haloxylon persicum* Bge. are very interesting. The region under investigation is the Karakum Desert in Soviet Central Asia (Gunin, Ishankuliev & Togisaev, 1972). Under the canopies of *H. aphyllum*, the depth of moistening and the amount of soil moisture (2–4%) are considerably higher than under canopies of *H. persicum* (0.5–1%). Under *H. aphyllum*, even at the end of summer, some available moisture persists at depths greater than 40 cm, but in the case of *H. persicum* the soil may have no available moisture even at the beginning of summer. This phenomenon may be explained by the fact that *H. aphyllum* derives moisture from the ground water, while *H. persicum* derives it from rainfall and from condensation. Besides that, stem flow is twice as great in *H. aphyllum* as in *H. persicum*. At the same time, in contrast to *H. persicum*, active roots of *H. aphyllum* ramify, in general, in the lower soil horizons. It must be added that the top soil horizon, which prevents physical evaporation, is better developed under *H. aphyllum*.

As many investigations have shown, the most favourable water régime for vegetation occurs in sandy soils. This is caused by the high infiltration capacity of sands; lack of surface run-off losses; low water losses by evaporation; and by low values of the wilting point. The process of upward water distillation resulting from a temperature gradient is expressed most distinctly in desert sands. Kulik (1963) has established experimentally that, in sandy semi-desert soils (in the south-eastern region of the European part of the Soviet Union) seasonal transmission of water vapour amounts to between 15 and 25 mm. These properties described for sandy soils occur in all the deserts of the world. Not without reason do the peoples of central Asia have the proverb: 'Life is in sands'.

On compact, impervious rocks the speed and absolute values of surface run-off are greatest. Therefore the vegetative cover is extremely poor: the surface is often covered by a nearly sterile crust of salt or clay. Finely divided particulate material is exported by wind and water. Deflation is a most characteristic process of deserts. The removal of fine particles from a surface covered with rock fragments leads to formation of a specific

Table 17.4 *The water budget of major soil types of semi-desert. Average for 10 years.* (Rode & Pol'ski, 1962)

Soils	Moisture income during growing season						Moisture losses (mm)				
	Total precipitation during cold period (mm)	Depth of penetration (cm)	Spring increase in water storage	Precipitation during warm period	Moisture income from underground waters	Total	Outflow in underground waters	Evapotranspiration	Total	Moisture turnover (mm)	Autumn deficiency of moisture[1] (mm)
Solonetz alkaline	136	35	80	108	30	218	0	210	210	428	−230
Light chestnut	135	82	144	131	30	305	7	290	297	602	−250
Dark meadow	132	257	332	128	30	490	62	422	484	974	−284

[1] Autumn deficiency of moisture – the difference between the moisture-storage corresponding to field capacity, and actual moisture-storage in the soil.

stony 'desert pavement'. Sometimes this pavement is formed not by broken fragments of rock but by concretions or blocks derived from pedological hardpans, formed in ancient pluvial epochs (that is, from the remains of ancient soils).

A fundamental study of the water régime and balance of semi-desert soils in relation to micro-relief (Table 17.4) was carried out in the north-western parts of the Caspian plain in the USSR (Rode & Pol'ski, 1962). Three components of the soil-cover complex were studied; solonchak–solonetz on micro-hills; light-chestnut soil on micro-slopes; and dark-coloured soils of low micro-depressions. Owing to redistribution of snow and melt waters among the micro-relief elements, solonetz soils receive 80 mm of winter precipitation, less than the norm. Micro-slopes receive the whole amount of annual precipitation, and the micro-depressions receive additionally nearly 200 mm of moisture on account of run-off from micro-hills. As a result, the soils of micro-depressions have a periodical deep penetration of water to the ground water table, but the solonetz soils are soaked only to the lower surface of the alkali horizon, and this moisture is lost very quickly by evapo-transpiration. The soil horizons occurring at depths between 50 and 100 cm are constantly devoid of physiologically available water. Within the second metre, moisture increases down to the capillary fringe of ground-water. Moisture increasing downwards through the profile creates a suction gradient which supports the constant ascent of solutions upwards. Thus a non-leaching type of water régime for the upper part is combined with an exudative (evaporating) régime for the lower part of the profile. Transpiration of the vegetation is the main factor supporting this régime.

The water régime of micro-slopes of semi-desert soils is of the non-leaching type. Soil is wetted in spring to a depth of 50–100 cm. As in the solonetz soils, there is a constant moisture flow from the soil ground-water; however, it does not penetrate the solum, but ceases at its lower surface, where it is intercepted by plant roots. Here available moisture is absent during the whole year.

Weathering and clay formation

However slow weathering in arid soils may be, the products of weathering gradually and constantly accumulate in it. Frequent fluctuations of temperature and moisture, combined with prolonged periods of drought, lead to prevalence of physical weathering. In short wet periods, however, in arid soils the ordinary processes of weathering – oxidation, dissolution and hydrolysis – proceed very intensively, and result in degradation of primary minerals and formation of soluble salts, calcium and magnesium carbonates, soluble silicates and secondary alumino-silicates. Silicate

447

efflorescences were observed, for instance, on the rock surfaces in deserts of Sudan, and there are reports of secondary crystalline silica in the Egyptian deserts. Solutions of mobile silica migrate like salts, and accumulate on slopes and in depressions.

Weathering of primary minerals is also accompanied by a weak argillosynthesis. In the middle part of the profile of grey-brown desert and brown semi-desert soils in central Asia, a horizon is formed which is marked by accumulation of a clay fraction, often not accompanied by an increase in sesquioxides (Lobova, 1960). Newly-formed argillaceous material is fixed *in situ* owing to its firm aggregation, which is caused by high concentration of calcium carbonates (Rozanov, 1951). The limit of argillosynthesis in deserts coincides with the limit of distribution of the main mass of roots and microorganisms – that is, with the part of profile most regularly wetted. In this way, the most favourable conditions occur here for the biochemical weathering of primary minerals and new synthesis of clay. Argillosynthesis is confirmed by micromorphological investigations, which have found weathered sericitized grains of felspars, weathered fragments of mica, accumulations of ferrimorphic products and clay minerals. Illite and to a smaller degree montmorillonite are dominant in the clay fraction (Lobova, 1960). In other areas arid soils are characterized by the presence of consolidated and cemented horizons, which are known as pans or duripans. To all appearance they are relict horizons of past hydromorphic stages.

The slight ferruginization of desert soils is considered as one of the peculiarities of weathering which is displayed in deserts. Lobova (1960) considers this weak ferruginization as a result of processes analogous to rubefication and ferrallitization. Outwardly, ferruginization appears as a weak reddening caused by the prevalence of dehydrated forms of ferric oxides. The ferric oxides are distinguished as pellicles or films enveloping the minerals, or separate scales resting on the fragments of biotite and white mica. The basic materials for formation of iron hydroxide are micas. Ferruginization develops in the crust and in the horizon where finer particles accumulate. This process apparently takes place during the short period when, after spring moistening of the soil, rapid heating to a temperature of 50–70 °C takes place. The combination of sufficiently high humidity with intense heating, followed by abrupt drying, results in disruption of the crystal lattice of micas, loss of iron from the crystal lattice and formation of hydroxide pellicles.

There is a possible role for organic matter in this process, particularly for fulvic acids, which are capable of extracting iron in a neutral or mildly alkaline medium. It has been experimentally determined that ferruginous pellicles appear on the transparent mineral grains only when the grey mica sands are heated – to a temperature between 70 and 100 °C. In the presence of organic matter under natural conditions, this process takes place more intensely and surface horizons of soils and sands assume a yellowish-ochric colour.

In the automorphic desert soils of ancient terraces which had been under the influence of ground waters in the past during pluvial epochs, ferruginization is a relict indication, and takes the form of dispersed concretions or even hardpan and laterite (the soils of high ancient Nile terraces in Egypt).

Crust formation on the soil surface

A highly peculiar feature of desert and semi-desert pedogenesis is the formation of a porous dense crust on the soil surface underlain by a micro-horizon of flaky character. This crust is especially characteristic of arid soils in temperate climates, but it is also noticed in the subtropics and tropics (Miller & Brown, 1938; Skujinš, 1975*a*, *b*). The thickest crust (up to 8 cm) is developed in desert soils; in semi-desert soil it is not so thick, but the flaky type of subhorizon is better developed. The crusts of arid soils are usually somewhat sandy. This results from the accumulation of sand particles shifted from surrounding areas of coarser-textured soil.

The mechanism of crust formation in arid soils is unclear. Probably it may be explained by weak development of root-mass in the surface horizon, high calcareousness of the soils, and the seasonal contrast in the hydrothermal régime. When after moistening the soil mass is quickly heated and dried, rapid precipitation of calcium carbonate occurs with liberation of carbon dioxide. Numerous pores are formed, carbonates cement the soil mass and give firmness to the sides of the pores. This process has been experimentally reproduced by Paletskaya, Lavrov & Kogan (1958). A definite role in crust formation may be played by bio-chemical processes. In the surface layer of automorphic arid soils a considerable biomass of algae and lichens occurs, and production of oxygen and carbon dioxide by microorganisms reaches a maximum (Bolyshev, 1968; Skujinš, 1975*a*).

Three types of crust were noted by Skuninš (1975*b*) in the semi-arid areas of North Africa:

(*a*) *Crusts of physico-chemical origin.* These become established by wind-sorting of soil components and cementation as described above.

(*b*) *Crusts of mechanical origin.* These are due to an occasional cultivation of the soil in years with heavier rainfall. The soil is compacted at ploughing depth; in a dry season the loosened, sandy, arable layer is removed by wind action, and the hard, compacted layer is exposed.

(*c*) *Crusts of biological origin.* These are mostly due to fungal and, to a lesser extent, algal activity. In sandy soils these are rather fragile crusts; a harder crust, including lichen cover, develops on clay-containing soils (Skujinš, 1975a).

It was noted that the three types of crust in semi-arid sandy areas of North Africa had a similar type of fungal microflora, distinct from that of the non-crusted areas. It would appear that lower animals (insects) may play a major role here in transporting and mixing available litter with soil – that is, supplying the fungi with a source of energy.

It is not unlikely that the flaky structure of the undercrust horizon is connected with processes of winter freezing. The deeper and longer the soil freezes, the better, as a rule, will the flaky character of the horizon be expressed.

Accumulation and conservation of excess soluble salts
Gypsum and calcium carbonate

All the arid soils of the world are characterized by active processes of salt accumulation, not only in hydromorphic, but in automorphic landscapes too. This is due to the poor development of surface run-off and slight leaching of products of weathering and soil formation. In Central Asia, Latin America and the Arabian deserts there is practically no leaching of excess soluble salts (chlorides and sulphates), and they are preserved in desert soils for an indefinite time. Especially is this true of the weakly soluble salts, gypsum, and calcium and magnesium carbonates.

The vegetation cover (xerophytes and halophytes) favours the accumulation of carbonates and other soluble salts in the upper part of profile of automorphic desert soils. A definite role is also played by the aeolian dust. The roots and above-ground parts of halo-xerophytic vegetation of deserts and semi-deserts are characterized by high ash content (15–40% ash); halophytic shrubs carry chlorides, sulphates and carbonates up to the surface, which leads to the salinization and alkalinization of the soil.

The influence of *Haloxylon aphyllum*, *H. persicum* and other species on soil properties has been studied in the south-eastern part of the Karakum Desert (Bazilevich, Chepurko, Rodin & Miroshnichenko, 1972). The total quantity of salt added annually to the soil in the litter of *H. aphyllum* reaches 80 g m^{-2}, and more than 90% of it consists of alkali carbonates. Chlorides, sulphates and sodium carbonate accumulate in the upper part of the profile under *H. aphyllum*; alkalinity increases here to give a pH between 8.5 and 9.0 Simultaneously with the excess of soluble salts, more than 50 g m^{-2} of calcium and magnesium carbonates is added annually under *Haloxylon* spp.; up to 18% of calcium and magnesium carbonates accumulates in the crust, and up to 13% in the horizon beneath the crust, whereas in the parent rocks the carbonate content does not exceed 4%. Thus, the biological cycling of the elements leads to an active accumulation of carbonates and other soluble salts in the upper part of an automorphic soil profile. In conditions of extreme dryness the salts accumulated as a result of weathering and biological cycling move downwards very slowly and will in the main be recycled to the surface. Very often lateral movement of salt solutions occurs more intensively than vertical movement.

It is necessary to stress that a considerable part of the biogenic salts contained in plant ash consists of sodium carbonate and bicarbonate. Thus, up to 42 g m^{-2} of sodium and 32 g m^{-2} of potassium may be added annually under *H. aphyllum* by decomposition of plant debris (Bazilevich, Chepurko, Rodin & Miroshnichenko, 1972). Soil alkalinization and sorption of exchangeable sodium on the absorbing complex proceeds intensively. In a surface crust under *H. aphyllum*, from 20% to 45% of exchange capacity is represented by sodium. In such conditions the soil mass is highly dispersed, the clay material becomes mobile, and the upper part of the soil profile is clearly differentiated. Eluvial and illuvial clay horizons are formed; the lower limit of the *B*-horizon is at the depth corresponding to soil wetting.

Biochemical processes in soils

An important role in profile formation in desert soils is played by various biochemical processes. Their activity in arid soils is relatively great during the short periods of seasonal rains. Investigations of arid soils in the Great Basin desert of the United States have shown a sharp difference between the biochemical activity in the surface soil horizon (0–3 cm) and in the rest of the soil mass (Skujinš, 1974).

The cycling of organic matter, depending on processes of biochemical decomposition, reaches a considerable intensity in the surface horizon; the deeper portions of the soil are more inert. Thus, carbon dioxide evolution (soil respiration) from the 0–3 cm horizon is on average two to three times higher than it is in the 5–10 cm horizon, and five times higher than at a depth of 100–200 cm. The surface soil on average loses carbon dioxide at a rate of about 40 μmol g^{-1} min^{-1}. Dehydrogenase activity (which characterizes biological activity as a whole in the soil) is one order of magnitude higher in the surface layer than in the next horizon, and at a depth of 110–130 cm it is hardly perceptible. The same regularities apply in general to proteolytic activity, characterizing the ability of the soil to decompose proteins. On the other hand, phosphatase activity is about the same throughout the whole soil profile. It is noteworthy that the horizon of maximal biological activity (to a depth of 3 cm) does not coincide with

451

the horizon of maximal accumulation of microorganisms (between the depths of 5 and 20 cm). Only algae and lichens have their maximal development in the surface horizon. Biological activity is not dependent on the quantity of microorganisms as determined by methods generally used (Skujinš, 1972, 1974).

Nitrogen turnover has been studied in the arid soils of the Great Basin desert (subtropical brown semi-deserts) (Skujinš, 1975a). Like carbon, nitrogen has a maximal accumulation in the surface horizon of these soils, reaching 0.3%. In lower horizons, its content falls to 0.04%. The maximal nitrogen content in the soil occurs during the wet periods – April–May, and October–November. During the wet months of spring and autumn the nitrogen-containing soil organic matter is rapidly decomposed, and in summer and winter its content in the soil decreases. In the course of litter mineralization the greater part of nitrogen is lost, and less than 10% is converted into ammonium ions. Organic compounds constitute more than 99% of nitrogen; less than 1% is in the form of ammonium and nitrate nitrogen. The maximal content of ammonium nitrogen (at a depth of 0–3 cm) is 104 ppm. This maximum is attained in autumn and in late spring; in early spring and in summer its concentration decreases. The high concentration of ammonium in the autumn is caused by the overall nitrogen input due to fixation of nitrogen by blue-green algae and litter fall. As some of the plants contain allelochemics and exert inhibitory effects on several processes in the nitrogen cycle, a temporary accumulation of ammonium occurs. Eventually, most of the ammonium present is lost by volatilization or by nitrification followed by denitrification (Skujinš, 1975a); some may be fixed by clay particles. The leaching of nitrogen compounds into lower horizons of desert soils is not of great importance because the amount of precipitation is insignificant and depth of moistening limited.

The turnover of nitrogen, and that of other elements to a more limited extent, has been studied by Charley (1968) in desert areas at Broken Hill in south-eastern Australia. The community studied was dominated by *Atriplex vesicaria* Hew. ex Benth., and occurred in a saline desert on subtropical soil. In the first place, nitrogen limits development of the *A. vesicaria* community, through both the total nitrogen content of the soil, and also its rate of cycling. If the nitrogenous nutrition is improved, the transpiration loss by halophytic shrubs per unit of organic matter produced decreases by approximately one-third (Trumble & Woodroffe, 1954).

In a study of soil nitrogen distribution beneath and about a single bush of *Atriplex vesicaria*, it was found that nitrogen withdrawal from surrounding soil had resulted in an addition of approximately 7 g of this element to the soil directly beneath canopy projection, most of it to the top 12 cm of the profile. The extra amount accumulated in the upper 12 cm of soil beneath the canopy represented a 38% increase in nitrogen concentration of this layer.

Soil properties are affected to an important extent not only by the return of nitrogen in litter, but also by the return of calcium and magnesium, promoting the coagulation of soil colloids. The return of sodium is approximately three times greater than that of calcium-plus-magnesium. If the absorbing complex of the soil studied were equal to 0.4 meqg^{-1}, sodium could completely saturate the soil absorbing complex within nine years. But this has not happened, thanks to the influence of calcium and magnesium. Chloride is returned with the litter of *A. vesicaria* to a greater extent than any other ion, but this ion is comparatively little-accumulated in soil; the capillary movement of water transports it laterally to neighbouring areas having more rapid physical evaporation and covered by sparse vegetation or wholly bare.

Litter from halophytic shrubs is decomposed very rapidly, maybe completely during a single year. Oxidation of nitrogen-containing soil organic matter to give nitrates is performed by the microorganisms of the genera *Nitrosomonas*, *Nitrosococcus* and *Nitrobacter*, which are more tolerant of high temperature and lack of moisture than higher plants. It has been established that soil-drying considerably accelerates mineralisation and nitrification when followed by subsequent wetting. The outburst of microbial activity after preliminary soil drying may be explained by partial sterilization, by physiological youth of the surviving microorganisms, by free enzymes in soil, by destruction of inhibiting agents, and by physical change of vegetational debris, which becomes more susceptible to decomposition. Frequent repetition of the drying–wetting cycle leads to the rapid mineralization of nitrogen-containing material. With every cycle, however, less mineral nitrogen is formed, because in the course of decomposition the plant debris become impoverished of readily-decomposed organic nitrogen compounds. Abrupt changes in moistening and drying conditions are particularly characteristic of the surface horizon of arid soils where mineralization is most active and mineral nitrogen accumulates most rapidly.

The peculiar rhythm of precipitation and soil-moistening plays an essential role in nitrogen cycling. Precipitation events ineffective for plant growth are here in question. Desert plants can only use the moisture of precipitation events exceeding 12 mm, after which the surface horizon remains moist for several days. The growth of new roots of *Atriplex vesicaria*, which are involved in the uptake of moisture and nutrient elements, begins only 3–4 days after soil wetting (Cowling, 1969). Microorganisms, on the other hand, are already active several hours after rainfall (Funke & Harris, 1968), so that they are able to use the moisture of 'ineffective' precipitation. Activity of microorganisms in desert soils

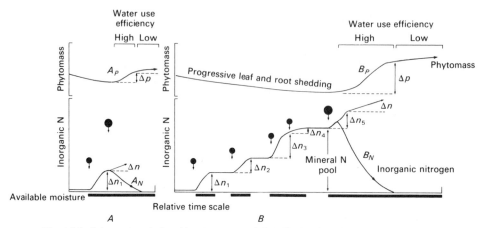

Fig. 17.3. Schematic relationships between rainfall distribution, inorganic nitrogen pool of the soil, and vegetation production efficiency with respect to water use. Key: ●, effective rainfall; ●, ineffective rainfall.

in the absence of nitrogen uptake by plants is thus responsible for accumulation of mineral nitrogen.

On the basis of data concerning nitrogen cycling in an *Atriplex vesicaria* community, Charley (1968) proposes the simple functional process model of Fig. 17.3. Changes in the inorganic nitrogen pool of the soil are shown for two wetting–drying cycles: the first (cycle *A*) is composed of one ineffective and one effective fall of rain, while the second (cycle *B*) is comprised of four ineffective rainfall events and one effective event. Horizontal segments of the curve B_N represent periods when the soil surface is dry and has no available moisture. Curves A_P, B_P and A_N, B_N represent phytomass and inorganic soil nitrogen responses to the *A* and *B* rainfall sequences respectively (circles); Δp and Δn show changes in phytomass and the inorganic nitrogen pool of the soil respectively.

The beginning of sequence *A* reflects the condition when available moisture was absent, the soil-surface dry, and phytomass and mineral nitrogen in the soil decreasing compared with the previous amounts built up during an effective rainfall period. The vegetation does not respond to the first ineffective rainfall and phytomass continues to decrease by leaf- and root-shedding. However, microorganisms respond to this rain almost immediately and their activity leads to a small accumulation of mineral nitrogen in the soil (Δn_1). Subsequently, however, if an effective rain occurs, mineralization continues, but at a somewhat slower rate because the most readily decomposable organic nitrogen has already been mineralized. Then, several days after the effective rain, growth of higher plants begins, at first very rapidly, but more slowly as the mineral nitrogen pool (A_N) is exhausted and they become dependent on the relatively slow rate of background mineralization of resistant organic nitrogen (Δn). As the previously accumulated mineral nitrogen pool was small, the period of rapid growth and high water-use efficiency shown by A_P is short in this cycle.

In sequence B the first ineffective rainfall is followed by further ineffective falls, each of which calls forth an outbreak of microorganism activity and an increase in mineral nitrogen content of the soil if the soil surface has been dry for some time between falls; such dry phases between rains appear to render organic nitrogen more susceptible to mineralization in following wet phases, and the length and temperature of the dry period is significant in this regard. Thus the increment after the fourth ineffective rain of the sequence is minimal as there has been no dry phase between rains to enhance subsequent decomposition of remaining organic nitrogen residues.

During the period of rain ineffective for plants, the foliage and roots continue to die off and nitrogen reserve in the phytomass is reduced. Finally, an effective rainfall event occurs and a significant increase in phytomass and plant nitrogen content begins (B_P). At first this increase is rapid and water-use efficiency high, but afterwards, as the inorganic nitrogen reservoir in the soil is depleted (B_N), the nitrogen nutrition of the vegetation suffers because it becomes dependent on the rate of mineralization of resistant residues. Rate of growth and water-use efficiency decline accordingly.

For a short time after the final effective rain an increase in the mineral nitrogen pool is observed because mineralization is proceeding but the vegetation has yet to begin significant active uptake of nitrogen.

It follows from the suggested model that the total growth increment resulting from a given effective rain should be intimately related to the preceding sequence of rainfall events, not just the rain to which the vegetation is currently responding.

The fate of carbon in soils of arid lands has been the subject of considerably less study. The state of organic matter in soil is reasonably well understood but not the processes of its transformation.

Sparse vegetation cover, low phytomass production, extremely long periods of biological rest, and litter decomposition in oxidizing conditions indicate a low accumulation of humus and nutrient elements (Table 17.5). A high rate of mineralization of plant residues and humus is characteristic. As an index of this process one may use the ratio of reserve carbon in humus to that in roots. In arid soils this ratio in the uppermost horizon does not exceed 3–4:1 (Makhmudova, 1972), whereas in the same layer in chernozem it reaches 25:1. One has every reason to suppose that, in humification of plant debris in desert soils, the most important role is played by actinomycetes, which are adapted better than other organisms to desert conditions (Rybalkina & Kononenko, 1957).

The humus content in desert soils oscillates within the limits of 0.1–0.7%,

Soil processes

Table 17.5. *Nitrogen and phosphorus content in soils of humid and arid regions of Australia.* (Charley & Cowling, 1968)

	Nitrogen		Phosphorus	
Soil	Number of samples	%	Number of samples	ppm
Arid	77	0.06	70	240
Humid	138	0.22	208	620

very seldom reaching 1%. In semi-deserts it is two or three times higher. The ratio of carbon to nitrogen in arid soils is narrow. In grey-brown desert soils of Asia it ranges from 4:1 to 5:1 (Lobova, 1960), in brown semi-desert soils from 8.3:1 to 9.5:1 (Titova, 1972), in the subtropical desert saline soils of Australia from 5:1 to 8:1, gradually decreasing to a depth of 60 cm (Charley & Cowling, 1968). According to the data of Skujinš (1972), in semi-desert soils of the Great Basin (USA) it ranges between 6:1 and 12:1. The value of the carbon:nitrogen ratio decreases from the surface down to a depth of 5–10 cm, then remains uniform to a depth of 1 m, whereafter it increases considerably again. This distribution is explained by the presence in surface horizons of a quantity of undecomposed plant residues, poor in nitrogen as compared with humus. At great depths where biological activity is low, undecomposed roots also poor in nitrogen constitute a considerable proportion of the organic matter. The relatively high nitrogen content in humus of arid soils is explained by the fact that microbial protoplasm forms a large part of the humus.

Humification leads to the formation mainly of low-polymer fractions – that is, fulvic acids. The content of fulvic acids in most arid soils is 3–4 times higher than that of humic acids. A high bitumen content in humus is characteristic of arid soils, this being caused by specific biochemical plant compounds in these regions. Species of the genera *Artemisia* and *Atriplex* contain much oil, wax, resins, volatile oils and other substances enabling the plant to resist temperature fluctuations, deficiencies in moisture, and other unfavourable influences.

Investigations by Ponomareva (1956) have shown that the fulvic acids of desert soils, in comparison with those of steppe soils, have a simpler composition. She was able to separate a fraction of fulvic acid which passes into the anode chamber in electrodialysis, and has a low carbon content (about 40%). Fulvic acids of the arid zone are associated with iron and aluminium to a greater extent than with calcium, in spite of the high calcareousness of the soils. Perhaps this may be due to simplified structure of the fulvic acids.

Pedogenesis in hydromorphic landscapes

As mentioned, there are characteristic active processes of salt accumulation, caused by climate and insufficient drainage, in arid lands throughout the world. Processes of salt movement and accumulation are the main peculiarity of pedogenesis in the deserts. Contemporary processes of evaporation may account for the formation of halomorphic soils and brackish ground-waters in arid areas, but these processes should be considered against a background of more ancient geochemical cycles of easily soluble salts. In the course of millions of years, the geochemical stream of salt solutions is maintained from regions of tectonic uplift to lowland regions through mechanical and chemical redistribution by surface run-off and by lateral movement of underground waters.

The processes of soil salinization are most striking in hydromorphic landscapes of arid lands, where soils are influenced by intensive evaporation of saline underground waters, recharged every year by new inflows carrying new supplies of salts. The salt concentration of subsoil and surface waters is particularly high in extremely arid climates, and reaches striking values of 100, 250, and 300 gl^{-1}. Among the salts, the most soluble ones are most prominent – sodium chloride and sulphate, magnesium chloride and sulphate, and calcium sulphate (Kovda, 1946–7, 1971).

Solonchak formation

Processes in the formation of saline soils, their dynamics and productivity are considered in Kovda's monographs (Kovda, 1937, 1946–7, 1971).

Processes of current salt accumulation in soils and the salt budget of the landscape are determined by the balance of ground-water. The simplest varieties of ground-water balance are the following:

(*a*) the influx is compensated by losses;
(*b*) the influx exceeds losses; or
(*c*) the losses exceed influx.

In the first case the level of ground-waters remains approximately the same; in the second case their level rises; in the third it sinks.

The salt balance of soils is controlled not only by the overall balance of the ground-waters, but, to an even greater degree, by the processes of influx and loss. In natural non-irrigated landscapes, the role and ratio of ground-water outflow, the rate of transpiration and the rate of evaporation are of decisive importance. The outflow of ground-water is accompanied by leaching of salts, and therefore in all cases reduces salt accumulation. Losses of ground-water by evaporation are a main factor in salt accumulation. If the income items of the ground-water balance are compensated

457

by evaporation, there will be a marked salinization of soil and water-bearing horizons, and increasing mineralization of the ground-water. If the capillary fringe reaches the surface, salt accumulation leads to the formation of the most pronounced form of saline soils with a crust or a fluffy saline layer on the surface (so-called 'solonchak').

In extremely arid areas, evaporation of soil waters between the surface and a depth of 0.5–1.0 m reaches 1500 to 2000 mm yr^{-1}. At a depth of 2 m, this value decreases to 100 mm, and at a depth of 3–4 m loss of ground-water by evaporation from the soil surface has practically ceased. In this case, only internal evaporation is possible, in which case the intensity of ground-water evaporation is very low, and can practically be neglected. Under these circumstances, salinization of the solum goes on very slowly. Loss of ground-water by transpiration is a process associated with the production of phytomass. However, transpiration intensifies the general process of increasing the concentration of ground-water and salt accumulation; in this case, however, the accumulation occurs not on the surface, but in the whole of the root zone, and particularly in the capillary fringe from which the plants draw most of their water.

Thus, the most widespread and active factor in the formation of saline soils is the process of evaporation and transpiration of ground-water. Insufficient drainage of the landscape and slow outflow of ground-water is at least as important. Contemporary salt accumulation in deserts may also be due to evaporation of surface, colluvial, sea and irrigation waters. Evaporation leads both to an increase in mineralization and a change in composition of ground-waters. As concentration proceeds, the less soluble compounds precipitate and the content of the most soluble salts in the ground-water increases. At first the solution is saturated with sesquioxides and silica, mixtures of which are deposited following the evaporation of ground-water in soils of all climatic zones, particularly arid zones. Afterwards the ground-water and soil solution become saturated with calcium and magnesium carbonates. They may precipitate within the water-bearing horizon and in the capillary fringe above the ground-water; this process is promoted by increases in temperature. As the solution rises nearer to the surface, calcium bicarbonate is deposited as calcium carbonate. As a result, some soil strata become strongly cemented by lime and silica (hardpan or crust).

The next stage is the saturation of ground-water with gypsum. Gypsum is deposited above the carbonate zone, forming the next salt horizon. After this, solutions enriched with the most soluble compounds – sodium sulphate, chloride and nitrate – reach the soil surface. Such a process of differentiation of soluble substances is observed in lateral movements of ground-water from elevated places to low-lying depressions as well. On a larger scale, regional geochemical differentiation of soluble salts can be observed occurring from the top of hills, along the slopes towards the intracontinental lowlands. The ground waters in this direction become gradually more enriched with highly soluble salts and relatively impoverished of slightly soluble ones. The solutions of chlorides and nitrates reach the lowermost sections of the lowlands.

Salt distribution in relation to micro-relief elements in arid lands is of an opposite type. Strong accumulation of highly mobile salts is observed on micro-elevated spots; micro-inclinations, which are heated and dried more rapidly, play the role of wicks, sucking salt solutions from surrounding areas. Charley & McGarity (1964) have established the interesting fact there is a considerable accumulation of nitrates in the bare, highly saline soils that typically separate the depressions of gilgai micro-relief in arid Australia.

The salt distribution in natural waters of continents is subject to approximately the same regularities in connection with increasing climatic aridity as salt redistribution in internal continental depressions. The drier the climate, the richer in salts are the soils and ground-waters. In groundwaters and salt crusts of arid lands, such salts as carbonates, sulphates, chlorides, nitrates and borates usually accumulate to a considerable extent (Table 17.6).

The composition and dynamics of the soil solution of upper soil horizons in hydromorphic soils of arid lands are determined by annual meteorological conditions, and by the composition and the régime of ground-water. The higher the concentration of salts in ground-water, the higher the concentration of soil solutions. The salt concentration in some areas reaches $400–500 \, \text{gl}^{-1}$. In this case some less-soluble salts saturate the solution and are deposited in a solid phase in the soil. The composition of the soil solution fluctuates considerably during the year. In the rainy period a part of the deposited salts passes back into solution. Decreases of temperature results in precipitation of some salts whose solubility decreases in cold conditions (sodium sulphate and carbonate).

In the solid phase of the soil the less-soluble components (clay minerals, silica compounds, sesquioxides, calcium carbonates, gypsum) accumulate, forming concretions or cemented layers. In arid-climate conditions, accumulated masses of salts, both soluble and slightly soluble, have a tendency to long-term conservation after the ground-waters have disappeared and active salt-accumulation processes have ceased. Thus were created the widespread relict salt and calcareous crusts, and relict salted soils, in great alluvial plains of ancient arid lands.

Surface and river waters, as well as ground-water, play a great role in redistribution and accumulation of salts in soils of arid lands. In absolute deserts, where precipitation does not occur every year, the transportation and redistribution of salts by colluvial waters, small local rivers and

459

Table 17.6. *Salt accumulation in Eurasia in connection with natural conditions*

Landscapes	Average annual rainfall (mm)	Average annual evaporation (mm)	Relative moisture of dry period (%)	Residual salinity of sedimentary deposits	Maximal concentration of ground waters (g l⁻¹)	Maximal amounts of easily soluble salts in solonchaks (g l⁻¹)	The most important salts
Deserts	50–100	2000–2500	20	Common	200–350	25–75	$NaCl$, KNO_3, $NaNO_3$, $MgSO_4$, $CaSO_4$, $CaCl_2$, $MgCl_2$
Semi-deserts	200–300	1000–1500	20–30	Frequent	100–150	5–8	$NaCl$, Na_2SO_4, $CaSO_4$, $MgSO_4$
Steppes	300–450	800–1000	35–45	Rare	50–100	2–3	Na_2SO_4, $NaCl$, Na_2CO_3, $NaHCO_3$
Wood-steppe	350–500	500–800	40–45	Rare	1–3	0.5–1	$NaHCO_3$, Na_2CO_3, Na_2SO_4, Na_2SiO_3

springs, have special importance (deserts of west China, Arabia, Peru, Chile, etc.). After episodic heavy showers, the temporary streams wash away the salt-bearing rocks on the slopes and carry away the dissolved salts together with silt. In the course of long periods of geological time, the influx and evaporation of colluvial solutions provokes the development of saline soils on the lower parts of colluvial plains.

The salt content in the upper horizons of saline soils of extremely arid areas reaches 10–20%, and sometimes 30–75%. Desert soils of west China and Chile are covered by a salt crust which commonly have a thickness of 30–80 cm, and sometimes 3–5 m. These salts consist mainly of chlorides, sulphates and often of nitrates. Sometimes the salt dust forms enormous dunes and barkhans tens of metres high (so-called pseudosand).

If current salt accumulation mainly depends on evaporating groundwater, the role of plant litter in it is insignificant. Thus, if ground-waters occur at a depth of 0.5–1 m, their annual evaporation reaches 10 000 $m^3 ha^{-1}$. As a result the soil may receive 50–100 $t ha^{-1}$ of salts per annum. But the biogenic salt influx to the soils from the litter of halophytes does not exceed 200–500 $kg ha^{-1}$.

The low yield of halophytes on saline soils, sparseness of vegetative cover, and coarse root texture, are the reasons for the slight accumulation of organic matter and biophilic elements. Solonchaks are poor in carbon, nitrogen and phosphorus.

Pedogenesis in the wadis (beds of temporary streams)

Besides the soils receiving supplementary amounts of moisture and material from ground water, in arid lands there are soils formed in shallow flat beds under influence of additional inflow of run-off waters. Some processes characterizing these soils have been studied by Hillel & Tadmor (1962) in the central Negev Highlands of Israel.

Thanks to superficial flow from surrounding areas, the wadis receive several times as much water as the amount of rainfall. The depth of water penetration in the soils of gravelly wadis attains several metres. In soils of coarse texture, however, the moisture reserves in the root zone are very small. The gravelly soils of wadis, therefore, represent dry habitats. The water régime in soils of loessial wadis is considerably more favourable. They are also wetted to a depth of several metres, but moisture reserves during periods of rainfall increase by 400 mm and more. Of this, about 160 mm is available water.

As these areas could receive such additions of moisture several times during the growing season, the whole reserve of available water may amount to 250–500 $mm yr^{-1}$ (Table 17.3). In consequence, wadi soils are covered by a carpet of luxuriant grasses and legumes with numerous

461

shrubs, the roots of which are able to use the deep moisture reserves and continue growth until the late autumn. The soils are clearly of meadow type.

Process of takyr formation

Takyrs are desert soils with a bare, parquet-like surface, broken up by a network of splits into numerous polygonal aggregates. They are typical landscape elements of the deserts of central Asia. Takyr-like formations (claypans) are also found in deserts of Australia, Iran and North Africa.

Takyrs have no higher vegetation. They have on the surface a compact crust horizon 1–8 cm thick, of porous structure, with a scaly horizon beneath. The horizon of salt is located deeper.

Takyrs are situated in the lower parts of piedmont plains, on ancient deltas and on local depressions among sands and low plateaux. The formation of takyrs requires a seasonal flooding of the surface by a thin layer of water, carrying suspended clay material and soluble salts, and also a deep ground-water table.

The processes of takyr formation have been studied by many Soviet investigators (Gerassimov, 1931; Bolyshev, 1955; Bazilevich, Degopic & Krukov, 1956; Kovda *et al.*, 1956). The surface-water régime of takyrs is very peculiar and sharply contrasting. If rains in the mountains of central Asia are greater than 8–9 mm, surface flow of water occurs and extends on to the piedmont plains of the deserts. The volume of run-off is sometimes as much as $25\,000 \text{ m}^3\,\text{km}^{-2}$. In Turkmenia, for instance, during the spring the water on takyr plains forms very shallow temporary lakes, with a water reserve of the order of several millions of cubic metres (Bogdanov, 1954). The salt concentration in the water is most often from $1–2 \text{ g l}^{-1}$; the salts consist mainly of sodium chloride and sulphate. The formation of takyr lakes depends considerably on their low water-infiltration capacity. In early spring, when the surface of the takyr is flooded, the soil gets thoroughly wetted to a depth of 10–40 cm. Because of this shallow infiltration, the major part of the accumulated water evaporates. Precipitation water does not penetrate further than 40 cm, and beyond this depth no moisture is available to plants. In the upper part of the takyr profile, moisture remains available only until the month of April or May. Later, the soil becomes completely dry until the autumn, when new precipitation and surface run-off lead to a new seasonal wetting of the takyr. In the most favourable time of spring, the reserve of available water in the takyr does not exceed 30 mm. In summer, the soil is air-dry.

The salt régime of takyrs is correlated with their moisture régime. Early in the spring a seasonal soil desalinization to a depth of 10–18 cm is observed (in the upper part of the soil there remains not more than 0.4%

of salts, mainly sodium carbonate), and alkalinity is strongly increased (pH increases up to 8.5 or 9.0). In summer, on the contrary, a seasonal salinization of the uppermost horizon takes place with capillary and perched moisture; salts, illuviated during the winter and spring to some depth, return again to the surface. The salt content increases 2 to 3 times compared with spring level; among salts, chlorides are dominant.

The seasonal recurrence of salinization and desalinization processes causes development of alkalinization, peptization, and even solodization of the soil. Colloids are destroyed in the uppermost stratum; their content decreases by a factor of two to three, compared with underlying horizons. Humus becomes highly dispersed; more than half of it enters the colloidal fraction, and is illuviated very actively into the subcrustal *B*-horizon. In the colloidal fraction of the illuvial horizon, alumina, magnesia, and silica accumulate; their content here is 2–5 times as much as in the crust horizon.

Algae play an important part in takyr formation, green algae and diatoms forming a pellicle 2–5 mm in thickness on the surface of the takyr. The algae appear capable of increasing considerably the alkalinity of the takyr crust. It has been experimentally determined that, in the course of five days, the activity of the algae on the surface of the takyr resulted in an increase in titratable alkalinity of the surface water from 0.2 to 2.52 meq l^{-1}; during the day-time, when photosynthetic activity is high, algae increased the pH of surface water from 7.3 up to 9.0 and increased the content of carbonate by more than 2 meq l^{-1} (Fig. 17.4).

The algae are very active in breaking down alumino-silicates in the soil by their biological secretions. After half a year of cultivation of blue-green algae and diatoms on different takyr horizons, the quantity of extractable silica and sesquioxides was several hundred times as much as in the control (Bolyshev, 1968).

Algae also play a part in the formation of the porous crust of the takyr; producing oxygen and consuming carbon dioxide in the process of photosynthesis, they promote change of calcium bicarbonate into carbonate, and the cementation of crusts. Formation of bubbles of oxygen by algae might be the main reason for the porosity of the crust. Probably they are also responsible for the high content of nitrogen in takyr humus.

The pedogenetic role of plants in the process of accumulating humus and mineral elements in takyrs is small. The phyto-biomass reserve on takyrs is not more than 100–300 kg ha^{-1}, which results in an increase in mineral elements of not more than 10–20 kg ha^{-1} yr^{-1}. Salt importation by surface run-on reaches about 1 t ha^{-1}.

The major part of the humus in the takyr is not the product of pedogenesis in the takyr itself, but is brought from the surrounding areas by waters of surface run-off. Characteristic features of this humus are the

463

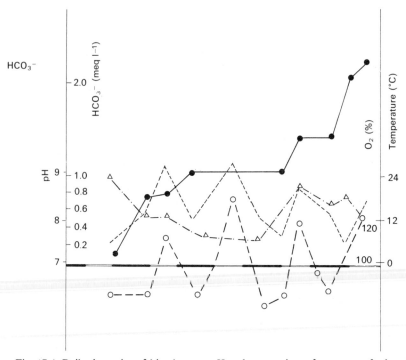

Fig. 17.4. Daily dynamics of bicarbonate, pH and oxygen in surface-water of takyr during the vegetation of algae over the period 29/9–3/10. Symbols: - - - - - -, pH; O– – – –O, O_2; △– · – · – · △, temperature; ●—●, bicarbonate. Dark bars on baseline, night; light bars, day.

dominance of fulvic acids over humic acids (the ratio ranging from 1.5:1 to 5.0:1), simplified structure of humic and fulvic acids (carbon content in the former is 50%, in the latter 40%), and humus enrichment with nitrogen (C:N = 4:7). Total humus content does not exceed 1% in the crust, gradually decreasing down the profile; the ratio of humic and fulvic acids increases, and the carbon:nitrogen ratio becomes narrower (Ponomareva, 1956).

Neoautomorphic landscapes

Formation of solonetz (alkaline soils with structural B-horizon)

Tectonic lifting and erosional dissection of former lowlands leads to sinking of the water table. The factors leading to salt accumulation are excluded, and the salting processes cease completely. In an arid climate, however, the accumulated masses of salts remain in soils and subsoils for a very long time. The desalinization processes of the surface stratum go on very slowly, still depending on the amount of precipitation and natural drainage conditions. For this reason, the desalinization processes are considerably more effective in semi-desert regions which are more humid. If sodium salts predominate among the soluble salts, the process of desalinization is accompanied by a process of alkalinization and afterwards by the formation of solonetz (columnar black alkali) soils. Under the influence of grass vegetation, solonetz soils may be transformed into chestnut and brown steppe soils.

As a rule, chestnut and brown soils have spots of typical solonetz. As classical examples of such semi-desert steppes we may cite the Caspian lowland, and the south Ukraine in Europe, North Kazakhstan in Asia, the Great Basin in North America, and arid regions of Australia. Considerably less solonetz-alkalinization of soil is found in extremely arid desert conditions; still, many soils there show traces of columnar structure, high pH and other solonetz features.

At the beginning of desalinization first the chlorides, being most soluble, then sulphates, and lastly the carbonates of alkalis and alkaline earths are leached. After the more or less considerable quantities of chlorides, sodium sulphate and gypsum have been washed out as a result of alkaline hydrolysis of organic and mineral soil colloids saturated with sodium, the reaction of the solutions becomes much more alkaline (pH reaches 9–9.5). The alkaline reaction, the saturation of the colloids with sodium (20–30% of exchange capacity) and the decrease of the electrolyte content in the soil solution finally cause peptization and mobilization of colloids, their migration downwards through the soil profile, and coagulation there. In the A-horizon, destruction of primary and secondary alumino-silicates takes place. Silica, iron and aluminium oxides are converted into mobile compounds and migrate downwards through the profile, forming the illuvial horizon B.

The migration of silicic acid is particularly active. The content of silica in the form of colloidal associations in the soil solution of the most alkaline horizons (pH 9–10) reaches several hundred milligrams per litre. By conversion of silicic acid into a gel, soil in the B-horizon becomes cemented and impermeable to water roots. In such conditions, neosynthesis of montmorillonite and other minerals with a mobile crystal lattice takes place. The soil profile becomes sharply differentiated. In desalinization of the upper part of the profile, a highly organic A-horizon from 10 cm to 20 cm deep is formed. Below this is located a columnar B-horizon (from 15 cm to 30 cm deep). In the deeper part of the profile, a residual saline horizon remains. This residual salinity within the solonetz subsoil continues for a very long time. Even with very deep ground-waters (deeper than 6–7 m) the profile of a solonetz in a semi-desert climate has a gradient of soil-water suction permitting salinity of the subsoil between the first and third metre of profile to be maintained (Kovda, 1937; Rode & Polski,

Soil processes

1962). This fact results in a slow, but permanent, ascending flow of salt solutions with a capillary fringe. Only after further lowering of the water table below 9–10 m do the processes of salinization gradually cease completely; in any case this does not affect the layer occupied by roots (root penetrability).

The process of formation of steppe soils (steppization)

Cessation of ascending flows, which carry salts upwards, and, in connection with this, colonization by various herbs (grasses and legumes) instead of halophytes, results:

(a) in loss by the soils of salinity and alkalinity features;
(b) in replacement of exchangeable sodium by biogenic exchangeable calcium, magnesium and potassium; and
(c) in the accumulation of humus and the disappearance of a marked B-horizon.

This transformation of solonetz and takyrs into zonal soils of arid lands could be called steppization.

The associations of succulent halophytes characteristic of solonchak are involved in the biological cycling of a great amount of soluble salts, with a comparatively low content of biophilic elements (nitrogen, phosphorus, potassium). The high ash content of these plants, attaining 45–50%, mainly consists of chlorides and in smaller degree of sulphates. Therefore the succulent halophytes maintain the process of salt accumulation, although they are not a principal decisive factor in it.

After the water table sinks, the place of succulent halophytes is taken by semi-halophytic, xerophytic vegetation and *Artemisia* spp. Their ash content is 20–30%, sulphates being dominant in the ash over chlorides; the content of calcium, magnesium and potassium is greater than in typical halophytes. The amount of salts annually involved in biological cycling by communities of semi-halophytes and xerophytes is small in comparison with the succulent halophytes; but the role of the former in maintaining the soil salinity is high, since in the absence of an influence of saline ground-waters they become the principal and only factor supporting salinization.

In the course of further desalinization, and with a deeper water table (to a depth of 10–20 m), grasses, legumes, Compositae, and other steppe plants dominate in the vegetative cover. In these plant groups the content of mineral substances is not higher than 5–7% and of this figure only 0.5% consists of chlorides and sulphates. The sum of calcium, magnesium and potassium is 5–20 times the sodium content. Compared with halophytes the content of silicon, sesquioxides and phosphorus increases abruptly.

466

The biological turnover under the canopy of herbaceous vegetation does not promote the processes either of salinization or of alkalinization. On the contrary, the high content of calcium, magnesium and potassium in the ash of this vegetation promotes a gradual exclusion of exchangeable sodium from the soil absorbing complex, and disappearance of alkalinity (Kovda, 1937).

Furthermore, the developed, ramified, mainly surface root system of grasses is a considerably more powerful influence in the accumulation of humus than the root systems of halophytes and xerophytes. Under the influence of these plants, solonetz soils and takyrs change into neo-automorphic soils: chestnut, brown semi-desert soils, and grey-brown earths of the deserts.

References

Bazilevich, N. I., Degopik, I. Ya. & Kryukov, P. A. (1956). Elementy gidrologicheskogo rezhima i khimizma vod takyrnykh ravnin. In: *Takyry Zapadnoĭ Turkmenii i puti ikh sel'skokhozyaĭstvennogo osvoeniya*, pp. 91–104. Izd-vo AN SSSR. Translated title: Hydrological régime and water chemistry of takyr plains. In: *Takyrs of West Turkmenia and ways of their agricultural mastering*, pp. 91–104. USSR Academy of Science, Moscow. (In Russian.)

Bazilevich, N. I., Chepurko, N. L., Rodin, L. E. & Miroshnichencko, Yu, M. (1972). Biogeokhimiya i produktivnost' chernosaksaul'nikov yugo-vostochnikh Karakumov. *Problemy osvoeniya pustyń*, **5**, 3–9. Translated title: Biogeochemistry and productivity of *Haloxylon aphyllum* communities in South-East Karakum. *Problems of mastering deserts*, **5**, 3–9. (In Russian.)

Bogdanov, V. V. (1954). Vremennyĭ poverkhnostnyĭ stok na takyrakh. In: *Pustyni SSSR i ikh osvoenie*, (T) vol. 2, pp. 408–507. Moscow: Izd-vo AN SSSR. Translated title: Temporary surface run-off on takyrs. In: *Deserts of the USSR and their development*, vol. 2, pp. 488–507. USSR Academy of Science, Moscow. (In Russian.)

Bolyshev, N. N. (1955). *Proiskhozhdenie i evolyutsiya pochv takyrov*, pp. 1–95. Moscow: Izd-vo M.G.U. Translated title: *Origin and evolution of takyr-soils*, pp. 1–95. Moscow University Press, Moscow. (In Russian.)

Bolyshev, N. N. (1968). *Vodorosli i ikh rol' v obrazovarii pochv*. Izd-vo M.G.U. Translated title: *Algae and their role in pedogenesis*. Moscow University Press, Moscow. (In Russian.)

Brown, C. N. (1956). The origin of caliche on the North-Eastern Liano–Estacado, Texas. *Journal of Geology*, **64**, 1–15.

Butzer, K. W. (1959). Naturlandschaft Agyptens während der Vorgeschichte und des dynastischen Zeitalters. *Abhandlungen Akademie der Wissenschaften und der Literatur in Mainz Mathematisk-Naturwissenschaftliche Klasse*, **2**, 43–122.

Charley, J. L. (1968). The role of shrubs in nutrient cycling. In: *Wildland Shrubs – Their Biology and Utilization* (eds. C. M. McKell, J. P. Blaisdell and J. R. Goodin), pp. 182–203, USDA Forest Service General Tech. Report INT-1.

Charley, J. L. & Cowling, S. W. (1968). Changes in soil nutrient status resulting from overgrazing and their consequences in plant communities of semi-arid areas. *Proceedings of the Ecological Society of Australia*, **3**, 28–38.

Soil processes

Charley, J. L. & McGarity, J. W. (1964). High soil-nitrate levels in patterned salt bush communities. *Nature (London)*, **201**, 1351–2.

Cowling. S. W. (1969). 'A study of vegetation activity patterns in a semi-arid environment.' Ph.D. Thesis, University of New England, Australia.

Durand, J. H. (1963). Les croûtes calcaires et gypseuses en Algérie; formation et âge. *Bulletin de la Société Géologique de France, Serie 7*, **5**, 959–68.

Funke, B. E. & Harris, J. O. (1968). Early respiratory responses of soil treated by heat and drying. *Plant & Soil*, **28**, 38–48.

Gerasimov, I. P. (1931). O takyrakh i protsesse takyroobrazovaniya. *Pochvovedenie*, **4**, 5–11. Translated title: About the 'takyrs' and the process of takyr formation. *Pochvovedenie*, **4**, 5–11. (In Russian.)

Gile, L. H. (1967). Soils of an ancient basin floor near Las Cruces, New Mexico. *Soil Science*, **103** (4), 265–76.

Glazovskaya, M. A. (1971). Landshaftno–geokhimicheskie relikty Avstralii. *Vestnik Moskovskogo Gosudarstvennogo Universitata, Seriya geografiya*, **1**, 45–52. Translated title: Landscape–geochemical relicts of Australia. *Vestnik MGU Series Geography*, **1**, 45–52. (In Russian.)

Gunin, P. D., Ishankuliev, M. & Togyzaev, R. (1972). O fitotsenologicheskoĭ slozhnosti vostochnykh Karakumov. In: *Opyt izucheniya i osvoeniya Vostoch nykh Karakumov*, pp. 23–38. Ylym, Ashkhabad. Translated title: About phytocenological complexity of East Karakums, In: *Experiments on the study and development of the East Karakums*, pp. 23–38. Ylym, Ashkhabad. (In Russian.)

Hillel, D. & Tadmor, N. (1962). Water regime and vegetation in the Central Negev Highlands of Israel. *Ecology*, **43** (1), 33–41.

Kaiser, E. (1926). *Die Diamantenwüste Südwest Africas*. Berlin.

Kassas, M. & Imam, M. (1957). Climate and Microclimate in the Cairo desert. *Bulletin de la Société de Géographie d'Egypte*, No. xxx, 25–52.

Khamzin, Kh. V. (1965). Dinamika vlazhnosti pochv osnovnykh rastitel'nykh soobshchestv yugo-zapadnykh Kyzylkumov. In. *Voprosy ratsional'nogo ispol'zovaniya i luchsheniya pustynnykh pastbishch*, pp. 73–80. Nauka, Tashkent, Uz SSR. Translated title: Dynamics of soil water in general plant associations of South-West Kizil-Kum. *Nauka, Tashkent, USSR*. (In Russian.)

Kovda, V. A. (1937). *Solonchaki i solontsy*. Moskva-Leningrad: Izd-vo AN SSSR. *Translated title: Solonchaks and solonetzes*. USSR Academy of Science, Moscow, Leningrad. (In Russian.)

Kovda, V. A. (1946–47). *Proiskhozhdenie i rezhim zasolennykh pochv*, T (vols 1 & 2) Moskva-Leningrad: Izd-vo AN SSSR. Translated title: *Origin and regime of saline soils*, Vols. I & II. USSR Academy of Science, Moscow, Leningrad. (In Russian.)

Kovda, V. A. (1954). *Geokhimiya pustyn' SSSR*. Moskva: Izd-vo AN SSSR. Translated title: Geochemy of deserts of USSR. USSR Academy of Science, Moscow, Leningrad. (In Russian.)

Kovda, V. A. (1971). *Origins of saline soils and their regime*. Israel Programme for Scientific Translations, Washington and Jerusalem.

Kovda, V. A., Letunov, P. A., Zemskiĭ, P. M., Budakova, A. A., Shavrygin, P. I. & Kuznetsova, T. V. (1956). Elementry rezhima vlazhnosti takyrov. In: *Takyry Zapadnoĭ Turkmenii i puti ikh sel'skokhozyaĭstvennogo osvoeniya*, pp. 489–522. Moskva: Izd-vo AN SSSR. Translated title: Elements of moisture regime of takyrs. In: *Takyrs of West Turkmenia and methods for their agricultural development*, pp. 489–522. USSR Academy of Science, Moscow. (In Russian.)

Kulik, N. F. (1963). Nekotorye osobennosti vodnogo rezhima peskov polupustynnoĭ zony. In: *Prirodnye usloviya zhivotnovodstva i kormovaya baza pustyn'*. Ylym: Ashkhabad. Translated title: Some peculiarities of water regime of sands of the semi-desert zone. In: *Natural conditions of cattle-breeding and fodder basis of deserts*. Ylym, Ashkhabad. (In Russian.)

Lobova, E. V. (1960. *Pochvy pustynnoi zony SSSR*. Moskva, Leningrad: Izd-vo AN SSSR. Translated title: *Soils of the desert-zone of USSR*. USSR Academy of Science, Moscow, Leningrad. (In Russian.)

Makhmudova, D. G. (1972). Gumusoobrazova nie v osnovnykh pochvakh pustynnoĭ zony Karshinskoĭ stepi. *Problemy osvoeniya pustyn*, 3, 63–6. Translated title: Humus formation in principal types of the Karshe steppe desert zone. *Problems of mastering Deserts*, 3, 63–6. (In Russian.)

Miller, J. T. & Brown, I. C. (1938). Observations regarding soils of Northern and Central Mexico. *Soil Science*, **46** (6), 427–51.

Owen, H. B. (1954). *Bauxite in Australia*. Commonwealth of Australia. Department of National Development, Bureau of Mineral Resources, Geological and Geophysics Bulletin 24, Canberra.

Paletzkaya, A. N., Lavrov, A. P. & Kogan, Sh.; I. (1958). K voprosu ob obrazovanii poristosti takyrnykh korok. Translated title: To the problem of the formation of porosity in takyr crust. *Pochvovedenie*, 3, 34–41. (In Russian.)

Perelman, A. I. (1959). *Protsessy migratsii soleĭ ne ravninakh Vostochnoĭ Turkmenii i Zapadnogo Uzbekistana v neogene*. Moskva: Izd-vo AN SSSR. Translated title: *Process of salt-migration on the plains of East Turkmenia and West Kazakhstan during Neogene time*. USSR Academy of Science, Moscow. (In Russian.)

Petrov, M. P. (1973). *Pustyni zemnogo shara*. Translated title: *Deserts of the World*. Nauka, Leningrad. (In Russian.)

Ponomareva, V. V. (1956). Gumus takyrov. In: *Takyry Zapadnoĭ Turkmenii i puti ikh sel'skokhozyaĭstvennogo osvoeniya*, pp. 411–39. Moskva: Izd-no AN SSSR. Translated title: *Humus of takyrs of West Turkmenia and ways of their agricultural development*, pp. 411–39. USSR Academy of Science. (In Russian.)

Rybalkina, A. V. & Kononenko, E. V. (1957). Aktivnaya mikroflora pochv. In: *Mikroflora pochv Evropeĭskoĭ chasti SSSR*, pp. 174–248. Moskva: Izd-vo AN SSSR. Translated title: Active microflora of soils. In: *Microflora of Soils of the European part of the USSR*, pp. 174–248. USSR Academy of Science, Nauka, Moscow. (In Russian.)

Rode, A. A. & Pol'ski, M. M. (1962). Vodnyĭ rezhim i balans tsellinnykh pochv solontsovogo kompleksa. Translated title: Water regime of soils of a solonetzic complex. *Pochvovedenie*, 3, 1–15. (In Russian.)

Rozanov, A. N. (1951). *Serozemy Sredneĭ Azii*. Moskva: Izd-vo AN SSSR. Translated title: *Sierozems (grey desert soils) of Middle Asia*. USSR Academy of Science, Moscow. (In Russian.)

Saa, G. (1963). *Captation de agua de la neblina*. Universal del Norte, Filis VCV. Antofagasta.

Skujinš, J. (1972). *Nitrogen dynamics in desert soils*. US/IBP Desert Biome Research Memorandum. RM 72–40.

Soil processes

Skujinš, J. (1974). Dehydrogenase: an indicator of biological activities in arid soils. *Transactions 10th International Congress of Soil Science, Moscow, 1974*, **3**, 101–7. Nauka, Moscow.

Skujinš, J. (1975*a*). Nitrogen cycle in clay-containing cold desert soils. *Transactions 10th International Congress of Soil Science, Moscow, 1974*, **12**. Nauka, Moscow.

Skujinš, J. (1975*b*). *Soil microbiological and biochemical investigations. III. Tunisian Presaharan Project.* Annual Report, 1974. US/IBP Desert Biome. Utah State University Press, Logan.

Stephens, C. G. (1964). Silcretes of Central Australia. *Nature (London)*, **203**, 1407.

Titova, N. A. (1972). Priroda gumusa i formy ego svyazi s mineral'noĭ chast'yu tselinnykh i osvoennykh pochv sukhostepnogo ryada Yugo-Vostoka Evropeĭ skoĭ chasti SSSR. In: *Organicheskoe veshchestro tselinnykh i osvoennykh pochv*, pp. 70–99. Nauka, Moskva. Translated title: Nature of humus and forms of its connections with the mineral part of virgin and developed soils of the dry-steppe series of south-east part of USSR. In. *Organic matter of virgin and developed soils*, pp. 70–99. Nauka, Moscow. (In Russian.)

Trumble, H. C. & Woodroffe, K. (1954). The influence of climatic factors on the reaction of desert shrubs to grazing by sheep. In: *Biology of deserts* (ed. J. L. Cloudsley-Thompson) pp. 129–47. Institute of Biology, London.

United States Department of Agriculture (1970). *Soil taxonomy of the National Cooperative soil survey.* (Selected chapters.) Soil survey conservation service. U.S. Department of Agriculture, Washington, D.C.

Manuscript received by the editors May 1975

470

Plant processes

18. Introduction

R. K. GUPTA

Ecosystems of the arid lands are characterized by variations of rainfall both in time and space, high extremes of temperatures and wind velocity, and low plant and animal production. While temperature, solar radiation and soil nutrient inputs to the ecosystem are fairly continuous over the years, the precipitation usually comes in discrete and discontinuous packages. From the foregoing description of the atmospheric processes, it is clear that the inputs driving the ecosystem come in pulses of very short duration relative to the periods of zero input between them. It is only during these periods that life, both of plants and of animals, is activated. Thus, these systems are primarily water-controlled systems (Noy-Meir, 1973).

Plants are capable of fixing solar energy, along with carbon dioxide and water, so as to produce the plant and animal proteins so vital for human nutrition. In spite of the abundance in the arid lands of sunshine and space for cropping, agricultural production is limited by the availability of soil moisture. Superimposed on this situation is mismanagement and over-exploitation of the land resources relative to their carrying capacity. The trends in the growth of animal and plant populations during the past few decades have shown that, in the arid lands, over-exploitation is at least as prevalent as in other biomes where conditions of climate and soil are far more favourable for high production. For proper utilization and management of land resources in arid lands, it is essential to understand the various processes involved which govern the ecosystems. Particularly in arid lands, the environment being relatively hostile, it is of prime importance to understand the processes by which the plants adapt themselves to the rigours of the arid environment.

It may be worth pointing out here that farmers in the arid zone, during periods of good rainfall, as in many other regions save and store food grains whenever there is a good harvest to cover the risk of adverse climatic conditions. The farmer has to depend for requirements of fodder, fuel, fibre and other items on the natural ecosystems. Perhaps this has a strong bearing on environmental degradation, particularly in arid lands where the resources are limited and have deteriorated with increased demand. It is evident that many of the arid lands enjoyed a high level of civilization and culture in the past, and that present conditions were caused by over-exploitation of both renewable and non-renewable resources in those regions. The role of natural ecosystems for sustained productivity over

473

long periods could be understood if adequate attention were paid to these lands in future programmes of research.

Work under the International Biological Programme constituted a beginning for such research. During the IBP, observations on key ecological processes (runoff, soil moisture dynamics, plant water-use dynamics, efficiency of water use, animal consumption), were performed at a number of sites. Simulation models were built which attempted to use climatic data, together with the known state of the system at a fixed point in time, to predict changes in soil moisture, and plant and animal productivity. The data from the IBP sites are being used to test and improve such models. Once reliable prediction is achieved, the models may be used to predict production in other sites.

The reviews in this Section are aimed at integrating studies of plant processes under the IBP with research outside it and with previously existing knowledge, to provide a basis for understanding the role of plant processes in the dynamics of arid-land ecosystems as a whole, and hence contribute to the management of such ecosystems.

In this Section, the various plant processes, from seed dormancy, germination and establishment, through the activities of the established growing plant (photosynthesis, respiration, water and ionic uptake, translocation, and vegetative growth), to reproduction, together with litter fall and death, are surveyed in sequence. Each chapter includes information on the nature of the processes, factors affecting their rates and the form of relations between them, with special emphasis on new knowledge obtained during the IBP period, though knowledge of these processes prior to 1967 as background information has not been excluded. Attempts have been made to pinpoint the gaps in our knowledge of these processes. Co-ordination in these studies has been achieved mainly through the co-operation of the various Chapter authors among themselves and with scientists of different disciplines from various countries.

From the various chapters contributed in this section on plant processes, it is evident that very little information is available from the arid regions of developing nations such as the Indo-Pakistan subcontinent, African and Latin American countries. Most of the examples cited by the authors describing the different plant processes relate mainly to Australian or North American deserts, while a few come from the Middle East and erstwhile French Colonial countries. In the developing countries the most urgent concern today is with agricultural production for food, fodder, fibre, fuel etc., and not much attention has been paid in their research programmes to the study of natural ecosystems. As might be expected, much of the research effort is directed towards crop improvement in agro-ecosystems in the strict sense. Nevertheless, natural ecosystems, though they do not find a prominent place in the research programmes of some of the developing countries, are of fundamental importance from the viewpoint of soil and water conservation, and the management of natural environment and land resources. This situation is being increasingly appreciated. It is hoped that these systems will receive adequate attention in addition to agro-ecosystems if the basic concepts of land capability, and sustained economic returns from the land, are of any value.

I am grateful to all the authors who have responded to our invitations to contribute chapters regarding different aspects of plant process studies.

Reference

Noy-Meir, I. (1973). Desert ecosystems: environment and producers. *Annual Review of Ecology and Systematics*, **4**, 25–52.

Manuscript received by the editors May 1975

19. Germination and seedling behavior of desert plants

F. W. WENT

Basically, the seed is a structure for reproduction. This is true both for annual plants and perennials. But for annuals seeds are the *only* mechanism by which they survive the inclement winter or drought season; in perennials survival depends mainly on the vegetative state and seeds are only a subsidiary method of reproduction. This means that in the case of annuals we should look upon seeds not primarily as *dispersal* units, but as *survival* units, and that the problem of seed *germination* is absolutely central to the existence of annual plants. If we add to this that, the more arid a climate is, the larger is the proportion of annuals in the vegetation, then we see that in deserts germination and seedling survival are among the most important elements in understanding the vegetation and describing the ecosystem.

The growing season in the desert is restricted to a short period during which sufficient moisture is available; consequently germination of seeds is also severely restricted by many different types of germination control, such as dormancy, hardseededness, or the need for scarification, heat and cold treatments, or leaching. Another consequence of the reproduction of annuals solely by seed is that 'the final floristic composition of the (desert) vegetation is controlled by seed germination' (Batanouny, 1965). This means the germination behavior of plants is basic to an understanding of desert vegetation.

Considering the significance of germination control in desert plants, the following quotation can be taken from Koller (1969): 'The survival value of seed dormancy may be evaluated by at least the two following criteria. A regulatory mechanism should be one which prevents germination from taking place in an unfavourable environment, without impairing viability of the seed and its capacity to germinate subsequently, under the proper circumstances. A more difficult criterion to determine is the actual reduction in survival potential which would be incurred in a species which is well adapted to a certain habitat, by eliminating from its genetical complement the germination-regulating mechanism being studied. Should it be possible to produce such mutants, it would be advisable to remember that they should be tested not under the average environmental conditions of the habitat, but under the most extreme which may be encountered in it, even at intervals of several years.'

477

Plant processes

Germination

A very complete review on seed germination in general was provided by Koller (1972), and the present paper will only try to add a few reviews of recent papers on germination in desert environment, and especially some work carried out under IBP auspices.

The most important publication about germination and development of desert plants which appeared in the last decade is the book by Evenari, Shanan & Tadmor (1971). This book deals with a particular desert, the Negev in southern Israel. It consists largely of a description of pre-Christian agriculture in an area of low rainfall (about 100 mm yr^{-1}), until recently almost completely disregarded as an agricultural possibility. Archeological, botanical and agricultural research by Evenari and his colleagues has shown that, by application of age-old methods of collection of run-off rainwater in appropriate catchment basins, annual crops and fruit trees can be grown in such low-rainfall areas without additional irrigation water.

In the course of this archeo-agricultural research, Evenari collected a wealth of information on germination of the native flora (Evenari *et al.*, 1971, pp. 261–263, 269, 273, 281–291), completing his own and Koller's work in this particular desert. Let me quote from p. 261: 'Perhaps the most exciting aspect of our biological desert research had been the discovery, step by step, of the full harmony between environment and germination behavior. For a number of years we recorded in detail the life cycles of most of the plants belonging to the three main dwarf-shrub associations. This included counting and measuring seed germination, seedling growth, mortality, and survival for a number of years in 1-meter-square observation plots. Some plots received varying amounts of artificial irrigation, especially in the summer season, imitating supplemental and unseasonal rain. However, this artificial rain did not induce the germination of even one single seed of shrubs, dwarf shrubs, or any other desert plant, even when the irrigation was quite considerable.' *Artemisia herba-alba* Asso 'cannot be fooled by unnatural summer rains'. Whereas in years with good summer rains (1964 and 1965) germination was abundant, and most seedlings survived, in the worst drought year (1963) not one *Artemisia* seed germinated. 'All the other desert dwarf shrubs behaved in a similar manner.'

This germination and seedling-survival behavior of shrubs should result in very definite age groups in nature. This is clearly true in all deserts, and was proven in the case of *Zygophyllum dumosum* Boiss., of which all plants in two areas of the Negev desert belonged to eight or ten groups covering a 57-year period.

The germination behavior of biennial (or biseasonal, as Evenari calls them) desert plants, especially of *Salsola inermis* Forssk., differs radically

478

from that of the desert shrubs described above. In 1965, a year with abundant rains, they germinated in great numbers, but not a single seedling survived the following summer drought, whereas all seedlings which developed in the previous drought year survived.

Seed dispersal

Among annuals, Evenari *et al.* (1971) describe the germination behavior of *Gymnarrhena micrantha* Desf., a composite studied in detail by Koller & Roth (1964). This is a typical example of a plant with antitelechoric behavior, in which seeds have a mechanism preventing their dispersal. The mother plant produces two kinds of flowers: subterranean and above-ground. The seeds produced in the subterranean flower are larger and are not dispersed by wind, as are the achenes from the above-ground flowers. Thus they germinate after rain inside the dead mother plant. Their seedlings are much more drought-resistant, and grow into larger plants. They have the advantage that the mother plant has already prepared with her taproot a channel in the soil through which rainwater penetrates more easily and which can be used by the daughter plant for its roots.

I would like to interject here some observations of my own on an American desert annual, *Chorizanthe rigida* (Torr.) T. & G. Just before this polygonaceous species matures, all its tissues, from roots and stems to fruits, become lignified. Since its involucres are very spiny, it becomes very painful to handle, and its complete lignification keeps the plant from disintegration. Thus most of its woody involucres, each containing one seed, remain attached to the mother plant, and the seeds will not germinate because they are firmly enclosed in the woody involucre. In the course of two to three years, or rather several rainy periods, the lignified involucres, stems, and roots are attacked by fungi, and partially disintegrate. The enclosed seeds will then germinate, and the old disintegrating plants will become surrounded by *Chorizanthe rigida* seedlings, many of them following the old taproot with their own roots. The fungi living on the decaying woody roots of the mother plant connect with the roots of the young plants to act as their root-hairs.

In many other desert plants we find seed heteroblasty and antitelechoric mechanisms. An interesting case is that of *Aegilops ovata* emend. Willd., described by Datta, Evenari & Gutterman (1970) and Datta, Gutterman & Evenari (1972). In wild wheat there is an enormous spread in caryopsis weight depending on its location in the spikelet. The more basal caryopses are much heavier than the more apical ones (by a factor of 6). The caryopsis weight is slightly correlated with the weight of the daughter plant developing from it; the smallest caryopses germinate poorly, especially when the mother plants were grown under cool conditions. Of special

479

importance for the survival of the species is that the caryopses within the individual spikelets differ very much in their germinability, and that the smaller caryopses germinate very much later than the bigger ones. Therefore no single germination event causes all seeds to produce plants, and a reserve of viable seeds always remains after a period of major germination.

Quite different again is the germination behavior of *Blepharis persica* (Burm. f.) Ktze (Gutterman, Witztum & Evenari, 1967, 1969), a desert species of the Acanthaceae which ejects its seeds with jaculators, after water has penetrated through the apex of the capsule. After the seeds are wetted the hairs of their coat swell, lifting the seed to the right position for root penetration into the soil.

Root systems of seedlings

As Evenari *et al.* (1971) have shown for annuals in the Negev desert (see their Figure 175), and as Kooper (1927) has described for annuals developing during the dry season in Java, their seedlings produce only very small and scanty root systems. This is very different from shrub seedlings, which usually during the first months of growth produce taproots five to ten times as long as their shoots. The root systems of the annuals investigated by Kooper increased by a factor of four during the wet season. In the North American deserts too, the roots of winter annuals penetrate 5 cm or slightly deeper, with only a dozen or fewer lateral rootlets, and usually few or no root-hairs. Yet these rootlets have a well-developed rhizosphere, where a network of hyphae surrounds them. The hyphae belong to a much larger mycelium which penetrates all through the desert soil, consisting of predominantly dark-colored hyphae, the mycelia either being sterile, or producing dictyospores (*Ulocladium*) or pycnidia (*Phoma* and *Macroventuria*) in culture. The hyphae of these mycelia surround all sand grains and are the major force causing cohesion of the desert soil (Went & Stark, 1968). They may also bring water from the deeper soil layers to the superficial roots of the small seedlings and annuals. When an upper layer of desert soil 5–10 cm thick is lifted off with the roots of the annuals largely intact, these annuals wilt within a few hours, indicating that their water supply is cut off. Although part of this water transport may pass through individual hyphae, probably most moves through rhizomorphs or hyphal bundles, which are very common in desert soils, even though fruiting bodies of these fungi are rare (Went, 1973).

Seedling populations and seed production

Germination in the desert occurs mainly after rains of 25 mm or more (Went, 1949; Soriano, 1953; Juhren, Went & Phillips, 1956), although in the Negev desert dew seems to be a sufficient water supply for a number of summer germinators. After initial germination a number of seedlings (5%–50%) die when their position in the soil prevents their roots from penetrating sufficiently to absorb moisture (Went, 1973). A relatively small number are removed by herbivores; this removal becomes important only after the seedlings have reached an edible size, or when they have proceeded from the rosette to the erect state (for instance, *Atrichoseris platyphylla* Gray). There is no indication that any seedlings of annuals die because of interspecific or intraspecific competition (Went, 1973). On the contrary, all seedlings in a particular area grow at the same rate and form a remarkably even stand.

Under extreme desert conditions, such as in the center of Death Valley, with an annual rainfall of 43 mm, there is little plant growth. In most years there is barely enough rain for very limited germination of annuals only, and these produce only just enough seeds to replace those that germinated (Went, 1973). But in adjoining deserts with higher rainfall (100 mm or over), seed production per plant is much greater. On an average each germinated seed there produced 10–20 viable seeds (Went, 1973).

The viability of those seeds can be tested only if their germination controls are known. This was tested specifically for a number of Death Valley plants after a poor growing season, and only a number of *Cryptantha* species had about 100% germinability, with lower percentages for others. When seeds have ripened early in the season, before temperatures have risen to 40 °C, their viability is high (e.g. in *Geraea canescens* (Torr.) T. & G.).

Seed reserves in soil

In a very interesting series of studies, Goodall and his co-workers (Goodall, Childs & Wiebe, 1972; Childs & Goodall, 1973; Goodall & Morgan, 1974) have counted the seed reserves in soils of North American deserts. The seeds were separated by sieve, by flotation liquids (specifically, a solution of potassium carbonate with a density of 1.6), and finally by eye; the recovery was 80–100% for most species. There was considerable difference in the depth at which these seeds were found. Whereas many seeds were concentrated on the surface (such as *Agropyron cristatum* Gaertn., *Bromus tectorum* L., and other grasses with long glumes), other seeds were predominantly found 1–2 cm deep (for instance, *Camelina microcarpa* Andrz. in the Great Basin, *Festuca octoflora* Walt. in the

481

Plant processes

Mohave, and *Descurainia pinnata* (Walt.) Britton in the Chihuahuan Desert) or deeper (e.g. *Polygonum douglasii* in the Great Basin, *Astragalus nuttallianus* DC. in the Sonoran and *Chenopodium* sp. in the Chihuahuan). This seems to be a function of the size of the seed, with the smallest seeds predominating in the deeper soil layers. At the 37 sites in Curlew Valley (in the northern part of the Great Basin desert, better described as steppe) the number of seeds of the commoner plants varied from 2 to 100 dm^{-2}. A weighted average for the Mohave Desert sites sampled (in Rock Valley, Nevada) shows a total seed population of 4.3 seeds dm^{-2}; the corresponding figure for the Sonoran Desert sites was 331, and those for three areas in the Chihuahuan Desert were 13.8, 229 and 395 seeds dm^{-2}. This is typical for the number of seeds present in deserts, as determined by germination tests carried out by Went and his collaborators in Death Valley in the northern Mohave, and the Joshua Tree National Monument in the southern Mohave desert. After adequate rain most of the viable seeds will germinate, and the number of seedlings varies from 1 to 500 dm^{-2}.

That, after a rainfall of 25 mm or more, most of the viable seeds present in the desert will germinate is shown in the first place by the observation that a second rainfall of 25 mm, occurring before the seedlings of the first rain have produced seeds, results in very limited further germination, or none at all. In an unpublished experiment I watered artificially 30 plots in the Las Vegas area, in a winter with hardly any natural rain. Germination was fair on the plots which received 100 mm of artificial rain (35.2 seedlings per plot), and poor on the plots which had less than 30 mm artificial precipitation (3.5 plants per plot only). In the former plots most seeds present had germinated, for the rain in the succeeding year brought out only 1.7 seedlings, whereas the plots with low 'precipitation' and poor germination produced 4.3 seedlings the following year.

Seedling behavior

The most extensive work on seed germination and seedling survival anywhere was carried out by Beatley (1967, 1974*b*). She worked in the northern Mohave desert on or around the Nevada Nuclear Test Site for a 10-year period, and established and checked about 100 plots, each with its rain gauge, which enabled her to correlate rainfall with subsequent germination and seedling growth. After a heavy September rain (40–50 mm) in 1963 a number of winter annuals germinated, but survival was poor (less than 40%) in spite of another 25 mm rain during their stage of vegetative growth. On the same site, rains totalling 85 mm during the spring of 1965 caused a comparable degree of germination, with a much higher survival percentage (60%).

Mortality of the seedlings was seldom due to browsing, and occurred

482

usually in the early stages of growth, before stem elongation had started. Beatley believes that most of the seedling mortality was due to insufficient water in the soil.

In another paper Beatley (1974b) summarizes her ten years of work with annuals on the Nuclear Test Site. In accordance with the predominantly autumn and winter rains of this area, there is practically no mention of summer germinators, so common in the southern parts of the Mohave Desert, and in Arizona and New Mexico. In a complicated flow diagram summarizing her observations she shows that all rains of more than 25 mm in October and November result in flowering and fruiting of annuals, whether or not followed by further rain during the winter, whereas less than 25 mm in autumn, followed by less than 25 mm of rain later in the winter season, produces essentially no growth of annuals.

The situation Beatley describes differs from that in Death Valley, where September and October rains of 25 mm induce germination of perennials like *Larrea tridentata* Cov. *Franseria dumosa* Gray and *Tidestroemia oblongifolia* Standl. and of annuals like *Chorizantha rigida*, *Oenothera clavaeformis* T. & F., and *Geraea canescens* T. & G., but not of *Gilia* spp., *Monoptilon bellioides* Hall or *Nemacladus* spp. which need late-autumn rains for germination.

Seed viability

Very little is known about retention of viability of seed under natural desert conditions. Therefore a study by Winkworth (1971) is of interest. He buried hundreds of batches of seeds of *Cenchrus ciliaris* L. (an annual grass) in the central Australian desert near Alice Springs, and tested them for germinability over a five-year period. Whereas seed in laboratory storage increased in germinability, under desert conditions germination decreased in a two-year period to about 10%, more than sufficient for establishment of the species after appropriate rains. Both in the desert and the laboratory, germination of recently harvested and consequently dormant seed increased sharply over a one-year period.

Under completely dry storage conditions (in vacuum) there was no decrease in viability of seeds over a 20-year period. When stored under room conditions (20%–50% r.h.) the same seeds lost their germinability almost completely in 10 years; seeds from plants from the most arid regions retained their viability for the longest period (Went, 1969).

The germination behavior of a number of annual plants from the Kyzyl-kum (a desert in west-central Asia) was investigated by Shatskaya (1973). All of them were largely or completely dormant upon collection. Their dormancy had worn off in six months, faster at a storage temperature of 50 °C–60 °C than at 18 °C–24 °C. All of them are winter annuals; consequently many of them germinated poorly in summer in the germination tests. These low-temperature germinators were: *Taeniatherum crinitum* (Schreb.) Nevski, *Cerastium inflatum* Link in Desf., *Silene conica* L., *Drabopsis verna* C. Koch, *Heteranthelium piliferum* Hochst. ex Jaub & Spach, *Bromus* spp, and *Malcolmia africana* (L.) R.Br. in Ait. Some other winter annuals germinated well even under high temperatures, such as *Aegilops* spp. and *Poa bulbosa* L.

Much ecological work on desert plants has been carried out under the auspices of the US Atomic Energy Commission at the Nevada Test Site in the southwestern United States; this research has been summarized by Wallace & Romney (1972).

Seeds and seedlings of many desert shrubs were subjected to gamma radiation from a radiocobalt (^{60}Co) source; as expected, seedlings were more sensitive than seeds. Seedlings with large nuclei (*Artemisia tridentata* Nutt., *Lycium andersoni* Gray and *Yucca schidigera* Roezl) were far more sensitive to gamma radiation than those with smaller nuclei (*Larrea tridentata* or *Franseria dumosa*). Unfortunately the nuclear volume data as reported on p. 48 differ radically from those reported on p. 397 of the same report, making the interpretation somewhat questionable.

Most desert perennial and shrub species showed fair germination in the laboratory without special treatments, with only a few needing chilling or scarification.

The viability of seeds can of course best be determined by direct germination tests. These may give misleading results if the seeds are dormant, and can germinate only after scarification, stratification, leaching, after-ripening, heat treatment or other means. In most cases the germination restraints are located in the seed-coat, and removal of the seed-coat causes immediate development of the embryos. With the seeds of desert plants, which have so many mechanisms to prevent premature germination (Koller, 1969) seed-coat removal is probably the simplest method of establishing viability. A frequently-used test for seed viability is the tetrazolium method (Porter, Durrell & Romm, 1947), in which the viable embryos are stained when placed in a dilute solution of 2,3,5-triphenyl-tetrazolium chloride.

An extensive and excellent study of seed viability of arid-zone plants was recently conducted by Mott (1972). In a general study of annual plants in the arid zone of Western Australia, Mott studied seed dormancy, germination, and early establishment of annuals. Field and laboratory tests were correlated, and the existence of two distinct floras of annuals was connected with low and high temperatures following rains. Grasses, like the genera *Aristida*, *Eriachne* and *Eragrostis*, which produce a late-summer vegetation, germinated predominantly at 25 °C–30 °C, whereas dicotyledons, like the genera *Crassula*, *Calandrinia*, *Helichrysum*, and *Helip-*

terum, common as spring annuals, germinated best at 15 °C–20 °C. This agrees closely with my own observations in the laboratory and in southern California deserts, where summer annuals (*Pectis papposa* Harv. & Gray, *Amaranthus fimbriatus* and grasses like *Bouteloua* spp. and *Aristida* sp.) germinated at high temperatures (26 °C), and winter annuals (*Calandrinia ambigua* Howell, *Gilia* spp., *Plantago insularis* Eastw.) germinated at 17 °C or lower (Went, 1949). Mott (1972) established that seeds of these Western Australian annuals were all dormant immediately after ripening, but germinated well after a storage period of from one to several months. For a detailed study of germination behavior and seed dormancy, Mott selected field-collected seed of the summer annual *Aristida contorta* F. Muell. and the spring annuals *Helipterum craspedioides* W. V. Fitzg. and *Helichrysum cassinianum* Gaudich. The optimum germination temperature for *A. contorta* was 30 °C in light, for *H. craspedioides* it was 15 °C in light, and for *H. cassinianum* 20 °C both in light and darkness. This meant that only the latter species germinated when its seeds were buried 1 cm deep; the others did not germinate but retained much of their viability while buried. Mott found that the surface quality of the seeds had a significant effect on their germination. 'The copious mucilage produced by the seed coat of *Helichrysum* on wetting, and the long epidermal hairs of *Helichrysum* seed, both increase the seed–soil contact, enabling better water uptake, as well as anchoring the seed.'

These Australian desert annuals have few or none of the polymorphic seed characters as described by Zohary (1937) or Evenari *et al.* (1971) for the Near-East annual flora, very much like their absence in the deserts of south-western North America. And similarly, little viable seed remained in the soil after optimal germination conditions occurred. In his biochemical studies Mott found that the absolute requirement for oxygen in his seeds may be due to a diffusion barrier, and not to removal of an inhibitor.

The role of animals

It has been established that, over an 8-year period of observation of fifteen desert plots, there is a tenfold to twentyfold increase in the number of viable seeds after each germination event (Went, 1973). Under ideal growing conditions a desert plant produces far more than ten to twenty viable seeds, as shown by Abdel Rahman & Batanouny (1959). Disregarding the seedlings which did not become established for one reason or another, they found in the Egyptian desert along the Cairo–Suez road that seed production ranged from 40 seeds per plant up to 70 000. I, myself, found that there was no decrease in viability of seeds under the dry desert conditions, and there were no indications of their disappearance by rotting or other microbial or biochemical means. Nor do they disappear by germination and subsequent death of the seedlings. Since there is no accumulation of viable seeds on the desert floor, these seeds must disappear in some other way. This is by collection and digestion by rodents, harvester ants, and birds, and to a very limited extent by lizards (in whose stomachs desert plant seeds are found).

Chew & Butterworth (1964) and Mauer (1967) produced valuable information about the role of rodents in the desert ecosystem, and Tevis (1958), Whitford (1973), and Went, Wheeler & Wheeler (1972) published information about the role of ants in desert energy flow. In good seed years ants remove only a small proportion of all available seeds. But both rodent and ant populations fluctuate greatly from year to year. Whitford (1973) found that, in a good seed year, harvester ants in New Mexico had a small impact on seed reserves in general, but some species such as *Eriogonum trichopes* Torr. and *Bouteloua barbata* Lag. were significantly affected.

Mauer (1967) did much live-trapping of seed-eating rodents in California in the Deep Canyon and Death Valley areas, studying cheek-pouch contents of kangaroo rats (*Dipodomys* spp.) and pocket mice (*Perognathus* spp.). They collected apparently indiscriminately all seeds available and easily digestible (not *Franseria dumosa* or *Chorizantha rigida*, preferred by ants). Yet the seed caches of these rodents, which they make in years of abundant seed production, contain only one single species of seeds, such as *Plantago insularis*. Mauer found that in spring during their reproductive season seed-eaters also collected herbage as well as seeds.

Germination conditions and dormancy

In addition to the specific information on germination of desert seeds discussed thus far, there are many other facts which should be recorded. Batanouny & Ziegler (1971a, 1971b, 1972) have investigated the Egyptian species *Zygophyllum coccineum* L. in much detail. Light inhibition can be largely overcome by kinetin at a concentration of 5×10^{-5} M or higher; it is restored by abscisic acid. This suggests that a germination inhibitor related to abscisic acid is involved in the light inhibition, especially since the seeds germinate better after soaking. Once germinated, the seeds cannot stand redrying. But when the seeds are kept moist at temperatures too low (4 °C) or too high (40 °C) for germination, they will sprout as soon as they are brought to 25 °C. This is quite generally true. For this reason seeds can remain dormant for many seasons even while moist, provided temperature or other conditions prevent germination. But once germinated they have lost all resistance against drought. This is true not only for desert seeds, but also for seeds from plants from temperate regions. Thus, weed seeds prevented from germinating by being buried too deep may retain

486

their viability for scores of years. A desert seed which has seed inhibitors is *Zilla spinosa* (Turra) Prantl (Batanouny, Lendzian & Ziegler, 1972). Extracts made of them inhibit not only *Zilla spinosa* but also *Lepidium sativum* L. In addition the *Zilla spinosa* seeds contain germination stimulators. As the seeds become older the inhibitor activity decreases; at the same time the mechanical strength of the seedcoat decreases (through abrasion and microbiological activity?). This is interpreted by the authors as providing a better chance for survival of the seedlings, which in time become better anchored in the soil.

In an article by Sankari & Barbour (1972), the germination behavior of *Salsola vermiculata* L., a perennial forage plant from the Middle East and North Africa, was studied. In nature the seeds mature in autumn, and can germinate immediately after autumn rains, when the temperatures (12 °C–18 °C) are optimal for germination. But with its very wide range of effective germination conditions the occurrence of this plant seems to be in no way limited by its germination behavior.

The germination and seedling behavior of the commonest desert shrub of the North American deserts, *Larrea tridentata*, has been the subject of several investigations (Barbour, 1968; Sheps, 1973; Beatley, 1974a). It requires high temperatures for germination, and therefore is found as seedlings only after summer rains. The seeds either do not germinate or soon die when in the vicinity of established shrubs of the same species; this is *not* due to competition for water (Sheps, 1973). Early growth is definitely stimulated by the presence of organic matter in the soil. Beatley found that at the limits of the distribution range of *L. tridentata* the viability of seed was positively correlated with rainfall in a dry year (1963) but negatively in a wet year (1965).

References

Abdel Rahman, A. A. & Batanouny, K. H. (1959). Germination of desert plants under different environmental conditions. *Bulletin de l'Institut du Désert*, **9**, 21–40.

Barbour, M. G. (1968). Germination requirements of the desert shrub *Larrea divaricata*. *Ecology*, **49**, 915–23.

Batanouny, K. H. (1965). *Germination and plant cover in different microhabitats in Wadi Hoff*. Bulletin No. 39, Faculty of Science, Cairo University.

Batanouny, K. H. & Ziegler, H. (1971a). Ecophysiological Studies on Desert Plants. II. Germination of *Zygophyllum coccineum* L. seeds under different conditions. *Oecologia*, **8**, 52–63.

Batanouny, K. H. & Ziegler, H. (1971b). Eco-Physiological Studies on Desert Plants. III. Respiration of negatively photoblastic *Zygophyllum coccineum* L. seeds during germination. *Oecologia*, **8**, 64–77.

Batanouny, K. H. & Ziegler, H. (1972). Oekophysiologische Untersuchungen an Wüstenpflanzen. IV. Die Wirkung von Kinetin und Abscisinsäure auf die

Plant processes

Keimung der negativ photoblastischen Samen von *Zygophyllum coccineum* L. *Biochemie und Physiologie der Pflanzen*, **163**, 241–9.

Batanouny, K. H., Lendzian, K. & Ziegler, H. (1972). Oekophysiologische Untersuchungen an Wüstenpflanzen. VI. Hemmstoffe für Keimung und Wachstum in den Früchten von *Zilla spinosa* Prantl. *Oecologia*, **9**, 12–22.

Beatley, J. C. (1967). Survival of winter annuals in the Northern Mojave desert. *Ecology*, **48**, 745–50.

Beatley, J. C. (1974). Effects of rainfall and temperature on the distribution and behavior of *Larrea tridentata* (creosote-bush) in the Mojave Desert of Nevada. *Ecology*, **55**, 245–61.

Beatley, J. C. (1974*b*). Phenological events and their environmental triggers in Mojave desert ecosystems. *Ecology*, **55**, 856–63.

Chew, R. M. & Butterworth, B. B. (1964). Ecology of rodents in Indian Cove (Mojave Desert) Joshua Tree National Monument, Calif. *Journal of Mammalogy*, **45**, 203–25.

Childs, S. & Goodall, D. W. (1973). *Seed reserves of desert soils*. US/IBP Desert Biome Research Memorandum RM 73–5. Logan, Utah.

Datta, S. C., Evenari, S. C. & Gutterman, Y. (1970). The heteroblasty of *Aegilops ovata*. *Israel Journal of Botany*, **19**, 463–83.

Datta, S. C., Gutterman, Y. & Evenari, M. (1972). The influence of the origin of the mother plant on yield and germination of their caryopses in *Aegilops ovata*. *Planta*, **105**, 155–64.

Evenari, M. L., Shanan, L. & Tadmor, N. (1971). *The Negev: The Challenge of a Desert*. Harvard University Press, Cambridge, Mass.

Goodall, D. W. & Morgan, S. (1974). *Seed reserves in desert soils*. US/IBP Desert Biome Research Memorandum RM 74–16. Logan, Utah.

Goodall, D. W., Childs, S. & Wiebe, H. (1972). *Methodological and validation study of seed reserves in desert soils*. US/IBP Desert Biome Research Memorandum RM 72–8. Logan, Utah.

Gutterman, Y., Witztum, A. & Evenari, M. (1967). Seed dispersal and germination in *Blepharis persica* (Burm.) Kuntze. *Israel Journal of Botany*, **16**, 213–34.

Gutterman, Y., Witztum, A. & Evenari, M. (1969). Physiological and morphological differences between populations of *Blepharis persica* (Burm.) Kuntze. *Israel Journal of Botany*, **18**, 89–95.

Juhren, M., Went, F. W. & Phillips, E. (1956). Ecology of desert plants. IV. Combined field and laboratory work on germination of annuals in the Joshua Tree National Monument, Calif. *Ecology*, **37**, 318–30.

Koller, D. (1969). The physiology of dormancy and survival of plants in desert environments. In: *Dormancy and Survival*, XXIII Symposium of Society of Experimental Biology, pp. 449–69. Cambridge University Press, Cambridge.

Koller, D. (1972). Environmental control of seed germination. In: *Seed Biology* (ed. T. T. Kozlowski), vol. 2, pp. 1–101. Academic Press, New York.

Koller, D. & Roth, M. (1964). Studies on the ecological and physiological significance of amphicarpy in *Gymnarrhena micrantha* (Compositae). *American Journal of Botany*, **51**, 26–35.

Kooper, W. J. C. (1927). Sociological and ecological studies on the tropical weed-vegetation of Pasuruan (Java). *Recueil des Travaux Botaniques Néerlandais*, **24**, 1–255.

Mauer, R. (1967). 'Ecology of *Perognathus formosus* and associated rodents in an arid desert canyon in the Southern Mohave desert.' Ph.D. Thesis, University of Nevada.

488

Mott, J. J. (1972). 'The autecology of annuals in an arid region of Western Australia.' Ph.D. Thesis, University of Western Australia.

Porter, R. H., Durrell, M. & Romm, H. J. (1947). The use of 2,3,5-Triphenyltetrazoliumchloride as a measure of seed germinability. *Plant Physiology*, **22**, 149–59.

Sankari, M. N. & Barbour, M. G. (1972). Autecology of *Salsola vermiculata* var. *villosa* from Syria. *Flora*, **161**, 421–39.

Shatskaya, M. G. (1973). Semennaya produktivnost' polukustarnikov i zapasy semyan v pochve. In: *Teoreticheskie osnovy i metody fitomelioratsii pustyn nykh pastbishch Yugo-Zapadnogo Kyzulkuma*, pp. 87–94. Translated title: Seed production of semi-shrubs and seed reserves in the soil. In: *Theoretical bases and methods for plant improvement in desert pastures of the south-western Kyzylkum*. Taskent. (Cited by Rodin, L. E. (1977). *Productivity of vegetation in arid zone of Asia*. (Synthesis of the Soviet studies for the IBP, 1965–74). Nauka, Leningrad.)

Sheps, L. O. (1973). Survival of *Larrea tridentata* seedlings in Death Valley National Monument, California. *Israel Journal of Botany*, **22**, 8–17.

Soriano, A. (1953). Estudios sobre germinacion I. *Revista de Investigaciones Agricolas*, **7**, 315–40.

Tevis, Jr. L. (1958). Interrelations between the harvester ant, *Veromessor pergandei* (Mayr), and some desert ephemerals. *Ecology*, **39**, 695–704.

Wallace, A. & Romney, E. M. (1972). *Radioecology and ecophysiology of desert plants at the Nevada Test Site*. US Atomic Energy Commission, Report No. TID–25954.

Went, F. W. (1949). Ecology of desert plants. II. The effect of rain and temperature on germination and growth. *Ecology*, **30**, 1–13.

Went, F. W. (1969). A long-term test of seed longevity. II. *Aliso*, **7**, 1–12.

Went, F. W. (1973). Competition among plants. *Proceedings of the National Academy of Sciences of the United States of America*, **70**, 585–90.

Went, F. W. & Stark, N. (1968). The biological and mechanical role of soil fungi. *Proceedings of the National Academy of Sciences of the United States of America*, **60**, 497–504.

Went, F. W., Wheeler, J. & Wheeler, G. C. (1972). Feeding and digestion in some ants (*Veromessor* and *Manica*). *BioScience*, **22**, 82–8.

Whitford, W. G. (1973). *Demography and bioenergetics of herbivorous ants in a desert ecosystem as functions of vegetation, soil type and weather variables*. US/IBP Desert Biome Report, vol. 3, 2.3.3.2., pp. 1–63. Logan, Utah.

Winkworth, R. E. (1971). Longevity of buffel grass seed sown in an arid Australian range. *Journal of Range Management*, **24**, 141–5.

Zohary, M. (1937). Die verbreitungsökologischen Verhältnisse der Pflanzen Palästinas. *Beihefte zum botanischen Centralblatt*, **56**, 1–155.

Manuscript received by the editors December 1974

20. Water uptake and translocation, stomatal movements and transpiration

H. MEIDNER

Introduction

This chapter attempts to summarise the nature of processes involved in the movement of water into and through plants and of water vapour out of plants. Several atmospheric and soil processes are relevant and the reader is referred particularly to Chapters 15 and 17 above; these chapters provide information about the environmental conditions upon which water movements depend. Chapter 23 on root growth and activity is also relevant.

The main body of the present chapter describes in general terms the principles underlying the water relations of higher plants and the movement of water into and through them. In an Appendix, techniques used in the study of these processes are outlined and some hypothetical examples are introduced to illustrate the principles involved.

It must be understood that ionic uptake, dealt with in Chapter 24 below, is deliberately left out of account in dealing with water movement in plants. Active ion transport is practically independent of water movements, provided water is present for the ions to move in. Ionic movements can influence water movements and make them more complex, but reference will be made to these only when essential.

No metabolic process is known which is directly concerned with the movement of water. Water movement in plants occurs as a consequence of physico-chemical conditions, while metabolic processes contribute towards the creation and maintenance of such conditions. Thus, structural features such as membrane systems, or the synthesis, translocation and distribution of solutes, are the result of metabolic activity: water movement follows as a consequence of such active metabolism – in itself it is not an active process.

The movement of water into seeds, seedlings and established plants is at all times the result of the existence of a gradient between the water potential of the soil and that of the plant. The term 'water uptake' is misleading; water is not 'taken up', it moves into the plant. The soil water potential (ψ_s) depends on the osmotic properties of the soil solution making up its solute potential (π_s) and on the adsorptive properties of soil

Plant processes

constituents, often colloidal, making up its matric potential (τ_s); the latter is usually the more important in dry soils and arid regions. The sum of the solute and matric potentials is the soil water potential (Equation [1], in Appendix).

Plant water potentials depend also on solute and to a lesser extent on matric potentials but in addition to these, pressure forces (turgor) must be taken into account. The sum of solute, matric and pressure (turgor) potentials is the plant water potential (Equation [2], in Appendix). The following has been written with arid lands in mind although the principles discussed apply generally.

Water movement

Seeds

In the case of seeds, vital for the survival of the species, the whole body of the seed can be regarded as colloidal matter with matric potentials even lower than those of comparatively dry soils, and therefore with enormous imbibitional properties. The movement of water into seeds is almost entirely due to the process of imbibition – that is, the water moves down the water potential gradient into the seed with its very low seed water potential. Even in arid zones the soil water potential must, at certain times of the year, be higher than the seed water potential to allow germination to occur (Chapter 19). Investigations under the IBP (Hironaka & Tisdale, 1971) established that the two months' ripening period required by seeds of *Sitanion hystrix* (Nutt.) J. G. Sm. caused field germination to be delayed until conditions for survival were more favourable, and that then germination was rapid. It may be relevant that Heydecker (pers. comm.) has recently demonstrated that prolonged anaerobic submersion of seeds in solutions of −12 bar solute potential at temperatures between +5 °C and +15 °C for several weeks promoted rapid and consistent germination in common horticultural species.

Seedlings

In the case of the young seedling containing vacuolated cells, the imbibitional properties of the seed have largely been lost, and the movement of water into such a seedling depends mainly on the osmotic properties of the sap in its vacuolated cells especially in the root-hair zone (disregarding the non-vacuolated meristematic cells in the root tip, which have, in addition to their solute potential, a considerable matric potential).

Solute potentials in root cells can be low, but they do not reach the low levels of seed matric potentials, so that for water movement into the seedling to occur the soil water potential must be higher than the minimum

492

which permits germination; seasonal conditions, even in arid zones, usually allow for this. However, as soon as above-ground parts of the seedling are present, and especially green leaf-like parts, an additional factor can contribute towards lowering the seedling water potential below that of the soil water potential, so that water movement into the seedling will occur. This additional factor is the effect of water vapour loss (transpiration) from the above-ground parts on the overall seedling water potential. This aspect of plant water relations is dealt with below when the established plant is under consideration.

There remains one feature of water movement into plants, especially seedlings, which must be mentioned, namely, the forces which act *against* water movement into plants or more strictly into plant cells. These forces are pressure (turgor) potentials (P) which develop gradually as water moves into a plant. For the assessment of the plant water potential they must be added to the solute potential (Equation [2] in Appendix).

As water moves into the seedling from the soil the solute potential will be slightly raised because the sap is being diluted; however, more importantly, a pressure (turgor) potential will gradually develop, counteracting the effect of the solute potential. Whilst these changes occur the gradient between soil water potential and plant water potential becomes less and less steep until the two potentials have become equal, and as a consequence net movement of water ceases. The plant will be at its highest degree of turgor under the particular environmental conditions (see Example [2] in Appendix).

Mature plants

As indicated above the water potential of established plants is the resultant of two forces: (*a*) the solute potential of the sap in its cells (neglecting matric potentials due to cellulosic and cytoplasmic constituents) and (*b*) the pressure potential of the plant tissues. On occasion the pressure potential will in effect counteract water movement into the plant by raising the plant water potential and decreasing the gradient between soil and plant (see Example [2] in Appendix). This will be the case in the absence of, or at very low rates of, transpiration, and it occurs at dusk and during the night. During the day, however, and especially in arid regions, the pressure potentials change into tensions and assume quite a different role, unless other processes intervene, such as stomatal movements which are dealt with below (p. 497).

Far from counteracting water movement into the plant as positive pressures do, such tensions greatly reinforce solute potentials and contribute to a very substantial reduction in the plant water potential, depressing it considerably below that of the soil water potential and

Plant processes

steepening the gradient from soil to plant. Xylem water columns are known to be able to withstand these very considerable tension forces and plant stems are known to react to the existence of such tensions by diurnal changes in stem diameter. Thus, the required gradient for water movement into the plant is provided largely as a consequence of transpiration; if water is available it will move into the plant (see Example 3 in Appendix).

This effect of transpirational water vapour loss on the plant water potential is often referred to as 'transpiration pull'. Like 'water uptake' this term, although descriptive enough, conceals the basic energy relations as they were stated at the beginning of the chapter: water moves into the plant, it is not 'taken up' nor 'pulled in', it moves down a water potential gradient. When rates of transpiration exceed rates of water movement into the plant, the plant water potential decreases, and the gradient between soil and plant steepens; therefore reservoirs of water hitherto unavailable become available, and the plant survives. In addition plant saps become more concentrated as transpirational loss of water vapour proceeds, and solute potentials will decrease, thereby contributing towards a reduction of plant water potential and a steepening of the gradient between soil and plant. However, this effect is comparatively small.

Factors affecting water movement into the plant

For a discussion of factors affecting water movement into plants it must be assumed that water is available; if it is not, this circumstance will be the overriding factor and no other can influence the process.

Temperature

Given a reasonably constant soil-water potential, changes in temperature will only slightly affect the rate of water movement into plants by their effects on diffusion, imbibition and osmosis.

More important, changes in temperature will affect membrane permeability, which between 0 °C and +4 °C remains very low and gradually increases as the temperature rises. The phenomenon of 'physiological drought' is indeed due partly to this membrane property. The effect of temperature on general metabolism ($Q_{10} = 2$–3) has indirect consequences for water movement into plants. At temperatures below +5 °C there occurs in many plant tissues a change from insoluble storage products to soluble substances, especially sugars. This is usually regarded as a frost-protection mechanism; however, it also depresses the plant water potential, steepening the gradient for water movement into the plant, and possibly diminishing the effects of 'physiological drought' at temperatures where membrane permeability is low. Decreased rates of metabolism due to low

494

temperatures also adversely affect rates of active ion intake: as a consequence solute potentials will be raised, water potential gradients will be less steep, and water movement will slow down.

However, during daylight the most pronounced effect of a change in temperature is on the gradients in water vapour pressure between the plant and the atmosphere, because it is these which determine rates of transpiration (leaving stomatal control out of account for the present). Transpirational loss of water vapour in its turn has the most decisive effect on pressure potentials in the plant, as has already been mentioned. Suffice it to state here that increases in temperature will almost always be accompanied by increases in transpiration rates, and, after a lag period, plant water potentials will decrease so that rates of water movement into the plant increase. Conversely, decreases in temperature will almost always be accompanied by decreased rates of transpiration and, after a lag period, increasing pressure potentials will develop, thus causing rates of water movement into the plant to become slower.

Wind

Basically, wind affects evaporation rates. Even when stomata are closed and plants do not transpire in the narrower sense of the term, their aerial parts will lose water vapour by evaporation especially in warm winds. The water content of cuticles and underlying tissues will be depleted, and this will be followed by the inevitable lowering of the plant water potential, making possible increased rates of water movement into the plant.

When stomatal transpiration occurs the effects of wind are the same, but under these conditions even slight air movements ($0.5\ \mathrm{m\,s^{-1}}$) are sufficient to cause considerable increases in transpiration rates with the consequences outlined above. In arid regions it is important to remember that 'still' air will allow plants to surround themselves with their own micro-climate of relatively high water vapour pressure, and therefore low transpiration rate, whereas air movements will expose the plant to conditions demanding much greater water use which can only be met if rates of water movement into the plant are speeded up.

Light

The influence of light on water movement into plants is due to its effects on stomata, leaf temperature and transpiration, as well as to its effect on metabolism, especially photosynthesis, translocation and growth. All these effects make for increased rates of water movement into plants provided water is available.

Stomata open in light and thus open the major pathway for water vapour

495

out of the plant. Leaf temperatures rise owing to leaves being illuminated, thereby causing an increase in the saturation water vapour pressure in the internal air-spaces of the leaves, and hence increased rates of transpiration. The process of water evaporation from cell walls into the internal air-spaces is a major cooling mechanism; but it cannot, as a rule, prevent leaf temperatures from rising above air temperatures, especially in arid regions.

Photosynthesis produces solutes with osmotic properties, and these are translocated vigorously; they contribute to a decrease in the plant water potential and a steepening of the gradient between soil and plant. Plant growth, as measured by dry-weight increase, is stimulated in light: newly formed tissues appear to have particularly low water potentials, so that water moves preferentially to sites of active growth. This again leads to a lowering of the whole plant water potential, and hence increased rates of water movement into the plant.

Translocation of water

Water movement into the roots of a plant will contribute towards the development of pressure potentials within the plant unless there is a continued upward movement of water at the same rate as its rate of entry, or faster. In the absence of transpiration this happens, and the maximum pressure potential that develops will be of a similar magnitude to the pressure under which water moves into the plant (see previous section). This does in fact happen commonly and leads to guttation during the early hours of the morning; so-called root pressure, measurable on decapitated plants or on branches of intact plants, is another result of water movement into the plant in the absence of transpirational losses of water vapour.

It is well to remember in this connection that, even if the pressure under which water moves into a plant is only 1 bar, this is in theory sufficient to raise the water to a height of 10 m. Thus, since the predominant vegetation of the earth (grasslands, steppes, bush, scrub and arid-zone vegetation) is less than 10 m high, water supply to these types of vegetation would be assured in the absence of transpiration and occurrence of the 'transpiration pull'. However, translocation of water would be very limited, and the water content of plants would be practically stagnant. Transpiration has been called an 'unavoidable evil'; viewed in the light of the translocation or turn-over of the plant's water content, this description is thoughtless. Transpirational loss of water vapour is the major outlet for water that moves into the plant; thus it provides the mechanism for water translocation, together with the vertical and lateral distribution of a considerable amount of solutes and dissolved gases. Unrestricted loss of water vapour would, however, become damaging and cause insurmountable stress were it not for the provision of a substantial measure of control by stomatal movements (see next section).

Factors affecting translocation of water – resistances

The translocation of water with its dissolved content occurs vertically in the xylem vessels and laterally in the parenchyma rays which extend into the phloem. In these tissues resistances have to be overcome. The resistances affect the rate of translocation; therefore, when transpiration rates are moderately high, resistances contribute to the development of tensions, and thus reduce the water potential in the xylem from a possible value of zero in the early morning (when one of the components of the plant water potential was a positive pressure potential) to values as low as −30 bar later in the day. These low potentials do not disappear suddenly when the rate of transpiration slows down or stops altogether. Water continues to be translocated upwards for a considerable time in response to the existence of these potentials. It must be remembered that low potentials developed in the first place because the rate of water movement into the plant could not keep pace with the rate of water vapour loss from the plant. These low potentials are raised only gradually, depending on the rate at which water can enter the plant, until in the early morning they may have disappeared.

Stomatal movements

Open stomatal pores provide the main path for water vapour diffusion from internal air-spaces to the atmosphere. Stomatal size, number and distribution are such that the diffusion path allows for rates of transpiration in excess of rates of water movement into the plant, with the consequences discussed in previous sections. However, of the resistances to the movement of water and of water vapour, the stomatal resistance alone is variable and it is situated where any variation in the resistance is most effective in influencing the rate of water vapour movement out of the plant.

Water movement into the plant and water translocation within the plant occur because of the existence of water potential gradients between soil and plant and between root tissue, stem tissue, leaf tissue and bud tissue respectively. Evaporation of water from cell walls into leaf air-spaces occurs also because of water potential gradients. In the cell walls the potential is high because walls are permeated by relatively pure liquid water, since solutes are retained within cell membranes. The colloidal nature of the wall constituents exerts only a mild matric potential under conditions of moderate transpiration. Opposed to this is the 'water potential' of the *vapour* in the air spaces adjacent to cell walls; this is several orders of magnitude lower than that of liquid water in the cell walls, thus providing a very steep gradient indeed. Evaporation must therefore occur, and the air-spaces will become saturated with water vapour at the prevailing leaf temperature. Exceptions to this state of affairs will be discussed below under transpiration. Thus the stomata are situated between an air-space saturated with water vapour and the atmosphere which is as a rule not saturated, especially in arid zones.

Stomatal control of vapour diffusion out of the leaf is measurable over the whole range of their openings; this is especially true in conditions of moving air. The degree of control diminishes as the opening increases but it does not disappear. In 'still' air, stomatal control becomes unimportant once pores are about half open, because the outside boundary layer assumes a controlling influence.

Factors affecting stomatal movements

General

Stomatal movements occur as a consequence of changes in the turgor relations between epidermal and guard cells. In addition to water supply, factors like light, carbon dioxide concentration, wind, temperature, humidity and polluting gases such as ozone and sulphur dioxide affect stomatal movements (Meidner & Mansfield, 1968); but only water supply need concern us here.

Stomata open, or are disposed to open, in the early hours of the morning before sunrise owing to an endogenous rhythm in guard-cell metabolism. When the sun rises the stomata of those leaves facing the sun open rapidly, usually to their maximum aperture. As the day progresses a partial stomatal closure often occurs as water stress develops. During the afternoon a second opening movement may take place, followed by final closure as the sun begins to set. In plants with crassulacean acid metabolism (CAM, see Chapter 21 below) stomata open during the night and remain practically closed during the day. If the night atmosphere is moist several non-CAM plants have also been reported to open their stomata at night, especially if the preceding day produced water stress (Gindel, 1970).

Water supply and humidity

Since stomatal movements are due to changes in the turgor relations between epidermal and guard cells, water supply must be an important factor affecting stomata. Whilst the terms 'hydroactive' and 'hydropassive' do not elucidate causes of changes in turgor relations that give rise to certain stomatal movements, they focus attention on those with which we are here concerned.

498

The stomata of a water-stressed plant with a low water potential may not respond fully to the usual opening stimuli, and the open stomata of a transpiring plant becoming gradually water-stressed may respond with partial stomatal closure. Thus, IBP work confirmed that stomata respond more directly to light than to water stress unless the latter becomes severe (Ting, Johnson, Szarek & Brun, 1972).

Even under severe water stress it would be an over-simplification to postulate that water stress *per se* is the cause of this stomatal behaviour, because the turgor relations between epidermal and guard cells may, but do not of necessity, change in favour of the epidermal cells when water stress develops. Indeed, it is known that plants undergoing water stress produce progressively more abscisic acid and other hormones, which are exceedingly effective in causing stomatal closure. The effect lasts for some time so that stomata of water-stressed plants may be prevented from opening fully for one or several days, thus aiding in the recovery from stress. Other factors such as increased respiratory release of carbon dioxide may also contribute towards temporary closure in plants under water stress. Partial stomatal closure will, of course, cause a decreased rate of transpiration and allow the plant to recover provided water is available.

Truly (hydro)passive stomatal movements are also known, though it is perhaps unlikely that they are as common in nature as they are in the laboratory. When a transpiring plant becomes rather suddenly exposed to conditions causing greatly increased rates of transpiration (hot wind, for instance), leaves may wilt. Under these circumstances stomata may temporarily open very fully, because the epidermal cells seem to lose their turgor more rapidly than the better protected guard cells. Such passive or transient opening on wilting lasts for about 10 min and is followed by closure unless oscillations set in (see below). Conversely, if a transpiring plant is suddenly exposed to a sharp rise in its water potential (flooding of an irrigation channel), open stomata may temporarily close partially, when the epidermis gains full turgor before the guard cells are supplied with water. Such passive or transient closure on recovery from stress also lasts for a few minutes only before a new equilibrium aperture is established.

The establishment of an equilibrium aperture does not always occur. As a consequence of sudden changes in rates of water-vapour loss or water supply, feed-back effects of stomatal control can set in motion so-called stomatal oscillations with periods of between 15 and 40 minutes. Laboratory studies, often using plants with their roots in culture solution, have shown this phenomenon very clearly; but it is not certain that stomatal oscillations are as frequent and as pronounced in nature as they can be in the laboratory. Nevertheless, the effects of stomatal control on water translocation and water movement into the plant are real enough.

Plant processes

Low atmospheric humidity has been reported to cause stomatal closure in some desert species whilst moist air permitted opening; this was despite the fact that leaf water stress increased and the soil water content remained low (Schulze *et al.*, 1972).

Transpiration

Water movement from soil to atmosphere through the plant is due to the enormous difference in water potential between the soil water and atmospheric water vapour. The change in phase from liquid to vapour occurs in the leaf air-spaces, and involves a substantial expenditure of energy – hence the important cooling effect of the process.

When dealing with the diffusion of water vapour from leaf air-spaces into the atmosphere it is difficult to adhere to the water potential terminology, because the measurement of such potentials is so much more difficult than the measurement of differences in vapour pressures or vapour densities; the latter are accordingly preferred.

The vapour pressure in leaf air-spaces is a function of leaf temperature. For each leaf temperature there is a maximum vapour pressure known as the saturation water-vapour pressure. Except under special circumstances to be discussed below, it is generally assumed that leaf air-spaces are near saturation vapour pressure. Unless there is mist, fog or rain the atmosphere is rarely saturated; therefore, vapour will diffuse down the pressure gradient from leaf air-space to atmosphere. The main path for this vapour diffusion (transpiration) is provided by open stomatal pores; a parallel path offering a much higher resistance is through the cuticle. The most convenient way to express the pressure under which vapour diffuses out of the leaf is the difference in vapour pressure between leaf air-space and the outside atmosphere, measured in mbar or Nm^{-2}. This difference is identical with the water-vapour pressure deficit of the atmosphere when leaf and air temperatures are the same (see Appendix, Example 4(*a*)). It cannot be over-emphasised that a knowledge of the leaf temperature *and* the air temperature is essential for transpiration studies. Differences of less than 0.5 °C in leaf temperatures have a considerable effect on the saturation water-vapour pressure in the leaf air-spaces (see Appendix, Examples 4 (*b*), (*c*), (*d*)).

Leaves are surrounded by boundary layers of varying dimensions depending on air movements. The vapour pressure in the boundary layer is higher than in the atmosphere at some distance from the leaf, but it is impossible to estimate accurately the vapour pressure difference between leaf air-space and this boundary layer surrounding the leaf. Some kind of mean estimate must be used.

500

Factors affecting transpiration rates

Humidity and temperature

The amount of water vapour present in unit volume of air – that is, its density – determines the prevailing water vapour pressure. However, this must be related to the temperature of the atmosphere. This is achieved by determining the difference between the prevailing water vapour pressure and the saturation water vapour pressure at the temperature of the atmosphere; this difference is the water-vapour pressure deficit of the atmosphere, and represents without question the most important factor influencing the rate of transpiration (see Appendix, Example 4), provided the leaf air-space is nearly saturated with water vapour.

Stomata, boundary layers and wind

Rates of transpiration do not depend on the gradient in water vapour pressure alone, but also on the resistance to diffusion offered by the path. The variable stomatal diffusion resistance therefore often controls the rate of transpiration. All factors which influence stomatal movements (see previous section) will indirectly influence transpiration. The other highly influential resistance is the thickness of the boundary layer, which depends on the degree of air movement.

Soil moisture

Diminishing available soil moisture influences transpiration rate, in that it contributes to lessening the gradient in potential from soil to plant. It will also cause further reductions in plant water potentials; the latter may affect stomata or cause changes in water vapour pressure in leaf air-spaces (see below). Sammis, Qashu, Ryan & Thames (1972) reported that transpiration rates in riparian vegetation diminished linearly in proportion to the ratio between available water and that present at field capacity. This did not seem to correlate with changes in stomatal opening alone.

Plant exposure in the field

Transpiration rates of isolated leaves or plants will differ from those of plants in a field, although overall atmospheric factors may appear to be the same. In reality, atmospheric factors will, of course, not be the same, because above a field or within a canopy there exists a distinct micro-climate which exercises the most direct influence on transpiration rates, and overall atmospheric conditions are less important.

Plant processes

Water vapour pressure in the leaf air-space

It has been assumed so far that the leaf air-spaces are nearly saturated with water vapour for the particular leaf temperature; in temperate climates this appears to be a wholly reasonable assumption. However, it follows from what has been said that any variation in the water vapour pressure prevailing in the leaf air-spaces would have profound effects on the rate of transpiration. Such variations have been postulated, and have been referred to as 'incipient drying' of leaves and 'changes in mesophyll resistance'. Measurements have been made of such changes in mesophyll resistance (Meidner, 1965: Jarvis & Slatyer, 1970). Sudden changes in transpiration rate at constant stomatal opening have been observed, but it is not possible to measure the water vapour pressure in the leaf air-spaces itself – hence the reality of this factor remains in doubt. IBP work has, it appears, added data which remove some of these doubts – especially in arid zones where one would expect 'incipient drying' to occur (Bamberg, Wallace, Kleinkopf & Vollmer, 1972; Caldwell, Moore, White & De Puit, 1972; Bamberg, Wallace, Kleinkopf & Vollmer, 1973). Thus, there are several records of increasing photosynthesis rates and decreasing transpiration rates for *Larrea divaricata* Cav., *Eurotia lanata* (Pursh.) Moq. and *Atriplex confertifolia* (Torr & Frém.) Wats. These changes in rates cannot be explained by the recorded changes in environmental factors or in stomatal conductivity. The most striking example is for *Eurotia lanata* for which the photosynthesis rate, in terms of carbon dioxide uptake per unit dry weight, ranged between 120 and 160 μg g^{-1} min^{-1} while transpiration rate (loss of water per unit dry weight) changed from only 1 mg min^{-1} to virtually zero.

Concentration of leaf sap

Reference to this topic is made only to show that its influence on transpiration rate is negligible. Although it is true that the osmotic concentration of the leaf sap increases as a consequence of a transpiration rate in excess of the rate of replenishment of leaf water content, such increases in concentration affect the water vapour pressure in the leaf air-space system only very slightly.

The relation between water vapour pressure and concentration of the solution above which the vapour pressure is measured is based on Raoult's Law:

$$\frac{\text{Lowering of vapour pressure}}{\text{Vapour pressure of pure solvent}} = \frac{\text{Moles of solute}}{\text{Moles of solvent} + \text{moles of solute}}$$

That is, for 1 mol solute in 1 l water $= \dfrac{1}{1000/18 + 1}$

$$= 18/1018$$

$$= 0.0176$$

Thus, for a molar solution the vapour pressure is reduced by 1.76%. Since a molar solution has a solute potential of -22.6 bar, a decrease of 1 bar in the solute potential will lower the vapour pressure by $0.0176/22.6 = 0.0008$ or 0.08%. Even if the sap were to be concentrated so that its $\pi = 100$ bar the effect on evaporation would amount to only 8% compared with that of pure water. And even these considerations do not really apply since the water in the cell walls which evaporates is not the cell sap but almost solute-free water.

Appendix: Relationships, measurements and estimates

Soil water potentials

Soil water potential is the algebraic sum of the solute potential of the soil solution and the matric potential conferred by soil constituents. It is, however, not practicable to measure the two potentials separately, for they are interdependent. The direct measurement of soil water potentials rests on the measurement of the vapour pressure associated with the soil. Extremely accurate temperature control is essential. Psychrometry is the most reliable method for vapour pressure determinations, provided temperature control is adequate (Slatyer, 1967; Kozlowski, 1968).

Instead of a vapour-pressure method, indirect methods can be used. The most elementary is a bio-assay using osmotically calibrated seeds, preferably the seeds under consideration (Meyer & Anderson, 1952; Meidner & Sheriff, 1976). One set of weighed seed samples is immersed in a series of osmotic solutions, the other in the soil, and both are weighed after suitable intervals of time. Percentage gains in weight can then be matched to assess the water potential of the soil in relation to the solute potential of the solution. Plotting percentage changes against solute potentials will give more refined estimates.

Gravimetric measurements, resistance blocks, thermal conductivity and neutron probe methods measure soil water content, not soil water potential, and must be calibrated for each individual soil (Kramer, 1969; Wiebe *et al.*, 1971; Meidner & Sheriff, 1976).

The expression for soil water potential shown below is the algebraic sum of matric and solute potentials. Care must be taken to observe the correct signs of the individual terms in the equation. Both matric and solute potentials carry negative signs, therefore their sum, the soil water

503

Plant processes

potential, will be a negative term also. The unit of measurement of water potentials is the bar.

$$\psi_s \quad = \quad \tau_s \quad + \quad \pi_s \qquad [1]$$

ψ_s	τ_s	π_s
Total soil water potential directly measured by vapour-pressure method (psychrometry).	Matric potential conferred by soil constituents.	Solute potential of soil solution.

Neither can be measured individually, since they depend on one another.

Example 1

Order of magnitude of individual terms as estimated in desert environment:

$\tau_s = -10$ to -43 bar   at 15 and 30 cm depth
$\pi_s = \quad -2$ to $\quad -3$ bar

$\psi_s = -12$ to -46 bar   at 15 and 30 cm depth

Plant water potential

Plant water potential is the algebraic sum of the solute potential of the sap (neglecting separate matric potentials) plus the pressure potential (either hydrostatic or turgor). The solute potentials of plant tissues can be measured by plasmolytic methods or by determinations of the depression of freezing point. Measurements of pressure potentials are not easily accomplished.

Direct measurements of plant water potentials are possible by vapour-pressure methods such as psychrometry; however, extremely accurate temperature control is essential. For certain material such as stems, branches, twigs and petiolate leaves a pressure bomb may be used to measure plant water potentials; but unless it is correctly used the results may be misleading. Plant water potentials of leaf strips, mesocarp tissue, swollen root tissue, tuber and corm tissue can be assessed directly and accurately by immersion in a series of osmotic solutions and determination of changes in either weight or dimensions at regular intervals *until equi-librium has been attained.* Plotting percentage changes against solute potentials of the solutions allows a reliable assessment of the plant water potential.

Equation [2] below shows how the pressure under which water will move into a rooted plant may be estimated. It is the algebraic sum of pressure potential (hydrostatic or turgor), the solute potential of the sap (neglecting tissue matric potentials) and the soil water potential. Great care

504

must be taken to use the correct signs for these terms: solute and soil water potentials carry negative signs, the pressure potential may be positive (pressure) or negative (tension): it is by far the most variable factor in plant water relations and therefore the most decisive.

Pressure under which water moves into plant =

$$P_p \qquad + \qquad \pi_p \qquad - \qquad \psi_s \qquad [2]$$

Pressure potential, not readily measured.   Solute potential, measured by plasmolytic method or depression of freezing point   Soil water potential.

Together making up the plant water potential, ψ_s, measurable by vapour-pressure method or immersion of tissue in graded osmotic solutions.

Example 2

Likely situation during the night:

$P_p = +12$ bar   Maximum pressure potential for this plant in this soil.
$+\pi_p = -20$ bar

$\psi_p = -8$ bar $\Big\{$ Soil water potential equal to plant water potential
$-\psi_s = -8$ bar $\Big\{$ therefore no gradient – no net movement of water. Pressure under which water moves into plant = zero.

Example 3

Likely situation during day:

$P_p = -6$ bar $\Big\{$ Pressure potential has assumed negative sign representing tension build-up in xylem as a result of transpiration.

$+\pi_p = -24$ bar $\Big\{$ Sap concentrated as a result of transpiration, therefore lowering of solute potential of sap.

$\psi_p = -30$ bar $\Big\{$ Plant water potential reduced by a factor of almost four compared with situation at night (cf. Example 2) mainly owing to change in pressure potential.

$-\psi_s = -10$ bar $\Big\{$ Soil water potential lowered owing to evaporative loss and plant water use.

$= -20$ bar

Pressure under which water moves into plant from soil $= 20$ bar   Soil water potential in excess of plant's water potential by 20 bar.

Plant processes

The pressure under which water moves into the plant is given by the difference between two potentials (both negative), and is quoted as a numerical value without sign. In this case, the difference between -30 and -10 is 20.

Water vapour pressure (WVP) gradients

The loss of water (as vapour) from the plant is determined by the gradient in water vapour pressure between leaf and atmosphere. The following example illustrates, for hypothetical situations, the relationship between this quantity and the temperature and humidity conditions which determine it.

Example 4

(*a*) Temperate climate, no sun, WVP of the air 70% of saturation pressure (SWVP):

Leaf Temp. 15 °C, SWVP	17.0 mbar
Air Temp. 15 °C, prevailing WVP	12.0 mbar

Pressure under which water vapour diffuses out of leaf	5.0 mbar = Water vapour pressure deficit of atmosphere when leaf and air temp. equal

(*b*) Temperate climate, mild sun, hence leaf temperature raised above air temperature and vapour pressure of air slightly reduced to 65% of SWVP.

Leaf Temp. 16.8 °C, SWVP		19.0 mbar
Air Temp. 16.0 °C, prevailing WVP	11.7 mbar

Pressure under which water vapour diffuses out of leaf	7.3 mbar

(*c*) Hot climate, moderate sun, WVP of air 45% of saturation pressure:

Leaf Temp. 36 °C, SWVP		59.5 mbar
Air Temp. 30 °C, prevailing WVP	19.2 mbar

Pressure under which water vapour diffuses out of leaf	40.3 mbar

(*d*) Hot climate, moderate sun but humid air at 78% of saturation pressure, therefore less steep gradient, lower transpiration rate and therefore smaller cooling effect, hence raised leaf temperature:

506

Leaf Temp. 38 °C,   SWVP   65.6 mbar
Air Temp.   30 °C,   prevailing WVP 33.2 mbar

Pressure under which water vapour   32.4 mbar
diffuses out of leaf

References

Bamberg, S., Wallace, A., Kleinkopf, I. G., Vollmer, A. (1972). *Gaseous exchange in the Mohave Desert shrubs*. US/IBP Desert Biome Research Memorandum. RM 72–21. Logan, Utah.

Bamberg, S., Wallace, A., Kleinkopf, G. & Vollmer, A. (1973). *Plant productivity and nutrient interrelationships of perennials in the Mohave Desert*. US/IBP Desert Biome Reserch Memorandum. RM 73–10. Logan, Utah.

Caldwell, M. M., Moore, R. T., White, R. S. & DePuit, E. J. (1972). *Gas exchange of Great Basin shrubs*. US/IBP Desert Biome Research Memorandum. RM 72–20. Logan, Utah.

Gindel, I. (1970). The nocturnal behaviour of xerophytes. *New Phytologist*, **69**, 399–404.

Hironaka, M. & Tisdale, E. W. (1971). *Growth and development of* Sitanion hystrix. US/IBP Desert Biome Report of Progress 2.3.1.4 (Research Memorandum RM 71–14). Logan, Utah.

Jarvis, P. G. & Slatyer, R.O. (1970). The role of the mesophyll cell wall in transpiration. *Planta*, **90**, 303–22.

Kozlowski, T. T. (ed.) (1968). *Plant water relationships*. Academic Press, London and New York.

Kramer, P. J. (1969). *Plant and soil water relations. A modern synthesis*. McGraw-Hill, New York.

Meidner, H. (1965). Stomatal control of transpirational water loss. In: *The state and movement of water in living organisms*. Symposia of the Society for Environmental Botany, XIX. pp. 185–204. Cambridge University Press, Cambridge.

Meidner, H. & Mansfield, T. A. (1968). *The physiology of stomata*. McGraw-Hill, New York.

Meidner, H. & Sherriff, D. W. (1976). *Water and plants*. Blackie, Glasgow.

Meyer, B. S. & Anderson, D. B. (1952. *Plant physiology*. Van Nostrand, New York, London & Toronto.

Sammis, T., Qashu, H., Ryan, J. & Thames, J. (1972). *Water balance techniques*. US/IBP Desert Biome Research Memorandum. 72–13. Logan, Utah.

Schulze, E. D., Lange, O. L., Buschbom, U., Kappen, L. & Evenari, M. (1972). Stomatal response to changes in humidity. *Planta*, **108**, 259–70.

Slatyer, R. O. (1967). *Plant water relationships*. Academic Press, London & New York.

Ting, I. P., Johnson, H. B., Szarek, S. R. & Brun, G. D. (1972). *Gas exchange and productivity in* Opuntia spp. US/IBP Desert Biome Research Memorandum. 72–19. Logan, Utah.

Wiebe, H. H., Campbell, G. S., Gardner, W. H., Rawlins, S. L., Gary, J. W. & Brown, R. W. (1971). *Measurement of plant and soil water status*. Utah Agricultural Experiment Station, Bulletin 484.

Manuscript received by the editors February 1975

21. Photosynthesis and respiration of plants in the arid ecosystem

E. J. DEPUIT

Introduction

For obvious reasons, a comprehension of plant-exchange processes is fundamental for an understanding of ecosystem function. The balance between plant photosynthesis and respiration determines plant primary production, which is the basic source of carbon and energy for the ecosystem. All biological processes of the ecosystem are ultimately affected by plant gas exchange. In recent studies of arid ecosystems (such as those under the US/IBP Desert Biome program), much emphasis has accordingly been placed on studies of plant gas exchange. The purpose of this chapter is to synthesize results of pertinent research, providing a general definition of the state of knowledge on this subject at the present time.

Most photosynthetic studies in the IBP program have dealt with net carbon dioxide intake – that is, net carbon gain after any losses due to mitochondrial or peroxisomal respiration during photosynthesis. This emphasis on net rather than gross photosynthesis is perhaps justifiable since, in the final analysis, a knowledge of net gain or loss of carbon dioxide under varying natural conditions may be acceptable within the framework of the whole research program. Finer breakdown of net photosynthesis into its component parts of gross photosynthesis, 'dark' respiration and photorespiration is not only technically difficult at present, but perhaps would be an over-detailed analysis for the purposes envisaged. Respiration measurements in ecosystem studies usually refer to respiratory processes under varying conditions in darkness.

Research in the field of photosynthesis has undergone a rapid expansion in the past decade, with three biochemical pathways now recognised: the pentose carbon pathway (C_3 plants), the dicarboxylic carbon pathway (C_4 plants) and crassulacean acid metabolism (CAM plants) (Björkman, 1973; Black, 1973). Two major respiratory processes are now known for plants: mitochondrial (dark) respiration and peroxisomal (photo) respiration (Jackson & Volk, 1970; Beevers, 1971). The nature of these biochemical pathways in relation to gas exchange in the arid ecosystem will be considered later in this chapter.

A number of approaches to the description of photosynthesis have been developed. One of the more useful of these involves an electrical

509

Plant processes

resistance analog in which various resistances, in series and parallel, to carbon flow from the atmosphere to sites of carboxylation within the plant are conceptualized. The concentration gradient of carbon dioxide between the atmosphere and the sites of carboxylation thus becomes the driving force of the reaction under conditions of light saturation of photosynthesis. Gaastra (1959) defined three major resistances to the flow of carbon dioxide: plant boundary-layer resistance (r_a'); stomatal diffusion resistance (r_s'); and mesophyll resistance (r_m'). Subsequent workers have refined these concepts considerably, particularly with respect to the mesophyll resistance, which is in actuality a composite term including diffusional resistance within the mesophyll; chemical resistance to carboxylation; and, in some cases, losses of carbon by respiration concurrent with photosynthesis (Lake, 1967; Gifford & Musgrave, 1970; Jones & Slatyer, 1972). In view of recent advances in understanding of this resistance, Gifford & Musgrave (1972) renamed it residual resistance (r_r'). These resistances, or their reciprocal conductances, may be expected to vary with changes in physical or biological factors; this variation is then reflected in changes in patterns and magnitudes of net photosynthesis.

Rates of photosynthesis and respiration under natural conditions are governed by a number of physical factors (James, 1953; Talling, 1961), to which must be added interactive effects of biological factors. Noy-Meir (1973) stated that water availability was the dominant physical factor controlling biological processes in arid ecosystems, in view of the generally scarce and sporadic nature of precipitation in such ecosystems. Water availability influences plant gas exchange through direct effects on the biochemical processes themselves, and indirectly through effects on stomatal behavior and plant phenological development. Other physical factors affecting rates of gas exchange include temperature, irradiation, humidity, and, to a smaller extent, wind. Gas-exchange effects of plant factors such as phenology and morphology may be superimposed upon those of physical factors (DePuit, 1974), and differences in response to physical factors may be expected between plants with differing bio-chemical pathways of photosynthesis and respiration (Björkman, 1973). In the following sections the nature of the effects of these various factors on gas exchange in the arid ecosystem will be examined.

Factors affecting the rates of the processes

Water availability

The generally low and sporadic nature of precipitation in desert eco-systems makes water availability the major limiting factor for most bio-logical processes (Noy-Meir, 1973). A strong direct correlation has commonly been noted between water availability on the one hand, and the primary productivity and morpho-phenologic development of desert plants

510

on the other (e.g. Chew & Chew, 1965; West, 1969; Dunn, 1970; Oechel, Strain & Odening, 1972; Detling & Klikoff, 1973; Bamberg *et al.*, 1974; Beatley, 1974; West & Gunn, 1974); indeed, primary production of certain desert annuals may not occur at all except during episodic periods of adequate soil moisture (Patten & Smith, 1974). Perennial plant species in arid ecosystems frequently are exposed to and survive astonishingly low water potentials. Halvorson & Patten (1974), for example, reported minimum plant water potentials as low as -85 bar for *Franseria deltoidea*. Gas-exchange activity for desert species under such conditions, however, is usually very low, although Moore (1971) found active net photosynthesis in *Atriplex confertifolia* at water potentials as low as -60 bar. With few exceptions, research has shown a decline in net photosynthesis with decreasing water potential (Slatyer, 1967; Hellmuth, 1968; Troughton, 1969; Boyer, 1970a, 1970b, 1971; Kriedemann & Smart, 1971; Schultz & Gatherum, 1971; DePuit & Caldwell, 1973; Plaut & Bravdo, 1973; Bamberg *et al.*, 1974; Caldwell *et al.*, 1974; DePuit, 1974; Odening, Strain & Oechel, 1974; Ting, Johnson, Yonkers & Szarek, 1974), although there is a wide variation among, and even within, species with respect to rate of decline. This intra- and interspecific variability in rate of decline with water stress makes attempts to model photosynthetic response quite difficult at the community level.

Three major modes of water-potential effects on net photosynthesis may be recognized (Slatyer, 1967; Crafts, 1968; DePuit, 1974):

(*a*) hydroactive closing of the stomata, bringing about a reduced supply of carbon dioxide to the mesophyll (affecting r_s');

(*b*) effects of water deficit on the biochemical processes involved in photosynthesis (affecting r_r');

(*c*) effects of water deficit on processes of respiration in light (affecting r_r' if respiration is included in the term).

Stomatal closure (i.e. increased r_s') under conditions of low available moisture is the major cause of reduced net photosynthesis in many species under water stress (Troughton, 1969; Boyer, 1970b, 1971; Stevenson & Shaw, 1971; Biscoe, 1972; Teare & Kanemasu, 1972; Beadle *et al.*, 1973; Beardsell, Mitchell & Thomas, 1973; DePuit & Caldwell, 1973; Harris, 1973; Jones, 1973a; Moldau, 1973; Pasternak & Wilson, 1974). A relatively high degree of stomatal control of gas exchange has been considered to be of adaptive significance to xerophytic species in terms of plant water conservation (Neales, Patterson & Hartney, 1968); Whiteman & Koller (1967b) postulated that the optimal leaf-resistance characteristics for successful xerophytes would include low r_r' values and relatively high, sensitive r_s' values, thereby maximizing gain in carbon dioxide relative to water loss.

Although some workers (Teare & Kanemasu, 1972; DePuit & Caldwell,

1973; DePuit, 1974) have noted direct correlations between depressed water potentials in plant tissue and lowered net photosynthesis, many other studies have found no such correlation. Dunn (1970) for example, working with evergreen sclerophylls, found somewhat elevated tissue water potentials concurrent with drought-induced stomatal closure and reduction in net photosynthesis, as did Hodges (1967) with coniferous species. Such stomatal control of tissue water potential would be advantageous to plants adapted to endure drought (Jones, 1974). In general, the best correlations between depressed net photosynthesis and decreasing water potential have been obtained when soil or substrate water potentials are used (e.g. Bamberg *et al.*, 1974; Morrow & Mooney, 1974; Reid, 1974); this is supported by the fact that in many studies on well-watered plants no significant reduction in net photosynthesis was noted under conditions of high but transient values for tissue water stress (Wilson, 1967; Turner & Begg, 1973). Therefore, in attempts to relate net photosynthesis and growth to water potential, soil rather than plant water potential may be the best correlative parameter (Campbell & Harris, 1974).

However, increases in stomatal diffusion resistance with decreases in water potential do not always completely, or even largely, account for depressions in net photosynthesis, as is evident from studies where net photosynthesis was depressed under water stress even when stomata were open (Boyer & Bowen, 1970; Jones, 1973b; Ting *et al.*, 1974). Hellmuth (1969) found relatively little stomatal regulation of net photosynthesis for the Australian desert shrub *Acacia craspedocarpa* under extreme water stress, and attributed regulation of net photosynthesis to other factors (r_r', for instance). Many studies have shown that residual resistances to assimilation of carbon dioxide increase with decreases in water potential (Gale, Kohl & Hagan, 1966; Hellmuth, 1969; Troughton, 1969; Boyer & Bowen, 1970; Redshaw & Meidner, 1971; Beadle *et al.*, 1973; DePuit, 1974; Ting *et al.*, 1974). Such increases in r_r' may be due to increases in intracellular chemical or diffusional resistances to carbon dioxide transfer (Troughton, 1969), or may reflect indirect effects on apparent r_r' due to increases of respiration in light relative to photosynthesis as water stress increases (Kramer, 1969; Levitt, 1972).

General declines in rates of dark respiration with decreases in water potential are commonly recognized (e.g. Dunn, 1970; Boyer, 1971; Schultz & Gatherum, 1971), although somewhat increased respiration rates at lower water potentials following initial declines have been noted for certain species (Brix, 1962; Pallas, Michel & Harris, 1967; Mooney, 1969; DePuit, 1974). At extremely low water potentials, respiration may be practically nil, suggesting direct drought injury to plants under such conditions (Kaul, 1966; Crafts, 1968; Levitt, 1972). Both Levitt (1972) and Kramer (1969) have pointed out that although both gross photosynthesis and respiration may decline with decreasing water potentials, the rate of decline of photosynthesis may be more rapid than that of respiration, resulting in a further depression of net photosynthesis (e.g. through respiratory effects on apparent r_i). This is supported by the fact that, in a number of studies of desert and other species under extreme heat and water stress, net photosynthesis has become negative, indicating higher respiration rates than gross photosynthesis rates (Slatyer, 1967; Hellmuth, 1968; Troughton & Cowan, 1968; Strain, 1969; Dunn, 1970; Raschke, 1970; DePuit, 1974). Negative net photosynthesis under such conditions must in large part be due to dark respiratory processes in light, since it is unlikely that photorespiration, as presently understood, could exceed gross photosynthesis for any length of time (Beevers, 1971).

Biome studies have shown seasonal gas exchange to be correlated with patterns of water potential. Bamberg and his collaborators (Bamberg, Wallace, Kleinkopf & Vollmer, 1973; Bamberg *et al.*, 1974) found seasonal patterns and magnitudes of net uptake of carbon dioxide for three Mohave Desert species, *Ambrosia dumosa*, *Krameria parvifolia* and *Larrea divaricata*, to be directly related to the favorability of the moisture regime. Ting and his co-workers (Ting, Johnson, Szarek & Brum, 1972; Ting, Johnson, Yonkers & Szarek, 1973, 1974), and Patten & Nisbet (1973) have noted general declines in productivity and metabolic activity of CAM-pathway species with decreases in available moisture. Cunningham, Balding & Syvertsen (1973) observed that the resistance of grass leaves to diffusion of carbon dioxide increased to a variable extent with increasing water stress. Caldwell *et al.* (1973, 1974) have reported that net assimilation and dark respiration rates in the cool desert shrubs *Atriplex confertifolia*, *Ceratoides lanata*, *Artemisia tridentata* and *Gutierrezia sarothrae* decreased as water stress increased.

The degree of depression of primary productivity with water stress, however, varies widely among species adapted for survival in the arid ecosystem. Different species exhibit differing morpho-phenological, physiological and biochemical 'strategies' for enduring or avoiding environmental stresses (Pourrat & Hubac, 1974). Some species, such as many desert annuals (e.g. Patten & Smith, 1974), simply die or become dormant during periods of low water-availability, while other perennial species, such as many desert shrubs and cacti (Bamberg *et al.*, 1974; Caldwell *et al.*, 1974; Ting *et al.*, 1974), exhibit varying degrees of decreased metabolic activity. These various adaptive strategies will be reviewed in greater detail later in this chapter. Obviously, no generalizations are possible regarding the responses of individual species to water potential, although at a community level the comments in the preceding paragraphs may perhaps be applied. It should also be emphasized that effects of water potential on plant gas exchange in the arid ecosystem, although of paramount

513

importance in themselves, should always be considered in conjunction with effects of other factors comprising the environmental complex.

Temperature

Effects of temperature on plant gas-exchange in the arid ecosystem may be second in importance only to those of water potential. Daytime temperatures in desert areas during the growing season may become very high, whereas at night surprisingly low temperatures may prevail. Such wide diurnal fluctuations in temperature are a characteristic of arid ecosystems. In many deserts, especially 'cool' deserts at higher latitudes or elevations, there is also wide seasonal fluctuation in mean temperatures. Therefore, effects of varying temperatures on plant gas-exchange activity should be pronounced in desert ecosystems.

Most research on photosynthesis has indicated a definite effect of even moderate temperature fluctuation on net assimilation rates (e.g. Wilson, 1967; Ludlow & Jarvis, 1971; Helms, 1972; Hari & Luukkanen, 1973, 1974). Most investigators have found that there is an optimum temperature for net photosynthesis, above and below which assimilation rates are reduced (Kriedemann & Smart, 1971; Ludlow & Wilson, 1971a; Fryer & Ledig, 1972; Moore, Miller, Albright & Tieszen, 1972; Hari & Luukkanen, 1974). In arid ecosystems, much research has been conducted on the temperature optimum of net photosynthesis (Mooney, West & Brayton, 1966; Strain & Chase, 1966; Hellmuth, 1968, 1969, 1971; Lange, Koch & Schulze, 1969; Strain, 1969; Adams, 1970; Björkman, Pearcy, Harrison & Mooney, 1972; Bamberg *et al.*, 1973, 1974; Caldwell *et al.*, 1973, 1974; DePuit & Caldwell, 1973; McPherson & Slatyer, 1973; DePuit, 1974; Lange *et al.*, 1974; Pearcy & Harrison, 1974; Pearcy, Berry & Bartholomew, 1974; Pearcy, Harrison, Mooney & Björkman, 1974), with optimum temperatures ranging from 15 °C to 47 °C. Absolute values of the temperature optimum of net photosynthesis may depend in part upon the biochemical pathway of photosynthesis involved, C_4 species generally exhibiting higher optimum temperatures than C_3 species (Björkman, 1973; Black, 1973).

The temperature optimum of net photosynthesis may also depend upon the thermal environment to which plants are exposed, since temperature acclimation generally acts to promote net photosynthesis at prevailing temperatures (Caldwell, 1972). In general, species or ecotypes of species growing in warmer climates tend to have higher optimum temperatures for net photosynthesis. This is supported by studies which have shown elevated temperature optima in warm-grown vs cool-grown ecotypes of the same species (e.g. Mooney & Billings, 1961; Mooney & West, 1964; Strain & Chase, 1966). Pearcy & Harrison (1974), for example, found substantial differences in temperature optima of net photosynthesis between individuals of *Atriplex lentiformis* from coastal and desert habitats, the desert ecotype exhibiting a much higher optimum temperature (44 °C) than the coastal ecotype (32 °C). A temporary acclimation of net photosynthesis to temperature may also accompany seasonal changes in environmental temperatures, although there is much variation among species in occurrence of this phenomenon, depending on specific differences in morphological and physiological plasticity (Mooney *et al.*, 1966; Strain & Chase, 1966; Mooney & Shropshire, 1967; Strain, 1969; White, Moore & Caldwell, 1971; Caldwell, 1972; DePuit & Caldwell, 1973). Lange *et al.* (1974) found optimum temperatures and upper compensation points of net photosynthesis of two desert species to be lower in spring and fall, and highest during summer. However, although Hellmuth (1968, 1969) found the temperature optimum of net photosynthesis to shift somewhat through the season for *Acacia craspedocarpa* and *Rhagodia baccata*, he later (Hellmuth, 1971) found little seasonal change in optimum temperatures or compensation points for several other Australian desert shrubs. Clearly, occurrence of seasonal temperature acclimation is largely dependent upon individual characteristics of the species involved.

Rates of dark respiration generally increase with increases in temperature (James, 1953), a pattern universally confirmed by recent studies. Recent evidence has suggested that rates of photorespiration, relative to photosynthesis, may also increase with temperature (e.g. Hew, Krotkov & Canvin, 1969; Hofstra & Hesketh, 1969; Döhler & Przybylla, 1973). Some studies have shown overall decreases in respiration in plants under warmer growing conditions (DePuit & Caldwell, 1973: Bamberg *et al.*, 1974; DePuit, 1974; Pearcy & Harrison, 1974), which suggests the possibility of a temperature acclimation of respiration.

The nature of temperature effects on plant gas exchange is complex. There is some agreement at present that temperature effects are closely interrelated with those of irradiation and water potential (Meidner & Mansfield, 1968; Hari & Luukkanen, 1973, 1974), and sometimes humidity (Schulze *et al.*, 1974). Temperature effects on stomatal diffusion resistance (r_s') may well be exerted through the temperature response of gross photosynthesis, where increases in rate of gross photosynthesis may induce decreases in r_s' due to effects on the potassium-pump mechanism of the guard cells (Zelitch, 1971). However, in situations of limited water availability r_s' may increase with increasing temperature in species which exercise close stomatal control, thus conserving plant water resources (Downes & O'Connor, 1973). A pattern of higher r_s' values with increasing temperatures has often been observed (e.g. Whiteman & Koller, 1967a; DePuit, 1974), whereas other studies have shown decreases in r_s' at higher temperatures (e.g. Björkman *et al.*, 1972). Raschke (1970) noted a varying response of r_s' to temperature. Effects of temperature on stomata, there-

515

fore, appear to follow no set pattern, but vary according to species involved and prevalent environmental conditions.

Residual resistance to assimilation of carbon dioxide (r_r') may also increase at elevated temperatures, particularly if effects of respiration in light are included in the term. Decreases in net photosynthesis at high temperatures with no stomatal closure (El-Sharkaway & Hesketh, 1964; Hodges, 1967; Raschke, 1970) attest to the importance of r_r' in such situations. Increases in r_r' at higher temperatures may be due to such things as lowered enzyme activities or efficiencies (Decker, 1959; Hew *et al.*, 1969), or to effects of increased respiration relative to photosynthesis (Hari & Luukkanen, 1973). Again, both dark respiration and photorespiration rates tend to increase with temperature, although mitochondrial ('dark') respiration rates in light may be somewhat lower than rates in darkness. Elevated respiration rates due to high temperatures, when coupled with the effects of water stress on the ratio of gross photosynthesis to total respiration in light (see the previous section), may cause the negative net photosynthesis often observed under conditions of heat and water stress.

Seasonal effects of temperature on magnitude of net photosynthesis are not as clear-cut as effects of water potential, presumably because of the close interdependence of temperature effects on water availability. If water is not limiting, some studies (El-Sharkaway & Hesketh, 1964; Chew & Chew, 1965; Mooney & Shropshire, 1967; Oechel *et al.*, 1972) have shown higher absolute rates of net assimilation of carbon dioxide concurrent with higher temperatures. If water is limiting, the reverse may hold true.

Irradiation

Energy from incident irradiation in the visible portion of the spectrum (400–700 nm) provides the driving force for the light reactions of photosynthesis. If other factors are non-limiting, a consistent increase in rates of photosynthesis occurs as photosynthetically active irradiation increases until saturation light intensities are reached, after which photosynthetic rates remain unaffected by further increases in irradiation. There is much interspecific variation in light saturation intensity, corresponding to differences between species in efficiency of utilizing solar energy (Hesketh & Moss, 1963). These differences in saturation intensity, together with variation in the units and methodology used in research devoted to irradiation effects, make extrapolation of light response curves of photosynthesis for the arid ecosystem as a whole quite difficult. Relatively low saturation light intensities (Hellmuth, 1969) in some species may allow maximal photosynthetic rates for longer periods each day, and would partially explain the early diurnal maximum for photosynthetic rates observed in a number of studies (Dunn, 1970; Mika & Antoszewski, 1972; DePuit & Caldwell, 1973; DePuit, 1974; Pearcy, Berry & Bartholomew, 1974), although unfavorable temperature and moisture conditions later in the day may also have been involved. Other species, including many plants with C_4 metabolism, may be capable of utilizing a higher proportion of solar energy (Cartledge & Connor, 1973; Woledge, 1971).

In addition to the dependence of the photochemical reactions of photosynthesis on irradiation intensity, irradiation may affect net photosynthesis through effects on stomata, although the nature of such effects is somewhat complicated. Effects of irradiation on gas exchange through changes in stomatal aperture may be largely dependent on other physical factors, i.e. temperature and water potential. A number of studies have indicated decreases in r_s' with increases in irradiation (e.g. Ehrler & Van Bavel, 1968; Biscoe, Littleton & Scott, 1973), whereas other studies have shown just the reverse relationship (e.g. Slatyer & Bierhuizen, 1964; Whiteman & Koller, 1967a; Akita & Moss, 1973). Evidence also exists pointing to differences between C_3 and C_4 plants in stomatal response to irradiation (Akita & Moss, 1972; Pasternak & Wilson, 1973), stomata of C_4 species generally being more responsive to changes in irradiation and other environmental factors.

Effects of irradiation on net photosynthesis are closely coupled with those of temperature and water stress (Meidner & Mansfield, 1965, 1968). When water stress is minimal, net photosynthesis can be explained successfully in terms of irradiation and temperature (Ludlow & Wilson, 1971a; Helms, 1972; DePuit & Caldwell, 1973). At lower water potentials net photosynthesis does not correlate so well with irradiation (DePuit & Caldwell, 1973; DePuit, 1974). Hari & Luukkanen (1974) defined a term for physiological water stress, incorporating effects of temperature, water potential and intrinsic plant factors, which explained patterns of net photosynthesis quite well when coupled with irradiation.

Irradiation also affects the processes of respiration in light. Photorespiration, being largely dependent upon photosynthesis (Beevers, 1971), might be expected to have nearly the same response pattern to irradiation as photosynthesis (Holmgren & Jarvis, 1967; Brix, 1968). Considerable evidence exists for a substantial reduction of mitochondrial respiration in light (see reviews by Jackson & Volk, 1970 and Raven, 1972b) although a considerable portion of this apparent reduction may be due to photosynthetic reassimilation of respired carbon dioxide. Much recent evidence has suggested, however, that mitochondrial respiration may also be directly inhibited by photosynthetic intermediates in light (Jackson & Volk, 1970; Raven, 1972a). Therefore, mitochondrial respiration rates in light may be substantially lower than rates reported under dark conditions, a fact to be remembered in any attempts to estimate levels of mitochondrial

517

Plant processes

respiration in light by extrapolation from experimental data. Raven (1972a) stated that mitochondrial respiration in light ranges from 25% to 100% of respiration in dark, depending upon species and environmental conditions.

Humidity

In addition to effects of water potential, temperature and irradiation, some workers have investigated possible effects of atmospheric humidity on gas-exchange processes (Tranquillini, 1963; Lange et al., 1969; Lange, Lösch, Schulze & Kappen, 1971; Stevenson & Shaw, 1971; Bamberg et al., 1974; Davies & Kozlowski, 1974; Schulze et al., 1974). Crafts (1968) pointed out that low temperature and high humidity (i.e. low vapor pressure deficit) may tend to ameliorate effects of water stress on net assimilation of carbon dioxide, whereas under opposite conditions – high temperature and low humidity – water-stress effects may be accentuated. Experimental data have partially supported this hypothesis (Lange et al., 1969, 1971). The primary way in which photosynthesis responds to humidity appears to be through its effects on stomatal diffusion resistance (r_s'). Schulze et al. (1974) found humidity and temperature to be the dominant factors controlling daily patterns of r_s' for Prunus armeniaca. Increases in humidity (i.e. decreases in leaf-to-air vapor pressure deficit) generally induced stomatal opening, as did increasing temperatures if water stress was low. Open stomata during periods of high atmospheric humidity would tend to maximize intake of carbon dioxide relative to transpirational loss of water, since the driving force of transpiration, leaf-to-air vapor pressure deficit, would be lowered under such conditions, and higher efficiency of photosynthesis in terms of water use is very advantageous to plants under drought conditions. It is interesting to note that maximum daily temperatures, which would tend to increase both uptake of carbon dioxide and loss of water, generally coincided with minimum daily humidities which induced stomatal closure, thus preventing excessive loss of water during hot afternoon periods.

To be sure, relative humidities in arid environments are in general rather low; effects of high humidity on net assimilation of carbon dioxide in the arid ecosystem may thus at best be infrequent in most situations. However, the possibility certainly exists that seemingly minor diurnal fluctuations in humidity (for instance, from early morning to midday) could change plant gas-exchange patterns.

Plant factors

In addition to effects of physical factors on plant gas exchange, relationships involving various characteristics of the plant species themselves affect gas exchange in the arid ecosystem. These plant factors can be arbitrarily placed in two general classes: (*a*) factors related to differing biochemical pathways of gas exchange; and (*b*) factors related to morphology and phenology.

Biochemical pathways

In many succulent plants a specific series of biochemical reactions takes place leading to non-autotrophic fixation of carbon dioxide, these reactions being collectively termed crassulacean acid metabolism (CAM). In brief, this pathway involves net assimilation of carbon dioxide by green tissues in the dark, leading to a distinct accumulation of organic acids, L-malic acid in particular. During subsequent light periods, organic acid levels decrease as carbon dioxide, from decarboxylated malate, is refixed photosynthetically. Thus, pronounced diurnal fluctuations in organic acids are a characteristic of CAM species. Ting (1971) provides a more complete description of the metabolic pathway.

Patten & Dinger (1969) found that the temperature of the plant tissue, rather than that of the air, is most important in affecting metabolic rates of certain CAM species. Typically, CAM activity is highest where night temperatures are low and day temperatures are high. Such a thermal regime stimulates stomatal opening at night and closure during the day; low night temperatures may also accelerate organic acid build-up through effects on specific enzymes involved. Photoperiod also affects CAM metabolism, highest CAM activity occurring when day lengths are shortest. Thus, maximum CAM activity usually takes place under conditions of widely fluctuating temperatures, high by day and low by night, concurrent with short photoperiods (Ting, 1971). If cool temperatures with little diurnal fluctuation occur when photoperiods are long, significant uptake of carbon dioxide may take place in light. The preceding generalizations on CAM metabolism have been largely verified for desert succulents by studies under the IBP (Patten, 1971, 1972; Ting *et al.*, 1972, 1973, 1974; Patten & Nisbet, 1973); highest rates of net carbon dioxide assimilation in CAM species typically occur during cool months with relatively short photoperiods.

A decline in net assimilation of carbon dioxide by CAM succulents has been noted with decreasing water potential (Ting *et al.*, 1972, 1973, 1974; Bartholomew, 1973; Patten & Nisbet, 1973; Szarek, Johnson & Ting, 1973). Ting *et al.* (1974) found decreased nocturnal assimilation of carbon

519

Plant processes

dioxide during drought to be associated with high stomatal and mesophyll (or residual) resistances. Lack of stomatal opening during drought may result in continuous internal recycling of endogenously produced carbon dioxide, with little exogenous gas exchange (Szarek *et al.*, 1973), which also reflects the generally high cuticular resistance to gas flux exhibited by CAM species (Ting *et al.*, 1973). However, species with CAM metabolism may be capable of a rapid favorable response to decreased water stress even after considerable periods of drought, as is evidenced by rapid increases in net assimilation of carbon dioxide following rainfall (Szarek *et al.*, 1973; Ting *et al.*, 1974). In general, CAM species are well adapted for an existence in arid environments on account of the remarkably high efficiency of photosynthesis in relation to water use (Neales *et al.*, 1968; Mooney, 1972; Meinzer & Rundel, 1973).

Some temperature acclimation may take place with CAM species through the course of a growing season (Patten & Nisbet, 1973), with changes in compensation point temperatures lagging slightly behind seasonal temperature changes. Nisbet & Patten (1974) found similar rates of assimilation of carbon dioxide for *Opuntia phaeacantha* var. *discata* at higher temperatures in summer and lower temperatures in winter, although lower temperatures still tended to increase assimilation rates in warm-acclimated plants.

The C_4-dicarboxylic pathway of photosynthesis is a second pathway distinct from C_3 (pentose) photosynthesis. Species exhibiting C_4 photosynthesis typically possess a conspicuous *Kranz* leaf anatomy (Laetsch, 1971, 1974), which facilitates function of the C_4 pathway. In brief, *Kranz* anatomy is characterized by a layer of chloroplast-rich, relatively impervious, bundle-sheath cells surrounding the vascular tissue. Carbon dioxide is initially fixed into C_4 organic acids in the mesophyll, as in dark fixation of carbon dioxide by CAM plants, which are then transported to the bundle-sheath cells and decarboxylated. The carbon dioxide released is then refixed in the bundle-sheath cells by means of the Calvin cycle (Hatch, 1971). C_4 and CAM metabolism are thus quite similar; Ting (1971) observed that with CAM metabolism initial and final carboxylation reactions are separated by time, whereas with C_4 metabolism they are separated spatially by means of *Kranz* anatomy.

A number of species indigenous to warm and/or dry regions have been found to possess the C_4-dicarboxylic acid pathway of photosynthesis (see, for instance Welkie & Caldwell, 1970; Downton, 1971; Williams & Markley, 1973 and Osmond, 1974). Although the C_4 pathway may be inherently less efficient energetically than the C_3 (pentose) pathway (Hatch, 1971; Pearcy *et al.*, 1974), C_4 species may be in many ways ideally suited for an existence in arid ecosystems (Björkman, 1971; Caldwell, 1972; McWilliam & Mison, 1974). Features with adaptive value in this

520

environment, shown by most C_4 species (Björkman, 1973; Black, 1973), include (*a*) they show little or no photorespiration; (*b*) the potential absolute rate of net photosynthesis is efficient in terms of water use; (*c*) the optimum temperature for photosynthesis is relatively high; (*d*) the saturation light intensity is relatively high; and (*e*) the minimum carbon concentration for net photosynthesis (CO_2 compensation point) is low.

The generally higher efficiency of photosynthesis in relation to water use which characterizes C_4 species may be due to the high intrinsic efficiency of utilization of low carbon dioxide concentrations and lack of oxygen inhibition of photosynthesis (Björkman, 1971), resulting in lower residual resistances to uptake of carbon dioxide, coupled with typically high and responsive stomatal diffusion resistances (e.g. Slatyer, 1970; Akita & Moss, 1972). Whitman & Koller (1967*b*) also considered that high water-use efficiencies through relatively low r_r' and stress-sensitive r_s' values would be of adaptive significance for desert species.

Although photosynthetic rates per unit leaf material are usually higher for C_4 than for C_3 species, net carbon gain by the plant as a whole may not necessarily follow a similar pattern. The absolute amount of photosynthetic tissue available, for instance, may affect whole-plant productivity just as much as differences in rates associated with differing photosynthetic pathways. Slatyer (1970), for example, found that although leaf photosynthetic rates of the C_4 *Atriplex spongiosa* were indeed higher than those of the C_3 *Atriplex hastata*, *A. hastata* ultimately showed higher whole-plant growth rates on account of its greater leaf area. Differences in root growth and development characteristics between C_3 and C_4 species may also be reflected in patterns of total plant growth. Data of Caldwell & Camp (1974) and Fernandez (1974) suggest that C_4 shrubs have longer periods of root growth and more rapid rates of root turnover than C_3 shrubs in cool desert ecosystems; when water becomes limiting, such root-development characteristics in C_4 species may make possible longer periods of net photosynthesis. Clearly, phenological and morphological effects on gas exchange should be considered, as well as those of the various photosynthetic pathways, in any discussion of plant processes.

Morphological and phenological factors

Most studies of plant gas exchange have been primarily concerned with leaf tissue, and the possibility of significant gas-exchange activity by other above-ground plant organs has frequently been ignored. Some gas exchange undoubtedly does occur in stems, buds and reproductive organs of all species, although the significance of such activity no doubt varies widely among species. Stem tissue may be particularly important in whole-shoot gas exchange of certain species (Thorne, 1959; Ludlow &

521

Plant processes

Wilson, 1971a). Considerable net photosynthesis in stems of deciduous tree and shrub species has been reported (e.g. Pearson & Lawrence, 1958; Strain & Johnson, 1963; Zelawski, Riech & Stanley, 1970; Perry, 1971). The presence and possible significance of chlorophyll in stems of desert species has long been noted (Cannon, 1908; Fahn, 1964); DePuit & Caldwell (1975) discuss at length the possibility of significant gas exchange in stems of desert species. Wiebe, Al-Saadi & Kimball (1974) reported chlorophyll content and photosynthetic capacity in anomalous secondary wood in stems of *Atriplex confertifolia*. Perhaps the most striking example of stem photosynthetic activity reported for desert plants involves the drought-deciduous *Cercidium floridum*. Studies have shown green stems of *C. floridum* to account for up to 40% of total yearly photosynthetic production (Adams, Strain & Ting, 1967; Adams & Strain, 1968, 1969) DePuit & Caldwell (1975) similarly found substantial photosynthesis in the green stems of the half-shrub *Gutierrezia sarothrae*. However, not all desert species possessing chlorophyllous stems exhibit significant stem net photosynthesis, as is shown by the studies of Mooney & Strain (1964) on *Fouquieria splendens* and DePuit & Caldwell (1975) on *Artemisia tridentata*. When they have been studied, response patterns of net photosynthesis by stems to physical factors have in most cases been found to be roughly similar to those of net photosynthesis by leaves, although absolute rates for stems are usually lower than for leaves (Ludlow & Wilson, 1971a; DePuit, 1974; DePuit & Caldwell, 1975). Thus, for certain species stem net photosynthesis may provide an important contribution to whole-shoot carbon gain, particularly during stress periods when many species shed leaves. Neglect of possible stem photosynthesis and respiration may result in a misrepresentation of true leaf rates for the processes if gas exchange rates of entire shoots are expressed per unit of leaf material (DePuit & Caldwell, 1975).

Leaf age and plant canopy structure may affect plant gas exchange. Research has indicated a general decline in rates of photosynthesis with increasing age after the leaf has expanded fully (Hopkinson, 1966; Elmore, Hesketh & Muramoto, 1967; Dickmann, 1971; Eagles, 1971; Woledge, 1973), and this decline may be attributed either to increased stomatal diffusion resistance (Ludlow & Wilson, 1971b; McPherson & Slatyer, 1973; Turner & Begg, 1973) or to increased residual resistance (Obendorf & Huffaker, 1970; Ludlow & Wilson, 1971b; Osman & Milthorpe, 1971) to transport of carbon dioxide in older leaves. Adverse effects of leaf age on net photosynthesis would be expected to become progressively more pronounced through the growing season, since most new leaves usually mature early in the season. Leaf position and crown form may also influence the photosynthetic capacity of the leaves. Leaves which have developed in open, high-irradiation microenvironments tend to exhibit higher maximum photosynthetic rates than leaves from closed, shaded microenvironments (Beuerlein & Pendleton, 1971; Woledge, 1971, 1973; Mika & Antoszewski, 1972).

Phenological changes in leaf morphology may affect photosynthetic capacities of leaves at different times of the season. Cunningham & Strain (1969) found lower photosynthetic rates in smaller, denser late-season leaves of *Encelia farinosa*; DePuit (1974) noted a similar phenomenon with *Artemisia tridentata* and *Gutierrezia sarothrae*. Eagles (1971) observed a reduction in rates of net photosynthesis concurrent with reduced leaf-area ratios (that is, leaf area/leaf weight), which generally declined with time, for *Dactylis glomerata*. Hellmuth (1968) noted differences in leaf morphology at different times of the season for *Acacia craspedocarpa*, and found differences in patterns and absolute magnitudes of gas exchange between different types of leaves.

Temporal phenological changes in leaf age and morphology may be important, in conjunction with changes in physical factors, in seasonal acclimation patterns of plants (Caldwell, 1972; Orshan, 1972).

Patterns of gas exchange in the arid ecosystem

The interaction of the various physical and biological factors described in the preceding sections result in the diurnal and seasonal patterns of gas exchange shown by plants in arid ecosystems. In general, factors exerting the greatest effect on these processes are those which are most limiting; effects of a factor which is farthest from optimal (such as low water potential, or high temperature) may supersede effects of other less limiting process factors. This principle should be remembered when apparently inconsistent relationships between rates of gas exchange and the values of individual, non-limiting factors are encountered.

Diurnal patterns of gas exchange

When water stress is low, the daily pattern of net photosynthesis has been found to be mainly governed by irradiation and temperature through the course of the day (Wilson, 1967; Helms, 1972; Hari & Luukkanen, 1973, 1974), although in certain situations humidity may also have an effect (Lange *et al.*, 1971; Schulze *et al.*, 1974). For some desert species under such conditions, rates of net photosynthesis have been shown to parallel the daily course of irradiation, peaking at midday, under clear conditions, as long as temperatures are not prohibitive (Moore, 1971; DePuit & Caldwell, 1973; DePuit, 1974; Pearcy & Harrison, 1974). However, in other cases a morning peak in net photosynthesis rates has been observed, followed by a leveling off or decline in rates (e.g. DePuit & Caldwell, 1973;

523

Plant processes

DePuit, 1974); the morning peaks of net photosynthesis may either reflect relatively low light saturation intensities for photosynthesis, or effects of supra-optimal temperatures later in the day. Under conditions of limited water availability, depression of net photosynthesis at midday is far more widespread (Whiteman & Koller, 1967b; West, 1969; Dunn, 1970; Bamberg *et al.*, 1973; DePuit & Caldwell, 1973; DePuit, 1974; Pearcy *et al.*, 1974), and with certain species a bi-modal pattern of net photosynthesis (that is, morning and late afternoon peaks) has been observed (Hellmuth, 1968, 1971; Lange *et al.*, 1969; Strain, 1970; Moore, 1971). A midday depression of net photosynthesis under conditions of limiting water availability may be related to either supra-optimal temperatures, or to high transient plant–soil water stresses. It should be recognized, however, that exceptions to the above generalizations have been observed for plants in arid ecosystems. Björkman *et al.* (1972) and Hellmuth (1969) found essentially no midday depression of net photosynthesis for certain desert species, even under conditions of severe water stress. Clearly, there may be important interspecific differences in the effects of irradiation, temperature and water potential on daily patterns of net assimilation.

Night respiration patterns of plants are generally correlated with the course of temperature throughout the dark period, higher rates occurring at higher temperatures. Bamberg *et al.* (1973) reported that the highest dark respiration rates generally occur early in the evening, with lower rates thereafter.

Endogenous diurnal rhythms in gas-exchange activity have been reported for a number of species (e.g. Barrs, 1968; Chia-Looi & Cumming, 1972; Jones & Mansfield, 1972). The endogenous rhythm phenomenon, however, appears to be peculiar to certain species, since for many species investigated no internally controlled rhythms in net gas exchange have been observed.

Seasonal patterns of gas exchange

As noted previously, seasonal patterns of gas exchange for plants in the arid ecosystem are correlated best with water availability and temperature. Maximum seasonal rates of net photosynthesis and respiration generally occur during periods when water and heat stress are lowest, a fact borne out by numerous studies on plants in arid regions (Chew & Chew, 1965; Hellmuth, 1968; West, 1969; Dunn, 1970; Patten, 1971, 1972; Caldwell, Moore, White & DePuit, 1972; Oechel *et al.*, 1972; Ting *et al.*, 1972, 1973, 1974; Bamberg *et al.*, 1973, 1974; Caldwell *et al.*, 1973, 1974; Patten & Nisbet, 1973; Lange *et al.*, 1974; Mooney & Chu, 1974; Odening *et al.*, 1974; Pearcy *et al.*, 1974). Effects of plant factors must be considered in conjunction with water potential and temperature, however, since the magnitude and reversibility of effects of the latter depend in large part upon the phenological, morphological, and biochemical characteristics of the species.

Seasonal morpho-phenological changes in desert plants are most often triggered by water potential (Beatley, 1974), although photoperiod and temperature regime may also be involved. Adaptive morpho-phenological 'strategies' used by desert species to survive in an environment characterized by low and sporadic water availability are reviewed by Noy-Meir (1973) and discussed at length by Bamberg *et al.* (1973), Odening *et al.* (1974), and DePuit (1974). More complete descriptions of the phenology of desert species are provided elsewhere in this volume. In general, annual species in arid ecosystems are relatively ephemeral, germinating only when physical conditions are suitable and exhibiting relatively high rates of primary production prior to dormancy and death. Perennial species may be drought-deciduous, winter-deciduous, or evergreen. Deciduous species generally have relatively high leaf net photosynthesis rates during favorable periods, but lose their leaves and become largely dormant during stress periods (Mooney & Dunn, 1970; Bamberg *et al.*, 1973; DePuit, 1974); the green stems of certain deciduous species may also be capable of significant net photosynthesis, which would be of adaptive significance during leafless periods (e.g. Adams & Strain, 1969; DePuit, 1974). Evergreen perennial species typically have somewhat lower net photosynthesis rates, but retain the capacity for net assimilation, in varying degrees, throughout stress periods. Such species commonly show some seasonal leaf dimorphism, producing different types of leaves morphologically suited to the environmental conditions prevailing at different seasons (Cunningham & Strain, 1969; DePuit & Caldwell, 1973; Odening *et al.*, 1974). Some perennial evergreen species possess the C_4 or CAM pathways of photosynthesis, which may be of benefit under stress conditions for reasons cited previously. A few species can maintain almost their full gas-exchange capacity even under extreme environmental stress, such as the C_4 plant *Tidestromia oblongifolia* in Death Valley, California (Björkman *et al.*, 1972). Odening *et al.* (1974) studied three perennial desert shrubs with differing adaptations for avoiding water stress. *Larrea divaricata*, an evergreen species, maintains net photosynthesis throughout the year regardless of water stress by means of a high protoplasmic tolerance to drought, whereas *Encelia farinosa* prolongs periods of net photosynthesis under water stress by means of seasonal leaf variability and a drought-deciduous habit. The phreatophytic *Chilopsis linearis* is most sensitive to low water potentials, and hence is usually confined to habitats offering sufficient sub-surface water.

Plant processes

Existing gaps in knowledge

An accurate estimate of the net gas exchange of the whole plant obviously requires an understanding of gas-exchange patterns and responses of all plant organs with a capacity for photosynthesis or respiration. As stated previously, most research has been conducted on leaf gas exchange, whereas gas exchange of other above-ground plant organs, most notably stems, may in some cases be significant. Although some research has been conducted on stem gas exchange (for instance, Bamberg *et al.*, 1974; Caldwell *et al.*, 1974), much more effort is needed in this area. Net respiratory activity of below-ground plant biomass must also be taken into account when attempting to predict the net gas exchange of the whole plant. Research in this area has developed rather slowly, owing to technical difficulties associated with measuring root respiration. Preliminary experimentation has suggested substantial respiration by the root system (Caldwell *et al.*, 1974); measurements of root respiration in the arid ecosystem are in progress (Bamberg *et al.*, 1974; Caldwell *et al.*, 1974), and more are certainly needed.

Another area of potential importance in evaluation of net gas exchange of the whole plant or the community is the effect of leaf canopy structure on net gas exchange. Photosynthetic measurements have generally been conducted on well-illuminated, exposed leaf tissue, and the resulting estimates of net photosynthesis are commonly applied to leaves in all parts of the canopy when attempts are made to predict net photosynthesis under ambient conditions. In fairly open plant communities, such an approach may not be too inaccurate, but in communities where a substantial proportion of the leaf biomass is shaded, and thus is exposed to or has developed under limited irradiation, the net photosynthesis rates of the community may be considerably over-estimated. A greater understanding of the effects of mutual shading on the net photosynthesis rates of the community is therefore needed.

The ultimate goal of gas-exchange research within an ecosystem study is a capability of accurately predicting the gas exchange and primary productivity of the plant community as a whole. Since most gas-exchange research has measured photosynthesis and respiration rates over short time periods, and expressed the results per unit plant material, there is a need to integrate these rates over a longer time period and to express them per unit land area. These conversions require a knowledge of the biomass and density of the plant community; a knowledge of community species composition is also needed, so that the large differences in gas-exchange rates and responses between species may be taken into account. If rates of net gas exchange or primary production for longer periods of time are required, a feasible means of integrating the effects of variable

526

factors on this longer time scale must be developed. Such estimates of total net gas exchange will be required if the total carbon balance of the arid ecosystem (Mooney, 1972; Caldwell *et al.*, 1974) is to be ascertained.

Acknowledgments

Sincere appreciation is extended to Dr Martyn M. Caldwell, Utah State University, for his review and assistance in the preparation of this chapter. Facilities and personnel required for manuscript preparation were provided by the Department of Animal and Range Sciences, Montana State University.

References

Adams, M. S. (1970). Adaptations of *Aplectrum hyemale* to the environment. Effects of preconditioning temperature on net photosynthesis. *Bulletin of the Torrey Botanical Club*, **97**, 219–24.

Adams, M. S. & Strain, B. R. (1968). Photosynthesis in stems and leaves of *Cercidium floridum*: spring and summer diurnal field responses and relation to temperature. *Oecologia Plantarum*, **3**, 285–97.

Adams, M. S. & Strain, B. R. (1969). Seasonal photosynthetic rates in stems of *Cercidium floridum* Benth. *Photosynthetica*, **3**, 55–62.

Adams, M. S., Strain, B. R. & Ting, I. P. (1967). Photosynthesis in chlorophyllous stem tissue and leaves of *Cercidium floridum*: assimilation and distribution of ^{14}C from $^{14}CO_2$. *Plant Physiology*, **42**, 1797–9.

Akita, S. & Moss, D. N. (1972). Differential stomatal response between C_3 and C_4 species to atmospheric CO_2 concentration and light. *Crop Science*, **12**, 789–93.

Akita, S. & Moss, D. N. (1973). Photosynthetic responses to CO_2 and light by maize and wheat leaves adjusted for constant stomatal apertures. *Crop Science*, **13**, 234–7.

Bamberg, S., Wallace, A., Kleinkopf, G. & Vollmer, A. (1973). *Plant productivity and nutrient interrelationships of perennials in the Mohave Desert*. US/IBP Desert Biome Research Memorandum, RM 73–10. Logan, Utah.

Bamberg, S., Wallace, A., Kleinkopf, G., Vollmer, A. & Ausmus, B. (1974). *Plant productivity and nutrient interrelationships of perennials in the Mohave Desert*. US/IBP Desert Biome Research Memorandum, RM 74–8. Logan, Utah.

Barrs, H. D. (1968). Effect of cyclic variations in gas exchange under constant environmental conditions on the ratio of transpiration to net photosynthesis. *Physiologia Plantarum*, **21**, 918–29.

Bartholomew, B. (1973). Drought response in the gas exchange of *Dudleya farinosa* (Crassulaceae) grown under natural conditions. *Photosynthetica*, **7**, 114–20.

Beadle, C. L., Stevenson, K. R., Neumann, H. H., Thurtell, G. W. & King, K. M. (1973). Diffusive resistance, transpiration and photosynthesis in single leaves of corn and sorghum in relation to leaf water potential. *Canadian Journal of Plant Science*, **53**, 537–44.

Beardsell, M. F., Mitchell, K. J. & Thomas, R. G. (1973). Effects of water stress under contrasting environmental conditions on transpiration and photosynthesis in soybean. *Journal of Experimental Botany*, **24**, 579–86.

Beatley, J. C. (1974). Phenological events and their environmental triggers in Mojave Desert ecosystems. *Ecology*, **55**, 856–63.

Beevers, H. (1971). Photorespiration: assessment. In *Photosynthesis and Photorespiration* (eds. M. D. Hatch, C. B. Osmond & R. O. Slatyer), pp. 541–3. Wiley–Interscience, New York.

Beuerlein, J. E. & Pendleton, J. W. (1971). Photosynthetic rates and light saturation curves of individual soybean leaves under field conditions. *Crop Science*, **11**, 217–19.

Biscoe, P. V. (1972). The diffusion resistance and water status of leaves of *Beta vulgaris*. *Journal of Experimental Botany*, **23**, 930–40.

Biscoe, P. V., Littleton, E. J. & Scott, R. K. (1973). Stomatal control of gas exchange in barley awns. *Annals of Applied Biology*, **75**, 285–97.

Björkman, O. (1971). Comparative photosynthetic CO_2 exchange in higher plants. In: *Photosynthesis and Photorespiration* (eds. M. D. Hatch, C. B. Osmond & R. O. Slatyer), pp. 18–32. Wiley–Interscience, New York.

Björkman, O. (1973). Comparative studies on photosynthesis in higher plants. *Photophysiology*, **8**, 1–64.

Björkman, O. & Berry, J. (1973). High efficiency photosynthesis. *Scientific American*, **229** (10), 80–93.

Björkman, O., Pearcy, R. W , Harrison, A. T. & Mooney, H. A. (1972). Photo synthetic adaptation to high temperature in Death Valley, California. *Science*, **175**, 786–9.

Black, C. C. (1973). Photosynthetic carbon fixation in relation to net CO_2 uptake. *Annual Reviews of Plant Physiology*, **24**, 253–86.

Boyer, J. S. (1970*a*). Leaf enlargement and metabolic rates in corn, soybean, and sunflower at various leaf water potentials. *Plant Physiology*, **46**, 233–4.

Boyer, J. S. (1970*b*). Differing sensitivity of photosynthesis to low leaf water potentials in corn and soybean. *Plant Physiology*, **46**, 236–9.

Boyer, J. S. (1971). Nonstomatal inhibition of photosynthesis in sunflower at low leaf water potentials and high light intensities. *Plant Physiology*, **48**, 532–6.

Boyer, J. S. & Bowen, B. L. (1970). Inhibition of oxygen evolution in chloroplasts isolated from leaves with low water potentials. *Plant Physiology*, **45**, 612–15.

Brix, H. (1962). The effect of water stress on the rates of photosynthesis and respiration in tomato plants and loblolly pine seedlings. *Physiologia Plantarum*, **15**, 10–20.

Brix, H. (1968). Influence of light intensity at different temperatures on rate of respiration of Douglas-fir seedlings. *Plant Physiology*, **43**, 389–93.

Caldwell, M. M. (1972). Gas exchange of shrubs. In *Wildland Shrubs – Their Biology and Utilization* (eds. C. M. McKell, J. P. Blaisdell & J. R. Goodin), pp. 260–70. U.S. Department of Agriculture, Forest Service General Technical Report INT-1. Washington, D.C.

Caldwell, M. M. & Camp, L. B. (1974). Below-ground productivity of two cool desert communities. *Oecologia*, **17**, 123–30.

Caldwell, M. M., Moore, R. T., White, R. S. & DePuit, E. J. (1972). *Gas exchange of Great Basin shrubs*. US/IBP Desert Biome Research Memorandum, RM 72–20. Logan, Utah.

Caldwell, M. M., Wiebe, H. H., DePuit, E. J., Fernandez, O. A., Camp, L. B. & Fareed, M. (1973). *Gas exchange and root growth of cold desert plants*. US/IBP Desert Biome Research Memorandum, RM 73–13. Logan, Utah.

Photosynthesis, respiration and biochemical transformations

Caldwell, M. M., DePuit, E. J., Fernandez, O. A., Wiebe, H. H. & Camp, L. B. (1974). *Gas exchange, translocation, root growth, and soil respiration of Great Basin plants.* US/IBP Desert Biome Research Memorandum, RM 74–9. Logan, Utah.

Campbell, G. S. & Harris, G. A. (1974). *Effect of soil water potential on soil moisture absorption, transpiration rate, plant water potential, and growth of* Artemisia tridentata. US/IBP Desert Biome Research Memorandum, RM 74–44. Logan, Utah.

Cannon, W. A. (1908). *The topography of the chlorophyll apparatus in desert plants.* Carnegie Institution, Washington, Publication 98.

Cartledge, O. & Connor, D. J. (1973). Photosynthetic efficiency of tropical and temperate grass canopies. *Photosynthetica,* **7**, 109–13.

Chew, R. M. & Chew, A. E. (1965). The primary productivity of a desert shrub (*Larrea tridentata*) community. *Ecological Monographs,* **35**, 355–75.

Chia-Looi, A. & Cumming, B. G. (1972). Circadian rhythms of dark respiration, flowering, net photosynthesis, chlorophyll content, and dry weight changes in *Chenopodium rubrum. Canadian Journal of Botany,* **50**, 2219–26.

Crafts, A. S. (1968). Water deficits and physiological processes. In: *Water Deficits and Plant Growth* (ed. T. T. Kozlowski), Vol. II, Chapter 3. Academic Press, New York.

Cunningham, G. L. & Strain, B. R. (1969). An ecological significance of seasonal leaf variability in a desert shrub. *Ecology,* **50**, 400–8.

Cunningham, G. L., Balding, F. R. & Syvertsen, J. P. (1973). *A model of net CO_2 exchange rate for C_4 grasses.* US/IBP Desert Biome Research Memorandum, RM 73–15. Logan, Utah.

Davies, W. J. & Kozlowski, T. T. (1974). Stomatal responses of five woody angiosperms to light intensity and humidity. *Canadian Journal of Botany,* **52**, 1525–34.

Decker, J. P. (1959). Some effects of temperature and carbon dioxide concentration on photosynthesis of *Mimulus. Plant Physiology,* **34**, 103–6.

DePuit, E. J. (1974). 'Gas exchange studies of arid land plants.' Ph.D. Dissertation, Utah State University, Logan, Utah.

DePuit, E. J. & Caldwell, M. M. (1973). Seasonal pattern of net photosynthesis of *Artemisia tridentata. American Journal of Botany,* **60**, 426–35.

DePuit, E. J. & Caldwell, M. M. (1975). Stem and leaf gas exchange of two arid land shrubs. *American Journal of Botany,* **62**, 954–61.

Detling, J. K. & Klikoff, L. G. (1973). Physiological response to moisture stress as a factor in halophyte distribution. *American Midland Naturalist,* **90**, 307.

Dickmann, D. I. (1971). Photosynthesis and respiration by developing leaves of cottonwood (*Populus deltoides* Burtr.). *Botanical Gazette,* **132**, 353–4.

Döhler, G. & Przybylla, K. R. (1973). Photorespiration in the blue-green alga *Anacystis nidulans* at different temperatures. *Planta,* **110**, 153–8.

Downes, R. W. & O'Connor, D. J. (1973). Effect of growth environment on gas exchange characteristic of brigalow (*Acacia harpophylla* F. Muell.). *Photosynthetica,* **7**, 34–40.

Downton, W. J. S. (1971). Check list of C_4 species. In: *Photosynthesis and Photorespiration* (eds. M. D. Hatch, C. B. Osmond & R. O. Slatyer), pp. 554–6. Wiley–Interscience, New York.

Dunn, E. L. (1970). 'Seasonal patterns of carbon dioxide metabolism in evergreen sclerophylls in California and Chile.' Ph.D. Thesis, University of California, Los Angeles, California.

Eagles, C. F. (1971). Changes in net assimilation rate and leaf-area ratio with time in *Dactylis glomerata*. *Annals of Botany*, **35**, 63–74.

Ehrler, W. L. & Van Bavel, C. H. M. (1968). Leaf diffusion resistance, illuminance, and transpiration. *Plant Physiology*, **43**, 208–14.

Elmore, C. D., Hesketh, J. D. & Muramoto, H. (1967). A survey of rates of leaf growth, leaf aging and leaf photosynthetic rates among and within species. *Journal of the Arizona Academy of Science*, **4**, 215–19.

El-Sharkaway, M. A. & Hesketh, J. D. (1964). Effects of temperature and water deficit on leaf photosynthetic rates of different species. *Crop Science*, **4**, 514–18.

Fahn, A. (1964). Some anatomical adaptations of desert plants. *Phytomorphology*, **14**, 93–102.

Fernandez, O. A. (1974). 'The dynamics of root growth and the partitioning of photosynthates in cool desert shrubs.' Ph.D. Dissertation, Utah State University, Logan, Utah.

Fryer, J. A. & Ledig, F. T. (1972). Microevolution of the photosynthetic temperature optimum in relation to the environmental complex gradient. *Canadian Journal of Botany*, **50**, 1231–5.

Gaastra, P. (1959). Photosynthesis of crop plants as influenced by light, carbon dioxide, temperature and stomatal diffusion resistance. *Mededelingen Landbouwhogeschool Wageningen*, **59**, 1–68.

Gale, J., Kohl, H. C. & Hagan, R. M. (1966). Mesophyll and stomatal resistances affecting photosynthesis under varying conditions of soil, water and evaporation demand. *Israel Journal of Botany*, **15**, 64–71.

Gifford, R. M. & Musgrave, R. B. (1970). Diffusion and quasi-diffusion resistances in relation to the carboxylation kinetics of maize leaves. *Physiologia Plantarum*, **23**, 1048–56.

Gifford, R. M. & Musgrave, R. B. (1972). Activation energy analysis and limiting factors in photosynthesis. *Australian Journal of Biological Science*, **25**, 419–23.

Halvorson, W. L. & Patten, D. T. (1974). Seasonal water potential changes in Sonoran Desert shrubs in relation to topography. *Ecology*, **55**, 173–7.

Hari, P. & Luukkanen, O. (1973). Effect of water stress, temperature, and light on photosynthesis in alder seedlings. *Physiologia Plantarum*, **29**, 45–53.

Hari, P. & Luukkanen, O. (1974). Field studies of photosynthesis as affected by water stress, temperature and light in birch. *Physiologia Plantarum*, **32**, 97–102.

Harris, D. G. (1973). Photosynthesis, diffusion resistance and relative plant water content of cotton as influenced by induced water stress. *Crop Science*, **13**, 570–72.

Hatch, M. D. (1971). Mechanism and function of the C_4 pathway of photosynthesis. in: *Photosynthesis and Photorespiration* (eds. M. D. Hatch, C. B. Osmond & R. O. Slatyer), pp. 139–152. Wiley–Interscience, New York.

Hellmuth, E. O. (1968). Ecophysiological studies on plants in arid and semi-arid regions in Western Australia. I. Autecology of *Rhagodia baccata*. *Journal of Ecology*, **56**, 319–44.

Hellmuth, E. O. (1969). Ecophysiological studies on plants in arid and semi-arid regions in Western Australia. II. Field physiology of *Acacia craspedocarpa*. *Journal of Ecology*, **57**, 613–34.

Hellmuth, E. O. (1971). Ecophysiological studies on plants in arid and semi-arid regions in Western Australia. III. Comparative studies on photosynthesis, respiration and water relation of ten arid zone and two semi-arid zone plants under winter and late summer climatic conditions. *Journal of Ecology*, **59**, 225–60.

Helms, J. A. (1972). Environmental control of net photosynthesis in naturally growing *Pinus ponderosa* Laws. *Ecology*, **53**, 92–101.

Hesketh, J. D. & Moss, D. N. (1963). Variation in the response of photosynthesis to light. *Crop Science*, **3**, 107–10.

Hew, C. S., Krotkov, G. & Canvin, D. T. (1969). Effects of temperature on photosynthesis and CO_2 evolution in light and darkness by green leaves. *Plant Physiology*, **44**, 671–7.

Hodges, J. D. (1967). Patterns of photosynthesis under natural environmental conditions. *Ecology*, **48**, 234–42.

Hofstra, G. & Hesketh, J. D. (1969). Effects of temperature on the gas exchange of leaves in the light and dark. *Planta*, **85**, 228–37.

Holmgren, P. & Jarvis, P. G. (1967). Carbon dioxide efflux from leaves in light and darkness. *Physiologia Plantarum*, **20**, 1045–51.

Hopkinson, J. M. (1966). Studies on the expansion of the leaf surface. VI. Senescence and the usefulness of old leaves. *Journal of Experimental Botany*, **17**, 762–70.

Jackson, W. A. & Volk, R. J. (1970). Photorespiration. *Annual Reviews of Plant Physiology*, **21**, 385–432.

James, W. O. (1953). *Plant Respiration*. Clarendon Press, Oxford.

Jones, H. G. (1973a). Moderate-term water stresses and associated changes in some photosynthetic parameters in cotton. *New Phytologist*, **72**, 1095–1105.

Jones, H. G. (1973b). Photosynthesis by thin leaf slices in solution. II. Osmotic stress and its effects on photosynthesis. *Australian Journal of Biological Science*, **26**, 25–33.

Jones, H. G. (1974). Assessment of stomatal control of plant water status. *New Phytologist*, **73**, 851–9.

Jones, M. B. & Mansfield, T. A. (1972). A circadian rhythm in the level of CO_2 compensation in *Bryophyllum feldtschenkoi* with zero values during the transient. *Planta*, **103**, 134–46.

Jones, H. G. & Slatyer, R. O. (1972). Estimation of the transport and carboxylation components of the intracellular limitation to leaf photosynthesis. *Plant Physiology*, **50**, 283–8.

Kaul, R. (1966). Effect of water stress on respiration of wheat. *Canadian Journal of Botany*, **44**, 623–32.

Kramer, P. J. (1969). *Plant and Soil Water Relationships: A Modern Synthesis*. McGraw-Hill, New York.

Kriedemann, P. E. & Smart, R. E. (1971). Effects of irradiance, temperature, and leaf water potential on photosynthesis of vine leaves. *Photosynthetica*, **5**, 6–15.

Laetsch, W. M. (1971). Chloroplast structural relationships in leaves of C_4 plants. In: *Photosynthesis and Photorespiration* (eds. M. D. Hatch, C. B. Osmond & R. O. Slatyer), pp. 323–49. Wiley–Interscience, New York.

Laetsch, W. M. (1974). The C_4 syndrome: a structural analysis. *Annual Reviews of Plant Physiology*, **25**, 27–52.

Lake, J. V. (1967). Respiration of leaves during photosynthesis. II. Effects on the estimation of the mesophyll resistance. *Australian Journal of Biological Science*, **20**, 495–9.

Lange, O. L., Koch, W. & Schulze, E. D. (1969). CO_2-gas exchange and water relationships of plants in the Negev Desert at the end of the dry period. *Berichte der Deutschen Botanischen Gesellschaft*, **82**, 39–61.

Lange, O. L., Lösch, R., Schulze, E. D. & Kappen, L. (1971). Responses of stomata to changes in humidity. *Planta*, **100**, 76–86.

Lange, O. L., Schulze, E. D., Evenari, M., Kappen, L. & Buschbom, U. (1974). The temperature-related photosynthetic capacity of plants under desert conditions. I. Seasonal changes of the photosynthetic response to temperature. *Oecologia*, **17**, 97–110.

Levitt, J. (1972). *Responses of Plants to Environmental Stresses*. Academic Press, New York.

Ludlow, M. M. & Jarvis, P. G. (1971). Photosynthesis in Sitka spruce (*Picea sitchensis* (Bong.) Carr). I. General characteristics. *Journal of Applied Ecology*, **8**, 925–53.

Ludlow, M. M. & Wilson, G. L. (1971a). Photosynthesis of tropical pasture plants. I. Illuminance, carbon dioxide concentration, leaf temperature, and leaf–air vapour pressure difference. *Australian Journal of Biological Science*, **24**, 449–70.

Ludlow, M. M. & Wilson, G. L. (1971b). Photosynthesis of tropical plants. III. Leaf age. *Australian Journal of Biological Science*, **24**, 1077–87.

McPherson, H. G. & Slatyer, R. O. (1973). Mechanisms regulating photosynthesis in *Pennisetum typhoides*. *Australian Journal of Biological Science*, **26**, 329–39.

McWilliam, J. R. & Mison, K. (1974). Significance of the C_4 pathway in *Triodia irritans* (spinifex), a grass adapted to arid environments. *Australian Journal of Plant Physiology*, **1**, 171.

Meidner, H. & Mansfield, T. A. (1965). Stomatal responses to illumination. *Biological Review*, **40**, 483–509.

Meidner, H. & Mansfield, T. A. (1968). *Physiology of Stomata*. McGraw-Hill, New York.

Meinzer, F. C. & Rundel, P. W. (1973). Crassulacean acid metabolism and water use efficiency in *Echeveria pumila*. *Photosynthetica*, **7**, 358–64.

Mika, A. & Antoszewski, R. (1972). Effect of leaf position and tree shape on the rate of photosynthesis in the apple tree. *Photosynthetica*, **6**, 381–6.

Moldau, H. (1973). Effects of various water regimes on stomatal and mesophyll conductances of bean leaves. *Photosynthetica*, **7**, 1–7.

Mooney, H. A. (1969). Dark respiration of related evergreen and deciduous Mediterranean plants during induced drought. *Bulletin of the Torrey Botanical Club*, **96**, 550–55.

Mooney, H. A. (1972). The carbon balance of plants. *Annual Review of Ecology and Systematics*, **3**, 315–46.

Mooney, H. A. & Billings, W. D. (1961). Comparative physiological ecology of arctic and alpine populations of *Oxyria digyna*. *Ecological Monographs*, **31**, 1–29.

Mooney, H. A. & Chu, C. (1974). Seasonal carbon allocation in *Heteromeles arbutifolia*, a California evergreen shrub. *Oecologia*, **14**, 295–306.

Mooney, H. A. & Dunn, E. L. (1970). Photosynthetic systems of mediterranean-climate shrubs and trees of California and Chile. *American Midland Naturalist*, **104**, 447–53.

Mooney, H. A. & Shropshire, F. (1967). Population variability in temperature related photosynthetic acclimation. *Oecologia Plantarum*, **2**, 1–13.

Mooney, H. A. & Strain, B. R. (1964). Bark photosynthesis in ocotillo. *Madroño*, **17**, 230–33.

Mooney, H. A. & West, M. L. (1964). Photosynthetic acclimation of plants of diverse origin. *American Journal of Botany*, **51**, 825–7.

Mooney, H. A., West, M. L. & Brayton, R. (1966). Field measurements of the metabolic response of bristlecone pine and big sagebrush in the White Mountains of California. *Botanical Gazette*, **127**, 105–13.

Moore, R. T. (1971). 'Transpiration of *Atriplex confertifolia* and *Eurotia lanata* in relation to soil, plant and atmospheric moisture stresses.' Ph.D. Dissertation, Utah State University, Logan, Utah.

Moore, R. T., Miller, P. C., Albright, D. & Tieszen, L. L. (1972). Comparative gas exchange characteristics of three mangrove species during the winter. *Photosynthetica*, **6**, 387–93.

Morrow, P. A. & Mooney, H. A. (1974). Drought adaptations in two California evergreen sclerophylls. *Oecologia*, **15**, 205–22.

Neales, T. F., Patterson, A. A. & Hartney, V. J. (1968). Physiological adaptation to drought in the carbon assimilation and water loss of zerophytes. *Nature* (London), **219**, 469–72.

Nisbet, R. A. & Patten, D. T. (1974). Seasonal temperature acclimation of a prickly-pear cactus in south-central Arizona. *Oecologia*, **15**, 345–52.

Noy-Meir, I. (1973). Desert ecosystems: environment and producers. *Annual Review of Ecology and Systematics*, **4**, 25–51.

Obendorf, R. L. & Huffaker, R. C. (1970). Influence of age and illumination on distribution of several Calvin cycle enzymes in greening barley awns. *Plant Physiology*, **45**, 574–82.

Odening, W. R., Strain, B. R. & Oechel, W. C. (1974). The effect of decreasing water potential on net CO_2 exchange of intact desert shrubs. *Ecology*, **55**, 1086–95.

Oechel, W. C., Strain, B. R. & Odening, W. R. (1972). Tissue water potential, photosynthesis, ^{14}C-labeled photosynthate utilization, and growth in the desert shrub *Larrea divaricata* Car. *Ecological Monographs*, **42**, 127–41.

Orshan, G. (1972). Morphological and physiological plasticity in relation to drought. In: *Wildland Shrubs – Their Biology and Utilization* (eds. C. N. McKell, J. P. Blaisdell & J. R. Goodin), pp. 245–54. U.S. Department of Agriculture, Forest Service General Technical Report INT-1. Washington, D.C.

Osman, A. M. & Milthorpe, F. L. (1971). Photosynthesis of wheat leaves in relation to age, illuminance and nutrient supply. II. Results. *Photosynthetica*, **5**, 61–70.

Osmond, C. B. (1974). Leaf anatomy of Australian saltbushes in relation to photosynthetic pathways. *Australian Journal of Botany*, **22**, 39–44.

Pallas, J. E., Michel, B. E. & Harris, D. G. (1967). Photosynthesis, transpiration, leaf temperatures and stomatal activity of cotton plants under varying water potentials. *Plant Physiology*, **42**, 76–88.

Pasternak, D. & Wilson, G. L. (1973). Illuminance, stomatal opening, and photosynthesis in sorghum and cotton. *Australian Journal of Agricultural Research*, **24**, 527–32.

Pasternak, D. & Wilson, G. L. (1974). Differing effects of water deficit on net photosynthesis of intact and excised sorghum leaves. *New Phytologist*, **73**, 847–50.

Patten, D. T. (1971). *Productivity and water stress in cacti*. US/IBP Desert Biome Research Memorandum, RM 71–12. Logan, Utah.

Patten, D. T. (1972). *Productivity and water stress in cacti*. US/IBP Desert Biome Research Memorandum, RM 72–17. Logan, Utah.

Patten, D. T. & Dinger, B. E. (1969). CO_2 exchange patterns of cacti from different environments. *Ecology*, **50**, 686–8.

Plant processes

Patten, D. T. & Nisbet, R. A. (1973). *Productivity and water stress in cacti*. US/IBP Desert Biome Research Memorandum, RM 73–11. Logan, Utah.

Patten, D. T. & Smith, E. M. (1974). *Phenology and function of Sonoran Desert annuals in relation to environmental changes*. US/IBP Desert Biome Research Memorandum, RM 74–12. Logan, Utah.

Pearcy, R. W. & Harrison, A. T. (1974). Comparative photosynthetic and respiratory gas exchange characteristics of *Atriplex lentiformis* (Torr.) Wats. in coastal and desert habitats. *Ecology*, **55**, 1104–11.

Pearcy, R. W., Berry, J. A. & Bartholomew, B. (1974). Field photosynthetic performance and leaf temperatures of *Phragmites communis* under summer conditions in Death Valley, California. *Photosynthetica*, **8**, 104–8.

Pearcy, R. W., Harrison, A. T., Mooney, H. A. & Björkman, O. (1974). Seasonal changes in net photosynthesis of *Atriplex hymenelytra* shrubs growing in Death Valley, California. *Oecologia*, **17**, 111–21.

Pearson, L. C. & Lawrence, D. B. (1958). Photosynthesis in aspen bark. *American Journal of Botany*, **45**, 383–7.

Perry, T. O. (1971). Winter season photosynthesis and respiration by twigs and seedlings of deciduous and evergreen trees. *Forest Science*, **17**, 41–3.

Plaut, Z. & Bravdo, B. (1973). Response of carbon dioxide fixation to water stress. Parallel measurements on isolated chloroplasts and intact spinach leaves. *Plant Physiology*, **52**, 28–32.

Pourrat, Y. & Hubac, C. (1974). Comparison of drought-resistance mechanisms in two desert plants *Artemisia herba-alba* Asso. and *Carex pachystylis* Asch. and Graebn. *Physiologia Vegetale*, **12**, 135–47.

Raschke, K. (1970). Temperature dependence of CO_2 assimilation and stomatal aperture in leaf sections of *Zea mays*. *Planta*, **91**, 336–63.

Raven, J. A. (1972a). Endogenous inorganic carbon sources in plant photosynthesis. I. Occurrence of the dark respiratory pathways in illuminated plant cells. *New Phytologist*, **71**, 227–47.

Raven, J. A. (1972b). Endogenous inorganic carbon sources in plant photosynthesis. II. Comparison of total CO_2 production in the light with measured CO_2 evolution in the light. *New Phytologist*, **71**, 995–1014.

Redshaw, A. J. & Meidner, H. (1971). Effects of water stress on the resistance to uptake of CO_2 in tobacco. *Journal of Experimental Botany*, **23**, 229–40.

Reid, C. P. P. (1974). Assimilation, distribution, and root exudation of ^{14}C by ponderosa pine seedlings under induced water stress. *Plant Physiology*, **54**, 44–9.

Schultz, R. C. & Gatherum, G. E. (1971). Photosynthesis and distribution of assimilate of scotch pine seedlings in relation to soil moisture and provenance. *Botanical Gazette*, **132**, 91–6.

Schulze, E. D., Lange, O. L., Evenari, M., Kappen, L. & Buschbom, U. (1974). The role of air humidity and leaf temperature in controlling stomatal resistance of *Prunus armeniaca* L. under desert conditions. I. Simulation of the daily course of stomatal resistance. *Oecologia*, **17**, 159–70.

Slatyer, R. O. (1967). *Plant Water Relationships*. Academic Press, New York.

Slatyer, R. O. (1970). Comparative photosynthesis, growth, and transpiration of two species of *Atriplex*. *Planta*, **93**, 175–89.

Slatyer, R. O. & Bierhuizen, J. F. (1964). Transpiration from cotton leaves under a range of environmental conditions in relation to internal and external diffusive resistances. *Australian Journal of Biological Science*, **17**, 115–30.

534

Photosynthesis, respiration and biochemical transformations

Stevenson, K. R. & Shaw, R. H. (1971). Diurnal changes in leaf resistance to water vapor diffusion at different heights in a soybean canopy. *Agronomy Journal*, **63**, 17–19.

Strain, B. R. (1969). Seasonal adaptations in photosynthesis and respiration in four desert shrubs growing *in situ*. *Ecology*, **50**, 511–13.

Strain, B. R. (1970). Field measurements of tissue water potential and carbon dioxide exchange in the desert shrubs *Prosopis juliflora* and *Larrea divaricata*. *Photosynthetica*, **4**, 118–22.

Strain, B. R. & Chase, V. C. (1966). Effect of past and prevailing temperatures on the carbon dioxide exchange capacities of some woody desert perennials. *Ecology*, **47**, 1043–5.

Strain, B. R. & Johnson, P. L. (1963). Corticular photosynthesis and growth in *Populus tremuloides*. *Ecology*, **44**, 581–4.

Szarek, S. R., Johnson, H. B. & Ting, I. P. (1973). Drought adaptation in *Opuntia basilaris*. Significance of recycling carbon through crassulacean acid metabolism. *Plant Physiology*, **52**, 539–84.

Talling, J. F. (1961). Photosynthesis under natural conditions. *Annual Review of Plant Physiology*, **12**, 133–54.

Teare, I. D. & Kanemasu, E. T. (1972). Stomatal diffusion resistance and water potential of soybean and sorghum leaves. *New Phytologist*, **71**, 805–10.

Thorne, G. N. (1959). Photosynthesis of lamina and sheaths of barley leaves. *Annals of Botany*, **23**, 365–70.

Ting, I. P. (1971). Nonautotrophic CO_2 fixation and crassulacean acid metabolism. In: *Photosynthesis and Photorespiration* (eds. M. D. Hatch, C. B. Osmond & R. O. Slatyer), pp. 169–85. Wiley–Interscience, New York.

Ting, I. P., Johnson, H. B., Szarek, S. R. & Brum, G. D. (1972). *Gas exchange and productivity for* Opuntia *spp.* US/IBP Desert Biome Research Memorandum, RM 72–19. Logan, Utah.

Ting, I. P., Johnson, H. B., Yonkers, T. A. & Szarek, S. R. (1973). *Gas exchange and productivity for* Opuntia *spp.* US/IBP Desert Biome Research Memorandum, RM 73–12. Logan, Utah.

Ting, I. P., Johnson, H. B., Yonkers, T. A. & Szarek, S. R. (1974). *Gas exchange and productivity for* Opuntia *spp.* US/IBP Desert Biome Research Memorandum, RM 74–11. Logan, Utah.

Tranquillini, W. (1963). Die Abhängigkeit der Kohlensäureassimilation junger Lärchen, Fichten and Zirben von der Luft – und Bodenfeuchte. *Planta*, **60**, 70–94.

Troughton, J. H. (1969). Plant water status and carbon dioxide exchange of cotton leaves. *Australian Journal of Biological Science*, **22**, 289–302.

Troughton, J. H. & Cowan, I. R. (1968). Carbon dioxide exchange in cotton: some anomolous fluctuations. *Science*, **161**, 281–3.

Turner, W. C. & Begg, J. E. (1973). Stomatal behavior and water status of maize, sorghum and tobacco under field conditions. I. At high water potential. *Plant Physiology*, **51**, 31–6.

Welkie, G. W. & Caldwell, M. M. (1970). Leaf anatomy of species in some dicotyledon families as related to the C_3 and C_4 pathways of carbon fixation. *Canadian Journal of Botany*, **48**, 2135–46.

West, M. L. (1969). 'Physiological ecology of three species of *Artemisia* in the White Mountains of California.' Ph.D. Dissertation, University of California, Los Angeles, California.

Plant processes

West, N. E. & Gunn, C. (1974). *Phenology, productivity and nutrient dynamics of some cool desert shrubs*. US/IBP Desert Biome Research Memorandum, RM 74–7. Logan, Utah.

White, R. S., Moore, R. T. & Caldwell, M. M. (1971). Seasonal trends in photosynthetic activity of two desert halophytes. *Bulletin of the Ecological Society of America*, **52**, 39.

Whiteman, P. C. & Koller, D. (1967a). Interactions of carbon dioxide concentration, light intensity and temperature on plant resistances to water vapour and carbon dioxide diffusion. *New Phytologist*, **66**, 463–73.

Whiteman, P. C. & Koller, D. (1967b). Species characteristics in whole plant resistances to water vapour and CO_2 diffusion. *Journal of Applied Ecology*, **4**, 363–77.

Wiebe, H. H., Al-Saadi, H. A. & Kimball, S. L. (1974). Photosynthesis in the anomolous secondary wood of *Atriplex confertifolia* stems. *American Journal of Botany*, **61**, 444–8.

Williams, G. J. & Markley, J. L. (1973). The photosynthetic pathway type of North American shortgrass prairie species and some ecological implications. *Photosynthetica*, **7**, 262–70.

Wilson, J. W. (1967). Effects of seasonal variation in radiation and temperature on net assimilation and growth rates in an arid climate. *Annals of Botany*, **31**, 41–57.

Woledge, J. (1971). The effect of light intensity during growth on the subsequent rate of photosynthesis of leaves of tall fescue. *Annals of Botany*, **35**, 311–22.

Woledge, J. (1973). The photosynthesis of ryegrass leaves grown in a simulated sward. *Annals of Applied Biology*, **73**, 229–37.

Zelawski, W., Riech, F. P. & Stanley, R. G. (1970). Assimilation and release of internal carbon dioxide by woody plant shoots. *Canadian Journal of Botany*, **48**, 1351–4.

Zelitch, I. (1971). *Photosynthesis, Photorespiration and Plant Productivity*. Academic Press, New York.

Manuscript received by the editors March 1975

22. Translocation of assimilates and creation, distribution and utilization of reserves

M. J. TRLICA and J. S. SINGH

Introduction

Carbon is the vehicle by which organisms store and transfer energy by chemical binding (Mooney, 1972). Higher plants assimilate carbon through the process of photosynthesis in their green tissues, mainly the leaves. The carbon thus fixed is utilized for a variety of plant functions, such as respiration, elaboration of new vegetative and reproductive structures, and storage. Since survival and growth of a plant and of different organs within the plant body depend upon these functions, the carbon fixed through photosynthesis must be transported to various organs. This transport from the site of synthesis to the sites of utilization is called translocation. The sites or organs where the translocated material is utilized or stored are called sinks.

Reserve substances in plants are normally considered to include carbohydrates, fats, oils and some proteins. However, all organic compounds of plants contain energy and most could probably be metabolized for maintenance or growth under certain circumstances. Cook (1966a) stated that reserve substances consist largely of carbohydrates. Weinmann (1948) found that the percentage of fat in the roots of grasses was not significantly affected by herbage removal and concluded that fats probably did not function as reserves. Smith & Silva (1969) found that, following defoliation of alfalfa (*Medicago sativa* L.), the roots lost a greater proportion of their total nonstructural carbohydrates than their nitrogen. McIlvanie (1942) found that total nitrogen in roots of *Agropyron spicatum* (Pursh.) Scribn. & Smith was depleted by 53% during early vegetative growth, whereas carbohydrates were depleted by 70%. He considered carbohydrates to be the most important reserve substances. Since carbohydrates appear to be the major forms of carbon for translocation and reserve storage, they will be considered in more detail than other organic plant constituents.

Carbon assimilated by green plants in excess of demands for maintenance, growth and reproduction may be considered as surplus carbon constituting a carbohydrate reserve. These reserve compounds may be stored and later utilized during periods when there are high construction demands (Mooney, 1972). In most climates these demands come when conditions are favorable for growth or regrowth. However, demands may also come at unpredictable times when shoots are partially or entirely destroyed through defoliation by herbivores or fire. In some cases, the construction of reproductive organs may also occur from reserves rather than from current photosynthate. Further, some plants of arid areas, such as *Agave* sp., store reserves for many years before committing them to a costly reproductive apparatus (Mooney, 1972).

Jameson (1964) believed that carbohydrate reserves were only needed for the production of new photosynthetic tissue. Once a plant became a net producer of carbohydrate he found no evidence to indicate that the growth rate was affected by the concentration of stored carbohydrates. May (1960) and Alcock (1964) have also questioned the role of plant reserves for growth, as most evidence for their use in growth was indirect and there was little evidence of controls and mechanisms for the trans-location and utilization of carbohydrates in regrowth. However, apical growth of perennial plants is believed by many to take place at the expense of stored materials, whereas cambial growth may rely on current photosynthate (Kozlowski & Keller, 1966).

The pattern of carbohydrate utilization often varies with the species and environmental conditions. The environment can affect the ratio of currently-produced carbohydrates to stored carbohydrates that are used in primary growth (Merrill & Kilby, 1952; Mochizuki & Hanada, 1958). For some species, internode elongation is so rapid that it is completed before the leaves are fully expanded. When this occurs, utilization of stored materials is a necessity (Kozlowski & Keller, 1966). Similarly, initiation of new root growth in grasses during early growth before the beginning of leaf expansion must come from stored reserves (Singh & Coleman, 1975). The older leaves in many evergreen species provide food for the expanding shoots (Kozlowski, 1964; Kozlowski & Clausen, 1965; Kozlowski & Winget, 1964).

Unfortunately, many of the results obtained in experiments to determine utilization of carbohydrate reserves for apical growth are inconclusive. Many of these tests relied on indirect methods of measurement or on techniques, such as stripping of leaves and girdling of stems, which altered the normal behavior of the plant. These studies usually did not distinguish between utilization of currently-produced carbohydrates or of stored carbohydrates. They also did not define the period during which stored material was produced and reutilized.

The mechanism of translocation

Several monographs and reviews on this subject have been published in recent years (Crafts, 1961; Kursanov, 1963; Richardson, 1968; Wardlaw, 1968a; Canny, 1971, 1973; Crafts & Crisp, 1971). Consequently, it is not necessary here to do more than outline the state of knowledge.

It is well established that most translocation between organs takes place in the phloem, and that sucrose is the predominant form in which carbohydrates are translocated. The mass-flow theory of Münch (1930) is now widely accepted as probably the most important mechanism for transport in the phloem, though some form of activated diffusion (Mason & Phillis, 1937) seems also to operate. Translocation is an energy-demanding process (particularly in transport into and out of the phloem), is selective, and often operates against diffusion gradients. The mechanisms supplying the energy needed for translocation depend on trans-formations between adenosine triphosphate and adenosine diphosphate. For details of the mechanisms involved in the translocation process, and the evidence on which the above statements are based, the reader is referred to the references listed in the preceding paragraph.

Rates of translocation

Measured translocation rates are generally quite rapid (see Table 22.1). The rates measured as specific mass transfer of dry matter per unit area of phloem range from 0.14 to 4.8 g cm^{-2} h^{-1} and the translocation velocities range from 1.5 to 7200 cm h^{-1}. The translocation velocity of 39 to 109 cm h^{-1} as reported by Wardlaw (1965) for wheat may be taken, according to Canny (1971), as the center of a distribution of velocities measured by many people in many ways. Some examples of these rates are given in Table 22.1. Different compounds also seem to move at different rates. For example, Biddulph & Cory (1957) reported that, in *Phaseolus vulgaris* L., sucrose moved at a rate of 107 cm h^{-1}, while tritiated water moved at the rate of 87 cm h^{-1}. Similarly, Nelson & Gorham (1959) reported translocation rates for amino acids ranging from 370 (asparagine, glutamine) to 1370 cm h^{-1} (alanine, serine).

Factors affecting translocation

Water

The conducting tissue, representing a complex and well-organized osmo-meter, is affected by the water balance of the plant (Crafts & Crisp, 1971). Weatherley, Peel & Hill (1959) and Plaut & Reinhold (1965) reported that water deficiency reduced assimilate movement. However, McWilliam

Table 22.1. *Some measured rates of assimilate translocation for several species*

Plant species	Specific mass transfer, in dry matter per unit area of phloem ($g\,cm^{-2}h^{-1}$)	Reference
Cucurbita pepo	4.8	Colwell (1942)
Gossypium hirsutum	0.14–0.64	Mason & Maskell (1928)
Kigeha africana	2.6	Clements (1940)
Solanum tuberosum	4.5	Dixon & Ball (1922)
Tropaeolum najus	0.7	Crafts (1931)
	Velocity ($cm\,h^{-1}$)	
Glycine max	17.0	Thrower (1965)
Heracleum mantegazzianum	35–70	Ziegler & Vieweg (1961)
Saccharum officinarum	150	Hartt & Kortschak (1963)
Salix sp.	1.5–2.0	Canny (1961)
Triticum aestivum	39–69	Wardlaw (1965)

(1968) demonstrated continued movement of assimilates from the green stem to the roots of *Phalaris tuberosa* L. after defoliation resulting from severe water deficit, thereby illustrating the stability of the conducting system in plants under water stress. Roberts (1964) and Wiebe & Wihrheim (1962) reported that high water-stress resulted in greater acropetal movement as compared with plants under low water-stress. Wardlaw (1967) also observed an increased movement of assimilates from the lower leaves to the ear in water-stressed wheat (*Triticum aestivum* L.) plants. Working with *Lolium temulentum* L., Wardlaw (1968b) found that the velocity of assimilate movement through a water-stressed leaf could be maintained at normal rates if adjacent leaves were removed to increase the relative demand for assimilates from the stressed leaf. Therefore, the reduced velocity of assimilate movement in plants under water stress seems to be an indirect effect resulting from reduced growth. Wardlaw (1967) had earlier observed with water-stressed wheat plants that when growth was not affected by water stress, as during grain development, the velocity of assimilate movement was not reduced. It appears, therefore, that under most conditions the effects of water stress on photosynthesis and growth outweigh those on translocation.

Sosebee & Wiebe (1971) studied the influence of soil water stress and defoliation on translocation in *Agropyron cristatum* (L.) Gaertn. and barley (*Hordeum vulgare* L.). They found that translocation in plants grown without adequate soil water was chiefly to the underground portions of the plants. This relative downward movement of assimilates seemed to be especially influenced by defoliation. In plants with adequate soil water, clipping appeared to stimulate upward movement of assimilates. They postulated that it was most likely that limited water reduced the activity of the shoot meristems and cell enlargement, thereby reducing the demand for translocation to the shoot. They believed that increased accumulation of reserves in perennating organs such as roots and crowns might be an effective survival mechanism, allowing plants of arid regions to utilize reserves for increased growth when moisture conditions improved.

Temperature

Usually warmer soil temperatures are more congenial for translocation to roots (Fujiwara & Suzuki, 1961). Burr *et al.* (1958) reported that cooling the roots of sugarcane (*Saccharum officinarum* L.) reduced assimilate transport by 50% in 24 h and 82% in 80 h. Habeshaw (1973) also demonstrated reduced translocation to cooled roots. Whitehead, Sansing & Loomis (1959) found reduced or no assimilate transfer to roots in tomato (*Lycopersicum esculentum* Mill.) when the stem was cooled to 5 °C. Ford & Peel (1967) reported that increased viscosity of sap when young shoots of *Salix* sp. were cooled resulted in decreased assimilate movement. The slowing of exudation when isolated parts of the inflorescence stalk of *Yucca flaccida* Engelm. were cooled was also attributed to increased viscosity (Tammes, Vonk & Die, 1969). Geiger (1966) and Swanson & Geiger (1967) also found that when a 2 cm portion of petiole of *Beta vulgaris* L. was cooled, the assimilate transport was reduced by 65%–95%. However, this inhibition was temporary, and with continued treatment normal rates were resumed. Swanson & Geiger (1967) proposed that increased turgor pressure as the sugar potential built up in the source leaf resulted in metabolic loading of sieve tubes, and the passive mass flow of assimilates in sieve tubes was resumed.

Light

Rohrbaugh & Rice (1949) found that translocation was greater during the light than in the dark period. According to Kursanov (1963), translocation of assimilates to roots in young pumpkin (*Cucurbita pepo* L.) was not affected by darkness, but in old plants this translocation occurred only during dark periods. Nelson & Gorham (1957) fed sugars labeled with radiocarbon (^{14}C) to primary leaves of soybean (*Glycine max* (L.) Merr.) seedlings, and reported that only 4% of the total uptake was translocated to roots in the light, as compared to 16% in the dark. Fujiwara & Suzuki (1961) reported a direct correlation between the length of the photoperiod and the translocation rate. Butcher (1965) also reported decreased translocation of assimilates in *Beta vulgaris* during the dark period as compared with the light period. In wheat, Nelson (1963) reported increased root:shoot ratios with increasing light intensity; under low light intensities, stem growth may compete with grain production (Carr & Wardlaw, 1965). Thus, different plants seem to react differently with regard to the effect of light on translocation.

Oxygen

Mason & Phillis (1936) indicated the necessity of oxygen for phloem transport. Willenbrink (1957) and Ullrich (1961), however, could find no evidence for any effect of anoxia on the transport of fluorescein through the petiole. Geiger & Christy (1971) found a rapid decline in the rate at which labeled assimilates were imported when the sink region was subjected to anoxia. More recently, Qureshi & Spanner (1973) have also supported the findings of Mason & Phillis. They found that anoxia imposed on the stolon connecting the sink with the source greatly reduced the assimilate transfer.

Inhibitors

Bieleski (1960) found that certain metabolic inhibitors inhibited the loading and unloading of phloem, thus reducing or blocking assimilate transfer, though others like 2,4-dichlorophenoxyacetic acid (2,4-D), amitrole, picloram, dalapon and maleic hydrazide (MH) are known to be transported (Kursanov, 1963). However, the results to date on the effect of inhibitors on phloem transport are not conclusive (Crafts & Crisp, 1971).

Partitioning of assimilates, and source–sink relations

Organs that have no chloroplasts and lead an essentially heterotrophic existence can be termed sinks. Examples of below-ground sinks are roots, rhizomes, tubers and other storage organs. Above-ground sinks are stems, buds, flowers, fruits and young developing leaves. The activity and demand of sinks are controlled by phenology and environmental factors.

The young shoots are relatively more efficient than older ones in carbon fixation (Dahlman & Kucera, 1968, 1969; Singh & Coleman, 1975). During early growth, there is also greater retention of the assimilates in the shoots. Thus, Singh & Coleman (1975) found that retention of photoassimilated radiocarbon in shoots of a semi-arid shortgrass species (*Bouteloua gracilis*

Table 22.2. *Partitioning of photoassimilated radiocarbon (^{14}C) in short-grass prairie, dominated by* Bouteloua gracilis *(H.B.K.) Lag. ex Steud, three days after labeling (% of total recovered in plants).* (Singh & Coleman, 1975)

Plant part	May	July	September
Shoots	31.2	20.5	14.6
Crown	31.1	21.0	14.4
Roots	37.7	58.5	71.0

(H.B.K.) Lag.) three days after labeling was 31% during early growth, 20% retention during maturity, and only 15% retention during later stages of growth. Balasko & Smith (1973) reported that in *Phleum pratense* L. the loss of radioactivity from leaf blades by translocation and respiration within the first week after labeling was 70% at initiation of stem elongation, 66% at ear emergence, and 67% at anthesis.

A majority of reports on the distribution of assimilates into various plant organs concern laboratory or culture conditions. In *Lolium perenne* L. and *Lolium temulentum*, Ryle (1970*a*) found that 44%–50% of radiocarbon moved to roots. In *Lolium multiflorum* Lam. (Marshall, 1966) and in wheat (Doodson, Manners & Myers, 1964) up to one-half of the labeled carbon which left the source leaf was found in roots. Annual plants, in general, transfer less assimilate to roots (Ryle, 1970*b*). In a semi-arid mixed-grass prairie under natural conditions, Warembourg & Paul (1973) reported that 46%–54% of the photofixed radiocarbon moved to below-ground parts. Results from a semi-arid shortgrass prairie indicated that from 38% to 71% of the total plant radiocarbon was located in roots three days after labeling (Table 22.2). Bamberg, Wallace, Kleinkopf & Vollmer (1972) estimated that only 10%–20% of the annual production of photosynthate was translocated to root systems of eight desert species. They found only 4%–22% of the originally fixed radiocarbon in the roots of these desert plants.

Sinks also compete with each other for their supply of assimilates. Thus, Wardlaw (1965) found that when two-thirds of the developing grains in wheat were removed the translocation to crowns and roots increased markedly. In general, the upper leaves form the source of assimilates for flowers, fruits or developing stems, while lower leaves supply the crowns and roots. However, if the local demand is intense, all leaves may supply only one sink (Kursanov, 1963). Clipping or grazing generally results in an initial reduction of assimilate transfer to roots, because demands by the regrowing shoots are dominant (White, 1973).

Plant processes

Numerous interactions among abiotic and biotic factors can cause changes in the source and sink relationships. For example, any factor which favours high rates of photosynthesis and production of assimilates will increase the amount of material available for export to sinks. Any factor which inhibits assimilate production will reduce the concentration of carbohydrates at the source.

As growth and phenological development progress, tissue which was at one time a sink may become a source of carbohydrate production (Wardlaw, 1968a). Reserve carbohydrates in plant storage organs may be utilized for new growth of above-ground plant parts (Cook, 1966a). Hence, these storage organs represent a source of available energy for plant growth. However, once photosynthate is produced in excess of demand, these same storage organs may be considered as a sink for receiving the excess carbohydrates. Therefore, the relationships among sources and sinks are quite complex and never static.

Transformation of translocates within the sinks

Transformation of translocates within sinks often occurs. Sugars translocated to underground parts may be converted into starch or fructosans (Weinmann, 1952). McCarty (1938) found that cool autumn temperatures resulted in the transformation of reserve carbohydrates to more soluble forms in *Bromus carinatus* Hook. & Arn. Sucrose concentration increases at the expense of starch reserves in the autumn. Dodd & Hopkins (1958) found similar transformations in *Bouteloua gracilis*. Smith & Leinweber (1971) showed that, in tillers of *Schizachyrium scoparius* (Michx) Nash, sucrose concentration in leaves and starch concentration in roots were the best physiological indicators of changes in morphological stages of development.

Many factors can influence the conversion of one carbohydrate to another. Suzuki (1971) found that potassium played an important role in the accumulation of fructosan in *Phleum pratense.* He also found that defoliation stimulated the decomposition of long-chain fructosans to sugars without noticeable accumulation of shorter-chain fructosans. Several enzymes play an important role in the transformation of carbohydrates within plants. The types of resulting carbohydrates formed depend upon the kinds and amounts of enzymes present. Enzyme activity can be affected both by external environmental factors such as light, water, temperature and nutritional status, and by internal conditions such as concentration of certain sugars, cellular hydration and pH. Just as enzymes are formed in the plant, they may likewise be inactivated by formation of internal inhibitors (Kramer & Kozlowski, 1960).

The form of carbohydrates stored varies among plant species. Perennial

544

grasses native to temperate latitudes appear to accumulate fructosans and sucrose in their stem bases and rhizomes (Weinmann & Reinhold, 1946; Ojima & Isawa, 1967). Perennial grasses native to semi-tropical or tropical areas appear to store starch and sucrose (DeCugnak, 1931; Hunter, McIntyre & McIlroy, 1970). However, the view of DeCugnak (1931) that grass species which accumulate sucrose and starch do not accumulate fructosan is not supported by work of Okajima & Smith (1964), who found that fructosan was the principal storage carbohydrate in several North American grass species studied, except for *Bromus inermis* Leyss. where sucrose was predominant. In all of the other species except *B. inermis*, starch was present to the extent of 3%–6% of the dry matter. The principal reserve substances of grasses are, therefore, sugars, fructosans, dextrins and starch (Weinmann, 1952; Smith & Grotelueschen, 1966). The principal reserve substances of two semi-arid cultivated species, alfalfa and cotton (*Gossypium hirsutum*), were sugars and starch (Eaton & Ergle, 1948; Lechtenberg, Holt & Youngberg, 1971).

Distribution and utilization of reserves

Nonstructural reserve carbohydrates may be stored temporarily in most perennating plant parts. Most storage occurs in living parenchyma cells. Storage organs for carbohydrate reserves occur both above and below ground. These organs include roots, rhizomes, tubers, stolons, seeds, crowns, leaf bases and stem bases of herbaceous species, and also stems and twigs of woody species (Cook, 1966*a*).

Quantities of carbohydrate involved in storage can be significant. According to Mooney (1972), at the end of the growing season, as much as 60% of the dry matter in underground storage organs such as rhizomes may consist of carbohydrate. Mooney also reported that in *Aesculus californica* (Spach.) Nutt., a drought-deciduous tree of southern California, available carbohydrates might form as much as 40% of the dry matter in new bark and wood. Carbohydrates were stored in virtually all parts of the plant to provide reservoirs for new growth in the spring, as well as for a large commitment to fruit development after leaf fall.

Balasko & Smith (1973) identified organs for accumulation of non-structural carbohydrates in *Phleum pratense* by feeding radiocarbon to plants at three phenological stages. If the plants were exposed to labeled carbon dioxide at initiation of stem elongation, roots and leaves were the primary recipients of labeled carbohydrates when measured one week later. Stems and inflorescences accumulated most of the labeled carbo-hydrates when plants were fed the labeled carbon at the time of inflor-escence emergence. One week following feeding at anthesis, stems and roots contained 73% of the total radiocarbon.

545

Plant processes

Bamberg *et al.* (1972) believed that small stems or twigs were the major storage sites for carbon in *Ambrosia dumosa* (Gray) Payne, *Atriplex canescens* (Nelson) H. & C., *Atriplex confertifolia* (Torr. & Frem.) Wats., *Ephedra nevadensis* S. Wats., *Eurotia lanata* (Pursh) Meg., *Larrea divaricata* Cav., *Lycium andersonii* Gray and *Lycium pallidum* Miers. Stored reserves in the stems were mobilized and were used in early development of new growth when environmental conditions became favorable.

Optimal growth requires a balance between supplies of carbohydrate for energy, and a readily-available source of protein for synthesis of new protoplasm. Sheard (1968) suggested that water-insoluble protein nitrogen in the tertiary shoots of *Phleum pratense* was a significant factor in the initiation of early spring growth, along with carbohydrate reserves.

Priestly (1962) stated that the absolute amount of carbohydrate reserves in storage organs would often be more relevant than their concentrations. Sprague & Sullivan (1950) found in some grasses that, although roots had lower concentrations of carbohydrate reserves than other storage organs, the total quantity of carbohydrates stored in roots was greater because the mass of roots was greater.

Diurnal variations in nonstructural carbohydrates

Since single carbohydrate fractions in plant storage organs may be transformed from one form to another, a determination of total available carbohydrates (TAC) or total nonstructural carbohydrates (TNC) may have more value in distinguishing among factors influencing source and sink relationships than determinations of individual constituents. These carbohydrates can be utilized as readily-available sources of energy (Smith, Paulsen & Raguse, 1964). They include reducing and nonreducing sugars, starch, dextrins and fructosans. They do not include the structural carbohydrates, hemicellulose, cellulose, or pentosans.

Diurnal variations of total nonstructural carbohydrates (TNC) in several organs of *Panicum virgatum* L. were studied by Greenfield & Smith (1973). They found that there was no diurnal change in the concentration of reducing sugar in any shoot component. Total sugar percentages reflected changes in the concentration of nonreducing sugars. Percentages increased from 06.00 to 18.00 hours, and then decreased for all shoot parts, except for the lower three internodes which had similar percentages at 12.00, 18.00 and 24.00 hours. Starch percentages were also highest at 18.00 hours in the inflorescence, leaf blades, and top leaf sheath and internode. Second and third leaf sheaths were similar in starch content at 18.00 and 24.00 hours, but starch was most abundant in the bottom two sheaths and all internodes, except the top one, at 24.00 hours. Highest percentages of nonstructural carbohydrates occurred at 18.00 hours in the inflorescence,

546

leaf blades, leaf sheaths, sheaths, and top two internodes. The bottom three internodes were highest in TNC at 24.00 hours.

Diurnal variations in nonstructural carbohydrates have also been observed in alfalfa (Lechtenberg *et al.*, 1971). All nonstructural carbohydrates in alfalfa began to accumulate after 06.00 hours. It was noted that hexoses increased first in leaves and then in stems, followed by sucrose and then starch. These reserves were depleted in the same order in the afternoon and at night. Diurnal variations in the starch content of stems were relatively small. However, starch appeared to act as a temporary storage product in leaves, as daily fluctuations in content were observed.

Diurnal cycles in the concentration of carbohydrate reserves were studied by Weinmann & Reinhold (1946), Holt & Hilst (1969) and Lechtenberg, Holt & Youngberg (1971, 1972). Changes in individual carbohydrate fractions and total nonstructural carbohydrates were related. The cycles usually began with a low carbohydrate level in the morning hours, a peak in the afternoon, and a decline during the evening and night. In general, there was a conversion of simple sugars to disaccharides and then conversion from disaccharides to starch or inulin. Holt & Hilst observed that almost one-third of the daily production of total nonstructural carbohydrates in *Bromus inermis* was utilized during the night.

Redistribution and utilization of reserves

Carbohydrate reserves act as energy sources and as precursors for structural carbohydrates, proteins, and fats. Carbohydrate reserves can also be used for respiration and limited growth during the winter (Cook, 1966a). Reserves are needed for initiation of early spring growth and for regrowth in the fall. They are also required for regrowth after foliage removal and at any time that photosynthesis cannot meet the demands of the plant (Menke, 1973).

A broad review of nitrogen distribution and utilization in plants is given by Taylor (1967). There is ample evidence that nitrogen is stored in various tissues, mobilized, and translocated to growing points during periods of high demands. It also appears that, during periods of synthesis, nitrogen may be translocated as amino acids to some metabolic sink, built into protein and then be hydrolyzed and retransported back to storage regions before the organ is shed.

Abiotic factors affecting redistribution and utilization of reserves

The level of carbohydrates in storage organs of plants is constantly changing. Diurnal and seasonal variations have been observed by numerous investigators and have been associated with the natural phenological

Plant processes

development of species, and partially explained by various abiotic factors affecting growth such as temperature, soil water, and soil nutrients.

Temperature

Near-optimum daytime temperatures that promote growth or regrowth tend to reduce the levels of carbohydrate reserves (Alberda, 1957; Brown & Blaser, 1965, 1970; 'Auda, Blaser & Brown, 1966; Blaser, Brown & Bryant, 1966; Colby, Drake, Oohara & Yoshida, 1966; Smith, 1968; Davidson, 1969). This indicates that sub-optimum temperatures might restrict growth more than photosynthesis (Blaser et al., 1966). High temperatures increase respiration rates, and consequently cause reductions in available carbohydrates.

During active spring growth, temperature was found to be the most important factor affecting the carbohydrate reserves of *Dactylis glomerata* L. (Colby *et al.*, 1966). Low temperatures promoted the accumulation of carbohydrates, whereas high temperatures caused declines in the reserves. Clipping to low stubble heights permitted increases of soil temperature and resulted in lowered carbohydrate reserves. Feltner & Massengale (1965) found that maximum temperatures could account for more of the variability in TNC levels than any other single measure of temperature. The deleterious effects of frequent defoliations on TNC reserves were greatest during periods of warm temperatures.

Water

Periods of water stress tend to increase the level of carbohydrate reserves in plants (Eaton & Ergle, 1948; Brown & Blaser, 1965, 1970; Blaser *et al.*, 1966; Maranville & Paulsen, 1970; Sosebee & Wiebe, 1971; Trlica, 1971; Dina & Klikoff, 1973). Drought appeared to depress carbohydrate utilization to a greater extent than photosynthesis in cotton plants (Eaton & Ergle, 1948).

Carbohydrates increased in the herbage of *Cynodon dactylon* (L.) Pers. and in the stubble and herbage of *Dactylis glomerata* when growth was retarded by water stress (Blaser *et al.*, 1966). Fall regrowth of *Agropyron cristatum* and *Elymus junceus* Fisch, two grasses of arid rangelands, was stimulated either by natural rainfall or irrigation, causing reductions in reserves (Trlica & Cook, 1972). Favorable soil water conditions that promote plant growth or regrowth tend to lower carbohydrate reserves.

Brown & Blaser (1970) indicated that an increase in percentage of carbohydrate under water stress might be caused by a decrease in the protein and amino acid content of a storage organ. Their study of several species showed that water stress reduced protein formation or caused degradation of protein already formed. Therefore, with decreases in other constituents, the percentage of carbohydrates would be increased.

Dina & Klikoff (1973) studied the effects of plant water stress on carbohydrate and nitrogen reserves of *Artemisia tridentata* Nutt. They found that the starch content did not change significantly in water-stressed plants, although the sugar content significantly increased in leaves, stems and roots. Leaf nitrogen content significantly decreased, while the stem nitrogen content increased. They believed that sugar increases in the leaves, stems, and roots and nitrogen accumulation in the stems of these plants might be of significance, as this might protect the RNA–DNA complex, as well as enzymes, during water stress. Also, if the concentration of sugars did not increase, cellular injury might occur. They also suggested that the nitrogen changes were an adaptation for conservation of nitrogen through storage in the stem during periods of water stress, analogous to the decline in synthesis associated with the onset of dormancy. They believed that as water stress became less severe, the nitrogen pool within the stems might be mobilized and utilized for renewed cellular growth.

If accumulation of sugar is an important factor in the resistance of plant organs to water stress, then continued translocation would appear to be important in survival of storage organs such as rhizomes and roots which are distant from the site of assimilation. However, protection of the photosynthetic apparatus would necessitate a slowing down in the transfer of assimilates away from the chloroplasts (Santarius, 1967; Santarius & Heber, 1967). It could be that the balance of retention of sugars by the chloroplasts and the transfer of sugars to the conducting system will in part dictate the response of the plants to water stress.

Nutrients

Nutrient enrichment of soils that promotes growth or regrowth often lowers carbohydrate reserves (Benedict & Brown, 1944; Burton, Jackson & Knox, 1959; Brown & Blaser, 1965; Adegbola & McKell, 1966a; Blaser et al., 1966; Colby et al., 1966; Paulsen & Smith, 1968; Reynolds, 1969; Zanoni, Michelson, Colby & Drake, 1969; Lechtenburg et al., 1972). Adegbola & McKell (1966a) found that the concentration of sucrose and fructosan in stems, stolons, roots and rhizomes of *Cynodon dactylon* decreased with increasing rates of nitrogen fertilization; during the active growth phase, sucrose was possibly as important a source of reserves for regrowth as was fructosan. Adegbola & McKell (1966b) stated that the regrowth potential of *C. dactylon* was closely associated with the level of carbohydrate reserves available at the beginning of the growing season. Regrowth of plants fertilized the previous season was closely related to the content of reserve carbohydrates present in the stubble and rhizomes.

When heavy application of nitrogen to *C. dactylon* was followed by a period of hot, dry weather, carbohydrate reserves often were reduced to critical levels (Colby *et al.*, 1966). Poor recovery of plant growth and serious injury resulted. Increasing the rate of nitrogen fertilization caused reserves to be reduced even further. Turner (1969) found that nitrogen fertilization of *Agropyron repens* (L.) Beav. resulted in increased rates of utilization of carbohydrates in the rhizomes.

Some investigators have reported that nutrient enrichment of soils has little or no effect on the carbohydrate reserves of plants, or that over long time periods it increased their carbohydrate reserves (Barnes, 1960; Matches, 1960; Bommer, 1966; Paulsen & Smith, 1968; Zanoni *et al.*, 1969; White, Brown & Cooper, 1972). The concentration of TNC in the roots of alfalfa increased with increasing rates of potassium fertilization (Matches, 1960). Nitrogen fertilization of grasses resulted in increases in the carbohydrate reserves of stubble and underground organs (Bommer, 1966).

In some recent studies, nitrogen fertilization has been found to result in decreased carbohydrate reserves during early growth, but increased reserve levels after more photosynthetic tissue has been produced. Pettit & Fagan (1974) found that nitrogen fertilization decreased TNC reserves in *Buchloe dactyloides* (Nutt.) Engelm. during vegetative and reproductive growth, but that TNC accumulated more rapidly during later phenological stages in plants that had received heavy nitrogen applications (90–120 kgN ha^{-1}). In *Bromus inermis*, nitrogen fertilization resulted in greater depletion of TNC after defoliation, but had no effect on the maximum level of carbohydrates accumulated (Paulsen & Smith, 1968). Probably the greater photosynthetic areas produced by fertilized plants enabled the initial depletion to be replaced by the time they were sampled. Nitrogen fertilization caused a decrease in total nonstructural carbohydrates in stem bases of *Stipa viridula* Trin. only from the time of growth initiation until the second leaf was formed (White *et al.*, 1972).

Plants endowed with a large capacity to store carbohydrates may be better adapted for survival during unfavorable environmental conditions (Wilson, 1944). McCarty & Price (1942) found that high concentrations of sugars in the storage organs of plants were associated with cold resistance and survival. Smith (1964) found a positive relationship between carbohydrate reserves and winter survival; plants low in reserves could not develop a high level of frost hardiness. Hanson & Stoddart (1940) showed that plants with root systems low in carbohydrate reserves were more susceptible to drought injury. Survival of alpine species near their

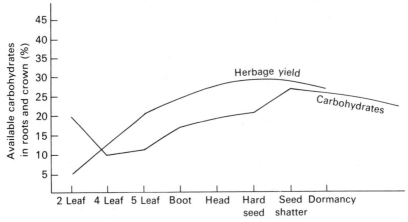

Fig. 22.1. Carbohydrate balance and herbage yield of a typical grass species throughout the annual cycle. (From Cook, 1966a.)

lower altitudinal limits was shown by Mooney & Billings (1965) to be enhanced by large amounts of stored nonstructural carbohydrates.

Biotic factors affecting redistribution and utilization of reserves

Numerous comprehensive reviews concerning carbohydrate reserves of plants in relation to phenological development, vigor, production and defoliation have been published (Graber, 1931; Weinmann, 1948, 1961; Troughton, 1957; May, 1960; Priestly, 1962; Jameson, 1963, 1964; Cook, 1966a, b; Coyne, 1969; White, 1973). Depletion of reserves by excessive defoliation results in reduced vigor and herbage growth, and in extreme cases can lead to death of the plants (Weinmann, 1948).

Growth and phenological development

The level of carbohydrate reserves in storage organs of plants varies during the annual growth cycle, in relation to phenological stages of development. Generally, however, carbohydrate reserve levels in storage organs of perennial plants follow what might be termed a V- or U-shaped annual cycle. Theoretical V- and U-shaped cycles are illustrated in Figs. 22.1 and 22.2 respectively. Plants that exhibit somewhat of a V-shaped seasonal cycle in carbohydrate reserve levels usually have rapid drawdown of reserves for initiation of spring growth followed by a rapid accumulation of reserves after the low point in reserve levels has been reached (Fig. 22.1). Plants that have a U-shaped carbohydrate reserve cycle normally maintain low levels of reserves during active growth, with reserve stores being re-

551

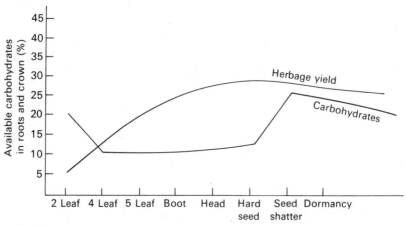

Fig. 22.2. Carbohydrate level and herbage yield of a forage species that does not replenish its reserves appreciably until seed formation. (From Cook, 1966*b*.)

plenished only after growth rates decline as plants approach maturity (Fig. 22.2). However, the seasonal variation of carbohydrate reserves differs with climatic conditions and among species. For many species the lowest reserve levels occur during early growth, but in other species the reserve level is lowest after seed ripening (Jameson, 1963). The changes through a year in carbohydrate reserve levels are similar in all perennial grasses but may be influenced by the growth behavior of the species and by weather (Weinmann, 1952).

Carbohydrate reserves usually undergo significant drawdown during initiation of spring growth. McCarty & Price (1942) observed, in mountain forage plants, that approximately 75% of the total carbohydrates stored in autumn were consumed in winter respiration and in the production of the first 10% of spring herbage growth. Mooney & Billings (1960) found that 50% of the reserves in rhizomes of the alpine plant *Polygonum bistortoides* L. were used in a one-week period during early growth. Kimura (1969) calculated that, during early growth of an evergreen conifer species, carbohydrate reserves were depleted by a quantity equal to 40% of the yearly production. McCarty (1938) and McIlvanie (1942) found that from 10% to 45% of the annual growth was produced before root reserves ceased to decline. Donart (1969) related carbohydrate reserve cycles of six mountain species to growth and development. Minimum root reserves were reached during early spring growth after approximately 13% of the total annual growth had been produced.

The seasonal course of carbohydrate storage in forage plants is often inversely related to herbage growth (Aldous, 1930; Sampson & McCarty, 1930; McCarty, 1935, 1938; Weinmann, 1940; McIlvanie, 1942; Kinsinger,

1953; Mooney & Billings, 1960; McConnell & Garrison, 1966; Coyne & Cook, 1970; Menke, 1973). After the low point in reserves is reached, some species immediately start replenishing their carbohydrate reserves throughout the remainder of the growing season until they reach maturity or become dormant (Fig. 22.1). Carbohydrates begin to accumulate when the photosynthetic rate surpasses the carbohydrate utilization rate. McDonough (1969) found that the carbohydrate content of the caudices of *Mertensia arizonica* Greene continually increased until shoot senescence. An upward trend in root reserves of *Coronilla varia* L. was maintained from late spring through summer (Langille & McKee, 1968).

Total available carbohydrates in the storage regions of *Agropyron cristatum* attained a maximum at the time of flowering, and decreased steadily during the remainder of the year (Trlica & Cook, 1972; Sosebee & Wiebe, 1973). Although the downward translocation of assimilates was most rapid during the fall, the amount being accumulated was apparently less than that utilized in root and tiller growth (Sosebee & Wiebe, 1973). In contrast, McConnell & Garrison (1966) and Menke (1973) found that TNC in roots of *Purshia tridentata* (Pursh.) DC. declined until seed formation and then accumulated until leaf fall. Menke (1973) also found that reserves in the roots of *Opuntia* sp. reached a minimum at the flowering stage of development.

Many species of plants exhibit additional drawdown in reserves prior to flowering or during fall regrowth. In *Agropyron cristatum*, there was a decrease in carbohydrate reserves just prior to flowering (Hyder & Sneva, 1959). Seven of the eight salt-desert species studied by Coyne & Cook (1970) exhibited a drawdown in carbohydrate reserves during fall regrowth. This same trend was also evident in *A. cristatum* and *Elymus junceus* (Trlica & Cook, 1972). However, the general trend of reserve accumulation usually continued upward until plants became quiescent or dormant.

Oechel, Strain & Odening (1972) studied photosynthate utilization in the desert shrub *Larrea divaricata*, one of the most abundant and widespread evergreen xerophytic shrubs in the hot deserts of North America. *L. divaricata* produced photosynthate throughout the year in the formation of new leaves and stem tissue. Labeling experiments with radiocarbon ($^{14}CO_2$) indicated that materials fixed at different times were used similarly for growth and maintenance of the plant, and that stored materials were not important in providing energy during periods of increased growth. These data and those of Strain (1969) indicated that currently-produced photosynthate was primarily used by *L. divaricata* for current growth and maintenance of the terminal stem and leaf tissue. A small but reasonably constant proportion of photosynthate went into reserve materials. Although the reserves might be important during extended periods of adverse

Plant processes

conditions, they did not appear to play much part in the carbon economy of the plant during the study period, except possibly as a temporary transitional pool of reserve assimilates. Because *L. divaricata* was never dormant and always metabolically active, it responded quickly to short-term fluctuations in the environment. Because its growth and productivity patterns are flexible and dependent on existing environmental conditions, this species has apparently adapted to growth in areas with varying seasonal precipitation and temperature patterns.

Mooney (1972) indicated that the most productive plant systems combined a high capacity for carbon gain with a high capability for carbon redistribution, to permit the formation of more photosynthetic tissue. Coyne (1969) studied seasonal trends in total available carbohydrates with respect to phenological stage of development for eight salt-desert range species, and concluded that plant vigor depended upon the amount of carbohydrate reserves stored at the end of the growing season.

Translocation of reserves to storage sites is generally more active in autumn when plants are completing their annual cycle. There is usually a decline in stored reserves during the quiescent or dormant period because of respiration and slight growth (Cook, 1966a). A considerable proportion of stored carbohydrates may be lost to respiration both during periods of quiescence or dormany and during formation of new tissue (Weinmann, 1961).

Grazing and defoliation

A number of studies on the effects of defoliation on plant vigor, production, and carbohydrate reserves have established that frequency, intensity, and season of defoliation can explain most plant responses to defoliation (Aldous, 1930; Sampson & McCarty, 1930; Graber, 1931; Biswell & Weaver, 1933; Bukey & Weaver, 1939; Hanson & Stoddart, 1940; McCarty & Price, 1942; McIlvanie, 1942; Sullivan & Sprague, 1943, 1953; Weinmann, 1943, 1949; Holscher, 1945; Smith & Graber, 1948; Blaisdell & Pechanec, 1949; Sprague & Sullivan, 1950; Waite & Boyd, 1953; Thaine, 1954; Brougham, 1956; Neiland & Curtis, 1956; Welch, 1968; Trlica, 1977). In general, too heavy, too early, or too frequent grazing or defoliation resulted in declining vigor of vegetation (Hedrick, 1958).

Immediately after severe defoliation, photosynthesis and carbohydrate reserves may not meet the demand for growth. Other organic constituents, possibly proteins, may be remobilized and utilized in growth (Davidson & Milthorpe, 1965). Sullivan & Sprague (1943) found evidence for hydrolysis of proteins in *Lolium perenne* placed in the dark after defoliation. In addition, they found that the content of soluble carbohydrates continued to decline in the dark after defoliation, almost to the point of exhaustion.

554

Defoliation at any time during the year usually affects the levels of carbohydrate reserves. Plants are, however, affected more by defoliation at certain phenological stages of development than at others, and it is desirable to know at what stages important arid and semi-arid forage species can be utilized without severe depletion of reserve carbohydrates.

Donart & Cook (1970) found that 90% defoliation of two mountain grasses and two forbs early in the growing season, when carbohydrate reserves were low, was more detrimental than defoliation late in the growing season, when carbohydrate reserves were high. This was the case, however, only if there was opportunity for regrowth before fall dormancy. Defoliation of two browse species appeared to lower the carbohydrate reserves more when it took place late in the growing season at a time when carbohydrate reserves were high.

Agropyron sibericum (Willd.) Beauv. and *A. cristatum* were found to be tolerant of spring grazing, but *Agropyron inerme* (Scribner & Smith) Rydb. and its close relative *A. spicatum* were sensitive to spring grazing (Hyder & Sneva, 1963b). *Agropyron cristatum* and *A. sibericum* accumulated total water-soluble carbohydrates several weeks earlier than did *A. inerme.*

Cooper & Watson (1968) found that frequent cutting of alfalfa and sainfoin (*Onobrychis viciaefolia* Serp.) was not detrimental if the last cutting took place early enough to provide time for carbohydrate storage in the autumn before killing frosts. Late clipping of *Andropogon gerardii* Vitman decreased reserves available for winter dormancy, and resulted in subsequent depression of spring regrowth (Owensby, Paulsen & McKendrick, 1970).

Trlica & Cook (1971, 1972) and Menke (1973) found that severe defoliation of numerous semi-arid range species was especially detrimental if defoliation occurred when plants were rapidly replenishing their reserves, usually near maturity. Plants that were defoliated late in the growing season usually produced little regrowth, hence little photosynthetic tissue was present during the normal period for carbohydrate storage.

Bouteloua gracilis and *Agropyron smithii* Rydb., under several clipping treatments, were found to be tolerant of defoliation to stubble heights of 5 cm and 7.5 cm respectively (Fisher, 1966). Everson (1966) found that the concentration and absolute quantity of soluble sugars and starch in storage organs of *A. smithii* were lower under intense clipping treatments. Cook, Stoddart & Kinsinger (1958) found that roots of *Agropyron cristatum* plants clipped at a low stubble height contained a lower percentage of reducing sugars. Roots from plants clipped frequently had lower concentrations of reducing sugars, sucrose and fructose in the roots. However, Kinsinger & Hopkins (1961) reported that moderately-clipped plants of *A. smithii* had higher carbohydrate reserves than did unclipped plants.

555

Plant processes

Willard & McKell (1973) found that clipping *Chrysothammus viscidiflorus* (Hook) Nutt. and *Symphoricarpos vaccinoides* Rydb. caused reduction in carbohydrate reserves, the reduction being greater as the intensity of defoliation increased from 30% foliage removal through 60% to 90%. Greatest reductions in reserves were noted when plants were clipped during the summer growth period. However, one complete year of rest following clipping in the summer was sufficient to allow full recovery of reserves.

One year of rest after severe defoliation may not be sufficient for recovery of many semi-arid and arid range species. Menke (1973) found that defoliated plants of *Atriplex canescens* (Pursh.) Nutt., *Artemisia frigida* Willd. and *Purshia tridentata* required more than one year of rest for recovery of vigor and reserves. Cook & Child (1971) showed that desert plants, when defoliated to the extent that vigor was moderately reduced, required more than seven years of nonuse for recovery of vigor.

The TNC in storage organs in alfalfa in the autumn was reduced by a single cutting treatment in fall more than by three cuttings per year prior to fall (Kust & Smith, 1961). There was a direct relationship between the amount of TNC present in the storage organs in the fall and the yield of alfalfa hay obtained the next year. Ogden & Loomis (1972) reported that growth during the fall enabled *Agropyron intermedium* (Host) Beauv., clipped during the summer, to recover total water-soluble carbohydrate and root weight to very nearly the same level as control plants.

Robinson & Massengale (1968) found in alfalfa that the leaf area attained before harvesting was correlated with the acid-hydrolyzable carbohydrates in roots. Reynolds (1971) reported that after two years of uniform harvest schedules for alfalfa, the two-cut, three-cut, and four-cut treatments had vigorous and productive stands. The greatest decline in carbohydrate levels usually occurred after the first harvest each year. Reserve carbohydrates in alfalfa roots were highest when the interval between cuttings was greatest and when the stubble left after cutting was tallest (Wolf, Larson & Smith, 1962). The vigor of regrowth following a dormant period or defoliation is often correlated with the status of the plant in respect of carbohydrate reserves (Baker & Garwood, 1961; Ward & Blaser, 1961; Reynolds, 1962; Smith, 1962; Hyder & Sneva, 1963a; Alcock, 1964; Alberda, 1966; Wolf, 1967; Alburquerque, 1968; Steinke & Booysen, 1968; Laycock & Conrad, 1969; Ueno & Smith, 1970; Greub & Wedin, 1971b, Trlica & Cook, 1971, 1972). In general, the rate of regrowth is slower and the amount of regrowth is less for plants with lower levels of carbohydrate reserves.

Poor regrowth of *Bromus inermis* and *Phleum pratense* after the first harvest appeared to be associated with low carbohydrate reserves and inactive basal buds (Reynolds, 1962). Regrowth after defoliation of

Phalaris arundinacea L. was correlated with the levels of carbohydrate reserves in the plant (Wolf, 1967). When all leaves were removed tiller regrowth rates for *Festuca arundinacea* (Scrib.) Celek. were correlated with the concentration of carbohydrate reserves (Alburquerque, 1968). Tillers of *Dactylis glomerata* with high carbohydrate reserves produced more total dry matter for the first 25 days after defoliation than did tillers with low carbohydrate reserves (Ward & Blaser, 1961).

Davidson & Milthorpe (1965) stated that labile carbohydrate reserves contributed significantly to growth only during the first few days following defoliation. They believed that the extent of the contribution of carbohydrate reserves to growth depended upon the severity of defoliation and on the level of the environmental factors influencing growth and photosynthesis. The size of the reserve pool could affect subsequent regrowth indirectly for a significant period of time by influencing the rate of formation of new photosynthetic tissue. Davidson (1969) found evidence that root growth rates might be proportional to concentrations of total soluble carbohydrates in roots.

Regrowth potential of *Agropyron repens* was related to carbohydrate reserves and the number of dormant buds on rhizomes (Schirman & Buckholtz, 1966). Treatments that reduced apical dominance and stimulated dormant buds resulted in enhanced shoot growth. Activation of buds and vigorous regrowth caused a rapid depletion of carbohydrate reserves.

Several researchers have reported a positive correlation between the vigor of sprouting and the level of carbohydrate reserves in roots of woody plants (Baker, 1918; Aldous, 1935; Jones & Laude, 1960; Tew, 1970). However, Wright & Stinson (1970) showed that, in the roots of *Prosopis glandulosa* DC., regrowth following cutting was not in direct proportion to the total carbohydrate reserves.

Steinke (1969) found that defoliated plants of *Eragrostis curvula* (Schrad.) Nees translocated labeled materials from storage organs to all new leaves, where these materials were utilized as the respiratory substrate and for the production of structural material. On the basis of his results, he speculated that immediately after defoliation the reserves were utilized to produce photosynthetic material. Once these first few leaves had been produced, the plant drew on its reserves no longer. However, until downward translocation from new photosynthetic material had begun, the roots were deprived of their regular supply of carbohydrates (Steinke & Booysen, 1968). It was only when the plant was not using carbohydrates in excess of current requirements for growth and respiration that re-storage of reserves could take place. Steinke (1969) suggested, therefore, that carbohydrate reserves were important only in determining initial regrowth, but that it was the general carbohydrate status of the plant which determined the overall response to defoliation.

557

Plant processes

Other researchers have questioned the role of root carbohydrate reserves for regrowth of perennial grasses after defoliation (Mitchell, 1954; Baker, 1963; Moore & Biddiscombe, 1964; Marshall & Sagar, 1965). They believed that reserve carbohydrates were of little importance for shoot regrowth.

Pearce, Fissel & Carlson (1969) studied the deposition and redistribution of radiocarbon during growth of alfalfa plants. Individual alfalfa plants were allowed to assimilate labeled carbon dioxide at weekly intervals. The plants were then defoliated, and redistribution of radiocarbon was followed during subsequent regrowth. After defoliation, radiocarbon changes in alfalfa plants best fitted a sigmoid curve. The greatest changes occurred between 3 and 15 days after defoliation. During the 28 days of regrowth, 45% of the radiocarbon was lost to respiration, leaching and sloughing from the plant, whereas 19% had moved into top growth. Large roots had lost 70% of their original radiocarbon content.

In an elegant study, Smith & Marten (1970) found that carbohydrates labeled with radiocarbon which had been stored in roots and crowns of alfalfa were readily redistributed to developing shoots during foliar regrowth. Greatest redistribution occurred at the early vegetative stage and decreased with advancing maturity. Approximately 40% of the initially stored nonstructural carbohydrates was found in the shoots at the early vegetative regrowth stage, whereas only 13% of the labeled carbohydrates remained in the shoots at the reproductive stage. A maximum of 9% was utilized in the synthesis of structural tissues in the developing shoots. Respiratory utilization of labeled carbohydrates by the entire plant increased from 26% at the young vegetative stage to 71% at a reproductive stage. Smith & Marten concluded that the metabolic roles of these carbohydrates were somewhat analogous to that of the endosperm in starchy seeds. The reserves were utilized for structural components and retained in an available state, and served as readily-available respiratory substrates. What initiated the mobilization of these reserves for foliar regrowth of alfalfa following harvest, and the magnitude of critical levels of stored carbohydrates to maintain maximum rates of shoot development and dry matter production, were not known.

Conditions optimal for regrowth of *Lolium perenne* after repeated defoliation often gave rise to a depletion of the carbohydrate reserves (Alberda, 1957). Factors, such as optimal temperature or high nitrogen fertilization, which promoted leaf growth tended to lower the soluble carbohydrates after repeated defoliation. Factors which tended to reduce rapid leaf growth, or which increased apparent photosynthesis, caused increases in carbohydrate reserves.

558

Conclusions and future needs for research

The primary products of photosynthesis are carbohydrates. These carbohydrates are distributed throughout the plant to be utilized later in metabolism, formation of structural components, or as reserve substances. Translocation is necessary to move these assimilates from photosynthetically-active tissue to active sinks where they can be utilized in metabolism, or to storage organs for subsequent storage and utilization. This review has underlined the need for proper understanding of the translocation mechanism and for more quantitative information on translocation rates in relation to driving variables. This information is necessary not only for proper understanding of the plant functions, but also for management practices where translocation may be manipulated to increase the harvestable yield from the system.

Carbohydrates are the major forms of carbon which are created, translocated and stored within green plants. Although other forms of carbon, such as fats, oils, or proteins, may also be involved, their importance as readily-available sources of energy for metabolism is less. Carbohydrates usually considered as reserve constituents are sugars, starch, inulin, and fructosans. They are normally stored in the perennating organs of plants. The amounts of carbohydrates accumulated as reserve substances is determined by many internal and external factors. These reserves are important for growth of perennial plants following dormancy or quiescence, or for regrowth following defoliation or other extreme stresses (Sosebee & Wiebe, 1971).

Any factor affecting production or utilization of carbohydrates for metabolic processes will affect the level of carbohydrate reserves (Menke, 1973). Depletion of carbohydrate reserves during regrowth after foliage removal, particularly if defoliation is frequent and severe, can be a primary cause of deterioration of the forage resource, with depressed vigor and herbage productivity (Weinmann, 1948; Cook, 1966*a*; Menke, 1973). Plants are, however, affected more by defoliation at certain phenological stages of development than at others. Therefore, studies designed to establish relationships among the seasonal changes in carbohydrate reserves, growth and phenological stage of development, and to determine at what stages plants are most detrimentally affected by defoliation, are desirable. In addition, it would be desirable to know the period of rest required to regain normal vigor, herbage productivity and adequate carbohydrate reserves following defoliation.

Some investigators have questioned the role of carbohydrates in regrowth following defoliation (May & Davidson, 1958; May, 1960; Jameson, 1963; Alcock, 1964; Davidson & Milthorpe, 1965, 1966; Humphreys & Robinson, 1966; Greub & Wedin, 1971*a*). May & Davidson (1958) suggested that the decrease in the proportion of nonstructural carbo-hydrates after defoliation may have been caused largely by its use as respiratory substrate. Carbohydrate reserves were believed to be of minor importance as a substrate for synthesis at new growing points. However, some recent studies utilizing radiocarbon have given direct evidence of the use of carbohydrate reserves for regrowth (Pearce, Fissel & Carlson, 1969; Smith & Marten, 1970).

Plants which heavily deplete reserves during their annual growth cycle have a considerable amount of capital to repay during the growing season (Cook, 1966a; Mooney, 1972). If the season is short, poor weather could significantly reduce the pool of carbohydrates available for subsequent years. Depletion of reserves in palatable perennials by grazing could shift the competitive balance toward nonpalatable species and result in a change in community composition (Cook, 1966a; Trlica, 1977).

Plants which are equal with respect to their growth forms, efficiency of carbon gain, and in the amounts of reserves they store for subsequent regrowth could have dissimilar competitive capacities, dependent upon the time at which a commitment is made for initiation of regrowth and carbohydrate utilization (Mooney, 1972). The time of commitment of reserves is certainly as important in competition as the initial carbon-gaining capacity of the plants. If unfavorable biotic or abiotic conditions prevail following investment of carbohydrate reserves for growth initiation, then the plant's health or vigor may be impaired.

May (1960) stated that the use of the term 'reserve' may foster false conceptions of the role of carbohydrates which accumulate in plants. He concluded that a dearth of information on mobilizing hormones, trans-location mechanisms, and use of carbohydrates at meristems precluded an accurate evaluation of the function of reserves for regrowth. This statement is still valid today.

References

Adegbola, A. A. & McKell, C. M. (1966a). Effect of nitrogen fertilization on the carbohydrate content of coastal Bermudagrass (*Cynodon dactylon* (L.) Pers.). *Agronomy Journal*, **58**, 60–4.

Adegbola, A. A. & McKell, C. M. (1966b). Regrowth potential of coastal Bermuda grass as related to previous nitrogen fertilization. *Agronomy Journal*, **58**, 145–6.

Alberda, T. (1957). The effects of cutting, light intensity, and night temperature on growth and soluble carbohydrate content of *Lolium perenne* L. *Plant and Soil*, **8**, 199–230.

Alberda, T. (1966). The influence of reserve substances on dry-matter production after defoliation. *Proceedings of the 10th International Grassland Congress*, Helsinki, 1966, pp. 140–7.

Alburquerque, H. E. (1968). Leaf area, and age, and carbohydrate reserves in the regrowth of tall fescue (*Festuca arundinacea* Schreb.) tillers. *Dissertation Abstracts*, Section B., **28**, 3968B.

Alcock, M. B. (1964). The physiological significance of defoliation on the subsequent regrowth of grass-clover mixtures and cereals. In: *Grazing in Terrestrial and Marine Environments* (ed. D. J. Crisp), pp. 25–41. Blackwell Scientific, Oxford.

Aldous, A. E. (1930). Effect of different clipping treatments on the yield and vigor of prairie grass vegetation. *Ecology*, **11**, 752–9.

Aldous, A. E. (1935). *Management of Kansas permanent pastures*. Kansas Agricultural Experimental Station Bulletin 272.

Auda, H., Blaser, R. E. & Brown, R. H. (1966). Tillering and carbohydrate contents of orchardgrass as influenced by environmental factors. *Crop Science*, **6**, 139–43.

Baker, F. S. (1918). Aspen reproduction in relation to management. *Journal of Forestry*, **16**, 389–98.

Baker, H. K. (1963). Recent research in grassland. In: *Vistas in Botany* (ed. W. B. Turrill), vol. 2, Applied Botany, pp. 36–61. Pergamon, Oxford.

Baker, H. K. & Garwood, E. A. (1961). Studies on the root development of herbage plants. v. Seasonal changes in fructosan and soluble-sugar contents of cocksfoot herbage, stubble, and roots under two cutting treatments. *Journal of the British Grassland Society*, **16**, 263–7.

Balasko, J. A. & Smith, D. (1973). Carbohydrates in grasses. v. Incorporation of ^{14}C into plant parts and nonstructural carbohydrates of timothy (*Phleum pratense* L.) at three developmental stages. *Crop Science*, **13**, 19–22.

Bamberg, S., Wallace, A., Kleinkopf, G. & Vollmer, A. (1972). Gas exchange and assimilate distribution in Mojave desert shrubs. *US/IBP Desert Biome Research Memorandum* RM 73.10. Utah State University, Logan, Utah.

Barnes, D. L. (1960). Growth and management studies on *Sabi Panicum* and star grass. Part i. *Rhodesia Agricultural Journal*, **57**, 399–411.

Benedict, H. M. & Brown, G. B. (1944). The growth and carbohydrate response of *Agropyron smithii* and *Bouteloua gracilis* to changes in nitrogen supply. *Plant Physiology*, **19**, 481–94.

Biddulph, O. & Cory, R. (1957). An analysis of translocation in the phloem of the bean plant using HTO, P^{32} and ^{14}CO$_2$. *Plant Physiology*, **32**, 608–19.

Bieleski, R. L. (1960). The physiology of sugarcane. iv. Effects of inhibitors on sugar accumulation in storage tissue slices. *Australian Journal of Biological Sciences*, **12**, 221–31.

Biswell, H. H. & Weaver, J. E. (1933). Effect of frequent clipping on the development of roots and tops of grasses in prairie sod. *Ecology*, **14**, 368–89.

Blaisdell, J. P. & Pechanec, J. F. (1949). Effects of herbage removal at various dates on vigor of bluebunch wheatgrass and arrowleaf balsamroot. *Ecology*, **30**, 298–305.

Blaser, R. E., Brown, R. H. & Bryant, H. T. (1966). The relationship between carbohydrate accumulation and growth of grasses under different microclimates. *Proceedings of 10th International Grassland Congress*, Helsinki, 1966, pp. 147–50.

Bommer, D. F. R. (1966). Influence of cutting frequency and nitrogen level on the carbohydrate reserves of three grass species. *Proceedings of 10th International Grassland Congress*, Helsinki, 1966, pp. 156–60.

Plant processes

Brougham, R. W. (1956). The effect of intensity of defoliation on regrowth of pastures. *Australian Journal of Agricultural Research*, **7**, 377–87.

Brown, R. H. & Blaser, R. E. (1965). Relationship between reserve carbohydrate accumulation and growth rate in orchardgrass (*Dactylis glomerata* L.) and tall fescue (*Festuca arundinacea*). *Crop Science*, **5**, 577–82.

Brown, R. H. & Blaser, R. E. (1970). Soil moisture and temperature effects on growth and soluble carbohydrates of orchardgrass (*Dactylis glomerata*). *Crop Science*, **10**, 213–16.

Bukey, F. S. & Weaver, J. E. (1939). Effects of frequent clipping on the underground food reserves of certain prairie grasses. *Ecology*, **20**, 246–52.

Burr, G. O., Hartt, C. E., Tanimoto, T., Takahashi, T. & Brodie, H. W. (1958). The circulatory system of the sugarcane plant. In: *International Conference on Radioisotopes in Scientific Research, Proceedings of the First (UNESCO) International Conference* (ed. R. C. Extermann), pp. 351–68. Pergamon Press, New York.

Burton, G. H., Jackson, J. E. & Knox, F. E. (1959). The influence of light reduction upon the production, persistence and chemical composition of coastal Bermudagrass, *Cynodon dactylon*. *Agronomy Journal*, **51**, 537–42.

Butcher, H. C. (1965). The kinetics of carbon-14 translocation in sugar beet: An effect of illumination. *Dissertation Abstracts*, **25**, 7350.

Canny, M. J. (1961). Measurements of the velocity of translocation. *Annals of Botany* (New Series), **25**, 152–67.

Canny, M. J. (1971). Translocation: mechanisms and kinetics. *Annual Review of Plant Physiology*, **22**, 237–60.

Canny, M. J. (1973). *Phloem Translocation*. Cambridge University Press, Cambridge.

Carr, D. J. & Wardlaw, I. F. (1965). The supply of photosynthetic assimilates to the grain from the flag leaf and ear of wheat. *Australian Journal of Biological Sciences*, **18**, 711–19.

Clements, H. F. (1940). Movement of organic solutes in the sausage tree, *Kigelia africana*. *Plant Physiology*, **15**, 689–700.

Colby, W. G., Drake, M., Oohara, H. & Yoshida, N. (1966). Carbohydrate reserves in orchardgrass. *Proceedings of 10th International Grassland Congress*, Helsinki, 1966, pp. 151–5.

Colwell, R. N. (1942). The use of radioactive phosphorus in translocation studies. *American Journal of Botany*, **29**, 798–807.

Cook, C. W. (1966a). Carbohydrate reserves in plants. *Utah Agricultural Experimental Station Research Series 31*.

Cook, C. W. (1966b). The role of carbohydrate reserves in managing range plants. *Utah Agricultural Experiment Station Mimeograph Series 499*.

Cook, C. W. & Child, R. D. (1971). Recovery of desert plants in various states of vigor. *Journal of Range Management*, **24**, 339–43.

Cook, C. W., Stoddart, L. A. & Kinsinger, F. E. (1958). Responses of crested wheatgrass to various clipping treatments. *Ecological Monographs*, **28**, 237–72.

Cooper, C. S. & Watson, C. A. (1968). Total available carbohydrates in roots of sainfoin (*Orobrychis viciaefolia* Scop.) and alfalfa (*Medicago sativa* L.) when grown under several management regimes. *Crop Science*, **8**, 83–5.

Coyne, P. I. (1969). Seasonal trend in total available carbohydrates with respect to phenological stage of development in eight desert range species. Ph.D. Dissertation, Utah State University, Logan, Utah.

Coyne, P. I. & Cook, C. W. (1970). Seasonal carbohydrate reserve cycles in eight desert range species. *Journal of Range Management*, **23**, 438–44.

Crafts, A. S. (1931). Movement of organic materials in plants. *Plant Physiology.* **6**, 1–41.

Crafts. A. S. (1961). *Translocation in Plants.* Holt, Rinehart and Winston, New York.

Crafts, A. S. & Crisp, C. E. (1971). *Phloem Transport in Plants.* W. H. Freeman, San Francisco.

Dahlman, R. C. & Kucera, C. L. (1968). Tagging native grassland vegetation with carbon-14. *Ecology,* **49**, 1119–1203.

Dahlman, R. C. & Kucera, C. L. (1969). Carbon-14 cycling in the root and soil components of a prairie ecosystem. In: *Second National Symposium on Radioecology Proceedings* (eds. D. J. Nelson & F. C. Evans), pp. 652–60. Ann Arbor, Michigan.

Davidson, J. L. & Milthorpe, F. L. (1965). Carbohydrate reserves in the regrowth of cocksfoot (*Dactylis glomerata* L.). *Journal of the British Grassland Society,* **20**, 15–18.

Davidson, J. L. & Milthorpe, F. L. (1966). The effect of defoliation on the carbon balance in *Dactylis glomerata. Annals of Botany* (New Series), **30**, 186–98.

Davidson, R. L. (1969). Effects of edaphic factors on the soluble carbohydrate contents of roots of *Lolium perenne* L. and *Trifolium repens* L. *Annals of Botany* (New Series), **33**, 579–89.

De Cugnak, A. (1931). Recherches sur les glucides des graminées. *Annales des Sciences Naturelles,* **13**, 1–129.

Dina, S. J. & Klikoff, L. G. (1973). Effect of plant moisture stress on carbohydrate and nitrogen content in big sagebrush. *Journal of Range Management,* **26**, 207–9.

Dixon, H. H. & Ball, N. G. (1922). Transport of organic substances in plants. *Nature* (*London*), **109**, 236–7.

Dodd, J. D. & Hopkins, H. H. (1958). Yield and carbohydrate content of blue grama grass as affected by clipping. *Transactions of the Kansas Academy of Science,* **61**, 280–87.

Donart, G. B. (1969). Carbohydrate reserves of six mountain plants as related to growth. *Journal of Range Management,* **22**, 411–15.

Donart, G. B. & Cook, C. W. (1970). Carbohydrate reserve content of mountain range plants following defoliation and regrowth. *Journal of Range Management,* **23**, 15–19.

Doodson, J. K., Manners, J. G. & Myers, A. (1964). The distribution pattern of [14]carbon assimilated by the third leaf of wheat. *Journal of Experimental Botany,* **15**, 96–103.

Eaton, F. M. & Ergle, D. R. (1948). Carbohydrate accumulation in the cotton plant at low moisture levels. *Plant Physiology,* **23**, 169–87.

Everson, A. C. (1966). Effects of frequent clipping at different stubble heights on western wheatgrass (*Agropyron smithii* Rydb.). *Agronomy Journal,* **58**, 33–5.

Feltner, K. C. & Massengale, M. A. (1965). Influence of temperature and harvest management on growth, level of carbohydrate in roots and survival of alfalfa (*Medicao sativa* L.). *Crop Science,* **5**, 585–8.

Fisher, A. G. (1966). 'Seasonal trends of root reserves in blue grama and western wheatgrass.' M.S. Thesis. Colorado State University, Fort Collins.

Ford, J. & Peel, A. J. (1967). Preliminary experiments on the effect of temperature on the movement of ^{14}C-labeled assimilates through the phloem of willow. *Journal of Experimental Botany,* **18**, 406–15.

Fujiwara, A. & Suzuki, M. (1961). Effects of temperature and light on the translocation of photosynthetic products. *Tohoku Journal of Agricultural Research*, **12**, 363–7.

Geiger, D. R. (1966). Effect of sink region cooling on translocation rate. *Plant Physiology*, **41**, (Supplement): xx.

Geiger, D. R. & Christy, A. L. (1971). Effect of sink region anoxia on translocation rate. *Plant Physiology*, **47**, 172–4.

Graber, L. F. (1931). Food reserves in relation to other factors limiting the growth of grasses. *Plant Physiology*, **6**, 43–72.

Greenfield, S. B. & Smith, D. (1973). Diurnal variations of non-structural carbohydrates in each part of a shoot of switchgrass (*Panicum virgatum* L.). *Agronomy Abstracts*, p. 25.

Greub, L. J. & Wedin, W. F. (1971a). Leaf area, dry matter accumulation, and carbohydrate reserves in alfalfa and birdsfoot trefoil under a three-cut management. *Crop Science*, **11**, 341–4.

Greub, L. J. & Wedin, W. F. (1971b). Leaf area, dry matter production, and carbohydrate reserve levels of birdsfoot trefoil as influenced by cutting height. *Crop Science*, **11**, 734–8.

Habeshaw, D. (1973). Translocation and the control of photosynthesis in sugar beet. *Planta*, **110**, 213–26.

Hanson, W. R. & Stoddart, L. A. (1940). Effects of grazing upon bunch wheatgrass. *Journal of the American Society of Agronomy*, **32**, 278–89.

Hartt, C. E. & Kortschak, H. P. (1963). Tracing sugar in the cane plant. *Proceedings of the 11th Congress of the International Society of Sugar Cane Technologists*, pp. 323–34.

Hedrick, D. W. (1958). Proper utilization – a problem in evaluating the physiological response of plants to grazing use: A review. *Journal of Range Management*, **11**, 34–43.

Holscher, C. E. (1945). The effects of clipping bluestem wheatgrass and blue grama at different heights and frequencies. *Ecology*, **26**, 148–56.

Holt, D. A. & Hilst, A. E. (1969). Daily variations in carbohydrate content of selected forage crops. *Agronomy Journal*, **61**, 239–42.

Humphreys, L. R. & Robinson, A. R. (1966). Interrelations of leaf area and nonstructural carbohydrate status as determinants of the growth of sub-tropical grasses. Proceedings of *10th International Grassland Congress*, Helsinki, 1966, pp. 113–16.

Hunter, R. A., McIntyre, B. L. & McIlroy, R. J. (1970). Water-soluble carbohydrates of tropical pasture grasses and legumes. *Journal of the Science of Food and Agriculture*, **21**, 400–405.

Hyder, D. N. & Sneva, F. A. (1959). Growth and carbohydrate trends in crested wheatgrass. *Journal of Range Management*, **12**, 271–6.

Hyder, D. N. & Sneva, F. A. (1963a). Morphological and physiological factors affecting the grazing management of crested wheatgrass. *Crop Science*, **3**, 267–71.

Hyder, D. N. & Sneva, F. A. (1963b). *Studies of six grasses seeded on sagebrush–bunchgrass range: Yield, palatability, carbohydrate accumulation, and developmental morphology*. Oregon Agricultural Experimental Station Technical Bulletin 71.

Jameson, D. A. (1963). Responses of individual plants to harvesting. *Botanical Review*, **29**, 532–94.

Jameson, D. A. (1964). Effect of defoliation on forage plant physiology. In: *Forage plant physiology and soil range relationships*, pp. 67–80. American Society of Agronomy, Special Publication 5, Madison, Wisconsin.

Jones, M. B. & Laude, H. M. (1960). Relationship between sprouting in chamise and the physiological condition of the plant. *Journal of Range Management*, **13**, 210–14.

Kimura, M. (1969). Ecological and physiological studies on the vegetation of Mt. Shimagare. VII. Analysis of production processes of young *Abies* stand based on the carbohydrate economy. *Botanical Magazine*, **82**, 6–19.

Kinsinger, F. E. (1953). 'Forage yield and carbohydrate content of underground parts of grasses as affected by clipping.' M.S. Thesis, Kansas State College, Fort Hays.

Kinsinger, F. E. & Hopkins, H. H. (1961). Carbohydrate content of underground parts of grasses as affected by clipping. *Journal of Range Management*, **41**, 9–12.

Kozlowski, T. T. (1964). Shoot growth in woody plants. *Botanical Review*, **30**, 335–92.

Kozlowski, T. T. & Clausen, J. J. (1965). Food relations in shoot growth of woody plants. *Ecological Society of America Bulletin*, **46**, 92.

Kozlowski, T. T. & Keller, T. (1966). Food relations of woody plants. *Botanical Review*, **32**, 294–382.

Kozlowski, T. T. & Winget, C. H. (1964). The role of reserves in leaves, branches, and roots on shoot growth of red pine. *American Botanist*, **51**, 522–9.

Kramer, P. J. & Kozlowski, T. T. (1960). *Physiology of Trees*. McGraw-Hill, New York.

Kursanov. A. L. (1963). Metabolism and the transport of organic substances in the phloem. *Advances in Botanical Research*, **1**, 209–78.

Kust, C. A. & Smith, D. (1961). Influence of harvesting management on level of carbohydrate reserves, longevity of stands and yields of hay and protein from Vernal alfalfa. *Crop Science*, **1**, 267–9.

Langille, A. R. & McKee, G. W. (1968). Seasonal variation in carbohydrate root reserves and crude protein and tannin in crown vetch forage, *Coronilla varia* L. *Agronomy Journal*, **60**, 415–19.

Laycock, W. A. & Conrad, P. W. (1969). How time and intensities of clipping affect tall bluebell. *Journal of Range Management*, **22**, 299–303.

Lechtenberg, V. L., Holt, D. A. & Youngberg, H. W. (1971). Diurnal variation in nonstructural carbohydrates, *in vitro* digestibility, and leaf to stem ratio of alfalfa. *Agronomy Journal*, **63**, 719–24.

Lechtenberg, V. L., Holt, D. A. & Youngberg, H. W. (1972). Diurnal variation in nonstructural carbohydrates in *Festuca arundinacea* (Schreb.) with and without N fertilizer. *Agronomy Journal*, **64**, 302–5.

McCarty, E. C. (1935). Seasonal march of carbohydrates in *Elymus ambiguus* and *Muhlenbergia gracilis* and their reaction under moderate grazing use. *Plant Physiology*, **10**, 727–38.

McCarty, E. C. (1938). *The relation of growth to the varying carbohydrate content in mountain brome*. United States Department of Agriculture, Technical Bulletin 598. Washington, D.C.

McCarty, E. C. & Price, R. (1942). *Growth and carbohydrate content of important mountain forage plants in central Utah as affected by clipping and grazing*. United States Department of Agriculture Technical Bulletin 818. Washington, D.C.

McConnell, B. R. & Garrison, G. A. (1966). Seasonal variations of available carbohydrates in bitterbrush. *Journal of Wildlife Management*, **30**, 168–72.

McDonough, W. T. (1969). Carbohydrate reserves in *Mertensia arizonica* as related to growth, temperature and clipping treatments. *Ecology*, **50**, 429–32.

Plant processes

McIlvanie, S. K. (1942). Carbohydrate and nitrogen trends in bluebunch wheatgrass, *Agropyron spicatum*, with special reference to grazing influences. *Plant Physiology*, **17**, 540–57.

McWilliam, J. R. (1968). The nature of the perennial response in Mediterranean grasses. II. Senescence, summer dormancy, and survival in *Phalaris*. *Australian Journal of Agricultural Research*, **19**, 397–409.

Maranville, J. W. & Paulsen, G. M. (1970). Alteration of carbohydrate composition of corn (*Zea mays* L.) seedlings during moisture stress. *Agronomy Journal*, **62**, 605–8.

Marshall, C. (1966). 'Studies on the organization of the vegetative grass plant.' Ph.D. Thesis. University College of North Wales, Bangor.

Marshall, C. & Sagar, G. R. (1965). The influence of defoliation on the distribution of assimilates in *Lolium multiflorum* Lam. *Annals of Botany*, **29**, 365–72.

Mason, T. G. & Maskell, E. J. (1928). Studies on the transport of carbohydrates in the cotton plant. II. The factors determining the rate and the direction of movement of sugars. *Annals of Botany*, **42**, 571–636.

Mason, T. G. & Phillis, E. (1936). Further studies on transport in the cotton plant. V. Oxygen supply and the activation of diffusion. *Annals of Botany*, **50**, 455–99.

Mason, T. G. & Phillis, E. (1937). The migration of solutes. *Botanical Review*, **3**, 47–71.

Matches, A. G. (1960). The development of carbohydrate reserves by alfalfa during the initial season of establishment. *Dissertation Abstracts*, **21**, 17.

May, L. H. (1960). The utilization of carbohydrate reserves in pasture plants after defoliation. *Herbage Abstracts*, **30**, 239–45.

May, L. H. & Davidson, J. L. (1958). The role of carbohydrate reserves in regeneration of plants. *Australian Journal of Agricultural Research*, **9**, 767–77.

Menke, J. W. (1973). 'Effects of defoliation on carbohydrate reserves, vigor, and herbage yield for several important Colorado range species.' Ph.D. Dissertation. Colorado State University, Fort Collins.

Merrill, S. & Kilby, W. W. (1952). Effect of cultivation, irrigation, fertilization and other cultural treatments on growth of newly planted tung trees. *Proceedings of the American Society for Horticultural Science*, **58**, 69–81.

Mitchell, K. J. (1954). Influence of light and temperature on the growth of ryegrass (*Lolium* spp.). III. Pattern and rate of tissue formation. *Physiologia Plantarum*, **7**, 51–65.

Mochizuki, T. & Hanada, S. (1958). The effect of nitrogen on the formation of the anisophylly on the terminal shoots of apple trees. *Soil and Plant Food*, **4**, 68–74.

Mooney, H. A. (1972). The carbon balance of plants. *Annual Review of Ecology and Systematics*, **3**, 315–46.

Mooney, H. A. & Billings, W. D. (1960). The annual carbohydrate cycle of alpine plants as related to growth. *American Journal of Botany*, **47**, 594–8.

Mooney, H. A. & Billings, W. D. (1965). Effects of altitude on carbohydrate content of mountain plants. *Ecology*, **46**, 750–1.

Moore, R. M. & Biddiscombe, E. F. (1964). The effects of grazing on grasslands. In: *Grasses and Grasslands* (ed. C. Barnard), pp. 221–235. Macmillan, London.

Münch, E. (1930). *Die Stoffbewegungen in der Pflanze*. Gustav Fischer, Jena

Neiland, B. B. & Curtis, J. (1956). Differential response to clipping of six prairie grasses in Wisconsin. *Ecology*, **37**, 355–65.

Nelson, C. D. (1963). Effect of climate on the distribution and translocation of assimilates. In: *Environmental Control of Plant Growth* (ed. L. T. Evans), pp. 149–74. Academic Press, New York.

Nelson, C. D. & Gorham, P. R. (1957). Uptake and translocation of ^{14}C-labelled sugars applied to primary leaves of soybean seedlings. *Canadian Journal of Botany*, **35**, 339–47.

Nelson, C. D. & Gorham, P. R. (1959). Translocation of ^{14}C-labelled amino acids and amides in the stems of young soybean plants. *Canadian Journal of Botany*, **37**, 431–8.

Oechel, W. C., Strain, B. R. & Odening, W. R. (1972). Tissue water potential, photosynthesis, ^{14}C-labeled photosynthate utilization, and growth in the desert shrub *Larrea divaricata* Cav. *Ecological Monographs*, **42**, 127–41.

Ogden, P. R. & Loomis, W. E. (1972). Carbohydrate reserves of intermediate wheatgrass after clipping and etiolation treatments. *Journal of Range Management*, **25**, 29–32.

Ojima, K. & Isawa, T. (1967). Physiological studies on carbohydrates of forage plant. II. Characteristics of carbohydrate composition according to species of plant. *Journal of the Japanese Society of Grassland Science*, **13**, 39–50.

Okajima, H. & Smith, D. (1964). Available carbohydrate fractions in the stem bases and seeds of timothy (*Phleum pratensis*) smooth brome grass (*Bromus inermis*) and several other northern grasses. *Crop Science*, **4**, 317–20.

Owensby, C. E., Paulsen, G. M. & McKendrick, J. D. (1970). Effect of burning and clipping on big bluestem reserve carbohydrates. *Journal of Range Management*, **23**, 358–62.

Paulsen, G. M. & Smith, D. (1968). Influence of several management practices on growth characteristics and available carbohydrate content of smooth bromegrass. *Agronomy Journal*, **60**, 375–9.

Pearce, R. B., Fissel, G. & Carlson, G. E. (1969). Carbon uptake and distribution before and after defoliation of alfalfa. *Crop Science*, **9**, 756–9.

Pettit, R. D. & Fagan, R. E. (1974). Influence of nitrogen and irrigation on carbohydrate reserves of buffalograss. *Journal of Range Management*, **27**, 279–82.

Plaut, Z. & Reinhold, L. (1965). The effect of water stress on ^{14}C sucrose transport in bean plants. *Australian Journal of Biological Sciences*, **18**, 1143–55.

Priestly, C. A. (1962). *Carbohydrate resources within the perennial plant; their utilization and conservation.* Commonwealth Bureau of Horticulture and plantation Crops, Technical Communication 27. Commonwealth Agricultural Bureaux, Farnham Royal, Bucks. England.

Qureshi, F. A. & Spanner, D. C. (1973). The effect of nitrogen on the movement of tracers down the stolon of *Saxifraga sarmentosa*, with some observations on the influence of light. *Planta*, **110**, 131–44.

Reynolds, J. H. (1962). Morphological development and trends of carbohydrate reserves in alfalfa, smooth bromegrass and timothy under various cutting schedules. *Dissertation Abstracts*, **23**, 1855–6.

Reynolds, J. H. (1969). Carbohydrate reserve trends in orchardgrass (*Dactylis glomerata* L.) grown under different cutting frequencies and nitrogen fertilization levels. *Crop Science*, **9**, 720–3.

Reynolds, J. H. (1971). Carbohydrate trends in alfalfa roots under several forage harvest schedules. *Crop Science*, **11**, 103–6.

Richardson, M. (1968). *Translocation in Plants.* St Martin's Press, New York.

Roberts, B. R. (1964). Effects of water stress on the translocation of photosynthetically assimilated carbon-14 in yellow poplar. In: *The Formation of Wood*

Plant processes

in Forest Trees (ed. M. H. Zimmerman), pp. 273–88. Academic Press, New York.

Robinson, G. D. & Massengale, M. A. (1968). Effect of harvest management and temperature on forage yield, root carbohydrates, plant density and leaf relationships in alfalfa. *Crop Science*, **8**, 147–51.

Rohrbaugh, L. M. & Rice, E. L. (1949). Effect of application of sugar on the translocation of sodium 2,4-dichlorophenoxyacetate by bean plants in the dark. *Botanical Gazette*, **111**, 85–9.

Ryle, G. J. A. (1970*a*). Distribution patterns of assimilated ^{14}C in vegetative and reproductive shoots of *Lolium perenne* and L. *temulentum*. *Annals of Applied Biology*, **66**, 155–67.

Ryle, C. J. A. (1970*b*). Partition of assimilates in an annual and a perennial grass. *Journal of Applied Ecology*, **7**, 217–27.

Sampson, A. W. & McCarty, E. C. (1930). The carbohydrate metabolism of *Stipa pulchra*. *Hilgardia*, **5**, 61–100.

Santarius, K. A. (1967). Das Verhalten von CO_2-Assimilation, NADP- und PGS-Reduktion und ATP-Synthese intakter Blattzellen in Abhängigkeit vom Wassergehalt. *Planta*, **73**, 228–42.

Santarius, K. A. & Heber, U. (1967). Das Verhalten von Hill-Reaktion und Photophosphorylierung isolierter Chloroplasten in Abhängigkeit vom Wassergehalt, II, Wasserentzug über Ca Cl$_2$. *Planta*, **73**, 109–37.

Schirman, R. & Buckholtz, K. P. (1966). Influence of atrazine on control and rhizome carbohydrate reserves of quackgrass. *Weeds*, **14**, 233–6.

Sheard, R. W. (1968). Relationship of carbohydrate and nitrogen compounds in the haplocorn to the growth of timothy (*Phleum pratense* L.). *Crop Science*, **8**, 658–60.

Singh, J. S. & Coleman, D. C. (1975). Evaluation of functional root biomass and translocation of photoassimilated carbon-14 in a shortgrass prairie ecosystem. In: *The Belowground Ecosystem: A Synthesis of Plant Associated Processes* (ed. J. K. Marshall). Dowden, Hutchinson & Ross, Stroudsburg, Pennsylvania.

Smith, A. E. & Leinweber, C. L. (1971). Relationship of carbohydrate trend and morphological development of little bluestem tillers. *Ecology*, **52**, 1052–7.

Smith, D. (1962). Carbohydrate root reserves in alfalfa, red clover and birdsfoot treefoil under several management schedules. *Crop Science*, **2**, 75–8.

Smith, D. (1964). Winter injury and the survival of forage plants. A review. *Herbage Abstracts*, **34**, 203–9.

Smith, D. (1968). Carbohydrates in grasses. IV. Influence of temperature on the sugar and fructosan composition of timothy plant parts at anthesis. *Crop Science*, **8**, 331–4.

Smith, D. & Graber, L. F. (1948). The influence of top growth removal on the root and vegetation development of biennial sweetclover. *Journal of the American Society of Agronomy*, **40**, 818–31.

Smith, D. & Grotelueschen, R. D. (1966). Carbohydrates in grasses. I. Sugar and fructosan composition of the stem bases of several northern adapted grasses at seed maturity. *Crop Science*, **6**, 263–6.

Smith, D & Silva, J. P. (1969). Use of carbohydrate and nitrogen root reserves in regrowth of alfalfa from greenhouse experiments under light and dark conditions. *Crop Science*, **9**, 464–7.

Smith, D., Paulsen, G. M. & Raguse, C. A. (1964). Extraction of total available carbohydrates from grass and legume tissue. *Plant Physiology*, **29**, 960–2

568

Smith, L. H. & Marten, G. C. (1970). Foliar regrowth of alfalfa utilizing ^{14}C-labeled carbohydrates stored in roots. *Crop Science*, **10**, 146–51.

Sosebee, R. E. & Wiebe, H. H. (1971). Effect of water stress and clipping on photosynthate translocation in two grasses. *Agronomy Journal*, **64**, 14–17.

Sosebee, R. E. & Wiebe, H. H. (1973). Effect of phenological development on radiophosphorus translocation from leaves in crested wheatgrass. *Oecologia*, **13**, 102–12.

Sprague, V. G. & Sullivan, J. T. (1950). Reserve carbohydrates in orchardgrass clipped periodically. *Plant Physiology*, **25**, 92–102.

Steinke, T. D. (1969). The translocation of ^{14}C-assimilates in *Eragrostis curvula*: An autoradiographic survey. *Proceedings of the Grassland Society of Southern Africa*, **4**, 19–34.

Steinke, T. D. & Booysen, P. de V. (1968). The regrowth and utilization of carbohydrate reserves of *Eragrostis curvula* after different frequencies of defoliation. *Proceedings of the Grassland Society of Southern Africa*, **3**, 105–10.

Strain, B. R. (1969). Seasonal adaptations in photosynthesis and respiration in four desert shrubs growing *in situ*. *Ecology*, **50**, 511–13.

Sullivan, J. T. & Sprague, V. G. (1943). Composition of the roots and stubble of perennial ryegrass following partial defoliation. *Plant Physiology*, **18**, 656–70.

Sullivan, J. T. & Sprague, V. G. (1953). Reserve carbohydrates in orchardgrass cut for hay. *Plant Physiology*, **28**, 304–13.

Suzuki, M. (1971). Behavior of long-chain fructosan in the basal top of timothy as influenced by N, P, and K and defoliation. *Crop Science*, **11**, 632–5.

Swanson, C. A. & Geiger, D. R. (1967). Time course of low temperature inhibition of sucrose translocation in sugar beets. *Plant Physiology*, **42**, 751–6.

Tammes, P. M. L., Vonk, C. R. & van Die., J. (1969). Studies on phloem exudation from *Yucca flaccida* Haw. VII. The effect of cooling on exudation. *Acta Botanica Neerlandica*, **18**, 224–9.

Taylor, B. K. (1967). Storage and mobilization of nitrogen in fruit trees: A review. *Journal of the Australian Institute of Agricultural Science*, **33**, 23–9.

Tew, R. K. (1970). Root carbohydrate reserves in vegetative reproduction of aspen. *Forest Science*, **16**, 318–20.

Thaine, R. (1954). The effect of clipping frequency on the productivity of root development of Russian wild ryegrass in the field. *Canadian Journal of Agricultural Science*, **34**, 299–304.

Thrower, S. L. (1965). Translocation of labelled assimilates in the soybean. IV. Some effects of low temperature on translocation. *Australian Journal of Biological Sciences*, **18**, 449–61.

Trlica, M. J., Jr. (1971). 'Defoliation and soil moisture regime effects on plant regrowth and carbohydrate reserve utilization and storage in eight desert range species.' Ph.D. Dissertation, Utah State University, Logan.

Trlica, M. J., Jr. (1977). Effects of frequency and intensity of defoliation on primary producers of arid and semi-arid rangelands. In: *Proceedings of the 2nd U.S./Australia Rangeland Panel, Adelaide*, (1972). Australian Rangeland Society, Perth.

Trlica, M. J., Jr. & Cook, C. W. (1971). Defoliation effects on carbohydrate reserves of desert species. *Journal of Range Management*, **24**, 418–25.

Trlica, M. J., Jr. & Cook, C. W. (1972). Carbohydrate reserves of crested wheat-grass and Russian wildrye as affected by development and defoliation. *Journal of Range Management*, **25**, 430–5.

Troughton, A. (1957). *The underground organs of herbage grasses*. Commonwealth

Bureau of Pastures and Field Crops Bulletin 44. Commonwealth Agricultural Bureaux, Farnham Royal, Bucks. England.

Turner, D. J. (1969). The effects of shoot removal on the rhizome carbohydrate reserves of couch grass (*Agropyron repens* (L.) Beauv.). *Weed Research*, **9**, 27–36.

Ueno, M. & Smith, D. (1970). Growth and carbohydrate changes in the root wood and bark of different sized alfalfa plants during regrowth after cutting. *Crop Science*, **10**, 396–9.

Ullrich, W. (1961). Zur Sauerstoffabhängigkeit des Transportes in den Siebröhren. *Planta*, **57**, 402–29.

Waite, R. & Boyd, J. (1953). The water-soluble carbohydrates of grasses. II. Grasses cut at grazing height several times during the growing season. *Journal of the Science of Food and Agriculture*, **4**, 257–61.

Ward, C. V. & Blaser, R. E. (1961). Carbohydrate food reserves and leaf area in regrowth of orchardgrass. *Crop Science*, **1**, 366–70.

Wardlaw, I. F. (1965). The velocity and pattern of assimilate translocation in wheat plants during grain development. *Australian Journal of Biological Sciences*, **18**, 269–81.

Wardlaw, I. F. (1967). The effect of water stress on translocation in relation to photosynthesis and growth. I. Effect during grain development in wheat. *Australian Journal of Biological Sciences*, **20**, 25–39.

Wardlaw, I. F. (1968a). The control and pattern of movement of carbohydrates in plants. *Botanical Review*, **34**, 79–105.

Wardlaw, I. F. (1968b). The effect of water stress on translocation in relation to photosynthesis and growth. II. Effect during leaf development in *Lolium temulentum* L. *Australian Journal of Biological Sciences*, **22**, 1–16.

Warembourg, F. R. & Paul, E. A. (1973). The use of $^{14}CO_2$ canopy techniques for measuring carbon transfer through the plant-soil system. *Plant & Soil*, **38**, 331–45.

Weatherley, P. E., Peel, A. J. & Hill, G. P. (1959). The physiology of the sieve tube: Preliminary experiments using aphid mouth parts. *Journal of Experimental Botany*, **10**, 1–2.

Weinmann, H. (1940). Seasonal changes in the roots of some South African highveld grasses. *Journal of South African Botany*, **6**, 131–45.

Weinmann, H. (1943). Root reserves in South African highveld grasses in relation to fertilizing and frequency of clipping. *Journal of South African Botany*, **10**, 37–54.

Weinmann, H. (1948). Underground development and reserves of grasses. A review. *Journal of the British Grassland Society*, **3**, 115–40.

Weinmann, H. (1949). Productivity of Marandellas sandveld pastures in relation to frequency of cutting. *Rhodesia Agricultural Journal*, **46**, 175–89.

Weinmann, H. (1952). Carbohydrate reserves in grasses. *Proceedings of VIth International Grassland Congress*, **1**, 655–60.

Weinmann, H. (1961). Total available carbohydrates in grasses and legumes. *Herbage Abstracts*, **31**, 255–61.

Weinmann, H. & Reinhold, L. (1946). Reserve carbohydrates in South African grasses. *Journal of South African Botany*, **12**, 57–73.

Welch, T. G. (1968). Carbohydrate reserves of sand reedgrass under different grazing intensities. *Journal of Range Management*, **21**, 216–20.

White, L. M. (1973). Carbohydrate reserves of grasses: A review. *Journal of Range Management*, **26**, 13–18.

White, L. M., Brown, J. H. & Cooper, C. S. (1972). Nitrogen fertilization and clipping effects on green needlegrass (*Stipa viridula* Trin.). III. Carbohydrate reserves. *Agronomy Journal*, **64**, 824–8.

Whitehead, C. W., Sansing, N. G. & Loomis, W. E. (1959). Temperature coefficient of translocation to tomatoes. *Plant Physiology*, **34** (Supplement), xxi.

Wiebe, H. H. & Wihrheim, S. E. (1962). The influence of internal moisture stress on translocation. In: *Proceedings of Symposium on Use of Radioisotopes in Soil–Plant Nutrition Studies*, pp. 279–88. IAEA, Vienna.

Willard, E. E. & McKell, C. M. (1973). Simulated grazing management systems in relation to shrub growth responses. *Journal of Range Management*, **26**, 171–4.

Willenbrink, J. (1957). Über die Hemmung des Stofftransports in den Siebröhren durch lokale Inaktivierung verschiedener Atmungsenzyme. *Planta*, **48**, 269–342.

Wilson, H. K. (1944). Control of noxious plants. *Botanical Review*, **10**, 279–326.

Wolf, D. D. (1967). *Characteristics of stored carbohydrates in reed canarygrass as related to management, feed value and herbage yield.* Connecticut Agricultural Experiment Station Bulletin 402.

Wolf, D. D., Larson, K. L. & Smith, D. (1962). Grass-alfalfa yields and food storage of associated alfalfas as influenced by height and frequency of clipping. *Crop Science*, **2**, 363–4.

Wright, H. A. & Stinson, K. J. (1970). Response of mesquite to season of top removal. *Journal of Range Management*, **23**, 127–8.

Zanoni, L. J., Michelson, L. F., Colby, W. G. & Drake, M. (1969). Factors affecting carbohydrate reserves of cool season turfgrass. *Agronomy Journal*, **61**, 195–8.

Ziegler, H. & Vieweg, G. H. (1961). Der experimentelle Nachweis einer Massenströmung im Phloem von *Heracleum mantegazzianum* Somm. et Lev. *Planta*, **56**, 402–8.

Manuscript received by the editors April 1975

23. Root development and activities

M. C. DREW

Introduction

The habitat of plants growing in the arid and semi-arid regions of the world is characterized at least during part of the season by low and variable rainfall, low humidity, high insolation and high soil temperatures. All these factors combine to decrease the storage or availability of soil water, which often becomes a dominant factor in controlling the growth and distribution of plant species. Soils of low moisture content provide a medium particularly unfavourable to the normal growth and activity of roots: movement of water and nutrients to root surfaces becomes negligible; the resistance offered by the dry or cemented particles of soil can restrict root penetration; and with exposure to desiccation cells may lose their turgidity and die.

Despite this unfavourable environment many plant life-forms are to be found, ranging from ephemeral annuals to substantial shrubs. What special aspects of root growth and function enable plants to survive under conditions which are only occasionally favourable? Roots in any soil, under any climate, are continuously subject to the stresses of the soil environment, since temperature or water supplies rarely remain within the narrow limits optimal for growth. Arid conditions merely provide exceptional problems since the stresses are more extreme or of longer duration, so that many root functions, particularly those dependent upon concomitant root growth, are confined to comparatively short periods by water availability and season.

This chapter describes some aspects of the growth and physiological activities of roots, the manner in which these are affected by soil environmental conditions, and adaptations which may contribute to plant survival under arid conditions.

Although root systems vary greatly in their form and distribution in soil as a result of genetic and environmental factors, certain basic features of their growth and function are common to all annual and perennial plants. Roots function in:

(*a*) absorption and translocation of water and inorganic nutrients;
(*b*) synthesis and transport of organic compounds, including growth regulators;
(*c*) storage of metabolites, and sometimes water; and
(*d*) anchoring the plant in the soil.

Plant processes

Two aspects seem particularly relevant to the present chapter. The first concerns the dual requirements of resistance to desiccation, combined with unimpaired ability to absorb water and mineral nutrients. After roots have completed extension growth, some centimetres behind the growing root-tip, a succession of barriers resisting water loss begins to be laid down in the endodermis, hypodermis (or exodermis), and epidermis (where it persists), through deposition of lignin and hydrophobic lamellae of suberin over primary cell walls. Later the periderm, comprising layers of suberized cork cells, develops in roots of woody angiosperms and gymnosperms, most herbaceous dicotyledons and some monocotyledons, and tissues external to the periderm are shed (Esau, 1965; Borger, 1973). Mucigel, a mucilaginous material produced by the root cap, invests the outer surface of the root tip and may retard desiccation of the apical meristem and younger tissues before they become suberized. Some regions of the root may continue their absorptive functions despite the development of these structures; this will be discussed later (pp. 589–90).

The second aspect concerns the influence of hormones produced by roots on the metabolism of shoots, proposed long ago by Went (1938) and Chibnall (1939). Only during the last decade has substantial progress been made in this field. Evidence now suggests that roots synthesize cytokinins and possibly gibberellins, growth regulators which are essential for normal shoot growth and development. Cytokinins have been identified in the xylem exudates of a wide range of monocotyledons and dicotyledons, both annuals and woody perennials (Weiss & Vaadia, 1965; Kende & Sitton, 1967; Carr & Burrows, 1968; Vaadia & Itai, 1969; Short & Torrey, 1972; Skene & Antcliff, 1972). It seems likely that the synthesis of cytokinins in roots occurs in growing apices where normal cell division and elongation are able to continue (Weiss & Vaadia, 1965; Short & Torrey, 1972). It is of particular significance, therefore, that soil environmental conditions which interfere with the normal processes of root growth also reduce the amounts of growth regulators transported to shoots. Such effects have been observed under conditions of high salinity and water stress (Vaadia & Itai, 1969), unfavourable temperatures (Atkin, Barton & Robinson, 1973), and short periods of reduced aeration (Burrows & Carr, 1969; Reid, Crozier & Harvey, 1969). Increased amounts of abscisic acid (ABA) and other inhibitors are found in xylem exudates of roots subjected to unfavourable temperatures or water stress; but it is still not clear whether these compounds originate from roots or shoots. Indolyl acetic acid (IAA) and other compounds with auxin activity found in xylem exudates from roots are probably of both shoot and root origin (Scott, 1972).

Since roots transport ions and water and synthesize growth regulators which are essential for normal shoot metabolism, and roots in turn receive carbohydrates and growth regulators from the shoot, a close interdepen-

574

dence exists between root and shoot growth. The detailed mechanisms remain to be elucidated, but it is evident that the activities of the root system cannot be considered in isolation from those of the shoot. It is well established that the distribution of carbon between shoots, roots and other organs can be greatly modified according to environmental conditions both above and below ground (Leonard, 1962).

The distribution of roots in the soil

Types of root

The broad division of root systems into 'tap root' (as in most dicotyledons and gymnosperms) and 'fibrous' (as in most monocotyledons) needs little elaboration (see Esau (1965) for descriptions). The tap root and its laterals are usually supplemented by adventitious roots which develop from the stem base and, most importantly, from dormant and newly initiated primordia from deep within relatively old roots which have undergone secondary thickening (Eames & MacDaniels, 1947; Esau, 1965). The highly branched laterals which form dense networks in the soil fail to undergo secondary thickening and are often short-lived (Head, 1973). These laterals, together with adventitious roots, are sometimes referred to as feeder roots during their early growth before extensive discolouration occurs (indicating periderm formation), but the term is unsatisfactory, for all roots in their primary state, including those which are elongating rapidly (the extension roots) are probably acting as 'feeder roots'. Chance events may dictate those which persist and later form the major skeleton of the root system, which functions more in conduction and anchorage than absorption (see Leshem (1965) for discussion).

Classification of root systems

Attempts to classify root systems in more detail (for example by Cannon, 1949) have not met with great support. Environmental factors can exert an overriding influence on root extension, branching, orientation and longevity, resulting in wide differences in root form between individuals within a species. Zohary (1961) distinguished at least ten main types of root system in Near Eastern desert plants, differing in their depth, production of laterals and specialized modifications, but few of these correspond to the types described by Cannon (1949).

One way of regarding the 'strategy' of root distribution in arid-land soils, recognising that water is the major factor controlling root growth, is to consider the length of time water remains available at different depths, and the types of root system and life cycle best suited to intercept this efficiently (Noy-Meir, 1973). The frequency with which available water

575

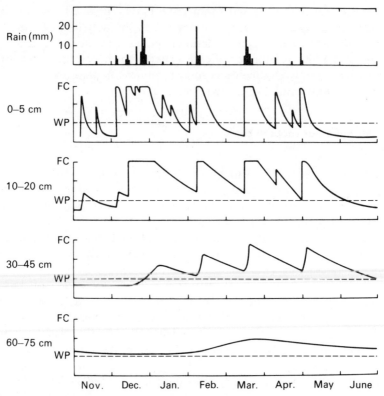

Fig. 23.1. Replenishment and depletion of available water at different depths in desert shrubland during the season. FC, WP – field capacity and wilting point. (From Noy-Meir, 1973.)

is replenished to different depths in a desert soil and lost by evapotranspiration is illustrated in Fig. 23.1: for most habitats the depth of water penetration does not exceed the rooting zone. On this basis, four categories of root systems can be distinguished.

Shallow-rooting ephemerals

Much of the water from light rains penetrating the soil to a depth of 10–30 cm may be lost by evaporation, but its duration of several weeks may be sufficient for roots of fast-growing annuals and herbaceous perennials to complete their life cycle. The root systems of these plants are often shallow and poorly branched (Evenari, Shanan & Tadmor, 1971; Chapter 19 above). With deeper wetting of soil, the roots of some ephemerals may penetrate to depths of 50 cm or more; but completion of the life cycle of these 'drought evaders' does not usually depend on this.

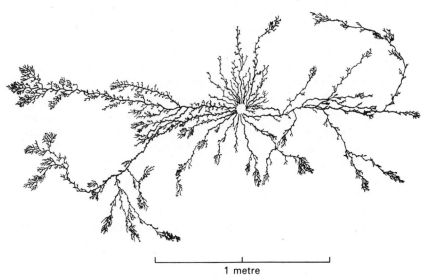

Fig. 23.2. Plan of surface roots of *Opuntia camanchica*. The entire system was between 2.5 and 10 cm below the soil surface, with three to five vertical roots descending 60–90 cm. (From Weaver & Clements, 1938.)

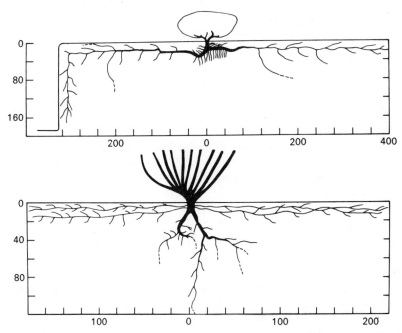

Fig. 23.3. Diagrams of root systems of Negev Desert shrubs. Upper, *Zygophyllum dumosum*. Lower, *Retama raetam*; Dimensions in centimetres. (From Evenari *et al.*, 1971.)

577

Plant processes

Shallow-rooting perennials

Roots of cacti such as *Opuntia fulgida, Ferocactus wislizeni* and *Carnegiea gigantea* are often located no more than a few centimetres beneath the soil surface even in deep soil, and therefore benefit from the lightest rains (Cannon, 1911). It appears that the exposed surfaces of the roots remain absorptive, despite subjection to extreme temperatures and desiccation, for rehydration of shoot tissues and the onset of atmospheric carbon assimilation occur within hours of a rainfall following prolonged drought (Szarek, Johnson & Ting, 1973). Lateral roots may branch to the fourth or fifth order, effectively intercepting rain over a large area (see Fig. 23.2). Shallow root systems also occur in *Artemisia herba-alba, Zygophyllum dumosum* (see Fig. 23.3) and *Statice pruinosa* through abortion of apical meristems, even in the same soil profile as deep-rooting species, in Near-Eastern deserts (Zohary, 1961).

Deep-rooting perennials with superficial laterals

Shrub survival depends, during prolonged droughts, upon deeper stores of water (see Fig. 23.1) reached by a well-developed tap root or vertically orientated laterals. Water is stored at sufficient depth to avoid loss by evaporation over long periods, but survival of shrubs depends upon replenishment at least once every 1 to 2 years by 40–100 mm of rain falling in a short period (Noy-Meir, 1973). There is usually a well-developed lateral root system which, together with adventitious roots, can utilize the more frequent rains penetrating only 10 to 30 cm (see Figs. 23.3, 23.4). Other examples of root systems of arid-land plants in this category are described by Tabler (1964) for *Larrea* sp., Jones & Hodgkinson (1970) for *Atriplex* sp., and Orshan (1972) for *Artemisia monosperma* and other species. Although the root systems excavated by Hellmers, Horton, Juhren & O'Keefe (1955) (see Fig. 23.4) contrasted in their relative depth and extensiveness, both the types illustrated may be considered *deep* rooting in the present context.

Competition in the upper zones can be intense between the superficial laterals of shrubs, summer annuals and germinating seedlings (Negbi & Evenari, 1961; Zohary, 1961; Noy-Meir, 1973). and result in the virtual disappearance of the ephemerals in dry years.

A striking adaptation among the desert shrubs is the development of an extensive root system. Roots as far as 30 m from the stem have been recorded in the Near-East deserts for *Tamarix aphylla* (Zohary, 1961). In *Prosopis* sp., roots extending 15 m (Cannon, 1911) and possibly up to 30 m (McGinnies, 1972) have been recorded for rain-fed plants in the Arizona

578

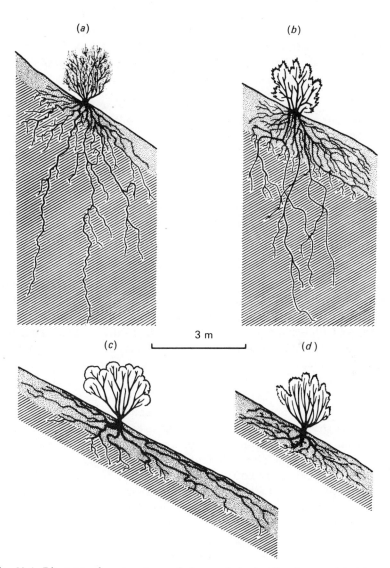

Fig. 23.4. Diagrams of root systems of chaparral shrubs. Species are: (*a*) *Adenostoma fasciculatum*; (*b*) *Quercus dumosa*; (*c*) *Arctostaphylos glauca*; (*d*) *Ceanothus crassifolius*. Roots of *Adenostoma* and *Quercus* penetrated through fractured rock to a depth of 8–9 m. Roots of *Arctostaphylos* and *Ceanothus* were predominantly in the top soil, although some penetrated weathered rock to depths of 2.6 m (*Arctostaphylos*) and 1.4 m (*Ceanothus*). (From Hellmers *et al.*, 1955.)

579

Plant processes

desert uplands. Roots of *Larrea divaricata* grow up to 6 m from the stem in the Argentinian steppe (Oppenheimer, 1960).

An extensive root system can also develop in perennial grasses, forming a network just beneath the surface of sands. Individual roots of *Aristida* sp. extend 10–20 m from the stem (Price, 1911; Zohary, 1961), while vertical roots may penetrate several metres to stored water.

Deep-rooting perennials depending on a water table (phreatophytes)

Plants which develop roots reaching to the water table are rendered independent of water supplies from rainfall. Their laterals often branch copiously in the capillary fringe above the water table. It is clear, however, that the soil environment must be favourable for extended periods to allow roots to penetrate to considerable depths, and for this reason phreatophytes are usually restricted to dune areas, alluvial soils and habitats receiving water from run-off. Remarkable rooting depths have been recorded for this category of plants. Roots of *Prosopis* sp. have been found at a depth of 53 m near Tucson, Arizona (Phillips, 1963), and *Zizyphus lotus* is claimed to grow to depths of 60 m in southern Morocco (Le Houérou, 1972). These may be extreme, but *Retama raetam* penetrates to depths of 20 m and *Atriplex halimus* to 8 m in the deserts of the Near East (Zohary, 1961).

Phreatophytes can act as useful indicators of the depth of the saturated zone, and sometimes of water quality. Because of their ability to transpire without restraint, vast quantities of water are passed into the atmosphere: estimates of 2000 m^3 ha^{-1} yr^{-1} have been made for *Tamarix gallica*. Other phreatophyte species important in parts of the south-western United States include *Salix* sp. *Prosopis* sp. and *Populus* sp. These plants can constitute an economic problem because of the loss of water in the vicinity of watercourses, and their establishment in the beds of streams which they block during periods of rapid run-off (McCleary, 1968; Davis, 1974).

A number of reviews have emphasised the dominating influence of soil texture on water penetration, storage and the establishment of root systems in arid and semi-arid regions (Zohary, 1961; Noy-Meir, 1973; Walter & Stadelmann, 1974). In clay soils, because of their high field-capacity, water penetration is comparatively shallow, and it is soon lost by evaporation. In coarse-textured soils water may penetrate 5–10 times more deeply, with little evaporative loss from depth. Because of poor infiltration much more run-off occurs from clays than from sands and rocks. Thus clay soils are the driest habitats for plants in arid regions, and vegetation is usually more dense and vigorous on sandy or rocky soils receiving the same rainfall, producing the 'inverse-texture' effect (Chapter 17, above).

580

With the exception of succulents and xerohalophytes, rain-fed plants persisting in arid zones develop high root:shoot or root:leaf ratios, implying that the collecting system is comparatively large in relation to the transpiring surfaces (Kassas, 1966; Anderson, Perry & Leigh, 1972; Walter & Stadelmann, 1974). Ratios of 30 or more have been recorded for some species; but the weights may include large quantities of woody tissues and storage organs, and the fraction of the root system which functions in absorption is unknown. In mesophytes, root:shoot ratios increase under *uniform* conditions of inadequate soil water, deficiency of mineral nutrients and unfavourable temperature (Davidson, 1969; Mooney, 1972) – usually because root growth is less retarded than that of the shoot. When the top soil becomes dry but deeper layers remain moist, an acceleration of root extension occurs in the deeper layers. This has sometimes led to the misleading view that root growth is increased in dry soil, the nature of the moisture regimes at depth having been overlooked. Similar factors doubtless contribute to root distribution in desert plains.

Specialized morphological and anatomical adaptations to arid conditions

Aspects of root physiology of particular importance in the survival of perennials after available water throughout most of the rooting depth has been depleted are: (*a*) the ability of the root systems to resist severe desiccation; and (*b*) the ability to take up water and ions following replenishment of available water. Many workers have drawn attention to the production of adventitious roots, which probably occurs in all perennials and biseasonal annuals, following periods of rain when temperatures are high (Cannon, 1911; Migahid, 1961; Jones & Hodgkinson, 1970; Evenari *et al.*, 1971; Charley, 1972; Orshan, 1972; Grenot, 1974). These adventitious roots have been termed 'rain roots'. Copious production of adventitious roots in response to moistening of the soil also occurs on the buried stems of psammophyte shrubs which tolerate moving sands (Shields, 1953; Petrov, 1972).

The development of 'rain roots' can be rapid: Walter & Stadelmann (1974) describe observations of various cacti, watered after 6 months' continuous drought. Adventitious roots emerged in *Opuntia puberula* after 8 hours; among other cacti 50% of the plants developed adventitious roots after 24 hours. In *Atriplex* sp. 3–4 days may elapse so that only substantial rains are said to be effective in rehydration and ion uptake (Cowling, 1969, cited by Charley, 1972). It is often assumed that 'rain roots' are essential for water and ion uptake; but roots of cacti seem able to take up water after prolonged desiccation without forming them, and other instances of absorption thickened suberized roots are described below. Such observations raise questions, however, concerning the pathways of

581

water movement across tissues previously subject to prolonged desiccation. A better understanding of the role of ephemeral adventitious roots, including perhaps their production of growth regulators, is clearly needed.

In the roots of some xeric grasses growing in sandy, well-aerated soil, the cortex forms an aerenchyma or remains intact for only a short distance behind the growing tip. Cells in the mid-cortex collapse and disintegrate leaving an outer ring of cells connected to the stele by the remains of broken cell walls (Beckel, 1956; Killian & Lemée, 1956). Examples of such 'sheath roots' among plants of the Near East desert are cited in Zohary (1961). The sheath is thought to reduce desiccation, particularly on roots exposed by winds in dune habitats.

Many have drawn attention to the presence of encrusting coats of soil particles or sand grains which appear to be cemented around roots by a zone of mucigel, or strongly attached to root hairs and mycorrhizal hyphae (Price, 1911; Zohary, 1961; Went & Stark, 1968; Petrov. 1972). Marked production of mucigel by the root cap and epidermal cells is thought to allow root growth through dry media without desiccation injury, the mucigel ensuring close contact with the sand to facilitate water uptake (Price, 1911). Increased production of mucigel and soluble exudates also takes place in the roots of agricultural crops and forest trees under conditions of moisture stress and mechanical impedance (Barley, 1970; Barber & Gunn, 1974; Tesche, 1974; Nambiar, 1975) Nambiar noted that roots of wheat in contact with dry soil exuded more mucilage compared with parts of the same root system in wet soil, so that an annulus of soil up to 3.5 mm in diameter was strongly retained around the root. In a recent study using the scanning electron microscope (Sprent, 1975), increased amounts of sand were found to adhere to roots of soybean (*Glycine max*) under conditions of water stress, apparently by means of mucigel.

Such modifications to the anatomy of roots, and their contact with the soil, are likely to influence the radial movement of ions and water towards root surfaces. Discontinuities in partly degenerated cortices would be expected greatly to increase resistance to flow, and delay the re-establishment of continuous films of water when roots are remoistened after a period of drought. Further information is clearly needed on whether thin layers of mucigel, air spaces, or encrusting soil could confer much protection against desiccation and high temperatures.

Potential barriers to desiccation which deserve further attention are the interxylary periderm and the suberization of dormant root tips. In the stem of *Artemisia tridentata* and in species of *Sedum* and *Salvia* a band of cork cells is laid down in the summer surrounding the xylem produced during the previous season's growth (Diettert, 1938). Comparable interxylary bands of cork cells are laid down in the roots of herbaceous perennials

(Moss, 1934) and are thought to protect against desiccation and attack by pathogenic organisms, but there seems little information on the prevalence of this adaptation on roots and stem bases of xerophytes (Killian & Lemée, 1956).

Roots of pines (*Pinus halepensis, P. resinosa*) which cease growing in response to arid soil conditions enter a dormant state in which cells near the surface of the root cap form layers of suberin in continuity with the endodermis, a process known as 'metacutinization' (Leshem, 1965; Wilcox, 1968). Leshem sampled roots in the pine forests in Israel at depths of 25–30 cm where, following winter rains, temperatures approached 27–28 °C during the summer months and soil dried well below the wilting point. Metacutinization occurred as the soil water potential decreased towards −7 bar (Leshem, 1970), but the meristems could rupture the suberized layer and resume extension within a period of a few days when rewetted. Although Leshem threw doubt upon the effectiveness of the suberized layer as a protection against desiccation or heat shock, his assessment of root survival depended upon dehydrogenase activity – a test which is not widely accepted (Sator, 1973) – and this interesting topic deserves reappraisal with more reliable techniques.

Methods of measuring root distribution

Apart from the gross distribution of roots within the soil profile, information is often required on the distribution of active roots with depth, microsite or season, and in relation to changing soil conditions. A variety of methods for estimating root distribution are now available but most have been designed for agricultural crops and have yet to be tested in less favourable soils. Some of the problems have been reviewed elsewhere (Danielson, 1967; Barley, 1970; Ellis & Barnes, 1973).

Earlier work concerned with the distribution of plant root systems relied upon the excavation of soil around roots which were exposed upon the vertical walls of trenches (Weaver, 1926). The method is time-consuming and labour-intensive, but it is unlikely to be supplanted when knowledge of depth and extent of roots of individual plants is required. In comparatively uniform stands of vegetation, sampling procedures can be used where representative or quantitative approaches are required. One approach has been to remove a soil block or monolith from the side of the trench by inserting a pinboard to retain the exposed roots when the soil is subsequently washed away (Schuurman & Goedewaagen, 1971). Soil blocks have also been successfully obtained in soils of low natural cohesion by freezing them with liquid nitrogen. Soil cores obtained with a powered sampler can be used to sample roots in soils of suitable texture, free of rocks. Roots are subsequently washed out of the soil.

Plant processes

Loss of fine laterals is always a risk in washing, and may result in serious underestimation of total length and dry weight. Length can be estimated by Newman's method (Newman, 1966) or by semi-automated procedures using an image-analysing computer or a simpler device designed by Rowse & Phillips (1974) which employs a photoelectric cell. Root distribution can also be determined *in situ* on a micro-scale: Melhuish & Lang (1968) impregnated blocks of soil with resin, and observed root positions under the microscope in small thin sections of prepared faces. Another *in situ* method involved the use of autoradiography (Baldwin, Tinker & Marriott, 1971). Shoots were injected with radiophosphorus (^{32}P) which was translocated into the roots. By inserting X-ray film (supported by steel backing plates) into the soil, cut ends of roots labelled with radiophosphorus were located from the position of spots on the films. From the number of roots crossing a plane in the soil, equations based on statistical probability were used to estimate root length per unit volume at that point. Inter-penetrating root systems of different plants can be distinguished by autoradiography with suitable pairs of isotopes, for example radiophosphorus isotopes (^{32}P and ^{33}P) emitting beta particles of contrasting energy (Baldwin & Tinker, 1972) or by supplying carbon dioxide labelled with radiocarbon (^{14}C) to shoots (Ellern, Harper & Sagar, 1970).

A method used extensively with agricultural crops has been to inject stem bases with rubidium-86. The relative distribution of physiologically active roots within the soil profile is then determined by extracting soil cores and assaying for translocated rubidium using gamma-spectrometry (Russell & Ellis, 1968; Ellis & Barnes, 1973). This method has the particular advantage that the labelled roots can be assayed without being extracted from the soil cores. Methods using radiocarbon suffer from the disadvantage that roots need to be washed from the soil before assay is carried out.

Soil-injection techniques with radioisotopes have also been used to give a relative measure of the ability of plants to extract nutrients from different locations in the soil (Fox & Lipps, 1960; Nye & Foster, 1961). Carrier-free radiophosphorus (^{32}P) is commonly used for this purpose. Although most experience has been gained in agricultural soils with crop plants, the method is sufficiently sensitive to demonstrate shifts in uptake by roots from deeper soil layers following surface drought (Newbould, 1969) and has also been used with comparatively large woody plants (Huxley, Patel, Kabaara & Mitchell, 1974). Water extraction from different depths by roots can be followed in suitable soils using the neutron moisture meter.

Underground root laboratories (rhizotrons) have the advantage of allowing continuous observations of the same root segment through glass windows set against vertical or horizontal walls (Rogers & Head, 1969; Head, 1973; Klepper, Taylor, Huck & Fiscus, 1973) but such installations seem justifiable only when seasonal activity or the effects of changing soil conditions with time or depth are an important aspect of the study. A drawback to this approach is the destruction of natural soil structures down the profile adjacent to the excavated surface. Fibre optics to observe root activities in soil with the minimum of disturbance (Waddington, 1971) have not yet been widely used.

Root biomass, and the total amount of carbon transported into roots, are still difficult to estimate. Substantial shedding, decomposition and replacement of roots occurs in perennials (Head, 1973). Little is known concerning the quantity of carbon lost as root exudates from woody plants, but recent estimates for young cereals suggest that amounts equivalent to more than 30% of the final weight of the shoot may be lost as mucigel and soluble exudates (Barber & Martin, 1976).

Supply of nutrient ions and water to absorbing root surfaces in the soil

There is sometimes a need to evaluate or predict the conditions under which soil water content restricts the growth of vegetation. The importance of this aspect in relation to the yield of irrigated crops needs no emphasis, but the requirement of natural vegetation for survival may be much less exacting. For example, shrubs which persist through the summer drought, particularly species which shed leaves or branches (Chapter 26), can greatly reduce transpiration, so that slow delivery of water from the soil may be sufficient to maintain an adequate water balance.

The maximum amounts of water and nutrients which can be made available to the plant depend ultimately on the overall volume of soil occupied by the root system. It is only in recent years that attention has been directed to the detailed processes controlling the *rates* of supply to roots from within the rooting volume. Dissolved substances move to absorbing root surfaces by mass flow (convection) and diffusion (Barber, 1962; Olsen & Kemper, 1968; Nye, 1969; Tinker, 1969).

In mass flow, solutes are swept along with the soil water drawn towards roots in response to transpiration. The amounts supplied in this way can be approximately gauged by the product of the transpiration ratio (the amount of water transpired per gram of tissue produced by the plant) and the average concentration of the solute in the soil solution. This amount can then be compared with the average concentration of the solute in the plant tissue. Calcium, magnesium, sodium and chloride ions are usually in sufficiently high concentration in soil solution to be carried predominantly by mass flow. A marked build-up in the concentrations of these

585

ions occurs around roots where absorption is slower than supply by mass flow (Barber, 1962; Barber, Walker & Vasey, 1963), and this may contribute further to salinity problems (Sinha & Singh, 1974).

For ions like phosphate which are present in the soil solution in very low concentration, supply by mass flow is insignificant. Diffusion then becomes predominant, the solute moving down a concentration gradient towards the root surface in response to absorption by the plant (Drew & Nye, 1970). Nutrients such as potassium and phosphate which react with the soil diffuse only very slowly and, depending on their diffusion coefficient, ions more than a few millimetres away from a root surface are unlikely to be absorbed.

Information on the relative contribution of mass flow and diffusion to supply is important. Solutes carried predominantly by mass flow may move to individual roots from distances of 10 cm or so, commensurate with those from which water is drawn. Nitrate moves mainly by mass flow in fertile agricultural soils (Barber, 1962; Barber *et al.*, 1963), so that roots compete much more readily for nitrate (as they do for water) than for potassium and phosphate (Cornforth, 1968; Andrews & Newman, 1970). But in arid-land soils the average concentrations of nitrate are usually low, and some plants (for example, succulents) grow with unusually low transpiration ratios, making it difficult to generalize about nitrate movement to roots without quantitative data for specific situations.

When the soil water content decreases, a high resistance is offered to the movement of solutes and water along the thin films of moisture and the narrow capillaries which remain water-filled (see Slatyer, 1967; Scotter, 1974). The distances that nutrients and water move to roots then greatly decrease. Theoretical flux equations can be used to calculate the approximate magnitude of these effects, including competition between roots, in influencing rates of supply of ions and water to root systems under somewhat idealized conditions (Nye, 1966; Gardner, 1968; Barley, 1970; Baldwin, Nye & Tinker, 1973). Few experiments have yet attempted to confirm the gradients of water potential and ion concentration predicted from theory (Farr & Vaidyanathan, 1972; Dunham & Nye, 1974), and the technical difficulties are formidable. In addition to considerations of supply, the absorptive ability of the roots may become impaired, either directly from loss of cell turgidity (or other form of desiccation injury), or indirectly through the shoot ceasing to transpire or grow.

Uptake of soil water and nutrients, particularly when their movement is restricted to short distances, will clearly be influenced by branching patterns, and the presence of viable root hairs and mycorrhizae, since these determine in effect the volume of soil brought into close proximity to root surfaces. The ability of fine laterals to explore soil peds, the entry of root hairs into soil aggregates, and the continuing extension of new

586

roots into untapped zones all contribute to the function of the root as a 'collecting system' but it is doubtful whether all these detailed processes can be incorporated into a meaningful *mechanistic* model.

The important question of water-potential gradients around absorbing roots in relatively dry soil remains unresolved. It has been argued on theoretical grounds that, for the densities of roots commonly encountered in crop plants, the average water flux into individual root segments (deduced from transpiration data) must be so low that the resistance of the soil to water flow can be neglected, at least until the soil water potential approaches the permanent wilting point (Hansen, 1974; Newman, 1974; Williams, 1974).

According to this view, resistance of roots to radial water flow, rather than soil resistance, exerts a major limitation to water uptake by plants in a drying soil. There is little doubt that the endodermis is the location of the principal resistance to water flow across absorbing roots, and that this variable resistance, by modifying water flow through the intact plant, exerts an important indirect influence upon stomatal behaviour and transpiration (see p. 221 in Slatyer, 1967).

Most calculations concerning the significance of soil resistance to water flow towards roots have assumed that all parts of the root system are equally capable of water absorption. But the various barriers to water loss, described on p. 574, will exert their limitations to water entry (see p. 589). Furthermore, the combined effects of low rainfall, and intense competition for water between roots located near the soil surface, may result in water absorption being sustained by relatively few roots in the deeper soil during periods of drought. There is, therefore, some uncertainty over realistic values of water flux into those parts of the root system which are able to contribute *under natural conditions*. Few measurements have been made of rates of water extraction by known amounts of roots at various depths in the soil. In a paper using this approach, Taylor & Klepper (1975) found that root resistance far exceeded the resistance of a loamy fine sand when the soil water potential was high. When the water potential decreased to between -0.5 and -0.3 bar, increasing soil resistance probably imposes a limitation on water uptake. For woody plants growing in adverse soil environments with low root densities, earlier suberization of roots, and possibly only part of the root system in contact with available water, water uptake by individual roots may be sufficiently rapid for soil resistance to water flow to become significant at soil water potentials well above -15 bar.

A further area of uncertainty concerns the degree of contact between root surfaces and the soil; the topic is reviewed by Cowan & Milthorpe (1968) and Newman (1974). In comparatively moist, finely structured soils, water films are probably continuous between soil particles and much of the root surface. But as the soil dries it may shrink away from the root. Diurnal contraction in diameter has been observed for roots growing in air spaces when the shoots are rapidly transpiring (Huck, Klepper & Taylor, 1970; Hansen, 1974). Root hairs and mucigel may help maintain contact between the root and soil, allowing a continuing flow of ions and water and aiding the re-establishment of moisture films following rewetting of the soil. Calculations suggest that significant transfer of water could occur as vapour across air-gaps (Cowan & Milthorpe, 1968), but Newman (1974) suggests that the movement of water through the root hairs which may bridge such gaps would greatly exceed the vapour transfer. Where growth occurs down fissures and in coarse-textured soils, a significant portion of the total root surface may fail to be in contact with moisture films, but quantitative data are lacking.

The roots of mesophytes show little ability to lower soil water potentials much below -15 bar, and the rate of supply of water to root surfaces becomes too slow to prevent permanent wilting of leaves. For some perennial plants in arid zones however, soil moisture can be reduced to -100 bar and less (Slatyer, 1967; Moore, White & Caldwell, 1972). In finely textured soils, significant quantities of water may be slowly released at this potential, supply being sufficient to offset transpiration losses.

Adverse soil environments which restrict extension and branching reduce the effectiveness of the root as a 'collecting system' for ions and water, but plants are efficient in tapping favourable soil micro-sites and heterogeneities. The period when growth of perennial plants in arid regions is most likely to be limited by root activities is during the seedling stage, when roots may be exposed to adverse conditions in the superficial layers. Once roots become established, the drying of the surface soil layers probably stimulates more rapid extension and branching in favourable zones at depth, as it does in crop plants (El Nadi, Brouwer & Locher, 1969; Klepper *et al.*, 1973). In laboratory experiments with Gramineae, compensatory growth of this type has been observed in response to various stress conditions – for example, unfavourable temperature, desiccation, mechanical impedance, nutrient deficiency, and injury to root tips.

When the entire rooting depth becomes subject to desiccation, collection of water may depend upon water held in micro-sites (for example beneath stones (Evenari *et al.*, 1971)) or slowly released from peds not penetrated by roots. The role of mycorrhizae when the soil water potential is low remains virtually unexplored.

No consideration of the supply of water and ions to roots can neglect the question of which regions of the root system predominantly contribute to absorption. Although it is widely assumed that only the extreme apical regions of young roots absorb ions and water, the various suberized barriers being least developed there, this simple view can no longer be sustained. The earlier work of Kramer and his co-workers (Kramer, 1969) indicated that regions up to 5 cm behind the root tip were effective in transport of ions to shoots in both monocotyledons and dicotyledons. It is now clear that the older portions of seminal axes of cereals, situated up to 50 cm or more behind the root tips, can continue to absorb and translocate phosphate and potassium, provided roots have not suffered damage from desiccation or attack by pathogens (Clarkson & Sanderson, 1971). The finer lateral branches can be as effective, per unit volume, as the main roots in absorption and translocation, and since they comprise a high proportion of the root systems in plants more than a few weeks old they provide an overwhelming contribution to the nutrition of the plant.

The suberized Casparian band of the endodermis, which is formed within a few mm of the root-tip, constitutes the inner limit to the free space, for at this point water and ions must pass through cell membranes to reach the conducting tissues of the stele. The deposition of suberized lamellae in the endodermis does not restrict the movement of potassium and phosphate across the root into the xylem, but calcium transport is markedly reduced. Such observations are consistent with the view that radial movement of the phosphate and potassium (but not calcium) into the stele occurs in the symplast, the numerous plasmodesmata in pits in the thickened inner tangential wall of the endodermis providing a pathway through to the stele (Robards, Jackson, Clarkson & Sanderson, 1973; Clarkson, 1974).

There seems general agreement that the zone of maximum absorption of water by roots of monocotyledons and dicotyledons occurs from close behind the tip up to a region some 10 cm or so further back, where there is increased resistance to water flow as a result of suberization and lignification of walls (see Kramer (1969) for a review of earlier work). Yet with increased transpiration the resistance of roots of water flow decreases, and the region of maximal water uptake may shift towards the suberized basal region. In a study by Graham, Clarkson & Sanderson (1973) the regions of maximal absorption in barley and *Cucurbita pepo* were located in tissues no more than 2–3 days old. In both species, water flux was reduced to about 15% of the maximum when suberin lamellae were first laid down in the endodermis, but the flux was thereafter undiminished, even over the older parts of the root system as far as 50 cm from the root apex. Plasmodesmata probably provide a passage through the suberized barrier (Clarkson, Robards & Sanderson, 1971). The pathways taken by water through the basal region in response to increased transpiration have yet to be determined.

In the view of Kramer & Bullock (1966) and Kramer (1969), the absorption of water, and possibly solutes, in perennial plants must occur through older roots which have developed a periderm. Such roots display a significant permeability to water, and because they constitute most of the root system in mature plants they probably make a predominant contribution to water uptake. Numerous references to the earlier literature are cited by these authors, in which it was shown that water and ion uptake took place through roots of woody plants when most or all of the roots appear to have developed a periderm. The conspicuous lenticels which occur in the periderm (Eames & MacDaniels, 1947) are thought to provide a pathway through the layers of cork cells; but this important aspect, and the question of whether there is selective control of the movement of solutes into the xylem, have not been directly investigated with modern techniques.

The role of the hypodermis has received even less attention. Like the endodermis, the hypodermis develops Casparian bands, and later deposition of suberin lamellae and lignin (van Fleet, 1961). However, phosphate uptake and transport in roots of *Zea mays* was restricted in the basal regions, coinciding with the deposition of suberin lamellae in the hypodermis. Micro-autoradiography showed that radiophosphorus (^{32}P) then failed to penetrate beyond the epidermis (Ferguson, 1976).

Information is meagre concerning the effects of progressive desiccation and rewetting on absorptive activities of roots, and no studies have followed concurrent changes in water status of the tissue and fine structure. Root systems subjected to severe water stress show a lower average permeability to water for several days after rewetting (Kramer, 1969; Hansen, 1974), but it is not known whether recovery depends upon the growth of new unsuberized roots. Root tips of wheat (*Triticum aestivum*), rapidly desiccated to water potentials as low as -24 bar, initially accumulated radiochlorine (^{36}Cl) at a low rate when rewetted, but within 18 hours their absorptive ability was restored (Cole & Alston, 1974). No information was given on changes in root structure during this period, but root tips of *Zea mays* lost almost 70% of their water, with disruption of membranes and fine structure, without appearing to cause lethal damage: upon rehydration, existing cell structures were restored (Nir, Klein & Poljakoff-Mayber, 1969).

When the basal regions of barley roots (which do not form a hypodermis) were desiccated to the extent that the entire cortex collapsed, no ion uptake took place on subsequent immersion in nutrient solution, although the ability to translocate ions through the desiccated region to the shoot from other parts of the same root was unimpaired (Clarkson, Sanderson & Russell, 1968).

The possibility that transient changes in the ability to absorb ions can occur without direct injury to roots is raised by recent work of Pitman, Lüttge, Läuchli & Ball (1974). When shoots were subjected to a brief period of water stress from which they soon recovered, the transport of ions by roots freshly excised from the plants was strongly depressed. Ion transport by roots gradually recovered in intact plants, the rate of recovery depending on the duration of the previous water stress. It was suggested that ABA produced in the stressed shoots was translocated to roots and reduced their transport of ions, but no analysis of endogenous growth regulators was reported.

Effects of soil environmental factors on root growth and function

In recent years considerable progress has been made in understanding the way in which adverse soil conditions can exert a profound influence upon root distribution and metabolism, and upon shoot growth. Detailed information has been obtained almost exclusively with crop plants, often under controlled conditions in the laboratory, but the conclusions are clearly relevant to plants under natural conditions.

Despite the complexity of the soil environment, its ultimate properties, in so far as they influence root metabolism, must be the prevailing water potential and temperature, mechanical resistance to growth, the composition of the soil atmosphere (Shaw, 1952), together with the chemical environment. New experimental methods have reduced difficulties in the measurement of these properties in the field, although steep gradients, for example in water potential, may occur in the vicinity of the root.

Aeration requirements are not considered in this chapter although they may be important in the establishment and survival of some desert shrubs (Lunt, Letey & Clark, 1973). Inadequate gas exchange becomes critical only as the soil approaches water saturation, and such occurrences in arid zones are restricted to depressions and watercourses.

Soil water potential

The preferential growth of roots in wetter zones of the soil profile (Wiersum, 1958; Zahner, 1968) is of considerable importance to plant survival in arid zones. Water content varies irregularly between different locations due to accumulation of run-off, natural water repellency of the soil, or interception by foliage and stem flow (Pressland, 1973; Walter & Stadelmann, 1974). Highly branched roots occur in moist pockets of soil under stones (Evenari *et al.*, 1971), in cracks in bed-rock and isolated pockets of clay or organic matter which retain water (Hellmers *et al.*, 1955; Batanouny & Abdel Wahab, 1973).

Although there have been reports from time to time concerning the transport of water by roots from wet soil and exudation into dry soil (Russell, 1961; Thorup, 1969), the significance of these findings still remains obscure. Roots of crop plants can penetrate into soils drier than −15 bar only for short distances, possibly a few millimetres (Wiersma, 1959; Russell, 1961; Cullen, Turner & Wilson, 1972); but the lower limit of water potential at which root growth is arrested is difficult to define with confidence. Earlier attempts to determine this (Klute & Peters, 1969) showed that comparatively small decreases in matric potential (less than 2 bar) retarded root extension in some soils. Such reports can probably be discounted, for they fail to take account of the inevitable relation between the water content of a material and its strength properties. As the water content of the soil decreases, its shear strength rises and provides a greater mechanical resistance to root extension (see, for example, Mirreh & Ketcheson, 1972, 1973). Studies have been made of the growth of roots in solutions in which the water potential has been controlled with osmolytes such as polyethylene glycol, but suspicions remain that these substances penetrate cells or damage them in some way.

Some experiments have been designed to take into account changes in soil strength with soil water potential by measuring the resistance of the soil to penetrometers (Eavis & Payne, 1969; Taylor & Ratliff, 1969; Greacen & Oh, 1972). These studies indicate that soil water potentials as low as −12 bar have no direct influence on root extension. Greacen & Oh (1972) concluded from their data that expanding cells behind the root tip are able to adjust to dry soil by compensatory increases in the osmotic potential of their vacuolar sap, and this interesting possibility needs confirmation.

Roots are often said to grow in search of water, but there is no clear evidence of any hydrotropic responses. Most observations can be explained by roots extending preferentially into media of lower mechanical resistance (and therefore higher water content).

Temperature

Soil temperature can be modified by plant cover, orientation of slopes, surface colour and texture (Chapter 17 above). Shifts in the temperature regime by only a few degrees towards the optimum for root activities can have a marked effect upon the establishment of seedlings and the growth of perennials when soil water is readily available. Near the optimum temperature, roots extend most rapidly, branch frequently, show a high permeability to water, and (according to studies of excised roots) absorb ions most rapidly (Nielson & Humphries, 1966; Kramer, 1969).

Some of these effects however may be partially offset at lower temperatures. Bowen (1970) found that absorption of phosphate along individual roots of pine seedlings could proceed, as the root aged, for a longer

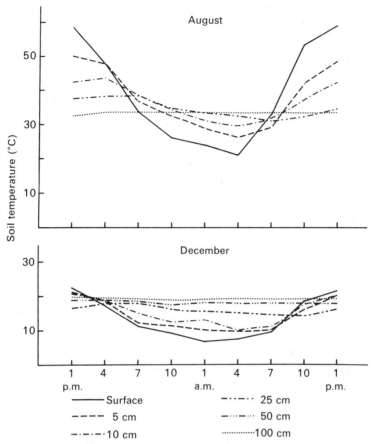

Fig. 23.5. Diurnal variation in soil temperature at different depths in the desert near Cairo. (From Migahid, 1961.)

time at low temperatures, partially compensating for faster extension, branching and uptake rates which occurred at higher temperatures.

Wide differences exist between species from contrasting climates with respect to the comparatively narrow temperature range which is optimal for root growth and function. Whereas the optimum for roots of temperate grasses may be 10 °C, roots of *Opuntia* spp. barely begin extension at 16 °C, reach an optimum at 30 °C and decline sharply at temperatures above 34 °C (Cannon, 1916). The root response in *Opuntia* appears ideally adapted to prevailing conditions, for the period of summer rains in its natural habitat coincides with the time when surface soil temperatures reach the optimum. But there must be sustained periods when superficial roots, particularly exposed portions receiving incident radiation, are raised to temperatures above the optimum. The diurnal range of temperatures at different depths in a desert soil in summer and winter is shown in Fig. 23.5. The temperature amplitude decreases with depth, so that deeper roots in summer may be able to continue normal functions provided phloem activity in proximal parts of the roots is unimpaired. Instances where high surface soil temperatures may cause injury to roots are cited by Kramer (1969). In winter the temperature trend is reversed, the deeper soil now being at a higher temperature. Little is known about the way in which root systems integrate the effects of wide ranges of temperature between different zones. However, if growth occurs predominantly within the most favourable thermal zone at the expense of other zones, as it does in cereals (Crossett, Campbell & Stewart, 1975), there is little doubt that most other functions, for example water and ion uptake, will also be concentrated there.

The influence of the temperature of the rooting zone on plant growth is best shown by experiments in which shoot and root temperatures have been varied separately. Data from a large number of experiments on this aspect have been collected by Cooper (1973). Comparatively small changes in root temperatures can, when all other conditions favour growth, exert a large effect on the shoots. In *Zea mays* an increase in root temperature from 18 to 19 °C caused a 40% increase in the dry weight of the shoots maintained at 25 °C (Walker, 1969). This response can in part be attributed to the behaviour of the shoot meristem, which in Gramineae is initially close to the soil surface. The temperature of the transpiration stream reduces (or raises) the temperature of the meristem by conduction, and so controls the immediate rate of leaf expansion (Watt, 1971).

Root temperatures may also influence shoot growth through their effect on the synthesis of growth regulators by roots, although the evidence on this is indirect. In *Zea mays* the amounts of cytokinin- and gibberellin-like substances in the xylem exudates of decapitated plants decreased at temperatures which were sub-optimal for shoot and root growth, while amounts of unidentified inhibitors increased (Atkin *et al.*, 1973). A brief heat treatment applied to roots (2 min at 26 °C) caused a decrease in the rate of leaf growth which was associated with decreased amounts of cytokinins, and increases in ABA, in the xylem exudates carried towards the shoots (Itai, Ben-Zioni & Ordin, 1973). Decreased production of growth regulators is also implicated in causing thermal injury to shoots when supra-optimal temperatures (40 °C) are maintained around roots (Rameshewar & Steponkus, 1969; Gur, Bravdo & Mizrahi, 1972).

Temperatures can exert a marked effect upon root distribution by altering geotropic response. Soil temperatures of 17 °C caused radicles of *Zea mays* to grow at an angle close to the horizontal (10°) but above and

594

below this temperature (over the range 10–30 °C) roots grew progressively closer to the vertical (Onderdonk & Ketcheson, 1973). Such responses may partly explain the tendency for roots to extend in more vertical directions later in the season; an additional factor encouraging more vertical orientation may be the increased resistance offered by a drying topsoil.

Mechanical impedance

Soils in arid zones almost always provide severe mechanical constraints to root development. Sands and gravels often include a range of particle sizes in which the finer particles pack tightly in voids between the larger ones; surface crusts, hardpans and rocky pavements frequently occur (Lutz, 1952; Chapter 17 above), and compact horizons of clay may become impenetrable. Even favourable soils may become resistant as their water content decreases. Roots have no ability to reduce the dimensions of their apical meristems and so pass through rigid narrow pores in tightly packed sands (Wiersum, 1957): roots must either extend through pores and fissures at least as great as their own diameter, or create and enlarge cavities to a suitable size. Failure to do so results in the abortion of root tips and root systems may remain shallow or, as is often observed, produce long laterals which may eventually find a fissure in the impeding zone above which they are spreading, and then continue downward extension. Survival of the plant may then depend on whether the rooting zone is sufficiently deep (Taylor, 1974). Zones of constriction can sometimes be observed on roots where they have passed through a hardpan but these involve impeded cambial or secondary growth. The ability of confined plant organs to exert considerable force is well known, but it should be remembered that the *rate* of expansion is greatly reduced under such conditions.

Whenever the root tip displaces soil particles, it experiences some degree of mechanical stress, by reaction, from the resistance of the particles to compression (Barley & Greacen, 1967). Detailed information on the magnitude of the stresses around the root tip which influence its growth and function is essential to understanding how roots respond to mechanical constraints. Experiments in artificial media indicate that relatively low stresses around root tips, little more than 0.2 bar, are sufficient to halve extension rates when pores are being enlarged (Gill & Miller, 1956; Abdalla, Hettiaratchi & Reece, 1969; Goss & Drew, 1972). Considerable modification to root morphology can subsequently occur; for example, impedance to seminal roots results in increased initiation of fine laterals, which grow at an accelerated rate if pore size is large enough to

595

provide no constraints. By using smaller pore sizes, the extension of laterals as well as main roots can be impeded, producing a small distorted root system (Goss & Drew, 1972).

Whether the sensitivity of root growth to mechanical stress when water supplies are adequate is best explained by considerations of osmotic forces, or growth regulation at the apical meristem, remains an open question. Where a soil becomes increasingly resistant through loss of water, desiccation of the roots may also take place. Turgor may decrease to such an extent that little stress can be exerted by expanding cells to overcome the resistance of their cell walls and the external medium.

There is no clear evidence that roots of different species differ much in their ability to elongate in a resistant medium, although detailed studies have been restricted to crop plants. In practice, perennials are often able to contend with hardpans, probably because the chances of roots discovering fissures increases with time and rooting density; the age of lateral roots of pine above and below a hardpan was found to differ by eight years (Faulkner & Malcolm, 1972).

Roots appear to minimize the effects of friction around their tips by the production of mucigel and by the continuous sloughing-off of cap cells. Because the pathways of least mechanical resistance are followed, roots are often found in old root channels and in fissures and cracks between the major soil peds. Whether such roots can make much contribution to absorption of ions and water is doubtful because of poor or variable contact with the soil.

Soil solutes

Pronounced localized concentrations of inorganic nutrients, particularly nitrogen, can occur near the surface in some arid soils, due to the localized accumulation and mineralization of organic matter (Charley, 1972). The proliferation of roots in the more fertile pockets of soil is well recognized (Wiersum, 1958). Favourable concentrations of nitrate in only a small part of the rooting zone cause a direct, localized stimulation of lateral root initiation and extension in cereals (Drew, Saker & Ashley, 1973; Drew & Saker, 1975). It would be of interest to know whether similar responses contribute to localized patterns of root distribution around arid-land shrubs when soil water is favourable.

Phytotoxins from leachates of leaves or exuded from roots, or from decomposing organic matter, can modify root distribution and plant establishment (Woods, 1960; Muller, 1966; Whittaker & Feeney, 1971). Various phenolic acids, at the concentrations at which they occur in soil, rapidly but reversibly inhibit ion uptake, suggesting a direct effect on

cell-membrane properties (Glass, 1974). The important question of tolerance of high salinity is considered elsewhere (Chapter 24 below).

Soil microflora

Much remains to be known about the ways in which the soil microflora
may contribute to plant survival under arid soil conditions. Laboratory
experiments suggest that micro-organisms can influence plant growth,
both by the effect of microbial metabolites on plant metabolism, and by
modifying the supply of inorganic nutrients to roots. Thus, non-infecting
micro-organisms have been shown to alter mechanisms of ion uptake and
transport as well as root growth and development (Bowen & Rovira, 1969),
and compete with roots for a limited supply of phosphate (Benians &
Barber, 1974). The dense clusters of fine laterals (proteoid roots) in the
Proteaceae, which appear to be elicited under natural conditions by
non-infecting rhizosphere micro-organisms in soil of low nutrient status
(Malajczuk & Bowen, 1974), provide an extreme example. The resulting
mats of root probably assist in efficient collection of phosphate and
other immobile ions. The possibility of nitrogen fixation by free-living
rhizosphere micro-organisms, under conditions which promote root
exudation (Döbereiner, 1974), has recently aroused much interest but
the significance to the nitrogen economy of vegetation in arid zones has
yet to be assessed.

Production of potentially protective layers of mucigel, and other exudates, around the root tips of crop plants is probably stimulated by the
presence of rhizosphere bacteria, some of which may synthesize additional
quantities of mucilaginous compounds, using root exudates as their predominant source of carbon (Darbyshire & Greaves, 1973): more observations are needed for native plants with their normal rhizosphere
populations. Bacterial isolates from the rhizosphere (Brown, 1974), as
well as mycorrhizal fungi, can synthesize cytokinin- and gibberellin-like
compounds in pure culture, but apart from possible involvement in modifying extension and branching in ectomycorrhizae (Slankis, 1973), the
significance to plant metabolism has yet to be established.

In nature, roots of most plants eventually become infected with mycorrhizal fungi, and their occurrence on plants from arid environments
appears to be widespread (Went & Stark, 1968; Khan, 1974). Vesicular–
arbuscular mycorrhizae and ectomycorrhizae contribute to increased efficiency of phosphate uptake from nutrient-poor soils, in part by the growth
of external hyphae from the host into the soil (Sanders & Tinker, 1971;
Mosse, 1973; Gerdemann, 1974). Mycelial strands exploit large volumes
of soil between roots and have been shown to translocate phosphate to

Plant processes

mycorrhizae over distances of up to 12 cm in field studies (Skinner & Bowen, 1974).

Although the significance of mycorrhizae to mineral nutrition is now well established, their influence on plant water relations has received far less attention. There are indications that mycorrhizae have a more prolonged persistence, and a greater resistance to desiccation, than non-mycorrhizal roots (Harley, 1969): the presence of mycorrhizae may assist in some way the survival of seedling trees under arid conditions (Muttiah, 1972). Clearly more widespread information on this topic is required, employing modern techniques for investigating the water status of plant tissues and the soil. There is little direct information, too, as to whether mycorrhizae are more efficient in extracting water from dry soil than non-mycorrhizal roots, but suggestions that mycorrhizal fungi grow well at low water potentials (Mexal & Reid, 1973) deserve further detailed investigation in this connexion.

References

Abdalla, A. M., Hettiaratchi, D. R. P. & Reece, A. R. (1969). The mechanics of root growth in granular media. *Journal of Agricultural Engineering Research*, **14**, 236–48.

Anderson, D. J., Perry, R. A. & Leigh, J. H. (1972). Some perspectives on shrub-environment interactions. In: *Wildland Shrubs – their Biology and Utilization* (eds. C. M. McKell, J. P. Blaisdell & J. R. Goodin), pp. 172–181. USDA Forest Service, Ogden, Utah.

Andrews, R. E. & Newman, E. I. (1970). Root density and competition for nutrients. *Oecologia Plantarum*, **5**, 319–34.

Atkin, R. K., Barton, G. E. & Robinson, D. K. (1973). Effect of root-growing temperature on growth substances in xylem exudates of *Zea mays*. *Journal of Experimental Botany*, **24**, 457–87.

Baldwin, J. P., Nye, P. H. & Tinker, P. B. (1973). Uptake of solutes by multiple root systems from soil. III. A model for calculating the solute uptake by a randomly dispersed root system developing in a finite volume of soil. *Plant and Soil*, **38**, 621–35.

Baldwin, J. P. & Tinker, P. B. (1972). A method of estimating the lengths and spatial patterns of two interpenetrating root systems. *Plant and Soil*, **37**, 209–13.

Baldwin, J. P., Tinker, P. B. & Marriott, F. H. C. (1971). The measurement of length and distribution of onion roots in the field and the laboratory. *Journal of Applied Ecology*, **8**, 543–54.

Barber, D. A. & Gunn, K. B. (1974). The effect of mechanical forces on the exudation of organic substances by the roots of cereal plants grown under sterile conditions. *New Phytologist*, **73**, 39–45.

Barber, D. A. & Martin, J. K. (1976). The release of organic substances by cereal roots into soil. *New Phytologist*, **76**, 69–80.

Barber, S. A. (1962). A diffusion and mass-flow concept of soil nutrient availability. *Soil Science*, **93**, 39–49.

Barber, S. A., Walker, J. W. & Vasey, E. H. (1963). Mechanisms for the movement of plant nutrients from the soil and fertilizer to the plant root. *Journal of Agricultural and Food Chemistry*, **11**, 204–7.

Barley, K. P. (1970). The configuration of the root system in relation to nutrient uptake. *Advances of Agronomy*, **22**, 159–201.

Barley, K. P. & Greacen, E. L. (1967). Mechanical resistance as a soil factor influencing the growth of roots and underground shoots. *Advances in Agronomy*, **19**, 1–43.

Batanouny, K. H. & Abdel Wahab, A. M. (1973). Eco-physiological studies on desert plants. VIII. Root penetration of *Leptadenia pyrotechnica* (Forsk.) Decne. in relation to its water balance. *Oecologia*, **11**, 151–61.

Beckel, D. K. B. (1956). Cortical disintegration in the roots of *Bouteloua gracilis*. *New Phytologist*, **55**, 183–90.

Benians, G. J. & Barber, D. A. (1974). The uptake of phosphate by barley plants from soil under aseptic and non-sterile conditions. *Soil Biology and Biochemistry*, **6**, 195–200.

Borger, G. A. (1973). Development and shedding of bark. In: *Shedding of Plant Parts* (ed. T. T. Kozlowski), pp. 205–236. Academic Press, New York.

Bowen, G. D. (1970). Effects of soil temperature on root growth and on phosphate uptake along *Pinus radiata* roots. *Australian Journal of Soil Research*, **8**, 31–42.

Bowen, G. D. & Rovira, A. D. (1969). The influence of micro-organisms on growth and metabolism of plant roots. In: *Root Growth* (ed. W. J. Whittington), pp. 170–99. Butterworths, London.

Brown, M. E. (1974). Seed and root bacterization. *Annual Review of Phytopathology*, **12**, 181–97.

Burrows, W. J. & Carr, D. J. (1969). Effects of flooding the root system of sunflower plants on the cytokinin content in the xylem sap. *Physiologia Plantarum*, **22**, 1105–12.

Cannon, W. A. (1911). *Root Habits of Desert Plants*. Carnegie Institution of Washington, Publication 131.

Cannon, W. A. (1916). Distribution of cacti with special reference to the role played by the root response to soil temperature and soil moisture. *American Naturalist*, **50**, 435–42.

Cannon, W. A. (1949). A tentative classification of root systems. *Ecology*, **30**, 542–8.

Carr, D. J. & Burrows, W. J. (1968). Evidence of the presence in xylem sap of substances with kinetin-like activity. *Life Sciences*, **5**, 2061–77.

Charley, J. L. (1972). The role of shrubs in nutrient cycling. In: *Wildland Shrubs – their Biology and Utilization* (eds. C. M. McKell, J. P. Blaisdell & J. R. Goodin), pp. 182–203. USDA Forest Service, Ogden, Utah.

Chibnall, A. C. (1939). *Protein Metabolism in the plant*. Yale University Press, New Haven, Connecticut.

Clarkson, D. T. (1974). *Ion Transport and Cell Structure in Plants*. McGraw-Hill, New York.

Clarkson, D. T. & Sanderson, J. (1971). Relationship between the anatomy of cereal roots and the absorption of nutrients and water. In: *Agricultural Research Council Letcombe Laboratory Annual Report for 1970*, pp. 16–25. Wantage, Oxfordshire, England.

Clarkson, D. T., Sanderson, J. & Russell, R. S. (1968). Ion uptake and root age. *Nature* (London), **220**, 805–6.

Clarkson, D. T., Robards, A. W. & Sanderson, J. (1971). The tertiary endodermis in barley roots: fine structure in relation to radial transport of ions and water. *Planta*, **96**, 292–305.

Cole, P. J. & Alston, A. M. (1974). Effect of transient dehydration on absorption of chloride by wheat roots. *Plant and Soil*, **40**, 243–7.

Cooper, A. J. (1973). *Root temperature and plant growth*. Commonwealth Agricultural Bureaux Research Review No. 4. Farnham Royal, Bucks, England.

Cornforth, I. S. (1968). Relationships between soil volume used by roots and nutrient accessibility. *Journal of Soil Science*, **19**, 291–301.

Cowan, I. R. & Milthorpe, F. L. (1968). Plant factors influencing the water status of plant tissues. In: *Water Deficits and Plant Growth* (ed. T. T. Kozlowski), Vol. 1, pp. 137–93. Academic Press, New York.

Crossett, R. N., Campbell, D. J. & Stewart, H. E. (1975). Compensatory growth in cereal root systems. *Plant and Soil*, **42**, 673–83.

Cullen, P. W., Turner, A. K. & Wilson, J. H. (1972). The effect of irrigation depth on root growth of some pasture species. *Plant and Soil*, **37**, 345–52.

Danielson, R. E. (1967). Root systems in relation to irrigation. In: *Irrigation of Agricultural Lands* (eds. R. M. Hagan, H. R. Haise & T. W. Edminster), pp. 390–424. American Society of Agronomy, Madison, Wisconsin.

Darbyshire, J. R. & Greaves, M. P. (1973). Bacteria and protozoa in the rhizosphere. *Pesticide Science*, **4**, 349–60.

Davidson, R. L. (1969). Effects of soil nutrients and moisture on root/shoot ratios in *Lolium perenne* L. and *Trifolium repens* L. *Annals of Botany*, **33**, 571–6.

Davis, S. N. (1974). Hydrogeology of arid regions. In: *Desert Biology* (ed. G. W. Brown), Vol. 2, pp. 1–30. Academic Press, New York.

Diettert, R. A. (1938). The morphology of *Artemisia tridentata* Nutt. *Lloydia*, **1**, 3–74.

Döbereiner, J. (1974). Nitrogen-fixing bacteria in the rhizosphere. In: *The Biology of Nitrogen Fixation* (ed. A. Quispel), pp. 86–120. North-Holland Publishing, Amsterdam.

Drew, M. C. & Nye, P. H. (1970). The supply of nutrient ions by diffusion to plant roots in soil. III. Uptake of phosphate by roots of onion, leek and ryegrass. *Plant and Soil*, **33**, 545–63.

Drew, M. C. & Saker, L. R. (1975). Nutrient supply and the growth of the seminal root system in barley. II. Localised, compensatory increases in lateral root growth and rates of nitrate uptake when nitrate supply is restricted to only part of the root system. *Journal of Experimental Botany*, **26**, 79–90.

Drew, M. C., Saker, L. R. & Ashley, T. W. (1973). Nutrient supply and the growth of the seminal root system in barley. I. The effect of nitrate concentration on the growth of axes and laterals. *Journal of Experimental Botany*, **24**, 1189–1202.

Dunham, R. J. & Nye, P. H. (1974). The influence of soil water content on the uptake of ions by roots. II. Chloride uptake and concentration gradients in soil. *Journal of Applied Ecology*, **11**, 581–96.

Eames, A. J. & MacDaniels, L. H. (1947). *An Introduction to Plant Anatomy*, 2nd edition. McGraw-Hill, New York.

Eavis, B. W. & Payne, D. (1969). Soil physical conditions and root growth. In: *Root Growth* (ed. W. J. Whittington), pp. 315–36. Butterworths, London.

Ellern, S. J., Harper, J. L. & Sagar, G. R. (1970). A comparative study of the distribution of the roots of *Avena fatua* and *A. strigosa* in mixed stands using a ^{14}C-labelling technique. *Journal of Ecology*, **58**, 865–8.

Ellis, F. B. & Barnes, B. T. (1973). Estimation of the distribution of living roots of plants under field conditions. *Plant and Soil*, **39**, 81–91.

El Nadi, A. H., Brouwer, R. & Locher, J. Th. (1969). Some responses of the root and shoot of *Vicia faba* plants to water stress. *Netherlands Journal of Agricultural Science*, **17**, 133.

Esau, K. (1965). *Plant Anatomy*, 2nd edition. Wiley, New York.

Evenari, M., Shanan, L. & Tadmor, N. H. (1971). *The Negev: the Challenge of a Desert*. Harvard University Press, Cambridge, Massachusetts.

Farr, E. & Vaidyanathan, L. V. (1972). The supply of nutrient ions by diffusion to plant roots in soil. IV. Direct measurement of changes in labile phosphate content in soil near absorbing roots. *Plant and Soil*, **37**, 609–16.

Faulkner, M. E. & Malcolm, D. C. (1972). Soil physical factors affecting root morphology and stability of Scots Pine on upland heaths. *Forestry*, **45**, 23–36.

Ferguson, I. B. (1976). Ion uptake by roots in relation to the development of a hypodermis. *New Phytologist*, **77**, 11–14.

Fox, R. L. & Lipps, R. C. (1969). Distribution and activity of roots in relation to soil properties. *Transactions 7th International Congress Soil Science*, **3**, 260–7.

Gardner, W. R. (1968). Availability and measurement of soil water. In: *Water deficits and Plant Growth* (ed. T. T. Kozlowski), Vol. I, pp. 107–35. Academic Press, New York.

Gerdemann, J. W. (1974). Mycorrhizae. In: *The Plant Root and its Environment* (ed. E. W. Carson), pp. 205–17. University Press of Virginia, Charlottesville.

Gill, W. R. & Miller, R. D. (1956). A method for the study of the influence of mechanical impedance and aeration on the growth of seedling roots. *Soil Science Society of America Proceedings*, **20**, 154–7.

Glass, A. D. M. (1974). Influence of phenolic acids upon ion uptake. III. Inhibition of potassium absorption. *Journal of Experimental Botany*, **25**, 1104–13.

Goss, M. J. & Drew, M. C. (1972). Effect of mechanical impedance on growth of seedlings. *Agricultural Research Council Letcombe Laboratory Annual Report for 1971*, pp. 35–42. Wantage. Oxfordshire, England.

Graham, J., Clarkson, D. T. & Sanderson, J. (1973). *Agricultural Research Council Letcombe Laboratory Annual Report for 1972*, pp. 9–12. Wantage, Oxfordshire, England.

Greacen, E. L. & Oh, J. S. (1972). Physics of root growth. *Nature New Biology* (London), **235**, 24–5.

Grenot, C. J. (1974). Physical and vegetational aspects of the Sahara Desert. In: *Desert Biology* (ed. G. W. Brown), Vol. 2, pp. 103–64. Academic Press, New York.

Gur, A., Bravdo, B. & Mizrahi, Y. (1972). Physiological responses of apple trees to supra-optimal root temperatures. *Physiologia Plantarum*, **27**, 130–8.

Hansen, G. K. (1974). Resistance to water transport in soil and young wheat plants. *Acta Agriculturae Scandinavica*, **24**, 37–48.

Harley, J. L. (1969). *The Biology of Mycorrhiza*, 2nd edition. Leonard Hill, London.

Head, G. C. (1973). Shedding of roots. In: *Shedding of Plant Parts* (ed. T. T. Kozlowski), pp. 237–93. Academic Press, New York.

Hellmers, H., Horton, J. S., Juhren, G. & O'Keefe, J. (1955). Root systems of some chaparral plants in Southern California. *Ecology*, **36**, 667–73.

Huck, M. G., Klepper, B. & Taylor, H. M. (1970). Diurnal variations in root diameter. *Plant Physiology* (Lancaster), **45**, 529–30.

Huxley, P. A., Patel, R. Z., Kabaara, A. M. & Mitchell, H. W. (1974). Tracer studies with ^{32}P on the distribution of functional roots of Arabica coffee in Kenya. *Annals of Applied Biology*, **77**, 159–80.

Itai, C., Ben-Zioni, A. & Ordin, L. (1973). Correlative changes in endogenous

601

hormone levels and shoot growth induced by short heat treatments to the root. *Physiologia Plantarum*, **29**, 355–60.

Jones, R. & Hodgkinson, K. C. (1970). Root growth of rangeland chenopods: morphology and production of *Atriplex nummularia* and *Atriplex vesicaria*. In: *The Biology of Atriplex* (ed. R. Jones), pp. 77–85. CSIRO, Canberra.

Kassas, M. (1966). Plant life in deserts. In: *Arid Lands – a geographical appraisal* (ed. E. S. Hills), pp. 145–180. Methuen, London.

Kende, H. & Sitton, D. (1967). The physiological significance of kinetin- and gibberellin-like root hormones. *Annals of the New York Academy of Sciences*, **144**, 235–43.

Killian, Ch. & Lemée, G. (1956). Les xérophytes: leur économie d'eau. In: *Handbuch der Pflanzenphysiologie. III. Pflanzen und Wasser* (ed. W. Stocker), pp. 787–824. Springer, Berlin.

Khan, A. G. (1974). The occurrence of mycorrhizas in halophytes, hydrophytes and xerophytes, and of *Endogone* spores in adjacent soils. *Journal of General Microbiology*, **81**, 7–14.

Klepper, B., Taylor, H. M., Huck, M. G. & Fiscus, E. L. (1973). Water relations and growth of cotton in drying soil. *Agronomy Journal*, **65**, 307–10.

Klute, A. & Peters, D. B. (1969). Water uptake and root growth. In: *Root Growth* (ed. W. J. Whittington), pp. 105–132. Butterworths, London.

Kramer, P. J. (1969). *Plant and Soil Water Relationships*. McGraw-Hill, New York.

Kramer, P. J. & Bullock, H. C. (1966). Seasonal variations in the proportions of suberized and unsuberized roots of trees in relation to the absorption of water. *American Journal of Botany*, **53**, 200–4.

Le Houérou, H. N. (1972). Africa – the mediterranean region. In: *Wildland Shrubs – their Biology and Utilization* (eds. C. M. McKell, J. P. Blaisdell & J. R. Goodin), pp. 26–36. USDA Forest Service, Ogden, Utah.

Leonard, E. R. (1962). Inter-relations of vegetative and reproductive growth, with special reference to indeterminate plants. *Botanical Review*, **28**, 353–410.

Leshem, B. (1965). The annual activity of intermediary roots of the Aleppo pine. *Forest Science*, **11**, 291–8.

Leshem, B. (1970). Resting roots of *Pinus halepensis*: structure, function, and reaction to water stress. *Botanical Gazette*, **131**, 99–104.

Lunt, O. R., Letey, J. & Clark, S. B. (1973). Oxygen requirements for root growth in three species of desert shrubs. *Ecology*, **54**, 1356–62.

Lutz, J. F. (1952). Mechanical impedance and plant growth. In: *Soil Physical Conditions and Plant Growth* (ed. B. T. Shaw), pp. 43–71, American Society of Agronomy, Monograph 2. Academic Press, New York.

McCleary, J. A. (1968). The biology of desert plants. In: *Desert Biology* (ed. G. W. Brown), Vol. 1, pp. 141–94. Academic Press, New York.

McGinnies, W. G. (1972). North America. In: *Wildland Shrubs – their Biology and Utilization* (eds. G. M. McKell, J. P. Blaisdell & J. R. Goodin), pp. 55–66. USDA Forest Service, Ogden, Utah.

Malajczuk, N. & Bowen, G. D. (1974). Proteoid roots are microbially induced. *Nature* (London), **251**, 316–17.

Melhuish, F. M. & Lang, A. R. G. (1968). Quantitative studies of roots in soil. I. Length and diameters of cotton roots in a clay-loam soil by analysis of surface-ground blocks of resin impregnated soil. *Soil Science*, **106**, 16–22.

Mexal, J. & Reid, C. P. P. (1973). The growth of selected mycorrhizal fungi in response to induced water stress. *Canadian Journal of Botany*, **51**, 1579–88.

Migahid, A. M. (1961). The drought resistance of Egyptian desert plants. In: *Plant Water Relationships in Arid and Semi-arid Conditions. UNESCO Arid Zone Research*, **16**, 213–33.

Mirreh, H. F. & Ketcheson, J. W. (1972). Influence of soil bulk density and matric pressure on soil resistance to penetration. *Canadian Journal of Soil Science*, **52**, 477–83.

Mirreh, H. F. & Ketcheson, J. W. (1973). Influence of soil water matric potential and resistance to penetration on corn root elongation. *Canadian Journal of Soil Science*, **53**, 383–8.

Mooney, H. A. (1972). The carbon balance of plants. *Annual Review of Ecology and Systematics*, **3**, 315–46.

Moore, R. T., White, R. S. & Caldwell, M. M. (1972). Transpiration of *Atriplex confertifolia* and *Eurotia lanata* in relation to soil, plant, and atmospheric moisture stresses. *Canadian Journal of Botany*, **50**, 2411–18.

Moss, E. H. (1934). Rings of cork in the wood of herbaceous perennials. *Nature* (London), **133**, 689.

Mosse, B. (1973). Advances in the study of vesicular-arbuscular mycorrhiza. *Annual Review of Microbiology*, **11**, 171–96.

Muller, C. H. (1966). The role of chemical inhibition (allelopathy) in vegetational composition. *Bulletin of the Torrey Botanical Club*, **93**, 332–51.

Muttiah, S. (1972). Effect of drought on mycorrhizal associations of *Pinus caribaea*. *Commonwealth Forestry Review*, **51**, 116–20.

Nambiar, E. K. S. (1975). Mobility and plant uptake of micronutrients in relation to soil water content. In: *Trace elements in soil–plant–animal systems* (eds. D. J. D. Nicholas & A. R. Egan), pp. 151–63. Academic Press, New York.

Negbi, M. & Evenari, M. (1961). The means of survival of some desert summer annuals. In: *Plant–Water Relationships of Arid and Semi-Arid Conditions. UNESCO Arid Zone Research* **16**, 249–59.

Newbould, P. (1969). The absorption of nutrients by plants from different zones in the soil. In: *Ecological Aspects of the Mineral Nutrition of Plants* (ed. I. H. Rorison), pp. 177–90. Blackwell Scientific, Oxford.

Newman, E. I. (1966). A method of estimating the total length of root in a sample. *Journal of Applied Ecology*, **3**, 139–45.

Newman, E. I. (1974). Root and soil water relations. In: *The Plant Root and its Environment* (ed. E. W. Carson), pp. 363–440. University Press of Virginia, Charlottesville.

Nielsen, K. F. & Humphries, E. C. (1966). Effects of root temperature on growth. *Soils and Fertilizers*, **29**, 1–7.

Nir, I., Klein, S. & Poljakoff-Mayber, A. (1969). Effect of moisture stress on submicroscopic structure of maize roots. *Australian Journal of Biological Science*, **22**, 17–33.

Noy-Meir, I. (1973). Desert ecosystems: environment and producers. *Annual Review of Ecology and Systematics*, **4**, 25–51.

Nye, P. H. (1966). The effect of the nutrient intensity and buffering power, size and root hairs of a root, on nutrient absorption by diffusion. *Plant and Soil*, **25**, 81–105.

Nye, P. H. (1969). The soil model and its application of plant nutrition. In: *Ecological Aspects of the Mineral Nutrition of Plants* (ed. I. H. Rorison), pp. 105–14. Blackwell Scientific, Oxford.

Nye, P. H. & Foster, W. N. M. (1961). The relative uptake of phosphorus by crops and natural fallow from different parts of their root zone. *Journal of Agricultural Science*, **56**, 299–306.

Plant processes

Olsen, S. R. & Kemper, W. D. (1968). Movement of nutrients to plant roots. *Advances in Agronomy*, **20**, 91–151.

Onderdonk, J. J. & Ketcheson, J. W. (1973). Effect of soil temperature on direction of corn root growth. *Plant and Soil*, **39**, 177–86.

Oppenheimer, H. R. (1960). Adaptation to drought: xerophytism. In: *Plant Water Relationships in Arid and Semi-Arid Conditions. Reviews of Research, UNESCO Arid Zone Research*, **15**, 105–38.

Orshan, G. (1972). Morphological and physiological plasticity in relation to drought. In: *Wildland Shrubs – their Biology and Utilization* (eds. C. M. McKell, J. P. Blaisdell & J. R. Goodin) pp. 245–54. USDA Forest Service, Ogden, Utah.

Petrov, M. P. (1972). Asia. In: *Wildland Shrubs – their Biology and Utilization* (eds. C. M. McKell, J. P. Blaisdell & J. R. Goodin), pp. 37–50. USDA Forest Service, Ogden, Utah.

Phillips, W. S. (1963). Depth of roots in soil. *Ecology*, **44**, 424.

Pitman, M. G., Lüttge, U., Läuchli, A. & Ball, E. (1974). Effect of previous water stress on ion uptake and transport in barley seedlings. *Australian Journal of Plant Physiology*, **1**, 377–85.

Pressland, A. J. (1973). Rainfall partitioning by an arid woodland (*Acacia aneura* F. Muell.) in south-western Queensland. *Australian Journal of Botany*, **21**, 235–45.

Price, J. R. (1911). The roots of some North African desert grasses. *New Phytologist*, **10**, 328–40.

Rameshewar, A. & Steponkus, P. L. (1969). Reduction of high temperature injury in intact plants. *Plant Physiology* (Lancaster), **44**, supplement, abstract 7.

Reid, D. M., Crozier, A. & Harvey, B. M. R. (1969). The effects of flooding on the export of gibberellins from the root to the shoot. *Planta*, **89**, 376–9.

Robards, A. W., Jackson, S. M., Clarkson, D. T. & Sanderson, J. (1973). The structure of barley roots in relation to the transport of ions into the stele. *Protoplasma*, **77**, 291–311.

Rogers, W. S. & Head, G. C. (1969). Factors affecting the distribution and growth of roots of perennial woody species. In: *Root Growth* (ed. W. J. Whittington), pp. 280–92. Butterworths, London.

Rowse, H. R. & Phillips, D. A. (1974). An instrument for measuring the total length of root in a sample. *Journal of Applied Ecology*, **11**, 309–14.

Russell, E. W. (1961). *Soil Conditions and Plant Growth*, 9th edition. Longmans, London.

Russell, R. S. & Ellis, R. B. (1968). Estimation of the distribution of plant roots in soil. *Nature* (London), **217**, 582–3.

Sanders, F. E. & Tinker, P. B. (1971). Mechanism of absorption of phosphate from soil by *Endogone* mycorrhizas. *Nature* (London), **233**, 278–9.

Sator, C. (1973). Methodological studies to distinguish functional from non-functional roots. (Translated title). *Landbauforschung Voelkenrode*, **22**, 87–92.

Schuurmann, J. J. & Goedewaagen, M. A. J. (1971). *Methods for the examination of root systems and roots*. 2nd edition. Centre for Agricultural Publications and Documentation, Wageningen.

Scott, T. K. (1972). Auxins and roots. *Annual Review of Plant Pysiology*, **23**, 235–58.

Scotter, D. R. (1974). Salt and water movement in relatively dry soil. *Australian Journal of Soil Research*, **12**, 27–35.

Shaw, B. T. (Ed.) (1952). *Soil Physical Conditions and Plant Growth*, American Society of Agronomy, Monograph 2. Academic Press, New York.

604

Shields, L. M. (1953). Gross modification in certain plants tolerant of calcium sulphate dunes. *American Midland Naturalist*, **50**, 224–37.

Short, K. C. & Torrey, J. G. (1972). Cytokinins in seedling roots of pea. *Plant Physiology* (Lancaster), **49**, 155–60.

Sinha, B. K. & Singh, N. T, (1974). Effect of transpiration rate on salt accumulation around corn roots in a saline soil. *Agronomy Journal*, **66**, 557–60.

Skene, K. G. M. & Anticliff, A. J. (1972). A comparative study of cytokinin levels in bleeding sap of *Vitis vinifera* (L.) and the two grapevine root stocks, Salt-Creek and 1613. *Journal of Experimental Botany*, **23**, 283–93.

Skinner, M. F. & Bowen, G. D. (1974). The uptake and translocation of phosphate by mycelial strands of pine mycorrhizas. *Soil Biology and Biochemisty*, **6**, 53–6.

Slankis, V. (1973). Hormonal relationships in mycorrhizal development. In: *Ectomycorrhizae, their Ecology and Physiology* (ed. G. C. Marks and T. T. Kozlowski), pp. 231–298. Academic Press, New York.

Slatyer, R. O. (1967). *Plant–Water Relationships*. Academic Press, New York.

Sprent, J. I. (1975). Adherence of sand particles to soybean roots under water stress. *New Phytologist*, **74**, 461–3.

Szarek, S. R., Johnson, H. B. & Ting, I. P. (1973). Drought adaption in *Opuntia basilaris*. Significance of recycling carbon through crassulacean acid metabolism. *Plant Physiology* (Lancaster), **52**, 539–41.

Tabler, R. D. (1964). The root system of *Artemisia tridentata* at 9500 ft in Wyoming. *Ecology*, **45**, 633–6.

Taylor, H. M. (1974). Root behaviour as affected by soil structure and strength. In: *The Plant Root and its Environment* (ed. E. W. Carson), pp. 271–91. University Press of Virginia, Charlottesville.

Taylor, H. M. & Klepper, B. (1975). Water uptake by cotton root systems: an examination of assumptions in the single root model. *Soil Science*, **120**, 57–67.

Taylor, H. M. & Ratliff, L. F. (1969). Root elongation rates of cotton and peanuts as a function of soil strength and soil water content. *Soil Science*, **108**, 113–19.

Tesche, M. (1974). The effect of water stress on the exudation of carbohydrates by the roots of *Picea abies* (L). Karst. and other young conifers. *Flora*, **163**, 26–36.

Thorup, R. M. (1969). Root development and phosphorus uptake by tomato plants under controlled soil moisture conditions. *Agronomy Journal*, **61**, 808–11.

Tinker, P. B. (1969). The transport of ions in the soil around plant roots. In: *Ecological Aspects of the Mineral Nutrition of Plants* (ed. I. H. Rorison), pp. 135–47. Blackwell Scientific, Oxford.

Vaadia, Y. & Itai, C. (1969). Inter-relationships of growth with reference to the distribution of growth substances. In: *Root Growth* (ed. W. J. Whittington), pp. 65–77. Butterworths, London.

Van Fleet, D. S. (1961). Histochemistry and function of the endodermis. *Botanical Review*, **27**, 165–220.

Waddington (1971). Observation of plant roots *in situ*. *Canadian Journal of Botany*, **49**, 1850–2.

Walker, J. M. (1969). One-degree increments in soil temperatures affect maize seedling behaviour. *Soil Science Society of America Proceedings*, **33**, 729–36.

Walter, H. & Stadelmann, E. (1974). A new approach to the water relations of desert plants. In: *Desert Biology* (ed. G. W. Brown), Vol. 2, pp. 213–310. Academic Press, New York.

605

Plant processes

Watt, W. R. (1971). Role of temperature in the regulation of leaf extension in *Zea mays. Nature* (London), **229**, 46–7.

Weaver, J. E. (1926). *Root Development of Field Crops*. McGraw-Hill, New York.

Weaver, J. E. & Clements, F. E. (1938). *Plant Ecology*, 2nd edition. McGraw-Hill, New York.

Weiss, C. & Vaadia, Y. (1965). Kinetin-like activity in root apices of sunflower plants. *Life Sciences*, **4**, 1323–6.

Went, F. W. (1938). Specific factors other than auxin affecting growth and root formation. *Plant Physiology* (Lancaster), **13**, 55–80.

Went, F. W. & Stark, N. (1968). The biological and mechanical role of soil fungi. *Proceedings of the National Academy of Sciences*, **60**, 497–504.

Whittaker, R. H. & Feeney, P. P. (1971). Allelochemics: chemical interactions between species. *Science*, **171**, 757–70.

Wiersma, D. (1959). The soil environment and root development. *Advances in Agronomy*, **11**, 43–51.

Wiersum, L. K. (1957). The relationship of the size and structural rigidity of pores to their penetration by roots. *Plant and Soil*, **9**, 75–85.

Wiersum, L. K. (1958). Density of root branching as affected by substrate and separate ions. *Acta Botanica Neerlandica*, **7**, 174–90.

Williams, J. (1974). Root density and water potential gradients near the plant root. *Journal of Experimental Botany*, **25**, 669–74.

Woods, F. W. (1960). Biological antagonisms due to phytotoxic root exudates. *Botanical Reviews*, **26**, 546–67.

Wilcox, H. E. (1968). Morphological studies of the root of red pine, *Pinus resinosa*, I. Growth characteristics and patterns of branching. *American Journal of Botany*, **55**, 247–54.

Zahner, R. (1968). Water deficits and growth of trees. In: *Water Deficits and Plant Growth* (ed. T. T. Kozlowski), Vol. 2, pp. 191–254. Academic Press, New York.

Zohary, M. (1961). On hydro-ecological relations of the near east desert vegetation. In: *Plant–Water Relationships in Arid and Semi-Arid Conditions. UNESCO Arid Zone Research*, **16**, 199–212.

Manuscript received by the editors February 1975

24. Ion uptake, transport and excretion

C. B. OSMOND

Introduction

The plant processes of ion uptake, transport and excretion in arid and semi-arid shrub vegetation interact to produce and maintain some of the most striking examples of patterned mineral distribution in soils (Gates, Stoddart & Cook, 1956; Charley & McGarity, 1964; Charley, 1972). These patterns are no doubt highlighted by the low levels of nutrient anions (NO_3^- and $H_2PO_4^-$) and the high levels of non-nutrient anions (Cl^- and HCO_3^-) found in these soils, as well as by the pattern of rainfall which controls soil microbial activity and contributes to the concentration of available nutrients at the soil surface (Charley & Cowling, 1968; Charley, 1972). However, the plant processes which determine the ability of arid-zone vegetation to accumulate high levels of inorganic ions and to absorb nutrient ions in the presence of high concentrations of non-nutrient ions deserve particular attention.

Arid-zone vegetation may contain concentrations of inorganic ions higher by a factor of 2 to 5 than vegetation of other regions (Table 24.1). These ions largely account for the osmotic component of the low tissue water potential measured in arid-zone vegetation, which presumably determines the ability of these plants to withstand soil water potentials below -50 bar. In laboratory experiments and in the field, the absorption of ions to high concentration has been related to improved water relations and growth under arid conditions. For example, the growth stimulation due to sodium chloride frequently observed in *Atriplex* spp. in culture solutions is dependent on relative humidity (Gale, Naaman & Poljakoff-Mayber, 1970). Evidently the addition of salt and its absorption by *Atriplex halimus* L. facilitated water uptake in the face of the increased transpirational demand at low external humidity. Kaplan & Gale (1972) showed that salt uptake improved water balance in this species, reducing water loss from the leaves with relatively little change in photosynthesis. Field studies suggest that the higher ion concentrations in *Atriplex confertifolia* compared to *Eurotia lanata* are related to the prolonged physiological activity and carbon gain in the former species during dry, late summer months (Moore, Breckle & Caldwell, 1972).

For the purposes of this review it is assumed that most of the ion-absorption activity of plants in the arid zone will be confined to periods

607

Table 24.1. *Inorganic ion content of leaves from species growing in different environments* (Data of Rodin & Bazilevich, 1965)

Vegetation type	Ion content (% of dry matter)
Tropical forest	4.40 (28)
Coniferous mixed forests	1.77 (26)
Deciduous forests	4.77 (19)
Desert vegetation	10.09 (14)

Number of specimens analysed is shown in parenthesis; specimens include trees, shrubs and herbaceous species.

following sufficient rainfall to initiate new root activity (Chapter 23 above) during which ion concentrations in soil solution and soil water potentials probably exceed values which limit ion absorption of plants in more mesic environments. Estimation of ion activity in soil solution remains a complex exercise (Adams, 1974) but it is likely that the saturation extract may range up to 150 mmol l^{-1} soluble salts in saline soils, and contain limiting nutrients such as phosphorus ($H_2PO_4^-$) at less than 1 μmol l^{-1} concentration. Soil water potentials in arid-land soils may decline to values less than -50 bar, but in these soils it is improbable that ion absorption by plants is significant. Under these conditions, changes in ion transport and availability in the soil are likely to overshadow plant processes. The absorption of ions by roots in dry soil (contact exchange and related phenomena (Jenny, 1966)) is unlikely to make a substantial contribution to the ionic relations of arid-zone plants.

For these reasons, then, this chapter briefly summarizes current knowledge of ion uptake, transport and excretion in plants as a function of external ion concentration and water potential. Some emphasis will be given to factors which may permit the absorption of ions to higher than usual concentrations within the plant. In this context, ion *uptake* embraces the ion relations of cells and tissues, ion *transport* is largely restricted to the movement of ions between root and shoot, and ion *excretion* confined almost exclusively to the activity of salt glands. The term ion *absorption* is used in the general sense, as for example in the case of studies with intact plants.

Compartments and fluxes, an essential framework

The absorption of ions by higher plants may be examined at several levels, with varying degrees of oversimplification and compromise. At each level, however, it is important to identify the relationship between ion

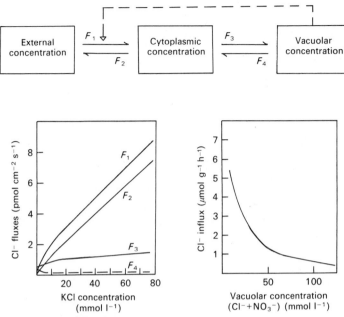

Fig. 24.1. Schematic model of compartments and fluxes involved in ion uptake to vacuole of plant cells. An example of the relationship between external concentration and the fluxes of chloride ions in barley roots is shown (lower left, from Cram, 1973*a*). The negative feedback control of plasma membrane influx (F_1) by vacuolar concentration is shown by a dashed line. An example of this relationship for chloride influx in barley roots is shown (lower right, Cram, 1973*b*).

concentration (strictly, ion activity) in specific compartments, and its relationship to a specific flux of this ion between adjacent compartments. This approach does not differ in principle from that applied in nutrient cycling or in systems analysis, and it does permit the simulation of relatively complex systems (Pitman, 1969). The groundwork of the compartment and flux approach was set out in Briggs, Hope & Robertson (1961), but has been largely ignored in some recent texts (Epstein, 1972; Waisel, 1972). The progress and problems of this approach have been discussed in reviews (MacRobbie, 1971; Anderson, 1972, 1973; Lüttge & Pitman, 1976), and specific applications are discussed below. The compartment and flux approach is strictly applicable only to steady-state systems, and difficulties may arise with cells of growing plants.

Ion uptake by plant cells

Uptake to the vacuole of root cortical cells

Ion uptake to the vacuole of plant cells involves the interaction of bi-directional fluxes across two cell membranes and the activity of ions in the external solution, the cytoplasm and the vacuole (Fig. 24.1). Compartmental analysis of this relatively complex system is based on techniques developed for single cells of coenocytic algae (MacRobbie, 1971). In spite of shortcomings, these methods permit the most adequate appraisal now available of cell ionic relations.

The relationship between external concentration and the absorption of ions to the vacuole of plant cells has been a major preoccupation of ion-uptake physiologists in the last decade. In nearly all tissues examined this relationship is described by at least two hyperbolic functions, one saturating at below 1 mmol l^{-1} external concentration and another saturating in the region of 50 mmol l^{-1} (Epstein, 1972; Lüttge, 1973). Interpretation of these isotherms, usually based on the assumption that the isotherms describe a uni-directional flux at the plasma membrane (at least at low concentrations), has far outdistanced understanding of the kinetic relationship. The experimental methods used measure net flux to the vacuole, and the results are therefore a complex function of several component processes. As pointed out by Cram (1973a), the hyperbolic relationship between external concentration and uptake to the vacuole is purely fortuitous, for none of the fluxes at the plasma membrane or tonoplast are of this form (Fig. 24.1). At low concentrations, influx to the vacuole is limited by the plasma membrane influx (F_1); and at higher concentrations influx at the tonoplast (F_3) limits uptake to the vacuole, as predicted by Osmond & Laties (1968) and Laties (1969). Cram's analysis takes pains to isolate conclusions regarding the kinetics of the ion-uptake system from conclusions regarding the mechanisms of component uptake processes (Cram, 1973a). Complex analysis of the hyperbolic isotherm (Nissen, 1974) and analogies with enzyme systems of isolated membranes (Hodges, 1973) do not seem to be justified at this time.

Although the hyperbolic relationship may be fortuitous, it remains a useful description of the relationship between external concentration and net uptake on two grounds:

(a) The concentration at half the maximal velocity of uptake in the low concentration range (the apparent affinity for ion uptake) is usually lower than the average concentration of ions in soil solutions (Table 24.2). The isotherm thus reflects a property of ion uptake in roots which may account for ion absorption in most soils.

(b) Absorption isotherms show that ion uptake by roots may be quite specific, and insensitive to high concentrations of other ions. For example, absorption of potassium ions from solutions of low concentration is insensitive to high levels of sodium ions (Epstein, 1972), and phosphate ($H_2PO_4^-$) uptake is insensitive to chloride ions (Carter & Lathwell, 1967). These data suggest that root-cell uptake of essential

610

Table 24.2. *Apparent affinity of ion uptake processes in excised roots compared with ion concentrations in soil solution.* (Data taken from Epstein, 1972)

Ion	Species	Apparent affinity mmol l^{-1}	Soil Solution[1] mmol l^{-1}
K+	*Hordeum vulgare*	0.02	0.5–5.0 (87%)
	Agropyron elongatum	0.01	
NO_3^-	*Zea mays*	0.02	0.8–3.2 (86%)
$H_2PO_4^-$	*Zea mays*	0.006	0.001–0.005 (74%)

[1] Percentage of all analyses falling in this range is indicated in parenthesis.

ions such as potassium and phosphate may be little influenced by soil salinity (Rains, 1972).

Although the apparent affinity described by the hyperbolic isotherm may have some qualitative significance, the rate parameters do not. Very high rates of ion transport in barley roots with a low concentration of salt but high in sugar are not sustained by these roots for any significant period, and do not reflect the rate of transport in roots grown in the presence of inorganic ions (Pitman, Courtice & Lee, 1968). Further, the ion concentration in the cell cytoplasm or vacuole appears to exert control over ion influx (F_1) at the plasma membrane (Fig. 24.1). Pretreatment of discs of beet tissue (*Beta vulgaris*) with unlabelled solutions reduced the subsequent influx of labelled ions, with kinetics consistent with cytoplasmic filling (Osmond & Laties, 1968). Cram (1973b) used a more plausible measure of plasma membrane influx, and found that influx of chloride ions was most highly correlated with the ($Cl^- + NO_3^-$) concentration in the vacuole (Fig. 24.1). Chloride influx did not respond to the internal concentration of malate, sodium or potassium. Influx of nitrate ions also responded to internal chloride concentration.

Earlier studies related the reduction in net flux as tissues approach flux equilibrium to increased efflux (F_2 and F_4 in Fig. 24.1). The above observations (Cram, 1973b) suggest a more sophisticated, rather specific form of control of ion uptake, and consequently of vacuolar ion concentration and hydrostatic pressure, in growing cells (Cram, 1974). If these observations can be generalised, they imply that most plant cells would attain a similar vacuolar concentration of ions. The relationship between influx and vacuolar ion concentration in cells capable of absorbing ions to high concentrations presumably differs from that in Fig. 24.1, but has yet to be investigated.

Plant processes

Uptake to the vacuole of leaf cells

Leaf tissues may exert some control over the transport processes delivering ions via the xylem stream (p. 616 below) but the compartmental and flux analysis of ion uptake in leaf cells is otherwise similar to that of other tissues (Robinson, 1971). Some of the limitations involved in studies with leaf slices have been described (Osmond, 1968), but in respect of characteristics such as free space (Pitman, Lüttge, Kramer & Ball, 1974) and hyperbolic isotherms (Epstein, 1972) leaves are generally similar to other tissues.

Leaf tissues usually contain higher concentrations of ions than root tissues, so that studies of ion uptake as a function of external concentration are not strictly comparable with those of low-salt roots of cereals (Epstein, 1972). This high-salt status may account for the observation that uptake of monovalent cations in leaf slices is often associated with substantial efflux of complementary cations (Osmond, 1968; Smith & Robinson, 1971). The relationship between internal concentration and influx of ions in leaf cells has not been examined, but rates of potassium uptake by leaf slices apparently decrease with increasing salt content (for instance, in slices of *Zea mays* (Smith & Epstein, 1964) and *Avicennia marina* (Rains & Epstein, 1967)). This and other aspects of ion uptake in leaf cells deserve further attention, for they may determine features such as the extracellular accumulation of ions in leaf tissues (Oertli, 1968), the availability of ions to gland systems (p. 618 below), and the production of hormones regulating ion transport (p. 616 below).

Ion uptake and cell water relations

Accumulation of inorganic ions in the vacuole, usually as salts of carboxylic acids (p. 619), is the principal means of turgor regulation in the cells of higher plants (Cram, 1974). Thus a solute requirement for expansion growth may be described, and osmotic adjustment by solute uptake is the common basis for adjustment of plant water relations during mild salinity stress.

Ion uptake to the cell vacuole is thus a central feature of plant water relations and it is significant that the uptake processes are relatively insensitive to changes in cell turgor induced by externally applied osmotica (non-plasmolysing treatments).

Ion transport within the plant

In the intact plant the ionic relations of cells in the root and shoot are connected and controlled by the translocation stream in the xylem and the

612

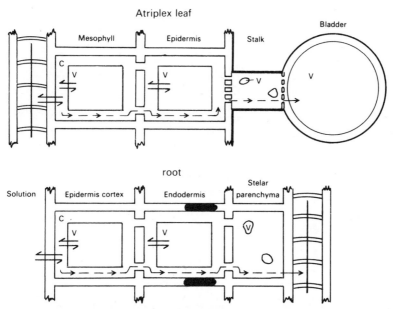

Fig. 24.2. Simplified model of the symplast pathway ($\rightarrow \rightarrow \rightarrow$) involved in transport across the root to the stele and across the leaf to a salt gland. Reproduced, with permission, from Structure and Function of Plant Glands, *Annual Review of Plant Physiology*, volume 22. Copyright © 1971 by Annual Reviews Inc. All rights reserved.

recirculation system of the phloem. It seems likely that bulk flow or exchange of ions through the free space is restricted by the suberisation of endodermal cells at the interface of the root cortex and stele. Absorption of ions into the transport system commences at the plasma membrane of root cortical cells, and transport thus competes with uptake for ions absorbed at this membrane. There is general agreement that the symplast of the root (the connected cytoplasmic compartments of root cortical cells) is the operational compartment from which ions are transferred to the xylem stream (Fig. 24.2). Biophysical evidence for the symplastic network has been reviewed by Spanswick (1976) and the theoretical basis for symplast function has been assessed by Tyree (1970).

The symplast thus provides an intracellular path connecting tissues of the root which are not connected by a free-space pathway. The symplast in leaves serves an equally important role in ion excretion (Fig. 24.2; see also Luttge, 1971), and the symplast is presumably involved in retranslocation in the phloem, but this role is not well understood. The processes by which ions are transferred from the symplast to the xylem stream are disputed. Laties (1969) argues for a passive release of ions into non-living xylem vessels, whereas Anderson (1972) favours the involvement of living xylem parenchyma cells.

613

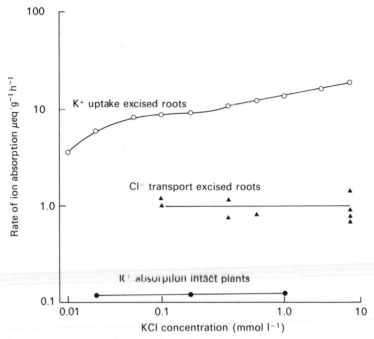

Fig. 24.3. Comparisons of rate and form of response to external KCl concentration for uptake of potassium ions by excised low salt barley roots, from Epstein, Rains & Elzam (1963); transport of chloride ions from barley roots, from Pitman (1971) and uptake of potassium ions by intact barley plants under steady-state conditions, from Johansen, Edwards & Loneragan (1968).

Transport and external concentration

Ion transport will be dependent on ion activity in the cytoplasmic compartment of root cortical cells, and Pitman (1971) described a model based on symplast theory in which the specific activity of labelled ions transported to the shoot may be related to the specific activity of the cytoplasmic phase calculated from fluxes into root cells. Early experiments which suggested that transport displayed a hyperbolic isotherm at low external concentrations only (Laties, 1969), and the interpretation of these isotherms, have been questioned (Anderson, 1972). Subsequent studies indicate that transport of chloride ions from barley roots is rather insensitive to external concentration (Pitman, 1971). It seems likely that transport, regulated according to uptake and demand in the shoot, is an important rate-limiting step in ion absorption by intact plants. Few steady-state experiments have been conducted with whole plants, but these show, for example, that absorption of potassium ions is saturated at relatively low external concentration, and that uptake and transport in the intact plant do not display the hyperbolic isotherm typical of the isolated processes

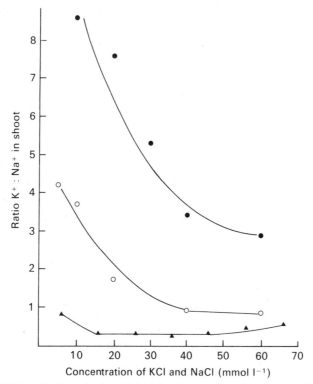

Fig. 24.4. Selectivity for potassium (K^+:Na^+ ratio) as a function of external concentration of equimolar (KCl+NaCl) solution. *Hordeum vulgare* (●, from Pitman (1965)); *Sinapis* (○, from Pitman (1966)) and *Atriplex halimus* (▲, from Mozafar, Goodin & Oertli (1970)).

(Johansen, Edwards & Loneragan, 1970). Fig. 24.3 compares data from the literature for the rate of potassium *uptake* into low salt barley roots, the rate of chloride *transport* from barley roots, and steady-state rate of potassium *absorption* by barley plants, each as a function of the external concentration of potassium chloride. The 'pacemaker' role of transport is obvious in this comparison, and the independence of transport from external concentration presumably reflects properties associated with ion accumulation in the symplasm (Pitman, 1971).

Although the rate of transport bears little relationship to the rate of uptake by isolated root cells, ion specificity of root uptake is largely preserved during transport to the shoot. In isolated roots, potassium uptake is relatively insensitive to sodium ions at low concentrations, but the two ions appear to compete during uptake at high concentrations. This phenomenon is reflected in a decrease in potassium:sodium ratio as total external concentration increases; this is illustrated in Fig. 24.4 by data for shoots of *Hordeum vulgare*, *Sinapis alba* and *Atriplex halimus*, species

Plant processes

which differ markedly in selectivity for potassium. The potassium selectivity of root uptake processes is modified during transport by transpiration rate (Pitman, 1965) and by selective retranslocation of potassium (Greenway & Pitman, 1965) from the shoot. Although halophytes are rather less selective for potassium, a component of potassium uptake and transport in these plants is insensitive to extraordinarily high levels of sodium chloride (Ashby & Beadle, 1957; Black, 1960; Waisel, 1972).

Transport and water stress

Ion transport from root to shoot is markedly depressed by water stress in the external medium. Greenway & Klepper (1968) showed that transport of previously absorbed sodium and phosphate ($H_2PO_4^-$) ions was reduced by a decrease in external osmotic potential of as little as 5.4 bar. Much of the reduction in transport may have been due to reduced water flow, but this variable was eliminated in studies by Pitman, Lüttge, Läuchli & Ball (1974a) in which water stress was induced by a short wilting of the shoot. Transport in roots excised from these plants was inhibited for several hours after resumption of normal transpiration. These authors propose that the synthesis of abscisic acid (ABA), a well-established hormone response of water stress, may provide a mechanism for the control of transport to the shoot (Pitman, Lüttge, Läuchli & Ball, 1974b).

Transport and growth rate

In most plants the concentration of ions in the shoot remains relatively constant during growth, implying that ion transport is closely geared to growth rate. Pitman (1972) showed that transport of potassium ions in barley was most closely correlated with the relative growth rate of the shoot. Regulation of transport might be achieved by regulation of uptake at the plasma membrane of leaf cells, or by retranslocation via the phloem. Fig. 24.5 illustrates the components and potential regulatory steps involved in these processes. Under some conditions provision of energy to the root might be a simple regulator of ion uptake and transport. Under other conditions the concentration of ions in leaf cell vacuoles may limit influx into these cells (Fig. 24.1), and result in the extracellular and symplastic accumulation of ions (Oertli, 1968). This may result in loss of turgor in leaf cells and in the production of ABA, as in response to water stress, and this hormone may in turn regulate transport as described above (Pitman, 1972; Pitman et al., 1974b).

Retranslocation probably plays a minor role in the regulation of the net flux of ions from root to shoots, and of the ion content of shoots. Greenway, Gunn & Thomas (1966) concluded that retranslocation of

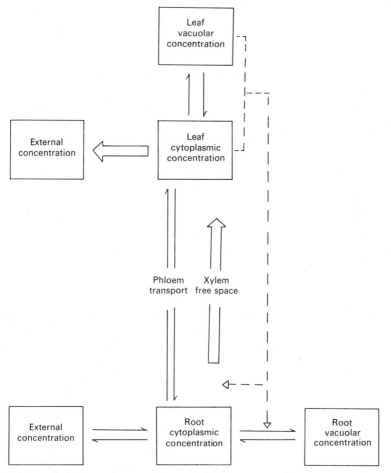

Fig. 24.5. Schematic model of compartments and fluxes involved in ion transport from root to shoot. The major transport pathway is via the xylem free space and is controlled by fluxes from the root and into the shoot symplast. Transport is shown as uni-directional, as is the ion excretion flux. The feedback control due to ion content of the shoot (or to the relative concentrations of ions in shoot free space, symplast and vacuole) is shown by the dashed line.

sodium and chloride ions from shoots was similar in salt-tolerant and salt-sensitive species. Thus the ability of arid-zone plants to accumulate high concentrations of ions in shoot tissues may not involve reduced retranslocation. Rather, these species may show different relationships between ion transport and external concentration or growth rate. Many of these plants have well developed salt-excretion systems in leaf tissue, which provide a further means of regulation of ion uptake in leaf cells and consequently of ion transport from the root.

Plant processes

Ion excretion

Excretion of ions from plants other than by the shedding of senescent tissues may be an important part of the mineral cycle in some systems. Excretion may occur from roots to soil, and qualitative studies show that even the relatively immobile ions such as calcium may move from leaf to soil (Epstein, 1972). Quantitative studies of root excretion appear to have been neglected. Loss of ions from shoots may involve relatively non-specific leaching (Tukey, 1970) or complex salt glands (Lüttge, 1971; Waisel, 1972). The excretory function of gland systems is analogous to the transport function from the root stele. Both systems maintain a steady-state flux of ions between compartments (Anderson, 1972), and this analogy is particularly well illustrated by Fig. 24.2 (Lüttge, 1971).

The gland may excrete ions to the exterior of the leaf or, as in the case of *Atriplex* spp., may accumulate salt in specialized epidermal bladders (Osmond *et al.*, 1969). The walls of cells adjacent to embedded glands, or the walls of the epidermal bladder, are suberized, so that free space diffusion of ions in the region of the gland is restricted (Lüttge, 1971). Salt-excreting glands appear to draw ions from the symplasm of leaf mesophyll cells (Lüttge & Osmond, 1970), and this intracellular pathway again connects two otherwise isolated compartments. Judging by the extraordinarily high concentrations of salts excreted by gland systems (from 1 mol l^{-1} to 10 mol l^{-1} in bladders of *Atriplex* spp.), the flux of salt through the gland is much less sensitive than uptake and transport processes to the concentration of ions in the final compartment.

Few gland systems have been studied in sufficient detail for the contribution of excretion to the overall ionic balance of the shoot to be quantitatively assessed. Secretion is the principal component of the regulation of ion content in leaf cells of the mangrove *Aegialitis annulata* R.Br. (Atkinson *et al.*, 1967). In *Atriplex* spp., more than half the chloride content of leaves is excreted to the epidermal bladders (Table 24.3). For these two systems at least, it is clear that the salt-excreting glands are responsible for a large reduction of the salt load imposed on leaf cells. Leaf cells are the principal centres of metabolic activitiy in the plant, and it is not surprising that symptoms of nutrient deficiency or toxicity are first observed in leaf tissues.

Ion absorption and plant metabolism
Ion absorption and intermediary metabolism

Absorption of mineral elements by plant cells is coupled to intermediary metabolism in several ways. During ion uptake the balance of cation and anion absorption in plant cells is maintained by carboxylic acid synthesis

618

Table 24.3. *Chloride concentration in bladders and laminae of leaves of* Atriplex *spp.* (*meq per g dry weight*) (Osmond, unpublished data)

Species	Tissue	NaCl concentration in culture solution (mmol/l)		
		5 or 10	50	250
Atriplex vesicaria	Bladder	0.87	1.43	1.56
	Lamina	0.38	0.46	0.75
Atriplex nummularia	Bladder	0.62	1.04	1.44
	Lamina	0.35	0.43	0.49
Atriplex spongiosa	Bladder	> 0.1	0.49	2.14
	Lamina	0	0.23	1.08
Atriplex inflata	Bladder	0	—	2.01
	Lamina	> 0.07	—	0.63

or consumption in the cytoplasm and the transport of the organic anion across the tonoplast (Osmond, 1976). Although high concentrations of many organic-acid anions may accumulate in the vacuole of plant tissues, the formation and removal of these anions from the metabolic compartment is a slow process relative to the total metabolic carbon flux.

In growing tissues the apparent excess of inorganic cation uptake over inorganic anion uptake is largely a result of the metabolic incorporation of the nutrient anions nitrate (NO_3^-) and phosphate ($H_2PO_4^-$). Reduction of these anions during metabolism is compensated by the stoichiometric synthesis of organic-acid anions. For example, the high level of soluble oxalate found in leaf tissues of many Chenopodiaceae appears to be produced to balance cations remaining after nitrate reduction. Cation excess, oxalate content and reduced nitrogen levels are highly correlated during leaf growth in *Atriplex* (Osmond, 1967).

When the balance of inorganic cations and anions is considered for the whole plant, it is frequently found that the sum of reduced anions exceeds the content of cations (De Wit, Dijkshoorn & Noggle, 1963). Presumably the excess anion absorption involves the exchange of additional nitrate for hydroxyl ions arising in the metabolic incorporation of nitrate. Benzioni, Vaadia & Lips (1971) propose further that exchange processes of this type may also occur during ion transport. They envisage that retranslocation of potassium salts of organic acids from shoots and their metabolism in roots provides a mechanism for additional uptake and transport of potassium nitrate. These hypotheses are largely based on experiments in fertilised pasture; it remains to be determined whether these relationships are found under natural conditions.

Plant processes

Ion absorption and salinity tolerance

Ion absorption in relation to salinity tolerance embraces most aspects of ion absorption covered in this chapter. Recent reviews (Goodin & Mozafar, 1972; Rains, 1972; Waisel, 1972; Jefferies, 1973; Caldwell, 1974) suggest that the ionic relations of halophytes are similar to those of other plants; but increasing evidence indicates that halophytes are better able to regulate ionic concentration in metabolic compartments while accumulating high concentrations of salt to the vacuole. There are two important metabolic features of salinity tolerance which must be considered. Firstly, in higher plants it seems improbable that salinity tolerance involves the production of an unusually resistant metabolic machinery, as is the case in halophilic bacteria. There is reasonable evidence that the interaction between inorganic ions and enzymes *in vitro* is the same, whether the enzymes are derived from salt-sensitive or salt-tolerant species (Queen, 1974; Osmond, 1976). Secondly, intracellular regulation of inorganic ion concentration implies that the metabolic provision of compatible solutes such as proline or sugar alcohols may play an important role in cytoplasmic osmotic relationships.

The principal difficulty in all aspects of salinity tolerance is specification of the ionic activity in different cellular compartments. Jefferies (1973) described a first approach to this problem in applying compartmental and flux analysis to data for *Triglochin maritima* L. This study emphasised the ability of the halophyte to maintain a high potassium:sodium ratio in the cytoplasm against low ratios externally. The significance of this ratio in metabolic or other terms remains to be assessed.

Ion absorption and energy metabolism

Each of the processes of uptake, transport and excretion may involve movement of ions against an electrochemical potential gradient and the expenditure of metabolic energy ('active uptake'). Although metabolic poisons may make it possible to assign this metabolic coupling to particular steps of energy metabolism in specific cases (Lüttge & Pitman, 1976), it is likely that in practice ion transport may call on whatever energy source is available (Johansen & Lüttge, 1974). The expenditure of energy on ion absorption may be very small in comparison to that expended on other processes. At flux equilibrium, the cells of coenocytic algae probably expend less than 10% of respiratory energy on active ion transport (N. A. Walker, personal communication); and the photosynthetic production of adenosine triphosphate by cells of an expanding leaf may exceed by a factor of one thousand the molar rate of ionic uptake (respectively about 10^3 and 1 μmol h^{-1} per gram fresh weight). In non-autotrophic tissues

620

of halophytes the active uptake of ions could conceivably be a major respiratory drain. Caldwell & Camp (1974) showed that the root biomass of arid-zone shrubs may exceed that of shoots by a factor of ten. Although only a small part of this root system would be active in ion absorption under favourable conditions, maintenance of vacuolar ion content in root cells may involve considerable expenditure of energy (Caldwell, 1974).

Speculations and conclusions

In the last decade, increasing attention to the properties of ion absorption in complex tissues and organisms has led to a better understanding of key processes involved in ion uptake under natural conditions. For example, whatever the nature and location of the ion-uptake processes in plant roots, they have a demonstrably high affinity for most ions and may adequately account for ion absorption from most soil solutions. The uptake of important ions such as potassium and phosphate ($H_2PO_4^-$) is not substantially hindered by high concentration of other ions such as sodium and chloride. Of particular interest in relation to plants from arid regions, it is now possible to specify the processes likely to distinguish these plants from others and permit the absorption of ions to high internal concentrations.

Two feedback loops appear to play a vital role in the regulation of ion absorption in plants. The first of these, the negative feedback of vacuolar ion concentration on plasma membrane influx (Fig. 24.1), if cut or substantially modified, could have the effect of modifying the feedback system regulating ion transport to the shoot (Fig. 24.5). If the uptake feedback control was less sensitive to vacuolar ion concentration, presumably all cells of the organism would be capable of absorbing ions to higher concentrations. Such a plant could in theory sustain a higher transport flux to the shoot, for leaf cells would be capable of maintaining higher vacuolar ion concentrations and of postponing the generation of hormonal regulators of transport. If the leaf had well-developed salt glands, then these could effectively cut the feedback control (shown in Fig. 24.3) by maintaining ion concentrations in free space and symplast in an equilibrium with vacuolar ion concentration such that the hormonal regulators were not produced.

These speculations are at present without direct experimental support, and the best available comparisons between species capable of accumulating high levels of ions on the one hand, and species such as barley (*Hordeum vulgare*) and beans (*Phaseolus vulgaris*) on the other, remain unsatisfactory (Greenway & Osmond, 1970). However, it is probable that the 'luxury uptake' of ions by plants such as *Atriplex* spp. (Black, 1960; Osmond, 1966) represents a significant and most interesting departure from the conventional processes of ion absorption. Although the ionic relations of this genus have been investigated in some detail, this review serves only to emphasise our present ignorance. A systematic reappraisal of ion uptake, transport and excretion in species of this genus to which a modest amount of research has been directed could given new insights to the physiology of arid-land plants and greatly augment fundamental knowledge of the physiology of ion absorption.

References

Adams, F. (1974). Soil solution. In: *The Plant Root and Its Environment* (ed. E. W. Carson), pp. 441–82. University Press of Virginia, Charlottesville.

Anderson, W. P. (1972). Ion transport in cells of higher plant tissues. *Annual Review of Plant Physiology*, **23**, 51–72.

Anderson, W. P. (ed.) (1973). *Ion transport in Plants*. Academic Press, London & New York.

Ashby, W. C. & Beadle, N. C. W. (1957). Studies in halophytes III. Salinity factors in the growth of Australian saltbushes. *Ecology*, **38**, 344–52.

Atkinson, M. R., Findlay, G. P., Hope, A. B., Pitman, M. G., Saddler, H. D. W. & West, K. R. (1967). Salt regulation in the mangroves *Rhizophora mucronata* Lam. and *Aegialitis annulata* R.Br. *Australian Journal of Biological Sciences*, **20**, 589–99.

Benzioni, A., Vaadia, Y. & Lips, H. (1971). Nitrate uptake by roots as regulated by nitrate reduction products of the shoot. *Physiologia Plantarum*, **24**, 288–90.

Black, R. F. (1960). Effects of NaCl on the ion uptake and growth of *Atriplex vesicaria* Heward. *Australian Journal of Biological Sciences*, **13**, 249–66.

Briggs, G. E., Hope, A. B. & Robertson, R. N. (1961). *Electrolytes and Plant Cells*. Blackwell, Oxford.

Caldwell, M. M. (1974). Physiology of desert halophytes. In: *Ecology of Halophytes* (ed. R. J. Reimold and W. H. Queen), pp. 355–78. Academic Press, London & New York.

Caldwell, M. M. & Camp, L. B. (1974). Belowground productivity of two cool desert communities. *Oecologia*, **17**, 123–30.

Carter, O. G. & Lathwell, D. J. (1967). Effect of chloride on phosphorous uptake by corn roots. *Agronomy Journal*, **59**, 250–53.

Charley, J. L. (1972). The role of shrubs in nutrient cycling. In: *Wildland Shrubs – Their Biology and Utilisation* (eds. C. M. McKell, J. P. Blaisdell & J. R. Goodin), pp. 182–203. USDA Forest Service, Ogden, Utah.

Charley, J. L. & Cowling, S. W. (1968). Changes in soil nutrient status resulting from overgrazing and their consequences in plant communities of semi-arid areas. *Proceedings of the Ecological Society of Australia*, **3**, 28–38.

Charley, J. L. & McGarity, J. W. (1964). High soil nitrate levels in patterned saltbush communities. *Nature (London)*, **201**, 1351–2.

Cram, W. J. (1973a). Chloride fluxes in cells of the isolated root cortex of *Zea mays*. *Australian Journal of Biological Sciences*, **26**, 757–79.

Cram, W. J. (1973b). Internal factors regulating nitrate and chloride influx in plant cells. *Journal of Experimental Botany*, **24**, 328–41.

Cram, W. J. (1974). The regulation of concentration and hydrostatic pressure in cells in relation to growth. In: *Mechanisms of Regulation of Plant Growth* (eds. R. L. Bieleski, A. R. Ferguson and M. M. Cresswell), Bull. 12, pp. 183–89. Royal Society of New Zealand, Wellington.

De Wit, C. T., Dijkshoorn, W. & Noggle, J. C. (1963). Ionic balance and the growth of plants. *Verslagen van Landbouwkundige Onderzoekingen, Wageningen*, **69** (15), 1–68.

Epstein, E. (1972). *Mineral Nutrition of Plants: Principles and Perspectives*, Wiley, New York.

Epstein, E., Rains, D. W, & Elzam, O. E. (1963). Resolution of dual mechanisms of potassium absorption by barley roots. *Proceedings National Academy Science of USA*, **49**, 684–92.

Gale, J., Naaman, R. & Poljakoff-Mayber, A. (1970). Growth of *Atriplex halimus* in sodium chloride salinated culture solutions as affected by the relative humidity of the air. *Australian Journal of Biological Sciences*, **23**, 947–52.

Gates, D. H., Stoddart, L. A. & Cook, C. W. (1956). Soil as a factor influencing plant distribution. *Ecological Monographs*, **26**, 151–75.

Goodin, J. R. & Mozafar, A. (1972). Physiology of salinity stress. In: *Wildland Shrubs – Their Biology and Utilisation* (eds. C. M. McKell, J. P. Blaisdell & J. R. Goodin), pp. 255–259. USDA Forest Service, Ogden, Utah.

Greenway, H. & Klepper, B. (1968). Phosphorus transport to the xylem and its regulation by water flow. *Planta*, **83**, 119–36.

Greenway, H. & Osmond, C. B. (1970). Ion relations, growth and metabolism of *Atriplex* at high external electrolyte concentrations. In: *The Biology of Atriplex* (ed. R. Jones), pp. 49–56. CSIRO, Melbourne.

Greenway, H. & Pitman, M. G. (1965). Potassium retranslocation in seedlings of *Hordeum vulgare*. *Australian Journal of Biological Sciences*, **18**, 237–47.

Greenway, H., Gunn, A. & Thomas, D. A. (1966). Plant response to saline substrates VIII. Regulation of ion concentrations in salt-sensitive and halophytic species. *Australian Journal of Biological Sciences*, **19**, 741–56.

Hodges, T. K. (1973). Ion absorption by plant roots. *Advances in Agronomy*, **25**, 163–207.

Jefferies, R. L. (1973). The ionic relations of seedlings of the halophyte *Triglochin maritima* L. In: *Ion Transport in Plants* (ed. W. P. Anderson), pp. 297–321. Academic Press, London & New York.

Jenny, H. (1966). Pathways of ions from soil into root according to diffusive models. *Plant and Soil*, **25**, 265–89.

Johansen, C., Edwards, D. G. & Loneragan, J. F. (1970). Potassium fluxes during potassium absorption by intact barley plants of increasing potassium content. *Plant Physiology*, **45**, 601–3.

Johansen, C. & Lüttge, U. (1974). Respiration and photosynthesis as alternative energy sources for chloride uptake by *Tradescantia albiflora* leaf cells. *Zeitschrift für Pflanzenphysiologie*, **71**, 189–99.

Kaplan, A. & Gale, J. (1972). Effect of sodium chloride salinity on the water balance of *Atriplex halimus*. *Australian Journal of Biological Sciences*, **25**, 895–903.

Laties, G. G. (1969). Dual mechanisms of salt uptake in relation to compartmentation and long-distance transport. *Annual Review of Plant Physiology*, **20**, 89–116.

Lüttge, U. (1971). Structure and function of plant glands. *Annual Review of Plant Physiology*, **22**, 23–44.

Lüttge, U. (1973). *Stofftransport der Pflanzen*, Springer, Berlin.

Lüttge, U. & Osmond, C. B. (1970). Ion absorption in *Atriplex* leaf tissue III. Site of metabolic control of light-dependent chloride secretion to epidermal bladders. *Australian Journal of Biological Sciences*, **23**, 17–25.

Plant processes

Lüttge, U. & Pitman, M. G. (eds.) (1976). *Ion transport in cells and tissues*, Encyclopedia of Plant Physiology, New Series. Springer, Berlin.

MacRobbie, E. A. C. (1971). Fluxes and compartmentation in plant cells. *Annual Review of Plant Physiology*, **22**, 72–96.

Moore, R. T., Breckle, S. W. & Caldwell, M. M. (1972). Mineral ion composition and osmotic relations of *Atriplex confertifolia* and *Eurotia lanata*. *Oecologia*, **11**, 67–78.

Mozafar, A., Goodin, J. R. & Oertli, J. J. (1970). Sodium and potassium interactions in increasing the salt tolerance of *Atriplex halimus* L. II. Na$^+$ and K$^+$ uptake characteristics. *Agronomy Journal*, **62**, 481–4.

Nissen, P. (1974). Uptake mechanisms; inorganic and organic. *Annual Review of Plant Physiology*, **25**, 53–79.

Oertli, J. J. (1968). Extracellular salt accumulation, a possible mechanism of salt injury in plants. *Agrochimica*, **12**, 461–9.

Osmond, C. B. (1966). Divalent cation absorption and interaction in *Atriplex*. *Australian Journal of Biological Sciences*, **19**, 37–48.

Osmond, C. B. (1967). Acid metabolism in *Atriplex*. I. Regulation of oxalate synthesis by the apparent excess cation absorption in leaf tissue. *Australian Journal of Biological Sciences*, **20**, 575–87.

Osmond, C. B. (1968). Ion absorption in *Atriplex* leaf tissue I. Absorption by leaf mesophyll cells. *Australian Journal of Biological Sciences*, **21**, 1119–30.

Osmond, C. B. (1976). Ion absorption and carbon metabolism in cells of higher plants. In: *Ion Transport in Cells and Tissues*, Encyclopedia of Plant Physiology, New Series, eds. U. Lüttge & M. G. Pitman. Springer, Berlin.

Osmond, C. B. & Laties, G. G. (1968). Interpretation of the dual isotherm for ion absorption in beet tissue. *Plant Physiology*, **43**, 747–55.

Osmond, C. B., Lüttge, U., West, K. R., Pallaghy, C. K. & Shacher-Hill, B. (1969). Ion absorption in *Atriplex* leaf tissue II. Secretion of ions to epidermal bladders. *Australian Journal of Biological Sciences*, **22**, 797–814.

Pitman, M. G. (1965). Transpiration and the selective uptake of potassium by barley seedlings (*Hordeum vulgare* cv. 'Bolivia'). *Australian Journal of Biological Sciences*, **18**, 987–98.

Pitman, M. G. (1966). Uptake of potassium and sodium by seedlings of *Sinapis alba*. *Australian Journal of Biological Sciences*, **19**, 257–69.

Pitman, M. G. (1969). Simulation of Cl$^-$ uptake by low salt barley roots as a test of models of salt uptake. *Plant Physiology*, **44**, 1417–27.

Pitman, M. G. (1971). Uptake and transport of ions in barley seedlings I. Estimation of chloride fluxes in cells of excised roots. *Australian Journal of Biological Sciences*, **24**, 407–21.

Pitman, M. G. (1972). Uptake and transport of ions in barley seedlings III. Correlation between transport to the shoot and relative growth rate. *Australian Journal of Biological Sciences*, **25**, 905–19.

Pitman, M. G., Courtice, A. C. & Lee, B. (1968). Comparison of potassium and sodium uptake by barley roots at high and low salt status. *Australian Journal of Biological Sciences*, **21**, 871 81.

Pitman, M. G., Lüttge, U., Kramer, D. & Ball, E. (1974). Free space characteristics of barley leaf slices. *Australian Journal of Plant Physiology*, **1**, 65–75.

Pitman, M. G., Lüttge, U., Lauchli, A. & Ball, E. (1974a). Effect of precious water stress on ion uptake and transport by barley seedlings. *Australian Journal of Plant Physiology*, **1**, 377–85.

Pitman, M. G., Lüttge, U., Lauchli, A. & Ball, E. (1974b). Action of abcisic acid on ion transport as affected by root temperature and nutrient status. *Journal of Experimental Botany*, **25**, 147–55.

Queen, W. H. (1974). Physiology of coastal halophytes. In: *Ecology of Halophytes* (eds. R. J. Reimold & W. H. Queen), pp. 345–54. Academic Press, London & New York.

Rains, D. W. (1972). Salt transport by plants in relation to salinity. *Annual Review of Plant Physiology*, **23**, 367–88.

Rains, D. W. & Epstein, E. (1967). Preferential absorption of potassium by leaf tissue of the mangrove *Avicennia marina*: an aspect of halophytic competence in coping with salt. *Australian Journal of Biological Sciences*, **20**, 847–57.

Robinson, J. B. (1971). Salinity and the whole plant. In: *Salinity and Water Use* (eds. T. Talsma & J. R. Philip), pp. 193–206. Macmillan, London.

Rodin, L. E. & Bazilevich, N. I. (1965). *Production and mineral cycling in terrestrial vegetation* (English translation ed. G. E. Fogg), pp. 288. Oliver & Boyd, Edinburgh.

Smith, F. A. & Robinson, J. B. (1971). Sodium and potassium influx into citrus leaf slices. *Australian Journal of Biological Sciences*, **24**, 861–71.

Smith, R. C. & Epstein, E. (1964). Ion absorption by shoot tissue: kinetics of potassium and rubidium absorption by corn leaf tissue. *Plant Physiology*, **39**, 992–6.

Spanswick, R. M. (1975). Symplastic transport in tissues. In: *Ion Transport in Cells and Tissues* (eds. U. Lüttge & M. G. Pitman), Encyclopedia of Plant Physiology, New Series. Springer, Berlin.

Tukey, H. B. (1970). The leaching of substances from plants. *Annual Review of Plant Physiology*, **21**, 305–24.

Tyree, M. T. (1970). The symplast concept, a general theory of symplastic transport according to the thermodynamics of irreversible processes. *Journal of Theoretical Biology*, **26**, 181–214.

Waisel, Y. (1972). *The Biology of Halophytes*, Academic Press, London & New York.

Manuscript received by the editors February 1975

25. Flowering, seed formation and dispersal

J. J. MOTT with an Appendix by P. CHOUARD

Introduction

As a higher plant matures it is capable of shifting from vegetative to reproductive growth, with the initiation of flowers, development of fruits and production of a new generation of seed. Each of these steps can be under the control of more or less systematic physiological mechanisms, and these in turn can be affected by environmental variables. In mesic environments, the flowering process is usually adapted to the seasonal climatic cycle, and individuals have a high probability of completing a successful reproductive cycle. However, desert environments are characterised by a rainfall which is not only scarce, but also frequently extremely irregular, both in timing and the amount it eventually contributes to soil moisture. As a result, water in amounts necessary to complete the reproductive cycle may become available without the seasonal periodicity that characterises wetter habitats. This variation in time can impose considerable constraints on the ability of the individual to produce seed successfully.

In considering the role of flowering in desert species, one must take into account the two main survival strategies of plants growing in arid conditions: drought tolerance, normally exhibited by perennial species; and drought avoidance, a strategy common in annual species (Levitt, 1972). An adequate supply of soil moisture is usually only available for relatively short periods in arid conditions, expecially in relation to the time required to complete the complex processes involved in flowering and the formation of new seeds (Salisbury, 1963; Amen, 1968). Under conditions of limited moisture the problems of annual plants are more pronounced than those for perennial species, as annuals must complete their entire life cycle before flowering. Among the annuals, emphasis has been placed on the role of selection for germination, and heterogeneity of the seed population, as being of prime importance for the survival of the populations in arid regions (Went, 1953; Koller, 1969; see also Chapter 19 above). In species with these adaptations, the reproductive capacity of the individual is considered to be incapable of being exhausted in a single attempt at establishment, allowing another chance for successful reproduction. However, in the case of some annual species from an arid area in Australia, once the requirements for germination had been satisfied the

627

majority of the seed store germinated, leaving little seed for further attempts at establishment, and thus emphasising the importance of successful reproduction in the survival of the population (Mott, 1972a, 1973).

Although rainfall is considered to be the overriding variable in arid lands, flowering can be under the control of other environmental agents, such as photoperiod and temperature. These variables and their possible interaction with soil moisture must be taken into account when the reproduction of desert species is considered.

Flowering responses to environmental variables may take two forms. One type of response may be represented by a step function – flowering does not occur until the controlling factor passes a certain threshold value, but when it does so the extent of the flowering response may be independent of this factor, and be controlled by others. The other type of response, usually termed 'quantitative', is represented by a continuous function, the quantity of flowers formed increasing continuously as the level of the factor changes. Both types of response may be combined, of course, the plant showing a quantitative response once a threshold value is exceeded.

Control of flowering by temperature and light

Arid zones are usually defined as areas where potential evaporation exceeds the average annual precipitation. Deserts are not confined to any particular latitude belt or position on a continent, but occur from the equator to well into the mid-latitudes with a consequent range of photoperiodic and temperature conditions (McGinnies, Goldman & Paylore, 1968).

In the Sonoran Desert, Went (1953) and Beatley (1967, 1974) reported a vernalisation requirement for several species of winter annuals, Beatley stating that the winter annuals 'do not differ in any known respect from winter annuals in humid regions of the continent'. Similar patterns were also found in the case of several herbaceous perennials. Thus, for optimum reproduction, the species must commence growth during autumn rains, and undergo some vernalisation during the winter months before flowering during the spring and summer. If autumn rains do not occur then little growth takes place in these species. However, rainfalls during late winter and early spring can give rise to reproductive growth in many shrubs and perennial grasses, indicating that vernalisation in these latter species is not obligatory. Winter rains can also lead to some successful germination and fruiting for the winter annuals, but generally winter temperatures are too low for successful germination. Evenari & Gutterman (1966) found no sign of obligate vernalisation in eighteen species of winter annuals from the Negev Desert of Israel, photoperiod apparently being the controlling factor. Zakharyants (1972) and Yu, Nasyrov, Labedeva & Kichitov (1972) reported a quantitative response to lower temperatures in winter annuals growing in Central Asian deserts, with optimal growth at 10 °C to 15 °C. Phenological studies in the field of a wide range of perennial grasses and shrubs growing in the warmer winters of the Australian arid zone also did not show any obligate requirement for vernalisation (Williams, 1971; Davies, 1973), and similar results were obtained in studies of winter annuals by Mott (1972b), although in some species there was a quantitative response to lower temperatures (Mott & McComb, 1975).

With summer rainfall, growth takes place in the warmer months. Negbi & Evenari (1962) reported the growth of five species of bi-seasonal annuals which germinate in winter, but do not flower until the following summer. These species appear to have a quantitative high-temperature requirement for flowering, as well as some photoperiodic control. Growth in some summer-germinating annuals from central Asia was also quantitatively stimulated by high temperatures (Yu *et al.*, 1972), and Mott & McComb (1975) found a quantitative decrease in the time to flowering at high temperature for a species growing after summer rainfall in Australia.

The importance of photoperiodic control of flowering has been reviewed by several authors and a variety of responses noted, usually relating to the environment under which the plant grows (Salisbury, 1963; Evans, 1969). In desert plants, phenological studies have shown that there is a wide variation in the flowering response to photoperiodic changes. Williams (1971) and Davies (1973) report that flowering occurs over a number of months for many perennial species in Australia, and Kassas (1966), Mott (1972b) and Davies (1973) noted species which may flower at any time throughout the year, depending only on availability of soil moisture. Beatley (1974) indicated that many perennials flower through the summer months, presumably in response to long days, but the ability of some grasses to flower during late autumn indicates a quantitative response. In the Appendix to this chapter (p. 640), Chouard reports studies on the photoperiodic responses of two species of the North African and Middle Eastern deserts, one of which (*Scrophularia arguta* Sol.) is of special interest in that it bears two morphologically distinct types of shoot which differ completely in their photoperiodic reactions.

Definitive studies of the photoperiodic responses of desert plants under controlled light duration are not common. Lewis & Went (1946) found a quantitative long-day response in seven winter annuals from Californian deserts, but all plants older than 100 days flowered, even under a photoperiod of 8 hours. Similar results were obtained by Evenari & Gutterman (1966), with twenty-one species of annuals from the Negev. Seventeen species had a quantitative photoperiodic response, fifteen winter annuals being long-day plants and two summer-growing species responding to short days. Another four winter annuals behaved as long-day plants under glasshouse conditions, but as day-neutral plants in the field. Joswik (1970) working on the perennial summer grasses *Astrebla* spp. in Australia, also reported a facultative response to photoperiodic changes, in this case to short days.

The facultative nature of both thermoinduction and photoinduction of flowering in many desert species has obvious advantages for their reproduction in an environment which has an erratic timing of the commencement of growth, as it enables plants to flower over a wide seasonal range of temperature and photoperiod, given sufficient soil moisture. However, the definite response of most species to some photoperiodic regime does not confirm Evenari's (1962) observation that light intensity may be critical in the control of flowering. Indeed, taking into consideration account the high radiation generally occurring throughout the year in tropical and Mediterranean deserts, it is difficult to conceive that light intensity may be important in the control of flowering in a population, although there may be some control of individuals in specific micro-environments where the light intensity is low due to shading.

The interaction between temperature and photoperiod can be an important factor in determining the flowering response. Evenari & Gutterman (1966) reported that, in two bi-seasonal species of *Salsola*, flowering was controlled by a quantitative response to both short days and high temperatures. Thus plants germinating during autumn or winter rains would not flower until late summer. In the case of *Hordeum bulbosum*, a perennial grass from semi-arid Mediterranean climates, there is a specialised interaction between environment and the type of regeneration (Ofir, Koller & Negbi, 1967; Ofir & Koller, 1974). The plant can flower after the winter growing season, and growth is resumed at the onset of the next growing season from specialised regeneration buds. The reproductive phase, which includes the formation of regeneration buds, requires both vernalisation and long days, thus occurring during late winter or spring. The regeneration buds, once formed, initially will not sprout under high temperatures. As time progresses growth will take place at higher temperatures, with the rate of activation increasing with temperature. In the field this temperature-sensitive dormancy of the regeneration bud prevents growth after summer storms, but allows growth under early autumn rainfall.

This interaction of photoinduction and thermoinduction of flowering is also well illustrated by the flowering responses of some annual species from an arid annual community in Australia. The species grow in a region which has a discrete summer and winter rainfall, leading to the formation of two distinct annual populations, a predominantly dicotyledon flora resulting from winter rains, while grasses form the majority of the species

630

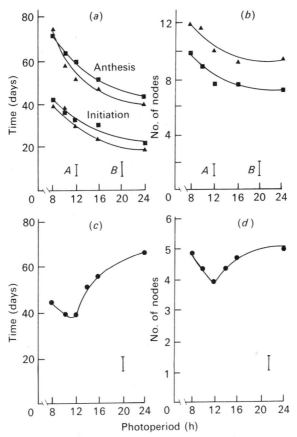

Fig. 25.1. The effect of photoperiod on time to anthesis and the number of nodes to first flower for (*a*) and (*b*) *Helichrysum cassinianum* (▲) and *Helipterum craspedioides* (■); (*c*) and (*d*) *Aristida contorta* (●). The vertical bars show the least significant differences (*P* = 0.05). In (*a*) and (*b*) L.S.D. for plants grown at photoperiods of 8–15 h are shown (*A*) and from 16–24 h (*B*). (From Mott & McComb, 1975.)

growing in summer (Mott, 1972*a*, 1973). The three species studied were the summer grass *Aristida contorta* and the two winter composites *Helipterum craspedioides* and *Helichrysum cassinianum*, which contributed the major part of the biomass. In all three species the response to photoperiod was quantitative, the composites exhibiting a long-day response, while the grass was an intermediate-day species with flowering delayed by either long or short photoperiod (Fig. 25.1). When plants were grown under a constant photoperiod of 16 hours, low temperatures accelerated the flowering process in the composites, reducing the number of nodes to flowering, although there was no obligate requirement for vernalisation. In *Aristida contorta*, low temperatures slowed growth and delayed flow-

Table 25.1. *Effect of temperature on number of nodes, shoot dry weight and time to anthesis for* Helipterum craspedioides, Helichrysum cassinianum *and* Aristida contorta

	Temperature régime (°C)						
Species	15	20	25	30	18/23	23/28	
	Number of nodes to first flower						
H. craspedioides	13.0	13.7	19.2	20.0	20.0	17.4	***
H. cassinianum	10.5	14.5	18.6	—	18.1	20.4	***
A. contorta	—	—	5.1	4.8	5.3	4.7	N.S.
	Days to anthesis						
H. craspedioides	59.4	49.9	54.9	60.0	49.7	60.0	N.S.
H. cassinianum	53.9	52.9	63.8	> 80.0	59.3	70.2	***
A. contorta	> 80.0	> 80.0	64.7	61.4	65.0	56.6	**
	Shoot dry weight at anthesis (mg)						
H. craspedioides	223	363	277	185	323	281	***
H. cassinianum	256	350	462	—	400	598	***
A. contorta	—	—	140	233	127	161	***

Each value is the mean of ten replicates. The photoperiod was 16 hours, and where alternating temperatures were used a 12-hour alternation was maintained.

Significance levels for the differences between temperature régimes (analysis of variance): *** $P < 0.001$; ** $P < 0.01$; N.S. not significant.

ering, and high alternating temperatures gave the shortest time to anthesis (Table 25.1).

Although the photoperiodic responses of the winter composites and the summer grass were quite different, photoperiodic requirements alone would not preclude flowering of the species at any time of the year in the field. Temperature is clearly important; the lower temperatures of winter and spring promoted the flowering of the composites, while the higher temperatures of summer favoured the development of the grass. On several occasions some 'out-of-season' plants occurred in the field, and after abnormally low soil temperatures during a summer rainfall event a considerable number of winter annuals germinated. However, even although soil moisture remained high for several weeks, there was almost total mortality among the unseasonal winter annuals, and no individuals survived to set seed, the only dicotyledons seeding in autumn being those which normally grew during the summer months (Table 25.2). Thus, even though plants could grow for some time in the field, the long period needed for anthesis under the high summer temperatures meant that plants died of moisture stress before flowering. Strict germination requirements for the annuals (Mott, 1972*a*, 1973) ensure that, with rare exceptions, the plants germinate at the season which provides the most satisfactory conditions for subsequent vegetative and reproductive growth.

Table 25.2. *Germination and survival to anthesis of annual plants in run-on and run-off areas in the Murchison region of Western Australia* (*totals from 20 quadrats of 1 dm²*) (From Mott, 1972)

Site	1969 (Winter)		1970 (Winter)		1971 (Summer)		1971 (Winter)	
	Number germi-nated	% Survival	Number germi-nated	% Survival	Number germi-nated	% Survival	Number germi-nated	% Survival
			Run-off plain					
Monocotyledons	27	26	70	87[1]	116	89	0	0
Dicotyledons	574	8	440	11	98	10	316	38
			Run-on channel					
Monocotyledons	22	27	12	100[1]	108	78	2	0
Dicotyledons	673	44	596	36	157	12	379	45

[1] Includes plants which had germinated following the initial count at germination.

The term 'ephemeral' has been applied to all annual plants growing in an arid region (Shreve, 1951), and many reviewers have emphasised the short-lived nature of desert annuals, implying that they all germinate and set seed within a short period of time (Shreve, 1951; Evenari, 1962; Kassas, 1966; Arnon, 1972). The general view is that the brevity of the life cycle enables plants to avoid moisture stress. However, although a few species do appear to be truly ephemeral, with a life cycle of 3 to 6 weeks (Cloudsley-Thompson & Chadwick, 1964), the majority of annuals require much longer before seeding occurs. Tevis (1958a), Klikoff (1966) and Beatley (1967, 1974), in studies on annuals growing in the deserts of North America, found that winter annuals took from 5 to 8 months before setting seed, while summer annuals had a life cycle of at least 8 to 10 weeks before seed-set. Negbi & Evenari (1962) and Evenari & Gutterman (1966) found that winter annuals in the Negev take from 6 to 8 months to set seed. Mott (1972b) found that winter annuals in the Australian arid zone took at least 3 to 4 months to set seed, and summer annuals from 8 to 10 weeks before the first seeds matured. In many cases it appears that annuals need more time to set seed than one could expect the soil to remain moist, and thus they may have to undergo some moisture stress before the end of their life cycle.

Soil moisture, flowering and seed production

The importance of rainfall events in determining flowering of both annual and perennial plants in arid regions has been documented by many authors (Went, 1953, 1955; Evenari, 1962; Kassas, 1966; Koller, 1969). Rainfall events have often been found to lead to the flowering of perennials, and to the germination and subsequent flowering of annuals, provided that the seasonal requirements mentioned in the previous section have been satisfied. However, the irregularity of rainfall in both amount and timing would appear to lead to a high probability that plants will undergo some moisture stress during the reproductive cycle.

Field observations on perennials have shown that in some cases moisture deficit can delay flowering (Bykov, 1974). This delay can be for a considerable period, and Bykov found that flowering of *Artemisia pauciflora* could be delayed for up to 4 weeks. In extremely dry years, complete failure of successful fruiting, or both flowering and fruiting, has been reported for the perennials of many areas (Zohary, 1962; Davies, 1968, 1973; Kassas, 1966; Sankary & Barbour, 1972; Beatley, 1974; Bykov, 1974).

There is only a limited amount of information on the influence of moisture stress on the flowering of desert plants, and most of this concerns annuals (Tevis, 1958a; Klikoff, 1966; Mott, 1972b, 1973). However, Davies (1968, 1973) reported long-term phenological observations on several perennial species in an arid area of Australia. In the case of the dominant perennial shrub *Acacia aneura* Davies found that, although flowering could occur after rainfall in any season, only those flowers resulting from summer rainfall produced fruit, and that a significant quantity of mature fruit resulted only when good rains occurred in the following winter.

Preece (1971), working on another population of *A. aneura*, tested the effects of irrigation on individuals in the field, and although the results were equivocal they agreed with those of Davies. Using the criterion that summer rainfall followed by winter falls was necessary for successful reproduction, Preece analysed approximately 80 years of rainfall data for several sites and found that only in 10% to 15% of these years would seeding take place.

The great variation in size of mature individuals in populations of desert annuals has often been commented on (Evenari, 1962; Kassas, 1966; Arnon, 1972), and it is generally accepted that the main cause is moisture stress, although there may be some subsidiary factors such as genetic differences between individuals. Evenari (1962) put forward the hypothesis that the variation in size may be due, not to a generalised stress on the whole plant, but to a hormonal control of growth, as he had observed that young seedlings developed size differences even while growing in areas with similar soil moisture content. He raised the possibility that the depth of water penetration may be the controlling factor; once growing roots have encountered a dry zone, they may exert some hormonal control of the vegetative apex. Although this type of control remains an hypothesis, I have noted a similar variation in size of seedlings growing in areas with a high soil-moisture content in an annual community in

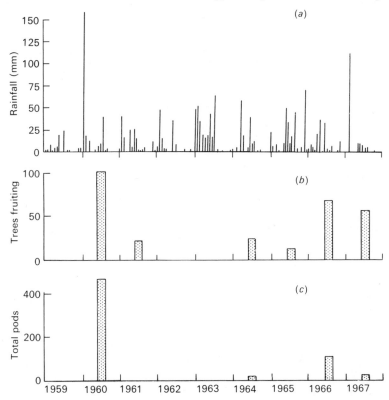

Fig. 25.2. Fruit production in *Acacia aneura* in an arid area of Western Australia. (*a*) Rainfall in 20-day periods. (*b*) Percentage of marked trees in September each year. (*c*) Total number of pods collected in 0.6 m × 0.6 m trays beneath twenty-five marked trees each year. No observations were made of the trees in 1962 and 1963. (From Davies, 1968.)

Australia (Mott & McComb, 1974). In this case the variation in size could be correlated with different nutrient content between the sites, and laboratory experiments supported this hypothesis (Mott, 1972*b*).

Went (1948, 1953) emphasised the importance of environmental conditions at germination for the survival of desert annuals, and concluded that, once germinated, individuals usually reach maturity if only as depauperate and barely reproductive individuals. He also stated that 'after heavy rains the plants remain vegetative for some time, and start to flower only after a considerable size is reached. After the lightest rain which just allows germination, the plants almost immediately change over to the reproductive stage, and thus remain diminutive', implying that moisture stress may reduce the interval to reproduction. For annual plants growing under the dry conditions of arid areas, any reduction in the time to anthesis as a response to moisture stress would appear to have the

635

Table 25.3. *Effect of water stress on the number of nodes to first flower,
time to anthesis, seedling and senescence of* Helipterum craspedioides,
Helichrysum cassinianum *and* Aristida contorta

	Soil moisture content (Field capacity)			L.S.D. ($P = 0.05$)
	15%	10%	7%	
	Number of nodes to first flower			
H. craspedioides	10.4	10.4	10.0	0.5
H. cassinianum	10.8	10.5	9.2	0.6
	Days to anthesis			
H. craspedioides	43.8	42.0	46.6	4.6
H. cassinianum	49.4	56.0	49.0	10.6
A. contorta	51.2	47.4	56.2	6.6
	Days to start of seedling			
H. craspedioides	68.0	67.6	64.8	4.4
H. cassinianum	111.8	106.0	101.0	12.5
A. contorta	114.4	100.0	113.6	5.1
	Days to senescence of leaves			
H. craspedioides	107.2	102.2	78.8	5.1
H. cassinianum	99.6	89.9	81.4	9.5
A. contorta	132+[1]	132+[1]	123.2	

[1] Plants had not senesced at the end of the experiment.
Each value is the mean of 10 replicates grown under glasshouse conditions with a
photoperiod of 18 hours. L.S.D. is least significant difference.

selective advantage of increasing the likelihood of satisfactory seed-set.
But Koller (1969) points out that there are no indications that the onset
of soil moisture stress may promote flowering.

The majority of definitive experiments concerned with the effect of
moisture stress have been carried out using crop plants, and have been
reported in reviews by Salter & Goode (1967) and Slatyer (1969, 1973).
Few data are available on native species and these are mainly from humid
environments (Jarvis, 1963; Newman, 1965, 1967). These studies have
shown that moisture stress has little effect on the time to initiation, or
slightly delays it, but may decrease the physiologic age of the plant at
initiation. In a few species a slight decrease in the time from initiation
to anthesis has been noted, but normally there is an increase in the time
from initiation to flowering. Klikoff (1966), in a detailed field study of the
annual *Plantago insularis* in the Sonoran Desert, found that under high
moisture stress there was a slight delay in the time to flowering. Mott
(1972b) noted no significant change in the time to seeding for plants under
moisture stress in the field, and Bykov (1974) reported similar results for
desert annual communities near the Caspian Sea.

Table 25.4. *Effect of water stress on numbers of seeds, weight of seeds, and seed germinability in* Helipterum craspedioides, Helichrysum cassinianum *and* Aristida contorta

	Soil moisture content (Field capacity)			L.S.D. ($P = 0.05$)
	15%	10%	7%	
	Number of seeds per plant			
H. craspedioides	37.4	18.2	8.0	16.5
H. cassinianum	21.4	13.8	9.4	7.1
A. contorta	13.6	27.0	4.6	6.7
	Weight of individual seeds (mg)			
H. craspedioides	3.1	3.1	2.4	0.4
H. cassinianum	8.2	9.5	6.5	0.9
A. contorta	2.4	2.5	2.2	0.3
	Percentage germination			
H. craspedioides	12	12	6	1.3
H. cassinianum	18	26	5	1.8
A. contorta	40	42	0	4.9

Each value is the mean of 10 plant replicates or, in germination trials, of four replicates each of 25 seeds. L.S.D. is least significant difference.

The effects of moisture stress on flowering were investigated under laboratory conditions of constant soil moisture with the three annual species *Helipterum craspedioides, Helichrysum cassinianum* and *Aristida contorta* (Table 25.3). There was no reduction in the time to anthesis or the commencement of seeding in any of the three species, even although the level of stress used had marked effects on relative turgidity and plant growth. The only change was a slight decrease in the number of nodes formed – that is, a reduction in the physiologic age – at the commencement of anthesis in one of the composites.

The reduction of seed production under drought conditions has been noted for field populations of many arid-zone annuals, and a similar reduction was found for the two composites under all levels of moisture stress imposed in the laboratory (Table 25.4). An increase was noted in the number of seeds formed by *Aristida contorta* under mild moisture stress, and it appears that this species does not grow well at the moisture levels near field capacity maintained in the unstressed controls. However, at the highest stress a reduction in seed production similar to that in the two composites was observed. In all these species the main effect of soil moisture stress was on the number of primordia formed. This is similar to the effect of moisture stress on a number of cereals (Aspinal, Nicholls & May, 1964; Wells & Dubetz, 1966; Bingham, 1967). The early death of

637

the plants would contribute to the lower total number of flowers and eventually seeds, but this is a subsidiary cause of reduced seed production in these species, not the major factor as found by Newman (1967) with *Teesdalia nudicaulis*. This high moisture stress also greatly reduced the dry matter production, and in all species seeds set by the plants growing under high moisture stress were found to have significantly lower germination percentages than those produced by unstressed plants. The reduction in seed weight was similar to that reported in cereals (Aspinall *et al.*, 1964; Salter & Goode, 1967).

There are a number of physiological differences between desert plants and those growing in more mesic environments, and these could help the individuals to withstand some degree of moisture stress (for instance, ability to hold water at low leaf water potentials (Slatyer, 1960; Connor & Tunstall, 1968); photosynthetic activity at high moisture stress (Hellmuth, 1971; Kappen *et al.*, 1972)). However, it appears that there are few specific adaptations evident in the reproductive processes of arid-zone species, the response to moisture stress being essentially the same as that exhibited by plants growing in more mesic environments. Some recent work by Dina & Klikoff (1974) does indicate that there may be a more rapid accumulation of carbohydrate reserves in the desert annual *Plantago insularis* than in annuals native to wetter regions. This more rapid accumulation would allow the earlier formation of mature seeds once successful fertilization had taken place. But generally it appears that the success of reproduction depends on some moisture being available throughout the cycle. In this respect the spatial redistribution of water after rainfall could be important in yielding areas of higher moisture content, producing more favourable conditions for growth. This movement of water has been reported for many desert areas (Zohary, 1962; Kassas, 1966; Koller, 1969), and in an annual community in Australia it appears that the redistribution of rainfall is essential in maintaining the population in some drought years (Mott, 1973; Mott & McComb, 1974). The concentration of water into washes enabled plants in these more favourable environments to set seed, although few individuals in the rest of the community matured. As most of the soil store of seed had germinated in the initial rains, the wetter sites acted as 'reservoir areas' and plants recolonised the drier run-off areas by wind-blown seed.

Seed dispersal

A large number of seed-dispersal mechanisms have been described in the course of studies on the germination behaviour of arid-zone species. These mechanisms involve vectors which are common to those operating in more mesic environments, including wind (Cloudsley-Thompson & Chadwick,

1964; Koller, 1969), water (Went, 1955) and animals (Fahn & Werker, 1972), particularly ants (Tevis, 1958b; Nordhagen, 1959). Seed dispersal in arid communities falls into two classes: widespread dispersal, often of large numbers of seeds, to enable the exploitation of a number of potential sites; and little movement of seed from the parent plant, facilitating the utilisation of a habitat proved to be favourable by the ability of the parent plant to set viable seed. Secondary dispersal of plants can be under the control of allelopathic restriction of germination by parental or other individuals (Knipe & Herbel, 1966).

The interaction of two dispersal types enabling survival over a wide range of conditions is shown in two amphicarpic annual species. These species are *Gymnarrhena micrantha* (Koller & Roth, 1964; Koller, 1969) and *Scrophularia arguta* (studied by Chouard and his students and reported in the Appendix to this chapter, p. 640). Both species have two morphologically distinct inflorescences which in turn produce two types of seed, one adapted to germinating in close proximity to the parental plant, lacking dormancy and ensuring survival in drought conditions, while the other seeds are dispersal units adapted for widespread aerial dispersal during favourable rainfall.

Finally, as noted in the previous section, effective seed dispersal, especially in annuals, may enable a population to exploit an area with only a few sites suitable for reproduction during drought, by means of recolonisation of the drier areas from seed formed by plants growing on reservoir sites with more favourable soil moisture.

Conclusion

It appears that, in many arid-zone species, there is little obligate temperature or photoperiodic requirement for flowering. Thus anthesis can take place over a wide seasonal range, limited only by the availability of soil moisture. However, as in many mesic species, moisture stress tends to retard flowering and reduce the reproductive output of the individual, which shows no specific adaptation of reproduction to an environment where moisture stress is the limiting factor. Thus, under arid conditions several years may elapse between successful reproductive events in perennial species, and many individuals in annual populations may die before seed is set.

In contrast with the extensive literature concerning mechanisms for controlling germination in arid-zone species (Barton, 1965; Koller, 1964, 1969, 1972), little work has been carried out on the control of the flowering process by the environment. Field observation can be difficult in view of the possibility of a long time interval between successive flowering events under drought conditions, and definitive studies under controlled conditions are also difficult because of the problems involved in the study of plants growing under the stressed conditions frequently occurring in low-rainfall regions. However, reasons for the success or otherwise of reproduction can be essential to the understanding of the dynamics of plant populations, especially those of annual species, and it is important to continue autecological studies of important species as well as long-term studies on the phenology and production of field populations.

Appendix: flowering and morphogenesis in two desert species

Scrophularia arguta Sol.

Little detailed work has been carried out on amphicarpic plants. However, one species, *Scrophularia arguta* Sol., has been studied in some depth. This plant is an annual, growing on the sheltered north side of rocks and in small fissures in the semi-arid and arid areas of the northern Sahel and Sahara.

In this species, buds forming in the axils of cotyledons and basal leaves produce long slender plagiotropic stems, bearing alternate, thin, sessile bracts (microphylls), and one flower head, yielding very small seeds. The main stem of the plant is strong and erect, bearing opposite leaves with long petioles (macrophylls), and terminating in a large inflorescence forming non-dormant seeds, which can germinate throughout the year. Normally the seeds formed in the apical inflorescences are widely dispersed by the wind, but in droughts seeds are only formed in the basal inflorescences, and these seeds are deposited in the niches in which the plant grows. These seeds then germinate and grow in the same site as the parent plant.

Early information was obtained using simple controlled environments (Chouard & Lourtioux, 1959). Under these conditions the plagiotropic microphyllous stems were day-neutral in their flowering response, while the macrophyllous apical inflorescences had a quantitative long-day requirement under high light intensities, and an obligate long-day response under low-intensity light. Thus, two different photoperiodic requirements occurred in a single individual on different stems.

If the plant is decapitated, even close to the cotyledons, the highest pair of buds remaining grow to form a macrophyllous-type inflorescence with a long-day response. This metamophosis occurs even if the buds would normally have formed plagiotropic lower stems, and inflorescences indifferent to photoperiod. When decapitation takes place after the formation of slender lower stems and day-neutral flowers, these basal stems progressively change into a macrophyllous stem with a long-day requirement for flowering.

More detailed work has been carried out by Miginiac (1970, 1973) using excised portions of seedlings cultured *in vitro*. Fragments containing the cotyledons, their axillary buds and 5 mm of epicotyl and hypocotyl were cultured in agar. Miginiac observed that, if adventitious roots had formed on the hypocotyl, then the stems formed from the cotyledonary buds were small and erect, resembling macrophyllous stems, and with the same long-day requirement for flowering. However, if the adventitious roots were cut as soon as possible, then microphyllous stems with day-neutral flowers resulted. Since the plants were cultured *in vitro*, material absorbed by the adventitious roots could have no effect on growth, and it appears that the roots influenced growth by hormones released from the growing apices. Further work showed that cytokinins could cause a similar change in the shoot apex to that caused by intact adventitious roots.

If the apical bud is present in such preparations, then a macrophyllous stem results, and the auxin formed by the apical bud counteracts the morphogenetic effects of roots on the basal buds.

Thus, developmental changes as well as growth correlations can be caused by hormone production and translocation. Further examples are given by Miginiac (1970). Another short-day plant in which decapitation experiments were effective in preventing flowering was *Chenopodium polyspermum* L., a mesic plant growing on the borders of ponds in temperate areas.

Artemisia herba-alba Asso.

The perennial shrub *Artemisia herba-alba* Asso. is an important fodder species in the semi-deserts on the northern side of the Sahara–Sind desert, and in arid areas of Spain. Pourrat (1974), working under controlled conditions, found a short-day requirement for flowering, and that the leaf shape could vary greatly, depending on the environment in the phytotron and the age of the plant. In the field the plants are normally long-day plants, flowering during autumn, because of the large number of long days required for induction (*cf. Inula glutinosa* Pers. in the Mediterranean countries), as well as delays due to drought. Dormancy in the seed changes with maturation of the caryopsis, and the timing and amount of winter rainfall.

References

Amen, R. D. (1968). A model of seed dormancy. *Botanical Review*, **34**, 1–31.
Arnon, I. (1972). *Crop production in Dry Regions, vol. 1. Background and principles*. Leonard Hill, London.
Aspinall, D., Nicholls, D. & May, L. (1964). The effects of soil moisture stress on the growth of barley. *Australian Journal of Agricultural Research*, **15**, 729–45.

Plant processes

Barton, L. V. (1965). Seed dormancy: general survey of dormancy types in seeds and dormancy imposed by external agents. In: *Encyclopedia of Plant Physiology* (ed. W. Ruhland), **15** (2), 699–720.

Beatley, J. C. (1967). Survival of annuals in the northern Mojave Desert. *Ecology*, **48**, 745–50.

Beatley, J. C. (1974). Phenological events and their environmental triggers in Mojave Desert ecosystems. *Ecology*, **55**, 856–63.

Bingham, J. (1967). Investigations on the physiology of yield in winter wheat by comparisons of varieties and by artificial variation in grain numbers per ear. *Journal of Agricultural Science*, **68**, 411–22.

Bykov, B. A. (1974). Fluctuations in the semidesert and desert vegetation of the Turanian plain. In: *Vegetation Dynamics* (ed. R. Knapp), *Handbook of Vegetation Science* vol. 8. Junk. The Hague.

Chouard, P. & Lourtioux, A. (1959). Corrélations et réversions de mise à fleurs chez la plante amphicarpique *Scrofularia arguta* Sol. *Compte Rendu de l'Académie des Sciences, Paris*, **249**, 889–91.

Cloudsley-Thompson, J. L. & Chadwick, M. J. (1964). *Life in Deserts*. Dufour Editions, Philadelphia.

Connor, D. J. & Tunstall, B. R. (1968). Tissue water relations for brigalow and mulga. *Australian Journal of Botany*, **16**, 487–90.

Davies, S. J. J. F. (1968). Aspects of a study of emus in semi-arid Western Australia. *Proceedings of the Ecological Society of Australia*, **3**, 160–66.

Davies, S. J. J. F. (1973). Environmental variables and the biology of native Australian animals in the mulga lands. *Tropical Grasslands*, **7**, 127–34.

Dina, S. J. & Klikoff, L. G. (1974). Carbohydrate cycle of *Plantago insularis* var. *fastigiata*, a winter annual from the Sonoran Desert. *Botanical Gazette*, **135**, 13–18.

Evans, L. T. (1969). *The induction of flowering*. Cornell University Press, Ithaca, New York.

Evenari, M. (1962). Plant physiology and arid zone research. *The problems of the arid zone. Proceedilngs of the Paris Symposium*, pp. 175–95. UNESCO, Paris.

Evenari, M. & Gutterman, Y. (1966). The photoperiodic responses of some desert plants. *Zeitschrift für Pflanzenphysiologie*, **54**, 7–27.

Fahn, A. & Werker, E. (1972). Anatomical mechanisms of seed dispersal. In: *Seed Biology* (ed. T. T. Kozlowski), pp. 151–221. Physiological Ecology series. Academic Press, London & New York.

Hellmuth, E. O. (1971). Ecophysiological studies on plants in arid and semi-arid regions in Western Australia. III. Comparative studies on photosynthesis, respiration and water relations of ten arid zone and two semi-arid zone plants under winter and late summer climatic conditions. *Journal of Ecology*, **59**, 225–59.

Jarvis, M. S. (1963). A comparison between the water relations of species with contrasting types of geographical distribution in the British Isles. In *The water relations of plants*, pp. 289–312 (ed. A. J. Rutter and F. H. Whitehead). Blackwell Scientific, Oxford.

Jozwik, F. X. (1970). Response of Mitchell grasses (*Astrebla* F. Muell.) to photo period and temperature. *Australian Journal of Agricultural Research*, **21**, 395–405.

Kappen, I., Lange, O., Schulze, E., Evenari, M. & Buschbaum, U. (1972). Extreme water stress and photosynthetic activity of the desert plant *Artemisia herba-alba*. *Oecologia (Berl.)*, **10**, 177–82.

Kassas, M. (1966). Plant life in deserts. In: *Arid Lands: A geographical appraisal* (ed. E. Hills), pp. 145–80. Methuen, London.

Klikoff, L. G. (1966). Competitive response to moisture stress of a winter annual of the Sonoran Desert. *American Midland Naturalist*, **75**, 383–91.

Knipe, O. D. & Herbel, C. H. (1966). Germination and growth of some semi-desert grassland species treated with aqueous extract from creosote bush. *Ecology*, **47**, 775–81.

Koller, D. (1964). The survival value of germination-regulating mechanisms in the field. *Herbage Abstracts*, **34**, 1–7.

Koller, D. (1969). The physiology of dormancy and survival of plants in desert environments. In: *Dormancy and Survival* (ed. H. W. Woolhouse). Symposia of the Society of Experimental Biology, XXIII, 449–69. Cambridge University Press, Cambridge.

Koller, D. (1972). Environmental control of seed germination. In: *Seed Biology* (ed. T. T. Kozlowski), vol. 2, pp. 1–101. Physiological Ecology Series. Academic Press, London & New York.

Koller, D. & Roth, N. (1964). Studies on the ecological and physiological significance of amphicarpy in *Gymnarrhena micrantha* (Compositae). *American Journal of Botany*, **51**, 26–35.

Levitt, J., (1972). *Response of plants to environmental stresses*. Physiological Ecology Series. Academic Press, London & New York.

Lewis, H. & Went, F. W. (1946). Plant growth under controlled conditions. IV. Response of California annuals to photoperiod and temperature. *American Journal of Botany*, **32**, 1–12.

McGinnies, W. G., Goldman, B. J. & Paylore, P. (eds.) (1968). *Deserts of the World. An appraisal of research into their physical and biological environments*. University of Arizona Press, Tucson.

Miginiac, E. (1970). Influence des corrélations entre organes sur la croissance et le développement floral des bourgeons cotylédonaires chez la *Scrofularia arguta* Sol. *Biologia plantarum*, **12**, 64–70.

Miginiac, E. (1973). 'Mise à fleurs et corrélations entre organes chez la *Scrofularia arguta* Sol.' Thèse Doct. ès Sc., Paris VI (CNRS, A.O. 82 42).

Mott, J. J. (1972*a*). Germination studies on some annual species from an arid region of Western Australia. *Journal of Ecology*, **60**, 293–304.

Mott, J. J. (1972*b*). 'The autecology of annuals in an arid region of Western Australia.' Ph.D. Thesis, University of Western Australia, Perth.

Mott, J. J. (1973). Temporal and spatial distribution of an annual flora in an arid region of Western Australia. *Tropical Grasslands*, **7**, 89–97.

Mott, J. J. & McComb, A. J. (1974). Patterns in annual vegetation and soil microrelief in an arid region of Western Australia. *Journal of Ecology*, **62**, 115–16.

Mott, J. J. & McComb, A. J. (1975). The role of photoperiod and temperature in controlling the phenology of three annual species from an arid region of Western Australia. *Journal of Ecology*, **63**, 633–41.

Negbi, M. & Evenari, M. (1962). The means of survival of some desert summer annuals. In: *Plant–work relationships in arid and semi-arid conditions. Proceedings of the Madrid Symposium*, pp. 249–57. UNESCO, Paris.

Newman, E. I. (1965). Factors affecting the seed production of *Teesdalia nudicaulis*. 1. Soil moisture in spring. *Journal of Ecology*, **53**, 211–32.

Newman, E. I. (1967). Response of *Aira praecox* to weather conditions. 1. Response to drought in spring. *Journal of Ecology*, **55**, 539–66.

Plant processes

Nordhagen, R. (1959). Remarks on some new or little known myrmecochorous plants from North America and East Asia. *Bulletin of the Research Council of Israel*, 7D 184–9.

Ofir, M. & Koller, D. (1974). Relationships between thermoinduction and photo-induction of flowering and dormancy in *Hordeum bulbosum* L., a perennial grass. *Australian Journal of Plant Physiology*, **1**, 259–70.

Ofir, M., Koller, D. & Negbi, M. (1967). Studies on the physiology of regeneration buds of *Hordeum bulbosum*. *Botanical Gazette*, **128**, 25–34.

Polunin, N. (1960). *Introduction to plant geography and some related sciences*. Longmans, Green, London.

Pourrat, Y. (1974). 'Propriétés d'écophysiologie associées à l'adaptation d'*Artemisia herba-alba*, plante d'intérêt pastoral en milieu désertique.' Univ. Paris VI, Thèse de Physiologie végétale.

Preece, P. B. (1971). Contributions to the biology of mulga. 1. Flowering. *Australian Journal of Botany*, **19**, 21–38.

Salisbury, F. B. (1963). *The Flowering Process*. Pergamon, Oxford.

Salter, P. J. & Goode, J. E. (1967). *Crop responses to water at different stages of growth*. Commonwealth Bureau of Horticultural and Plantation Crops. East Malling, Maidstone, Kent.

Sankary, M. N. & Barbour, M. G. (1972). Autecology of *Haloxylon articulatum* in Syria. *Journal of Ecology*, **60**, 697–712.

Shreve, F. (1951). *Vegetation of the Sonoran Desert*. Carnegie Institution of Washington Publication No. 591, Washington D.C.

Slatyer, R. O. (1960). Aspects of tissue water relationships of an important arid zone species (*Acacia aneura* F. Muell.) in comparison with two mesophytes. *Bulletin of the Research Council of Israel*, **8D**, 159–68.

Slatyer, R. O. (1969). Physiological significance of internal water relations to crop yield. In: *Physiological aspects of Crop Yield*, pp. 53–8. The American Society of Agronomy and Crop Science Society of America, Madison, Wisconsin.

Slayter, R. O. (1973). The effect of internal water status on plant growth, development and yield. Plant response to climatic factors. *Proceedings of Uppsala symposium*, pp. 177–91. UNESCO, Paris.

Tevis, L. (1958a). Germination and growth of ephemerals induced by sprinkling a sandy desert. *Ecology*, **39**, 681–8.

Tevis, L. (1958b). Interrelations between the harvester ant *Veromessor pergandei* Mayr and some desert ephemerals. *Ecology*, **39**, 695–704.

Wells, S. A. & Dubetz, S. (1966). Reaction of barley varieties to soil water stress. *Canadian Journal of Plant Science*, **46**, 507–12.

Went, F. W. (1948). Ecology of Desert Plants. 1. Observations on germination in the Joshua Tree National Monument, California. *Ecology*, **30**, 1–13.

Went, F. W. (1953). The effects of rain and temperature on plant distribution in the desert. In: *Desert Research*, pp. 232–37. Research Council of Israel, Special Publication No. 2.

Went, F. W. (1955). The Ecology of Desert Plants. *Scientific American*, **193**, 68–72.

Williams, O. B. (1971). Phenology of species common to three semi-arid grasslands. *Proceedings of the Linnean Society of New South Wales*, **96**, 193–203.

Yu, S., Nasyrov, G. P., Labedeva, V. K. & Kichitov (1972). Photosynthesis in desert plants of Tajikistan. In: *Ecophysiological foundation of ecosystems productivity in arid zone*, pp. 9–11. Nauka, Leningrad.

Zakharyants, I. L. (1972). Characteristic features of photosynthesis in Kyzyl-kum Desert plants. In: *Ecophysiological foundation of ecosystems productivity in arid zone*, pp. 6–9. Nauka, Leningrad.

Zohary, M. (1962). On hydro-ecological relations of the Near East desert vegetation. In: *Plant water relationships in arid and semi-arid conditions*. Proceedings of the Madrid symposium, pp. 199–210. UNESCO, Paris.

Manuscript received by the editors March 1975

26. Formation, distribution and function of plant litter in desert ecosystems

N. E. WEST

Introduction

Plant litter plays important roles in terrestrial ecosystems, especially in nutrient cycling and energy flow (Wiegert, Coleman & Odum, 1970). Litter also modifies the microclimate and chemical characteristics of the soil. All these functions influence the productivity and regeneration of ecosystems (Medwecka-Kornas, 1970, 1971). For these reasons litter has been studied extensively in the more mesic environments of the world, especially forests (Bray & Gorham, 1964). The structure and function of the litter component of desert ecosystems have, however, been little investigated and the literature has not been comprehensively reviewed heretofore.

Rodin & Bazilevich (1967) have reviewed the available literature on phytomass and standing crops of different elements. Their data include estimates of litter production for Syrian and Russian deserts. Until interest in various ecophysiological and nutrient-cycling phenomena began to emerge in recent years, particularly in integrated ecosystem research programs under the IBP, little attention was given elsewhere in the world to desert plant litter.

Definitions

Although many think of plant litter as synonymous with fallen leaves, in a broader sense litter is the accumulation of *all* dead remains of plants, before it is converted into humus.

In practice, the term litter is usually applied only to the *horizontal* accumulation of organic matter recognizable as to origin and lying on the soil surface. Dead material which has not yet fallen is usually called 'standing dead'. These restrictions of definition cause some special problems in deserts. For instance, underground litter from aerial plant organs is rarely mentioned in the literature, but can be an important component of desert ecosystems (Holmgren & Brewster, 1972).

The Soviet literature, summarized by Rodin & Bazilevich (1967), includes as litter the dead wood in standing live trees and shrubs, and all dead non-functioning roots, attached or not. Independent vertical standing-dead

647

material is also sometimes considered as part of the litter component of ecosystems since it similarly fits the concepts of energy flow and nutrient cycling. Because the term is so ill-defined, one must carefully consider the authors' definition of litter whenever making comparisons between published results.

The standing crop of litter or necromass is that amount present at any particular time in a given area. It is usually measured at the end of a distinct season of production, for instance after leaf fall during a drought period. Litter production constitutes the gross rate of input to the litter compartment. Decomposition, animal consumption, wind transport, and harvest by man continually cause losses from the standing crop, the net accumulation or accretion rate being the balance between input and the sum of these outputs.

By 'litter fall' is meant the transfer of plant material from the living to non-living state. Of the net primary production, a part is used as increments to the living plant structure; part is lost through herbivory, in which lagomorphs, rodents and insects usually play the largest part in the absence of domestic livestock; leaching and volatilization also lead to small losses; the remainder constitutes the input to the plant litter compartment. Trampling and wastage may accelerate litter production.

Litter is consumed by a variety of invertebrate detritivores. If left in place, it eventually disappears by weathering and the activities of decomposer organisms. In deserts, litter is macerated rather than humified, and rapid oxidation occurs.

Litter may be divided as to its age and degree of decay into: L, fresh organic material; F, partly decomposed litter; and H, amorphous litter layers. These layers were previously designated $A_{0'}$, $A_{0''}$, and $A_{0'''}$ respectively (Medwecka-Kornas, 1971). The American convention is to distinguish 01 and 02 horizons. The origin of organic matter is recognizable with the naked eye in the former horizon, but not in the latter (Soil Survey Staff, 1960). When plant parts become unrecognizable as to origin, the litter is regarded as having been converted into soil organic matter or humus, and one speaks of the soil surface (A horizons).

Character of desert litter

In desert regions litter is usually sparse, rarely forming a continuous surface layer. It is derived mostly from shrubs and herbaceous plants, particularly annuals. Ordinarily, litter consists of dead leaves, bud scales, woody twigs, herbaceous stems, bark and inflorescences. Pollen, fruit and fallen seeds are also sometimes included in the litter fraction. Cryptogamic plant inputs have rarely been considered, but should be included if a complete assessment is desired.

Table 26.1. *Distribution of plant litter in a community in southeastern Washington dominated by* Artemisia tridentata *(Rickard & Cline, 1970)*

Mean±standard deviation; sample size, 22 plots	
Litter between shrubs (67% of ground area) 15.72 g m^{-2}±16.04	Litter beneath shrubs (23% of ground area) 234.65 g m^{-2}±113.47

Although similar processes go on beneath the soil surface, rates of belowground death and deterioration have rarely been studied. We will confine further discussion to aboveground litter. The reader is referred to Chapter 23 where Drew has reviewed what is known about belowground plant biomass dynamics in deserts.

Litter patterns

Spatial patterns

The low stature and widely scattered nature of individual plants in most desert communities has made the estimation of standing crops and production of litter more difficult than in other more heavily vegetated ecosystems. Leaves and flowers are usually small and wind readily disperses them. As a result, most litter accumulates in wind-protected areas around the bases of shrubs or in depressions in the soil surface, where overland flow of water also augments accumulation. Rickard & Cline (1970) illustrate this phenomenon with data from an area dominated by *Artemisia tridentata* Nutt. in southwestern Washington, USA (Table 26.1). A further example of this type of ecosystem pattern is the plant and litter cover of a site dominated by *Atriplex confertifolia* (Torr. & Frém.) Wats. on the northern edge of the Great Salt Lake Desert, Utah, USA (illustrated in Fig. 26.1) (Gasto, 1969).

Production patterns and their movement

Two main approaches to estimating litter production may be taken (Medwecka-Kornas, 1971):

(a) continuous trapping of the material shed in an ecosystem with safeguards against its disappearance (litter-trap method); and
(b) single or repeated estimation of the amount of litter on the soil surface (ground-litter sampling).

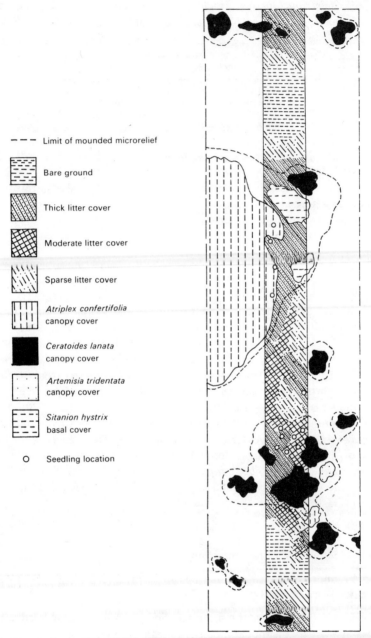

Limit of mounded microrelief

Bare ground

Thick litter cover

Moderate litter cover

Sparse litter cover

Atriplex confertifolia
canopy cover

Ceratoides lanata
canopy cover

Artemisia tridentata
canopy cover

Sitanion hystrix
basal cover

O   Seedling location

Fig. 26.1. A site dominated by *Atriplex confertifolia*. Sketch of relationship between ground cover, microrelief and seedling distribution in a 2.2 m segment of a permanent transect. The areas between the two central continuous lines represent a 15 cm central transect where detailed seedling data were recorded (Gasto, 1969).

Although it has been recommended that litter production in deserts be estimated from successive observation of plots (Sukacev & Dylis, 1966), the process of disappearance must be taken into account. American experience favors trap methodology.

Rather than position litter traps at random as forest ecologists do in their studies of litter production, desert ecologists have usually had to resort to traps constructed either around or between plants. High side-walls are required to prevent excessive losses by wind. Remezov, Rodin & Bazilevich (1963) designed traps of netting for use in the Eurasian deserts. Mack (1971), West (1972) and West & Fareed (1973) have used similar techniques to study litter production by North American cool-desert shrubs. Litter production is related by regression analysis to canopy cover, volume, or weight or density so that the results can be extrapolated to give estimates per hectare.

By periodically removing litter, seasonal patterns of litter production can be established. Periods of rapid phenological change need more attention than periods of dormancy. Several years of study are recommended to characterize an average sequence of seasonal changes. The more erratic the precipitation, the less dependable is the timing of litter production (Maconochie & Lange, 1970). Fig. 26.2 presents graphically an example of annual pattern of litter production, using data for *Atriplex confertifolia* in Curlew Valley, Utah, USA (West, 1972).

Function

Water conservation

Litter fall from desert plants is intimately related to drought resistance. Natural shedding of leaves and other plant parts reduces the transpiring surface during periods of soil drying, often preventing dehydration of plants to lethal levels and thus enhancing survival (Kozlowski, 1973). Leaf shedding generally begins with the oldest leaves, and progresses to younger ones. From circumstantial evidence, it appears that water is translocated from old to young leaves before the former are shed. Leaves abscise, are reduced to stipules, or replaced by brachyblasts. Desert shrubs may reduce the weight of their young shoots through abscission, this reduction ranging from 33% to well over 75% (Orshan, 1972).

Tissues other than leaves are often lost by desert plants. Zohary (1954) and Orshan (1954) have classified drought-resistant plants of arid zones according to the parts that are shed. Orshan (1972) separated:

(*a*) leaf shedders – plants which seasonally shed only leaves and inflorescences;
(*b*) branch shedders – plants which seasonally shed only parts of their branches;

Plant processes

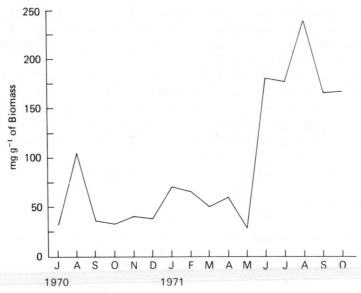

Fig. 26.2. Monthly pattern of litter fall from *Atriplex confertifolia* in Curlew Valley, Utah, USA; July, 1970 to October, 1971 (West, 1972).

(*c*) whole-shoot shedders – plants which seasonally shed all aboveground parts; and

(*d*) annuals – plants which seasonally are entirely renewed.

Seasonal polymorphism of leaves and twigs, common in deserts, results from shedding and growth of various types of branches and leaves, and has the effect that litter fall takes place during a longer period of the year than in strictly deciduous vegetation (Orshan, 1963; Kozlowski, 1973).

Nutrient conservation

Structural polymorphism, along with the evergreen habit (Monk, 1966), may be adaptations favoring nutrient as well as moisture conservation. Another mechanism for conserving nutrients is the translocation of nutrients from the parts to be shed. For instance, Beale (1971) and Winkworth (1973) found that the concentration of nitrogen and phosphorus in fallen phyllodes of *Acacia aneura* in central Australia decreased markedly at times of major phyllode fall, while amounts of the more abundant potassium, calcium, magnesium and sodium showed little or no consistent change. Furthermore, shedding rates were increased by an order of magnitude when rains of over 25 mm broke drought dormancy and initiated new phyllode growth (Wilcox, 1960, 1974; Burrows, 1972).

Mack (1971) found that leaves of *Artemisia tridentata*, in varying degrees of senescence in summer, show a steady decrease in phosphorus and potassium content as the leaves approach death and drop from the plant. He concluded that redistribution of these minerals may be a conservation mechanism, allowing the plants to reuse them in flowering, and possibly overcoming the need for additional ion uptake during a period when soil moisture is approaching depletion. Dina & Klikoff (1973) found that the leaf nitrogen content of this species declines as water stress develops, and the nitrogen is transferred to twigs. *A. tridentata* loses its larger leaves in early summer, and retains only small leaves through the dry summer and into the next spring. Desert halophytes also transfer nutrients before litter fall. Charley (1959) and Cowling (1969) observed transfers of nitrogen and phosphorus out of leaves and fruits of *Atriplex vesicaria* before shedding.

Litter differs greatly in its chemical content. These differences are summarized by Rodin & Bazilevich (1967). Litter must decompose before the inorganic nutrients return in forms available for plant growth. The rate of disappearance of litter may be measured by several techniques (Cromack, 1973). Marking a pair of matched plots, to be harvested at two different dates, might seem best suited to deserts since the microclimates influencing decomposition are least altered; however, extreme heterogenity between plots makes it difficult to match pairs. In practice, the mesh-bag technique is most commonly employed (Mack, 1971; Comanor & Prusso, 1973). Decomposition rates can be faster than often surmised for deserts, and the organisms involved are different from those of more mesic systems. These topics will be reviewed in more detail in volume 2.

Salts and allelochemical substances

In addition to the usual problems of cycling essential nutrients, desert plants possess other chemical components that affect ecosystem function. Desert halophytes accumulate excess salts (Rickard & Keough, 1968), and their litter decomposes more slowly (Fireman & Hayward, 1952) than that of glycophytes. This results in a salt-pumping effect, which, with time, increases the salt content of soils in the vicinity of such plants (Roberts, 1950).

Leaves of shrubs of many desert genera such as *Artemisia* contain large amounts of phenolic compounds which have been found to inhibit certain microbiological processes such as nitrogen fixation and nitrification (Skujins & West, 1973). Although it has often been suspected, shrub litter with high phenolic content has not yet been found to inhibit seed germination of a wide array of species (Knipe & Herbel, 1966). Seedlings of some desert shrubs are found in the zone of greatest litter accumulation near the parent

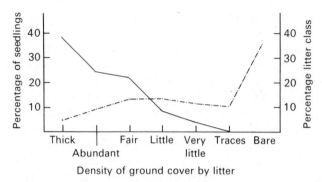

Fig. 26.3. Proportion of *Ceratoides lanata* seedlings in different litter density classes. Curlew Valley, Utah, USA, 1968–70 (Gasto, 1969).

shrubs (Gasto, 1969; Bowns, 1973). An illustration of this positive relationship is given in Fig. 26.3. An interaction of more favorable soil moisture, temperature moderation and higher nutrient reserves under litter than in bare, open spaces is suspected.

In other cases (Wallace & Romney, 1972; Sheps, 1973) field observations of seedling occurrences point to a negative relationship between seedlings and mature desert shrubs. Whether these are species with autotoxic substances volatilizing or leaching from live plants or their litter remains to be definitely proven.

Although animals such as sheep can be detritivores when they eat fallen leaf accumulations on the ground (Wilcox, 1971), plant litter in desert ecosystems would appear to have little overall effect on the distribution of vertebrate animals. Litter distribution, however, plays a decided role in the distribution of smaller animals, especially invertebrates. Tenebrionidae (Rickard & Haverfield, 1965) and mites (Wallwork, 1972) thrive in litter, and populations are usually higher where litter biomass is highest (C. Gist, personal communication).

Comparative fluxes

Rodin & Bazilevich's (1967) data indicate that, in desert communities, an average of 30% to 60% of the total organic mass (more in communities with ephemerals) is contained in the annual litter fall. This makes them similar to grasslands where 45% to 60% of the net primary production reaches the litter compartment each year. In forests, on the other hand, only 1% to 4% of the biomass on average goes into annual litter fall.

If root remains are considered part of litter, as in the Soviet literature (Rodin & Bazilevich, 1967), litter can account for 80% to 90% of the total annual net primary production. This explains the high values reported for

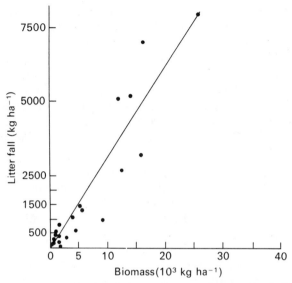

Fig. 26.4. Litter production in relation to biomass of vegetation in Syrian and Eurasian deserts. (Redrawn from Rodin & Bazilevich (1967); in the original, the ordinate scale is given in 'kg/ha', which appears by comparison with their Table 44 to be a mistake for 'cntr/ha'.)

relative and absolute litter production by Soviet investigators, compared with the literature from other countries.

The trend elsewhere is to relate litter production to aboveground standing crops. For instance, Charley & Cowling (1968) calculate that, on the average, 46% of the aboveground organic matter of *Atriplex vesicaria* Heward becomes litter. Orshan & Zand (1962) found that from 70% to 90% of the spring weight of desert chamaephytes in Israel may be lost during the summer drought. The actual proportion varies widely, depending on climatic conditions. A much higher percentage becomes litter at the start of a drought period following climatic conditions more favorable than average (Maconochie & Lange, 1970).

The absolute amount of litter fall depends directly on the total mass of organic matter and fluctuates widely (Fig. 26.4). Among the data collected by Rodin & Bazilevich (1967) the subtropical Syrian deserts produce the least whereas shrub steppes with annuals produce the most. Herbaceous *Artemisia* deserts in Russia yield 1200 to 2500 kg ha^{-1}yr^{-1} of litter fall. Those deserts with ephemerals yield up to 10000 kg ha^{-1}yr^{-1}, as much as or more than litter fall in forests (Rodin & Bazilevich, 1967).

Mack (1971) found that *Artemisia tridentata*, a long-lived perennial woody shrub which is dominant in the cool deserts of eastern Washington, USA, produced 34 kg ha^{-1} of leaves and 28 kg ha^{-1} of inflorescences annually. Branch and bark losses appeared to be negligible. Approximately

655

Plant processes

250 g m⁻² of wood was lying on the ground under this vegetation. West (1972) and West & Fareed (1973) found similar values of litter productivity for *A. tridentata* in northern Utah. In addition, they studied litter production by *Atriplex confertifolia* and *Ceratoides lanata* (Pursh) J. T. Howell in the same area. The latter two species are smaller, shorter-lived and more suffrutescent than *Artemisia tridentata*, but had a more rapid turnover of biomass and mineral content, so that litter productivity was about the same as in the *Artemisia*-dominated ecosystems. Charley & Cowling (1968) found that *Atriplex vesicaria* in western New South Wales produced an annual contribution to litter consisting, on average, of 684 kg ha⁻¹ of leaves, 361 kg ha⁻¹ of fruits and 49 kg ha⁻¹ of wood. Burrows (1972) observed a highly variable rate of litter production by *Eremophila gilesii* F.v.M. in southwestern Queensland, averaging around 500 kg ha⁻¹ yr⁻¹. Wilcox (1960) found that *Acacia aneura* F.v.M. ex Benth. produced about half this quantity of litter.

More results from Soviet research became available later. Togyzaev & Miroschnichenko (1972) found that the litter produced by two species of *Haloxylon* in the Karakum desert amounts to around 440 kg ha⁻¹ yr⁻¹. Kurochkina & Borovskaya (1970) report an annual aboveground litter production of 920 kg ha⁻¹ and belowground litter production of 4950 kg ha⁻¹ in an association dominated by *Eurotia ceratoides*. In another association dominated by *Artemisia terrae-albae*, they found that 1280 kg ha⁻¹ of aboveground and 2290 kg ha⁻¹ of belowground litter was produced.

Conclusions

Two contrasting patterns of leaf litter fall seem to be emerging for cool and warm desert shrubs. Cool desert shrubs, although predominantly evergreen, show a tendency to deciduousness through varying degrees of aestival reduction in the quantity of foliage carried by the plant. Ephemeral leaves are shed once soil moisture is depleted. Smaller leaves are retained over winter and shed when replacements appear in the spring. Warm deserts have some tropophytes, such as the Fouquieriaceae in North America. The prevailing pattern, however, is for leaves to be retained, even if dead, until drought dormancy is broken and new foliage develops. The more irregular the precipitation pattern, the more irregular the leaf shedding pattern.

Litter from inflorescences is produced even more irregularly in both kinds of deserts. Although no data on production rates are available, the contribution of woody portions to litter is probably added very slowly. Wind and rain in both types of desert, and hailstorms and snow in the cooler deserts, are physical agents causing occasional pulses of litter formation.

Formation, distribution and function of plant litter

The greater the standing crop biomass, the greater the production of litter. The less woody the vegetation, the higher the proportion of the net primary production that finishes as litter each year. Standing crops and rates of production of desert plant litter, in proportion to living phytomass, are high compared with other ecosystems. This is primarily due to drought-induced mortality and relatively slow decomposition rates. Desert plant litter is highly patterned. This patterning is of considerable importance in influencing seedling establishment, nutrient cycling and invertebrate activity in desert ecosystems.

Acknowledgment

The work on which this report is based was carried out as a part of the US-IBP Desert Biome, and was supported in part by National Science Foundation Grant No. GB-15886.

References

Beale, I. F. (1971). 'The productivity of two mulga (*Acacia aneura* F. Muell.) communities after thinning in south-west Queensland.' M. Agr. Sci. thesis, University of Queensland, Brisbane.

Bowns, J. E. (1973). 'An autecological study of blackbrush (*Coleogyne ramosissima* Torr.) in southwestern Utah.' Ph.D. dissertation. Utah State University, Logan.

Bray, J. R. & Gorham, E. (1964). Litter production in forests of the world. *Advances in Ecological Research*, 2, 101–57.

Burrows, W. H. (1972). Productivity of an arid zone shrub (*Eremophila gilesii*) community in south-western Queensland. *Australian Journal of Botany*, 20, 317–29.

Charley, J. L. (1959). 'Soil salinity–vegetation patterns in western New South Wales.' Ph.D. dissertation. University of New England, Armidale, New South Wales.

Charley, J. L. & Cowling, S. W. (1968). Changes in soil nutrient status resulting from overgrazing and their consequences in plant communities of semi-arid zones. *Proceedings of the Ecological Society of Australia*, 3, 28–38.

Comanor, P. L. & Prusso, D. C. (1973). Decomposition and mineralization in an *Artemisia tridentata* community in northern Nevada. US/IBP Desert Biome Research Memo. RM 73–39. University of Utah, Logan.

Cowling, S. W. (1969). 'A study of vegetation activity patterns in a semi-arid environment.' Ph.D. dissertation. University of New England, Armidale, New South Wales.

Cromack, K. (1973). 'Litter production and decomposition in a mixed hardwood watershed and a white pine watershed at Coweeta Hydrologic Station, North Carolina.' Ph.D. dissertation. University of Georgia, Athens.

Dina, S. J. & Klikoff, L. G. (1973). Effect of plant moisture stress on carbohydrate and nitrogen content of big sage brush. *Journal of Range Management*, 26, 207–9.

Fireman, M. & Haywood, H. E. (1952). Indicator significance of some shrubs in the Escalante Desert, Utah. *Botanical Gazette*, 114, 143–55.

Plant processes

Gasto, J. (1969). 'Comparative autecological studies of *Eurotia lanata* and *Atriplex confertifolia*.' Ph.D. dissertation. Utah State University, Logan.

Holmgren, R. C. & Brewster, S. F., Jr. (1972). *Distribution of organic matter reserve in a desert shrub community*. USDA Forest Service Research Paper. INT–130. Ogden, Utah.

Knipe, D. & Herbel, C. H. (1966). Germination and growth of some semidesert grassland species treated with aqueous extract from creosotebush. *Ecology*, **47**, 775–81.

Kozlowski, T. T. (1973). Extent and significance of shedding of plant parts. In: *Shedding of plant parts* (ed. T. T. Kozlowski), pp. 1–37. Academic Press, London & New York.

Kurochkina, L. Ya. & Borovskaya, T. A. (1970). Kharakteristika pochv i rastitelnosti zarastayushchikh peskov Yugo-Vostochnykh Taukumov. In: *Pastbischa i senokosy Kazakstana*, pp. 30–47. Alma-Ata. (Cited by Rodin, 1977).

Mack, R. N. (1971). 'Mineral cycling in *Artemisia tridentata*.' Ph.D. dissertation. Washington State University, Pullman.

Maconochie, J. R. & Lange, R. T. (1970). Canopy dynamics of trees and shrubs with particular reference to arid zone top feed species. *Transactions of the Royal Society of South Australia*, **94**, 243–8.

Mcdwecka-Kornaś, A. (1970). Litter production. In: *Methods of study in soil ecology* (ed. J. Phillipson), pp. 139–43. UNESCO, Paris.

Medwecka-Kornaś, A. (1971). Plant litter. In: *Methods of study in quantitative soil ecology: population, production and energy flow* (ed. J. Phillipson), pp. 24–33. IBP Handbook No. 18. Blackwell Scientific, Oxford.

Monk, C. D. (1966). An ecological significance of evergreenness. *Ecology*, **47**, 504–5.

Orshan, G. (1954). Surface reduction and its significance as a hydroecological factor. *Journal of Ecology*, **42**, 442–4.

Orshan, G. (1963). Seasonal dimorphism of desert and Mediterranean chamaephytes and its significance as a factor in their water economy. In: *The water relations of plants* (eds. A. J. Rutter & F. H. Whitehead), pp. 206–22. Blackwell, Oxford.

Orshan, G. (1972). Morphological and physiological plasticity in relation to drought. In: *Wildland Shrubs – Their biology and utilization* (eds. C. M. McKell, J. P. Blaisdell & J. R. Goodin), pp. 245–54. USDA, Forest Service, Ogden, Utah.

Orshan, G. & Zand, G. (1962). Seasonal body reduction of certain desert half-shrubs. *Bulletin of the Research Council of Israel*, **110**, 35–42.

Remezov, N. P., Rodin, L. E. & Bazilevich, N. I. (1963). Metodicheskie ukazaniya k izucheniyu biologicheskogo krugovorota zol'nykh veshchestv i azota nazemnykh rastitel'nykh soobshchestv v osnovnykh prirodnykh zonakh umerennogo poyasa. *Botanicheskii Zhurnal*, **46**, 869–77.

Richard, W. H. & Cline, J, F. (1970). Litter fall. In *US IBP Desert Biome Plant Specialists Meeting*, pp. 57–60. Jan. 2–3, 1970; Las Vegas, Nevada.

Rickard, W. H. & Haverfield, L, E. (1965). A pitfall trapping survey of darkling beetles in desert steppe vegetation. *Ecology*, **46**, 873–5.

Rickard, W. H. & Keough, R. F. (1968). Soil–plant relationships of two steppe desert shrubs. *Plant and Soil*, **29**, 205–13.

Roberts, R. C. (1950). Chemical effects of salt-tolerant shrubs on soils. *Transactions of the IVth International Congress of Soil Science*, **1**, 404–6.

Rodin, L. E. (ed.) (1977). *Produktivnost rastitel'nosti aridnoi zony Azii.* Nauka, Leningrad.

Rodin, L. E. & Bazilevich, N. I. (1967). *Production and mineral cycling in terrestrial vegetation.* (English translation ed. by C. E. Fogg.) Oliver & Boyd, Edinburgh.

Sheps, L. O. (1973). Survival of *Larrea tridentata* S. & M. seedlings in Death Valley National Monument, California. *Israel Journal of Botany*, **22**, 8–17.

Skujins, J. J. & West, N. E. (1973). *Nitrogen dynamics in stands dominated by some major cold-desert shrubs.* US/IBP Desert Biome Research Memorandum RM 73–25. Logan, Utah.

Soil Survey Staff (1960). *Soil classification: A comprehensive system (7th approximation).* Soil Conservation Service U.S. Department Agriculture, Washington, D.C.

Sukacev, W. & Dylis, N. (1966). Programma i metodika biogeotsenologicheskikh issledovanii. Academy of Sciences of the USSR, Nauka, Moscow.

Togyzaev, R. K. & Miroshnichenko, Yu. M. (1972). Zapas i dinamika opada v cherno-i belosaksaul'nikakh vostochnykh Karakumov. *Problemy Osvoeniya Pustyn*, **3**, 51–5. English summary in *Biological Abstracts*, **55**, 048176.

Wallace, A. & Romney, E. M. (1972). *Radioecology and ecophysiology of desert plants at the Nevada Test Site.* Report No. TID-25954, NTIS. U.S. Atomic Energy Commission, Springfield, Virginia.

Wallwork, J. A. (1972). Distribution patterns and population dynamics of the micro-arthropods of a desert soil in Southern California. *Journal of Animal Ecology*, **41** (2), 291–310.

West, N. E. (1972). *Biomass and nutrient dynamics of some major cold-desert shrubs.* US/IBP Desert Biome Research Memorandum RM 72–15. Logan, Utah.

West, N. E. & Fareed, M. (1973). *Shoot growth and litter fall processes as they bear on primary production of some cool desert shrubs.* US/IBP Desert Biome Research Memorandum RM 73–9. Logan, Utah.

Wiegert, R. G., Coleman, D. C. & Odum, E. P. (1970). Energetics of the litter-soil subsystem. In: *Methods of study in soil ecology* (ed. J. Phillipson), pp. 93–8. UNESCO, Paris.

Wilcox, D. G. (1960). Studies in the mulga pastoral zone. 2. Some aspects of the value of mulga scrub. *Journal of Agriculture of Western Australia*, **1**, 581–6.

Wilcox, D. G. (1974). Morphogenesis and management of woody perennials in Australia. In: *Plant morphogenesis as the basis for scientific management of range resources*, pp. 60–71. USDA. Miscellaneous Publication 1271, Washington, D.C.

Winkworth, R. E. (1973). The ecophysiology of mulga (*Acacia aneura*). *Tropical Grasslands*, **7**, 43–8.

Zohary, M. (1954). Hydro-economical types in the vegetation of Near East deserts. In: *Biology of Deserts* (ed. J. Cloudsley-Thompson), pp. 56–67. Institute of Biology, London.

Manuscript received by the editors January 1975

27. Integration

R. K. GUPTA

Natural propagation, growth and yield of plants in arid areas are restricted by diverse limiting factors such as low precipitation, frequent drought spells, intense radiation and poor soil conditions such as an inadequate moisture régime in the soil profile due to lower moisture-holding capacity, high infiltration rates and low organic carbon. It is, therefore, important to understand the various processes which combine in nature to constitute the whole dynamics of the individual and of the plant population.

Shortage of water is one of the main hindrances to plant production in arid lands. Most of these areas suffer from low and erratic rainfall. The drought conditions may prevail at various stages of plant life. In some years rains fail completely, while in other there may be initial drought at the seedling stage, resulting in large-scale mortality, poor plant density and thus low yields. The water deficit may also occur at different growth stages leading to poor production. Adjustment of various plant processes during its life cycle make it possible for the plant to survive adverse climatic conditions.

Desert life-forms

Desert plants have been broadly classified as drought-evading and drought-enduring. The first category includes ephemerals that germinate just after the effective monsoon showers in the hot deserts. During dry periods, they maintain no photosynthetically active parts but only special resistant reserve organs – the seed or other storage organs like the bulb, rhizome, etc. – from which a new pulse of growth is initiated and which in turn are replenished from it. Transfer between the two phases may be subject to a certain lag in response to the rainfall, but the growth pulse is still closely tied to transients of available soil moisture in the upper soil layer (5 to 30 cm). This category of plants comprises the majority of the desert flora. The two sub-types generally recognized are the annuals and the perennial ephemeroids (geophytes and hemicryptophytes). The only reserve in the annuals is the seed, which stores energy and nutrients but not water, and hence depends for reactivation on external water. Both activation and storage are irreversible processes, once they have been triggered. The reserve biomass is small as compared to the peak active biomass, the latter being built up mostly from its own production. In perennial ephemeroids, storage organs such as bulbs and rhizomes contain a water reserve as well

661

as a reserve of carbohydrates and proteins. Hence the active biomass can be built up rapidly upon the signal of a rainy season, and flowering can be independent of the rainfall. Reactivation and storage flows may be more flexible and reversible than in the annuals.

The drought-enduring or persistent group includes all perennials which maintain some photosynthesis during dry periods; they must have both water and energy to provide for the inevitable transpiration and respiration of the active tissues. The energy reserves in woody plants, both above and below ground, are an adaptation to the arid environment. External and internal reserves of water are required. The many special adaptations of these true xerophytes have been the subject of many morphological and physiological studies. They vary in the level of activity maintained in drought, and hence in their dependence on reserves. The drought-enduring group of trees and shrubs may reduce their photosynthetically active biomass and transpiring surface considerably during dry periods by shedding most of the leaves or stems or replacing them with smaller, dense leaves with lower gas-exchange rates. The root system is also reduced by shedding rootlets in the upper dry soil layer. Thus, while residual activity is maintained, water and energy losses are low and relatively small water reserves (in soil and plant) are sufficient. In certain trees and shrubs the green biomass is maintained at a nearly constant level throughout the year. Plants belonging to this group require a larger and more reliable water reserve, as well as tight control of cuticular and stomatal transpiration, high efficiency (ratio of assimilation to transpiration), and tolerance of low internal water potential and of high internal temperatures resulting from suppression of transpiration. All or most of these are characteristics of true drought-enduring plants.

Evergreen shrubs may be sclerophyllic, leafless with green stems or xerohalophytes with succulent leaves, Many of them take water from soil beyond − 100 bar and/or have specialized root systems. These attributes enable them to utilize slowly and efficiently the external water reserves in deep saline, rocky layers that are not available to other plants. Succulents, like many cacti, often have shallow roots and thus little external water reserve. On the other hand, they accumulate large internal water reserves from which the green cortex is maintained during drought. There are indications that in both evergreens and succulents, even though the green biomass fluctuates it shows little net increase during the short favourable periods; thus most production must be translocated to reserves. In these and other desert perennials and ephemerals, translocation, storage and mobilization of reserves are important; and still very little is known about the regulation of these processes.

Germination and seedling behaviour

Seed germination studies have been reviewed by Went (Chapter 19). The seeds are not only the dispersal unit for the plant, but a survival unit in the annuals which form the bulk of arid vegetation, since the growing season is restricted to short periods. The process of germination is controlled by many factors like dormancy and hard-seededness, the need for scarification, heat and cold treatment, etc. The regulatory mechanism controlling the process of germination is adapted to harmonize germination behaviour with the environment. Studies in many places have shown that artificial rain does not induce germination (Chapter 19). The germination and seedling behaviour of shrubs should result in definite age groups in nature. Some annuals may show *antitelechoric* behaviour where seeds have a mechanism to prevent their dispersal such as in *Gymnarrhena micrantha* (Koller & Roth, 1964; Evenari, Shanan & Tadmor, 1971) and *Chorizanthe rigida*; heteroblasty is also frequent. Seedlings of annuals during the dry season produce small and scanty root systems, differing in this from shrub seedlings which during the first month of growth produce tap roots 5 to 10 times as long as the shoots. Root systems of annuals in the wet season are about four times larger than those of the summer population.

Another important aspect of germination in desert plants is that the process starts only after rains of 25 mm or so (Went, 1959; Soriano, 1953). I have myself recorded similar observations from the Indian arid zone (Gupta, 1975). This phenomenon in the arid zone is important since it marks the initiation of much other biological activity. Interestingly enough, all seedlings of annuals in a particular area grow at the same rate, forming a remarkably even stand.

Germinability in seeds of most arid plants increases after storage in laboratory, while under desert conditions germination decreases to about 10% over two years. Both in the desert and in the laboratory, germination of recently harvested and consequently dormant seed increased sharply over a period of one year (Winkworth, 1971). Under vacuum storage, there was no decrease in viability of seeds over 20 years; but when stored under room conditions (20% to 50% r.h.), the same seeds lost their germinability almost completely in 10 years (Went, 1969). In some of the plants which produce seeds in very large quantity, viz., *Haloxylon salicornicum*, the seeds are viable for only a very short period, which again indicates an adaptation to the soil moisture conditions prevailing in arid lands. Glumes of certain grasses are reported to contain inhibitors restricting germination of the enclosed seeds (Lahiri & Kharbanda, 1963). These inhibitors are mostly water-soluble. Arid-land plants not infrequently have dimorphic seeds (Lahiri & Kharbanda, 1961), the larger seeds producing faster growing seedlings.

663

Plant processes

Water uptake, stomatal behaviour and transpiration

Water movement in plants occurs as a consequence of physico-chemical conditions, while metabolic processes contribute towards the creation and maintenance of such conditions. The movement of water into seeds and seedlings is the result of the existence of a gradient between the water potential of the soil and that of the plant. However, in seedlings (turgor) pressure potential, which develops gradually as the water moves into the plant, is a force which act against water movement into plant cells. Quick water uptake by seeds is a basic requirement for successful establishment in the desert, and is entirely due to the process of imbibition. Some grasses successful in arid lands are provided with hygroscopic glumes, which help their germination (when inhibitors are removed), particularly in the optimum temperature range of 30 °C to 35 °C. Most tree species have a long germinative period extending over a month. Absence of favourable soil moisture for such prolonged periods, particularly in the surface soil, poses problem for their natural regeneration. Limited success of large-scale aerial sowings in many deserts could perhaps thus be explained. Unstabilized sand dunes where no vegetation exists, and which are the sources of blown sand, may contain abundant moisture within a metre or two of the surface. Strategy of successful seedling establishment indicates that such places are best suited for tree species.

The total amount of water taken up and transpired by plants depends mostly on what remains after unavoidable losses by runoff, drainage and surface evaporation, and also on the rate of uptake from the soil layer between 5 and 40 cm in competition with evaporation. The rate of water flow through the soil–plant–atmosphere path depends upon the difference in water potential between soil and atmosphere and on the resistances to transfer between them, among which the stomatal resistance is most frequently dominant. Plants are able to regulate the stomatal resistance (and hence the transfer) rather tightly in response to changes in water demand and supply. This mechanism is essential for optimization of water use in arid conditions. Increased soil resistance due to drying around roots, seems to be compensated by root growth (Qashu, Evans & Wheeler, 1972). However, this is not the appropriate place to discuss these processes and the factors affecting water uptake by seeds, seedlings and mature plants, such as temperature, wind, light, which have been discussed by Meldner (Chapter 20).

Whether transpiration (and growth) is a linear or step function of soil water content has long been controversial. It is now clear that the shape of the curve depends upon the water demand and the root density or, more precisely, on the effectiveness of the plant in adjusting water supply to demand. Over a wide range, transpiration may be linear with soil water

664

potential. In crop plants, transpiration or wilting point is reached at -10 to -13 bar; but ability to use soil moisture down to -100 (or -150) bar seems to be common in the perennials, xerohalophytes, sclerophyllous shrubs and grasses of the arid zone (Slatyer, 1967; Winkworth, 1970; Kappen *et al.*, 1972; Moore, White & Caldwell, 1972). Local differences in root density and uptake are yet another source of horizontal or vertical patterns in soil moisture dynamics about which little is known, and which could be important in arid communities (Qashu *et al.*, 1972).

The rate of translocation of water is affected by resistances in flow or diffusion paths – when transpiration rates are moderately high, resistances contribute to development of tensions, and thus reduce water potential in the xylem from a possible value of zero in early morning to values as low as -30 bar during the following day. Stomatal pores provide the main path for water diffusion from the internal air-spaces to the atmosphere. Stomatal size, number and distribution are such that the diffusion path permits rates of transpiration in excess of rates of water movement into the plants. Theoretically, if the pressure under which the water moves into a plant is 1 bar, it is sufficient to raise water to a height of 10 m. The water supply in arid-zone vegetation types (predominantly grasslands, steppe, and shrublands) would be assured even without the occurrence of 'transpiration pull', though translocation of water would be limited, and the water content of plants would be practically stagnant.

Photosynthesis, respiration and biochemical transformation

A strong correlation between the primary productivity of desert plants on the one hand, and their morpho-phenologic development and water status on the other, has been reported. Indeed primary productivity of certain desert annuals may not occur at all except during episodic periods of adequate soil moisture. Perennial plants are exposed to, and survive in, low water potentials. In annuals, the net above-ground primary productivity is recorded to vary between 30 and 200 gm^{-2} in the arid zone and between 100 and 600 gm^{-2} in the semi-arid zone (Chew & Chew, 1965; Orshan & Diskin, 1968; Beatley, 1969; Nechayeva, 1970; Golley & Golley, 1972; Gupta, Saxena & Sharma, 1971, 1972; Burrows, 1972; Le Houérou, 1972; Rodin, 1972; Rodin, Bazilevich & Miroshnichenko, 1972; West, 1972, Gupta, 1975). These data are directly related to precipitation and suggest that a fair proportion of variation in productivity in the arid ecosystem could be accounted for by a linear regression on precipitation.

To estimate the gas exchange of the plant as a whole requires understanding of the gas-exchange pattern and responses for all plant organs with a capacity for photosynthesis or respiration. At present, most research is on the gas exchange of leaves. In certain situations and in certain species, other above-ground plant parts, such as stems, may show significant gas exchange. Net respiratory activity or below-ground plant biomass must also be recognized when attempting to predict the gas exchange of the whole plant.

Three biochemical pathways, namely the pentose carbon pathway (C_3 plants), the dicarboxylic pathway (C_4 plants), and crassulacean acid metabolism (CAM plants), are now recognized. Two major respiratory processes now known for plants are mitochondrial (dark) respiration and peroxysomal (photo)respiration. The nature of these biochemical pathways in relation to gas exchange in arid ecosystem has been ably described above (DePuit, Chapter 21). Rates of photosynthesis and respiration under natural conditions are governed by a number of physical factors, to which must be added interactive effects and biological factors; among these, the sparse and sporadic nature of precipitation in the arid zone is the most important limiting factor. The effects of temperature may be second in importance to those of water potential. Energy from the incident irradiation in the visible portion of spectrum (400–700 nm) provides the driving force for the light reactions of photosynthesis. If other factors are non-limiting, a consistent increase in rates of photosynthesis with increases in phytosynthetically active irradiation occurs until saturation light intensity is reached, after which photosynthetic rates level off regardless of further increases in irradiation. Though there is much interspecific variation in light-saturation intensity, corresponding to difference between species in efficiency of utilizing solar energy, effects of irradiation are closely coupled with those of temperature and water stress.

An understanding of the biochemical processes in plants has led one to believe that adequate nitrogen can help the plants to maintain normal metabolism under heat stress, which is of concern in arid areas. It was found (Lahiri, Singh & Kackar, 1973) that proteins are degraded under hyperthermia to form large quantities of amino acids and other soluble nitrogenous compounds. Damage to plants occurs due to the accumulation of ammonia, which is ultimately formed as a result of metabolic derangements. Plants which produce more aspartic and glutamic acids can withstand this environmental rigour by neutralizing this toxic ammonia to form amides, which are not harmful. Under conditions of high fertility, protein and enzyme systems become more stable under heat stress. The mechanism of this action is still obscure.

Root development

Root growth and activity has been reviewed by Drew in Chapter 23. The principal functions of root systems are absorption and transport of ions and water, and synthesis and transport of organic compounds, particularly the growth regulators. These functions, particularly those dependent upon concomitant root growth, are sensitive to adverse conditions (stresses) in the soil. Arid conditions provide exceptional problems since stresses are more extreme or of longer duration, with the result that root functions are confined to comparatively short periods while water is available.

Drew gives examples of the distribution of root systems under arid conditions, mostly from direct excavation. Existing knowledge of morphological and anatomical adaptations to the arid environment is surveyed; there is considerable scope for study of the distribution of living or active root tissues with depth and season, or in response to soil environment, using techniques developed in recent years using radioisotopes in the field.

Considerable progress has been achieved during this period in understanding the details of processes involved in transport to root surfaces under idealized conditions: the high resistance offered to ion and water movement in thin water films; the distance ion and water move to roots; and inter-root competition. The importance of roots as collecting systems, and contributions made by extension and branching, root hairs, and mycorrhizae under favourable conditions, is becoming clear. In practice, under favourable conditions, when root activities are most critical, there is still uncertainty about the location and distribution of 'absorbing zones' on roots; root survival or regeneration; the importance of mucigel, rhizophere organisms, root hairs and contact with soil. It has been concluded that, despite the genetic control of root activities, soil environment overwhelmingly modifies root growth and function; the features of the soil environment in question, water, mechanical impedance, temperature, inorganic ions, soil atmosphere and biological aspects, including effects of mycorrhizae and other micro-organisms, pathogenic and non-pathogenic and allelopathy are most important. For each environmental factor, aspects of root functions are discussed including modifications to absorbing zones, compensatory absorption and root growth mechanisms. It has further been shown how the combined effects of the soil environment ultimately determine which parts of the soil profile provide nutrients to plants and constitute limiting factors to growth.

Ion uptake, transport and excretion

The principles governing the distribution and movements of ions in a single plant cell, a whole plant or within a plant community are basically similar; they are reviewed by Osmond in Chapter 24. At each level, the system can be divided into a series of compartments in which the concentration, or more specifically the activity, of ions largely determines the rate of the processes which connect one compartment with another.

In the arid environment, plant ionic relations are qualified by several

Plant processes

constraints such as the availability of water limiting the period of root activity and of availability of ions. Perennials thus show a complex pattern of ionic uptake, while annuals may be subjected to short periods of uptake and to high concentration of the same ions. Concentrations of nutrient ions in the arid environment are usually low and other ions frequently high, depending on the parent material and the rates of physical and biological processes. Therefore, knowledge of the periodicity and concentration of available ions is essential before one can assess the significance of various plant factors such as ionic uptake by roots, movement of ions within plants, ion excretion, and salinity tolerance. The IBP witnessed several important developments in our understanding of the basic ion absorption processes such as (a) the functions relating concentration to rate of ion uptake (isotherms of Epstein and Laties) have been explained in terms of fluxes at the plasma membrane and the tonoplast, and (b) the symplast theory of ion movements across the root cortex to the xylem has been developed.

There has been substantial development during the IBP in understanding of salt-excretion processes in arid plants. It has been well recognized that salinity tolerance involves regulation of internal distribution of ions rather than a particularly tolerant form of metabolism. This has been discussed by Osmond (Chapter 24) who gives an account of the ionic relations of halophytes, and provides evidence against salt-tolerance in cytoplasm.

Translocation of reserves

The primary products of phytosynthesis are carbohydrates, which are distributed throughout the plant to be utilized in metabolism, construction of structural components, and as reserve. The translocation mechanism, and quantitative information on translocation rates in relation to driving variables, have been reviewed by Trlica & Singh in Chapter 22.

It is well established that most translocation between organs takes place in the phloem, and that sucrose is the predominant form in which carbohydrates are translocated. The mass flow theory of Münch (1930) is now widely accepted as probably the most important mechanism for transport in the phloem, through some form of activated diffusion (Mason & Phillis, 1937) seems also to operate. Translocation is an energy-demanding process (particularly transport into and out of the phloem), is selective, and often operates against diffusion gradients. The mechanisms supplying the energy needed for translocation depend on transformations between ATP and ADP.

Though carbohydrates are the major compounds of carbon which are created, translocated and stored within green plants, other carbon compounds of lesser importance are oils and proteins. Carbohydrates are considered as reserve constituents normally stored in perennating plant organs, which are important for growth of perennial ephemeroids. Any factor affecting production or utilization of carbohydrates in the plant for metabolic processes will affect the level of carbohydrate reserves. It has further been emphasized that depletion of carbohydrate reserves during regrowth after foliage removal can be a primary cause of deterioration of the forage resource. If the reserves have been heavily depleted during the annual growth cycle, the plants have a considerable amount of capital to repay during growing season. If the season is short, poor weather could significantly reduce the pool of average carbohydrate for subsequent years. Depletion of reserves in palatable perennials by grazing could shift the competitive balance towards non-palatable species and result in a change in community composition. The time of commitment for initiation of regrowth and carbohydrate utilization is as important in competition as the initial capacity of plants to gain carbon. If unfavourable biotic and abiotic conditions prevail following investment of carbohydrate reserves for growth initiation, then the health of the plant may be impaired. However, dearth of information even today on mobilizing hormones, translocation mechanisms, and use of carbohydrates at meristems, preclude an accurate evaluation of the function of reserves for regrowth.

Flowering, seed formation and dispersal

In arid-zone species, obligate photoperiodic or temperature requirements for flowering are uncommon. Anthesis can take place over a wide seasonal range, limited only by availability of soil moisture. However, in mesic species moisture stress tends to retard flowering and reduce reproductive output of the individual, and the same may often be true of arid-zone species which show no specific adaptation of reproduction to an environment where moisture stress is the limiting factor. Thus, under arid conditions there may be several years between successful reproductive events in perennial species, and many individuals in annual population may die before seed is set.

In contrast with the extensive literature concerning mechanisms for controlling germination in arid-zone species, little work has been carried out to study control of the flowering process by the environment (Mott, Chapter 25). Field observations can be difficult in view of the possibility of long intervals between successive flowering events under drought conditions. Definitive studies under controlled conditions are also difficult because of the problems involved in the study of plants growing under the stressed conditions which frequently occur in low-rainfall regions. However, success or otherwise of reproduction can be an essential feature in the dynamics of plant populations, especially those of annual species.

669

Plant processes

It is important to continue autecological studies of important species, as well as long-term studies on phenology and production of field populations. Similarly, studies on *Scrophularia arguta*, a plant of rocky fissures in the Sahara, have shown the role of cytokinins in affecting flowering (see Appendix by Chouard to Chapter 25).

Litter formation and distribution

The production of leaf litter, surveyed by West (Chapter 26) has two contrasting patterns for cool- and warm-desert shrubs. Cool-desert shrubs, although predominantly evergreen, show a tendency to deciduousness through varying degrees of aestival reduction in the quantity of foliage carried by the plant. Ephemeral leaves are shed once soil moisture is depleted. Smaller leaves are retained over winter, and shed when replacements appear in spring. Warm deserts have some tropophytes. The prevailing pattern is for the leaves to be retained even if dead, until drought dormancy is broken and a new set develops. The more irregular the precipitation pattern, the more irregular the leaf-shedding pattern.

Litter from inflorescences is even more sporadically produced in both kinds of deserts. Although no data on production rates are available, contributions of woody portions to litter may be expected to be added only very slowly. Wind and rain are physical agents causing occasional pulses of litter formation. Spatially, also, desert plant litter is highly patterned, which is of considerable importance in influencing seedling establishment, nutrient cycling and invertebrate activity in desert ecosystems.

As is evident, the greater the standing crop biomass, the greater is litter production. The less woody the vegetation the higher the proportion of net primary production that ends up as litter each year. The ratio of litter production and standing crop to living phytomass is high in deserts as compared to other ecosystems. This is primarily due to drought-induced mortality and relatively slow decomposition rates.

Competition and interaction between plant populations

Plant processes described above affect the primary productivity, biomass and spatial interactions between plant populations depending on the intensity of extreme environmental conditions. There are different views expressed on the role of arid environment controlling plant density. In many situations, periods between disasters are long enough for plant densities to build up to levels where intense competition for water does occur. Sometimes the root systems in shrub communities may occupy most of the area though the canopy cover may be hardly 3–5%; while at times there may be a regular spatial pattern, thus showing inter-species competition. In a study of competition in populations of *Cenchrus ciliaris* and *Tephrosia purpurea*, carried out by the present author at Jodhpur, it was shown that subsequent to the monsoon season when all the nutritious and palatable species are selectively grazed by animals, *Tephrosia purpurea* attains dominance. Of all the ratios tried in pots, a grass:legume ratio of 4:6 has been found to cause maximum loss in dry-matter production for the grass *Cenchrus ciliaris*. Mortality due to competition for water has been widely indicated in desert annuals (Beatley, 1967; Satyanarayan & Gaur, 1967; Gupta & Sharma, 1973). In some desert shrubs allelopathic substances inhibiting germination and growth of other species have been reported, but the significance of these in the field could not be proved (Muller, 1953).

Studies of variation in the floristic composition of monsoonal vegetation of alluvial plains of the Indian arid zone have shown (Satyanaryan & Gaur, 1967) that, during the monsoon period of 30th July to 22nd September, perennials except *Cenchrus ciliaris* increase in number of colonies and decrease in number of individuals. Among annuals, *Cenchrus biflorus*, *Digitaria adscendens*, *Aristida adscensionis* and *Eragrostis ciliaris* behave like perennials. Forbs rapidly increase in number but perennial weeds germinate more slowly. Ephemerals like *Urochloa panicoides* and *Tragus biflorus* do not stand competition with other species. Highest percentage cover and density of annuals are found in the middle of the monsoon, while for perennials it may be the end of the monsoon. Mortality in annuals is due to their short life period, poor establishment and lack of competitive power. Some of the plants like *Aristida adscensionis*, *Cenchrus biflorus*, *Digitaria adscendens* and *Tribulus terrestris* may behave as annuals, as bienniels, or as perennials depending upon the environmental conditions.

In another study (Gupta & Sharma, 1973), phytosociological variations for a period of five years were recorded at Jodhpur in the Indian arid zone, and it was noticed that perennial grasses were the most prominent contributors to basal cover in all the seasons. Ephemerals and therophytes contribute relatively less after the post-monsoon season, due to heavy loss of moisture by evaporation and downward penetration to subsoil layers. Annual grasses suffer heavily during successive droughts. A decrease in total percentage basal cover was recorded under exclosure without any utilization. Perennials remained alive during adverse soil-moisture conditions due to their relatively deeper root system. Vapour condensation into the lower subsoil layer provides an interesting enrichment in its moisture content.

Salinization of the soil surface by salt accumulation, with consequent inhibition of non-halophytes, is apparently common (Litav, 1957; Charley, 1959). Positive effects of shrubs and trees on other plants, as expressed in spatial association, are often observed in the desert (Agnew & Haines,

671

Plant processes

1960; Mott, 1972). This may partly be due to micro-environmental modifications – for instance atmospheric, due to reduction of radiation, temperature, wind and evaporation; or edaphic, such as increased organic nutrient content, accumulation of wind-blown sand and silt. Sometimes mechanisms like concentration of wind-blown seeds near a plant clump, or growth of seedlings in a clump as a result of protection from grazing – for instance, *Euphorbia caducifolia* in *Salvadora oleoides, Acacia senegal* etc. – are peculiar to desert conditions.

The periods for each of the plant processes such as germination, flowering and seed-setting are short and uncertain in the deserts, depending upon the fluxes of rainfall. Thus, in the arid zone, a major problem is how to regulate these processes, particularly time and intensity of flowering. In desert annuals seed longevity, seed diversification and maximum utilization of environmental fluxes are frequent adaptive strategies (Negbi & Evenari, 1961; Cohen, 1966, 1967; Gutterman, Witztum & Evenari, 1967; Koller, 1972). Even when vegetative growth is limited, one of the adaptations is to produce some seeds (at least one per plant), while heavy seeding and dispersal in favourable periods allow both for continued occupation of safe microhabitats and search for new ones.

In desert perennials, successful reproduction may occur less frequently. Seed longevity is less critical. For a few perennials, germination follows a strategy of trial and error almost every year, while in some it depends on climatic sequences which occur once in several years and which probably are correlated with a high probability of successful establishment.

Irregular fluctuations, superimposed on both an increasing trend and an eventual steady state, have been found in plant population dynamics in the arid zone (Hall, Specht & Eardly, 1965). These fluctuations, with periods of three to five years, seem to be in response to sequences of wet and dry years. In some populations turnover is recorded as fairly rapid, while in others there was no change even in 40 years.

These features in the desert make succession and climax problematic in desert communities. Kassas (1966) distinguished successional changes in desert vegetation from seasonal and accidental changes. Thus climax is defined to include those irregular fluctuations in competition. Succession (i.e. long-term trends) has been considered as allogenic in response to geomorphic processes (Chaudhuri, 1960; Kassas, 1966; Gupta, 1968; Gaussen, Legris, Gupta & Meher-Homji, 1971). Autogenic succession occurs in dune stabilization and in formation of mounds around shrubs. Changes in human and stock pressure may induce drastic successional and degradational trends in arid communities (Hastings & Turner, 1965; Gupta, 1968; Gupta & Sharma, 1973).

672

References

Agnew, A. D. Q. & Haines, R. W. (1960). Studies on the plant ecology of the Jazira of Central Iraq. *Bulletin of the College of Science, University of Baghdad*, **5**, 41–60.

Beatley, J. C. (1967). Survival of winter annuals in the northern Mojave Desert. *Ecology*, **48**, 745–50.

Beatley, J. C. (1969). Biomass of desert winter annual populations in southern Nevada. *Oikos*, **20**, 261–73.

Burrows, W. H. (1972). Productivity of an arid zone shrub (*Eremophila gulesii*) community in south-west Queensland. *Australian Journal of Botany*, **20**, 317–30.

Charley, J. L. (1959). 'Soil salinity–vegetation patterns in western New South Wales and their modification by overgrazing.' Ph.D. thesis. University of New England, Armidale, New South Wales.

Chaudhuri, I. I. (1960). Succession of vegetation in the arid regions of West Pakistan Plains. In: *Proceedings of the Symposium on soil erosion and its control in arid and semi-arid zones*, pp. 141–55. Karachi Food and Agricultural Council.

Chew, R. M. & Chew, A. E. (1965). The primary productivity of a desert shrub (*Larrea tridentata*) community. *Ecological Monographs*, **35**, 355–75.

Cohen, D. (1966). Optimizing reproduction in a randomly varying environment. *Journal of Theoretical Biology*, **12**, 119–29.

Cohen, D. (1967). Optimizing reproduction in a randomly varying environment when a correlation may exist between the conditions at the time a choice has to be made and the subsequent outcome. *Journal of Theoretical Biology*, **16**, 1–14.

Evenari, M., Shanan, L. & Tadmor, N. (1971). *The Negev: the challenge of a desert*. Harvard University Press, Cambridge, Mass.

Gaussen, H., Legris, P., Gupta, R. K. & Meher-Homji, V. M. (1971). *International map of vegetation and environmental conditions. Sheet Rajputana I.C.A.R.* Section Scientifique et Technique. Hors Travaux Série No. 17. Institut Française, Pondicherry.

Golley, P. & Golley, F. B. (1972). *Symposium on tropical ecology with an emphasis on organic productivity*. Athens, Georgia.

Gupta, R. K. (1968). Anthropogenic influences on the vegetation of W. Rajasthan. *Vegetatio*, **16** (1–4), 79–94.

Gupta, R. K. (1975). Plant life in the Thar Desert. In: *Environmental analysis of the Thar Desert* (eds. R. K. Gupta & I. Prakash), pp. 202–36. English Book Depot, Dehra Dun, India.

Gupta, R. K. & Sharma, S. K. (1973). Phytosociological changes in an enclosed area on old alluvial flats of Jodhpur in the Indian arid zone during a period of five years. *Journal of Indian Botanical Society*, **52**, 99–108.

Gupta, R. K., Saxena, S. K. & Sharma, S. K. (1971). Aboveground productivity of grasslands at Jodhpur, India, *Proceedings of the Symposium on tropical ecology with an emphasis on organic productivity*, pp. 75–93. Compiled by P. M. & F. B. Golley.

Gupta, R. K., Saxena, S. K. & Sharma, S. K. (1972). Aboveground productivity of three promising desert grasses at Jodhpur under different rainfall conditions. In: *Eco-physiological foundation of ecosystems productivity in arid zone* (ed. L. E. Rodin), pp. 134–7. Nauka, Leningrad.

Plant processes

Gutterman, Y., Witztum, A. & Evenari, M. (1967). Seed dispersal and germination in *Blepharis persica*. *Israel Journal of Botany*, **16**, 213–34.

Hall, E. A., Specht, R. L. & Eardley, C. M. (1964). Regeneration of the vegetation on Koonamore vegetation reserve, 1926–1962. *Australian Journal of Botany*, **12**, 205–64.

Hastings, J. R. & Turner, R. M. (1965). *The changing mile: an ecological study of vegetation change with time in the lower mile of an arid and semi-arid region.* University of Arizona Press, Tucson.

Kappen, L., Lange, O. L., Schulze, E. D., Evenari, M. & Buschbom, V. (1972). Extreme water stress and photosynthetic activity of the desert plant *Artemisia herba-alba. Oecologia*, **10**, 177–82.

Kassas, M. (1966). Plant life in deserts. In: *Arid Lands* (ed. E. S. Hills), pp. 145–80. Methuen, London.

Koller, D. (1972). Environmental control of seed germination. In: *Seed Biology* (ed. T. T. Kozlowski), pp. 1–101. Academic Press, London & New York.

Koller, D. & Roth, M. (1964). Studies on the ecological and physiological significance of amphicarphy in *Gymnarrhena micrantha* (Compositae). *Annals of Botany*, **51**, 26–35.

Lahiri, A. N. & Kharbanda, B. C. (1961). Dimorphic seeds in some arid zone grasses and the significance of growth differences in their seedlings. *Science and Culture*, **27**, 448–50.

Lahiri, A. N. & Kharbanda, B. C. (1963). Germination studies on arid zone plants. II. Germination inhibitors in the spikelet glumes of *Lasiurus sindicus*, *Cenchrus ciliaris* and *C. setigerus. Annals of Arid Zone*, **1**, 115–26.

Lahiri, A. N., Singh, S. & Kackar, N. D. (1973). Studies on plant–water relationships. VI. Influence of nitrogen level on the performance of nitrogen content of plants under drought. In: *Physiological strategies for maximization in arid areas* (ed. A. N. Lahiri), *Proceedings of the Indian National Science Academy*, B, **39**, 77–94.

Le Houérou, H. N. (1972). An assessment of the primary and secondary production of the arid grazing land ecosystems of North Africa. In: *Ecophysiological foundation of ecosystems productivity in arid zone* (ed. L. E. Rodin), pp. 168–72. Nauka, Leningrad.

Litav, M. (1957). The influence of *Tamarix aphylla* on soil composition in the Northern Negev of Israel. *Bulletin of the Research Council of Israel*, **D6**, 38–45.

Mason, T. G. & Phillis, E. (1937). The migration of solutes. *Botanical Review*, **3**, 47–71.

Moore, R. T., White, R. S. & Caldwell, M. M. (1972). Transpiration of *Atriplex confertifolia* and *Eurotania lanata* in relation to soil, plant and atmospheric moisture stresses. *Canadian Journal of Botany*, **50**, 2311–8.

Mott, J. J. (1972). Germination studies on some annual species from an arid region of Western Australia. *Journal of Ecology*, **60**, 293–304.

Muller, C. H. (1953). The association of desert annuals with shrubs. *American Journal of Botany*, **40**, 53–60.

Münch, E. (1930). *Die Stoffbewegungen in der Pflanze*. Gustav Fischer, Jena.

Nechayeva, N. T. (ed.) (1970). Rastitel'nost' tsentral'nykh Karakumov i eě produotivnost. Ylym, Ashkhabad.

Negbi, G. & Evenari, M. (1961). The means of survival of some desert summer annuals. *Arid Zone Research*, **16**, 249–59.

Orshan, G. & Diskin, S. (1968). Seasonal changes in productivity under desert conditions. In: *Functioning of terrestrial ecosystems* (ed. F. E. Eckhardt), pp. 191–201. Proceedings of UNESCO, Paris.

Qashu, H. K., Evans, D. D. & Wheeler, M. (1972). *Soil factors influencing water uptake by plants under desert conditions.* US/IBP Desert Biome Research Memorandum RM 72–37. Logan, Utah.

Rodin, L. E. (ed.) (1972). *Ecophysiological foundation of ecosystems productivity in arid zone.* Nauka, Leningrad.

Rodin, L. E., Bazilevich, N. I. & Miroshnichenko, Y. M. (1972). Productivity and biogeochemistry of *Artemisieta* in the Mediterranean area. In: *Ecophysiological foundation of ecosystems productivity in arid zone* (ed. L. E. Rodin), pp. 193–8. Nauka, Leningrad.

Satyanarayan, Y. & Gaur, Y. D. (1967). Phytosociological variations in floristic composition of the vegetation in the arid zone. 1. Monsoonal vegetation of the alluvial plants. *Annals of Arid Zone,* 6 (2), 178–99.

Slayter, R. O. (1967). *Plant–water relationships.* Academic Press, London & New York.

Soriano, A. (1953). Estudios sobre germinacio. I. *Revista de Investigaciones Agricolas,* 7, 315–40.

Went, F. W. (1959). Ecology of Desert Plants. II. The effect of rain and temperature on germination and growth. *Ecology,* 30, 1–13.

Went, F. W. (1969). A long-term test of seed longevity. II. *Aliso,* 7, 1–12.

West, N. E. (1972). *Biomass and nutrient dynamics of some major cold-desert shrubs.* US/IBP Desert Biome Research Memorandum 72-15. Logan, Utah.

Winkworth, R. E. (1970). The soil water regime of an arid grassland (*Eragrostis eriopoda* Benth.) community in central Australia. *Agricultural Meteorology,* 7, 387–99.

Winkworth, R. E. (1971). Longevity of Buffel grass seed sown in an arid Australian range. *Journal of Range Management,* 24, 141–5.

Manuscript received by the editors March 1975

Animal processes

28. Introduction

D. W. GOODALL

Though animal biomass in arid lands is far less than that of the vegetation, the animals can on occasion have far-reaching effects on the dynamics of the ecosystems. This is more often true of domestic livestock than of native animals, which over the long term are normally in equilibrium with other components of the ecosystem.

In the chapters of this section, various aspects of animal life in the deserts are discussed, in terms of processes involving the individual or the unispecific population, where other elements of the system may be treated as playing a rather passive role.

The second chapter deals with the processes leading to the ingestion of food, including diet selection, both by herbivores and carnivores. The following chapter deals with the utilization of ingested food – the processes of assimilation, respiration and excretion; in this chapter, invertebrates and vertebrates have been treated separately. The fourth chapter cover the processes of exchange of water and energy by desert animals – the ways in which they adapt to the two most important constraints of the desert environment.

The fifth chapter covers aspects of the spatial distribution of desert animals, especially as dependent on behaviour, and the temporal distribution of their activity. This is followed by a chapter on reproduction and development, and an account of the processes of disease and death completes the section.

29. Food selection and consumption

O. J. REICHMAN, I. PRAKASH and V. ROIG

Introduction

Scattered throughout the literature on both deserts and consumers are references to what desert consumers ingest, how much they ingest, and from what sources they obtain their food. There are, however, no reviews on the topic, although Brown's volumes (1968, 1974) are very pertinent. This chapter is an effort to bring together works in the literature which have specifically or incidentally dealt with the diets of desert organisms, and recent work done under the IBP.

Naturally, the material included reflects both our own past and present research propensities and interests and the geographic areas in which we have worked. In addition to our own work, the information presented has depended on the studies published by other scientists and hence reflect those desert areas best known and most extensively studied. Thus, for example, the North American deserts are probably over-represented, and little or no information was available to us on the Gobi Desert.

As will be seen, the diets of desert organisms are frequently determined by the need to maintain water balance. Many of the data on consumers come from literature on water-balance phenomena, although the data were also obtained from sources such as incidental observations, and taxonomic accounts. With this framework in mind, the data will be presented by animal group, and synthesized at the end of the chapter.

Special groups of animals, often rather specialized, are found in the limited aquatic environments in the desert. No attempt will be made to cover these in the present chapter, which will be confined to consumers in terrestrial environments. One may, however, draw attention to a detailed survey of the diets of the invertebrate fauna of a stream in the Great Basin Desert of North America (Koslucher & Minshall, 1973), and to a review by Deacon & Minckley (1974) covering the fish of desert waters.

Feeding habits of different taxonomic groups

Aschelminthes

Nematoda

As in all biomes, the ecology of nematodes in deserts is poorly known. Healey (1973) found *Protospirura numidica* Quentin in *Peromyscus* sp. (a rodent) *Melanoplus femur* (a grasshopper) and *Gryllus* sp. (a cricket) in

Animal processes

the sagebrush desert of Utah. Nine species of nematodes were found on *Distichlis spicata* (L.) Greene, eight on *Sarcobatus vermiculatus* (Hook) Torr., and eight on *Artemisia tridentata* Nutt. at 1300 m in the deserts of Utah (Havertz, 1962).

Recent work begun by Freckman, Sher & Mankau (1974) indicates that in several deserts in southwest North America there are a number of fungal feeders (three species), plant parasites (approximately fifteen species), predator–omnivores (three species), and microbivores (three species), constituting collectively a considerable biomass. The diversity of these feeding guilds was greatest in the top 10 cm of the soil, perhaps indicating that most of the food resources used by these animals are concentrated at this level.

Mollusca

Snails (Gastropoda: Pulmonata)

Very few mollusks are known from desert areas. However, Schmidt-Nielsen, Taylor & Shkolnik (1972) and Yom-Tov (1970) have noted that in areas of the Negev Desert small white snails dot the desert surface. Snails of the genus *Helicella* feed primarily on the leaves of higher plants, while *Sphincterochila* spp. feed on surface mud and ignore the higher plants. Presumably, the mud contains sufficient amounts of detritus to maintain the snails.

Arthropoda

Arachnida

Mites (*Acari*)

In many areas of the North American deserts, numerous large, bright red mites can be observed crawling over the desert floor after summer rains. In a study of the ecology of these mites (*Dinothrombium pandorae*) in the Mohave Desert, Tevis & Newell (1962) found only two individuals, out of hundreds observed, associated with food items. These individuals were astride termites and applying their pedipalps and chelicerae in preparation for sucking the termites dry. The emergence of the mites is apparently correlated with the emergence of the termites after appropriate rains. The association is a tenuous one, as the termites rapidly lose their wings after emergence and within an hour are hidden from mite predation.

Wallwork (1972), studying microarthropods in the Mohave Desert, found that, generally, species of the Cryptostigmata and Astigmata were herbivorous and Prostigmata and Mesostigmata were carnivorous. More specifically, the stomachs of *Joshuella striata* Wallwork, a Cryptostig-

682

matan, contained primarily fungal hyphae and spores, with some decomposed leaf litter. An Astigmatan mite, *Glycyphagus* sp., also ate fungi in the active stage, but did not feed in the hypopial stage. *Aphelacarus acarinus* (Berl.) was primarily herbivorous, but ate mostly plant detritus and some fungal hyphae.

Scorpions

Stanhke (1966) noted that scorpions would eat most small animals, both vertebrates and invertebrates, which they could subdue. These prey included spiders, centipedes, and a 200 mm lizard, although Isopoda seemed to be avoided. Hadley & Williams (1968), working in the deserts in northwestern Mexico on the scorpions *Hadrurus hirsutus* (Wood), *Centruroides sculpturatus* Ewing, and *Vejovis* spp., found the animals to be actively foraging only at night. Only 1–5% of those individuals observed were actually pursuing or ingesting prey, which were usually spiders, beetles, Lepidoptera and Orthoptera. A few solpugids (Arachnida: Solifugae) were eaten, and cannibalism was occasionally observed. The scorpions would attempt to eat anything they could immobilize, usually using only their large pedipalps, as stinging actually increased the escape activity of some prey (mice and lizards, for instance). In laboratory studies (Hadley & Williams, 1968) two species of *Hadrurus* preyed on mice (*Peromyscus* sp., *Perognathus* sp.) and lizards (species of *Cnemidophorus*, *Uta*, *Sceloporus*, *Coeleonyx* and *Dipsosaurus*). Millipedes, Isopoda and *Eleodes* spp. were generally avoided. The prey were eaten at the capture locality and not taken elsewhere.

Pseudoscorpions

Pseudoscorpions are almost exclusively carnivorous, feeding on Collembola, Psocoptera, Thysanoptera, Diptera, Symphyla, and other Arachnida (Cloudsley-Thompson, 1968). These Arachnida are occasionally cannibalistic when 'pressured', and will rob other pseudoscorpions of their food after short battles (Cloudsley-Thompson, 1968).

Solpugids (*Solifugae*)

The diets of solpugids are difficult to determine, as the ingested material is usually masticated to a liquid, or finely ground. However, it has been noted that these Arachnida are voracious feeders, frequently stalking and ambushing their prey, and occasionally feeding until they are too gorged to move (Muma, 1966). Muma (1951) has noted that these animals, which are not known to possess toxins, have been observed to kill birds and small

Animal processes

mammals. He also noted that they ate lizards and many different kinds of insects. They are occasionally cannibalistic, especially when in a confined space, or during and after conspecific combat (Muma, 1951). In a study of 18 North American species, Muma (1966) observed that larvae and early nymphs do not feed, but live on the residue in the egg. Second instar nymphs may participate in communal feeding. In addition, nocturnal solpugids will not feed during daylight hours. However, they may actively chase, stalk and ambush prey at night, using sight, touch and terrestrial vibrations to detect the prey. Muma (1966) presents evidence that solpugids ingest Orthoptera, Dermaptera, Coleoptera, Hemiptera, Lepidoptera, Diptera, Isoptera, Neuroptera, Odonata, Hymenoptera, and Araneida. Among the most common dietary items are termites, flies, moths, scarab beetles, maggots and gnats, the solpugids apparently selecting the items on the basis of size and degree of scleratization (for instance, the smallest solpugids tend to eat small, soft prey).

Spiders (Araneae)

Somewhat surprisingly, relatively little information is available on the feeding ecology of spiders in deserts, Cloudsley-Thompson (1968) states that they primarily feed on other arthropods. Bristow (1941) noted that spiders feed on various qualities and sizes of prey, depending on the season and prey size available. One of us (OJR) has seen tarantulas feeding on ants in the Chihuahuan Desert. Others (D. W. Davidson, personal communication) have also noted spider predation on species of the ant genera *Novomessor*, *Pogonomyrmex*, and *Veromessor* in the deserts of southwest North America.

Chew (1961) suggests that spiders on *Larrea divaricata* Cav. in the southwestern United States may feed on Chermidae, causing a decline in the population densities of the prey. He also suggests that spiders ingest small flies and Homoptera, and are occasionally cannibalistic, but tend to avoid beetles and Lepidoptera.

Insecta

Much of the desert in North and South America is covered by species of *Larrea*, and therefore consumers of these shrubs could be of considerable importance.

Werner & Olsen (1973) found several insects which depended on *L. divaricata*, either as adults or as larvae. These include Orthoptera (*Bootettix punctatus* Sardder, *Ligurotettix coquilletei kunzei* Caudell., *Insara covilleae* and *Diapheromera covilleae* Rehn & Hebard); Lepidoptera (*Thyridopteryx meadi* Hy. Edw., *Semiothisa pallidata* Packard and *Syn-*

684

glochris perumbrari Hulst.); Coleoptera (*Eupagoderes marmoratus* and *Eptcauta lauta* (Hon.); Homoptera (*Tachardiella larrea* (Comstock) and a mealybug (Family Pseudococcidae), and Diptera (a gall fly, probably *Asphondylia auripila* Felt). In addition, *I. covilleae* occasionally fed on *Asphondylia* galls. Personal observations (OJR) indicate that many kinds of bees are associated with flowers of *L. divaricata*, apparently gathering nectar and/or pollen.

In another IBP volume, Shultze (1975) has listed and discussed in great detail many of the predators found on *Larrea* spp., both in North and South America. The work includes information on the season of foraging, diet breadth, specific food, feeding guild, hiding substrates, and oviposition sites.

In a study on another dominant shrub in the deserts of North America, *Prosopis juliflora*, Riazance & Whitford (1974) found that *Oncideres* spp., which girdle the branches, did not have an effect on the biomass of the plants they attacked. Although the stem sections distal to the girdling died, growth proximal to the damage increased to compensate for the damage. These authors also noted that stem borers, family Bostrichidae, bored into and killed both small stems and leaves of *P. juliflora*, producing in one plant a loss of 1% stem biomass and 53% leaf biomass. Riazance & Whitford (1974) also found from 26% to 57% of the seed crop of *P. juliflora* damaged by the weevil *Bruchus prosopis*.

A major shrub in the Great Basin Desert of North America is *Artemisia tridentata* Nutt., and an important consumer of this plant is the leaf-eating *Aroga websteri*. Hsiao and his coworkers (Hsiao & Kirkland, 1973; Hsiao & Green, 1974) determined that *A. websteri* larvae ingested 40 mg (dry weight) of sagebrush during their development. They also found that approximately 80% of the foliage of *A. tridentata* was destroyed by *A. websteri* in the Curlew Valley in 1972, but that all except 20–30% of the plants recovered that fall. Using estimates based on foliage consumption and insect densities, it was estimated that one kilogram of *A. tridentata* could support 240 defoliators.

A major group of insects in deserts are ants. Werner (1973) states that the leaf cutter ant, *Acromyrmex versicolor* Pergrande, gathers leaves of *Larrea divaricata* in the Sonoran Desert. However, this ant species also uses many other items, including leaves and petals of various plants gathered from the ground. Various kinds of grasses (blades are preferred over stems), *Allionia incarnata*, *Haplopappus tenuisectus*, *Prosopis juliflora*, three species of *Opuntia*, *Acacia greggii*, *Cercidium floridum*, *Euphorbia melandenia*, *Proboscidea arenaria*, *Tidestromia lanuginosa*, and *Zinnia pumila* are gathered by the ants and taken underground to ingest or use as a base for cultivation of fungi. *Prosopis juliflora* is probably the most important leaf material, as the nests are usually near plants of this

685

species and much of it is used when its leafs out early in the spring. When the plants are flowering, the blooms are favored over the leaves. In addition to leaves, *A. versicolor* occasionally collected feces of moths, grasshoppers and birds, especially during the summer.

Some desert ants are apparently carnivorous. Creighton (1964) noted that, except in one instance, *Pheidole clydei* Gregg brought only arthropods or their remains back to the nest. The one exception was a flower anther, the ants otherwise using spiders, flies, termite nymphs and other *Pheidole* species. The author surmised that, although this Mohave Desert species is carnivorous, it is primarily a scavenger rather than a predator.

Many ant species in the desert appear to be granivorous. Creighton & Creighton (1960) found *Pheidole militicida* Wheeler to use grass seeds almost exclusively. Whitford (1973) determined that three species of *Pogonomyrmex* in the Chihuahuan Desert fed on the most abundant seed species, shifting preferences as various kinds became available. Seeds of *Eriogonum* spp. made up over one-half of the diet, with *Chenopodium* spp. also being used. Composites (such as *Bahia absinthifolia* and *Baileya multiradiata*) were not important items in the diets, although they were highly represented in the seed production. *Pogonomyrmex desertorum* foraged heavily on grass seeds, especially *Tridens pulchellus* and *Bouteloua barbata*. Insects and other animal items made up a relatively small portion of the items used by these ants.

Although most ants appear to prefer certain items for forage use, many are scavengers, taking what is available to them. Whitford & Kay (1974) noted that over 50% of the diet of *Novomessor cockerelli* in the Chihuahuan Desert consisted of termites and other insect remains. The remainder of the diet was made up of seeds, this species showing the same preference as *Pogonomyrmex* spp. for the abundant seeds of *Eriogonum* spp. (Whitford, 1973). Tevis (1958) states that although *Veromessor pergandei* (Mayr) in the Mohave Desert feeds primarily on seeds (68–92% in different seasons), other items are also frequently taken (such as insects, flowers, and miscellaneous non-edible material). The major seeds used by this species were *Pectocarya recurvata* Johnston and *Plantago insularis* Morris (Jeps.) (Tevis, 1958). Went, Wheeler & Wheeler (1972) demonstrated that workers of *Veromessor pergandei* brought almost anything they could transport back to the nest. This included sticks, leaves, insects, and both good and aborted seeds (especially *Franseria dumosa* Gray, *Hymenoclea salsola* T. & G., *Atriplex hymenelytra* (Torr.) Wats., *Larrea divaricata* and *Chorizanthe brevicornii* Torr.) Apparently the seed embryos were digested out of the hard seeds by enzymes. Carrol & Janzen (1973) state that many ants are scavengers, and that most groups store seeds and have the capacity to use 'honey dew'. Wheeler (1908) noted that *Myrmecocystus* sp. produced 'honey' for the workers. Went *et al.*

(1972) found these ants in Deep Creek, Mohave Desert, to be very specialized feeders, collecting 'nectar' from *Euphorbia* spp. and ingesting mycorrhizal fungi. They also suggest that, rather than the workers of *Veromessor* spp. and *Manica* spp. feeding the young, the young may digest the proteinaceous material with enzymes and feed the workers. Shaeta & Kaschef (1971) found foragers of *Messor aegyptiacus* Emery in Egypt foraging primarily on plant material (seeds, stems and leaves), but the foragers also retrieved animal and non-edible material.

Among the least known of desert consumers are the termites. However, recent studies by Nutting and his coworkers (Nutting, Haverty & LaFaze (1974); Haverty & Nutting (1975)) reveal the use of various types of wood by termites (*Heterotermes aureus*, *Gnathmitermes perplexus*, *Paraneotermes simplicicornis*, and *Amitermes* spp.) in a desert grassland of the Sonoran Desert. The kind and amount of wood eaten by the termites varied, but dead wood from *Acacia greggii*, *Cercidium floridum*, *Opuntia* spp., and *Prosopis juliflora* were major species attacked. These plant species make up over 97% of the dead wood available, and Haverty & Nutting (1975) suggest that, in the Sonoran Desert, the termites do not compete for food, but rather divide up the resource based on different modes of attack and specific wood preferences.

Harris (1970) noted that *Psammotermes hybostome* Desneux in the Sahara Desert survives on the wind-blown debris and animal droppings along the sand dunes. In some very dry areas, they may exist on exposures of relics of Pleistocene flora. In areas which support more vegetation, this termite species will feed on almost all shrub species, even those known to be toxic to mammals (Harris, 1970). Sands (1965) found that harvester termites stored food, but that scavengers and browsers did not.

Bees of many kinds feed on the nectar produced by desert plants. Alcorn, McGregor, Butler & Kurtz (1958) describe the various bees which are attracted to succulent cacti in the Sonoran Desert, and outline the times at which some of these feed. Grant & Grant (1968) also mention the use of desert plant nectar by bees.

Insects of most groups occur in deserts, and many apparently have adapted successfully to arid environmental regimes. Wallwork (1972), working in the Mohave Desert, identified Collembola adults as being primarily herbivorous, while beetles of the families Staphilinidae and Carabidae were carnivorous. A psammophilous beetle (*Lepidochora argentogrisea*) in the Namib Desert has been found to feed on wind-blown detritus (Louw, 1972). While working in sand dunes in the Mohave Desert, Hawke & Farley (1973) discovered that the desert cockroach, *Arenivaga* sp., fed on decaying vegetation and roots, particularly the mycorrhizae associated with roots of *Prosopis juliflora*. Only rarely did the cockroach eat insects. Mosquitoes are common in various deserts where there are

687

Animal processes

oases or intermittent rain pools. These insects require a blood meal before the females can reproduce, and they apparently feed on a variety of mammals and birds, including man (Cloudsley-Thompson, 1968).

Centipedes (Chilopoda)

Cloudsley-Thompson (1968) briefly mentions that centipedes are carnivorous and predatory, but that they will feed on vegetation.

Millipedes (Diplopoda)

At certain times of the year, soon after summer rains, the Sonoran Desert floor can be covered with millipedes. Crawford & Wooten (1973), in an IBP study of the millipede *Orthoporus ornatus* (Girard), have assessed the role of this animal in a desert ecosystem in Big Bend National Park, Texas, and near Albuquerque, New Mexico (Crawford, 1974). *Orthoporus ornatus* frequently uses almost any kind of dead plant material and the superficial tissue of shrubs. Material from *Opuntia* spp. was important in use in Texas, *Salsola* sp. near Albuquerque, and *Ephedra* sp. and *Prosopis juliflora* in southern New Mexico; *Larrea divaricata* was rarely eaten (Crawford, 1974). Ingestion of moist soil was apparently a prerequisite for the ingestion of *Ephedra* sp. The millipedes will infrequently use new plant shoots and animal feces. Hoffman & Payne (1969) suggest that carnivory may be more widespread in the diets of millipedes than is currently believed.

Cordata: Vertebrata
Amphibia

By their very nature of dependence on water, few amphibians occur in arid regions. Generally, frog tadpoles are adapted to ephemeral ponds; they feed on algae and other vegetation, as well as organic debris from the bottom of the ponds (Mayhew, 1968). Calaby (1960) suggests that adult frogs will generally take any insect of the correct size. In South Africa *Pyxicephalus* sp. eats nocturnal insects and termites whereas *Breviceps* sp. feeds on diurnal insects and termites (Fitzsimmons, 1935). *Pyxicephalus* is also known in captivity to eat other frogs, mice and ducklings, and small snakes in the field (Rose, 1962). *Bufo alvarius* has been shown to eat young *Scaphiopus* (Cole, 1962). The adults of some genera (such as *Bufo* and *Pyxicephalus*) are occasionally cannibalistic (Bragg, 1956; Cunningham, 1961). In addition, tadpoles are occasionally cannibalistic, especially when they are late in metamorphosing (Bragg, 1956). In fact, Bragg (1956) noted that seven of several hundred larvae of *Scaphiopus*

688

bombifrons Cope had different mouthparts ('beaks') and jaw muscles, the apparent dimorphism allowing these individuals to ingest conspecific tadpoles should other food become scarce.

Reptilia

Turtles (*Testudines*)

Incidental statements concerning the diet of a North American desert tortoise, *Gopherus agassizi* (Cooper), have mentioned on the one hand that the reptile is a strict vegetarian (Miller, 1955), and on the other that captive *G. agassizi* would eat snails (Nichols, 1953). A more complete study by Woodbury & Hardy (1948) indicates that, although the animal is primarily a vegetarian, it does occasionally ingest insects, and will eat insects and rabbit meat in captivity. *G. agassizi* in southern Utah were found to eat mostly grass, flowers of *Encelia canescens* and *Erodium cicutarium* (Woodbury & Hardy, 1948). The turtle may respond to specific color clues for food choice. *G. agassizi* rarely drinks, apparently getting most of its water from the food it eats.

Lizards (*Squamata: Sauria = Lacertilia*)

Reptiles in general, and lizards specifically, seem to be well adapted for desert existence. Lizard species diversity is high in a number of deserts (Pianka, 1973) and they eat a variety of foods (Pianka, 1971*b*). Most desert lizards are insectivorous, some of them specializing on particular types of insects. Aspland (1967) noted that many of the lizards in Baja California, Mexico, were broadly insectivorous, feeding on termites, beetles, sawflies, moths, butterflies and Orthoptera. The genus *Sceloporus* appear to be very generalized insect feeders. *Sceloporus magister* Hallowell feeds on a wide variety of arthropod prey, with ants, adult beetles and insect larvae being most important, in terms of numbers eaten (Parker & Pianka, 1973). *Sceloporus olivaceus* eats mostly Orthoptera, Lepidopterous larvae and Hemiptera (Kennedy, 1956). The relatively small species *Sceloporus occidentalis* ingests ants, termites, Diptera and Coleoptera (Johnson, 1966), while the larger *Sceloporus pointsetti* feeds on Orthoptera and some plant material (Smith & Milstead, 1971). Related Iguanid lizards are also broadly insectivorous. *Urosaurus ornatus* in southeast Arizona feeds primarily on Isoptera, Homoptera, Hemiptera and ants in trees and shrubs (Aspland, 1964). *Callisaurus draconoides* in southwestern North America varies its diet geographically and seasonally, but is known to eat spiders, scorpions, ants (and other Hymenoptera), grasshoppers, mantids, beetles, termites, Homoptera, Hemiptera, Diptera, Lepidoptera, insect eggs and larvae, and other lizard species (Pianka & Parker, 1972).

Animal processes

Generalized insect feeders from other lizard groups include Teiid lizards of the genus *Cnemidophorus*. *Cnemidophorus tigris* forages actively during the day, searching under bushes for larvae and adult insects. In the southern part of its range, *C. tigris* eats many termites, while to the north it ingests fewer (Pianka, 1970). This species shifts its diet seasonally, feeding primarily on termites and beetles in the spring, and changing to grasshoppers in summer (Pianka, 1970). Pianka (1970) noted that *Uta stansburiana* and *Callisaurus draconoides* in the Sonoran and Mohave Deserts also switched to grasshoppers at the same time as *Cnemidophorus tigris*. Pianka (1970) and Milstead (1965) found that the diets of *Cnemidophorus tigris* included spiders, scorpions, solpugids, ants and other Hymenoptera, grasshoppers, cockroaches, mantids, beetles, ant-lion adults, termites, Homoptera, Hemiptera, butterflies, insect eggs and larvae, lizards and incidental vegetation.

Agamid lizards of the genus *Amphibolurus* have been shown to have a varied insect diet (Tyler, 1960; Pianka, 1971a). Representatives of the genus *Ctenotus* are opportunistic insectivores, the larger species eating larger insects than smaller species (Pianka, 1969). Isopods made up a major portion of the diet (up to 69%), but other items ingested include gastropods, centipedes, spiders, scorpions, Rhaphidoidea, Thysanura, ants and other Hymenoptera, locusts, Blattidae, mantids, Neuroptera, Coleoptera, Isoptera, Diptera, Homoptera, Hemiptera, eggs and larvae of insects, lizards, floral plant parts (up to 10%) and miscellaneous vegetation (Pianka, 1969).

Some lizards of dry areas have evolved to ingest common insects of their area, particularly ants. Members of the Lacertid lizard genus *Eremias* are known to prey on ants (Fitzsimmons, 1935). The Agamid *Moloch horridus* Gray in Australia feeds almost entirely on ants (Davey, 1923; White, 1949). Pianka & Pianka (1970) have found that the stomachs of this species contain mostly ants, although there are apparently other items incidentally ingested which the ants were carrying at the time of their capture. Approximately 24–45 ants were eaten per minute, with up to 2500 ants (in this case, *Iridomyrmex* spp.) being eaten by one lizard at a single feeding (Pianka & Pianka, 1970). Although *M. horidus* eats many kinds of ants, stinging ants were frequently avoided (Pianka & Pianka, 1970). The Iguanid horned lizards (*Phrynosoma* spp.) of the New World also feed primarily on ants (Norris, 1949; Reeve, 1952), and their fecal pellets consist of digested ant carcasses.

There are a number of lizards which have specialized in eating termites, including *Ichnotropis* sp., *Eremias* sp. and *Palmatogecko* sp. (Fitzsimmons, 1935) and *Cnemidophorus hyperthyrus beldingi* (Bostic, 1966). Two species of legless, fossorial skinks (*Typhlosaurus lineatus* and *Typhlosaurus gariepensis*) in the Kalahari Desert have specialized on termites,

690

with the larger species, *T. lineatus*, feeding on the largest termites (Huey, Pianka, Egan & Coons, 1974). Termites are very abundant in the area and make up 84–97% of the diets of these lizards, although they also ingest beetles, ants, Arachnida and insect eggs and larvae (Huey *et al.*, 1974).

Very few lizards are primarily herbivorous, although there are some which specialize on vegetation. The Agamid genus *Uromastix* in the Old World is herbivorous as an adult (Schmidt & Inger, 1957), but the young have different teeth and may be insectivorous (Pope, 160; Mertens, 1960). In the New World, two Iguanid lizard genera, *Sauromalus* and *Dipsosaurus*, are primarily herbivorous. Early work indicated the herbivorous nature of *Sauromalus* spp. (Woodbury, 1931; Shaw, 1939, 1945), and more recent work has described the degree of herbivory. Hansen (1974) found *Sauromalus obesus* near the west end of the Grand Canyon, Arizona to feed mainly on leaves of *Sphaeralcea ambigua* (66%) and *Franseria dumosa* (9%) while *Acacia greggii*, *Lotus strigosus* and soft grasshopper larvae were also ingested. In an extensive study in the Mohave Desert, Nagy (1973) found only one insect and a small amount of feces in stomachs of *S. obesus*, which otherwise contained only vegetation. Leaves were important in the diets in spring, but flowers of *Larrea divaricata* were increasingly used during the summer; leaves of this species were not used frequently, but leaves of *Oenothera clavaeformis* and *Franseria dumosa* were. The lizards shifted their diet from annuals in the spring to perennials in the summer, eventually using to some degree approximately 50% of the plant species available. Many of the plants not used were grasses (Nagy, 1973). Mayhew (1963) noted that *Sauromalus orcutti* preferred yellow flowers, and suggested that this might influence its food choice. *Dipsosaurus dorsalis* is a common lizard in the deserts of North America, and Norris (1953) noted that its range closely corresponds to the range of *Larrea divaricata*. This lizard feeds primarily on vegetation (94.2%, according to Pianka (1971*a*) and Minnich & Shoemaker (1970), especially flowers of *Larrea divaricata* (Norris, 1953; Pianka, 1971*a*). Some mammalian fecal pellets occur in the diet, and there are also some insects, especially in the summer (Norris, 1953); Aspland (1967) suggests that juveniles may feed primarily on insects.

Several lizard species appear to be highly opportunistic, with the capacity to feed on both vegetation and insects. *Aporosaura anchietae* in the Namib Desert feeds on kelp flies where it lives near the sea, and on wind-blown seeds in nearby barren sand dunes (Louw, 1972). In Nevada, USA, *Crotaphytus wislizenii* Baird & Girard feeds on seeds, blossoms and leaves (12%), berries of *Lycium* sp. (22%), insects (55%; mostly moths and termites, and a few ants), and lizards (3.5%, including species of *Callisaurus*, *Cnemidophorus*, *Uta*, *Sceloporus* and *Phrynosoma*) (Tanner & Krogh, 1974).

Animal processes

A few desert lizards are primarily carnivorous or predatory. Perhaps the best known of these is *Heloderma suspectum* Cope, one of the two lizard species known to be poisonous. *H. suspectum* feeds on the eggs of reptiles and birds, and small or young rodents (Hensley, 1949; Bogert & Del Campo, 1956; Pianka, 1966).

Cannibalism has been noted in several desert lizards, including *Hemidactylus flaviviridis* (Rao, 1924; Mahendra, 1936), *Xantusia vigilis* (Heimlich & Heimlich, 1947), *Varanus griseus* (Daudin) (Flower, 1933), *Phrynosoma douglassi* (Dodge, 1938), *Sceloporus orcutti* (Mayhew, 1963), *Crotaphytus wislizenii silus* Stejneyer (Montanucci, 1965) and *Uma notata* (Shaw, 1950).

Snakes (*Sguamata: Serpentes = Ophidia*)

All known desert snakes feed on animals or animal matter (Mayhew, 1968), and there is a tendency for proportion of mammals to lizards in snake diets to increase as the size of the snakes increases. Some very small snakes concentrate on Insects and other invertebrates. *Prosymna* spp. (Fitzsimmons, 1962) and *Chionactis occipitalis* (Klauber, 1951) eat mostly insects, while *Typhlops* spp. (Fitzsimmons, 1962) and *Leptotyphlops* spp. (Klauber, 1940) feed primarily on termites.

Many snakes, including *Psammophis* spp. (Fitzsimmons, 1962) and *Bitis peringueyi* (Louw, 1972; Fitzsimmons, 1962), feed on lizards. *Arizona elegans* (Miller & Stebbins, 1964) and *Crotalus* spp. (Klauber, 1956) have been killed by having the sharp horns of *Phrynosoma* spp. puncture their intestines after ingestion. In addition, many snakes are ophiophagous; *Naja* sp. is known to eat *Psammophis* spp. (Fitzsimmons, 1938), *Masticophis* spp. have eaten *Crotalus* spp. (Stebbins, 1954; Miller & Stebbins, 1964), *Hypsiglena torquata* eats *Leptotyphlops dulcis* (Dundee, 1950) and *Arizona elegans* eats *Phyllorhynchus* sp. (Klauber, 1935). The small Colubrid *Chionactis occipitalis* is preyed on by *Masticophis* spp., *Lampropeltis* spp., *Salvadora hexalepis*, *Arizona elegans* and *Rhinocheilus lecontei* (Klauber, 1951). *Diadophis punctatus* in Texas eats lizards and snakes, as well as earthworms (Gehlback, 1974).

As might be expected, many pit vipers (such as *Crotalus* spp.) feed on warm-blooded animals, using their heat-sensing pits to detect prey (Klauber, 1956), although some species tend to eat lizards which are smaller and easier to swallow (Klauber, 1956). Many kinds of homeotherms are used; *Crotalus cerastes lateropens* has been shown to eat fifteen species of mammals (ranging in size from *Notiosorex crawfordi* to *Neotoma* spp.), four bird species, nine lizard species, and four species of snakes (Funk, 1965). Funk (1964) also noted that *Crotalus molossus* ingested mice and, on one occasion, *Heloderma suspectum*. The Australian desert python feeds on wallabies and kangaroos (Leopold, 1961).

692

Birds (Aves)

Because of their vagility, birds which periodically inhabit the desert can seasonally or daily move out of it or move to areas (such as water holes) which are more equable, thereby avoiding some of the stresses incurred by other desert animals. Most of the birds associated with deserts are insectivorous (Miller, 1951). However, there are many other modes of feeding. In North America the doves (Columbidae), *Carpodacus mexicanus* (Müller), *Pipilo fuscus* Swainson and *Amphispiza bilineata* (Cassin) tend to be granivorous (Tomoff, 1974) as do the budgerigar (*Melopsittacus undulatus*) in Australia (Cade & Dybas, 1962) and *Pterocles alchata* in the Negev (Shkolnik, 1971). In addition, *P. alchata* is known to fly great distances carrying water on its breast feathers to give to the young on the nest (Cade & Maclean, 1967; Sholnik, 1971).

Other granivorous birds include *Taeniopygia castanotis* in Australia, *Lophortyx gambelii* and *Cyrtonyx montezumae* in North America (Bartholomew & Cade, 1963) and *Erythrina sinaiaca* in Israel (Shkolnik, 1971). Bartholomew & Cade (1963) suggest that desert Fringillids and most desert birds require green vegetation or free water to augment their diet of dry seeds. Serventy (1971) considers *Amphispiza bilineata* to be the best desert-adapted bird in North America, and this species must add greenery and insects to its dry seed diet for proper water balance. Although desert birds do not appear to be able to maintain weight on completely dry diets, as some mammals can, birds do maintain weight when the dry diet is supplemented with succulent vegetation (Lowe, 1955; Bartholomew & Cade, 1956; Bartholomew, 1960; Guilliou, 1960; Smyth & Bartholomew, 1966).

Although many desert birds use green vegetation, relatively few of them are almost entirely herbivorous. The ostrich (*Struthio camelus*) in the Namib feeds mostly on the grasses *Bohenia* sp. and *Stipagrostis uniplumus* and cannot maintain itself on dry food (Louw, 1972). Desert hummingbirds, while not feeding on the vegetation *per se*, ingest quantities of nectar (Grant & Grant, 1968) from plants such as *Fouquieria splendens*, *Castilleja* spp., *Allionia* spp. and *Agave* spp. Succulent vegetation provides much water for nestlings (Gordon, 1934), and doves will drink water and regurgitate it to their young (Salt & Zeuthen, 1960). *Auriparus flaviceps* (Sunderall) in the Sonoran Desert frequently eats the seed pods of *Cercidium* spp., *Olneya tesota* Guy and *Prosopis* spp., but does not eat the seeds themselves (Taylor, 1971). Occasionally, this bird will also ingest the berries of *Lycium exsertum* (Taylor, 1971).

Whereas some birds supplement dry diets with green vegetation, probably many more get their moisture from eating insects. Tomoff (1974) has listed several insectivorous bird species from the Sonoran Desert, and describes from which microhabitat they get their prey. Birds which are largely granivorous (such as *Amphispiza bilineata* (Serventy, 1971)) augment their diet with insects, apparently for moisture. Insects are also a water source for such birds as *Salpinctes absoletus* (Say.), *Auriparus flaviceps* and seed-eating sparrows (Dawson & Bartholomew, 1968). Taylor (1971) describes the diet of *Auriparus flaviceps* in the Sonoran Desert, including such items as caterpillars, spiders, Hemiptera, Homoptera, Coleoptera, Diptera, Hymenoptera, and some Orthoptera. Swallows and swifts in Africa are known to eat swarming termites, as are nightjars (Serventy, 1971), although these birds apparently still have to drink free water to maintain water balance (Serventy, 1971). Irwin (1956) found very few insectivorous passerines around a water hole in Bechuanaland, again indicating that desert birds can fulfil most of their water requirements through dietary preferences.

Some intermediate-sized birds apparently may eat mainly invertebrates when small, but change to a diet predominantly of vertebrates as they get larger. Ligon (1968) described the diet of the owl *Micrathene whitneyi* in the Sonoran Desert to be almost entirely of arthropods (including Chilopoda, Arachnida and insects), although one lizard (*Sceloporus jarrovi*) and one snake (*Leptotyphlops dulcis*) were taken by an adult owl. *Geococcyx californianus* in the Sonoran Desert feeds on arthropods and lizards (especially *Cnemidophorus* spp., which are diurnal); but as the birds grow older, lizards make up almost the entire diet (Bryant, 1916; Ohmart, 1973).

Predatory birds in deserts apparently all get enough moisture from their carnivorous diet (Dawson & Bartholomew, 1968) to sustain their activity. In fact, some birds live and reproduce in very harsh desert conditions (for instance, peregrine and sooty falcons, in the deserts of North Africa (Bartholomew & Cade, 1963)). No doubt a variety of prey are taken by predatory birds in the desert, from lizards to rodents and rabbits. A collection of pallets from the owl *Bubo virginianus* in the Chihuahuan Desert contained the skulls of 234 mammals (117 *Mus musculus*, 35 *Notiosorex crawfordi*, 27 *Peromyscus eremicus*, 25 *Sigmodon hispidus*, 22 *Reithrodontomys* sp., 2 *Dipodomys merriami*, 2 *Peromyscus* sp. and 1 *Macrotus californicus* (Bradshaw & Howard, 1960)). *Falco peregrinus babylonicus* has been shown to prey on bats (Bartholomew & Cade, 1963) and one of us (OJR) has observed *Bubo virginianus* taking bats in the Chihuahuan Desert.

Mammalia
Marsupialia

The diets of desert marsupials are poorly known. The mulgara (*Dasycercus cristicauda*) of the central Australian desert is primarily carnivorous, feeding on insects, small reptiles and small rodents (Schmidt-Nielsen,

1964). The red kangaroo (*Megaleia rufa* Desmarest) in central Australia limits its range to shrubby areas, which during drought may be only along water courses, feeding mostly on green shrubs and grasses, especially *Eragrostis* spp. (Chippendale, 1962; Newsome, 1965).

Insectivora

The insectivore *Notiosorex crawfordi* of the American deserts is almost entirely insectivorous, feeding on insect larvae, crickets, grasshoppers, flies, moths and centipedes (Fisher, 1941; Hoffmeister & Goodpaster, 1962). There are several species of insectivores which live in the arid regions of India, and the diets of two of these have been fairly completely studied. Stomach contents of 30 hedgehogs, *Hemiechinus auritus*, revealed that almost 54% of the diet was made up of insects (including Coleoptera, Orthoptera, Isoptera and Neuroptera). In addition, amphibians, reptiles, miscellaneous mammalian remnants and eggshells were found in the stomach (Krishna & Prakash, 1956). At various times of the year, these hedgehogs have been shown to ingest a variety of insects, toads, lizards and other hedgehogs (Prakash, 1956, 1959a, 1959b).

Primates

The langur, *Presbytis entellus*, is a leaf-eating monkey found in the southeastern deserts of India. It feeds on a variety of leaves from trees and other vegetation, and recently has become an agriculture pest by eating fruits from cultivated orchards (Mohnot, personal communication).

The baboon (*Papio hamadryas*) of east Sudan, Somaliland and southwest Arabia is an omnivore. Its preferred dietary item is leaves and flowers of *Acacia* spp. but it will also ingest grass seeds and fruits when available. Large quantities of locusts are ingested when they are abundant, and one female baboon was observed carrying the carcass of a small dik-dik (antelope), which was later found with only small portions eaten (Kummer, 1968).

Chiroptera

Most of the Microchiropteran bats in the North American deserts are insectivorous. In Arizona *Eumops perotis* (Schinz) eats mostly Hymenoptera (58%), but also many other insects (Ross, 1961). In the same area *Tadarida brasiliensis* (Saussure) ate many Lepidopteran insects, and a few Hymenoptera and Hemiptera (Ross, 1961). *Antrozous pallidus* (Le Conte) was noted to be a very generalized feeder, ingesting Orthoptera, Homoptera, Hemiptera, Neuroptera, Coleoptera and Lepidoptera (Ross, 1961).

695

Animal processes

One of us (OJR) has captured foraging *A. pallidus* in mouse-traps on the ground, and also carrying a 150 mm centipede to a night roost.

Nectar provides energy and nutrition for several very specialized bats in the deserts of North America and Mexico. Nectar makes up approximately 75% of the diet of *Leptonycteris sanbomis* with pollen and occasional insects making up the remaining 25% (Carpenter, 1969; Howell, 1973). Near the sea in the arid regions of Baja California, Mexico, the bats of the genus *Pizonyx* feed on fish which they catch with the sharp claws on their hind feet (Carpenter, 1969).

In the deserts of India, the Indian fruit bat *Pteropus giganteus* roosts in trees of *Ficus* spp. and *Tamarindus indica*, feeding on figs of *F. religiosa* and *F. bengalensis* (Prakash, 1959*b*). They also show a strong preference for other fruit such as mango (*Mangifera indica*), guava (*Psidium guajava*) and blackberries (*Rubus* spp.) (Prakash, 1959*b*). Microchiropteran diets are poorly known, except that they eat moths, Neuropterous insects and beetles. The Indian bat *Megaderma lyra* has frequently been observed to feed on other bats such as *Rhinopoma* sp. and *Taphozous perforatus* (Prakash, 1959*c*). The heads of the victims are always ingested, with the body frequently being left uneaten (Prakash, 1959*c*). In addition to the bats, lizards (*Hemidactylus flaviridis*), birds and insects are eaten in the wild, and captive *M. lyra* will eat sparrows, gerbils, mice, rats and other bats (Prakash, 1959*c*).

Edentata

Armadillos are occasionally found in arid regions in North America, where they eat eggs, insects, snakes, lizards, and amphibians (Walker, 1968). One of us (VR) has shown that desert edentates in South America (such as *Zaedyus* spp., *Chaetophractus* spp., and *Chlamyphorus* spp.) have a varied diet. Analysis of the stomach contents of 211 *Zaedyus* spp. from north Patagonia (Fig. 29.1) indicate that vegetation and fruit made up from 40% to 90% of the diet seasonally, with insects being the next most important item eaten. Snakes, lizards and mammals were also occasionally eaten.

Rabbits (*Lagomorpha*)

Early studies from North America mention that rabbits of the genus *Lepus* feed on succulent herbs when available, but may switch to *Opuntia* spp. during dry periods (Vorhies, 1933) and may even eat *Larrea divaricata* (Jaeger, 1948). Chew & Chew (1970) show that *Lepus californicus* Gray and *Sylvilagus auduboni* (Baird) feed primarily on shrub browse and herbs. *Lepus* spp. have also been noted to eat fresh grass, leaves of *Prosopis*

696

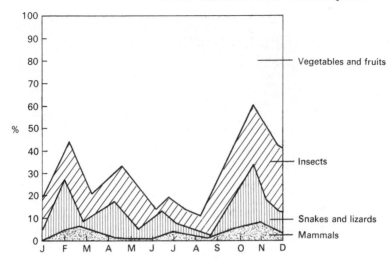

Fig. 29.1. Constituents of the diet of *Zaedyus pichy* from north Patagonia.

spp., and cactus pads during dry seasons (Schmidt-Nielsen, 1964). In more recent studies north of Phoenix, Arizona, Turkowski & Reynolds (1974) found that *S. auduboni* ingested 46 species of plants, and miscellaneous arthropods. Grasses, especially *Tridens pulchellus*, *Bromus* spp. and *Eragrostis* spp. were major constituents of the diet, with forbs such as *Plantago purshii*, *Cryptantha* spp. and *Lupinus sparsiflorus* also being used. The diets varied considerably seasonally, with plant species important in the diet during one season all but absent in a subsequent season (Turkowski & Reynolds, 1974). In addition, some plant species were sampled by a considerable portion of the population, but made up a small part of the whole diet. Turkowski & Reynolds (1974) suggest that these lagomorphs are able to adapt to use a variety of foodstuffs as they become available, consuming 75% of the grass and forb genera and 66% of the shrub genera available to them. The rabbits apparently prefer early growth stages of the plants, as older stages were frequently ignored.

Shoemaker, Nagy & Costa (1974) found that *Lepus californicus* fed primarily on annuals (64%), particularly *Salsola iberica*, in the Mohave Desert. The major perennial eaten was *Larrea divaricata*, with *Ambrosia* (= *Franseria*) *dumosa* also being favored.

Lepus nigricollis in India appears to be a true herbivore, consuming a variety of grasses, shrubs and tree seedlings. Identifiable plant species in stomach contents include *Cenchrus ciliaris*, *Lasiurus sindicus*, *Cynodon dactylon*, *Indigofera cordifolia*, and leaves of *Albizzia lebbek* and *Oropetium thomaem* (Prakash, unpublished data).

697

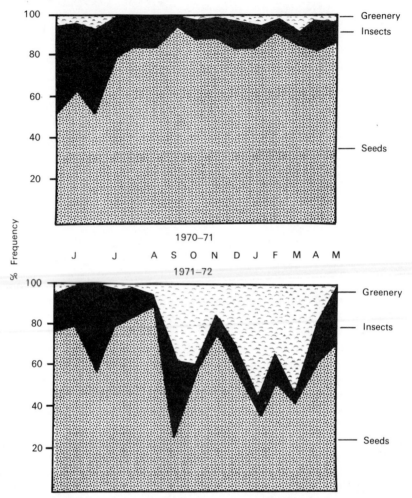

Fig. 29.2. Frequency of occurrence of the constituents of the diet of *Dipodomys merriami* during two years. There were two sampling periods in June, July and August. (From Reichman *et al.*, 1975.)

Rodentia

The family Heteromyidae includes some of the most desert-adapted animals yet studied. These rodents, particularly the genera *Dipodomys*, *Perognathus* and *Microdipodops*, maintain themselves primarily on a diet of dry seeds, only rarely, if ever, drinking free water (Hall & Linsdale, 1929; Schmidt-Nielsen, 1964). Although these rodents primarily ingest seeds, they will also ingest green vegetation when it periodically becomes available (Reichman, 1975; Reichman & Van De Graaff, 1975; Reichman,

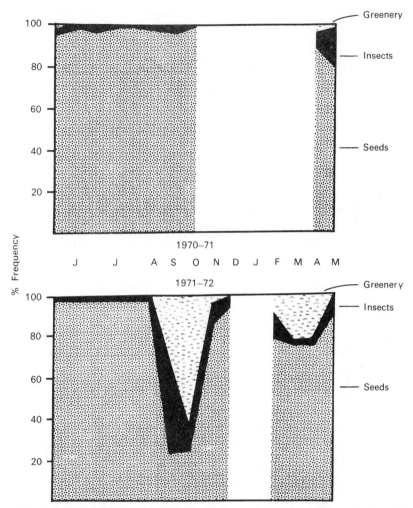

Fig. 29.3. Frequency of occurrence of the constituents of the diet of *Perognathus amplus* during two years. There were two sampling periods in June, July and August. (From Reichman *et al.*, 1975.)

1978). In addition to the seeds and greenery used, various heteromyid species use a proportion of insects in their diets, over 17% in the case of *Dipodomys merriami* Mearns in the Sonoran Desert (Reichman *et al.*, 1975). Forbs provided from 28% to 78% of the diets of four Heteromyid species, with shrubs and grass seeds being variously used (Figs 29.2, 29.3). The availability of food items broadly determines the diets of the Heteromyidae, but specific preferences determine the exact quantities eaten (Reichman, 1975, 1978). It has been shown that Heteromyidae ranging in size from 1 g to 40 g require from 60 to 325 seeds of various species per night, respectively, to fulfill their energy requirements (Reichman, 1977). A peculiar anatomical feature of *Dipodomys microps* (Merriam) allows it to eat a potentially toxic halophyte in the Great Basin Desert. This species uses its chisel-shaped teeth to strip the salt-containing cells from the leaf surfaces of *Atriplex* spp., rendering the remainder edible (Kenagy, 1973).

Rodents of the genera *Notomys* and *Leggadina* in Australia are even more adept than Heteromyidae at maintaining themselves on a dry diet (MacMillen & Lee, 1967, 1969). These rodents are primarily granivorous, and can tolerate salt-containing vegetation (Findlayson, 1940; MacMillen & Lee, 1967, 1969).

The majority of rodents inhabiting arid regions of the world are herbivorous. Fossorial pocket gophers (*Thomomys bottae* (Edyoux & Gervais)) inhabiting Rock Valley in the Mohave Desert ate approximately one-third of their weight per day in vegetation, preferring the perennial *Lycium* spp. and the annual *Eriogonum* spp. (Dingman & Byers, 1974). *Larrea divaricata* was ingested, but was not a preferred item. The Springhaas in the arid regions of Africa ingests a variety of vegetation, including bulbs, fleshy roots, stems and grass, although insects will occasionally be taken (Walker, 1968). These rodents will also travel up to 32 km to find water.

Woodrats of the genus *Neotoma* frequently are found in the deserts of North America, but, unlike the Heteromyidae, they require moisture to maintain themselves. Various authors have reported the woodrats to eat few insects (less than 1% of their diet, according to Vorhies & Taylor (1940)), seeds, fruits, greenery (especially species of *Prosopis*, *Acacia*, *Cereus*, *Eriogonum*, *Artemisia* and *Opuntia*) (Vorhies & Taylor, 1940; Finley, 1958; Schmidt-Nielsen, 1964; MacMillen, 1964; Ryan, 1968). Woodrats apparently have the capacity to eat large quantities of *Opuntia* spp., physiologically ignoring the toxic oxalates contained in these plants (Schmidt-Neilsen, 1964). Some authors have suggested that woodrats eat *Larrea divaricata* (Jaeger, 1948; Ryan, 1968). Some Old World counterparts of the woodrats, the gerbils (*Psammomys* spp.), eat many succulent plants, even those containing salt, and also have the ability to tolerate oxalates in their diets (Schmidt-Nielsen, 1964). Petter (1961) noted that *Psammomys* spp. ingested very succulent Chenopodiaceae which contained from 78% to 89% water. A related gerbil, *Meriones animaleus*, also is primarily herbivorous. Observations by one of us (VR) on South American rodents show that *Lagostomus maximus*, a member of the Chinchillidae, is primarily herbivorous. Two members of the Caviidae, *Dolichotis patagonica* and *Microcavia australis*, are also both herbivorous, the former occasionally feeding on *Prosopanche americana*, a parasite of *Prosopis* spp. and the latter on *Larrea* sp. The South American

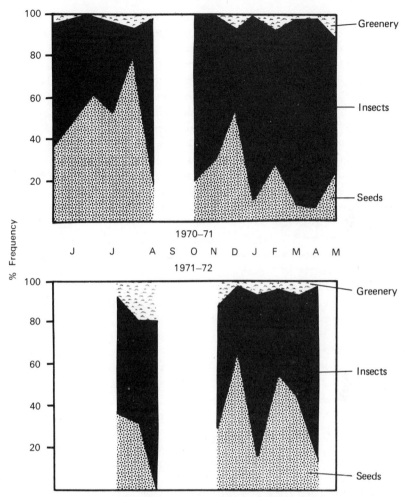

Fig. 29.4. Frequency of occurrence of the constituents of the diet of *Peromyscus eremicus* during two years. There were two sampling periods in June, July and August. (From Reichman *et al.*, 1975.)

fossorial rodent, *Ctenomys* sp., feeds on all parts of various bushes, including *Larrea* sp.

Many arid-region rodents are omnivorous, depending on both vegetation and insects at various times of the year to maintain their energetic and nutritional requirements. In India, the northern palm squirrel, *Funambulus pennanti* W. Houghton, consumes fruits, insects, insect larvae and bird eggs (Prakash, 1959*b*). This squirrel eats a considerable number of locusts during the summer months when little vegetation or fruit is available (Prakash & Kametkar, 1969).

In North American deserts, ground squirrels are conspicuous members of the diurnal desert fauna, and because they are active during the day they face a number of water-balance problems (Bartholomew & Hudson, 1961). Members of the genus *Spermophilus* (*Citellus*) are highly omnivorous, feeding on seeds, greenery, stems, roots, carrion and insects, some of which they store (Walker, 1968; Bartholomew & Hudson, 1961; Hudson, 1962). *Spermophilus nelsoni* tends to avoid inappropriate (in terms of moisture) vegetation until no other greenery is available, and tends to be insectivorous during the summer and fall (Hawbreaker, 1947).

One of us (VR) has found that *Akodon* spp. in the central deserts of Argentina, eat a number of items, including vegetation, seeds, insects and Oligochaeta. Reichman (1978) studied the diet of the North American desert Cricetid rodent, *Peromyscus eremicus* (Baird); this species eats mostly insects (56%), but also ingests numerous seeds and green vegetation when it is available (Fig. 29.4).

Among the most versatile mammals in terms of diet are the gerbils. These rodents are known to eat seeds, leaves, stems, fruits and insects in several deserts in which they occur (Shkolnik, 1971; Louw, 1972). Extensive studies of the stomach contents of two gerbils (*Meriones hurrianae* Jerdon and *Tatera indica*) show considerable seasonal disparity in their feeding propensities. In addition, *M. hurrianae* feeds during the day and *T. indica* during the night. The fluctuations in food items used are reflections of seasonal changes in availability and quantity. Seeds are least important in the diets in June and July, while showing maximum use in December and January, the range being from 10% to 60% for *M. hurrianae* and nil to 40% for *T. indica*. Stems and rhizomes in the diet of *T. indica* show less fluctuation (15–30%) than in that of *M. hurrianae* (10% in January and 45% in June). Leaves and flowers in the diet of *T. indica* range from 20% to 30% throughout the year, but in the case of *M. hurrianae* their use goes down to 5% in May and reaches 40% in October. Insects are not used by *M. hurrianae* except in the months when locusts are available, but they form a regular food for *T. indica* and in July reach a maximum of 40% in the diet (Prakash, 1962, 1969).

Buxton (1923) reports about a very close relationship between the halophilous *Suaeda* sp. and a dwarf gerbil (*Dipodilus dasyurus*) in Iraq. *Suaeda* sp. grows in salt patches in the deserts; a few bushes of *Atriplex* sp. and *Salsola* sp. were the only plants found associated with it, and they were not common. Several insect species lived on the *Suaeda* sp., and the dwarf gerbils lived on any insects they could catch and on the succulent leaves of the plant. The rodents required water in captivity, and there is little doubt that they are entirely dependent on this plant, and the insects found upon it, for food and water.

Members of the family Dipodidae, the jerboas, inhabit many arid regions in north Africa, Asia Minor and southern Asia, where their diets include succulent plants, seeds and insects (Walker, 1968).

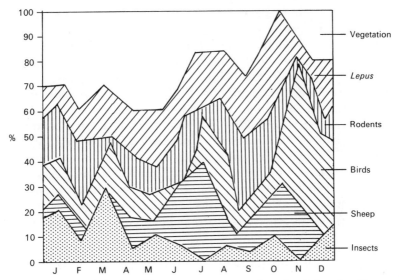

Fig. 29.5. Constituents of the diet of *Dusicyon gymnocercus* from South America. (Crespo, personal communication to V. R.)

Several species of rodents inhabiting arid regions are primarily insectivorous, among them being *Onychomys* spp. of the North American deserts. These animals eat a variety of insects, and ingest those mammals and birds which they can subdue (up to 89% of the diet is animal material) (Bailey & Sperry, 1929; Schmidt-Nielsen & Haines, 1964; Flake, 1973). Other carnivorous mice are in the genus *Acomys*. A major portion of the diet of these rodents in the Negev Desert consists of snails (Shkolnik & Borut, 1969; Shkolnik, 1971).

Carnivora

All North American carnivore families except bears are represented in arid regions, apparently getting sufficient moisture from their food (Bartholomew & Hudson, 1968). Coyotes (*Canis latrans* Say) show a great variety of feeding behavior, from carnivory (only 2% vegetation in diet, Sperry (1941)) to a diet including a considerable amount of vegetation (80% of scats containing plant material, Murie (1951)). Murie (1951) found the stomachs of coyotes to contain plant material (*Opuntia* spp., *Prosopis* spp., *Acacia* spp.), beef, javelina (*Tayassu tajaçu* (Linn.)), coyotes, rodents, rabbits, birds, grasshoppers and beetles. The stomachs of 230 *Dusicyon* sp. from the pampas of South America (Fig. 29.5) indicated a diet which was highly seasonal and contained vegetation, rabbits, rodents, birds, insects and domestic sheep (Crespo, personal communication).

Remains at the burrow entrance of a kit fox (*Vulpes macrotis* Merriam) in the Great Basin Desert indicate that this individual had eaten eighteen young and fourteen adults of *Lepus* spp., two individuals of *Sylvilagus* sp., five *Peromyscus* spp., three *Dipodomys merriami*, one *D. microps*, one *Onychomys* sp., four *Eremophila alpestris*, one pigeon (*Columba livia*), and three unidentified birds (Egoscue, 1962). *Vulpes vulpes* in the Indian deserts feeds primarily on the desert gerbil (*Meriones hurrianae*) (Blanford, 1888–1891). One of us (IP) has examined the stomachs of a number of these foxes and found them to contain berries and seeds of *Zizyphus* spp. and *Citrullus* spp., insects, scorpions and gerbils. The Bengal fox, *Vulpes bengalensis*, occurs along with *V. vulpes* but is not so common. It feeds on ground birds and lizards, but small mammals also form part of its diet. Beetles, grasshoppers and termites are also eaten in fair numbers (Pocock, 1941). Stomachs examined were full of scorpions, seeds of melon (*Citrullus vulgaris*), and parts of *Tatera indica* (Prakash, 1969).

The jackal, *Canis aureus aureus* is the common scavenger of India, feeding on offal or dead carcasses of cattle, sheep and other livestock. It sometimes attacks sick sheep and their lambs. Ailing or injured gazelles are also hunted by packs of jackals. The examination of stomach contents of a few jackals revealed that they were almost full with the berries of *Zizyphus nummularia*, chitinous parts of scorpions and beetles (*Helicopris buciphalus*, *Juliodes atkinsoni*, *Anthia sexuttata*). The stomach of a female contained bony pieces of the desert gerbil, *Meriones hurrianae*, and fur of a mongoose, *Herpestes auropunctatus pallipes* (Prakash, 1969). In the irrigated parts of the desert the jackals damage the crops of sugar cane (*Saccharum officinarum*) and maize (*Zea mays*). In some areas of Rajasthan, jackals and foxes appear to consume more leaves and vegetation than most desert carnivores (Prakash, 1959b).

The fennec (*Fennecus zerda*) in the Sahara survives on a mainly carnivorous diet, consuming insects, lizards, mammals and varying amounts of vegetation (Schmidt-Nielsen, 1964).

Desert Mustelid carnivores such as the badger (*Taxidea taxus* (Schreber)) ingest *Citellus* spp., *Thomomys* spp., rabbits, lizards and insects (Martin, Zim & Nelson, 1951). Arid-region skunks have diets greatly determined by the availability of vertebrates, invertebrates and vegetation. *Mephitis mephitis* (Schreber) ingests insect larvae, adult insects, spiders, frogs, lizards, mice, eggs of birds, *Opuntia* spp. and *Prosopis* spp. *Mephitis mucroura* (Lichtenstein) and *Conepatus mesoleucus* (Lichtenstein) have similar diets, but ingest more vegetation.

The Indian mongoose, *Herpestes edwardsi ferrugineus*, a fairly common carnivore in the Indian desert, is well known as a 'rat-killer'. It has been introduced in Jamaica, the Phillipines and several other islands to save the sugar cane crops from rat damage. In the desert, however, its stomachs contained feathers of the partridge *Francolinus pondicerianus*, incisors of a rodent, skin of *Varanus griseus* and remains of termites (*Anacanthotermes macrocephalus*), other insects, and a scorpion (Prakash, 1969).

The small Indian Mongoose, *Herpestes auropunctatus pallipes*, feeds mostly upon insects. Stomachs of two mongooses contained *Helicopris buciphalus*, *Anthia sexguttata*, *Blaps orientalis*, *Onthophagus longicornis*, *Gryllus saggilatus* and scorpions. One was observed feeding upon an unidentified lizard (Prakash, unpublished data).

The Indian desert cat, *Felis libyca ornata*, is one of the carnivores which has been reported to feed on the gerbils *Meriones hurrianae* and *Tatera indica*. Their stomachs, however, contained termites, *Periplaneta* sp., *Hirodula codurcota*, *Gryllus saggilatus*, and other unidentifiable insects. Nocturnal and capable of climbing trees, it also feeds upon pigeons and ring doves, *Streptopelia decaocto* (Prakash, 1969).

North American Felids which range into arid regions include *Lynx rufus* (Schreber), which ingests a number of animal species and relatively little vegetation (4.5%, according to Young (1958)), and *Felis concolor* (Kerr), which eats rodents, rabbits, deer and carrion (Young, 1946).

Artiodactyla

Many large ungulates avoid many problems of food and water in arid environments by moving or migrating to the most appropriate regions. Others maintain water balance by manipulating their diet to ensure sufficient moisture intake (Schmidt-Nielsen, 1964). Javelinas (*Tayassu tajaçu* (Linn.)) in the Sonoran Desert eat a variety of vegetation, particularly fruit of *Opuntia* spp. (and pads when fruits are not available), beans of *Prosopis* spp. and bases of *Agave* spp. Annual forbs are important seasonally in the diet, as are fruits of *Cereus giganteus*; very few insects are eaten (Eddy, 1961). Other authors have noted the dependence on *Opuntia* spp., showing that it makes up 84.5% of the volume of material eaten, while grass makes up 8.6% and seeds of *C. giganteus* (indicating that the fruit had been eaten) only 0.6% of the diet (Sowls, 1958; Neal, 1959).

Mule deer (*Odocoileus hemionus* (Rafinesque)) in the Sonoran Desert feed on succulent forbs and shrubs, and usually require free water (Elder, 1956). Pronghorn antelopes (*Antilocapra americana*) in the Chihuahuan Desert ate 168 species of forbs, 56 species of browse shrubs and 18 species of grasses, the proportion used in each season depending on availability (Buechner, 1950). Wild sheep (*Ovis canadensis* Shaw) feed primarily on shrubs, especially *Coleogyne ramosissima*. They also eat a number of forbs (*Stanleya* sp., *Astragalus* spp., *Bassia* sp.) and grasses (especially *Hilaria* spp.) (Russo, 1956; Wilson, 1968; Irvine, 1969). Most of the vegetation ingested was succulent, but occasionally they were

Table 29.1. *Primary dietary habits (X) and known dietary habits (×) of the animals discussed in this chapter*

Herb. = primarily vegetation in diet; Gran. = primarily seeds in diet; Omni. = variety of items in diet; Insect. = primarily insects in diet; Carn. = primarily animal matter other than insects in diet; Detri. = primarily decaying matter in diet; Scav. = primarily detritus in diet; Can. = known to be occasionally cannibalistic.

Animal group			Herb.	Gran.	Omni.	Insect.	Carn.	Detri.	Scav.	Can.
Nematoda			X					X		
Mollusca	Gastropoda (*snails*)		X		X			X		
Arthropoda	Acarina (*mites*)		X[1]	X	X	X	X	X	X	
	Scorpionidae					X	X			×
	Pseudoscorpionidae					X	X			×
	Solifugidae					X	X			×
	Araneida (*spiders*)					X	X			×
	Chilopoda (*centipedes*)		X				X			
	Diplopoda (*millipedes*)		X				X[2]			
Insecta			X			X	X			×
Amphibia			X[3]			X[3]	X			×
Reptilia	Chelonia (*turtles*)		X	X	X	X	X			
	Squamata (*lizards*)			X		X	X		×	×
	(*snakes*)					X	X		×	×
Aves			X	X	X	X	X		×	
Mammalia	Lagomorpha (*rabbits*)		X	X						
	Rodentia		X	X	X	X				
	Carnivora	Canidae			X		X		×	
		Felidae					X		×	
	Artiodactyla		X							
	Marsupialia		X		X	X	X		×	
	Insectivora					X	X			
	Primates		X		X		X			
	Chiroptera		X[4]			X		X		
	Edentata		X		X	X				

[1] Includes fungi.   [2] Includes animal feces.   [3] Larvae and adults are almost completely different in their dietary habits.   [4] Mostly fruit.

forced to eat dried leaves of *Calochortus* spp., *Streptanthus* spp., *Cirsium* spp., and *Hymenoxys* spp. (Wilson, 1968).

In the dry regions of its range, the giraffe (*Giraffa cameleopardalis*) ingests large quantities of leaves of *Acacia* spp., as does *Gazella dorcas*, which shows no need to drink water on this diet (Carlisle & Ghorbial, 1968). Taylor (1968) has discussed the exceptional morphological adaptations of *Gazella granti* and *Oryx beisa* which allow them to exist by feeding at night on hygroscopic food, when it contains the most moisture. These animals feed on the leaves of plants which contain only 1% water during the day, but contain 30% water nocturnally, allowing the ungulates to take in over five liters of water per night with their food (Taylor, 1968). In the Negev, gazelles (*Gazella* spp.) cannot live on food alone, although they ingest a considerable amount of vegetation, and must find free water to drink (Shkolnik, 1971).

As mentioned in the Introduction to this Chapter, many desert animals have been ignored or neglected because of the paucity of data concerning their diets. Table 29.1, however, presents a summary of the dietary modes of the animals discussed in this Chapter, indicating both the major habit and other known habits.

Synthesis

The use of the majority of items ingested by desert consumers probably depends on the moisture requirements imposed on the organism by the generally low-moisture and high-temperature regimes of deserts. Thus, certain types of food (such as herbaceous material and insects) are superior to others because of the moisture provided, without requiring the animals to have special adaptations to the use of the item. Other items, such as seeds, probably require the consumer to have a particular capacity to choose those seed species which will yield appropriate amounts of metabolic water.

As is often the case elsewhere, desert consumers frequently use those dietary items which are most abundant. Thus, for example, many desert consumers use insects. If the insect prey items exhibit seasonal or diel activity patterns the consumers may mirror this trait, as do lizards and bats. In other cases, insect-consumers such as kangaroo rats may ingest different kinds of insects, and may forage for active adult insects during the warm season and for larvae during other seasons (Reichman, 1975; Reichman, 1978). Of course, the feeding of many animals, particularly poikilotherms, is regulated by environmental conditions, especially temperature, as well as by food availability. Thus both environmental constraints and temporal patterns of availability of appropriate foods force desert consumers to adjust their seasonal and diel activity patterns and

Animal processes

their dietary preferences. This can even occur seasonally within a species (for instance, rodents are active late at night during the hottest part of the summer, and earlier during winter; and gazelles and oryx feed at a time of night when the greatest amount of hygroscopic water is available). These modifications in diet and foraging behavior allow many species to mitigate what appears, to a human investigator, to be an unfavorable environment and take advantage of seasonal bursts of productivity and diversity.

References

Alcorn, S. M., McGregor, S. E., Butler, G. D. & Kurtz, E. B. (1958). Pollination requirements of the sahuaro (*Carnegia gigantea*). *Cactus and Succulent Journal*, **31**, 39–41.

Aspland, K. K. (1964). Seasonal variation in the diet of *Urosaurus ornatus* in a riparian community. *Herpetologica*, **20**, 91–4.

Aspland, K. K. (1967). Ecology of the lizards in the relictual Cape Flora, Baja California. *American Midland Naturalist*, **77**, 462–75.

Bailey, V. E. & Sperry, C. C. (1929). *Life history and habits of grasshopper mice, genus* Onychomys. U.S. Department of Agriculture Technical Bulletin No. 145, pp. 1–20. Washington, D.C.

Bartholomew, G. A. (1960). The physiology of desert birds. *Anatomical Record*, **137**, 338.

Bartholomew, G. A. & Cade, T. J. (1956). Water consumption of house finches. *Condor*, **58**, 406–12.

Bartholomew, G. A. & Cade, T. J. (1963). The water economy of land birds. *Auk*, **80**, 504–39.

Bartholomew, G. A. & Dawson, J. W. (1961). Desert ground squirrels. *Scientific American*, **205**, 107–16.

Bartholomew, G. A. & Hudson, J. W. (1968). Temperature regulation in desert mammals. In: *Desert Biology* (ed. G. W. Brown), vol. 1, pp. 395–421. Academic Press, New York & London.

Blanford, W. T. (1888–91). *Fauna of British India, Mammalia*. Taylor & Francis, London.

Bogert, C. M. & del Campo, M. (1956). The gila monster and its allies. *Bulletin American Museum of Natural History*, **109**, 1–238.

Bostic, D. L. (1966). Food and feeding behaviour of the teiid lizard, *Cnemidophorus hyperthyrus beldingi*. *Herpetologica*, **22**, 23–31.

Bradshaw, G. & Howard, B. (1960). Mammal skulls recovered from owl pellets in Sonora, Mexico. *Journal of Mammalogy*, **41**, 282–3.

Bragg, A. N. (1956). Dimorphism and cannibalism in tadpoles of *Scaphiopus bombifrons* (Amphibia, Salientia). *Southwestern Naturalist*, **1**, 105–8.

Bristow, W. S. (1941). *The family of spiders*. B. Quaritch, London.

Brown, G. W. (ed.) (1968). *Desert Biology*, vol. I. Academic Press, New York & London.

Brown, G. W. (ed.) (1974). *Desert Biology*, vol. II. Academic Press, New York & London.

Bryant, H. C. (1916). Habits and food of the roadrunner in California. *University of California Publications in Zoology*, **17**, 21–50.

708

Buechner, H. K. (1950). Life history, ecology, and range use of the pronghorn antelope in Trans-Pecos Texas. *American Midland Naturalist*, **43**, 257–354.

Buxton, P. A. (1923). *Animal life in deserts*. Arnold, London.

Cade, T. J. & Dybas, J. A. (1962). Water economy of the budgerygah. *Auk*, **79**, 345–64.

Cade, T. J. & MacLean, G. L. (1967). Transport of water by adult sandgrouse to their young. *Condor*, **69**, 323–43.

Calaby, J. H. (1960). A note on the food of Australian desert frogs. *Western Australian Naturalist*, **7**, 79–80.

Carlisle, D. B. & Ghorbial, L. I. (1968). Food and water requirement of Dorcas gazelle in the Sudan. *Mammalia*, **32**, 570–76.

Carpenter, R. E. (1969). Structure and function of the kidney and the water balance of desert birds. *Physiological Zoology*, **42**, 288–302.

Carroll, C. R. & Janzen, D. H. (1973). Ecology of foraging ants. *Annual Review of Ecology and Systematics*, **4**, 231–58.

Chew, R. M. (1961). Ecology of the spiders of a desert community. *Journal of the New York Entomological Society*, **69**, 5–41.

Chew, R. M. & Chew, A. E. (1970). Energy relationships of the mammals of a desert shrub (*Larrea tridentata*) community. *Ecological Monographs*, **40**, 1–20.

Chippendale, G. (1962). Botanical examination of kangaroo stomach contents and cattle rumen contents. *Australian Journal of Science*, **25**, 21–2.

Cloudsley-Thompson, J. (1968). *Spiders, scorpions, centipedes, and mites*. Pergamon Press, Oxford, New York.

Cole, C. J. (1962). Notes on the distribution and food habits of *Bufo alvarius* at the eastern edge of its range. *Herpetologica*, **18**, 172–5.

Crawford, C. S. (1974). *The role of* Orthoporus ornatus *millipedes in a desert ecosystem*. US/IBP Desert Biome Research Memorandum, RM 74–34. Logan, Utah.

Crawford, C. S. & Wooten, R. C. (1973). *The role of* Orthoporus ornatus *millipedes in a desert ecosystem*. US/IBP Desert Biome Research Memorandum, RM 73–31. Logan, Utah.

Creighton, W. S. (1964). The habits of *Pheidole* (*Ceratopheidole*) *clydei* Gregg (Hymenoptera: Formicidae). *Psyche*, **71**, 169–73.

Creighton, W. S. & Creighton, M. P. (1960). The habits of *Pheidole militicida* Wheeler (Hymenoptera: Formicidae). *Psyche*, **66**, 1–12.

Cunningham, J. D. (1961). Observations on the natural history of the California toad, *Bufo californicus* Camp. *Herpetologica*, **17**, 255–60.

Davey, H. W. (1923). The moloch lizard, *Moloch horridus* Gray. *Victorian Naturalist*, **40**, 58–60.

Dawson, W. R. & Bartholomew, G. A. (1968). Temperature regulation and water economy of desert birds. In: *Desert Biology* (ed. G. W. Brown), vol. I, pp. 357–94. Academic Press, New York & London.

Deacon, J. E. & Minckley, W. L. (1974). Desert fishes. In: *Desert Biology* (ed. G. W. Brown), vol. II, pp. 385–488. Academic Press, New York & London.

Dingman, R. E. & Byers, L. (1974). *Interaction between a fossorial rodent (the pocket gopher,* Thomomys bottae) *and a desert plant community*. US/IBP Desert Biome Research Memorandum, RM 74–22. Logan, Utah.

Dodge, N. N. (1938). Amphibians and reptiles of the Grand Canyon National Park. *Grand Canyon Natural History Association Natural History Bulletin*, **9**, 1–55.

Dundee, H. A. (1950). Additional records of *Hypsiglena* from Oklahoma with notes on the behaviour and the eggs. *Herpetologica*, **6**, 28–30.

Animal processes

Eddy, T. A. (1961). Foods and feeding patterns of the collared peccary in southern Arizona. *Journal of Wildlife Management*, **25**, 248–57.

Egoscue, H. J. (1962). Ecology and life history of the kit fox in Tooele County, Utah. *Ecology*, **43**, 481–97.

Elder, H. B. (1956). Watering patterns of some desert game animals. *Journal of Wildlife Management*, **20**, 368–78.

Findlayson, H. H. (1940). On central Australian mammals – I. The Muridae. *Transactions of the Royal Society of South Australia*, **64**, 125–36.

Finley, R. B. (1958). The wood rats of Colorado; distribution and ecology. *University of Kansas Publications, Museum of Natural History*, **10**, 213–552.

Fisher, H. I. (1941). Notes on shrews of the genus *Notiosorex*. *Journal of Mammalogy*, **22**, 262–9.

Fitzsimmons, V. F. M. (1935). Scientific results of the Vernay–Lang Kalahari expedition, March to September, 1930. Reptilia and Amphibia. *Annals of the Transvaal Museum*, **16**, 295–397.

Fitzsimmons, V. F. M. (1938). Transvaal Museum expedition to Southwest Africa and Little Namaqualand, May to August, 1937. *Annals of the Transvaal Museum*, **19**, 153–209.

Ftizsimmons, V. F. M. (1962). *Snakes of Southern Africa*. MacDonald, London.

Flake, L. D. (1973). Food habits of four species of rodents on a short-grass prairie in Colorado. *Journal of Mammalogy*, **54**, 636–47.

Flower, S. S. (1933). Notes on the recent reptiles and amphibians of Egypt, with a list of species recorded from that kingdom. *Proceedings of the Zoological Society of London*, **106**, 735–851.

Freckman, D. W., Sher, S. A. & Mankau, R. (1974). *Biology of nematodes in desert ecosystems*. US/IBP Desert Biome Research Memorandum, RM 74–35. Logan, Utah.

Funk, R. S. (1964). On the food of *Crotalus molossus molossus*. *Herpetologica*, **20**, 134.

Funk, R. S. (1965). Food of *Crotalus cerastes lateropens*. *Herpetologica*, **21**, 15–17.

Gehlbach, F. R. (1974). Evolutionary relations of southwestern ringneck snakes (*Diadophis punctatus*). *Herpetologica*, **30**, 63–72.

Gordon, S. (1934). The drinking habits of birds. *Nature* (London), **133**, 436–7.

Grant, K. A. & Grant, V. (1968). *Hummingbirds and their flowers*. Columbia University Press, New York.

Guillion, G. W. (1960). The ecology of Gambel's quail in Nevada and the arid southwest. *Ecology*, **41**, 518–36.

Hadley, N. F. & Williams, S. C. (1968). Surface activities of some North American scorpions in relation to feeding. *Ecology*, **49**, 726–34.

Hall, E. R. & Linsdale, J. M. (1929). Notes on the life history of the kangaroo mouse (*Microdipodops*). *Journal of Mammalogy*, **10**, 298–305.

Hansen, R. M. (1974). Dietary of the chuckwalla, *Sauromalus obesus*, determined by dung analysis. *Herpetologica*, **30**, 120–23.

Harris, W. V. (1970). Termites of the Palearctic Region. In: *Biology of termites* (eds K. Krishna & F. M. Weesner), vol. II, pp. 295–312. Academic Press, New York & London.

Haverty, M. I. & Nutting, W. L. (1975). Natural wood preferences of desert termites. *Annals of the Entomological Society of America*, **68**, 533–6.

Havertz, R. (1962). 'The distribution of free living nematodes in selected plant communities of the Wasatch Mountains.' Ph.D. Thesis, University of Utah, Salt Lake City.

Hawbreaker, A. C. (1947). Food and moisture requirements of the Nelson antelope ground squirrel. *Journal of Mammalogy*, **28**, 115–25.

Hawke, S. D. & Farley, R. D. (1973). Ecology and behaviour of the desert burrowing cockroach, *Arenivaga* sp. (Dictyoptera, Polyphagidae). *Oecologia*, **11**, 263–79.

Healey, M. C. (1973). 'The influence of intermediate hosts on the infection pattern of *Protospirura numidica* in the Bonneville Basin, Utah.' MS Thesis, University of Utah, Logan.

Heimlich, E. M. & Heimlich, M. G. (1947). A case of cannibalism in captive *Xantusia vigilis*. *Herpetologica*, **3**, 149–50.

Hensley, M. M. (1949). Mammal diet of *Heloderma*. *Herpetologica*, **5**, 152.

Hoffman, R. L. & Payne, S. A. (1969). Diplopods as carnivores. *Ecology*, **50**, 1096–8.

Hoffmeister, D. F. & Goodpaster, W. W. (1962). Life history of the Desert Shrew *Notiosorex crawfordi*. *Southwestern Naturalist*, **7**, 236–52.

Howell, D. J. (1973). Bats and pollen: physiological aspects of the syndrome of chiropterophily. *Comparative Biochemistry and Physiology*, **48**A, 263–76.

Hsiao, T. H. & Green, T. W. (1974). *Demographic studies of sagebrush insects as fluctuations of various environmental factors*. US/IBP Desert Biome Research Memorandum, RM 74–29. Logan, Utah.

Hsiao, T. H. & Kirkland, R. L. (1973). *Demographic studies of sagebrush insects as functions of various environmental factors*. US/IBP Desert Biome Research Memorandum, RM 73–34. Logan, Utah.

Hudson, J. W. (1962). The role of water in the biology of the antelope ground squirrel, *Citellus leucurus*. *University of California (Los Angeles), Publications in Zoology*, **64**, 1–56.

Huey, R. B., Pianka, E. R., Egan, M. E. & Coons, L. W. (1974). Ecological shifts in sympatry: Kalahari fossorial lizards (*Typhlosaurus*). *Ecology*, **55**, 304–16.

Irvine, C. A. (1969). *The desert bighorn sheep of southeast Utah*. Utah State Division of Fish and Game Publication No. 69–12.

Irwin, M. P. S. (1956). Notes on the drinking habits of birds in semi-arid Bechuanaland. *Bulletin of the British Ornithological Club*, **76**, 99–101.

Jaeger, E. C. (1948). Who trims the creosote bush? *Journal of Mammalogy*, **29**, 187–8.

Johnson, D. R. (1966). Diet and estimated energy assimilation of three Colorado lizards. *American Midland Naturalist*, **76**, 504–9.

Kenagy, G. J. (1973). Daily and seasonal patterns of activity and energetics in a heteromyid rodent community. *Ecology*, **54**, 1201–19.

Kennedy, J. P. (1956). Food habits of the rusty lizard, *Sceloporus olivaceus* Smith. *Texas Journal of Science*, **8**, 328–49.

Klauber, L. M. (1935). *Phyllorhynchus*, the leaf-nosed snake. *Bulletin of the Zoological Society of San Diego*, **12**, 1–31.

Klauber, L. M. (1940). The worm snakes of the genus *Leptotyphlops* in the United States and Mexico. *Transactions of the San Diego Society of Natural History*, **9**, 87–162.

Klauber, L. M. (1951). The shovel-nosed snake, *Chionactis*, with descriptions of two new subspecies. *Transactions of the San Diego Society of Natural History*, **11**, 141–204.

Klauber, L. M. (1956). *Rattlesnakes*. University of California Press, Berkeley.

Koslucher, D. G. & Minshall, G. W. (1973). Food habits of some benthic invertebrates in a Northern cool-desert stream (Deep Creek, Curlew Valley,

Animal processes

Idaho–Utah). *Transactions of the American Microscopical Society*, **92**, 441–52.

Krishna, D. & Prakash, I. (1956). Hedgehogs of the desert of Rajasthan. Pt. 2. Food and feeding habits. *Journal of the Bombay Natural History Society*, **53**, 362–6.

Kummer, H. (1968). *Social organization of the Hamadryas baboons: A field study.* Karger, Basle.

Leopold, A. S. (1961). *The Desert.* Time, Inc., New York.

Ligon, J. D. (1968). The biology of the elf owl, *Micrathene whitneyi. Miscellaneous Publications of the Museum of Zoology, University of Michigan*, **136**, 1–70.

Louw, G. N. (1972). The role of advective fog in the water economy of certain Namib Desert animals. *Symposia of the Zoological Society of London*, **31**, 297–314.

Lowe, D. H. (1955). Gambel quail and water supply on Tiburon Island, Sonora, Mexico. *Condor*, **57**, 244.

MacMillen, R. E. (1964). Population ecology, water relations, and social behaviour of a southern California semidesert rodent fauna. *University of California Publications in Zoology*, **71**, 1–66.

MacMillen, R. E. & Lee, A. K. (1967). Australian desert mice: Independence of exogenous water. *Science*, **158**, 383–5.

MacMillen, R. E. & Lee, A. K. (1969). Water metabolism of Australian hopping mice. *Comparative Biochemistry and Physiology*, **28**, 493–514.

Martin, A. C., Zim, H. S. & Nelson, A. L. (1951). *American wildlife and plants.* Dover, New York.

Mahendra, B. C. (1936). Contributions to the bionomics, anatomy, reproduction, and development of the Indian house-gecko, *Hemidactylus flaviviridus* Ruppel. Part I. *Proceedings of the Indian Academy of Sciences*, **4**, 250–81.

Mayhew, W. W. (1963). Biology of the granite spiny lizard, *Sceloporus orcutti. American Midland Naturalist*, **69**, 310–27.

Mayhew, W. W. (1968). Biology of desert amphibians and reptiles. In: *Desert Biology* (ed. G. W. Brown), vol. I, pp. 195–356. Academic Press, New York & London.

Mertens, R. (1960). *The world of amphibians and reptiles.* McGraw-Hill, New York.

Miller, A. H. (1951). An analysis of the distribution of the birds of California. *University of California Publication in Zoology*, **50**, 531–644.

Miller, A. H. & Stebbins, R. C. (1964). *The lives of desert animals in Joshua Tree National Monument.* University of California Press, Berkeley.

Miller, L. (1955). Notes on the desert tortoise, *Gopherus agassizi*, of California. *Copeia* (1955), 113–18.

Milstead, W. W. (1965). Changes in competing populations of whiptail lizards (*Cnemidophorus*) in southwestern Texas. *American Midland Naturalist*, **73**, 75–80.

Minnich, J. & Shoemaker, V. II. (1970). Diet, behavior and water turnover in the desert iguana, *Dipsosaurus dorsalis. American Midland Naturalist*, **84**, 496–509.

Montanucci, R. R. (1965). Observations on the San Joaquin leopard lizard, *Crotaphytus wislizenii silus* Stejneger. *Herpetologica*, **21**, 270–83.

Muma, M. H. (1951). The arachnid order Solpugida in the United States. *Bulletin of the American Museum of Natural History*, **97**, 35–144.

712

Muma, M. H. (1966). Feeding behaviour of North American Solpugida (Arachnida). *Florida Entomologist*, **49**, 199–216.

Murie, A. (1951). Coyote food habits on a southwestern cattle range. *Journal of Mammalogy*, **32**, 291–5.

Nagy, K. (1973). Behavior, diet and reproduction in a desert lizard, *Sauromalus obesus*. *Copeia* (1973), 93–102.

Neal, B. J. (1959). A contribution on the life history of the collared peccary in Arizona. *American Midland Naturalist*, **61**, 177–90.

Newsome, A. E. (1965). The abundance of red kangaroos, *Megaleia rufa* (Desmaret) in central Australia. *Australian Journal of Zoology*, **13**, 269–87.

Nichols, U. G. (1953). Food habits of the desert tortoise, *Gopherus agassizii*. *Herpetologica*, **9**, 65–9.

Norris, K. S. (1949). Observations on the habits of the horned lizard *Phrynosoma m'calli*. *Copeia* (1949), 176–80.

Norris, K. S. (1953). The ecology of the desert iguana *Dipsosaurus dorsalis*. *Ecology*, **34**, 265–87.

Nutting, W. L., Haverty, M. I. & LaFage, M. I. (1974). *Colony characteristics of termites as related to population density and habitat*. US/IBP Desert Biome Research Memorandum, RM 74–33. Logan, Utah.

Ohmart, R. D. (1973). Observations on the breeding adaptations of the road-runner. *Condor*, **75**, 140–49.

Parker, W. S. & Pianka, E. R. (1973). Notes on the ecology of the iguanid lizard, *Sceloporus magister*. *Herpetologica*, **29**, 143–52.

Petter, F. (1961). Répartition géographique et écologique des rongeurs désertiques du Sahara occidental à l'Iran oriental. *Mammalia*, **25**, 1–219.

Pianka, E. R. (1966). Convexity, desert lizards and spatial heterogeneity. *Ecology*, **47**, 1055–9.

Pianka, E. R. (1969). Sympatry of desert lizards (*Ctenotus*) in western Australia. *Ecology*, **50**, 1012–30.

Pianka, E. R. (1970). Comparative autecology of the lizard *Cnemidophorus tigris* in different parts of its geographic range. *Ecology*, **51**, 703–20.

Pianka, E. R. (1971a). Comparative ecology of two lizards. *Copeia* (1971), 129–38.

Pianka, E. R. (1971b). Lizard species diversity in the Kalahari Desert. *Ecology*, **52**, 1024–9.

Pianka, E. R. (1973). The structure of lizard communities. *Annual Review of Ecology and Systematics*, **4**, 53–74.

Pianka, E. R. & Parker, W. S. (1972). Ecology of the iguanid lizard *Callisaurus draconoides*. *Copeia* (1972), 493–508.

Pianka, E. R. & Pianka, H. D. (1970). Ecology of *Moloch horridus* (Lacertilia: Agamidae) in Western Australia. *Copeia* (1970), 90–103.

Pocock, R. I. (1941). *Fauna of British India, Mammalia*. Taylor & Francis, London.

Pope, C. H. (1960). *The reptile world*. Knopf, New York.

Prakash, I. (1956). Studies on the ecology of the desert hedgehogs. *Proceedings of the Rajasthan Academy of Science*, **6**, 30–42.

Prakash, I. (1959a). Foods of certain insectivores and rodents in captivity. *University of Rajasthan Studies (B)*, **6a**, 1–18.

Prakash, I. (1959b). Foods of Indian desert mammals. *Journal of Biological Sciences*, **21**, 100–109.

Prakash, I. (1959c). Food of the Indian false vampire. *Journal of Mammalogy*, **40**, 545–7.

713

Prakash, I. (1962). Ecology of gerbils of the Rajasthan Desert India. *Mammalia*, **26**, 311–31.

Prakash, I. (1969). Eco-toxicology and control of Indian desert gerbillae, *Meriones hurrianae* Jerdon, v. Food preference in the field during monsoon. *Journal Bombay Natural History Society*, **65**, 581–9.

Prakash, I. & Kametkar, L. R. (1969). Bodyweight, sex and age factors in populations of the northern palm squirrel, *Funambulus pennanti* Wroughton. *Journal Bombay Natural History Society*, **66**, 99–115.

Rao, L. (1924). A note on cannibalism in a gecko. *Journal Bombay Natural History Society*, **30**, 228.

Reeve, W. L. (1952). Taxonomy and distribution of the horned lizard genus *Phrynosoma*. *University of Kansas Science Bulletin*, **34**, 817–960.

Reichman, O. J. (1975). The relation of desert rodent diets to available resources. *Journal of Mammalogy*, **56**, 731–51.

Reichman, O. J. (1977). Optimization of diets through food preferences by Heteromyid rodents. *Ecology*, **58**, 454–7.

Reichman, O. J. (1978). *Ecological aspects of the diets of Sonoran Desert rodents*. Museum of Northern Arizona Research Paper Series 20. Museum of Northern Arizona, Flagstaff.

Reichman, O. J. & Van De Graaff, K. (1975). Association between ingestion of green vegetation and desert rodent reproduction. *Journal of Mammalogy*, **56**, 503–6.

Riazance, J. & Whitford, W. G. (1974). *Studies of wood borers, girdlers and seed predators of mesquite*. US/IBP Desert Biome Research Memorandum, RM 74–30. Logan, Utah.

Rose, W. (1962). *The reptiles and amphibians of South Africa*. Maskew Miller, Cape Town.

Ross, A. (1961). Notes on food habits of bats. *Journal of Mammalogy*, **42**, 66–71.

Russo, J. P. (1956). *The desert bighorn sheep in Arizona*. State of Arizona Game and Fish Department.

Ryan, R. M. (1968). *Mammals of Deep Canyon, Colorado Desert, California*. The Desert Museum, Palm Springs.

Salt, G. W. & Zeuthen, E. (1960). The respiratory system. In: *Biology and Comparative Physiology of Birds* (ed. A. J. Marshall), vol. I, pp. 363–409. Academic Press, New York & London.

Sands, W. A. (1965). A late development and colony foundation in five species of Trinervitermes (Isoptera, Nasutitermitinae) in Nigeria, West Africa. *Insectes Sociaux*, **12**, 117–30.

Schmidt, K. P. & Inger, R. F. (1957). *Living reptiles of the world*. Doubleday, New York.

Schmidt-Nielsen, K. (1964). *Desert animals*. Oxford University Press, Oxford, New York.

Schmidt-Nielsen, K. & Haines, H. B. (1964). Water balance in a carnivorous desert rodent, the grasshopper mouse. *Physiological Zoology*, **37**, 259–65.

Schmidt-Nielsen, K., Taylor, C. R. & Shkolnik, A. (1972). Desert snails: Problems of survival. *Symposia of the Zoological Society of London*, **31**, 3–13.

Serventy, D. L. (1971). Biology of desert birds. In: *Avian Biology* (eds. D. S. Farner & J. R. King), vol. I, pp. 287–339. Academic Press, New York & London.

Shaeta, M. N. & Kaschef, A. B. (1971). Foraging activities of *Messor aegyptiacus* (Hymenoptera: Formidicidae). *Insectes Sociaux*, **18**, 215–26.

714

Shaw, C. E. (1939). Food habits of the chuckwalla, *Sauromalus obesus*. *Herpetologica*, **1**, 153.

Shaw, C. E. (1945). The chuckwallas, genus *Sauromalus*. *Transactions San Diego Society of Natural History*, **10**, 296–306.

Shaw, C. E. (1950). Lizards in the diet of captive *Uma*. *Herpetologica*, **6**, 36–7.

Shkolnik, A. (1971). Adaption of animals to desert conditions. In: *The Negev. The Challenge of the desert* (eds. M. Evenari. L. Shanon & N. Tadmor), pp. 301–23. Harvard University Press, Cambridge, Mass.

Shkolnik, A. & Borut, A. (1969). Temperature and water relations in two species of spiny mice (*Acomys*). *Journal of Mammalogy*, **50**, 245–54.

Shoemaker, V. H., Nagy, K. A. & Costa, W. R. (1974). *The consumption, utilization and modification of nutritional resources by the jackrabbit* (Lepus californicus) *in the Mojave Desert*. US/IBP Desert Biome Research Memorandum, RM 74–25. Logan, Utah.

Shultze, J. C. (1975). *Larrea* as a habitat component for desert invertebrates. In: Larrea *and its Role in Desert Ecosystems* (eds. T. J. Mabry & J. Hunziker). IBP–SES program. Dowden, Hutchinson & Ross, New York.

Smith, D. D. & Milstead, W. W. (1971). Stomach analysis of the crevice spiny lizard (*Sceloporus pointsetti*). *Herpetologica*, **27**, 147–9.

Smyth, M. & Bartholomew, G. A. (1966). The water economy of the black-throated sparrow and the rock wren. *Condor*, **68**, 447–58.

Sowls, L. K. (1958). Experimental feeding and measurement of water consumption of captive javalina. *Arizona University Cooperative Wildlife Research Unit Report*, **8**, 14–16.

Sperry, C. C. (1941). Food habits of the coyote. *United States Fish and Wildlife Service Research Bulletin*, **4**, 1–69.

Stahnke, H. L. (1966). Some aspects of scorpion behaviour. *Bulletin of the Southern California Academy of Science*, **65**, 65–80.

Stebbins, R. C. (1954). *Amphibians and reptiles of western North America*. McGraw-Hill, New York.

Tanner, W. W. & Krogh, J. E. (1974). Ecology of the leopard lizard, *Crotaphytus wislizenii*, at the Nevada Test Site, Nye County, Nevada. *Herpetologica*, **30**, 63–72.

Taylor, C. R. (1968). Hygroscopic food: A source of water for desert antelope? *Nature (London)*, **219**, 181–2.

Taylor, W. K. (1971). A breeding biology study of the verdin, *Aureparus flaviceps*, in Arizona. *American Midland Naturalist*, **85**, 289–328.

Tevis, L. (1958). Interrelations between the harvester ant *Veromessor pergandei* (Mayr) and some desert ephemerals. *Ecology*, **39**, 695–704.

Tevis, L. & Newell, I. M. (1962). Studies on the biology and seasonal cycle of the giant red velvet mite, *Dinothrombium pandorae* (Acari, Thrombidiidae). *Ecology*, **43**, 497–505.

Tomoff, C. S. (1974). Avian species diversity in desert scrub. *Ecology*, **55**, 396–403.

Turkowski, F. J. & Reynolds, H. G. (1974). *Annual nutrient and energy intake of the desert cottontail*, Sylvilagus auduboni, *under natural conditions*. US/IBP Desert Biome Research Memorandum, RM 74–24. Logan, Utah.

Tyler, M. J. (1960). Observations on the diet and size variation of *Amphibolurus adelaidensis* (Gray) (Reptilia: Agamidae) on the Nullarbor Plain. *Transactions of the Royal Society of South Australia*, **83**, 111–17.

Vorhies, C. T. (1933). The life history and ecology of jackrabbits, *Lepus alleni* and *Lepus californicus* in relation to grazing in Arizona. *University of Arizona Agriculture Experiment Station Technical Bulletin*, **49**, 471–587.

Vorhies, C. T. & Taylor, W. P. (1940). Life history and ecology of the white-throated woodrat, *Neotoma albigula* Hartley, in relation to grazing in Arizona. *University of Arizona College of Agriculture Technical Bulletin*, **86**, 445–529.

Walker, E. P. (1968). *Mammals of the world.* Johns-Hopkins University Press, Baltimore.

Wallwork, J. A. (1972). Distribution patterns and population dynamics of the micro-arthropods of a desert soil in southern California. *Journal of Animal Ecology*, **41**, 291–310.

Went, F. W., Wheeler, J. & Wheeler, G. C. (1972). Feeding and digestion in some ants (*Veromessor* and *Manica*). *Bioscience*, **22**, 82–8.

Werner, F. G. (1973). *Foraging activity of the leaf-cutter ant*, Acromyrmex versicolor, *in relation to season, weather and colony condition.* US/IBP Desert Biome Research Memorandum, RM 73–28. Logan, Utah.

Werner, F. G. & Olsen, A. R. (1973). *Consumption of* Larrea *by chewing insects.* US/IBP Desert Biome Research Memorandum, RM 73–32. Logan, Utah.

Wheeler, W. M. (1908). Honey ants with a revision of the American Myrmecocysti. *Bulletin of the American Museum of Natural History*, **24**, 345–97.

White, S. R. (1949). Some notes on the netted dragon lizard. *Western Australian Naturalist*, **1**, 157–61.

Whitford, W. G. (1973). *Demography and bioenergetics of herbivorous ants in a desert ecosystem as functions of vegetation, soil types and weather variables.* US/IBP Desert Biome Research Memorandum, RM 73–29. Logan, Utah.

Whitford, W. G. & Kay, C. A. (1974). *Demography and role of herbivorous ants in a desert ecosystem as functions of vegetation, soil and climate variables.* US/IBP Desert Biome Research Memorandum, RM 74–31. Logan, Utah.

Wilson, L. O. (1968). *Distribution and ecology of the desert bighorn sheep in southeastern Utah.* Utah State Division of Fish and Game, Publication No. 68–5.

Woodbury, A. M. (1931). A descriptive catalog of the reptiles of Utah. *Bulletin University of Utah*, **21**, 1–129.

Woodbury, A. M. & Hardy, R. (1948). Studies of the desert tortoise, *Gopherus agassizi. Ecological Monographs*, **18**, 145–200.

Yom-Tov, Y. (1970). The effects of predation on population densities of some desert snails. *Ecology*, **51**, 907–11.

Young, S. P. (1946). *The puma – mysterious American cat.* Dover, New York.

Young, S. P. (1958). *The bobcat of North America.* Wildlife Management Institute, Washington, D.C.

Manuscript received by the editors February 1975

30. Assimilation, respiration and production: *(a)* Invertebrates

C. S. CRAWFORD

Introduction

Desert invertebrates must contend with a food base limited by low productivity and with a climate that frequently restricts the opportunity to acquire that food. Chief among the climatic constraints is a low and often irregular rainfall affecting not only primary production, but also the conditions under which many invertebrates can function without undergoing a negative water balance. The physiological and behavioral adaptations to desert conditions of arthropods in particular have been studied and reviewed, most recently by Cloudsley-Thompson (1975).

In contrast, the energetics characteristic of desert invertebrates have hardly been explored. Desert vertebrates seem to have received considerably more attention in this regard (Chapter 30*b*). In the present review aspects of the assimilation, respiration, and production of desert invertebrates are examined, as are annual energy budgets of two desert species relative to those of some non-desert arthropods. Aquatic invertebrates are not considered, nor for the most part are social insects. Practically all pertinent research has been done on arthropods and snails.

Assimilation

Ecologists working with invertebrates frequently measure assimilation in the manner outlined by Petrusewicz & Macfadyen (1970) and discussed by Johnson & Schreiber in Chapter 30*b*. However, physiologists interested in insect nutrition have developed a somewhat different set of notations used in estimating food utilization. This approach is discussed extensively by Waldbauer (1968), whose term 'approximate digestibility' (*AD*) is similar to 'assimilation efficiency' as described by Conover (1966) for zooplankton. Assimilation efficiency employs measurements of ash-free dry-weight ratios of food and feces; this seems to be unnecessary in calculating *AD*.

Under experimental conditions efficiency of food utilization varies with external factors and physiological states, as well as with diet. Thus, in the desert locust *Schistocerca gregaria* Forsk, Norris (1961) found that *AD* increased among crowded adults, although Brennière *et al.* (1949, cited by Waldbauer, 1968) did not detect such an increase in the fourth-instar

717

gregarious phase. The same insect displays a greater *AD* during somatic growth than during ovarian growth when on a preferred bran diet (Mordue & Hill, 1970).

Table 30.1 gives values of assimilation efficiencies or *AD*s for five desert arthropods. Assimilation efficiency has been measured in only two of these species. The desert millipede *Orthoporus ornatus* Girard is primarily a detritivore; its efficiency varies directly with temperature, is essentially the same when superficial tissues of two desert shrubs are eaten, and is higher than the 6% to 15% range reported for most millipedes (Wooten & Crawford, 1975). The relatively high efficiency of this species may be related to its pronounced ability to digest cellulose (Nunez, 1974), and is probably of considerable adaptive value because of its short feeding season.

However, the assimilation efficiency of the desert scorpion *Urodacus yaschenkoi* Birula (Table 30.1) is very high (Shorthouse, 1971), which accords with the expectation of Kozlovsky (1968) and others for carnivores.

Three primary consumers of living vegetation are listed in Table 30.1. Similarities in their *AD*s are apparent. Yet the sagebrush defoliator *Aroga websteri*, studied recently by Hsiao & Kirkland (1973), has a relatively low *AD* when compared with other species of Lepidoptera listed by Waldbauer (1968). Sagebrush leaves have a high (42% to 53%) dry-matter content, which may result in low *AD* values (Soo Hoo & Fraenkel, 1966). The *AD* values given for *Schistocerca gregaria* and *Locusta migratoria* in Table 30.1 were calculated from similar stages feeding on grass. When the same individuals of *S. gregaria* were fed bran, which presumably contained much less water, the *AD* value was only 1% lower (Dadd, 1960), so it may be that ability to convert food to tissue varies more with dry-matter content in some insect groups than in others.

Respiration

Energy costs of poikilotherms and homeotherms are likely to differ for several reasons, one being that thermoregulation by homeotherms at temperatures below body optima is an energy-requiring function. Maintenance of a high body temperature when physical activity is unnecessary, particularly in a small animal, is energetically costly (Heinrich, 1974) However, even though poikilotherms have by definition no physiological mechanisms for regulating body temperature, seasonal changes in their rates of oxygen consumption do not necessarily follow seasonal changes in environmental temperature. This is especially noticeable in insect diapause (Beck, 1968).

Scholander, Flagg, Walters & Irving (1953) found that non-dormant

Table 30.1. *Assimilation efficiencies and approximate digestibility coefficients (AD) of desert arthropods*

General classification	Species and stage	Temperature (°C)	Food	Assimilation efficiency (%)	Approximate digestibility coefficient (%)	Reference
Moth (herbivore)	*Aroga websteri* (instars IV and V)	30	Leaves of *Artemisia tridentata*	—	34.9±1.8	Hsiao & Kirkland, 1973
Locust (herbivore)	*Locusta migratoria* (instar V)	32	Grass	—	39.0	Dadd, 1960
Locust (herbivore)	*Schistocerca gregaria* (instar V)	32	Grass	—	39.0	Dadd, 1960
Millipede (herbivore–detritivore)	*Orthoporus ornatus* (adult)	20	Bark of *Ephedra* sp.	20.3±2.5	—	Wooten & Crawford, 1975
		24	Bark of *Ephedra* sp.	31.4±2.3	—	
		30	Bark of *Ephedra* sp.	37.6±3.5	—	
		20	Bark of *Prosopis* sp.	21.7±4.1	—	
		25	Bark of *Prosopis* sp.	34.0±4.6	—	
Scorpion (carnivore)	*Urodacus yaschenkoi*	20	Cockroaches	92.4	—	Shorthouse, 1971

terrestrial poikilotherms, when compared to aquatic poikilotherms, showed little tendency to maintain temperature-independent metabolic rates. These authors concluded that three possible means exist by which poikilotherms can achieve metabolic homeostasis in the face of changing temperatures: (*a*) by lateral displacement of the *RT* curve relating metabolic rate to temperature; (*b*) by maintenance of low Q_{10}; and (*c*) by selection of a constant thermal environment. The latter phenomenon has been well documented for a number of desert invertebrates (Tenebrionid beetles (Edney, 1971; Hamilton, 1971); scorpions (Alexander & Ewer, 1958; Hadley, 1970*a*); millipedes (Wooten, Crawford & Riddle, 1975); snails (Yom-Tov, 1971)) and will not be discussed here.

There is now evidence that some desert invertebrates can displace *RT* curves and maintain low Q_{10} values. Metabolic compensation at high temperatures has been demonstrated in the Sonoran Desert wolf spider *Lycosa carolinensis* by Moeur & Eriksen (1972). They showed that its oxygen consumption stabilizes within three days following exposure to an acute temperature increase of 22 °C to 39 °C, and that acclimation is even faster for a smaller temperature increase. A relative reduction in metabolic rate is simultaneously effected, suggesting that natural acclimation is accompanied by a relative reduction in energy expenditure as days become warmer. Furthermore, this spider's *RT* curve shifts to the right between January and June in the 29 °C to 45 °C range, and rises more gradually between 29 °C and 39 °C in June than in January.

Respiratory Q_{10} values were low (1.00 to 1.54) between 31 °C and 39 °C in June specimens of *L. carolinensis*; they rose much faster above that temperature range (Moeur & Eriksen, 1972). In the tarantula *Aphonopelma* sp. from southeastern Arizona Q_{10} values declined from 1.93 to 1.11 between 30 °C and 40 °C (Seymour & Vinegar, 1973). Below 23 °C the tarantula is inactive and its Q_{10} values increase considerably as temperature drops. The same theme is evident in *Orthoporus ornatus* millipedes from southern New Mexico. Large and small specimens acclimated to 25 °C showed moderate and stable Q_{10} values (1.45 to 1.44 and 2.28 to 2.06, respectively) when the temperature was raised from 25 °C to 35 °C in two hours (Wooten & Crawford, 1974). However, when the temperature was lowered from 25 °C to 15 °C, the Q_{10} increased significantly in the larger specimens and showed a tendency to increase in the smaller animals. From the three examples given above it appears that low values for respiratory Q_{10} over habitat temperature ranges are energy-conserving adaptations in certain desert invertebrates.

A second major distinction between the energetics of homeotherms and poikilotherms has been suggested – that, whereas the latter are more efficient producers of biomass, they are simultaneously less efficient in assimilating food (Engelmann, 1966). This conclusion was modified by

Table 30.2. *Oxygen consumption by large, long-lived, arid-land arthropods at 20 °C*

General classification	Species	Month or season	N	Oxygen consumption (μl g^{-1} h^{-1})	Reference
Centipede	*Scolopendra polymorpha*	October	9	68.7 ± 5.3	Crawford, Riddle & Pugach, 1975
Millipede	*Orthoporus ornatus*	May	15	51.5 ± 3.7	Wooten, 1973
Scorpion	*Centuroides sculpturatus*	Unknown	15	61.5 ± 14.3 (♀)	Hadley & Hill, 1969
			15	75.1 ± 14.3 (♂)	
Scorpion	*Diplocentrus spitzeri*	October	8	92.1 ± 19.1	Crawford & Riddle, 1975
Scorpion	*Euscorpius carpathicus*	Unknown	Unknown	69.8	Dresco-Derouet, 1964
Scorpion	*Paruroctonus aquilonalis*	Summer	> 100	32–52	Riddle (In press)
Scorpion	*Urodacus yaschenkoi*	Unknown	119	54 (est.)	Shorthouse, 1971
Spider	*Aphonopelma* sp.-B	Summer	6	30–50 (est.)	Seymour & Vinegar, 1973
Spider	*Lycosa carolinensis*	January	9	180 (est., 23 °C)	Moeur & Eriksen, 1972
Spider	*Lycosa lenta*	Unknown	80	94 ± 5	Anderson, 1970

Animal processes

McNeill & Lawton (1970), who presented data suggesting that long-lived poikilotherms, because of relatively unproductive older individuals in their populations, have higher respiratory costs at any level of production than do short-lived poikilotherms.

Large, long-lived arthropods are often conspicuous and abundant components of desert faunas. A listing of recorded rates of oxygen consumption at 20 °C for some of these (Table 30.2) suggests they are characterized by relatively low metabolic rates. None listed are insects. Large, short-lived insects (including resting individuals of *Schistocerca gregaria*) generally exhibit much higher metabolic rates (Miller, 1964). However, it is misleading to suggest a causal relation between metabolic rates and body dimensions in arthropods possessing different means of ventilation. For example, there is considerable evidence that spiders with tracheal systems have higher metabolic rates than spiders with book-lungs (Anderson, 1970).

Therefore, an explanation for the low rates observed in certain large, long-lived desert arthropods would probably have to include reference to their non-tracheated or weakly tracheated ventilatory systems. For non-flying poikilotherms such systems are satisfactory.

Aside from ventilatory-system structure, inherently low rates of oxygen consumption alone should be adaptive in many desert invertebrates. Anderson (1970) argues that ancient arachnid predators moving from aquatic to terrestrial habitats, as well as modern forms inhabiting unstable environments, would be well adapted to inconsistent food availability by having low metabolic rates. Support for this contention is provided by Ettershank & Whitford (1973), using the perhaps unlikely example of harvester ants. They showed that two desert species of *Pogonomyrmex* have lower rates of oxygen consumption than another *Pogonomyrmex* species from a more mesic region.

The value of reduced oxygen consumption (and consequent reduced ventilation) to the conservation of body water should also be noted. Ahearn (1970) concluded that well-regulated spiracular control contributed to the success of Tenebrionid beetles in desert habitats. In the desert scorpion *Hadrurus arizonensis* (Hadley, 1970*b*) and in a semimontane scorpion from the south-western United States, *Diplocentrus spitzeri* (Crawford & Wooten, 1973), respiratory transpiration does not appear to be a major pathway of water loss at moderate temperatures, but may become so at temperatures approaching upper lethal limits.

The rate of oxygen consumption may also be related to atmospheric humidity. Kay & Whitford (1975) found that two out of five desert ant species greatly increased their oxygen consumption with increasing vapor pressure deficit. Their activity and death rates also increased markedly in dry air relative to those of the other species. In these instances higher rates of oxygen consumption may have been related to increased water stress. *Pogonomyrmex rugosa*, but not *Pogonomyrmex maricopa*, reacts in the same way to increased vapor pressure deficit, and may be elevating its metabolism to produce needed metabolic water (Ettershank & Whitford, 1973). On the contrary, oxygen consumption in the desert snail *Rabdotus schiedeanus* (Pfeiffer) rose with increasing humidity, suggesting that stored energy reserves are conserved during seasonal dry periods (Riddle, 1975). Hadley (1970*b*) noted the same response in *Hadrurus arizonensis*.

Some desert invertebrates appear to spend most of their lives in a state of dormancy. In order to survive during such long periods of food deprivation, not only must metabolic rates be lowered, but products of earlier ingestion and assimilation must serve as energy sources.

Survival without food can take place for four years in the desert Tenebrionid beetle *Blaps requieni* (Cloudsley-Thompson, 1960). Starvation is known to depress metabolism in certain non-desert spiders (Anderson, 1974),* in millipedes (Gromysz-Kalkowska, 1970), and in shore crabs (Marsden, Newell & Ahsanulla, 1973). In the absence of direct evidence to the contrary one can speculate that the same effect occurs also in many desert invertebrates.

Circumstantial evidence supporting this idea is seen in certain pulmonate snails. In the dormant desert snail *Sphincterochila boisseri*, metabolism is so low that tissues can be used for several years as the sole energy source (Schmidt-Nielsen, Taylor & Shkolnik, 1971). Horne (1973) calculated tissue utilization in the arid-land snail *Bulimulus dealbatus mooreanus* to be 21.5 mg per gram of dry weight during 60 days of aestivation at 22 °C. During aestivation that snail also reduced its metabolic rate (by 16%) and exhibited a respiratory quotient (RQ) of 0.82 while metabolizing mainly protein and carbohydrate. A relative increase in utilization of lipid and protein probably occurs in dormant desert millipedes, *Orthoporus ornatus*, which have an RQ of 0.90 in the feeding season and only 0.77 to 0.78 while in dormancy (Wooten & Crawford, 1974).

Production and annual energy budgets

Production can be regarded most conveniently as the net balance between assimilation and respiration during a given period. Modifications of this definition consider actual changes in biomass or energy, together with loss of materials or non-respiratory energy (Petrusewicz & Macfadyen, 1970). Phillipson (1971) points out that definitions of production may or may not include the weight of reproductive products.

Poikilotherms are considered more efficient producers of biomass than

* On the other hand, Myrcha & Stejgwiłło-Laudanska (1973) found an increase in three Lycosid species.

are homeotherms; that is, ratios of production to assimilation or consumption in poikilotherms are relatively large (Wiegert & Evans, 1967; Petrusewicz & Macfadyen, 1970). Ants (and perhaps termites as well) also expend relatively small amounts of assimilated energy for production; reasons given include the need for colony maintenance and the high annual replacement of workers (Hadley, 1972; Petal, 1972).

Little is known about production in desert invertebrates. Noting that biomass ratios of spiders (predators) to insects (prey) ranged between 13.3% and 47.2% in different desert shrubs, Chew (1961) concluded that the insects must have much greater rates of production in order to serve as a food base for the spiders. Limited information on production of alate termites trapped during the summer in the Sonoran Desert was presented by Nutting, Haverty & LaFage (1974). They gave values of 44.27 g ha^{-1} for *Gnathamitermes perplexus* and 3.28 g ha^{-1} for *Heterotermes aureus*.

An estimate of feeding-season production (dry weight) for the millipede *Orthoporus ornatus* in the Chihuahuan Desert approximated 0.85 kg ha^{-1} (Crawford, 1976). This is equivalent to about 0.20 kcal m^{-2}, which is nearly two orders of magnitude less than an estimate made for a warm-temperate forest species (Saito, 1967), but not much different from the estimate of O'Neill (1968) for a deciduous forest millipede. Annual production of the Australian desert scorpion *Urodacus yaschenkoi* was estimated at 0.224 kcal m^{-2} (Shorthouse, 1971).

Production or growth efficiencies (ratios of production to assimilation) have been calculated for a variety of non-desert poikilotherms; for purposes of comparison some are listed in Table 30.3 with efficiencies calculated for two desert arthropods. That of *Urodacus yaschenkoi* is about 37%, which is close to other values given in the literature for carnivorous poikilotherms (Shorthouse, 1971). Estimates for *Orthoporus ornatus* (Crawford, 1976) suggest that net growth efficiency of this millipede is similar to that of a Japanese millipede studied by Saito (1967).

The figures given for *O. ornatus* substantiate McNeill & Lawton's (1970) assumption that when a proportion of a poikilotherm population exceeds two years in age and probably experiences at least two periods of high respiration cost without production, its annual production efficiency will be low.

Shorthouse (1971) reworked the poikilotherm data collated by McNeill & Lawton (1970) and others, and distinguished two trends relating annual respiration and annual production in poikilotherms. One trend represents mainly long-lived aquatic detritivores with high rates of annual production. The other applies to data from terrestrial poikilotherms generally, including those for *Orthoporus ornatus* and *Urodacus yaschenkoi*, both long-lived desert poikilotherms.

Table 30.3 summarizes annual energy flow in selected arthropod popu-

Table 30.3. *Annual energy flow (kcal m^{-2}) in desert arthropods and other selected species*

General classification	Species	Assimilation[1]	Respiration	Production	Net growth efficiency (%)	References
Beetle (carnivore)	*Nebria brevicollis*	0.79	0.42	0.37	47.1	Manga, 1972
Locust (herbivore)	*Encoptolophus sordidus costalis*	2.95	1.72	1.23	41.7	Bailey & Riegert, 1973
		2.96	1.58	1.38	46.6	
Locusts (herbivores)	Chiefly *Melanopus* sp.	1.76	1.12	0.64	36.4	Wiegert, 1965
		0.97	0.60	0.37	38.1	
		13.26	8.69	4.57	34.5	
Millipede (detritivore)	*Japonaria laminata armigera*	57.8	30.9	26.9	46.5	Saito, 1967
Millipede[3] (herbivore–detritivore)	*Orthoporus ornatus*	3.01	1.51	1.50	49.8	Crawford, 1976
		0.45	0.25	0.20	44.4	
Scorpion[3] (carnivore)	*Urodacus yaschenkoi*[2]	0.60	0.38	0.22	36.7	Shorthouse, 1971
Spider (carnivore)	*Pardosa lugubris*	1.10	0.80	0.30	27.2	Edgar, 1971

[1] Calculated from published values of annual respiration and production.   [2] Calculated on the basis of a 2440 m^2 sampling area.
[3] Desert arthropods. Values for *O. ornatus* for feeding season only.

lations. With population energy flow defined as the sum of respiratory energy loss and energy stored as secondary production (Wiegert, 1965), values listed under 'Assimilation' suggest that energy flow in desert invertebrates may be minimal relative to energy flow in invertebrates occupying similar trophic positions in other ecosystems.

Concluding remarks

Clearly, there is need for an increased number of detailed studies of the energetics of desert invertebrates before definitive statements can be made about the roles of these animals in desert ecosystems. In particular, greater emphasis should be placed on understanding the function of those soil-dwelling desert invertebrates which account for the major release of nutrients tied up in dead organic material. Aside from recent studies on soil micro-arthropods by Wallwork (1972) and by Edney, McBrayer, Franco & Phillips (1974), on termites by Nutting *et al.* (1974), on ants by Whitford & Kay (1974), and on nematodes by Freckman, Shor & Mankau (1974) – most of which have been initiated under the IBP and have not yet been published – there is very little literature on the dynamics of these potentially significant animals.

Acknowledgments

Appreciation is extended to W. A. Riddle for his critical review and to D. J. Shorthouse for kindly making available his Ph.D. thesis.

References

Ahearn, G. A. (1970). The control of water loss in desert Tenebrionid beetles. *Journal of Experimental Biology*, **53**, 573–95.

Alexander, A. J. & Ewer, D. W. (1958). Temperature adaptive behaviour in the scorpion *Opisthophthalmus latimanus* Koch. *Journal of Experimental Biology*, **35**, 349–59.

Anderson, J. F. (1970). Metabolic rates of spiders. *Comparative Biochemistry and Physiology*, **33**, 51–72.

Anderson, J. F. (1974). Responses to starvation in the spiders *Lycosa lenta* Hentz and *Filistata hibernalis* (Hentz). *Ecology*, **55**, 576–85.

Bailey, C. G. & Riegert, P. W. (1973). Energy dynamics of *Encoptolophus sordidus costalis* (Scudder) (Orthoptera. Acrididae) in a grassland ecosystem. *Canadian Journal of Zoology*, **51**, 91–100.

Beck, S. D. (1968). *Insect photoperiodism.* Academic Press, New York & London.

Chew, R. M. (1961). Ecology of spiders in a desert community. *Journal of the New York Entomological Society*, **69**, 5–41.

Cloudsley-Thompson, J. L. (1960). Notes on Arachnida, 35. A scorpion eaten by a beetle. *Entomologists' Monthly Magazine*, **95**, 223.

Cloudsley-Thompson, J. L. (1975). Adaptations of Arthropoda to arid environments. *Annual Review of Entomology*, **20**, 261–83.

Conover, R. J. (1966). Assimilation of organic matter by zooplankton. *Limnology and Oceanography*, **1**, 338–45.

Crawford, C. S. (1976). Feeding-season production in the desert millipede *Orthoporus ornatus* (Girrard) (Diplopoda). *Oecologia* (Berlin), **24**, 265–76.

Crawford, C. S. & Riddle, W. A. (1975). Overwintering physiology of the scorpion *Diplocentrus spitzeri*. *Physiological Zoölogy*, **48**, 84–92.

Crawford, C. S. & Wooten, R. C., Jr. (1973). Water relations in *Diplocentrus spitzeri*, a semimontane scorpion from the southwestern United States. *Physiological Zoölogy*, **46**, 218–29.

Crawford, C.. S., Riddle, W. A. & Pugach, S. (1975). Overwintering physiology of the centipede *Scolopendra polymorpha*. *Physiological Zoology*, **48**, 290–94.

Dadd, R. H. (1960). Observations on the palatability and utilization of food by locusts, with particular reference to the interpretation of performances in growth trials using synthetic diets. *Entomologia Experimentalis et Applicata*, **3**, 283–304.

Dresco-Derouet, P. L. (1964). Le métabolism respiratoire des scorpions. II. Mesures de l'intensité respiratoire chez quelques espèces à différentes températures. *Bulletin du Muséum National D'Histoire Naturelle*, **36**, 97–9.

Edgar, W. D. (1971). Aspects of the ecological energetics of the wolf spider *Pardosa* (*Lycosa*) *lugubris* (Walckenaer). *Oecologia* (*Berl.*), **7**, 136–54.

Edney, E. B. (1971). The body temperature of Tenebrionid beetles in the Namib Desert of Southern Africa. *Journal of Experimental Biology*, **55**, 253–72.

Edney, E. B., McBrayer, J. F., Franco, P. J. & Phillips, A. W. (1974). *Distribution of soil arthropods in Rock Valley, Nevada*. US/IBP Desert Biome Research Memorandum, RM 74-32, Logan, Utah.

Engelmann, M. D. (1966). Energetics, terrestrial field studies, and animal productivity. *Advances in Ecological Research*, **3**, 73–115.

Ettershank, G. & Whitford, W. G. (1973). Oxygen consumption of two species of *Pogonomyrmex* harvester ants (Hymenoptera: Formicidae). *Comparative Biochemistry and Physiology*, **46A**, 605–11.

Freckman, D. W., Sher, S. A. & Mankau, R. (1974). *Biology of nematodes in desert ecosystems*. US/IBP Desert Biome Research Memorandum, RM 74–35, Logan, Utah.

Gromysz-Kalkowska, L (1970). The influence of body weight, external temperature, seasons of the year and fasting on respiratory metabolism in *Polydesmus complanatus* (L.) (Diplopoda). *Folia Biologica*, **18**, 311–26.

Hadley, M. (1972). Perspectives in productivity studies, with special reference to some social insect populations. *Ekologia Polska*, **20**, 174–84.

Hadley, N. F. (1970a). Micrometeorology and energy exchange in two desert arthropods. *Ecology*, **51**, 434–44.

Hadley, N. F. (1970b). Water relations of the desert scorpion, *Hadrurus arizonensis*. *Journal of Experimental Biology*, **53**, 547–58.

Hadley, N. F. & Hill, R. D. (1969). Oxygen consumption of the scorpion *Centuroides sculpturatus*. *Comparative Biochemistry and Physiology*, **29**, 217–26.

Hamilton, W. J. (1971). Competition and thermoregulatory behavior of the Namib Desert Tenebrionid beetle genus *Cardiosis*. *Ecology*, **52**, 810–22.

Heinrich, B. (1974). Thermoregulation in endothermic insects. *Science*, **185**, 747–56.

Horne, F. R. (1973). The utilization of foodstuffs and urea production by a land snail during estivation. *Biological Bulletin*, **144**, 321–30.

727

Animal processes

Hsiao, T. S. & Kirkland, R. L. (1973). *Demographic studies of sagebrush insects as functions of various environmental factors.* US/IBP Desert Biome Research Memorandum, RM 73-34. Logan, Utah.

Kay, C. A. & Whitford, W. G. (1975). Influence of temperature and humidity on oxygen consumption of five Chihuahuan Desert ants. *Comparative Biochemistry and Physiology*, **52A**, 281–6.

Kozlovsky, D. G. (1968). A critical evaluation of the trophic level concept. (1) Ecological efficiencies. *Ecology*, **49**, 48–60.

McNeill, S. & Lawton, J. H. (1970). Annual production and respiration in animal populations. *Nature*, **225**, 472–4.

Manga, N. (1972). Population metabolism of *Nebria brevicollis* (F.) (Coleoptera: Carabidae). *Oecologia (Berl.)*, **10**, 223–42.

Marsden, I. D., Newell, R. C. & Ahsanulla, M. (1973). The effect of starvation on the metabolism of the shore crab, *Carcinus meanas. Comparative Biochemistry and Physiology*, **45A**, 195–213.

Miller, P. L. (1964). Respiration – aerial gas transport. In: *The Physiology of Insecta* (ed. M. Rockstein), vol. III, pp. 557–615. Academic Press, New York & London.

Moeur, J. E. & Eriksen, C. H. (1972). Metabolic responses to temperature of a desert spider, *Lycosa (Pardosa) carolinensis* (Lycosidae). *Physiological Zoölogy*, **45**, 290–301.

Mordue, A. J. & Hill, L. (1970). The utilization of food by the adult female desert locust, *Schistocerca gregaria. Entomologia Experimentalis et Applicata*, **13**, 352–8.

Myrcha, A. & Stejgwiłło-Laudanska, B. (1973). Changes in the metabolic rate of starved Lycosidae spiders. *Bulletin de L'Académie Polonaise des Sciences; Série des Sciences Biologiques*, **21**, 209–19.

Norris, M. J. (1961). Group effects on feeding in adult males of the desert locust, *Schistocerca gregaria* (Forsk.), in relation to sexual maturation. *Bulletin of Entomological Research*, **51**, 731–53.

Nuñez, F. S. (1974). 'The digestive tract and digestive enzymes of the desert millipede *Orthoporus ornatus* (Girard) (Spirostreptidae). Ph.D. Dissertation, The University of New Mexico, Albuquerque.

Nutting, W. L., Haverty, M. I. & LeFage, J. P. (1974). *Colony characteristics of termites as related to population density and habitat.* US/IBP Desert Biome Research Memorandum, RM 74–28. Logan, Utah.

O'Neill, R. V. (1968). Population energetics of the millipede, *Narceus americanus* (Beauvois). *Ecology*, **49**, 803–9.

Petal, J. (1972). Methods of investigating the productivity of ants. *Ekologia Polska*, **20**, 9–22.

Petrusewicz, K. & Macfadyen, A. (1970). Productivity of terrestrial animals. In: *IBP Handbook No. 13* (ed. J. Phillipson). Blackwell Scientific, Oxford.

Phillipson, J. (1971). Other arthropods. In: *IBP Handbook No. 13* (ed. J. Phillipson), pp. 262–87. Blackwell Scientific, Oxford.

Riddle, W, A. (1975). Water relations and humidity-related metabolism of the desert snail *Rabdotus schiedeanus* (Pfeiffer) (Helicidae). *Comparative Biochemistry and Physiology*, **51A**, 579–83.

Riddle, W. A. (1978). Respiratory physiology of the desert grassland scorpion *Paruroctonus aquilonalis. Journal of Arid Environments*, (In Press).

Saito, S. (1967). Productivity of high and low density populations of *Japonaria laminata armigera* (Diplopoda) in a warm-temperate forest ecosystem. *Researches on Population Ecology*, **9**, 153–66.

728

Assimilation, respiration and production (a) Invertebrates

Schmidt-Nielsen, K., Taylor, C. R. & Shkolnik, A. (1971). Desert snails: problems of heat, water and food. *Journal of Experimental Biology*, **55**, 385–98.

Scholander, P. F., Flagg, W., Walters, V. & Irving, L. (1953). Climatic adaptation in arctic and tropical poikilotherms. *Physiological Zoölogy*, **26**, 67–92.

Seymour, R. S. & Vinegar, A. (1973). Thermal relations, water loss and oxygen consumption of a North American tarantula. *Comparative Biochemistry and Physiology*, **44A**, 83–96.

Shorthouse, D. J. (1971). 'Studies on the biology and energetics of the scorpion *Urodacus yaschenkoi* (Birula 1904).' Ph.D. Thesis, Australian National University, Canberra.

Soo Hoo, C. F. & Fraenkel, G. (1966). The consumption, digestion and utilization of food plants by a polyphagous insect, *Prodenia eridania* (Cramer). *Journal of Insect Physiology*, **12**, 711–30.

Waldbauer, G. P. (1968). The consumption and utilization of food by insects. In: *Advances in Insect Physiology* (eds. J. W. L. Beament, J. E. Treherne & V. B. Wigglesworth), vol. 5, pp. 229–98. Academic Press, New York & London.

Wallwork, J. A. (1972). Distribution patterns and population dynamics of the micro-arthropods of a desert soil in southern California. *Journal of Animal Ecology*, **41**, 291–310.

Whitford, W. G. & Kay, C. A. (1974). *Demography and role of herbivorous ants in a desert ecosystem as functions of vegetation, soil and climate variables.* US/IBP Research Memorandum, RM 74–31. Logan, Utah.

Wiegert, R. G. (1965). Energy dynamics of the grasshopper populations in old field and alfalfa field ecosystems. *Oikos*, **16**, 161–76.

Wiegert, R. G. & Evans, F. C. (1967). Investigations of secondary productivity in grasslands. In: *Secondary productivity of terrestrial ecosystems (principles and methods)* (ed. K. Petrusewicz), pp. 499–518. Warszawa-Krakow.

Wooten, R. C. (1973). 'Physiological energetics of the desert millipede *Orthoporus ornatus*.' Ph.D. Dissertation, The University of New Mexico, Albuquerque.

Wooten, R. C. & Crawford, C. S. (1974). Respiratory metabolism of the desert millipede *Orthoporus ornatus* (Girard) (Diplopoda). *Oecologia (Berl.)*, **17**, 179–86.

Wooten, R. C. & Crawford, C. S. (1975). Food, ingestion rates, and assimilation in the desert millipede *Orthoporus ornatus* (Girard) (Diplopoda). *Oecologia (Berl.)*, **20**, 231–6.

Wooten, R. C., Crawford, C. S. & Riddle, W. A. (1975). Behavioural thermoregulation of *Orthoporus ornatus* (Diplopoda: Spirostreptidae) in three desert habitats. *Zoological Journal of the Linnean Society*, **57**, 49–74.

Yom-Tov, Y. (1971). Body temperature and light reflectance in two desert snails. *Proceedings of the Malacological Society of London*, **39**, 319–25.

Manuscript received by the editors January 1975

30. Assimilation, respiration and production: *(b)* Vertebrates

D. R. JOHNSON and R. K. SCHREIBER

Introduction

Physiological and behavioral adaptations to a desert existence have been the focus of extensive investigation and frequent review (Schmidt-Nielsen, 1964; Brown, 1968; Maloiy, 1972). Summaries of progress and techniques in energetics are also available (Slobodkin, 1962; Engelmann, 1966; Petrusewicz, 1967; Petrusewicz & Macfadyen, 1970). A definitive review of avian energetics has been made by Gessaman (1973). The energetics of desert anurans is unexplored. In view of this, we have examined some of the aspects of assimilation, respiration and production of North American mammals and reptiles, particularly rodents and lizards, based on the literature available through 1973. We have summarized some of the individual energy budgets, and suggested the likely course of future research involving the energy metabolism of xerophilous vertebrates.

Methods

In developing energy budgets, investigators can utilize either direct or indirect methods. The direct method uses doubly-labeled water ($D_2{}^{18}O$) to estimate carbon dioxide production (and hence metabolism) from the difference in turnover rates of the two isotopes. This method provides a means of integrating metabolic rate over a period of time during which the animal lives in the wild under natural conditions. Its disadvantages include the high cost of instrumentation and time-consuming analysis (Mullen, 1973). While the $D_2{}^{18}O$ method has been used in energetics studies of birds and mammals, we are not aware of such a study involving reptiles or amphibians.

Energy budgets can also be developed indirectly by summing the energy costs of basal metabolism, activity, digestion, reproduction, growth, and, in homeotherms, thermogenesis. Most of these estimates are based upon data obtained from captive animals, and it is assumed that these are adequate to describe the field situation. Mullen & Chew (1973) have found rather close agreement in comparing the energy metabolism of a pocket mouse (*Perognathus formosus* Merriam) as measured by the $D_2{}^{18}O$ method with that estimated indirectly from laboratory-based metabolic studies. They caution, however, that such an agreement is not likely for species

731

which demonstrate behavioral patterns in captivity which differ from those in the wild.

Assimilation

Assimilation (A_q) represents that portion of the food ingested which is digested and retained. Hence consumption $(C_q) = A_q + F_q$ where F_q is the energy loss in the feces. Since the food assimilated is utilized in both respiration (maintenance) and in production (growth and elaboration of products), $A_q = R_q + P_q$.

Assimilation can be calculated either by (*a*) food consumption experiments using captive animals in which the energy loss by the rejecta (feces and urine) is subtracted from that ingested; or (*b*) through summation of the energy costs of respiration and production. The food-consumption method has been favored in avian energetics, while indirect calorimetry has been employed in most mammalian studies (see Gessaman (1973) for a recent review).

The assimilation:consumption ratio (A_q/C_q) represents assimilation efficiency. Several factors affect this parameter, including (*a*) the proportion of roughage in the diet, since lignin and fiber reduce efficiency; (*b*) the plane of nutrition, which at higher levels increases the rate of passage and hence reduces efficiency; (*c*) the frequency of feeding, since repeated low-level intake increases efficiency; and (*d*) adaptation to the diet, since – in ruminants at least – an abrupt change may upset microbial balance, reducing efficiency.

Some investigators have made both elegant calculations of the energy cost of respiration, and faulty estimates of consumption, because they lacked accurate measurements of assimilation efficiency. Fortunately, a technique is available which provides a measurement of asssimilation efficiency of the free-living animal on a natural diet. Since ash is a naturally occurring component of all diets, and since its level is maintained within narrow limits within the body, ash provides a suitable tracer (indicator) with which to measure assimilation efficiency. If the animal remains in mineral balance, ash intake (measured as the non-combustible portion of the food ingested) will equal ash loss in the rejecta. Johnson & Groepper (1970) have shown that, in rodents at least, the ash tracer method effectively measures assimilation of gravid, lactating and juvenile individuals despite their increased mineral demands.

Assimilation efficiency is calculated as

$$1 - [(1/y_r - 1)/(1/y_0 - 1)]$$

where y_0 is the ash content of the food and y_r is that of the rejecta. This method has been used to measure assimilation efficiencies of zooplankton

Table 30.4. *Assimilation efficiencies of desert rodents and lizards*

| | Assimilation efficiency (%) | | |
Species	Wild	Laboratory	Reference
Rodents			
Spermophilus townsendi Bachman	—	83.7–94.4	Schreiber, 1973
Eutamias minimus (Bachman)	87.6	78.9–90.8	Schreiber, 1973
Dipodomys ordii Woodhouse	94.3	95.1–97.7	Schreiber, 1973; Johnson & Groepper, 1970
D. microps (Merriam)	91.3	—	Schreiber, 1973
D. merriami Mearns	87.0	85.1–95.5	Soholt, 1973
Perognathus parvus (Peale)	90.1	84.5–94.5	Schreiber, 1973
Peromyscus maniculatus (Wagner)	87.9	77.0	Schreiber, 1973; Johnson & Groepper, 1970
Onychomys leucogaster (Wied–Neuwied)	89.7	86.2	Schreiber, 1973
Reithrodontomys megalotis (Baird)	85.6	87.7–91.8	Schreiber, 1973
Lizards			
Crotaphytus collaris (Say)	—	74.0–93.9	Essghaier, 1972
C. wislizenii Baird & Girard	77.8	84.3–98.5	Essghaier & Johnson, 1975
Cnemidophorus tigris Baird & Girard	79.8	—	Essghaier & Johnson, 1975
Uta stansburiana Baird & Girard	84.6	—	Essghaier & Johnson, 1975
Sceloporus occidentalis Baird & Girard	—	91.6	Essghaier, 1972
Sceloporus graciosus Baird & Girard	—	91.3	Essghaier, 1972
Phrynosoma platyrhinos Girard	—	92.2–99.3	Essghaier, 1972
Phrynosoma douglassi Bell	—	78.5–92.1	Essghaier, 1972
Ctenosaura pectinata	—	82.0	Throckmorton, 1971
Sauromalus obesus Baird	—	50.0–55.0	Nagy, personal communication
Dipsosaurus dorsalis (Baird & Girard)	—	51.0	Nagy, personal communication

(Conover, 1966), terrestrial snails (Mason, 1970), a lagomorph (Johnson & Maxell, 1966), grassland rodents (Johnson & Groepper, 1970), and desert vertebrates including rodents (Schreiber, 1973; Soholt, 1973) and lizards (Essghaier & Johnson, 1975).

Assimilation efficiencies of desert rodents on natural diets range from 85% to 95%, similar to those measured on laboratory diets (Table 30.4). Granivorous species (*Perognathus* spp., *Dipodomys* spp.) show a higher efficiency than that demonstrated by omnivores (*Eutamias* spp., *Peromyscus* spp., *Reithrodontomys* spp., *Onychomys* spp.). There is no evidence that desert-dwelling populations are more efficient than others of the same species inhabiting more mesic environments. *Peromyscus maniculatus* (Wagner) assimilated about 91% of its natural diet under mesic conditions, while *Dipodomys ordii* Woodhouse averaged 92% assimilation (Johnson & Groepper, 1970), values similar to those for desert populations of the same species (Table 30.4).

Few data are available for other mammals from desert environments. Captive peccaries (*Tayassu tajaçu* (L.)) assimilated about 81% of the material from *Opuntia* spp. ingested (Zervanos & Hadley, 1973). We are aware of only one study of the assimilation efficiency of desert-dwelling hares or rabbits. Shoemaker, Nagy & Costa (1974) found that penned individuals of *Lepus californicus* Gray assimilated 73% of a diet of green spring annuals and 53% of a diet of shrubby perennials and green material of *Salsola* sp. Assimilation efficiency was reduced to 25% when this species was fed a diet consisting of the same shrubs and dried annuals.

Great Basin lizards, which are primarily insectivorous, are somewhat less efficient than rodents at assimilation (Table 30.4). On low-chitin laboratory diets, however, assimilation is much increased. *Sceloporus graciosus* Baird and Girard and *Sceloporus occidentalis* Baird & Girard assimilated 83% of a mealworm diet (Mueller, 1970). Other Great Basin Iguanids show similar assimilation on mealworm diets (Table 30.4).

Respiration

The energy cost of respiration occurs as a result of basal metabolism, thermoregulation, digestion and activity. Predictive equations of basal metabolic rate as a function of body weight have been developed for passerine and non-passerine birds, metatherian and eutherian mammals (Poczopko, 1971), and lizards (Bartholomew & Tucker, 1964). McNab (1970) has reviewed the relationships of basal metabolic rate in mammals to climate and food habits. Burrowing rodents from a variety of climatic regions, including deserts, exhibit a basal rate below that predicted for mammals of equivalent body size. MacMillen & Lee (1970) have proposed that this adaptation in desert rodents serves primarily to reduce heat storage, although the saving of respiratory water represents a coincidental benefit.

Accurate estimates of the proportion of time spent active, at rest, and in torpor, both daily and seasonally, are difficult to obtain. Activity patterns have been monitored by automatic photographic recorders (Pearson, 1960a), and by tagging mice with miniaturized dosimeters (French, Maza & Aschwanden, 1966), electronic transmitters (Osgood & Weigl, 1972; Marten, 1973) and radioactive wires (Kenagy, 1973). Estimates of the nocturnal pattern of above-ground activity can also be gained by frequent inspection of live traps (Chew & Butterworth, 1964; Kenagy,

1973). Many desert rodents are active above ground for 4 to 5 hours nightly during favorable weather, although *Perognathus formosus* may spend as much as 30 to 40% of its time above ground during the summer months (French *et al.*, 1966). *Dipodomys merriami* Mearns is active for 5 to 6 hours daily within an environmental chamber under simulated desert conditions (Wirtz, personal communication).

The above-ground activity of heliothermic lizards is greatly influenced by weather factors, particularly solar radiation and wind (Kay, 1970). The activity patterns of *Uta stansburiana* Baird & Girard show marked seasonal differences (Alexander & Whitford, 1968). During the year, a population in New Mexico spent 25% of the time above ground and 75% in the burrow. Winter activity above ground was directly related to soil surface temperatures. A large literature has developed on the thermal ecology of lizards, and the relationship of body temperature to activity (reviewed by Brattstrom, 1965). Heath (1964) has criticized the methods used in gathering much of these data and hence the conclusions drawn from them.

A reasonable estimate of the energy available for activity can be obtained by comparing active and resting metabolic rates (metabolic scope of activity). During peak periods of activity the metabolic rate of the western harvest mouse (*Reithrodontomys megalotis* (Baird)) was six times the basal rate, although the integrated cost of daily activity probably exceeds the basal level by only 50% (Pearson, 1960b). McNab (1963) used an intermediate level of 1.5 times the basal rate in calculating the energy budgets for three species of *Peromyscus*. Chew & Chew (1970) estimated the energy cost of activity by averaging the mean daily maximum rates of eight species of pocket mice as measured in a respirometer. The energetic cost of running by small desert mammals is from 2 to 6 times that at rest (Taylor, Schmidt-Nielsen & Raab, 1970; Yousef, Robertson, Dill & Johnson, 1970, 1973).

Maximum metabolic rates of Varanid lizards under electrical stimulation were about 6 times the minimum rates at 20 °C, and about 2.5 times the average minimum rate at 40 °C (Bartholomew & Tucker, 1964). Metabolic rate during activity was increased 27%, 36% and 31% over that at rest in *Uta stansburiana* at 15°, 25° and 35 °C respectively (Alexander & Whitford, 1968). That of *Cnemidophorus tigris* Baird & Girard under electrical stimulation was 6 to 7 times the metabolic rate at rest (Asplund, 1970). Dawson & Bartholomew (1958) measured a metabolic scope of 3.6 for *Dipsosaurus dorsalis* (Baird & Girard) at temperatures of 20° to 35 °C. The difficulties in obtaining reliable estimates of both the pattern and intensity of activity by indirect methods like those described emphasize the usefulness of the $D_2^{18}O$ method in calculating the energy cost of respiration.

Production

The elaboration of any product, whether it is body tissue, eggs, hair, feathers, antlers or milk, represents production. In homeotherms almost all of the energy assimilated (A_q) is used in respiration (R_q), only about 2% appearing as production (P_q) (Golley, 1968; Turner, 1970). Ecological efficiency (P_q/C_q) is of course even less. It is evident that errors in measuring homeotherm production are of much less consequence than those occurring in the measurement of respiration.

Production efficiency ($100\ P_q/A_q$) is the ratio of the energy value of tissue produced to that assimilated (McNeill & Lawton, 1970). Production efficiency varies with the food ration and the product elaborated. In cattle, for example, the energetic value of milk is 20% greater than that of fat with equivalent costs of production (Kleiber, 1961, p. 291). Production efficiencies of 12 species of desert-dwelling mammals appear in Table 30.5.

We are not aware of measurements of the energy cost of pregnancy and lactation in desert mammals. There is indirect evidence, in certain rodents at least, that the increased energy demands of pregnancy and lactation are met by both hyperphagia and improved assimilation (Johnson & Groepper, 1970).

In lizards, like other poikilotherms, a much greater proportion of the assimilated energy is used in production. Although no data are available for desert species, ecological and production efficiencies have been calculated for *Lacerta vivipara* Jacquin (Avery, 1971) and *Anolis carolinensis* Voigt (Kitchell & Windell, 1972). These authors cite literature confirming high efficiencies of growth for snakes as well. Similar data are needed for populations living in the wild to corroborate these findings. There is indirect evidence that certain lizards meet the increased energy demands of egg production by hyperphagia (Johnson, 1966; Essghaier & Johnson, 1975).

Annual energy budgets

Energy flow (kcal yr^{-1}) for adults of *Reithrodontomys megalotis* (Baird), *Perognathus parvus* (Peale), *Peromyscus maniculatus* (Wagner) and *Onychomys leucogaster* (Wied-Neuwied) as reported by Schreiber (1973), and those for eight other species of desert rodents and lagomorphs as reported by Chew & Chew (1970), are summarized in Table 30.5. There is rather close agreement in the values reported, a finding that is expected since similar methods were used in calculating energy costs in both studies.

Seasonal torpor in the pocket mice (*Perognathus* spp.) results in a considerable energy saving in comparison with other species of similar

736

Table 30.5. *Energy flow in desert mammals and lizards*

Species	Metabolic body size[3]	Assimila-tion (kcal yr^{-1})	Respira-tion (kcal yr^{-1})	Produc-tion (kcal yr^{-1})	Net growth efficiency (%)
Mammals[1]					
Perognathus flavus Baird	0.023	1175	1145	30	2.5
Reithrodontomys megalotis (Baird)	0.034	3324	3295	29	0.9
Perognathus parvus (Peale)	0.048	2070	2024	46	2.2
Peromyscus maniculatus (Wagner)	0.052	5141	5090	51	1.0
Peromyscus eremicus (Baird)	0.053	4294	4187	107	2.5
Onychomys torridus (Coues)	0.061	3770	3693	77	2.0
Onychomys leucogaster (Wied-Neuwied)	0.062	4857	4792	65	1.3
Dipodomys merriami Mearns	0.088	5046	4952	94	1.9
Spermophilus spilosoma Bennet	0.188	6056	5900	156	2.6
Ammospermophilus harrisi (Audubon & Bachman)	0.207	6141	6019	122	2.0
Sylvilagus auduboni (Baird)	0.902	48955	47955	1000	2.0
Lepus californicus Gray	1.17	116050	113775	2275	2.0
Tayassu tajaçu (L.)	4.27	—	246740	—	—
Lizards[2]					
Uta stansburiana Baird & Girard	0.033	—	58	—	—

[1] Modified from Chew & Chew (1970), Schreiber (1973), and Zervanos & Hadley (1973).
[2] From Alexander & Whitford (1968).
[3] For mammals this is $W^{.75}$, for lizards $W^{.62}$, where W is the body weight in kg.

body size (Table 30.5). The survival value of torpor in Heteromyidae has already received considerable attention (see, for instance, Brown & Bartholomew, 1969). Based on data reported by Tucker (1966), a pocket mouse weighing 23 g saves about 135 mg of food for each hour it spends in torpor. Certain populations of Heteromyid rodents undoubtedly face periodic shortages despite assiduous efforts in caching food (Soholt, 1973). Torpor and food hoarding are only parts of the behavioral repertoire of desert rodents which better insures survival in a harsh environment (Bartholomew & Dawson, 1968).

Energy flow in lizards is of a low order, perhaps 1% of that for homeotherms of equivalent body size (Table 30.5). Alexander & Whitford (1968) calculated that a lizard (*Uta stansburiana*) must assimilate 58 kcal in order to survive one year in a desert scrub community in New Mexico. Obviously, more studies are desirable. Use of the $D_2{}^{18}O$ method would provide a means of independently evaluating estimates made by indirect methods.

Future studies

For some, energetics was once little more than calorimetry. This simplistic approach assumed that a knowledge of the caloric density of ecological materials was about all that was necessary in order to develop an energy budget. For others energetics was a rather harmless pastime because of its descriptive rather than predictive approach. We believe that both views are in error.

Calorimetry became *passé*, not because it was inadequate, but because it became complete. The literature is replete with energy values. Investigators lacking certain caloric densities can readily estimate them with considerable accuracy based on those available for related materials. The challenges are elsewhere.

One promising avenue of research is that of assessing the effects of nutrient quality on physiological processes, reproduction for example. The nutrient quality of the food is more likely to be critical for herbivores than for other consumers (Boyd & Goodyear, 1971). There is abundant evidence that reproduction in Heteromyid rodents which are primarily granivorous coincides with the availability of green forage (Van de Graaff & Balda (1973), and the literature cited there). Are some dietary components, apparently not available in seeds, necessary for successful reproduction? Do populations artificially supplied with food, or those with sufficient hoarded food, continue reproduction? With respect to insectivores, how is insect abundance, and hence reproduction in certain lizards and rodents, related to the pattern and intensity of rainfall? In securing answers to these and other questions, we can eventually develop models which predict the responses of desert vertebrate populations to changes in variables both within and outside the system (Goodall, 1972).

References

Alexander, C. E. & Whitford, W. G. (1968). Energy requirements of *Uta stansburiana. Copeia*, **4**, 678–83.

Asplund, K. K. (1970). Metabolic scope and body temperatures of whiptail lizards (*Cnemidophorus*). *Herpetologica*, **26**, 403–10.

Avery, R. A. (1971). Estimates of food consumption by the lizard *Lacerta vivipara* Jacquin. *Journal of Animal Ecology*, **40**, 351–65.

Bartholomew, G. A. & Cade, T. J. (1957) Temperature regulation, hibernation, and aestivation in the little pocket mouse, *Perognathus longimembris. Journal of Mammalogy*, **38**, 60–72.

Bartholomew, G. A. & Dawson, W. R. (1968). Temperature regulation in desert mammals. In: *Desert Biology* (ed. W. G. Brown, Jr.), vol. 1, pp. 395–421. Academic Press, London & New York.

Bartholomew, G. A. & Tucker, V. A. (1964). Size, body temperature, thermal conductance, oxygen consumption, and heart rate in Australian varanid lizards. *Physiological Zoology*, **37**, 341–54.

Boyd, C. E. & Goodyear, C. P. (1971). Nutritive quality of food in ecological systems. *Archives of Hydrobiology*, **69**, 256–70.

Brattstrom, B. H. (1965). Body temperatures of reptiles. *American Midland Naturalist*, **73**, 376–422.

Brown, G. W., Jr. (ed.) (1968). *Desert Biology*, vol. 1. Academic Press, London & New York.

Brown, J. H. & Bartholomew, G. A. (1969). Periodicity and energetics of torpor in the kangaroo mouse, *Microdipodops pallidus*. *Ecology*, **50**, 705–9.

Chew, R. M. & Butterworth, B. B. (1964). Ecology of rodents in Indian Cove (Mojave Desert), Joshua Tree National Monument, California. *Journal of Mammalogy*, **45**, 203–25.

Chew, R. M. & Chew, A. E. (1970). Energy relationships of the mammals of a desert shrub (*Larrea tridentata*) community. *Ecological Monographs*, **40**, 1–21.

Conover, R. J. (1966). Assimilation of organic matter by zooplankton. *Limnology and Oceanography*, **11**, 338–45.

Dawson, W. R. & Bartholomew, G. A. (1958). Metabolic and cardiac responses to temperature in the lizard *Dipsosaurus dorsalis*. *Physiological Zoology*, **31**, 100–111.

Engelmann, M. D. (1966). Energetics, terrestrial field studies, and animal productivity. In: *Advances in Ecological Research* (ed. J. B. Cragg), vol. 3, pp. 73–115. Academic Press, London & New York.

Essghaier, M. F. (1972). 'Bioenergetics of Great Basin lizards.' M.S. thesis, University of Idaho, Moscow, Idaho.

Essghaier, M. F. & Johnson, D. R. (1975). Aspects of the bioenergetics of Great Basin lizards. *Journal of Herpetology*, **9**, 191–5.

French, N. R., Maza, B. G. & Aschwanden, A. P. (1966). Periodicity of desert rodent activity. *Science*, **154**, 1194–5.

Gessaman, J. A. (1973). Methods of estimating the energy cost of free existence. In: *Ecological energetics of homeotherms* (ed. J. A. Gessaman), pp. 3–31. Vol. 20 of Monograph series. Utah State University Press, Logan.

Golley, F. B. (1968). Secondary productivity in terrestrial communities. *American Zoologist*, **8**, 53–9.

Goodall, D. W. (1972). Potential applications of biome modelling. *Terre et la Vie*, 1972, 118–38.

Heath, J. E. (1964). Reptilian thermoregulation: evaluation of field studies. *Science*, **146**, 784–5.

Johnson, D. R. (1966). Diet and estimated energy assimilation of three Colorado lizards. *American Midland Naturalist*, **76**, 504–9.

Johnson, D. R. & Groepper, K. L. (1970). Bioenergetics of North Plains rodents. *American Midland Naturalist*, **84**, 537–48.

Johnson, D. R. & Maxell, M. H. (1966). Energy dynamics of Colorado pikas. *Ecology*, **47**, 1059–61.

Kay, F. R. (1970). Environmental responses of active lizards at Saratoga Springs, Death Valley, California. *Great Basin Naturalist*, **30**, 146–65.

Kenagy, G. J. (1973). Daily and seasonal patterns of activity and energetics in a heteromyid rodent community. *Ecology*, **54**, 1201–19.

Kitchell, J. F. & Windell, J. T. (1972). Energy budget for the lizard, *Anolis carolinensis*. *Physiological Zoology*, **45**, 178–88.

739

Animal processes

Kleiber, M. (1961). *The fire of life.* Wiley, New York.

MacMillen, R. E. & Lee, A. K. (1970). Energy metabolism and pulmocutaneous water loss of Australian hopping mice. *Comparative Biochemistry and Physiology,* **35,** 355–69.

McNab, B. K. (1963). A model of the energy budget of a wild mouse. *Ecology,* **44,** 521–32.

McNab, B. K. (1970). Body weight and the energetics of temperature regulation. *Journal of Experimental Biology,* **53,** 329–48.

McNeill, S. & Lawton, J. H. (1970). Annual production and respiration in animal populations. *Nature (London),* **225,** 472–74.

Maloiy, G. M. O. (Ed.) (1972). *Comparative physiology of desert animals.* Symposia of the Zoological Society of London No. 31. Academic Press, London & New York.

Marten, G. G. (1973). Time patterns of *Peromyscus* activity and their correlations with weather. *Journal of Mammalogy,* **54,** 169–88.

Mason, C. F. (1970). Food, feeding rates and assimilation in woodland snails. *Oecologia,* **4,** 358–73.

Mueller, C. F. (1970). Energy utilization in the lizards *Sceloporus graciosus* and *S. occidentalis. Journal of Herpetology,* **4,** 131–34.

Mullen, R. K. (1973). The $D_2{}^{18}O$ method of measuring the energy metabolism of free-living animals. In: *Ecological energetics of homeotherms* (ed. G. A. Gessaman), pp. 32–43. Vol. 20 of Monograph series. Utah State University Press, Logan.

Mullen, R. K. & Chew, R. M. (1973). Estimating the energy metabolism of free-living *Perognathus formosus*: a comparison of direct and indirect methods. *Ecology,* **54,** 633–7.

Osgood, D. W. & Weigl, P. D. (1972). Monitoring activity of small mammals by temperature telemetry. *Ecology,* **53,** 738–40.

Pearson, O. P. (1960a). Habits of harvest mice revealed by automatic photographic recorders. *Journal of Mammalogy,* **41,** 58–74.

Pearson, O. P. (1960b). The oxygen consumption and bioenergetics of harvest mice. *Physiological Zoology,* **33,** 152–60.

Petrusewicz, K. (Ed.) (1967). *Secondary productivity of terrestrial ecosystems* (two vols.). Panstwowe Wydawnictwo Naukowe, Krakow.

Petrusewicz, K. & Macfadyen, A. (1970). *Productivity of terrestrial animals.* IBP Handbook No. 13 (ed. J. Phillipson). Blackwell Scientific, Oxford.

Poczopko, P. (1971). Metabolic levels in adult homeotherms. *Acta Theriologica,* **16,** 1–21.

Schmidt-Nielsen, K. (1964). *Desert animals.* Oxford University Press, Oxford.

Schreiber, R. K. (1973). 'Bioenergetics of rodents in the northern Great Basin Desert.' Ph.D. dissertation, University of Idaho, Moscow.

Shoemaker, V. H., Nagy, K. A. & Costa, W. R. (1974). *The consumption, utilization and modification of nutritional resources by the jackrabbit* (Lepus californicus) *in the Mohave Desert.* US/IBP Desert Biome, Research Memorandum RM 74–25. Logan, Utah.

Slobodkin, L. B. (1962). Energy in animal ecology. In: *Advances in ecological research* (ed. J. B. Cragg), vol. 1, pp. 68–101. Academic Press, New York & London.

Soholt, L. F. (1973). Consumption of primary production by a population of kangaroo rats (*Dipodomys merriami*) in the Mojave Desert, *Ecological Monographs,* **43,** 357–76.

740

Taylor, C. R., Schmidt-Nielsen, K. & Raab, J. L. (1970). Scaling of energetic cost of running to body size in mammals. *American Journal of Physiology*, **219**, 1104–7.

Throckmorton, G. S. (1971). Digestive efficiency in the herbivorous lizard *Ctenosaura pectinata*. *Herpetological Reviews*, **3**, 108. (Abstract.)

Tucker, V. A. (1966). Diurnal torpor and its relation to food consumption and weight changes in the California pocket mouse (*Perognathus californicus*). *Ecology*, **47**, 245–52.

Turner, F. B. (1970). The ecological efficiency of consumer populations. *Ecology*, **51**, 741–42.

Van De Graaff, K. M. & Balda, R. P. (1973). Importance of green vegetation for reproduction in the kangaroo rat, *Dipodomys merriami merriami*. *Journal of Mammalogy*, **54**, 509–12.

Yousef, M. K., Robertson, W. D., Dill, D. B. & Johnson, H. D. (1970). Energy expenditure of running kangaroo rats, *Dipodomys merriami*. *Comparative Biochemistry and Physiology*, **36**, 387–93.

Yousef, M. K., Robertson, W. D., Dill, D. B. & Johnson, H. D. (1973). Energetic cost of running in the antelope ground squirrel *Ammospermophilus leucurus*. *Physiological Zoology*, **46**, 139–47.

Zervanos, S. M. & Hadley, N. F. (1973). Adaptational biology and energy relationships of the collared peccary (*Tayassu tajacu*). *Ecology*, **54**, 759–74.

Manuscript received by the editors May 1975

31. Thermal and water relations of desert animals

N. F. HADLEY

Introduction

No area of 'environmental physiology' has received more attention in the past decade than has the study of animals living in hot dry environments. The variety of adaptations employed by animals to cope with temperature extremes and water deficits encountered in desert habitats have stimulated the investigative curiosity of scientists throughout the world. As a result, a rather extensive literature is now available on the thermal and water relations of desert species. Much of this information has been summarized in review-type articles which make reference to desert animals, or which are contained in proceedings of symposia specifically concerned with xeric-adapted species (Brown, 1958; Whittow, 1970, 1971; Maloiy, 1972a; Yousef, Horvath & Bullard, 1972).

A complete review of thermal and water relations of desert animals is neither possible nor necessary in the present chapter. Instead I have selected certain topics in which there is interesting information or which warrant further investigation. These topics, discussed from a comparative standpoint, include the general categories of thermoregulatory mechanisms, water and salt metabolism, and energy relationships. Emphasis will be placed on application of new techniques, instrumentation, and attempts to monitor physiological responses of free-roaming desert animals.

Thermal relations

Temperature tolerance and heterothermy

Desert-adapted animals often have an extended upper temperature range at which their metabolic activities can function. This extension probably reflects a combination of seasonal acclimatization, and genetic differences between xeric species and their mesic congeners. With the exception of amphibians, upper lethal temperatures for terrestrial desert animals range between 40 and 50 °C. Generally arthropods (solpugids, scorpions, beetles) exhibit the greatest tolerance, surviving temperatures approaching 50 °C (Hadley, 1972); however, the pulmonate desert snail, *Sphincterochila boissieri*, tolerates temperatures between 50 and 55 °C, depending upon length of exposure (Schmidt-Nielsen, Taylor & Shkolnik, 1971). Upper

743

lethal temperatures are usually lower for aquatic forms, but here too thermal adaptation to warm desert waters is evident. The highest values recorded for temperature tolerance in fish (44.6±0.05 °C) were obtained for *Cyprinodon macularius* collected from Quitobaquito Spring in the Arizona Sonoran Desert (Lowe & Heath, 1969), and for the minnow *Cyprinodon atroros*, which was observed active in water at 47.2 °C in the Cuatro Cienegas Basin, Coahuila, Mexico (W. L. Minckley, personal communication). Wickstrom & Castenholz (1973) reported that ostracods of the genus *Potamocypris* from the Great Basin Desert survived 5 h at 49±0.5 °C, and the LD_{50} for a 1 min exposure was 55.12 °C.

A frequently observed adjustment to desert temperature extremes by endotherms involves the relaxation of limits for thermoregulatory homeostasis. One form of heterothermic behavior can involve a drop in body temperature during cooler evening hours (nocturnal hypothermia). Another type of heterothermic behavior involves a rise of body temperature several degrees above normothermic levels during the hottest portion of the day, the stored heat being dissipated by non-evaporative means during the night or in burrows where climatic conditions are milder; this behavior, termed facultative hyperthermia, is exhibited by a number of desert birds and mammals. Benefits of hyperthermia include a reduction in the rate of heat gain because of the reduced temperature gradient between the environment and the animal, and savings of water and energy because of the reduced demand for evaporative cooling.

The periodicity and extent of hyperthermy depends, in part, on the animal's size, its hydration state, and its metabolism during hyperthermy. Different strategies of temperature regulation are employed by desert mammals of various size classes (Taylor, 1970, 1971). Large mammals such as the eland (*Tamotragus oryx*), with low ratios of surface area to mass and low weight-specific metabolic rates, experience a slow rise in body temperature from hypothermic morning levels. These mammals significantly reduce the time during which evaporative cooling must be employed, and may not acquire a body temperature which necessitates sweating or panting. Smaller mammals, in contrast, gain heat rapidly and soon reach the point where body temperatures approach and even exceed ambient temperature. Under the latter conditions the direction of heat flow is reversed and the animal is able to utilize physical methods of heat transfer such as radiation and convection. Both strategies imply a reduced hydration state and a need for further conservation of critical body water supplies. When water is plentiful, these animals may not undergo hyperthermia, but simply maintain constant body temperatures by sweating or panting. Reduced metabolism during hyperthermia also increases its effectiveness. Hart (1971) reported that the desert rodents *Spermophilus leucurus* and *Spermophilus tereticaudatus* tolerate hyperthermia without a concomitant increase in metabolism. This reduces both the hyperthermia itself and the requirement for evaporative cooling.

Whereas the existence and adaptive significance of a labile body temperature in desert birds and mammals is readily apparent, the physiological processes which effect this increased thermolability are unknown. Bligh (1972) proposed several possible explanations involving dehydration and its relation to thermoregulatory control. These include reduced effectiveness of evaporative cooling through the reduction of fluid secretion onto the evaporative surface, the possibility of dehydration causing a shift in the 'set-point' of body temperature, or the existence of two distinct threshold levels, one for evaporative heat loss and one for heat production. Investigations designed to test these hypotheses clearly are needed if we are fully to understand the nature of this physiological adaptation to heat and aridity, and use domestic species more effectively in these habitats (Bligh, 1972).

Cardiovascular adjustments in thermoregulation

The role of the cardiovascular system in thermoregulatory processes of desert animals has been an area of active and fruitful research. Paramount in these studies have been investigations of the basis and adaptive significance of temperature differences between head and body, and changes in blood flow and cardiac function which alter the rate of heat gain or loss. Of the animal groups examined in this respect, desert lizards and large mammals have received the bulk of attention.

Initial experimentation to determine the morphological and physiological basis for temperature differences between head and body began with Heath's (1964, 1966) studies of the horned lizard, *Phrynosoma coronatum*. He proposed a countercurrent heat-exchange system whereby warm venous blood draining the head via the internal jugular lost heat to the cool arterial blood entering the head via the internal carotid. When a preferred temperature was reached, contraction of the internal jugular constrictor muscle shunted blood arriving from the body into the external jugular vein. Since no countercurrent arrangement exists in association with this vessel, the head now received the cooler body blood and the temperature differential diminished. Differences in head and body temperatures have since been reported in a number of lizards and snakes (see Webb, Johnson & Firth (1972) for a comprehensive list). Webb *et al.* (1972) have extended Heath's findings, suggesting that precise temperature regulation of the head depends upon a combination of 'circulatory adjustments' in which the animal increases its activity and heart rate, and 'respiratory adjustments' which are characterized by increased ventilation rates, panting, and in some instances gular flutter.

Animal processes

A countercurrent heat-exchange system apparently is responsible for a similar temperature differential between the brain and body in desert mammals, the brain temperature often being several degrees lower than the rectal temperature. Selective cooling of the brain has been demonstrated in the sheep, *Ovis aries* (Baker & Hayward, 1968), and in gazelles (*Gazelle thomsonii*) and oryx (*Oryx beisa*) (Taylor, 1969; Taylor & Lyman, 1972). The exchange system operates basically as follows. Arterial blood supplying the brain passes through hundreds of small arteries (carotid rete mirabilis) which lie in a venous pool (cavernous sinus). Venous blood cooled by evaporation from walls of the nasal passages drains through the cavernous sinus and allows for an exchange of heat between venous and arterial blood (Taylor, 1969). This heat-exchange system in desert mammals (and possibly certain avian species) represents an important physiological mechanism for permitting heat storage and tolerating hyperthermia during periods of maximum activity or under high environmental heat loads.

Considerable research has also centered on blood flow and cardiac function as they relate to heating and cooling rates. Kluger & Heath (1970) demonstrated that vasodilation in the wing of the bat, *Eptesicus fuscus*, was an important mechanism for heat dissipation, particularly during flight. A series of investigations have shown that in lizards cutaneous vasodilation occurs with localized heating, and vasoconstriction with cooling (Morgareidge & White, 1969; Weathers, 1971; Weathers & Morgareidge, 1971; Baker, Weathers & White, 1972). As a result of this differential blood shunting, lizards gain heat more rapidly than they cool and are able to remain near or at their preferred temperature for longer periods. A summary of many of the probable circulatory and behavioral correlates of temperature regulation in lizards has been presented by White (1973) (Fig. 31.1).

Cardiovascular adjustments in thermoregulation are not unique to vertebrates. The sphinx moth, *Manduca sexta*, relies on circulatory heat transfer to maintain rather precise thoracic temperatures during flight over a wide range of ambient temperatures (Heinrich, 1970, 1971). By ligating the dorsal vessel and subsequently removing insulating scales covering the thorax, Heinrich determined that heat generated in the thorax during flight was transferred to the blood pumped from the comparatively cool abdomen and eventually dissipated when blood returned to the abdomen. This mechanism of heat transfer appears to require no additional heat production or water loss, a feature important in the adaptation of the moth to desert regions (Heinrich, 1971).

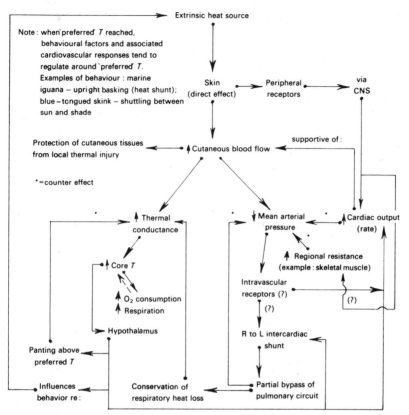

Fig. 31.1. Summary of some major factors known or suspected of involvement in the thermoregulation of body temperature in lizards. (From White, 1973.)

Coloration and its thermal consequences

The paradox between the seemingly disproportionate number of desert species with black coloration and the apparent thermal problems created by dark pigmentation has continued to attract the interest of desert biologists. Various hypotheses and explanations have been advanced to explain this paradox and, in many cases, quantitative data have been offered in support of a particular argument. Among invertebrates, beetles continue to be the favorite experimental test animals of investigators. Hadley (1970a), Edney (1971a) and Hamilton (1973) measured body temperatures of black and white Tenebrionid beetles under natural and simulated desert conditions. The white beetles included naturally occurring species found in the Namib Desert of East Africa, as well as black individuals with their elytra painted white for purposes of comparison. Results generally indicated that black beetles do indeed absorb more

747

incident radiation (visible and near-infrared) than white individuals and, therefore, are likely to exhibit slightly higher body and/or subelytral temperatures. The extent of the exaggerated heat load due to dark coloration in these beetles, however, must be considered in association with the many factors known to influence energy exchange – body size, surface texture, orientation, activity cycles, etc.

Hamilton (1973) proposed a mechanism whereby black coloration might be thermally advantageous to these desert beetles. Dark individuals, by maximizing absorption of incident solar radiation during early morning and late afternoon hours, could increase the time for surface activity before temperature extremes encountered during midday forced their retreat into shade or burrows. In support, Hamilton points out that white beetles, because of the increased reflectivity and reduced thermal load, can be, and indeed are, active during the middle portion of the day when dark beetles have retreated. His arguments, although sound from the standpoint of energetics, are not without objections. Also one still must consider possible advantages of dark coloration in protection or concealment which may have been selected for at the expense of thermal consequences. His objective treatment, however, does expose certain fallacies regarding coloration in desert animals, and provides guidelines for future research in this area.

Black coloration and its thermal consequences have also been explored in a variety of ectothermic and endothermic vertebrates. Norris's (1967) comprehensive paper correlating coloration and energy relations in reptiles showed that a desert iguana, *Dipsosaurus dorsalis*, in the dark condition had a net energy gain of 92.4 cal min^{-1} as against 71.2 cal min^{-1} for light-colored individuals, a difference of 0.42 °C in rate of heat gain due to metachrosis. Hamilton & Heppner (1967) proposed that dark or black coloration in birds and mammals might reduce the metabolic cost of homeothermy by maximizing absorption of radiant solar energy. Support for this hypothesis comes from several subsequent studies on birds. Heppner (1970) found that black-dyed zebra finches (*Poephila castanotis*) absorbed 3.1 cal min^{-1} more than white birds, while white birds had a metabolic heat production 2.7 cal min^{-1} greater than black birds. Ohmart & Lasiewski (1971) reported substantial energy savings in desert road-runners (*Geococcyx californianus* (Lesson)) which were able to elevate body temperatures to normothermic levels by exposing black plumage and naked black skin to solar radiation during sunning behavior. Finally, Marder (1973) found that black plumage surface heated up more than light-colored feathers of *Corvus corax ruficollis* in the Negev Desert of Israel. During summer heat loads, high surface temperatures would enhance heat dissipation to the environment via convection and radiation, and also reduce the rate of heat gain from the environment because of the reduced temperature gradient.

748

Responses to cold

Physiologists studying adaptations of animals to desert conditions have typically concentrated on mechanisms employed to circumvent or counteract stresses imposed by high temperatures and desiccating atmospheres. This is to be expected, as these factors constitute the two basic problems faced by warm-desert species. In many deserts, however, cold can also be a limiting factor either diurnally or seasonally. This is particularly true in high-latitude deserts or in deserts which contain mountains within their boundaries.

Studies of responses of desert homeotherms to cold have been primarily directed towards the phenomenon of torpidity and its adaptive significance. Bartholomew & Dawson (1968) and Dawson & Hudson (1970) discuss this in their reviews of desert birds and mammals respectively, and mention was made of this phenomenon in the section on heterothermy above. Responses to seasonal changes in the absence of 'hibernation' were examined for the collared peccary, *Tayassu tajaçu* (Linn.), in the Arizona Sonoran Desert (Zervanos & Hadley, 1973). In contrast to summer conditions, peccaries during winter months increased heat production and reduced heat loss. Major periods of activity were shifted to daytime hours, with much time spent basking. At night animals sought shelter and huddled together to reduce heat loss. Pelage density increased in winter, which reduced convective heat loss; however, the improvement in insulation was not enough to compensate for colder ambient temperatures. Thus, in winter peccaries increased metabolic rates to augment heat production. The increased metabolism was reflected in the animal's food intake; energy requirements in winter averaged 93.4 kcal kg^{-1} d^{-1} compared to 72.2 kcal kg^{-1} d^{-1} in summer.

More spectacular adjustments to cold temperature such as freezing resistance and supercooling, typically associated with high-latitude and polar species, have also been demonstrated in a number of desert organisms. Lowe, Heed & Halpern (1967) observed *Drosophila nigrospiracula* to be capable of supercooling to between $-5\,°C$ and $-6\,°C$ (LD_0), a feature which allows the species to remain active on the surface and breed throughout winter months in the Sonoran Desert. Cloudsley-Thompson & Crawford (1970) obtained a mean supercooling point of $-11.8\,°C$ for the Tenebrionid beetle *Eleodes* sp., and $-5.8\,°C$ for the scorpion *Vejovis* sp. Subsequent investigations have provided supercooling values ranging from $-3.8\,°C$ in adult desert locusts, *Schistocerca gregaria* (Forsk.), to $-10.4\,°C$ in the African desert Tenebrionid beetle, *Ocnera hispida* (Cloudsley-Thompson, 1973). Supercooling limits and freezing-point temperatures for 45 reptilian species, many of which are desert forms, were recorded by Lowe, Lardner & Halpern (1971). Mean supercooling limits for lizards and snakes ranged between $-3.89\,°C$ and $-7.44\,°C$.

Animal processes

For some species the capacity to supercool would provide protection against freezing weather encountered in their habitat during colder months. Minimum temperatures of $-5.1\,°C$ were recorded immediately above the tops of rotting sahuaro cactus (*Cereus giganteus*) which serves as the host plant for *Drosophila nigrospiracula* (Lowe *et al.*, 1967), and subzero cold can be encountered in rock crevices and burrows selected as hibernacula by desert reptiles. In other species the capacity to supercool is greater than necessary to survive climatic extremes in a particular desert region, and may be a taxonomic rather than an adaptive feature (Cloudsley-Thompson, 1973).

Water relations

Components of water loss

The problem of dehydration in desert species reflects both increased drying power of the air and the use of evaporative cooling to prevent overheating. Water is lost as both liquid and vapor, and losses occur through a variety of avenues depending on the species in question and its hydration state. Major pathways of water loss are basically similar in all groups – integumentary and respiratory transpiration. Generally, integumentary transpiration predominates at lower temperatures and respiratory transpiration at higher temperatures, although integumentary water loss continues to increase as ambient temperatures rise. Water loss associated with defecation, elimination of nitrogenous waste products, extra-renal salt removal, and emergency cooling mechanisms such as 'salivation' make up the remaining components, and may surpass transpiratory water loss in importance. Components of water loss and their relative contributions to total water loss for the beetle *Eleodes armata* are shown in Fig. 31.2

Most desert-adapted arthropods exhibit relatively low integumentary transpiration rates. This reduction in the rate of outward passage of water is generally attributed to a wax or grease layer deposited on the cuticular surface, although the tanned chitin-protein complex of the exocuticle or extensions of the lipid material into the underlying cuticular layers may also be effective in this process. Support for the view that an epicuticular lipid is primarily responsible for waterproofing qualities of the integument is derived from the following: (*a*) cuticles from which surface lipids are removed, either mechanically or chemically, are relatively permeable to water; (*b*) a similar degree of waterproofing can be produced when extracted cuticular lipids are deposited on artificial membranes or insect wings; (*c*) a marked increase in cuticular permeability to water occurs in many species at a specific temperature (transition temperature) which corresponds to a possible phase shift in the lipid layer; and (*d*) restoration

750

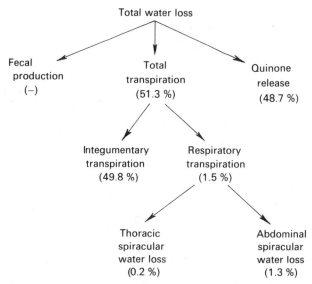

Fig. 31.2. Components of water loss and their percentage contribution to total water loss in the desert Tenebrionid beetle, *Eleodes armata*, at 25 °C and near 0% r.h. The absence of fecal production and the relatively high water loss attributed to quinone basically reflect experimental conditions, and may not accurately represent the contributions of these components in nature. (After Ahearn, 1970.)

of the epicuticular lipid in a previously abraded insect once again confers resistance to desiccation (Edney, 1967; Hadley, 1970*b*; Jackson & Baker, 1970).

The structural arrangement and composition of this layer is still subject to controversy. The existence of tightly-packed molecules in a lipid monolayer as proposed by Beament (1961) is not fully supported by ultrastructural evidence (Locke, 1965), or by the chemical composition of insect waxes analyzed thus far (Hackman, 1964). Application of modern techniques such as gas chromatography, nuclear magnetic resonance, mass spectrometry, scanning electron microscopy and isotopic labelling are needed to provide answers. Especially valuable would be investigations of structural and compositional changes which occur at the transition temperature, correlation of lipid composition with thermal regimes and degree of water impermeability, and sites and pathways for the biosynthesis of cuticular waxes.

Terrestrial desert vertebrates do not possess an integumentary barrier to water movement comparable to the epicuticular lipid layer characteristic of many arthropods, although the formation of a cocoon by several amphibian species during estivation no doubt greatly enhances the water impermeability of their integument (Lee & Mercer, 1967; McClanahan, 1967). Lack of sweat glands in reptiles and birds, and the relatively

Animal processes

impermeable appearance of their integument, suggested that evaporation from the skin of these species represented only a small fraction of total evaporative water loss. The relatively high rates of cutaneous water loss observed in reptiles (Bentley & Schmidt-Nielsen, 1966; Dawson, Shoemaker & Licht, 1966; Claussen, 1967) and birds (Bernstein, 1971) have necessitated re-examination of this earlier assumption. The functional significance of reptilian scales in reducing cutaneous water loss was also questioned by Licht & Bennett (1972), who compared a scaleless gopher snake, *Pituophis melanoleucus catenifer*, with a normal individual of similar size. Even though the scaleless snake lacked the outer 'superficial' dermal layer and possessed a much thinner keratin layer, the rate of water loss for the scaleless snake was comparable to that of the normal individual. The role of the mammalian integument in reducing water loss has also received attention. Ghobrial (1970a) suggested that the thinness of the unkeratinized epidermis and its horny layer in the jerboa (*Jaculus jaculus*) and gazelle (*Gazella dorcas dorcas*) may permit a greater loss of water by transpiration than observed in the camel (*Camelus dromedarius*) which has a comparatively thick epidermis. However, Hattingh (1972) found a poor correlation between epidermal thickness and 'transepidermal water loss' in nine mammalian skins, and suggested that some other integumentary feature or process was responsible for the barrier function.

Specialized avenues of moisture uptake

Scarcity of bulk supplies of surface water imposes a serious problem for desert inhabitants who must continually replenish body water, especially during hot summer months when rates of water loss by evaporation are high and reduced activity of prey organisms can eliminate the major source of water. During these periods exploitation of more restricted water sources may be essential. Two potential sources are atmospheric and substrate moisture. Their availability depends, in part, on the geographical location of the desert and the time of day or year. In most deserts the relative humidity at the surface is almost 100% during early morning hours (Hadley & Williams, 1968; Hadley, 1970a), and advective fogs are frequent in some coastal desert regions (Louw, 1972). Burrow microenvironments may also provide conditions in which moisture uptake from burrow air or surrounding soil is possible.

Uptake of water vapor from subsaturated atmospheres has been demonstrated in a variety of arthropods; most of the known cases are listed by Noble-Nesbitt (1969). For many species absorption is only possible at high relative humidities; however, moisture uptake by booklice (Psocoptera) of the genus *Liposcellis* has been reported at relative humidities approaching 50% (Knülle & Spadafora, 1969), and between 45% and 47.5% for the Thysanuran *Ctenolepisma terebrans* (Edney, 1971b). The exact site and mechanism of uptake are still obscure. The general body surface including both cuticle and epidermis has been commonly thought to be involved; however, Noble-Nesbitt (1970) found that atmospheric uptake ceased when he occluded the anus of the Thysanuran *Thermobia domestica*. Rectal absorption of moisture, in turn, has been disputed by Okasha (1971) who contends that anal blockage results in nervous inhibition of moisture uptake since there are stretch receptors located in the anus that are concerned with volume regulation.

In spite of impressive evidence for atmospheric moisture uptake in a variety of species, its occurrence in truly desert forms is rare and its adaptive significance questionable. I am aware of only two investigations which have confirmed this phenomenon in desert arthropods – Edney's (1971b) study mentioned above and an earlier study (Edney, 1966) on the cockroach *Arenivaga* sp., which inhabits sand dunes in low-altitude deserts in southern California. Investigations of desert scorpions (Hadley, 1970b; Crawford & Wooten, 1973) and desert Tenebrionid beetles (Ahearn, 1970) failed to show significant water gain via this avenue. It appears that the cuticular layer or layers so important in reducing transpiration rates in these species also function to prevent inward movement of water vapor, although the possibility of the latter cannot be discounted in all desert species. Louw (1972) also reported that water resulting from condensation of fog on the elytra of Tenebrionid beetles in the Namib Desert was not absorbed through the cuticle, but may enter the digestive tract and subsequently become incorporated into the hemolymph.

Utilization of substrate moisture by desert species appears to be no better developed than their ability to absorb moisture from subsaturated atmospheres. Desert amphibians which rely on integumental moisture uptake to maintain water balance are an important exception. Species such as the spadefoot toad, *Scaphiopus couchii*, remain in burrows for 10 months of the year, during which time they can lose 72% of their normal body weight (McClanahan, 1967). They emerge following summer rains and can rapidly replenish body water by simply being in contact with free-standing water. Although rehydration apparently takes place across the entire integument, in the toad *Bufo punctatus* certain regions such as the ventral pelvic integument absorb water more rapidly than other areas, and can account for as much as 70% of the uptake rate across the total integument (McClanahan & Baldwin, 1969). Moisture uptake from the soil while in the burrow is also possible as long as the osmotic pressure of body fluids is higher than soil water tension. By elevating the osmotic pressure of the blood through urea storage, desert toads are able to maintain a favorable gradient for continued moisture uptake from the surrounding soil even when soil water tensions reach very low levels (Shoemaker, McClanahan & Ruibal, 1969).

Regulation of body fluid concentration and ionic constituents during dehydration

In spite of behavioral and physiological mechanisms for reducing water loss in desert species, extreme temperatures and dry air often produce severe water deficits. During these periods it is essential that osmotic pressure and concentration of certain body fluids do not reach levels which are incompatible with biological functioning. In most insects the osmotic pressure of hemolymph is regulated during dehydration despite a reduction in hemolymph volume (Edney, 1968; Wall, 1970; Okasha, 1973). Osmotic regulation implies removal of solutes, particularly sodium and potassium ions, from the hemolymph. The role of the Malpighian tubules and the rectum in this process is discussed in detail by Shaw & Stobbart (1972). Possible mechanisms for ionic regulation during desiccation and subsequent rehydration are diagrammatically represented in Fig. 31.3.

Toleration of increased urea and electrolyte concentration in body fluids of toads and frogs in burrows, and its significance in providing for more favorable concentration gradients between the animal and surrounding soil, have been mentioned. Among reptiles the desert iguana, *Dipsosaurus dorsalis*, showed no evidence of dehydration or accumulation of electrolytes even after six-month drought (Minnich, 1970). Elimination of excess electrolytes, which resulted from dietary intake and the concomitant evaporation of ion-free water, was accomplished by renal production of urate salts and, to a lesser extent, by excretions of the salt gland. Nagy (1972) found that, during drought, the lizard *Sauromalus obesus* became dehydrated, but fractional fluid volumes and electrolyte concentrations in the plasma were maintained at normal levels. As in the case of the iguana, the major means of electrolyte excretion in *S. obesus* were salt-gland secretions and urate pellets, both of which require little water.

Renal structure and function in birds and mammals

Physiological responses to dehydration and osmotic stress in birds and mammals are closely linked with renal structure and function. These vertebrate groups are unique in that they are capable of producing urine hyperosmotic to blood plasma. Bird kidneys are generally not as efficient in this respect as those of mammals, producing a maximum urine concentration approximately 2 to 3 times that of the plasma (Carey & Morton, 1971; Krag & Skadhauge, 1972). Partial compensation for this lower

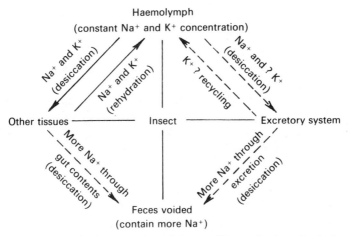

Fig. 31.3. Diagrammatic representation of the possible mechanisms for ionic regulation during one cycle of 3 days' desiccation and 1 day rehydration. Solid arrows indicate likely pathways, broken arrows indicate possible pathways. (From Okasha, 1973.)

ability to concentrate solutes is provided by the elimination of nitrogenous end-products in the form of uric acid, a semi-solid suspension which requires little water, and in some xeric species by the presence of functional salt glands which secrete concentrated solutions of electrolytes such as sodium and potassium chloride. In contrast, electrolyte concentrations in urine as high as 26 times those in plasma have been recorded for some desert rodents (MacMillen & Lee, 1967), making them virtually independent of exogenous water. Electrolyte concentrations of urine, and urine:plasma ratios, are given for selected birds and mammals in Table 31.1.

Differences in concentrating ability between birds and mammals can be largely attributed to structural differences. The avian kidney is structurally similar to the reptilian kidney, although it contains nephrons of both mammalian and reptilian type (respectively with and without loop structure). Urine concentration in birds is accomplished by a countercurrent multiplier system functionally identical to that operative in mammalian kidneys (Johnson & Mugaas, 1970; Emery, Poulson & Kinter, 1972); however, because of the limited number of mammalian-type nephrons which are available to participate in this process, the capacity for urine concentration is less (Braun & Dantzler, 1972).

Structural differences in kidneys are often responsible for increased efficiency of particular species and subspecies occupying xeric environments. Among birds, poor concentrators have short straight medullary units while xeric species have longer units which are extensively curved (Johnson & Ohmart, 1973). Similar morphological differences are seen

755

Table 31.1 *Urine electrolyte and osmotic concentrations, and urine:plasma (U/P) ratios in selected birds and mammals. Values are means ± standard deviation*

Species	Na$^+$ (meq l^{-1})	K$^+$ (meq l^{-1})	Cl$^-$ (meq l^{-1})	Urea (mmol l^{-1})	Osmotic concentration (mOsm l^{-1})[1]	U/P ratio	Remarks	Reference
Birds								
Budgerigar (*Melopsittacus undulatus*)	58.0±24.1	73.2±69.9	34.0±7.3	—	348.0±112	2.3	Dehydrated 3–32 days	Krag & Skadhauge (1972)
Sage Sparrow (*Amphispiza belli nevadensis*)	267.3±17.9	—	307.0±15.3	—	644.1±46.6	2.4	Maintained on 0.25 M NaCl drinking solution	Moldenhauer & Wiens (1970)
California Quail (*Lophortyx californicus*)	321.6	—	310.0	—	750.9	2.1	Maintained on 0.3 M NaCl drinking solution	Carey & Morton (1971)
Gambel's Quail (*Lophortyx gambelii*)	493.4	—	421.3	—	962.4	2.9	Maintained on 0.3 M NaCl drinking solution	Carey & Morton (1971)
Mammals								
Australian Hopping Mouse (*Notomys alexis*)	—	—	—	5430	9370	24.6	Maximum values; diet of dry grain	MacMillen & Lee (1971)
Canyon Mouse (*Peromyscus crinitus stephensi*)	30	—	—	1958	3150	9.0	Deprived of water	Abbot (1971)
Collared Peccary (*Tayassu tajacu*)	57±17	155±44	68±17	—	1182	3.4	Dehydrated summer animals	Zervanos & Hadley (1973)
Somali Donkey (*Equus asinus*)	11	278	170	202	1384	4.5	22–40 °C; minimum water	Maloiy (1970)
Camel (*Camelus dromedarius*)	6.0±0.75	630.0±28.6	153.0±22.6	954.0±66.1	2230.0±68.5	6.3	Minimum water	Maloiy (1972 b)

[1] 'Osm' is the abbreviation for Osmole, the mass of 6.023×10^{23} osmotically active particles, and is almost equivalent to 'mole' for a non-electrolyte at high dilution.

between mesic-adapted and xeric-adapted mammals. In view of the fact that the greater the length of loops participating in countercurrent activity the greater the urine-concentrating ability, a strong correlation should be expected between medullary thickness, urine-concentrating ability, and water availability in the habitat of each species. Heisinger & Breitenbach (1969) found such a correlation among subspecies of cottontail rabbits; desert rabbits, *Sylvilagus audubonii baileyi* showed the highest relative medullary thickness of any of the subspecies studied. Similar correlations of medullary thickness with habitat dryness have been found in Cricetid rodents (Heisinger, King, Halling & Fields, 1973).

Kidneys need not be adapted to maximize water conservation and salt elimination in all desert mammals. The desert bat, *Leptonycteris sanborni*, is a nectar feeder. This diet provides large quantities of water, but little protein and almost no salt. Carpenter (1969) found the kidney of this species to have a highly developed cortex with many convoluted tubules, and a thin renal medulla with poorly developed papillae – morphological features which promote the reabsorption of salts and the production of a hypo-osmotic urine. In comparison to two other desert bats investigated, *L. sanborni* has the lowest ability to conserve water through urine production, but is the only species that is independent of free water in a desert environment (Carpenter, 1969).

Lower glomerular filtration rates (GFR) and concomitant reduced urine flow are two additional responses to dehydration observed in birds. Braun & Dantzler (1972) reported that desert quail (*Lophortyx gambelii* Gambel) responded to acute osmotic stress with a 20% reduction in GFR. In dehydrated budgerigars (*Melopsittacus undulatus*), GFR decreased by 37% from 4.43 μlg^{-1}min^{-1} to 3.24 μlg^{-1}min^{-1}, while urine flow rates (UFR) decreased from 105 nlg^{-1}min^{-1}, to 28 nlg^{-1}min^{-1} (Krag & Skadhauge, 1972). The factor believed responsible for the decline in GFR is a rise in the osmotic pressure of the plasma, which causes constriction of the afferent arterioles in the reptilian-type glomeruli, reducing the number of functioning nephrons and shunting blood around the glomeruli through bypass vessels. Mammalian-type (medullary) nephrons continue filtering during dehydration to provide for continued maintenance of concentrating ability (Braun & Dantzler, 1972).

Reduction of GFR and UFR in mammals can also result in a considerable savings of water and electrolytes. Filtration rates of fully hydrated camels average 0.66 mlkg^{-1}min^{-1}, but drop by two-thirds to 0.22 mlkg^{-1}min^{-1} after 10 days without water (Siebert & MacFarlane, 1971). This results in a drop of nearly 90% in sodium excretion, and 66% for potassium. Urine flow rates likewise exhibit a marked decrease, ranging from 2 to 6 mlmin^{-1} in hydrated camels, while in dehydrated camels the rates were from 0.5 to 1.2 mlmin^{-1} (Siebert & MacFarlane, 1971). Reduced UFR as an

Animal processes

adaptive response to water shortage has been demonstrated in a number of xeric-adapted mammals, including the Somali donkey, *Equus asinus* (Maloiy, 1970), *Gazella dorcas dorcas* (Ghobrial, 1970*b*), and *Tayassu tajaçu* (Zervanos & Hadley, 1973). Species which lack the ability to reduce urine volume when water intake is restricted, such as the waterbuck (*Kobus defassa ugandae*), may be limited to habitats where water is plentiful (Taylor, Spinage & Lyman, 1969).

Radioisotope applications

The use of radioisotopes to study the nature and rates of physiological processes in desert-adapted species has been a most effective tool for providing data on the complex inter-relationships between the animal and its environment. Radioisotopes can be measured when present in minute amounts, and their movement can be followed at the cellular, organismal and ecosystem level. In the past radiotracer studies have been primarily confined to the laboratory, because of difficulties involved in controlling experimental conditions and variables. Although useful data have been obtained in this manner, laboratory conditions are often highly artificial and can lead to ecologically meaningless interpretation of data. The extension of radioisotope techniques to free-roaming animals in their natural habitats counteracts some of these difficulties and provides a check on laboratory data obtained previously.

Tritiated water (THO) is most commonly used to determine body water and rates of water turnover in desert animals. The former determination relies on the isotope dilution factor, the latter on the biological half-life of tritium. To my knowledge, there have been no isotopic determinations of either aspect of water relations in free-living desert invertebrates, partly because of body size and difficulties in recapture of tagged individuals. However, our preliminary results using desert scorpion indicate that such a measurement is possible and should provide valuable data. Several papers have reported water turnover in free-living desert lizards using THO (Minnich & Shoemaker, 1970, 1972; Green, 1972; Nagy, 1972). Rates varied from a minimum of 5.5 $mg d^{-1}$ per gram live weight for *Varanus gouldii* in winter (Green, 1972) to 30 $mg d^{-1}$ per gram live weight for *Dipsosaurus dorsalis*, a value corrected to zero weight loss (Minnich & Shoemaker, 1970). Using the THO method in birds, Ohmart, Chapman & MacFarland (1970) reported that desert-dwelling roadrunners exhibited a turnover of 41.8 $ml d^{-1}$ under moderate conditions, but only 26.2 $ml d^{-1}$ under simulated desert conditions.

Tritiated water has been used to study the water dynamics of mammals of various sizes and habitat preferences, under simulated and actual desert conditions. Results of these studies generally indicate that water transfer

758

rates are positively correlated with the availability of water in the natural habitat of the species (Kennedy & MacFarlane, 1971; Holleman & Dieterich, 1973). These studies, and previous ones mentioned on other vertebrate groups, have also led to questions regarding the validity of the technique and assumptions involved. Haines, Howard & Setchell (1973), in their examination of several Australian desert rodents, tested the assumption that THO equilibrates with all body tissues. They found that THO reached equilibrium in all tissues except unshorn skin, in which there was approximately 15% less activity than in other tissues. The existence of this difference was confirmed by determining THO concentrations in evaporate collected separately from the head and trunk regions, and suggests a system of more than one compartment for body water (Haines *et al.*, 1973). It is likely that, as more studies are performed, critical data on the technique and methods employed as well as on water relations of the species involved will be forthcoming.

Although measurement of metabolism is a relatively simple laboratory procedure, data obtained in this manner may not accurately reflect an animal's metabolism in its natural habitat, where its activity varies and environmental parameters such as temperature and relative humidity are continually changing. To overcome these difficulties, isotope techniques have also been employed to measure energy metabolism of field populations. The most promising of these, and one which has been field-tested on desert species, is that employing doubly-labelled water ($D_2^{18}O$). This method has been discussed by Johnson & Schreiber in the previous chapter, and the reader is referred there for further information.

Energy relations

Energy-exchange budgets

The exchange of energy between a desert species and its environment is dependent upon a variable array of transactions, which include metabolic and nutritional factors, and physical methods of heat transfer such as radiation, conduction, convection and evaporation. The latter mechanisms provide the foundation for 'heat-exchange budgets' or 'energy-exchange budgets', in which components contributing to heat gain are listed on one side of an equation and those resulting in heat loss are listed on the opposite side. Quantification of these components, especially in free-roaming animals under natural desert conditions, has provided useful information on the relative contributions of various exchange mechanisms employed by organisms to remain in thermodynamic equilibrium with their environment.

Complete heat-exchange budgets for desert arthropods active on the desert surface under mild loads of radiation and heat have been constructed for two Tenebrionid beetles (Hadley, 1970*a*; Edney, 1971*a*). In both studies the primary components of the energy equation were heat gained from radiation absorption and heat lost by convection. Neither metabolism, evaporation, nor conduction contributed enough to the heat balance to warrant inclusion in the final equation. In fact, Edney (1971*a*) reduced the determination of body temperature under the above conditions to the simple expression:

$$R_n = h_c \Delta T,$$

where R_n is net radiation load, h_c the convection coefficient, and ΔT the temperature excess of the beetle over ambient air.

Although there has been no construction of a complete energy budget for desert reptiles under natural conditions, there are considerable data available concerning one or more of the components comprising such a budget. Norris's (1967) study discussed earlier in reference to coloration and its thermal consequences provides an analysis of each component under a set of arbitrarily established environmental circumstances. Similarly detailed investigations on the arboreal lizard *Sceloporus occidentalis* (Bartlett & Gates, 1967) and the American alligator *Alligator mississippiensis* (Spotila, Soule & Gates, 1972) provide methodology and techniques which can be utilized in desert field studies. The design and use of radiotelemetric devices for monitoring movement, body temperature, and other physiological processes (Stebbins & Barwick, 1968; Osgood, 1970; Kroll, Clark & Albert, 1973) should facilitate the acquisition of data on non-captive animals in their natural environment.

There is a long history of partitional calorimetric investigations on man in the desert (Gagge, 1972), but detailed analyses of total heat exchange for other homeotherms is limited to a few species only. Yarbrough (1971) discusses some of the difficulties of obtaining accurate energy budgets for birds, citing temporal variations in effective body surface, and peripheral and appendicular blood circulation, as factors which hinder the accurate apportionment of heat exchange. Time and energy budget calculations on avian species have shown how different bird activities result in different partitioning of the avenues for heat exchange, and exemplify the difficulties cited by Yarbrough (1971).

Quantification of thermal exchange under field conditions has perhaps been more successful in mammals, particularly larger species. Finch (1972) investigated the modes of heat gain and loss in two East African antelopes, the eland, which relies on sweating, and the hartebeest, *Alcelaphus buselaphus*, which primarily uses panting as a means of evaporative cooling. Heat absorbed at the fur surface, of which over one-half was due to long-wave radiation from ground and atmosphere, was approximately 9 times metabolic heat production. Approximately 66% (eland) and 75%

760

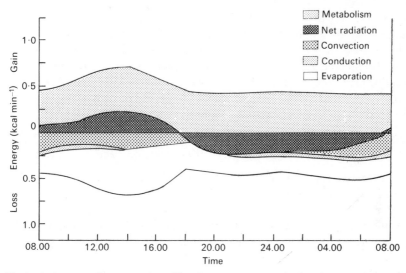

Fig. 31.4. Avenues of energy gain and loss for summer peccaries in a desert enclosure during July. (From Zervanos & Hadley, 1973.)

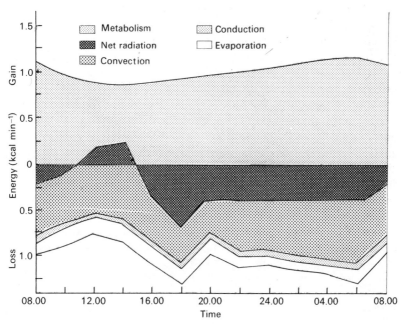

Fig. 31.5. Avenues of energy gain and loss for winter peccaries in a desert enclosure during December (From Zervanos & Hadley, 1973.)

Animal processes

(hartebeest) of this absorbed heat load was dissipated by long-wave radiation, while evaporation accounted for 31% in the eland and 20% in the hartebeest of total heat dissipation during peak periods of radiation. Convectional heat loss was small in both species (Finch, 1972). Zervanos & Hadley (1973) determined the total energy flux for the collared peccary, *Tayassu tajaçu*, at thermal equilibrium for a period of 24 h during summer and winter in a desert enclosure, using the following equation:

Metabolic heat + Absorbed Radiation =
Re-radiation + Convection + Evaporation ± Conduction.

Avenues of energy gain and loss for peccaries during both seasons are shown in Figs. 31.4 and 31.5. Metabolism was the major source of heat gain during both summer and winter, and was supplemented by a net absorption of radiation during daytime hours. Counterbalancing heat gain was radiative cooling, especially during clear night-time hours, and convective and evaporative heat transfer, the former predominating during winter, the latter during summer. Conduction was responsible for dissipating only a small proportion of the total heat load during either season.

Future research

In spite of numerous studies conducted thus far on xeric-adapted organisms, our knowledge concerning the nature of adaptive mechanisms and animal–environment interactions is far from complete. I have selected only a few of the many areas of research currently being actively pursued. Also deserving mention in the preceding discussion are recent advances in the following: hormonal control of water and electrolyte balance; respiratory and metabolic adaptations and their relation to water conservation; diurnal and seasonal rhythms in behavior which provide for amelioration of climatic extremes; and enzyme function and temperature compensation in aquatic and terrestrial forms. Some of these subjects are discussed elsewhere in this volume. Future research in all areas should stress the continued application of scientific disciplines such as radiochemistry and biophysics, and should employ mathematical models to predict behavioral and physiological parameters and provide groundwork for experimental testing. Wherever possible field-oriented studies on non-captive animals should be attempted, to confirm laboratory findings and provide the investigator with ecologically significant data.

Acknowledgments

I thank Dr Robert Ohmart for critically reviewing the manuscript and making suggestions for its improvement. Appreciation is also extended to

Drs Greg Ahearn, A. Y. K. Okasha, and Fred White for their permission to include previously published material. This paper was written while my research was supported by a grant from the National Science Foundation (GB 31444).

References

Abbott, K. D. (1971). Water economy of the canyon mouse *Peromyscus crinitus stephensi. Comparative Biochemistry & Physiology*, **38**A, 38–52.

Ahearn, G. A. (1970). The control of water loss in desert Tenebrionid beetles. *Journal of Experimental Biology*, **53**, 573–95.

Baker, L. A., Weathers, W. W. & White, F. N. (1972). Temperature induced peripheral blood flow changes in lizards. *Journal of Comparative Physiology*, **80**, 313–23.

Baker, M. A. & Hayward, J. N. (1968). The influence of the nasal mucosa and the carotid rete upon hypothalamic temperature in sheep. *Journal of Physiology, London*, **198**, 561–79.

Bartlett, P. N. & Gates, D. M. (1967). The energy budget of a lizard on a tree trunk. *Ecology*, **48**, 315–22.

Bartholomew, G. A. & Dawson, W. R. (1968). Temperature regulation in desert mammals. In: *Desert Biology* (ed. G. Brown), vol. I, pp. 395–421. Academic Press, New York & London.

Beament, J. W. L. (1961). The water relations of insect cuticle. *Biological Review*, **36**, 281–320.

Bentley, P. J. & Schmidt-Nielsen, K. (1966). Cutaneous water loss in reptiles. *Science*, **151**, 1547–9.

Bernstein, M. H. (1971). Cutaneous and respiratory evaporation in the painted quail, *Excalfactoria chinensis*, during ontogeny of thermoregulation. *Comparative Biochemistry & Physiology*, **38**A, 611–17.

Bligh, J. (1972). Evaporative heat loss in hot arid environments. In: *Comparative Physiology of Desert Animals* (ed. G. M. O. Maloiy), pp. 357–69. Academic Press, New York & London.

Braun, E. J. & Dantzler, W. H. (1972). Function of mammalian-type and reptilian-type nephrons in kidney of desert quail. *American Journal of Physiology*, **222**, 617–29.

Brown, G. (Ed.) (1968). *Desert Biology*, vol. I. Academic Press, New York & London.

Carey, C. & Morton, M. L. (1971). A comparison of salt and water regulation in California quail (*Lophortyx californicus*) and Gambel's quail (*Lophortyx gambelii*). *Comparative Biochemistry & Physiology*, **38**A, 75–101.

Carpenter, R. E. (1969). Structure and function of the kidney and the water balance of desert bats. *Physiological Zoology*, **42**, 288–302.

Claussen, D. L. (1967). Studies of water loss in two species of lizards. *Comparative Biochemistry & Physiology*, **20**, 115–30.

Cloudsley-Thommpson, J. L. (1973). Factors influencing the super-cooling of tropical Arthropoda, especially locusts. *Journal of Natural History*, **7**, 471–80.

Cloudsley-Thompson, J. L. & Crawford, C. S. (1970). Lethal temperatures of some arthropods of the southwestern United States. *Entomologist's Monthly Magazine*, **106**, 26–9.

Crawford, C. S. & Wooten, R. C. (1973). Water relations in *Diplocentrus spitzeri*,

763

a semimontane scorpion from the southwestern United States. *Physiological Zoology*, **46**, 218–29.

Dawson, W. R. & Hudson, J. W. (1970). Birds. In: *Comparative Physiology of Thermoregulation* (ed. G. C. Whittow), vol. I, pp. 223–310. Academic Press, New York & London.

Dawson, W. R., Shoemaker, V. H. & Licht, P. (1966). Evaporative water losses of some small Australian lizards. *Ecology*, **47**, 589–94.

Edney, E. B. (1966). Absorption of water vapour from unsaturated air by *Arenivaga* sp. (Polyphagidae, Dictyoptera). *Comparative Biochemistry & Physiology*, **19**, 387–408.

Edney, E. B. (1967). The impact of the atmospheric environment on the integument of insects. In: *Biometeorology, III. Proceedings of the 4th Biometeorology Congress (1966)* (eds. S. W. Tromp & W. H. Weihe), pp. 71–82. Swets & Zeitlinger, Amsterdam.

Edney, E. B. (1968). The effect of water loss on the haemolymph of *Arenivaga* sp. and *Periplaneta americana*. *Comparative Biochemistry & Physiology*, **25**, 149–58.

Edney, E. B. (1971a). The body temperature of Tenebrionid beetles in the Namib Desert of southern Africa. *Journal of Experimental Biology*, **55**, 253–72.

Edney, E. B. (1971b). Some aspects of water balance in Tenebrionid beetles and a Thysanuran from the Namib Desert of southern Africa. *Physiological Zoology*, **44**, 61–76.

Emery, N., Poulson, T. L. & Kinter, W. B. (1972). Production of concentrated urine by avian kidneys. *American Journal of Physiology*, **223**, 180–87.

Finch, V. A. (1972). Energy exchanges with the environment of two East African antelopes, the eland and the hartebeest. In: *Comparative Physiology of Desert Animals* (ed. G. M. O. Maloiy), pp. 315–26. *Symposium of the Zoological Society of London, 31*. Academic Press, New York & London.

Gagge, A. P. (1972). Partitional calorimetry in the desert. In: *Physiological Adaptations: Desert and Mountain* (eds. M. K. Yousef, S. M. Horvath & R. W. Bullard), pp. 23–51. Academic Press, New York & London.

Ghobrial, L. I. (1970a). A comparative study of the integument of the camel, Dorcas gazelle and jerboa in relation to desert life. *Journal of Zoology, London*, **160**, 509–21.

Ghobrial, L. O. (1970b). The water relations of the desert antelope *Gazella dorcas dorcas*. *Physiological Zoology*, **43**, 249–56.

Green, B. (1972). Water losses of the sand goanna (*Varanus gouldii*) in its natural environments. *Ecology*, **53**, 452–7.

Hackman, R. H. (1964). Chemistry of the insect cuticle. In: *The Physiology of Insecta* (ed. M. Rockstein), vol. 3, pp. 471–506. Academic Press, New York & London.

Hadley, N. F. (1970a). Micrometeorology and energy exchange in two desert arthropods. *Ecology*, **51**, 434–4.

Hadley, N. F. (1970b). Water relations of the desert scorpion, *Hadrurus arizonensis*. *Journal of Experimental Biology*, **53**, 547–58.

Hadley, N. F. (1972). Desert species and adaptation. *American Scientist*, **60**, 338–47.

Hadley, N. F. & Williams, S. C. (1968). Surface activities of some North American scorpions in relation to feeding. *Ecology*, **49**, 726–34.

Haines, H., Howard, B. & Setchell, C. (1973). Water content and distribution of tritiated water in tissues of Australian desert rodents. *Comparative Biochemistry & Physiology*, **45**A, 787–92.

Hamilton, W. J. (1973). *Life's Color Code*. McGraw-Hill, New York.

Hamilton, W. J. & Heppner, F. (1967). Radiant solar energy and the function of black homeotherm pigmentation: an hypothesis. *Science*, **155**, 196–7.

Hart, J. S. (1971). Rodents. In: *Comparative Physiology of Thermoregulation* (ed. G. C. Whittow), vol. II, pp. 1–149. Academic Press, New York & London.

Hattingh, J. (1972). The correlation between transepidermal water loss and the thickness of epidermal components. *Comparative Biochemistry & Physiology*, **43**A, 719–22.

Heath, J. E. (1964). Head–body differences in horned lizards. *Physiological Zoology*, **37**, 273–9.

Heath, J. E. (1966). Venous shunts in the cephalic sinuses of horned lizards. *Physiological Zoology*, **39**, 30–5.

Heinrich, B. (1970). Thoracic temperature stabilization by blood circulation in a free-flying moth. *Science*, **168**, 580–2.

Heinrich, B. (1971). Temperature regulation of the sphinx moth, *Manduca sexta*. II. Regulation of heat loss by control of blood circulation. *Journal of Experimental Biology*, **54**, 153–66.

Heisinger, J. F. & Breitenbach, R. P. (1969). Renal structural characteristics as indexes of renal adaptation for water conservation in the genus *Sylvilagus*. *Physiological Zoology*, **42**, 160–72.

Heisinger, J. F., King, T. S., Halling, H. W. & Fields, B. L. (1973). Renal adaptations to macro- and micro-habitats in the family Cricetidae. *Comparative Biochemistry & Physiology*, **44**A, 767–74.

Heppner, F. (1970). The metabolic significance of differential absorption of radiant energy by black and white birds. *Condor*, **72**, 50–59.

Holleman, D. F. & Dieterich, R. A. (1973). Body water content and turnover in several species of rodents as evaluated by the tritiated water method. *Journal of Mammalogy*, **54**, 456–65.

Jackson, L. L. & Baker, G. L. (1970). Cuticular lipids of insects. *Lipids*, **5**, 239–46.

Johnson, O. W. & Mugaas, J. N. (1970). Quantitative and organizational features of the avian renal medulla. *Condor*, **72**, 288–92.

Johnson, O. W. & Ohmart, R. D. (1973). The renal medulla and water economy in vesper sparrows (*Pooecetes gramineus*). *Comparative Biochemistry & Physiology*, **44**A, 655–61.

Kennedy, P. M. & MacFarlane, W. V. (1971). Oxygen consumption and water turnover of the fat-tailed marsupials *Dasycercus cristicauda* and *Sminthopsis crassicaudata*. *Comparative Biochemistry & Physiology*, **40**A, 723–32.

Kluger, M. J. & Heath, J. E. (1970). Vasomotion in the bat wing: a thermoregulatory response to internal heating. *Comparative Biochemistry & Physiology*, **32**, 219–26.

Knülle, W. & Spadafora, R. R. (1969). Water vapor sorption and humidity relationships in *Liposcelis* (Insecta: Psocoptera). *Journal of Stored Products Research*, **5**, 49–55.

Krag, B. & Skadhauge, E. (1972). Renal salt and water extraction in the budgerygah (*Melopsittacus undulatus*). *Comparative Biochemistry & Physiology*, **41**A, 667–83.

Kroll, J. C., Clark, D. R., Jr. & Albert, J. W. (1973). Radiotelemetry for studying thermoregulation in free-ranging snakes. *Ecology*, **54**, 454–6.

765

Lee, A. K. & Mercer, E. H. (1967). Cocoon surrounding desert-dwelling frogs. *Science*, **157**, 87–8.

Licht, P. & Bennett, A. F. (1972). A scaleless snake: tests of the role of reptilian scales in water loss and heat transfer. *Copeia* (1972), 702–7.

Locke, M. (1965). Permeability of insect cuticle to water and lipids. *Science*, **147**, 295–8.

Louw, G. N. (1972). The role of advective fog in the water economy of certain Namib Desert animals. In: *Comparative Physiology of Desert Animals* (ed. G. M. O. Maloiy), pp. 297–314. *Symposium of the Zoological Society of London, 31*. Academic Press, New York & London.

Lowe, C. H. & Heath, W. G. (1969). Behavioral and physiological responses to temperature in the desert pupfish *Cyprinodon macularius*. *Physiological Zoology*, **45**, 54–9.

Lowe, C. H., Heed, W. B. & Halpern, E. A. (1967). Supercooling of the saguaro species *Drosophila nigrospiracula* in the Sonoran Desert. *Ecology*, **48**, 984–5.

Lowe, C. H., Lardner, P. J. & Halpern, E. A. (1971). Supercooling in reptiles and other vertebrates. *Comparative Biochemistry & Physiology*, **39**A, 125–35.

McClanahan, L., Jr. (1967). Adaptations of the spadefoot toad, *Scaphiopus couchi*, to desert environments. *Comparative Biochemistry & Physiology*, **20**, 73–99.

McClanahan, L., Jr. & Baldwin, R. (1969). Rate of water uptake through the integument of the desert toad, *Bufo punctatus*. *Comparative Biochemistry & Physiology*, **28**, 381–9.

MacMillen, R. E. & Lee, A. K. (1967). Australian desert mice: independence of exogenous water. *Science*, **158**, 383–5.

Maloiy, G. M. O. (1970). Water economy of the Somali donkey. *American Journal of Physiology*, **219**, 1522–7.

Maloiy, G. M. O. (ed.) (1972*a*). *Comparative Physiology of Desert Animals. Symposium of the Zoological Society of London, 31*. Academic Press, New York & London.

Maloiy, G. M. O. (1972*b*). Renal salt and water excretion in the camel (*Camelus dromedarius*). In: *Comparative Physiology of Desert Animals* (ed. G. M. O. Maloiy), pp. 243–59. *Symposium of the Zoological Society of London, 31*. Academic Press, New York & London.

Marder, J. (1973). Body temperature regulation in the brown-necked raven (*Corvus corax ruficollis*). II. Thermal changes in the plumage of ravens exposed to solar radiation. *Comparative Biochemistry & Physiology*, **45**A, 431–40.

Minnich, J. E. (1970). Water and electrolyte balance of the desert iguana, *Dipsosaurus dorsalis*, in its natural habitat. *Comparative Biochemistry & Physiology*, **35**, 921–33.

Minnich, J. E. & Shoemaker, V. H. (1970). Diet, behaviour and water turnover in the desert iguana, *Dipsosaurus dorsalis*. *American Midland Naturalist*, **84**, 496–509.

Minnich, J. E. & Shoemaker, V. H. (1972). Water and electrolyte turnover in a field population of the lizard, *Uma scoparia*. *Copeia* (1972), 650–59.

Moldenhauer, R. R. & Wiens, J. A. (1970). The water economy of the sage sparrow, *Amphispiza belli nevadensis*. *Condor*, **72**, 265–75.

Morgareidge, K. R. & White, F. N. (1969). Cutaneous vascular changes during heating and cooling in the Galapagos marine iguana. *Nature* (*London*), **223**, 587–91.

Nagy, K. A. (1972). Water and electrolyte budgets of a free-living desert lizard, *Sauromalus obesus*. *Journal of Comparative Physiology*, **79**, 39–62.

Noble-Nesbitt, J. (1969). Water balance in the firebrat, *Thermobia domestica* (Packard). Exchanges of water with the atmosphere. *Journal of Experimental Biology*, **50**, 745–69.

Noble-Nesbitt, J. (1970). Water balance in the firebrat, *Thermobia domestica* (Packard). The site of uptake of water from the atmosphere. *Journal of Experimental Biology*, **52**, 193–200.

Norris, K. S. (1967). Color adaptation in desert reptiles and its thermal relationships. In: *Lizard Ecology: A Symposium* (ed. W. W. Milstead), pp. 162–229. University of Missouri Press, Columbia.

Ohmart, R. D. & Lasiewski, R. C. (1971). Roadrunners: energy conservation by hypothermia and absorption of sunlight. *Science*, **172**, 67–9.

Ohmart, R. D., Chapman, T. E. & McFarland, L. Z. (1970). Water turnover in roadrunners under different environmental conditions. *Auk*, **87**, 787–93.

Okasha, A. Y. K. (1971). Water relations in an insect, *Thermobia domestica*. I. Water uptake from sub-saturated atmospheres as a means of volume regulation. *Journal of Experimental Biology*, **55**, 435–48.

Okasha, A. Y. K. (1973). Water relations in an insect, *Thermobia domestica*. III. Effects of desiccation and rehydration on the haemolymph. *Journal of Experimental Biology*, **58**, 385–400.

Osgood, D. W. (1970). Thermoregulation in water snakes studied by telemetry. *Copeia* (1970), 568–71.

Schmidt-Nielsen, K., Taylor, C. R. & Shkolnik, A. (1971). Desert snails: problems of heat, water and food. *Journal of Experimental Biology*, **55**, 385–98.

Shaw, J. & Stobbart, R. H. (1972). The water balance and osmo-regulatory physiology of the desert locust (*Schistocerca gregaria*) and other desert and xeric arthropods. In: *Comparative Physiology of Desert Animals* (ed. G. M. O. Maloiy), pp. 15–38. *Symposium of the Zoological Society of London*, *31*. Academic Press, New York & London.

Shoemaker, V. H., McClanahan, L., Jr. & Ruibal, R. (1969). Seasonal changes in body fluids in a field population of spadefoot toads. *Copeia* (1969), 585–91.

Siebert, B. D. & MacFarlane, W. V. (1971). Water turnover and renal function of dromedaries in the desert. *Physiological Zoology*, **44**, 225–40.

Spotila, J. R., Soule, O. H. & Gates, D. M. (1972). The biophysical ecology of the alligator: heat energy budgets and climate spaces. *Ecology*, **53**, 1094–102.

Stebbins, R. C. & Barwick, R. E. (1968). Radiotelemetric study of thermoregulation in a lace monitor. *Copeia* (1968), 541–7.

Taylor, C. R. (1969). The eland and the oryx. *Scientific American*, **220**, 88–95.

Taylor, C. R. (1970). Strategies of temperature regulation: effect on evaporation in East African ungulates. *American Journal of Physiology*, **219**, 1131–5.

Taylor, C. R. (1971). Ranching arid lands: physiology of wild and domestic ungulates in the desert. *Proceedings of the conference on sustained production from semi-arid areas*, pp. 167–185. Govt. Printer, Gabarone.

Taylor, C. R. & Lyman, C. P. (1972). Heat storage in running antelopes: independence of brain and body temperatures. *American Journal of Physiology*, **222**, 114–17.

Taylor, C. R., Spinage, C. A. & Lyman, C. P. (1969). Water relations of the waterbuck, an East African antelope. *American Journal of Physiology*, **217**, 630–34.

Wall, B. J. (1970). Effects of dehydration and rehydration on *Periplaneta americana*. *Journal of Insect Physiology*, **16**, 1027–42.

Weathers, W. W. (1971). Some cardiovascular aspects of temperature regulation in the lizard *Dipsosaurus dorsalis. Comparative Biochemistry & Physiology,* **40**A, 503–15.

Weathers, W. W. & Morgareidge, K. R. (1971). Cutaneous vascular responses to temperature change in the spiny-tailed iguana, *Ctenosaura hemilopha. Copeia* (1971), 548–51.

Webb, G. J., Johnson, C. R. & Firth, B. T. (1972). Head–body temperature differences in lizards. *Physiological Zoology,* **45**, 130–42.

White, F. N. (1973). Temperature and the Galapagos marine iguana – insights into reptilian thermoregulation. *Comparative Biochemistry & Physiology,* **45**A, 505–13.

Whittow, G. C. (ed.) (1970). *Comparative Physiology of Thermoregulation. Vol. I. Invertebrates and Non-mammalian Vertebrates.* Academic Press, New York & London.

Whittow, G. C. (ed.) (1971). *Comparative Physiology of Thermoregulation. Vol. II. Mammals.* Academic Press, New York & London.

Wickstrom, C. E. & Castenholz, R. W. (1973). Thermophilic ostracod: aquatic metazoan with the highest known temperature tolerance. *Science,* **181**, 1063–4.

Yarbrough, C. G. (1971). The influence of distribution and ecology on the thermo-regulation of small birds. *Comparative Biochemistry & Physiology,* **39**A, 235–66.

Yousef, M. K., Horvath, S. M. & Bullard, R. W. (eds.) (1972). *Physiological Adaptations: Desert and Mountain.* Academic Press, New York & London.

Zervanos, S. M. & Hadley, N. F. (1973). Adaptational biology and energy relationships of the collared peccary (*Tayassu tajacu*). *Ecology,* **54**, 759–74.

Manuscript received by the editors March 1974

32. Spatial and temporal distribution and behaviour

W. A. LOW

Introduction

'Populations of living organisms are rarely distributed at random over the space available to them.' This generalization made in 1946 by L. C. Cole can be broadened to include time as well. Such a basic statement seems a good place to start this review.

Discontinuity and alteration of animal populations in both time and space has long been recognized (Elton, 1927). However, the factors which control the use of space by an animal or a species, and their quantitative relationships to distribution and behaviour, are still imperfectly known. This is particularly true of semi-arid and arid regions where traumatic changes occur in animal populations in response to catastrophic climatic changes.

Wilbur, Tinkle & Collins (1974) have discussed environmental certainty and its relationship to resource availability, and evolution of life histories to adapt to the degree of stability of the resource. In arid and semi-arid lands, it is probably more appropriate to use the terms instability or uncertainty (Low, 1975), as events are usually irregular in time and intensity. Barclay (1975) has shown in models that species in uncertain environments have a high probability of evolving r-type life histories. It is in this basic setting that arid-land animals exist.

The basic questions are:

(a) How do populations of animals change in density, age and sex ratios, and behaviour in arid areas? (What are the dynamics of the state variables in the system?)

(b) What are the important factors which cause the populations to change?

(c) What are the quantitative relationships which define the interactions between populations and the factor or factors causing the changes, and are they of predictive value? (What are the processes?)

In this review, I have attempted to gather data on the functional relationship of environmental factors to the intensity and pattern of use or occupation of habitat by the animal, and at the same time point out some of the phenomena of population and distribution dynamics.

The geographical coverage of this review has, in the main, been restricted to the arid lands of the subtropics and continental interiors, as

769

Animal processes

defined by Logan (1968). Australian literature has been most extensively used, further information coming from African and North American sources. Few papers concerning arid lands in other continents and regions have been consulted. Indeed, little information appears to be available except from the three continents mentioned. The grasslands generally border the true desert areas (Logan, 1968), and applicable information has accordingly been included from the relatively large body of data collected under the US/IBP Grassland Biome programme.

Nature of factors and their influence on processes

Pianka (1974), Bledsoe & Jameson (1969), and Kendeigh (1961) among others, have discussed the environmental factors which affect distribution and density of animal populations and their presumed importance in eco-system processes. The factors may be organized in a number of ways. I have chosen to organize them under two main groups: physical (abiotic) and biotic factors. There are interactions between the two groups and commonly the physical factors control the biotic. In most cases, the biotic factors tend to be less random in their influence than are the physical factors, probably a reflection of their dependence on physical driving functions and their relationship with other biotic factors (Bledsoe & Jameson, 1969; Low, 1975).

Each type of arid land has a characteristic magnitude and range for each of the controlling factors (Logan, 1968). These characteristics determine the role and effect of derived physical factors and biotic factors in determining the distribution, dynamics and behaviour of animal populations.

Physical factors

Physical (abiotic) factors include both extrinsic and intrinsic or derived variables. The main extrinsic variables ('forcing functions' of Bledsoe & Jameson, 1969) include factors which on an annual basis are relatively invariable for a given area, such as photoperiod, radiation (0.5% variation), and substrate; moderately variable, such as air temperature and wind; and markedly variable, such as precipitation (300% variation) and humidity (Rasmussen, 1971).

The dependent (derived or intrinsic) variables are determined by the extrinsic factors and hence are fairly predictable once the latter are known. Included are soil moisture, run-off or surface water, soil temperature, evaporation rate and soil nutrient status; fires, too, can be predicted from the extrinsic variables, though in a stochastic sense only.

770

Photoperiod and radiation

Photoperiod and radiation have a profound influence on animal behaviour, particularly in subtropic desert areas where the clear air permits maximum penetration of radiation (Logan, 1968). There are two rhythmic patterns, seasonal and circadian, resulting from the regular orbital movement and rotation of the Earth. The major influence of these factors in determining annual reproductive activity as well as daily maintenance activities have long been known (Kendeigh, 1961).

Animal populations have generally become adapted to the average conditions which prevail in their habitat (Wilbur *et al.*, 1974). Since excessive insolation, with its heating effects, is a limiting factor in desert areas, the adaptations required by animals are those that assist in avoiding excess radiation (see Chapter 31). Hence activity is generally crepuscular or nocturnal during the hot summer periods, but may become diurnal in the cooler winters (Bodenheimer, 1957; Bigalke, 1972; Russell, 1974*a*; Clark, 1978; Packard, 1977).

Crepuscular and nocturnal animals need concern us no further with regard to radiation, but diurnal animals must overcome exposure to radiation and excess heat loads. In arid areas only introduced animals and some insects and birds remain active during the day in summer. Cattle (*Bos taurus* L.) seek shade when the air temperature reaches temperatures close to body temperature (Yeates & Schmidt, 1974). Raptors, although exposed to radiation, fly in the cool air above the intense level of reradiated energy (Logan, 1968). Some ants, however, are active when soil temperatures exceed 45 °C (Whitford, 1973; Briese, 1974).

A behavioural and physical adaptation of the North American desert bird the road runner, *Geococcyx californianus* (Lesson), has enabled it to become hypothermic and to use solar radiation to warm itself when the air temperature is below its thermo-neutral zone (Ohmart & Lasiewski, 1971). These birds save energy calculated at 551 cal h^{-1} during their hypothermic sunning. This energy conservation is probably important during the winter when the food supply is limited.

Habitat selection in hot, arid areas may result from attempts to avoid high levels of solar radiation. Dawson (1972, 1974) has reviewed the features of thermoregulation and behaviour in red kangaroos (*Megaleia rufa* (Desmarest)) and euros (*Macropus robustus* (Gould)), and has shown that, in the rock shelters they use on hot summer days, euros have a much reduced heat load compared to the habitat they normally use in cooler periods.

Russell (1974*a*) has discussed the daily distribution of kangaroos, and found that during the hot summer days red kangaroos seek shaded areas

771

exposed to wind. Dawson & Denny (1969) found that the thermal load in these sheltering sites was much less than in surrounding open areas; and Dawson (1972) has shown that an animal lying down is exposed to less re-radiation of infra-red energy than one standing.

The influence of photoperiodicity on animal behaviour is not usually important *per se* in arid areas, where rainfall and food production are the usual keys to activity. Only in some introduced animals has photoperiod been found to control reproduction (Bodenheimer, 1957; Williams & Thwaites, 1974). In sheep (*Ovis aries* (Erxleben)), when the Border Leicester breed from high latitudes was exposed to equatorial photoperiodicity, only 37% of the ewes came into oestrus; presumably they were insensitive to the limited change in day length (Williams & Thwaites, 1974).

Briese (1974) has found that, among the ants in his study, two out of fifteen species were completely nocturnal, and nine out of fifteen species changed their activity pattern with seasons. Competition apparently determined the major activity period, which was modified in some species by radiation.

Precipitation

Precipitation is, by definition, the most important extrinsic factor in arid areas. Although arid areas are characterized by irregularity of time and amount of rainfall, there is a wide range in predictability dependent on the type of desert (Logan, 1968). Life in any particular desert is necessarily adapted to the set of conditions existing there.

Activity of arid-land amphibians is controlled by rainfall. Some North American species will breed after appropriate rains in the spring or summer (see, for instance, Stebbins (1954), Packer (1963) and Chapter 33). Woody & Thomas (1968; cited by Thomas, Cameron & Holmes, 1970) have shown that the spadefoot toad *Scaphiopus bombifrons* Cope will not breed unless at least 1.8 mm of rain have fallen, the temperature is about 10 °C, and the barometric pressure is low. These conditions will apparently ensure that the eggs and tadpoles will have time to hatch and metamorphose. Activity is so tied to rainfall, that adult individuals of *Scaphiopus bombifrons* may be active for only 1 or 2% of the year (Thomas *et al.*, 1970). In Australia, arid-land frogs breed after suitable rains (Low, 1975).

Considerable work has been done on locusts in attempting to predict population outbreaks (Uvarov, 1957; Clark, 1978). Basically, rainfall is indirectly essential through providing soil moisture for egg-laying, survival and hatching and permitting forage to grow to enable development and reproduction of the nymph and adult. Clark (1978) found in the east-central arid area of Australia that over 60% of adult Australian plague locusts (*Chortoicetes terminifera* Walker) moved from areas where no rain had fallen to areas where rain had fallen by being blown into low pressure areas. Total numbers of locusts were determined by the proximity and size of favourable wet areas, their ability to find the area, and reproduction and survival of young. If rain fell over less than 30% of the area then the populations declined. A twenty-fold increase in population resulted following a twelve-month period of adequate rainfall and soil moisture.

Watson (1978) has shown that adult dragonflies disperse after rainfall provides breeding areas.

Harris (1971) reported, in comparisons of seven different sites in the US/IBP Grasslands Biome studies, that there was a direct relationship between the biomass of rodents in an area and the rainfall. For each 1 cm increase in mean annual rainfall, there was a 16 g increase in rodent biomass. However, the relationship did not hold in comparing desert grasslands and less arid grasslands.

Carstairs (1974) has related plagues of rats (*Rattus villosissimus* (Waite)) in central Australia to rainfall years. The relationship is complex and involves season of rainfall, flooding, suitable habitat and food. During favourable periods, defined in terms of rainfall, but dependent on plant growth, rat populations have been estimated to spread into previously uninhabited land at rates of 1.6 to 3 km per day. The rats spread from their drought refuge areas in the grassland of mid-north Australia for many hundreds of kilometres taking up to two or three years and several generations to exploit suitable habitat when it is available.

Waterfowl in Australian arid lands are dependent on water, but again indirectly, as food supply and habitat are the proximate factors controlling nomadic movements and breeding (Frith, 1967). Serventy & Whittell (1951) report an analysis of the breeding behaviour of 50 bird species from an arid area in Western Australia which showed that 33 species nested opportunistically in any season after sufficient rainfall. However, Davies (1974) has shown that the effective breeding period in one of these species, the zebra finch, *Taeniopygia guttata* (Vieillot), is during the spring when the greatest proportion of nestlings are fledged. Marshall & Disney (1957) have shown for the red-billed weaver finch (*Quelea quelea* L.) in Tanzania that sufficient rain must fall to allow vegetation to grow to sufficient length to permit the finches to weave nests. Presumably conditions suitable to produce such vegetation will ensure that food will be available for a sufficient time to enable young to be raised.

Although many studies have shown that rainfall is the ultimate factor controlling the use of space by an animal and its population numbers, few studies have determined the quantitative relationship. Animals directly dependent on rainfall, such as amphibians and aquatic insects, are more directly dependent on surface water and will be treated below. Most animals are only indirectly dependent on rainfall and the proximate factors

773

Animal processes

are usually food or habitat; these are also treated below. For purposes of modelling ecosystems, existing data expressing population distribution and numbers as functions of proximate factors need to be related to the ultimate factors for more direct predictability. Bodies of data such as those accumulated by the US/IBP Grassland and Desert Biomes are probably adequate for this purpose, but the relationships need to be calculated.

Atmospheric humidity

Humidity is important to animal populations primarily as the factor largely determining evaporation (Bledsoe & Jameson, 1969). It is difficult to separate the role of humidity from that of evaporation, but evaporation is the proximate factor controlling animal processes. For that reason, humidity will be treated in the section on evaporation.

Air temperature

Air temperature is easily measured and widely recorded. Unfortunately air temperature is usually not the temperature directly affecting the rates of biological processes (Holm & Edney, 1973). Derived quantities such as ground surface temperature or soil temperature are more directly relevant. The air temperature combines with net radiation and other factors to define the heat load on the animal (see Chapter 31), which is the determinant of behaviour.

Studies of the influence of temperature on speed of development, fecundity, longevity, and dispersal have been popular for many years, and the literature is extensive (Allee *et al.*, 1949; Andrewartha & Birch, 1954; MacFadyen, 1957; Chapter 33 below). Spomer (1973) has pointed out that the temperature of an organism frequently changes independently of air temperatures, and that at moderate temperatures the atmosphere is usually neither a source nor a sink of heat. From this it can be inferred that it is usually the extremes which affect the distribution of an organism. Each species has a characteristic range of temperatures within which it can be active, and minima and maxima which are lethal. By behavioural means, the animal may avoid the extremes so that its distribution in time and space will be limited by its tolerance and selection of favourable climatic ranges. Happold (1973) found that energy expenditure of the gregarious rodent *Notomys alexis* was reduced by 38% in a group of individuals huddled together, as compared with an isolated individual, during a period when the burrow temperature reached a minimum of 10 °C. In studies over a period of two years in a semi-arid ecosystem dominated by Chenopodiaceae, Briese (1974) found that climatic variables had little influence on

774

ant populations, but that they did affect the assemblage of ant species that were active at any particular time. Varying seasonal and diurnal patterns of activity limited the direct competition among the 22 species present. Light, temperature and moisture were all involved, but influenced the different species in varying ways. Briese found that species active during the day changed from unimodal activity patterns in the cooler seasons to bimodal patterns during the summer. Similar shifts in activity patterns have been observed in lizards in Australia (Pianka, 1973) and Kenya (Western, 1974), Tenebrionid beetles in the Namib Desert (Holm & Edney, 1973), cattle in central Australia (Yeates & Schmidt, 1974; W. A. Low, unpublished data) and collared peccaries (*Tayassu tajaçu* (Linn.)) in the Sonoran desert (Bigler, 1974) and southern Texas (Low, 1970). These activity periods are related to comfort zones, which differ between breeds and species (Brody, 1956). Daws & Squires (1974) showed experimentally that air temperatures up to 38 °C increased water intake in a linear manner and hence reduced forage intake of sheep (Squires & Wilson, 1971). Two breeds studied differed in this respect, Merinos being better adapted to hot dry conditions than Border Leicester. Daily activity periods for large mammals generally become limited when the ambient temperature approaches 35° to 38 °C.

Similarly, P. Greenslade (1974) in a study of epigaeic fauna in semi-arid Australia found the activity of various species of Collembola restricted to certain seasons. While rainfall was a major factor, the temperature régime determined the complex of species that was active.

The polar and high-altitude deserts are primarily heat-limited, since it is the coldness that prevents adequate moisture being held by the air (Logan, 1968). It is primarily food scarcity as a result of cold that limits animal density in these deserts, as effectively as heat in subtropical deserts limits food and the animals dependent on it (Bliss *et al.*, 1973).

Clark (1978) determined that the Australian migratory locust will not take off unless the temperature is at least 17.5 °C, and will not sustain their night dispersal flights unless the temperatue is 21 °C. The size of locust populations is also controlled by high summer temperatures, as the eggs succumb in the absence of summer rains.

These few examples from an extensive literature show the variety of effects that temperature has on various kinds of animals. If the distribution of a species includes a certain area, it must be able to tolerate or behaviourally avoid the temperature range that exists there, and it is usually some other proximate factor that controls its numbers and distribution. The temperature, unless outside the normal range, will usually only determine the temporal or seasonal pattern of use of the area.

Animal processes

Wind

The important role of wind in dispersing flying insects has long been known (Uvarov, 1957). Clark's (1978) work on Australian migratory locusts shows that the migration of flying locusts is predictable to the extent that the winds are predictable. At wind speeds below 1.8 m s^{-1} the direction of flight of locusts capable of flying at 3.2 m s^{-1} is variable. Wind speeds greater than 3 m s^{-1} result in the locusts flying with the wind. As mentioned earlier, strong winds are usually associated with atmospheric depressions which frequently result in rainfall. Hence, by being blown downwind, the locusts have a greater chance of finding an area favourable for foraging and egg-laying.

It is interesting to speculate that this technique may also be used by various nomadic birds in finding favourable feeding and nesting areas in the arid and semi-arid areas of central Australia. Anecdotal reports on myriads of birds appearing soon after rains are legion (Serventy & Whittell, 1951), however, the mechanism by which the birds find the wet areas has not been elucidated.

The direct effects of wind speeds greater than 30 km h^{-1} in blowing ants about the surface (Briese, 1974) are probably of little importance in ecosystem dynamics.

Observations on daily behaviour of cattle in central Australia have revealed that wind is apparently important in determining cattle distribution only under extreme temperature conditions (W. A. Low, unpublished data). During very hot days, cattle seek exposed areas, presumably for increased evaporative cooling due to winds. In the winter, however, when temperatures are close to freezing, the cattle seek shelter from strong winds in the lee of hills and trees. Sheltering behaviour has also been observed in red kangaroos (Russell, 1974a).

A feature apparent from satellite imagery is the heavier grazing in the windward side or corner of fenced paddocks throughout the semi-arid sheep-grazing areas of Australia (Graetz et al., 1977). The factors responsible for movement by both sheep and cattle into the wind during grazing have not been closely examined.

The combined effects of wind and other factors such as temperature and evaporation are generally of importance in determining activity periods and distribution. The direct role of wind is mainly dispersal of passive insects, and modification of distribution of mobile animals.

Substrate

Like the other extrinsic abiotic factors, the substrate is a major determinant of distribution and activity of animals, particularly of the sedentary and less mobile species. In addition to a direct role, it has also an indirect role through determining the distribution of habitat, both forage and cover. The relationship of substrate to habitat and animal distribution has been well studied (Kendeigh, 1961; Smith, 1966; Wallwork, 1970) and has become the basis of management for many wildlife species (Giles, 1969).

Kirkham & Fisser (1972), using a method of multivariate analysis, found that the harvester ant *Pogonomyrmex occidentalis* (Cresson) had higher densities on sandy soils, due to the ease of establishing colonies there as opposed to the heavier clay soils. Greenslade & Greenslade (1973) found ant faunas to be richer and denser on sandy soils than on clay soils. Textured soils were, however, preferred over structureless sands (Greaves, 1971; Greenslade, 1974*b*). Although soil type influenced distribution of nest sites, it did not influence foraging areas (Greenslade, 1974*a*).

Surprisingly, Wallwork (1972) has found a greater number of micro-arthropods living in mineral soil than in litter in a Californian desert. Acari, particularly, are more abundant in the soil, although Collembola were more evenly distributed.

Soil type has been shown to affect the distribution of the spadefoot toad, but few other amphibians and reptiles have been studied in this regard (see review by Thomas *et al.*, 1970). Western (1974), working in northern Kenya, found that lizard species had preferred substrates and habitats, but that the average biomass density of all species of 0.7 to 0.8 kg ha^{-1} did not vary as greatly as did that of large mammals (9.5 to 124 kg ha^{-1}, Watson (1969)) when alluvial valley bottoms were compared with lava hills. The differences must be related to forage differences which are determined by the substrate. Since 72% of the mammal species in deserts are subter-ranean (Bodenheimer, 1957), the extent of favourable substrates must be a major factor limiting their distribution.

Lewis's (1971) survey of rodents in North American grasslands showed that Geomyids and Heteromyids preferred easily worked soils, while four other families, including Cricetids, showed little preference. However, Newsome & Corbett (1975) found that population outbreaks of *Mus musculus* and *Rattus villosissimus* in central Australia occurred only if the soil was friable and suitable for building nests at the same time that food and predators were not limiting. When the area dried off, *Rattus villosissimus* was found to exist in refuge areas, where soils were sandy, in greater numbers than in the black cracking clays.

The same situation is known to occur in Australian arid-land rabbits (*Oryctolagus cuniculus* (L.)) which use textured stony soils as refuge areas during drought, whereas during good periods expansion into sandy-soil habitats is rapid (Myers & Parker, 1965).

The rôle of minerals and trace elements in controlling the distribution of habitats and animals has not been examined in arid areas. Weir (1971*b*),

777

working in central Africa, found that elephants (*Loxodonta africana* (Blumenbach)) in the semi-arid Wankie National Park, Rhodesia, concentrated in localized areas with a high sodium concentration during the seven-month dry period.

It appears that substrate properties have a profound rôle in determining distribution of animals, either directly or indirectly. Its relevance to animals actually living in the substrate is self-evident, and its control of the surface habitat determines the niches available for animals living above the soil surface.

Dependent factors
Soil moisture

The indirect effects of soil moisture through interactive habitat control probably influence the distribution or behaviour of the majority of animals in arid areas. The most direct effects are on subterranean and litter-dwelling fauna.

The basic principles of development and survival in arid lands of soil arthropods (Uvarov, 1957; Pradhan, 1957) as well as the activity and distribution of subterranean mammals, which make up 72% of those living in the deserts, have been known for some time (Bodenheimer, 1957; Schmidt-Nielsen, 1964). A few recent studies have amplified the data base and provided some rate-control data. Briese (1974) found immediately after rain a sharp increase in the proportion of harvester ant nests which were active. During the hot summer, when soil moisture decreased from 14.6% to 2.7%, the number of active nests in his study site, which contained 165 viable colonies, decreased from 35 to 14. A simple experiment with three species of harvester ants showed that raising the soil moisture to 4% resulted in 100% and 60% activity respectively in two species of *Pheidole*, but was not sufficient to cause activity in *Chelaner* (sim. *whitei* Emery).

Clark (1978) determined that both hatching and egg laying of the Australian locust *Chortoicetes terminifera* were controlled by soil moisture. Eggs must absorb 2.25 times their weight of water before hatching, but can only extract moisture from the soil while water potentials are greater than -9 or -10 bar. If the water potential is below this level, the eggs become dormant or die.

It appears that threshold values exist for both development and activity. When the soil moisture level drops below the critical level either life or activity stops.

Surface water

Animals which are dependent on free water for drinking are naturally restricted in their distribution by the time which they can survive between drinks and the distance they can travel during that time. Many arid-land animals obtain most or all of their water requirements from suitable dietary intake (forage, seeds or animal matter), either from water actually contained in the food, or water produced in the course of metabolism. These species are dependent on free water only during stress periods such as drought, when diets or body reserves are inadequate to provide the water required (Schmidt-Nielsen, 1964). Surface water may be required by other animals for breeding, feeding or as a living habitat.

Because of their requirement for evaporative cooling the distribution of many birds is restricted to areas with drinking water available. Immelmann (1965) states that the distribution of zebra finches in arid Australia is patchy since the main factor limiting their distribution is water. Indeed, several arid-land finches have evolved a sucking habit of drinking, as pigeons do, so as to obtain water quickly. However, the ability of birds to fly long distances fairly quickly allows them to be distributed over a much larger area than water-dependent mammals (Schmidt-Nielsen, 1964). The distances moved by Australian waterfowl in finding breeding and feeding grounds (Frith, 1967) have already been mentioned. Little quantitative information is available, although Braithwaite (1974) has provided additional data for the grey teal. The water requirements of large mammals, particularly domestic livestock, have been well studied in temperate areas (Hafez, 1962, 1968; Schmidt-Nielsen, 1964; Wilson, 1975; Siebert, 1978); it is of practical importance, since provision of water is a tool used in controlling the distribution of domestic stock in arid rangelands. Richmond, Langham & Trujillo (1962) found that the water turnover of mammals, in litres per day, could be expressed as $aw^{0.8}$ where w is the bodyweight in kilograms and a takes the value of 0.09 for marsupials, 0.123 for eutherians. In the light of this, Dawson (1974) showed that kangaroos would have a water turnover one-quarter of that for sheep. Siebert (1978) has compared a wide range of desert-adapted vertebrates and, using the similar expression $a'w^{0.82}$ has found values of a' ranging from 0.012 in Amphibia (Warburg, 1972) to 0.502 in the budgerigar (*Melopsittacus undulatus* Shaw) (Shadhuage, 1972) in temperate conditions. However, when water is restricted, water turnover can be reduced to one-half or one-third in many desert-adapted forms (Taylor, 1968).

Quality of the water or of forage is also important in determining how much water is required and hence the frequency with which an animal must drink. Wilson (1978) found that a salt content greater than 1.5% to 2%

779

in drinking water decreased forage intake and increased water intake by 40% to 50%. Wilson (1975), in reviewing water requirements of domestic stock, found that during the dry season the drinking frequency of cattle was daily, sheep every one or two days, and kangaroos only occasionally. Ealey (1967) found in a dry summer that 2% of euros (*Macropus robustus*) drank more than twice a day and that 28% did not drink at all. On the average, euros drank once every 3 to 10 days and consumed about 2.3 l wk^{-1}. African antelopes such as the eland (*Taurotragus oryx* (Blainville)), oryx (*Oryx beisa* (Ruepell)), Grant's gazelle (*Gazella granti* (Brooke)) and Thomson's gazelle (*Gazella thomsoni* (Gunther)) rarely drink under natural conditions, but get their moisture from forage (Taylor, 1968). Cattle of British breeds in central Australia will forage as far as 29 km from water in the winter and 14.5 km in the summer; but the average distance out from water to the main feeding areas was less than 3 km (Low, Hodder & Abel, 1978). This compares with 3 to 8 km for cattle on the shadeless grasslands of the Barkly Tablelands in north-central Australia (Yeates & Schmidt, 1974). The distance was influenced by availability of forage and by temperatures, and both these factors influenced the frequency of drinking. During the hot summer with good forage conditions, 55% of the cattle observed in the area of abundant shade watered every day, whereas in the winter only 27% watered every day (Low *et al.*, 1978). On the shadeless Barkly Tablelands most of the cattle watered every day during the hot summer (Yeates & Schmidt, 1974).

The migration of the antelope of the East African plains is seen as an adaptation to the alternation of wet seasons and dry seasons (Estes, 1974). Animals concentrate around available water when feed is dry during the dry season; when the wet season returns, they move back to the green feed of the essentially waterless grasslands. Skerman (1975) has found that, if the Masai did not move their cattle in the same manner, cattle production could decrease by 80%; the factors responsible were salt and forage together with water supply.

Soil temperature

Ground temperature as a derived quantity often exercises more direct control over animal activity than does air temperature. Briese's (1974) work has already been discussed. He found that different ant species were active at different soil temperatures, and interpreted the adaptations of the different species as a means of decreasing competition. *Melophorus* spp. were active only when soil temperatures exceeded 37 °C; but there was a definite range (10 °C to 55 °C) below and above which all the 15 species of ants studied were inactive.

Wallwork (1972) found there was no significant difference in density of micro-arthropods, in either litter or mineral soil, between areas exposed to direct sunlight and shaded areas. Although temperatures or duration of exposure were not noted, one must assume that the substrate insulation had adequately overcome insolation.

High ground temperatures with their resultant high re-radiation have serious effects on calves in the shadeless Barkly Tablelands of Australia (Yeates & Schmidt, 1974). Calves have a higher heat load per unit mass than cows, and their cooling mechanism is occasionally insufficient to keep their body temperature within safe limits. Calves which had rectal temperatures as high as 45 °C, as a result of standing or lying on ground at a temperature of 55 °C to 66 °C, were found dead a day later (Yeates & Schmidt, 1974). In central Australia, cattle usually rest in the shade when air temperatures approach 38 °C (W. A. Low, unpublished data). On hot days, afternoon grazing began at ambient temperatures two or three degrees higher if the cattle had had the opportunity of resting in the shade than if they had been exposed to full sunshine (Yeates & Schmidt, 1974).

Evaporation

Evaporation rate, saturation deficit and relative humidity have all been used as measures of the rate of water loss from an animal. The consequent cooling or dehydration of the animal affects its behaviour, and consequently its distribution.

Clark (1978) found that the Australian plague locust will fly at any humidity within the range of 9 to 70%, provided temperature and wind speed are also in the appropriate range. Whitford (1973) found that foraging ants were inactive when the saturation deficit exceeded a limit which varied between 37 and 69 mbar (25 and 45 $g\,m^{-3}$) in different species. However, Briese (1974) analyzed the behaviour of five species of harvester ants to determine the relative importance of saturation deficit and surface temperature in affecting activity. *Chelaner* (sim. *rothsteini* Emery) and a species of *Pheidole* were more affected by temperature, *Chelaner* (sim. *whitei*) was intermediate and two other species of *Pheidole* were more affected by moisture status.

Nel (1965) found that the temperate-zone ant *Iridomyrmex detectus* (Smith) transpired more on cold winter and spring days than on hot days. His observations suggested that this was due to increased activity on cool days and the abraded state of the cuticle in the winter, although he could not isolate the mechanisms.

Breeding of many arid-land birds after rain appears to be a means of overcoming the high moisture loss associated with courting and egg production by concentrating reproduction in a period when relative humidity is high and evaporative loss low (Immelmann, 1963).

781

Animal processes

Happold (1973) found that desert rodents seek to avoid excessive loss of moisture by behaviourally avoiding air which has a high saturation deficit. She found that the desert-adapted rodents *Notomys alexis* and *Pseudomys albocinereus* (Gould), which are nocturnal and fossorial, plugged entrances and huddled in groups to decrease the evaporation rate. Huddling is also a feature of behaviour of the collared peccary (*Tayassu tajaçu*) of middle American deserts (Low, 1970; Sowls, 1974) and camels (*Camelus dromedarius* L.) (Gauthier-Pilters, 1974). Although this behaviour has not been experimentally examined, it appears to decrease thermal stress and high evaporative loss.

Russell (1974*a*) suggests that restlessness in red kangaroos and euros at high environmental temperatures promotes heat loss through evaporative cooling of forelimbs and chest which have been dampened with saliva.

Apart from the work by Briese (1974) and Clark (1978), the influence of moisture loss on animal behaviour and distribution has rarely been quantified. Behaviour patterns have been described and attributed to moisture loss, but process curves showing rates of change in activity due to changing moisture loss are unavailable.

Fire

Fire has been recognized as a natural feature of many ecosystems (Dyksterhuis, 1949; Vines, 1975). In semi-arid and temperate areas of North America, the influence of fire on animal populations has been studied for many years, and fire has been used as a means of population control (see, for review, Kirsch & Kruse (1973)). However, in arid lands the effects of fire on animal populations are known mainly from anecdotes relating to incineration of animals and destruction of habitat. Controlled observations before and after fire, such as those of Winkworth (1970) on spinifex hummock grasslands in central Australia, will be required before prescribed burning can become a management tool in the arid lands. Survival and re-invasion rates, at least for the animals important in energy cycling, are urgently required.

Biotic factors

In this review I have been concerned with biotic factors influencing animal distribution through habitat (primarily shelter) and food. Other biotic interactions, such as competition, reproduction, predation and disease, which may also affect animal distribution, are treated elsewhere.

Biotic aspects of habitat

The biotic portion of the habitat consists mainly of the plants which provide, among other things, shelter, feeding sites, nesting areas and display sites.

Briese (1974) compared the populations of harvester ants in an eco-system dominated by salt-bush (*Atriplex* spp.) with those in the same ecosystem converted into a grassland by sheep grazing. Since the diets of the ants were generalized, forage-plant changes had little influence. However, total specific diversity decreased as a result of removal of the salt-bush canopy as a foraging site. Aggressive interactions and colony spacing were the most important factors in controlling the specific composition of the ant community. The increased abundance of harvester ants in the grassland may be compared with the increase in density of termites (*Drepanotermes perniger* Froggat) which followed conversion to grassland of vegetation dominated by mulga (*Acacia aneura* F. Muell.) in southwest Queensland (Watson, Lendon & Low, 1973).

Whitford & Ettershank (1972) have shown that colony density of herbi-vorous ants in a desert in the southwestern United States appears to be a function of cover and diversity of vegetation, as well as of competition between ant species. Whitford (1973) also found that foraging effort decreased as an exponential decay function with increasing distance of forage from the nest.

Western (1974) has discussed the biomass density of large mammals, small mammals, and lizards in an arid area in northern Kenya. The biomass densities of mammals were approximately tenfold greater in an alluvial valley bottom than on a lava hillside, but those of lizards approxi-mately equal in the two areas. These results could be explained in terms of suitable cover and foraging sites. Kikkawa (1974) found that clutch sizes in birds were larger and more variable in subtropical semi-arid open habitats than in closed subtropical forests. Moreover, species diversity was greater in the semi-arid region, and species associations were some-what looser, as calculated using Furuike's (1965) index of fidelity. The unpredictable environment and the greater diversity of habitats were the primary reasons for the differences found in the arid area.

Lewis (1971) discussed the differences in bird populations on several grazed and ungrazed areas in North American semi-arid grasslands, and found that the scaled quail (*Callipepla squamata* (Vig.)) and loggerhead shrike (*Lanius ludovicianus* L.) occurred only in the grazed sites, and the density of the horned lark (*Eremophila alpestris* (L.)) was up to ten times greater in the grazed site. He suggests that habitat differences result in more favourable feeding conditions in the grazed area for these three species, but pointed out that the grasshopper sparrow (*Ammodramus*

Animal processes

savannarum (Gmelin)) existed only in the ungrazed sites. Newsome & Corbett (1977) suggest that introduction of cattle and rabbits to central Australia has resulted in removal of habitat as well as competition for shelter, and that seven out of ten marsupials of medium to large size have been reduced in numbers as a result (see also Newsome (1971)). It seems possible that some of these rare marsupials and rodents are susceptible to drought, and that the species survive during long droughts only in suitable refugia, as Noy-Meir (1974) suggests with his theory of low persistence and high resilience in arid-land biota. Undoubtedly the number of refugia have declined with the introduction of domestic stock and rabbits.

Von Richter (1972) has pointed out that, on several African semi-arid ranges, habitat destruction has occurred, in part through population pressure, in part through human action, and that in consequence the populations have diminished greatly through mortality or emigration.

Food availability

Food availability has been widely studied as a factor controlling distribution and behaviour of animals. Probably owing to difficulties in sampling both animal populations and their food, the processes are not well defined. Food selection itself is discussed by Reichmann in Chapter 29.

Whitford (1973), Whitford & Kay (1974) and Briese (1974) have found a positive correlation between numbers of foraging ants and the availability of food in semi-arid areas. The degree of satiation of the colony (Whitford & Kay, 1974) and the presence of larvae (Briese, 1974) also affects the intensity of foraging activity. Carroll & Janzen (1973) have reviewed the ecology of foraging ants and found that, when food supply was sparsely distributed and unpredictable in time and location, the average foraging distance and search time were long. The feeding activity of termites is also largely dependent on availability of forage, but temperature and humidity conditions also control the feeding periods (Lendon, 1974). However, as Lee & Wood (1971, p. 193) point out, evidence based on activity of these insects is non-quantitative and samples only a certain proportion of the population.

Clark (1978) found that green feed was required for development of the Australian plague locust and that 56% of the variance in average density of adult locusts was due to variation in the cumulative precipitation during the three-week period when nymphs were hatching. However, direct evidence of the degree of control by the green forage is lacking.

Little information is available on the influence of food on lizard activity. In a review of lizard community structure Pianka (1973) considered that in North America food was the major dimension separating niches of

784

lizards, but in the Kalahari Desert place and time separated the niches. However, in Australia, food, place and time are all important for niche separation. The differences are due primarily to species richness and the need to diversify niches to decrease competition.

Russell (1974*b*) thought that food was important in regulating numbers of kangaroos, though other factors were also involved. Newsome (1965) showed that green forage was the main factor influencing the distribution of red kangaroos in central Australia. Low, Birk, Lendon & Low (1973) have examined the distribution of red kangaroos based on plant-community preferences, and Low (1972) has shown that the foraging distribution of cattle in central Australia changes progressively as forage dries off following rain.

Wilson (1978) found that high salt-content of forage limits the distance that sheep can forage from water. Merino sheep grazing on salt-bush (*Atriplex* spp.) water twice a day, whereas those grazing on *Danthonia* grassland only water once a day. Lynch (1974) found in semi-arid range-land in Australia that, during forage scarcity, sheep are scattered throughout the large paddocks and that group structure breaks down.

A number of studies in two symposium volumes (Louw & Malan, 1972; Geist & Walther, 1974) discuss the influence of forage and habitat on ungulate distribution and behaviour. Estes (1974), in his survey of the social behaviour of Bovids on the African plains, attributes their migratory movements to lack of green feed with sufficient water content to allow the animals to be relatively independent of water holes. During the dry season they migrate to favourable areas, and during the wet season they migrate back to the grass plains. Bliss *et al.* (1973) also point out that it is lack of available food in the Arctic tundra that causes birds and caribou to migrate.

The diets of mammals have been particularly well studied, but the influence of food on their spatial and temporal distribution has usually been only a side issue. This is understandable with domestic animals in limited-choice situations. However, under the extensive conditions of arid lands, distribution of food regulates the distribution of mobile animals, both domestic livestock and wild-life.

Discussion

Occasionally a single limiting factor in the environment may have an overwhelming control over an animal's distribution or behaviour (Shelford, 1911; Odum, 1953). Such a feature as presence or absence of drinking water, for example, determines whether finches will exist in arid regions (Immelmann, 1963). More frequently simple climatic control of, say, food supply is the main factor controlling population distribution or

785

abundance. However, as Russell (1974*b*) points out with reference to the marsupial quokka (*Setonix brachyurus* Quoy & Gainard) in Western Australia, lack of shelter, water shortage and space limitations have been found to interact with food supplies to determine mortality rates. Where factors are closely correlated, it is difficult to separate their relative contribution to control. Indeed it may not be meaningful or useful to do so.

A number of strategies have evolved to allow species to survive traumatic periods. Drought evaders avoid drought either temporally or spatially. Temporal evasion through physiological adaptations such as diapause, aestivation or hibernation are found in invertebrates, frogs, lizards, and some small mammals. Spatial evasion is possible, either through migration as found in waterfowl and large raptors, or in suitable refuges. These refuges may be temporary and actively selected, a situation found in mobile mammals such as red kangaroos moving to areas where local showers have ameliorated forage conditions; or they may be relatively permanent, where a nucleus population of a species, such as *Rattus villosissimus*, can survive a drought and re-radiate during favourable periods. Some animals combine both strategies; frogs, for instance, may dig down to suitable refuges and also reduce their metabolic rates. Drought tolerators such as cattle passively exist (or die) through drought. The drought-survival strategies are graphically shown in Fig. 32.1.

Likewise, strategies for increasing the populations of an area where a resource has suddenly become available are reproduction and immigration. Semi-arid and arid-land animals have evolved life-history 'strategies' that enable them to re-occupy the environment (Wilbur *et al.*, 1974; Low, 1975). The *K*-strategy employed by species that exist near the carrying capacity of the environment and the *r*-strategy employed by species which frequently experience population expansions (MacArthur & Wilson, 1967; Pianka, 1970, 1972) are both found in arid-land animals, but the latter is most prevalent (Andrewartha & Birch, 1954; Barclay, 1975). The *r*-strategy enables a species to quickly repopulate areas in which local populations may have become extinct or numbers much reduced during droughts, and Noy-Meir (1974) suggests that this is normal.

While various strategies are used to survive in or repopulate arid areas, the basic strategy depends on an animal's trophic position and environmental predictability. The strategy of migration is usually used in conjunction with reproduction, but is most important for mobile animals like locusts, birds and large mammals. However, emigration from rapidly expanding populations is also a feature of small mammal populations which form plagues (Carstairs, 1974; Newsome & Corbett, 1975). Migration is also related to the seasonal availability of food and water. Where the seasons are regular, as in the African grasslands (Estes, 1974) and the

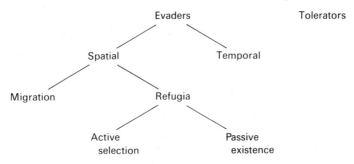

Fig. 32.1. Drought-survival strategies.

Arctic tundra (Bliss *et al.*, 1973), migration is a feature of large mammals and of many bird populations. Where seasons are irregular, as in the semi-arid and arid sub-Saharan region of Africa (Estes, 1974) and in Australia (Davies, 1974), nomadism is a feature of the mobile animal populations. Since, however, the nature of controls is understood only very imperfectly, information on climatic changes cannot yet be used with any confidence in the management of animals within natural ecosystems.

It appears that most animals adapted to arid-land conditions have nearly divorced themselves from a need for free water, thus freeing themselves from the main constraint affecting distribution. The exceptions are mainly mobile animals such as birds and large mammals.

Gaps in knowledge

Data have been collected on a variety of aspects of population dynamics, distribution and behaviour. In many cases the environmental factors that influence the performance of animal populations have been identified. However, the majority of studies stop at that point and do not go on to determine the functional relationship that exists between the factor and the aspect it controls.

The relationship between a process and a factor influencing it can usually be expressed in the form of a curve, adequate definition of which requires data for several points. Among the studies surveyed in this chapter, few have provided more than one or two points for this purpose.

Studies under the US/IBP Desert and Grassland Biome programmes over the last seven years have made great strides in organizing studies of animal populations in arid and semi-arid rangelands, and describing the biotic and abiotic factors which affect them. A considerable body of data is now available and needs integrating to the point where the functional relationships can be determined and the information used in management. Aspects of spatial distribution and social behaviour may have considerable

787

Animal processes

local influence on rangelands; hence, the processes by which these aspects of behaviour are controlled by environmental factors may need to be determined. Little information is available on these processes in arid-land animals (W. A. Low, 1977; Cowling, 1977).

Weir (1971a) has sounded a word of warning as a result of his studies on distribution of wildlife in southern Rhodesia. The distribution of animals during dry periods may be effectively regulated through providing water-holes, but the long-term processes of biogenic environmental differentiation are not well known or understood. Hence the derived environmental factors may counter the manipulative location of water-holes.

A basic problem is that population surveys are frequently difficult to compare because of differences in the time of the year and population cycle during which the survey was made. Further complications are caused by differences in types of habitat, and habitat requirements and population biology need to be known before accurate assessment can be made of population density, distribution or behaviour. A recent example is discussed by B. S. Low (personal communication). She found that the utilization by red kangaroos of a range of communities in central Australia showed a regular seasonal pattern despite irregular climatic changes. She suggested that surveys of kangaroo densities at different times of the year would yield biased estimates of population changes.

Conclusions

In general it appears that most studies have only reached the goal of defining the dynamics of spatial and temporal distribution and behaviour of animal populations. A few have isolated the main factors controlling processes, and fewer yet have reached the stage of defining the process itself in terms of quantitative effects of the environmental factors on the dynamics of the state variables. In some studies, notably those of the US/IBP Desert and Grassland Biome programs, the potential exists for successful conclusion of the projects; but this will not be achieved until the mass of data collected has been synthesized to determine the quantitative relationships between environmental factors and the state variables describing animal distribution and behaviour.

Pieper (1969) has pointed out that 'Consumer populations tend to vary tremendously both in time and space and hence their impact on other eco system components varies considerably. These variations make evaluation of the role of consumers very difficult since sampling techniques must be designed to measure these variations.' These same variations make evaluation of the influence of environmental factors on the consumer populations equally difficult, and sampling techniques still appear to be the main limitation to obtaining adequate data to describe the processes.

788

Acknowledgments

I wish to express my appreciation of early discussions with the noted sheep behaviourist Dr Justin J. Lynch, which led to the approach adopted in this review.

References

Allee, W. C., Emerson, A. E., Park, O., Park, T. & Schmidt, K. P. (1949). *Principles of Animal Ecology*. Saunders, Philadelphia.

Andrewartha, H. C. & Birch, L. C. (1954). *The distribution and abundance of animals*. University of Chicago Press, Chicago, Illinois.

Barclay, H. (1975). Population strategies and random environments. *Canadian Journal of Zoology*, **53**, 160–5.

Bigalke, R. C. (1972). Observations on the behaviour and feeding habits of the springbok, *Antidorcas marsupialis*. *Zoologica Africana*, **7** (1), 331–59.

Bigler, W. J. (1974). Seasonal movements and activity patterns of the collared peccary. *Journal of Mammalogy*, **55** (4), 851–4.

Bledsoe, L. J. & Jameson, D. A. (1969). Model structure for a grassland ecosystem. In: *The grassland ecosystem: a preliminary synthesis* (eds. R. L. Dix & R. G. Beidleman), pp. 410–37. Colorado State University, Fort Collins, Range Science Department, Science Series No. 2.

Bliss, L. C., Courtin, G. M., Pattie, D. L., Riewe, R. R., Whitfield, D. W. A. & Widdon, P. (1973). Arctic tundra ecosystems. *Annual Review of Ecology & Systematics*, **4**, 359–400.

Bodenheimer, F. S. (1957). The Ecology of mammals in arid zones. In: *UNESCO Arid Zone Research, Reviews of Research, vol. VIII, Human & Animal Ecology*, pp. 100–37. UNESCO, Paris.

Braithwaite, L.W. (1974). Environment and timing of reproduction and flightlessness in two species of Australian ducks. *International Ornithological Congress Canberra, August 1974, Abstracts*, **16**, 36.

Briese, D. T. (1974). 'Ecological studies of an ant community.' Ph.D. Thesis, Australian National University, Canberra.

Brody, S. (1956). Climatic physiology of cattle. *Journal of Dairy Science*, **39**, 715–25.

Carroll, C. R. & Janzen, D. H. (1973). Ecology of foraging ants. *Annual Review of Ecology & Systematics*, **4**, 231–57.

Carstairs, J. L. (1974). The distribution of *Rattus villosissimus* (Waite) during plague and non-plague years. *Australian Wildlife Research*, **1**, 95–106.

Clark, D. P. (1978). The significance of the availability of water in limiting invertebrate numbers. In: *Studies of the Australian Arid Zone: 3. Water in Rangelands* (ed. K. M. W. Howes). CSIRO, Melbourne.

Cole, L. C. (1946). A theory for analyzing contagiously distributed populations. *Ecology*, **27**, 329–41.

Cowling, S. W. (1977). Effects of herbivores on nutrient cycling and distribution in rangeland ecosystems. In: *The impact of herbivores on arid and semi-arid rangelands*. Proceedings 2nd Workshop United States/Australian Rangelands Panel. Adelaide, 1972. Australian Rangeland Society, Perth.

Davies, S. J. J. F. (1974). Environmental variables and the biology of Australian arid-zone birds. *International Ornithological Congress, Canberra, August 1974, Abstracts*, **16**, 36.

789

Animal processes

Daws, G. T. & Squires, V. R. (1974). Observations on the effects of temperature and distance to water on the behaviour of Merino and Border Leicester sheep. *Journal of Agricultural Science, Cambridge*, **82** (3), 383–90.

Dawson, T. J. (1972). Thermoregulation in Australian desert kangaroos. *Symposium of the Zoology Society of London*, **31**, 133–46.

Dawson, T. J. (1974). Recent advances in marsupial physiology (non-reproductive). *Australian Mammalogy*, **1** (2), 181–7.

Dawson, T. J. & Denny, M. J. S. (1969). A bioclimatological comparison of the summer day microenvironments of two species of arid zone kangaroo. *Ecology*, **50**, 328–32.

Dyksterhuis, E. J. (1949). Condition and management of rangeland based on quantitative ecology. *Journal of Range Management*, **2**, 104–15.

Ealey, E. H. M. (1967). Ecology of the euro, *Macropus robustus* (Gould) in north-western Australia. II. Behaviour, movements and drinking patterns. *CSIRO Wildlife Research*, **12**, 27–51.

Elton, C. S. (1927). *Animal Ecology*. Sidgwick and Jackson, London. (Macmillan, New York 3rd edition, 1947.)

Estes, R. G. (1974). Social organization of the African Bovidae. In: *Behaviour of ungulates and its relation to management* (eds. V. Geist & F. Walther). International Union for Conservation of Nature Publication, new series, No. 24, 166–205. Morges, Switzerland.

Frith, H. J. (1967). *Waterfowl in Australia*. Angus & Robertson, Sydney.

Furuike, H. (1965). Expression of fidelity by means of the information theory. *Japanese Journal of Ecology*, **15**, 43–7.

Gauthier-Pilters, H. (1974). The behaviour and ecology of camels in the Sahara, with special reference to nomadism and water management. In: *Behaviour of ungulates and its relation to management* (eds. V. Geist & F. Walther). International Union for Conservation of Nature Publication, new series, No. 24, 542–51. Morges, Switzerland.

Geist, V. & Walther, F. (eds.) (1974). *Behaviour of ungulates and its relation to management*. International Union for the Conservation of Nature Publication, new series, No. 24, vol. 2, 942 pp. Morges, Switzerland.

Giles, R. H. (ed.) (1969). *Wildlife Management Techniques* (3rd revised edition). The Wildlife Society, Washington, D.C.

Graetz, R. D., Carnegie, D. M., Hacker, R., Lendon, C. & Wilcox, D. G. (1976). A qualitative evaluation of LANDSAT imagery of Australian rangelands. *Australian Rangeland Journal*, **1** (1), 53–9.

Greaves, T. (1971). The distribution of the three forms of the meat ant, *Iridomyrmex purpureus* (Hymenoptera: Formicidae) in Australia. *Journal of the Australian Entomological Society*, **10**, 15–21.

Greenslade, P. (1974). Phenology of some microarthropods of arid pasture. *First Australasian Conference on the ecology of grassland invertebrates, Armidale, 1974*, pp. 45–6. (Abstract.) CSIRO, Armidale, N.S.W.

Greenslade, P. J. M. (1974a). Ants of a semi-arid site in South Australia I. The summer fauna. Unpublished manuscript. CSIRO, Division of Soils, Adelaide.

Greenslade, P. J. M. (1974b). Some relations of the meat ant, *Iridomyrmex purpureus* (Hymenoptera: Formicidae) with soil in South Australia. *Soil Biology and Biochemistry*, **6**, 7–14.

Greenslade, P. J. M. & Greenslade, P. (1973). Ants of a site in arid southern

790

Australia. *Proceedings of the International Union for the study of social insects, Congress* VII, pp. 40–9.

Hafez, E. S. E. (ed.) (1962). *Behaviour of domestic animals.* Bailliére, Tindall & Cox, London.

Hafez, E. S. E. (ed.) (1968). *Adaptations of domestic animals.* Lea and Febiger, Philadelphia.

Happold, M. (1973). 'The social behaviour of conilurine rodents.' Ph.D. Thesis, Department of Zoology, Monash University, Melbourne.

Harris, L. D. (1971). Small mammal studies and results in the Grassland Biome. In: *Preliminary analysis of structure and function in grasslands* (ed. N. R. French). Colorado State University, Fort Collins, Range Science Department, Science Series No. 10, pp. 213–40.

Holm, E. & Edney, E. B. (1973). Daily activity of Namib Desert arthropods in relation to climate. *Ecology,* **54,** 45–56.

Immelmann, K. (1963). Drought adaptations in Australian desert birds. *Proceedings of the International Ornithological Congress, Ithaca, New York (1962),* **13,** 649–57.

Immelmann, K. (1965). *Australian Finches in Bush and Aviary.* Angus & Robertson, Sydney.

Kendeigh, S. C. (1961). *Animal Ecology.* Prentice Hall, Englewood Cliffs, New Jersey.

Kikkawa, J. (1974). Comparison of avian communities between wet and semi-arid habitats of eastern Australia. *Australian Wildlife Research,* **1** (2), 107–16.

Kirkham, D. R. & Fisser, H. G. (1972). Rangeland relations and harvester ants in north-central Wyoming. *Journal of Range Management,* **25,** 55–60.

Kirsch, L. M. & Kruse, A. D. (1973). Prairie fires and wildlife. *Proceedings of Tall Timbers Fire Ecology Conference,* **12,** 284–303.

Lee, K. E. & Wood, T. G. (1971). *Termites and soils.* Academic Press, New York & London.

Lendon, C. (1974). Dietary selection of the foraging termite, *Amitermes vitiosus,* in captive colonies and mulga rangeland. *1st Australasian Conference on the ecology of grassland invertebrates, Armidale, 1974,* pp. 43–4 (Abstract). CSIRO, Armidale, New South Wales.

Lewis, J. K. (1971). The Grassland Biome: a synthesis of structure and function. In: *Preliminary analysis of structure and function in grasslands* (ed. N. R. French). Proceedings of Symposium 'The Grassland Biome: Analysis and synthesis of first year data', Colorado State University, Fort Collins, Range Science Department, Science Series No. 10, 317–87.

Logan, R. F. (1968). Causes, climates and distribution of deserts. In: *Desert Biology* (ed. G. W. Brown), pp. 21–50. Academic Press, New York & London.

Louw, G. N. & Malan, M. E. (Eds.) (1972). Symposium on Animal Behaviour. Proceedings held at Durban, South Africa, July 1971. *Zoologica Africana,* **7** (1), 1–412.

Low, B. S. (1975). The evolution of amphibian life histories in the desert. In: *Evolution of Desert Biota* (ed. D. W. Goodall), pp. 149–95. University of Texas Press, Austin.

Low, B. S., Birk, E., Lendon, C. & Low, W. A. (1973). Community utilization by cattle and kangaroos in mulga near Alice Springs, N.T. *Tropical Grasslands,* **17** (1), 149–56.

Low, W. A. (1970). 'The influence of aridity on reproduction of the collared

791

peccary (*Dictoyles tajacu* [Linn.]) in Texas.' Ph.D. Thesis, University of British Columbia, Vancouver. (Abstract in *Dissertation Abstracts International*, 1970, 7692–B.)

Low, W. A. (1972). Community preference by free-ranging shorthorns in the Alice Springs District. *Proceedings of Australian Society of Animal Production*, **9**, 381–6.

Low, W. A. (1977). Behaviour of herbivores (except sheep) influencing rangelands. In: *The impact of herbivores on arid and semi-arid rangelands*, pp. 165–77. Proceedings 2nd Workshop United States/Australian Rangelands Panel, Adelaide, 1972. Australian Rangeland Society, Perth.

Low, W. A., Hodder, R. M. & Abel, D. E. (1978). Watering behaviour of British breed cattle in central Australia. In: *Studies of the Australian arid zone. 3. Water in rangelands* (ed. K. M. W. Howes). CSIRO, Melbourne.

Lynch, J. J. (1974). Merino sheep, some factors affecting their distribution in very large paddocks. In: *Behaviour of ungulates and its relation to management* (eds. V. Geist & F. Walther), pp. 679–707. International Union for the conservation of nature publication, new series, No. 24. Morges, Switzerland.

MacArthur, R. H. & Wilson, E. D. (1967). *The theory of island biogeography*. Princeton University Press, Princeton, N.J.

MacFadyen, A. (1957). *Animal Ecology*. Pittman and Sons, London.

Marshall, A. J. & Disney, H. J. de S. (1957). Experimental induction of the breeding season in a xerophilous bird. *Nature (London)*, **180**, 647–9.

Myers, K. & Parker, B. S. (1965). A study of the biology of the wild rabbit in climatically different regions in eastern Australia. I. Patterns of distribution. *CSIRO, Wildlife Research*, **10**, 1–32.

Nel, J. J. C. (1965). Influence of temperature and relative humidity on water loss in the workers of the meat ant *Iridomyrmex detectus* (Smith) (Dolichoderinae: Hymenoptera). *Australian Journal of Zoology*, **13**, 301–15.

Newsome, A. E. (1965). The distribution of red kangaroos, *Megaleia rufa* (Desmarest) about sources of persistent food and water in central Australia. *Australian Journal of Zoology*, **13**, 289–99.

Newsome, A. E. (1971). Competition between wildlife and domestic livestock. *Australian Veterinary Journal*, **47**, 577–86.

Newsome, A. E. & Corbett, L. K. (1976). Outbreaks of rodent plagues in central Australia: Their causes, consequences and evolutionary significance. In: *Rodents in desert environments* (eds. I. Prakash & P. Ghosh)). Monographiae Biologicae, vol. 28, 117–54. Junk, The Hague.

Newsome, A. E. & Corbett, L. K. (1977). The effects of native, feral and domestic animals on the productivity of the Australian Rangelands. In: *The impact of herbivores on arid and semi-arid rangelands*, pp. 331–56. Proceedings 2nd Workshop United States/Australian Rangelands Panel, Adelaide, 1972. Australian Rangeland Society, Perth.

Noy-Meir, I. (1974). Stability in arid ecosystems and the effects of man on it. *Proceedings 1st International Congress of Ecology The Hague, Netherlands, September 1974*, pp. 220–25.

Odum, E. P. (1953). *Fundamentals of Ecology* (1st edition), Saunders, London.

Ohmart, R. D. & Laslewski, R. C. (1971). Roadrunners: energy conservation by hypothermia and absorption of sunlight. *Science*, **172**, 67–9.

Packard, R. L. (1977). Effects of herbivores on seed production, seed distribution and on reproduction from seed. In: *The impact of herbivores on arid and semi-arid rangelands*, pp. 211–26, Proceedings 2nd Workshop United States/

Australian Rangelands Panel, Adelaide, 1972. Australian Rangeland Society, Perth.

Packer, W. C. (1963). Dehydration, hydration and burrowing behaviour in *Helioporus eyrei* (Gray) (Leptodactylidae). *Ecology*, **44**, 643–51.

Pianka, E. R. (1970). On *r* and *K* selection. *American Naturalist*, **104**, 592–7.

Pianka, E. R. (1972). *r* and *K* selection or *b* and *d* selection? *American Naturalist*, **106**, 581–8.

Pianka, E.R. (1973). The structure of lizard communities. *Annual Review of Ecology & Systematics*, **4**, 53–74.

Pianka, E. R. (1974). *Evolutionary Ecology*. Harper & Row, New York.

Pieper, R. D. (1969). Section III, Consumers, Introduction. In: *The grassland ecosystem: a preliminary synthesis* (eds. R. L. Dix & R. G. Beidleman), p. 242. Colorado State University, Fort Collins, Range Science Department, Science Series No. 2.

Pradhan, S. (1957). The ecology of arid zone insects (excluding locusts and grasshoppers). In: *UNESCO Arid Zone Research, Reviews of Research, vol. VIII, Human and Animal Ecology*, pp. 199–240.UNESCO, Paris.

Rasmussen, J. L. (1971). Abiotic factors in grassland ecosystem analysis and function. In: *Preliminary analysis of structure and function in grasslands* (ed. N. R. French). Colorado State University, Fort Collins, Range Science Department, Science Series No. 10, pp. 11–34.

Richmond, C. R., Langham, W. H. & Trujillo, T. T. (1962). Comparative metabolism of tritiated water by mammals. *Journal of Cellular and Comparative Physiology*, **59**, 45–53.

Russell, E. M. (1974*a*). Recent ecological studies on marsupials. *Australian Mammalogy*, **1** (2), 189–211.

Russell, E. M. (1974*b*). The biology of kangaroos (Marsupialia – Macropodidae). *Mammal Review*, **4** (1/2), 1–59.

Schmidt-Nielsen, K. (1964). *Desert animals, physiological problems of heat and water*. Clarendon Press, Oxford.

Serventy, D. L. & Whittell, H. M. (1951). *A handbook of the birds of Western Australia*. (2nd edition.) Paterson Brokensha, Perth.

Shelford, V. E. (1911). Physiological animal geography. *Journal of Morphology*, **22**, 551–618.

Siebert, B. D. (1978). Function, regulation and comparative use of water in vertebrates. In: *Studies of the Australian Arid Zone. 3. Water in Rangelands* (ed. K. M. W. Howes), pp. 153–64. CSIRO, Melbourne.

Skadhuage, E. (1972). Salt and water excretion in xerophilic birds. *Symposia of the Zoological Society of London*, **31**, 113–29.

Skerman, P. J. (1975). Nomadism overseas and cattle management in northern Australia. In: *Proceedings III World Conference on Animal Production* (ed. R. L. Reid), pp. 264–7. Sydney University Press, Sydney.

Smith, R. L. (1966). *Ecology and Field Biology*. Harper and Row, New York.

Sowls, L. K. (1974). Social behaviour of the collared peccary *Dicotyles tajacu* (L.). In: *Behaviour of ungulates and its relation to management* (eds. V. Geist & F. Walther), pp. 144–65. International Union for the Conservation of Nature Publication, new series, No. 24. Morges, Switzerland.

Spomer, G. G. (1973). The concepts of 'interactions' and 'operational environment' in environmental analyses. *Ecology*, **54** (1), 200–204.

Squires, V. R. & Wilson, A. D. (1971). Distance between food and water supply and its effects on drinking frequency, and food and water intake of Merino and Border Leicester sheep. *Australian Journal of Agricultural Research*, **22**, 283–90.

Stebbins, R. C. (1954). *Amphibians of Western North America*. McGraw-Hill, New York.

Taylor, C. R. (1968). The minimum water requirements of some East African bovids. *Symposia of Zoological Society of London*, **21**, 195–206.

Thomas, B. O., Cameron, R. E. & Holmes, J. D. (1970). The importance and role of amphibians and reptiles in grassland ecosystems. In: *The grassland ecosystem: a preliminary synthesis* (eds. R. L. Dix & R. G. Beidleman). Colorado State University, Fort Collins, Range Science Department, Science Series No. 2 (supplement), 307–1–23.

Uvarov, B. P. (1957). The aridity factor in the ecology of locust and grasshoppers of the Old World. In: *UNESCO Arid Zone Research, Vol. VIII, Human and animal ecology*, pp. 164–98. UNESCO, Paris.

Vines, R. G. (1975). Bushfire research in CSIRO. *Search*, **6** (3), 73–8.

von Richter, W. (1972). Remarks on present distribution and abundance of some South African carnivores. *Journal of the South African Wildlife Management Association*, **2** (1), 9–16.

Wallwork, J. A. (1970). *Ecology of soil animals*. McGraw-Hill, New York & Sydney.

Wallwork, J. A. (1972). Distribution patterns and population dynamics of the micro-arthropods of a desert soil in southern California. *Journal of Animal Ecology*, **41**, 291–310.

Warburg, M. R. (1972). Water economy and thermal balance of Israeli and Australian amphibia from xeric habitats. *Symposia of Zoological Society of London*, **31**, 79–106.

Watson, J. A. L. (1978). Water balance in the insects of arid lands. In: *Studies of the Australian Arid Zone: 3: Water in Rangelands* (ed. K. M. W. Howes). CSIRO, Melbourne.

Watson, J. A. L., Lendon, C. & Low, B. S. (1973). Termites in mulga lands. *Tropical Grasslands*, **7** (1), 121–6.

Watson, R. M. (1969). The South Turkana Expedition: Scientific Papers II. A survey of the large mammal population in South Turkana. *Geography Journal* **135**, 529–46.

Weir, J. S. (1971*a*). The effect of creating additional water supplies in a central African National Park. *British Ecological Society Symposium*, **11**, 367–85.

Weir, J. S. (1971*b*). Spatial distribution of elephants in an African National Park in relation to environmental sodium. *Oikos*, **23**, 1–13.

Western, D. (1974). The distribution, density and biomass density of lizards in a semi-arid environment of Northern Kenya. *East African Wildlife Journal*, **12**, 49–62.

Whitford, W. G. (1973). *Demography and bioenergetics of herbivorous ants in a desert ecosystem as functions of vegetation, soil type and weather variables.* US/IBP Desert Biome Research Memorandum RM 73–29, Logan, Utah.

Whitford, W. G. & Ettershank, G. (1972). *Demography and role of herbivorous ants in a desert ecosystem as functions of vegetation, soil and climate variables.* US/IDP Desert Biome Research Memorandum RM 72–32. Logan, Utah.

Whitford, W. G. & Kay, C. A. (1974). *Demography and role of herbivorous ants in a desert ecosystem as functions of vegetation, soil and climate variables.* US/IBP Desert Biome Research Memorandum RM 74–31. Logan, Utah.

Wilbur, H. M., Tinkle, D. W. & Collins, J. P. (1974). Environmental certainty, trophic level, and resource availability in life history evolution. *American Naturalist*, **108** (964), 805–17.

Williams, H. L. & Thwaites, C. J. (1974). The reproductive performance of Border Leicester ewes in contrasting photoperiodic environments. *Journal of Agricultural Science, Cambridge*, **83** (1), 101–4.

Wilson, A. D. (1975). Water requirements and productivity of animal populations. In: *Proceedings III World Conference on Animal Production* (ed. R. L. Reid), pp. 268–72. Sydney University Press, Sydney.

Wilson, A. D. (1978). Water requirements of sheep. In: *Studies of the Australian Arid Zone: 3. Water in Rangelands* (ed. K. M. W. Howes). CSIRO, Melbourne.

Winkworth, R. E. (1970). Regeneration in a hard spinifex (*Triodia basedowii*) community. In: *Working papers of the Australian Arid Zone Research Conference, Broken Hill, New South Wales, May 1970*, section 6, 20–22. CSIRO, Melbourne.

Woody, J. R. & Thomas, B. O. (1968). Study of certain meteorological influences on the emergences and breeding of the plains spadefoot toad (*Scaphiopus bombifrons*). *Journal of Colorado–Wyoming Academic Science*, **6**(1), 11 (abstract). (Cited by Thomas *et al.*, 1970.)

Yeates, N. T. M. & Schmidt, P. J. (1974). *Beef cattle production*. Sydney, Butterworth.

Manuscript received by the editors May 1975

33. Development and reproduction in desert animals

S. E. RIECHERT

Introduction

In attempting to write a chapter on a topic as broad as development and reproduction in desert animals, one has to limit the subject matter in some way. I have chosen to view these processes only as they are modified or limited by idiosyncracies of the desert environment. The discussion presented herein represents bits and pieces from a tremendous variety of works ranging in content from natural-history accounts to more comprehensive studies on population dynamics and experimentation on embryonic development. For the most part, literature dealing expressly with these processes is not available. This stands in marked contrast to the wealth of material in the literature on morphological and physiological adaptations to survival in the desert. Since ultimately an animal's fitness is measured by its reproductive success, this chapter demonstrates the need for more emphasis on understanding reproductive processes in desert animals.

General relationships

Fecundity in desert animals is limited both by temperature extremes, and by the vagaries of precipitation and associated food availability. Of the eggs produced by oviparous forms, many will succumb to temperature extremes and desiccation. Hatchlings face similar problems, with the addition of food limitation. Along this entire progression from initiation of reproduction to incorporation of offspring into the populations, adaptation buffers the stresses imposed by the environment on the organisms.

This paper is divided into sections dealing with fecundity and early development. Emphasis will be placed on general patterns of adaptations across taxonomic boundaries, in an attempt to make some general statements concerning the reproductive and developmental strategies best fitting animals to a desert environment.

Fecundity

Environmental limitations

Breeding and initial production of offspring is strongly influenced by the desert environment. Although no inherent trend in decreased or increased sizes of clutches or litters can be detected across taxonomic lines in animals inhabiting desert regions, there is a marked annual variability in clutch size and fecundity in desert populations which is not observed elsewhere. For instance, the desert roadrunner *Geococcyx californianus* (Aves: Cuculidae) exhibits a much more variable clutch size than does its relative the lesser roadrunner, *G. velax*, a more tropical species (Ohmart, 1973). For many animals fecundity is reduced in drought years or during dry seasons (insects (Key, 1959), lizards (Bodenheimer, 1954; Miller, 1954; Marshall & Hook, 1960; Mayhew, 1963, 1965*a*, 1966*a*, *b*, 1967; Wilhoft, 1963; Chapman & Chapman, 1964; Sweifel & Lowe, 1966; Hoddenbach & Turner, 1968; Turner, Medica, Lannon & Hoddenbach, 1969; Turner, Hoddenbach, Medica & Lannon, 1970; Kay, Miller & Miller, 1970; Turner, Medica & Smith, 1973, 1974; Nagy, 1973), birds (Keast, 1959; Immelmann, 1963; Dawson & Bartholomew, 1968; Vielliard, 1970; Ohmart, 1973; Russell, Gould & Smith, 1973; Noy-Meir, 1974), marsupials (Newsome, 1964, 1966; Sadlier, 1965; Myers, 1968; Brown, 1974), and rodents (Beatley, 1969; Bradley & Mauer, 1971; Balda, Bateman & Vaughan, 1972; Franz, Reichman & Van De Graaf, 1973; Hungerford, Lowe & Madson, 1973, 1974; Shubin, 1974)).

Breeding itself often is limited or curtailed. The lizard *Sauromalus obesus* Baird abandons social behavior and reproductive activity altogether during drought years in the Mohave Desert (Nagy, 1973). Cessation of reproductive activity during drought years probably occurs in desert snails, nematodes and millipedes where rain is required for feeding activity and breeding (Schmidt-Nielsen, Taylor & Shkolnik, 1971; Manku, Sher & Freckman, 1973; Crawford, 1974). Ephemeral insects requiring an aquatic larval stage and microcrustaceans can be added to this group, since their populations will be represented entirely by encysted eggs during drought periods (Rzóska, 1961; Cole, 1968). Important also are Amphibia, as best exemplified by the genus *Scaphiopus*. Most members of a spade-foot toad population, though exhibiting some cyclic activity in their burrows, will not emerge to feed and breed prior to a 'good' rainfall (Bragg, 1950*a*, 1956, 1965; Stebbins, 1951; Gosner & Black, 1955; Mayhew, 1962*a*, 1965*b*; Ruibal, Tevis & Roig, 1969). These and other Amphibia breed in temporary pools. During drought periods such pools are not available and breeding cannot take place. Breeding may be limited in endotherms as well. The classic mammalian example is seen in some desert marsupials, which require rainfall for inception of estrus (Newsome, 1964, 1966; Sadlier, 1965). Breeding is, thus, severely reduced in drought years.

798

Other taxa, while not halting reproductive activities altogether, may exhibit a decrease in frequency of clutch or litter during dry periods (aquatic insects (Toth & Chew, 1972), Amphibia (Main, Littlejohn & Lee, 1959), lizards (Johnson, 1960; Turner *et al.*, 1973, 1974), birds (Keast, 1959), marsupials (Newsome, 1964, 1966; Sadlier, 1965; Brown, 1974) and rodents (Franz *et al.*, 1973; Hungerford *et al.*, 1973, 1974)), or produce smaller-sized clutches (lizards (Marshall & Hook, 1960; Mayhew, 1963, 1966*a*; Wilhoft, 1963), birds (Ohmart, 1973; Ricklefs, 1965) and rodents (Hungerford *et al.*, 1974)). A smaller number of young produced might reflect the resorption of incompletely developed ova as seen in some reptiles (Zweifel & Lowe, 1966) or a high percentage of preimplantation losses in mammals. Prakhash, Rana & Jain (1973) found this to be the case in the rat *Rattus cutchicus cutchicus*, which loses an average of 44% of the ova produced before implantation. This percentage was found to be even higher during hot-dry periods experienced in the Indian deserts.

The high temperatures associated with desert summers and drought periods can interfere with the reproductive process, though temperature extremes appear to affect fewer taxa than does precipitation or the lack of it. Butler (1970) found that temperature affected the number of eggs laid by lygus bugs, Miridae; as temperature increased, egg laying was reduced. Temperature also interfered with reproduction in white rats raised under desert conditions through its adverse effect on food consumption (Morag, Kali & Furman, 1969). In another study, Licht (1973) reported that temperature influences the testicular cycle of *Dipsosarus dorsalis* Baird & Girard and *Xantusia vigilis* Baird, while Turner *et al.* (1974) suggested that temperature is influential in the timing of clutches of the Iguanid *Uta stansburiana*. For the majority of desert animals, however, rainfall and its effect on the growth of vegetation and support of insect populations is the factor that influences the reproductive process most. The physical lack of breeding pools and moisture directly limits reproduction of Amphibia, snails and aquatic invertebrates. The influence of precipitation on reproduction in many reptiles, birds and mammals may be less direct. In these animals reproduction and even breeding requires increased water and energy consumption. During periods of prolonged drought, and to a lesser extent during the annual dry season, excess food and water is often not available. A limited supply of water has been found to affect the number of birds breeding at any given time (Vielliard, 1970), whereas several workers have shown that failure to breed, or reproduction at a lower level, during dry periods is related to poor nutritional state of the adult members of the population (Bodenheimer, 1954; Miller, 1954; Marshall & Hook, 1960; Mayhew, 1963, 1965*a*, 1966*a*, *b*, 1967; Wilhoft, 1963; Chapman & Chapman, 1964; Frith & Sharman, 1964; Sadlier, 1965; Zweifel & Lowe, 1966; Hoddenbach & Turner, 1968; Turner *et al.*, 1969, 1973; Kay, Miller & Miller, 1970;

Animal processes

Bradley & Mauer, 1971; Hungerford *et al.*, 1973; Nagy, 1973). The poor nutritional state, in turn, is related to the failure of rains to stimulate annual vegetation growth.

In species with an annual cycle the lack of available food or dietary requirements might result in a failure to reach reproductive maturity in dry years. Even if reproductive maturity is reached, individuals may not have achieved enough biomass to incorporate a portion of it into eggs. At an individual level, this is demonstrated in populations of the funnel-web spider in south-central New Mexico (Riechert & Tracy, 1975). Individuals occupying poor web-sites (little insect availability) do not achieve reproductive maturity in time to lay their egg sacs before the advent of the summer rains. At this time most of the active spiders are drowned in floods, whereas the embryos survive in the egg sacs which are impermeable to water (Riechert, 1974). Thus, only those spiders that maximize their food intake at good web locations during the driest and hottest part of the year contribute offspring to the succeeding generation (Riechert & Tracy, 1975). Maturation of the desert locust *Schistocerca gregaria* (Forsk) is also delayed during dry periods, but by low availability of gibberellin and oils in its diet, rather than by quantity of food.

Just as specific dietary components are important to the maturation and reproductive success of spiders and locusts, so is the presence of invertebrates and green plant material in the diet of many lizards and rodents. The period of rapid reproductive development in lizards, for instance, coincides with the dominance of Diptera and plants in the diet (Mayhew, 1965*a*, 1966*a*, *b*, 1967; Hoddenbach & Turner, 1968; Turner *et al.*, 1969; Fenton *et al.*, 1970). The nutritional state and amount of growth observed in the lagomorphs *Sylvilagus audubonii* (Baird), *Lepus californicus* Gray and *Lepus alleni* (Mearns) are also related to the availability of green vegetation. Here, too, reproduction is correlated with nutritional state (Hungerford *et al.*, 1973, 1974). The mechanism by which nutrition and reproduction are integrated has been identified by experimental work with white rats (*Rattus norvegicus*). Before or during early pregnancy in rats, Morag, Kali & Furman (1969) found that growth of maternal tissue has priority in the use of available food sources. Thus, maternal weights increased at the expense of new embryos which were, as a result, rarely implanted under desert conditions. The mother, apparently, must reach a threshold weight or nutritional level before food is made readily available to the developing ova.

Green plants may be important to some animals for the water they provide. Beatley (1969) suggested that *Dipodomys merriami* Mearns requires the extra water which green plants offer to cover the increased activity associated with mating. It has even been suggested that an estrogenic substance in green plants stimulates estrus in female *Dipo-*

domys spp. and marsupials, and that estrus will not ocur if the animals are not able to forage on fresh vegetation (Newsome, 1966; Bradley & Mauer, 1971). Thus, precipitation either directly or indirectly affects the reproductive success of the majority of desert animals.

Adaptations

Strategies to lessen the impact of temperature extremes and the ephemeral nature of precipitation can involve: (*a*) selection of more favorable micro-environments or patches of greater food availability; (*b*) migration in and out of areas as they provide favorable or increasingly more unfavorable habits; (*c*) timing of breeding to fit local rainfall patterns; and (*d*) physio-logical and morphological adaptations to avoid heat stress and water loss.

Habitat selection

At least one desert spider, the funnel-web building spider (*Agelenopsis aperta* (Gertsch)) actively selects web-sites which provide protection from the thermal environment and are located in areas of high prey density (Riechert, 1973, 1976; Riechert & Tracy, 1975). The nutritional state of the animals and subsequent production of offspring (number and biomass) are linearly related to food intake and, thus, to web location (Riechert & Tracy, 1975). This species is able to maximize energy intake during the hottest and driest time of the year (a necessity to continuation of the population, since annual summer rains flood the area, resulting in 97% mortality to existing individuals). In an artificially irrigated area, Turner *et al.* (1973) observed both growth and successful reproduction in the Iguanid lizard *Uta stansburiana* during a dry year when, elsewhere in the habitat, individuals exhibited less growth and failed to reproduce. Active selection by lizards of areas with more favorable moisture regimes has to my knowledge, yet to be demonstrated. Local habitat selection to allow growth and reproduction in an otherwise unfavorable environment is perhaps a viable adaptation only in invertebrates, where use can be made of variation at the microhabitat level.

Migration

Migratory birds and locusts can increase their chances of reproductive success by seeking rains and moving in and out of areas in accordance with existing local conditions at any given time. Thus, the major repro-ductive advantage birds and locusts have over other animals inhabiting deserts is their greater mobility. Although Russell, Smith, Gould & Austin

Animal processes

(1972) found the doves *Zenaida asiatica* and *Zenaida macroura* to breed in a Sonoran Desert study area, most of their food was obtained from agricultural areas to the east. In the same study area, ten out of twenty-two species of birds nesting there were visitors which timed their arrival with the summer rains. The nests of these visiting birds account for the greatest peak in bird breeding activity in this desert (Russell *et al.*, 1972). The migrants are present only during the nesting season and go elsewhere for the remainder of the year. For the most part, birds inhabiting Old-World deserts have a dual breeding range wherein only one brood is raised in the desert habitat (Ohmart, 1969). This can be observed in *Aimophila cassinii* in North America. This sparrow breeds in the spring in the Great Plains and after the summer rains breeds again in the Sonoran Desert (Ohmart, 1969).

Desert locusts have also been observed to migrate in relation to available precipitation. They apparently either follow barometric pressure gradients, or move downwind, which enables them to locate and breed in areas where rain is highly probable (low barometric pressure (Cloudsley-Thompson & Chadwick, 1964); or areas of wind convergence (Rainey, 1951)).

Timing

The timing of reproduction to fit local rainfall patterns appears to be important in a wide range of taxa. Peaks in reproductive activity are often associated with rainy periods. For some this implies breeding just prior to the rains, thus ensuring adequate food for the young, while others wait until after the onset of the rains. Short (1974) noted that parrots and woodpeckers nest just prior to the summer rains in the Sonoran Desert, and make the best use they can of the limited food available at that time. The young in these cases are fledged at a time when the food supply is greatly augmented by emerging insects. Females of the spider *Agelenopsis aperta* in a desert-grassland area in south-central New Mexico also lay their eggs just prior to the rains. Most of the adults suffer mortality with the advent of the rains and resultant flooding, but the embryos survive in the protected environment of the egg sac (Riechert, 1974). These spiderlings emerge concurrently with a tremendous increase in available prey associated with annual rains (Cloudsley-Thompson & Idris, 1964; Ghilarov, 1964, Ahearn, 1971; Riechert & Tracy, 1975).

On the other hand, populations of *Agelenopsis aperta* inhabiting other desert areas less subject to flooding, breed first in August and September (after the onset of the summer rains). This pattern appears to be characteristic of most desert animals, including other spiders inhabiting the desert grassland mentioned above (Riechert, unpublished data). Reproductive flights of alates in the leaf-cutter ant *Acromyrmex versicolor* in

802

the Chihuahuan Desert (Werner & Murray, 1972) and oviposition in the Tanganyikan locust *Nomadacris septem fasciata* (Woodrow, 1965), are both initiated by annual rains. Various birds, rodents, and most Amphibia also breed only after the rains have arrived.

Some of the taxa mentioned above limit their breeding activity to specific seasons, whereas others breed whenever rains are associated with moderate temperatures. The larks (Alaudidae) in the Namib Desert, which breed principally following summer rains (Willoughby, 1971), and North American desert spiders belong to the former group, while the desert snails *Eremina desertorum*, *Sphincterochila boissieri*, and *Trochoidea seetzeni* are representative of the latter group (Cloudsley-Thompson & Chadwick, 1964; Schmidt-Nielsen *et al.*, 1971; Yom-Tov, 1972). A few Amphibia can become sexually active and breed at any time of the year in water made available by rains (*Limnodynastes ornatus*, *Heleioporus pictus* and *Cyclorama platycephalus* (Buxton, 1923)). In addition, rain triggers the breeding seasons of a number of African birds, and Australian birds and marsupials (Keast & Marshall, 1954; Serventy & Marshall, 1957; Keast, 1959; Newsome, 1966; Brown, 1974). The very sight of rain in Australia stimulates birds to courtship (Immelmann, 1963). These birds are capable of immediate reproduction, since they maintain tonic gonadotropic activity in the hypothalamus–hypophysial axis (Dawson & Bartholomew, 1968).

Some of the rainy-weather breeders remain sexually active for most of the year, the rains merely being associated with increased breeding activity. Desert Amphibia which require permanent water are often included in this category, in that they exhibit extended breeding seasons in which they periodically lay clutches, water temperature and rainfall permitting (Main *et al.*, 1959; Bragg, 1965). A number of terrestrial desert insects can also be included in this category: they breed continuously, but show a marked numerical increase during periods of rainfall (grasshoppers (Chapman, 1962), the Lepidopteran *Aroga websteri* (Hsiao & Kirkland, 1973) and others (Riechert, unpublished data, 1971–74)). Some rodents are also capable of producing litters all the year round, but exhibit peaks in breeding activity corresponding to spring and times of annual rainfall, as exemplified by the Indian gerbil, *Tatera indica indica*, in the Rajasthan Desert (Prakash, Jain & Purohit, 1971). Red kangaroos (*Megaleia rufa* Desmaret) and euros (*Macropus robustus*) can breed continuously because they have an embryonic diapause and *post partum* estrus and mating (Frith & Sharman, 1964; Sadlier, 1965). This particular feature allows the animals to reproduce whenever nutritional well-being allows, and is not seen in temperate marsupials (Brown, 1974). The animals mentioned above are what one might consider opportunistic breeders (Ewer, 1968).

On a less dynamic scale, extended breeding seasons have been observed in Sonoran Desert birds which make a second attempt at nesting following the summer rains only if an earlier attempt in the spring has failed (Short, 1974). Given good rainfall, *Lepus alleni* also exhibits a lengthened breeding season in North American desert areas (Hungerford *et al.*, 1974).

In regions characterized by two periods of rainfall, such as the Indian deserts and the Sonoran and Chihuahuan Deserts of North America, animals may respond to one or both of the seasons with reproductive activity. Animals in the North American deserts which breed principally following winter rains include those which rely on green vegetation for nutrition; in the spring, nutritional health improves, fat is stored, and breeding takes place. This is especially characteristic of reptiles (Marshall & Hook, 1960; Saint Girons, 1962; Mayhew, 1963, 1965*a*, 1966*a*, *b*, 1967, 1968; Wilhoft, 1963; Lofts,Phillips & Tam, 1966; Zweifel & Lowe, 1966; Hoddenbach & Turner, 1968; Turner *et al.*, 1969, 1974; Kay *et al.*, 1970; Shammakov, Ataev & Kamalova, 1973). In desert habitats, the North American lagomorphs *Lepus alleni, L. californicus* and *Sylvilagus auduboni* also exhibit the greatest reproductive activity after the inception of winter rain, though earlier than seen in the reptiles (Sowls, 1957; Stout, 1970; Hungerford *et al.*, 1974). On the other hand, desert representatives of the Heteromyid genera *Perognathus* and *Dipodomys* and the Cricetid genus, *Peromyscus*, first breed in early summer (Reichman & Van De Graaf, 1973). Resident birds usually breed in spring following the winter rains (Russell *et al.*, 1972; Russell *et al.*, 1973; Short, 1974). Although nutritional state influences reproductive activity in some taxa, it appears less important in others. *Ambystoma tigrinum* Green, for instance, breeds in the spring, irrespective of whether the past winter was favorable (Webb, 1969) and six species of Indian rodents exhibit both spring and post-monsoonal peaks in reproductive activity (Prakash, 1971), independent of nutritional condition. Spring breeding activity in these animals and others is apparently triggered by day length rather than by available moisture or nutritional state.

Some of the animals mentioned here will breed again following the summer rains. Resident Sonoran birds often start second nests at this time (Russell *et al.*, 1972), and if there is rain the tiger salamander will breed again (Webb, 1969). Of the resident birds only *Aimophila carpalis* (Coutts) (Short, 1974), *Geococcyx californianus* (Lesson) (Ohmart, 1969), *Pipilo fuscus* Swainson, and *Toxostoma curvirostre* (Swainson) (Ohmart, 1973) exhibit a definite bimodality in breeding. As mentioned earlier, other North American desert birds maintain a lengthened breeding season with one attempt at summer breeding, if the spring attempt fails.

Although some lizards and snakes will produce additional clutches following the summer rains (Lowe, 1942; Klauber, 1956; Blair, 1960; Johnson, 1960; Chapman & Chapman, 1964; Mayhew, 1971), the females of other species are refractory to stimulation of the estrus cycle at this

804

time, since fat bodies are needed for yolk production (Darveskii, 1960; Hahn & Tinkle, 1965; Tinkle & Irwin, 1965; Zweifel & Lowe, 1966; Hahn, 1967). This inhibition of fall breeding may increase chances for survival to the next spring, at which time there is a greater probability of reproductive success (Zweifel & Lowe, 1966; Mayhew, 1968; Tinkle, 1969).

One other variation in the timing of reproduction is observed in desert animals. Some species stagger reproductive activities, so that all females are not ready to breed at the same time (the Amphibia *Scaphiopus couchi* Baird (Strecker, 1908), *Bufo punctatus* (Tevis, 1966), *Bufo woodhousei* Girard (Bragg, 1940*a, b*; Clark & Bragg, 1950)). For desert spiders such staggering might reflect individual variations in feeding success, which, if great enough, will affect the timing of maturity and breeding activity (Riechert, personal observations).

Heat stress

Desert animals exhibit numerous behavioral and physiological adaptations to ensure survival under temperature extremes (see Chapter 31 above). Some of the mechanisms developed against temperature stress are associated with the reproductive system as well. The genital systems of some desert lizards, for instance, are tolerant of high temperatures. Spermatogenesis in the lizards *Dipsosaurus dorsalis* (Mayhew, 1971) and *Uma scoparia* (Licht & Basu, 1967) can occur at higher temperatures than for other vertebrates. Spermatogenesis may also be limited to cool nights during the summer months (Mayhew, 1968). This phenomenon is observed in some desert birds as well (Riley, 1937).

At least in the marsupials, physiological and morphological mechanisms have developed which maintain testes temperature within a tolerable range. Male euros and red kangaroos are capable of breeding throughout the year, since they possess retia mirabilia which reduce hypoxia and heat-induced sterility (Sadlier, 1965); blood flow can thus be increased to the testes when testicular temperature rises (Setchell & Thorburn, 1969). Mayhew (1968), in a review of reproduction in desert lizards, expresses the view that there is little correlation between breeding and temperature in this group. Lizards are described as being heliothermic, in that they can modify temperature stresses by behavioral means (Cowles & Bogert, 1944; Bogert, 1949; Norris, 1953; Cowles, 1962; Mayhew, 1962*b*). One need only look in the literature on adaptive behavior for reducing and avoiding temperature stresses in desert animals (see Chapters 31 and 32), to realize that temperature problems which might arise in the act of reproduction or breeding can probably be behaviorally avoided. Those animal taxa which are unable to tolerate or behaviorally avoid temperature extremes during summer months for the most part estivate or undergo torpor. These

805

Animal processes

animals clearly will not be engaged in reproductive activities during this period. For instance the cactus mouse, *Peromyscus eremicus* Baird, estivates for 6 to 8 weeks in the summer, when its lowered metabolic rate allows escape from water and nutritional demands during the hottest months (MacMillen, 1965). This and other estivating mammals are in a state of torpor and do not carry out any normal activities.

Development

In general, the young of most animals are more susceptible to environmental stresses than are the adults. Desert animals are no exception to this generalization (Noy-Meir, 1974). While adults can avoid temperature and water stresses by means of behavior and associated movements, the behavioral repertoire and motor coordination of the young are inadequate to allow for such avoidance behavior. In the developing embryo, it is absent altogether. Since the desert environment is not only harsh, but highly variable and unpredictable, survival to maturity must be improbable for any given individual. Tinkle (1967) found a juvenile survivorship of over 20% to be rare in the lizard *Uta stansburiana*, and less than 10% of the population was estimated to live more than one year. The average life span of any given individual of *U. stansburiana* is only 18.5 weeks. The mortality rate is at least as high as this during the development of Amphibia, where temporary pools frequently dry up before metamorphosis is completed (Bragg, 1950*b*).

In this kind of environment, hatching and developmental success must depend, at least in part, on the selection of suitable nesting sites by the parents, and on any care or benefits they may offer the young during development. There must also be selection for rapid development in animals inhabiting the desert. Finally, morphological and physiological mechanisms may be developed to limit temperature and water stress.

Parental action

Nutritional state

Hatching and developmental success is first influenced by the nutritional state of the females. In some taxa of reptiles and mammals, embryos are reabsorbed and the female does not come into estrus if she is not in good nutritional health. It appears, however, that invertebrates and Amphibia will initiate reproductive activities without the accumulation of fat reserves. In the spider *Agelenopsis aperta* there is a linear relationship between the fat reserves built up by the females and the amount of yolk provided to each egg (Riechert & Tracy, 1975). Since the young spiderlings rely on the yolk for food while in the egg sac and before the first capture

806

attempt, it is to be expected that additional yolk will increase the probability of survival for individuals possessing it. These individuals can live for a longer period without prey, and are probably larger and stronger at the time of their first attempt to capture prey than are spiderlings receiving less yolk. The difference between these spiders which reproduce somewhat independently of nutritional health, and the higher vertebrates in which reproduction is more closely coupled to nutritional state, is a matter of life strategy. In an annual animal, such as a spider, it is probably better to reproduce, even though poorly, than not at all. On the other hand, an animal with a longer life-span may succeed better by ensuring survival of members of its reproductive class, and producing offspring only at times when they are most likely to survive. This subject has been considered at length by Tinkle (1969) and others in relation to the evolution of life histories of the lizard group, some of which are short-lived and others long-lived.

Nest-site selection

The placement of eggs and nests must surely influence the survival of the young. Most desert animals are fairly selective both in choosing a habitat in which to carry out normal activity and in selecting a nesting or breeding location. Mayhew (1968) presents an extensive review of Amphibian selection of breeding sites; some species require permanent pools for breeding, others prefer temporary pools, and some even make use of terrestrial habitats. Following a rain, the males of the frog genus *Heleioporus* dig burrows in which eggs are laid in a frothy mass at the bottom (Parker, 1940; Main, Lee & Littlejohn, 1958; Lee, 1967; Mayhew, 1968). Members of the genus *Breviceps* lay eggs in burrows, lined with mucus (De Villiers, 1929; Fitzsimons & Van Dam, 1929; Rose, 1962; Poynton, 1964), and *Pseudophryne occidentalis* lays its eggs in tunnels beneath the ground litter (Main, 1965). The type of habitat chosen reflects the developmental needs of the larvae of the various species. Zweifel (1968) found embryonic development in the frog *Rana pipiens* to be the slowest of all the species studied. The adults of this species breed only in permanent pools. On the other hand, spadefoot toads, *Scaphiopus* spp., have a very short metamorphosis time and adults of this genus breed in temporary rain pools. In the terrestrial frogs, rain may or may not be necessary to complete development (Fitzsimons & Van Dam, 1929; De Villiers, 1929; Main *et al.*, 1959), depending on the species. *Pseudophryne occidentalis* and *Heliophora* sp. require flooding for successful development, while *Breviceps parvus* needs no water.

Egg-laying sites in some invertebrate species are correlated with embryonic needs as well. Breeding desert locusts, *Schistocerca gregaria*,

807

actively seek areas where rain is probable (Rainey, 1951; Cloudsley-Thompson & Chadwick, 1964). The eggs of this locust require moist conditions for development (Hunter-Jones, 1964), and eggs are not laid unless such conditions are available (Norris, 1968).

With the exception of the ostrich, *Struthio camelus* (Buxton, 1923), few birds have eggs which can withstand exposure to the sun. Owls, doves and swifts inhabiting desert areas nest only in caves or in holes in large cacti. Russell *et al.* (1972) found that nesting success in a Sonoran Desert study area was correlated with the amount of protection afforded the eggs. Birds either nesting in holes or having enclosed nests, *Colaptes chrysoides*, *Myiarchus tyrannulus*, *Auriparus flaviceps*, and *Otus asio*, had more offspring hatching and surviving to fledge than did other species.

Parental care

Parental care of the offspring is common in desert birds and mammals. Almost all the young of two desert marsupials, the red kangaroo and euro, survive to leave the pouch (Brown, 1974). In part, this success is related to the fact that breeding is limited to times when the mother is in a good nutritional state, and also to the protection afforded by the brood pouch. The capability of the mother to carry her offspring with her must also benefit the young.

Birds which do not typically nest in shaded areas in desert habitats demonstrate behavior which tends to lower egg temperature. Ponomareva & Grazhdankin (1973) found that, although sixteen bird species used different types of behavior to protect the young on the nest, the end result in all cases was to prevent external factors from affecting nest temperature. A ground-dwelling bird of the north African deserts, *Pterocles* spp., presents a unique example of this phenomenon. The parent dampens the eggs and soil around the nest with its breast feathers which become wetted while the bird drinks (Buxton, 1923; Cloudsley-Thompson & Chadwick, 1964). The white-winged dove, *Zenaida asiatica* (L.), an inhabitant of the Sonoran Desert, frequently builds its nest on cholla, *Opuntia* sp. and on the peripheral branches of trees. In such places, the nests may receive considerable solar radiation. The adult birds have unusually low body temperatures, and the brood patch serves as a heat sink to the eggs (Russell, 1969). The male exhibits a lower body temperature than the female, and it is he that tends the eggs during the hottest part of the day. The eggs of another Sonoran bird species, *Geococcyx californianus*, are also relatively exposed in nests in *Opuntia versicolor*. Since adaptations to avoid heat are not developed in the hatchlings until they are 3 to 5 days old, the adults must tend them continuously until this stage (Ohmart, 1973; Lowe & Hinds, 1969). Coinciding with the development of thermoregulatory mechanisms in the young is the increasing need for the adults to spend the warmer part of the day in search of lizards to feed them.

It is apparent from this discussion that the degree of parental care and nest-site selection are inversely related. Bird species nesting in shaded or protected locations offer the eggs and young less constant attention than do those with exposed nests. Since predation by snakes is a major source of mortality in the nest (Russell *et al.*, 1972), perhaps nest-tending serves two adaptive functions in species with more exposed nests.

Physiological and morphological adaptations

Adaptations exhibited by embryos and juvenile animals can be grouped into three categories: (*a*) severe conditions can be avoided by quiescence or dormancy, embryonic development continuing when favorable conditions become available; (*b*) the speed of development can be increased, thereby exposing the most susceptible stage of the life cycle to stress conditions for as short a period as possible; or (*c*) there may be morphological or physiological adaptations which either permit avoidance of stresses or make the developmental stages more tolerant to these conditions.

Suspended development

Suspended development with decreased activity and metabolism is common in the life cycles of many desert invertebrates, including most aquatic crustacea (Rzóska, 1961; Cole, 1968), many insects (Shulov & Pener, 1963; Jaeger, 1965; Wallace, 1968; Huque & Juleel, 1970), mites (Wallace, 1970, 1971) and nematodes (Mankau *et al.*, 1973). Dormancy is also known for at least one fish genus. The eggs of the cyprinodont, *Nothobranchius*, in East Africa can survive desiccation for several seasons, and upon introduction of water reach sexual maturity within 8 to 10 weeks (Peters, 1963). Although desert grasshoppers and various locusts are known to survive 3 years in the egg stage (Jaeger, 1965; Schmoller, 1970), the capacity for quiescence reaches its culmination, perhaps, in members of the Branchiopod order Notostraca (tadpole shrimps), whose eggs can stay in dust for up to 15 years (Buxton, 1923). For the organisms mentioned above, the egg stage is more tolerant to adverse conditions than is any other stage. Nematodes, for instance, are basically aquatic organisms which, while inhabiting the soil, require a film of water around them. Adult nematodes are, thus, under osmotic stress during the dry season in the desert, whereas the eggs resist desiccation completely (Mankau *et al.*, 1973). In the diapause state, arthropod eggs are also resistant to heat. Laboratory experiments have shown that the eggs of *Triops granarius* can survive temperatures up to 98 °C for sixteen hours (Carlisle, 1968). The capacity of the egg stage to undergo quiescence alleviates the necessity for timing of reproductive activity to fit a favorable environment, and is observed in taxa which reproduce continuously under favorable conditions. In some arthropods, larvae are also capable of tiding over harsh times through cryptobiosis. Although larvae of *Polypedilum vanderplancki* Hint. cannot withstand exposure to temperatures exceeding 43 °C for any length of time, in the cryptobiotic state they are capable of surviving brief exposures to temperatures between 102 °C and 104 °C (Hinton, 1960).

Developing eggs and larval stages of other desert animals are far less resistant to desiccation. Although turtle eggs can resist water loss through a leathery shell, most lizard eggs require high humidity at least, and some need water as well (*Sceloporus orcutti* (Mayhew, 1963, 1968), *Crotaphytus collaris* (Clark, 1946)). As in lizards, many snake eggs require moisture (Stebbins, 1954; Mendelssohn, 1963, 1965; Dmi'el, 1967). Increases in size and weight observed in incubating lizard and arthropod eggs are thought to be the result of water intake (Simkins & Asama, 1930; Bellairs, 1959; Mulherkar, 1962; Bustard, 1966; Pandha & Thapliyal, 1967; Browning, 1969). (In desert locusts, at least, water can be absorbed against an osmotic gradient (Browning, 1969)). An external water supply appears to be necessary for egg development in these taxa; eggs of *Sceloporus undulatus* showing an increase of less than 50% in size fail to complete development (Cunningham & Hurwitz, 1936; Cunningham & Huene, 1938). Larval development of desert grasshoppers and locusts also ceases when the environment becomes dry (Hunter-Jones & Lambert, 1961; Hunter-Jones, 1964; Shulov, 1970).

Rate of development

The eggs of desert animals appear to develop more rapidly than those inhabiting other biomes. For instance the desert Copepoda *Metacyclops minutus* and *Metadiaptomus mauretanicus* reach adulthood in two days of the existence of a pool, Phyllopoda achieve medium size in a week in African temporary pools and Conchostraca mature in 5 days (Rzóska, 1961; Cole, 1968). Desert Amphibia also develop rapidly. Most amphibian eggs hatch in a matter of hours, and in some metamorphosis is reached in a little over a week (Mayhew, 1968; Zweifel, 1968).

The rapid development of desert embryos is, at least in part, related to temperature. Increased temperature within a tolerable range was found to increase significantly the rate of development of eggs of dragonflies (Hodgkin & Watson, 1958), Amphibia (Zweifel, 1968) and the desert locust, *Schistocerca gregaria* (Husain, 1937; Hamilton, 1950; Hunter-Jones, 1970). In general, the relationship between temperature and growth in insects is best represented by a simple sigmoid curve, with the relationship inverted when the temperature is above an optimum (Stinner, Gutierrez & Butler, 1974), though work with desert locusts indicates that the relationship is linear in this species until a critical thermal maximum is reached (Hunter-Jones, 1970). Many Amphibia spend their larval lives in temporary pools. As these pools dry, water temperature rises, which in turn increases the rate of development of the larvae, allowing some to reach metamorphosis before the pool dries entirely (Brown, 1967; Zweifel, 1968).

In endothermic animals, characteristics conferring survival value on the juvenile develop early. The relatively exposed young of *Geococcyx californianus* rapidly develop features which facilitate thermoregulation. A favorable surface–mass ratio, black skin, gular flutter and salt-secreting nasal glands are functioning between the third and fifth day after hatching (Lowe & Hinds, 1969; Ohmart, 1973). These features permit the young to maintain a fairly balanced temperature while the parents are out procuring lizards during the morning hours (Ohmart, 1973).

The nestlings of some Old World desert bird species exhibit early behavioral and physiological thermoregulation as well. Ponomareva & Grazhdankin (1973) found the young of open-nesting species to tolerate short-term hypothermia and fluctuations in body temperature of up to 12°. The nestlings of the turtle dove, *Streptopelia senegalensis* were alone able to handle long-term heat stress, presumably through energy expenditure in pharynx quivering. The tympanic bullae and hind limbs of the jerboa *Jaculus jaculus butleri* develop rapidly at the expense of the rest of the body. These two features are already of adult size by the time the animal is ready to leave the nest. Happold (1970) suggests that acute hearing and locomotion are needed to escape the heavy predation pressures on young jerboas in the desert, where little cover is available. Growth in *Dipodomys merriami* Mearns is much more uniform than in the jerboa. This animal attains 82% of adult size within fifteen days after birth (Butterworth, 1961). Allometric ontogenetic growth contributes to this noted post-natal growth (Van De Graaf, 1973).

Temperature tolerance

Physiological and morphological adaptations to increased temperatures experienced during embryonic development have been studied largely in researches on desert Amphibia. Since most Amphibia require water for embryonic development, and natural desert habitats offer a limited supply of permanent pools in which breeding can take place, the larval stages of many species will encounter high and varied temperatures in temporary rain pools. Zweifel (1968) lists three adaptations to temperature in embryos of desert Amphibia: (*a*) there is a tolerance at early embryonic stages to

811

a temperature range which is species-specific; (*b*) this range of tolerance increases as development proceeds; and (*c*) egg masses exhibit various absorbing properties to solar radiation. Individual species might exhibit any combination of these adaptations. As a general rule, the more temporary the pool that is selected for breeding, the more tolerant are the larval stages to high temperatures. Solar radiation will penetrate these shallow pools and greatly increase the temperature in them as compared to springs or eddy pools in desert streams. Spadefoot toads, *Scaphiopus*, all breed in temporary pools, can tolerate high temperatures, and develop rapidly (Zweifel, 1968). *Rana pipiens*, however, requires permanent waters, its larvae are intolerant to temperature extremes, and development is slow (Zweifel, 1968).

Most desert Amphibia exhibit an increased tolerance to temperature extremes with developmental age. Delson & Whitford (1973) found that *Ambystoma tigrinum* exhibits an increasingly higher thermal maximum with development to the neotonic adult stage. Zweifel (1968) found this to be the case in most of the species he tested. This increase in temperature tolerance occurs at both ends of the temperature range, resulting in a broader range of tolerance in later larval stages (Atlas, 1935; Schechtman & Olson, 1941; Moore, 1942; Brown, 1967; Herreid & Kinney, 1967; Zweifel, 1968). Acclimation may account for some of the observed increases in tolerance. In all of the species mentioned above, acclimation temperatures and lethal temperatures are positively correlated (Brown, 1969). Thus there appears to be a direct relationship between the previous thermal history of an organism and its heat resistance (Fry, 1958). It follows that thermal tolerance would be expected to increase independently of age as water temperatures rise in drying rain pools.

Zweifel (1968) also observed some species differences in the pigmentation of amphibian eggs, which he thought might have some adaptive significance. The dark melanin of the ovum of *Rana pipiens* might increase the absorptivity to solar radiation and thus help raise embryonic temperature in cold permanent pools (Zweifel, 1968). However, he also noted that eggs of *Scaphiopus couchii* are darkly pigmented. In this inhabitant of temporary pools, melanin possibly serves to shield the embryos from ultraviolet radiation. The adaptive significance of melanin to embryonic development in desert amphibians has yet to be fully understood.

Overview

It is clear from this presentation that the physical environment of the desert has strongly influenced the reproductive and developmental processes exhibited by animal inhabitants. Although the daily extremes in temperature place limits on development, it is the unpredictability of precipitation that most interferes with the process of reproduction in the desert habitat. The response of animal inhabitants has been to obtain as flexible a reproductive schedule as possible, given the existing alternatives within various taxonomic groups. We can consider this flexibility analogous to the open genetic system proposed by Mayr (1964, 1974) to account for the modification of behavior by experience in some animal groups. Desert animals appear to possess a reproductive program with sufficient checks and flexibility to allow adjustment to existing environmental conditions.

Adjustments to environment may occur at different steps in the reproductive process in the various taxa. For instance, breeding itself is curtailed during drought years in many groups through the absence of some stimulus related to rainfall. Reproduction may also be regulated at the level of implantation, in that the probability of reabsorption of the embryos is dependent on the physical state of the dam, which is indirectly related to the stimulation of vegetation growth by rainfall. The production of offspring in some long-lived lizards and many desert rodents appears to be controlled in this manner. Following hatching, there may be some mechanism developed for differential survival of the offspring in the event that the environment proves unfavorable. Such a facultative system has been observed in the desert roadrunner, *Geococcyx californianus* (Ohmart, 1973). This bird exhibits an asynchronous production of eggs. Older hatchlings are better able to compete for food than are their younger siblings and, if food is in short supply, these older birds receive more food. The parents are, in a sense, able to adjust clutch size behaviorally to conditions existing in any given nesting season; the smaller nestlings are eventually eaten by the parents, if there is a food shortage. Finally, reproductive efforts may be renewed given failure in prior attempts. Animals exhibiting continuous or extended breeding seasons are facultative in this respect.

No real correspondence exists between the type of facultative mechanism utilized and phylogenetic position. For instance, certain insects, amphibian and bird species may all exhibit continuous breeding. It is fitting that animals respond to a highly variable environment with reproductive flexibility. Local extinctions would be of frequent occurrence, if this were not the case.

References

Ahearn, G. A. (1971). Ecological factors affecting population sampling of desert Tenebrionid beetles. *American Midland Naturalist*, **86**, 385–406.

Atlas, M. (1935). The effect of temperature on the development of *Rana pipiens*. *Physiological Zoology*, **8**, 290–310.

Balda, R. P., Bateman, G. C. & Vaughan, T. A. (1972). *Diets, food preferences,* and reproductive cycles of some desert rodents. US/IBP Desert Biome Research Memorandum, R.M. 72–29, 1–32. Logan, Utah.

Beatley, J. C. (1969). Dependence of desert rodents on winter annuals and precipitation. *Ecology*, **50**, 721–4.

Bellairs, A. de'A. (1959). Reproduction in lizards and snakes. *New Biology*, **30**, 73–90.

Blair, W. F. (1960). *The Rusty Lizard, a Population Study*. University of Texas Press, Austin.

Bodenheimer, F. S. (1954). Problems of physiology and ecology of desert animals. In: *Biology of Deserts* (ed. J. L. Cloudsley-Thompson). Institute of Biology, London.

Bogert, C. M. (1949). Thermoregulation and eccritic body temperatures in Mexican lizards of the genus *Sceloporus*. *Anales Del Instituto de Biologia Universidad Nacional Autonoma de Mexico*, **20**, 415–26.

Bradley, W. G. & Mauer, R. A. (1971). Reproduction and food habits of Merriam's kangaroo rat, *Dipodomys merriami*, *Journal of Mammalogy*, **52** (3), 497–507.

Bragg, A. N. (1940a). Observations on the ecology and natural history of Anura. II. Habits, habitat, and breeding of *Bufo woodhousei* Girard in Oklahoma. *American Midland Naturalist*, **24**, 306–21.

Bragg, A. N. (1940b). Observations on the ecology and natural history of Anura. III. The ecological distribution of Anura of Cleveland County, Oklahoma, with notes on the habits of several species. *American Midland Naturalist*, **24**, 322–35.

Bragg, A. N. (1950a). Salientian breeding dates in Oklahoma. In: *Researches on the Amphibia of Oklahoma*. University of Oklahoma Press, Norman, Oklahoma.

Bragg, A. N. (1950b). Some adaptations of survival value in spadefoot toads. In: *Researches on the Amphibia of Oklahoma*. University of Oklahoma Press, Norman, Oklahoma.

Bragg, A. N. (1856). In quest of the spadefoots. *New Mexico Quarterly*, **25**, 345–58.

Bragg, A. N. (1965). *Gnomes of the Night*. University of Pennsylvania Press, Philadelphia.

Brown, G. D. (1974). The biology of marsupials of the Australian arid zone. *Australian Mammalogy*, **1**, 269–88.

Brown, H. A. (1967). High temperature tolerance of the eggs of a desert anuran, *Scaphiopus hammondii*. *Copeia*, 265–70.

Brown, H. A. (1969). The heat resistance of some anuran tadpoles (Hylidae and Pelobatidae). *Copeia*, 1969, 138–47.

Browning, T. O. (1969). Permeability to water of the shell of the egg of *Locusta migratoria migratorioides* with observations on the egg of *Teleogryllus commodus*. *Journal of Experimental Biology*, **51**, 99–105.

Bustard, H. R. (1966). Notes on the eggs, incubation and young of the bearded dragon, *Amphibolurus barbatus barbatus* (Cuvier). *British Journal of Herpetology*, **3**, 252–9.

Butler, G. (1970). Terrestrial invertebrate specialists meeting (minutes), US/IBP Desert Biome Invertebrate Meeting.

Butterworth, B. B. (1961). A comparative study of growth and development of the kangaroo rats, *Dipodomys deserti* Stephens and *Dipodomys merriami* Mearns. *Growth*, **25**, 127–39.

Buxton, P. A. (1923). *Animal Life in Deserts*. Arnold, London.

Carlisle, D. B. (1968). *Triops* (Entomostraca) eggs killed only by boiling. *Science*, **161**, 279–80.

Chapman, R. F. (1962). The ecology and distribution of grasshoppers in Ghana. *Proceedings of the Zoological Society of London*, **139**, 1–66.

Chapman, B. M. & Chapman, R. F. (1964). Observations on the biology of the lizard *Agama agama* in Ghana. *Proceedings of the Zoological Society of London*, **143**, 121–32.

Clark, C. B. & Bragg, A. N. (1950). A comparison of the ovaries of two species of *Bufo* with different ecological requirements. In: *Researches on the Amphibia of Oklahoma*. University of Oklahoma Press, Norman, Oklahoma.

Clark, H. (1946). Incubation and respiration of eggs of *Crotaphytus c. collaris* (Say). *Herpetologica*, **3**, 136–9.

Cloudsley-Thompson, J. L. & Chadwick, M. J. (1964). *Life of Deserts*. Dufour, Philadelphia.

Cloudsley-Thompson, J. L. & Idris, B. E. M. (1964). The insect fauna of the desert near Khartoum: seasonal fluctuation and the effect of grazing. *Proceedings of the Royal Entomological Society of London* (A), **39**, 41–6.

Cole, G. A. (1968). Desert Limnology. In: *Desert Biology* (ed. G. W. Brown, Jr.), vol. I, pp. 423–86. Academic Press, New York & London.

Cowles, R. B. (1962). Semantics in biothermal studies. *Science*, **135**, 670.

Cowles, R. B. & Bogert, C. M. (1944). A preliminary study of the thermal requirements of desert reptiles. *Bulletin of the American Museum of Natural History*, **83**, 265–96.

Crawford, C. S. (1974). *The role of Orthoporus ornatus millipedes in a desert ecosystem*. US/IPB Desert Biome Research Memorandum, R.M. 74–34, pp. 77–88. Logan, Utah.

Cunningham, B. & Huene, E. (1938). Further studies on water adsorption by reptile eggs. *American Naturalist*, **72**, 380–85.

Cunningham, B. & Hurwitz, A. P. (1936). Water adsorption by reptile eggs during incubation. *American Naturalist*, **70**, 590–95.

Darevskii, I. A. (1960). Sezonnye izmeneniya zhirovykh tel i gonad u nekotorykh yashcherits doliny reki Araks v Armenii. *Zoologicheskii Zhurnal*, **39**, 1209–17.

Dawson, W. R. & Bartholomew, G. A. (1968). Temperature regulation and water economy of desert birds. In: *Desert Biology* (ed. G. W. Brown, Jr.), Vol. I, pp. 357–94. Academic Press, New York & London.

Delson, J. & Whitford, W. G. (1973). Critical thermal maxima in several life history stages in desert and montane populations of *Ambystoma tigrinum*. *Herpetologica*, **2**, 352–5.

De Villiers, C. (1929). Some features of the early development of *Breviceps*. *Annals of the Transvaal Museum*, **13**, 151–2.

Dmi'el, R. (1967). Studies on reproduction, growth, and feeding in the snake *Spalerosophis cliffordi* (Colubridae). *Copeia*, 332–46.

Ewer, R. F. (1968). A preliminary survey of the behaviour in captivity of the dasyurid marsupial, *Sminthopsis crassicaudata* (Gould.). *Zeitschrift für Tierpsychologie*, **25**, 319–65.

Fitzsimons, V. F. M. & Van Dam, G. (1929). Some observations on the breeding habits of *Breviceps*. *Annals of the Transvaal Museum*, **13**, 152–3.

Franz, C. E., Reichman, O. J. & Van De Graaf, K. M. (1973). *Diets, food preferences and reproductive cycles of some desert rodents*. US/IBP Desert Biome Research Memorandum, R.M. 73–24, pp. 1–128. Logan, Utah.

Frith, H. J. & Sharman, G. B. (1964). Breeding in wild populations of the red kangaroo *Megaleia rufa*. *CSIRO Wildlife Research*, **9**, 86–114.

Animal processes

Fry, F. E. J. (1958). Temperature compensation. *Annual Review of Physiology*, **20**, 207–24.

Ghilarov, M. S. (1964). Osnovnye napravleniya prisposoblenii nasekomykh k zhizni v pustyne. *Zoologicheskii Zhurnal*, **43**, 443–54.

Gosner, K. L. & Black, J. H. (1955). The effects of temperature and moisture on the reproductive cycles of *Scaphiopus h. holbrooki*. *American Midland Naturalist*, **54**, 192–203.

Hahn, W. E. (1967). Estradiol-induced vitellinogenesis and concomitant fat mobilization in the lizard *Uta stansburiana*. *Comparative Biochemistry & Physiology*, **23**, 83–93.

Hahn, W. E. & Tinkle, D. W. (1965). Fat body cycling and experimental evidence for its adaptive significance to ovarian follicle development in the lizard *Uta stansburiana*. *Journal of Experimental Zoology*, **158**, 79–86.

Hamilton, A. G. (1950). Further studies on the relation of humidity and temperature to the development of two species of African locusts – *Locusta migratoria migratorioides* (R. and F.) and *Schistocerca gregaria* (Forsk.). *Transactions Royal Entomological Society of London, Series A*, **101**, 1–58.

Happold, D. C. D. (1970). Reproduction and development of the Sudanese jerboa, *Jaculus jaculus butleri* (Rodentia, Dipodidae). *Journal of Zoology, London*, **162**, 505–15.

Herreid, C. F., II & Kinney, S. (1967). Temperature and development of the wood frog, *Rana sylvatica*, in Alaska. *Ecology*, **48**, 579–90.

Hinton, H.E. (1960). Cryptobiosis in the larva of *Polypedilum vanderplanki* Hint. *Journal of Insect Physiology*, **5**, 286–300.

Hoddenbach, G. A. & Turner, F. B. (1968). Clutch size of the lizard *Uta stansburiana* in southern Nevada. *American Midland Naturalist*, **80**, 262–5.

Hodgkin, E. P. & Watson, J. A. L. (1958). Breeding of dragon flies in temporary waters. *Nature (London)*, **181**, 1015–16.

Hsiao, T. H. & Kirkland, R. L. (1973). *Demographic studies of sagebrush insects as functions of various environmental factors*. US/IBP Desert Biome Research Memorandum, R.M. 73–34, pp. 1–28. Logan, Utah.

Hungerford, C. R., Lowe, C. H. & Madson, R. L. (1973). *Population studies of the desert cottontail* (Sylvilagus auduboni) *and black-tailed jackrabbit* (Lepus californicus) *in the Sonoran Desert*. US/IBP Desert Biome Research Memorandum, R.M. 73–20, pp. 1–15. Logan, Utah.

Hungerford, C. R., Lowe, C. H. & Madson, R. L. (1974). *Population studies of the desert cottontail* (Sylvilagus auduboni), *blacktailed jackrabbit* (Lepus californicus) *and Allen's jackrabbit* (Lepus alleni) *in the Sonoran Desert*. US/IBP Desert Biome Research Memorandum, R.M. 74–23, pp. 73–93. Logan, Utah.

Hunter-Jones, P. (1964). Egg development in the desert locust (*Schistocerca gregaria* Forsk.) in relation to the availability of water. *Proceedings of the Royal Entomological Society of London* (A), **39**, 25–33.

Hunter-Jones, P. (1970). The effect of constant temperature on egg development in the desert locust *Schistocerca gregaria* (Forsk.). *Bulletin of Entomological Research*, **59**, 707–18.

Hunter-Jones, P. & Lambert, J. G. (1961). Egg development of *Humbe tenuicornis* Schaum in relation to availability of water. *Proceedings of the Royal Entomological Society of London* (A), **36**, 75–80.

Huque, H. & Juleel, M. A. (1970). Temperature-induced quiescence in the eggs of the desert locust. *Journal of Economic Entomology*, **63**, 1398–1400.

Husain, M. A. (1937). A summary of investigations on the desert locust, *Schistocerca gregaria*, at Lyallpur during 1934–35. *Fourth International Locust Conference, Cairo*, Appendix 31.

Immelmann, K. (1963). Drought adaptations in Australian desert birds. *Proceedings of the 13th International Ornithological Congress, Ithaca, New York, 1962*, pp. 649–57.

Jaeger, E. C. (1965). *The California Deserts*. Stanford University Press, Stanford, California.

Johnson, C. (1960). Reproductive cycle in females of the greater earless lizards, *Holbrookia texana*. *Copeia* (1960), 297–300.

Kay, F. R., Miller, B. W. & Miller, C. L. (1970). Food habits and reproduction of *Callisaurus draconoides* in Death Valley, California. *Herpetologica*, **26**, 431–6.

Keast, A. (1959). Australian birds: their zoogeography and adaptations to an arid continent. In: *Biogeography and Ecology in Australia* (eds. A. Keast, R. L. Crocker & C. S. Christian) Monographiae Biologicae, vol. 8, 89–114. Junk, The Hague.

Keast, A. & Marshall, A. J. (1954). The influence of drought and rainfall on reproduction in Australian desert birds. *Proceedings of the Zoological Society of London*, **124**, 493–9.

Key, K. H. L. (1959). The ecology and biogeography of Australian grasshoppers and locusts. In: *Biogeography and Ecology in Australia* (eds. A. Keast, R. L. Crocker & C. S. Christian). Monographiae Biologicae, vol. 8, 192–210. Junk, The Hague.

Klauber, L. M. (1956). *Rattlesnakes*. University of California Press, Berkeley, California.

Lee, A. K. (1967). Studies in Australian Amphibia. II. Taxonomy, ecology, and evolution of the genus *Heleioporus* Gray (Anura: Leptodactylidae). *Australian Journal of Zoology*, **15**, 365–439.

Licht, P. (1973). Environmental influences on the testis cycles of the lizards *Dipsosaurus dorsalis* and *Xantusia vigilis*. *Comparative Biochemistry & Physiology*, **45**, 7–20.

Licht, P. & Basu, S. L. (1967). Influence of temperature on lizard testes. *Nature (London)*, **213**, 672–4.

Lofts, B., Phillips, J. G. & Tam, W. H. (1966). Seasonal changes in the testis of the cobra *Naja naja*. *General and Comparative Endocrinology*, **6**, 466–75.

Lowe, C. H. (1942). Notes on the mating of desert rattlesnakes. *Copeia* (1942), 261.

Lowe, C. H. & Hinds, D. S. (1969). Thermoregulation in desert populations of roadrunners and doves. In: *Physiological Systems in Semiarid Environments* (eds. C. C. Hoff and M. L. Riedesal). University of New Mexico Press, Albuquerque, New Mexico.

MacMillen, R. E. (1965). Aestivation in the cactus mouse, *Peromyscus eremicus*. *Comparative Biochemistry & Physiology*, **16**, 227–48.

Main, A. R. (1965). *Frogs of southern Western Australia*. Western Australian Naturalists' Club: Handbook No. 8.

Main, A. R., Lee, A. K. & Littlejohn, M. J. (1958). Evolution in three genera of Australian frogs. *Evolution*, **12**, 224–33.

817

Main, A. R., Littlejohn, M. J. & Lee, A. K. (1959). Ecology of Australian frogs. In: *Biogeography and Ecology in Australia* (eds. A. Keast, R. C. Crocker & C. S. Christian). Monographiae Biologicae, vol. 8, 396–411. Junk, The Hague.

Mankau, R., Sher, S. A. & Freckman, D. W. (1973). *Biology of nematodes in desert ecosystems.* US/IBP Desert Biome Research Memorandum, R.M. 73–7, pp. 1–22.

Marshall, A. J. & Hook, R. (1960). The breeding biology of equatorial vertebrates: reproduction of the lizard *Agama agama lionotus* Boulenger at latitude 0° 01′ N. *Proceedings of the Zoological Society of London,* **134**, 197–205.

Mayhew, W. W. (1962a). *Scaphiopus couchi* in California's Colorado Desert. *Herpetologica,* **18**, 153–61.

Mayhew, W. W. (1962b). Temperature preferences of *Sceloporus orcutti. Herpetologica,* **18**, 217–33.

Mayhew, W. W. (1963). Reproduction in the granite spiny lizards, *Sceloporus orcutti. Copeia* (1963), 144–52.

Mayhew, W. W. (1965a). Reproduction in the sand-dwelling lizard *Uma inornata. Herpetologica,* **21**, 39–55.

Mayhew, W. W. (1965b). Adaptations of the amphibian *Scaphiopus couchi* to desert conditions. *American Midland Naturalist,* **74**, 95–109.

Mayhew, W. W. (1966a). Reproduction in the psammophilous lizard *Uma scoparia, Copeia,* 1966, 114–22.

Mayhew, W. W. (1966b). Reproduction in the arenicolous lizard *Uma notata. Ecology,* **47**, 9–18.

Mayhew, W. W. (1967). Comparative reproduction in three species of the genus *Uma.* In: *Lizard Ecology: A Symposium* (ed. W. W. Milstead), pp. 48–61. University of Missouri Press, Columbia, Missouri.

Mayhew, W. W. (1968). Biology of desert amphibians, and reptiles. In: *Desert Biology* (ed. G. W. Brown, Jr.), vol. I, pp. 195–356. Academic Press, New York & London.

Mayhew, W. W. (1971). Reproduction in the desert lizard *Dipsosaurus dorsalis. Herpetologica,* **27** (1), 57–77.

Mayr, E. (1964). The evolution of living systems. *Proceedings of the National Academy of Science,* **51**, 934–41.

Mayr, E. (1974). Behavior programs and evolutionary strategies. *American Scientist,* **62**, 650–59.

Mendelssohn, H. (1963). On the biology of the venomous snakes of Israel. Part I. *Israel Journal of Zoology,* **12**, 143–70.

Mendelssohn, H. (1965). On the biology of the venomous snakes of Israel. Part II. *Israel Journal of Zoology,* **14**, 185–212.

Miller, M. R. (1954). Further observations on reproduction in the lizard *Xantusia vigilis. Copeia* (1954), 38–40.

Moore, J. A. (1942). Embryonic temperature tolerance and rate of development in *Rana catesbeiana. Biological Bulletin (Woods Hole),* **83**, 375–88.

Morag, M., Mali, J. & Furman, M. (1969). The effect of a desert climate on the lactation and on the fertility of the nursing rat. *International Journal of Biometeorology,* **13**, 61–8.

Mulherkar, L. (1962). Studies on the absorption of water by the eggs of the garden lizard *Calotes versicolor* (Daud) using Trypan Blue. *Proceedings of the National Institute of Science, India, B,* **28**, 94–9.

Myers, K. (1968). Physiology and rabbit ecology. *Proceedings of the Ecological Society of Australia*, **3**, 17.

Nagy, K. A. (1973). Behavior, diet and reproduction in a desert lizard, *Sauromalus obesus*. *Copeia*, 1973, 93–102.

Newsome, A. E. (1964). Anoestrus in the red kangaroo, *Megaleia rufa* (Desmarest). *Australian Journal of Zoology*, **12**, 9–17.

Newsome, A. E. (1966). The influence of food on breeding in the red kangaroo in Central Australia. *CSIRO Wildlife Research*, **11**, 187–96.

Norris, K. S. (1953). The ecology of the desert iguana *Dipsosaurus dorsalis*. *Ecology*, **34**, 265–87.

Norris, M. J. (1968). Laboratory experiments on oviposition responses of the desert locust *Schistocerca gregaria* (Forsk.). *Anti-Locust Bulletin*, **43**, 1–47.

Noy-Meir, I. (1974). Desert ecosystems: higher trophic levels. *Annual Review of Ecology & Systematics*, **5**, 195–214.

Ohmart, R. D. (1969). Dual breeding ranges in Cassin sparrow (*Aimophila cassini*). In: *Physiological Systems in Semiarid Environments* (eds. C. Clayton Hoff and Marvin L. Riedesel). University of New Mexico Press, Albuquerque, New Mexico.

Ohmart, R. D. (1973). Observations on the breeding adaptations of the road-runner. *Condor*, **75**, 140–49.

Pandha, S. K. & Thapliyal, J. P. (1967). Egg laying and development in the garden lizard, *Calotes versicolor*. *Copeia*, 1967, 121–5.

Parker, H. W. (1940). The Australian frogs of the family Leptodactylidae. *Novitates Zoologicae*, **42**, 1–106.

Peters N., Jr. (1963). Embryonale Anpassungen oviparer Zahnkarpfen aus periodisch austrocknenden Gewässern. *International Review of Hydrobiology*, **48**, 257–313.

Ponomareva, T. S. & Grazhdankin, A. V. (1973). Adaptatsiya ptentsov pustynnykh ptits k teplovomu vozdeistviyu sredy. *Zoologicheskii Zhurnal*, **52**, 1528–36.

Poynton, J. C. (1964). The amphibia of southern Africa. *Annals of the Natal Museum*, **17**, 1–334.

Prakash, I. (1971). Breeding season and litter size of Indian desert rodents. *Zeitschrift für Angewandte Zoologie*, **58**, 441–54.

Prakash, I., Jain, A. P. & Purohit, K. G. (1971). A note on the breeding and post-natal development of the Indian gerbil *Tatera indica indica* in Rajasthan Desert. *Säugetierkundliche Mitteilungen*, **19**, 375–80.

Prakash, I., Rana, B. D. & Jain, A. P. (1973). Reproduction in the cutch rock rat *Rattus cutchicus cutchicus* in the Indian Desert. *Mammalia*, **37**, 457–67.

Rainey, R. C. (1951). Weather and the movement of locust swarms: a new hypothesis. *Nature (London)*, **168**, 1057–60.

Reichman, O. J. & Van De Graaf, K. M. (1973). Seasonal activity and reproductive patterns of some species of Sonoran Desert rodents. *American Midland Naturalist*, **90**, 118–26.

Ricklefs, R. F. (1965). Brood reduction in the curve-billed thrasher. *Condor*, **67**, 505–10.

Riechert, S. E. (1973). 'The effects of thermal balance and prey availability on distribution patterns of the desert spider, *Agelenopsis aperta* (Gertsch).' Ph.D. Thesis. University of Wisconsin, Madison, Wisconsin.

Riechert, S. E. (1974). The pattern of local web distribution in a desert spider: mechanisms and seasonal variation. *Journal of Animal Ecology*, **43**, 733–45.

Animal processes

Riechert, S. E. (1976). Web-site selection in a desert spider. *Oikos*, **26**, 1–5.

Riechert, S. E. & Tracy, C. R. (1975). Thermal balance and prey availability: bases for a model relating web-site characteristics to spider reproductive success. *Ecology*, **56**, 265–84.

Riley, G. M. (1937). Experimental studies on spermatogenesis in the house sparrow, *Passer domesticus* (L.). *Anatomical Record*, **67**, 327–51.

Rose, W. (1962). *The Reptiles and Amphibians of southern Africa*. Maskew Miller, Capetown.

Ruibal, R., Tevis, L., Jr. & Roig, V. (1969). The terrestrial ecology of the spadefoot toad *Scaphiopus hammondi*. *Copeia*, 571–84.

Russell, S. M. (1969). Regulation of egg temperatures by incubant white-winged doves. In: *Physiological systems in Semiarid Environments* (eds. C. Clayton Hoff & Marvin L. Riedesel). University of New Mexico Press, Albuquerque, New Mexico.

Russell, S. M., Smith, E. L., Gould, P. & Austin, G. (1972). *Studies on Sonoran birds*. US/IBP Desert Biome Research Memorandum, RM 72–31, pp. 1–6. Logan, Utah.

Russell, S. M., Gould, P. J. & Smith, E. L. (1973). *Population structure, foraging behavior and daily movement of certain Sonoran Desert Birds*. US/IBP Desert Biome Research Memorandum, R.M. 73–27, pp. 1–20. Logan, Utah.

Rzóska, J. (1961). Observations on tropical rainpools and general remarks on temporary waters. *Hydrobiologia*, **17**, 265–86.

Sadlier, R. M. F. S. (1965). Reproduction in two species of kangaroo *Macropus robustus* and *Megaleia rufa* in the arid Pilbara region of Western Australia. *Proceedings of the Zoological Society of London*, **145**, 239–61.

Saint Girons, H. (1962). The reproductive cycle of the horned viper *Cerastes cerastes* (L.) in nature and in captivity. *Bulletin de la Société Zoologique de France*, **87**, 41–51.

Schechtman, A. M. & Olson, J. B. (1941). Unusual temperature tolerance of an amphibian egg (*Hyla regilla*). *Ecology*, **22**, 409–10.

Schmidt-Nielsen, K., Taylor, C. R. & Shkolnik, A. (1971). Desert snails: problems of heat, water and food. *Journal of Experimental Biology*, **55**, 385–98.

Schmoller, R. R. (1970). Terrestrial desert arthropods: fauna and ecology. *Biologist*, **52**, 77–98.

Serventy, D. L. & Marshall, A. J. (1957). Breeding periodicity in Western Australian birds: with an account of unseasonable nestings in 1953 and 1955. *Emu*, **57**, 99–126.

Setchell, B. P. & Thorburn, G. D. (1969). The effect of local heating on blood flow through the testes of some Australian marsupials. *Comparative Biochemistry and Physiology*, **31**, 675–7.

Shammakov, S. Sh., Ataev, Ch. A. & Kamalova, Z. Ya. (1973). Ekologiya za raspiiskoi krugogolivki v Turkmenii. *Ekologiya*, **4**, 80–83.

Short, L. L. (1974). Nesting of southern Sonoran birds during the summer rainy season. *Condor*, **76** (1), 21–32.

Shubin, I. G. (1974). Ekologiya zheltoi pestrushki (*Lagurus luteus*) v Zaisanskoi Kotlovine. *Zoologicheskii Zhurnal*, **53**, 272–7.

Shulov, A. S. (1970). The development of eggs of the red locust *Nomadacris septemfasciata* (Serv.), and African migratory locust *Locusta migratoria migratorioides* (R. and F.), and its interruption under particular conditions of humidity. *Anti-Locust Bulletin*, 1–22.

Shulov, A. & Pener, M. P. (1963). Studies on the development of eggs of the desert locust *Schistocerca gregaria* (Forsk.) and its interruption under particular conditions of humidity. *Anti-Locust Bulletin*, 41–59.

Simkins, C. S. & Asama, J. J. (1930). Observations on *Calotes versicolor*. *Journal of Tennessee Academy of Science*, **5**, 69–75.

Sowls, L. K. (1957). Reproduction in the Audubon cottontail in Arizona. *Journal of Mammalogy*, **38** (2), 234–43.

Stebbins, R. C. (1951). *Amphibians of Western North America*. Berkeley, University of California Press, Berkeley, California.

Stebbins, R. C. (1954). *Amphibians and Reptiles of Western North America*. McGraw Hill, New York.

Stinner, R. E. Gutierrez, A. P. & Butler, G. D. Jr. (1974). An algorithm for temperature dependent growth rate simulation. *Canadian Entomologist*, **106**, 159–524.

Stout, G. A. (1970). The breeding biology of the desert cottontail in the Phoenix region, Arizona. *Journal of Wildlife Management*, **34**, 47–51.

Strecker, J. K. (1908). Notes on the life history of *Scaphiopus couchi* Baird. *Proceedings of the Biological Society of Washington*, **21**, 199–206.

Tevis, L., Jr. (1966). Unsuccessful breeding by desert toads (*Bufo punctatus*) at the limit of their ecological tolerance. *Ecology*, **47**, 766–75.

Tinkle, D. W. & Irwin, L. N. (1965). Lizard reproduction: refractory period and response to warmth in *Uta stansburiana* females. *Science*, **148**, 1613–14.

Tinkle, D. W. (1967). The life and demography of the side-blotched lizard, *Uta stansburiana*. *University of Michigan Museum of Zoology Miscellaneous Publication*, **132**, 5–174.

Tinkle, D. W. (1969). The concept of reproductive effort and its relation to the evolution of life histories of lizards. *American Naturalist*, **103**, 501–16.

Toth, R. & Chew, R. M. (1972). Development and energetics of *Notonecta undulata* during predation on *Culex tarsalis*. *Annals of the Entomological Society of America*, **65**, 1270–79.

Turner, F. B., Medica, P. A., Lannom, J. R. & Hoddenbach, G. A. (1969). A demographic analysis of fenced populations of the whiptail lizard, *Cnemidophorus tigris* in southern Nevada. *Southwest Naturalist*, **14** (2), 189–202.

Turner, F. B., Hoddenbach, G. A., Medica, P. A. & Lannon, J. R., Jr. (1970). The demography of the lizard, *Uta stansburiana* Baird and Girard, in southern Nevada. *Journal of Animal Ecology*, **39**, 505–519.

Turner, F. B., Medica, P. A. & Smith, D. D. (1973). *Reproduction and survivorship of the lizard,* Uta stansburiana, *and the effects of winter rainfall, density and predation on these processes*. US/IBP Desert Biome Research Memorandum, R.M. 73–26, pp. 1–19. Logan, Utah.

Turner, F. B., Medica, P. A. & Smith, D. D. (1974). *Reproduction and survivorship of the lizard,* Uta stansburiana, *and the effects of winter rainfall, density and predation on these processes*. US/IBP Desert Biome Research Memorandum, R.M. 74–26, pp. 117–27. Logan, Utah.

Van De Graaf, K. M. (1973). Comparative developmental osteology in three species of desert rodents, *Peromyscus eremicus, Perognathus intermedius* and *Dipodomys merriami*. *Journal of Mammalogy*, **54**, 3.

Vielliard, J. (1970). La distribution du casarca roux *Tadorna ferruginea* (Pallas). *Alauda*, **38**, 87–119.

Wallace, M. M. H. (1968). The ecology of *Sminthurus viridis* (L.) (Collembola). II. Diapause in the aestivating egg. *Australian Journal of Zoology*, **16**, 871–83.

Animal processes

Wallace, M. M. H. (1970). Diapause in the aestivating egg of *Halotydeus destructor* (Acari: Eupodidae). *Australian Journal of Zoology*, **18**, 295–313.

Wallace, M. M. H. (1971). The influence of temperature and moisture on diapause development in the eggs of *Bdellodes lapidaria* (Acari: Bdellidae). *Journal of Australian Entomological Society*, **10**, 276–80.

Webb, R. G. (1969). Survival adaptation of tiger salamanders (*Ambystoma tigrinum*) in the Chihuahuan Desert. In: *Physiological Systems in Semiarid Environments* (eds. Clayton Hoff and Marvin L. Riedesel). University of New Mexico Press, Albuquerque, New Mexico.

Werner, F. G. & Murray, S. C. (1972). *Demography, foraging activity of leaf-cutter ants*, Acromyrmex versicolor, *in relation to colony size and location, season vegetation, and temperature*. US/IBP Desert Biome Research Memorandum, R.M. 72–33, pp. 1–10. Logan, Utah.

Willoughby, E. J. (1971). Biology of larks (Aves: Alaudidae) in the central Namib Desert. *Zoologica Africana*, **6**, 133–76.

Wilhoft, D. C. (1963). Reproduction in the tropical Australian skink, *Leiolopisma rhomboidalis*. *American Midland Naturalist*, **70**, 442–61.

Woodrow, D. F. (1965). Observations on the red locust (*Nomadacris septemfasciata* Serv.) in the Rukwa Valley, Tanganyika, during its breeding season. *Journal of Animal Ecology*, **34**, 187–200.

Yom-Tov, Y, (1972). Field experiments on the effect of population density and slope direction on the reproduction of the desert snail *Trochoidea* (*xerocrassa*) *seetzeni*. *Journal of Animal Ecology*, **41** (**1**), 17–22.

Zweifel, R. G. (1968). Reproductive biology of anurans of the arid Southwest, with emphasis on adaptation of embryos to temperature. *Bulletin of the American Museum of Natural History*, **140**, 1–64.

Zweifel, R. G. & Lowe, C. H. (1966). The ecology of a population of *Xantusia vigilis*, the desert night lizard. *American Museum Novitates*, **2247**, 1–57.

Manuscript received by the editors May 1975

34. Longevity, mortality and disease

G. T. AUSTIN and M. J. O'FARRELL

Introduction

Demographic studies of natural populations are important in determining the role played in the community by each taxon. Of particular interest are the survival rates on a temporal basis with regard to age structure. In this chapter we shall deal with mortality (the reciprocal of survival), longevity, and factors which may effect mortality (such as disease).

Desert ecosystems present a rigorous environment in which to live, yet afford a wide variety of ecological niches to occupy. Consequently it is not unusual to encounter a diversity of animals seldom found in more predictable environments. Although deserts offer a unique natural laboratory to study demographic parameters under such diverse conditions, there is a dearth of comprehensive studies in the literature. Thus we must draw heavily on the literature from other communities to arrive at generalizations which may or may not apply to desert communities. For the most part we limit our discussion to methodologies and generalizations and then present the data available for North American deserts.

In many studies of animal popuations there is an attempt to determine age structure and mortality. In many taxa and stages of the life cycle, however, information is scanty. Life tables have been constructed for many game animals (see for instance, Green & Evans, 1940; Leopold, Sperry, Feeney & Catenhusen, 1943; Murie, 1944; Caughley, 1966; Bradley & Baker, 1967), but in general there are relatively few such studies on small mammals (see review in Caughley, 1966), small birds (see review in Lack, 1954), other vertebrates (see review in Deevey, 1947) or invertebrates (see review in Harcourt, 1969). Mortality rates during the nestling period of altricial birds are well known (Ricklefs, 1969). The availability of longevity and mortality data depends largely on the ability to sample and age individuals of a population. The occurrence and incidence of disease are even less well known unless the information is of importance to man.

Throughout, daily mortality rates are calculated (Ricklefs, 1969) by:

$$m = \frac{-(\log_e P)}{T}$$

where P is the proportion surviving until time T (in days).

Animal processes

Insect mortality

Little is known concerning mortality of desert insects. The construction of life tables based on demographic data on field populations is mainly restricted to agricultural pests (Harcourt, 1969). The construction of insect life tables requires a sampling procedure that includes a wide variety of growing conditions and the measurement of the mortality factors involved. A detailed account of procedures and calculations is given by Harcourt (1969).

Mortality in the moth, *Plutella maculipennis* in Ottawa, Canada, has been summarized by Harcourt (1969). Loss of eggs was small (1.2%), whereas loss between hatching and the 4th instar rose to 47.0%. Mortality then declined until cocoon formation at which time it increased to 51%. The major mortality factors were rainfall, parasitism and predation, but their relative importance depended on the life stage.

Mortality over a 14-year period in *Bupalus piniarus* (Lepidoptera) in the Netherlands has been summarized by Klomp (1966). Loss of eggs was moderate (36.7%) increasing in the first instar to 53.5%. Mean mortality during intermediate instars was from 17% to 22%, but then increased for prepupal stages (36% to 40%). Mean mortality by midwinter was very low (5.4%) but reached a maximum of 53.3% by spring. Again, factors that affected mortality varied in importance depending on season and stage in the life cycle. Also, vast differences occurred from year to year depending on fecundity and density-independent factors.

The examples given above may give some indication as to the variability in mortality rates in insects. Unfortunately, no such studies exist for desert-dwelling insects. Preliminary mortality data on the lepidopteran *Aroga websteri*, reared in the laboratory, have been collected by Hsiao & Green (1974). Mortality followed trends similar to those illustrated above with high losses in early larval stages (58% to 66%), whereas losses decreased to 18% prior to pupation. Pupal mortality amounted to 43.2%. The total loss attributed to parasitism amounts to 20.2%, but the major mortality appeared to arise from other causes, for all life stages examined. The laboratory data gathered so far represent good comparative information but point to the dearth of knowledge concerning desert insects.

It is apparent that many factors, singly or in some combination, affect mortality in insects. Differential mortality is found at different life-stages, and density of the population may account for its severity during earlier stages. The methods for determining and analyzing the various factors influencing mortality in insect populations have been discussed by Solomon (1964).

Amphibians

Much of our knowledge of demography of frogs and toads has been summarized by Turner (1962). Life tables for a genus of salamanders have been established by Organ (1961). Survival in adults has been studied by recapture of marked individuals and of larvae by estimates of number surviving from the estimated number of eggs laid. Anuran mortality is relatively poorly known. Mortality of larvae is high (probably averaging more than 90% of eggs laid) and appears to be governed by rainfall, site of oviposition and permanence of the water source (Bannikov, 1948; Martof, 1956a; Turner, 1960; Herreid & Kinney, 1966; Tevis, 1966). More data are available for adult mortality. Conservative estimates of adult mortality to the first year after initial capture ranged from about 40% to 90% in various species (Bannikov, 1950; Blair, 1953; Jameson, 1955, 1956b; Pearson, 1955, 1957; Martof, 1956b; Turner, 1959, 1960; Kelleher & Tester, 1969). Mortality appears to be age-specific, at least in some species, with juveniles and older adults experiencing greater mortality than first-year adults (Bannikov, 1950; Jameson, 1956b; Kelleher & Tester, 1969). Jameson (1955) found greater mortality during the summer than winter in *Syrrhophus marnocki*.

Studies of desert anurans are few (Table 34.1). Turner (1959) estimated an annual adult mortality of 56% (0.22% per day) for *Bufo punctatus* in Death Valley. High mortality rates of larval stages of the same species were noted in another California desert site by Tevis (1966). Toads of the genus *Scaphiopus* are well-adapted to and widespread in North American deserts. Although there have been no studies of desert populations, an investigation of a member of this genus in Florida indicated an annual adult mortality rate of less than 40% (Pearson, 1955). Desert species are probably similar.

The most important factor which affects anuran mortality appears to be the availability and, especially in arid lands, permanence of water (Bragg, 1940; Jameson, 1956a, b; Martof, 1956b; Turner, 1960; Tevis, 1966). Other mortality factors include abnormalities in development, fungal infestations, temperature (Herreid & Kinney, 1966), predation (Bragg, 1940; Jameson, 1956b), crowding, and pollution (Bragg, 1940). Pearson (1955) found the greatest survival of adults of *Scaphiopus h. holbrooki* at intermediate densities, suggesting that density-dependent factors may be involved.

Longevity of captive anurans ranges from 11 years in Pelobatidae and 16 years in Hylidae and Ranidae to more than 30 years in Bufonidae (Goin & Goin, 1962). Natural longevity is considerably less (Table 34.1) with values of about 9 years in Pelobatidae (Pearson, 1955), 3 to 4 years or more in Bufonidae (Hamilton, 1955; Thornton, 1960; Tevis, 1966), 3 to 5 years

Table 34.1. *Mortality and longevity of some desert amphibians and reptiles*

Species	Annual mortality of adults (%)	Daily mortality rates (%)			Maximum natural longevity	Average age of breeding population (months)	Location	Source
		First week	Juveniles (age)	Adults (age)				
Amphibia								
Pelobatidae								
Scaphiopus couchi	47	—	—	0.17 (1–2 yr)	>2 yr	—	Texas	Jameson, 1956a
Bufonidae								
Bufo woodhousei	—	—	—	—	>4 yr	—	Texas	Thornton, 1960
Bufo punctctus	56	—	—	0.22 (1–2 yr)	>4 yr	—	California	Turner, 1959; Tevis, 1966
Microhylidae								
Gastrophryne olivacea	—	—	—	—	7–8 yr	—	Kansas	Fitch, 1956b
Reptilia								
Testudinidae								
Gopherus agassizi	5	—	—	—	>30 yr	—	Utah	Woodbury and Hardy, 1948
Iguanidae								
Sauromalus obesus	5–25	—	—	<0.01	—	—	California	Berry, 1974
Crotaphytus collaris	55	—	0.30 (<10 m)	0.20 (>10 m)	—	—	Kansas	Fitch, 1956a
Crotaphytus wislizenii	38	—	0.40 (<8 m)	0.13 (>8 m)	7–8 yr	—	Nevada	Turner et al., 1969
Crotaphytus wislizenii	57	—	0.52 (<8 m)	0.23 (>8 m)	7–8 yr	—	Nevada	Turner et al., 1969
Sceloporus magister	—	—	1.11 (0–1 yr)	0.33 (>1 yr)	>6 yr	—	Nevada	Tanner and Krogh, 1973
Sceloporus undulatus	71	—	1.34 (0–1 yr)	0.35 (>1 yr)	>3 yr	—	New Mexico	Vinegar, 1975
Sceloporus undulatus	72	—	—	—	—	—	New Mexico	Vinegar, 1975
Uta stansburiana	91	6.15	1.70 (2–8 wk)	0.54 (8–52 wk)	22 m	9	Texas	Tinkle, 1967

Species							Location	Reference
Uta stansburiana	91	6.82	2.16 (2–8 wk)	0.54 (8–52 wk)	32 m	9	Texas	Tinkle, 1967
Uta stansburiana	78	—	0.78 (2–10 wk)	0.41 (> 10 wk)[1]	—	12	Colorado	Tinkle, 1967
Uta stansburiana	78	—	0.66 (< 8 m)	0.40 (> 8 m)[2]	44 m	12	Nevada	Turner et al., 1970
Uta stansburiana	67	—	0.35 (< 8 m)[3]	0.30 (> 8 m)[4]	—	11+	Nevada	Turner et al., 1974
Uta stansburiana	—	—	0.79 (< 8 m)	—	—	—	Nevada	Turner et al., 1974
Xantusiidae								
Xantusia vigilis	29	—	—	0.09 (36–72 m)	—	—	California	Zweifel and Lowe, 1966
Xantusia vigilis	50–95	—	—	0.18–0.82 (72–108 m)	—	—	California	Zweifel and Lowe, 1966
Teiidae								
Cnemidophorus tigris	43	—	0.27 (< 8 m)	0.15 (> 8 m)	7 yr	22	Nevada	Turner et al., 1969a
Cnemidophorus tigris	41	—	—	—	—	—	Nevada	Tanner and Jorgensen, 1963
Colubridae								
Masticophis taeniatus	—	—	—	0.23[5]	—	—	Utah	Hirth, 1966
Viperidae								
Crotalus viridis	78	—	0.29 (< 2 yr)	0.05 (> 3 yr)	> 10 yr	—	Utah	Woodbury et al., 1951

[1] Based on annual survival rate from overwinter survival of juveniles (6 m) and recaptures of adults in their second season (12 m).
[2] Females from Table 8, Turner et al., 1970
[3] Enclosures with predatory *Crotaphytus wislizenii* excluded.
[4] Average from Table 10, Turner et al., 1974.
[5] From overwinter survival.

Animal processes

in Hylidae (Jameson, 1956a; Green, 1957) and 5 to 12 years in Microhylidae and Ranidae (Fitch, 1956b; Martof, 1956a; Turner, 1960).

Reptiles

Data on mortality in lizard populations are obtained mainly through marking and subsequent recovery. Mortality rates are known from many intensive studies (Stebbins & Robinson, 1946; Fitch, 1954, 1956a, 1958; Crenshaw, 1955; Blair, 1960; Hirth, 1963; Zweifel & Lowe, 1966; Tinkle, 1967; Brooks, 1967; Turner, Lannom, Medica, & Hoddenbach, 1969; Turner, Medica, Lannom & Hoddenbach, 1969a, b; Turner, Hoddenbach, Medica & Lannom, 1970; Turner, Medica & Smith, 1973, 1974). Most of these concern species whose ranges include the desert, although some studies were of non-desert populations (Table 34.1). Annual mortality rates vary considerably from a nearly annual turnover in some populations of *Uta stansburiana* (Tinkle, 1967) to an annual mortality of less than 30% during the first few years of life in *Xantusia vigilis* (Zweifel & Lowe, 1966), and between 5% and 25% in *Sauromalus obesus* (Berry, 1974). Variation also exists between populations of a single species and in successive years as illustrated by *Uta stansburiana* (Tinkle, 1967; Turner *et al.*, 1970, 1974). Studies of non-desert species indicate similar ranges of annual mortality (Kramer, 1946, cited by Lack, 1954; Crenshaw, 1955; Kennedy, 1958; Fitch, 1958, 1967; Hirth, 1963; Sexton, Heatwole & Meseth, 1963; Storr, 1965; Brooks, 1967).

Mortality of eggs and newly hatched young is poorly known. Blair (1960) reported a (maximum) 76.6% nest mortality (2.42% mortality per day assuming a 60-day incubation period). Of eggs which survived the incubation period, 6.4% failed to hatch (0.10% per day). Thus mortality during incubation averaged 78% (2.52% per day). In contrast, about 50% of eggs laid by *Crotaphytus collaris* hatched (Fitch, 1956a). During the first few days after hatching mortality rates of *Uta stansburiana* were high (> 6% per day (Tinkle, 1967)); this decreased in juveniles to a level somewhat higher than in adults (Table 34.1).

Predation by other lizards, snakes and occasional mammals and birds appear to be the major mortality factor in lizards (Blair, 1960; Tinkle, 1967; Brooks, 1967; Turner *et al.*, 1974). At least in some species, mortality is density-dependent (Turner, Lannom, Medica & Hoddenbach, 1969; Turner *et al.*, 1973). Severe winter weather accounted for deaths of about 25% of a *Uta stansburiana* population (Tinkle, 1967).

Longevity is known for several species, mostly from captive individuals. Available data indicate that potential longevity averages about 6 to 7 years in Agamidae and Gekkonidae, 15 years in Iguanidae and Teiidae and 20 years in Scincidae and Helodermatidae (Altman & Dittmer, 1962). Actual

828

longevity in the wild averages 3 to 8 years in Iguanidae and 7 years in Teiidae (Table 34.1). Average age of a population of *Uta stansburiana* was estimated as 18.5 weeks (Tinkle, 1967). Average age of the breeding population increases with decreasing annual mortality (Table 34.1). An adult population of *Sceloporus magister* in Nevada consisted mainly of individuals 3 to 5 years old (Tanner & Krogh, 1973), indicating a low annual mortality rate.

Data for reptiles other than lizards are few. Woodbury & Hardy (1948) estimated mortality at less than 5% per year for *Gopherus agassizi*. Snake mortality was heaviest during the first 1 or 2 years of life, declining to very low rates among sub-adults and adults (Fitch, 1949; Woodbury *et al.*, 1951). Overall mortality rates for three species of snakes during approximately 7 months of hibernation averaged 0.23% per day (Hirth, 1966). Of two species which range into the Great Basin Desert, *Masticophis taeniatus* averaged 0.23% mortality per day and *Crotalus viridis* 0.19% per day.

Tortoises are long-lived, but longevity of *Gopherus agassizi* appears unknown although it is in excess of 30 years (Patterson & Brattstrom, 1972). Longevity of captive snakes is in excess of 20 years (from summarization by Goin & Goin (1962)).

Birds

Adult mortality and longevity

Adult mortality rates for birds have been obtained mainly through banding individuals of known age and their subsequent recovery as recaptures, census of marked individuals returning to a specified area to breed, or recoveries of dead birds. Adult mortality in stationary populations can be derived from the number of new breeding birds each year by assuming that replacements equal adult mortality. Adult mortality rates are known for a number of species of birds (see reviews by Hickey (1952, 1955), Lack (1954), Farner (1955), Boyd (1962), Ashmole (1971) and Botkin & Miller (1974)). Among passerines of the temperate zone, annual adult mortality averages 40% to 60% (Lack, 1954), while that for gallinaceous species averages 50% to 80% (Hickey, 1955). Annual adult mortality rates among desert passerines appear slightly lower, judging from the few data available for North American species: about 40% in *Auriparus flaviceps* (based on the proportion of first-year birds at the beginning of the breeding season (Austin, 1977), about 39% in *Campylorhynchus brunneicapillus* (based on the mean approximate proportion of year-old individuals in the male population (Anderson & Anderson, 1973)) and about 48% in *Toxostoma curvirostre* (based on loss of winter-banded birds (Anderson & Anderson, 1973).

Numerous data are available on longevity of birds, both in captivity and

829

Table 34.2. *Nesting success of birds in North American deserts. (Fledging success = percent eggs laid to fledge; nest success = percent nests built to fledge at least one young)*

Species	Fledging success	Nest success	Number of nests	Habitat	Year	Location	Source
Columbidae							
Zenaida macroura	32.4	26.1	46	Desert grassland	1970–71	Arizona	Austin, unpublished data
	14.3	15.0	20	Desert scrub	1971–72	Arizona	Russell *et al.*, 1972, 1973
Zenaida asiatica	40.9	41.7	24	Desert scrub	1948–49	Arizona	Hensley, 1954
Paridae							
Auriparus flaviceps	44.1	54.2	48	Desert grassland	1970–71	Arizona	Austin, 1977
	29.7	36.0	25	Desert scrub	1965–66	Arizona	Taylor, 1971
	82.1	80.0	15	Desert scrub	1948–49	Arizona	Hensley, 1954
	83.2	100.0	25	Desert riparian	1969–70	Nevada	Austin, 1977
	56.9	—	18	Desert scrub	1965	New Mexico	Moore, 1965
Troglodytidae							
Campylorhynchus brunneicapillus	47.8	55.7	61	Desert grassland	1970–71	Arizona	Austin, unpublished data
	54.3	66.0	53	Desert scrub	1939–59	Arizona	Anderson & Anderson, 1973
	64.6	68.8	154	Desert scrub	1963–68	Arizona	Anderson & Anderson, 1973
	82.6	80.0	20	Desert scrub	1948–49	Arizona	Hensley, 1954
	31.7	46.2	13	Desert scrub	1971–72	Arizona	Russell *et al.*, 1972, 1973
Mimidae							
Mimus polyglottos	21.6	21.4	14	Desert grassland	1970–71	Arizona	Austin, unpublished data
	24.2	24.4	45	Desert grassland	1970–71	Arizona	Austin, unpublished data
Toxostoma curvirostre	24.4	20.9	86	Desert scrub	1963–68	Arizona	Anderson & Anderson, 1973
	72.5	80.0	15	Desert scrub	1948–49	Arizona	Hensley, 1954
	30.8	31.8	22	Desert scrub	1971–72	Arizona	Russell, *et al.*, 1972, 1973
Sylviidae							
Polioptila melanura	0.0	28.6[1]	14	Desert grassland	1970–71	Arizona	Austin, unpublished data
	20.0	5.0	20	Desert scrub	1971–72	Arizona	Russell *et al.*, 1972, 1973
Icteridae							
Molothrus ater	22.7[2]	—	—	Desert grassland	1970–71	Arizona	Austin, unpublished
Fringillidae							
Carpodacus mexicanus	80.5	80.0	10	Desert scrub	1948–49	Arizona	Hensley, 1954
Pipilo fuscus	44.0	42.5	40	Desert grassland	1970–71	Arizona	Austin, unpublished data
Aimophila carpalis	42.0	39.0	41	Desert grassland	1970–71	Arizona	Austin, unpublished data
Aimophila cassinii	62.5	63.6	11	Desert grassland	1970–71	Arizona	Austin, unpublished data
Amphispiza bilineata	58.3	60.0	10	Desert grassland	1970–71	Arizona	Austin, unpublished data
Spizella breweri	—	19.4	31	Desert scrub	1972	Utah, Idaho	Balph, 1973

[1] Successfully raised *Melothrus ater*.
[2] From nests of *Polioptila melanura*, *Vermivora luciae*, *Aimophila carpalis*, *Aimophila cassinii*, and *Amphispiza bilineata*.

Table 34.3. *Mortality rates of North American desert birds (percent per day)*

Species	Egg	Nestling	Post-fledging[1]	Adult	Location	Year	Source
Columbidae							
Zenaida macroura	5.95	1.07	—	—	Arizona	1970–71	Austin, unpublished data
	6.18	7.96	—	—	Arizona	1971–72	Russell *et al.*, 1972, 1973
Zenaida asiatica	2.81	0.87	—	—	Arizona	1948–49	Hensley, 1954
Paridae							
Auriparus flaviceps	2.56	1.86	0.87	—	Arizona	1970–71	Austin, 1977
	3.77	2.88	—	—	Arizona	1965–66	Taylor, 1971
	0.19	0.88	—	—	Arizona	1948–49	Hensley, 1954
	0.34	0.66	—	—	Nevada	1969–70	Austin, 1977
	—	—	—	0.13[2]	North American deserts	—	Austin, 1977
Troglodytidae							
Campylorhynchus brunneicapillus	1.66	2.11	0.84	—	Arizona	1970–71	Austin, unpublished data
	2.30	1.02	—	—	Arizona	1939–59	Anderson & Anderson, 1973
	1.01	1.22	2.21[3]	0.14[4]	Arizona	1963–68	Anderson & Anderson, 1973
	2.19	3.65	—	—	Arizona	1971–72	Russell *et al.*, 1972, 1973
	0.82	0.17	—	—	Arizona	1948–49	Hensley, 1954
Mimidae							
Mimus polyglottos	4.44	7.21	—	—	Arizona	1970–71	Austin, unpublished data
Toxostoma curvirostre	4.13	4.71	1.92	—	Arizona	1970–71	Austin, unpublished data
	4.03	5.63	6.35[5]	0.19[6]	Arizona	1963–68	Anderson & Anderson, 1973
	2.09	5.08	—	—	Arizona	1971–72	Russell *et al.*, 1972, 1973
	0.51	1.43	—	—	Arizona	1948–49	Hensley, 1954
Icteridae							
Molothrus ater	8.18	3.06	—	—	Arizona	1970–71	Austin, unpublished data
Fringillidae							
Carpodacus mexicanus	1.55	0.00	—	—	Arizona	1948–49	Hensley, 1954
Pipilo fuscus	2.50	3.82	—	—	Arizona	1970–71	Austin, unpublished data
Aimophila carpalis	4.71	1.95	1.80	—	Arizona	1970–71	Austin, unpublished data
Aimophila cassinii	1.28	3.08	—	—	Arizona	1970–71	Austin, unpublished data
Amphispiza bilineata	2.70	1.34	—	—	Arizona	1970–71	Austin, unpublished data

[1] To 30 days post-fledging.
[2] Based on immature-adult ratios.
[3] Based on Figure 16–2, Anderson & Anderson (1973).
[4] Based on proportion of first year males in male population, Anderson & Anderson (1973).
[5] Based on Anderson & Anderson (1973), data on p. 185.
[6] Based on Table 18.1 assuming four months between banding and breeding season, Anderson & Anderson (1973).

Animal processes

in the wild. Potential longevity of small land birds averages 15 to 20 years in captivity and about 10 years in the wild (from summarization by Altman & Dittmer (1962)). Average age of most small land birds in the wild, however, is approximately 1 to 2 years (Lack, 1954). Among desert species, *Campylorhynchus brunneicapillus* lives at least 5 years in the wild and attain an average age of 1.5 to 2 years, and two individuals of *Toxostoma curvirostre* lived through at least six breeding seasons (Anderson & Anderson, 1973).

Nesting mortality

Mortality during the nesting stage of birds is determined by direct observation of the fate of eggs and nestlings. Nesting success and mortality rates of eggs and young are better known than adult mortality rates, both for birds in general (reviews by Kalmbach (1939), Kendeigh (1942), Lack (1954), Hickey (1955), Nice (1957), Skutch (1966) and Ricklefs (1969)) and for desert species (Tables 34.2, 34.3). In deserts, nesting success is, on the average, lower than the average 55 to 60% for most temperate and arctic species (nest success as cited by Ricklefs (1969, 1973)) but comparable with 21% nest success in a temperate non-desert scrub habitat (Nolan, 1963), 35% fledgling success in a temperate grassland site (Wiens, 1973) and 31% nest success in a humid tropical site (Ricklefs, 1969). Because nestling periods are generally shorter in arid regions (Table 10 in Ricklefs (1969)), mortality rates are, on average, greater.

Considerable variation exists between sites, even in the same desert (Table 34.4), and between years (Marchant, 1960; Lloyd, 1960; Russell, Smith, Gould & Austin, 1972; Russell, Gould & Smith, 1973; Austin, unpublished data). Seasonal variation also exists; in Sonoran Desert grassland, overall nesting success was, on the average, greater after the summer rains than before (Austin, unpublished data). Other factors affecting nesting success in deserts include nest-type (enclosed nests more successful than open nests (Russell *et al.*, 1972; Austin, unpublished data) as in other communities (Ricklefs, 1969)), and nest-orientation (Austin, 1974, 1976).

Mortality factors for eggs and nestlings have been analyzed for a number of passerine species (Ricklefs, 1969), with predation accounting for nearly 55% of egg losses and 56% of nestling losses. In Sonoran Desert grassland, predation accounted for about 30% of egg losses and about 65% of nestling losses (Austin, unpublished data), while other important sources of egg losses were hatching failure, brood parasitism and desertion. In Sonoran Desert scrub, predation (37%) and brood parasitism (22%) were the important causes of nest failure (Russell *et al.*, 1973).

Post-fledging mortality is poorly known for birds as a whole. Mortality

Table 34.4. *Average*[1] *success and mortality of open-nesting birds of arid lands*

Hatching success = percent eggs laid to hatch; nestling success = percent eggs hatched to fledge; fledging success = percent eggs laid to fledge; nest success = percent nests built to fledge at least one young.

Location	Average hatching success	Average nestling success	Average fledging success	Average nest success	Average daily mortality rates of eggs & nestlings (%)	Source
Arizona (desert grassland)	48.9 (9)[2]	69.8 (8)	34.2 (9)	38.2 (8)	3.86 (8)	Austin, unpublished data
Arizona (desert scrub)	72.8 (3)	89.5 (3)	64.6 (3)	67.2 (3)	1.70 (3)	Hensley, 1954
Arizona (desert scrub)	43.4 (3)	60.2 (3)	21.7 (3)	17.3 (3)	5.68 (3)	Russell *et al.*, 1972, 1973
S.W. Ecuador (semiarid)	73.2 (11)	70.1 (11)	46.0 (11)	51.6 (11)	3.07 (11)	Marchant, 1960
Iraq	43.9 (8)	59.5 (8)	26.3 (8)	26.9 (7)	4.92 (8)	Marchant, 1963

[1] Mean of values for each species. [2] Number of species involved in calculation.

Table 34.5. *Mortality rate of some desert mammals*

Species	Annual mortality of adults (%)	Mortality rate per day (%)	Age class	Location	Source
Vespertilionidae					
Eptesicus fuscus	—	0.26	< 1 yr	Minnesota,	Beer, 1955
	—	0.11	1–2 yr	Wisconsin	
	23	0.07	2–10 yr		
Canidae					
Urocyon cinereoargenteus	—	0.27	< 9 m	Georgia,	Wood, 1958
	—	0.33	9–21 m	Florida	
	50	0.19	> 21 m		
Leporidae					
Lepus californicus	—	0.58[1]	< 10 m	California	Lechleitner, 1959
	60	0.25[2]	> 10 m		
Lepus californicus	—	0.50	first yr	Utah	Gross *et al.*, 1974
	80	0.44	adult		
Heteromyidae					
Dipodomys merriami	75	0.38	—	Nevada	French *et al.*, 1967[3]
Dipodomys microps	84	0.50	—		
Perognathus longimembris	62	0.27	—		
Perognathus formosus	70	0.33	—		
Perognathus formosus	58	0.24	> 1 m	Nevada	French *et al.*, 1974[4]
Perognathus formosus	71	0.34	winter adult	Nevada	Chew *et al.*, 1973
	75	0.39	summer adult		
Perognathus parvus	75	0.38	1–2 yr	Washington	O'Farrell, Olson, Gilbert & Hedlund, 1975
Bovidae					
Ovis canadensis ♂	—	0.42	< 1 yr	Nevada	Bradley & Baker,
	—	0.01	1–8 yr		1967
	—	0.06	8–12 yr		
	—	0.25	> 12 yr		

[1] Estimated from calculated annual mortality for adults and age structure in August.
[2] Estimated from age structure in February (i.e. 60% of adults replaced in one year).
[3] From survival curves 10–30 months, plot *A*.
[4] From survival curves through 2 years, plot *A* and *C*.

between fledging and independence appears to be lower than mortality in the nest but greater than adult mortality (Table 34.3; see also Lack (1954), Ricklefs (1969, 1973)).

Mammals

Methods for obtaining mortality data for mammals are given by Caughley (1966). Mortality is known for various groups of mammals, but there are insufficient data at present to classify these into discrete patterns.

834

Table 34.6. *Disappearance rates (maximal mortality) of some adult desert rodents*

Species	Maximum annual mortality rate (%)	Maximum daily mortality rate (%)	Location	Source
Ammospermophilus nelsoni	60	0.25	California	Hawbacker, 1958
Dipodomys merriami	60	0.25	Arizona	Chew & Chew, 1970
Dipodomys merriami	84	0.51	California	Chew & Butterworth, 1964
Perognathus longimembris	69	0.32	California	Chew & Butterworth, 1964
Peromyscus eremicus	99	1.16	Arizona	Chew & Chew, 1970
Onychomys torridus	77	0.40	Arizona	Chew & Chew, 1970

Demographic parameters are well known for several big-game species (Deevey, 1947; Caughley, 1966; Bradley & Baker, 1967), but the most detailed studies of small mammals have been on laboratory populations (Leslie & Ranson, 1940; Leslie, Tener, Vizoso & Chitty, 1955). Annual mortality rates vary considerably. Rodents generally have high rates of mortality, often with nearly annual population turnover (Linduska, 1947, 1950; Howard, 1949). Annual mortality of lagomorphs is only slightly lower (Green & Evans, 1940; Linduska, 1947; Lechleitner, 1959; Meslow & Keith, 1968; Gross, Stoddart & Wagner, 1974). Bats, carnivores and ungulates experience considerably lower annual mortality (Bourlière, 1947; Deevey, 1947; Beer, 1955; Wood, 1958; Caughley, 1966).

Annual mortality of desert mammals appears similar to figures previously obtained for related species in other temperate communities (Tables 34.5, 34.6). An exception to this is certain Heteromyid rodents (*Perognathus* spp.) that are long-lived and show a relatively low annual mortality for such small mammals (Chew & Butterworth, 1964; French, Maza & Aschwanden, 1967). This has been attributed to their seasonal activity and periods of torpor (Tucker, 1962, 1966; Chew & Butterworth, 1964; French *et al.*, 1967). Periodic torpor during periods of severe weather conditions in the high desert may account for longer life-spans and somewhat decreased mortality in other rodents (e.g., *Dipodomys* spp.).

Prenatal mortality is sometimes estimated by a comparison of numbers of corpora lutea and surviving embryos, and analyzed separately for the pre- and post-implantation periods (Lechleitner, 1959). Few data are available for this category of mortality for mammals in general. In the jackrabbit (*Lepus californicus*) Lechleitner (1959) reported 6% pre-implantational loss and 41.4% post-implantational loss. In the same species, Gross *et al.* (1974) reported a loss of 8% of ova before implantation, and 3% of embryos between implantation and birth. Preweaning

835

Table 34.7. *Longevity and mean age of populations of some mammals which occur in North American deserts*

Species	Sex	Maximum Longevity		Mean age of free-living populations	Source
		Captive	Free-living		
Phyllostomaticae					
Macrotus californicus	—	—	40 m	—	Paradiso & Greenhall, 1967
Vespertilionidae					
Myotis lucifugus	—	—	24 yr	—	Griffin & Hitchcock, 1965
Myotis thysanodes	♀	—	11 yr	—	Paradiso & Greenhall, 1967
Myotis velifer	—	—	6 yr	—	Paradiso & Greenhall, 1967
Myotis yumenensis	—	35 m	—	—	Orr, 1958
Pipistrellus hesperus	♂	—	4 yr	—	Paradiso & Greenhall, 1967
Eptesicus fuscus	♂	—	19 yr	—	Paradiso & Greenhall, 1967
Plecotus townsendii	♀	—	16 yr 5 m	—	Paradiso & Greenhall, 1967
Antrozous pallidus	—	8 yr 3 m	—	—	Orr, 1958
Lasiurus cinereus	—	15 m	—	—	Orr, 1958
Molossidae					
Tadarida brasiliensis	♂	4 yr 5 m	—	—	Orr, 1958
Tadarida brasiliensis	—	—	4 yr 6 m	—	Paradiso & Greenhall, 1967
Procyonidae					
Bassariscus astutus	—	8 yr	—	—	Flower, 1931
Mustelidae					
Mephitis mephitis	—	6 yr 1 m	—	—	Flower, 1931
Spilogale putorius	—	9 yr 10 m	—	—	Egocue, Bittmen & Petrovich, 1970
Taxidea taxus	—	13 yr 10 m	—	11 yr	Flower, 1931
Mustela vison	—	10 yr	—	—	Palmer, 1954
Canidae					
Canis latrans	—	15 yr	—	—	Manville, 1953
Urocyon cinereoargenteus	—	>8 yr 5 m	—	—	Flower, 1931
Felidae					
Felis concolor	—	16 yr	—	9 yr	Flower, 1931
Lynx rufa	—	15 yr	—	—	Flower, 1931
Leporidae					
Lepus californicus	—	>7 yr	—	—	Haskell & Reynolds, 1947
Heteromyidae					
Perognathus longimembris	♀	7 yr 6 m	—	—	Orr, 1939
Perognathus longimembris	—	8 yr 1 m	—	—	Edmonds and Fertig, 1972
Perognathus longimembris	Both	—	5 yr 1 m	3.8-4.4 m[1]	French et al., 1967

Perognathus formosus	Both	—	35+ m	3.7–5.0 m[1]	French et al., 1967
Perognathus formosus	—	—	45+ m	—	Chew et al., 1973
Perognathus flavus	♀	5 yr	—	—	Aldous, 1930
Perognathus parvus	♀	4 yr 6 m	—	—	Huey, 1959
Perognathus parvus	Both	—	>3 yr	—	O'Farrell et al., 1975
Perognathus fallax	♂	8 yr 4 m	—	—	Huey, 1959
Microdipodops megacephalus	—	5 yr 5 m	—	—	Egoscue et al., 1970
Dipodomys agilis	—	6 yr 3 m	—	—	Rabb, 1960
Dipodomys deserti	—	5 yr 5 m	—	—	Brattstrom, 1960
Dipodomys heermanni	Both	—	12 m	—	Fitch, 1948
Dipodomys heermanni	♂	—	35 m	—	Fitch, 1948
Dipodomys merriami	Both	—	35+ m	3.9–4.7 m[1]	French et al., 1967
Dipodomys merriami	—	7 yr 9 m	—	—	Egoscue et al., 1970
Dipodomys microps	Both	—	35+ m	4.9 m[1]	French et al., 1967
Dipodomys ordii	—	7 yr 5 m	—	—	Egoscue et al., 1970
Cricetidae					
Reithrodontomys megalotis	—	>29 m	—	—	Egoscue et al., 1970
Reithrodontomys megalotis	—	—	—	11 m[2]	Svihla, 1931
Peromyscus boylii	—	—	18 m	6.8 m	Brown, 1964
Peromyscus crinitus	—	7 yr 8 m	—	—	Egoscue et al., 1970
Peromyscus californicus	—	3 yr 6 m	—	—	Egoscue et al., 1970
Peromyscus maniculatus	♂	8 yr 4 m	—	—	Dice, 1933
Peromyscus truei	—	5 yr 2 m	—	—	Egoscue et al., 1970
Onychomys leucogaster	—	4 yr 2 m	—	—	Egoscue et al., 1970
Neotoma lepida	—	5 yr 1 m	—	—	Egoscue et al., 1970
Neotoma lepida	—	5 yr 7 m	—	—	Rabb, 1960
Lagurus curtatus	—	23 m	—	—	Egoscue et al., 1970
Tayassuidae					
Tayassu tajacu	♂	>9 yr 4 m	—	—	Flower, 1931
Cervidae					
Odocoileus hemionus	—	15 yr	—	8 yr	Flower, 1931
Antilocapridae					
Antilocapra americana	—	15 yr	—	8 yr	Flower, 1931
Bovidae					
Ovis canadensis	♂	17 yr 4 m	16 yr	9 yr 7 m	Bradley & Baker, 1967
Ovis canadensis	♀	—	16 yr	7 yr 3 m	Bradley & Baker, 1967

[1] After logarithmic transformation, data from fenced plots *A* and *C*.
[2] Captive population.

mortality is unknown for natural populations but has been estimated as 17% based on laboratory data for *Peromyscus* spp. (French & Kaaz, 1968). Juvenile mortality is also poorly known. In *Lepus californicus*, 80% mortality was reported between birth and March of the following year (Gross *et al.*, 1974). Juvenile mortality in *Lepus* spp. also appears to exceed that of adults (Lechleitner, 1959; Meslow & Keith, 1968). In *Ovis canadensis* juvenile mortality exceeds 70% (Bradley & Baker, 1967).

Longevity, especially in captive mammals, is well known (Table 34.7). Bats are long-lived in the wild, maximum free-living longevities averaging 15 to 20 years. Maximum rodent longevity (in captivity) averages 4 to 7 years; but free-living longevity appears on the average to be less than 2 years, although significant percentages of free-living populations of *Perognathus* spp. may approach potential longevity (Chew & Butterworth, 1964; French *et al.*, 1967).

Disease

The subject of disease naturally follows a discussion of mortality. There are, however, few diseases limited to desert-dwelling animals; therefore, we shall discuss diseases that are common to desert animals yet may be widely spread in other environments. In addition, we are excluding parasitic diseases, inasmuch as a separate chapter would be needed adequately to cover the vast literature on the organisms responsible.

Only three diseases could be considered as specifically 'desert diseases': (*a*) coccidioidomycosis, (*b*) desert sore, and (*c*) West Nile infection (histoplasmosis) (Lowe, 1958). The most serious of the three is coccidioidomycosis, also known as San Joaquin Valley Fever. The disease occurs in all the low-scrub deserts in North and South America and is limited usually, but not exclusively, to the Lower Sonoran Life Zone or its equivalent (Lowe, 1968). This is a highly infectious disease characterized by single or multiple pulmonary and thoracic lymph node granulomas and a tendency to disseminate to other tissues (Merck Veterinary Manual, 1973). *Coccidioides immitis* is the causal, air-borne fungus. As a primary infection it is usually not fatal. However, as a secondary, disseminated lesion it may occur in any organ of the body in any combination of suppuration, necrosis and granuloma. It is the secondary form which may be most important as a factor in mortality. The most recent hypothesis for growth and infection by *C. immitis* involves the intense heating and sterilization of surface soils and seasonal rains promoting rapid germination, growth and reentry of the fungus to the upper soil surface (Lowe, 1968). Dust storms promote the distribution of the infectious spores and their subsequent inhalation by desert animals.

Desert sore is a bacterial skin ulceration usually associated with skin abrasions and poor hygiene (Lowe, 1968). It is of questionable importance in desert animals. West Nile infection is a mosquito-borne arbovirus throughout the desert regions of the Middle East (Lowe, 1968). It is primarily associated with children, and likewise of questionable importance to desert animals in general.

Histoplasmosis is a widespread pulmonary fungal disease similar to coccidioidomycosis caused by *Histoplasma capsulatum* (Merck Veterinary Manual, 1973). This disease is characterized by pulmonary nodules, ulceration of the mucous membranes, and lymphadenopathy. Infection is acquired by inhalation. Chronic infections are not usually fatal; however, acute disseminated histoplasmosis is usually fatal.

There are numerous eye diseases, bacterial and viral, that result in inflammation of the conjunctiva and are collectively termed conjunctivitis. Although this disease is prevalent in human populations it has been found in a variety of other animals (Lowe, 1968; Merck Veterinary Manual, 1973).

Tularemia is a widespread bacterial disease common in rodents and lagomorphs (Lowe, 1968). The causative agent is *Francisella tularensis*, and is spread mainly by ticks. This disease is characterized by fever, lethargy, and lesions of the lymph nodes, liver and spleen (Merck Veterinary Manual, 1973). It may reach epizootic proportions, and may be a periodically important factor in mortality of some small mammals.

Finally, numerous forms of encephalomyelitis can occur in desert animals. Of these, the primary diseases are rabies, Venezuelan equine encephalitis and Western equine encephalitis. These diseases may occur in a variety of desert animals but at present there are no data to assess their impact as a mortality factor.

In summary, there are numerous diseases that occur in desert organisms, but information on them is, in the main, restricted to their relationship to human medicine and general public health. Little is known on the role of these diseases as a factor in mortality of free-living populations.

Conclusions

In general, mortality patterns in free-living animals are poorly known, except for species considered economically important and for nesting mortality in birds. Much of this lack of knowledge is due to the difficulty of studying dispersing populations and thus the low probability of recovering a marked individual, and the length of time necessary to establish mean values of survival in variable ecosystems such as the desert. Certain aspects of mortality of free-living populations (preweaning mortality in rodents, for instance) will nearly always have to be extrapolated from laboratory populations or, at best, populations in enclosures.

Within the limits of our knowledge, desert animals follow mortality patterns established for other communities, although there may be more annual variation than elsewhere. Nesting mortality of desert birds appears higher than in some other temperate communities. The lower nesting success may be compensated by a longer potential breeding season, at least in the warmer deserts. Desert rodents of the genus *Perognathus* have a longer life span and lower mortality rate than other rodents, owing apparently to a relatively low basal metabolism, and periodic torpor at times of food shortage and cold.

Acknowledgments

We thank F. R. Kay, J. S. Miller, K. Moor and D. Thomas for critically reading the manuscript and offering helpful suggestions, F. I. Smith pro vided interpretation and permission to use certain data on birds from the Sonoran Desert of Arizona. We are grateful to W. G. Bradley for providing us the time and facilities for the completion of the manuscripts.

References

Aldous, S. E. (1930). A silky pocket mouse in captivity. *Journal of Mammalogy,* **11**, 80–81.

Altman, P. L. & Dittmer, D. S. (eds.) (1962). *Growth.* Federation of the American Society of Experimental Biology, Washington, D.C.

Anderson, A. H. & Anderson, A. (1973). *The Cactus Wren.* University of Arizona Press, Tucson.

Ashmole, N. P. (1971). Sea bird ecology and the marine environment. In: *Avian Biology* (eds. D. S. Farner & J. R. King), vol. 1, pp. 223–86. Academic Press, New York & London.

Austin, G. T. (1974). Nesting success of the cactus wren in relation to nest orientation. *Condor,* **76**, 216–17.

Austin, G. T. (1976). Behavioral adaptations of the verdin to the desert. *Auk,* **93**, 245–62.

Balph, D. F. (1973). *Curlew Valley validation site report.* US/IBP Research Memorandum, RM 73–1, 218–30. Logan, Utah.

Bannikov, A. G. (1948). On the fluctuation of anuran populations. *Doklady Akademii Nauk SSSR,* **61**, 131–4.

Bannikov, A. G. (1950). Age distribution of a population and its dynamics in *Bombina bombina* L. *Doklady Akademii Nauk SSSR,* **70**, 5549–56.

Beer, J. R. (1955). Survival and movements of banded big brown bats. *Journal of Mammalogy,* **36**, 242–8.

Berry, K. H. (1974). The ecology and social behaviour of the chuckwalla, *Sauro-*

malus obesus obesus Baird. *University of California Publications Zoology*, **101**, 1–60.

Blair, W. F. (1953). Growth, dispersal, and age at sexual maturity of the Mexican Toad (*Bufo valliceps* Wiegman). *Copeia* (1953), 208–12.

Blair, W. F. (1960). *The Rusty Lizard – a population study*. University of Texas Press, Austin.

Botkin, D. B. & Miller, R. S. (1974). Mortality rates and survival of birds. *American Naturalist*, **108**, 181–92.

Bourlière, F. (1947). Longévité moyenne et longévité maximum chez les vertébrés. *Année Biologique*, **50**, 249–70.

Boyd, H. (1962). Mortality and fertility of European Charadrii. *Ibis*, **104**, 368–87.

Bradley, W. G. & Baker, D. P. (1967). Life tables for Nelson Bighorn Sheep on the Desert Game Range. *Desert Bighorn Council, 1967 Transactions*, pp. 142–70.

Bragg, A. N. (1940). Observations on the ecology and natural history of Anura. I. Habits, habitat and breeding of *Bufo cognatus* Say. *American Naturalist*, **74**, 424–38.

Brattstrom, B. H. (1960). Longevity in the Kangaroo Rat. *Journal of Mammalogy*, **41**, 404.

Brooks, G. R. (1967). Population ecology of the Ground Skink, *Lygosoma laterale* (Say). *Ecological Monographs*, **37**, 71–87.

Brown, L. N. (1964). Dynamics in an ecologically isolated population of the brush mouse. *Journal of Mammalogy*, **45**, 436–42.

Caughley, G. (1966). Mortality patterns in mammals. *Ecology*, **47**, 906–18.

Chew, R. M. & Butterworth, B. B. (1964). Ecology of rodents in Indian Cove (Mohave Desert), Joshua Tree National Monument, California. *Journal of Mammalogy*, **45**, 203–25.

Chew, R. M. & Chew, A. E. (1970). Energy relationships of the mammals of a desert shrub (*Larrea tridentata*) community. *Ecological Monographs*, **40**, 1–21.

Chew, R. M., Turner, F. B., August, P., Maza, B. G. & Nelson, J. (1973). *Effect of density on the population dynamics of* Perognathus formosus *and its relationships within a desert ecosystem*. US/IBP Desert Biome Research Memorandum, RM 73–18. Logan, Utah.

Crenshaw, J. W. (1955). The life history of the southern spiny lizard, *Sceloporus undulatus undulatus* Latreille. *American Midland Naturalist*, **54**, 257–98.

Deevey, E. S. (1947). Life tables for natural populations of animals. *Quarterly Review of Biology*, **22**, 283–314.

Dice, L. R. (1933). Longevity in *Peromyscus maniculatus gracilis*. *Journal of Mammalogy*, **14**, 147–8.

Edmonds, V. W. & Fertig, D. S. (1972). Longevity of the pocket mouse, *Perognathus longimembris*. *Southwestern Naturalist*, **17**, 300–301.

Egoscue, H. J., Bittmenn, J. G. & Petrovich, J. A. (1970). Some fecundity and longevity records for captive small mammals. *Journal of Mammalogy*, **51**, 622–3.

Farner, D. S. (1955). Bird banding in the study of population dynamics. In: *Recent Studies in Avian Biology* (ed. A. Wolfson), pp. 397–449. University of Illinois Press, Urbana.

Fitch, H. S. (1948). Habits and economic relationships of the Tulare Kangaroo Rat. *Journal of Mammalogy*, **29**, 5–35.

Fitch, H. S. (1949). Study of snake populations in central California. *American Midland Naturalist*, **41**, 513–79.

Animal processes

Fitch, H. S. (1954). Life history and ecology of the Five-lined Skink, *Eumeces fasciatus*. *University of Kansas Publications Museum of Natural History*, **8**, 1–156.

Fitch, H. S. (1956a). An ecological study of the collared lizard (*Crotaphytus collaris*). *University of Kansas Publications Museum of Natural History*, **8**, 213–74.

Fitch, H. S. (1956b). Early sexual maturity and longevity under natural conditions on the Great Plains narrow-mouthed Frog. *Herpetologica*, **12**, 281–2.

Fitch, H. S. (1958). Natural history of the six-lined Racerunner (*Cnemidophorus sexlineatus*). *University of Kansas Publications Museum Natural History*, **11**, 11–62.

Fitch, H. S. (1967). Ecological studies on the University of Kansas Natural History Reservation. In: *Lizard Ecology, A Symposium* (ed. W. W. Milstead), pp. 30–44. University of Missouri Press, Columbia.

Flower, S. S. (1931). Longevity of mammals in captivity. *Proceedings Zoological Society* (*London*) (1931), 145–234.

French, N. R. & Kaaz, H. W. (1968). The intrinsic rate of increase of irradiated *Peromyscus* in the laboratory. *Ecology*, **49**, 1172–9.

French, N. R., Maza, B. G. & Aschwanden, A. P. (1967). Life spans of *Dipodomys* and *Perognathus* in the Mohave Desert. *Journal of Mammalogy*, **48**, 537–48.

French, N. R., Maza, B. G., Hill, H. O., Aschwanden, A. P. & Kaaz, H. B. (1974). A population study of irradiated desert rodents. *Ecological Monographs*, **4**, 45–72.

Goin, C. J. & Goin, O. B. (1962). *Introduction to herpetology* (2nd edition). W. H. Freeman, San Francisco. 353 pp.

Green, N. B. (1957). A study of the life history of *Pseudacris brachyphona* (Cope) in West Virginia with special reference to behavior and growth of marked individuals. *Dissertation Abstracts*, **17**, 23692.

Green, R. G. & Evans, C. A. (1940). Studies on a population cycle of Snowshoe Hares on the Lake Alexander area. II. Mortality according to age groups and seasons. *Journal of Wildlife Management*, **4**, 267–78.

Griffin, D. R. & Hitchcock, H. B. (1965). Probable 24-year longevity record for *Myotis lucifugus*. *Journal of Mammalogy*, **46**, 332.

Gross, J. E., Stoddart, L. C. & Wagner, F. H. (1974). Demographic analysis of a northern Utah jackrabbit population. *Wildlife Monographs*, No. 40, 68 pp.

Hamilton, W. J. (1955). Notes on the ecology of the Oak Toad in Florida. *Herpetologica*, **11**, 205–10.

Harcourt, D. G. (1969). The development and use of life tables in the study of natural insect populations. *Annual Review of Entomology*, **14**, 175–96.

Haskell, H. S. & Reynolds, H. G. (1947). Growth, developmental food requirements and breeding activity of the California Jack Rabbit. *Journal of Mammalogy*, **28**, 129–36.

Hawbacker, A. C. (1958). Survival and home range in the Nelson Antelope Ground Squirrel. *Journal of Mammalogy*, **39**, 207–15.

Hensley, M. M. (1964). Ecological relations of the breeding bird population of the desert biome of Arizona. *Ecological Monographs*, **24**, 185–207.

Herreid, C. F. & Kinney, S. (1966). Survival of Alaskan Woodfrog (*Rana sylvatica*) larvae. *Ecology*, **47**, 1039–41.

Hickey, J. J. (1952). *Survival studies of banded birds*. United States Department of Interior, Fish and Wildlife Service Science Report, Wildlife No. 15, Washington, D.C.

Hickey, J. J. (1955). Population research on gallinaceous birds. In: *Recent*

Studies in Avian Biology (ed. A. Wolfson), pp. 326–96. University of Illinois Press, Urbana.

Hirth, H. F. (1963). The ecology of two lizards on a tropical beach. *Ecological Monographs*, **33**, 83–112.

Hirth, H. F. (1966). Weight changes and mortality of three species of snakes during hibernation. *Herpetologica*, **22**, 8–12.

Howard, W. E. (1949). Dispersal, amount of inbreeding and longevity in a local population of Prairie Deermice on the George Reserve, Southern Michigan. *Contributions Laboratory of Vertebrate Biology, University of Michigan*, **43**, 1–50.

Hsiao, T. Y. & Green, T. W. (1974). Demographic studies of sagebrush insects as functions of various environmental factors. US/IBP Desert Biome Research Memorandum, RM 74–29. Logan, Utah.

Huey, L. M. (1959). Longevity notes on captive *Perognathus*. *Journal of Mammalogy*, **40**, 412–15.

Jameson, D. L. (1955). The population dynamics of the Cliff Frog, *Syrrhophus marnocki*. *American Midland Naturalist*, **54**, 342–81.

Jameson, D. L. (1956a). Survival of some central Texas frogs under natural conditions. *Copeia* (1956), 55–7.

Jameson, D. L. (1956b). Growth, dispersal and survival of the Pacific Tree Frog. *Copeia* (1956), 25–9.

Kalmbach, E. R. (1939). Nesting success: Its significance in waterfowl reproduction. *Transactions North American Wildlife Conference*, **4**, 591–604.

Kelleher, K. E. & Tester, J. R. (1969). Homing and survival in the Manitoba Toad, *Bufo hemiophrys*, in Minnesota. *Ecology*, **50**, 1040–8.

Kendeigh, S. C. (1942). Analysis of losses in the nesting of birds. *Journal of Wildlife Management*, **6**, 19–26.

Kennedy, J. P. (1958). The biology of the Eastern Fence Lizard, *Sceloporus undulatus hyacinthinus*. Ph.D. Dissertation, University of Texas, Austin.

Klomp, H. (1966). The dynamics of a field population of the Pine Looper, *Bupalus piniarius* L. (Lep., Geom.). In: *Advances in Ecological Research*, **3**, 207–305.

Kramer, G. (1946). Veränderungen von Nachkommenziffer und Nachkommengrösse sowie der Altersverteilung von Inseleidechsen. *Zeitschrift für Naturforschung*, **1**, 700–710. (Cited by Lack, 1954.)

Lack, D. (1954). *The natural regulation of animal numbers*. Clarendon Press, Oxford.

Lechleitner, R. R. (1959). Sex ratio, age classes, and reproduction of the Black-tailed Jack Rabbit. *Journal of Mammalogy*, **40**, 63–81.

Leopold, A., Sperry, T. M., Feeney, W. S. & Catenhusen, J. S. (1943). Population turnover on a Wisconsin pheasant refuge. *Journal of Wildlife Management*, **7**, 383–94.

Leslie, P. H. & Ranson, R. M. (1940). The mortality, fertility and rate of natural increase of the vole (*Microtus agrestis*) as observed in the laboratory. *Journal of Animal Ecology*, **9**, 27–52.

Leslie, P. H., Tener, T. S., Vizoso, M. & Chitty, H. (1955). The longevity and fertility of the Orkney Vole, *Microtus orcadensis*, as observed in the laboratory. *Proceedings of the Zoological Society of London*, **125**, 115–25.

Linduska, J. P. (1947). Longevity of some Michigan game farm mammals. *Journal of Mammalogy*, **28**, 126–9.

Linduska, J. P. (1950). 'Ecology and land-use relationships of small mammals on a Michigan farm.' Ph.D. Dissertation, Michigan State University, East Lansing.

Lloyd, M. (1960). Statistical analysis of Marchant's data on breeding and clutch-size. *Ibis*, **102**, 600–611.

Lowe, C. H. (1968). Fauna of desert environments. In: *Deserts of the World: An appraisal of research into their physical and biological environments* (eds. W. G. McGinnies, B. J. Goldman & P. Paylore), pp. 569–645. University of Arizona Press, Tucson.

Manville, R. H. (1953). Longevity of the Coyote, *Journal of Mammalogy*, **34**, 390.

Marchant, S. (1960). The breeding of some S.W. Ecuadorian birds. *Ibis*, **102**, 349–82, 584–99.

Marchant, S. (1963). The breeding of some Iraqi birds. *Ibis*, **105**, 516–57.

Martof, B. (1956*a*). Growth and development of the Green Frog, *Rana clamitans*, under natural conditions. *American Midland Naturalist*, **55**, 101–17.

Martof, B. (1956*b*). Factors influencing the size and composition of populations of *Rana clamitans*. *American Midland Naturalist*, **56**, 224–45.

Merck Veterinary Manual (4th edition) (1973). Merck, Rahway, New Jersey.

Meslow, E. C. & Keith, L. B. (1968). Demographic parameters of a Snowshoe Hare population. *Journal of Wildlife Management*, **32**, 812–34.

Moore, D. R. (1965). 'Breeding biology and nest usage of the Verdin in southern New Mexico.' Masters Thesis. New Mexico State University, Las Cruces.

Murie, A. (1944). The wolves of Mount McKinley. In: *Fauna of National Parks*, Series 5. United States Printing Office, Washington, D.C.

Nice, M. M. (1957). Nesting success in altricial brids. *Auk*, **74**, 305–21.

Nolan, V. Jr. (1963). Reproductive success of birds in a deciduous scrub habitat. *Ecology*, **44**, 305–13.

O'Farrell, T. P., Olson, R. J., Gilbert, R. O. & Hedlund, J. D. (1975). A population of Great Basin Pocket Mice, *Perognathus parvus*, in the shrub-steppe of south-central Washington. *Ecological Monographs*, **45**, 1–28.

Organ, J. A. (1961). Studies on the local distribution, life history and population dynamics of the salamander genus *Desmognathus* in Virginia. *Ecological Monographs*, **31**, 189–220.

Orr, R. T. (1939). Longevity in *Perognathus longimembris*. *Journal of Mammalogy*, **20**, 505.

Orr, R. T. (1958). Keeping bats in captivity. *Journal of Mammalogy*, **39**, 339–44.

Palmer, R. S. (1954). *The mammal guide. Mammals of North America, north of Mexico*. Doubleday, New York.

Paradiso, J. L. & Greenhall, A. M. (1967). Longevity record for American bats. *American Midland Naturalist*, **78**, 251–2.

Patterson, R. & Brattstrom, B. (1972). Growth in captive *Gopherus agassizi*. *Herpetologica*, **28**, 169–71.

Pearson, P. G. (1955). Population ecology of the Spadefoot Toad, *Scaphiopus h. holbrooki* Harlan. *Ecological Monographs*, **25**, 233–67.

Pearson, P. G. (1957). Further notes on the population ecology of the Spadefoot Toad. *Ecology*, **38**, 580–86.

Rabb, G. B. (1960). Longevity records for mammals at the Chicago Zoological Park. *Journal of Mammalogy*, **41**, 113–14.

Ricklefs, R. E. (1969). An analysis of nesting mortality in birds. *Smithsonian Contributions in Zoology*, **9**, 1 48.

Ricklefs, R. E. (1973). Fecundity, mortality, and avian demography. In: *Breeding Biology of Birds* (ed. D. S. Farner), pp. 366–447. Proceedings of a Symposium on breeding behavior and reproductive physiology in birds, Denver.

Russell, S. M., Gould, P. J. & Smith, E. L. (1973). *Population structure, foraging behavior and daily movements of certain Sonoran Desert birds.* US/IBP Desert Biome Research Memorandum, RM 73–27. Logan, Utah.

Russell, S., Smith, E., Gould, P. & Austin, G. (1972). *Studies on Sonoran birds.* US/IBP Desert Biome Research Memorandum, RM 72–31. Logan, Utah.

Sexton, O. J., Heatwole, H. & Meseth, E. H. (1963). Seasonal population changes in the lizard, *Anolis limifrons*, in Panama. *American Midland Naturalist*, **69**, 482–91.

Skutch, A. F. (1966). A breeding census and nesting success in Central America. *Ibis*, **108**, 1–16.

Solomon, M. E. (1964). Analysis of processes involved in the natural control of insects. In: *Advances in Ecological Research*, **2**, 1–58.

Stebbins, R. C. & Robinson, H. B. (1946). Further analysis of a population of the lizard *Sceloporus graciosus gracilis*. *University of California Publications Zoology*, **48**, 149–68.

Storr, G. M. (1965). The *Amphibolurus maculatus* species-group (Lacertilia, Agamidae) in Western Australia. *Journal Royal Society of Western Australia*, **48**, 45–54.

Svihla, R. D. (1931). Notes on Desert and Dusky Harvest mice (*Reithrodontomys megalotis megalotis* and *R. m. nigrescens*). *Journal of Mammalogy*, **12**, 363–5.

Tanner, W. W. & Jorgensen, C. D. (1963). *Reptiles of the Nevada Test Site*. Brigham Young University Science Bulletin, Biological Series III.

Tanner, W. W. & Krogh, J. E. (1973). Ecology of *Sceloporus magister* at the Nevada Test Site, Nye County, Nevada. *Great Basin Naturalist*, **33**, 133–46.

Taylor, W. K. (1971). A breeding biology study of the Verdin, *Auriparus flaviceps* (Sundevall) in Arizona. *American Midland Naturalist*, **85**, 289–328.

Tevis, L., Jr. (1966). Unsuccessful breeding by desert toads (*Bufo punctatus*) at the limit of their ecological tolerance. *Ecology*, **47**, 766–75.

Thornton, W. A. (1960). Population dynamics in *Bufo woodhousei* and *Bufo valliceps*. *Texas Journal of Science*, **12**, 176–200.

Tinkle, D. W. (1967). The life and demography of the Side-blotched Lizard, *Uta stansburiana*. *Miscellaneous Publications, Museum of Zoology, University of Michigan*, No. 132.

Tucker, V. A. (1962). Diurnal torpidity in the California Pocket Mouse. *Science*, **136**, 380–81.

Tucker, V. A. (1966). Diurnal torpor and its relation to food consumption and weight changes in the California Pocket Mouse, *Perognathus californicus*. *Ecology*, **47**, 245–52.

Turner, F. B. (1959). Some features of the ecology of *Bufo punctatus* in Death Valley, California. *Ecology*, **40**, 175–81.

Turner, F. B. (1960). Population structure and dynamics of the Western Spotted Frog, *Rana p. pretiosa* Baird & Girard, in Yellowstone Park, Wyoming. *Ecological Monographs*, **30**, 251–78.

Turner, F. B. (1962). The demography of frogs and toads. *Quarterly Review of Biology*, **37**, 303–14.

Turner, F. B., Lannom, J. R., Medica, P. A. & Hoddenbach, G. A. (1969). Density and composition of fenced populations of Leopard Lizards (*Crotaphytus wislizenii*) in southern Nevada. *Herpetologica*, **25**, 247–57.

Turner, F. B., Medica, P. A., Lannom, J. R. & Hoddenbach, G. A. (1969a). A demographic analysis of fenced populations of the Whiptail Lizard, *Cnemidophorus tigris* in southern Nevada. *Southwestern Naturalist*, **14**, 189–201.

Turner, F. B., Medica, P. A., Lannom, J. R. & Hoddenbach, G. A. (1969b). A demographic analysis of continuously irradiated and non-irradiated populations of the lizard, *Uta stansburiana*. *Radiation Research*, **38**, 349–56.

Turner, F. B., Hoddenbach, G. A., Medica, P. A. & Lannom, J. R. (1970). The demography of the lizard, *Uta stansburiana* Baird & Girard, in southern Nevada. *Journal of Animal Ecology*, **39**, 505–19.

Turner, F. B., Medica, P. A. & Smith, D. D. (1973). *Reproduction and survivorship of the lizard,* Uta stansburiana, *and the effects of winter rainfall density and predation on these processes.* US/IBP Desert Biome Research Memorandum, RM 73–26. Logan, Utah.

Turner, F. B., Medica, P. A. & Smith, D. D. (1974). *Reproduction and survivorship of the lizard,* Uta stansburiana, *and the effects of winter rainfall, density and predation on these processes.* US/IBP Desert Biome Research Memorandum, RM 74–26. Logan, Utah.

Vinegar, M. B. (1975). Life history phenomena in two populations of the lizard, *Sceloporus undulatus*, in southwestern New Mexico. *American Midland Naturalist*, **93**, 388–402.

Wiens, J. A. (1973). Pattern and process in grassland bird communities. *Ecological Monographs*, **43**, 237–70.

Wood, J. E. (1958). Age structure and productivity of a Gray Fox population. *Journal of Mammalogy*, **39**, 74–86.

Woodbury, A. M. & Hardy, R. (1948). Studies of the Desert Tortoise, *Gopherus agassizi*. *Ecological Monographs*, **18**, 145–200.

Woodbury, A. M., Vetas, B., Julian, G., Glissmeyer, H. R., Heyrend, F. L., Call, A., Smart, E. W. & Sanders, R. T. (1951). Symposium: A snake den in Tooele County, Utah. *Herpetologica*, **7**, 1–52.

Zweifel, R. G. & Lowe, C. H. (1966). The ecology of a population of *Xantusia vigilis*, the desert night lizard. *American Museum Novitates*, **2247**, 1–57.

Manuscript received by the editors November 1975

35. Animal Processes – Integration

D. W. GOODALL

Most groups of air-breathing animals are to be found in the arid lands. Mammals, birds and reptiles are all obvious components of the fauna, and even the Amphibia are far from negligible. Most orders of insects and other Arthropod classes are to be found. The pulmonate Gastropods are prominent in places, and Nematoda and Protozoa are ubiquitous in the soil of arid lands as elsewhere.

As is clear from the preceding chapters, knowledge of processes in populations of desert animals is patchy. Reflecting the anthropocentric character of much biological investigation, mammals seem to be better known than other vertebrates, and vertebrates better than arthropods, while the nematodes and protozoa of the deserts are almost unknown.

Knowledge of the subject seems best developed for the deserts of North America and Australia, with those of South America, Africa and Asia lagging far behind. To some extent this may be a biased view, reflecting the fact that most of the writers in this Section are American; but there is little doubt that expanded research effort in the deserts of the other continents – encompassing most of the world's arid areas – would be rewarding.

For animals, the arid lands pose special problems which differ in some ways from those with which plants are faced. The mobility of animals, and their independence of sunlight, mean that they are not necessarily exposed to the full rigours of the desert environment – they can escape from it behaviourally. On the other hand, desert plants can retreat into dormancy (in the seed stage, at least) to an extent which is not possible for most animal groups. Water relations, too, differ. Plants need water in much greater quantity (per unit biomass) than animals, and obtain it in the main by using their root systems to explore the soil, often to considerable depth. Many animals can satisfy their needs for water by that contained in their food (or derived from it by metabolism); water taken in through the body surface is generally negligible, and, apart from food as a source, animals must depend on the availability of liquid water in drinkable quantities.

The most important adaptations of animals to the arid environment thus involve protection from excessive insolation, and the hyperthermia and dehydration which may result, and limitation in the intake of liquid water. The high intensity of radiation, together with a shortage of water for cooling purposes, makes thermoregulation particularly difficult and important for desert animals, and a number of special mechanisms (behavioural and physiological) have been developed for this purpose. Lack of water also presents special problems for those animals which produce liquid excreta; and the osmotic difficulties are intensified when the water available – and perhaps plant food too – is saline. Physiological devices to overcome these difficulties are an important feature of the desert fauna.

Another feature of the arid environment is that the biomass of food (plants for herbivores, or prey for predators) is often small in quantity and widely scattered. It also occurs patchily, through the patchy distribution of rainstorms. For larger animals, this puts a premium on mobility.

Periods of quiescence, when environmental conditions are particularly unfavourable, are often observed in desert fauna. In some (for instance, nematode eggs), the degree of dormancy and the ability to survive adverse conditions rival those of plant seeds. But in most groups limited metabolic activity must continue despite seasonal torpor or aestivation, or enclosure in a cocoon or egg-shell. During normal activity, too, respiratory losses can be restricted – sometimes by behavioural adaptation, sometimes by physiological mechanisms (acclimatization, or modified temperature coefficients) or by morphological features (e.g. the alternative gas-exchange structures of arachnids).

The decomposer cycle, though slow (as witness the abundance of dead woody material above ground in many deserts), is probably as important as cycling through herbivores. Some animals, notably termites and soil micro-arthropods, are important elements in the decomposer cycle; but knowledge of them is very limited.

For reproduction, the critical feature of the desert environment is its unreliability and variability from season to season and year to year. Years when reproduction is impossible or unsuccessful are common. In consequence, longevity and the ability to make a quick reproductive response to favourable conditions when they occur are particularly advantageous for desert animals.

Longevity and mortality of desert animals are poorly known, and could be a rewarding subject for research. Reproduction, on the other hand, has been studied in detail in certain groups of arid-zone animals. There are, for instance, numerous examples of how reproduction may be timed to give it the greatest chance of success – particularly in respect of the availability of food (green plant material or insects), and (for Amphibia particularly) the presence of liquid water. Juvenile phases may be particularly sensitive to the rigours of the desert environment, and special adaptations, either of the juveniles themselves or of parental behaviour, are common.

The smaller plant biomass and the high variability of the desert environment suggest that the niche breadth for animals is likely to be greater than in more mesic situations – they need to survive in a wider range of environmental conditions, and are likely to be advantaged by an ability to use a wider range of foods. Though these statements seem self-evident, comparative studies to confirm them have yet to be made.

Index

Page references in italic type are to tables and figures

Index

Agave lecheguilla, *34*, 40
Agelenopsis aperta, 800, 801, 802, 806–7
Agropyron, 35, 38, 246, *286*
Agropyron cristatum, 481, 540–1, 548, 553, 555
Agropyron elongatum, *611*
Agropyron fragile, 278, 279, 296; litter fall, *288*; phytomass, *282*
Agropyron inerme, 555
Agropyron intermedium, 556
Agropyron repens, 550, 557
Agropyron sibericum, 555
Agropyron smithii, 555
Agropyron spicatum, 537, 555
Aimophila carpatis, 804; mortality and longevity data, *830, 831*
Aimophila cassinii, 801; mortality and longevity data, *830, 831*
air flow, *see* atmospheric transport processes
Aizoaceae, 119, 423–4; *see also* Mesembryanthemaceae and individual genera
Aizoanthemum mossamedense, 120
Aizoon, 123
Akodon, 702
Ala Shan Desert (Ala-Chan), 10, 15, 307
Alaudidae (larks), 131, 803
albedo, *see* surface albedo
Albizzia amara, 256, 257
Albizzia latorum, 256
Albizzia lebbek, 697
Alcelaphus buselaphus (bubal hartebeest), 100, 760, 762
Alchemilla cryptantha, 237
Aleppo pine, 98
alfalfa, *see* Medicago sativa
algae, 285, 289, 290, 444, 450, 452, 463, 464
Algeria, 90, *103*, 104, *105*; arid zones of, *84*; rainfall data, *86, 87*
Alhagi maurorum, 242, 245, 247
Alice Springs, Australia: rainfall data, 153, 161, 419, *420*; radiation data, 352, *353*, *355–6*
alkaline soils (solonetz), *see* soil types
alkalinity and alkalinization, 450–1, 463, 465–7
allelochemics, 452
Allenrolfea, 41, 43
Alligator mississippiensis, 760
Allionia, 693
Allionia incarnata, 685
Allium, 252, 253, *312*
alluvial soils, *see* soil types
Aloe, 120, 310
Aloe dichotoma, 122
Alyssum desertorum, 278
Amaranthus fimbriatus, 485
Ambrosia dumosa, 513, 546, 697
Ambystomidae, *52*
Ambystoma tigrinum (tiger salamander), *52*, 804, 812
Amellus strigosus, 121
America, North, deserts of, 16, 19, 21–69, *304*, 351–2, 356, 367; boundaries of, *22*, 61–4; climate of, 25–6, *27*, *28*; fauna of, *see* fauna; and man's influence in, 64–9; physiography of, 10, 21–5; radiation, (global solar) *355–6*, *362*, 363, *364*, 366, (net), *369*; rainfall, 374, 376,

378, 380, 383, 386; soils of, 13, 26, 28–30; sunshine, 350, *351*, vegetation of, *see* vegetation; *see also* individual deserts (Chihuahuan, Great Basin, Mohave and Sonoran)
America, South, arid regions of, *305*, 356, 383
Amitermes, 687
amitrole, translocation in plants, 542
Ammodendron argenteum, 278; annual production of, *286*, 296; litter fall data, 285, *288*; phytomass and dead organic matter, 281, *282*
Ammodendron conollyi, 276
Ammodramus savannarum, 783–4
Ammosperma cinereum, 99
Ammospermophilus harrisii (antelope squirrel), *48*, 59, 63, *737*
Ammospermophilus interpres, 57, 58
Ammospermophilus leucurus, *48*, 62
Ammospermophilus nelsoni, *835*
Ammotragus lervia lervia (Barbary sheep), 100
Amphibia, 60, 188, 333, 751, 772, 779; development of, 806, 807, 810, 811, 812; diet and feeding habits of, 688–9, *706*; moisture uptake, 753–4; mortality and longevity of, 825–8; in North American deserts, *52–3*, 58; reproduction of, 798, 799, 803, 805, 806; and thermoregulation, 743; *see also* individual taxa
Amphibolurus, 690
Amphispiza belli (sage sparrow), *50*, 53, *756*
Amphispiza bilineata (black-throated sparrow), *50*, 60, 693, 694, *830, 831*
Amygdalus, 246, 253–4
Amygdalus brahuica, 254
Amygdalus eburnea, 254
Amygdalus erioclada, 254
Amygdalus scoparia, 251
Anabasetea, 241
Anabasis, 241, 244, 251, 254
Anabasis aphylla, *249*
Anabasis articulata, 99, 244
Anabasis hausknechtii, *249*
Anabasis macroptera, 253
Anabasis oropediorum, 98
Anabasis salsa, 278; annual production, *286*; litter fall, *288*; phytomass and dead organic matter, *282*
Anabasis setifera, 244, 252, 253
Anacampseros spp., 120
Ancanthotermes macrocephalus, 705
Anacardiaceae, *34*; *see also* individual genera
Andrachne rotundifolia, 252
Andropogon gerardii, 555
Anemone, *312*
Angola, 122, 137
Angolosaurus skoogi, 125, 130
animals, *see* fauna
Anisantha tectorum, 281
Anisotes trisulcus, 237
An Nafud (Nefud), 14
annual production of vegetation, in central Asia 284–5, *287–8*, 296
annuals, 627, 639, 661, 663, 665, 668; flowering of, and factors affecting, (photoperiod), 629–30, (soil moisture), 632–3, 633–8, (temperature), 630–2; vernalization requirements of, 628–9; *see also* ephemerals

Index

Index

Index

Index

Index

Index

Index

Malye Barsuki, central Asia, 274, *275*, 276, 278; annual production in, *286*; phytomass and dead organic matter, 281, *282*, 285, *288*

Mammalia, *737*, 752; behaviour and distribution dynamics of, 777, 778, 779, 783, 786, 787; in Africa, 100–1, 132–6; in North America, *48–9*, 58; in Asia, 260–3, 291, *293*, 294; in Australia, 167, 188; development of, 806, 808; dispersion patterns of, 59–61, 62, 63; fecundity of, 798, 799; feeding habits of, 694–707, 785; mortality and longevity of, 834–8; renal structure and function of, 754–8; species diversity, 329–32; thermal regulation of, 744, 745, 746, 760, 762; *see also* individual taxa

Mammillaria, 32, *312*

Manduca sexta, 746

Mangifera indica, 696

Manica, 687

man's influence, in desert ecosystems, 64–9, 102–5, 167, 168, 190–1, 258–9, 314–15

maquis, 231

Marsupialia, 167, 694–5, *706*, 779, 784; fecundity of, 798, 799, 803, 805; *see also* individual families and genera

Masileh-Karir salt-desert basin, 216

mass and heat transport, by air flow above vegetation, 398–401

mass-flow theory, of transport in phloem, 539, 668

Masticophis (whipsnakes), 51, *53*, 692

Masticophis bilineatus, *53*

Masticophis flagellum (coachwhip), *53*

Masticophis taeniatus, 51, 62, *827*, 829

matorral, as degraded forest, 95, 98

Matthiola, 257

Matthiola odoratissima, 257

Mausolea eriocarpa, 280

Mayo culture, of Coastal Mexico, 68

meadows, in arid North Africa, 96

Mecas, 51

mechanical impedance of soils, and effects on root growth and function, 595–6

Medicago, 175, 254

Medicago aschersoniae, 240

Medicago sativa, 537, 547, 558

Megaderma lyra, 696

Megaleia rufa (red kangaroo), 166, 172, 176, 188, 695; behaviour and distribution of, 771–2, 785, 786, 788; development and reproduction of, 803, 808

Melanophis femur, 681

Melanopus, *725*

Mellivora capensis (honey badger), 133

Meloidae, 51, 54

Melophorus, 780

Melopsittacus undulatus (budgerigar), 693, 757, 756, 779

Mephitis macroura, 704

Mephitis mephitis, 704, *836*

Merino sheep, 168, 172, 176, 775, 785; wool growth rates and reproduction, 174, 176, 185–6

Meriones animaleus, 700

Meriones hurricanae, 702, 704, 705

Meriones libycus, 101

Meriones shawi, 101

Merriam's kangaroo rat, *see Dipodomys merriami*

Mertensia arizonica, 553

mesas, remnants of former plateaux, 228

Mesembryanthemaceae, 118, 119, 121, 122; *see also* Aizoaceae and individual genera

Mesembryanthemum cryptantham, 120

mesophyll resistance, *see* resistance, residual

mesophytes, 581, 588

Mesopotamian Province, 306, 307; vegetation of, 246

Mesostigmata, 682

Mesozoic era, *66*, 214, 217

mesquite, *see Prosopis glandulosa*

Messor aegyptiacus, 687

metabolic rates, of vertebrates, 735; *see also* respiration

metabolism, salt, in desert fauna: ionic regulation during dehydration, 754, *755*; renal structure and function in birds and mammals, 754–8

metabolism, water, in desert fauna: moisture uptake, 752–4; and use of radioisotopes, 758–9; water loss, components of, 750–2

metacutinization, of roots, 583

Metacyclops minutus, 810

Metadiaptomus mauretanicus, 810

Mexico, *23*, 24–5, 42, 44, 374

Micrathene whitneyi (elf owl), *50*, 694

Microcaeculus namibensis, 150

Microcavia australis, 700

microclimate and evaporation in desert regions, 258–9, 209–30, 435–6; energy balance, 409–10; leaves and canopies, energy balance of, 422–6; radiation balance of desert landscapes, 411–14; temperature and heat transfer, 414–22; transpiration, 501

Microcolus vaginatus, 285

Microdipodops, *48*, 57, 58, 62, 63, 698

Microdipodops megacephalus, 57, 62, *837*

Microdipodops pallidus, 57

microdunes, *see* rheboub

microfungi, soil, 291, *293*

Microhylidae, *826*; *see also* individual genera

microorganisms, soil, 289, 291, 293, 294, 309; and effects on root growth and function, 597–8; and nitrogen cycle, 452, 453–4, 454

microphyllous desert scrub of the Chihuahuan Desert, 40

microrelief, effects on water and salt distribution, 447, 459

Micruroides euryxanthus (Arizona coral snake), *53*

Middle East, 213, 215–16, *219*; geology and geomorphology of, 213–16; hydrology of, 223–4, *225*; livestock data, *264*, *265*, 266; soils of, 227–32; vegetation of, 241–2; *see also* individual countries

millipedes, *see* Diplopoda

Mimidae, *830*, *831*; *see also* individual genera

Mimosa biuncifera, 40

Mimulus, 44

Mimus polyglottos (mockingbird), *50*; mortality and longevity data of, *830–1*

minnow, *see Cyprinodon atrorus*

Miocene Period, 42, 58, *66*, 214

Index

night snake, *see Hypsiglena torquata*
Nitraria retusa, 243
Nitraria sibirica, 281
nitrate: absorption of, by roots, 586, *611*, 619; accumulation in desert soils, 459, 460, 461
Nitrobacter, 453
nitrification, 452–3
nitrogen: cycle, 451–6; distribution and utilization in plants, 547, 549, 596, 652; distribution in soil, 452–6; fertilization of soil, effects of, 549–50; fixation, 452; losses by volatilization, 452; mineralization, 453–6; plant responses to, 452, 549–50
Nitrosococcus, 453
Nitrosomonas, 453
Noea mucronata, 245, 246, 250
Nolina, *312*
Nomadacris septum fasciata, 803
north Africa, *see* Africa, north
North America, *see* America, North
Northern Hemisphere, arid zones of, *362*, 363, *364*, 366, *369*, 390
Nothobranchius, 809
Notiosofex crawfordi (desert shrew), *48*, 692, 694, 695
Notomys, 700
Notomys alexis (Australian hopping mouse), *756*, 774, 782
Notostraca, 809
Novomessor, 684
Novomessor cockerelli, 686
Nubo-Arabian massif, 215
Nubian Desert, 306
Nubian ibex, *see Capra ibex nubiana*
Nubian sandstone uplands, 215
Nubo-Sindian province, 237
nullahs, 309
nutrient ions, in soil, 585–91, 668; and effects on root growth and function, 596–7; *see also* ion absorption, transport and uptake
Nyctaginaceae, *33*
Nymphoides indica, 242

Ocnera hispida, 749
ocotillo, *see Fourquieria splendens*
Odocoileus hemionus, 705, *837*
Odonata, 684
Odyssea pancinervis, 124
Oedibasis apiculata, 279
Oenothera, *33*
Oenothera clavaeformis, 483, 691
Olea chrysophylla, 237
Olea cuspidata, 257
Olea europaea, 97, 98
Olea laperini, 100
Oligocene Period, 42, 66, 217
Olneya, 39, *312*
Olneya tesota, *32*, 33, 39, 693
Oman, *219*, 221, 262
Onagraceae, *33*
Oncideres, 685
Onobrychis viciaefolia, 555
Onobryens, 251
Ononis, 94

Ononis natrix, 247
Onosma spp., 257
Onthophagus longicornis, 705
Onychomys, 48, 49, 58, 703, 704, 733
Onychomys leucogaster, 48, 59, 63, *733*, 736, 737, *837*
Onchomys torridus, 48, 59, 62, 737, *835*
Ophidia, *see* snakes
Ophioglossum polyphyllum, 123
Opisthophthalmus, 129
Opisthophthalmus concinnus, 125
Opuntia, 687, 705, 734, 808; in North America, *32*, 33, 34, 40, 61, 685, 688, 700; carbohydrate reserves, 553; and soil temperature, 593–4
Opuntia acanthocarpa, 47
Opuntia basilaris (beavertail cactus), *33*
Opuntia bigelovii, *31*
Opuntia camanchica, 577, 578
Opuntia fulgida, 578
Opuntia leucotricha, 40
Opuntia phaeacantha var. *discata*, 520
Opuntia puberula, 581
Opuntia ramosissima, 47
Opuntia streptacantha, 40
Opuntia versicolor, 808
Ordos Desert, 10, 15, 306, 307
Oreoscoptes montanus (sage thrasher), *50*, 53
Oreoscoptes spp., 58
Oreotragus oreotragus (klipspringer), 134
organic matter in soils, 451–6
organpipe cactus, *see Cereus (Lemaireocereus) thurberi*
Ormenis lonadioides, 99
Ornithodorus savigny (sand tampan), 130
orographic and general convergence precipitation, 379–80
Oropetium capensis, 122
Oropetium thomaem, 697
Orthoporus ornatus, 55, 688; assimilation of, 718, 719; production of, 724, *725*; respiration of, 720, *721*, 723
Orthoptera, 54, 684, 688; *see also* grasshoppers, locusts and individual genera
Orycteropus afer (aardvark), 133
Oryctolagus cuniculus (European rabbit), 169, 178, 187, 777
Oryx algazel (*Oryx tao*), 100
Oryx beisa, 707, 780
Oryx gazella, 134, *135*
Oryx leucoryx (long-horned Arabian oryx), 260, *261*, 262
Oryx tao, see *Oryx algazel*
Oryzopsis, 35
osmotic regulation in insects, during dehydration, 754, *755*
osmotic relations, of plants, 491–507
ostrich, *see Struthio camelus*
Othonna, 120
Otus asio, 808
oueds, *see* wadis
Ovis aries, *see* sheep
Ovis canadensis, 705; mortality and longevity data, *834*, *837*
owl, 49

870

Index

872

Index

Index

Index

878

Index